Red Hat Linux

UNLEASHED

Kamran Husain, Timothy Parker, Ph.D., et al.

SAMS
PUBLISHING

201 West 103rd Street
Indianapolis, IN 46290

This one is for my dad, Dr. Bilal Husain. May he rest in peace.

—Kamran Husain

This one is for Roy MacLean and his wife, Geety. I've been lucky to have such a good friend for so many years. On top of that, he's one heck of a Foosball player! Amicus usque ad aras.

—Tim Parker

Copyright © 1996 by Sams Publishing

Publisher and President	Richard K. Swadley
Acquisitions Manager	Greg Wiegand
Development Manager	Dean Miller
Managing Editor	Cindy Morrow
Marketing Manager	John Pierce
Assistant Marketing Manager	Kristina Perry

Acquisitions and Development Editor
Dean Miller

Software Development Specialist
Cari Skaggs

Production Editor
James Grass

Copy Editors
David Bradford
Kristine Simmons

Technical Reviewer
Rob Pfister
Stephen Tallon

Editorial Coordinator
Bill Whitmer

Technical Edit Coordinator
Lynette Quinn

Resource Coordinator
Deborah Frisby

Formatter
Frank Sinclair

Editorial Assistants
Carol Ackerman
Andi Richter
Rhonda Tinch-Mize

Cover Designer
Tim Amrhein

Book Designer
Gary Adair

Copy Writer
Peter Fuller

Production Team Supervisor
Brad Chinn

Production
Mary Ann Abramson, Stephen Adams, Gina Brown, Michael Brumitt, Bruce Clingaman, Jason Hand, Michael Henry, Louisa Klucznik, Clint Lahnen, Ryan Oldfather, Casey Price, Laura Robbins, Bobbi Satterfield, Ian Smith, Laura A. Smith, Andrew Stone, Tim Tate

Part VIII Advanced Programming Topics

Part IX Appendixes

Contents

Part II Using Linux

Part V Linux for Programmers

Part VI Linux for System Administrators

Part VIII   Advanced Programming Topics

Part IX Appendixes

Acknowledgments

Of course, many thanks to Uzma, Haya, and Hana for putting up with long schedules, missed vacations, and skating lessons.

Kamran Husain

This book was much easier to write than most, primarily because we did all the work for previous versions of Linux Unleashed. Still, there was a lot of time and frantic effort making sure we had everything ready for the Red Hat version. Dean Miller and Grace Buechlein at Sams helped coordinate things at their end.

Each chapter of this book had to be checked for accuracy, a task performed very well by our technical editors. The chapters that we rewrote and modified had to be done under extreme time pressures, and we thank our families and friends for understanding why we couldn't take "just one night off."

On a personal level, thanks to Yvonne for understanding why I had to work like mad every night. Thanks to my parents who didn't get their promised visit because I had another book to do (I'll visit real soon. I promise!) And thanks to all my friends for keeping my morale up during the long nights.

Tim Parker

About the Authors

Kamran Husain is a software consultant with experience in Windows UNIX system programming. He has dabbled in all sorts of software for real-time systems, applications, telecommunications, seismic data acquisition and navigation, X Windows/Motif and Microsoft Windows applications. He refuses to divulge any more of his qualifications. Kamran offers consulting services and teaches training classes through his company, MPS Inc., in Texas. He is an alumnus of the University of Texas at Austin. You can reach Kamran through Sams Publishing, Web http://www.ikra.com, or via e-mail at khusain@ikra.com or mpsi@aol.com.

Tim Parker is a consultant and technical writer based in Ottawa, Canada. He is Technical Editor for *SCO World Magazine*, and Contributing Editor for *UNIX Review, Advanced Systems Magazine*, and *Canadian Computer Reseller*. He has written more than 800 feature articles and two dozen books. When not writing, Tim is a private pilot, scuba diver, white-water kayaker, and general adrenaline junkie.

Uzma Husain is an alumna of the New Jersey Institute of Technology, where she received her Masters in computer science. Her work experience is in the financial software and MIS arena.

Peter McKinnon is a software developer with Bell-Northern Research in Ottawa, Canada. He has a degree in Mathematics from Dalhousie University and a Computer Science degree from the Technical University of Nova Scotia. His current work involves the development of reverse-engineering tools.

Rick McMullin is a computer consultant with Brierly, Doucette, and Simpson Consulting Ltd. of Ottawa, Canada. He specializes in object-oriented systems development and computer security. Rick has been teaching UNIX courses for several years and has been a strong enthusiast and supporter of Linux since its early releases.

Ed Treijs is a technical writer and consultant based in Toronto, Canada. When not writing technical manuals, Ed tinkers with his three classic Firebirds.

Rob Pfister is a software engineer specializing in very large database applications. He holds a degree in computer science from the University of Maine. Rob has been a Linux enthusiast since he installed version 0.96 in early 1992.

Introduction to *Red Hat Linux Unleashed*

Red Hat Linux Unleashed grew out of our popular *Linux Unleashed* book, now in its second edition, which featured SlackWare's version of Linux. The last year has a seen a growing number of users attracted by the Red Hat Linux version. Red Hat's Linux offers a number of different features from SlackWare's features we thought were important enough to deserve focus in a Linux Unleashed book of its own.

Red Hat Linux is quite different from SlackWare's Linux, primarily in the installation and package maintenance routine. Red Hat's user-friendly installation and easy X configuration make it especially attractive to first-time Linux users. The actual behavior of either version of Linux, once installed, is virtually the same, through.

The contents of much of this book are similar to those in our Linux Unleashed book, although we have made a few changes to reflect Red Hat Linux's nature. The first few chapters dealing with installation and configuration have been revised to reflect Red Hat's procedures, and the chapter on LILO has been rewritten to clear up some issues. The chapter on Perl has also been rewritten to present the latest version of Perl. The rest of the book's contents have been checked for accuracy and timeliness against the Red Hat software.

We hope you enjoy this book and find it a gentle introduction to the wonderful world of Linux!

Introduction

If imitation is the most sincere form of flattery, UNIX should be proud indeed. The Linux project was begun several years ago as a public domain version of the popular UNIX operating system—the most widely used operating system in the world. Linux made it possible for anyone to obtain a full-featured version of UNIX for their own pleasure and education, with a minimum of monetary outlay. (With commercial versions of UNIX costing many hundreds of dollars, this was a very important aspect of Linux's popularity.)

Although begun by a single programmer, Linux quickly blossomed into a project organized by people around the world, each contributing ideas, code, and effort for the good of the project and no recompense. The environment in many ways recalled the excitement and dedication the nascent personal computer industry experienced years ago.

This book was an interesting project right from the start. It combined the expertise of several veteran UNIX and Linux users with a complete distribution version of Linux supplied on CD-ROM. This is, essentially, one-stop shopping for a Linux system. The CD-ROM coupled with the installation chapters of this book help you install the complete Linux software system software on your PC, then you can read through the subjects that interest you in the book, working through with the examples on your machine.

For those who have never used Linux (or UNIX) before, you will find the operating system both engrossing and confusing. UNIX has a long and evolved history, leading inevitably to some idiosyncrasies with the operating system. On the other hand, UNIX and Linux are a powerful multitasking operating system that can take your PC far beyond the limitations of the DOS operating system.

We sincerely hope you enjoy reading this book, and that you find the information useful, educational, and beneficial. The book covers many aspects of Linux, not all of which you will care about. However, we set out to create the most complete introduction to Linux that we could, and we think we've accomplished that task.

Enjoy!

Kamran Husain and Tim Parker

Conventions Used in This Book

The following typographic conventions are used in this book:

- Code lines, commands, statements, variables, and any text you type or see on the screen appears in a `computer` typeface. When lines of input and output are shown together, **bold computer** typeface is often used to show the user's input.

- Placeholders in syntax descriptions appear in an *italic computer* typeface. Replace the placeholder with the actual filename, parameter, or whatever element it represents.

- *Italics* highlight technical terms when they first appear in the text and are sometimes used to emphasize important points.

- Pseudocode, a way of explaining in English what a program does, also appears in *italics.*

- A special icon ➥ is used before a line of code that is really a continuation of the preceding line. Sometimes a line of code is too long to fit as a single line in the book, given the book's limited width. If you see the ➥ before a line of code, remember that you should interpret that "line" as part of the line immediately before it.

Introduction

PART

I

Introduction to Linux

1

*by Kamran
Husain and
Tim Parker*

Welcome to Linux.

This book is about Linux, a clone of the UNIX operating system that runs on machines with an Intel 80386 processor or better, as well as Intel-compatible CPUs, such as AMD and Cyrix.

This first chapter introduces you to the major features of Linux and helps get you acquainted with them. It does not go into great detail or cover any advanced topics, as this is done in later chapters. Instead, it is intended to give you a head start in understanding what Linux is, what Linux offers you, and what you need to run it.

Don't be afraid to experiment. The system won't bite you. You can't destroy anything by working on it. UNIX has some amount of security built in, to prevent "normal" users (the role you will now assume) from damaging files that are essential to the system. The absolute worst thing that can happen is that you'll delete all of your files and have to go back and reinstall the system. So, at this point, you have nothing to lose.

One word of caution when reading this chapter: At times it will delve into topics that may seem very alien to you, especially if you are new to UNIX and Linux. Don't despair. As you go through this book, you will become more and more familiar with the topics introduced here. Linux is not an easy system to pick up in one day, so don't try to do it. There is no substitute for experience, so relax and learn Linux at your own pace.

What This Book Is Not

This book makes several assumptions about you, the reader. I hope we can safely assume that you have some working knowledge of PCs and Microsoft's Disk Operating System (MS-DOS). (In some Linux documentation, MS-DOS is also referred to as "messy DOS," but I'll let you be the judge of that!) If you are not familiar with DOS or computers in general, now would be a good time to pick up a book to introduce yourself to PCs. Even so, you should be able to follow this book without needing any extra material.

Some readers of this book will be familiar with UNIX. If that's the case, a lot of the early material will be familiar to you, especially when we talk about the shells. If you are new to UNIX, don't be concerned: This book was written with you in mind and should guide you through your early hesitant sessions at the console and show you everything you need to know. Pretty soon, you'll be an expert! Now, let's get started with Linux.

What Is Linux?

Linux is a free, UNIX work-alike designed for Intel processors on PC architecture machines. Linux is not UNIX, as UNIX is a copyrighted piece of software that demands license fees when any part of its source code is used. Linux was written from scratch to avoid license fees entirely, although the operation of the Linux operating system is based entirely on UNIX. It shares UNIX's command set and look-and-feel, so if you know either UNIX or Linux, you know the other, too.

Linux supports a wide range of software, from TeX (a text formatting language) to X (a graphical user interface) to the GNU C/C++ compilers to TCP/IP networking. Linux is also compliant with the POSIX.1 standard, so porting applications between Linux and UNIX systems is a snap.

New users of UNIX and Linux may be a bit intimidated by the size and apparent complexity of the system before them. There are many good books on using UNIX out there, for all levels of expertise ranging from novice to expert. However, few (if any) of these books cover, specifically, the topic of using Linux. Although 95 percent of using Linux is exactly like using other UNIX systems, the most straightforward way to get going on your new system is with a book tailored for Linux (such as this one, amazingly enough!).

How to Pronounce Linux

Pronouncing the word *Linux* is one of the great controversies of the Linux world. Americans pronounce the proper name Linus with a long *i* sound, as in *style*. However, because Linux was originally based on a small, PC-based implementation of UNIX called *Minix* (pronounced with a short *i*), the actual pronunciation of Linux preserves this characteristic: It's officially pronounced "LIH nucks."

Linux Versus UNIX

UNIX is a trademark of X/Open. Linux is not a trademark, and has no connection to the trademark UNIX or X/Open.

UNIX is one of the most popular operating systems worldwide because of its large support base and distribution. It was originally developed as a multitasking system for minicomputers and mainframes in the mid-1970s, but it has since grown to become one of the most widely used operating systems anywhere, despite its sometimes confusing interface and lack of central standardization.

UNIX is a multitasking, multiuser operating system. This means that there can be many people using one computer at the same time, running many different applications. (This differs from MS-DOS, where only one person can use the system at any one time.)

Under UNIX, for users to identify themselves to the system, they must log in, which entails two steps: Entering your login name (the name by which the system identifies you), and entering your password, which is your personal secret key to logging in to your account. Because only you know your password, no one else can log in to the system under your username.

In addition, each UNIX system has a hostname assigned to it. It is this hostname that gives your machine a name, gives it character, class, and charm. The hostname is used to identify individual machines on a network, but even if your machine isn't networked, it should have a hostname.

Versions of UNIX exist for many systems, ranging from personal computers to supercomputers. Most versions of UNIX for personal computers are quite expensive and cumbersome. Where does Linux fit in? Well, Linux is free (solves the expensive part), very powerful, and easy to install and maintain by an individual (so much for the cumbersome part).

What Do I Get with a Linux System?

Linux is a freely distributable version of UNIX developed primarily by Linus Torvalds at the University of Helsinki in Finland. Linux was further developed with the help of many UNIX programmers and wizards across the Internet, allowing anyone with enough know-how and gumption to hack a custom UNIX kernel the ability to develop and change the system.

UNIX and its clones have long been perceived as large, resource-hungry, disk-devouring systems. Linux is not such a beast. It is small, fast, and flexible.

Linux has been publicly available since around November of 1991. v0.10 went out in November of 1991, v0.11 in December of 1991. There are very few small bugs now, and in its current state Linux is mostly useful for people who are willing to port code and write new code. Because Linux is very close to a reliable and stable system, Linus decided that v0.13 will be known as v0.95.

So what are some of the important features of Linux that make it so unique? Here are a few:

- **Full multitasking and 32-bit support.** Linux, like all other versions of UNIX, is a real multitasking system, allowing multiple users to run many programs on the same system at once. Linux is also a full 32-bit operating system, utilizing the special protected-mode features of Intel 80386 and later processors and their work-alikes.

- **The X Window System.** The X Window System is the *de facto* industry-standard graphics system for UNIX machines. A complete version of the X Window System, known as XFree86, is available for Linux. The X Window System is a very powerful graphics interface, supporting many applications.

- **TCP/IP (Transmission Control Protocol/Internet Protocol) support.** This is the set of protocols that links millions of university and business computers into a worldwide network known as the Internet. With an Ethernet connection, you can have access to the Internet or to a local area network from your Linux system. Using SLIP (Serial Line Internet Protocol) or PPP (Point to Point Protocol), you can access the Internet over phone lines with a modem.

- **Virtual memory and shared libraries.** Linux can use a portion of your hard drive as virtual memory, expanding your total amount of available RAM. Linux also implements shared libraries, allowing programs that use standard subroutines to find the code for these subroutines in the libraries at runtime. This saves a large amount of space on your system; each application doesn't store its own copy of these common routines.

■ **The Linux kernel uses no code from AT&T or any other proprietary source.** Much of the software available for Linux is free. In fact, a large number of utilities in Linux are developed by the GNU project at the Free Software Foundation in Cambridge, Massachusetts. However, Linux enthusiasts, hackers, programmers, and recently even commercial companies from all over the world have contributed to the growing pool of Linux software.

■ **Linux supports (almost) all of the features of commercial versions of UNIX.** In fact, some of the features found in Linux may not be available on other proprietary UNIX systems.

■ **GNU software support.** Linux supports a wide range of free software written by the GNU Project, including utilities such as the GNU C and C++ compiler, `gawk`, `groff`, and so on. Many of the essential system utilities used by Linux are GNU software.

■ **Linux is compatible with the IEEE POSIX.1 standard.** Linux has been developed with software portability in mind, thus supporting many important features of other UNIX standards.

■ **Virtual memory support.** Linux utilizes all of your system's memory, without memory limits or segmentation through the use of a virtual memory manager.

■ **Built-in support for networking, multitasking, and other features.** You'll see this touted as "New Technology" in systems such as Windows NT. In fact, UNIX (and now, Linux) has implemented this "new technology" for more than 15 years.

■ **Linux is cheaper to get than most commercially available UNIX systems and UNIX clones.** If you have the patience and access to the Internet, the only price you pay for Linux is your time. Linux is freely available on the Internet. For a nominal fee of anywhere from US $30 to US $90, you can save yourself some time and get CD-ROM or floppy-disk distributions from several commercial vendors (or from this book).

Arguably, the most important advantage of using Linux is that you get to work with an honest-to-goodness kernel. All of the kernel source code is available for Linux, and you have the ability to modify it to suit your needs. Looking at the kernel code is an educational experience in itself.

Undoubtedly, the development of Linux has been so rapid because of the availability of the source code. Also, with an ever-expanding group of hackers who want to get their hands dirty with their own system, Linux has grown steadily into the fully packed operating system that it is today.

> **NOTE**
>
> Linux uses the Intel 80386 chip's protected mode-functions extensively, and is a true 32-bit operating system. CPUs before the 80386 will not run Linux as they lack protected modes.

The Downside of Linux and the Reason for This Book

Linux is a hacker's project, written by a multitude of gifted programmers for the sheer joy of programming and sharing the code. This hacker attitude can be a daunting experience for someone not familiar with UNIX, and its side effects are sometimes noticed quite easily (such as a lack of documentation, obtuse commands, and dependencies on other programs that are not clear). Luckily, there is little problem with stable Linux software because it has been worked on by many people; it's the early releases of new software that tend to show these holes.

Help with Linux is generally not a phone call away as it is with a commercial version of UNIX. You can get help from the Internet newsgroups and other members of the Linux community via e-mail. However, when it's midnight and your system just won't boot like the README file said it would, you do feel a sense of despair.

There is a huge distinction between commercial versions of UNIX and Linux: Commercial versions of UNIX are designed for customers and will work out of the box, whereas Linux is not guaranteed to work at all on your system. You are indeed on your own.

Actually, the only problem for new users is a lack of basic UNIX system-administrative knowledge. Setting up and running your own UNIX system is something most UNIX users never get to do, even after years of experience. Yes, you get to do it yourself, but it ain't that easy. You might actually consider being nice to your local UNIX system administrator after installing Linux for the first time.

Here are some other parts of Linux that you should be warned about:

- Some of the features on your favorite UNIX system may not be available for your Linux system. Your choice in this matter is to either write the application yourself, convince someone else to write it, or find an alternative process (the easiest out in most cases).

- As with software, some of the hardware in your machine may not be supported by Linux. Again, your choices are to either write the driver software yourself or get it from somewhere else.

■ You do have to spend some time and effort managing your Linux machine. You do develop a knack for fixing problems from experience. However, only with experience can you learn to recognize common problems and find or develop solutions.

Even with standard Linux distributions, there are sometimes little quirks that need to be fixed by hand in order for everything to work correctly. If you have previous UNIX experience, it should be easy to find these problems. However, if you're new to UNIX, it would serve you well to read up on using and running a UNIX system before you dive in.

To reiterate, Linux isn't for everyone. Many users can get in over their heads when starting with Linux. To keep your head above water, I strongly encourage you to find a good book on using UNIX system administration.

About Linux's Copyright

Ah, yes—that old topic of copyrights. Compared to death and taxes, Linux copyrights are a mere annoyance.

Actually, Linux is copyrighted under the GNU General Public License, sometimes called the GPL or copyleft. (Note the *left* instead of *right*.) This copyleft license was developed by the Free Software Foundation to enable programmers to write "free software," where "free" refers to freedom, not just cost. The GPL provides for the protection of such free software in a number of ways:

■ It allows the original author to retain the software's copyright.

■ It allows others to take the software and modify it, or even base other programs on it.

■ It allows others to redistribute or resell the software, or modified versions of the software. Note that you can even resell the software for profit. However, in reselling or redistributing the software, you cannot restrict any of these rights from the party you're selling it to.

> **NOTE**
>
> Also, if you sell the software, you have to be able to provide at no cost the full source code so that others can modify the software and resell it if they wish. You cannot hold back the source of your modifications.

The original authors of the Linux software may never see a dime of these revenues. This is allowed by the GNU GPL because the point of free software isn't to make money. This is simply an understanding between the authors of the software and those using or selling it.

One other thing: Free software, as covered by the GNU GPL (which includes Linux), comes with absolutely no warranty. However, individual vendors may provide support for the software, which usually includes a warranty. Unless you purchased such support, the assumption is that the software comes with no such warranty, and if you use a piece of free software that goes haywire and wipes everything on your system, neither the authors nor those who distributed the software to you are liable.

Free software as covered by the GPL is not shareware, nor is it in the public domain. Neither of these terms correctly describes what free software really is. The complete GNU GPL is printed in Appendix E, "Copyright Information." To sum it all up, you can freely distribute Linux as much as you like, and you can even modify it and distribute your own version of Linux. But in doing so, you can't take away those rights from others. In short, you must attribute the original authors of the work.

> **CAUTION**
>
> Please note that there are absolutely no warranties with any of the software you get with Linux. If an application goes awry and wipes your disk, you have no one's neck to wring. Unless someone explicitly gives you a warranty in writing on their software, do not assume any warranty whatsoever for anything other than what is explicitly written in the warranties.

Hardware Requirements

Now that you know a little about the good and bad points of Linux, let's see what's required in terms of hardware.

Unlike some other versions of UNIX for the PC, Linux is very small. You can run an entire system from a single, high-density 5.25-inch floppy. However, to run a complete Linux system, there are other hardware requirements.

Linux, by its very nature, is continuously expanding, and more features are added every day. However, hardware compatibility is limited to that hardware the developers themselves have access to. For instance, if none of the Linux developers has access to the WhizBang Slice-O-Matic T3222 Ethernet card from a no-name manufacturer, then chances are it isn't supported.

On the other hand, there are many generic drivers for hardware, such as the IDE disk driver, which should work with all IDE hard drives and adapters regardless of manufacturer. Of course, the developers of the drivers couldn't test their software against every IDE device on the market, so they assume the IDE standards are followed by manufacturers. If a device doesn't work, it's probably because the manufacturer deviated from the standards, or added features the generic drivers can't handle.

A good place to look on the CD-ROM is in the /docs/howto directory for the Hardware-HOWTO file. This file will list a lot of the supported hardware for Linux.

If your favorite peripheral isn't supported by Linux, all that's required is to write a kernel driver for it. This may be easy or difficult, depending on the hardware and the technical specifications that are available. For example, some hardware developers prefer to write their own drivers for MS-DOS and Windows, and not release specifications for third parties to write their own. Therefore, writing drivers for Linux will be difficult, if not impossible.

The following is a rough guideline of some hardware requirements for Linux. You do not have to follow them directly, but this list should give you a rough idea of what's required:

> **TIP**
>
> If you're in the market for a new system, you should heed the following recommendations.

- An Intel 80386 or better CPU (the faster and more powerful the better, of course). You don't need a math coprocessor, although it's strongly recommended as it speeds up a lot of graphics operations, especially under X. If you have an 80386 chip, 80387 math coprocessors are available separately and are installed in a socket on your motherboard. If you have a 80486 processor, the math coprocessor is on the 486 chip itself. (The exception is the 80486SX, which is a 486 chip without the coprocessor components.) Pentium and Pentium Pro CPUs have the coprocessor built in.

  If you don't have a math coprocessor, the Linux kernel will emulate floating-point math for you. If you do have one, however, floating-point math will be handled by the hardware, which for some applications is a real plus.

- Your system must be either an ISA, EISA, PCI, or local bus architecture machine. These terms specify how the CPU communicates with hardware, and are a characteristic of your motherboard. Most existing systems use the ISA bus architecture.

> **NOTE**
>
> MicroChannel architecture (MCA) machines, such as the IBM PS/2 line, are *not* currently supported.

- At least 4MB of RAM.

  Memory is speed, so if you have more RAM you'll thank yourself for it later. If you're a power user, 8MB should be more than enough for most applications. If you want to run X Window, your system will require at least 8MB of RAM.

- A hard drive with space available for installing Linux. The amount of space required depends on the amount of software you're installing and how much free space you wish to leave yourself. You can install Linux in very small amounts of disk space, but a realistic minimum is about 150MB. For a full system with X and development tools, much more is required. The complete installation can use up 250MB, with more useful for data files.

- A Hercules, CGA, EGA, VGA, or Super VGA video card and monitor. In general, if your video card and monitor work under MS-DOS or Microsoft Windows, then Linux should be able to use them without any problem. However, if you're going to use the X Window system (either Metro-X or Xfree86), some video configurations are not supported.

Other Hardware Requirements

Linux will also run on a number of laptop machines (some laptops use certain software interrupts to power the memory, and Linux doesn't work well with these systems to date). The best way to find out if Linux will run on your hardware is just to try it out.

> **NOTE**
>
> At the time of writing, Linux doesn't run on an IBM PS/2 computer. Stay tuned to the Internet for details.

There are other hardware drivers currently under development for Linux. To use these drivers, however, you usually have to patch them into your kernel code, which assumes that you already have a running Linux system (a kind of chicken-and-egg problem if you have not already installed Linux). In such cases, you can install whatever Linux you happen to have and then apply the patches with the Linux `patch` command.

Then there is the issue of tape drives for Linux. There is a working QIC-02 device driver for Linux, supporting Everex/Wangtek cards. There are additional patches for the QIC-02 to support Archive SC402/499R. You can find them in `/pub/linux/alpha/qic-02` directory at `tsx-11.mit.edu` server. (There have been reports of some bugs in the driver, but you can back up and restore.)

Most of the newer tape drivers are all for SCSI drives, so if you have a SCSI tape drive, chances are that it is supported.

Special Requirements for X

Your 4MB of RAM will make X run very slowly. You should have at least 8MB of RAM for running programs in X. You will need another 6MB to 10MB of disk space for the GCC compiler in addition to X if you want to develop applications for X.

CAUTION

Do not try to bring up an Xserver that does not support your hardware. There have been cases where damage has resulted from pushing the monitor (especially fixed-frequency monitors) beyond its capabilities.

As far as mice go, Linux supports both serial and Bus varieties. For the serial mice, you can use Logitech, Microsoft, MouseSystems, or compatibles. The following Bus mice are known to work: Logitech, Microsoft, ATI_XL, and PS/2 (aux).

There you have it, a brief introduction to an operating system that could very well change the way you program. Now for getting yourself ready for Linux.

Before You Get Started

Assuming that you have hardware compatible with Linux, obtaining and installing the system is not difficult. But be prepared to be a bit frustrated at first, if you are new to UNIX or Linux. The two best defenses against frustration with using Linux are the following:

1. Get organized.
2. Educate yourself about Linux and UNIX.

TIP

Experience with my bad memory has forced me to keep an indexed log of all the bugs, quirks, and symptoms in Linux. I have a dog-eared notebook of all the weird features of Linux.

Summary

In this chapter we learned about Linux and some of its more prominent features:

- UNIX is a trademark of X/Open. Linux is not a trademark, and has no connection to the trademark UNIX or X/Open.
- Linux is designed to run on Intel 80386 and faster CPUs and their compatibles.
- Linux has most of the UNIX-like features and applications built in to it. These features include a Virtual File System (VFS), networking, multitasking and multiuser capabilities along with a host of applications such as Xfree86, Metro-X, TeX, and the GNU utilities.
- You will learn a lot about operating systems when working with Linux.

- Linux is copyrighted under the GNU copyleft agreement. See Appendix E for the complete text.

- The hardware requirements for Linux include at least an 80386 processor, a minimum of 100MB of disk space, 4MB of RAM and a 3.5-inch floppy drive.

- The more memory you have, the faster Linux will run.

- The swap space on Linux is an area on the disk used by Linux as a scratch area when working with lots of processes.

- You will need 8MB of RAM to get X Window to run with an acceptable degree of performance.

- You will need to educate yourself a little on Linux and UNIX before you start the installation procedure. This is especially important if you are new to UNIX.

- There are several ways of finding help on topics in Linux: The Linux Documentation Project, via FAQs, INFO-SHEETS, and from the files on the CD-ROM itself.

- The `Hardware-HOWTO` document contains a lot of information about all the devices supported by Linux.

- It's best to check the Linux Hardware Compatibility List on the CD-ROM before starting your installation process or buying anything for your PC.

Types of Linux Available

2

by Kamran Husain and Tim Parker

This chapter covers the many types of Linux systems and distributions available. I strongly recommend that you read this chapter at least once before starting the installation process. Included in this chapter are the following topics:

- The various distribution types in Linux
- The types of disk sets for each distribution
- Which distribution sets are important for you
- How to look for files on the CD-ROM
- How to get Linux from FTP sites
- How to get Linux from BBS sites
- How to find FTP sites where you can get Linux updates

Linux Releases

There are many independent releases of Linux, each with its own list of unique features. Some of these releases are available free of charge if you have access to the Internet. Some releases are available for a nominal fee ($20 to $90) for distribution on CD-ROM or disks. Typically, the CD-ROM versions are cheaper and are easier to use than the floppy-disk distributions because the cost of one CD-ROM is less than the cost of 30 or more floppy disks. Another plus for the CD-ROM is the convenience of having everything on one source media. It beats swapping disks!

What's a Linux Release?

A Linux *release* is a set of files for a complete Linux system. Various changes made by the Linux community are incorporated into each release.

Linux releases are identified by numbers. These numbers are of the form *X.YY.ZZ*, where *X* is between 0 and 9, and *YY* and *ZZ* are numbers between 0 and 99. Generally, the higher the number, the newer the release. Some release numbers also include *pNN*, where *NN* is a number between 1 and 20. These refer to patches to a specific Linux version (a *patch* is a fix or an update to the software). For example, 0.99p15 would mean the fifteenth patch to the Linux release 0.99.

A release consists of several components called *series of disks*, or a collection of disks. For example, the X series of disks comes on 10 disks. Each series is referred to by its name. A name generally tells you who put the software together and what its date is.

Some of the releases of Linux are as follows:

- *The Red Hat Software Inc. Release*

  This is a release of Linux from Red Hat Software Inc. The latest version is 3.0.3, which is included on the CD-ROM at the back of this book.

The highlight of the installation package is the Red Hat Packet Manager (RPM). Using the RPM enables you to safely install and uninstall packages. By far, the uninstall capability of the package is the best feature because most upgrades to critical packages require a complete Linux installation. Red Hat Linux is also notable for the ability to install from an X session, assuming the video card and monitor are supported by Linux.

■ *Slackware*

This is a popular release of Linux included with this book's sister books: *Linux Unleashed Second Edition* and *Linux System Administrator's Survival Guide.* You can get versions of this release on CD-ROM from various vendors for about $25.

The primary distributor for this release is Patrick Volkerding, who can be reached at `volkerdi@mhdl.moorhead.msus.edu`.

■ *The Softlanding Linux System Release (SLS)*

This release consists of about 23 disks for Linux and 10 for X11. The first disk (`a1`) must be "rawritten" (using `rawrite.exe` in Chapter 3, "Installing and Updating Linux") on floppies, and the rest of the images must be put onto DOS-formatted floppies using the DOS `copy` command. This release contains all the software package(s) you need to get started with Linux, and for newcomers it is easy to install.

The SLS release can also be found at `tsx-11.mit.edu` in the directory `/pub/linux/packages/SLS` and on `sunsite.unc.edu` in the directory `/pub/Linux/SLS`. By snail mail, SLS is available from

Softlanding Software
910 Lodge Ave.
Victoria, B.C.
Canada V8X-3A8
(604) 360-0188

■ *The TAMU (Texas A&M University) Linux Release*

This release is supposedly like the SLS release, but it has some different software packages and a different installation procedure than SLS. The installation procedure is the main difference from SLS. A single boot diskette, which boots directly into an automated installation program, is used. This installation program asks a few questions about the desired configuration and sets up everything, including your file systems, booting from the hard drive with LILO (see Chapter 5, "Odds and Ends") and a simplified X configuration.

This release is a full-featured package, including X Window, `emacs`, networking tools, boot utilities, and a list of sources for all installation programs without any use restrictions. TAMU is available from `sc.tamu.edu` in `pub/free_unix4`.

■ *H.J. Lu's bootable rootdisk*

This is a release of the Linux kernel and basic binaries on a single floppy. It, along with Lu's `gccdisk`, `libdisk`, and so on, is good for upgrading or installing a basic

Linux system by hand. It's not recommended for newcomers, because there's no real install script; it's mostly meant as an upgrade of the basic system software.

H.J. Lu's bootable rootdisk release is found at `tsx-11.mit.edu:` in the directory `/pub/linux/packages/GCC`.

■ *The Manchester Computing Centre Interim Release*

This is the fabled MCC-Interim Linux release, which was originally the *de facto* standard Linux distribution. This release has almost all of the important Linux software, such as Slackware, but does not contain `emacs` or X Window.

MCC-Interim can be found on `sunsite.unc.edu` in the directory `/pub/Linux/distributions/MCC` and also at `ftp.mcc.ac.uk` in the directory `/pub/linux/mcc-interim`.

■ *Trans-Ameritech*

This is available only on CD-ROM. The CD-ROM offers a complete, uncompressed, bootable Linux file system. This feature has two distinct advantages: You have instant access to the file of your choice without having to uncompress or unzip any archives, and it saves the disk space that you would use uncompressing these archives.

The CD-ROM is based on the Slackware distribution of Linux with all the source code, an uncompressed file system, and NetBSD source and binary distribution.

To minimize the possibility of hardware conflicts, many extra kernels are provided for different configurations. They are usable for installation and normal use. Many online documents are provided for quick reference, including the Linux Documentation Project files in `source`, `dvi`, and `ps` formats. This distribution also includes the FlexFax, a package that enables you to send and receive faxes on either class 1 or class 2 fax modems.

To help first-time Linux users, many of the provided documentation files are readable from DOS even before Linux is installed.

All source files for Linux are available on the CD-ROM. The most often needed source code files are uncompressed and can be used directly from the CD-ROM. An uncompressed Linux file system is available for reference and disk-space conservation. You can run programs directly from the CD-ROM. There is a large information directory, including many man pages, for online reference.

For a hacker's reference, an uncompressed FreeBSD source tree is provided. You can order by phone (408) 727-3883, or e-mail at `roman@trans-am.com`.

■ *The Linux Support Team Erlang Distribution (LST)*

This release is for you if you speak German. The menus, manuals, and installation instructions are in German. You can get this release from `ftp.uni-erlangen.de` under `/pub/Linux/LST.distribution`.

■ *Yggdrasil Plug-and-Play Linux*

This is a complete CD-ROM distribution of the Linux operating system. It includes a great deal of software covering nearly every package that you would expect to find on a complete UNIX system. A complete file list is available via FTP from `yggdrasil.com`.

They also offer The Linux Bible, a full library of Linux and UNIX documentation, including three books from the Linux Documentation Project, their Yggdrasil installation manual, and the complete set of Linux HOWTO guides.

Yggdrasil's Plug-and-Play Linux is named for *plug-and-play operation,* which means that you can place a floppy in drive A, turn the computer on, and answer all the questions. That's all there is to installation. The reality is a little more complicated, because you have to know whether your hardware is compatible before you begin.

The login screen lists a number of preconfigured usernames, including `install`, which installs the system, giving paragraphs of explanation about every question it asks the user.

The `install` script even searches for a modem, and upon finding it, configures mail and UUCP so that mail sent to an Internet address is transparently delivered through a bulletin-board system at Yggdrasil. Some people might not like this, so don't say that I didn't warn you!

The X Window configuration is automated, too, with forms to fill in as you run X for the first time, as well as a graphical control panel that enables additional forms for configuration of networking, SLIP, outgoing UUCP, the printer, and so on. You can call them, toll-free, in the U.S. at (800) 261-6630 or e-mail them at `info@ygg-drasil.com`.

Yggdrasil Computing, Incorporated
4880 Stevens Creek Blvd., Suite 205
San Jose, CA 95129-1034

■ *InfoMagic Developer's Resource CD-ROM Kit*

This is a complete snapshot of the `sunsite.unc.edu` and `tsx-11.mit.edu` archives. It also includes the complete GNU software collection (in source form). The following Linux distributions are included on the discs: Slackware, Debian, SLS, TAMU, MCC, and JE (Japanese Extensions).

The Linux HOWTO documents have been formatted for use with the Microsoft Multimedia Viewer (which is included) to allow browsing and full text search under Microsoft Windows. You can contact them at (800) 800-6613 or via e-mail at `Orders@InfoMagic.com`.

The contents of the CDs can also be found at the site `InfoMagic.com` in the directory `/pub/Linux` or `ftp.uu.net` in the directory `/vendor/InfoMagic/cd-roms/linux`.

There you have it. This list of locations where you can get Linux from is incomplete. In fact, I should apologize to the folks whose company names didn't get listed here. There was not enough time for me to fully review all the distributions before this book went to press. If you would like a more complete list, please look at the newsgroups `comp.os.linux.announce` and `comp.os.linux.misc`.

The document `Distribution-HOWTO` is archived on a number of Linux FTP sites, including `sunsite.unc.edu` in `pub/Linux/docs/HOWTO`.

Other Linux Information Sources

If you like magazines, you will love *The Linux Journal*, a monthly publication covering the Linux community. Most material in *LJ* is new (that is, derived from a bunch of USENET newsgroup topics). Each issue includes columns and articles on Linux programming, GNU, Free Software Foundation issues, systems administration, questions and answers, interviews, and more. This is a darn good magazine. You can reach the publishers at

> *Linux Journal*
> P.O. Box 85867
> Seattle, WA 98145-1867
> (206) 527-3385

If you want to keep up-to-date with the latest releases of Linux, try to get quarterly updates to your Linux system via a subscription to Morse Telecommunication, Inc.'s *Linux Quarterly CD-ROM*. Each CD contains the complete contents of `tsx-11.mit.edu`. This is one of the most popular Internet Linux sites. It provides both source and binary files of major Linux distributions, utilities, source code, and documentation. This quarterly update includes Slackware, SLS, MCC, and Debian releases of Linux. Get information through e-mail from `order@morse.net`.

Lastly, the Linux Systems Labs (`dirvin@vela.acs.oakland.edu`) can also provide commercial software for Linux, including manuals, database applications, and other applications software not in the shareware or public domain. You can contact Linux Systems Labs at (800) 432-0556.

Finding Linux Updates on the Internet

As I mentioned previously, a CD-ROM is not the only place for you to get Linux or information about Linux. After all, you might not have a CD-ROM reader. If you don't, you aren't out of luck. You can still get Linux goodies from the Internet sites in the following listing. The catch is that you have to be on the Internet.

So, you may well ask, why am I showing you how to get Linux from the Internet when you already have it on a CD? Well, some of the files on the CD might be different a year from now. In fact, some of the locations you see listed here might be different, too. By showing you how to find out more, you can use the `archie` method at a later time to locate updates to Linux and more information easily.

If you want to learn more about the Internet and `archie`, read *The Internet Unleashed* (Sams Publishing, 1994).

I used the `telnet` program to log into `archie.internic.net`, a good site from which to use the `archie` program. The `archie` program is a searching utility for locating files on the Internet by specifying keywords. I logged in with the name `archie` and didn't have to provide a password. (See Listing 2.1.)

The `archie>` prompt is where I issued the `find Linux` command. The `search type of sub` means that we'll ask `archie` to search for all strings in its database with the word *Linux* anywhere in it.

The output from Listing 2.1 shows only a few files. I have edited it to fit in the book. Your listing won't match.

Listing 2.1. Using `archie` to find Linux.

```
$ telnet archie.internic.net
...
login: archie

********************************************************************

        Welcome to the InterNIC Directory and Database Server.

********************************************************************
# Bunyip Information Systems, 1993, 1994

# Terminal type set to 'vt100 24 80'.
# 'erase' character is '^?'.
# 'search' (type string) has the value 'sub'.
archie> find Linux
# Search type: sub.
# Your queue position: 1
# Estimated time for completion: 16 seconds.
working...

Host unix.hensa.ac.uk    (129.12.43.16)
Last updated 23:37 22 Nov 1994

    Location: /pub/sunsite/pub
        DIRECTORY    drwxr-xr-x    1024 bytes  21:32 16 Nov 1994  Linux


Host unix.hensa.ac.uk    (129.12.43.16)
Last updated 23:37 22 Nov 1994

    Location: /pub/walnut.creek/XFree86/binaries
        DIRECTORY    drwxr-xr-x    1536 bytes  20:26 13 Nov 1994  Linux
```

continues

Listing 2.1. continued

```
Host romulus.ucs.uoknor.edu     (129.15.10.20)
Last updated 18:31 16 Nov 1994

    Location: /
        FILE    -rwxrwxrwx      13 bytes  15:05 12 Nov 1994  Linux

Host ftp.germany.eu.net    (192.76.144.75)
Last updated 23:39  6 Nov 1994

    Location: /pub/os
        DIRECTORY    drwxrwxr-x     512 bytes  01:44  5 Nov 1994  Linux

Host csc.canberra.edu.au    (137.92.1.1)
Last updated 03:23  6 Nov 1994

    Location: /pub/ise
        DIRECTORY    drwxr-xr-x    1024 bytes  18:49 31 Oct 1994  Linux

Host power.ci.uv.es    (147.156.1.3)
Last updated 21:12 23 Nov 1994

    Location: /pub/linux/docs/faqs
        FILE    -r--r--r--  96319 bytes  16:25 30 Oct 1994  Linux-FAQ


Host ftp.ncsa.uiuc.edu    (141.142.20.50)
Last updated 20:06 11 Nov 1994

    Location: /HDF/contrib
        DIRECTORY    drwxrwxr-x     512 bytes  01:02 30 Oct 1994  Linux
[24;1H[K:[24;1H[24;1H[K

Host romulus.ucs.uoknor.edu    (129.15.10.20)
Last updated 18:31 16 Nov 1994

    Location: /mirrors/Linux/docs/faqs
        FILE    -rwxrwxrwx      15 bytes  00:56 30 Oct 1994  Linux-FAQ

Host monu1.cc.monash.edu.au    (130.194.1.101)
Last updated 21:27 17 Oct 1994

    Location: /pub/linux/docs/faqs
        FILE    -rw-r--r--  96568 bytes  23:39 21 Sep 1994  Linux-FAQ


Host dutiws.twi.tudelft.nl    (130.161.156.11)
Last updated 03:10 23 Nov 1994

    Location: /pub
        DIRECTORY    drwxrwxr-x     512 bytes  10:31 29 Aug 1994  Linux


Host telva.ccu.uniovi.es    (156.35.31.31)
Last updated 22:27 23 Nov 1994
```

```
        Location: /uniovi/mathdept/src
            DIRECTORY     drwxr-xr-x     1024 bytes   10:36 28 Jul 1994   Linux


    Host neptune.ethz.ch     (129.132.101.33)
    Last updated 17:38 15 Nov 1994

        Location: /pub/Oberon
            DIRECTORY     drwxrwxr-x      512 bytes   07:31 22 Jul 1994   Linux


    Host ftp.germany.eu.net     (192.76.144.75)
    Last updated 23:39  6 Nov 1994

        Location: /pub/os/Linux/Local.EUnet/Kernel/Linus/net-source
            DIRECTORY     drwxr-xr-x      512 bytes   04:23 19 Jul 1994   Linux


archie> find LDP
# Search type: sub.
# Your queue position: 1
# Estimated time for completion: 16 seconds.
working...

Host hpcsos.col.hp.com     (15.255.240.16)
Last updated 18:49 13 Nov 1994

        Location: /mirrors/.scsi0/linux/docs
            FILE      -rwxr-xr-x       17 bytes   20:42  4 Nov 1994   LDP


Host romulus.ucs.uoknor.edu     (129.15.10.20)
Last updated 18:31 16 Nov 1994

        Location: /mirrors/Linux/docs
            FILE      -rwxrwxrwx       17 bytes   23:14 24 Oct 1994   LDP


Host mcsun.eu.net     (192.16.202.2)
Last updated 20:32 10 Nov 1994

        Location: /os/linux/doc
            FILE      -rwxrwxrwx       12 bytes   14:22 18 Sep 1994   LDP

archie>quit
```

Common Extensions for Filenames

Table 2.1 is a list of common filename extensions for the files you will see in Linux archives. The fname in the following table implies the filename with which you want to work.

Table 2.1. File extensions used in Linux releases.

Extension	Used By
.Z	compress/uncompress. Use uncompress *fname* foo.Z to uncompress the file, where *fname* is the name of the file that was uncompressed.
.z, .gz gzip.	gzip is now used by many archive sites instead of compress. If you don't have gzip on your system, get it! To uncompress one of these files, use gzip -d *fname*.z. .gz is the new gzip extension.
.tar	Tar file. Use tar xvf *fname*.tar to unpack it. Or you can use tar tvf *fname*.tar to get an index listing of the tar file.
.taz	Compressed tar file. You can do something such as zcat *fname*.taz ¦ tar xvf - or tar xvfz *fname*.taz to unpack it (some versions of tar don't have the z option).
.tpz, .tgz	gzipped tar file. If you have gzip, zcat is linked to it, so you can do zcat foo.tpz ¦ tar xvf to unpack it.
.tpz	The old extension. All gzipped tar files should now end in .tgz instead.

Most distributions use gzipped tar files with the tgz extension.

Obtaining Linux from BBSs

A *bulletin board system* (BBS) enables you to transfer messages and files via your phone line. All you need is a computer with communications software and a modem. Some BBSs transfer messages among each other, forming large computer networks similar to USENET. The most popular of these in the U.S. are FidoNet and RIME.

Linux is available from various BBSs worldwide. Some of the BBSs on FidoNet carry comp.os.linux as a FidoNet conference.

> **NOTE**
>
> While you are installing Linux, you might get the error You may have inserted the wrong disk when you insert the next disk in a series.
>
> Each disk has a small file on it that contains the name of the disk. For example, the SLS a3 disk has a file on it called diska3. If it doesn't exist, or is named something else (such as diska3.z), create it or rename it. If you copied the files to the SLS floppies using copy *.*, you probably missed the diska3 file because it doesn't have an extension in the filename.

Also, the last disk in a series (for example, the a4 or b5 disk) has a file on it called `install.end`. You need this file as well. These files are used by the installation programs to keep track of when to stop installing a package.

Accessing DOS Files from Linux

Linux supports several features that you can use to access your DOS files from Linux. With the `mtools` package, included with most distributions of Linux, you can use commands such as `mcopy` and `mdir` to access your DOS files. Another option is to mount a DOS partition or floppy directly under Linux, which gives you direct access to your files by way of the DOS file system.

You will find the `mtools` package indispensable if you have to swap files between DOS and Linux. When you first start Linux from a DOS machine, it's comforting to know that you can transfer files easily between two machines that are running different operating systems, so don't worry; you will not have to give up your familiar DOS environment.

Why use `mtools` if you can just mount a DOS drive? `mtools` is good if you want to do something quickly—for example, if you want to get directories on a bunch of floppies. The mount procedure requires you to mount the drive, get a directory, and then `umount` it. With `mtools` you can get the directory with one command.

`mtools` also comes with the Slackware release of Linux and is available in source-code form on most Linux FTP sites. This `mtools` source tree can prove to be interesting reading, especially if you are a programmer.

There is also DOS Emulator available for Linux, and work is beginning on a Microsoft Windows emulator to run under the X Window system. The DOS Emulator isn't perfect, so don't expect to play DOOM on it—Dosemu is still in the development stages. You can use it to run some standard applications such as WordPerfect 5.1, Quicken, and Lotus 1-2-3. At the time I wrote this, Dosemu was slow and crashed frequently. However, you can work with it for some quick tasks.

Summary

This chapter has given you a whirlwind tour of what's actually available for Linux. You also learned about Linux releases and how to interpret the release numbers. Each Linux release consists of several disk sets. Some of these files in a disk set are just labels, and some are called packages. A *package* is generally a compressed tar archive containing binary files and directory trees.

Finally, for DOS fans, Linux provides a host of tools to read or write DOS disks and files. There is even an experimental DOS emulator for you to run DOS programs under Linux. Any DOS partitions can be mounted to appear as directory trees, so you can still work with your data on DOS disks.

Installing and Updating Linux

3

by Tim Parker

IN THIS CHAPTER

The process of installing Red Hat Linux is straightforward, although there are lots of little problems scattered throughout the process that can cause hassles. Red Hat Linux is much easier to install than many other versions of Linux, so you will find the installation goes quite easily. Common errors that you might make are handled nicely by the Red Hat installation program, and the system is versatile enough to handle most configuration requirements.

The essential steps for installing Red Hat Linux are as follows:

1. Create boot and root disks.
2. Boot Linux from floppies.
3. Partition the hard disk.
4. Create a swap file.
5. Create a Linux file system.
6. Install the Linux software.
7. Configure the kernel.
8. Set the boot process.
9. Reboot into Linux from your hard disk.

The process is similar whether you are installing from a CD-ROM or from a diskette (which may have come from an FTP site, for example). Because the CD-ROM is the most common form of installation (and the one included with this book), it is used as the example in this chapter.

If you are installing from a floppy and have downloaded the distribution files from an FTP site or copied them from a CD-ROM, you will need a DOS-formatted floppy for each disk in the distribution disk set. You can use standard DOS copy commands to copy the disk set files to the floppy, one floppy for each file in the distribution set. The files are all numbered so you know which floppy is in which set, and what their order should be.

Installing Red Hat Linux

Unlike some versions of Linux, Red Hat gives you a number of methods of installing its operating system that offer versatility and ease of use. For most people, installation will be a very simple task with most of the process automated by the Red Hat installation routines. Users with some special hardware or disk-layout problems will have to perform a more typical manual installation of Linux. This chapter covers all the steps you need to install Linux manually, as well as the brief instructions you need to allow an automated installation.

If you want to try an automated installation of Red Hat Linux, there are two ways to go. One is called *floppyless*, as it uses a routine on the CD-ROM to install itself. This step simply saves you the trouble of making floppy diskettes; the rest of the installation process is exactly the same.

The alternative to floppyless installation is to create boot and root floppies and use those to start up the system and access the CD-ROM. The following sections discuss both floppyless and floppy-based methods in more detail.

Floppyless Installation

If your hard disk already has an operating system like DOS, or one that produces a DOS window, you can try installing directly from the CD-ROM. Boot into your existing operating system, change to the CD-ROM drive, and issue the command

REDHAT

at the DOS prompt. You will be asked a series of questions by the program that help it determine the best images for the boot kernel. You can also provide any special startup installation commands during this stage.

> **NOTE**
>
> Do not run the floppyless installation process from inside a Windows or OS/2 session. Boot your system into DOS or DOS emulation and run it from there.

The floppyless installation routine guides you through the kernel determination process by displaying all possible choices on menus and prompting you for your answers. The process is intuitive and can be used by anyone who knows the type of hardware installed on their system. If you are not exactly sure of hardware, you can still try the floppyless installation; the worst that can happen is you must try again with different settings.

If the installation process detects some hardware-configuration issues, it may offer you advice on setting parameters or making changes. These bits of advice are, for the most part, just that: advice. You don't have to heed the advice if you don't want. In some cases, the advice makes a lot of sense (such as resolving IRQ conflicts), in which case you should take care of the issue.

Floppy-Based Installation

A floppy-based installation requires you to produce three floppies: one for the boot (kernel) image, and two for the root or swap images. The following section, entitled "Boot and Root Floppies," looks at the production of these floppies in detail. After these disks have been produced, your system is booted with the boot floppy in drive A:. After the kernel has been read and some diagnostics have been performed, you are prompted for the first of the root or swap floppies, then the second floppy, and then the installation procedure is started.

> **TIP**
>
> A quick word of advice when using floppies: Red Hat Linux is particularly sensitive to fast floppy changes. If you hit the Return key too quickly and the floppy is not in the drive, you will probably get errors and have to start the boot process all over again. This occurs when booting and Red Hat asks for the first and second swap or root floppies. Make sure the diskette is in the drive, wait a few seconds, then hit Return to prevent any problems. The disk-change process is not as forgiving as DOS or Windows!

After the boot and root floppies have been loaded, the normal Red Hat Linux installation routine is started.

The Red Hat Installation Routine: A Quick Guide

> **NOTE**
>
> This section gives you a quick overview of the installation routine and can be used by those experienced with Linux or very simple hardware setups. If you run into any problems at all during the installation process, check the more detailed sections later in this chapter.

After you have successfully loaded your boot and root images either from disk or CD-ROM, you are launched into the installation routine. The Red Hat Linux distribution has a very useful menu-driven installation routine that is much more forgiving of errors than many other Linux versions. For the most part, you need only read the screens and make logical choices to have the installation process continue properly. Many of the steps are automated and occur without your intervention.

If something happens with the automated installation routine that causes an error, a warning on the screen is displayed and you will be dropped into a manual installation routine. This can be used just as easily as the automated routine; it just takes a little longer. Again, menu-driven options make the process painless.

You can probably install Red Hat Linux on your system based entirely on the automated installation routine. If this is the case, you can move on to other chapters in this book. The rest of this chapter covers some of the most important steps in setting up and installing a Linux system in more detail. If you encounter problems during the installation, or want to make changes to your configuration, you can check the respective sections later in this chapter. For now, you can take a quick look at each of the steps in the automated installation process.

Choosing Text or Graphics Installation

Red Hat Linux gives you two choices for installation: text-based or X-based. If you have installed Linux before or are familiar with operating systems, you can use either with equal confidence. The graphical interface installation using X is a more visually pleasant installation process, and it is a neat aspect of Red Hat Linux.

On the other hand, the text-based installation process is more traditional and familiar to veteran Linux users. If you are unsure of how to use X, or not sure of your system configuration with respect to mouse and video card, you should stay with the text-based installation. It guides you through each step with full descriptions on the screen.

Setting Up Your Hard Drive

If you have not set up Linux on your system before, or you need to allocate partitions for Linux on your system, you will need to use a disk-partitioning scheme. Red Hat Linux gives you a choice of two disk partitioning utilities: fdisk and cfdisk. The fdisk utility is similar to the DOS FDISK program. It is covered in more detail later in this chapter, in the section entitled, "Installing the Linux Partitions."

The cfdisk utility is similar to fdisk but is a little more friendly. Many people find cfdisk easier to use than fdisk, as it uses simple mnemonic commands to perform each function. The choice of partitioning utility is entirely up to you: they both do the same job.

If you have set new partitions on your hard disk for Linux, you will have to reboot your system to make them effective (don't forget to write the partition table to disk when you exit either fdisk or cfdisk!). After a reboot, start the installation process again either from your boot floppies or the CD-ROM, and the new disk partitions will be recognized by Linux.

Formatting the Partitions

After the disk partitions are set, Red Hat will try to detect your swap partition. The installation routine will display a window with the device names of all your swap partitions listed. To format the swap partition, choose one of the partitions listed (or the only entry if you set up only one swap partition) and choose Yes from the menu to start the formatting. The process takes about a minute, depending on the size of the swap partition.

After the swap partition has been formatted and made available to the kernel, the installation routine detects any Linux data partitions. These are displayed with the option to format them. For a new installation, you should format the Linux partition using this screen.

Setting Up Ethernet

During the swap and Linux data-formatting process, Red Hat asks if you want to install Ethernet now. If you have an Ethernet card in your machine and want to set it up while the installation process is running, you can do so. If you don't have an Ethernet card or want to delay the installation for later, that's fine, too; you can skip a few steps.

If you elect to set up Ethernet now, you are asked for a machine name and a domain name. After that, you are asked for the IP address of your machine and the subnet mask (which is generated automatically and probably doesn't need changing). A few other configuration settings based on the IP address may be displayed. Again, the default settings are fine for almost every system.

You will be asked if your machine uses a gateway. If you use a separate machine to access the Internet or another network, answer Yes. If you use a gateway, you will be asked for its identification.

You will also be asked if there is a nameserver to be used by this machine. If your network has a DNS (Domain Name System) server that performs IP address conversions, answer Yes and supply its identification. Otherwise, answer No. You can always add a nameserver later, after the system is up and running.

Setting Up the Mouse

After a message about the Metro-X server supplied with Red Hat Linux and a selection of the type of graphics card to use (if in doubt, select standard VGA or SVGA), you are asked for the type of mouse attached to your system. Select the entry that matches the type of mouse you use, or one that is compatible with your mouse.

You are then asked which device your mouse is attached to. In most cases, the mouse is attached to COM1 (/dev/ttyS0) or COM2 (/dev/ttyS1). Select the proper entry. If you are not sure which port your mouse uses, select COM1; it is the most common configuration.

Configuring X

If you have selected the X-based installation routine, Red Hat Linux tries to determine your video system so it can start X. If you are using the text-based installation routine, this process is skipped for now.

In most cases, Red Hat Linux will try to set up the X system by checking the type of video card you have. You will probably see a message asking if you want the installation routine to "autoprobe," which means it will try to determine the type of video card and video chipset installed on your machine. If you have a particular reason for not autoprobing (some video cards will hang if they are sent the wrong sequence), you will have to manually supply the configuration information. If you are unsure whether or not autoprobing should be allowed, let it go ahead and try. The worst that can happen (usually) is that the system will hang and you have to reboot.

After autoprobing, the installation routine displays the type of video chipset it found and the amount of memory it thinks is on the card. For most systems, accept the defaults unless you know exactly what type of chipset and on-board RAM you have.

After answering all the questions properly, X will start and you will see the X-based installation procedure.

Selecting Packages to Install

Whether you are using X or text-based installation, you will see a screen that lists all the packages on the Linux CD-ROM. You can select which packages are to be installed during the setup process. You can install as many or as few of these packages as you want. You can delay the installation of many of them until later, if you want.

After selecting the packages to be installed, you will see a message asking if you want to have individual package contents displayed for selection. This lets you select only portions of the more generic packages for installation. If you select this option, you will have to wait by your screen and provide input at regular intervals. If you want Linux to install all the components in a package, answer No to this prompt and you can leave the system to install by itself.

After you have selected the packages to be installed, Red Hat's installation routine will start installing the software. You will see status messages on the screen as the process goes along.

Using LILO

After the installation process has formatted the drive partitions and copied all the software packages you selected to the data partition, you are asked if you want to run LILO to set up the boot system for this drive. If you have a disk drive devoted only to Linux, or it is a split DOS/Linux drive, you can run LILO and set the drive to boot into either operating system.

If you are running another operating system, such as UNIX or OS/2, you may elect not to use LILO and create a boot floppy instead. LILO is covered in much more detail in Chapter 4, "LILO."

Boot and Root Disks

Even if you are installing from CD-ROM, you need three high-capacity floppies (either 1.2MB or 1.44MB). These are a single-boot floppy and two root (also called swap) floppies. The boot floppy holds the kernel used to start Linux the first time. The root or swap floppies hold a small file system that includes utilities needed for the installation.

In most cases, the boot and root floppies are copied from existing files that are called *images*. The image is a precompiled version of the system that you duplicate onto the floppies, eliminating the need to start from scratch. CD-ROM and FTP distributions will have directories for several boot and root images. You must select the image that matches your hardware as much as possible, copy them to the diskettes, and start your system with the diskettes.

You can do most of these steps from DOS, although you can't use the DOS copy command to create the boot and root floppies. The floppies must be created with a utility that ignores DOS formatting. This utility, commonly called RAWRITE.EXE, is included with most Linux software distributions.

Selecting a Boot Kernel and Root Image

The Red Hat Linux CD-ROM has a directory under the root directory called images which contain the boot and root images. You should run DOS either from a floppy or a partition on your hard disk to examine the CD-ROM. If you are copying your files from an FTP site, you can select the boot and root images you need while connected to the remote FTP machine and transfer only the images you need to your local machine.

The types of boot kernels usually available are described in a file in the kernel image directories. The Red Hat Linux CD-ROM accompanying this book has a number of directories under the images directory:

- ▓ 1213—Contains the standard boot images
- ▓ 1357—Contains experimental boot images with a new kernel
- ▓ custom—Contains boot-disk images of a specialized nature

Under the images directory there is also a directory called floppies, which contains mirror images of the floppy distribution set for Red Hat Linux. Among the three subdirectories that hold images, there are many hundreds of images. If you are not familiar with Linux or don't want to play around with special kernels and hardware configurations, stick to the 1213 directory. It has boot images that will handle most systems.

In the \images\1213 directory there is a file called IMAGE.TXT, which lists the makeup of each image. A typical entry looks like this:

```
image # 0021:
   SCSI    : Adaptec, Buslogic
   Ethernet: SMC
   CD-ROM  : IDE/ATAPI or SCSI
```

For each image in the 1213 directory the IMAGE.TXT file lists the image name (the file for the preceding entry is called BOOT0021.IMG), the type of controller card used for the disk drives (a SCSI controller made by, or compatible with those by, Adaptec or Buslogic), the type of Ethernet card (SMC in this example), and the type of CD-ROM drive on the system (an IDE or SCSI CD-ROM drive, in this case).

After you have selected the proper image that most closely matches your hardware setup, you can copy it to a floppy. You will also need the two root-disk images, which are in the \images\1213 directory as RAMDISK1.IMG and RAMDISK2.IMG. If you choose the boot image incorrectly, don't worry. All that will happen is you won't be able to install Linux, and you can start the process again.

If you obtained your boot and root images from an FTP or BBS site, the files may be compressed and archived. If they are, they will end with the file type .gz. Before you can install the images to a floppy, they must be uncompressed with the gzip utility.

Creating the Boot and Root Floppies

You can create the boot and root floppies either from DOS or from a running UNIX or Linux system. If you don't run DOS yet, or don't have a DOS boot disk, you will have to use another machine to create the floppies. Because the DOS-based floppy creation is the most common, we can deal with it first. This uses a utility called RAWRITE.EXE, which is included on the CD-ROM in the \DOSUTILS directory.

To create the boot and root floppies, you must use a utility program to write the image to diskette. If your image files are compressed (they will have a .gz) extension, they must first be uncompressed with the gzip utility. If you are working from CD-ROM, you will have to copy the files to a DOS hard disk since you can't write the uncompressed image to the CD-ROM. To uncompress a .gz file, issue the command

```
gzip -d filename
```

where *filename* is the name of the compressed file (including the .gz extension). The -d option tells gzip to decompress the file. When it is completed, the .gz file will have been erased and only the uncompressed file will remain (with the same filename, less the .gz extension). You should uncompress the boot and root images.

The three floppies you need for Red Hat Linux don't have to be blank, as the RAWRITE utility used to copy the image to the floppies doesn't respect DOS formatting conventions. The two floppies must be high density. The disks must be formatted using the DOS format program. The boot diskette must be the correct size for your system's boot floppy drive (A: in DOS terms).

To use the RAWRITE program, enter its name at the DOS prompt with the full path to the utility, such as:

```
D:\DOSUTILS\RAWRITE
```

if your CD-ROM is drive D (or you can copy the files to a directory on your hard disk). RAWRITE will prompt you for the name of the file to copy and then destination drive letter. RAWRITE will then copy the images. Label the disks when the process is finished.

If you have access to a UNIX or Linux system, you can create the boot disks from within that operating system. You will need to put the image files on the UNIX or Linux system and use the dd utility to copy them to floppy. First, make sure the images are uncompressed (no .gz extension). If they are not, uncompress them with the gunzip utility.

To uncompress files in UNIX or Linux, issue the command

```
gunzip filename
```

where *filename* is the name of the image file, with its .gz extension. The gunzip utility will erase the compressed file and leave an uncompressed version in its place.

To copy the images to a floppy, you need to know the device name of the floppy within the operating system. For most systems, the first floppy drive is /dev/fd0 and the second floppy drive is /dev/fd1. (Some systems treat the floppy drives as a raw device, which have the names /dev/rfd0 and /dev/rfd1.) Copy image files to the floppy with the command

```
dd if=filename of=/dev/fd0 obs=18k
```

where *filename* is the name of the uncompressed image. The dd command converts file formats. The if and of parts of the command indicate the input and output filenames or devices. The obs portion of the command indicates the output block size (in this case, 18KB).

For example, to copy the BOOT0023.IMG image to the first floppy (3.5-inch 1.44MB), issue the command:

```
dd if=boot0023.img of=/dev/fd0 obs=18k
```

If you already have a Linux system, an easy way to make the boot and root floppies for Red Hat Linux is with a utility supplied on the CD-ROM. There is a Perl program called MKFLOPPIES.PL in the IMAGES subdirectory that can do the entire task for you. A series of questions will help you determine the proper images.

Partitioning the Hard Disk

Hard disks are divided into partitions or areas dedicated to an operating system. A hard disk can have up to four primary partitions, with some partitions being further divided into more logical drives by the operating system software.

Linux prefers to have two partitions: one for the Linux swap space, and one for the Linux software file system itself. The swap space is used as an extension of your machine's physical RAM and can be quite small. The Linux file-system partition tends to be quite large, as it must hold all the Linux software. You can have several Linux file-system partitions, although one must be designated as the boot partition (where the kernel and primary utilities are located).

If you are using an existing hard disk that has an operating system already installed on it, you will have to repartition your hard disk to make room for Linux. This tends to be a destructive process, meaning that anything on your hard disk will be destroyed. Make backups of your existing data if you want to keep it!

Partitioning of a hard disk is done with the `fdisk` utility from DOS or Linux, or interactively during the Red Hat Linux installation. You don't need to partition the drives before installing Red Hat Linux, but if you do partition during the installation routine you will have to reboot to make the changes effective. If you have used `fdisk` in DOS, the Linux version does the same task (although the menus are completely different and much more complicated). Many PC-based UNIX systems also use `fdisk` to partition hard drives.

> **NOTE**
>
> A DOS utility called `FIPS` sometimes allows nondestructive changes to your partitions, assuming no data is on the areas that will be repartitioned. `FIPS` is available from many sources, including most of the Linux FTP sites and some Linux CD-ROMs. However, you should make backups, just in case!

You must decide how much space to allocate to the different partitions before you start, as changing your mind later will mean destroying all the data you have saved to disk. The Linux swap-space partition size will depend on the amount of RAM in your system, the number of users you expect, and the type of development you will do.

If you are going to maintain a DOS partition on the same disk, you will have to balance the disk-space requirements of both operating systems against your total disk capacity. A minimum Linux file-system partition will be about 20MB, although closer to 200MB is needed for a full X-based installation.

Linux Swap-Space Partition

How big should the swap-space partition be? No single number works for all installations, unfortunately. Generally, because the swap space is used as an extension of physical RAM, the more RAM you have, the less swap space is required. You can add the amount of swap space and the amount of RAM together to get the amount of RAM Linux will use. For example, if you have 8MB of RAM on your machine's motherboard, and a 16MB swap-space partition, Linux will behave as though you had 24MB of total RAM.

Linux uses the swap space by moving pages of physical RAM to the swap space when it doesn't need that page at the moment, and vice versa when it needs the memory page. So why not make a very large swap space and let Linux think it's in heaven? Because the swap space is much slower in access time than RAM, and there is a point at which the size of the swap space acts against your Linux system's efficiency, instead of for it.

Swap space may not be needed if you have lots of RAM. For example, if you have 16MB of physical RAM and don't intend to do any application development or run X, you won't make much use of the swap space because Linux can fit everything it needs into the 16MB. (You still should have a small swap space, just in case.)

If you are running X, developing applications, or running memory-hog applications like databases, swap space is crucial even if you have lots of physical RAM. Even 16MB RAM is not enough for X, so you need swap space.

A good rule is to create a swap space with a size of 16MB. Unless you have a very small capacity hard disk, this won't be a major drain on your resources and it does give Linux plenty to work with. If you don't want to allocate this much space, a good rule is to have a total of 16MB RAM (swap space plus physical RAM). Don't eliminate the swap space completely, though, unless you really have a lot of RAM. At a minimum, set up a 4MB swap space. Running out of RAM can cause Linux to totally lock up or crash, which isn't a pretty sight!

Setting Up Partitions

Because the versions of `fdisk` in DOS, OS/2, UNIX, and Linux all differ, all the steps aren't explained here. The `fdisk` utility is very easy to use, so if you have used PC machines for a while this will not be a problem for you. Remember, though, that `fdisk` will destroy existing data on your disk! You can set up your Linux disk partitions either from DOS or from within Linux. It really doesn't matter which approach you use, although the DOS `fdisk` program is a little easier to use than the Linux version. If you are using DOS `fdisk` to repartition a DOS area on your drives, you may as well use it to set up the Linux swap space and file-system partitions, too. The DOS version of `fdisk` has one problem, though: it can't set the partition type numbers. Linux's `fdisk` lets you set the partition types to be recognized more easily (type 82 for Linux swap and type 83 for Linux data).

To set up partitions for Linux, remove any existing partitions first (unless you want to keep them as they are). If you intend to use DOS on the same system as Linux, DOS should be the first partition on the disk so it can boot. (There are a few ways to get by this using LILO, but it is still a good rule to leave DOS as the first partition.) If you are keeping an existing DOS partition, it should be the first partition.

You should create a DOS boot disk that can reformat and transfer the DOS kernel to the hard drive, regardless of whether you are leaving an existing DOS partition or creating a new one. To create the boot diskette, use the DOS command

```
format a: /s
```

(assuming A: is the drive the diskette is in). The `/s` option transfers the operating system kernel. Next, copy the utilities `FDISK`, `FORMAT`, `SYS`, and `CHKDSK` to the boot floppy. You should also copy an editor, such as `EDIT`, and your existing `CONFIG.SYS` and `AUTOEXEC.BAT` files (although you could rename them). This disk will let you format any new DOS partitions. Alternatively, if you are starting from scratch with a new DOS partition, you can simply reload DOS from the original diskettes when ready to format the DOS partition.

If you are removing an existing DOS partition and re-creating a smaller one (as you would if your entire disk was DOS before Linux came into your life), follow these steps (after making a backup of your DOS data):

1. Remove the existing DOS partition.
2. Create a new primary DOS partition as the first partition.
3. Make the DOS partition active.
4. Reboot the system from your boot floppy (or DOS disks).
5. Format the DOS partition and transfer the DOS kernel (COMMAND.COM) and hidden .SYS files by using the DOS SYS command or using FORMAT /S.
6. Restore your backup files to the DOS partition (this can be done at any time).

Next, set up the Linux swap-space partition by creating a partition of the proper size. You can do this step either from DOS or when you have booted Linux from the boot and root floppies. For the sake of this chapter, we'll assume you are setting up the partitions from DOS (although the process is the same either way).

Most versions of fdisk enable you to enter the size of the partition in MB, with the utility calculating the sector numbers that apply to it. Set the size of the Linux swap space to whatever size you decided. Don't make the partition active or format it! You can set up the swap-space partition in an extended disk partition, but a primary partition is a better choice if your disk can support it.

Finally, create the Linux file-system partition to be whatever size you want, or the rest of the disk if that's the only partition missing. Again, don't activate or format the partition. When you are running the Linux installation routine, you will identify and format the swap space and file-system partitions properly.

Install the Linux Partitions

One of the first steps you are asked to do by the installation routine is to set up disk partitions. Red Hat Linux has two disk-partitioning utilities: fdisk and cfdisk. Both perform the same tasks, but cfdisk is a little easier to use. The fdisk utility, though, will be familiar to users of other Linux versions.

If you have more than one hard drive, you can place your Linux partitions on either drive. If you are planning on keeping a DOS partition, though, make sure it is the first partition on the first drive. Linux isn't so picky. If you want to boot Linux cleanly, place a Linux file system on the first drive. You can also create Linux file systems on the second drive. Linux swap partitions can be on either drive. If you have two drives, putting the swap space on the second drive and the bootable Linux data partition on the first should provide better performance.

Linux's *fdisk*

Linux's fdisk program is different from the one in DOS, so you should check the menus frequently to determine the proper commands. During the installation process the disk partitions are detected automatically, and you are placed in the fdisk program.

Alternatively, you can run fdisk at any time from a Linux prompt. You invoke the Linux fdisk in the same manner as that in DOS. If you don't specify a drive, fdisk will assume the first one in the system. Otherwise, you can specifically indicate which disk drive to partition by giving the device name on the command line, as in

fdisk /dev/hdb

which will invoke fdisk for the second drive. If your system has IDE, ESDI, or RLL drives, the first is /dev/hda and the second /dev/hdb. SCSI drives are /dev/sda, /dev/sdb, and so on. Because seven SCSI drives can be supported on a single controller, you could have up to /dev/hdg. (You can go even higher with another controller card, but few Linux systems will require this!)

As mentioned previously, Linux fdisk commands are different from the fdisk commands for DOS. Essentially, the commands you need to run the Linux fdisk utility are the following:

- d—Deletes an existing partition
- l—Lists all known partition types
- n—Creates a new partition
- p—Displays the current partition table
- q—Quits fdisk without saving changes
- t—Changes a partition's type code
- v—Verifies the partition table
- w—Writes current partition table to disk and exits

The process for setting up a partition is to first examine the partition table to make sure any existing partitions are correct. If you have a DOS partition on your drive, it should show in the partition table. If you created Linux swap and file-system partitions when you were in DOS's fdisk, they should appear in the partition table too, although the partition types will be incorrect.

Setting Up Linux Partitions

To create the Linux swap space, use the n command and give the starting sector number. Usually, this will be immediately after any existing DOS partition (or other operating systems you have installed). Linux's fdisk lets you specify the size of the partition either by supplying an end sector number or by giving a size in MB. The latter is much easier to work with, so just enter the number of MB you want to set your Linux swap-space partition to. The format is usually +*XX*M, where *XX* is the number of megabytes (such as +16M). You can also specify kilobytes, but you don't want to create a swap partition that is less than 1MB in size.

NOTE

Most PC BIOSs cannot handle more than 1024 cylinders on a disk drive. You may not be able to create DOS or Linux partitions or file systems that go beyond the 1,023th cylinder (numbering starts at zero). Some other operating systems, such as SCO UNIX, enable you to use anything beyond the 1,024 limit. Linux can use partitions beyond the 1,024 limit, but it can't boot from them. If you have a disk drive that has more than 1,023 cylinders, make sure your primary Linux partition ends before 1,023. You can create extra partitions following that cylinder and mount them as second file systems.

The `fdisk` program will ask you if you want to create a primary or an extended partition. If you are creating a primary partition it wants the number (one to four—remember a DOS partition has to be number 1 to boot). In most cases you should create only primary partitions, unless you have a large disk drive. Extended partitions can be used to add logical drives inside them, as DOS creates logical drives. In Linux, extended partitions are not the same as extended file systems!

After you have created the Linux partition, you should assign its type. Some versions of `fdisk` prompt for this right away, whereas others let you select the option to assign file-system types from the `fdisk` menu. In either case, the letter l will display all known file-system types. Choose the one that designates a Linux swap space (number 82), and check the partition table. Your Linux swap-space partition should have the correct size and partition type displayed. Actually, Linux doesn't care about the partition-type numbers and ignores them completely, although it can make autodetection of the Linux partitions a little easier during installation. Some other operating systems do note them, though, so it's a good practice to label them correctly to prevent future problems. It also helps you keep the partition table nicely organized!

Next, create your primary Linux file-system partition in the same manner. If you want to use the rest of the disk drive for that partition, you can enter the end sector number of your drive (Linux's `fdisk` will tell you the range you can use). This would be the usual default if your hard drive has a DOS, Linux swap space, and Linux file-system partition on it. After you have created the Linux file system, you should identify its file type as 82, which is a "Linux native" type.

You should note the size of the swap-space and file-system partitions in blocks; you will need this information later. You can read this straight from the partition table.

After you've created the Linux partitions and are satisfied with the partition-table layout, save and exit `fdisk`. If you don't save the information, you will have to repeat the process again.

Enabling the Swap Space For Installation

When you have set up the disk partitions through the automated installation routine, you don't have to worry about enabling the swap space; it is performed automatically. If you are doing these steps manually, you will have to enable the swap space so Linux can use it.

If you have 4MB of RAM or less, you will have problems installing Linux unless you have the kernel use the swap space. (If you have only 4MB or less of RAM in your system, you should have a swap space of at least 8MB—preferably 16MB.) If you try to install Linux and get memory error messages, it's because there is not enough RAM and the swap space is needed.

> **NOTE**
>
> If you've turned the swap space on and still get error messages, you need either more physical RAM or a larger swap space. To increase the size of a swap-space partition, you may have to remove the existing Linux partitions and re-create them with `fdisk`.

If you have a small amount of RAM, you should enable the swap space to help the installation process. Even if you have lots of RAM, there's no reason not to enable the swap space now, anyway. To enable the swap space, issue the command

```
mkswap -c partition size
```

where `partition` is the name of the partition and `size` is the size of the partition in blocks. You may have noted this number earlier when setting up the partition table. If not, you can start `fdisk` again and read the size in blocks from the partition-table display.

For example, if you have set up the Linux swap space on partition `/dev/hda2` (the second primary partition on the first non-SCSI drive) and it has a size of 13,565 blocks, you would issue the command

```
mkswap -c /dev/hda2 13565
```

The `-c` option in the command line tells the `mkswap` utility to check for bad blocks in the partition. If this option is on, it will take a little longer to create the swap partition; however, a bad block in the swap partition can cause your entire system to crash, so it's worth the delay. If `mkswap` finds any errors in the swap space, it will generate an error message. However, because `mkswap` flags bad blocks to be left alone, you can ignore the messages unless there are a considerable number of them, in which case your hard drive has too many bad blocks!

When the swap partition has been formatted, you enable the Linux swap-space partition with the command `swapon`. Usually you will have to specify the partition, although some versions can figure the partition out automatically from the partition table. It never hurts to be explicit, though. To enable the swap partition just formatted, enter the command

```
swapon /dev/hda2
```

You will have to repeat the `format` and `swapon` commands for each swap partition, if you created more than one. As soon as the `swapon` command is executed, the Linux kernel will start to use the new swap space as an extension of the physical RAM.

Creating the Linux File-System Partition

When you have a swap space configured and working, you can set up the Linux file system. This step may be automated by some Linux installation scripts, or you may have to execute it yourself. Either way, this section explains what is going on.

You will have already allocated the partition table to support a Linux file system. Now you can create the file system with the `mkfs` (make file system) command. The exact format of the command depends on the type of file system you are setting up. The most popular file system (for reasons of speed and flexibility) is called the Second Extended file system (which has nothing to do with extended partitions on a hard disk). To create a Second Extended file system, issue the command

```
mke2fs -c partition size
```

where `partition` is the device name and `size` is the size of the partition in blocks (taken from the partition display in `fdisk`). The size doesn't have to be specified with `mke2fs` as it can figure it out from the partition information. For example, to create a file system in `/dev/hda3`, the command would be

```
mke2fs -c /dev/hda3
```

> **NOTE**
>
> When specifying the size of a partition, make sure you use blocks and not sectors or cylinders. Using the wrong value will result in errors or only a fraction of your partition being used.

The `mke2fs` utility will check the partition for bad blocks (the `-c` option) then set the file system up properly in that partition. If you are setting up a large partition, the disk check can take a few minutes—but you should not ignore it unless you know your disk is good.

The other file systems available to Linux are the Xia file system, the Extended file system, and the Minix file system. The Xia file system is good, but not as popular as the Second Extended. The Extended file system is an older version of Second Extended, whereas the Minix file system is compatible with the old Minix operating system. You can create these file systems with the following commands:

■ Extended—mkefs

■ Minix—mkfs

■ Xia—mkxfs

All three commands take the same arguments as the Second Extended file-system command. The Minix file system is limited to 64MB.

None of the mkfs commands format the filesystem—they simply set it up. You are prompted for a file-system format during the installation process.

Troubleshooting

There are many different problems that can occur while setting up and installing a Linux system, although most of them will be self-explanatory from error messages. A few commonly encountered problems can be easily dealt with, though, so we'll look at them briefly.

Software Installation

You may encounter a few errors when installing Linux. If you get the message device full, it means you have run out of disk space and need to install fewer components or allocate more hard disk space. If you haven't installed the basic system, you will need more disk space. You will have to delete your partitions and start the installation process again, allocating more to Linux.

Errors such as read error, file not found, and tar: read error are indicative of a problem with either the disk medium you are installing from, or an incomplete Disk Set. These problems usually occur with floppies, and they tend to indicate a bad diskette. All you can do in most cases is replace the diskette with a new one.

Hard Disk and Disk Controller

When Linux boots it displays a few messages, one of the most important being a partition check. You will see messages like this:

```
Partition check:
hda: hda1 hda2 hda3
hdb: hdb1 hdb2
```

In this example, the first non-SCSI disk has three partitions and the second disk has two. Your system's output will probably be different, of course. If you don't see any partition information, either the hard disk controller is not recognized properly, or the disk drives themselves are not accessible. There are a number of potential causes for these problems, including the obvious:

■ Check the cables inside the computer. The hard-disk cable should run from the adapter card to each drive's connector. Make sure the cables are connected in the proper manner (the red strip on the cable is at pin 1 on the connector).

■ Confirm that the power connector is attached to each disk drive. Without power, your drive won't spin up and Linux can't touch it.

■ Check the partition table to make sure you created a Linux partition properly.

After that, if the drive is not working properly with Linux but works fine when you boot DOS, a kernel driver for the hard disk is probably at fault. Some IDE drives, for example, are not as well-behaved (that is, conforming to the IDE standards) as others, and your IDE kernel driver may not be able to talk to your drives. Try using a different kernel image and see if the problem solves itself. If you are using a SCSI kernel and adapter and the drives are not recognized, use the utilities that came with the SCSI adapter card to force a check of the hard drives. They may have a SCSI ID set incorrectly.

Device Conflicts

One of the most commonly encountered problems is hardware not recognized properly. This can happen to a CD-ROM, a network card, and even a hard disk. Most of the time this is caused by a conflict in the IRQ (interrupt), DMA (Direct Memory Address), or I/O address settings. When two devices have the same settings on any one of the three characteristics, Linux and the BIOS may not be able to communicate with the device properly.

A symptom of this problem may be Linux hanging when it tries to find a specific device, as explained on the boot messages. When Linux boots up, it generates verbose messages on the console that explain what it is doing. If you see a message that it is trying to connect to the network card, for example, and it never gets past that point, chances are that the network card has a conflict with another device. (Totally failed cards are very rare and don't usually stop the boot process; Linux ignores devices it can't access. The problem with a working card with conflicting settings is that Linux is getting messages from two devices that don't act the same.)

To check for conflicts, you can run a diagnostic utility under DOS such as MSD or Norton Info. Windows 95 users can use the System icon in the Control Panel to obtain this information. These diagnostics can show you the current IRQ, DMA, and I/O addresses and pinpoint any conflicts. They can also be used for finding available settings.

Alternately, you will have to check the settings of every device in your system for conflicts. Usually, network cards will conflict with sound boards, non-SCSI tape driver cards, video cards, and similar add-on cards. Most cards use DIPs or jumpers to set these parameters, so check them against the documentation. To help isolate the problem, remove cards that are not necessary, such as a sound card, and see if the boot process moves past the device that caused the hang-up.

Another problem that can occur is with SCSI devices (and a few others, although much rarer) that must have specific settings in the kernel image. Some kernels were compiled with settings that are default values for adapters or disk drives; if the settings have been changed, the kernel will hang up. This is often the case with special-purpose kernels that have been developed for non-mainstream adapters. To check for this type of problem, you should investigate any documentation that came with the kernel image.

The most common devices in a PC (COM ports, parallel ports, and floppies) and their IRQ, DMA, and I/O addresses are shown in Table 3.1. These are the default values for a PC, but they may be changed by users. Because only two COM ports (serial ports) are usually supported by DOS, they share IRQ values. The I/O addresses are different, though. Both floppy disks share the same I/O addresses, IRQ, and DMA.

Table 3.1. Common IRQ, DMA, and memory address settings.

Device	*IRQ*	*DMA*	*I/O Address (Hex)*
COM 1 (`/dev/ttyS0`)	4	N/A	3F8
COM 2 (`/dev/ttyS1`)	3	N/A	2F8
COM 3 (`/dev/ttyS2`)	4	N/A	3E8
COM 4 (`/dev/ttys3`)	3	N/A	2E8
LPT 1 (`/dev/lp0`)	7	N/A	378-37F
LPT 2 (`/dev/lp1`)	5	N/A	278-27F
Floppy A (`/dev/fd0`)	6	2	3F0-3F7
Floppy B (`/dev/fd1`)	6	2	3F0-3F7

Network cards, SCSI adapters, sound boards, video cards, and other peripherals all must have unique IRQ, DMA, and I/O addresses, which can be difficult to arrange with a fully loaded system. For more information on available values, you should check your device or card-installation manual for recommended values and potential conflicts.

SCSI Problems

SCSI is one of the most versatile interfaces, and it pays for that versatility in potential problems. Linux is usually good about reporting problems with SCSI devices, although the error messages may leave you wondering about the real cause of the problem.

Table 3.2 lists many of the common SCSI errors and their probable causes. Find the message that closely matches the error message Linux displays in this table to determine your corrective steps.

Table 3.2. Common SCSI problems and their solutions.

Problem	Probable Solution
SCSI device at all possible IDs	One or more devices are at the same SCSI ID as the controller. Check and change device IDs. Controllers should be ID 7.
Sense errors	Probably caused by bad termination. Check that both ends of the SCSI chain are terminated. If that is not the problem, the cable is likely at fault.
Timeout errors	Usually caused by a DMA, IRQ, or I/O-address conflict. See the preceding section for more information.
SCSI adapter not detected	The BIOS is disabled or the SCSI adapter is not recognized by the kernel. Check the drivers.
Cylinders Beyond 1024	Your disk has more than 1,024 cylinders, which the PC BIOS can't handle. Linux can use more than 1,024 cylinders, but it can't boot from a partition that extends across that cylinder boundary.
CD-ROM drive not recognized	Some CD-ROMs require a CD in the drive to be recognized properly. Insert a CD and reboot.

Booting Linux

If you have installed Linux and the system won't boot properly from your hard disk, it may be a problem with LILO or with the partitions. If you created a boot floppy, boot from that. If that boots without a problem, check the partition table by executing `fdisk`. Make sure the Linux partition is active. If it is and you still can't boot from the hard disk, boot from the floppy and run LILO again to configure the boot sector. See Chapter 4 for more information on LILO.

A problem will sometimes occur when Linux can't find the main Linux partition. Boot from the floppy and hold down Shift or Ctrl. This produces a menu that enables you to specify the boot device explicitly. This problem can usually be corrected with LILO.

Summary

Much of this chapter will be familiar to you if you have installed Linux before, although some users really don't know what goes on during the automated installation script. Knowing the process, and staying on top of it, helps prevent problems with the Linux installation.

The next step is using LILO to properly configure the boot system—a commonly misunderstood and misused process. The next chapter looks at LILO.

LILO

4

*by Kamran
Husain and
Tim Parker*

IN THIS CHAPTER

Whenever you hear about Linux, you'll also hear about LILO. LILO is the boot loader used by Linux to load the operating system kernel. Whenever the Linux kernel is changed or moved, LILO must be invoked to rebuild a map of the kernel locations. LILO is versatile; it can boot Linux kernels from any type of file system, including floppy disk, as well as from other operating systems.

This chapter looks at LILO, the way hard disks are laid out with Linux, the boot process, and the most common boot processes and LILO's interactions with each. This should help you install and use LILO efficiently and effectively.

Using LILO to Boot Off the Hard Drive

LILO (which means *LInux LOader*) is a bit tricky to use if you are not familiar with it and its purpose. You need to install the *LILO* program, which changes the boot sector of your hard drive to allow you to choose between a DOS or a Linux partition as the boot source partition. LILO is included with Red Hat Linux and is installed automaically when you load the system from CD-ROM.

Some of the features of LILO include the following:

- It is independent of the file system. You can use LILO with DOS, UNIX, OS/2, and Windows NT.
- It can replace the master boot record on your hard drive.
- It can use up to 16 different boot images on several partitions on your hard drive. Each image can be protected by a password.
- It provides support for boot-sector, map-file, and boot images to reside on different disks or partitions.

Using LILO may seem risky at first; it can ruin your hard drive or leave you with a system that you cannot boot. To prepare yourself for this mishap, keep a boot disk handy. Also, you have to do this installation as `root`, so be careful.

If you have already installed Red Hat Linux, the LILO files will exist on your hard drive. If you are about to install Red Hat Linux, the LILO installation routine will be activated automatically as part of the installation process. If you want to redo the LILO system at any time, though, you can run the program `/sbin/liloconfig`.

The `liloconfig` program is easy to use and asks several questions about your system. The sheer number of possibilities cannot be completely covered here, but here are the terms with which you must be familiar:

- `/dev/hda` and `/dev/hdb` refer to both IDE hard drives 1 and 2 on your system. Individual partitions on each hard drive are referred to as `/dev/hda1`, `/dev/hda2`, `/dev/hda3`, and so on for drive 1. Similar to this are the partitions for drive 2: `/dev/dhb1` and so on.

- SCSI hard drives are referred to as /dev/sda and /dev/sdb for drive 1 and 2, respectively.

- The *Master Boot Record* (MBR) is the first boot sector of your drive that contains the partitioning information and boot-strap code. LILO will change this sector and make it incompatible with DOS. The DOS MBR program simply loads MS-DOS from the boot sector, which in turns loads command.com.

The liloconfig program asks you where you want to install LILO. If you are running multiple operating systems and plan to switch between them often, try installing on the Linux partition superblock. If you will use Linux primarily or only, install on the Master Boot Record. You will then be asked about the ability to load other operating systems from the boot prompt, and you get to identify each operating system and provide a name for it. This lets you start DOS, for example, from the boot prompt by entering the name you assigned to DOS partition.

After the liloconfig program has run, it will create a file called lilo.conf for you in the /etc directory. If you already have this file in your /etc directory, you can edit it manually using any ASCII editor. Of course, depending on how your system is set up, the contents of your Linux installation may vary. A sample lilo.conf file for a system containing both DOS and Linux looks like this:

```
boot=/dev/hda
map=/boot/map
install=/boot/boot.b
prompt
timeout=50
image=/vmlinuz
  root=/dev/hda2
  label=linux
other=/dev/hda1
  label=dos
  table=/dev/hda
```

In this lilo.conf file, you can see two different kernels that can be booted from /dev/hda. The first image is the default image, called vmlinuz. The other image is labeled DOS for the DOS partition. Typing **dos** at the boot prompt will boot this partition.

LILO Command-Line Arguments

The LILO configuration is written to disk using the /sbin/lilo command. The /sbin/lilo installer accepts several command-line options. A few of the more usual ones are listed here.

- -C <config_file>. Specifies the configuration file that is used by the map installer. If -C is omitted, /etc/lilo/config is used. In this example, you would use /etc/lilo.conf.

- -q. Lists the currently mapped files.

■ `-r <root_directory>`. Changes the directory to the specified directory before doing anything else. This is useful when running the map installer while the normal root file system is mounted somewhere else, for example, when recovering from an installation failure with an install disk.

■ `-t`. Test only. Performs the entire installation procedure without replacing the map file or writing the modified boot sector. This can be used in conjunction with the `-v` option to verify that LILO will use sane values.

■ `-v`. Be verbose about what it's doing. If you don't do this, the installation process will not display any messages or status information.

■ `-u [ device_name ]`. Restores the backup copy of the specified boot sector. The name is normally derived from its present name.

■ `-V`. Prints the version number and exits.

Configuration Parameters

The `/etc/lilo.conf` file can have the following parameters. All of these can be set from the command line, but storing them in a configuration file is more reliable. The following options are available to you:

■ `boot=<boot_device>`. Sets the name of the device that contains the boot sector. If `boot` is omitted, the boot sector is read from (and possibly written to) the device that is currently mounted as root.

■ `linear`. Generates linear sector addresses instead of sector/head/cylinder addresses. Linear addresses are translated at run time and do not depend on disk geometry. Note that boot disks, where `linear` is used, may not be portable.

■ `install=<boot_sector>`. Installs the specified file as the new boot sector. If `install` is omitted, `/etc/lilo/boot.b` is used as the default.

■ `disktab=<disktab_file>`. Specifies the name of the disk parameter table. The map installer looks for `/etc/lilo/disktab` if `disktab` is omitted.

■ `map=<map_file>`. Specifies the location of the map file. If `map` is omitted, the file `/etc/lilo/map` is used.

■ `message=<message_file>`. Specifies a file containing a message that is displayed before the boot prompt. No message is displayed when waiting for a Shift key after printing "LILO." The FF character ([Ctrl L]) clears the local screen. The size of the message file is limited to 65,535 bytes. The map file has to be rebuilt if the message file is changed or moved. The default file for messages is the `/etc/boot.message` file. Use this file to display boot options for your LILO configuration.

■ `verbose=<level>`. Turns on lots of progress reporting. Higher numbers give more verbose output.

■ `backup=<backup_file>`. Copies the original boot sector to `<backup_file>` (which may also be a device, such as `/dev/null`) instead of to `/etc/lilo/boot.<number>`.

- force-backup=<backup_file>. Like backup, but overwrites an old backup copy if it exists. backup=<backup_file> is ignored if force-backup appears in the same configuration file.

- prompt. Forces entering the boot prompt without expecting any prior key presses. Unattended reboots are impossible if prompt is set and timeout isn't.

- timeout=<tsecs>. Sets a time out (in tenths of a second) for keyboard input. If no key is pressed for the specified time, the first image is automatically booted. Similarly, password input is aborted if the user is idle for too long. The default timeout is infinite.

- serial=<parameters>. Enables control from a serial line. The specified serial port must be initialized, and LILO is accepting input from it and from the PC's keyboard. Sending a break on the serial line corresponds to pressing the Shift key on the console in order to get LILO's attention. All boot images should be password-protected if the serial access is less secure than access to the console—that is, if the line is connected to a modem. The parameter string has the syntax <port>,<bps><parity><bits>. The components <bps>, <parity>, and <bits> can be omitted. If a component is omitted, all following components have to be omitted as well. Additionally, the comma has to be omitted only if the port number is specified.

  <port>.   The number of the serial port, zero-based. 0 corresponds to COM1. alias /dev/ttyS0, alias /dev/ttys1, alias /dev/ttys2, alias /dev/ttys3.   All four ports can be used (if present).

  <bps>.   The baud rate of the serial port. The following baud rates are supported: 110, 150, 300, 600, 1200, 2400, 4800, and 9600 bps. Default is 2400 bps.

  <parity>.   The parity used on the serial line. LILO ignores input parity and strips the eighth bit. The following (upper- or lowercase) characters are used to describe the parity: n for no parity, e for even parity, and o for odd parity.

  <bits>.   The number of bits in a character. Only 7 and 8 bits are supported. Default is 8 if parity is none, 7 if parity is even or odd.

- If serial is set, the value of delay is automatically raised to 20. Example: serial=0,2400n8 initializes COM1 with the default parameters.

- ignore-table.   Tells LILO to ignore corrupt partition tables.

- fix-table.   Allows LILO to adjust 3-D addresses in partition tables. Each partition entry contains a 3-D (sector/head/cylinder) and a linear address of the first and the last sector of the partition. If a partition is not track-aligned and if certain other operating systems (such as PC/MS-DOS or OS/2) are using the same disk, the operating system may change the 3-D address. LILO can store its boot sector only on partitions where both address types correspond. LILO readjusts incorrect 3-D start addresses if fix-table is set.

> **CAUTION**
>
> `fix-table` does not guarantee that other operating systems might not attempt to reset the address later. It is also possible that this change has other, unexpected side effects. The correct fix is to repartition the drive with a program that does align partitions to tracks.

- `password=<password>`. Sets a password for all images.
- `unsafe`. This keyword is placed after a definition for a partition. The keyword tells LILO not to attempt to read the MBR or that disk's partition table entry. You can declare all the partitions in your system as a log of all exisiting partitions, then place the `unsafe` keyword entry to prevent LILO from reading it.

The kernel configuration parameters `append`, `ramdisk`, `read-only`, `read-write`, `root`, and `vga` can be set in the options section. They are used as defaults if they aren't specified in the configuration sections of the respective kernel images.

If the option `-q` is specified on the command line, the currently mapped files are listed. Otherwise, a new map is created for the images described in the configuration file `/etc/lilo/config` and they are written to in the boot sector.

The *boot:* Prompt

When the system boots up, after the keyboard test, press and hold down one of any one of these keys: Alt, Shift, or Ctrl (or you can set the Caps Lock or Scroll Lock key). If any of these keys are pressed, LILO displays the `boot:` prompt and waits for the name of a boot image. Pressing the Tab key or typing **?** gives you a list of names recognized by LILO. If you do not press any of these keys, LILO will boot up the first it finds in the `lilo.conf` file kernel (in this case, `vmlinuz.cd`) if there is no timeout specified in the `/etc/lilo.conf` file.

LILO can also pass command-line options to the kernel. *Command-line options* are words that follow the name of the boot image and are separated by spaces. Currently, the kernel recognizes the options `root=<device>`, `ro`, and `rw`, and all current `init` programs also recognize the option `single`, which boots the system in single-user mode. This bypasses all system-initialization procedures and directly starts a root shell on the console. Multiuser mode can be entered by exiting the single-user shell or by rebooting.

The option `vga` is processed by the boot loader itself. The option `vga=<mode>` alters the VGA mode that was set at startup. The legal values for mode are NORMAL, EXTENDED, ASK, or a decimal number for the BIOS `mode` command. You can get a list of available modes by typing `vga=ask` and pressing Enter.

The root=<device> option changes the root device. This overrides settings that may have been made in the boot image and on the LILO command line.

> <device> is either a hexadecimal device number or the full pathname of the device, such as /dev/hda3. (The device names are hard-coded in the kernel.)

> ro instructs the kernel to mount the root file system as read-only. rw mounts it as read-write. If neither ro nor rw is specified, the setting from the boot image is used.

> The no387 option disables using the hardware FPU.

Depending on the kernel configuration, some special configuration options for nonstandard hardware might be recognized as well. Some of these boot prompts include the following :

- For a Panasonic CD-ROM with SoundBlaster support, use sbpcd=0x340,SoundBlaster.
- For a bus mouse, use bmouse=irq.
- For reserving ports from being autoprobed by device drivers in special hardware device-conflict situations, you can use reserve=port,size. For example, reserve=0x200,8 will reserve 8 ports starting at 0x200 from being probed by device drivers.
- Ethernet cards usually take parameter from the ether=x,x,x,... command. The actual parameters sent depend on the type of card.
- For Mitsumi CD-ROM, use mcd=port,irq—for example, mcd=0x340,11.
- If your Ethernet card is not recognized, try ether=10,0x340 to probe for it at port 0x340 using interrupt 10. Note that the interrupt number here is given before the port number is given for the Mitsumi CD-ROM driver.

The parameters for each type of device will come with their documentation, so do not assume anything. Use only specified values. If you do follow instructions, you may wind up causing irrecoverable errors, which may lead to a corrupt file system.

Uninstalling LILO

In order to keep LILO from being invoked when the system boots, its boot sector has to be either removed or disabled. All other files belonging to LILO can be deleted after removing the boot sector, if desired.

LILO 0.14 (and newer) can be uninstalled with the lilo -u command.

If LILO's boot sector has been installed on a primary partition and is booted by the standard MBR or some partition-switching program, it can be disabled by making a different partition active. MS-DOS's FDISK, Linux's fdisk, or LILO's activate can do that.

If LILO's boot sector is the Master Boot Record (MBR) of a disk, it has to be replaced with a different MBR, typically MS-DOS's standard MBR. When using MS-DOS 5.0 or above, the MS-DOS MBR can be restored with FDISK /MBR. This alters only the boot loader code, not the partition table. LILO automatically makes backup copies when it overwrites boot sectors. They are named `/etc/lilo/boot.<nnnn>`, with `<nnnn>` corresponding to the device number—that is, 0300 is `/dev/hda`, 0800 is `/dev/sda`, and so on. Those backups can be used to restore the old MBR if no easier method is available.

The commands are

```
dd if=/etc/lilo/boot.0300 of=/dev/hda bs=446 count=1
```

or

```
dd if=/etc/lilo/boot.0800 of=/dev/sda bs=446 count=1
```

respectively.

> **NOTE**
>
> Some other operating systems (such as MS-DOS 6.0) appear to modify the MBR in their install procedures. It is therefore possible that LILO will cease to work after such an installation and Linux has to be booted from floppy disk. The original state can be restored by either rerunning `/etc/lilo/lilo` (if LILO is installed as the MBR) or by making LILO's partition active (if it's installed on a primary partition).
>
> Typically, the new operating system then has to be added to LILO's configuration (and `/etc/lilo/lilo` has to be rerun) in order to boot it.

Map Installer Errors

Some messages that indicate common errors when installing the maps are as follows:

- `Can't put the boot sector on logical partition <number>`

  You attempted to put LILO's boot sector on the current root file system partition, which is on a logical partition. This usually doesn't have the desired effect, because common MBRs can boot only primary partitions. This check can be bypassed by explicitly specifying the boot partition with the `-b` option or by setting the configuration variable `boot`.

- `Device 0x<number>: Got bad geometry <sec>/<hd>/<cyl>`

  The device driver for your SCSI controller does not support geometry detection. You have to use an `/etc/lilo/disktab` file.

- `Device 0x<number>: Invalid partition table, entry <number>`

  The 3-D and linear addresses of the first sector of the specified partition don't correspond. LILO can attempt to correct the problem; see variable `FIX-TABLE`.

■ `First sector of <device> doesn't have a valid boot signature`

The first sector of the specified device does not appear to be a valid boot sector. Check the device name.

■ `geo_comp_addr: Cylinder number is too big (<number> > 1023)`

A file is located beyond the 1024th cylinder of a hard disk. LILO can't access such files, because the BIOS limits cylinder numbers to the range 0-1023. Try moving the file to a different place, preferably a partition that is entirely within the first 1024 cylinders of the disk.

■ `<item> doesn't have a valid LILO signature`

The specified item has been located, but it is not part of LILO. If `<item>` is the first boot sector, you've probably forgotten to specify the `-i` option or the install variable to install the LILO boot sector.

■ `<item> has an invalid stage code (<number>)`

The specified item has probably been corrupted. Rebuild LILO.

■ `<item> is version <number>. Expecting version <number>`

The specified entity is either too old or too new. Make sure all parts of LILO (map installer, boot loaders, and chain loaders) are from the same distribution.

■ `Kernel <name> is too big`

The kernel image (without the setup code) is bigger than 512KB. LILO would overwrite itself when trying to load such a kernel. Try removing some unused drivers and compiling the kernel again.

■ `Partition entry not found`

The partition from which another operating system should be booted isn't listed in the specified partition table. This means either that an incorrect partition table has been specified or that you're trying to boot from a logical partition. The latter usually doesn't work. You can bypass this check by omitting the partition table specification (that is, omitting the variable `table`).

■ `Sorry, don't know how to handle device <number>`

LILO uses files that are located on a device for which there is no easy way to determine the disk geometry. Such devices have to be described in the file `/etc/lilo/disktab`.

LILO Error Codes

When LILO loads itself, it displays the word `LILO`. Each letter is printed before or after performing some specific action. If LILO fails at some point, the letters printed so far can be used to identify the problem. This is described in more detail in the technical overview.

Note that some hex digits may be inserted after the first `L` if a transient disk problem occurs. Unless LILO stops at that point, generating an endless stream of error codes, such hex digits do not indicate a severe problem. The following is the list of error messages you can see:

(nothing) No part of LILO has been loaded. LILO either isn't installed, or the partition on which its boot sector is located isn't active.

L<error> The first stage boot loader has been loaded and started, but it can't load the second stage boot loader. The two-digit error codes indicate the type of problem. (They are described in the next section.) This condition usually indicates a media failure or a geometry mismatch (that is, bad parameters in /etc/lilo/disktab).

LI The first-stage boot loader was able to load the second-stage boot loader but has failed to execute it. This can be caused either by a geometry mismatch or by moving /etc/lilo/boot.b without running the map installer.

LIL The second-stage boot loader has been started, but it can't load the descriptor table from the map file. This is typically caused by a media failure or a geometry mismatch.

LIL? The second-stage boot loader has been loaded at an incorrect address. This is typically caused by a subtle geometry mismatch or by moving /etc/lilo/boot.b without running the map installer.

LIL- The descriptor table is corrupt. This can be caused either by a geometry mismatch or by moving /etc/lilo/map without running the map installer.

LILO All parts of LILO have been successfully loaded.

There are also BIOS error codes that you might get while loading LILO. These are listed in Table 4.1.

Table 4.1. BIOS error codes.

Code	Value
0x00	Internal error. This code is generated by the sector-read routine of the LILO boot loader whenever an internal inconsistency is detected. This might be caused by corrupt files; try rebuilding the map file.
0x01	Illegal command. This shouldn't happen.
0x02	Address mark not found. This usually indicates a media problem. Try again several times.
0x03	Write-protected disk. This shouldn't happen.
0x04	Sector not found. This typically indicates a geometry mismatch. If you're booting a raw-written disk image, verify whether it was created for disks with the same geometry as the one you're using. If you're booting from a SCSI

Code	Value
	disk, you should check whether LILO has obtained correct geometry data from the kernel or whether the contents of your /etc/lilo/disktab file correspond to the real disk geometry. Removing compact may help too.
0x06	Change line active. This should be a transient error. Try booting a second time.
0x08	DMA overrun. This shouldn't happen. Try booting again.
0x09	DMA attempt across 64KB boundary. This shouldn't happen. Try omitting the -c option.
0x0C	Invalid media. This shouldn't happen and might be caused by a media error. Try booting again.
0x10	CRC error. A media error has been detected. Try booting several times, running the map installer a second time (to put the map file at some other physical location or to write good data over the bad spot), mapping out the bad sectors/tracks, and, if all else fails, replacing the media.
0x20	Controller error. This shouldn't happen.
0x40	Seek failure. This might be a media problem. Try booting again.
0x80	Disk timeout. The disk or the drive isn't ready. Either the media is bad or the disk isn't spinning. If you're booting from a floppy, you might not have closed the drive door. Otherwise, trying to boot again might help.

Using *BOOTLIN* Instead of LILO

The BOOTLIN package uses the DOS MBR to boot off the hard drive. To install this package, you must take the following steps:

1. From within Linux, copy a bootable kernel to your DOS partition.
2. Edit config.sys on the DOS partition to include two files: BOOT.SYS and BOOTLIN.SYS. The README files for these packages tell you how.
3. Reboot.

Now when you reboot, the BOOT.SYS and BOOTLIN.SYS files will boot into Linux for you.

To get back to running only DOS, remove the BOOTLIN.SYS and BOOT.SYS from your config.sys file.

The disadvantage of this approach is that you are limited to having DOS on your hard drive.

Restoring the MBR

If you want to restore the MBR to the original DOS MBR, you can use the following procedure:

1. Boot from a DOS floppy.
2. Run `fdisk /MBR` from the DOS prompt. (You can also use the command `SYS C:`.)
3. Reboot.

Summary

This chapter covered the topic of installing, configuring, and using LILO. It also covered some of the basic errors you can face and how to set up LILO using the `liloconfig` utility. The information you have learned from this topic should get you started in setting up LILO to boot Linux on your machine off the hard drive.

Odds and Ends

5

by Kamran Husain and Tim Parker

IN THIS CHAPTER

This chapter covers a variety of topics that basically could not fit in other chapters, nor could they justify a chapter by themselves. We cover these topics briefly and provide locations where you can get more information:

- Setting the default video mode
- How to mark bad blocks on a hard disk
- Loadable modules

Setting the Default Video Mode

You don't have to recompile the kernel to set the default video mode. Just use rdev with the -v switch to set the video mode in the kernel (either on your hard drive or on your boot floppy). For example, to change the kernel in /vmlinuz to prompt for the video mode on bootup, type the following:

```
rdev -v /vmlinuz -3
```

To change the kernel on your boot floppy, type

```
rdev -v /dev/fd0 {video-mode}
```

The valid video-mode options for the kernel are:

-3	Prompt the user for a response every time
-2	Extended VGA
-1	Normal VGA

The rdev program resides in /sbin. rdev is very handy and also is used to set the root and swap partitions, ramdisk size, and more in a compiled kernel. It means you don't have to recompile the kernel to make these changes. Use rdev -? for a list of options.

Identifying Bad Blocks on Your Hard Drive

If you are using a SCSI or IDE (and EIDE) drive, you don't have to worry about bad blocks as they are handled at the device level. On the other hand, if you have an older ESDI, RLL, or MFM drive (or other non-SCSI or non-IDE drive) you may need to scan your drive for bad blocks. Normally the bad blocks are identified and marked when the file system is created using mkefs, mke2fs, and mkxfs.

Unfortunately, the mkefs program cannot detect bad blocks on a hard drive. So if you create a file system over a part of your hard drive with bad blocks, things will eventually go wrong. What you need is a "bad block list" stored in a file; use the -l option on mkefs so it will flag those blocks when making a file system.

> **CAUTION**
>
> Do not check for bad blocks on a mounted system. Doing a check on a mounted file system will cause irreparable damage and/or loss of data. Unmount the file system first with the umount command. If you have to check the root file system, boot off a floppy disk, unmount the root file system if it is mounted, and then check for bad blocks.

mke2fs and mkxfs correctly flag bad blocks, so this only applies to mkfs and mkefs. This is also only needed for older RLL and MFM drives. SCSI and IDE drives have bad block logic on-board, so you are safe there.

How do you generate a bad block list? Generating a bad block list is only needed for older drives and older file system types (such as Minix and extfs). Your best bet is to use mke2fs or mkxfs, anyway.

Linux Loadable Modules

The Linux kernel (since version 1.2.0) supports loadable modules. Using loadable modules enables you to build a minimal kernel and add or remove modules to this kernel without requiring a kernel rebuild. A module could be support for a kernel function or a new feature.

To see what modules exist in your system, use the lsmod command. To install a module, use the insmod command. Some modules may require other modules. To check the dependencies, use the depmod command. To install a module (and its dependant modules), use the depmod command.

Summary

It's hard to summarize this chapter except to say that this has been a grab-bag of all the things that did not fit anywhere else. A lot of the information you need to configure Linux and install new kernels are included in separate chapters later in this book. Details on file systems are included in Part VI, "Linux for System Administrators."

IN THIS PART

Using Linux

II

PART

Getting Started with Linux

6

by Ed Treijs

Congratulations! Now that you have successfully installed Linux, you can start using it. In this chapter we will look at the steps you need to take to begin working with Linux, including the following:

- Starting and stopping Linux
- Logging in and out
- Creating a new user with adduser
- Changing your password
- Using virtual terminals
- Displaying system users with who

Starting (and Stopping!) Your Linux System

Depending on the setup you chose during Linux installation and configuration, either Linux starts automatically when you power on your computer, or it requires you to type something (such as Linux) to specify that you want to boot Linux.

As your Linux system starts up, you see quite a few Linux initialization messages scroll through your screen. When Linux has completed its startup, you should see the following prompt:

```
Welcome to Linux 1.2.13.
darkstar login:
```

> **WARNING**
>
> A Linux system must always be shut down properly. Improper shutdown, such as simply turning off your system, can cause serious damage to your Linux system! When you are finished using your Linux system, you must shut it down properly, as described in the next section. If you start to boot Linux, and then change your mind, you should let the system start up fully and then follow the shutdown procedure.

Because you know how to start Linux, it's even more important to know how to shut it down properly. Like many UNIX systems, if Linux is not powered down properly, damage to files can result. The easiest way to ensure a proper shutdown is to press the Ctrl, Alt, and Delete keys simultaneously. (This is the famous Ctrl-Alt-Delete "three-finger salute" used in DOS.)

Pressing Ctrl-Alt-Delete causes a number of advisory messages and Linux shutdown messages to be displayed. You must wait until the Linux shutdown procedure has finished, at which point your monitor shows the initial "power-on" screen, before turning your computer off.

What's This About "Logging In?"

Linux waits for a login. A login is simply the name that you supply to Linux to identify yourself to the operating system. Linux keeps track of which names are permitted to log in or access the system, and only allows valid users to have access.

> **NOTE**
>
> If you supplied a name to your system when installing Linux, the system name is used at the prompt. In the login shown earlier, the system has been called `darkstar`. The system name enables you to identify your machine to others when using networks or modem connections. Don't worry if you didn't name your system yet, because you can change the system's name at any time.

Every login name on the system is unique. Normally, a password is assigned to each login, too. This secret password is like the identification number you use with your bank card to prove that you really are who you say you are. Also, the things you can do with your login—the login's privileges—are controlled by Linux; different logins have different levels of privileges.

> **NOTE**
>
> Usually, login names reflect a person's real name. Although you can't have two identically named logins on your system, you can easily create logins for users with the same (real) name by having one or two characters different. So, for example, the login names `suej` and `suek` are treated by Linux as completely separate logins.
>
> Conversely, there is no reason that one human being (for instance, yourself) can't have two, three, or a dozen login names. In fact, because you will be the system administrator of your Linux system, you will have one or more administrative logins, and one or more regular user logins.

At the login prompt, try typing your name, your dog's name, or any other random name that occurs to you. None of these are valid logins (at least not yet). The system asks you for a password; it won't matter what you type, so just press Enter or type a random string of characters. Because the logins are not valid on the system, Linux won't let you in. It displays the message `Login incorrect` to tell you that either the name or the password you entered is not valid.

The only valid login on your Linux system after installation is the most powerful and dangerous login Linux offers: `root`. In the section "Creating a New Login," later in this chapter, we will create a safe login for you to use. This login can have your name, your dog's name, or whatever else you choose.

> **NOTE**
>
> The login prompt is actually produced by a program called `login` whose only task is to accept your user ID and password, verify it, and then display a message preventing your access or letting you through to the next program that starts your user session.

Why You Shouldn't Use the *root* Login

You will have to use the root login from time to time. Some things simply cannot be done on the Linux system without logging in as root. You should not, however, use the root login as your regular login. This is especially true if you are exploring the system, poking around, and trying out new commands that may not do what you thought they would!

Linux, as you already know, is a multiuser, multitasking operating system. Multiuser means that several people can be using Linux at the same time (of course, you have to add some additional terminals to your system, or it will get very crowded around the keyboard). Multitasking means that Linux can do more than one thing at a time. For example, you can spell-check a document while downloading information from some remote system. (Multiuser implies multitasking, because all users must be able to do their own work at the same time.) Linux, therefore, is very good at juggling all these tasks, keeping them from interfering with each other, and providing safeguards so that you cannot damage the system or another user's work.

> **WARNING**
>
> The root login does not restrict you in any way. With one simple command, issued either on purpose or by accident, you can destroy your entire Linux installation. For this reason, use the root login only when necessary. Avoid experimenting with commands when you do log in as root.

When you log in as root, you *become* the system. The root login is also sometimes called the *superuser* login, and with good reason. To use an analogy, instead of being a passenger on an airplane, you suddenly have all the privileges of the flight crew, the mechanics, and the cabin crew. "Hmm, what does this do?" becomes an extremely dangerous phrase when logged in as root.

One of the oldest stories in UNIX lore tells of new users who log in as root and, in ten keystrokes, destroy their system completely and irrevocably. But if you're careful to follow the steps given here, and stop and take a moment to think about the commands you are giving, none of the "How many new users does it take to nuke a system?" jokes will apply to you!

> **NOTE**
>
> System administrator is another term you will see often. A *system administrator* is the actual person who sets up and maintains the Linux system. The amount of work involved in system administration varies from system to system. A full-time system administrator may be required in an office for powerful machines that have many users, peripheral units such as printers and tape drives, and are connected to a network. Your Linux system will not require that level of dedication!
>
> System administration, because it deals with sensitive matters such as creating or deleting logins, requires superuser privileges. These privileges are provided by the root login. So, the system administrator is an actual person wielding superuser powers gained by logging in as root.

Your First Login

After all the cautions about using the root login, we're going to have you log in as root. Because root is the only authorized login on a newly installed Linux system, this is unavoidable. Also, we will be performing a couple of important procedures that require root privileges. However, after this first login, we will create a user ID that can prevent accidental damage to the operating system.

At the login prompt

```
darkstar login:
```

type

```
root
```

and press the Enter key.

```
Password:
```

Type in the root password that you set during installation and press the Enter key.

> **NOTE**
>
> Linux is *case-sensitive* (as are all UNIX versions). A capital R is, to Linux, a completely different letter from a lowercase r. When you type Linux commands, you must use the proper case or Linux will not understand them. The majority of Linux commands are typed in lowercase. This includes the login root; if you type Root or rOoT, Linux will reject the login.
>
> There is a curious exception, though. If you type the login IN ALL CAPITALS, the system will accept it—but from then on, everything on your screen will be in capital letters! This is left over from the days when some terminals only had uppercase letters. Although these terminals are now all gone or in museums, the login program retains this historical curiosity.

After you have logged in as root, the system starts up a user session for you. At this point you should see the following on your screen:

```
darkstar login: root
Last login: Sun Dec 11 17:26:18 on tty1
Linux 1.2.13.
You have mail.

If it's Tuesday, this must be someone else's fortune.
darkstar:~#
```

Linux tells you when the login for this user was last recorded (although this information may not appear the very first time you log in), and then provides you with some version information. Linux also tells you that this login has a mail message waiting to be read. Finally, if games were installed on your system, Linux gives you a witty saying or aphorism.

It is always good practice to scan the line that starts with Last login, and check that the time given is correct. This is especially important if your Linux system is accessed by other users or connected to other systems. If the time given does not look right, it could be that someone is using the login to break into your system, or using your username without your permission.

We will read the mail message later, after taking care of some important steps. If you are curious, the same mail message is sent by the install procedure when the operating system is installed. It concerns registration matters for Linux.

Your "fortune" is chosen randomly from a long list, so don't expect to see the same one shown in the previous example. If you didn't install the games package during the Linux installation routine, you won't see a fortune. You can install the games package at any time.

The final line you see on the screen is the system prompt. This tells you that Linux is waiting for you to type in your commands—it's prompting you for input. The system prompt also displays the following useful information:

- darkstar is the system name.
- The ~ character indicates your location in the file system (explained in Chapter 8, "The Linux File System").
- The # character usually specifically indicates that you're logged in as root (although the $ sign is used in some operating systems which makes it difficult to quickly ascertain whether you are logged in as root or a regular user). According to UNIX conventions, regular user prompts are either % or $, depending on the shell; while # is reserved for root. These symbols are called shell prompts because they are used by the shell to prompt you for commands.

Passwords

In Linux (and just about all other UNIX systems) the superuser login name is root. No matter how humble or huge the system, if you can log in as root, the system is wide open for you to do whatever you want. Obviously, letting just anyone log in as root is unacceptable because it exposes the system to too much potential for serious damage.

To prevent unauthorized access, the root login should always have a password, and that password should be *secure*. You may have noticed that the Red Hat installation requested that you set a root password during the installation process. Some Linux installations do not set the root password; it is set to a *null string*, which is a word with no characters. With root and any other login, Linux does not bother asking for the password if it's the null string.

The null string is the least secure password there is, because anyone who knows a valid username (such as root) can access the system. It is up to you to change the password. Linux lets you choose what the new password will be, and accepts it without complaint. Unfortunately, this can lead to a false sense of security.

It was noticed a long time ago that users chose passwords that they could easily remember: their dog's name, their birthday, their hometown, their spouse's name, and so on. The problem is that these passwords were also easy to break, either through guessing or by more sophisticated means. This led some system administrators to insist on difficult-to-break, randomly picked passwords (such as S8t6WLk). People could not remember these passwords at all, so they wrote them down on pieces of paper and stuck them on their desks. Others, who were trying to break into the system, would find these pieces of paper and gain use of that login.

The best passwords are ones with a combination of uppercase letters, lowercase letters, and numbers, that are still easy to remember. Fri13th, 22Skidoo, and 2Qt4U are just a few examples. These hard-to-guess passwords are known as *strong* passwords, while easy-to-guess ones are called *weak*.

Of course, you should never use these exact passwords, or any other published sample passwords, because they're so easy to guess. There are many mischievous minds out there who, on strolling by a Linux system, might try root and Fri13th for the fun of it. You don't want to be the one with the nightmare of getting your system broken into.

For the best security, passwords should be changed every so often. Many system administrators recommend once every two or three months as reasonable. This guards against dictionary-based guessing attacks, and also minimizes damage in cases in which the password has been broken but nothing has really been done with it yet.

> **NOTE**
>
> Don't leave your terminal unattended while you're logged in. The idly malicious may take the opportunity to make some changes to your files, or send a nasty mail message off to people you'd hate to alienate. Always log out or lock your terminal when you leave.

Of course, the amount of system security you require depends on how much access there is to your system, and how sensitive is the information found on it. The root password should always be a good, secure one. If nothing else, it will discourage you from casually logging on as root, especially if you leave your user logins with null passwords.

If you are using Linux at home for experimenting, much of the security worries mentioned previously may seem silly. However, it doesn't hurt to use good security, and the practice can be carried over to larger UNIX systems at work.

We must assign a password for the root login using the Linux command passwd. The spelling of the command has its history in the development of UNIX, when long commands, such as password, were avoided due to the number of characters that had to be typed! To change the root password at the system prompt, type the command passwd, and you see the following:

```
darkstar:~# passwd
Changing password for root
Enter new password:
```

At the prompt, type your new, secure password. What you type is not displayed on the screen. This keeps anyone looking over your shoulder (called "shoulder surfing") from reading the password you've entered.

> **WARNING**
>
> Make sure you type the password slowly and carefully! If any other user's password is lost or forgotten, it can be reset by the root login. But, if the root password is lost or forgotten, you must reinstall Linux.

Because it's so important that passwords are entered correctly, the system double-checks the spelling of the password for you by asking you to type it again:

```
Re-type new password:
```

Again, what you type is not displayed on the screen. If your two password entries match, you see the following:

```
Password changed.
darkstar:~#
```

The password is now changed in the system's configuration files. If the two entries do not match completely (remember, case is important), Linux gives you the message

```
You misspelled it.   Password not changed.
```

and changes are not made to the password. You need to start over with the passwd command.

> **WARNING**
>
> Do not forget your new root password! Chant it to yourself before going to sleep, if necessary. But don't write it down on a piece of paper and slip it under the keyboard, either!

> **TIP**
>
> If you want to leave a program right away and return to the shell prompt, try Ctrl-C (hold down the Ctrl key and press C; this is sometimes written as ^C). This usually terminates whatever program you're in (usually without ill effects), and redisplays the shell prompt.

Creating a New Login

Now that you have assigned a password for the root account, the next thing you should do is create a login with which you can safely explore the Linux system and try out some of the basic commands covered in the following chapters.

Login names are used by valid system users. You can create a login for yourself that you will use permanently, or you can create a temporary login for exploring the system and remove it later. Login names can be any character or number string you want. Typically, login names bear a resemblance to the user's real name, so Joe Smith's login name may be joe, jsmith, or joes.

Linux has a utility called adduser, which simplifies and automates the task of adding a new user to the system. (This isn't how they did it in the good old days. You should be glad. In the past, files had to be manually edited to add users, a tedious and error-prone process.)

To create a user, at the shell prompt type **adduser** and the username you want to add.

```
darkstar:~# adduser fido

Looking for first available UID… 505
Looking for first available GID… 507

Adding login: fido…done.
Creating home directory: /home/fido…done.
Creating mailbox: /var/spool/mail/fido…done.

Don't forget to set the password
```

To complete adding the user, you'll need to use the passwd command to set password.

```
Darkstar:~# passwd
```

The adduser command included with Red Hat automatically assigns the UID, GID, and the home directory for the user added. The adduser command included with other Linux distributions will prompt you for these parameters.

An even more user-friendly method of adding users is to use the "user and group management" portion of the control-panel available under X.

> **NOTE**
>
> The User ID is used by Linux whenever it is referring to something you have done. The operating system is designed to use a number rather than the full login name because it takes up less room and is easier to manipulate. The User ID is important, and each login on the system has its own unique number. By convention, UIDs of 500 or less are special system UIDs; root's UID is 0. Regular users get UIDs starting at 501.

Logging Out

Now that you have created a new user, you can use it in the next couple of chapters to explore Linux. To finish with your session as root, log out of the system by typing logout:

```
darkstar:~# logout

Welcome to Linux 1.2.13
darkstar login:
```

You see the login prompt displayed again. At this point, you can log back in as root, or as the new user you have just created.

Some systems enable you to log out with the Ctrl-D sequence. If the shell you are using supports Ctrl-D as a logout command, the login prompt reappears. Otherwise, you may see a message such as this:

```
Use "logout" to leave the shell.
```

If you have used other UNIX systems before, you may be used to using Ctrl-D to log out. The default shell used by Linux does not support Ctrl-D unless the keymappings are changed to allow it.

Trying Out Your New Login

Now we can try out our new login. We can also look at some of the interesting features and capabilities of Linux.

At the login prompt, type the login name you have just created. If you were conscientious and assigned a nonzero-length password to your new login, enter the password when prompted.

You should now see the following:

```
darkstar login: fido
Password:
Last login: Sun Dec 11 19:14:22 on tty1
Linux 1.2.13.

Quiet!  I hear a hacker....
darkstar:~$
```

Note that your prompt looks different from the root prompt. The $ prompt indicates that you are a regular user running under the bash shell (which was the default choice presented by the adduser program). Also, there is no You have mail message.

> **NOTE**
>
> Linux can be configured to automatically mail a message to all new users. This can be a greeting, or can give system information and etiquette.

To see an example of the difference between the root login and a regular user login, type adduser at the shell prompt and press Enter.

```
darkstar:~$ adduser
bash: adduser: command not found
```

The message you get looks somewhat cryptic. However, it has a typical Linux error message structure, so it's worth taking a little effort to understand it.

Linux Error Messages

First of all, the program that's giving you the message is your shell, bash. It therefore announces itself with bash:, somewhat like the character in a play script. Next is the shell's "monologue." Being the "strong and silent" type of character, bash's monologue is very terse and to the point. It declares the object that is causing it problems (adduser), and the problem with this object: the command (adduser) can't be found.

If the error message were expanded into real English, it would go something like this: "Hi, I'm bash. You know that adduser command you gave me? I looked everywhere for adduser but I couldn't find it, so I couldn't perform whatever actions adduser would have specified." With time, you will get quite good at understanding Linux error message grammar.

Search Paths

Why can root find adduser, but an ordinary user cannot? Linux has many directories, and each directory can hold many files (one of which can be the elusive adduser). In theory, Linux could go search through the file system until it found adduser. But if root accidentally mistyped adduser as aduser, Linux would have to rummage through every nook and cranny before finally giving up. This could take 10 or more seconds, and cause needless wear and tear on your hard drive.

Therefore, Linux has *search paths* for finding commands (discussed in Chapter 8). Usually, only a small part of the entire Linux file system is on the search path, which literally is the path along which Linux searches. Because root makes use of many system administration programs such as adduser, the directories that hold these programs are in root's search path. Ordinary users do not have system administration directories in their search path.

However, if you explicitly tell Linux where a file is located, it does not need to look through its search path. As it happens, adduser is found in the /sbin directory. Try running /sbin/adduser.

```
darkstar:~$ /sbin/adduser
bash: /sbin/adduser: Only root may add users to the system.
```

This time, bash could find adduser (because you told it exactly where to look), but discovered that an ordinary user does not have permission to run adduser. As you can see, Linux limits the actions of logins to their privilege level.

Virtual Terminals

Linux, as mentioned earlier, is a multiuser, multitasking system. This means that more than one login can access the system at the same time, and that each login can be doing one or more different things all at the same time. A serious multiuser system will have several terminals (consisting of a keyboard and a display screen) wired or networked to the main computer unit.

Although you probably don't have any terminals attached to your system, you still can log in several times under the same or different login names, using your single keyboard and screen! This magic is performed by using *virtual terminals*.

Press Alt-F2. When you do so, everything on your screen should disappear, to be replaced by the following:

```
Welcome to Linux 1.2.13
darkstar login:
```

Log in as your "regular" login (not root). When the shell prompt is displayed, type who at the prompt and press Enter. You should see the following:

```
darkstar:~$ who
fido      tty2      Dec 14 01:42
fido      tty1      Dec 14 01:40
```

When you run the Linux command who, your screen displays the names of all logins currently logged into the system, and where they are logged in from. (Your login name will appear, of course, instead of fido in the preceding example.)

By convention, tty1 is the main console screen. It is the "normal" one that appears after Linux has started up, so you don't have to do anything special to get it. If you have switched to any other virtual consoles, you can return to tty1 by pressing Alt-F1.

How many virtual screens are active on your system? Try going through all the Alt-F*n* keys. Alternatively, you can scroll through the virtual screens by using the Alt-right arrow combination to move up through the screens, or Alt-left arrow to move down.

Quite often you find yourself doing something, perhaps in a long and complicated program, and realize that you should have done something else first. Flip to another virtual terminal and do whatever it is.

Another handy use of virtual terminals is when, through experimentation or otherwise, your screen locks up or starts typing in strange symbols. From a different virtual terminal, you can try to fix things, or restart the system if necessary.

Linux also comes with a very powerful multitasking windowing environment called X. Installing and running X Window systems is described in Chapter 21, "Installing X Window on Linux."

Commands and Programs

"Run the who command" and "Run who" are much more common ways of saying "Type who at the prompt and press Enter." We will use the shorter expressions wherever their meaning is clear. Sometimes people familiar with Linux drop the word "run," so that one user might tell another, "I tried who but didn't see anything unusual." It's understood by the context that when they "tried who," they actually ran it.

Something else you will notice if you are reading carefully is that there seem to be both Linux *programs* and Linux *commands*. A command is what you type at the shell prompt. For this reason, the combination of the shell prompt and what you type after it is often called a *command line*. When you press the Enter key, Linux takes the command you've entered and tries to perform it. The Linux system has built-in responses to some commands; for other commands it finds the appropriately named program on your hard disk and executes that program.

In the strictest sense, then, the command is what you type, and the program is what performs your command. However, very simple programs with straightforward results, such as who, are often referred to as commands, although there is actually a who program on your hard disk. More complicated programs, usually interactive such as adduser, or open-ended such as a text editor, are called programs. So you might hear one experienced user tell another, "The adduser program worked fine. I tried the who command 15 minutes later and the new user had logged in already."

Summary

In this chapter, we assigned a password to the root login and created a new user ID to be used in the next few chapters. We tried out Linux multitasking, and we learned some useful Linux terminology tips that will serve us well in the future (we will try to avoid seeing too many error messages, though). At this point, you can either ensure that you have logged out of all virtual terminals, or move on to the following chapters.

In the next two chapters, we will become more familiar with using Linux. In Chapter 7, "Basic Linux Commands and Utilities," we try out a variety of Linux commands as we exercise our Linux muscles. In Chapter 8, we learn more about how Linux stores its programs and data, and explore some of the interesting terrain on your hard drive.

Basic Linux Commands and Utilities

7

by Ed Treijs

In this chapter, we will discover the following:

- How to modify the basic function of Linux commands by using command options
- How to run two or more Linux commands in tandem by using input and output re-direction
- How to use parameters, such as filenames, with Linux commands
- How to read and understand the notational shorthand used in Linux and UNIX documentation
- How to use Linux online man pages and help facilities
- How to use wildcards that fill in for one or more filenames
- How to check your environment variables
- How to list processes running on the Linux system
- How to kill processes
- How to temporarily become another user
- How to use grep (and understand what grep means!)

How Linux Commands Work

Most Linux commands are very flexible. When you enter a Linux command, there are several ways to tailor the basic command to your specific needs. We will look at the two main ways used to modify the effect of a command:

- Specifying or redirecting a command's input and output
- Using command options

A simple way to picture what a Linux command does is to imagine that it's a black box that is part of an assembly line. Items come down a conveyor belt, enter the black box, get processed in some way, come out of the black box, and are taken away on another conveyor belt. Command options let you fine-tune the basic process happening inside the black box. Command redirection lets you specify which conveyor belt will supply the black box with items and which conveyor belt will take away the resulting products.

Once you understand how redirection and command options work, you will be able to (at least in principle) use any Linux or UNIX command. This is because UNIX was based on a few simple design principles. Commands, therefore, should work in consistent ways. Of course, UNIX has grown and changed over the years, and the design principles can sometimes get buried under all the changes. But they still make up the foundation, so that UNIX-based systems such as Linux are quite coherent and consistent in how they work.

> **TIP**
>
> Pressing Ctrl-U at any point, right up to before you press Enter, lets you clear everything you've typed on the command line. You can use this whenever you spot an error at the very beginning of your typing, or when you decide you don't want to run a particular command after all. You can also use the Backspace key to "back up" by erasing characters (in fact, it can be almost a reflex action), but it's usually faster to just erase the whole command line and start again.
>
> Perhaps the most powerful keys to use at the command prompt are the arrow keys. The left and right arrows move the cursor non-destructively. If you make a typo early in the line, you can left-arrow your way to the character and type in a correction. Additionally, the up and down arrows enable you to jump through a list of the last several commands used (similar to DOS's DOSKEY utility).

Command Options

You can use command options to fine-tune the actions of a Linux command. Quite often, a Linux command will do almost—but not quite—what you want it to do. Instead of making you learn a second command, Linux lets you modify the basic, or default, actions of the command by using options.

The ls command is an excellent, and useful, example of a command that has a great many options. The ls command lists the files found on the Linux system's hard drive. This sounds simple enough, doesn't it? Try entering the command

```
darkstar:~$ ls
darkstar:~$
```

Well, nothing much seemed to happen.

Now try typing ls -a. Type it exactly as listed. The space between ls and -a is necessary, and there must be no space between the - and the a.

```
darkstar:~$ ls -a
./              .bash_history  .less          .term/
../             .kermrc        .lessrc
```

What you have done is modified what ls does by adding a command option—in this case, -a. By default, ls lists only files whose names don't begin with a period. However, -a tells ls to list all files, even ones that begin with a period. (These are usually special files created for you by Linux.) At present, all the files in your directory start with a period, so ls by itself does not list any files; you must add -a to see the files you have at present.

The ls command has many more options. You can use more than one option at a time. For example, try typing ls -al:

```
darkstar:~$ ls -al
total 10
drwxr-xr-x  3 fido      users       1024 Dec 21 22:11 ./
```

```
drwxr-xr-x   6 root      root       1024 Dec 14 01:39 ../
-rw-r--r--   1 fido      users        333 Dec 21 22:11 .bash_history
-rw-r--r--   1 fido      users        163 Dec  7 14:31 .kermrc
-rw-r--r--   1 fido      users         34 Jun  6  1993 .less
-rw-r--r--   1 fido      users        114 Nov 23  1993 .lessrc
drwxr-xr-x   2 fido      users       1024 Dec  7 13:36 .term/
```

You now get a listing with many more details about the files. (These will be explained in Chapter 8, "The Linux File System.") The l option can be used by itself; ls -l will give detailed descriptions of files that don't begin with a period. Sometimes filenames are so long they don't fit on a single line. Linux simply wraps the remainder to the next line.

> **NOTE**
>
> Strictly speaking, the dash (-) is not part of the command option. The dash simply tells Linux to understand each letter immediately following it as a command option. There *must* be a space before the dash, and there *must not* be a space between the dash and the letter or letters making up the command option. There *must* be a space after the command option if anything else is to be entered on the command line after it.
>
> You can type more than one command option after the dash, as we did with ls -al. In this case, we are specifying both the a and the l options. The order you specify options in usually doesn't matter; ls -al will give the same results as ls -la. Combining options doesn't work with all Linux commands, and then only with those that use a single letter to specify each option.
>
> Multiple options can also be specified individually, with each option preceded by a dash and separated from other options by spaces—for example, ls -a -l. This is usually done only when a particular option requires a further parameter.

By default, ls lists files in alphabetical order. Sometimes you might be more interested in when a file was created or last modified. The t option tells ls to sort files by date instead of alphabetically by filename, showing the newest files first. Therefore, typing ls -alt gives

```
darkstar:~$ ls -alt
total 10
drwxr-xr-x   3 fido      users       1024 Jan  2 13:48 ./
-rw-r--r--   1 fido      users        333 Dec 21 22:11 .bash_history
drwxr-xr-x   6 root      root       1024 Dec 14 01:39 ../
-rw-r--r--   1 fido      users        163 Dec  7 14:31 .kermrc
drwxr-xr-x   2 fido      users       1024 Dec  7 13:36 .term/
-rw-r--r--   1 fido      users        114 Nov 23  1993 .lessrc
-rw-r--r--   1 fido      users         34 Jun  6  1993 .less
```

The r option tells ls to produce a reverse output. This is often used with the t option. The following is an example of what you might get if you entered ls -altr:

```
darkstar:~$ ls -altr
total 10
-rw-r--r--   1 fido      users         34 Jun  6  1993 .less
```

```
-rw-r--r--   1 fido    users        114 Nov 23  1993 .lessrc
drwxr-xr-x   2 fido    users       1024 Dec  7 13:36 .term/
-rw-r--r--   1 fido    users        163 Dec  7 14:31 .kermrc
drwxr-xr-x   6 root    root        1024 Dec 14 01:39 ../
-rw-r--r--   1 fido    users        333 Dec 21 22:11 .bash_history
drwxr-xr-x   3 fido    users       1024 Jan  2 13:48 ./
```

Many other options can be used with `ls`, although we have now tried the most commonly used ones. The important thing to remember is that you can usually customize a Linux command by using one or more command options.

NOTE

As with basic Linux commands, case is important! For instance, `ls` has an R option (*recursive:* show files in subdirectories, too) that gives much different results from the r option.

TIP

You can think of a as the "all files" option, l as the "long list" option, t as the "sort by time" option, r as the "reverse sort" option, and so on. In fact, most options in Linux are *mnemonic*—the option letter stands for a word or phrase. Some option letters mean the same thing in many different Linux commands. For instance, v often means *verbose*—in other words, "Give me lots of detail."

However, do not assume that, on any unfamiliar command, certain options will work in the "usual" way! For instance, r is the recursive option for many Linux commands; however, in the case of `ls`, reverse sort is more commonly used, and therefore it gets the easier-to-type lowercase r, while recursive is left with the capital R. It might seem like not much extra effort to press the Shift key to get the capital letter, but try typing a string of four or five options, one of which is capitalized!

NOTE

You can easily find out which options are available for any Linux command by using the man command. See the section "The Linux Man Pages" later in this chapter.

Other Parameters

Linux commands often use parameters that are not actual command options. These parameters, such as filenames or directories, are *not* preceded by a dash.

For instance, by default ls lists the files in your current directory. You can, however, tell ls to list the files in any other directory simply by adding the directory to the command line. For instance, ls /bin will list everything in the /bin directory. This can be combined with command options, so that ls -l /bin gives you detailed listings of the files in /bin. Try this. You will be impressed by the number of files in the /bin directory!

You can also specify ls to list information about any particular file by entering its filename. For instance, ls -la .lessrc gives detailed information only about the .lessrc file.

Input and Output Redirection

Many Linux commands let you specify which file or directory they are to act upon, as we saw with the example ls -l /bin earlier.

You can also "pipe" the output from a command so that it becomes another command's input. This is done by typing two or more commands separated by the ¦ character. (This character normally is found on the same key as the \ character. You must hold down the Shift key or you will get \ instead of ¦). The ¦ character means "Use the output from the previous command as the input for the next command." Therefore, typing command_1¦command_2 does both commands, one after the other, before giving you the results.

Using our assembly-line metaphor, we are processing items through two black boxes instead of just one. When we use piping, it's like hooking up the first command's output conveyor belt to become the input conveyor belt for the second command.

> **TIP**
>
> Although Linux doesn't care whether ¦ is set off by spaces, if command_1 ¦ command_2 is easier for you to read and understand than command_1¦command_2, by all means use spaces around ¦.

You will have noticed that the output of ls -l /bin is many lines long, so that much of the information scrolls off the screen before you can read it. You can pipe this output to a formatting program called more, which displays information in screen-sized chunks. When you enter ls -l /bin ¦ more, you will see the following:

```
darkstar:~$ ls -l /bin ¦ more
total 1611
-rwxr-xr-x   1 root     bin          1248 Sep 17 04:25 arch*
-rwxr-xr-x   1 root     bin        295940 Sep  5 01:45 bash*
-rwxr-xr-x   1 root     bin          4840 Nov 24  1993 cat*
-rwxr-xr-x   1 root     bin          9220 Jul 20 12:06 chgrp*
-rwxr-xr-x   1 root     bin         13316 Jul 20 12:06 chmod*
-rwxr-xr-x   1 root     bin         13316 Jul 20 12:06 chown*
lrwxrwxrwx   1 root     root           17 Dec  7 13:37 compress -> /usr/bin/comp
➡ress*
-rwxr-xr-x   1 root     bin         21508 Jul 20 12:06 cp*
-rwxr-xr-x   1 root     bin         41988 May  1  1994 cpio*
lrwxrwxrwx   1 root     root            4 Dec  7 13:40 csh -> tcsh*
```

```
-rwxr-xr-x   1 root      bin          5192 Nov 24  1993 cut*
-rwxr-xr-x   1 root      bin         19872 Mar 23  1994 date*
-rwxr-xr-x   1 root      bin         17412 Jul 20 12:06 dd*
-rwxr-xr-x   1 root      bin         13316 Jul 20 12:06 df*
-rwxr-xr-x   1 root      bin         66564 Jun  9  1994 dialog*
-rwxr-xr-x   1 root      bin          1752 Sep 17 04:25 dmesg*
lrwxrwxrwx   1 root      root            8 Dec  7 13:37 dnsdomainname -> hostname*
-rwxr-xr-x   1 root      bin         13316 Jul 20 12:06 du*
-rwxr-xr-x   1 root      bin          3312 Mar 23  1994 echo*
-rwxr-xr-x   1 root      bin         36684 May  4  1994 ed*
-rwxr-xr-x   1 root      bin           326 Mar 23  1994 false*
--More--
```

The --More-- at the bottom of the screen tells you that there's more text to come. To go to the next screen of text, press the spacebar. Every time you press the spacebar, more displays another screenful of text. When the last screenful of text has been displayed, more returns you to the Linux prompt.

TIP

The more command can do many other things. For instance, to move back one screen at a time, type b for "back." Another useful command is q for "quit." This lets you leave immediately, without having to go through all the remaining screens of text.

While in more, type h for "help." This will list the commands available within more.

NOTE

The Linux system sometimes uses the command less instead of more. One difference you will notice is that, unlike more, less requires you to type q to return to the command line, even if you're at the end of the text to be displayed. This might seem cumbersome, but it prevents you from accidentally exiting the program by pressing the spacebar once too often.

The name less is a play on more. Originally, less was designed to have many features that more lacked. The version of more included in your Linux system has most of these features, however.

The Linux man program, discussed later, uses less to display text. Most other UNIX systems use more by default. Don't get confused. Remember to type q to exit from less!

Another thing you can do in Linux is to send output to a file instead of the screen. There are many different reasons why you might want to do this. You might want to save a "snapshot" of a command's output as it was at a certain time, or you might want to save a command's output for further examination. You might also want to save the output from a command that takes a very long time to run, and so on.

To send output to a file, use the > symbol (found above the period on your keyboard). For instance, you can place the output of the ls -1 /bin command into a file called test by typing ls -1 /bin > test. Again, spaces around > are optional and not strictly necessary, but they do make the command much more readable.

If you now do an `ls` or `ls -1`, you will see that you've created a new file called `test` in your own directory.

To see the contents of a file, you can again use the `more` command. Just specify the name of the file you want to look at. In this case, you would type `more test`.

> ### WARNING
>
> Be careful! When you use >, you completely overwrite the previous contents of the file you specify to take the output (if that file existed). For example, if we already had a file called `test` in our directory, its old contents would be completely replaced by the output from `ls -1 /bin`. Linux *will not* warn you that you are about to do this!
>
> Be particularly careful if you're not in your usual directory, or if you're logged in as root. You could, for instance, accidentally clobber the Linux program `test`, which exists as a file named `test`—fortunately, not in the directory where we created our `test` file! It's a good idea to check if the output file already exists before using >. In our example, we could have typed `ls -1 test` beforehand. If no information is displayed, the file does not exist.

You can specify that you want to add your output to the end of the file, rather than replace the file's contents, by using >>. Type `who >> test` to add the output of the `who` command to the end of the text already in the file `test`.

You can examine the results by using either `more` or `less` and paging through to the end of the file, or by using the Linux command `tail`, which displays the last few lines of the specified file. In this case, you would type `tail test` to see the last few lines of the file `test`. Try using `tail`!

> ### NOTE
>
> For a more detailed discussion of redirection and piping, see Chapter 10, "Using bash."

Notational Conventions Used to Describe Linux Commands

There is a set of accepted notational conventions used to describe, in a concise and consistent way, the correct syntax for any given Linux command. This specifies what options or parameters you must use, what options or parameters you can use or not use, and so on. Sometimes this set of conventions is used to give a complete and exhaustive listing of a command's syntax, showing every possible command and parameter. Sometimes it is used to make a particular example more general and the command's basic usage clearer.

If you remember the following six basic rules, you will be able, in principle, to understand the syntax of any Linux or UNIX command.

Six Basic Rules of Linux Notation

1. Any text standing by itself, and not within [ ], <>, or {}, must be typed exactly as shown.

2. Any text within square brackets ([ ]) is optional. You can type it or not type it. For instance, the syntax `ls [-l]` means you must type `ls` (per the first rule), while adding `-l` is optional, but not necessary. Do not type the square brackets themselves! In our example, type `ls` or `ls -l`. Don't type `ls [-l]`.

3. Angle brackets (<>) and the text within them must be replaced by appropriate text (usually a name or value). The text within the brackets usually indicates the nature of the replacement. For instance, the syntax `more <filename>` means that you should replace `<filename>` with the name of the file you wish to examine using `more`. If you want to look at the file `test`, you would type `more test`. Remember, do not use the angle brackets when you actually type the command!

4. Curly braces ({}) indicate that you must choose one of the values given within the braces. The values are separated by ¦ (which in this case means *or*, not *pipe!*). For example, the syntax `command -{a¦b}` means you must enter either `command -a` or `command -b`.

5. An ellipsis (...) means "and so on." It is normally used with parameters such as filenames, as described later.

6. The sixth basic rule states that the brackets can be combined as necessary. For instance, you don't have to type a filename with the `more` command. This would be indicated as `more [<filename>]`. The outer set of square brackets makes the entire parameter optional. If you do decide to use the parameter, replace the inner set of angle brackets with the appropriate value. Because the `more` command enables one or more filenames to be specified, the syntax becomes `more [<filename>...]`. The ellipsis means you can have as many `<filenames>` as you wish.

Online Help Available in Linux

Linux has help facilities available online. If you forget the exact use of a command, or you're looking for the right command to use, the answer might be available straight from Linux. The two help facilities we will try out are the `bash` shell's `help` command, and the `man` command, which is available on almost all UNIX systems, including Linux.

NOTE

If you have not installed the man pages package, you should do so now. Although it is possible to get by without man pages, they are a very valuable resource for both novice and expert Linux users.

The Linux Man Pages

The "man" in "man pages" stands for "manual." (As usual, the creators of UNIX shortened a long but descriptive word to a shorter, cryptic one!) Typing man *<command>* lets you view the manual pages dealing with a particular command.

Try typing man passwd to see what the Linux manual has to say about the passwd command.

The general layout of a man page is as follows:

```
COMMAND(1)              Linux Programmer's Manual           COMMAND(1)

NAME
      command - summary of what command does

SYNOPSIS
      <complete syntax of command in the standard Linux form>

DESCRIPTION
      More verbose explanation of what "command" does.

OPTIONS
      Lists each available option with description of what it does

FILES
      lists files used by, or related to, command

SEE ALSO
      command_cousin(1), command_spouse(1), etc.

BUGS
      There are bugs in Linux commands??

AUTHOR
      J. S. Goobly (goobly@hurdly-gurdly.boondocks)

Linux 1.0               22 June 1994                        1
```

The man page for passwd is actually quite understandable. Be warned, however, that man pages are often written in a very formal and stylized way that sometimes bears little resemblance to English. This is done not to baffle people, but to cram a great deal of information into as short a description as possible.

For example, try man ls. Notice how many options are available for ls and how long it takes to explain them!

Although it can take practice (and careful reading!) to understand man pages, once you get used to them, the first thing you'll do when you encounter a strange command is call up the man page for that command.

Finding Keywords in Man Pages

Sometimes you know what you want to do, but you don't know which command you should use to do it. You can use the keyword option by typing man -k *<keyword>*. The man program will return the name of every command whose name entry (which includes a very brief description) contains that keyword.

For instance, you can search on manual:

```
darkstar:~$ man -k manual
man (1)                      - Format and display the on-line manual pages
whereis (1)                  - Locate binary, manual, and or source for program
xman (1)                     - Manual page display program for the X Window System
```

You have to be careful to specify your keyword well, though! Using directory as your keyword isn't too bad, but using file will give you many more entries than you will want to wade through.

> **NOTE**
>
> You might have noticed that commands seem to be followed by numbers in brackets, usually (1). This refers to the manual section. Back in the days when UNIX manuals came in printed, bound volumes, normal commands were in Section 1, files used by administrators were in Section 5, programming routines were described in Section 3, and so on.
>
> Therefore, some man pages are not about commands at all, but rather about files or system calls used in Linux!
>
> If a particular entry shows up in more than one section, man will show you the lowest-numbered entry by default. You can see higher-numbered entries by specifying the section number. For instance, Section 5 has a manual entry on the passwd file. To see this rather than the manual entry for the passwd command type man 5 passwd.
>
> In general, man *<n> <entry>* will find the man page for *<entry>* in Section *<n>*.

The *bash* Shell *help* Facility

When you type a command at the prompt, the shell program takes what you've written, interprets it as necessary, and passes the result to the Linux operating system. Linux then performs the actions requested of it. Many Linux commands require Linux to find and start up a new program. However, the shell itself can perform a number of functions. These functions can be simple, often-used commands, so that the overhead of starting up separate programs is eliminated, or they can be facilities that make the shell environment friendlier and more useful. One of these facilities is the help command, which provides information on the bash shell's built-in functions.

Type help at the prompt. You will see at least some of the following:

```
GNU bash, version 1.14.6(1)
Shell commands that are defined internally. Type 'help' to see this list.
Type 'help name' to find out more about the function 'name'.
Use 'info bash' to find out more about the shell in general.

A star (*) next to a name means that the command is disabled.
```

```
%[DIGITS ¦ WORD] [&]              . [filename]
:                                [ arg... ]
alias [ name[=value] ... ]       bg [job_spec]
bind [-lvd] [-m keymap] [-f filena break [n]
builtin [shell-builtin [arg ...]] case WORD in [PATTERN [¦ PATTERN].
cd [dir]                         command [-pVv] [command [arg ...]]
continue [n]                     declare [-[frxi]] name[=value] ...
dirs [-l]                        echo [-neE] [arg ...]
enable [-n] [name ...]           eval [arg ...]
exec [ [-] file [redirection ...]] exit [n]
export [-n] [-f] [name ...] or exp fc [-e name] [-nlr] [first] [last
fg [job_spec]                    for NAME [in WORDS ... ;] do COMMA
function NAME { COMMANDS ; } or NA getopts optstring name [arg]
hash [-r] [name ...]             help [pattern ...]
history [n] [ [-awrn] [filename]] if COMMANDS; then COMMANDS; [elif
jobs [-lnp] [jobspec ...] ¦ jobs - kill [-s sigspec ¦ -sigspec] [pid
let arg [arg ...]                local name[=value] ...
logout                           popd [+n ¦ -n]
pushd [dir ¦ +n ¦ -n]            pwd
read [-r] [name ...]             readonly [-n] [-f] [name ...] or r
return [n]                       select NAME [in WORDS ... ;] do CO
set [—abefhknotuvxldHCP] [-o opti shift [n]
source filename                  suspend [-f]
test [expr]                      times
trap [arg] [signal_spec]         type [-all] [-type ¦ -path] [name
typeset [-[frxi]] name[=value] ... ulimit [-SHacdmstfpnuv [limit]]
umask [-S] [mode]                unalias [-a] [name ...]
unset [-f] [-v] [name ...]       until COMMANDS; do COMMANDS; done
variables - Some variable names an wait [n]
while COMMANDS; do COMMANDS; done { COMMANDS }
```

You will have to pipe the output of help to more (help ¦ more) to keep the first part from scrolling off your screen.

Wildcards: * and ?

In many a late-night card game, jokers are shuffled into the deck. The jokers are *wildcards* that can become any card of your choice. This is obviously very useful! Linux has wildcards also. They are, if anything, more useful than jokers in a card game.

Linux has several wildcards. Wildcards are used as a convenient and powerful shortcut when specifying files (or directories) that a command is to operate on. We will briefly look at the two most popular wildcards: * and ?.

The most commonly used wildcard is *, which stands in for any combination of one or more characters. For example, c* will match all filenames that begin with c. You can see this for yourself by typing ls /bin/c*.

What happens if you type ls /bin/c*t? How about ls /bin/*t?

The ? wildcard is more restrictive than *. It only stands in for any *one* character. You can see this by comparing ls/bin/d* with ls/bin/d?.

NOTE

Wildcards can only be used to match filenames and directory names. You can't, for example, type pass* at the Linux prompt and expect Linux to run the passwd program for you.

WARNING

Be very careful when using wildcards with dangerous commands, such as the ones used to permanently delete files! A good check is to run ls with the wildcards you plan to use and examine the resulting list of files to see if the wildcard combination did what you expected it to do. Also double-check that you typed everything correctly *before* pressing the Enter key!

Environment Variables

When you log in, Linux keeps a number of useful data items in the background ready for the system to use. The actual data is held in something called an *environment variable,* whose name is often descriptive or mnemonic. In fact, this is no different from the way you and I remember things. We know that there always is a piece of information called "day of the week" (the environment variable); however, we change the data in this variable, from Monday to Tuesday to Wednesday, and so on, as days go by.

To see the list of *exported* environment variables, type env. The environment variable's name is on the left, and the value held by the variable is on the right.

The most important variable to note is the PATH, whose value is your *search path.* As we will see in the next chapter, when you type a command, Linux will search every place listed in your search path for that command.

A longer list of environment variables, consisting of several new variables in addition to the ones you saw earlier, is displayed by the command set. The new variables are local: they have not been marked for export. For more information on exporting variables, see Chapter 10. You can think of local variables as items of information you need for only a certain time or location. For instance, remembering the variable "what-floor-am-I-on" becomes an unnecessary piece of information once you leave the building!

Processes and How to Terminate Them

In the previous chapter, we learned about the who command, which shows you the usernames of everyone who is logged into the system. The who program actually gets its information from the Linux system, which maintains and updates the list of the system's current users.

In fact, Linux keeps much more detailed records about what is happening on the system than just who is logged in. Because Linux is a multitasking system, in which many programs or program threads may be running simultaneously, Linux keeps track of individual tasks or *processes*.

Although these processes are usually well-behaved and well-managed by Linux, sometimes they might go out of control. This can happen if a program hits a bug or a flaw in its internal code or supplied data, or if you accidentally enter the wrong command or command option.

Being able to identify these misbehaving processes, and then being able to terminate or *kill* them, is an essential piece of knowledge for *all* Linux/UNIX users. (Obviously the world was a less kind and gentle place when the `kill` command was developed and named.) When you are your own system administrator, as in our case, it's doubly important!

The Process Status Command: *ps*

To find out what processes are running, we use the `ps` command. `ps` stands for "process status," not the "post script" you would write at the end of a letter.

Typing `ps` by itself gives you a concise listing of your own processes:

```
darkstar:~$ ps
  PID TTY STAT  TIME COMMAND
   41 v01 S<    0:00 -bash
  134 v01 R<    0:00 ps
```

The information in the first column, headed `PID`, is important. This is the Process ID number, which is unique, and which Linux uses to identify that particular process. You must know a process's PID to be able to kill it.

The `TTY` column shows you which terminal the process was started from.

The `STAT` column gives the status of the process. The two most common entries in the status column are `S` for *sleeping* and `R` for *running*. A sleeping process is one that isn't currently active. However, don't be misled. A sleeping process might just be taking a very brief catnap! In fact, a process might switch between sleeping and running many times every second.

The `TIME` column shows the amount of system time used by the process. Clearly, neither of our processes are taking up any appreciable system time!

Finally, the `COMMAND` column contains the name of the program you're running. This will usually be the command you typed at the command line. However, sometimes the command you type starts one or more *child* processes, and in this case, you would see these additional processes show up as well, without ever having typed them yourself. Your `login` shell will have a - before it, as in `-bash` in the previous example. This helps to distinguish this *primary* shell from any shells you might enter from it. These will not have the - in front.

> **NOTE**
>
> If you are logged in as root, you will see a list of *all* processes on the system. This is because the root username, being the superuser, owns everything that happens on the Linux system.
>
> If you are an "ordinary" user, but have also logged in on another terminal (including another virtual terminal you have selected by pressing Alt-F*n* as discussed in Chapter 6, "Getting Started with Linux"), you will see the processes you are running on the other terminal (or terminals) as well.

One useful option with ps is u. Although it stands for "user," as in "List the username as well," it actually adds quite a few more columns of information in addition to just the username:

```
darkstar:~$ ps -u
USER    PID %CPU %MEM SIZE  RSS TTY STAT START   TIME COMMAND
fido     41  0.1  6.8  364  472 v01 S<  23:19   0:01 -bash
fido    138  0.0  3.3   72  228 v01 R<  23:34   0:00 ps -u
```

In addition to the username in the USER column, other interesting new items include %CPU, which shows you what percentage of your computer's processing power is being used by the process, and %MEM, which shows you what percentage of your computer's memory is being used by the process.

If you want to see all processes running on the system, and not just the processes started by your own username, you can use the a command option. (The root login sees everyone's processes automatically and does not have to use a, so root can get the following output by simply typing ps.)

```
darkstar:~$ ps -a
 PID TTY STAT  TIME COMMAND
  62 v03 S<   0:00 /sbin/agetty 38400 tty3
  63 v04 S<   0:00 /sbin/agetty 38400 tty4
  64 v05 S<   0:00 /sbin/agetty 38400 tty5
  65 v06 S<   0:00 /sbin/agetty 38400 tty6
 330 v02 S<   0:00 -bash
 217 v01 S<   0:00 -bash
 217 v01 S<   0:00 ps -a
```

As you can see, quite a few "other" processes are happening on the system! In fact, most of the processes we see here will be running whether or not anyone is actually logged into the Linux system. All the processes listed as running on tty psf are actually system processes, and are started every time you boot up the Linux system. Processes of the form /sbin/agetty 38400 tty6 are login processes running on a particular terminal waiting for your login.

It can be useful to combine the a and u options (if you're not root).

```
darkstar:~$ ps -au
USER    PID %CPU %MEM SIZE  RSS TTY STAT START   TIME COMMAND
root     72  0.0  3.6  390  532 v01 S<  17:55   0:01 -bash
root     74  0.0  1.5   41  224 v03 S<  17:55   0:00 /sbin/agetty 38400 tty3
root     75  0.0  1.5   41  224 v04 S<  17:55   0:00 /sbin/agetty 38400 tty4
root     76  0.0  1.5   41  224 v05 S<  17:55   0:00 /sbin/agetty 38400 tty5
root     77  0.0  1.5   41  224 v06 S<  17:55   0:00 /sbin/agetty 38400 tty6
```

```
root          78  0.0  1.5   56   228  s00  S<   17:55   0:00 gpm -t mman
root          98  0.0  1.5   41   224  v02  S<   18:02   0:00 /sbin/agetty 38400 tty2
root         108 18.8  3.6  384   528  pp0  S<   18:27   0:01 -bash
```

A more technical `l` option can sometimes be useful:

```
darkstar:~$ ps -l
  F   UID   PID  PPID PRI NI SIZE  RSS WCHAN        STAT TTY    TIME COMMAND
  0   501    41     1  15  0  364  472 114d9c       S<   v01   0:00 -bash
  0   501   121    41  29  0   64  208 0            R<   v01   0:00 ps -l
```

The interesting information is in the PPID column. PPID stands for "Parent Process ID"—in other words, the process that started the particular process. Notice that the `ps -l` command was started by `-bash`, the `login` shell. In other words, `ps -l` was started from the command line. Notice also that the PPID for the login shell is PID 1. If you check the output from `ps -au` shown previously, you will see that the process with PID of 1 is `init`. The `init` process is the one that spawns, or starts, all other processes. If `init` dies, the system crashes!

> **NOTE**
>
> The Linux `ps` command has some quirks when it comes to options.
>
> First of all, the dash before the options is not necessary. In the earlier example, `ps 1` would work the same as `ps -l`. Because most Linux commands *do* require the use of dashes with their command options, and other versions of UNIX might require dashes when using `ps`, it's best to use the dash anyway.
>
> Second, the order in which you enter the options does matter, especially if you try to combine the `l` and `u` options! Try typing `ps -lu`, and then `ps -ul`. This behavior is not covered in the `ps` man page. The moral is twofold: First, use the minimum possible number of command options. Second, the man pages are, alas, not always correct and complete.

The Process Termination Command: *kill*

The `kill` command is used to terminate processes that can't be stopped by other means.

> **NOTE**
>
> Before going through the following procedure, if it's a program you're stuck in, make sure you can't stop or exit it by typing Ctrl-C or some other key combination.

1. Switch to another virtual console and log in as `root`.
2. Run `ps -u` and identify the offending process. You will use its PID in the next step.
3. Use the `kill` program by typing `kill <PID>`, where *PID* is the Process ID you wish to kill. Make sure that you have correctly identified the offending process! As root, you can kill any user process, including the wrong one if you misread or mistype the PID.

4. Verify that the process has been killed by using `ps -u` again. You can type `ps -u <PID>`, which shows you the status of only the specified PID. If there's a null result and you're just given the Linux prompt again, the PID is dead, so go to step 8. However, it's best to look at the complete `ps -u` list if it's not too long. Sometimes the offending process reappears with a new PID! If that is the case, go to step 6.

5. If the process is still alive and has the same PID, use `kill`'s 9 option. Type `kill -9 <PID>`. Check it as in step 4. If this does not kill the process, go to step 7. If the process is now dead, go to step 8.

6. If the offending process has reappeared with a new PID, that means that it's being created automatically by some other process. The only thing to do now is to kill the parent process, which is the true offender! You might also have to kill the parent process when `kill -9` does not work.

7. Use `ps -l` to identify the troublesome process's PPID. This is the PID of the parent process. You should check the parent's identity more closely by typing `ps -u <Parent PID>` before going ahead and killing it as described in step 3, using the PID of the *parent* in the `kill` command. You should follow through with step 4 and, if necessary, step 5, making sure the parent process has been killed.

8. The process is killed. Remember to log off. You should not leave `root` logged in on virtual consoles, because you will forget that the `root` logins are there!

NOTE

Sometimes processes are simply unkillable! In this case, you're best off shutting down the Linux system and rebooting.

Linux keeps ordinary users (as opposed to `root`) from killing other users' processes (maliciously or otherwise). For instance, if you are an ordinary user and you try to kill the `init` process, which always has PID=1, you will see

```
darkstar:~$ kill 1
kill:  (1) - Not owner
```

Actually, not even `root` can kill the `init` process, although there is no error message. The `init` process is one of those "unkillable" processes discussed earlier, because it's such a key process. That's all for the best!

Becoming Someone Else: The *su* Command

Usually, when you want to temporarily become a different user, you will simply switch to another virtual terminal, log in as the other user, log out when you're done, and return to your "home" virtual terminal. However, there are times when this is impractical or inconvenient. Perhaps all your virtual terminals are already busy, or perhaps you're in a situation (such as logged on via a telephone and modem) in which you don't have virtual terminals available.

In these cases, you can use the su command. "su" stands for "super user." If you type su by itself, you will be prompted for the root password. If you successfully enter the root password, you will see the root # prompt, and you will have all of root's privileges.

You can also become any other user by typing su *<username>*. If you are root when you type su *<username>*, you are not asked for that user's password since in principle you could change the user's password or examine all the user's files from the root login anyway. If you are an "ordinary" user trying to change to another ordinary user, you will be asked to enter the password of the user you are trying to become.

NOTE

Although su grants you all the privileges you would get if you logged on as that user, be aware that you won't inherit that login's exact environment or run that login's startup files (if any). This means that su is not really suited to doing extended work, and it's quite unsuitable for troubleshooting problems with that login.

The *grep* Command

"What on earth does grep mean?" you ask.

This is a fair question. grep must be the quintessential UNIX acronym, because it's impossible to understand even when it's spelled out in full!

grep stands for *Global Regular Expression Parser.* You will understand the use of this command right away, but when "Global Regular Expression Parser" becomes a comfortable phrase in itself, you should probably consider taking a vacation.

What grep does, essentially, is find and display lines that contain a pattern that you specify. There are two basic ways to use grep.

The first use of grep is to filter the output of other commands. The general syntax is *<command>* ¦ grep *<pattern>*. For instance, if we wanted to see every actively running process on the system, we would type ps -a ¦ grep R. In this application, grep passes on only those lines that contain the pattern (in this case, the single letter) R. Note that if someone were running a program called Resting, it would show up even if its status were S for sleeping, because grep would match the R in Resting. An easy way around this problem is to type grep " R ", which explicitly tells grep to search for an R with a space on each side. You must use quotes whenever you search for a pattern that contains one or more blank spaces.

The second use of grep is to search for lines that contain a specified pattern in a specified file. The syntax here is grep *<pattern> <filename>*. Be careful. It's easy to specify the filename first and the pattern second by mistake! Again, you should be as specific as you can with the pattern to be matched, in order to avoid "false" matches.

Summary

By this point you should have tried enough different Linux commands to start getting familiar (if not yet entirely comfortable) with typical Linux usage conventions.

It is important that you be able to use the man pages provided online by Linux. A very good exercise at this point is to pull up man pages for all the commands we have looked at in the past two chapters: login, passwd, who, adduser, and so on. If some of the commands listed under "See also:" look interesting, by all means take a look at their man pages too!

> **NOTE**
>
> Some man pages, such as the one for bash, are *extremely* long. Do not plan to read them all in one sitting!

In Chapter 8, we head out from "home" and poke around in the Linux filesystem. As system administrators, we should know what our hard drives contain! For instance, there are special "administrator-only" directories crammed with goodies.

Several more "essential" commands will be introduced. By the end of the next chapter, you will have seen and tried most of the important "user" Linux commands and will have had a taste of some of the "administrator" commands.

The Linux File System

8

by Ed Treijs

IN THIS CHAPTER

In this chapter, you learn about:

- Files: what they are, types of files, filenames
- Directories: what they are, parent directories and subdirectories, directory names, your home directory
- Absolute and relative file and directory names
- Moving between directories using the cd command
- Using the cat command to create a new file
- Creating directories
- Moving and copying files
- Removing files and directories
- File and directory ownership, using chown and chgrp to change ownership
- File and directory permissions, using chmod to change permissions
- Using the gunzip command to uncompress .gz files compressed by gzip
- The tar command
- The standard Linux directories and directory structure

To understand how Linux works, and to use the system beyond a superficial level, you must be familiar with the Linux notion of files and the file system into which they are organized.

Files: An Overview

The most basic concept of a file, and one you may already be familiar with from other computer systems, defines a *file* as a distinct chunk of information that is found on your hard drive. *Distinct* means that there can be many different files, each with its own particular contents. To keep files from getting confused with each other, every file must have a unique identity. In Linux, you identify each file by its name and location. In each location or *directory,* there can be only one file by a particular name. So, for instance, if you create a file called novel, and you get a second great idea, you will either have to call it something different, such as novel2, or put it in a different place, to keep from *overwriting* the contents already in your original novel.

Common Types of Files

Files can contain various types of information. The following three types will become the most familiar to you:

- User data: Information that you create and update. The very simplest user data is plain text or numbers. You learn to create these simple files later in this chapter. More complicated user data files might have to be *interpreted* by another program to make sense. For instance, a spreadsheet file looks like gibberish if you look at it directly. To work with a spreadsheet, you have to start up the spreadsheet program and read in the spreadsheet file.

■ System data: Information, often in plain text form, that is read and used by the Linux system—to keep track of which users are allowed on the system, for instance. As a system administrator, you are responsible for changing system data files. For instance, when you create a new user, you modify the file /etc/passwd, which contains the user information. Ordinary users of the system are usually not concerned with system data files, except for their private startup files.

■ Executable files: These files contain instructions that your computer can perform. This set of instructions is often called a *program*. When you tell the computer to perform them, you're telling it to *execute* the instructions given to it. To human eyes, executable files contain meaningless gibberish—obviously your computer doesn't think the way you do! Creating or modifying executable files takes special tools. You learn how to use these programming tools in Part V, "Linux for Programmers."

Filenames

Linux allows filenames to be up to 256 characters long. These characters can be lower- and upper-case letters, numbers, and other characters, usually the dash (-), the underscore (_), and the dot (.).

They can't include reserved *metacharacters* such as the asterisk, question mark, backslash, and space, because these all have meaning to the shell. We met some metacharacters when we discussed wildcards in the previous chapter. Other metacharacters will be introduced in the Linux shell chapters.

Directories: An Overview

Linux, like many other computer systems, organizes files in *directories*. You can think of directories as file folders and their contents as the files. However, there is one absolutely crucial difference between the Linux file system and an office filing system. In the office, file folders usually don't contain other file folders. In Linux, file folders *can* contain other file folders. In fact, there is no Linux "filing cabinet"—just a huge file folder that holds some files and other folders. These folders contain files and possibly other folders in turn, and so on.

Parent Directories and Subdirectories

Imagine a scenario in which you have a directory, A, that contains another directory, B. Directory B is then a *subdirectory* of directory A, and directory A is the *parent directory* of directory B. You will see these terms often, both in this book and elsewhere.

The Root Directory

In Linux, the directory that holds all the other directories is called the *root directory*. This is the ultimate parent directory; every other directory is some level of subdirectory.

From the root directory, the whole structure of directory upon directory springs and grows like some electronic elm. This is called a *tree structure* because, from the single *root* directory, directories and subdirectories branch off like tree limbs.

How Directories Are Named

Directories are named just like files, and they can contain upper- and lowercase letters, numbers, and characters such as -, ., and _.

The slash (/) character is used to show files or directories within other directories. For instance, usr/bin means that bin is found in the usr directory. Note that you can't tell, from this example, whether bin is a file or a directory, although you know that usr must be a directory because it holds another item—namely, bin. When you see usr/bin/grep, you know that both usr and bin must be directories, but again, you can't be sure about grep. The ls program shows directories with a following /—for example, fido/. This notation implies that you could have, for instance, fido/file; therefore, fido must be a directory.

The root directory is shown simply by the symbol / rather than mentioned by name. It's very easy to tell when / is used to separate directories and when it's used to signify the root directory. If / has no name *before* it, it stands for the root directory. For example, /usr means that the usr subdirectory is found in the root directory, and /usr/bin means that bin is found in the usr directory and that usr is a subdirectory of the root directory. Remember, by definition the root directory can't be a subdirectory.

The Home Directory

Linux provides each user with his or her own directory, called the *home* directory. Within this home directory, users can store their own files and create subdirectories. Users generally have complete control over what's found in their home directories. Because there are usually no Linux system files or files belonging to other users in your home directory, you can create, name, move, and delete files and directories as you see fit.

> **WARNING**
>
> Your home directory does not provide privacy! Normally, any user can go into another's home directory and read (and copy!) the files stored there (although he can't delete or change the files). When Linux creates your home directory, it in effect provides you with an open office cubicle whose desk and filing cabinet drawers are unlocked.
>
> You *must* lock up everything you want to keep private. (This topic is covered in the section "File Permissions and Ownership.") It is generally considered rude or nosy to poke around in someone else's home directory, just as it's rude or nosy to poke around in someone's office while they're away from their desk, but the world is full of nosy and rude people, so you must take precautions!
>
> Note that anyone logged in as root can read and manipulate *all* the files on the system, including files that users have locked up. If you can't trust the system administrator (who usually has the root password), don't use the system!

The location of a user's home directory is specified by Linux and can't be changed by the user. This is both to keep things tidy and to preserve system security.

Navigating the Linux File System

Fortunately, navigating the Linux file system is simple. There are only two commands to be learned, and one of them has absolutely no options or parameters!

The *pwd* Command: Where Am I?

Type pwd at the Linux command prompt. You see

```
darkstar:~$ pwd
/home/fido
darkstar:~$
```

This tells you that you're currently in the directory /home/fido. (If you are logged in under a different user name, you will see that name in place of fido.) This is your home directory. When you log in, Linux always places you in your home directory.

The letters "pwd" stand for "print working directory." Again, a command's name or function has been cut down to a few easy-to-type characters. (You will often see the term *current directory* used in place of *working directory*.)

You might be wondering what "working directory" or "being in a directory" really means. It simply means that Linux commands, by default, perform their actions in your working directory. For instance, when you run ls, you are shown only the files in your working directory. If you want to create or remove files, they will be created or removed in your working directory.

Absolute and Relative Filenames

If you specify only the name of a file, Linux looks for that file in your working directory. For example, more myfile lets you read the contents of the file myfile. But myfile must be in your current working directory, or the more command won't find it.

Sometimes you want to specify a file that isn't in your current directory. You would then specify the name of the directory the file is in, as well as the name of the file itself.

If, for instance, your current directory has a subdirectory called novel, which contains a file called chapter_1, you could type more novel/chapter_1, which tells more that it should look in the subdirectory novel for the file chapter_1. This is called a *relative filename*. You are specifying the location of chapter_1 *relative* to where you are now, in the subdirectory novel, which is found in your current directory. If you changed your working directory, the relative filename would no longer work.

Two special directory specifications are ".ᅠ" and "..".The specification "." always stands for the directory you are currently in, and ".." stands for the parent directory of your current directory.

(You see how "." and ".." are used later in this chapter.) Any filename that includes "." or ".." is, by definition, a relative filename.

A filename that is valid from any location is called an *absolute filename*. Absolute filenames always begin with /, signifying root. So if you specify a filename as /home/fido/novel/chapter_1, there is no doubt as to where the file is located. Every file on your system has a unique absolute filename.

Someone else on the system might also have a directory called novel in his or her home directory. Perhaps it even contains a file called chapter_1. In this case, you can't distinguish the two files by using the relative filename novel/chapter_1. However, the absolute filenames *will* be different—for instance, /home/fido/novel/chapter_1 as opposed to /home/mary/novel/chapter_1. The novel subdirectory in /home/fido is *not* the same directory as the novel directory in /home/mary! The two are in quite separate locations, and only coincidentally do they share the same name.

Going Places: The *cd* Command

The cd (change directory) command lets you change your working directory. You can think of it as moving to another directory.

The syntax of the cd command is

```
cd <directory specification>
```

There must be a space between cd and the directory specification.

The directory specification can be an absolute or relative one. For instance, type cd .. followed by pwd:

```
darkstar:~$ cd ..
darkstar:/home$ pwd
/home
darkstar:/home$ cd ..
darkstar:/$ pwd
/
darkstar:/$ cd ..
darkstar:/$ pwd
/
```

There is no parent directory for the root directory, so typing cd .. when in the root directory simply leaves you in the root directory.

Note that the Linux command prompt shows you which directory you are currently in, so you don't have to type pwd all the time. (I will continue to use pwd for clarity.)

You can also use absolute directory names.

```
darkstar:/$ cd /usr/bin
darkstar:/usr/bin$ pwd
/usr/bin
```

When you type an absolute directory name, you go to that directory, no matter where you started from. When you type cd .., where you end up depends on where you started.

To see the effect of changing your working directory, type ls. The list of files is so long that the first part scrolls off your screen. The ls command shows you the contents of your current directory (as always), but now your current directory is /usr/bin, which contains many more files than your home directory.

There's No Place Like Home

Type cd without any directory specification:

```
darkstar:/usr/bin$ cd
darkstar:~$ pwd
/home/fido
```

Typing cd by itself always returns you to your home directory. When exploring the file system, you sometimes wind up deep in a blind alley of subdirectories. Type cd to quickly return home, or type cd / to return to the root directory.

The ~ in your prompt is another special character. It stands for your home directory. There's no reason to type cd ~ when cd works just as well, and is much easier to type! However, try this:

When you type cd ~*<user>*, you move to that user's home directory. This is a very useful trick, especially on large systems with many users and more complicated directory structures than the simple /home/*<user>* on your Linux system.

TIP

When you're changing to a distant directory, it's often a good idea to take several steps. If you mistype a very long directory specification, you will have to retype the entire specification. Sometimes it might not even be clear why cd gave you an error! Taking a number of shorter steps means less retyping in case of an error. Consider this example:

```
darkstar:~$ cd /usr/docs/faq/unix
bash: /usr/docs/faq/unix: No such file or directory
```

You're pretty sure that this path is correct. Let's change directories one step at a time:

```
darkstar:~$ cd /usr
darkstar:/usr$ cd docs
bash: docs: No such file or directory
```

Aha! There's a problem with docs. The directory is actually named doc:

```
darkstar:/usr$ ls
bin/    doc/    games/    info/    man/    sbin/    spool/
darkstar:/usr$ cd doc
darkstar:/usr/doc$ cd faq/unix
darkstar:/usr/doc/faq/unix$ pwd
/usr/doc/faq/unix
```

Creating and Deleting Files

Linux has many ways to create and delete files. In fact, some of the ways are so easy to perform that you have to be careful not to accidentally overwrite or erase files!

WARNING

Go through the following sections very carefully. You should be logged in as your "ordinary" username, *not* as root! Only when you're sure you understand these sections thoroughly should you use these commands while logged in as root.

There is no "unerase" command in Linux! Be *sure* you know what you're doing!

Return to your home directory by typing cd. Make sure you're in your /home/<user> directory by running pwd.

In the previous chapter, you created a file by typing ls -l /bin > test. Remember, the > symbol means "redirect all output to the following filename." Note that the file test didn't exist before you typed this command. When you redirect to a file, Linux automatically creates the file if it doesn't already exist.

What if you want to type text into a file, rather than some command's output? The quick and dirty way is to use the command cat.

cat: That Useful Feline

The cat command is one of the simplest, yet most useful, commands in Linux. It certainly does more than any living feline!

The cat command basically takes all its input and outputs it. By default, cat takes its input from the keyboard and outputs it to the screen. Type cat at the command line:

```
darkstar:~$ cat
```

The cursor moves down to the next line, but nothing else seems to happen. Now cat is waiting for some input:

```
hello
hello
what
what
asdf
asdf
```

Everything you type is repeated on-screen as soon as you press Enter!

How do you get out of this? At the start of a line, type ^D (Ctrl-D). (In other words, hold down the Ctrl key and press D.) If you're not at the beginning of a line, you have to type ^D twice. ^D is the Linux "end of file" character. When a program such as cat encounters a ^D, it assumes that it has finished with the current file, and it goes on to the next one. In this case, if you type ^D by itself on an empty line, there is no next file to go on to, and cat exits.

> **NOTE**
>
> When you say that a program *exits,* you mean that it has finished running and that you are back at the Linux command prompt. It might seem odd to talk about the *program* exiting when, from your point of view as a user, you have exited the program. This turn of phrase goes back to the early days of UNIX, when it was coined by the people who were programming the system. They looked at things from the program's point of view, not the user's!

So how do you use cat to create a file? Simple! You redirect the output from cat to the desired filename:

```
darkstar:~$ cat > newfile
Hello world
Here's some text
```

You can type as much as you want. When you are finished, press ^D by itself on a line; you will be back at the Linux prompt.

Now you want to look at the contents of newfile. You could use the more or less commands, but instead, let's use cat. Yes, you can use cat to look at files simply by providing it with a filename:

```
darkstar:~$ cat newfile
Hello world
Here's some text
darkstar:~$
```

Neat! You can also add to the end of the file by using >>. Whenever you use >>, whether with cat or any other command, the output is always *appended* to the specified file. (Note that the ^D character does not appear on-screen. I show it in the examples for clarity.)

```
darkstar:~$ cat >> newfile
Some more lines
^D
darkstar:~$ cat newfile
Hello world
Here's some text
Some more lines
darkstar:~$
```

To discover what cat actually stands for, let's first create another file.

```
darkstar:~$ cat > anotherfile
Different text
^D
darkstar:~$
```

Now, try this:

```
darkstar:~$ cat newfile anotherfile> thirdfile
darkstar:~$ cat thirdfile
```

```
Hello world
Here's some text
Some more lines
Different text
darkstar:~$
```

cat stands for *concatenate*; cat takes all the specified inputs and regurgitates them in a single lump. This by itself would not be very interesting, but combine it with the forms of input and output redirection available in Linux and you have a powerful and useful tool.

Sometimes you want to change just one line of a file, or perhaps you are creating a large and complicated file. For this you should use one of the editing programs available in Linux. They are discussed in Chapter 16, "Text Editors."

Creating Directories

To create a new directory, use the mkdir command. The syntax is mkdir *<name>*, where *<name>* is replaced by whatever you want the directory to be called. This creates a subdirectory with the specified name in your current directory:

```
darkstar:~$ ls
anotherfile    newfile      thirdfile
darkstar:~$ mkdir newdir
darkstar:~$ ls
anotherfile    newdir/      newfile       thirdfile
```

> **TIP**
>
> The mkdir command is already familiar to you if you have used MS-DOS systems. In MS-DOS, you can abbreviate mkdir as md. You might think that md would work in Linux, because, after all, most of the commands we've seen have extremely concise names. However, Linux doesn't recognize md; it insists on the full mkdir.
>
> If you frequently switch between Linux and MS-DOS, you might want to use mkdir for both systems. However, be warned that you might start typing other Linux commands in MS-DOS—for example, typing ls instead of dir!

Moving and Copying Files

You often need to move or copy files. The mv command moves files, and the cp command copies files. The syntax for the two commands is similar:

```
mv <source> <destination>
cp <source> <destination>
```

As you can see, mv and cp are very simple commands. Here's an example:

```
darkstar:~$ ls
anotherfile    newdir/      newfile       thirdfile
```

```
darkstar:~$ mv anotherfile movedfile
darkstar:~$ ls
movedfile     newdir/        newfile        thirdfile
darkstar:~$ cp thirdfile xyz
darkstar:~$ ls
anotherfile   newdir/        newfile        thirdfile      xyz
```

You can use cat (or more or less) at any time to verify that anotherfile became movedfile, and that the contents of file xyz are identical to the contents of thirdfile.

It can get more confusing if you're moving or copying files from one directory to another. This is because a file's *real* name includes its absolute path—for instance, /home/fido/newfile. However, Linux lets you leave off parts of the file's name, because it's more convenient to refer to newfile rather than /home/fido/newfile.

For instance, suppose you want to move newfile into the newdir subdirectory. If you want the file to keep the same name, you type

```
darkstar:~$ mv newfile newdir/newfile
```

However, it's much more common to type

```
darkstar:~$ mv newfile newdir
```

Here, because you have typed a directory name for the destination, Linux assumes that you want the file to be placed in the specified directory.

You could also use cd to change to the directory you want to move the file to:

```
darkstar:~$ cd newdir
darkstar:~newdir$ copy ../newfile .
```

This example is a bit less intuitive than the first two! You specify that the source is ../newfile, which means "the file newfile in the current directory's parent directory." The destination you simply specify as ".", which is short for "the current directory." In other words, you're telling mv to "go up one level, grab newfile, and move it to right here." Because this is less intuitive, you might find yourself automatically *pushing* a file from your current directory to another directory rather than *pulling* a file from another directory into your current directory.

You can also change the name of the file while moving or copying it to another directory. The following is just one possible way:

```
darkstar:~$ cp newfile newdir/anothername
```

This would create a copy of newfile in the directory newdir and name the copied file anothername.

WARNING

When moving or copying files between directories, you should always double-check that the file's destination directory exists and verify the directory's name. Otherwise, the results of your command can be unexpected, as the following two examples show.

If in the example just shown you mistyped `newdir`—for instance, as `mv newfile mewdir`—you would wind up with a file called `mewdir` in your current directory and no file `newfile` in the `newdir` subdirectory!

Another way you would get an unexpected result would be to type `cp newfile newdir` if you didn't realize that the directory `newdir` existed. In this case, you would be expecting to create an identical file called `newdir` in your current directory. What you would actually do is create a copy of `newfile`, called `newfile`, in the subdirectory `newdir`.

The `mv` command is much more efficient than the `cp` command. When you use `mv`, the file's contents are not moved at all; rather, Linux makes a note that the file is to be found elsewhere within the file system's structure of directories.

When you use `cp`, you are actually making a second physical copy of your file and placing it on your disk. This can be slower (although for small files, you won't notice any difference), and it causes a bit more wear and tear on your computer. Don't make copies of files when all you really want to do is move them!

Moving and Copying with Wildcards

If you have 20 files in a directory, and you want to copy them to another directory, it would be very tedious to use the `cp` command on each one. Fortunately, you can use the wildcards `*` and `?` to copy more than one file at a time.

If you want to move or copy *all* files in a directory, use the wildcard `*`:

```
darkstar:~$ cp * /tmp
```

This command copies every file in your current directory to the directory `/tmp`.

You can use `*`, along with other characters, to match only certain files. For instance, suppose you have a directory that contains the files `book1`, `book_idea`, `book-chapter-1`, and `poem.book`. To copy just the first three files, you could type `cp book* /tmp`. When you type `book*`, you are asking Linux to match all files whose names start with `book`. In this case, `poem.book` does not start with `book`, so there is no way `book*` can match it. (Note that if your filename were `book.poem`, `book*` would match it.)

NOTE

As you saw at the outset, `mv` and `cp` are very simple commands. It's specifying the files that's the complicated part! If things still seem confusing, don't worry. Even experts sometimes mess up "simple" moves and copies. Follow the examples and try any different ways you think of. There is a definite logic as to how the files to be moved and copied should be specified. It takes a while to become familiar with this logic, and you will have to practice a while before these things become intuitive.

Moving Directories

To move a directory, use the mv command. The syntax is mv *<directory> <destination>*. In the following example, you would move the newdir subdirectory found in your current directory to the /tmp directory:

```
darkstar:~$ mv newdir /tmp
darkstar:~$ cd /tmp
darkstar:/tmp$ ls
/newdir
```

The directory newdir is now a subdirectory of /tmp.

> **NOTE**
>
> When you move a directory, all its files and subdirectories go with it.

Removing Files and Directories

Now that you know how to create files and directories, it's time to learn how to undo your handiwork.

To remove (or delete) a file, use the rm command (rm is a very terse spelling of *remove*). The syntax is rm *<filename>*. For instance:

```
darkstar:~$ rm dead_duck
```

removes the file dead_duck from your current directory.

```
darkstar:~$ rm /tmp/dead_duck
```

removes the file dead_duck from the /tmp directory.

```
darkstar:~$ rm *
```

removes all files from your current directory. (Be careful when using wildcards!)

```
darkstar:~$ rm /tmp/*duck
```

removes all files ending in duck from the /tmp directory.

> **WARNING**
>
> As soon as a file is removed, it is *gone!* Always think about what you're doing before you remove a file. You can use one of the following techniques to keep out of trouble when using wildcards.

1. Run `ls` using the same file specification you use with the `rm` command. For instance:

   ```
   darkstar:~$ ls *duck
   dead_duck     guiduck    lame-duck
   :~$ rm *duck
   ```

   In this case, you *thought* you wanted to remove all files that matched *duck. To verify that this indeed was the case, you listed all the *duck files (wildcards work the same way with all commands). The listing looked okay, so you went ahead and removed the files.

2. Use the `i` (interactive) option with `rm`:

   ```
   darkstar:~$ rm -i *duck
   rm: remove 'dead_duck'? y
   rm: remove 'guiduck'? n
   rm: remove 'lame-duck'? y
   darkstar:~$
   ```

   When you use `rm -i`, the command goes through the list of files to be deleted one by one, prompting you for the OK to remove the file. If you type y or Y, `rm` removes the file. If you type any other character, `rm` does not remove it. The only disadvantage of using this interactive mode is that it can be very tedious when the list of files to be removed is long.

Removing Directories

The command normally used to remove (delete) directories is `rmdir`. The syntax is `rmdir <directory>`.

Before you can remove a directory, it must be empty (the directory can't hold any files or subdirectories). Otherwise, you see

```
rmdir: <directory>: Directory not empty
```

This is as close to a safety feature as you will see in Linux!

TIP

This one might mystify you:

```
darkstar:/home$ ls
fido/    root/    zippy/
darkstar:/home$ ls zippy
core     kazoo      stuff
darkstar:/home$ rm zippy/*
darkstar:/home/zippy$ ls zippy
darkstar:/home$ rmdir zippy
rmdir: zippy: Directory not empty
darkstar:~$
```

The reason for the Directory not empty message is that files starting with . usually are special system files and are usually hidden from the user. To list files whose names start with ., you have to use ls -a. To delete these files, use rm .*:

```
darkstar:/home$ ls -a zippy
./   ../   .bashrc      .profile
darkstar:/home$ rm zippy/.*
rm: cannot remove '.' or '..'
darkstar:/home$ ls -a zippy
./   ../
darkstar:/home$ rmdir zippy
darkstar:/home$ ls
fido/    root/
darkstar:~$
```

You will most often come across this situation in a system administrator role.

Sometimes you want to remove a directory with many layers of subdirectories. Emptying and then deleting all the subdirectories one by one would be very tedious. Linux offers a way to remove a directory and all the files and subdirectories it contains in one easy step. This is the r (recursive) option of the rm command. The syntax is rm -r *<directory>*. The directory and all its contents are removed.

WARNING

You should use rm -r only when you really have to. To paraphrase an old saying, "It's only a shortcut until you make a mistake." For instance, if you're logged in as root, the following command removes all files from your hard disk, and then it's "Hello, installation procedure" time (do not type the following command!):

```
rm -rf /
```

Believe it or not, people do this all too often. Don't join the club!

File Permissions and Ownership

All Linux files and directories have ownership and permissions. You can change permissions, and sometimes ownership, to provide greater or lesser access to your files and directories. File permissions also determine whether a file can be executed as a command.

If you type ls -l or dir, you see entries that look like this:

```
-rw-r--r--   1 fido      users        163 Dec  7 14:31 myfile
```

The -rw-r--r-- represents the permissions for the file myfile. The file's ownership includes fido as the owner and users as the group.

File and Directory Ownership

When you create a file, you are that file's owner. Being the file's owner gives you the privilege of changing the file's permissions or ownership. Of course, once you change the ownership to another user, you can't change the ownership or permissions anymore!

File *owners* are set up by the system during installation. Linux system files are owned by IDs such as root, uucp, and bin. Do not change the ownership of these files.

Use the chown (change ownership) command to change ownership of a file. The syntax is chown `<owner> <filename>`. In the following example, you change the ownership of the file myfile to root:

```
darkstar:~$ ls -l myfile
-rw-r--r--   1 fido        users          114 Dec  7 14:31 myfile
darkstar:~$ chown root myfile
darkstar:~$ ls -l myfile
-rw-r--r--   1 root        users          114 Dec  7 14:31 myfile
```

To make any further changes to the file myfile, or to chown it back to fido, you must use su or log in as root.

Files (and users) also belong to *groups*. Groups are a convenient way of providing access to files for more than one user but not to every user on the system. For instance, users working on a special project could all belong to the group *project*. Files used by the whole group would also belong to the group project, giving those users special access. Groups normally are used in larger installations. You may never need to worry about groups.

The chgrp command is used to change the group the file belongs to. It works just like chown.

File Permissions

Linux lets you specify read, write, and execute permissions for each of the following: the owner, the group, and "others" (everyone else).

read permission enables you to look at the file. In the case of a directory, it lets you list the directory's contents using ls.

write permission enables you to modify (or delete!) the file. In the case of a directory, you must have write permission in order to create, move, or delete files in that directory.

execute permission enables you to execute the file by typing its name. With directories, execute permission enables you to cd into them.

For a concrete example, let's look at myfile again:

```
-rw-r--r--   1 fido        users          163 Dec  7 14:31 myfile
```

The first character of the permissions is -, which indicates that it's an ordinary file. If this were a directory, the first character would be d. There are also some other, more exotic classes. These are beyond the scope of this chapter.

The next nine characters are broken into three groups of three, giving permissions for owner, group, and other. Each triplet gives read, write, and execute permissions, always in that order. Permission to read is signified by an r in the first position, permission to write is shown by a w in the second position, and permission to execute is shown by an x in the third position. If the particular permission is absent, its space is filled by -.

In the case of myfile, the owner has rw-, which means read and write permissions. This file can't be executed by typing myfile at the Linux prompt.

The group permissions are r--, which means that members of the group "users" (by default, all ordinary users on the system) can read the file but not change it or execute it.

Likewise, the permissions for all others are r--: read-only.

File permissions are often given as a three-digit number—for instance, 751. It's important to understand how the numbering system works, because these numbers are used to change a file's permissions. Also, error messages that involve permissions use these numbers.

The first digit codes permissions for the owner, the second digit codes permissions for the group, and the third digit codes permissions for other (everyone else).

The individual digits are encoded by summing up all the "allowed" permissions for that particular user as follows:

read permission	4
write permission	2
execute permission	1

Therefore, a file permission of 751 means that the owner has read, write, and execute permission (4+2+1=7), the group has read and execute permission (4+1=5), and others have execute permission (1).

If you play with the numbers, you quickly see that the permission digits can range between 0 and 7, and that for each digit in that range there's only one possible combination of read, write, and execute permissions.

TIP

If you're familiar with the binary system, think of rwx as a three-digit binary number. If permission is allowed, the corresponding digit is 1. If permission is denied, the digit is 0. So r-x would be the binary number 101, which is 4+0+1, or 5. --x would be 001, which is 0+0+1, which is 1, and so on.

The following combinations are possible:

0 or ---: No permissions at all

4 or r--: read-only

2 or -w-: write-only (rare)

1 or - -x: execute

6 or rw-: read and write

5 or r-x: read and execute

3 or -wx: write and execute (rare)

7 or rwx: read, write, and execute

> **NOTE**
>
> Anyone who has permission to read a file can then copy that file. When a file is copied, the copy is owned by the person doing the copying. He or she can then change ownership and permissions, edit the file, and so on.

> **WARNING**
>
> Removing write permission from a file doesn't prevent the file from being deleted! It does prevent it from being deleted accidentally, since Linux asks you whether you want to override the file permissions. You have to answer y, or the file will not be deleted.

Changing File Permissions

To change file permissions, use the chmod (change [*file*] mode) command. The syntax is chmod *<specification> file*.

There are two ways to write the permission specification. One is by using the numeric coding system for permissions:

```
darkstar:~$ ls -l myfile
-rw-r--r--  1 fido     users        114 Dec  7 14:31 myfile
darkstar:~$ chmod 345 myfile
darkstar:~$ ls -l myfile
--wxr--r-x  1 fido     users        114 Dec  7 14:31 myfile
darkstar:~$ chmod 701 myfile
darkstar:~$ ls -l myfile
-rwx----x  1 root     users        114 Dec  7 14:31 myfile
```

This method has the advantage of specifying the permissions in an absolute, rather than relative, fashion. Also, it's easier to tell someone "Change permissions on the file to seven-five-five" than to say "Change permissions on the file to read-write-execute, read-execute, read-execute."

You can also use letter codes to change the existing permissions. To specify which of the permissions to change, type u (user), g (group), o (other), or a (all). This is followed by a + to add permissions or a - to remove them. This in turn is followed by the permissions to be added or removed. For example, to add execute permissions for the group and others, you would type

```
darkstar:~$ chmod go+r myfile
```

Other ways of using the symbolic file permissions are described in the chmod man page.

Changing Directory Permissions

You change directory permissions with chmod, exactly the same way as with files. Remember that if a directory doesn't have execute permissions, you can't cd to it.

> **WARNING**
>
> Any user who has write permission in a directory can delete files in that directory, whether or not that user owns or has write privileges to those files.
>
> Most directories, therefore, have permissions set to drwxr-xr-x. This ensures that only the directory's owner can create or delete files in that directory.
>
> It is especially dangerous to give write permission to all users for directories!

Miscellaneous File Commands

There are many Linux commands to manipulate files, directories, and the entire file system. Many of these commands are used only by system administrators. You will touch on a few that are also used by ordinary users. These and other important system administrator commands are further detailed in Chapter 37, "System Administration Basics."

Fear of Compression: The Zipless File

Most Linux files are stored on the installation CD-ROM in compressed form. This allows more information to be stored.

When you installed Linux, the installation program uncompressed many of the files it transferred to your hard drive. However, if you look, you will be able to find compressed files!

Any file ending in .gz—for example, squashed.gz—is a compressed file. To uncompress this particular type of file, type gunzip <file>. For this example, you would type gunzip squashed.gz. The gunzip program creates an uncompressed file and removes the .gz extension. Therefore, you would wind up with a normal file called squashed.

To compress a file, use the gzip command. Typing gzip squashed would compress squashed and rename it squashed.gz.

Another type of compressed file you might see ends with the extension .zip. Use unzip to uncompress these files. To create files of this type, use zip.

How to *tar* Without Feathering

In almost any location with several Linux or UNIX systems, sooner or later you will hear someone say, "Put that in a tar file and send it over."

They are referring to the output created by the tar program. Although tar stands for *tape archive,* it can copy files to floppy disk or to any filename you specify in the Linux file system. The tar command is used because it can archive files and directories into a single file and then recreate the files and even the directory structures later. It's also the easiest way to place Linux files on a floppy disk.

To create a tar file, you typically type tar cvf <destination> <files/directories>, where files/ directories specifies the files and directories to be archived, and destination is where you want the tar file to be created. If you want the destination to be a floppy disk, you usually type /dev/fd0 as the destination. This specifies your primary floppy drive (A: in MS-DOS). You can use a floppy disk that's been formatted under MS-DOS.

> **WARNING**
>
> When tar archives to a floppy disk, all the data already on the disk is destroyed. You have to reformat it to use it with MS-DOS again.

To extract a tar file, you typically type tar xvf <tar file>. For instance, to pull files from a floppy disk, you would type tar xvf /dev/fd0.

> **NOTE**
>
> Unlike gzip, tar doesn't remove, delete, or rename files it puts into the archive. However, when tar extracts archived files, it overwrites existing files with files of the same name from the archive.

Important Directories in the Linux File System

Most of the directories that hold Linux system files are "standard." Other UNIX systems will have identical directories with similar contents. This section summarizes some of the more important directories on your Linux system.

/

This is the root directory. It holds the actual Linux program, as well as subdirectories. Do not clutter this directory with your files!

/home

This directory holds users' home directories. In other UNIX systems, this can be the /usr or /u directory.

/bin

This directory holds many of the basic Linux programs. bin stands for *binaries*, files that are executable and that hold text only computers could understand.

/usr

This directory holds many other user-oriented directories. Some of the most important are described in the following sections. Other directories found in /usr include

docs	Various documents, including useful Linux information
man	The man pages accessed by typing man <command>
games	The fun stuff!

/usr/bin

This directory holds user-oriented Linux programs.

/var/spool

This directory has several subdirectories. mail holds mail files, spool holds files to be printed, and uucp holds files copied between Linux machines.

/dev

Linux treats *everything* as a file! The /dev directory holds *devices*. These are special files that serve as gateways to physical computer components. For instance, if you copy to /dev/fd0, you're actually sending data to the system's floppy disk. Your terminal is one of the /dev/tty files. Partitions on the hard drive are of the form /dev/hd0. Even the system's memory is a device!

A famous device is /dev/null. This is sometimes called the *bit bucket*. All information sent to /dev/null vanishes—it's thrown into the trash.

/usr/sbin

This directory holds system administration files. If you do an ls -l, you see that you must be the owner, root, to run these commands.

/sbin

This directory holds system files that are usually run automatically by the Linux system.

/etc

This directory and its subdirectories hold many of the Linux configuration files. These files are usually text, and they can be edited to change the system's configuration (if you know what you're doing!).

Summary

You should now feel more comfortable working in Linux. Understanding and being able to navigate the Linux file system is very important, since Linux really does consist simply of some files organized in a fairly standard way.

You still might find yourself stumped by certain file or directory problems. Remember that the online man pages can assist you. Linux gives you a lot of flexibility in creating files, specifying absolute or relative names, and setting permissions. Don't be afraid to experiment (as an ordinary user, in your home directory). There are too many different ways to perform tasks to list or exhaustively describe here. Don't cling to rigid recipes written on a piece of paper. You learn by trying!

You should go on to Chapters 9, "Introduction to the GNU Project Utilities," through 12, "Using tcsh," especially if you want to create programs or macros from system command files or learn more about the built-in user interface features in Linux shells. Chapter 16 has some very useful information about editing text files.

Once you are familiar with shells and have had some practice manipulating files and directories, you can move on to the advanced topics in Part III, "Editing, Typesetting, and More," through Part VIII, "Advanced Programming Topics," of this book.

Introduction to the GNU Project Utilities

9

by Peter MacKinnon

IN THIS CHAPTER

The GNU project, administered by the Free Software Foundation (FSF), seeks to provide software (in the form of source code) that is freely available to anyone who wants to use it. The project has a lengthy manifesto that explains the motivation behind this libertarian undertaking (for which we should all be thankful, since GNU has some of the best software around!). One of the key ideas within this manifesto is that high-quality software is an intrinsic human right, just as the air that we breathe is. Although GNU software is freely distributed, it is not public domain and is protected by the GNU General Public License. The main purpose behind the license is to keep GNU software free.

For more information on the FSF, you can write to them at

> Free Software Foundation
> 675 Massachusetts Avenue
> Cambridge, MA 02139

You can also request copies by sending e-mail to gnu@prep.ai.mit.edu.

The distribution of Linux on this book's CD-ROM comes with virtually all of the GNU programs that are currently available. They are archived using the tar program and compressed using the GNU gzip utility. gzip tends to compress better than the standard UNIX compression utility, compress. Files compressed with gzip end with a .gz suffix, whereas compress files end in .Z. However, gzip can uncompress compress files as well as its own.

Each of these compressed files has a version number included in its filename so that you can determine what version is most current. Once you decompress and un-tar the GNU file, the program can be compiled and installed on your system. Most of the files come with their own makefile. Most of the programs are refinements of standard Linux utilities such as make and bc.

GNU Software Currently Available

So much software, either developed by or made available through the Free Software Foundation (which develops the GNU products), is available that each program cannot be described in detail. The following sections have brief descriptions of the GNU utilities and programs that are included with this distribution of Linux. They are summaries based on the descriptions of the programs as supplied by GNU.

acm

acm is a multiplayer aerial combat game designed for the X Window system that can be played in a LAN environment. Players engage in simulated air-to-air combat against one another using missiles and cannons.

Autoconf

Autoconf generates shell scripts that can automatically configure source code packages (such as those for GNU). Autoconf creates a script for a software package from a file which lists the operating system features that the package can utilize. Autoconf requires GNU m4 to generate the required macro calls for its operation.

bash

The shell called bash is an enhancement of the Bourne shell (thus the name, which stands for Bourne Again SHell). It offers many of the extensions found in csh and ksh. The bash shell also has job control, csh-style command history, and command-line editing with Emacs and vi modes built in. See Chapter 10, "Using bash."

bc

bc is an algebraic language that can be used interactively from a shell command line, or with input files. GNU bc has a C-like syntax with several extensions including multicharacter variable names, an else statement, and full Boolean expressions. Unlike standard bc, GNU bc does not require the separate dc program, which is another GNU calculator utility.

BFD

The (BFD) library allows a program that operates on object files (such as ld or gdb) to support many different formats efficiently. BFD provides a portable interface, so that only BFD needs to know the details of a particular format. One result is that all programs using BFD will support formats such as a.out (default C executable) and COFF.

Binutils

Binutils includes a collection of development programs, including ar, c++filt, gprof, ld, nlmconv, objcopy, objdump, ranlib, size, strings, and strip.

Binutils Version 2.5.2 is completely rewritten to use the BFD library. The GNU linker ld emits source-line numbered error messages for multiply defined symbols and undefined references. nlmconv converts object files into Novell NetWare Loadable Modules (NLM). The objdump program can display data such as symbols from any file format understood by BFD.

Bison

Bison is an upwardly compatible replacement for the parser generator yacc. Bison takes a description of tokens in the form of a grammar and generates a parser in the form of a C program.

GNU C Compiler

Version 2.6 of the GNU C Compiler (gcc) supports three languages: C, C++, and Objective-C. The language selected depends on the source file suffix or a compiler option. The runtime support required by Objective-C programs is now distributed with gcc. The GNU C Compiler is a portable optimizing compiler that supports full ANSI C, traditional C, and GNU C extensions. GNU

C has been extended to support features such as nested functions and nonlocal goto statements. Also, gcc can generate object files and debugging information in a variety of formats. See Chapter 27, "Programming in C," for more detailed information about C language support.

GNU C Library

The GNU C library supports ANSI C and adds some extensions of its own. For example, the GNU stdio library lets you define new kinds of streams and your own printf formats.

GNU C++ Library

The GNU C++ library (libg++) is an extensive collection of C++ classes, a new iostream library for input/output routines, and support tools for use with g++. Among the classes supported are multiple-precision integers and rational numbers, complex numbers, and arbitrary-length strings. There are also prototype files for generating common container classes.

Calc

Calc is a desk calculator and mathematical tool that is used within GNU Emacs. Calc can be used as a basic calculator, but it provides additional features including choice of algebraic or Reverse Polish Notation (RPN), logarithmic functions, trigonometric and financial functions, complex numbers, vectors, matrices, dates, times, infinities, sets, algebraic simplification, differentiation, and integration.

GNU Chess

GNU Chess pits you against the computer in a full game of chess. It has regular-terminal, curses (a full-screen interface library for C), and X-terminal interfaces. GNU Chess implements many specialized features, including sophisticated heuristics that will challenge your best Bobby Fischer moves.

CLISP

CLISP is an implementation of Common Lisp, the list-processing language that is widely used in artificial-intelligence applications. CLISP includes an interpreter and a byte compiler and has user interfaces in English and German that can be chosen at compile time.

GNU Common Lisp

GNU Common Lisp (gcl) has a compiler and interpreter for Common Lisp. It is highly portable, extremely efficient, and has a source-level LISP debugger for interpreted code. gcl also has profiling tools and an Xlib interface.

cpio

cpio is a program that copies file archives to and from tape or disk. It can also be used to copy files into a larger archive file or to other directories.

CVS

The Concurrent Version System (CVS) manages software revision and release control in a multideveloper, multidirectory, multigroup environment. It works in conjunction with RCS, another source code control program.

dc

dc is an RPN calculator that can be used interactively or with input files.

DejaGnu

DejaGnu is a framework for writing scripts to test any program. It includes the embeddable scripting language Tcl and its derivative expect, which runs scripts that can simulate user input.

Diffutils

The Diffutils package contains the file-comparison programs diff, diff3, sdiff, and cmp. GNU diff compares files showing line-by-line changes in several formats and is more efficient than its traditional version.

ecc

ecc is an error-correction checking program that uses the Reed-Solomon algorithm. It can correct a total of three byte errors in a block of 255 bytes and can detect more severe errors.

ed

ed is the standard line-based text editor.

Elib

This is a small library of Emacs LISP functions, including routines for using doubly linked lists.

GNU Emacs

GNU Emacs is the second implementation of this highly popular editor developed by Richard Stallman. It integrates LISP for writing extensions and provides an interface to X. In addition to its own powerful command set, Emacs has extensions that emulate other popular editors such as vi and EDT (DEC's VMS editor). For more information on Emacs, please refer to Chapter 16, "Text Editors."

GNU Emacs 19

Emacs 19.30 is a richer version of the Emacs editor with extensive support for the X Window system. It includes an interface to the X resource manager, has X toolkit support, has good RCS support, and includes many updated libraries. Emacs 19 from the FSF works equally well on character-based terminals as it does under X.

es

es is a shell based on rc that has an exception system and supports functions that return values other than just numbers. It works well interactively or in scripts, particularly because its quoting rules are simpler than the C and Bourne shells.

Fileutils

Fileutils is a GNU collection of standard (and not-so-standard) Linux file utilities, including chgrp, chmod, chown, cp, dd, df, dir, du, install, ln, ls, mkdir, mkfifo, mknod, mv, mvdir, rm, rmdir, touch, and vdir.

find

find is a program that can be used both interactively and in shell scripts to find files given certain criteria and then execute operations (such as rm) on them. This program includes xargs, which applies a command to a list of files.

finger

finger displays information about one or more Linux users. GNU finger supports a single host that can act as the finger server host in sites that have multiple hosts. This host collects information about who is logged into other hosts at that site. Thus, a query to any machine at another site will return complete information about any user at that site.

flex

flex is a replacement for the lex scanner generator. The flex program generates more efficient scanners than does lex. The flex program also has the advantage that it generates C code. Scanners are used to identify tokens from input.

Fontutils

The Fontutils create fonts for use with Ghostscript or TeX. They also contain general conversion programs and other utilities. Some of the programs in Fontutils include bpltobzr, bzrto, charspace, fontconvert, gsrenderfont, imageto, imgrotate, limn, and xbfe.

gas

gas is the GNU assembler that converts assembly code into object files. Native assembly works for many systems, including Linux.

gawk

gawk is upwardly compatible with the awk program, which uses pattern-matching to modify files. It also provides several useful extensions not found in other awk implementations (awk, nawk), such as functions to convert the case of a matched string. For more detailed information, see Chapter 26, "gawk."

gdb

gdb is a debugger with a command-line user interface. Object files and symbol tables are read using the BFD library, which allows a single copy of gdb to debug programs of multiple object file formats. Other new features include command-language improvements, remote debugging over serial lines or TCP/IP, and watchpoints (breakpoints triggered when the value of an expression changes). An X version of gdb, called xxgdb, is also available.

gdbm

The gdbm library is the GNU replacement for the traditional dbm and ndbm database libraries. It implements a database using lookup by hash tables.

Ghostscript

Ghostscript is GNU's PostScript-compatible graphics language. It accepts commands in PostScript and executes them by writing directly to a printer, drawing in an X window, or writing to a file that you can print later (or to a bitmap file that you can edit with other graphics programs).

Ghostscript includes a graphics library that can be called from C. This allows client programs to use Ghostscript's features without having to know the PostScript language. For more information, consult Chapter 25, "Ghostscript."

Ghostview

Ghostview is as an X-based previewer for multipage files that are interpreted by Ghostscript.

gmp

GNU mp (gmp) is an extensive library for arbitrary precision arithmetic on signed integers and rational numbers.

GNats

GNats: GNU's A Tracking System is a problem-reporting system. It uses the model of a central site or organization that receives problem reports and administers their resolution by electronic mail. Although it is used primarily as a software bug-tracking system, it could also be used for handling system-administration issues, project management, and a variety of other applications.

gnuplot

gnuplot is an interactive program for plotting mathematical expressions and data. It handles both curves (two-dimensional) and surfaces (three-dimensional).

GnuGo

GnuGo plays the game of Go (also known as Wei-Chi).

gperf

gperf is a utility to generate "perfect" hash tables. There are implementations of gperf for C and C++ that generate hash functions for both languages.

GNU Graphics

GNU Graphics is a set of programs that produces plots from ASCII or binary data. It supports output to PostScript and the X Window system, has shell scripts examples using graph and plot, and features a statistics toolkit.

grep

This package contains GNU grep, egrep, and fgrep. These utilities, which search files for regular expressions, execute much faster than do their traditional counterparts.

groff

groff is a document-formatting system that includes drivers for PostScript, TeX dvi format, as well as implementations of eqn, nroff, pic, refer, tbl, troff, and the man, ms, and mm macros. Written in C++, these programs can be compiled with GNU C++ Version 2.5 or later.

gzip

gzip can expand LZW-compressed files but uses a different algorithm for compression that generally produces better results than the traditional compress program. It also uncompresses files compressed with the pack program.

hp2xx

GNU hp2xx reads HPGL files, decomposes all drawing commands into elementary vectors, and converts them into a variety of vector (including encapsulated PostScript, Metafont, and various special TeX-related formats, and simplified HPGL) and raster output formats (including PBM, PCX, and HP-PCL).

indent

GNU indent formats C source code according to the GNU coding standards but, optionally, can also use the BSD default, K&R, and other formats. It is also possible to define your own format. indent can handle C++ comments.

Ispell

Ispell is an interactive spell checker that suggests other words with similar spelling as replacements for unrecognized words. Ispell can use system and personal dictionaries, and standalone and GNU Emacs interfaces are also available.

m4

GNU m4 is an implementation of the traditional macroprocessor for C. It has some extensions for handling more than nine positional parameters to macros, including files, running shell commands, and performing arithmetic.

make

GNU make adds extensions to the traditional program that is used to manage dependencies between related files. GNU extensions include long options, parallel compilation, flexible implicit pattern rules, conditional execution, and powerful-text manipulation functions. Recent versions have improved error reporting and added support for the popular += syntax to append more text to a variable's definition. For further information about make, please see Chapter 51, "Source Code Control."

mtools

mtools is a set of public-domain programs that allow Linux systems to read, write, and manipulate files on an MS-DOS file system (usually a diskette).

MULE

MULE is a MULtilingual Enhancement to GNU Emacs 18. It can handle many character sets at once including Japanese, Chinese, Korean, Vietnamese, Thai, Greek, the ISO Latin-1 through Latin-5 character sets, Ukrainian, Russian, and other Cyrillic alphabets. A text buffer in MULE can contain a mixture of characters from these languages. To input any of these characters, you can use various input methods provided by MULE itself.

NetHack

NetHack is a display-oriented adventure game that supports both ASCII and X displays.

NIH Class Library

The NIH Class Library is a portable collection of C++ classes, similar to those in `Smalltalk-80`, that has been developed by Keith Gorlen of the National Institutes of Health (NIH) using the C++ programming language.

nvi

`nvi` is a free implementation of the `vi` text editor. It has enhancements over `vi` including split screens with multiple buffers, the capability to handle 8-bit data, infinite file and line lengths, tag stacks, infinite undo, and extended regular expressions.

Octave

`Octave` is a high-level language that is primarily intended for numerical computations. It provides a convenient command-line interface for solving linear and nonlinear problems numerically.

`Octave` does arithmetic for real and complex scalars and matrices, solves sets of nonlinear algebraic equations, integrates functions over finite and infinite intervals, and integrates systems of ordinary differential and differential-algebraic equations.

Oleo

`Oleo` is a spreadsheet program that supports X displays and character-based terminals. It can output encapsulated PostScript renditions of spreadsheets and uses `Emacs`-like configurable keybindings. Under X and in PostScript output, `Oleo` supports variable-width fonts.

p2c

`p2c` translates from Pascal code to C. It recognizes many Pascal variants including Turbo, HP, VAX, and ISO, and produces entirely usable C source code.

patch

`patch` is a program that takes the output from `diff` and applies the resulting differences to the original file in order to generate the modified version. It would be useful for developing a source code control system, if one were so inclined.

PCL

`PCL` is a free implementation of a large subset of `CLOS`, the Common Lisp Object System. It runs under `CLISP`, mentioned earlier.

perl

perl is a programming language developed by Larry Wall that combines the features and capabilities of sed, awk, shell programming, and C, as well as interfaces to system calls and many C library routines. It has become wildly popular for sophisticated applications that are not dependent on complex data structures. A "perl" mode for editing perl code comes with GNU Emacs 19.

ptx

GNU ptx is the GNU version of the traditional permuted index generator. It can handle multiple input files at once, produce TeX-compatible output, and produce readable KWIC (KeyWords In Context) indexes without needing to use the nroff program.

rc

rc is a shell that features C-like syntax (even more so than csh) and better quoting rules than the C and Bourne shells. It can be used interactively or in scripts.

RCS

The Revision Control System (RCS) is used for version control and management of software projects. When used with GNU diff, RCS can handle binary files such as executables and object files. For more information on RCS, please refer to Chapter 51.

recode

GNU recode converts files between character sets and usages. When exact transformations are not possible, it may get rid of any offending characters or revert to approximations. This program recognizes or produces nearly 150 different character sets and is able to transform files between almost any pair.

regex

regex is the GNU regular expression library whose routines have been used within many GNU programs. Now it is finally available by itself. A faster version of this library comes with the sed editor.

Scheme

Scheme is a language that is related to LISP. The chief difference is that Scheme can pass functions as arguments to another function, it can return a function as the result of a function call, and functions can be the value of an expression without being defined under a particular name.

screen

screen is a terminal multiplexer that runs several separate "screens" (ttys) on a single physical character-based terminal. Each virtual terminal emulates a DEC VT100 plus additional functions. screen sessions can be idled and resumed later on a different terminal type.

sed

sed is a non-interactive, stream-oriented version of ed. It is used frequently in shell scripts and is extremely useful for applying repetitive edits to a collection of files or to create conversion programs. GNU sed comes with the rx library, which is a faster version of regex.

Shellutils

Shellutils can be used interactively or in shell scripts and includes the following programs: basename, date, dirname, echo, env, expr, false, groups, id, nice, nohup, printenv, printf, sleep, stty, su, tee, test, true, tty, uname, who, whoami, and yes.

GNU Shogi

Shogi is a Japanese game similar to chess, with the exception that captured pieces can be returned to play. GNU Shogi is based on the implementation of GNU Chess: it implements the same features and uses similar heuristics. As a new feature, sequences of partial board patterns can be introduced in order to help the program play a good order of moves toward specific opening patterns. There are both character- and X-display interfaces.

Smalltalk

GNU Smalltalk is an interpreted object-oriented programming language system written in C. Smalltalk itself has become extremely popular among programmers recently and tends to be regarded as a "pure" object-oriented implementation language.

The features of GNU Smalltalk include a binary image save capability, the ability to invoke user-written C code and pass parameters to it, a GNU Emacs editing mode, a version of the X protocol that can be called from within Smalltalk, and automatically loaded per-user initialization files. It implements all of the classes and protocol in Smalltalk-80, except for the graphic user interface (GUI) related classes.

Superopt

Superopt is a function sequence generator that uses a repetitive generate-and-test approach to find the shortest instruction sequence for a given function. The interface is simple: you provide the GNU superoptimizer, gso, a function, a CPU to generate code for, and how many instructions you can accept.

tar

GNU `tar` is a file-archiving program that includes multivolume support, automatic archive compression/decompression, remote archives, and special features that allow `tar` to be used for incremental and full backups.

Termcap Library

The GNU `Termcap` library is a replacement for the `libtermcap.a` library. It does not place an arbitrary limit on the size of `Termcap` entries, unlike most other `Termcap` libraries.

TeX

`TeX` is a document-formatting system that handles complicated typesetting, including mathematics. It is GNU's standard text formatter. For more information on `TeX`, please refer to Chapter 19, "`TeX`."

Texinfo

`Texinfo` is a set of utilities that generates both printed manuals and online hypertext-style documentation (called "Info"). There are also programs for reading online Info documents. Version 3 has both GNU `Emacs` LISP and standalone programs written in C or shell script. The `texinfo` mode for GNU `Emacs` enables easy editing and updating of `Texinfo` files. Programs provided include `makeinfo`, `info`, `texi2dvi`, `texindex`, `tex2patch`, and `fixfonts`.

Textutils

The `Textutils` programs manipulate textual data and include the following traditional programs: `cat`, `cksum`, `comm`, `csplit`, `cut`, `expand`, `fold`, `head`, `join`, `nl`, `od`, `paste`, `pr`, `sort`, `split`, `sum`, `tac`, `tail`, `tr`, `unexpand`, `uniq`, and `wc`.

Tile Forth

`Tile Forth` is a 32-bit implementation of the `Forth-83` standard written in C. Traditionally, Forth implementations are written in assembler to use the underlying hardware as optimally as possible, but this also makes them less portable.

time

`time` is used to report statistics (usually from a shell) about the amount of user, system, and real time used by a process.

tput

`tput` is a portable way for shell scripts to use special terminal capabilities. GNU `tput` uses the `Termcap` database, instead of `Terminfo` as many others do.

UUCP

This version of UUCP (UNIX-to-UNIX copy) supports the f, g, v (in all window and packet sizes), G, t, e, Zmodem, and two new bidirectional (i and j) protocols. If you have a Berkeley sockets library, it can make TCP connections. If you have TLI libraries, it can make TLI connections.

uuencode/uudecode

uuencode and uudecode are used to transmit binary files over transmission media that support only simple ASCII data.

wdiff

wdiff is another interface to the GNU diff program. It compares two files, finding which words have been deleted or added to the first in order to create the second. It has many output formats and interacts well with terminals and programs such as more. wdiff is especially useful when two texts differ only by a few words and paragraphs have been refilled.

Summary

The GNU project provides UNIX-like software freely to everyone, with the provision that it remains free if distributed to others. GNU software can be compiled for many different types of systems, including Linux. Many GNU utilities are improvements of existing UNIX counterparts and include many new implementations of shells, the C compiler, and a code debugger. In fact, most Linux distributions make extensive use of GNU utilities. Other types of GNU software include games, text editors, calculators, and communication utilities. Each utility can be separately uncompressed, un-tarred, and compiled itself.

Using *bash*

10

*by Rick
McMullin*

This chapter looks at the shells in a little more detail. You'll start with bash (Bourne Again Shell), the default shell used by Linux and the most popular shell for new users. In this chapter you will learn

- What a shell is
- The most common shells used in Linux
- Command-line completion and wildcards
- Command history and aliases
- Redirection and pipes
- Changing prompts
- Job control
- How to customize your bash shell

You will also look at the most commonly used bash commands and the environment variables bash uses. By the end of this chapter, you should be able to work faster and more efficiently with bash.

Shells in a Nutshell

What is a shell, anyway? It seems to be a word used all the time in Linux, but the exact meaning is vague for many new users (and some veterans). This section explains exactly what a shell program is and why it is so important when using Linux.

What Is a Shell?

The shell is a program used to interface between you (the user) and Linux (or, more accurately, between you and the Linux kernel). Figure 10.1 illustrates the relationship between the user, the shell, and the Linux kernel. Every command you type at a prompt on your screen is interpreted by the shell, then passed to the Linux kernel.

> **NOTE**
>
> If you are familiar with MS-DOS, you will recognize this relationship as almost identical to the relationship between a DOS user and the COMMAND.COM program. The only real difference is that in the DOS world, no distinction is made between the COMMAND.COM program and DOS (or to be more accurate, the DOS kernel).

The shell is a command-language interpreter. It has its own set of built-in shell commands. The shell can also make use of all of the Linux utilities and application programs that are available on the system.

FIGURE 10.1.

The relationship between the user and the shell.

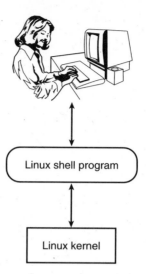

Whenever you enter a command it is interpreted by the Linux shell. For example, in earlier chapters when you were introduced to the Linux file- and directory-manipulation commands, all of the sample commands entered at the command prompt were interpreted by whichever Linux shell you were using.

Some of the commands, such as the print working directory (pwd) command, are built into the Linux bash shell. Other commands, such as the copy command (cp) and the remove command (rm), are separate executable programs that exist in one of the directories in the filesystem. As the user, you don't know (or probably care) if the command is built into the shell or is a separate program. Figure 10.2 shows how the shell performs this command interpretation.

FIGURE 10.2.

Command interpretation by the shell.

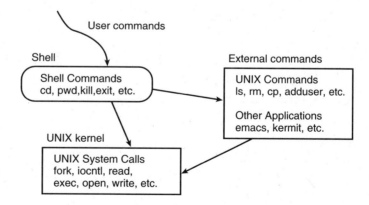

Figure 10.2 illustrates the steps that the shell takes to figure out what to do with user commands. It first checks to see if the command is one of its own built-in commands (like cd or pw(d). If the command is not one of these, the shell checks to see if it is an application program. *Application programs* can be utility programs that are part of Linux, such as ls and rm, or they can be application programs that are either purchased commercially, such as xv, or available as public domain software, such as ghostview.

The shell tries to find these application programs by looking in all of the directories that are in your search path. The *path* is a list of directories where executable programs can be found. If the command that was entered is not an internal shell command and it is not an executable file in your path, an error message will be displayed.

As the last step in a successful command, the shell's internal commands and all of the application programs are eventually broken down into system calls and passed to the Linux kernel.

Another important aspect of the shell is that it contains a very powerful interpretive programming language. This language is similar in function to the MS-DOS interpreted language, but is much more powerful. The shell programming language supports most of the programming constructs found in high-level languages, such as looping, functions, variables, and arrays.

The shell programming language is easy to learn, and once known it becomes a very powerful programming tool. Any command that can be typed at the command prompt can also be put into a executable shell program. This means that the shell language can be used to simplify repetitive tasks. See Chapter 13, "Shell Programming," for more information on shell programming.

How the Shell Gets Started

Earlier in this chapter you learned that the shell is the main method by which a user interacts with the Linux kernel. But how does this program get initialized to do so? The shell is started after you successfully log into the system, and it continues to be the main method of interaction between the user and the kernel until you log out.

Each user on your system has a default shell. The *default shell* for each user is specified in the system password file, called /etc/passwd. The *system password file* contains, among other things, each person's user ID, an encrypted copy of each user's password, and the name of the program to run immediately after a user logs into the system. The program specified in the password file does not have to be one of the Linux shells, but it almost always is.

The Most Common Shells

Several different kinds of shells are available on Linux and UNIX systems. The most common are the Bourne shell (called sh), the C shell (csh), and the Korn shell (ksh). Each of these three shells has its own advantages and disadvantages.

The *Bourne shell* was written by Steven Bourne. It is the original UNIX shell and is available on every UNIX system in existence. The Bourne shell is considered to be very good for UNIX shell programming, but it does not handle user interaction as well as some of the other shells available.

The *C shell*, written by Bill Joy, is much more responsive to user interaction. It supports features such as command-line completion that are not in the Bourne shell. The C shell's programming interface is thought by many not to be as good as that of the Bourne shell, but it is used by many C programmers because the syntax of its programming language is similar to that of the C language. This is also why it is named the C shell.

The *Korn shell* (ksh) was written by Dave Korn. He took the best features of both the C shell and the Bourne shell and combined them into one that is completely compatible with the Bourne shell. ksh is efficient and has both a good interactive interface and a good programming interface.

> **NOTE**
>
> There are many quality reference books about the Bourne, C, and Korn shells. If you want to use these shells instead of the three shells discussed in this and the next two chapters, you may want to find a good reference book on the particular shell you prefer. Because the shells included with Linux are used by most people, we will concentrate on those.

In addition to these shells, many other shell programs took the basic features from one or more of the existing shells and combined them into a new version. The three newer shells that will be discussed in this book are tcsh (an extension of csh), the Bourne Again Shell (bash, an extension of sh), and the Public Domain Korn Shell (pdksh, an extension of ksh). bash is the default shell on most Linux systems.

The Bourne Again Shell

The Bourne Again Shell (bash), as its name implies, is an extension of the Bourne shell. bash is fully backward-compatible with the Bourne shell, but contains many enhancements and extra features that are not present in the Bourne shell. bash also contains many of the best features that exist in the C and Korn shells. bash has a very flexible and powerful programming interface, as well as a user-friendly command interface.

Why use bash instead of sh? The biggest drawback of the Bourne shell is the way that it handles user input. Typing commands into the Bourne shell can often be very tedious, especially if you are using it on a regular basis and typing in a large number of commands. bash provides several features that make entering commands much easier.

Command-Line Completion

Often when you enter commands into bash (or any other shell), the complete text of the command is not necessary in order for the shell to be able to determine what you want it to do. For example, assume that the current working directory contains the following files and subdirectories:

```
News/  bin/  games/     mail/  samplefile  test/
```

If you want to change directories from the current working directory to the `test` subdirectory, you would enter the command

```
cd test
```

Although this command will work, `bash` enables you to accomplish the same thing in a slightly different way. Since `test` is the only file in the directory that begins with the letter *t*, `bash` should be able to figure out what you want to do after you type in the letter *t* alone:

```
cd t
```

After the letter has been typed, the only thing that you could be referring to is the `test` subdirectory. To get `bash` to finish the command for you, press the Tab key:

```
cd t<tab>
```

When you do this, `bash` finishes the command for you and displays it on the screen. The command doesn't actually execute until you press the Enter key to verify that the command `bash` came up with is the command that you really intended.

For short commands like this, you might not see very much value in making use of command-line completion. Using this feature may even slow you down when typing short commands. After you get used to using command-line completion, though, and when the commands that you are entering get a little longer, you will wonder how anyone lived without this feature.

So what happens if more than one file in the directory begins with the letter t? It would seem that this would cause a problem if you wanted to use command-line completion. Let's see what happens when you have the following directory contents:

```
News/  bin/   mail/      samplefile  test/  tools/ working/
```

Now you have two files in the directory that start with the letter t. Assuming that you still want to `cd` into the `test` subdirectory, how do you do it using command-line completion? If you type `cd t<tab>` as you did before, `bash` will not know which subdirectory you want to change to because the information you have given is not unique.

If you try to do this, `bash` will beep to notify you that it does not have enough information to complete the command. After beeping, `bash` will leave the command on the screen as it was entered. This enables you to enter more information without retyping what was already typed. In this case, you only need to enter an `e` and press the Tab key again. This will give `bash` enough information to complete the command on the command line for you to verify:

```
cd test
```

If instead you decided that you want to `cd` into the `tools` subdirectory, you could have typed

```
cd to<tab>
```

This would also give `bash` enough information to complete the command.

Whenever you press the Tab key while typing a command, bash will try to complete the command for you. If it can't complete the command, it will fill in as much as it can and then beep, notifying you that it needs more information. You can then enter more characters and press the Tab key again, repeating this process until bash returns the desired command.

Wildcards

Another way that bash makes typing commands easier is by enabling users to use wildcards in their commands. The bash shell supports three kinds of wildcards:

* * matches any character and any number of characters.

? matches any single character.

[...] matches any single character contained within the brackets.

The * wildcard can be used in a manner similar to command-line completion. For example, assume the current directory contains the following files:

```
News/  bin/  games/      mail/  samplefile  test/
```

If you want to cd into the test directory, you could type cd test, or you could use command-line completion:

```
cd t<tab>
```

This causes bash to complete the command for you. Now there is a third way to do the same thing. Because only one file begins with the letter t, you could also change to the directory by using the * wildcard. You could enter the following command:

```
cd t*
```

The * matches any character and any number of characters, so the shell will replace the t* with test (the only file in the directory that matches the wildcard pattern).

This will work reliably only if there is one file in the directory that starts with the letter t. If more than one file in the directory starts with the letter t, the shell will try to replace t* with the list of filenames in the directory that match the wildcard pattern and the cd command will cd into the first directory in this list. This will end up being the file that comes first alphabetically, and may or may not be the intended file.

A more practical situation in which to use the * wildcard is when you want to execute the same command on multiple files that have similar filenames. For example, assume the current directory contains the following files:

```
ch1.doc  ch2.doc  ch3.doc        chimp  config   mail/  test/  tools/
```

If you wanted to print all of the files that have a .doc extension, you could do so easily by entering the following command:

```
lpr *.doc
```

In this case, bash will replace *.doc with the names of all of the files in the directory that match that wildcard pattern. After bash performed this substitution, the command that would be processed would be:

```
lpr ch1.doc ch2.doc ch3.doc
```

The lpr command would be invoked with the arguments of ch1.doc, ch2.doc, and ch3.doc.

> **NOTE**
>
> Given the directory contents used in the previous example, there are several ways to print all of the files that have a .doc extension. All of the following commands would also work:
> ```
> lpr *doc
> lpr *oc
> lpr *c
> ```

The ? wildcard functions in an identical way to the * wildcard except that the ? wildcard only matches a single character. Using the same directory contents shown in the previous example, the ? wildcard could be used to print all of the files with the .doc extension by entering the following command:

```
lpr ch?.doc
```

The [...] wildcard enables you to specify certain characters or ranges of characters to match. To print all of the files in the example that have the .doc extension using the [...] wildcard, you would enter one of the following two commands:

```
lpr ch[123].doc
```

Using a command to specify a range of characters, you would enter

```
lpr ch[1-3].doc
```

Command History

bash also supports command history. This means that bash keeps track of a certain number of previous commands that have been entered into the shell. The number of commands is given by a shell variable called HISTSIZE. For more information on HISTSIZE, see the section "bash Variables" later in this chapter.

bash stores the text of the previous commands in a history list. When you log into your account, the history list is initialized from a history file. The filename of the history file can be set using the HISTFILE bash variable. The default filename for the history file is .bash_history. This file is usually located in your home directory. (Notice that the file begins with a period. This means that the file is hidden and will only appear in a directory listing if you use the -a or -A option of the ls command.).

Just storing previous commands into a history file is not all that useful, so bash provides several ways of recalling them. The simplest way of using the history list is with the up- and down-arrow keys, which scroll through the commands that have been previously entered.

Pressing the up-arrow key will cause the last command that was entered to appear on the command line. Pressing the up-arrow key again will put the command previous to that one on the command line, and so on. If you move up in the command buffer past the command that you wanted, you can also move down the history list a command at a time by pressing the down-arrow key. (This is the same process used by the DOS doskey utility.)

The command displayed on the command line through the history list can be edited, if needed. bash supports a complex set of editing capabilities that are beyond the scope of this book, but there are simple ways of editing the command line for small and easy changes. You can use the left and right arrow keys to move along the command line. You can insert text at any point in the command line, and can also delete text by using the Backspace or Delete key. Most users should find these simple editing commands sufficient.

> **NOTE**
>
> The complex set of editing commands that bash offers are similar to the commands used in the emacs and vi text editors.

Another method of using the history file is to display and edit the list using the history and fc (fix command) commands built into bash. The history command can be invoked using two different methods. The first method uses the command

history [*n*]

When the history command is used with no options, the entire contents of the history list are displayed. The list that is displayed on-screen might resemble the following sample list:

```
1  mkdir /usr/games/pool
2  cp XpoolTable-1.2.linux.tar.z /usr/games/pool
3  cd /usr/games/pool/
4  ls
5  gunzip XpoolTable-1.2.linux.tar.z
6  tar -xf XpoolTable-1.2.linux.tar
7  ls
8  cd Xpool
9  ls
10 xinit
11 exit
12 which zip
13 zip
14 more readme
15 vi readme
16 exit
```

Using the n with the history command causes the only last *n* lines in the history list to be shown. So, for example, history 5 shows only the last five commands.

The second method of invoking the history command is used to modify the contents of the history file, or the history list. The command has the following command-line syntax:

```
history [-r¦w¦a¦n] [filename]
```

In this form, the -r option tells the history command to read the contents of the history file and use them as the current history list. The -w option will cause the history command to write the current history list to the history file (overwriting what is currently in the file). The -a option appends the current history list to the end of the history file. The -n option causes the lines that are in the history file to be read into the current history list.

All of the options for the second form of the history command can use the filename option as the name of the history file. If no filename is specified, the history command will use the value of the HISTFILE shell variable.

The fc command can be used in two different ways to edit the command history. In the first way, the fc command would be entered using the following command-line syntax:

```
fc [-e editor_name] [-n] [-l] [-r] [first] [last]
```

where all options given in braces are optional. The -e editor name option is used to specify the text editor to be used for editing the commands. The first and last options are used to select a range of commands to take out of the history list. first and last can refer either to the number of a command in the history list or to a string that fc will try to find in the history list.

The -n option is used to suppress command numbers when listing the history commands. The -r option lists the matched commands in reverse order. The -l command lists the matched commands to the screen. In all cases except when the -l command option is used, the matching commands will be loaded into a text editor.

> **NOTE**
>
> The text editor used by fc is found by taking the value of editor name if the -e editor name option is used. If this option was not used, fc uses the editor specified by the variable FCEDIT. If this variable does not exist, fc will use the value of the EDITOR variable. Finally, if none of these variables exists, the editor that will be chosen is vi, by default.

Aliases

Another way that bash makes life easier for you is by supporting command aliases. *Command aliases* are commands that the user can specify. *Alias commands* are usually abbreviations of other commands, designed to save keystrokes.

For example, if you are entering the following command on a regular basis, you might be inclined to create an alias for it to save yourself some typing:

```
cd /usr/X11R6/lib/X11/config
```

Instead of typing this command every time you wanted to go to the sample-configs directory, you could create an alias called goconfig that would cause the longer command to be executed. To set up an alias like this you must use the bash alias command. To create the goconfig alias, enter the following command at the bash prompt:

```
alias goconfig='cd /usr/X11R6/lib/X11/configs
```

Now, until you exit from bash, the goconfig command will cause the original, longer command to be executed as if you had just typed it.

If you decide after you have entered an alias that you did not need it, you can use the bash unalias command to delete the alias:

```
unalias goconfig
```

There are a number of useful aliases that most users find helpful. These can be written in a file that you execute when you log in, to save you from typing them each time. Some aliases that you might want to define are the following:

- ■ `alias ll='ls -l'`
- ■ `alias log='logout'`
- ■ `alias ls='ls -F'`

If you are a DOS user and are used to using DOS file commands, you can use the alias command to define the following aliases so that Linux behaves like DOS:

- ■ `alias dir='ls'`
- ■ `alias copy='cp'`
- ■ `alias rename='mv'`
- ■ `alias md='mkdir'`
- ■ `alias rd='rmdir'`

NOTE

When defining aliases, you can't include spaces on either side of the equal sign, or the shell can't properly determine what you want to do. Quotation marks are necessary only if the command within them contains spaces or other special characters.

If you enter the alias command without any arguments, it will display all of the aliases that are already defined on-screen. The following listing illustrates a sample output from the alias command:

```
alias dir='ls'
alias ll='ls -l'
alias ls='ls -F'
alias md='mkdir'
alias net='term < /dev/modem > /dev/modem 2> /dev/null&'
alias rd='rmdir'
```

Input Redirection

Input redirection is used to change the source of input for a command. When a command is entered in bash, the command is expecting some kind of input in order to do its job. Some of the simpler commands must get all of the information that they need passed to them on the command line. For example, the rm command requires arguments on the command line. You must tell rm the files that you want it to delete on the command line, or it will issue a prompt telling you to enter rm -h for help.

Other commands require more elaborate input than a simple directory name. The input for these commands can be found in a file. For example, the wc (word count) command counts the number of characters, words, and lines in the input that was given to it. If you just type wc <enter> at the command line, wc waits for you to tell it what it should be counting. There will be a prompt on the command line asking for more information, but because the prompt is sometimes not easily identifiable, it will not necessarily be obvious to you what is happening. (It might actually appear as though bash has died, because it is just sitting there. Everything that you type shows up on-screen, but nothing else appears to be happening.)

What is actually occurring is that the wc command is collecting input for itself. If you press Ctrl-D, the results of the wc command will be written to the screen. If you enter the wc command with a filename as an argument, as shown in the following example, wc will return the number of characters, words, and lines that are contained in that file:

```
wc test
11 2 1
```

Another way to pass the contents of the test file to wc is to redirect the input of the wc command from the terminal to the test file. This will result in the same output. The < symbol is used by bash to mean "redirect the input to the current command from the specified file." So, redirecting wc's input from the terminal to the test file can be done by entering the following command:

```
wc < test
11 2 1
```

Input redirection is not used all that often because most commands that require input from a file have the option to specify a filename on the command line. There are times, however, when you will come across a program that will not accept a filename as an input parameter, and yet the input that you want to give exists in a file. Whenever this situation occurs, you can use input redirection to get around the problem.

Output Redirection

Output redirection is more commonly used than input redirection. *Output redirection* enables you to redirect the output from a command into a file, as opposed to having the output displayed on-screen.

There are many situations in which this can be useful. For example, if the output of a command is quite large and will not fit on the screen, you might want to redirect it to a file so that you can view it later using a text editor. There also may be cases where you want to keep the output of a command to show to someone else, or so you can print the results. Finally, output redirection is also useful if you want to use the output from one command as input for another. (There is an easier way to use the output of one command as input to a second command. This is shown in the "Pipelines" section in this chapter.)

Output redirection is done in much the same way as input redirection. Instead of using the < symbol, the > symbol is used.

> **NOTE**
>
> The best way to remember which symbol is input or output redirection is to think of the < as a funnel that is funneling input into the command (because the command receiving the input will be on the left-hand side of the <) and the > as a funnel that is funneling the output from the command into a file.

As an example of output redirection, you can redirect the output of the `ls` command into a file named `directory.out` using the following command:

```
ls > directory.out
```

Pipelines

Pipelines are a way to string together a series of commands. This means that the output from the first command in the pipeline is used as the input to the second command in the pipeline. The output from the second command in the pipeline is used as input to the third command in the pipeline, and so on. The output from the last command in the pipeline is the output that you will actually see displayed on-screen (or put in a file if output redirection was specified on the command line).

You can tell `bash` to create a pipeline by typing two or more commands separated by the vertical bar or pipe character, ¦. The following example illustrates the use of a pipeline:

```
cat sample.text ¦ grep "High" ¦ wc -l
```

This pipeline would take the output from the `cat` command (which lists the contents of a file) and send it into the `grep` command. The `grep` command searches for each occurrence of the word High in its input. The `grep` command's output would then consist of each line in the file that contained the word High. This output is then sent to the `wc` command. The `wc` command with the `-l` option prints the number of lines contained in its input.

To show the results on a real file, suppose the contents of `sample.text` was

```
Things to do today:
Low: Go grocery shopping
High: Return movie
High: Clear level 3 in Alien vs. Predator
Medium: Pick up clothes from dry cleaner
```

The pipeline would return the result 2, indicating that you had two things of high importance to complete today:

```
cat sample.text ¦ grep "High" ¦ wc -l
2
```

Prompts

bash has two levels of user prompt. The first level is what you see when bash is waiting for a command to be typed. (This is what you normally see when you are working with bash.)

The default first-level prompt is the $ character. If you do not like the $ character as the prompt, or you would prefer to customize your prompt, you can do so by setting the value of the PS1 bash variable. For example:

```
PS1="Please enter a command"
```

sets the bash shell prompt to the specified string.

The second level of prompt is displayed when bash is expecting more input from you in order to complete a command. The default for the second level prompt is >. If you want to change the second-level prompt, you can set the value of the PS2 variable, as in

```
PS2="I need more information"
```

In addition to displaying static character strings in the command prompts (as in the two preceding examples), you can also use some predefined special characters. These special characters place things such as the current time into the prompt. Table 10.1 lists the most commonly used special-character codes.

Table 10.1. Prompt special character codes.

Character	Meaning
\!	Displays the history number of this command.
\#	Displays the command number of the current command.
\$	Displays a $ in the prompt unless the user is root. When the user is root, it displays a #.
\\	Displays a backslash.
\d	Displays the current date.
\h	Displays the host name of the computer on which the shell is running.
\n	Prints a newline character. This will cause the prompt to span more than one line.
\nnn	Displays the character that corresponds to the octal value of the number nnn.
\s	The name of the shell that is running.
\t	Displays the current time.

Character	Meaning
\u	Displays the username of the current user.
\W	Displays the base name of the current working directory.
\w	Displays the current working directory.

These special characters can be combined into several useful prompts to provide you with information about where you are. (They can be combined in very grotesque ways, too!) Several examples of setting the PS1 prompt are:

```
PS1="\t"
```

This would cause the prompt to have the following appearance (there would not be a space after the prompt):

```
02:16:15
```

The prompt string

```
PS1=\t
```

would cause the prompt to have the following appearance:

```
t
```

This shows the importance of including the character sequence in quotation marks. The prompt string

```
PS1="\t\\ "
```

will cause the prompt to look like this:

```
02:16:30\ ·
```

In this case, there would be a space following the prompt because there was a space within the quotation marks.

Job Control

Job control refers to the ability to control the execution behavior of a currently running process. Specifically, you can suspend a running process and cause it to resume running at a later time. bash keeps track of all of the processes that it started (as a result of user input), and you can suspend a running process or restart a suspended one at any time during the life of that process.

Pressing Ctrl-Z suspends a running process. The bg command restarts a suspended process in the background, whereas the fg command restarts a process in the foreground.

These commands are most often used when a user wants to run a command in the background but by accident starts it in the foreground. When a command is started in the foreground, it locks the shell from any further user interaction until the command completes execution. This is usually no problem because most commands only take a few seconds to execute. If the command you are running is going to take a long time, though, you would typically start the command in the background so that you could continue to use bash to enter other commands in the foreground.

For example, if you started the command find / -name "test" > find.out (which will scan the entire filesystem for files named test and store the results in a file called find.out) in the foreground, your shell may be tied up for many seconds or even minutes, depending on the size of the filesystem and the number of users on the system. If you had issued this command and wanted to continue executing in the background so you could use the system again, you would enter the following:

```
control-z
bg
```

This would first suspend the find command, then restart it in the background. The find command would continue to execute, and you would have bash back again.

Customizing *bash*

Many ways of customizing bash have already been described in this chapter. Until now, the changes that you made affected only the current bash session. As soon as you quit, all of the customizations that you made will be lost. You can make the customizations more permanent by storing them in a bash initialization file.

You can put any commands that you want to be executed each time bash is started into this initialization file. Commands that are typically found in this file are alias commands and variable initializations.

The bash initialization file is named profile. Each user who uses bash has a .profile file in his home directory. This file is read by bash each time it starts, and all of the commands contained within it are executed.

The following code shows the default .profile file. This file is located in the /etc directory and is read when you start bash. If you want to add your own customizations to bash, you must copy this file into your home directory (if it is not already there) and call it .profile.

> **NOTE**
>
> Some setup programs make a copy of the .profile file in your home directory for you automatically when they create your login. However, not all routines do this, so you should check your home directory first. Remember that all files starting with a period are hidden and can only be displayed with the ls -A or ls -a command.

```
# commands common to all logins
export OPENWINHOME=/usr/openwin
export MINICOM="-c on"
```

```
export MANPATH=/usr/local/man:/usr/man/preformat:/usr/man:/X11/man:/usr/openwin
/man
export HOSTNAME="`cat /etc/HOSTNAME`"
PATH="$PATH:/usr/X11/bin:$OPENWINHOME/bin:/usr/games:."
LESS=-MM
# I had problems using 'eval test' instead of 'TERM=', but you might want to
# try it anyway. I think with the right /etc/termcap it would work great.
# eval 'tset -sQ "$TERM"'if [ "$TERM" = "" -o "$TERM" = "unknown"]; then
TERM=linux
fi
#PS1='`hostname`:`pwd`# '
if [ "$SHELL" = "/bin/pdksh" -o "$SHELL" = "/bin/ksh" ]; then
 PS1="! $"
elif [ "$SHELL" = "/bin/zsh" ]; then
 PS1="%m:%~%# "
elif [ "$SHELL" = "/bin/ash" ]; then
 PS1="$ "
else
PS1='\h:\w\$ '
fi
PS2='> '
ignoreeof=10
export PATH DISPLAY LESS TERM PS1 PS2 ignoreeof
umask 022
# set up the color-ls environment variables:
if [ "$SHELL" = "/bin/zsh" 1; then
  eval 'dircolors -z'
elif [ "$SHELL" = "/bin/ash" 1; then
  eval 'dircolors -s'
else
  eval 'dircolors -b'
fi
echo
fortune
echo
export TAPE="/dev/nftape"
```

bash Command Summary

Here are some of the most useful commands built into the bash shell:

alias: Used to set bash aliases (command nicknames that can be defined by the user).

bg: Background command. Forces a suspended process to continue to execute in the background.

cd: Change working directory. This command changes the current working directory to the directory specified as an argument.

exit: Terminates the shell.

export: Causes the value of a variable to be made visible to all subprocesses that belong to the current shell.

fc: Fix command. Used to edit the commands in the current history list.

fg: Foreground command. Forces a suspended process to continue to execute in the foreground.

help: Displays help information for bash built-in commands.

history: Brings up a list of the last *n* commands that were entered at the command prompt, where *n* is a configurable variable specifying the number of commands to remember.

kill: Used to terminate another process.

pwd: Print working directory. Prints the directory in which the user is currently working.

unalias: Used to remove aliases that have been defined using the alias command.

bash has many more commands than are listed here, but these are the most frequently used ones. To see the other commands bash offers and for more details of the commands listed, refer to the bash man page (type man bash).

bash Variables

Here are some of the most useful bash variables, including the variable name and a brief description:

EDITOR, FCEDIT: The default editor for the fc bash command.

HISTFILE: The file used to store the command history.

HISTSIZE: The size of the history list.

HOME: The HOME directory of the current user

OLDPWD: The previous working directory (the one that was current before the current directory was entered).

PATH: The search path that bash uses when looking for executable files

PS1: The first-level prompt that is displayed on the command line

PS2: The second-level prompt that is displayed when a command is expecting more input

PWD: The current working directory

SECONDS: The number of seconds that have elapsed since the current bash session was started

bash has many more variables than are listed here, but the most commonly used ones are shown. To find out what other variables bash offers, call the man page with the command man bash.

Summary

In this chapter you looked at some of the useful features of the Bourne Again Shell, bash. You have seen how command completion, aliasing, and job control can all combine to make you more productive and efficient when working with bash.

In the next chapter you will look at another popular Linux shell, the Public Domain Korn Shell (pdksh). It offers many useful features, too, providing you with a choice of shells.

Using pdksh

11

by
Rick McMullin

IN THIS CHAPTER

In the last chapter, you saw the Bourne Again Shell (bash) in some detail. Not everyone wants to use the bash shell, so several other shells are included with most Linux systems. One of them is pdksh, a variation on the Korn Shell.

In this chapter, we look at the pdksh shell and how it can be efficiently used. After reading this chapter, you will be familiar with the following topics:

- Command-line completion and wildcards
- Command history and aliases
- Input and output redirection
- Pipelines
- How to change your shell prompt
- Job control
- Key bindings

We will also look at how you can customize your copy of pdksh, as well as several of the important commands and variables used by the shell.

The Public Domain Korn Shell (*pdksh*)

The Korn shell, written by David Korn, was the third mainstream shell written for UNIX. Because of this, it incorporated many of the features of the Bourne and C shells (which were the first two shells). Because of the Korn shell's popularity among UNIX users, a version was developed for Linux called the Public Domain Korn Shell, or pdksh.

The current version of the Public Domain Korn Shell does not support all of the features that exist in the commercial version of the Korn shell. It does support most of the main features, however, and adds a few new features of its own.

Command-Line Completion

Often, when you are entering commands at the command line, the complete text of the command is not necessary in order for pdksh to be able to determine what you want to do. Command-line completion enables you to type in a partial command, and then by entering a key sequence, tell pdksh to try to finish the command for you.

pdksh does not default to allowing the user to perform command-line completion. You must enter a command to tell pdksh that you want to be able to use command-line completion. In order to enable command-line completion, enter one of the following commands:

```
set -o emacs
set -o vi
```

This causes pdksh to accept command editing that is similar to emacs or vi. Choose the editor that you are most familiar with, and use the basic editor commands for command-line editing.

NOTE

Most people find the emacs editing mode more user-friendly than the vi editing mode.

When using vi command-line editing, you must be in command mode when you enter any of the editing commands. You can enter command mode by pressing the Esc key. When command mode has been entered, you cannot type any characters onto the command line until you enter edit mode. There are many ways of doing this, but the usual way is by pressing the i (insert) key.

After the command-line completion function has been enabled, you can perform command-line completion by pressing the Esc key twice (when using emacs command-line editing), or by pressing \ (when using vi command-line editing). For example, if your current directory contains the files

```
News/        bin/        games/        mail/        sample.text        test/
```

and you want to edit the file sample.text using the vi text editor, you could enter the following command:

```
vi sample.text
```

After the s is typed, the only file that you could be referring to is sample.text, because it is the only file in the current directory that begins with the letter *s*. To get pdksh to finish the command when you are using emacs-style command editing, you must press the Esc key twice after you type the letter *s*:

```
vi s<escape><escape>
```

To get pdksh to finish the command when you are using vi command editing, you must press the \ key after you type the letter s:

```
vi s\
```

Either of these commands causes pdksh to finish the line for you and display the result on the screen. The command does not execute until you press the Enter key. This is done to give you a chance to confirm that the command pdksh came up with is the command that you really intended.

If the sample.text file is not the only file in the directory that begins with the letter s, pdksh completes the command as far as it can and then beeps, indicating that it needs more information to complete the command.

NOTE

The keyboard equivalent of pressing the Esc key is Ctrl-[, usually written as ^[. The caret (^) is the abbreviation for the Ctrl key. Pressing Esc twice using the Ctrl-[sequence would be written as ^[^[. You might see this convention in books or man pages.

Wildcards

The pdksh shell makes typing commands easier by enabling the user to use wildcards. pdksh supports the same wildcards that bash does:

> * matches any character and any number of characters.
>
> ? matches any single character.
>
> [...] matches any single character contained within the brackets.

The * wildcard can be used in a way that is similar to command-line completion. For example, if the current directory contains the files

```
News/          bin/          games/          mail/          sample.text          test/
```

and you want to edit the sample.text file using the vi text editor, you can perform this task by using the following wildcard:

```
vi s*
```

The * matches any character (and any number of characters), so pdksh replaces s* with sample.text (the only file in the directory that matches the wildcard pattern).

This works reliably if there is only one file in the directory that starts with the letter s. If more than one file starts with the same letter, the shell tries to replace s* with the list of filenames that match the wildcard pattern, and runs vi on the first file in this list. After you quit editing the first file, the second file in the list is loaded into vi, and so on for each file that matched the wildcard pattern. If you intended to edit more than one file, this would be fine, but if you only wanted to edit the sample.text file, this command would not work the way you expected it to.

A more practical situation in which to use the * wildcard is when you want to execute the same command on multiple files that have similar filenames. For example, assume that the current directory contains the following files:

```
News/          bin/          games/          mail/          sample.text          temp1.out
temp2.out      temp3.out     test/
```

If you want to delete all of the files with an .out extension, you can do it by entering the following command:

```
rm *.out
```

In this case, pdksh replaces *.out with the names of all of the files in the directory that match the wildcard pattern. After pdksh performs this substitution, the following command is processed:

```
rm temp1.out temp2.out temp3.out
```

The rm command is invoked with the arguments of temp1.out, temp2.out, and temp3.out.

The ? wildcard functions in a similar way to the * wildcard, except that the ? wildcard matches only a single character. Assuming the same directory contents as in the previous example, the ? wildcard can be used to delete all of the files with the .out extension by entering the following command:

```
rm temp?.out
```

The [...] wildcard enables you to specify characters or ranges of characters to match. To print all of the files in the previous example that have the .doc extension, enter one of the following two commands:

```
rm temp[123].out
rm temp[1-3].out
```

Command History

The pdksh shell supports a command history in much the same way as bash. The pdksh shell keeps track of the last HISTSIZE commands that have been entered (HISTSIZE is a user-definable pdksh variable).

pdksh stores the text of the last HISTSIZE commands in a history list. When you log in, the history list is initialized from a history file. The filename of the history file can be set using the HISTFILE pdksh variable. The default filename for the history file is .ksh_history. This file is located in your home directory. Notice that the file begins with a ., meaning that the file is hidden, and it appears in a directory listing only if you use the -a or -A option of the ls command.

The shell provides several ways of accessing the history list. The simplest way is to scroll through the commands that have been previously entered. In pdksh, this is done differently depending on whether you are using emacs or vi command editing.

If you are using emacs command editing, you scroll up through the history list by pressing Ctrl-p, and you scroll down through the list by pressing Ctrl-n. If you are using vi command-line editing, you scroll up through the history list by pressing either the k or - key, and you scroll down through the history list by pressing j or +.

> **NOTE**
>
> When using vi command editing, you must be in command mode for the key commands to work. You enter command mode by pressing the Esc key.

The command that is on the command line can be edited. The pdksh shell supports a complex set of editing capabilities (most of which are beyond the scope of this book). You can use the left and right arrow keys to move along the command line. You can insert text at any point and delete text from the command line by using the backspace or delete keys. Most users should find these simple editing commands sufficient; for those who do not, there are many other more complicated ways of editing the command line.

> **NOTE**
>
> The complex set of editing commands that pdksh offers is similar to the commands contained in the emacs or vi text editor (you can set either emacs or vi emulation by using the set -o emacs or set -o vi commands). If you are familiar with emacs (or vi), these commands will be familiar to you.

Another method of using the history file is to display and edit it using fc (fix command), the built-in pdksh shell command. If you read Chapter 10, "Using bash," you may remember that bash supported another command called history, which allowed you to view and modify the history file. The history command was left out of the pdksh shell because all of its functionality could be provided by the fc command.

> **TIP**
>
> Even though the history command is not built into pdksh, the command normally still works because it is usually set up as an alias to the fc -l command. For example, the .kshrc file usually contains a line such as alias history='fc -l', which provides behavior almost identical to the history command that is built into other shells.

The fc command is used to edit the command history. It has a number of options, as is illustrated in the following command syntax:

```
fc [-e ename] [-nlr] [first] [last]
```

All options given in braces are optional. The -e portion of the command can be used to specify the text editor that is to be used for editing the commands in the command history. The first and last options are used to select a range of commands to take out of the history list. First and last can refer either to the number of a command in the history list, or to a string that fc tries to find in the history list.

The -n option is used to suppress command numbers when listing the history commands that matched the specified range. The -r option lists the matched commands in reverse order. The -l command lists the matched commands to the screen. In all cases except for the -l option, the matching commands are loaded into a text editor.

The text editor used by fc is found by taking the value of ename if the -e option was used. If this option was not used, fc uses the editor specified by the variable FCEDIT. If this variable does not exist, fc uses the value of the EDITOR variable. Finally, if none of these variables exists, the editor chosen is vi.

If you enter the fc command with no arguments, it loads the last command that was entered into the editor. Remember that when you exit the editor, fc attempts to execute any commands that are in the editor.

The easiest way to understand what the `fc` command does is to look at a few examples:

> `fc` loads the last command into the default editor.
>
> `fc -l` lists the last 16 commands that were entered.
>
> `fc -l 5 10` lists the commands with history numbers between 5 and 10, inclusive.
>
> `fc 6` loads `history` command number 6 into the default editor.
>
> `fc mo` loads into the default editor the most recent command that starts with the string `mo`.

Aliases

Another way `pdksh` makes life easier for you is by supporting command aliases. Command aliases are commands that you can specify and execute. Alias commands are usually abbreviations of other commands.

You tell `pdksh` to execute a Linux command whenever it encounters the alias. For example, if you have a file in your directory that holds a list of things that you must do each day, and you typically edit the file every morning to update it, you might find yourself entering the following command on a regular basis:

```
vi things-to-do-today.txt
```

Because you are entering this command quite often, you might be inclined to create an alias for it to save yourself some typing. Instead of typing this command every time you want to edit the file, you can create an alias called `ttd` that causes the longer command to be executed.

To set up an alias such as this, you must use the `pdksh` `alias` command. To create the `ttd` alias, you enter the following command at the `pdksh` command prompt:

```
alias ttd='vi things-to-do-today.txt'
```

From the time that you enter the `alias` command until the time you exit from `pdksh`, the `ttd` command causes the longer command to be executed. If you decide after you enter an alias that you no longer want that alias, you can use the `pdksh` `unalias` command to delete the alias:

```
unalias ttd
```

After you use the `unalias` command to remove an alias, the alias no longer exists, and trying to execute it causes `pdksh` to report `Command not found`.

The following are some aliases that you might want to define:

```
alias ll='ls -l'
alias log='logout'
alias ls='ls -F'
```

If you are a DOS user and you prefer to use DOS file commands, you may also want to define the following aliases:

```
alias dir='ls'
alias copy='cp'
alias rename='mv'
alias md='mkdir'
alias rd='rmdir'
```

NOTE

When defining aliases, there must not be spaces on either side of the equal sign. The quotation marks are only necessary if the command within them contains spaces or other special characters.

If you enter the alias command without any arguments, it prints all of the aliases that are already defined to the screen. There is a way to make sure that all of your alias commands get executed each time you start pdksh. This is done by using an initialization file, which we will discuss in the "Customizing pdksh" section, later in this chapter.

Input Redirection

Input redirection is used to change the source of input for a command. Typically, when a command is entered in pdksh, the command expects some kind of input in order to do its job. Some of the simpler commands must get all of the information that they need passed to them on the command line. The rm command, for example, requires you to tell it on the command line which files you want to delete; if you do not specify any files it issues a prompt telling you to enter rm -h for help.

Other commands require more elaborate input than a simple directory name. The input for these commands is typically found in a file. For example, the wc (word count) command counts the number of characters, words, and lines in the input that was given to it. If you enter the wc command with a filename as an argument, wc returns the number of characters, words, and lines that are contained in that file. An example of this is

```
wc test
11 2 1
```

Another way to pass the contents of the test file to wc as input is to change (or redirect) the input of the wc command from the terminal to the test file. This results in the same output. The < character is used by pdksh to redirect the input to the current command from the file following the character. So, redirecting wc's input from the terminal to the test file is done by entering the following command:

```
wc < test
11 2 1
```

Input redirection is not used too often because most commands that require input from a file have an option to specify a filename on the command line. There are times, however, when you will come across a program that does not accept a filename as an input parameter, and yet the input that you want to give to the command exists in a file. Whenever this situation occurs, you can use input redirection to get around the problem.

Output Redirection

Output redirection is more commonly used than input redirection. Output redirection enables you to redirect the output from a command into a file, as opposed to having the output displayed on the screen.

There are many situations in which this capability can be very useful. For example, if the output of a command is quite large and does not fit on the screen, you might want to redirect it to a file so you can later view it using a text editor. Output redirection is done in much the same way as input redirection. Instead of using the < symbol, the > symbol is used.

To redirect the output of an ls command into a file named directory.out, the following command is used:

```
ls > directory.out
```

Pipelines

Pipelines are a way to string together a series of commands. This means that the output from the first command in the pipeline is used as the input to the second command. You can tell pdksh to create a pipeline by typing two or more commands separated by the ¦ character. The following is an example of using a pdksh pipeline:

```
cat test.file ¦ sort ¦ uniq
```

This is a fairly common pipeline. Here, the contents of test.file (the output from the cat command) are fed into the input of the sort command. The sort command, without any options, sorts its input alphabetically by the first field in the input. The sorted file is then piped into the uniq command. The uniq command removes any duplicate lines from the input. If test.file contains the lines

```
Sample dialog
Hello there
How are you today
Hello there
I am fine
```

the output from the pipeline is the following:

```
Hello there
How are you today
I am fine
Sample dialog
```

All of the lines in the file have been sorted by the first word in the line, and one of the Hello there lines has been removed because of the uniq command.

Shell Prompts

pdksh has three levels of user prompts. The first level is what the user sees when the shell is waiting for a command to be typed. (This is what you normally see when you are working with the shell.) The default prompt is the $ character. If you do not like the dollar sign as the prompt or prefer to customize the prompt to your own requirements, you can do so by setting the value of the PS1 pdksh variable.

To set a variable, give the name and equal sign, and the string you want to set it to. Make sure you do not place any spaces on either side of the equal sign, or the shell will not interpret your command properly. For example, the line

```
PS1="! Tell me what to do"
```

sets the shell prompt to the string ! Tell me what to do. The pdksh shell keeps track of how many commands have been entered since it was started. This number is stored into the shell variable called !. When you include the ! in the prompt, it displays the current command number in the prompt. The previous prompt command causes the command number followed by the string Tell me what to do to be displayed on the command line each time pdksh is expecting you to enter a command.

The second level of prompt is displayed when pdksh is expecting more input from you in order to complete a command. The default for the second level prompt is >. If you want to change the second level prompt, you can do so by setting the value of the PS2 pdksh variable, as in the following example:

```
PS2=" I need more information"
```

This causes the string I need more information to be displayed on the command line whenever pdksh needs something from you to complete a command.

pdksh does not support the advanced prompt options that bash supports. There is not a predefined set of escape codes that you can put in a pdksh prompt variable to display such items as the time or current working directory. You can, however, put other pdksh variables into a prompt variable. For example, the following two prompts are valid:

```
PS1=" (LOGNAME) "
PS1=' ($PW(D) '
```

The first example causes your prompt to be equal to your UNIX user name. The second example causes your prompt to be the current working directory. The single quotes are needed here so that the value of the PWD variable does not get assigned to the variable only the first time it is executed. If you use double quotes, the PWD variable is evaluated only when the command is first entered. (The prompt would always be the directory name of the directory that you are in when you enter the command.) The single quotes cause the value of the PS1 variable to be equal to the current value of the PWD variable. For more information on using these quotes, see Chapter 13, "Shell Programming."

Job Control

Job control is the capability to control the execution behavior of a currently running process. Specifically, you can suspend a running process and cause it to resume running at a later time. The pdksh shell keeps track of all of the processes that it started, and you can suspend a running process or restart a suspended one at any time during the life of that process.

Pressing the Ctrl-Z key sequence suspends a running process. The bg command restarts a suspended process in the background, and the fg command restarts a process in the foreground.

These commands are most often used when a user wants to run a command in the background but accidentally starts it in the foreground. When a command is started in the foreground, it locks the shell from any further user interaction until the command completes execution. This is usually not a problem, because most commands only take a few seconds to execute. If the command you are running is going to take a long time, you typically start the command in the background so that you can continue to use pdksh to enter other commands while it completes running.

If you start a command in the foreground that is going to take a long time, your shell may be tied up for several minutes. If you have done this and want to continue executing the command in the background, enter the following:

```
control-z
bg
```

This suspends the command and restarts it in the background. The command continues to execute, and you have the control of pdksh.

Key Bindings

One useful feature that pdksh supports, which is lacking in the Bourne Again Shell, is key bindings. This feature enables you to change the behavior of key combinations for the purpose of command-line editing.

If, for example, you do not like the fact that you have to use the emacs key sequence Ctrl-P to move up in the history buffer, you can change the key sequence for that command to something else. The syntax for doing the key binding is the following:

```
bind <key sequence> <command>
```

This feature effectively enables you to customize pdksh to have the exact feel that you want. One of the most commonly used key bindings is to bind the up, down, left, and right arrows to be used as they are in bash (for scrolling up and down the history list, and for moving left and right along the command line). This binding is typically found in your .kshrc file, which is the startup file for the shell (it is read whenever the shell starts).

The bind commands that are needed to create these bindings are as follows:

```
bind '^[['=prefix-2
bind '^XA'=up-history
bind "^XB'=down-history
```

```
bind '^XC'=forward-char
bind '^XD'=backward-char
```

The following list gives some of the most useful editing commands that you can use for binding keys, along with the default binding and a description of each. You can get a listing of all of the editing commands that pdksh supports by typing the bind command without any arguments.

abort (^G) is used to abort another editing command. It is most commonly used to stop a history list search.

backward-char (^B) moves the cursor backward one character. This command is often bound to the left arrow key.

backward-word (^[b) moves the cursor backward to the beginning of a word.

beginning-of-line (^A) moves the cursor to the beginning of the command line.

complete (^[^[) tells pdksh to try to complete the current command.

copy-last-arg (^[_) causes the last word of the previous command to be inserted at the cursor position.

delete-char-backward (ERASE) deletes the character that is to the left of the cursor.

delete-char-forward deletes the character to the right of the cursor.

delete-word-backward (^[ERASE) deletes the characters to the left of the cursor back to the first white space character that is encountered.

delete-word-forward (^[d) deletes the characters to the right of the cursor up to the first character that occurs after a whitespace character.

down-history (^N) moves down one line in the history list. This command is often bound to the down arrow key.

end-of-line (^E) moves the cursor to the end of the current line.

forward-char (^F) moves the cursor forward one character. This command is often bound to the right arrow key.

forward-word (^[F) moves the cursor forward to the end of a word.

kill-line (KILL) deletes the current line.

kill-to-eol (^K) deletes all of the characters to the right of the cursor on the current line.

list (^[?) causes pdksh to list all of the possible command names or filenames that can complete the word in which the cursor is currently contained.

search-history (^R) searches the history list backward for the first command that contains the inputted characters.

transpose-chars (^T) exchanges the two characters on either side of the cursor. If the cursor is at the end of the command line it switches the last two characters on the line.

up-history (^P) moves up one command in the history list. This command is often bound to the up arrow key.

Customizing Your *pdksh*

Many ways of customizing pdksh have been described in this chapter. Until now, though, the changes that you made only affected the current pdksh session. As soon as you quit pdksh, all of the customizations that you made are lost. There is a way of making the customizations more permanent.

This is done by storing all of your customizations in a pdksh initialization file. Users can put commands into this file that they want to be executed each and every time pdksh is started. Examples of commands that are typically found in this file are aliases and initializations of variables (such as the prompts).

In order to set up your customization file, you must tell pdksh where to look for the initialization file. This is different than with bash. The bash shell automatically knew where to look for its customization file. To tell pdksh where to look for the customization file, you must create a file in your home directory called .profile. This file is read and all of the commands in the file are executed each time you log into the system.

A sample of the commands that you should place in your .profile file are as follows:

```
export ENV=$HOME/.kshrc
EDITOR=emacs
```

The first line in the .profile file sets the ENV variable. This is the variable that pdksh looks at to find the initialization file that it should use. If you plan to customize pdksh, you should tell pdksh to look for a file in your home directory. The filename .kshrc is often used as the pdksh initialization filename, but you can pick another name if you want.

If you are not planning to customize pdksh, you can set the ENV variable to be equal to the system default pdksh initialization file. This file is in the /etc directory, and is called ksh.kshrc.

The second line in the .profile file sets the EDITOR variable. This is used by the .kshrc initialization file to determine what type of command-line editing commands to use for your session. If you prefer to use vi command-line editing, you can set this variable to be equal to vi.

Listing 11.1 shows most of what is contained in the system's default ksh.kshrc file. If you want to add your own customizations to pdksh, you should copy this file into your home directory and then add the customizations that you want to your own copy of the file.

TIP

Instead of copying the file to your home directory, you can create a new file in your home directory that calls the system default file, and then add customizations afterward.

Listing 11.1. Default `ksh.kshrc` file.

```
# NAME
#       ksh.kshrc - global initialization for ksh
#
# DESCRIPTION:
#       Each invocation of /bin/ksh processes the file pointed
#       to by $ENV (usually $HOME/.kshrc).
#       This file is intended as a global .kshrc file for the
#       Korn shell.  A user's $HOME/.kshrc file simply requires
#       the line:
#               . /etc/ksh.kshrc
#       at or near the start to pick up the defaults in this
#       file which can then be overridden as desired.
#
# SEE ALSO:
#       $HOME/.kshrc
#

# RCSid:
#       $Id: ksh.kshrc,v 1.6 93/09/29 08:57:50 sjg Exp $
#
#       @(#)Copyright (c) 1991 Simon J. Gerraty
#
#       This file is provided in the hope that it will
#       be of use.  There is absolutely NO WARRANTY.
#       Permission to copy, redistribute or otherwise
#       use this file is hereby granted provided that
#       the above copyright notice and this notice are
#       left intact.

case "$-" in
*i*)    # we are interactive
        # we may have su'ed so reset these
        # NOTE: SCO-UNIX doesn't have whoami,
        #        install whoami.sh
        HOSTNAME='hostname'
        USER='whoami'
        PROMPT="<$USER@$HOSTNAME:!>$ "
        PPROMPT='<$USER@$HOSTNAME:$PWD:!>$ '
        PS1=$PROMPT
        # $TTY is the tty we logged in on,
        # $tty is that which we are in now (might by pty)
        tty='tty'
        tty='basename $tty'

        set -o $EDITOR

        alias ls='ls -CF'
        alias h='fc -l ¦ more'
        # the PD ksh is not 100% compatible
        case "$KSH_VERSION" in
        *PD*)   # PD ksh
                case "$TERM" in
                xterm*)
                        # bind arrow keys
                        bind '^[['=prefix-2
                        bind '^XA'=up-history
                        bind '^XB'=down-history
```

```
                      bind '^XC'=forward-char
                      bind '^XD'=backward-char
                      ;;
            esac
            ;;
*)          # real ksh ?
            ;;
esac
case "$TERM" in
sun*)
            # these are not as neat as their csh equivalents
            if [ "$tty" != console ]; then
                    # ilabel
                    ILS='\033]L'; ILE='\033\\'
                    # window title bar
                    WLS='\033]l'; WLE='\033\\'
            fi
            ;;
xterm*)
            ILS='\033]1;'; ILE='\007'
            WLS='\033]2;xterm: '; WLE='\007'
            ;;
*)          ;;
esac
# do we want window decorations?
if [ "$ILS" ]; then
            ilabel () { print -n "${ILS}$*${ILE}"; }
            label () { print -n "${WLS}$*${WLE}"; }

            alias stripe='label "$USER@$HOST ($tty) - $PWD"'
            alias istripe='ilabel "$USER@$HOST ($tty)"'

            wftp () { ilabel "ftp $*"; "ftp" $*; eval istripe; }
            wcd () { "cd" $*; eval stripe; }
            wtelnet ()
            {
                    "telnet" "$@"
                    eval istripe
                    eval stripe
            }
            wsu ()
            {
                    "su" "$@"
                    eval istripe
                    eval stripe
            }
            alias su=wsu
            alias cd=wcd
            alias ftp=wftp
            alias telnet=wtelnet
            eval stripe
            eval istripe
            PS1=$PROMPT
fi
alias quit=exit
alias cls=clear
alias logout=exit
```

continues

Listing 11.1. continued

```
        alias bye=exit
        alias p='ps -l'
        alias j=jobs
        alias o='fg %-'

# add your favourite aliases here
;;
*)      # non-interactive
;;
esac
# commands for both interactive and non-interactive shells
```

pdksh Commands

Here are some of the most useful built-in pdksh commands:

. reads and executes the contents of the file. (This will be discussed in more detail in Chapter 13.)

alias is used to set aliases, command nicknames that can be defined by the user.

bg (background command) forces a suspended process to continue to execute in the background.

cd (change working directory) changes the current working directory to the directory specified.

exit terminates the shell.

export causes the value of a variable to be made visible to all subprocesses that belong to the current shell.

fc (fix command) used to edit the commands that are in the current history list.

fg (foreground command) forces a suspended process to continue to execute in the foreground.

kill is used to terminate another process.

pwd (print working directory) prints to the screen the directory in which the user is currently working.

unalias is used to remove aliases that have previously been defined using the alias command.

pdksh Variables

Some of the most useful pdksh variables are listed next, including the variable name, a short description, and default value (if one exists).

EDITOR, FCEDIT   The default editor for the fc bash command.

HISTFILE   The name of the file that is used to store the command history.

HISTSIZE   The size of the history list.

HOME   The HOME directory of the current user

OLDPWD   The previous working directory (the one that was current before the current directory was entered).

PATH   The search path that bash uses when looking for executable files.

PS1   The first level prompt that is displayed on the command line.

PS2   The second level prompt that is displayed when a command is expecting more input.

PWD   The current working directory.

SECONDS   The number of seconds that have elapsed since the current bash session was started.

Summary

We've looked at many of the features of the Public Domain Korn Shell (pdksh). It is similar to the Bourne Again Shell in many aspects, but it does add some new utilities.

In the next chapter, we look at tcsh, a version of the C shell that is available with Linux. After you have seen the features and the way you use the three shells, you should be able to decide which shell is best for you to use on a regular basis. Of course, you can use any shell at any time by simply typing its name.

Using *tcsh*

R

The last two chapters introduced you to the Bourne Again Shell (bash) and the Public Domain Korn Shell (pdksh). This chapter introduces a third shell, tcsh. This chapter shows you how tcsh supports the following:

- Command-line completion
- Command history and aliases
- Input and output redirection
- Pipelines
- Changing your prompts
- Job control
- Key bindings
- Spelling correction

In addition to these topics, we will see how you can customize tcsh to suit your tastes. You will also be introduced to several important tcsh commands and variables.

Rounding out the chapter is a section on neat little features that tcsh provides that are not available in any of the other shell programs we have discussed.

An Introduction to *tcsh*

tcsh is a modified version of the C shell (csh). It is fully backward-compatible with csh, but it contains many new features that make user interaction much easier. The biggest improvements over the csh are in the areas of command-line editing and history navigation.

Command Completion

Just like pdksh and bash, tcsh supports command-line completion. You invoke command-line completion in tcsh exactly the same way as you do in bash: by pressing the Tab key at any point while you are typing a command.

When you press the Tab key, tcsh tries to complete the command by matching what has been typed with any file in the directory that the command is referring to. For example, assume that you typed the following command and then pressed the Tab key:

```
emacs hello
```

Here, tcsh will try to match the letters hello with any file (or subdirectory) in the current directory. If there is a single file in the current directory that begins with the letters hello, tcsh fills in the rest of the filename for you. Now assume that you typed the following command and then pressed the Tab key:

```
emacs /usr/bin/hello
```

In this case, tcsh would try to match the letters hello with any file in the /usr/bin directory. From these examples, you can see that you must give tcsh something to go on before asking it to complete the command for you.

Another example of using command-line completion is as follows: Assume that the directory that you are currently in contains these files:

```
News/ bin/ mail/ sample.txt testfile ttd.txt
```

If you want to print the sample.txt file, you could type the following command:

```
lpr sample.txt
```

Using command-line completion, you could get away with typing the following command and then pressing the Tab key:

```
lpr s
```

At this point, tcsh attempts to complete the command and finds that the only file that can possibly match what was typed so far is the sample.txt file. tcsh would then complete the command by putting the following text on the command line:

```
lpr sample.txt
```

You can now either confirm that this is the intended command by pressing the Enter key, or you can edit the command if it isn't what you intended.

Wildcards

tcsh enables you to use wildcards in your commands. It supports the same three wildcards as bash and pdksh:

> * matches any character or any number of characters.
>
> ? matches any single character.
>
> [...] matches any single character contained within the brackets.

The * wildcard can be used to perform some of the same functions as command-line completion. If you entered a command like

```
cd t*
```

and only one subdirectory in the current directory begins with the letter t, this command would behave the same as if you had used command-line completion by pressing the Tab key.

The * matches any character or any number of characters, so the shell will replace the t* with the file in the directory that matches the wildcard pattern.

This will work reliably only if there is one file in the directory that starts with the letter t. If more than one file in the directory starts with the letter t, the shell will try to replace t* with the list of filenames in the directory that match the wildcard pattern, and the cd command will make the first directory in this list the working directory. This will end up being the file that comes first alphabetically and may or may not be the intended file.

A case that is more suited to using the * wildcard is if you want to perform the same operation on a number of files that have similar filenames. For example, assume the current directory contains the following files:

```
Mail/ atc1.stk atc2.stk bin/ borl.stk cdrom.txt lfi.stk temp/
```

If you want to print both of the files that start with atc and end with the .stk extension, you could do so by typing

```
lpr a*.stk
```

This command will do the job, because there are no other files in the directory that start with the letter a and have the .stk extension.

Using the ? wildcard, the following command will accomplish the same thing:

```
lpr atc?.stk
```

Using the [...] wildcard, you could enter the following command to get the same files to print:

```
lpr atc[12].stk
```

Command History

The tcsh shell provides a mechanism for accessing the command history that is similar to ones provided with bash and pdksh. The shell remembers the last history commands that have been entered into the shell (where history is a user-definable tcsh variable).

tcsh stores the text of the last history commands in a history list. When you log into your account, the history list is initialized from a history file. The default filename for the history file is .history, but you can change it using the histfile tcsh variable. This file is located in your home directory. Notice that the file begins with a period. This means that the file is a hidden file and will appear in a directory listing only if you use the -a or -A options of the ls command.

> **NOTE**
>
> In order for the history list to be saved in the history file, you must make sure that the savehist variable is set to the number of commands that you want to be saved. Refer to the .login file listing in the "Customizing tcsh" section of this chapter for an example of setting this variable.

The simplest way of using the history list is to use the up and down arrow keys to scroll through the commands that were entered earlier. Pressing the up arrow key will cause the last command entered to appear on the command line. Pressing the up arrow key again will put the command before that on the command line, and so on. If you move up in the command buffer past the command that you wanted, you can move down the history list one command at a time by pressing the down arrow key.

The command that is on the command line can be edited. You can use the left and right arrow keys to move along the command line, and you can insert text at any point. You can also delete text from the command line by using the Backspace or Delete keys. Most users should find these simple editing commands sufficient, but for those who do not, tcsh also supports a wide range of equivalent emacs and vi editing commands. See the "Key Bindings" section of this chapter for more information on vi and emacs command-line editing.

Another method of using the history file is to display and edit the history list using a number of other editing commands that tcsh provides. The history command can be invoked by any one of three different methods. The first method has the following command-line syntax:

history [-hr] [n]

This form of the history command displays the history list to the screen. The n option is used to specify the number of commands to display. If the n option is not used, the history command will display the entire history list. The -h option causes history to remove the command numbers and timestamps that are usually present in the output of the history command. The -r option tells history to display the commands in reverse order, starting with the most recent command. The following command displays the last five commands that were entered:

history 5

The second method of invoking the history command is used to modify the contents of the history file or the history list. It has the following command-line syntax:

history -S ¦ -L ¦ -M [*filename*]

The -S option writes the history list to a file. The -L option appends a history file to the current history list. The -M option merges the contents of the history file with the current history list and sorts the resulting list by the timestamp contained with each command.

NOTE

All of the options for the second form of the history command use the *filename* option as the name of the history file. If no filename is specified, the history command will use the value of the histfile variable. If the histfile variable isn't set, it will use the ~/.history (home directory) file.

The history command using the -c option clears the current history list.

In addition to the history command and its options, tcsh also contains many history navigation and editing commands. The following commands are used to navigate through the history list:

- !*n* re-executes the command with the history number of *n*.
- !-*n* re-executes the command that is *n* commands from the end of the history list.
- !! re-executes the last command that was entered.
- !c re-executes the last command in the history list that begins with the letter c.
- !?c? re-executes the last command in the history list that contains the letter c.

The history editing commands enable you to replace words and letters in previously entered commands as well as add words to the end of previously entered commands. More information on these editing commands can be found by referring to the tcsh man page. You can view this man page by entering the following command at the shell prompt:

```
man tcsh
```

Aliases

Command aliases are commands that you can specify and execute. Alias commands are usually abbreviations of other Linux commands. You tell tcsh to execute a Linux command whenever it encounters the alias. For example, if you entered the following alias command:

```
alias ls 'ls -F'
```

the ls -F command would be substituted for the ls command each time the ls command was used.

If you decide after you enter an alias that you don't need or want that alias to exist any longer, you can use the tcsh unalias command to delete that alias:

```
unalias cd
```

After you use the unalias command to remove an alias, the alias will no longer exist, and trying to execute that alias will cause tcsh to return a command not found error message.

Some aliases that you might want to define are:

- alias ll 'ls -l'
- alias ls 'ls -F'

If you are a DOS user and are accustomed to using DOS file commands, you might also want to define the following aliases:

- alias dir 'ls'
- alias copy 'cp'
- alias rename 'mv'

- `alias md 'mkdir'`
- `alias rd 'rmdir'`

> **NOTE**
>
> When you define aliases, quotation marks are necessary only if the command within them contains spaces or other special characters.

If you enter the `alias` command without any arguments, it will print to the screen all of the aliases that are already defined. The following listing illustrates sample output from the `alias` command:

```
alias ls 'ls -F'
alias dir 'ls'
alias ll 'ls -l'
alias md 'mkdir'
alias rd 'rmdir'
```

Input and Output Redirection

The standard input and output of a command can be redirected using the same syntax that is used by `bash` and `pdksh`. The < character is used for input redirection, and the > character is used for output redirection. The following command redirects the standard input of the `cat` command to the `.cshrc` file:

```
cat < .cshrc
```

In practice, input redirection isn't used very often because most commands that require input from a file support passing the filename as an argument to the command.

Output redirection is used much more frequently. The following command redirects the standard output of the `cat` command to the file named `cshenv` (which has the effect of storing the contents of the `.cshrc` and `.login` files in one file named `cshenv`):

```
cat .cshrc .login > cshenv
```

> **CAUTION**
>
> The file to which output is being redirected is created if it does not exist and is overwritten without warning if it already exists.

Pipelines

`tcsh` pipelines, just like `bash` and `pdksh` pipelines, are a way to string together a series of Linux commands. This means that the output from the first command in the pipeline is used as the input to the second command in the pipeline. The output from the second command in the pipeline is used as input to the third command in the pipeline, and so on. The output from the last command in the pipeline is the output that the user will actually see. This output will be displayed to the screen (or put into a file if output redirection was specified on the command line).

You can tell tcsh to create a pipeline by typing two or more commands separated by the ¦ character. The following command illustrates an example of using a tcsh pipeline:

```
cat file1 file2 ¦ wc -l
```

The cat command in this pipeline appends file2 to the end of file1 and passes the resulting file to the wc command. The wc command prints to the screen the total number of lines contained in the resulting file.

Prompts

tcsh has three levels of user prompts. The first-level prompt is what you see when tcsh is waiting for you to type a command. The default prompt is the % character. This prompt can be customized by assigning a new value to the prompt tcsh variable:

```
set prompt="%t$"
```

This example would change the first-level prompt to the current time followed by a dollar sign.

The second-level prompt is displayed when tcsh is waiting for input when in a while or for loop (used in shell programming, discussed in Chapter 13, "Shell Programming"). The default for the second-level prompt is %R?, where %R is a special character sequence that displays the status of the parser. You can change the second-level prompt by setting the value of the prompt2 tcsh variable. For example:

```
set prompt2="?"
```

changes the second-level prompt to a question mark.

The third-level prompt is used when tcsh displays the corrected command line when automatic spelling correction is in effect. This prompt is set using the prompt3 variable, and it has a default value of CORRECT>%R (y¦n¦e)?. See the "Correcting Spelling Errors" section for more information on this feature.

tcsh supports special character codes in its prompt variables. These codes are similar to the codes that bash supports in its prompts. The main difference between the two is that the syntax for using them is different. Table 12.1 lists the most commonly used special character codes.

Table 12.1. tcsh prompt special character codes.

Character Code	Meaning
%/	Displays the current working directory.

Character Code	Meaning
%h, %!, !	These codes all display the current history number.
%t, %@	These codes both display the time of day.
%n	Displays the username.
%d	Displays the current day of the week.
%w	Displays the current month.
%y	Displays the current year.

The following is an example of setting the prompt variable:

```
set prompt="%h %/"
```

This command sets the prompt to display the history number of the current command, followed by the current working directory.

Job Control

Job control refers to the ability to control the execution behavior of a currently running process. Specifically, you can suspend a running process and cause it to resume running at a later time. tcsh keeps track of all the processes that it starts as a result of user input. You can suspend a running process or restart a suspended one at any time during the life of that process.

Pressing the Ctrl-Z key sequence suspends a running process. The bg command restarts a suspended process in the background, and the fg command restarts a process in the foreground.

These commands are most often used when you want to run a command in the background but by accident start it in the foreground. When a command is started in the foreground, it locks the shell from any further user interaction until the command completes execution. This is usually fine because most commands take only a few seconds to execute. If the command you're running is going to take a long time, you would typically start the command in the background so that you could continue to use tcsh to enter other commands.

For example, if you started a command that was going to take a long time in the foreground, such as

```
find / -named "test" > find.out
```

your shell will be tied up for several minutes. If you have done this and want to cause the find command to continue executing in the background, you could enter the following:

```
control-z
bg
```

This would suspend the find command and then restart it in the background. The find command would continue to execute, and you would regain control of tcsh.

Key Bindings

Like the pdksh, tcsh provides the ability to change and add key bindings. The tcsh implementation of key bindings is more powerful than the way key bindings are done in pdksh.

With tcsh you can bind to things other than the built-in editor commands. This means that you can bind a key to a UNIX command, for example. tcsh also enables you to bind vi editing commands, whereas pdksh only allows the binding of emacs editing commands.

Key bindings can be very useful, especially if you're using a favorite editor other than emacs or vi. The basic syntax for defining key bindings is

```
bindkey [option] <instring or keyname> <outstring or command>
```

The options that bindkey supports are not discussed in this book. If you want to learn about the bindkey options, refer to the tcsh man page. The basic function of the bindkey command is to bind the key sequence contained in the first argument to the command contained in the second argument.

The following list gives some of the most useful editing commands that you can bind key sequences to, along with the default key binding for that command. You can list all the bindings that are defined in tcsh by typing the bindkey command without any arguments.

- beginning-of-line (^A): Moves the cursor to the beginning of the command line.
- backward-char (^B): Moves the cursor back one character.
- end-of-line (^E): Moves the cursor to the end of the command line.
- forward-char (^F): Moves the cursor forward one character.
- backward-delete-char (^H): Deletes the character to the left of the cursor.
- kill-line (^K): Deletes all of the characters to the right of the cursor.
- clear-screen (^L): Removes all of the text from the shell window.
- down-history (^N): Moves down one command in the history list.
- up-history (^P): Moves up one command in the history list.
- kill-whole-line (^U): Deletes all of the characters on the current line.

All of these commands are the same whether you're in emacs or vi insert mode. tcsh supports many more editing commands than are listed here. To see what these commands are, refer to the tcsh man page.

The following are examples of setting key bindings:

```
bindkey ^W kill-whole-line
bindkey ^S beginning-of-line
```

Other Neat Stuff

tcsh supports a few neat features that none of the other shells discussed in this book support. This section lists a few of the most useful of these extended features.

Correcting Spelling Errors

This feature, which is not available with any of the other shells discussed in this book, is a dream come true for many people (including me). If you're plagued by recurring typos, this feature might be enough to cause you to use tcsh over any of the other shells. You can tell tcsh to correct spelling errors in a command that you typed, and you also can tell it to automatically try to correct commands that it can't figure out.

The first function isn't quite as useful, because you must know that you have made a typing mistake before you actually execute the command. This feature is invoked by pressing Esc-S on the command line before you press Enter.

For example, suppose you wanted to change to the /usr/X11R6/X11 directory, so you typed the following command on the command line:

```
cd /usr/X11RT/bun
```

If you caught the typing errors before you executed the command (by pressing the Enter key), you could correct the errors by pressing Esc-S. tcsh will try to correct the spelling of the command. It would change the command to read

```
cd /usr/X11R6/bin
```

You could now press the Enter key, and the command would execute just as you wanted. Obviously this command has some limitations, because the shell can't (yet) read your mind, but for simple character transpositions or capitalization errors, it works very nicely.

The second method of instructing tcsh to perform spelling corrections on your commands is to set the correct tcsh variable. This variable, depending on what options you use, will tell tcsh to try to correct spelling errors in command names or anywhere in the command. The syntax for setting the correct variable is one of the following:

```
set correct=cmd
```

or

```
set correct=all
```

After you set the correct variable, whenever you enter a command that tcsh doesn't understand, it will automatically check to see if the command has any spelling errors. If it finds possible spelling errors, it gives you the corrected command and asks you if the new command is what you intended. For example, if you had set the correct variable with the all option and then entered the following command:

```
cd /usr/gmes
```

tcsh would respond with the following prompt on the command line:

```
CORRECT>cd /usr/games (y¦n¦e)?
```

If you respond to the prompt by pressing the y (yes) key, tcsh will execute the corrected command. If you respond to the prompt by pressing the n (no) key, tcsh will execute the command that you initially entered, which will in turn will cause an error message to be displayed.

If you respond to the prompt by pressing the e (edit) key, tcsh will put the command that you entered back on the command line and enable you to edit it.

Precommands

tcsh supports a way of executing a command prior to displaying each command prompt. This is done through the use of a special variable called precmd. If the precmd variable is set, the command that it is set to will be executed before the command prompt is displayed on-screen. For example, assume that you set the precmd variable using the following command:

```
alias precmd time
```

After this alias has been declared, the time command will always be executed before the command prompt is displayed on-screen.

Change Directory Commands

tcsh also supports change directory commands. These commands are executed only when the current directory changes (usually as a result of executing the cd command). This type of command is probably more useful than the precommands just mentioned, because there are times when you might want to know something about a directory that you just entered.

This feature is supported in the same way precommands are supported, only you must provide an alias for a different variable. The variable used for this is cwdcmd. If this variable is aliased to a command, that command will be executed each time you change current working directories.

A common use for this variable is to display the current directory to the screen. This can be done by entering the command

```
alias cwdcmd 'pwd'
```

This will display the name of the new directory each time a new directory is entered.

> **WARNING**
>
> You should not put a cd command into cwdcmd. Doing so could cause an infinite loop that would cause you to lose control of tcsh.

Monitoring Logins and Logouts

tcsh provides a mechanism that enables you to watch for any user who logs on or off the system. It does this through a tcsh variable named watch.

The watch variable contains a set of user ID and terminal number pairs. These pairs can contain wildcards and also can contain the word "any," which tells tcsh to match any user or terminal. The syntax for setting the watch variable is

```
set watch=(<user> <terminal>)
```

The *user* in this command refers to a Linux user ID. *terminal* refers to a Linux terminal device number.

Most people would use this capability to watch for friends logging onto the system. For example, if you were waiting for a person with the username jules to come to work in the morning, you could set the following watch variable:

```
set watch=(jules any)
```

This command would inform you when a person with the user ID jules logged into the system on any terminal. tcsh defaults to checking the defined watches every 10 minutes. If you want to know with greater or lesser frequency, you can change this default by passing the number of minutes to wait between checks as the first parameter to the watch variable. For example, to check every five minutes to see if jules has logged in, you would use the following watch variable:

```
set watch=(5 jules any)
```

This will do the same thing as the first command, except it will check every five minutes instead of every 10 to see if jules has logged in.

Customizing *tcsh*

I've discussed many ways of customizing tcsh in this chapter. If you just enter the commands that we have discussed at the command line, the changes you make will be lost every time you log out of the system. This section describes how to store these changes in a file that will be executed each time you start tcsh.

Two initialization files are important to tcsh. The first is called the login file. The commands in this file are executed when you first log into Linux. The contents of the default login file are shown in Listing 12.1.

Listing 12.1. Default csh.login file.

```
if ($?prompt) then
umask 022
  set cdpath = ( /usr/spool )
  set notify
  set history = 100
    setenv OPENWINHOME /usr/openwin
    setenv MANPATH /usr/local/man:/usr/man/preformat:/usr/man:/usr/X11r6/man:
    ➥/usr/openwin/man
    setenv MINICOM "-c on"
    setenv HOSTNAME "`cat /etc/HOSTNAME`"
    set path = ( $path /usr/X11r6/bin /usr/andrew/bin
    ➥$OPENWINHOME/bin /usr/games . )
```

continues

Listing 12.1. continued

```
endif
# I had problems with the Backspace key installed by 'tset,' but you might want
# to try it anyway, instead of the 'setenv term.....' below it.
# eval 'tset -sQ "$term"'
# setenv term  linux
#if ! $?TERM setenv TERM linux
# set to "linux" for unknown term type:
if ("$TERM" == "") setenv TERM linux
if ("$TERM" == "unknown") setenv TERM linux
set prompt = "%m:%~%# "
eval 'dircolors -t' # set up color-ls variables
alias ls 'ls -F'
if ( { tty —silent } ) then >& /dev/null
  echo "";fortune;echo ""
endif
```

This file, csh.login, can be found in the /etc directory. If you want to change any of the settings found in csh.login, you should copy it to your home directory and make the changes you want there.

The other file that tcsh makes use of is cshrc. The commands in this file are executed each time a copy of the tcsh program is run. Examples of the types of commands that usually appear in this file are aliases and variable declarations. This file, csh.cshrc, is also contained in the /etc directory. If you want to make changes to this file, you should copy it to your home directory and make your changes there.

When you first log in to Linux, tcsh executes the /etc/csh.cshrc file, followed by the /etc/ csh.login file. It then checks your home directory to see if you have a personal copy of the csh.cshrc file. This file can be named either .tcshrc or .cshrc. If you have one of these files in your home directory, tcsh will execute it next.

tcsh next checks to see if you have your own copy of the csh.login file in your home directory. This file must be named .login. If you do have a .login file in your home directory, it will be executed next.

Whenever you start another copy of tcsh after you log in to the system, it will execute the commands that are in the /etc/csh.cshrc file and then check your home directory to see if there is a .tcshrc or a .cshrc file there.

tcsh Command Summary

Here are some of the most useful tcsh commands:

- alias: Used to set and display aliases, command nicknames that can be set by the user.
- bg: Background command. Forces a suspended process to continue running in the background.
- bindkey: Enables users to change the editing actions that are associated with a key sequence.

- ■ `cd`: Changes the current working directory to the directory specified.
- ■ `exit`: Terminates the shell.
- ■ `fg`: Foreground command. Forces a suspended process to continue running in the foreground.
- ■ `history`: Enables users to display and modify the contents of the history list and the history file.
- ■ `kill`: Terminates another process.
- ■ `logout`: Terminates a login shell.
- ■ `set`: Used to set the value of `tcsh` variables.
- ■ `source`: Reads and executes the contents of a file. This command is discussed in more detail in Chapter 13.
- ■ `unalias`: Used to remove aliases that have been defined using the `alias` command.

tcsh Variables

Here are some of the most useful `tcsh` variables:

- ■ `autocorrect`: If this is set, `tcsh` will automatically try to correct command-line spelling errors.
- ■ `histfile`: The name of the file that is used to store the command history.
- ■ `history`: The size of the history list.
- ■ `home`: The user's home directory.
- ■ `path`: The search path that `tcsh` uses when looking for executable programs.
- ■ `prompt`: The first-level prompt that is displayed on the command line.
- ■ `prompt2`: The second-level prompt that is displayed when a `for`, `foreach`, or `while` loop is expecting input.
- ■ `prompt3`: The third-level prompt that is displayed when `tcsh` has attempted to correct a spelling error in a command.
- ■ `savehist`: This variable must be set to the number of history commands that you want to save, if you want `tcsh` to save the history list when you log out.
- ■ `watch`: Contains a list of user terminal pairs to watch for logins and logouts.

Summary

The last three chapters have presented the fundamental commands and concepts of the three most popular UNIX shells. `tcsh` is the most feature-rich shell of those presented, but that doesn't necessarily mean that it's the best shell for you to use. In the end, this decision will probably be based on your personal preference as opposed to what features are offered.

The next chapter looks at the programming languages that are provided by each of the shells we have discussed.

Shell Programming

13

by Rick McMullin

The previous three chapters described how to use the most common Linux shell programs. I mentioned that these shell programs have powerful interpretive programming languages built into them. Now it's time to look at them in more detail.

This chapter describes the fundamentals of shell programming and compares the bash, pdksh, and tcsh programming languages. This chapter covers the following topics:

- Creating and running shell programs
- Using shell variables
- The importance of quotes
- The test command
- Conditional statements
- Iteration statements

This chapter contains several small examples of shell programs. Each new concept or command that is introduced has some example code that further helps to explain what is being presented.

Creating and Running Shell Programs

At the simplest level, shell programs are just files that contain one or more shell or Linux commands. These programs can be used to simplify repetitive tasks, to replace two or more commands that are always executed together with a single command, to automate the installation of other programs, and to write simple interactive applications.

To create a shell program, you must create a file using a text editor and put the shell or Linux commands you want to be executed into that file. For example, assume you have a CD-ROM drive mounted on your Linux system. This CD-ROM device is mounted when the system is first started. If you later change the CD in the drive, you must force Linux to read the new directory contents. One way of achieving this is to put the new CD into the drive, unmount the CD-ROM drive using the Linux umount command, and then remount the drive using the Linux mount command. This sequence of steps is shown by the following commands:

```
umount /dev/cdrom
mount -t iso9660 /dev/cdrom /cdrom
```

Instead of typing both of these commands each time you change the CD in your drive, you could create a shell program that would execute both of these commands for you. To do this, put the two commands into a file and call the file remount (or any other name you want).

Several ways of executing the commands are contained in the remount file. One way to accomplish this is to make the file executable. This is done by entering the following command:

```
chmod +x remount
```

This command changes the permissions of the file so that it is now executable. You can now run your new shell program by typing remount on the command line.

NOTE

The remount shell program must be in a directory that is in your search path, or the shell will not be able to find the program to execute. Also, if you are using tcsh to write programs, the first line of the shell program must start with a # for tcsh to recognize it as a tcsh program file.

Another way you can execute the shell program is to run the shell that the program was written for and pass the program in as a parameter to the shell. In a tcsh program, this is done by entering the following command:

```
tcsh remount
```

This command starts up a new shell and tells it to execute the commands that are found in the remount file.

A third way of executing the commands in a shell program file is to use the . command (in pdksh and bash) and the source command in tcsh. This command tells the shell to execute all the commands in the file that is passed as an argument to the command. For example, the following command can be used to tell bash or pdksh to execute the commands in the remount file:

```
. remount
```

To do the same thing in tcsh, you would type the following command:

```
source remount
```

Another situation in which a simple shell program can save a lot of time is described in the following example. Assume you were working on three different files in a directory, and at the end of every day you wanted to back up those three files onto a floppy disk. To do this you would type a series of commands similar to the following:

```
mr dir /a
mount -t msdos /dev/fd0 /a
cp file1 /a
cp file2 /a
cp file3 /a
umount /a
```

As stated in the example, one way of doing this would be to mount the floppy drive and then type three copy commands, one for each file you wanted to copy. A simpler way would be to put the six commands into a text file called backup and then execute the backup command when you wanted to copy the three files onto the floppy drive.

NOTE

You will still have to ensure that the backup shell program is executable and is in a directory that is in your path before you run the command.

Using Variables

As is the case with almost any language, the use of variables is very important in shell programs. You saw some of the ways in which shell variables can be used in the introductory shell chapters. Two of the variables that were introduced were the PATH variable and the PS1 variable. These are examples of built-in shell variables, or variables that are defined by the shell program you are using. This section describes how you can create your own variables and use them in simple shell programs.

Assigning a Value to a Variable

In all three of the shells I have discussed, you can assign a value to a variable simply by typing the variable name followed by an equal sign and the value you want to assign to the variable. For example, if you wanted to assign a value of 5 to the variable count, you would enter the following command in bash or pdksh:

```
count=5
```

With tcsh you would have to enter the following command to achieve the same results:

```
set count = 5
```

> **NOTE**
>
> With the bash and pdksh syntax for setting a variable, you must make sure that there are no spaces on either side of the equal sign. With tcsh, it doesn't matter if there are spaces or not.

Notice that you do not have to declare the variable as you would if you were programming in C or Pascal. This is because the shell language is a non-typed interpretive language. This means that you can use the same variable to store character strings that you use to store integers. You would store a character string into a variable in the same way that you stored the integer into a variable. For example:

```
name=Garry          (for pdksh and bash)
set name = Garry    (for tcsh)
```

Accessing the Value of a Variable

Once you have stored a value into a variable, how do you get the value back out? You do this in the shell by preceding the variable name with a dollar sign ($). If you wanted to print the value stored in the count variable to the screen, you would do so by entering the following command:

```
echo $count
```

If you omitted the $ from the preceding command, the echo command would display the word count on-screen.

Positional Parameters and Other Built-In Shell Variables

The shell has knowledge of a special kind of variable called a positional parameter. Positional parameters are used to refer to the parameters that were passed to a shell program on the command line or a shell function by the shell script that invoked the function. When you run a shell program that requires or supports a number of command-line options, each of these options is stored into a positional parameter. The first parameter is stored into a variable named 1, the second parameter is stored into a variable named 2, and so forth. These variable names are reserved by the shell so that you can't use them as variables you define. To access the values stored in these variables, you must precede the variable name with a dollar sign ($) just as you do with variables you define.

The following shell program expects to be invoked with two parameters. The program takes the two parameters and prints the second parameter that was typed on the command line first and the first parameter that was typed on the command line second.

```
#program reverse, prints the command line parameters out in reverse #order
echo "$2" "$1"
```

If you invoked this program by entering

```
reverse hello there
```

the program would return the following output:

```
there hello
```

Several other built-in shell variables are important to know about when you are doing a lot of shell programming. Table 13.1 lists these variables and gives a brief description of what each is used for.

Table 13.1. Built-in shell variables.

Variable	Use
$#	Stores the number of command-line arguments that were passed to the shell program.
$?	Stores the exit value of the last command that was executed.
$0	Stores the first word of the entered command (the name of the shell program).
$*	Stores all the arguments that were entered on the command line ($1 $2 ...).
"$@"	Stores all the arguments that were entered on the command line, individually quoted ("$1" "$2" ...).

The Importance of Quotation Marks

The use of the different types of quotation marks is very important in shell programming. Both kinds of quotation marks and the backslash character are used by the shell to perform different functions. The double quotation marks (""), the single quotation marks (' '), and the backslash (\) are all used to hide special characters from the shell. Each of these methods hides varying degrees of special characters from the shell.

The double quotation marks are the least powerful of the three methods. When you surround characters with double quotes, all the whitespace characters are hidden from the shell, but all other special characters are still interpreted by the shell. This type of quoting is most useful when you are assigning strings that contain more than one word to a variable. For example, if you wanted to assign the string `hello there` to the variable `greeting`, you would type the following command:

```
greeting="hello there" (for bash and pdksh)
set greeting = "hello there" (for tcsh)
```

This command would store the `hello there` string into the `greeting` variable as one word. If you typed this command without using the quotes, you would not get the results you wanted. `bash` and `pdksh` would not understand the command and would return an error message. `tcsh` would assign the value `hello` to the `greeting` variable and ignore the rest of the command line.

Single quotes are the most powerful form of quoting. They hide all special characters from the shell. This is useful if the command that you enter is intended for a program other than the shell.

Because the single quotes are the most powerful, you could have written the `hello there` variable assignment using single quotes. You might not always want to do this. If the string being assigned to the `greeting` variable contained another variable, you would have to use the double quotes. For example, if you wanted to include the name of the user in your greeting, you would type the following command:

```
greeting="hello there $LOGNAME" (for bash and pdksh)
set greeting="hello there $LOGNAME" (for tcsh)
```

> **NOTE**
>
> Remember that the `LOGNAME` variable is a shell variable that contains the Linux username of the person who is logged in to the system.

This would store the value `hello there root` into the `greeting` variable if you were logged in to Linux as root. If you tried to write this command using single quotes it wouldn't work, because the single quotes would hide the dollar sign from the shell and the shell wouldn't know that it was supposed to perform a variable substitution. The `greeting` variable would be assigned the value `hello there $LOGNAME` if you wrote the command using single quotes.

Using the backslash is the third way of hiding special characters from the shell. Like the single quotation mark method, the backslash hides all special characters from the shell, but it can hide only one character at a time, as opposed to groups of characters. You could rewrite the greeting example using the backslash instead of double quotation marks by using the following command:

```
greeting=hello\ there (for bash and pdksh)
set greeting=hello\ there (for tcsh)
```

In this command, the backslash hides the space character from the shell, and the string `hello there` is assigned to the `greeting` variable.

Backslash quoting is used most often when you want to hide only a single character from the shell. This is usually done when you want to include a special character in a string. For example, if you wanted to store the price of a box of computer disks into a variable named `disk_price`, you would use the following command:

```
disk_price=\$5.00 (for bash and pdksh)
set disk_price = \$5.00 (for tcsh)
```

The backslash in this example would hide the dollar sign from the shell. If the backslash were not there, the shell would try to find a variable named `5` and perform a variable substitution on that variable. Assuming that no variable named `5` were defined, the shell would assign a value of `.00` to the `disk_price` variable. This is because the shell would substitute a value of null for the `$5` variable.

> **NOTE**
>
> The `disk_price` example could also have used single quotes to hide the dollar sign from the shell.

The back quote marks (``` `` ```) perform a different function. They are used when you want to use the results of a command in another command. For example, if you wanted to set the value of the variable `contents` equal to the list of files in the current directory, you would type the following command:

```
contents=`ls` (for bash and pdksh)
set contents = `ls` (for tcsh)
```

This command would execute the `ls` command and store the results of the command into the `contents` variable. As you will see in the section "Iteration Statements," this feature can be very useful when you want to write a shell program that performs some action on the results of another command.

The *test* Command

In `bash` and `pdksh`, a command called `test` is used to evaluate conditional expressions. You would typically use the `test` command to evaluate a condition that is used in a conditional statement or to evaluate the entrance or exit criteria for an iteration statement. The `test` command has the following syntax:

```
test expression
```

or

```
[ expression ]
```

Several built-in operators can be used with the test command. These operators can be classified into four groups: integer operators, string operators, file operators, and logical operators.

The shell integer operators perform similar functions to the string operators except that they act on integer arguments. Table 13.2 lists the test command's integer operators.

Table 13.2. The test command's integer operators.

Operator	Meaning
int1 -eq int2	Returns True if int1 is equal to int2.
int1 -ge int2	Returns True if int1 is greater than or equal to int2.
int1 -gt int2	Returns True if int1 is greater than int2.
int1 -le int2	Returns True if int1 is less than or equal to int2.
int1 -lt int2	Returns True if int1 is less than int2.
int1 -ne int2	Returns True if int1 is not equal to int2.

The string operators are used to evaluate string expressions. Table 13.3 lists the string operators that are supported by the three shell programming languages.

Table 13.3. The test command's string operators.

Operator	Meaning
str1 = str2	Returns True if str1 is identical to str2.
str1 != str2	Returns True if str1 is not identical to str2.
str	Returns True if str is not null.
-n str	Returns True if the length of str is greater than zero.
-z str	Returns True if the length of str is equal to zero.

The test command's file operators are used to perform functions such as checking to see if a file exists and checking to see what kind of file is passed as an argument to the test command. Table 13.4 lists the test command's file operators.

Table 13.4. The `test` command's file operators.

Operator	Meaning
-d filename	Returns True if `file`, `filename` is a directory.
-f filename	Returns True if `file`, `filename` is an ordinary file.
-r filename	Returns True if `file`, `filename` can be read by the process.
-s filename	Returns True if `file`, `filename` has a nonzero length.
-w filename	Returns True if `file`, `filename` can be written by the process.
-x filename	Returns True if `file`, `filename` is executable.

The `test` command's logical operators are used to combine two or more of the integer, string, or file operators or to negate a single integer, string, or file operator. Table 13.5 lists the `test` command's logical operators.

Table 13.5. The `test` command's logical operators.

Command	Meaning
! expr	Returns True if `expr` is not true.
expr1 -a expr2	Returns True if `expr1` and `expr2` are true.
expr1 -o expr2	Returns True if `expr1` or `expr2` is true.

The *tcsh* Equivalent of the *test* Command

The `tcsh` does not have a `test` command, but it supports the same function using expressions. The expression operators that `tcsh` supports are almost identical to those supported by the C language. These expressions are used mostly in the `if` and `while` commands, which are covered later in this chapter in the "Conditional Statements" and "Iteration Statements" sections.

The `tcsh` expressions support the same kind of operators as the `bash` and `pdksh` `test` command. These are integer, string, file, and logical expressions. The integer operators supported by `tcsh` expressions are listed in Table 13.6.

Table 13.6. The `tcsh` expression integer operators.

Operator	Meaning
int1 <= int2	Returns True if `int1` is less than or equal to `int2`.
int1 >= int2	Returns True if `int1` is greater than or equal to `int2`.
int1 < int2	Returns True if `int1` is less than `int2`.
int1 > int2	Returns True if `int1` is greater than `int2`.

The string operators that tcsh expressions support are listed in Table 13.7.

Table 13.7. The tcsh expression string operators.

Operator	Meaning
str1 == str2	Returns True if str1 is equal to str2.
str1 != str2	Returns True if str1 is not equal to str2.

The file operators that tcsh expressions support are listed in Table 13.8.

Table 13.8. The tcsh expression file operators.

Operator	Meaning
-r file	Returns True if file is readable.
-w file	Returns True if file is writable.
-x file	Returns True if file is executable.
-e file	Returns True if file exists.
-o file	Returns True if file is owned by the current user.
-z file	Returns True if file is of size 0.
-f file	Returns True if file is a regular file.
-d file	Returns True if file is a directory file.

The logical operators that tcsh expressions support are listed in Table 13.9.

Table 13.9. The tcsh expression logical operators.

Operator	Meaning
exp1 ¦¦ exp2	Returns True if exp1 is true or if exp2 is true.
exp1 && exp2	Returns True if exp1 is true and exp2 is true.
! exp	Returns True if exp is not true.

Conditional Statements

The bash, pdksh, and tcsh each have two forms of conditional statements. These are the if statement and the case statement. These statements are used to execute different parts of your shell program depending on whether certain conditions are true. As with most statements, the syntax for these statements is slightly different between the different shells.

The *if* Statement

All three shells support nested `if...then...else` statements. These statements provide you with a way of performing complicated conditional tests in your shell programs. The syntax of the `if` statement is the same for `bash` and `pdksh` and is shown here:

```
if [ expression ]
then
        commands
elif [ expression2 ]
then
        commands
else
        commands
fi
```

> **NOTE**
>
> The `elif` and `else` clauses are both optional parts of the `if` statement. Also note that `bash` and `pdksh` use the reverse of the statement name in most of their complex statements to signal the end of the statement. In this statement the `fi` keyword is used to signal the end of the `if` statement.

The `elif` statement is an abbreviation of `else if`. This statement is executed only if none of the expressions associated with the `if` statement or any `elif` statements before it were true. The commands associated with the `else` statement are executed only if none of the expressions associated with the `if` statement or any of the `elif` statements were true.

In `tcsh`, the `if` statement has two different forms. The first form provides the same function as the `bash` and `pdksh` `if` statement. This form of `if` statement has the following syntax:

```
if (expression1) then
        commands
else if (expression2) then
        commands
else
        commands
endif
```

> **NOTE**
>
> Once again, the `else if` and `else` parts of the `if` statement are optional.

The second form of `if` statement provided by `tcsh` is a simple version of the first `if` statement. This form of `if` statement evaluates only a single expression. If the expression is true, it executes a single command; if the expression is false, nothing happens. The syntax for this form of `if` statement is the following:

```
if (expression) command
```

This statement could be written using the first form of if statement by writing the if without any else or else if clauses. This form just saves a little typing.

The following is an example of a bash or pdksh if statement. This statement checks to see if there is a .profile file in the current directory:

```
if [ -f .profile ]
then
      echo "There is a .profile file in the current directory."
else
      echo "Could not find the .profile file."
fi
```

The same statement written using the tcsh syntax is shown here:

```
#
if ( { -f .profile } ) then
      echo "There is a .profile file in the current directory."
else
      echo "Could not find the .profile file."
endif
```

> **NOTE**
>
> Notice that in the tcsh example the first line starts with a #. This is required for tcsh to recognize the file containing the commands as a tcsh script file.

The *case* Statement

The case statement enables you to compare a pattern with several other patterns and execute a block of code if a match is found. The shell case statement is quite a bit more powerful than the case statement in Pascal or the switch statement in C. This is because in the shell case statement you can compare strings with wildcard characters in them, whereas with the Pascal and C equivalents you can compare only enumerated types or integer values.

Once again, the syntax for the case statement is identical for bash and pdksh and different for tcsh. The syntax for bash and pdksh is the following:

```
case string1 in
     str1)
            commands;;
     str2)
            commands;;
     *)
            commands;;
esac
```

string1 is compared to str1 and str2. If one of these strings matches string1, the commands up until the double semicolon (;;) are executed. If neither str1 nor str2 matches string1, the commands associated with the asterisk are executed. This is the default case condition because the asterisk matches all strings.

The tcsh equivalent of the bash and pdksh case statement is called the switch statement. This statement's syntax closely follows the C switch statement syntax. Here it is:

```
switch (string1)
     case   str1:
               statements
     breaksw
     case   str2:
               statements
     breaksw
     default:
               statements
     breaksw
endsw
```

This behaves in the same manner as the bash and pdksh case statement. Each string following the keyword case is compared with string1. If any of these strings matches string1, the code following it up until the breaksw keyword is executed. If none of the strings matches, the code following the default keyword up until the breaksw keyword is executed.

The following code is an example of a bash or pdksh case statement. This code checks to see if the first command-line option was -i or -e. If it was -i, the program counts the number of lines in the file specified by the second command-line option that begins with the letter i. If the first option was -e, the program counts the number of lines in the file specified by the second command-line option that begins with the letter e. If the first command-line option was not -i or -e, the program prints a brief error message to the screen.

```
case $1 in
   -i)
      count=`grep ^i $2 ¦ wc -l`
      echo "The number of lines in $2 that start with an i is $count"
      ;;
   -e)
      count=`grep ^e $2 ¦ wc -l`
      echo "The number of lines in $2 that start with an e is $count"
      ;;
   * )
      echo "That option is not recognized"
      ;;
esac
```

The same example written in tcsh syntax is shown here:

```
# remember that the first line must start with a # when using tcsh
switch ( $1 )
   case -i ¦ i:
      set count = `grep ^i $2 ¦ wc -l`
      echo "The number of lines in $2 that begin with i is $count"
   breaksw
   case -e ¦ e:
      set count = `grep ^e $2 ¦ wc -l`
      echo "The number of lines in $2 that begin with e is $count"
   breaksw
   default:
      echo "That option is not recognized"
   breaksw
endsw
```

Iteration Statements

The shell languages also provide several iteration or looping statements. The most commonly used of these is the for statement.

The *for* Statement

The for statement executes the commands that are contained within it a specified number of times. bash and pdksh have two variations of the for statement.

> **NOTE**
>
> The for statement syntax is the same in both bash and pdksh.

The first form of the for statement that bash and pdksh support has the following syntax:

```
for var1 in list
do
        commands
done
```

In this form, the for statement executes once for each item in the list. This list can be a variable that contains several words separated by spaces, or it can be a list of values that is typed directly into the statement. Each time through the loop, the variable var1 is assigned the current item in the list, until the last one is reached.

The second form of for statement has the following syntax:

```
for var1
do
        statements
done
```

In this form, the for statement executes once for each item in the variable var1. When this syntax of the for statement is used, the shell program assumes that the var1 variable contains all the positional parameters that were passed in to the shell program on the command line.

Typically this form of for statement is the equivalent of writing the following for statement:

```
for var1 in "$@"
do
        statements
done
```

The equivalent of the for statement in tcsh is called the foreach statement. It behaves in the same manner as the bash and pdksh for statement. The syntax of the foreach statement is the following:

```
foreach name (list)
        commands
end
```

The following is an example of the bash or pdksh style of for statement. This example takes as command-line options any number of text files. The program reads in each of these files, converts all the letters to uppercase, and then stores the results in a file of the same name but with a .caps extension.

```
for file
do
tr a-z A-Z < $file >$file.caps
done
```

The same example written in tcsh shell language is shown next:

```
#
foreach file ($*)
   tr a-z A-Z < $file >$file.caps
end
```

The *while* Statement

Another iteration statement offered by the shell programming language is the while statement. This statement causes a block of code to be executed while a provided conditional expression is true. The syntax for the while statement in bash and pdksh is the following:

```
while expression
do
       statements
done
```

The syntax for the while statement in tcsh is the following:

```
while (expression)
       statements
end
```

The following is an example of the bash and pdksh style of while statement. This program lists the parameters that were passed to the program, along with the parameter number.

```
count=1
while [ -n "$*" ]
do
       echo "This is parameter number $count $1"
       shift
       count=`expr $count + 1`
done
```

As you will see in the section titled "The shift Command," the shift command moves the command-line parameters over one to the left.

The same program written in the tcsh language is shown next:

```
#
set count = 1
while ( "$*" != "" )
       echo "This is parameter number $count $1"
       shift
       set count = `expr $count + 1`
end
```

The *until* Statement

The until statement is very similar in syntax and function to the while statement. The only real difference between the two is that the until statement executes its code block while its conditional expression is false, and the while statement executes its code block while its conditional expression is true. The syntax for the until statement in bash and pdksh is

```
until expression
do
        commands
done
```

The same example that was used for the while statement can be used for the until statement. All you have to do to make it work is negate the condition. This is shown in the following code:

```
count=1
until [ -z "$*" ]
do
        echo "This is parameter number $count $1"
        shift
        count=`expr $count + 1`
done
```

The only difference between this example and the while statement example is that the -n test command option (which means that the string has nonzero length) was removed, and the -z test option (which means that the string has zero length) was put in its place.

In practice the until statement is not very useful, because any until statement you write can also be written as a while statement.

> **NOTE**
>
> tcsh does not have an equivalent of the until statement other than rewriting it as a while loop.

The *shift* Command

bash, pdksh, and tcsh all support a command called shift. The shift command moves the current values stored in the positional parameters to the left one position. For example, if the values of the current positional parameters are

```
$1 = -r  $2 = file1  $3 = file2
```

and you executed the shift command

```
shift
```

the resulting positional parameters would be as follows:

```
$1 = file1  $2 = file2
```

You can also move the positional parameters over more than one place by specifying a number with the shift command. The following command would shift the positional parameters two places:

```
shift 2
```

This is a very useful command when you have a shell program that needs to parse command-line options. This is true because options are typically preceded by a hyphen and a letter that indicates what the option is to be used for. Because options are usually processed in a loop of some kind, you often want to skip to the next positional parameter once you have identified which option should be coming next. For example, the following shell program expects two command-line options— one that specifies an input file and one that specifies an output file. The program reads the input file, translates all the characters in the input file into uppercase, then stores the results in the specified output file.

> **NOTE**
>
> The following example was written using bash, pdksh syntax.

```
while [ "$1" ]
do
        if [ "$1" = "-i" ] then
                infile="$2"
                shift 2
        elif [ "$1" = "-o" ]
        then
                outfile="$2"
                shift 2
        else
                echo "Program $0 does not recognize option $1"
        fi
done

tr a-z A-Z <$infile >$outfile
```

The *select* Statement

pdksh offers one iteration statement that neither bash nor tcsh provides. This is the select statement. This is actually a very useful statement. It is quite a bit different from the other iteration statements because it actually does not execute a block of shell code repeatedly while a condition is true or false. What the select statement does is enable you to automatically generate simple text menus. The syntax for the select statement is

```
select menuitem [in list_of_items]
do
        commands
done
```

where square brackets are used to enclose the optional part of the statement.

When a `select` statement is executed, pdksh creates a numbered menu item for each element in the `list_of_items`. This `list_of_items` can be a variable that contains more than one item, such as `choice1 choice2`, or it can be a list of choices typed in the command. For example:

```
select menuitem in choice1 choice2 choice3
```

If the `list_of_items` is not provided, the `select` statement uses the positional parameters just as with the `for` statement.

Once the user of the program containing a `select` statement picks one of the menu items by typing the number associated with it, the `select` statement stores the value of the selected item in the `menuitem` variable. The statements contained in the `do` block can then perform actions on this menu item.

The following example illustrates a potential use for the `select` statement. This example displays three menu items, and when the user chooses one of them it asks whether that was the intended selection. If the user enters anything other than y or Y, the menu is redisplayed.

```
select menuitem in pick1 pick2 pick3
do
      echo "Are you sure you want to pick $menuitem"
      read res
      if [ $res = "y" -o $res = "Y" ]
      then
            break
      fi
done
```

A few new commands are introduced in this example. The `read` command is used to get input from the user. It stores anything that the user types into the specified variable. The `break` command is used to exit a `while`, `until`, `repeat`, `select`, or `for` statement.

The *repeat* Statement

tcsh has an iteration statement that has no equivalent in pdksh or bash. This is the `repeat` statement. The `repeat` statement executes a single command a specified number of times. The syntax for the `repeat` statement is the following:

```
repeat count command
```

The following is an example of the `repeat` statement. It takes a set of numbers as command-line options and prints that number of periods to the screen. This program acts as a very primitive graphing program.

```
#
foreach num ($*)
      repeat $num echo -n "."
      echo ""
end
```

> **NOTE**
>
> Any repeat statement can be rewritten as a while or for statement. The repeat syntax is simply more convenient.

Functions

The shell languages enable you to define your own functions. These functions behave in much the same way as functions you define in C or other programming languages. The main advantage of using functions as opposed to writing all of your shell code in line is for organizational purposes. Code written using functions tends to be much easier to read and maintain and also tends to be smaller, because you can group common code into functions instead of putting it everywhere it is needed.

The syntax for creating a function in bash and pdksh is the following:

```
fname () {
    shell commands
}
```

pdksh also allows the following syntax:

```
function fname {
    shell commands
}
```

Both of these forms behave in the exact same way.

Once you have defined your function using one of these forms, you can invoke it by entering the following command:

```
fname [parm1 parm2 parm3 ...]
```

> **NOTE**
>
> The tcsh shell does not support functions.

Notice that you can pass any number of parameters to your function. When you do pass parameters to a function, it sees those parameters as positional parameters, just as a shell program does when you pass it parameters on the command line. For example, the following shell program contains several functions, each of which is performing a task associated with one of the command-line options. This example illustrates many of the topics covered in this chapter. It reads all the files that are passed on the command line and—depending on the option that was used—writes the files out in all uppercase letters, writes the files out in all lowercase letters, or prints the files.

```
upper () {
      shift
      for i
      do
            tr a-z A-Z <$1 >$1.out
            rm  $1
            mv $1.out $1
            shift
      done; }

lower () {
      shift
      for i
      do
            tr A-Z a-z <$1 >$1.out
            rm $1
            mv $1.out $1
            shift
      done; }

print () {
      shift
      for i
      do
            lpr $1
            shift
      done; }

usage_error () {
      echo "$1 syntax is $1 <option> <input files>"
      echo ""
      echo "where option is one of the following"
      echo "p  — to print frame files"
      echo "u  — to save as uppercase"
      echo "l  — to save as lowercase"; }

case $1
in
      p | -p)     print $@;;
      u | -u)           upper $@;;
      l | -l)     lower $@;;
      *)          usage_error $0;;
esac
```

Summary

This chapter introduced you to many of the features of the bash, pdksh, and tcsh programming languages. As you become familiar with using Linux, you will find that you use shell programming languages more and more often.

Even though the shell languages are very powerful and also quite easy to learn, you might run into some situations where shell programs are not suited to the problem you are solving. In these cases you may want to investigate the possibility of using one of the other languages available under Linux. Some of your options are C and C++, which are described in Chapters 27, "Programming in C" and 28, "Programming in C++;" gawk, which is described in Chapter 26, "gawk;" and Perl, which is described in Chapter 29, "Perl."

Using Communication Tools Under Linux

14

by Uzma Husain

IN THIS CHAPTER

The communication tools discussed in this chapter include the following:

- ▓ write: For one-way communication with other users
- ▓ mesg: For controlling message reception from other users
- ▓ talk: For an interactive connection with other users
- ▓ e-mail: For sending and receiving messages
- ▓ telnet: For logging into remote sites
- ▓ ftp: For remote file transfers
- ▓ news: For reading news via nn and tin

This chapter discusses all of these communications tools in detail and gives you the basics of how to use them in Linux. With practice, you will soon begin to use these tools effectively.

Using the *write* Command

The write command is a communication tool that enables a user to interact directly with other users. If you want to ask your friend a simple question or ask her out to lunch, and you know that she is logged in, write is the tool to use. Unlike e-mail, which is discussed later, write pastes your message directly on the recipient's terminal. The recipient does not have to take any steps to receive it.

To use the write command, your terminal and that of the other user should have write permission. Having these permissions enables you to write messages on each other's terminals. To look at the terminal settings, you need to know which terminal you are on. To find your terminal number, use the tty command as shown here:

```
mpsi:~$ tty
/dev/tty2
mpsi:~$ ls -al /dev/tty2
crw--w--w-   1 calvin    users      4,   2 Jan 15 05:49 /dev/tty2
```

The preceding code sample shows that I am on /dev/tty2. Your output may be different, depending on which terminal you happen to be on. The output of the ls command shows that others have write permission available on your terminal. You can confirm this by using the mesg command as shown here:

```
mpsi:~$
mpsi:~$ mesg
Is y
```

The outcome of the mesg command shows that the terminal enables messages to be written to it. You can toggle the terminal settings on and off with the following command:

```
mpsi:~$ mesg n
mpsi:~$ mesg
Is n
```

The preceding segment turned the mesg off. Now you can't be disturbed by any other user. (You may miss out on lunch dates, though.)

A Description of the *write* Command

The write command enables you to write an actual message on the other terminal online. You have to issue the write command with the login ID of the user with whom you want to communicate. The write command informs the user at the other end that there is a message from another user. write pastes that message onto the other user's terminal if their terminal's write permissions are set. Even if they are in the middle of an edit session, write overwrites whatever is on the screen. The edit session contents are not corrupted; you can restore the original screen on most editors with Ctrl-L. write is mostly used for one-way communication, but you can have an actual conversation as well.

> **TIP**
>
> For the write command to work, mesg has to be turned on, so turn it back on.

A Sample *write* Session

Because you want your friend to be able to write to your tty as well, always begin by checking the status of the mesg command:

```
mpsi:~$
mpsi:~$ mesg
Is y
```

Let's see whether your friend Calvin is logged in. You can do this by using the who command and piping it to the grep program to search for Calvin, because you don't want the entire list of users to scroll down your terminal.

```
mpsi:~$ who | grep calvin
calvin    tty2      Jan 15 15:26
```

> **TIP**
>
> Don't forget to type /dev before the terminal name. Look at what happens when you don't type the /dev string:
>
> ```
> mpsi:~$ ls -l tty2
> ls: tty2: No such file or directory
> ```
>
> Oops! All the ttys are in /dev, so add /dev to tty2.

Now let's see whether he wants to be disturbed:

```
mpsi:~$ ls -al /dev/tty2
crw--w--w-   1 calvin   users      4,   2 Jan 15 15:28 /dev/tty2
mpsi:~$
```

This excerpt shows you that Calvin is indeed logged in. Now let's see whether he is interested in communicating with a write session:

```
mpsi:~$ write calvin
```

Calvin sees the following on his screen:

```
mpsi:~$
Message from laurel@mpsi on tty1 at 15:36 ...
```

Now you have to wait for Calvin's response to the request. He responds by typing the following on his terminal if he is interested in communicating with you:

```
mpsi:~$ write laurel
             How are you?
         Lunch tomorrow?
```

The following string appears on your terminal:

```
Message from calvin@mpsi on tty2 at 15:36 ...
             How are you?
         Lunch tomorrow?
```

You can answer Calvin by initiating another write session from your end and typing your message. You have to press Enter at the end of each line for it to be displayed at the other terminal. To simplify communications, you can type over at the logical end of your sentence. Calvin should do likewise.

write Etiquette

If you are waiting for the other party to respond to your write request, it is polite to let him reply while you wait. Only after he has accepted your invitation should the conversation begin. Also, let the called party have the first chance to reply by typing hello or any other salutation. Avoid typing until the other party stops or signals you to begin with an end-of-message word, such as over. Remember, only one person can speak at a time on this channel.

The *talk* Communication Tool

The write tool was nice for communicating one at a time. However, Linux enables you to type simultaneously with the talk tool.

talk is an interactive communication tool that enables you to have an actual conversation in real-time mode with another user. You can actually see the conversation being typed as the other user is typing it. For talk to work, the other user has to be logged in, just as in write.

`talk` can be very annoying and disturbing if someone wants to be pesky. If you don't want to be disturbed, just turn `talk` off by entering `mesg n` at the prompt.

A Sample *talk* Session

You can talk to somebody by typing `talk` followed by the user's login ID. To see if the user is logged in, you can use the `who` command just like you did for `write`. Let's try to talk to Calvin:

```
$  talk calvin
```

The computer responds with

```
[Waiting for your party to respond]
```

The user on the other end sees the following message even if he is in the middle of an edit session. The system beeps and displays the following message on the terminal:

```
Message from Talk_Daemon@mpsi at 13:08 ...
talk: connection requested by laurel@hobbes.com.
talk: respond with:  talk laurel@hobbes.com
```

To respond to this, type the command shown in the `respond with` message shown here. If your friend does not respond, the `talk` daemon persistently bothers him with the preceding message every 30 seconds.

At your terminal, you see the following messages:

```
[Ringing your party again]
[Ringing your party again]
[Ringing your party again]
[Ringing your party again]
```

Occasionally you will see the following message:

```
[Your party is refusing messages]
```

What happened? Your friend at the other end does not want to talk or be disturbed. After several of your interruptions, he has decided to turn his `mesg` off. That is why you got the message that your party is refusing messages.

Now let's look at a nicer scenario, when someone wants to talk to you. He has to respond with the following command:

`talk laurel.`

Then your terminal displays the following screen:

```
[Connection Established]




                    _____
```

The screen is divided horizontally with a dotted line, and you can type your message on the top half of the screen. This appears verbatim on the other terminal at the bottom half of the screen. You can type your messages, and the other user can type his, simultaneously.

The connection can be closed by entering Ctrl-C. The following line appears on the screen:

```
[Connection closing.Exiting]
```

You should now be back at your shell's command prompt.

talk Etiquette

The same etiquette applies to `talk` as in `write`. Always use lowercase letters, because CAPS LOCK conversations are considered loud and rude. Always finish your sentence by typing `over`. If you initiated the talk session, wait for the other party to respond with the `hello` first. To prevent both of you from typing at the same time, always read your message, wait for the `over`, type your own message, and then terminate it with `over`.

Electronic Mail

Electronic mail has taken the world by storm. E-mail, short for electronic mail, is a method of sending a message from a user on one computer to one or several recipients on another computer. E-mail provides fast and efficient transportation of data and documents. This mode of communication also eliminates the need to play telephone tag or to wait for a convenient or appropriate time to call someone. For someone with Internet access, e-mail provides the means to communicate with friends around the world.

Mailboxes and Agents

E-mail is stored in a file called the system mail in the mailbox. System mail has the same name as that of the user. For example, a user named Calvin will have a mailbox under Linux in `/var/spool/mail/calvin`.

E-mail originates in the form of a file on your computer created by a Mail User Agent (MUA). E-mail is then submitted to a mail router such as sendmail, after which it is handed over to a Mail Transporter Agent (MTA). E-mail is then appended to a mailbox. The MTA delivers it to the final delivery agent by traversing one or more hosts.

The MUA is used to read and send mail. The MUA is the user interface for the mail system. Mail can be composed by using simple MUAs such as `mail` or `mailx`, or sophisticated mail user agents such as `elm` or `pine`.

Understanding the Mail Message

A mail message includes two parts: a mail header and the text body.

The mail header is generated by the mail program automatically. A typical header in a mail message looks like this:

```
Date: Fri, 6 Jan 1995 13:27:00 -0600
From: "Calvin N. Hobbes" <calvin@hobbes.com>
To: laurel@hady.com
Subject: Format for a mail header

Hi, just checking the different parts in a mail message
```

`Date` specifies the date and time the message is sent.

`From` specifies both the sender's name in quotes and the address, which includes the login ID and the address of their machine, `hobbes.com`.

`To` is the recipient's mail address.

`Subject` is a one-line description of the mail message.

The mail header is followed by the body of the mail message. Here you type the message as text. The mail message is terminated by typing a period (.) as the first character on the last line. The mail handler responds with `EOT`, for End Of Text. This is the standard procedure for Berkeley mail; other mail handlers have their own way of ending message text entry.

Types of Mail User Agents

There are several types of mail user agents, some of which are listed here. A variety of different programs can be used for reading the mail. The two most common programs are `mail` and `Mail` (also called `mailx`). Because of the similarity of their names, `Mail` is also called `capmail` or Berkeley Mail. Berkeley Mail is far superior to `mail` because it is much easier to use.

This section covers the following types of mail user agents:

- `elm`
- Pine
- `mailx` (Berkeley Mail)

Using *elm*

`elm` stands for electronic mail and provides a full-screen interface mail program with a good help feature. `elm` is a pleasure to use when compared with Berkeley Mail because of its simplicity of use and functionality.

Start the `elm` system by typing `elm` at the command prompt:

$ elm

The screen is cleared, and the code shown in the following screen is displayed.

```
$ elm
   Mailbox is '/var/spool/mail/calvin' with 5 messages [ELM 2.4 PL25]


   N  1    Jan 12 Laurel N. Hardy     (15)    using el
   N  2    Jan 12 Laurel N. Hardy     (15)    2nd elm message
   N  3    Jan 12 Laurel N. Hardy     (16)    Using elm
   N  4    Jan 11 Laurel N. Hardy     (11)    Re: Format for a mail header
   N  5    Jan 11 Laurel N. Hardy     (11)    message # 1

    You can use any of the following commands by pressing the first character;
 d)elete or u)ndelete mail,  m)ail a message,  r)eply or f)orward mail,  q)uit
    To read a message, press <return>.  j = move down, k = move up, ? = help

 Command:
```

The top line on the screen is the mailbox and the number of messages it has in it. You may also see `elm`'s version number. This is followed by a list of all the messages in the mailbox, the date the messages were sent, the sender's name, and the subject of the message.

The current message is indicated by an arrow or inverse video.

One nice feature of `elm` is that it displays the sender's name instead of the login ID as Berkeley Mail does.

The bottom part of the screen lists the options available. At this point, you can reply to the message, delete or undelete a message, or forward the mail by entering the appropriate command. You can go up and down the message list by using k and j, just as in the `vi` editor.

Some of the actions available in `elm` are listed in Table 14.1.

Table 14.1. `elm` **actions.**

Command	elm 2.4 Action
Enter, Spacebar	Displays current message.
|	Pipes current message or tagged messages to a system command.
!	Shell escape.
?	This screen of information.
=	Sets current message to first message.
*	Sets current message to last message.
<NUMBER>, Enter	Sets current message to *<NUMBER>*.
/	Searches From/Subjects for pattern.
//	Searches entire message texts for pattern.
>	Saves current message or tagged messages to a folder.
<	Scans current message for calendar entries.
C	Copies current message or tagged messages.
c	Changes to another folder.
d	Deletes current message.
Ctrl-D	Deletes messages with a specified pattern.
e	Edits current folder.
f	Forwards current message.
g	Groups (all recipients') reply to current message.
h	Headers displayed with message.
J	Increments current message by one.
j, <DOWN>	Advances to next undeleted message.
K	Decrements current message by one.
k, <UP>	Advances to previous undeleted message.
l	Limits messages by specified criteria.
Ctrl-L	Redraws screen.
m	Mails a message.
n	Next message, displaying current, then increment.
p	Prints current message or tagged messages.
q	Quits, maybe prompting for deleting, storing, and keeping messages.

Let's try to send mail using elm.

To send mail, press m on the main screen. The header screen appears. elm prompts you to enter the name(s) of the recipient(s) of the mail. Enter calvin and root as recipients. Calvin is the primary recipient, and a copy of this message is sent to root as well.

elm then prompts for a subject. After entering the subject heading, elm puts you in the vi editor to enter the body of the mail message. After you are finished typing, use the vi command :wq to save and quit the vi editor. You can now send the message by pressing s.

You can also forward mail to others on the system with the f command or reply to a message with the r command.

To quit elm, type q at the main screen.

If elm is available on your system, try to use it. elm is very convenient and simple and can greatly improve your electronic mail interaction.

Using Pine

Pine, a trademark of the University of Washington, stands for Program for Internet News and E-mail. Pine offers the capability to send local and remote messages using a simple user interface as well as the capability to send documents and graphics.

You invoke Pine by entering pine on the command line. The screen shown here should appear.

```
$ pine
  PINE 3.91    MAIN MENU                          Folder: INBOX   1 Message


        ?      HELP             -  Get help using Pine

        C      COMPOSE MESSAGE  -  Compose and send a message

        I      FOLDER INDEX     -  View messages in current folder

        L      FOLDER LIST      -  Select a folder to view

        A      ADDRESS BOOK     -  Update address book

        S      SETUP            -  Configure or update Pine

        Q      QUIT             -  Exit the Pine program


      Copyright 1989-1994.  PINE is a trademark of the University of Washington.
                    [Folder "INBOX" opened with 1 message]
  ? Help                    P PrevCmd              R RelNotes
  O OTHER CMDS L [ListFldrs] N NextCmd              K KBLock
```

Pine is very easy to use, because it provides a full-screen interface with the up and down cursor controls. Simply select the item you want by using the arrow keys and press Enter at the selected line.

Let's send a message using Pine. Take the cursor to the Compose Message line and press Enter. The screen shown here appears.

```
   PINE 3.91    COMPOSE MESSAGE                      Folder: INBOX  1 Message

To      : "Laurel N. Hardy" <laurel@hobbes.com>
Cc      :
Attchmnt:
Subject : using pine
---- Message Text ----
Hi, I can do everything on one screen
.




Send message? [y] :
^G Get Help  ^X Send      ^R Rich Hdr  ^Y PrvPg/Top ^K Cut Line   ^O Postpone
^C Cancel    ^D Del Char  ^J Attach    ^V NxtPg/End ^U UnDel Line ^T To AddrBk
```

Pine takes you line-by-line through the mail header and the mail message. Press Ctrl-X to end the message as well as send it to the recipient. Just walk through all the options to get a feel for this mail system.

The last two lines on the screen tell you what commands are available for the current situation. Usually there are more commands than can be shown on two lines, so use the O key to see what other commands are available. The O is optional; you don't have to be able to see a command before you use it.

Pine creates a default configuration file, `.pinerc`, in your home directory. You can edit this file to select various options. Pine also creates a `mail` subdirectory for your saved-message folders. Type `?` from the Main Menu for more help.

Using *mailx* (Berkeley Mail)

This section is about `mailx`, another common mail program for Linux. This section covers the basics of `mailx`. `mailx` has many options and features, most of which are listed in its man pages. Discussing all these features would require a book in itself.

Let's see how to receive and send mail using `mailx`.

Receiving Mail

Suppose someone has sent you a mail message. How would you know about it? The `Mail` system deals with this by displaying a message when you log in. A sample login session is shown in the following screen.

```
Welcome to Linux 1.2.13.

mpsi login: laurel
Last login: Fri Jan  6 13:28:06 on tty1
Linux 1.2.13.
You have new mail.
```

To read the mail message, invoke the `Mail` handler by typing `mail` at the prompt. You will see the output shown in the following screen.

```
mpsi:~$ mail
Mail version 5.5-kw 5/30/95.  Type ? for help.
"/var/spool/mail/calvin": 1 message 1 new
>N  1 laurel@hobbes.com         Fri Jan  6 13:38   12/374   "just checking"
& 1
Message 1:
From laurel@hobbes.com Fri Jan  6 13:38:06 1995
Date: Fri, 6 Jan 1995 13:38:06 -0600
From: "Laurel N. Hardy" <laurel@hobbes.com>
To: calvin@hobbes.com
Subject: just checking

the body of the message
bye

& exit
You have mail in /var/spool/mail/calvin
```

In this example, the user Calvin has received a mail message from another user, Laurel. This message is the first message in the message queue and is declared as new, which means it has not been read yet. The message queue has an `>N`, indicating that it is a new message, followed by a message number (1), the sender's login ID (`laurel@hobbes.com`), the day of the week, the date and time the message was sent, and the subject of the message.

The ampersand (`&`) is the mail system prompt. You can now read the message by typing the message number at this prompt.

```
 & 1
Message 1:
From laurel@hobbes.com Fri Jan  6 13:38:06 1995
Date: Fri, 6 Jan 1995 13:38:06 -0600
From: "Laurel N. Hardy" <laurel@hobbes.com>
To: calvin@hobbes.com
Subject: just checking
```

```
the body of the message
bye

&
```

Mail Options

All the available options in the Mail system can be listed by typing a **?** after the **&**. The listed options are shown in Listing 14.1.

Listing 14.1. Mail options.

```
& ?

     Mail    Commands
t <message list>                type messages
n                               goto and type next message
e <message list>                edit messages
f <message list>                give head lines of messages
d <message list>                delete messages
s <message list> file           append messages to file
u <message list>                undelete messages
R <message list>                reply to message senders
r <message list>                reply to message senders and all recipients
pre <message list>              make messages go back to /usr/spool/mail
m <user list>                   mail to specific users
q                               quit, saving unresolved messages in mbox
x                               quit, do not remove system mailbox
h                               print out active message headers
!                               shell escape
cd [directory]                  chdir to directory or home if none given

A <message list> consists of integers, ranges of same, or user names separated
by spaces.  If omitted, Mail uses the last message typed.

A <user list> consists of user names or aliases separated by spaces.
Aliases are defined in .mailrc in your home directory.
&
```

Replying to a Message

Suppose you have three mail messages from different users and you want to reply to the one sent by Jeremy. Just invoke mail as before, as shown in Listing 14.2.

Listing 14.2. Three received messages.

```
mpsi:~$ mail
Mail version 5.5-kw 5/30/95.  Type ? for help.
"/var/spool/mail/laurel": 3 messages 3 unread
>U  1 calvin@hobbes.com       Fri Jan  6 13:27   12/429    "Format for a mail hea"
```

continues

Listing 14.2. continued

```
U   2  jeremy@hobbes.com        Sat Jan  7 15:25  72/23291  " Please reply soon"
U   3  calvin@hobbes.com        Wed Jan 11 12:29  12/373    "message # 3"
```

The U in front of the second message specifies that the message is still unread. You can read the message by typing the message number.

```
& 2
Message 2:
From jeremy@hobbes.com Sat Jan  7 15:25:00 1995
Date: Sat, 7 Jan 1995 15:25:00 -0600
From: "friend22" <jeremy@hobbes.com>
To: laurel@hobbes.com
Subject: Please reply soon

What's up?
```

You can reply to the message by typing r.

```
& r
To: jeremy@hobbes.com
Subject: Re: Please reply soon
Replying to your mail message # 2
I am too busy to reply to you now. Go away.
.
EOT
```

The Mail daemon automatically sets up the header in the reply mode, so all you have to do is type the text.

Sending and Forwarding Mail

Sending and forwarding mail can be done with the s and f commands, respectively. The procedures for creating the header and text of the message are similar to that of replying to a message.

The ~/signature file is appended to every mail message you send. You should place text in here that you want to send with every message. Some examples are your phone number or an alternative e-mail address (your recipient might not be able to reply to certain hosts). Mail etiquette requires that you keep you signature files short—four lines or less. Most recipients do not like to see pages of information about you in every mail message.

Using *news*

Using news is perhaps the best way of getting into what is probably the world's best online forum: the Usenet news service. There are literally thousands of giant bulletin boards for you to select topics from and post messages to. The number of subjects available can be quite overwhelming at times, since there are more than 13,000 newsgroup topics to choose from. (A newsgroup is one of the bulletin boards.) Newsgroups offer the best example of free speech and a forum for discussing just about any topic imaginable.

Topics range from the serious to the absurd. In the serious category you can talk about computer communications (`comp.dcom.telecom`), astronomy (`sci.astro`), and so forth. In the absurd corner you have `alt.tasteless`, `alt.barney.dinosaur.die.die.die`, and `alt.fan.oj-simpson.drive.faster`.

Usenet was started at Duke University in 1979 by two students, Tom Truscott and Jim Ellis, as an experiment to connect two computers between Duke and the University of North Carolina. From these two news sites in 1980, the number of news sites has grown to hundreds of thousands of sites in the 1990s, with millions of subscribers worldwide.

There are several news readers for Linux. I will cover two: `nn` and `tin`.

nn

The `nn` news reader stands for Net News. When you use `nn`, you decide which of the many news groups you are interested in. You unsubscribe those that do not interest you any more. `nn` lets you read all articles in each of the groups you subscribe to, using a menu-based article selection prior to reading the articles in the newsgroup.

When you enter a newsgroup in `nn`, you are presented with a screen that lists the most recent unread articles. Each item on this list contains at least the sender and subject. You are now in selection mode. You can select using the A through Z and 0 through 9 keys. When you select an article, it is displayed in a highlight color. If you press the spacebar, you go into read mode.

In read mode, `nn` presents you with each article. Press the spacebar to get to the next page of each article. If you are at the end of an article, the spacebar takes you to the next article.

When you have read all the selected articles in the current group, pressing the spacebar takes you to the next group.

Here are some of the other commands in `nn`:

- `?` or help gives a one-page overview of the commands available in the current mode. This is perhaps the most used command for beginners. The best way to learn about `nn` is by using this command.
- Ctrl-L or Ctrl-R redraws the screen.
- Ctrl-P shows the previous message.
- `!` is the shell escape command. You are prompted for a command if you do not type one after the `!`.
- `Q` quits `nn`.
- `V` prints release and version information (for debug).
- `:command` executes the command by name. This is used to invoke any of `nn`'s commands, including those that cannot be bound to a key.

The nn man pages provide about 600 lines of very detailed information about all the options and commands available to you. You do not have to use all of them—just use as many as necessary to customize your own environment.

tin

tin is a screen-oriented Net News reader. It can read news locally (/var/spool/news) or remotely (rtin or tin -r option) via an NNTP (Network News Transport Protocol) server. tin is based on the tass newsreader, which was developed by Rich Skrenta in March 1991. tass was itself heavily influenced by NOTES, which was developed at the University of Illinois by Ray Essick and Rob Kolstad in 1982. The most relevant author to date is Iain Lea (iain.lea@erlm.siemens.de). Check the long list of contributors in the man pages.

> **TIP**
>
> Use the h (help) command to view a list of the commands available at any level.

On startup, tin shows a list of the newsgroups found in $HOME/.newsrc. An arrow (->) or highlighted bar points to the first newsgroup. Move to a group by using the terminal arrow keys or j and k. Use Page Up and Page Down or Ctrl-U and Ctrl-D to page up and down. Select a newsgroup to read from by pressing Enter.

The Tab key advances to the next newsgroup that has unread articles and enters it.

To start and run tin, export NNTPSERVER to the address of your remote news server. Use the command

```
$ export NNTPSERVER=news.your.provider.com
```

Then run tin with the -r option to connect to this remote server.

A sample tin session is shown in Listing 14.3. It shows two newsgroups that I have subscribed to: alt.humor and tx.jobs.

When you select a message to read from and press either the right arrow or Enter key, you are shown the message itself, as shown in Listing 14.4.

Listing 14.3. A sample `tin` session.

```
                    Group Selection (news.neosoft.com  2)              h=help

      1   571   alt.humor
  u   2   398   tx.jobs
```

```
        <n>=set current to n, TAB=next unread, /=search pattern, c)atchup,
    g)oto, j=line down, k=line up, h)elp, m)ove, q)uit, r=toggle all/unread,
        s)ubscribe, S)ub pattern, u)nsubscribe, U)nsub pattern, y)ank in/out

Group tx.jobs ('q' to quit)...
```

Listing 14.4. Another sample `tin` session.

```
                      tx.jobs (368T 401A 0K 0H R)                    h=help

   171  +     US-TX-Dallas    MicroFocus Cobol Contract       Mark Allen
   172  +     CA-CLARIS HR, WINDOWS DEVELOPMENT POSITIONS A    CLARIS HR
   173  +     CA-CLARIS HR, DIRECTOR OF WORLDWIDE PRODUCT D    CLARIS HR
   174  +     CA-CLARIS HR, INTERNATIONAL WINDOWS ENGINEER     CLARIS HR
   175  +     CA, CLARIS CORP - TELECOMMUNICATIONS ANALYST     CLARIS HR
   176  +     CA- CLARIS HR, SYBASE PROGRAMMER/ANALYST AT C    CLARIS HR
   177  +     CA-CLARIS HR, DOCUMENTATION CONTROL SPECIALIST   CLARIS HR
   178  +     CA-CLARIS, SUPERVISOR, DIRECT ACCOUNT SERVICE    CLARIS HR
   179  +     CA-DEVELOPERS & TEST ENGINEERS - JAPANESE PRO    CLARIS HR
   180  +     CA-CLARIS HR, DATABASE INTERNALS ENGINEER POS    CLARIS HR
   181  +     CA, CLARIS CORPORATION - PRICING ANALYST         CLARIS HR
   182  +     WA-CLARIS HR, MAC & WINDOWS DEV'RS/ INTERFACE    CLARIS HR
   183  +     USA-TX-DALLAS -    Informix 4GL/ESQL             imi
   184  +     USA-TX-DALLAS - SONET Telephany Engineers        imi
   185  +     USA-TX-DALLAS - PowerBuilder                     imi
   186  +     USA-TX-DALLAS - Oracle DBAs                      imi
   187  +     USA-TX-DALLAS - CICS, Cobol, JCL, VSAM (ALC +    imi

   <n>=set current to n, TAB=next unread, /=search pattern, ^K)ill/select,
 a)uthor search, c)atchup, j=line down, k=line up, K=mark read, l)ist thread,
  |=pipe, m)ail, o=print, q)uit, r=toggle all/unread, s)ave, t)ag, w=post
```

In Listing 14.4, you see a list of subject headers and their index numbers. The + sign indicates that you have not read this message. For example, the SONET job for Dallas, Texas, has an index of 184 and is unread. To read this message, use the arrow keys to move to it, and then press Enter.

Command-Line Options

tin has several command-line options, some of which are listed in Table 14.2.

Table 14.2. tin's command-line options.

Option	Description
-c	Creates or updates index files for every group in $HOME/.newsrc or every file specified by the -f option and marks all articles as read.
-f file	Uses the specified file of subscribed newsgroups instead of $HOME/.newsrc.
-h	A help listing of all command-line options.
-m dir	The mailbox directory to use. The default is $HOME/Mail.
-n	Loads only groups from the active file that are also subscribed to in the user's .newsrc. This enables a noticeable speedup when connecting via a slow line.
-p program	Prints program with options.
-q quick	Starts without checking for new newsgroups.
-r read	News specified in the environment variable NNTPSERVER or contained in the file /etc/nntpserver.
-R read	News saved by -S option (not yet implemented remotely from the default NNTP server).
-s dir	Saves articles to a directory. The default is $HOME/News.
-v	Verbose mode for the -c, -M, -S, -u, and -Z options.

To add a new group, type g*groupname*. For example, gmisc.invest adds the newsgroup misc.invest.

tin offers an emacs-style editing facility for entering messages. The command strings include a history of commands to enable reuse of previous commands. The man pages for tin list all the commands available to you for editing, deleting, and removing messages.

tin uses the following important environment variables:

NNTPSERVER   The default NNTP server to remotely read news from. This variable needs to be set only if the -r command-line option is specified and the file /etc/nntpserver does not exist.

VISUAL   This variable overrides the default editor that is used in all editing operations within tin.

`tin` can pretty much be navigated by using the four arrow keys. The left arrow key goes up a level; the right arrow key goes down a level; the up arrow key goes up a line or page; and the down arrow key goes down a line or page. Most prompts within `tin` can be aborted by pressing Esc.

Using FTP

File transfer protocol (FTP) is a method of transferring files from one computer to another. FTP provides the capability of transferring files to and from a remote network site as well as means for sharing public files. In this section you go through a sample FTP session and follow the steps for finding and getting software from a remote site.

`ftp` is the user interface to the ARPANET standard FTP. The `ftp` service is the interface to the file transfer protocol. It lets a user connect to another site and send and receive files.

In this section you will try to get a file from the address `tsx-11.mit.edu` by logging in as anonymous. This anonymous use of FTP is very convenient and provides access to innumerable servers, providing a wealth of information. Publicly accessible FTP servers are called anonymous FTP servers.

Anonymous FTP

Anonymous FTP enables users to access remote sites without having an authorized user ID and password. Generally the login ID is anonymous and the password is `guest`. Most current systems require your e-mail address as the password instead of `guest`.

> **TIP**
>
> FTP stands for File Transfer Protocol; `ftp` is the program you run on Linux.

The client host with which `ftp` is to communicate may be specified on the command line. If this is done, `ftp` immediately attempts to establish a connection to an FTP server on that host. Otherwise, `ftp` enters its command interpreter and awaits instructions from the user. When `ftp` is awaiting commands from the user, the prompt `ftp>` is provided to the user. Enter `ftp` at the prompt, along with the site address:

`$ ftp hostname`

A hostname can be either a hostname or an Internet address. For example, you can use the following Internet address:

`mpsi$ ftp tsx-11.mit.edu`

If your system connects to the MIT server, the text shown in Listing 14.5 appears.

Listing 14.5. An `ftp` session.

```
220 tsx-11 FTP server (Version wu-2.4(3) Mon Jun 5 16:40:22 EDT 1995) ready.
Name (tsx-11.mit.edu:uzma): anonymous
331 Guest login ok, send your complete e-mail address as password.
Password:
230-Welcome, archive user!  This is an experimental FTP server.  If have any
230-unusual problems, please report them via e-mail to ftp-bugs@tsx-11.mit.edu.
230-If you do have problems, please try using a dash (-) as the first character
230-of your password -- this will turn off the continuation messages that may
230-be confusing your ftp client.
230-
230-The Linux archives are in /pub/linux/
230-
230-In most places, 'get <directory>.tar' will retrieve a tar file containing
230-that directory.  'get <file>.gz' gets a gzipped version of a files, and
230-'get <file>.Z' gets a compressed version of the file.  'get <dir>.tar.gz'
230-is possible, but not recommended.  'get <dir>.zip' will get a zip archive
230-with *NO* compression of the directory <dir>.
230-
230-If you find something on TSX-11 which doesn't work, or which you
230-believe is obsolete, please send mail to ftp-linux@TSX-11.MIT.EDU.
230-INCLUDE THE FULL PATHNAME OF THE FILE AND WHY YOU THINK IT IS OBSOLETE.
230-
230-                                - Ted and Michael
230-
230 Guest login ok, access restrictions apply.
Remote system type is UNIX.
Using binary mode to transfer files.
ftp>
```

The first line confirms that the connection is established. Line 220 indicates that the FTP server is ready. The system then prompts for a name, which is anonymous in this case, and a password. The password is not echoed, so any typing mistakes you make are not apparent. You are then connected to the remote FTP server, which awaits your commands.

ftp Commands

The `ftp` service enables the user to execute several commands. Some of the local commands are listed in Table 14.3.

Table 14.3. Some `ftp` commands.

Command	Description
[account [*passwd*]]	Supplies a supplemental password required by a remote system for access to resources once a login has been successfully completed. If no argument is included, the user is prompted for an account password in a non-echoing input mode.
ascii	Sets the file transfer type to network ASCII. This is the default type.

Command	Description
`bell`	Sounds a bell after each file transfer.
`binary`	Sets the file transfer type to binary mode.
`bye`	Terminates the FTP session with the remote server and then exits.
`cd remote-directory`	Changes the working directory on the remote machine to the remote directory.
`cdup`	Goes to the parent of the current remote machine's working directory.
`chmod mode file-name`	Changes the permission modes of the file.
`close`	Terminates the FTP session with the remote server.
`delete remote-file`	Deletes the remote file on the remote machine.
`dir [remote-directory]`	Prints a listing of the remote directory to the terminal.
`disconnect`	Same as `close`.
`get remote-file [local-file]`	Retrieves the remote file and stores it on the local machine. If the local filename is not specified, it is given the same name it has on the remote machine.
`hash`	While a file is being transferred, the hash sign (#) is printed for each data block transferred.
`help [command]`	Prints an informative message about the meaning of the command. If no argument is given, `ftp` prints a list of the known commands.
`lcd [directory]`	Changes the working directory on the local machine. If no directory is specified, the user's home directory is used.
`ls [remote-directory]`	Lists the contents of the remote directory.
`mdelete [remote-files]`	Deletes the remote files on the remote machine.
`mdir remote-files`	Like `dir`, except multiple remote files may be specified.
`mget remote-files`	Expands the remote files on the remote machine and does a `getfiles` based on regular expressions. For example, `mget f*.tar` will get all the files starting with the letter f.
`open host [port]`	Establishes a connection to the specified host FTP server on the optional port number.
`put local-file`	Stores a local file on the remote machine.
`pwd`	Prints the name of the current working directory on the remote machine.
`quit`	Same as `bye`.

continues

Table 14.3. continued

Command	Description
remotehelp [command-name]	Requests help from the remote FTP server. If a command name is specified, it is supplied to the server as well.
reset	Resets the communications connection.
rmdir directory-name	Deletes a directory on the remote machine.
size file-name	Returns the size of the file on the remote machine.
status	Shows the current status of ftp.
verbose	Displays all responses to the user.
? [command]	Same as help.

Some of the options that may be specified at the command line are listed as follows:

- -v   The verbose option. Gives a report on the transfer statistics and forces ftp to show all responses from the remote server.

- -n   Restrains ftp from attempting auto-login upon initial connection. In auto-login, ftp checks for the user's account on the remote machine.

- -I   Turns off interactive prompting during multiple file transfers.

- -d   Enables debugging.

Some ftp commands share the same name as Linux commands but perform a different function. For example, the ls command in ftp behaves like the ls -al command in Linux. To illustrate how this works, let's look at the directory listing command on a remote server:

> **NOTE**
>
> On some systems, ls at the ftp prompt will behave like the ls -F command.

```
ftp>
ftp> ls
200 PORT command successful.
150 Opening ASCII mode data connection for /bin/ls.
total 6
drwxrwxr-x   2 root      ftp-linu      512 Feb  8 1995  bin
drwxrwxr-x   2 root      wheel         512 Nov  5 1994  dev
drwxrwxr-x   3 root      wheel         512 Nov  9 17:22  etc
lrwxr-xr-x   1 tytso     wheel           1 Nov  5 02:17  ftp -> .
drwxrwx-wx   4 tytso     ftp-linu      512 Dec  8 07:44  incoming
drwxrwxr-x   9 tytso     ftp           512 Dec  1 22:35  pub
226 Transfer complete.
ftp>
```

As you can see, you did not have to type -al. You get the long listing from the ls command.

To abort a file transfer, use the terminal interrupt key (usually Ctrl-C). Sending transfers are immediately halted. Receiving transfers are halted by sending an `ftp ABOR` command to the remote server and discarding any further data received.

The ftp specification specifies many parameters that may affect a file transfer. The type may be `ascii`, `image` (binary), or `ebcdic`.

telnet

The `telnet` command is used to communicate with another host using the TELNET protocol. If `telnet` is invoked without the host argument, it enters command mode, indicated by its prompt, `telnet>`. Normally you would use

```
$ telnet hostname [port]
```

where *hostname* is the host you want to connect to and *port* indicates a port number (an application's address). If a number is not specified, the default telnet port is used.

telnet can log you in either one of two modes: character-by-character or line-by-line. In character-by-character mode, most text typed is immediately sent to the remote host for processing. In line-by-line mode, all text is echoed locally, and only completed lines are sent to the remote host.

While connected to a remote host, you can enter the `telnet` command mode by typing the telnet escape character, Ctrl-]. When in command mode, the normal terminal editing conventions are available.

The following commands are available under the command mode:

`close`	Closes a `telnet` session and returns to command mode.
`open host` `[[-l] user][-port]`	Opens a connection to the named host. If no port number is specified, `telnet` attempts to use the default port. The `[-l]` option may be used to specify the user name.
`quit`	Closes any open `telnet` session and exits `telnet`. An end-of-file (in command mode) will also close a session and exit.

Check the man pages for a list of long, detailed options for telnet.

Let's use `telnet` to do an Archie session. An Archie server is helpful for searching for files by giving a keyword in a title. See Listing 14.6.

Listing 14.6. Logging in via `telnet`.

```
$ telnet archie.internic.net
.
.
.
SunOS UNIX 4.1 (ds) (ttypa)
```

continues

Listing 14.6. continued

```
login: archie

*********************************************************************

              Welcome to the InterNIC Directory and Database Server.

*****************************************************************************

# Bunyip Information Systems, 1993, 1994

# Terminal type set to 'vt100 24 80'
# 'erase' character is '^?'.
# 'search' (type string) has the value 'sub'.
archie>
```

The archie> prompt is asking you for input. Let's look at some of the help information available for Archie. Type help at the archie> prompt. See Listing 14.7 for a sample output.

Listing 14.7. Help for Archie.

```
archie >help

These are the commands you can use in help:

                .       go up one level in the hierarchy

                ?       display a list of valid subtopics at the current level

<newline>
done, ^D, ^C     quit from help entirely

        <string>     help on a topic or subtopic
Eg.

        "help show"

will give you the help screen for the "show" command

        "help set search"

Will give you the help information for the "search" variable.

The command "manpage" will give you a complete copy of the archie manual page.
~
~
(END)
```

Now let's try to find a file on HylaFAX. Use the command find, as shown in Listing 14.8. The sub string indicates that you are searching for the word in the entire filename and are not looking for an exact match.

Listing 14.8. Finding by keyword.

```
archie> find hylafax
# Search type: sub.
# Your queue position: 1
# Estimated time for completion: 00:33
working... \
```

The results of the match are shown in Listing 14.9. You can scroll up and down with the k and j keys. The spacebar scrolls one page. The Enter key scrolls down one line at a time. You can stop the listing with the q key.

Listing 14.9. The output of the Archie command.

```
Host freebsd.cdrom.com     (192.153.46.2)
Last updated 11:06 30 Jan 1994

    Location: /.1/FreeBSD/FreeBSD-current/ports
      DIRECTORY    drwxr-xr-x    1024 bytes  01:17  4 Dec 1993  flexfax

    Location: /.1/FreeBSD/FreeBSD-current/ports/hylafax/man
      FILE     -rw-rw-r--   15254 bytes  15:45 31 Aug 1993  flexfax.1

    Location: /.1/FreeBSD/FreeBSD-current/ports/hylafax/dist
      FILE     -rw-rw-r--      17 bytes  15:40 31 Aug 1993  flexfax.alpha
      FILE     -rw-rw-r--    2671 bytes  15:40 31 Aug 1993  flexfax.spec

    Location: /.1/FreeBSD/FreeBSD-current/ports/hylafax/port/386bsd
      FILE     -rw-rw-r--    2828 bytes  15:45 31 Aug 1993  Makefile.flexfax

    Location: /.1/FreeBSD/FreeBSD-current/ports/hylafax/port/4.4bsd
      FILE     -rw-rw-r--    2839 bytes  15:45 31 Aug 1993  Makefile.flexfax

    Location: /.1/FreeBSD/FreeBSD-current/ports/hylafax/port/bsdi
      FILE     -rw-rw-r--    2837 bytes  15:46 31 Aug 1993  Makefile.flexfax

db/tmp/AAAa26919
```

After you are finished with Archie, you can log off the server. This closes the telnet connection. You can get your HylaFAX files via FTP from these sites.

Summary

The communication tools discussed in this chapter were write, talk, mesg, and mail. You also learned about nn and tin for reading news from the Internet. For getting files from remote sites, you learned how to use FTP. With the telnet session, you also learned a bit about Archie, an archival search utility.

As you can see, Linux offers a wide variety of communication tools. This chapter has merely introduced you to these tools. You have to work with each tool to learn its intricacies. Happy communicating.

Using the Linux Documentation

15

*by Tim Parker
and
Kamran Husain*

This chapter will take a brief look at the documentation that is available to you from the Linux CD-ROM, as well as alternative sources. You will see:

■ What documentation is available on the CD-ROM

■ Where to go on the Internet for more information

■ Linux newsgroups you should check for help

Hopefully, this book will provide most of the information you need to get going with Linux, but you may need to investigate other sources of information for a number of reasons (such as hardware support, troubleshooting, and so on).

The Linux Documentation Project

The first exposure most people get to Linux is a book like the one you are now reading or the Linux INFO-SHEET, a relatively short ASCII document that is available from Usenet, BBSes (bulletin board systems), and many user groups. The INFO-SHEET is a quick summary of Linux posted at regular intervals to the Linux newsgroups on Usenet.

As Linux was developed, several programmers started writing brief guides to their contributions, as well as wider areas of the operating system. These documents, while usually terse and awkward to read, did provide others with enough information to continue their own use of Linux. Over a short span, the documentation for Linux began growing rapidly, and a central organizing body became necessary to help keep it on track and avoid unnecessary duplication.

The Linux Documentation Project was created to provide a complete set of public domain documentation for Linux. From a few rough installation notes a couple of years ago, the documentation has expanded to include almost a thousand pages, some very good, some not. The following primary documents are currently available or soon to be released:

■ *Linux Installation* explains how to install and configure Linux.

■ The *Linux User's Guide* is a guide for first-time users.

■ The *Linux System Administrator's Guide* is a guide to various aspects of system administration.

■ The *Linux Network Administration Guide* explains how to set up and use networks.

■ The *Linux Kernel Hacker's Guide* is a guide to modifying the Linux kernel.

In addition to these primary documents, there are about a dozen smaller guides to specific or esoteric aspects of Linux. These smaller guides are called *How To* documents. Together they form a growing document suite that covers practically every aspect of Linux. These documents are available with most distributions of the software. Not all the documents are up to date, as changes to the operating system have occurred since they were first written. Several different people wrote the Linux documents, so the styles and layout are not consistent. A perfect-bound printed copy of the Linux Documentation Project is available from Linux Systems Labs and some bookstores.

> **NOTE**
>
> You can contact the Linux Systems Labs at 49884 Miller Court, Chesterfield, MI 48047. Their telephone number is (810) 716-1700, and their fax machine is at (810) 716-1703. You can get information about LSL from their e-mail address: info@lsl.com.

CD-ROM Documentation

The Red Hat CD-ROM that accompanies this book has a lot of documentation supplied. The primary location of information is the /doc directory of the CD-ROM, which contains several types of files. A directory listing of the /doc/HOWTO directory shows the following contents:

```
bash# ls /cdrom/doc/HOWTO/
BootPrompt-HOWTO        IPX-HOWTO               Printing-HOWTO
Bootdisk-HOWTO          Installation-HOWTO      Printing-Usage-HOWTO
Busmouse-HOWTO          Italian-HOWTO           SCSI-HOWTO
CDROM-HOWTO             JE-HOWTO                SCSI-Programming-HOWTO
Commercial-HOWTO        Java-HOWTO              Serial-HOWTO
Cyrillic-HOWTO          Kernel-HOWTO            Shadow-Password-HOWTO
DOSEMU-HOWTO            Keyboard-HOWTO          Sound-HOWTO
Danish-HOWTO            Keystroke-HOWTO         Sound-Playing-HOWTO
Distribution-HOWTO      MGR-HOWTO               TRANS.TBL
ELF-HOWTO              Mail-HOWTO               Term-HOWTO
Ethernet-HOWTO         NET-2-HOWTO             Tips-HOWTO
Firewall-HOWTO         NIS-HOWTO               UMSDOS-HOWTO
Ftape-HOWTO            News-HOWTO              UPS-HOWTO
German-HOWTO           PCI-HOWTO               UUCP-HOWTO
HAM-HOWTO             PCMCIA-HOWTO            XFree86-HOWTO
Hardware-HOWTO         PPP-HOWTO
Hebrew-HOWTO          Portuguese-HOWTO
```

Most of these files are extracted to your Linux hard drive if you select the documentation options when installing Linux through setup. The setup routine lets you choose which types of documentation will be moved from the installation CD-ROM to your hard drive, but you can't select individual entries in the sets. If you are limited in disk space, you should consider leaving most of the document on the CD-ROM and viewing it only on an as-needed basis.

A directory listing of this area shows a wealth of files:

```
bash# ls /usr/doc
ElectricFence-2.0.5-2   libc-5.2.18-1          sh-utils-1.12-4
FAQ                     libelf-0.5.2-2         slang-devel-0.99.24-2
HOWTO                   lilo-0.17-3            sliplogin-2.0.2-2
HTML                    linuxdoc-sgml-1.4      svgalib-1.2.9-3
SysVinit-2.58-2         m4-1.4-4              syslogd-1.3-1
XFree86-3.1.1-1         make-3.74-5           taper-6.0-2
bash-1.14.6-2          maplay-1.2-2          tcp_wrappers-7.3-1
bm2font-3.0-3          mawk-1.2.2-3          tcsh-6.06-7
bootpc-045-2          mb-5.0-5             tetex-0.3.3
cpio-2.4.1-3          mh-6.8.3-5            textutils-1.14-1
diffutils-2.7-3        multimedia-2.0-3      time-1.6-3
dosemu-0.60.4-3       mxp-1.0-2            tin-1.22-4
```

```
emacs-19.30-2          ncurses-1.9.6-6          tksysv-0.9-1
exmh-1.6.4-3           nfs-server-2.2beta4-6    umsdos_progs-0.8-4
fileutils-3.12-3       nslookup.help            uucp-1.06.1-4
findutils-4.1-5        nvi-1.49-4               words-2-2
fwhois-1.00-4          patch-2.1-3             wu-ftpd-2.4.2b9-1
gawk-2.15.6-3          pcmcia-cs-2.8.8-1        xfm-1.3.2-2
gcc-2.7.2-2            pdksh-5.2.3-2           xmailbox-2.2-2
getty_ps-2.0.7h-1      pidentd-2.5.1-4          xsysinfo-1.2-3
grep-2.0-3            playmidi-2.3-2          xv-3.10a-3
gzip-1.2.4-3          ppp-2.1.2d-4            yp-clients-2.2-2
inn-1.4unoff3-5        rcs-5.7-3              ypserv-0.15-2
ipfwadm-1.1-2         rdist-1.0-2            zoneinfo-95e-3
ispell-3.1.18-2       samba-1.9.15p8-2
less.hlp             sed-2.05-4
```

Each subdirectory in the preceding list contains more specific information about each tool. For example, if you want more specific information about the tape tool, look in the `/usr/doc/mt-st` directory for a README file for a listing of the contents.

HOWTO Documents

Let's face it. This one chapter (or text for that matter) cannot possibly hope to cover all the scenarios that you will encounter as you work with Linux. The number of combinations of hardware devices, software interfaces, and versions of Linux make it impossible to list them all here. That one specific CD-ROM or Ethernet card in your PC may not be listed here in this book, but may very well be supported under Linux. To get more specific information about specific topics, you have to read the HOWTO files for that topic.

Basically, a HOWTO file is compiled by someone who has tracked problems related to a specific issue. Topics include booting, printing, tape support, and so on. There are a number of HOWTO files included with the CD-ROM (and installed to the hard drive with most installations of Linux). If your mount point is `/cdrom`, the HOWTO files are found in `/cdrom/doc`. The files are in text format in that directory, so you can use any text editor to view them. A partial description of the files in the `/cdrom/doc/HOWTO` directory is shown here to help you get an idea of where to look for more information:

`Bootdisk-HOWTO`	This is the file you would read to get more information about creating boot and root disks for your machine.
`Busmouse-HOWTO`	This file contains information on installing and using a bus mouse with your Linux system.
`CDROM-HOWTO`	Linux supports a variety of CD-ROM drives. Unfortunately, not all the CD-ROM drives on the market are supported. Look in this file for more information about CD-ROM drive devices and Linux drivers.
`COPYRIGHT`	This file contains the copyright restrictions and information about Linux.
`Commercial-HOWTO`	Looking for commercial software available for Linux? Check out this file, which contains lists of companies and products for Linux.

DOSEMU-HOWTO	Linux has a DOS emulator called DOSemu. This HOWTO contains information about the Linux MS-DOS emulator.
Danish-HOWTO	How to configure Linux for use with the Danish character set.
Distribution-HOWTO	A general list of mail order distributions and other commercial services.
ELF-HOWTO	In the future, Linux binaries will be distributed in the Information on ELF binaries for Linux.
Ethernet-HOWTO	Information on Ethernet hardware compatibility for Linux.
Firewall-HOWTO	How to set up a firewall using Linux.
Ftape-HOWTO	Information on ftape drive compatibility with Linux.
German-HOWTO	Information on using Linux with German-specific features.
HAM-HOWTO	How to configure amateur radio software for Linux.
HOWTO-INDEX	Index of HOWTO documents about Linux.
Hardware-HOWTO	A list of hardware known to work with Linux.
INFO-SHEET	Generic introduction to the Linux operating system.
Installation-HOWTO	How to obtain and install the Linux software.
JE-HOWTO	Information on JE, a set of Japanese language extensions for Linux.
Kernel-HOWTO	Upgrading and compiling the Linux kernel.
META-FAQ	A listing of Linux sources of information.
MGR-HOWTO	Information on the MGR graphics interface for Linux.
Mail-HOWTO	Information on Linux-based mail servers and clients.
NET-2-HOWTO	How to configure TCP/IP networking, SLIP, PLIP, and PPP under Linux.
NIS-HOWTO	Linux NIS (Network Information Service) and YP (Yellow Pages).
News-HOWTO	Information on Usenet news server and client software for Linux.
PCI-HOWTO	Information on PCI-architecture compatibility with Linux.
PCMCIA-HOWTO	How to install and use PCMCIA Card Services.
PPP-HOWTO	Information on using PPP networking with Linux.
Printing-HOWTO	Information on how to set up printing under Linux.
Printing-Usage-HOWTO	How to use the printing system for a variety of file types and options.
SCSI-HOWTO	Linux SCSI drive tape CD-ROM HOWTO.
SCSI-Programming-HOWTO	Information on programming the generic Linux SCSI interface.

`Serial-HOWTO`	Information on use of serial devices and communications software.
`Sound-HOWTO`	Sound hardware and software for the Linux operating system.
`Term-HOWTO`	How to use the `term` communications package on Linux systems.
`Tips-HOWTO`	HOWTO on miscellaneous tips and tricks for Linux.
`UMSDOS-HOWTO`	How to install and use the UMSDOS file system.
`UPS-HOWTO`	Using Linux on a PC without a UPS will leave you vulnerable to the mercy of your electrical power company. Killing the power on a running Linux system can ruin your Linux box.
`UUCP-HOWTO`	Information on how to install and use the Taylor UUCP software for Linux.
`WRITING`	Check this file out if you are interested in writing your own HOWTO file.
`XFree86-HOWTO`	How to obtain, install, and configure XFree86 3.1.2 (X11R6).
`mini/`	Directory containing informal mini-HOWTOs.
`other-formats/`	Directory containing other formats of the HOWTOs.

Look at the preceding list carefully. If you see the topic of your interest here, you are in luck. The HOWTO file will be the best source for you to get more specific information. If you want to confirm that you have the latest HOWTO files, you can check the official repository of documents in the `tsx-11.mit.edu` site in the `/pub/linux/docs/HOWTO` directory for any updates.

Usenet Newsgroups

Usenet is a collection of discussion groups (called newsgroups) available to Internet users. The more than 13,000 newsgroups generate over 100MB of traffic every day. Of all these newsgroups (which cover every conceivable topic), several are dedicated to Linux. These newsgroups are a useful forum for information and answers to questions about Linux.

You can read Usenet newsgroups through newsreader software that accesses either the Internet or a local site that offers Usenet service (called a *newsfeed*). Many online services, such as CompuServe and Delphi, provide access to the newsgroups (sometimes at an additional cost), and some have their own forums for Linux users. BBSes dedicated to Linux in whole or in part are also appearing, and many excerpt the Usenet conversations for the BBS users who do not have access to Usenet.

Usenet newsgroups are divided into three categories: primary newsgroups that are readily available to all users, local newsgroups with a limited distribution (usually based on geography), and alternate newsgroups that may not be handled by all news servers due to the relaxed rules of etiquette on them. The primary newsgroups of interest to Linux users when this book was written are the following:

- Proponents of the Linux system sound off in `comp.os.linux.advocacy`.

- The `comp.os.linux.announce` newsgroup contains announcements important to the Linux community. This is a moderated newsgroup, which means someone approves the postings before you get to see them.

- The `comp.os.linux.answers` newsgroup contains questions and answers to problems about Linux.

- Ongoing work on Linux applications is discussed in `comp.os.linux.development.apps`.

- Ongoing work on the Linux operating system is discussed in `comp.os.linux.development.system`.

- The `comp.os.linux.hardware` newsgroup deals with issues concerning Linux and hardware support.

- Linux-specific (not just UNIX-specific) topics not covered by other groups are covered in `comp.os.linux.misc`.

- Linux-specific topics concerned primarily with X Window are covered in `comp.os.linux.x`.

- Linux networking issues are discussed in `comp.os.linux.networking`.

- The `comp.os.linux.setup` deals with Linux setup and installation problems.

These primary newsgroups should be available at all Usenet sites, unless the system administrator filters them out for some reason. The other Linux newsgroups tend to change frequently, primarily because they are either regional or populated with highly opinionated users. The `alt.` (alternate) newsgroups are the ones most likely to contain such users. One `alt.` newsgroup in operation when this book was written is

`alt.uu.comp.os.linux.questions`

To find the several different newsgroups about Linux, use your newsreader software to search for all newsgroups with the word *linux* in the title. If you have access to Usenet, regularly scan the newsgroup additions and deletions to check for new Linux newsgroups or existing groups that have folded. Notices about newsgroup changes are usually posted to all existing groups, but every now and again one gets through without fanfare. Online services that provide access to Usenet usually maintain lists of all active newsgroups that can be searched quickly.

The traffic on most of these Linux newsgroups deals with problems and issues people have when installing, configuring, administering, or using the operating system. A lot of valuable information passes through the newsgroups quickly, so check them regularly. The most interesting messages that deal with a specific subject (called a *thread*) are often collected and stored as an archive for access through an FTP site.

World Wide Web Sites

Not surprisingly, Linux has a good presence on the World Wide Web. There are several sites that have Linux information, and a few home pages are specifically dedicated for Linux business. Two of the more popular Linux Web sites are `http://sunsite.unc.edu/mdw/mdw.html` and `http://www.ssc.com/linux/linux.html`.

From the Linux home page at `www.ssc.com` you can link to other Linux sites, including those of commercial vendors of Linux products. These links are updated frequently, so they are a good place to start when navigating through the Web. One of the key utilities the `www.ssc.com` home page offers is access to the Linux Software Map (LSM), as complete an index to Linux software as you will find anywhere. The Linux Software Map includes all the software packages that were developed specifically for Linux, as well as utilities and applications that have been ported to Linux. The Linux Software Map window lets you search for keywords in online documents and indexes, and then displays the results to provide a fast, easy method of finding software and documents.

Another way to look for infomation about Linux is to use the WebCrawler through the Web site at `http::://www.webcrawler.com` and search for the word `Linux`. You will be rewarded with a list of names which contain information about Linux. (WebCrawler is a trademark owned by America Online, Inc.)

Also don't forget to check the Web site `www.yahoo.com` in the directory `Computers/Operating_Systems/Unix/Linux`.

Linux Journal

The *Linux Journal* is a commercial publication dedicated to Linux. It covers the entire gamut of Linux topics, ranging from material suitable for newcomers to the operating system to very complex programming. The *Linux Journal* has a home page, accessible through `www.ssc.com`. Some previously printed articles in electronic form are also found on the Web site.

> **NOTE**
>
> If you want more information about the *Linux Journal*, send e-mail to `subs@ssc.com`. You can also write to the publisher at P.O. Box 85867, Seattle, WA 98145, or telephone them at (206) 782-7733. Subscriptions cost $22 per year in the United States.

> **NOTE**
>
> Another online publication for more Linux information is the *Linux Gazette* at `http://www.redhat.com/lg`. It's a personal magazine in its infancy, but contains very good information for newbies and experts alike.

Summary

Because of the popularity of Linux, you are not left alone with a strange operating system and no support. If the files on the CD-ROM don't give you the answers you need, a visit to a Web site, Usenet newsgroup, or other Linux support vehicle should help get you straightened out. Every time you upgrade Linux or get a new CD-ROM, you should check the documentation files included to see if there have been any new additions that may interest you.

PART

Editing, Typesetting, and More

Text Editors

16

by Peter MacKinnon

IN THIS CHAPTER

It's time to look at editors. This chapter will show you

- What editors are and why you need one
- The basic editing functions
- The vi editor in more detail
- The emacs editor in more detail

What Are Editors and Why Do I Need One?

A *text editor* is one of the most essential tools provided with the Linux (or virtually any) operating system. With an editor, you can create and modify text files that have a wide variety of applications:

- User files such as .login and .cshrc
- System files
- Shell programs
- Documents
- Mail messages

These are but a few of the many different types of text files that you will use when working with Linux. Basically, editors enable you to insert, delete, move, and search text ranging from individual characters to thousands of lines.

Two of the most popular editors for the Linux system are emacs and vi. These editors are both full-screen text editors: Put simply, they use every row and column of your terminal screen to display the textual contents of a file. Both of these editors feature a rich set of commands. The essential commands for manipulating text can be learned reasonably quickly; the more sophisticated commands may take a little longer to master. However, you will likely appreciate this investment as you see how much time these powerful tools can save you.

Choosing one editor over another can be a matter of taste. Both emacs and vi are efficient and can handle virtually any size of file. The emacs editor is better suited to complex editing tasks and comes with an online help facility, but, for simple editing jobs, either editor is equally good. It really just comes down to whichever one you feel more comfortable using.

The Editing Functions

Although there are a variety of text editors for Linux that have different interfaces, they all basically do the same things. Any useful text editor should support the following features at a minimum.

Inserting and Deleting Text

The most intrinsic function of a text editor is to enable you to enter and erase characters as you see fit. This also implies that you have complete control over the movement of the cursor and its placement in the text.

Reading and Writing Files

Because you will want to save the text files that you create for future use and reuse, an editor can write your text to an external file. Whenever you need to make changes to your file, an editor can read the file from disk. A nice feature is that text editors are designed to accommodate ASCII formatted files, so an editor (such as emacs) can read any file written by another editor (such as vi), and vice versa.

Searching Text

Personally scanning line after line of a large file for instances of a particular word is either a great way to improve your powers of concentration or an exercise in self-torture. That is why text editors provide sophisticated search capabilities. These include the use of regular expressions as well as fixed strings. Remember that regular expressions include metacharacters (such as ., ?, and *) that replace and expand unknown text patterns.

Editors also support search-and-replace functions that enable you to change multiple instances of a string pattern with a single command.

Copying and Moving Text

Because there is no guarantee that the way text is initially typed into a file is the way it should forever remain, editors provide you with the means to copy, cut, and move (or paste) blocks of text. These blocks can range in size from several pages to a single character. The distinction between copying and cutting text is that cutting deletes the selected block of text after it has been copied to a buffer, whereas copying does not.

> **NOTE**
>
> Imagine having to retype Dickens's *A Tale of Two Cities* after realizing that you have somehow placed "It was the best of times, it was the worst of times" at the end of the file and not the start!

Editing Buffers

What is a buffer, you ask? *Buffers* are places in the memory of the editing program where text can reside as you make changes to a file. For example, the first time you edit a file, the text you have entered actually exists in a buffer that is written to an external file when you do a save. Buffers can also be used at other times in editing, particularly when it is necessary to temporarily move a block of text to memory as you make changes (in other words, cutting and pasting). Many editors enable you to manage multiple buffers simultaneously.

These editors have many commands that will not be fully detailed in this chapter. Before engaging in any long and arduous editing task, consult the man page for the editor you are using. There may be an easier way of doing whatever it is that you want to do. As you gain experience with an editor, you will discover convenient shortcuts and functions to perform your most tedious editing chores.

The *vi* Editor

The vi editor is installed with virtually every UNIX system in existence. Because of this, vi is considered by many to be the default text editor of the UNIX system (upon which Linux is based). vi has two modes of operation and terse commands, both of which make it a somewhat more difficult editor to learn than emacs. However, it is a useful editor to learn if emacs has not been installed on your Linux system.

Starting *vi*

You invoke vi from the command line by typing

```
vi
```

The screen will clear and a column of tildes (~) will appear in the leftmost column. You are now editing an empty, unnamed file. Whatever text you place in this file will exist in a buffer until you write the contents of the buffer to some named file. The tilde is vi's way of telling you that the line where the tilde appears is empty of text.

vi can also be started with a file or a list of files to edit:

```
vi filename1 filename2 filename3 ...
```

Typically, you will probably edit only one file per vi session. If you are editing a list of files, vi will edit each one in the sequence that they appear on the command line.

Alternatively, vi can be invoked from the command line as

```
vi +n filename
```

where *n* represents the line number where vi will place its cursor in *filename*. This is useful for programmers debugging large source code files who need to quickly jump to a known line containing an error.

Another example is useful in illustrating the vi editor. If you still have a vi session on your screen, exit it by pushing Esc, and then typing :q!. To start a new vi session, enter

```
vi asong
```

at the command line.

vi modes

At the bottom of the screen in the left corner, you will see

```
"asong" [NEW FILE] 1 line, 1 char
```

The messages displayed on this status line tell you what vi is doing or has just done. In this case, vi is telling you that it has opened an empty buffer whose contents will be saved (whenever you do a save) to the file asong.

At this moment, you are in the command mode of vi. This is the major conceptual leap required in working with this editor. When editing text, you must remember if you are in command mode or text mode. In *command mode,* any character sequences that you enter are interpreted as vi commands. In *text mode,* every character typed is placed in the buffer and displayed as text on-screen.

Four commands are echoed at the bottom of the screen on the status line:

/	Searches forward.
?	Searches backward.
:	An ex command (ex is a standalone line-based editor used within vi).
!	Invokes a shell command.

Each of these types of status-line commands must be entered by pressing Return. This is not true for other types of vi commands, such as the ones that do insertions.

> **TIP**
>
> To find out whether you are in command mode, use the set showmode preference described in the section entitled "Setting Preferences" later in this chapter.

Inserting Text

So, knowing that you are in command mode, let's insert some text. Basically, there are two commands for entering text on the current line: the letters i and a. These letters in lowercase insert (i) text to the left of the cursor or append (a) text to the right of the cursor. As with many vi commands, the uppercase versions of these letters have similar effects with subtle differences: uppercase I and A insert and append at the beginning and end of the current line, respectively.

After you type either of these letters, you will be placed in input mode. Any text entered after this point will be displayed on-screen.

Type an i and then type the following:

```
Down I walk<Enter>
by the bay,<Enter>
Where I can<Enter>
hear the water.<Enter>
Down we walk<Enter>
by the bay,<Enter>
My hand held<Enter>
by my daughter.<Enter>
```

To exit from input mode, press Esc. Notice that you did not see the letter i displayed before you entered the text, meaning that the i was correctly interpreted as a command. Also, it is important to note that it was not necessary to press Enter after pressing i for input mode.

Quitting vi

Now that you have some text for your file, let's quit the editor to see the results. The commands used for saving the file and exiting vi are slightly different from the i and d commands used in editing text: you must precede the command with a colon (:).

In this case, you want to do a save and exit, which are actually combined in one command. Type a :. At the bottom left of your screen, you will notice that a colon has appeared. vi has recognized that you are about to enter an ex command, and it will echo the remaining characters of the command after the colon. Type **wq** and press Return. vi quickly informs you that it has written the file to disk and tells you how many lines it contains. If the file is small and you have a fast system, this message may appear and be erased so quickly you won't catch it. Don't worry—the file has been saved if you issued the command properly. vi exits and you find yourself back at the shell prompt. Another way to save and exit is to type **ZZ**. The difference between this method and using wq is that ZZ will write the file only if it has been modified since the last save.

You can quit vi by typing **:q** if no changes have been made to the file you opened. This will not work if the file has been modified. If you are sure that you don't want to save what you have done, enter **:q!**. This command forces vi to quit, regardless of any edits.

To make sure that vi saved the file asong correctly, use the cat command to quickly view the file's contents:

```
$ cat asong
Down I walk
by the bay,
Where I can
hear the water.
Down we walk
by the bay,
My hand held
by my daughter.
$
```

Everything is exactly as you typed it in the file, so no surprises here.

Moving the Cursor

Moving the cursor around in vi essentially involves the following four keys:

- h   Moves the cursor one space to the left.
- j   Moves the cursor down one line.
- k   Moves the cursor up one line.
- l   Moves the cursor one space to the right.

These keys can perform their operations only when vi is in command mode. For convenience, most implementations of vi map these keys to their directional counterparts on the keyboard arrow keys.

vi enables you to move through a file in bigger "leaps" as well. Following are some commands for scrolling more than one line at a time:

Ctrl-U	Scrolls up a half-screen.
Ctrl-D	Scrolls down a half-screen.
Ctrl-F	Scrolls down one full screen.
Ctrl-B	Scrolls up one full screen.

The size of these movements largely depends on the terminal settings.

It is also possible to move the cursor to a specific line in a file. If you want to move to the tenth line, type **10G** or **:10** in command mode. G by itself will move the cursor to the end of the file. The cursor will not move if the number given is not applicable (for example, typing **:10** in a eight-line file will have no effect).

vi will also enable you to move the cursor a word at a time. A word is defined as any sequence of non-whitespace characters. To move to the beginning of the next word or punctuation mark on the current line, type **w**. Type **b** to move the cursor to the beginning of the current or previous word or punctuation mark.

Deleting Text

vi has commands for deleting characters, lines, and words. *Deletion* means that the selected text is removed from the screen but is copied into an unnamed text buffer from which it can be retrieved.

To delete a word, use the **dw** command. If you want to delete the word to the right of the cursor, type **dw**. If you are in the middle of a word, it will delete from the cursor position to the end. You can also delete several words at a time. For example, the command **4dw** will delete the next four words on the current line.

Lines can be deleted individually or by specifying a range of lines to delete. To delete the current line, type **dd**. The command **4dd** deletes four lines (the current line and three below it). **dG** will delete all lines from the current one to the end of the file.

On the current line, you can delete in either direction: **d^** will delete backward to the beginning of the line; **d$** (or **D**) will delete forward to the end of the line.

To delete individual characters, **x** deletes the character underneath the cursor, and **X** deletes the character to the left of the cursor. Both of these commands will accept a number modifier: For example, **4x** deletes the current character and the four characters to the right.

Unwanted changes such as deletions can be immediately undone by the **u** command. This "rolls back" the last edit made.

TIP

Not sure what command you just typed? When in doubt, press Esc and then enter the command again.

Copying and Moving Text

Moving sections of text around in a file basically requires three steps:

1. Yank the text into a buffer.
2. Move the cursor to where you want to insert the text.
3. Place the text from the buffer at the new location.

Yanking text means to copy it into either a named or unnamed buffer. The *unnamed buffer* is a temporary storage space in memory that is continually overwritten by successive yanks. vi has 26 named buffers that correspond to each letter of the alphabet.

To yank the current line into the unnamed buffer, the command is yy or Y. These commands can be modified by a number indicating how many lines beneath the cursor are to be yanked. For example, the command

```
3yy
```

in your file asong (with the cursor on the top line) yanks the following text into the temporary buffer:

```
Down I walk
by the bay,
Where I can
```

This text could also be yanked into the named buffer a by the following command:

```
"a3yy
```

The double quote (") tells the yank command to overwrite the contents of the named buffer a. If you had typed a capital A instead of a lowercase a, the three lines would have been appended to the end of the a buffer. This overwrite-versus-append concept works the same for all of the named buffers.

If you move the cursor to the end of the file using the :$ command, you can then paste the contents of the unnamed buffer to the end of the file. This is done using the p command, which pastes the contents of a buffer to the right of the cursor (P pastes to the left of the cursor). The paste command can also specify a named buffer in the same way as the yank command:

```
"ap
```

Yanks can also be performed on words using the command yw. This command can also use named buffers and accepts numeric modifiers.

Searching and Replacing Text

Text searches in vi can be performed in either direction: forward or backward. Searches are always started from the current cursor location and continue from the top or bottom of the file depending on which direction you use. In other words, searches "wrap around" the file.

You can use your file asong to illustrate searches. To search forward through asong for the word "bay," you would type

```
/bay
```

and press Return. Notice that this is a status-line command. The command /bay is echoed on the status line and the cursor is moved to the first occurrence it finds in the forward direction of the string "bay." Interested in finding another instance of "bay"? Enter a / character. This command continues the search for "bay" in the forward direction and places the cursor at the next instance of "bay." Each time you enter the / key, vi will try to find an instance of the previous string pattern. When it reaches the end of the file, vi will loop back and continue its search at the start of the file.

You can also search backward for strings in vi by using the ? command. It works in exactly the same manner as the / command, but in the opposite direction. Try it out by typing

?I

in asong, instructing vi to search back for instances of "I." This search can be repeated by typing ?, as you may have suspected. You can continue a search by pressing n, which always continues a search in the same direction as the previous search. However, typing N will use the same search string but in the opposite direction.

As I mentioned earlier, searches can be made very powerful through the use of regular expressions. The search command is supplied in the same fashion as described before (/ or ?), but square brackets are added to instruct vi to do a regular expression expansion of the enclosed characters. For example, search forward through asong from the first line for all strings containing the substring "er". Type

/er

vi's first matching string arrives at "Where." If you type n, vi will move the cursor to "where," and so on. You can also specify collections of characters or ranges of characters to match. Try typing the following:

/[a-z]y

This command used in asong will find the strings "by" and "my," as well as any word with these strings inside them (such as "bay"). This works because the range of characters given are treated as an enumerated range of ASCII values. Thus, you could also include a range of numbers (for example, 0-9). Now try the following command:

/[Mm]y

This will locate the strings "My" and "my."

In vi, searches without regular expressions will find only exact matches of the supplied pattern (including the case of the letters in the pattern). Clearly, regular expressions can be used to enhance many types of searches in which you may not know exactly how a pattern appears in a file.

One of the more common applications of a search is to replace instances of one word (or pattern) with another. This is done with an ex command that starts with a colon. To search the entire asong file for the string "Down" and replace it with the string "Up," type

:%s/Down/Up/g

The s indicates that this is a search operation, the % means that the entire file is to be searched, "Down" is the pattern to be found, "Up" is the new pattern, and the g tells vi that the search should continue until there are no more pattern matches. Without the g, vi would perform the replacement on only the first match it finds. This command also works with regular expressions appearing in the search pattern and the replacement pattern.

Setting Preferences

vi is *configurable*, which means that you can set options to control your editing environment. These options are initialized with default values that you can modify in vi at any time. vi is configured using the set command. The set command must be preceded by a colon and entered by pressing Return. For example, to display line numbers in the editor, you would issue

```
:set number
```

The following table describes a few of the more common set commands.

all	Displays a list of all available set options and their current status.
errorbells	Sounds the terminal bell when an error occurs.
ignorecase	Searches are case-insensitive.
number	Displays line numbers in the leftmost column of the screen (these are not written to the file).
showmode	An indication appears at the bottom right of the screen if you are in input mode, change mode, replace mode, and so on.

set commands that do not take a value can be switched off by inserting a "no" as a prefix to the set parameter. For example, the command

```
:set nonumber
```

switches line numbering off. The command

```
:set
```

shows only the options that you have changed.

The settings that you use in a vi session are (unfortunately) lost each time you exit vi. If you do not like the idea of resetting these options each time you use vi, there is an easier way to perform this initialization. Use the vi initialization file called .exrc. vi searches for this file in your home directory each time it is invoked. If it can't find this file, it uses the defaults set within the vi program. As you will see in the following example, the .exrc file can also be used to define vi macros.

A sample .exrc file would look something like this:

```
set number
set errorbells
set showmode
```

Note that the colon is not required before a set command in a .exrc file.

A Summary of Commands

The following is a summary of the more essential commands described in this chapter. You should consult the `vi` man page for more details on the many other `vi` commands.

i	Starts inserting text at the cursor.
h	Moves the cursor one character to the left.
j	Moves the cursor down one line.
k	Moves the cursor up one line.
l	Moves the cursor one character to the right.
C-f	Scrolls forward one screen.
C-b	Scrolls backward one screen.
*n*dd	Deletes the next *n* lines.
*n*yy	Yanks the next *n* lines into the unnamed buffer.
p	Puts the contents of the unnamed buffer to the right of the cursor.
u	Undoes the last change.
:wq	Writes changes and exits `vi`.
:q!	Exits `vi` without saving changes.
:set all	Shows all `set` parameters and their values.
/*string*	Searches forward for *string*.

The *emacs* Editor

emacs has become the editor of choice for many users because of its online help facility and its extensive collection of editing commands. For programmers, emacs is especially attractive because it can be configured to format source code for a variety of languages such as C, C++, and Lisp. emacs is somewhat easier to learn than `vi`, but it also features a much larger set of commands.

Starting *emacs*

emacs is invoked from the command line by entering

```
emacs
```

To start emacs with a file to be edited, enter

```
emacs filename
```

If you start emacs with a file, the screen will display the contents starting from the first line. Note the two lines at the bottom of the screen. The first of these lines, known as the *mode line,* displays the name of the file being edited and which part of the file that you are looking at (for example, TOP, 20%, BOT). The last line on the screen is the echo line, which emacs uses to display system messages and as a prompt for more input.

Control and Meta Keys

You are quite free at this point to start entering text into the edit buffer at the cursor location. However, you're probably wondering, "How do I move the cursor around?" Before I fill you in on this little detail, there are two keys that you should know about: the Control key (which I will refer to as C) and the Meta key (denoted by M). The Control key is used in most of the commands for emacs, but some use the Meta key instead. Commands in emacs consist of combinations of the Control or Meta key followed by some other character. It is necessary to hold down the Control key when pressing the next character, whereas the Meta key can be pressed and released before you enter the next character. For the PC, the Meta key is usually the Alt key.

> **NOTE**
>
> You may see the Control key abbreviated as C and the Meta key denoted by M.
>
> On the PC, you should use the Alt key for the Meta key.

Moving the Cursor

Now that you know about the Control key, we can talk about the cursor-movement commands. The basic ones that you need to remember are:

C-f	Moves the cursor forward one character.
C-b	Moves the cursor back one character.
C-p	Moves the cursor to the previous line.
C-n	Moves the cursor to the next line.
C-a	Moves the cursor to the beginning of the line.
C-e	Moves the cursor to the end of the line.

> **NOTE**
>
> When I refer to a command such as C-b, I mean press and hold the Control key while you press the letter b. The same is true for Meta commands such as M-v.

Most implementations of emacs conveniently map the first four movement commands to the arrow keys on the keyboard. Let's edit a new file called asong2. (If you are in the middle of a previous file, exit the editor by typing Ctrl-X, Ctrl-C.) Start up a new copy of emacs by entering the following command from the shell:

```
emacs asong2<Enter>
```

Now enter the following text into the buffer:

```
This is a file for edit
And you have to give emacs some credit
It's really quite swell
And all you have to do is spell
emacs works, if you let it!
```

Now use the C-b command to move back through this horrendous piece of poetry. Notice how the cursor jumps up to the end of each line after the reaching the beginning of the previous line. This works the same way in the opposite direction using the C-f command.

Another useful way of moving around is by scrolling through a file one screen at a time. The command C-v moves the cursor forward one screen at a time. The command M-v moves the cursor in the opposite direction.

Like vi, emacs treats a sequence of non-whitespace characters as a word. You can move the cursor forward one word at a time with the M-f command. The M-b command moves back one word.

Quitting *emacs*

At this time, you can stop editing to save the contents of the buffer to your file asong2. To do this, issue the command sequence C-x C-s. As you enter this command, notice how the command is displayed on the echo line as you type it. To quit emacs and return to the shell, enter the command C-x C-c. If you have made changes that haven't been saved using C-x C-s, emacs will ask for confirmation before quitting.

Deleting Text

You can delete text in several ways. The Backspace (or Delete) key is used to erase the character immediately preceding the cursor. The command C-d deletes the character underneath the cursor, and C-k deletes or "kills" all characters from the cursor to the end of the line. Words can be deleted also: M-d deletes the word the cursor is currently located over and M-Del (the Delete key) deletes the word previous to the current word.

If you ever find that you have committed an edit that you didn't really want, just type C-x u to undo the previous editing changes. You can repeat the undo command as many times as you want, rolling over all the changes you made. This is an advantage over vi, which can only undo the last change.

TIP

Change your mind about a command? Type C-g to abort the current command operation.

Working with Multiple Files

emacs enables you to edit several files in one session, each contained within its own buffer. To copy an external file into a new buffer, use the C-x C-f command. After entering this command, you will see the following prompt on the echo line:

```
Find file: ~/
```

emacs is smart when it looks for files. It supports *filename completion,* which means that you can simply type a few characters of a filename and emacs will attempt to match a file (or files) to what you have typed so far. To do this, type in the letters ".log" and press the Tab key. emacs expands this to ~/.login (or any other filename that matches). If two or more files match the pattern supplied, pressing the Tab key will cycle through them.

After you have loaded a new file into emacs, you can switch between buffers by using the C-x b command followed by the name of the buffer that you want. The buffer's name is that of the file that was loaded into it. The C-x b command also uses filename completion, so you can use the Tab key to cycle through your edit buffers after supplying a few relevant characters.

When you have finished editing a buffer, instead of saving the contents using the C-x C-s command, you may decide that you do not really want to keep the edits you have made. You can "kill" the current buffer by entering the command C-x k. emacs will prompt you for the name of the buffer to kill, but you can kill the current buffer by simply pressing Return. emacs will ask for confirmation, to which you can respond by typing yes (if you're sure) and press Return.

> **TIP**
>
> Whenever you are working with just two buffers, you can simply press Return after entering the C-x b command to switch to the other buffer.

Copying and Moving Text

In order to copy and move blocks of text in emacs, you must define the region of text by marking the beginning and end points of the text block. This is done by moving the cursor to where you want the block to begin and marking it using the C-Space command (in this case, Space means literally the spacebar). The end of the block is defined by wherever you place the cursor after that. To make a copy of the block, enter the command M-w. The text within the block is copied to emacs's internal clipboard, from which it can be pasted at another location using the C-y command. Alternatively, you can cut the block into the clipboard using C-w instead of M-w. Cutting, of course, deletes the text from its current location.

Let's try out some of these techniques on your buffer asong2. Use the M-< command to jump to the beginning of the buffer. Enter a C-Space to mark the start of the block and then use C-n to move down a line. Cut the block to the clipboard using C-w, move the cursor to the end of the buffer using M->, and paste it using C-y. The result should look like this:

```
It's really quite swell
And all you have to do is spell
emacs works, if you let it!
This is a file for edit
And you have to give emacs some credit
```

Searching and Replacing Text

You can search forward and backward through text using the C-s and C-r commands, respectively. These commands, like many in emacs, use *command completion*. This is the same concept as filename completion: you supply a few characters and emacs tries to fill in the rest. In this case, however, emacs moves the cursor to each instance it finds of the string supplied.

As you enter more characters, emacs narrows its search further. When you have found a correct match, press Return or use any of the cursor-movement commands to halt the search.

As with vi, searching in either direction wraps around the beginning or end of the file, depending on in which direction you are searching. However, when emacs reaches the top or bottom of the file, it will tell you that the search failed. You can keep searching by pressing C-s or C-r accordingly and emacs will continue using the current string.

To illustrate how searching in emacs works, let's search backward through your file asong2. Enter C-r and type an s. emacs moves the cursor to the "s" in "works". Now type a w. emacs now tries to find a pattern that matches the string sw. The cursor ends up on the "w" in "swell". You can edit the search string using the Backspace or Delete key. Delete the w and type a p. What happens?

Search-and-replaces are done by entering the query-replace command. This is qualified by the M-x command, which tells emacs that the text to follow is a full command and not a key combination. After you have entered the query-replace command, you will be prompted for the string to be found. Enter the string and press Return. emacs will then prompt you for the replacement string. Once you have entered the replacement string, emacs will search for every instance of the first string and, if it finds one, asks you if it should be replaced with the second string.

> **NOTE**
>
> emacs is actually composed of a set of explicit command names that are bound to key combinations. The query-replace command is bound to M-% in some implementations of emacs.

Using Modes with Buffers

emacs is versatile enough to handle many different types of editing chores. It enables you to associate modes to buffers so that you can have text formatting specific to your editing application. If you enter the command C-x m, emacs enters mail mode, which formats a buffer with To: and Subject: fields as well as a space for the body of the mail message. emacs can even send the mail message for you (by entering C-c C-c) after you have finished editing it.

emacs also supports modes for many different programming languages such as C. When a file with the extension .c (C source code) or .h (C header file) is loaded into emacs, the buffer is automatically set to C mode. This mode has knowledge of how C programs are formatted, and pressing the Tab key will indent a line correctly based on its place in the program (a for loop within another for loop, as an example).

Online Help in *emacs*

One of the best features of the emacs editor is that if you ever get stuck, or are just plain overwhelmed by it all, help is just a few keystrokes away—and lots of it! If you need a short emacs tutorial, just enter C-h t. If you would like to find out what function a particular key supports, type C-h k and then press the key. The help option has many different topics. Use C-h i to load the information documentation reader and read about all the types of help available.

A Summary of Commands

emacs, like the vi editor, has such a rich command set that we can cover only a portion of it in this chapter. The following table is a summary of the strictly essential commands that you will need for basic editing in emacs. The emacs man page should be consulted for a more comprehensive description of the full emacs command set.

C-b	Moves back one character.
C-d	Deletes the current character.
C-f	Moves forward one character.
C-g	Cancels the current command.
C-h	Enters emacs online help.
C-n	Moves forward to the next line.
C-p	Moves back to the previous line.
C-s	Searches forward for a string.
C-v	Scrolls forward one screen.
M-v	Scrolls backward one screen.
C-x u	Undoes the last edit.
C-x C-c	Exits emacs.
C-x C-s	Saves the buffer to a file.

Summary

There are many text editors available for the Linux system. Two of the most popular are `vi` (which is actually an alias to the `elvis` editor) and `emacs`. Both provide basic editing functions such as inserting and deleting text, reading and writing of external files, text searching, and copying and moving text. `vi` is a full-screen editor that has two modes: command mode and text mode. `emacs` is an extendible and powerful editor that is highly configurable to suit a variety of editing tasks (such as programming, document writing, and changing user or system files).

groff

17

by Tim Parker

This chapter looks at the groff text-formatting utility. Specifically, you will learn the following:

- What groff is
- How to do basic text formatting
- How to create macros
- What the mm macro package is

The groff program is the GNU version of nroff and troff, text-formatting languages that have been used in UNIX for many years. The groff system includes versions of troff, nroff, eqn, tbl, and other UNIX text-formatting utilities. The groff language is used primarily to compile man pages written and stored in groff/nroff format into a form that can be printed or displayed on-screen.

The nroff language was designed to provide text formatting in lineprinters, whereas troff was developed for phototypesetters. The commands in the two languages are identical, although some commands that cannot be processed by a lineprinter are ignored by nroff. In most cases, you don't use nroff or troff directly, but use a macro package to access them.

For the most part, nroff and troff have fallen into disuse with the development of powerful word processors and desktop-publishing packages. Their sole remaining use is for formatting man pages, which continue to be used widely.

Both nroff and troff have many commands that you will never require. Therefore, in this chapter we will look at the basic command set necessary for you to use the groff version of the two languages, and how they can be used for man page-specific applications. If you really want to use groff for advanced text formatting, you should pick up a dedicated book on the subject.

Embedding Commands

One aspect of groff that may take a little getting used to is that the way you type lines in the file isn't necessarily the way they will be displayed in the finished output. The groff system runs text lines together as much as possible. For example, the source file

```
This is fine stuff.
It is really interesting and
could keep me busy for hours.
```

covers three lines in the source, but when formatted, it's run together by groff to look like this:

```
This is fine stuff. It is really interesting and could keep me busy for hours.
```

with line breaks wherever necessary because of the page layout. This has an advantage in that you don't have to worry about making everything look properly formatted within the source. However, the disadvantage is that you might not have any idea what the output will look like until you see it!

A look at a groff source file shows that it is all ASCII characters that contain the usual text of the displayed output and a set of commands starting with a period, like this:

```
This is a bunch of text that will be displayed.
Here is even more text.
```

```
.ps 14
The line above is a groff command, identified by the
period in the first column of the line.
```

Most groff commands are on a line by themselves, although a few can be embedded anywhere on a line. These commands are usually prefaced by a backslash, much as the shell uses the backslash as an escape character. An example of a line with embedded commands is

```
This \fBline\fR has two embedded \fIgroff\fR commands.
```

Although there will be times when you want to use embedded commands, the majority are the commands on a single line, starting with a period.

Controlling Character Appearance

The groff language has a few commands for controlling the way characters look when printed or displayed. These include changing the size and line spacing of characters, as well as controlling fonts.

Sizes and Line Spacing

Character size and line spacing are not usually useful when displaying text on-screen, unless you are using a bitmapped terminal. They are used for printed documents, though. You can change the size of text with the .ps (point size) command:

```
This is the default 10-point size.
.ps 14
This is now in 14-point size.
.ps 20
This is a point size of 20.
.ps 6
And this is a really small point size of six.
```

NOTE

A point is 1/72 of an inch, so a 36-point character size is half an inch high. The 12-point size used most commonly is 1/6-inch high. Different versions of groff support different point sizes, but most versions support 6, 7, 8, 9, 10, 11, 12, 14, 16, 20, 24, 28, and 36 points. If you set a value that is not supported, it is rounded up to the next highest value (to a maximum of 36). The default point size is 10. If you use the .ps command without a value, groff reverts to the previous value.

Within a sentence, the point size can be changed with the line-embedded command \s followed by the point size. For example:

```
This is in 10-point, while \s20this is in
20, \s10 and back to 10 again.
```

The \s command should be followed by a legal point size. The special command \s0 causes groff to revert to its previous value. Relative changes are also supported, so you could embed commands such as \s+2 and \s-2, although only a single digit can be specified (so you can't change by more than nine points).

Line spacing is the vertical spacing between lines. Vertical spacing is not tied to point size, so it should be adjusted manually. As a general rule, use a vertical spacing about 20 percent larger than the point size. The default vertical spacing is 11.

Line spacing is controlled by the .vs (vertical space) command. In the next example, we change the point size and the vertical spacing to permit the characters to be printed clearly without overlap:

```
This is in normal 10-point, 11 vertical space size.
.ps 12
.vs 14
This is in 12-point with 14 vertical spacing.
```

If you use the .vs command without a value, groff reverts to the previous value.

If you want to force spacing for some reason, such as to separate sections of text, you can use the .sp (space) command. Used with no argument, .sp gives one blank line. It can also take arguments of i for inches and p for points:

```
This is default 10-point 11 vertical spaced text.
.sp

We have a blank line above this because of the command.
.sp 3.5i
```

```
This is three and a half inches below the previous line.
```

You can use fractions in most groff commands, as this example shows.

Fonts

Changing fonts requires the command `.ft` (font type). In the early days of `troff`, only four fonts were supported: Roman, Roman bold, Roman italic, and a set of special characters. Other fonts had to be specially loaded in the phototypesetter. For this reason, `groff` defaults to Roman.

To switch to Roman bold, you use the command `.ft B`, while `.ft I` switches, not surprisingly, to Roman italic. To return to the normal Roman font, the command `.ft R` is used, although on most systems, `.ft` by itself will suffice:

This is in normal Roman font.
.ft B
This is bold.
.ft I
This is italics.
.ft
This is back to normal Roman font.

You can switch fonts with a line-embedded command, too, using `\f` followed by either `I` or `B`, switching back with `R` to the normal font:

This is normal, `\fB`**bold**`\fR` and `\fI`*italics*`\fR`.

Because underline wasn't supported on most system printers, underlined text was converted to italic. The underline command `.ux` would italicize the next *x* lines of text.

Because we now have many thousands more fonts to work with than Roman, we must be able to change fonts within `groff`. The command to change fonts is `.fp` (font physically mounted), which also requires a number to indicate what position the font was mounted in the phototypesetter (old stuff, isn't it?). For example, if Helvetica were mounted in font position three and we referred to it by the font letter `H`, the command

.fp 3 H

would instruct the phototypesetter to switch to Helvetica in font position three. `groff` still retains these old-style commands.

Indenting and Line Length

The line length is set to default to 6.5 inches within `groff`. To override this value, the `.ll` (line length) command is used with an argument indicating the units. For example, the command

.ll 7i

switches `groff` to use a seven-inch line length. The maximum length accepted is usually about 7.5 inches, so to use paper wider than that you have to move the left margin over to compensate with the `.po` (page offset) command. The value `.po 0` sets the left margin as far over as is possible.

To indent text, you use the `.in` (indent) command. It takes a number and an indicator of the units as arguments, as the following example shows:

This is normal stuff.
```
.in 0.75I
```
        This is indented three-quarters of an inch.

To move the right margin to the left so that you can make a distinctive block of text within a normal chunk, you use the `.ll` (line length) command you saw earlier:

This is normal text, and goes on and on.
Even more text that continues the tradition.

```
.in 1i
.ll -1i
```
       This is now indented one inch to the left, and the right margin is indented one inch from the normal right margin. This makes the text stand out a little.

```
.in -1i
.ll +1i
```
And this is back to normal. The block will stand out nicely amongst all this normal text.

You will notice that we used relative movements of plus and minus a value in this example to make it easier. This way, we don't have to measure the page. You can revert to original values with the command `.in` and `.ll` with no arguments, as well.

An indent and line-length change is effective until the next command changes it. Sometimes you want to affect only a single line, though. If you want to indent only a single line, use the `.ti` (temporary indent) command:

This is really fine stuff. You can tell, 'cause I'm
still awake.
```
.ti 3i
```
        This line is temporarily indented by three inches, but the next line will be back to normal.

Tabs are used to set column output. Usually, tabs are used with `groff` only for unfilled text, which means material you would display in columns. Tab stops are set, by default, every half inch. To override these values, you use the `.ta` (tab) command. The command

```
.ta 1i 2i 3i 4i 5i 6i
```

sets the tabs at every inch instead. You can think of the setting of tabs within `groff` much as they are done on a typewriter, from left to right. Tabs are usually set for columns of numbers or tables, but the `groff` macro `gtbl` is much better at this. (You get a look at `gtbl` in the next chapter.)

Other Character Controls

The `groff` system has special instructions for controlling the size of individual letters, as well as formulas and special characters such as Greek letters. However, because it is unlikely that `groff` is used for this type of output these days, we'll ignore the capabilities. If you want more information on how to provide these special features, check the `groff` man pages or consult a good `troff` book.

Macros

A *macro* is a shorthand notation for a set of commands or strings. Many commands used to write man pages are macros. To give a practical example of a groff macro, suppose we want every paragraph to start with a blank line and a temporary indent of half an inch. The groff commands to do this are

```
.sp
.ti +.5i
```

Instead of typing these two lines every paragraph, we can define a macro of one character (or more) that does it for us.

To define the macro, we use the .de (define) command followed by the name of the macro and the commands. It would look like this, placed somewhere at the top of the source code:

```
.de PP
.sp
.ti +.5I
..
```

The last line with two periods indicates the end of the definition. Now, whenever we use the command .PP it will be executed as the lines in the macro.

> **WARNING**
>
> Make sure that you don't define a macro with the name of a reserved groff command, or the macro will not be executed.

Using *mm*

The mm (memorandum macros) package is not really part of nroff or troff, although both can use it. The mm program reads a source file much as groff does and translates it to output. Many of the mm macros are used for man pages. Indeed, many users find the nroff and troff commands too awkward or complicated, whereas mm is fully able to meet all their basic formatting needs.

To add mm commands, you use the period in the first column as with groff. The mm macros are usually quite simple, and easy to work with and use. We can look at the most important of them here.

Paragraphs and Headers

Like groff, mm runs text together when reformatting, regardless of line breaks in the source file. To force a new paragraph, use the .P command. It forces a line break and adds a blank line to the output. Paragraphs are usually formatted so that they are flush left.

Headings are created with the .H command. For example, the command

.H **This is a Heading**

will create a break, output the heading text in bold, and leave a bit of a space between the heading and the text that follows it.

There can be seven levels of headings; 1 is the highest and 7 is the lowest. To specify the heading level, add the number as the first argument after the `.H` command:

`.H 2` **This is a level 2 heading**

The mm heading macro will number the headings automatically, although you can suppress the numbering with the `.HU` (heading unnumbered) command. To reset the numbering (at a section break, for example), use the `.nr` (number register) command followed by the heading level and the number to use. For example, the command

```
.nr H2 1
```

will restart the numbering of second-level headings at 1.

Lists

Lists are easily created in mm with the `.LI` (list) command and the `.LE` (list end) command. This creates a bulleted list. For example, the command

```
.LI
thing 1
.LI
thing 2
.LE
thing 3
```

creates a bulleted list of the three bits of text. You can create a list with dashes instead of bullets using the `.DL` (dash list) command. The mark list command, `.ML`, creates a list with the character of your choice.

If you want a numbered list, use the `.AL` (automatic list) command. Lists with no arguments are created with Arabic numbers. To create an alphabetical list (A, B, C, and so on), use the macro command `.AL A`. Roman numerals (i, ii, iii, iv, v, and so on) can be used with the `.AL I` command.

You can nest list types as necessary. For example, the command

```
.AL I
.LI
groff
.AL
.LI
macros
.LI
mm
.LE
.LI
gtbl
.LI
geqn
.LE
```

will create output that looks like this:

```
I.   groff
        1. macros
        2. mm
II.   gtbl
III.  geqn
```

You have to be careful when terminating each list with an `.LE` command to ensure that you terminate the proper one. Experimentation and practice help you get the hang of this. You may have noticed that it takes a lot of commands to make a little list!

Font Changes

Changing fonts with mm is quite simple. When working from a period command, the command `.B` (bold) creates bold text until an `.R` (restore) command, while `.I` (italic) does the same until an `.R` command. If you want to bold or italicize only one word, you can do it after the period command, as this example shows:

This is normal text
`.B`
This is bold.
So is this.
`.R`
This is normal.
This is a single
`.Bbold`
word, though.

When you change only one word, you don't need a `.R` command.

Changes can be performed within text in the same manner as with groff:

```
This is an \fIitalics set of words\fR until here.
```

Footnotes

To create a footnote, use the `.FS` (footnote start) and `.FE` (footnote end) commands. Every footnote on a single page will be collected and printed at the bottom. Footnotes are automatically numbered unless you specify another character:

```
This is normal text.
.FS
```
This is a footnote with its proper number in front of it.
```
.FE
```
This is more normal text.
```
.FS *
```
But this is a footnote marked with an asterisk.
```
.FE
```
This is even more normal text. At the bottom of the page
will be a numbered footnote and an asterisked footnote.

You can use any valid character for the optional footnote mark, including special characters supported by groff.

Summary

As you might expect, there is a lot to both groff and mm that we haven't looked at. Because groff is seldom used these days, we covered only the most important aspects. As I said earlier, if you want to learn more about groff or mm, find a good reference book on the subject.

geqn and *gtbl*

18

by Tim Parker

Now that you are comfortable with groff, you can look at two useful add-ons for groff: geqn and gtbl. In this chapter, you learn the following:

- What are geqn and gtbl?
- How to create complex equations easily
- How to format tables for groff documents

In the last chapter, you saw how groff can be used to produce formatted documents to both screen and printer. Unfortunately, groff is not the easiest package to work with for complex problems such as tables and equations, so a set of macros for these tasks was developed.

The utilities gtbl and geqn are preprocessors, which means that you write the source code as usual, but then the gtbl and geqn programs scan through and replace their specific commands with groff commands. Except for the specific commands changed, no other changes to the text or groff commands are performed.

geqn

The geqn preprocessor is designed for formatting complex equations and printing special symbols. You need only use geqn if you are using groff to create a document with these kinds of characters embedded within them.

Although groff has enough power to provide simple equations, it is not particularly friendly, or powerful enough for more than single-line material. On the other hand, geqn is quite easy to work with. Most aspects of geqn are designed to look like equivalent English commands or words.

You can quickly move through a set of the important parts of geqn. As you will see, it is remarkably easy to work with.

Executing geqn

The geqn preprocessor is invoked before the groff formatter. Usually, this is accomplished with a simple pipe command:

geqn *filename* ¦ groff

This processes *filename* through geqn, which converts geqn commands to equivalent groff commands and then sends the result to groff for processing.

The command

geqn *file1 file2 file3* ¦ groff

processes three files and sends them all to groff.

Remember that many consoles can't display equations properly because they are not bitmapped and don't have the character set available. You may have to output the results to a printer to see any exercises you try.

Equations

You must tell geqn where equations begin and end by using the commands .EQ (equation start) and .EN (equation end). Within the two commands, anything typed is treated as an equation. For example, the command

```
.EQ
b=c*(d+x)
.EN
```

is formatted to the equation

```
b=c*(d+x)
```

If you try that line without the equation indicators, feeding it straight to groff, you don't receive the same output because groff can't interpret the characters properly.

You can number equations, as is often required in technical documents, by placing a number after the .EQ command. For example, the command

```
.EQ 15
b=c*(d+x)
.EN
```

places the number 15 in the left margin next to the equation.

Subscripts and Superscripts

To place superscripts and subscripts in an equation, use the commands sup and sub. The words sup and sub must be surrounded by spaces. For example, the command

```
E=mc sup 2
```

produces Einstein's most famous equation.

To indicate the end of a subscript or superscript and continue with normal characters, use a space or a tilde (~) character. For example, the command

```
x=(z sup 2)+1
```

gives you the finished output

$x=(z^{2)+1}$

which is probably not what you wanted. Instead, use one of the following commands:

```
x=(z sup 2 )+1
x=(z sup 2~)+1
```

In these commands, the space or the tilde indicates the end of the superscript. This gives you the following output:

$x=(z^2)+1$

You can subscript subscripts, and superscript superscripts, simply by combining the formats:

```
y sub x sub 3
```

You can also produce both subscript and superscript on the same character using the two commands together:

```
x sub y sup 3
```

Because a space is used to indicate the end of a subscript or superscript, this can cause a problem when you want spaces either as part of the equation, or to separate words to be converted. To get around this problem, use braces to enclose the subscript or superscript:

```
w sup {x alpha y}
```

This shows that the Greek letters are also available, as they are within groff. You can have braces within braces, as well:

```
omega sub { 2 pi r sup { 2 + rho }}
```

Try these commands for yourself, and experiment to see the output.

Fractions

To create a proper-looking fraction, use the keyword over. The geqn preprocessor automatically adjusts the length of the line separating the parts. For example, the command

```
a = 2b over {3c alpha}
```

produces an equation with a horizontal line separating the two components, just as if you were writing the equation out on paper.

You can, of course, combine all the other elements of geqn to create more complex-looking equations:

```
{alpha + beta * gamma sup 3} over {3 sub {4 + alpha}}
```

When you are combining sup and sub with over, geqn processes sup and sub first, and then it does over, much as you would when writing the equation.

Square Roots

To draw a square root symbol, use the keyword sqrt, and geqn ensures that the square root symbol is properly drawn to enclose all parts of the equation that are indicated as belonging to the square root. Very large square root signs that cover a lot of material on many lines, for example, do not look particularly good when printed. You should consider using the superscript 0.5 instead.

You can use sqrt quite easily. For example, the command

```
sqrt a+c - 1 over sqrt {alpha + beta}
```

has the first square root sign over a+c, and the second over the part in braces.

Summations, Set Theory, and Integrals

To produce a summation, use the keyword sum and the keywords from and to to show the upper and lower parts of the command. For example, use the command

```
sum from x=1 to x=100 x sup 2
```

to create the formula for summing x squared over the range 1 to 100. If you want to use a special word, use braces:

```
sum from x=1 to {x= inf} x sup 2
```

This is the same command, except summing from 1 to infinity. The braces ensure that the to component is properly interpreted. If no from or to component is specified, they are not printed.

To use integrals, the keyword int is used, and can again take a from argument:

```
lim from n=1 xy sup 3 = 9
```

Other reserved words for geqn are used with set theory. You can use the keywords union and inter for the union and intersect of sets.

Brackets, Bars, and Piles

As equations get more complicated, you need to use more brackets and braces. You can generate brackets ([ ]), braces ({}), and parentheses (()) as needed using the left and right commands:

```
left { b over d+1} = left ( alpha over {beta + gamma} )
```

This produces large braces, and parentheses are required to surround the terms. You can nest these, of course, with geqn adjusting the sizes properly. Braces are usually bigger than brackets and parentheses.

For floor and ceiling characters, use the left floor, right floor, left ceiling, and right ceiling commands. For example:

```
left ceiling x over alpha right ceiling > left floor beta over 2 right floor
```

draws the equation with the proper vertical bars and ceiling and floor markers.

To create a pile of elements, use the reserved word pile. The following example shows the usage best:

```
X = left [ pile { a above b above c } right ]
```

This produces output with the three elements a, b, and c stacked vertically within big braces.

Matrices

To make a matrix requires a little more work. You could probably make a matrix using the pile command, but if the elements are not of equal height, they will not line up. For that reason, use the keyword matrix. The general format is

```
matrix {
 ccol { elements }
 ccol { elements }
```

in which `ccol` produces centered columns. For left-adjusted columns, use `lcol`; `rcol` produces right-adjusted columns. The elements are specified individually. For example, the command

```
matrix {
 ccol { x sub 1 above y sub 1 }
 ccol { x sub 2 above y sub 2 }
```

produces the matrix

x_1 x_2
y_1 y_2

All matrices must have the same number of elements in each column or geqn can't process the matrix properly.

Quoted Text

Any characters placed within quotation marks are not interpreted by geqn. This is useful for text strings that may contain reserved words, such as the following:

```
italics "beta" = beta + gamma
```

Here, the word `beta` will appear in italic without being converted to the beta character.

Character Changes

You can change font and point size with geqn in much the same way as with groff. The default setting is usually Roman 10 point. If you want to set bold characters, use the keyword `bold`; `italic` sets italic font.

```
x=y bold alpha
```

You can also use the keyword `fat`, which widens the character (useful for things such as grad characters). These reserved words affect only what immediately follows, so you must use braces if the area to be changed is more than a single block of characters.

```
x=y*2 bold {alpha + gamma}
```

To change the size of characters, use the `size` keyword:

```
size 16 {alpha + beta}
```

This sets the enclosed text in 16-point size. Incremental changes are acceptable.

To affect the entire equation, you can use the `gsize` (global size) and `gfont` (global font) commands at the start of the geqn block:

```
.EQ
gsize 14
```

```
gfont H
....
```

This makes it easy to format the equations however you wish.

Using *geqn*

As you have seen, geqn is quite friendly and easy to use, especially if you are used to writing out equations longhand. You should play around with the system and learn the different features. There are more commands available within geqn, but the main ones have been shown to you. For more information, check the man pages or a good troff book that includes eqn.

gtbl

The gtbl routine is designed to help in the preparation of charts, multicolumn lists, and any other material presented in a tabular format. The gtbl commands are not difficult to work with, but can be awkward to learn, so studying examples is the best method.

To use gtbl, two special commands are used to indicate to groff that the area between the two commands is to be processed as gtbl instructions. These two key commands are .TS (table start) and .TE (table end). Commands between these two are processed by gtbl first, which converts the gtbl commands to groff commands; then, the source is passed to groff.

Tables are independent of each other with gtbl, meaning that each must contain all the information for formatting the data within the table and can't rely on a previous format. Tables contain three types of information: text for the table itself, options that control the behavior of gtbl, and formatting commands to lay out the table itself. The general format of a gtbl source code section is as follows:

```
.TS
options;
format.
data
.TE
```

Let's look at the important parts of the gtbl layout first, and then see how they are combined to produce finished tables.

Executing *gtbl*

Because gtbl is a preprocessor, it is invoked on the source file, and then the results are passed to groff. The simplest way to do this is with the command

```
gtbl filename ¦ groff
```

in which the gtbl preprocessor runs against the source in *filename* and then sends the output to groff. If you are processing more than one file at a time, or you need to send the output of gtbl to another preprocessor, such as geqn, you use piping slightly differently. The command

```
gtbl filename ¦ geqn ¦ groff
```

sends the output to geqn and then to groff.

Options

There can be a single line of options after a .TS command that affects the entire table. Any options must follow the .TS command. If more than one option is specified, they must be separated by spaces, commas, or tabs, and terminate in a semicolon. gtbl accepts the following options:

center	Centers the table (default is left-justified).
expand	Makes tables as wide as current line length.
box	Encloses the table in a box.
allbox	Encloses each element of the table in a box.
doublebox	Encloses the table in two boxes.
tab (*n*)	Uses *n* instead of a tab to separate data.
linesize (*n*)	Uses point size *n* for lines or rules.
delim (*mn*)	Uses *m* and *n* as equation delimiters.

When gtbl tries to lay out a table, it tries to keep the entire table on one page if possible, even if it has to eject the previous page only partially completed. This can sometimes cause problems because gtbl can make mistakes estimating the size of the table prior to generating it, especially if there are embedded line commands that affect spacing or point size. To avoid this problem, some users surround the entire table with the display macros .DS (display start) and .DE (display end). You can ignore this for most tables, unless you start embedding commands within the data.

Format

The format section of the table structure indicates how the columns are to be laid out. Each line in the format section corresponds to one line of data in the finished table. If not enough format lines are specified to match all the lines of data, the last format line specified is used for the remainder of the table. This lets you use a specific format for headers and a single format line for the rest of the table. The format section ends with a period.

Each line in the format section contains a keyletter for each column in the table. Keyletters should be separated by spaces or tabs for each column to enhance readability. Keyletters are case-independent (so you can use upper- or lowercase for the keyletters, or a mixture of the two, without affecting the layout). Supported gtbl keyletters are as follows:

l	Left-justified entry
r	Right-justified entry
c	Centered entry
n	Numeric entries lined up by units

a   Aligned on left so that widest entry is centered

s   Previous column format applies across rest of column

A sample format section consists of a letter for each column, unless the entry is repeated across the page. A sample format section looks like this:

```
c       s       s
l       n       n .
```

In this sample, the first line of the table is formatted with the first, second, and third columns centered (the s repeats the previous entry). The second and subsequent lines have the first entry left-justified, and the next two lined up as numbers. The period ends the format section. If you like, you can put all these format keyletters on a single line, using a comma to separate the lines:

```
c s s, l n n .
```

A table formatted by this set of commands looks like this (with random numbers inserted to show the lineup):

```
        Centered_Title
Entry1  12.23   231.23
Entry2   3.23    45.2
Entry3  45      123.2344
Entry4   3.2      2.3
```

Numeric data is usually aligned so that the decimal places are in a vertical column. However, sometimes you want to override this format by forcing a movement. The special character \& is used to move the decimal point. The special characters disappear when the table is printed. To show the effect of this special character, the following sample shows normal formatting and entries with the special character embedded (the first column is the source input, and the second is the generated output):

```
14.5            14.5
13              13
1.253            1.253
3\&1.21          31.21
53.2            53.2
6\&2.23          62.23
```

You can see that the numbers usually line up with the decimal point in a vertical row, except where moved over by the \& characters. Even if a number has no decimal point specified (as in the second line of the example), it is lined up as though one were present after the last digit.

The following are a few additional keyletters that can be used to create special formats and make the tables more attractive:

_   Horizontal line in place of column entry.

=   Double horizontal line in place of column entry.

¦   Between column entries, draws a vertical line between columns. Before the first keyletters, draws a line to the left of the table. After the last keyletters, draws a line to the right of the table.

¦¦	Between column entries, draws a double vertical line.
e/E	Sets equal width columns. All columns that have a keyletter followed by e or E are set to the same width.
f/F	Followed by a font name or number, changes the entry to the font specified.
n	Any number following a keyletter. Indicates the amount of separation between columns.
p/P	Followed by a number, changes the point size of the entry to the specified number. Increments acceptable.
t/T	Vertically spanned items begin at the top line. Normally, vertically spanning items (more than one line in the table) are centered in the vertical range.
v/V	Followed by a number, gives vertical line spacing.
w/W	Followed by a number, sets the width.

The order of these characters on the format line is not important, although the spacing between each format identifier must still be respected. Multiple letters can be used. The entry

```
np14w(2.5i)fi
```

sets the numeric entry (n) in italic (fi), with a point size of 14 (p14) and a minimum column width of 2.5 inches (w(2.5i)).

You may need to change the format of a table midway through—for example, to present summaries. If you must change the format, use the .T& (table continue) command.

Data

Data for the table is entered after all the format specifications have been completed. Data for columns is separated by tabs or any other character indicated in the tabs option. Each line of data is one line of the table. Long lines of data can be broken over several lines of source by using the backslash character as the last character in a line.

Any line starting with a period and followed by anything other than a number is assumed to be a groff command and is ignored by the preprocessor. If a single line of the data consists of only underscore or equal sign characters (single and double lines), it is treated as extending the entire width of the table.

You can embed a block of text within a table by using the text commands of T{ (start of text) and }T (end of text). This lets you enter something that can't be easily entered as a string separated by tabs.

Examples

The best way to understand how to use gtbl is to look at some simple examples. Here's a basic table command:

```
.TS
doublebox;
c c c, l l n.
Name          Dept          Phone
Joe           8A            7263
Mike          9F            2635
Peter         2R            2152
Yvonne        2B            2524
.TE
```

All of the entries in the data section are separated by tabs. This produces a table with three columns, the first line of which is centered text. The rest of the table has the first and second column left-justified, and the last column aligned by decimal point (there are none in this case). The entire table is surrounded by two boxes.

A slightly more complex example uses a table title, followed by a row of column headings, and then the data. Separate each element in the table by a box in this case:

```
.TS
allbox;
c s s
c c c
n n n .
Division Results
East          West          North
15            12            14
12            12            18
36            15            24
.TE
```

Try typing in these examples, or create your own, to see what effect the different commands have. When you've started using gtbl, it isn't that difficult.

Summary

Although word processors have made utilities such as geqn and gtbl less popular than they used to be, some diehard UNIX people still like to use them. There are times when you might not be able to produce an equation the way you want with your favorite word processor, so you might have to return to the basics. Also, because word processors capable of fancy formulas tend to be expensive, utilities such as geqn and gtbl are ideal for the occasional user who doesn't want to spend a lot of money on a seldom-used tool.

TeX

19

by Peter MacKinnon

IN THIS CHAPTER

This chapter looks at the following topics:

- What TeX is and why you would want to use it
- The differences between typesetting and writing
- The enhanced version of TeX called LaTeX
- What VirTeX and IniTeX are

What Is *TeX*?

TeX (pronounced *tech*) is a text formatting system invented by Donald Knuth. It lets you produce professionally typeset documents by embedding TeX commands within a normal ASCII text file. This text file can then be converted to what is known as a *DVI* (device-independent file), which can be either previewed on-screen using an X Window program called xdvi or converted to a printer-specific file format, such as PostScript, HP LaserJet, or for other popular printers.

TeX is a powerful program in that it enables you to define specific typesetting commands (such as font size, page size, or space between lines). It also works as a programming language that enables you to create macros for defining more abstract units of text such as documents, headings, and paragraphs. The benefit of these high-level macros is that they enable you to concentrate on the authoring of a document, not the typesetting. The key appeal of TeX for engineers and scientists is that it supports the typesetting of complex mathematical formulas.

Typesetting Versus Writing

The usefulness of a document can be limited by its appearance. Consider two documents: one that is well-organized with clearly defined units of text such as chapters, headings, and paragraphs, and another that has no paragraph breaks and no space between lines. The first document is much more appealing to the reader, whereas the second document is downright painful to read. So, despite the best efforts of an author to create a *magnum opus,* or even a recipe for strawberry jam, the meaning behind the words may get lost in a typographical abyss.

In book publishing, authors aren't usually responsible for anything beyond the genius of their words. They usually leave the design and crafting of the book to a book designer. This person then hands the design template to page layout technicians. TeX performs this book design and typesetting role for you, enabling you, the author, to be your own publisher. It gives you control over the publication of your own material while still permitting you to concentrate on what you're supposed to be writing about!

TeX

A TeX file can be created with any Linux text editor such as vi or Emacs. You can enter text into a file called arkana.tex like this:

```
Do you suppose that Alfred Hitchcock would have had as successful a directing
career if he did not have the considerable talents of actors Cary Grant and
James Stewart in his most popular films? That's a tough one to answer... \bye
```

After you have saved your file, use the TeX program to convert it to a DVI file using this command:

```
$ tex arkana
```

The resulting `arkana.dvi` file that is created contains your text. This file can be used by different output devices (hence the name) for viewing or printing. For example, if you want to print your DVI file to a PostScript printer, convert it to a `ps` format, and print it using the `dvi2ps` utility:

```
$ dvi2ps arkana.ps ¦ lp
```

This assumes that the default printer is PostScript-capable. If you want to just preview how the text looks, use the X application `xdvi`:

```
$ xdvi arkana.dvi &
```

The TeX command also produces a log file entitled `arkana.log`, containing any error and warning messages, and other information such as the number of pages of output. The beauty of all this indirect representation of TeX output is that the TeX source file and its resulting DVI are very portable, particularly from Linux to its ancestor UNIX.

Simple Text Formatting

Most of the work in creating a TeX document is putting in the words that discuss whatever you're writing about. As shown earlier, it is fairly simple to create an unadorned TeX file: The only special command you used was \bye. This command tells the TeX program that it has reached the end of the document. The \bye command uses one of several characters that TeX treats with special interest, specifically the backslash or *escape* character. Here is the set of special characters that TeX recognizes: \, {, }, ~, #, $, %, ^, &, and the space character. The meaning behind these characters will be discussed as you progress.

One of the main conveniences of TeX is the intelligent way it deals with text. Words are any sequence of characters separated by whitespace characters. The number of whitespace characters between words is immaterial because TeX treats them as one character. Sentences are recognized by the last word preceding a ., ?, !, or :. Paragraphs are distinguished by a blank line following a sentence. Much like the spaces between words, TeX treats excess blank lines as redundant and ignores them. Thus, the text

```
How do you compare
these two terrific leading men? James Stewart had that good-natured,
All-American        charm        mixed
with a surprising element of vulnerability, uncommon
among       other major Hollywood actors.


Cary Grant, on the other
hand, was versatile      enough to play the villain as well as the suave hero in
many films.
```

is formatted by TeX as follows:

```
How do you compare these two terrific leading men? James Stewart had that good-
natured, All-American charm mixed with a surprising element of vulnerability,
uncommon among other major Hollywood actors.

Cary Grant, on the other hand, was versatile enough to play the villain as well as
the suave hero in many films.
```

You can also insert comments into your TeX file using the `%` character. Text following a `%` character is treated as a comment and not made part of the TeX output. The text

```
From her% Nothing to do with Hitchcock
% ...nothing at all
e to there
```

is formatted as

```
From here to there
```

TeX has several commands for manipulating paragraphs. The `\par` command starts a new paragraph, which has the same effect as inserting a blank line.

```
From here \par to there
```

The preceding line is formatted as follows:

```
From here
to there
```

The `\noindent` command tells TeX not to indent the paragraph:

```
I grew up on Newcastle Street.

\noindent That was close to Hazlehurst.
```

This is output as follows:

```
        I grew up on Newcastle Street.
That was close to Hazlehurst.
```

You can also use the escape character before a space in order to force the insertion of an extra space:

```
I think that I need an extra\ \ \ space or two.
I'm sure        of it.
```

This becomes

```
I think that I need an extra   space or two.
I'm sure of it.
```

Fonts

Fonts are representations of characters that share similar size and style. The default font that TeX uses is Roman. You can override this by using the internal names that TeX associates with fonts that are externally loaded. You can also add new font definitions. The definitions that TeX knows about by default are: `\rm` (Roman), `\tt` (typewriter), `\bf` (bold), `\sl` (slanted), and `\it` (italic). TeX continues using whatever font was last specified (including the default) until it is instructed to do otherwise. Therefore, the text

```
This is roman, but I think I will switch to \tt typewriter for a while; then again,
maybe \it italic would be nice. Now back to \rm roman.
```

appears as follows:

This is roman, but I think I will switch to `typewriter for a while`; then again, maybe *italic would be nice. Now back to* Roman.

You can add a font and change its size using a command like this:

`\font \fontname=auxiliary font`

To use a 12-point roman font, redefine the `\rm` definition to use the `cmr12` auxiliary font, like this:

```
\font\rm=cmr12
We are changing from this font \rm to that font.
```

This formats as follows:

```
We are changing from this font to that font.
```

Fonts have up to 256 different symbols including the standard numeric, uppercase, and lowercase character symbols that you use most frequently. Symbols that are not represented on a standard keyboard can be accessed using the `\char` command. This command uses the integer that follows it as a character code index into a font's character table. For example, the text

```
TeX would interpret \char 37 as a comment symbol
but it would not
care about a \char 43 sign.
```

is processed by TeX as follows:

```
TeX would interpret % as a comment symbol but it would not
care about a + sign.
```

Controlling Spacing

You've seen how you can insert individual extra spaces in TeX files. Now, let's examine how you can have more control over the spacing of larger portions of text. TeX has a series of commands that recognize the following units of measurement:

Unit	Meaning
em	Approximately the width of the character M, depending on the font in use
in	Inches
pt	Points (1 inch equals 72 points)
mm	Millimeters (1 inch equals 25.4 millimeters)

These units are used with decimal numbers to specify the amount of spacing that you need. The `\hskip` command can insert a horizontal space on a line, like this:

```
\tt From here \hskip 0.5in to there
```

This produces the following output:

```
From here      to there
```

You can also supply a negative number, which moves the text following the \hskip command to the left (the negative direction). The \hfil command distributes horizontal space in a paragraph when space is available. The interesting thing about the \hfil command is the fact that TeX inserts one implicitly for each paragraph. Bearing this detail in mind, you can use this command to flush text left or right, or center it on a line, like this:

```
\noindent \hfil Some centered text. \par
```

This is output as follows:

```
                    Some centered text.
```

The \vskip command can insert a vertical space between paragraphs using a given unit of measurement (much like \hskip). The command

```
\vskip 40mm
```

places a vertical space of 40 millimeters between its preceding and succeeding paragraphs. TeX also provides vertical skipping commands in convenient units: \smallskip, \medskip, and \bigskip.

The vertical equivalent of \hfil is the \vfill command, which can distribute vertical spaces between paragraphs when extra space (nontext) is available. TeX assumes an implicit \vfill command at the end of a document.

You can also explicitly add line breaks and page breaks to your document with the \break command. If this command appears within a paragraph, TeX inserts a line break. If it appears between paragraphs, a page break is inserted. Conversely, you can specify points in your document where you want the text to be kept together and not broken across lines or pages. This is done by using the \nobreak command.

Page Layout

A page is composed of a header, footer, and body. The header and footer contain information such as chapter title, section heading, and page number. The body is where the main information in your document appears. By changing how this information is ordered in your TeX document, you are actually designing the look of the finished product.

The \headline and \footline commands both take arguments that specify their content. The format of these commands is as follows:

```
\headline={parameters}
```

The parameters could be a list of things such as a page number command and an \hfil command:

```
\headline={\hfil \the\pageno}
\footline={\hfil}
```

This pair of commands creates a right-justified page number and a blank footer on each page.

You can change the size of the text box that TeX uses for paragraphs by using the \hsize command. For instance, the text

```
\hsize=2in
This text is 2 inches wide but we could choose to make it wider or thinner.
```

produces the following:

```
This text is 2 inches wide but
we could choose to make it
wider or thinner.
```

Margins can be adjusted inward or outward using the \leftskip and \rightskip commands, respectively. By providing positive values to these commands, they move the margin inward, depending on which side you specify (left or right). As you may expect, negative values have the opposite effect: They move the margins outward. Indentation is controlled similarly using the \parindent command.

The \baselineskip and \parskip commands control the regular vertical spacing between lines and paragraphs, as in the following:

```
\baselineskip=0.15in
\parskip=0.3in
```

Baseline refers to the distance between the bottoms of characters (such as an *i*) on consecutive lines.

Using Groups

Normally, TeX continues using such things as fonts and text styles until you explicitly change the format. The grouping features of TeX enable you to define changes that are local to particular sections of text. The formatting originally specified is then restored after the group has been processed.

There are two ways to specify how text is grouped. One is to use the \begingroup and \endgroup command pair. The other is to use the braces { and }. Although both of these perform grouping roles, braces are also used to specify parameters to commands and, as such, must be used with care.

As an illustration of the use of groups in TeX, the text

```
Let's see \begingroup \it how {\bf this grouping stuff} really
works \endgroup, shall we?
```

produces the following:

```
Let's see how this grouping stuff really
works, shall we?
```

You may have noted from the example that, in fact, groups can contain other groups.

Mathematical Symbols

One of the most powerful features of TeX is its capability to generate correct mathematical notation for formulas with convenient commands. This is one of the key reasons behind TeX's popularity among engineers and scientists.

TeX distinguishes between formulas that must appear within regular text (inline formulas) and those that must appear on their own line (displayed formulas). You must use the $ symbol to denote inline formulas, as in

```
The equation $2+3=x$ must evaluate to $x=5$.
```

which is generated as the following:

```
The equation 2+3=x must evaluate to x=5.
```

However, displayed formulas are denoted using two consecutive $ symbols, as in

```
The equation $$2+3=x$$ must evaluate to $$x=5$$.
```

which produces the following:

```
        The equation

            2+3=x

must evaluate to

            x=5.
```

Table 19.1 shows some of the math symbols that TeX can generate, their associated commands, and their meaning.

Table 19.1. Some of the math symbols that TeX can generate.

Symbol	TeX *Command*	*Meaning*
Π	\pi	Pi
Σ	\sum	Sum
{	\{	Open bracket
}	\}	Close bracket
∫	\int	Integral
≤	\leq	Less than or equal to
≥	\geq	Greater than or equal to
≠	\neq	Not equal to
•	\bullet	Bullet
...	\ldots	Horizontal ellipsis
◆	\diamond	Diamond
Δ	\Delta	Delta

TeX uses particular fonts for the formulas it produces. These can be overridden in the usual fashion, but the changes are applicable only to letters and digits.

Using Figures in Your Document

Figures that are drawn outside of TeX can be inserted into their own space. This space "floats." In other words, TeX knows that it must keep track of the figure space as the text around it is added or deleted. This flexibility means that you, the writer, need not worry about exactly where in the document your figures will appear.

To insert a figure that must appear at the top of a page, use the following command:

```
\topinsert figure \endinsert
```

Here, *figure* can be an external reference or an internal definition. TeX tries to place the figure at the top of the next page with sufficient space.

You can also tell TeX that you want a figure to appear on its own page by using this command:

```
\pageinsert figure \endinsert
```

Macros

Macros have made TeX a highly extendible system. They essentially enable you to create new commands by associating existing commands and text sequences to a macro name. After they are defined, these macros can be used in other parts of your document to replace repetitive pieces of text, or to encapsulate abstract operations.

A macro is defined once, using the following format:

```
\def macroname {new text}
```

In this case, *macroname* is a name or TeX command preceded by a backslash character. Any reference to this macro name is replaced by the new text throughout the document. For example, the macro definition

```
\def\brg{burger}
Ham\brg, cheese\brg, lim\brg.
```

is output as follows:

```
Hamburger, cheeseburger, limburger.
```

Macros can refer to other macros, as in

```
\def\tig{a tigger }
\def\wond{a wonderful thing }
\def\pooh{\wond is \tig cause \tig is \wond}
\pooh\par
```

which produces the following:

```
a wonderful thing is a tigger cause a tigger is a wonderful thing
```

> **WARNING**
>
> You must be careful of recursive macro definitions—macros that refer to their own names within their definition. Such macro definitions cause TeX to continuously (and vainly) evaluate the macro, leading to an infinite loop. The following is an example of this:
>
> ```
> \def\itself{\itself}
> \itself
> ```

TeX macros have the added feature of being able to accept parameters when expanded, if a list of formal parameters has been specified in the macro definition. To create a macro using parameters, you would use this format:

```
\def macroname (list of formal parameters) {new text}
```

Here, the list of parameters is specified as #1, #1#2, #1#2#3, and so on. This is a powerful aspect of macros because it can change the output of an expanded macro based on the parameter in use. For example, the code

```
\def\parm#1{This is the #1 time I'll say this.}
\parm{first}
\parm{second}
\parm{last}
```

produces the following:

```
This is the first time I'll say this.
This is the second time I'll say this.
This is the last time I'll say this.
```

Each parameter that is used must be passed separately by enclosing it in braces, as in

```
\def\family#1#2{My #1 is #2.}
\family{wife}{Cindy}
\family{sister}{Sheila}
\family{father}{Myles}
```

which makes the following output:

```
My wife is Cindy.
My sister is Sheila.
My father is Myles.
```

You must specify an appropriate match of parameters in your macro definition. The macro definition

```
\def\mistake#1{This is wrong because of #2.}
```

is incorrect because it refers to a second parameter that is not specified in the formal parameter list.

Macros can be redefined in your document, but you should be aware that only the most recent definition will be applied. Also, macros defined within groups are only valid within the scope of the group.

Macro definitions can be nested within each other, as in the following:

```
\def\hey{Hey\def\hey{hey}}
\hey, \hey, \hey.
```

This has the following output:

```
Hey, hey, hey.
```

As with many topics within this book, we have examined only some of the highlights of TeX. There is much more to learn but, having covered the basics regarding macros, you can now look at the most popular extension of TeX, which uses macros to enhance the creation of documents. This extension is LaTeX.

LaTeX: An Enhancement of *TeX*

LaTeX is a collection of macros that build on the capabilities of TeX and provide a higher level of abstraction for the creation of documents. It is essentially a style library that encourages uniform formatting and typesetting across documents. LaTeX macros shift the emphasis away from the details of things such as "set text to 8-point slanted" to concepts that writers identify more readily with, such as the emphasis of a word or phrase. Thus, LaTeX macros have names that are more representative of the way writers *think* when they are writing.

Because LaTeX is an extension of TeX, you'll find it easy to become quickly productive in LaTeX, assuming that you have some experience in TeX. White space and spacing between paragraphs are handled in the same manner as in TeX. The special characters in TeX are the same in LaTeX, and comments are denoted using the % character.

The key differences between TeX and LaTeX become apparent as you learn more about the macros that define the layout of your document in a convenient fashion.

Defining a *LaTeX* Document

Every LaTeX document begins with the \documentclass command. The parameter passed to this command specifies what kind of document you want to write. The basic document classes are described in Table 19.2.

Table 19.2. Document classes.

Document Class	Description
article	Used for short reports, reference cards, presentations, scientific journals, and so on.
book	Used for complete books.
report	Used for reports having several chapters, theses, and so on.

To create a very basic LaTeX document, simply place some words between the two commands \begin{document} and \end{document}. The text that precedes the \begin{document} command is called the *preamble*, and the text that comes after is known as the *body*. So, you can create a very simple document such as the following:

```
\documentclass{article}
\begin{document}
What a small document this is.
\end{document}
```

To process this document (which you will edit in a file called gloves.tex), use the following command:

```
% latex gloves
```

This produces a DVI file and a log file in the same manner used by TeX. The DVI file can either be converted to PostScript, or viewed directly using xdvi.

You can specify options with the type of document in the \documentclass command using the following format:

```
\documentclass[option]{document class}
```

These options relate to the physical structure of the document. Some of the more common ones are listed in Table 19.3.

Table 19.3. \documentclass **options.**

Option	Description
10pt, 11pt, 12pt	The default font for the document, which is 10pt if not otherwise stated.
fleqn	Displays formulas as left-justified instead of centered.
leqno	Numbers formulas on the left side.
letterpaper, a4 paper	The paper size, which is letterpaper by default.
openright, openany	Starts the first page of a chapter on the right side, or on the next available page.
titlepage, notitlepage	Does or does not start a new page after the title.
twocolumn	Splits each page into two columns (useful for newsletters).
twoside, oneside	Generates double- or single-sided output.

Some of the differences between document classes are encapsulated by the defaults that they use for the options mentioned. For instance, articles and reports are single-sided by default, whereas books are not. Articles do not use the options for title pages and starting right-sided chapters because they do not understand what a chapter is. Thus, the document classes in LaTeX are smart enough to do the kind of layout that you expect for the type of document you need.

Packages

LaTeX also has the \usepackage command, which enables you to extend the capabilities of LaTeX even further by using an external *package* of features. The format is as follows:

\usepackage{*package name*}

package name can be any of several available packages. For instance, the doc package is used for the documentation of LaTeX programs, and the makeidx package provides support for the production of indexes.

You can also control what page styles LaTeX applies to your document by using the \pagestyle command. Table 19.4 describes the basic page styles available.

Table 19.4. Page styles.

Style	Description
empty	Sets the header and footers to be empty.
headings	Prints the current chapter heading and page number on each page with an empty footer.
plain	Prints the page number centered in the footer (the default page style).

You can also vary page styles in your document using the \thispagestyle command. This applies the supplied page style to the current page only.

Using Special Characters

LaTeX supports the use of international characters, such as umlauts (¨) and circumflexes (^). These characters are generated using a command variant on the letter itself. For example, the text

What a na\"\i ve ma^itre d' you are!

produces the following:

What a naïve mâitre d' you are!

International spacing can also be applied using the \frenchspacing command. This command tells LaTeX not to insert the usual extra space after a period.

Putting Structure into a *LaTeX* Document

LaTeX has commands that make it easy to enhance your document structurally, thus making it easier for the reader to digest. For the article document class, the commands are as follows: \section, \subsection, \subsubsection, \paragraph, \subparagraph, and \appendix. These commands, with the exception of \appendix, accept titles as arguments, and are declared before the body of text that they represent. LaTeX takes care of the rest; it sets the appropriate spacing between sections, section numbering, and title font. The \appendix command uses alphabetic increments in order to number succeeding appendix sections.

For the report and book classes, there are two additional commands: \part and \chapter. The \part command enables you to insert a section without affecting the numbering sequence of the chapters. You can suppress the appearance of a section in the table of contents by inserting a * character in the section command, as in the following:

```
\section*{I don't want to know about it}
```

You probably want to add a title to your document. This is done by specifying the arguments to the title commands and then calling the \maketitle command:

```
...
\title{Confessions of a LaTeX Enthusiast}
\author{Me}
\date
\begin{document}
\maketitle
...
```

To insert a table of contents in your document, issue the \tableofcontents command (big surprise) at the point where you want the table to appear. When you process your document with LaTeX, it needs two passes: one to make note of all the section numbers, and the other to build the table of contents from the information it collected in the first pass.

Adding Other Structural Elements

You can add cross-references to your document, which tie associated elements such as text, figures, and tables to text in other parts of your document. Use the \label command to set a point that you want to refer to, and give it an argument that is any name you choose. This name can then be referred to by the \ref and \pageref commands to generate a cross-reference containing the section number and page number that the section title appears on.

You can easily add footnotes using the \footnote command, which accepts the text of the footnote as an argument.

Structure is also enhanced by controlling the presentation of the text that appears between section titles. This can be easily managed by using LaTeX environments. Environments are specified by bounding a portion of text with \begin and \end commands, and passing an environment name to each command, as in the following:

```
\begin{hostileenvironment}
Looks like we're surrounded, said Custer.
\end{hostileenvironment}
```

LaTeX has many predefined environments for practical applications, as described in Table 19.5.

Table 19.5. Predefined environments.

Environment	Description
center	Centers text.
description	Used to present descriptive paragraphs.
enumerate	Used for numbered or bulleted lists.
flushleft	Paragraphs are left-aligned.
flushright	Paragraphs are right-aligned.
itemize	Used for simple lists.
quote	Used to quote single paragraphs.
quotation	Used for longer quotes that span several paragraphs.
tabular	Typesets tables with optional row and column separators.
verbatim	Produces typed text. Useful for representing programming code, for example.
verse	Used to control the linebreaks in poems.

Working with Figures and Tables

LaTeX also supports the variable placement (or "floating") of figures and tables in a document using the table and figure environments. A figure could be specified as follows:

```
\begin{figure}[!hbp]
\makebox[\textwidth]{\framebox[2in]{\rule{0pt}{2in}}}
\end{figure}
```

The options passed to the \begin{figure} command are placement specifiers that indicate your preferences for the location of the figure. LaTeX has to juggle the placement of floating figures and tables in a document by using these preferences, as well as internal guidelines such as the maximum number of floats allowed per page. In this example, you told LaTeX to keep the figure with its adjacent text (h), at the bottom of the next applicable page (b), or, failing that, on a special page with other floating figures (p). The ! character overrides LaTeX's best intentions for placing the figure, which may not necessarily jibe with what you are saying with the other placement specifiers.

Tables and figures can be labeled using the \caption command, which must be issued within the table or figure environment.

These are just some of the basics for using LaTeX, but hopefully they are sufficient to give you a place to start on the road to making your documents more visually appealing. You have probably noticed that LaTeX is somewhat easier to work with than TeX itself, because it hides much detail from you as an author.

VirTeX and IniTeX

Two other TeX-related programs work together but perform slightly different roles. The IniTeX program is used to create a TeX format (.fmt) file containing font definitions and macros. The VirTeX program can then quickly load this precompiled format file, much more quickly than TeX can. The command to use a format file is as follows:

```
$ virtex \&myformat sometexfile
```

The & character is necessary for VirTeX to recognize that it is loading a format file first; the & must be escaped using the \ character so as not to confuse the shell. The difference between VirTeX and IniTeX is that VirTeX can't be used to create TeX format files, but it executes much faster.

Summary

TeX is a document-formatting system for Linux that enables authors to produce their own high-quality publications. It produces documents that are portable among output devices such as printers or displays. TeX supports many typographical features and is particularly well-suited to the formatting of correct mathematical notation. It has macros that can be used to enhance the power of its basic command set. LaTeX, one of the most popular extensions to TeX, uses sophisticated macros to help you organize and typeset your documents based on its contents.

Printing

20

by Kamran Husain

IN THIS CHAPTER

This chapter introduces you to the topic of using the print facilities under Linux. We will cover the following topics:

- Printing files under Linux
- Getting the correct drivers for your hardware
- An introduction to printer device names
- Using the infamous `lpr`, `lpd`, and `lpc` commands
- Working with the `/etc/printcap` file
- How printing really works under Linux
- Using a PostScript printer with DVI support

Where To Start

If you are reading this chapter after being frustrated with the efforts of getting even a text file printed from Linux, you are at the right chapter.

On the other hand, if you have not even begun to deal with the act of printing from Linux to your printer, consider yourself lucky to have saved some time. Why, you ask? Well, chances are the default kernel you are booting with does not have printing enabled in it. If the capability is not there, you have to rebuild the kernel. How to rebuild and install the kernel has been dealt with in detail in Chapter 5, "Odds and Ends." All you have to remember is that you have to answer "y" (for yes) when asked whether you want printing enabled. The first time you build your kernel, the default is "n" (for no, don't build it). In later versions of the kernel, this option will be set to "y," but don't hold your breath just yet.

Once you have rebuilt and installed your kernel, you should be able to `cat` files to the `/dev/lp` or use the standard UNIX command `lpr` to print out the parallel or serial printer port on your PC.

If you have a serial printer, your printer will be one of the devices called `/dev/ttyS?`, `/dev/ttys?`, or `/dev/cua?`. If you have your printer hooked to the parallel, the devices would be `/dev/lp0`, and so on. Typing `cat file >/dev/????` should force what you type to the printer, where the question marks signify the device name. You may have to be logged in as `root` to be able to write to the printing device, because these ports usually have a restricted number of processes with write permission.

Printing Plain Text Files

Most plain text files in the UNIX world are boring. No page numbers, line breaks, formatting information, or logical page breaks. If you have a dot matrix printer, the output can cross over the perforations. The output on the pages can be flushed way to the left, making it look lopsided with extra spacing on the right side of the page.

For this reason, it's a good idea to send the text file through a program called a formatter. A simple formatter on Linux and UNIX is the `pr` command. The `pr` command is designed to format plain text for printing using a lineprinter. With `pr` you can add headers, footers, page numbers, date, margins, double-spaced lines, and so on. If you are a DOS user, you can think of the `pr` command as the `PRINT` command—in other words, a simple print utility.

Hardware and Drivers

We briefly touched the topic of printer drivers not being included in the default kernel. This section gives a little bit more detail on how to select your driver. There are two ways the kernel driver may be used to run the parallel printer ports. The first method, the original, is the polling driver. You will see this polling method used most often in most UNIX systems. The other method, the kernel driver, which may be used to run the parallel printer ports, is the interrupt driver. In principle, the interrupt driver only deals with the port when it gets an interrupt and should therefore be more efficient. In practice, people have found that efficiency depends on the type of machine. Selecting one or the other probably doesn't make too much difference in most situations.

For the polling driver, you may adjust its polling frequency with the program `tunelp` without kernel twiddling. The actual driver is in the kernel source file `lp.c`. To choose the interrupt driver instead of the polled, use the program `tunelp` to set it. You can get `tunelp` from the CD as part of the installation process or from the `sunsite` archives at `/pub/Linux/system/Printing /tunelp-1.3.tar.gz`.

Printer Device Names

On an XT bus system LPT1: becomes `/dev/lp0` (`major=6`, `minor=0`); on an AT system, LPT1: becomes `/dev/lp1` (`major=6`, `minor=1`). See Table 20.1 for device numbers for printers on Linux. See Chapter 53, "Writing Device Drivers," for a description of what major and minor mean. Basically, major refers to type of device and minor refers to the actual device if more than one device type can exist on the same machine. So if you have two parallel ports, the first is referred to with `major=6`, the next as `minor=0`.

Table 20.1. Device numbers for printers on Linux.

Name	Major	Minor	I/O address
lp0	6	0	0x3bc
lp1	6	1	0x378
lp2	6	2	0x278

For a serial printer, use the `/dev/ttyS?` or `/devttys?` device. Don't use the `/dev/cua?` device for serial printing, because these are usually reserved for modems. The `/dev/ttyS?` devices have `major=4` and the `/dev/cua?` devices have `major=5`.

The Infamous *lpr*, *lpd*, and *lpc* Commands

The `lpr`, `lpd`, and `lpc` commands are perhaps the programs hated the most by novices in the Linux community. If everything falls in place with these programs, you are set. If something is wrong, you have to know how these commands work together to get printing up and running.

You can always print directly to the printer by using the following command:

```
ls > /dev/lp0
```

Unfortunately, this command can interfere with other users trying to print. Also, this command may not even work if the computer is not able to time the sending of characters to the lineprinter correctly. On a slow printer, or a printer which is deselected or disconnected, this could cause your shell to hang.

What Linux does is spool the data. *Spooling* means collecting data into a file, and then starting up a background process to send the data to the printer. There is a spool area for each printer connected to your machine. Data designated for the printer is collected in the spool area at the rate of one file per print job. A background process—called the *printer daemon*—constantly scans the spool areas for new files to print. When one appears, the data is removed from the spool area and sent to the appropriate printer. When more than one file is waiting to be printed, they will be printed in the order they were completed. The spool area is really a queue.

The printer daemon needs the following information to do its job: the physical device to use, the spool area to look in, and if printing on a remote machine, the name of the remote machine and printer for remote printing. All this information is stored in a file called `/etc/printcap`.

There are five programs that use this information. These programs are in the `/usr/bin` and `/usr/sbin` directories: `lpr`, `lpq`, `lpc`, `lprm`, and `lpd`. The first four are used to submit, cancel, and inspect print jobs. The `/usr/sbin/lpd` program is the printer daemon. There are man pages for all these commands, which you should consult for more information.

The thing to remember is that by default `lpr`, `lprm`, `lpc`, and `lpq` operate on a printer called `lp`. You can define an environment variable called PRINTER to specify the printer name. For example, to print to the `hplj` printer, use `lp -Phplj` to override any setting of the PRINTER variable. Here is a quick introduction to some of the key commands related to printing under Linux:

- The `lpr` command submits a job to the printer.
- The `lpq` command shows you the contents of the spool directory for a given printer. Each file is specified by an ID and its location in the queue.
- The `lprm` command removes a job from the printer queue. You have to specify the ID returned for that job specified by `lpq`.
- The `lpc` command is the printer control command. This command lets you check the status of each printer and set its state. You can enable or disable printers and their queues. If no parameters are specified, `lpc` is in interactive mode, and you can type in your commands at a prompt. Replies to your commands are printed immediately. Type a ? for a list of commands you can use.

All these programs work off one directory, usually the /var/spool/lpd. Each printer has its own area under this directory to spool data in. For my ps printer, I have a /var/spool/lpd/ps directory.

The printer spool directories should belong to the *daemon* group and are both user and group read/writable, and world-*readable*. That is, the directory has to have permissions of -rwxrwxr-x (0775).

Each spool directory should contain four files: .seq, errs, lock, and status. These files should have the permissions -rw-rw-r-. The .seq file contains the job number counter for lpr to assign a job. The status file contains the message to be reported by lpc stat. The lock file is used by lpd to prevent itself trying to print two jobs to the same printer at once. The errs file is a log of printer failures and is not required. The status file has a text description of what the lpd program is doing with that file, for example printing, waiting, and so on.

The /etc/printcap File

The file /etc/printcap is a text file and is owned by root. The contents of /etc/printcap is not the easiest thing to read. Each entry in this file contains a description for a printer and how data is to be handled for that printer. For example, a printcap entry will define what physical device is to be used, what spool directory data for that device should be stored in, what preprocessing should be performed on the data, where errors on the physical device should be logged, and so forth. You can limit the amount of data that may be sent in a single job, or limit access to a printer to certain types of users.

You can have multiple printcap entries defining several different ways to handle data destined for the same physical printer. For example, a physical printer may support both PostScript and HP LaserJet data formats, depending on some setup sequence being sent to the physical printer before each job. It would make sense to define two printers, one of which preprocesses the data by prepending the HP LaserJet sequence, while the other prepends the PostScript sequence. Programs that generate HP data would send it to the HP printer, while programs generating PostScript would print to the PostScript printer.

Programs that change the data before it is sent to the physical printer are called *filters*. It is possible for a filter to send no data at all to a physical printer. An example of such a filter entry in a printcap file is shown in the following lines:

```
# Sample printcap entry with two aliases
myprinter¦laserwriter:\
# lp is the device to print to - here the first parallel printer.
    :lp=/dev/lp0: \
    # sd means 'spool directory' - where print data is collected
    :sd=/var/spool/lpd/myprinter:
```

Here's a brief summary of some of the entries in /etc/printcap. All fields in each entry are enclosed between a pair of colons and are denoted by a two-letter code. The two-letter code is followed by a value that depends on the type of field. There are three types of fields—string, boolean, and numeric. See Table 20.2 for a listing of some /etc/printcap fields.

Table 20.2. Some fields for `/etc/printcap`.

Code	Type	Description
lp	string	Specifies the device to print to, such as `/dev/lp0`
sd	string	Specifies the name of the spool directory for this printer
lf	string	Specifies the file to which errors on this printer are to be logged
if	string	Specifies the input filter name
rm	string	Specifies the name of a remote printing host
rp	string	Specifies the name of a remote printer
sh	boolean	Specifies this to suppress headers (banner pages)
sf	boolean	Specifies this to suppress end-of-job form feeds
mx	numeric	Specifies the maximum allowable print job size (in blocks)

Input filters are programs that take print data on their standard input and generate output on their standard output. A typical use of an input filter is to detect plain text and convert it into PostScript. That is, raw text is its input, and PostScript is its output.

When you specify an input filter, the printer daemon does not send the spooled print data to the specified device. Instead, it runs the input filter with the spooled data as standard input and the print device as standard output.

Sending your print data to a printer attached to another machine is done via the remote machine `rm` field and the remote printer `rp` field. Make sure that the print device field `lp` is empty. Note that data will still be spooled locally before being transferred to the remote machine, and any input filters you specify will also be run.

Suppressing form feeds (`sf`) is most useful if your printer is typically used for output from word-processing packages. Most WP packages create complete pages of data, so if the printer daemon is adding a form feed to the end of each job, you get a blank page after each job. If the printer is usually used for program or directory listings, however, having that form feed ensures that the final page is completely ejected, so each listing starts at the top of a new page.

The `mx` field enables you to limit the size of the print data to be spooled. The number you specify is in BUFSIZE blocks (1KB under Linux). If you specify zero, the limit is removed, enabling print jobs to be limited only by available disk space. Note that the limit is on the size of the spooled data, *not* the amount of data sent to the physical printer. If a user tries to exceed this limit, the file is truncated. The user will see a message saying `lpr: <filename>: copy file is too large`. This is useful if you have users or programs that may deliberately or accidentally create excessively large output. For PostScript physical printers, the limit is not useful at all because a very small amount of spooled PostScript data can generate a large number of output pages.

In order for any other machines to print using your printers, their names have to be registered in either the file `/etc/hosts.equiv` or `/etc/hosts.lpd`. Both files are simple text files with one host name per line. For security, add hosts to `/etc/hosts.lpd` only. Do not use `/etc/hosts.equiv` because that gives more access rights to tasks rather than simply sending print jobs out to the printer.

How It All Fits

Let's go through the steps of setting up printer support on /dev/lp1. Make sure you do this as root.

1. Create the spool directory for your printer, which we will call foobar for now. Make the permission -rwxrwxr-x.

```
mkdir /var/spool/lpd /var/spool/lpd/foobar
chown root.daemon /var/spool/lpd /var/spool/lpd/foobar
chmod ug=rwx,o=rx /var/spool/lpd /var/spool/lpd/foobar
```

2. In the directory /var/spool/lpd/foobar, create the necessary files and give them the correct permissions and owner:

```
cd /var/spool/lpd/foobar
touch .seq errs status lock
chown root.daemon .seq errs status lock
chmod ug=rw,o=r .seq errs status lock
```

3. Create the shell script input_filter in the directory /var/spool/lpd/foobar. You can have this as an empty file, too. Just be sure that the file is owned by root, group daemon, and is executable by anyone.

```
cd /var/spool/lpd/foobar
chmod ug=rwx,o=rx input_filter
```

4. Create the file /etc/printcap if it doesn't already exist. Remove all entries in it and add the test printcap entry given in Listing 20.1. Make sure the file is owned by root, and read-only to everyone else (-rw-r-r-).

Listing 20.1. A sample /etc/printcap file.

```
#
# Copyright (c) 1983 Regents of the University of California.
# All rights reserved.
#
# Redistribution and use in source and binary forms are permitted
# provided that this notice is preserved and that due credit is given
# to the University of California at Berkeley. The name of the University
# may not be used to endorse or promote products derived from this
# software without specific prior written permission. This software
# is provided "as is" without express or implied warranty.
#
# @(#)etc.printcap     5.2 (Berkeley) 5/5/88
#
# DecWriter over a tty line.
#lp|ap|arpa|ucbarpa|LA-180 DecWriter III:\
# :br#1200:fs#06320:tr=\f:of=/usr/lib/lpf:lf=/usr/adm/lpd-errs:
#lp:lp=/dev/lp0:sd=/var/spool/lp0:of=/usr/lib/lpf: lf=/usr/adm/lpd-errs
#
# Generic printer:
lp:lp=/dev/lp1:sd=/var/spool/lp1:sh
#
# typical remote printer entry
#ucbvax|vax|vx|ucbvax line printer:\
# :lp=:rm=ucbvax:sd=/var/spool/vaxlpd:lf=/usr/adm/lpd-errs:
#varian|va|Benson Varian:\
```

continues

Listing 20.1. continued

```
#  :lp=/dev/va0:sd=/var/spool/vad:mx#2000:pl#58:px#2112:py#1700:tr=\f:\
#  :of=/usr/lib/vpf:if=/usr/lib/vpf:tf=/usr/lib/rvcat:cf=/usr/lib/vdmp:\
#  :gf=/usr/lib/vplotf:df=/usr/local/dvif:\
#  :vf=/usr/lib/vpltdmp:lf=/usr/adm/lpd-errs:
#versatec¦vp¦Versatec plotter:\
#  :lp=/dev/vp0:sd=/var/spool/vpd:sb:sf:mx#0:pw#106:pl#86:px#7040:py#2400:\
#  :of=/usr/lib/vpfW:if=/usr/lib/vpsf:tf=/usr/lib/vcat:cf=/usr/lib/vdmp:\
#  :gf=/usr/lib/vplotf:vf=/usr/lib/vpltdmp:lf=/usr/adm/lpd-errs:\
#  :tr=\n\n\n\n\n\n\n\n\n\n\n\n\n\n\n\n\n\n\n\n\n\n\n\n\n\n\n\n\n\n\n\n\
#\n\n\n\n\n\n\n\n\n\n\n\n\n\n\n\n\n\n\n\n\n\n\n\n\n\n\n\n\n\n\n\n\
#\n\n\n\n\n\n\n\n\n\n\n\n\n\n\n\n\n\n\n\n\n\n\n\n\n\n\n\n\n\n\n:
#
#lp¦panasonic:lp=/dev/lp1:sd=/var/spool/lp/panasonic:lf=/usr/bin/mail:mc#1:\
#               ft=$$c$$p$$r$$f:hl#2:fl#3:ht=$$c$$n$$r$$t:sh:
#
# HP Laser jet plus
#lp¦hpj:\
#          :lp=/dev/lp1:\
#          :sd=/var/spool/lp1:\
#          :mx#0:\
#          :of=/var/spool/lp1/hpjlp:\
#          :lf=/var/spool/lp1/hp-log:
#
#lp¦Generic dot-matrix printer entry:\
#          :lp=/dev/lp1:\
#          :sd=/var/spool/lp1/lp:sh:\
#          :if=/usr/sbin/lpf:\
#          :df=/var/spool/lp1/filter.ps:\
#          :tf=/var/spool/lp1/filter.ps:\
#          :af=/var/spool/lp1/lp-acct:\
#          :lf=/var/spool/lp1/lp-err:
```

5. Start the lp daemon with the lpd command.

6. Do a test print using the command:

```
ls -l ¦ lpr -Pmyprinter
```

You can restrict remote users by group name by specifying the groups permitted, using one or more rg fields; for example, /etc/printcap - :rg=admin: restricts access to a printer to those users belonging to the group admin. You can also restrict access to those users with accounts on your system, by specifying the boolean flag :rs: in your /etc/printcap.

The Staircase Effect

The staircase effect results in lines printed one after another, with each line beginning where that last one ended. Usually, the output results in a few lines on the first page followed by many blank pages. An example of such an output is as follows:

one

two

three

four

Linux terminates each line of a file with a linefeed but not a carriage return. Therefore, the physical printing device should start each line below the end of the previous line. Some printers can be set to treat "linefeed" as "carriage return, linefeed," others cannot be set this way. If your printer can be set to treat "linefeed" as "carriage return, linefeed," then do that. If the printer cannot be modified, you should create a shell script filter that reads:

```
#!/bin/sh
if [ "$1" = -c ]; then
  cat
else
  sed -e s/$/^M/
fi
# the "echo -ne" assumes that /bin/sh is really bash
echo -ne \\f
```

Install this filter as the `if` filter by putting `:if=/usr/lib/lpf:` (or whatever) in your `/etc/printcap` entry for the printer.

Magic filters deduce their input files types from "magic numbers," which is a distinctive byte pattern at particular offsets. Magic filters are usually Perl scripts, Shell scripts, or C programs that simply identify the file type and then call the appropriate non-magic filter. A magic filter usage example is the "file" command which tries to interpret the type of file by reading the first few bytes.

PostScript Support

The Linux and UNIX community is completely PostScript dependent when it comes to documentation. If you don't have PostScript printing capability in your printer, there are times when you cannot even read documentation for software packages.

If you have access to a PostScript printer, no problem. Print all you want. On the other hand, if you want to save paper or do not have access to a PostScript printer, consider using Ghostscript. See Chapter 25, "Ghostscript," for more information about installing and using Ghostscript. In a nutshell, Ghostscript, which comes from the GNU project, is a PostScript interpreter that accepts PostScript input and generates output appropriate for X displays, printers, and some specialized display hardware and fax software.

There are a number of utilities that enable text to be printed to a PostScript device.

■ a2ps. This utility takes text and turns it into a PostScript document with headers and footers and page numbers. You can even print two pages on one sheet of paper.

- nenscript. The nenscript program is a clone of the commercial enscript program. The functionality is the same as that of a2ps.

- gslp. This is a PostScript program that comes with Ghostscript and is used to print a preamble to text files to convert the text files into PostScript. Check the man pages for gslp.ps.

Printing DVI Files

A DVI file is the processed output from a LaTeX or TeX input file. To print a DVI file to a PostScript printer, you can use dvips or eps. The dvips program converts DVI into PostScript. The output can be piped into Ghostscript or sent directly via lpr to a PostScript printer. eps is a program which converts DVI files directly into the standard Epson printer language. It is a DVI driver for Epson printers.

Summary

This chapter has given you a quick tour of the printing system under Linux. Armed with the information in this chapter, you should be able to get printing to work on your Linux machine.

IN THIS PART

PART

GUI

Installing X Window on Linux

21

by Kamran Husain

This chapter details the way to install X Window system for Linux. This version of X Window for Linux, called XFree86 Version 3.1.2, is an enhanced version of the X Window System Version 11 Release 6 with support for many versions of UNIX, including Linux. XFree86 supports considerably more hardware than the video hardware supported by the MIT standard release of X Window.

> **CAUTION**
>
> Please read this entire chapter *before* starting XFree86. If you are not careful, you could damage your hardware. Most important:
>
> XFree86 comes without a warranty of any kind. If you damage anything, even after reading these instructions, you are on your own.

Please note that even though I try to cover all the bases for installing X11 on your Linux system, I cannot cover all the hardware out there for PCs. In other words, this whole chapter is moot if you happen to have that one video card this version of XFree86 on Linux will smoke! So read all the items here carefully and see how they apply to your hardware. You could also check Chapter 2, "Types of Linux Available," for the listing of the hardware supported by this version of Linux. Check the HOWTO files for Hardware and Xfree86 for more up-to-date information.

> **NOTE**
>
> You can use the terms *X*, *XFree86*, *X11*, and *X Window* interchangeably, if you do not care about legal issues. Actually, however, XFree86 refers to the product of The XFree86 Project, Inc.

> **NOTE**
>
> You can also look at the installation documentation files and other manuals that come with XFree86 in your /usr/X11R6/lib/X11/etc directory. The main directory path is /usr/X11R6 for access to this tree, so that we are compatible with UNIX installations of X11R6.
>
> To read these documents, you need a working man program, as well as the groff package for formatting documents. Note that groff is required often to read man pages, so you should install the groff package, even though some distributions regard the groff package as optional.

This chapter covers the following:

- How to install X Window on Linux
- A brief introduction to XFree86

- Working with `XF86Config` and the `XConfig` file
- Running X Window system
- Introduction to X applications packages and compiling programs that use X

I also cover ways of finding information on X and XFree86 on the Internet and the ways to upgrade in the future. I discuss some of the problems you might have during installation, in addition to a list of the supported hardware.

Introduction to XFree86 and X11

X11 is a windowing system for UNIX clone operating systems. The X Window System with source code was issued by the MIT Consortium along with a set of original copyright notices. The X11 release on which XFree86.3.1.2 (or greater) is based is X11 Release 6.

The MIT Consortium's work is continued by the X Consortium, which just released an updated X called X11R6. Most commercial releases of Linux already include X11R6.

Some XFree86 servers are partly derived from X386 1.2, which was the X server distributed with X11R5. However, many servers have been developed in the past few years. Although the source and installation trees retain the X386 name—simplifying maintenance of the source trees—there is no connection between XFree86 and the commercial X386 product sold by SGCS. The XFree86 Project maintains technical contacts in an effort to keep changes that affect the user from diverging too radically from the workings of the products. Neither group is involved directly in the workings of the other.

The XFree86 Project, Incorporated

In the past, the XFree86 development team had several problems because it was not a legal organization, which made it impossible to become a member of the X Consortium, Inc. Not being a member was detrimental because new releases are provided only for members by the X Consortium before the official release date. This reason, along with several others, led to the founding of The XFree86 Project, Inc.

Installing XFree86

Xfree86 can be installed from the Red Hat CD-ROM using the RPM tool. The release is located in the `/RedHat/SRPMS` directory and is approximately 35MB. Installation from the CD-ROM or a hard drive is the only practical approach.

If you are downloading XFree from the Internet, the major files needed are listed in Table 21.1.

Table 21.1. Some distribution files for XFree86 available for FTP.

Filename	Description
X3128514.tgz	Server for 8514-based boards.
X312AGX.tgz	Server for AGX-based boards.
X312Ma32.tgz	Server for Mach32-based boards.
X312Ma8.tgz	Server for Mach8-based boards.
X312Mono.tgz	Server for monochrome video modes.
X312P9K.tgz	Server for P9000-based boards.
X312S3.tar.gz	Server for S3-based boards.
X312SVGA.tgz	Server for Super VGA-based boards.
X312VGA.tgz	Server for VGA/EGA-based boards.
X312W32.tgz	Server for ET4000/W32-based boards.
X312bin.tgz	The rest of the X11R6 binaries.
X312cfg.tgz	Config files for xdm, xinit, and fs.
X312doc.tgz	Documentation and manpages.
X312inc.tgz	Include files.
X312lib.tgz	Shared X libraries and support files.
X312fnt.tgz	Basic fonts.
X312ctrb.tgz	Selected contrib programs.
X312xtra.tgz	Extra XFree86 servers and binaries.
X312lkit.tgz	Server linkkit for customization.
X312fnt75.tgz	75-dpi screen fonts.
X312fnt100.tgz	100-dpi screen fonts.
X312fbig.tgz	Large Kanji and other fonts.
X312fscl.tgz	Scaled fonts (Speedo, Type1).
X312man.tgz	Manual pages.
X312pex.tgz	PEX binaries, includes, and libraries.
X312slib.tgz	Static X libraries and support files.

You can find the most recent versions on most Linux sites. You can find the C library (libc) and the dynamic loader (ld.so) in the GCC directory on the same Linux sites.

You can get the binary distributions of XFree86 for Linux via anonymous FTP from

```
tsx-11.mit.edu:/pub/linux/packages/X11/XFree86-3.1.2./binaries/Linux/els
```

or

```
sunsite.unc.edu:/pub/Linux/X11/XFree86-3.1.2
```

The files have names of the form X(ver)(name).tar.gz (version 3.1.2) or XF86-name .tar.gz where ver is the XFree86 version and name is the name of the package. If you already know which server you need to run, you should not get the *-svr* files. The filename form is XF86 servername.tar.gz, where servername is the name of the server to run.

The XFree86 distribution consists of several large gzipped tar files. You need the following setup to run XFree86. You have to have at least these versions.

Your computer needs main memory of at least 8MB and virtual memory of at least 16MB (that is, main memory plus swap memory). It is possible to run X on a 4MB machine if you take some precautions with memory usage.

In any event, your computer should have 16MB of virtual memory to run X Window. If you have 4MB of physical RAM, you should have 12MB of swap memory.

Because swapping is quite slow, you should have installed at least 8MB of RAM in your computer. With only 4MB of physical RAM, your X programs will run terribly slowly. If you want to run memory-hog programs from within X (for example, the C compiler gcc), you should have at least 16MB of main memory and another 16MB of swap memory.

The XFree86 distribution takes up about 17MB to 37MB of disk space depending on how many servers you install. You can save several megabytes of disk space by removing the X servers you do not need. However, if you plan to install more window managers than normal, you can expect to use about 35MB of disk space.

Before installing XFree86, you should make a backup of all files that you changed. They may not be usable, but they still hold a lot of information you might want to preserve. (Your old XConfig file will not be deleted, but it's always better to have a backup of this file.)

TIP

Do not use XFree86 3.1.*x* or earlier. From the Internet, you can get a copy of a version later than 3.1.1. Version 3.1.2 is on this book's CD-ROM.

There are two ways to install XFree86 on your machine: by using the setup utility or by using the manual procedure. The setup utility is the same menu-driven utility that you used in the original installation. The manual procedure is a bit more involved. It also requires attention to detail but enables you to have more control over every step. This procedure offers you the ability to stop and repeat steps instead of going through the complete installation process in the menu-driven option.

To avoid headaches, and get to sleep early, use the setup program and menus to do the installation process. If you really are in a foul mood, proceed with the following manual method.

To install the binary distribution manually, perform the following steps:

1. Log in as root or become root if you already are logged in.

2. Copy all the release's tar files to floppies or the hard drive, or know their location on the CD-ROM. If the CD-ROM or hard drive is not mounted, mount it now and ensure that you can get to the files from within Linux. Determine from Table 21.2 the name of the server type you need. For example, if you are using a color VGA monitor, you would want to use the XF86_SVGA server; for monochrome monitors including some EGA monitors (Do people still use them?), you might try XF86_Mono. You do not have to choose the server this minute, but realize that you can use only one of these servers.

3. Create the directory /usr/X11R6 (don't worry if it's already there).

4. Change your current working directory to /usr/X11R6 (cd /usr/X11R6).

5. Run umask 022 to make sure all the files are writable.

6. Run the following command on each *.tgz file to unzip and install its contents:

```
gzip -rc tarfilename | tar xvof -
```

Table 21.2. Types of servers in XFree86.

Type of server	Name
Color SVGA server	XF86_SVGA
16-color (S)VGA server	XF86_VGA16.
Monochrome server	XF86_Mono
S3 accelerated server	XF86_S3
8514/A accelerated server	XF86_8514
AGX support	XF86_AGX
Mach8 accelerated server	XF86_Mach8
Mach32 accelerated server	XF86_Mach32
Mach64 accelerated server	XF86_Mach64
ET4000/W32 accelerated server	XF86_W32

The flag (-r) for the gzip command tells it to recursively create all names and paths for the files in the tar file. The -c option will send the contents out to the standard output from where it will be piped to the tar command. The flags for the tar command tell tar to extract (x), be verbose (v), all files while preserving original ownership (o), from the file (f), designated by the standard input (-).

Repeat this step for all the tar files you have in your distribution.

The preceding step will overwrite all files from an older XFree86 version.

This step will not affect the `XF86Config` file, but the `XF86Config.eg` file will be overwritten. Most files in the distribution set will be overwritten. I repeat: Before installing XFree86, *back up every file you changed.*

After you finish installing XFree86, you have to configure it to match your system.

Setting Up Your XFree86 System

This section covers another one of the more difficult, time-consuming, and frustrating parts of installing XFree86: setting up a `XF86Config` file.

If you have XFree86 3.1.2 and your graphic card is listed in the `Hardware-HOWTO` file (see Chapter 1, "Introduction to Linux"), you should use the `XF86Config` program to do your configuration. This `XF86Config` program is a comfortable and safe way to set up your system. If your graphics card is not listed, you have some work ahead of you.

Your XConfig file is called `XF86Config.eg` and is in the `/usr/lib/x11` directory.

For more information, check the section called "The `XF86Config` File" in Chapter 22, "Configuring X Window on Linux."

One final check that you should do is to follow the link of `/usr/lib/X11/X` to the correct server. If you have an SVGA card, this link should be set, via an intermediate link if any, to `/usr/bin/X11/ XF86_SVGA`. If the link does not point to the right server, make it point to the correct server in `/usr/ bin/X11`.

Running X

At this point, you should be able to type `xinit` at the prompt and have X Window on your monitor. You have two options in starting X: Use the `xinit` program or use the `startx` shell script. The advantage to using the `xinit` program is that you can easily start X Window. The advantage to the `startx` script is that you can make modifications to how the environment variables are treated in bringing up X. With `xinit`, you are stuck with the defaults. In most cases, the defaults are what you want anyway. The `xinit` program executes statements in the order they are found in the `.xinitrc` file.

Once you have set up an XF86Config file, you probably want to run X. This is not done by running X, but by running startx. When running it for the first time, use the command

```
$ startx 2>&1 > Xstartup.log
```

This command gets a log file of the X startup by redirecting all output from stdout and stderr to a log file, Xstartup.log. If you encounter problems, the information in this file will help you get a clue as to what happened.

If you encounter any problems, please look at the XFree86 documentation files in /usr/X11R6/lib/X11/doc. These files provide a lot of information on what to do if problems occur. For more information, also look in the FAQs that are mentioned in those files.

Once you are in the environment of the window manager you chose in the .xinitrc file, you have to conform X Windows System's way of moving around. Please see the next few chapters to learn how to work with windows with three window managers: mwm, olwm, and fvwm.

Stopping X

To stop X and get back to the text-based console, you have to list the last application that was in the .xinitrc file. This last application could be the window manager, an xterm, or just about any application. When you quit X Window by stopping this application, you return to your character- or text-based terminal.

Another way to kill the window manager (and X) is to use the Ctrl-Alt-Backspace combination. This is not the preferred way of doing things because a more graceful way is to have the window manager be the last program started in the .xinitrc file, and exit from it to stop X and get back to console.

X Applications Packages

Several packages are related to X. I have mentioned the first two by name because they have a great influence on the look and feel of X.

■ XView. This package is included on the CD-ROM as part of the Slackware distribution. If you are installing from another source, you may want to read the next few paragraphs; otherwise skip to the next item.

The xview3L5.1.tar.gz package is a port to Linux of SUN's xview3.2 package by Kenneth Osterberg. It includes the xview toolkit, a set of extensions to X. The xview3L5.1.tar.gz gives you the look and feel of the OPEN LOOK extension to X (many recognize that from Open Windows from SUN). You can get it in the /pub/Linux/libs/X/Xview directory on sunsite.unc.edu.

To install XView, as root untar the tar file in any directory (/usr/src for example), read the documentation that comes with it (most importantly, the README), and run the INSTALL script. Note that you need about 25MB of free disk space to install XView completely (with examples). Some files are duplicated on this distribution. After running the INSTALL script and removing the xview3L5.1 directory, you need about 11MB. This would include all examples, which take about 2MB of disk space, along with 2.5MB for development libraries and files. If you do not want to compile any XView programs, you can spare this 4.5MB by removing the static (*.a) and stub (*.sa) libraries, as well as the examples.

> **TIP**
>
> Do not remove any shared (*.so) libraries while pruning the XView tree! Other applications may need these libraries in the future.

To run XView, you need at least 8MB of RAM, or even better, 16MB.

■ Motif. This is commercial software, so you will have to pay for it. You can find an advertisement from Metrolink (a company that provides a port to Linux) on tsx-11:/pub/linux/advertisements. There are companies other than Metrolink that sell Motif; every now and then advertisements will appear in the newsgroup comp.os.linux.announce.

■ Other Window managers. Both Motif and OPEN LOOK packages provide window managers different from the standard twm that comes with XFree86. XFree86 also includes the selection fvwm, a free window manager you may fall in love with. Many people do not like the twm window manager, so better window managers have been developed for XFree86. There are many X Window system managers available that run on Linux. A selection of these can be found on sunsite in the directory /pub/Linux/X11/window-managers.

■ Additional libraries. Sometimes you need additional libraries to run binary distributions or to compile an application. If the former is the case, you should find a pointer to that library in the README file of that package. If you do not have a pointer, you should look at the /pub/Linux/libs hierarchy at sunsite. Most libraries that work on Linux can be found there. If you cannot find it there and you have Internet access, follow the instructions on getting information in Appendix A, "Linux FTP Sites and Newsgroups."

■ Other X11 applications. There are many programs and applications available for X, way too many to list here. Look through the /pub/Linux/X11 hierarchy on sunsite.unc.edu for ports with many Linux packages. Most programs need no changes to run on Linux, so look at the generic X11 program archives, as well as at the Linux-specific sites. One of the largest X11 sites is ftp.x.org. In the /R5contrib directory you can find many programs for X11.

Compiling Programs That Use X

Please read the GCC-FAQ file. This is on the F series of the installation disks and CD-ROM. This file can also be found in the /pub/Linux/docs/faqs directories of sunsite before compiling any programs. Many questions on compiling programs with Linux are answered in this FAQ. Many Linux distributions include the most relevant FAQs in the directory /usr/doc, so you might look there first.

If you have the source code for a program that uses X11, it usually is shipped with an `Imakefile` instead of a `Makefile`.

`Imakefiles` are files that create `Makefiles` for your system. Discussing `Imakefiles` is beyond the scope of this book; however, you have to work with `Imakefiles` if you work at all with X sources. Just remember the shell script `xmkmf`, and you should be okay.

> **CAUTION**
>
> The `xmkmf` shell script actually runs the `imake` command with a set of arguments. The most common argument is the `-DUseInstalled` argument. If you examine `xmkmf`, (look in `/usr/ bin/X11/imake`), you will see that the `xmkmf` script is a basic wrapper around a call to `imake`. It's very tempting to use `imake` on a command line by itself. Do *not* do so. Run the `imake` command with the `-DUseInstalled` argument if you must run `imake` on the command line. If you do not use this argument, `imake` will behave as if it were re-creating the X Window system on your current directory.

Of course, before ever running `xmkmf`, you should have read the documentation that usually comes with such packages.

Run `xmkmf` in the directory that contains the `Imakefile`. If there is a hierarchy of directories with `Imakefiles`, you usually only have to run `xmkmf` in the `root` directory of that hierarchy.

The `xmkmf` command builds the `Makefiles` in all directories in the hierarchy.

Then you should run the `make` command with an argument to let `make` resolve its dependencies with the following command:

```
$ make depend
```

> **TIP**
>
> Don't be afraid if `include` files such as `stddef.h`, `varargs.h`, and so on, are not found. They are `gcc` proprietary header files and therefore not in the standard `include` directories.

After that, you can `make` the program by running `make`, and you can install your new utility (usually in `/usr/X11R6/bin`) by running

```
$ make install
```

The installation of the man pages is done by running

```
$ make install.man
```

Finding Information on X and XFree86 on the Net

There is an excellent document about XFree86 on the Internet by Matt Welsh, called "The Linux XFree86 HOWTO" document. This document will make an excellent resource for you as you install XFree86.

The ASCII version of this HOWTO document will be posted regularly to comp.os.linux.announce, comp.windows.x.i386unix, news.answers, and comp.answers. The latest version can be found on sunsite.unc.edu in the directory /pub/Linux/docs/HOWTO. This document will almost certainly be more current than any printed material because the electronic version is constantly updated.

For general X questions, you should read the FAQ and the FAQ-Xt. You can get these from ftp.x.org in the directory /R5contrib. Many Linux distributions include most relevant FAQs in the directory /usr/doc. Look on the CD-ROM for this directory.

If you have questions about the XFree86 package and cannot find an answer in the documentation files (XFree86, XF86Config, XF86_* manpages, or the README files in /usr/X11R6/lib/X11/doc), you may want to post a question to a newsgroup. The appropriate newsgroup for that purpose is comp.windows.x.i386unix. This newsgroup is dedicated to the XFree86 system. If you have a problem with the server and want to post a question to this newsgroup, you should provide enough information for those that want to help you. Here are some things that should be included in all postings concerning server problems:

- The operating system and which release you are running.
- Hardware you have (at least bus type [ISA/EISA/VLB/PCI], your graphic card including chip set, video RAM type #[D/VRAM], size, and speed).
- A concise description of the problem.
- A printout of the server startup (you can generate that by running startx 2>1 > Xerror.log or startx >& Xerror.log depending on whether you use a Bourne shell or C shell derivative.
- The used parts of the XF86Config. (It is not a good idea to include all lines commented out by a leading #.) This would be the largest part of your post, and most people will already know the copyright statements.
- A list of fixes you have already attempted.

Bug reports or questions on XFree86 can be sent directly to XFree86@Xfree86.org. This is the contact address of The XFree86 Project.

Newsgroups

There are some other newsgroups that cover X-related topics:

- comp.windows.x.apps—X applications
- comp.windows.x.intrinsics—X-intrinsic toolkit-related information

- ▦ `comp.windows.x.motif`—Motif extension to X

- ▦ `comp.windows.open-look`—OPENLOOK and the XView extension to X

Note that most of these groups have FAQ lists that are posted regularly to these groups. As always with regular postings, these can be obtained from `rtfm.mit.edu` via anonymous FTP.

Some Common Problems

Here are some of the problems you might see when you work with XFree86.

- ▦ No windows. All you get is a gray background and no windows. This is due to running without a window manager. Running X only starts the X server, not the window manager. You should use a script shown earlier in `startx`.

- ▦ Your Logitech serial mouse does not work. The keyword `Logitech` is reserved for older Logitech serial mice. Use the keyword `MouseMan` (or `Microsoft`) for newer mice. Logitech serial mice plugged into a PS/2 port require the keyword `PS/2`.

- ▦ You get errors about not finding any font files. First check the `XF86Config` file to see whether the directories in the font path are named correctly and contain fonts. If they are, run `mkfontdir` in each of those directories to set them up for use with X.

- ▦ After leaving X, your screen fonts are not restored. This is a known bug with some servers. There are utilities called `runx` or `restoretext` coming with `svgalib` that can help you in most cases. You can get them from `sunsite.unc.edu` in the file `/pub/Linux/libs/graphics/svgalib-1.2.10.tar.gz`.

- ▦ You will have some problems with the Diamond, Compaq AVGA, and S3 cards. This is what you have to live with when you are dealing with freeware.

- ▦ The server dies with the message `Cannot find a free VT`. XFree86 needs a free virtual terminal (VT) on which to run. So if you have put a `getty` process on every virtual console in your `/etc/inittab`, XFree86 is not able to start. The common practice is to leave `/dev/tty8` (for kernel messages) and `/dev/tty7` (for XFree86) free of a `getty` process.

This is not an exhaustive list. Please read the HOWTO documents in `/doc/HOWTO` on the CD-ROM for more information about other video card problems that are too specific to list here.

Supported Hardware

Currently, XFree86 Version 3.1.2 supports the following chip sets in the `XF86_SVGA` server. The list will be much much longer by the time this book hits the stands, so use the following list as a guideline:

Nonaccelerated chip sets:

- ▦ Tseng ET3000, ET4000AX, ET4000/W32

- ▦ Western Digital/Paradise PVGA1, WD90C00, WD90C10, WD90C11, WD90C24, and WD90C30

- Genoa GVGA
- Trident TVGA8800CS, TVGA8900B, TVGA8900C, TVGA8900CL, TVGA9000, TVGA9000i, TVGA9100B, TVGA9200CX, TVGA9320, TVGA9400CX, and TVGA9420
- ATI 28800-4, 28800-5, 28800-6, 28800-a
- NCR 77C22, 77C22E, 77C22E+
- Cirrus Logic CLGD6205, CLGD6215, CLGD6225, CLGD6235
- Compaq AVGA
- OAK OTI067, OTI077
- Cirrus CLGD5420, CLGD5422, CLGD5424, CLGD5426, and CLGD5428 chip sets
- Western Digital WD90C31 chip sets

These chip sets are all supported in 256-color (XF86_SVGA) and in monochrome mode (XF86_Mono) with the exception of the Cirrus chip sets, which are only supported in 256-color mode.

NOTE

If you have a grayscale display, you have to run the color server because grayscale behaves just like color, not like monochrome.

The monochrome server also supports generic VGA cards (using 64KB of the video memory as a single bank), the Hercules card, and the Hyundai HGC-1280. These drivers are not part of the XF86_Mono server by default. If you want to use these, you have to reconfigure your XF86_Mono server using the LinkKit, or of course, the source distribution—but the LinkKit needs less disk space and a shorter compile time.

XFree86 supports at least the following accelerated chip sets with separate servers:

- S3 86C911, 86C924, 86C801, 86C805, and 86C928 supported by the XF86_S3 server
- ATI mach8 supported by the XF86_Mach8 server
- ATI mach32 supported by the XF86_Mach32 server
- ATI Mach64 supported by the XF86_Mach64 server
- ET4000/W32 supported by the XF86_W32 server
- IBM 8514/a and true clones supported by the XF86_8514 server
- S3 Vision864 and Vision964.
- Weitek P9000.

The hardware that is not currently supported is:

- TIGA. TIGA will never be supported because it requires licensing materials from TI and may disallow source distributions.

- Microfield boards. Microfield boards will never be supported because they use proprietary and undocumented custom microcode interfaces.
- MGA chip sets (Matrox cards).

For some of these chip sets there are specific README files to be found in `/usr/X11R6/lib/X11/doc`. If there is one for the chip set you use, read it! In these READMEs, the specific options that can be used to configure the server are explained. Currently, there are special READMEs for ATI, Trident, Tseng, Western Digital, Cirrus, and manufacturer-specific chip sets.

More information on the servers can be found in their man pages. Another place to check is the `XFree86-HOWTO` file in the `sunsite` and `tsx-11` archives. The HOWTO document will generally be more up-to-date than any printed matter.

Summary

This section covered one of the hardest things you will have to do when installing a package on Linux—installing XFree86. Naturally, all of the possible problems you will face while installing this are too long to list here. After reading this chapter, though, you should have an idea of what you are getting yourself into and the general steps you have to take.

Do not despair if things don't work out just as the instructions say they will. You should be able to look at the configuration files to determine where the problem is and what might be done to fix it. If nothing works despite your best efforts, you have the recourse of knowing where to look for answers in FAQs, newsgroups, and FTP sites on the Internet for HOWTO and other documents on Linux.

Configuring X Window on Linux

22

by Kamran Husain

This chapter details the way to configure the X Window System for Linux. This version of X Window for Linux is called XFree86 Version 3.1.2.

This chapter covers the following topics with regard to configuring your X Window System:

- How to configure XFree86 on your system
- Working with `ConfigXF86` and the `XF86Config` file
- What the `.xinitrc file` is
- Your personal X resource file
- Using `xdm`
- Configuration of the window manager

Setting Up Your XFree86 System

This section covers another one of the most difficult, time-consuming, and frustrating parts of installing XFree86: setting up an `XF86Config` file.

If you have XFree86 3.1.2 and your graphic card is listed in the `Hardware-HOWTO` file (see Chapter 1, "Introduction to Linux"), you should use the `ConfigXF86` program to do your configuration. This `ConfigXF86` program is a comfortable and safe way to set up your system. If your graphics card is not listed, you have some work ahead of you.

The *XF86Config* File

To be able to set up an `XF86Config` file, you need to read from `/usr/X11R6/lib/X11/etc` these files: `README`, `README.Config`, `VideoModes.doc`, and `README.Linux`. You also need to read the man pages on the following topics: `XF86Config`, `XFree86`, `XFree86kbd`, and the server you are using.

The `XF86Config` file can be located in several places:

- `/usr/X11R6/lib/X11`. This is the standard location for the sample `XF86Config` file, but in some cases you cannot use it (for example, a read-only `/usr` partition).
- `/etc`.
- In your `home` directory.
- As `XF86Config.eg` in `/usr/X11R6/lib/X11`.

The Linux file system standard places the `XF86Config` file in `/etc/X11`. The XFree86 servers will not "expect" an `XF86Config` file at this location, so there must be a link from one of the places in the preceding list to `/usr/X11R6/lib/X11`. Find this link first and use it to access the file. This way, you can be sure your changes take effect.

To give you some hints, here is a list of what you need to set up the `XF86Config` file correctly:

- The server suitable for your system. To get a hint as to which is the correct one, run the `SuperProbe` program that comes with XFree86. It will identify your chip set, and you can look at the XFree86HOWTO file on the CD at the back of this book to see which server supports this chip set. Note that SuperProbe can detect far more hardware than XFree86 supports.

■ Your monitor's specifications, most importantly the maximum horizontal and vertical scan frequency ranges and the bandwidth. This information can be obtained from your monitor's datasheet.

■ The name of the chip set for your video card. For example, Tseng Labs, ET3000, ET4000, and so on.

■ The available dot clocks for your card or (if supported) the name of the programmable dot clock generator. Learn how to obtain these by reading the file /usr/X11R6/lib/X11/doc/ README.Config. Running XF86Config sets your system's dot clocks.

■ "Mouse type" refers to the protocol the mouse is using, not to the manufacturer. For example, a serial Microsoft mouse connected to the PS/2 port uses the PS/2 protocol, not the Microsoft protocol.

■ The type of device your mouse is connected to: serial or bus. (Usually you can use /dev/ mouse.)

■ Whether you want to use a national keyboard map or if you want to run the generic U.S. key table.

CAUTION

Do not share XF86Config files with people who do not have the same configuration (graphics card and monitor). By sharing, you could fry your monitor.

It isn't so hard to figure out modes for multisync monitors. Don't ever use a mode that you haven't verified as being within your monitor's specs. Even if you have exactly the same setup as the computer you're sharing the file with, check all modes before trying them. There are many people who run their computers from specs that may not damage their hardware but could damage yours.

Using *Xconfigurator*

Red Hat Linux comes with a utility called Xconfigurator. This is a menu-driven tool that will ask questions about your video card, monitor, and mouse, and then create an XF86Config file for you. Xconfigurator will ask some fairly in-depth questions about your video card and monitor. Gather up all your documentation about your machine's hardware before running Xconfigurator.

Examining the *XF86Config* File

The XF86Config file contains all the configuration parameters for your X Window installation. Space does not permit me to print the whole file. You will have to look in the directory /usr/lib/X11 for the XF86Config.eq file. Copy this XF86Config.eg file to XF86Config. Then edit the XF86Config file. The format of the XF86Config file consists of different sets that are listed in the following sections:

- Pathnames
- Font paths
- Keyboard type
- Mouse type
- Server type
- Video modes

Each of these sections describes your hardware configuration, location of files, or both, to the X server. Each section is enclosed by the words:

```
Section "SectionName"
< information for the section >
EndSection
```

The Pathnames

There is no reason to fiddle with the standard paths as provided in the sample XF86Config file. In fact, any distribution that provides a different path structure should have edited this section of the XF86Config.sample or the template XF86Config file for ConfigXF86. You do have to know where these paths are pointing to in case of difficulties.

Your XF86Config file should look similar to the lines from my XF86Config file, as shown in Listing 22.1.

Listing 22.1. Font paths.

```
#
# Multiple FontPath entries are allowed (which are concatenated together),
# as well as specifying multiple comma-separated entries in one FontPath
# command (or a combination of both methods)
#
FontPath        "/usr/X11R6/lib/X11/fonts/misc/"
FontPath        "/usr/X11R6/lib/X11/fonts/Type1/"
FontPath        "/usr/X11R6/lib/X11/fonts/Speedo/"
FontPath        "/usr/X11R6/lib/X11/fonts/75dpi/"
# FontPath      "/usr/X11R6/lib/X11/fonts/100dpi/"
```

To see whether these lines are correct, please look into each of the directories mentioned in Listing 22.1 to see whether they have files in them. If these directories are empty, you do not have the fonts installed, or they may be at another location.

The Keyboard Section

You should specify the `ServerNumlock` option. This is an easy way to specify your keyboard for XFree86. Otherwise, only those keyboard modifications needed for international keyboard support have to be set manually. In a typical `XConfig` file, this section looks like the one shown in Listing 22.2.

Listing 22.2. Keyboard selection.

```
#
# Keyboard and various keyboard-related parameters
#
Section "Keyboard"
  AutoRepeat 500 5
  ServerNumLock
# Xleds        1 2 3
# DontZap
#
# To set the LeftAlt to Meta, RightAlt key to ModeShift,
# RightCtl key to Compose, and ScrollLock key to ModeLock:
#
# LeftAlt      Meta
# RightCtl     Compose
# ScrollLock   ModeLock

# EndSection
```

The Pointer Section

The pointer section keyword is the name for the protocol the mouse uses. The available protocol names are listed in the `XF86Config` man page.

The Logitech serial mouse uses several keywords. The MouseMan uses the MouseMan keyword. The more recent Logitech serial mouse uses the Microsoft keyword. The older Logitech serial mouse uses the Logitech keyword.

Any mouse connected to the PS/2 port uses the PS/2 keyword even if it is in fact a serial mouse.

TIP

If you are not sure which kind of bus mouse you have, look at the kernel's startup messages. They identify the bus mouse type.

> **CAUTION**
>
> Ensure that the kernel bus mouse driver is using the same IRQ as the bus mouse. If not, you have to change the IRQ and rebuild the kernel. The IRQ for bus mouse devices is given in `/usr/src/linux/include/linux/busmouse.h`. The macro `MOUSE_IRQ` contains this IRQ and is set to `5` by default.

The following is a list of device names for the mouse selection:

- `/dev/inportbm` Use for the Microsoft bus mouse. Note that this uses the bus mouse protocol, not the Microsoft protocol.
- `/dev/logibm` Use this for the Logitech bus mouse. Note that this uses the bus mouse protocol, not the Logitech protocol.
- `/dev/psaux` Select for a PS/2 or quick port mouse. This uses the PS/2 protocol.
- `/dev/atibm` For the ATI XL bus mouse. Note that the ATI GU bus mouse is a Logitech or Microsoft bus mouse, depending on the version you have.
- Other supported mice are serial mice; therefore, the device names are the same as the serial devices (`/dev/ttyS?` or `/dev/ttyS??` for Linux).

> **TIP**
>
> If you have a two-button mouse, you might want to emulate the third button by setting `Emulate3Buttons` in the mouse section. Emulation is accomplished by pressing both buttons simultaneously. There are quite a number of other settings available, but they usually are not needed. Look at the `XF86Config` man page for a list of available settings.

You have to select one type of mouse and its baud rate if it's serial. Note in Listing 22.3 that I have "uncommented" the Microsoft mouse selection for my mouse and the 1200-baud rate line, and you will have to uncomment the line that matches your mouse selection. The 1200-baud rate seems to work fine with older mice and using the 9600 rate did not result in a speed difference for newer mice. Your results may vary.

Listing 22.3. Mouse selection.

```
#
Section "Pointer"
# Mouse definition and related parameters
#
#MouseSystems  "/dev/mouse"
Microsoft      "/dev/mouse"
#MMSeries      "/dev/mouse"
#Logitech      "/dev/mouse"
```

```
#MouseMan      "/dev/mouse"
#Busmouse      "/dev/mouse"
  BaudRate     1200
#  BaudRate    9600
#  SampleRate 150
#  Emulate3Buttons
... <deleted some stuff here > ...
EndSection
```

The Server Section

If you want to identify the chip set your graphics card uses, run `SuperProbe`, a program that comes with XFree86 and is capable of identifying a wide range of graphics hardware. Note that `SuperProbe` can probe far more hardware than XFree86 supports.

Listing 22.4 shows a plain setting for a 640×480 monitor for X with a virtual space of 800×600. A virtual space is an area where the display portion of your monitor is mapped onto. Your monitor is a window into this space.

Listing 22.4. Server selection.

```
#
# First the 8-bit color SVGA driver
#
vga256

#
# To disable SpeedUp, use NoSpeedUp
#
#  NoSpeedUp
#  Virtual    1152 900

  # Virtual   800 600
  Virtual     640 480
  ViewPort      0 0
  # Modes               "640x480" "800x600" "1024x768"
  # Modes               "640x480" "800x600"
  Modes                 "640x480"

#
# Next the 1-bit mono SVGA driver
#
vga2

  Virtual     800 600
  ViewPort      0 0
  Modes                 "640x480"
  # Modes         "800x600" "640x480"
```

Setting Up Video Modes

This is the hardest part. Please read `VideoModes.doc` before beginning. If you are using `ConfigXF86` (which I strongly recommend), and your monitor is not in the database, choose the generic modes and start making your own modes from there. If you do not have `ConfigXF86`, read the tutorial on building modes in the `README.Config` file.

> **NOTE**
>
> I know this entire chapter is full of warnings. Please do not be alarmed. Just be careful and read the instructions for each step before taking it.

`ConfigXF86` includes a neat utility to tune video modes. Because there is no check on the usability of a mode, you have to check the mode data against your monitor's specifications before testing the mode. The first line of the tuning modes screen gives you information on the specifications of the mode. You have to continuously check that these values are within your monitor's capabilities before testing that mode.

See Listing 22.5 for the common video modes for XFree86.

Listing 22.5. Video modes.

```
Section "Device"
    Identifier "Generic VGA"
    VendorName "Unknown"
    BoardName "Unknown"
    ChipSet "generic"
#   VideoRam 256
#   Clocks 25.2 28.3
EndSection

# ********************************************************************
# Screen sections
# ********************************************************************

# The color SVGA server

Section "Screen"
    Driver      "svga"
    Device      "Generic SVGA"
    Monitor     "Generic Monitor"
    Subsection     "Display"
        Depth       8
        Modes       "640x480"
        ViewPort    0 0
        Virtual     800 600
    EndSubsection
EndSection

# The 16-color VGA server
```

```
Section "Screen"
    Driver     "vga16"
    Device     "Generic VGA"
    Monitor    "Generic Monitor"
    Subsection "Display"
        Modes      "640x480"
        ViewPort   0 0
        Virtual    800 600
    EndSubsection
EndSection

# The Mono server

Section "Screen"
    Driver     "vga2"
    Device     "Generic VGA"
    Monitor    "Generic Monitor"
    Subsection "Display"
        Modes      "640x480"
        ViewPort   0 0
        Virtual    800 600
    EndSubsection
EndSection
```

The Mode line in a video section can have up to 10 values. Be very careful when modifying these values because a wrong setting may wind up destroying your monitor! It does not matter if these are not present because defaults can be used. A typical line to override defaults for a monitor would be:

```
"640x400"  28 640 480 728 776 480 480 482 494
```

The 10 values in order from left to right are shown in the following section. These values only make sense to video engineers or those folks who have to work with a monitor not defined in the default modes. Check your monitor's hardware specifications and get the values from there to fill in these ten parameters. The following are the fields to set:

- Label for screen resolution; for example, 640×480 or 1024×768.
- The clock frequency in mHz.
- The Horizontal Display End in number of visible dots per line on the screen.
- The Start Horizontal Retrace value. This specifies the number of pulses before the video sync pulse starts.
- The End Horizontal Retrace value defines the end of the sync pulse.
- The Horizontal Total value. This is the total number of dots per line invisible and visible.
- The Vertical Display End value. The number of visible lines on the screen.
- The Start Vertical Retrace value. The number of lines before the sync pulse starts.
- The End Vertical Retrace value is the number of lines at the end of the sync pulse.
- The Vertical Total value. The total number of lines, invisible plus visible, on the screen.

Multiscan monitors handle frequencies of 15 to 40 mHz. Some monitors work at 72 mHz vertical scan to prevent the flicker. You have to be able to calculate the frequency from the monitor's specification and come up with these numbers. A good place to start would be the XFree86-HOWTO document on how to get these values. Keep in mind that your video monitor is just a glorified television. You give it wrong values and you can fry it.

International Keyboard Layout for XFree86

XFree86 servers are able to read the key table from the Linux kernel, so you need to set up only one keyboard layout file (for the kernel). There are some restrictions, though; the kernel can support more keyboard functions than X11. X11 can only modify one of the four key tables. This modifier is called ModeShift.

Configurable keys for the ModeShift modifier are LeftAlt, RightAlt (=AltGr), RightCtl, and ScrollLock.

Usually the AltGr key is used for international keyboard modifications. To enable the XFree86 server to read the AltGr key table from the kernel, you should put the following line in the .olvwmrc file:

RightAlt "ModeShift"

Besides supporting only one additional key map, X11 cannot use *dead* keys. A key is called *dead* if when it is typed, it does not print a character until a second character is typed. A typical example is an accent key. Such keys are not supported by X11, so you need to replace all dead-key symbols with non-dead equivalents. Table 22.1 lists what you have to change.

Table 22.1. Key symbols.

Dead	*Non-Dead*
dead_tilde	ASCII tilde
dead_grave	grave
dead_circumflex	ASCII circum
dead_acute	apostrophe
dead_diaeresis	diaeresis

Instead of supporting dead keys, XFree86 supports a Compose key. This feature is described in the XFree86kbd man page and can be modified by assigning the Compose function to one of the keys. By default the ScrollLock key has the Compose function.

If you still want to have the dead keys on the console, you will have to use an xmodmap file to map the keys to the correct symbols under X. This is also the method that must be used with earlier versions of XFree86. On sunsite in the directory /pub/Linux/X11/misc, you can find sample xmodmap files for several languages. Note that you have to set the ModeShift modifier to get the right key table working.

Please read the `kbd.FAQ` that comes with the `kbd` package for Linux. You will find many hints for modifying your keyboard layout on the console, as well as for X.

The *.xinitrc* File

To use X, you need a startup file that calls the local modifications, the window manager, and an application you want to use right after X has started. If you are using `startx` (or `runx`) to start X, this startup file is called `xinitrc`. There is a standard `xinitrc` file, `/usr/lib/X11/xinit/xinitrc`, which is the traditional location for this file. The Linux file system standard places this file in `/etc/X11/xinit/xinitrc` in order to allow a read-only mounted `/usr partition`, so look in that location first.

If you are not content with what this file does (for instance, if you want to use a different window manager), you should copy it to the file `.xinitrc` in your home directory. After copying the file, you can edit it. Look at the man pages for `startx` and `xinit` for more information.

Note that both the `.xinitrc` and the `.Xresources` files must be readable and executable, so run the following commands on these files after editing them. You only have to run the `chmod` command once on the application.

```
$ chmod u+rx .xinitrc .Xresources
```

This command makes these files executable.

See Listing 22.6 for a sample `.xinitrc` file.

Listing 22.6. Sample `.xinitrc` file.

```
 1  #!/bin/sh
 2  # $XConsortium: xinitrc.cpp,v 1.4 91/08/22 11:41:34 rws Exp $
 3  # modified by obz

 4  userresources=$HOME/.Xresources
 5  usermodmap=$HOME/.Xmodmap
 6  sysresources=/usr/lib/X11/xinit/.Xresources
 7  sysmodmap=/usr/lib/X11/xinit/.Xmodmap

 8  # merge in defaults and keymaps

 9  if [ -f $sysresources ]; then
10      xrdb -merge $sysresources
11  fi

12  if [ -f $sysmodmap ]; then
13      xmodmap $sysmodmap
14  fi

15  if [ -f $userresources ]; then
16      xrdb -merge $userresources
17  fi
```

continues

Listing 22.6. continued

```
18 if [ -f $usermodmap ]; then
19     xmodmap $usermodmap
20 fi

21 # Set the background to a dull gray
22 if [ -f /usr/bin/X11/xsetroot ]; then
23 xsetroot -solid gray32
24 fi

25 if [ -f /usr/bin/X11/xclock ]; then
26         xclock -geometry 80x80 &
27 fi

28 olvwm &
29 # fvwm &

30 xterm  -e /bin/bash
```

The line numbers in this listing have been added for your benefit. Let's look at these lines in greater detail.

Lines 4 to 7 set the resource environment variables for the X Window installation for your system. Change these to the path of your system's X Window system distribution.

Lines 9 through 20 check for the existence of these resources and then run the appropriate program, xmodmap or xrdb, with these resources as parameters. I will cover xmodmap and xrdb in Chapter 23, "Using Motif." For now you can use this the way it stands.

Lines 22 to 24 check for the xsetroot program, and if present, execute it to set the background to a solid color, gray32.

The olvwm & command in line 28 starts the OPEN LOOK window manager for you. If you want to use fvwm instead of olvwm, uncomment line 29 and comment line 28 instead. The window manager must be run in the background if you have more commands following this one.

Line 30 starts a terminal to work with. Because this is the last line in the .xinitrc file, exiting this terminal causes your X session to stop. If you want to start more xterms, you can start them from within this xterm.

A simpler .xinitrc file to start with would be the following:

```
xterm -name Console &
olvwm
```

You can then enhance this .xinitrc file with what you want.

The Personal X Resource File

Sometimes you won't be content with default settings for applications that don't have a configuration file of their own. You can change some of these defaults by setting X resources in the .Xresources file in your home directory.

> **NOTE**
>
> You should know what effects setting the resources will have on the programs you use. Read the man pages for the program and for xrdb before editing the .Xresources file. See Chapter 2, "Types of Linux Available," and Chapter 25, "Ghostscript," for more information about X resources.

A resource file looks like an application default file. The difference is that in the resource file, resources for several applications are set. You should use the full names (*Progname.Resourcename*) instead of abbreviating the program name with an asterisk. Examples of application default files can be found in the /usr/X11R6/lib/X11/app-defaults directory. The resources available for a single application are usually shown in the man pages for that application.

If you are running a color server, you might want to put the following lines into your .Xresources file if some programs start in black and white:

```
#ifdef COLOR
*customization: -color
#endif
```

If this change is made, the program *foo* will read both the *Foo* and the *Foo-color* application default file from /usr/X11R6/lib/X11/app-defaults. The usual behavior is for *Foo* only to be read.

> **NOTE**
>
> If you *are* running a color server, the preceding code definitely should be added to the system .Xresources file. You might mention that to the person or entity who maintains the program you are running.

Note that the black-and-white color scheme of a program may be caused by the program rather than its resources.

The -xrm can be used with most X programs to override the parameters set in your .Xresources file. The usage is

```
-xrm "resource"
```

Alternatively, you can use xrdb <*filename*> command to enforce any changes you have made in <*filename*> apply to your current session.

Using *xdm*

If you want to run X on your system all the time, you could run xdm from the system startup. xdm is preconfigured on most systems, so you should not have to edit any of the xdm configuration files. Usually a run level is attached to an X-only system (look at /etc/inittab). All you have to do to get it working is change the default run level. On systems that use an init without run levels (run man init to see whether your system uses an init), you should look into the /etc/rc and /etc/rc.d/ rc.local files; you usually only have to remove comment signs at the beginning of a line that calls xdm. If no such line is present, you probably have a system that has no preconfigured xdm. In any event, xdm by default runs your .xinitrc file for you.

Configuration of the Window Manager

Window managers are a user- and site-specific issue. Several window managers are available for Linux. The configuration of one window manager is quite different from that of another. The window manager used in the configuration is usually explained in your .xinitrc file, so look there. The most commonly used window managers for Linux are

- ▪ olwm or olvwm for the OPEN LOOK Window manager. (It is on the CD at the back of this book.)
- ▪ mwm for the Motif window manager, possibly the most common commercial window manager. You have to buy it along with Motif.
- ▪ twm. (It is part of the XFree86 distribution on the CD at the back of this book.)
- ▪ fvwm. (This seems to be the most popular freely available window manager and is on the CD at the back of this book.)

I discuss some window managers in greater detail in the next few chapters on OPEN LOOK and Motif.

Compiling Programs That Use X

Before compiling any programs for X, please read the GCC-FAQ file. This file can be found in the pub/Linux/docs/faqs directories of sunsite. Many questions on compiling programs with Linux are answered in this FAQ. Many Linux distributions include the most relevant FAQs in the directory /usr/doc, so you might look there first.

If you have the source code for a program that uses X11, it is usually shipped with an Imakefile instead of a Makefile.

Imakefiles are files that create Makefiles for your system. Discussing Imakefiles is beyond the scope of this book; however, you will have to work with Imakefiles if you work at all with X sources. Just remember the shell script xmkmf, and you should be okay.

> **TIP**
>
> xmkmf is an abbreviation for X Make Makefile.

> **CAUTION**
>
> The xmkmf shell script actually runs the imake command with a set of arguments. The most common argument is the -DUseInstalled argument. If you examine xmkmf, (look in /usr/ X11R6/bin/); you will see that the xmkmf script is a basic wrapper around a call to imake. It's very tempting to use imake on a command line by itself. Do not do so. Run the imake command with the -DUseInstalled argument if you must run imake on the command line. If you do not use this argument, imake will behave as if it were re-creating the X Window system on your current directory.

Of course, before ever running xmkmf, you should read the documentation that usually comes with such packages.

Run xmkmf in the directory that contains the Imakefile. If there is a hierarchy of directories with Imakefiles, you usually only have to run xmkmf in the root directory of that hierarchy.

The xmkmf command builds the Makefiles in all directories in the hierarchy.

Then you should run the make command with an argument to let make resolve its dependencies, using the following command:

```
$ make depend
```

> **TIP**
>
> Don't be afraid if include files, such as stddef.h, varargs.h, and so on, are not found. They are gcc proprietary header files, and therefore not in the standard include directories.

After that, you can make the program by running make, and you can install your new utility (usually in /usr/X11R6/bin) by running this line:

```
$ make install
```

The installation of the man pages is accomplished by running

```
$ make install.man
```

Some Common Problems

Some of the problems you might see when you work with XFree86 are outlined in the following list.

- No windows—all you get is a gray background and no windows. This is due to running without a window manager. Running X only starts the X server, not the window manager. You should use a script shown earlier in startx in Chapter 21, "Installing X Window on Linux."

- Your Logitech serial mouse does not work. The keyword `Logitech` is reserved for older Logitech serial mice. Use the keyword `MouseMan` (or `Microsoft`) for newer mice. Logitech serial mice plugged into a PS/2 port require the keyword `PS/2`.

- You get errors about not finding any font files. First check the `XF86Config` file to see whether the directories in the font path are named correctly and contain fonts. If they are correct, run `mkfontdir` in each of those directories to set them up for use with X.

- After leaving X, your screen fonts are not restored. This is a known bug with some servers. There are utilities called `runx` or `restoretext` included with `svgalib` that can help you in most cases. You can get them from sunsite.unc.edu in the file `/pub/Linux/libs/graphics/svgalib-1.2.10.tar.gz`.

- You will have some problems on uncommon, extremely new, or extremely old cards. This is what you have to live with when you are dealing with freeware.

- The server dies with the message `Cannot find a free VT`. XFree86 needs a free virtual terminal (VT) on which to run. So if you have put a `getty` process on every virtual console in your `/etc/inittab`, XFree86 is not able to start. The common practice is to leave `/dev/tty8` (for kernel messages) and `/dev/tty7` (for XFree86) free of a `getty` process.

This is not an exhaustive list. Please read the `HOWTO` documents in `/usr/docs` on the CD-ROM for more information about other video card problems that are too specific to list here.

Compiling Sources for XFree86

You do not typically want to compile sources for XFree86 unless you really want to make changes to the sources because something is not working. You will need a lot of disk space and CPU time to do a complete build of the XFree86 system. Anything you need to know for compiling XFree86, you can find in the following files (in `/usr/X11R6/lib/X11/etc`): INSTALL, README, and README.Linux.

Note that you should not compile XFree86 to get rid of hardcoded restrictions (on the maximal pixel clock, for example) because without these restrictions, your hardware will probably break down.

To build a server that includes only those drivers you need, you should use the `LinkKit` instead of compiling the complete system. This is a little easier than trying to build it from scratch. The `LinkKit` package is specific and complicated and is therefore beyond the scope of this chapter.

Read `/usr/X11R6/lib/Server/README` for a description of how to use `LinkKit`. This file is not included in the standard XFree86 tar files but is part of the file that includes the `LinkKit`.

For adding drivers to the SVGA servers, you need the `LinkKit` only.

The documentation on how to build servers can be found in the `/usr/X11R6/lib/Server/VGADriverDoc` directory after installing the `LinkKit` package.

Summary

This chapter covered the topic of configuring the XFree86 system. After reading this chapter, you should have an idea of how to set up your `XF86Config` file to generate your X environment. Just remember to start with the basic configuration settings for VGA cards and then make enhancements. Keep backups of your work and do not change the video settings unless you know what you are doing. If nothing works despite your best efforts, you have the recourse of knowing where to look for answers in FAQs, newsgroups, and FTP sites on the Internet for HOWTO and other documents on Linux.

Using Motif

23

by Kamran Husain

In this chapter, you will cover the following topics:

- Installing Motif on your Linux machine.
- Some of the basic concepts required for using X Window. Displays, windows, screens, and the Client Server Architecture in X are introduced.
- An introduction to window managers, specifically the Motif Window Manager (mwm).
- Navigating in mwm windows with the keyboard and mouse.
- Widgets and their characteristics.
- Customizing your desktop with resource files and client applications, and how to set your environment to your liking.
- Using some standard X tools available in Linux.

The following assumptions are made about you, the reader, as we go further into this chapter:

- You have completely read Chapter 21, "Installing X Window on Linux," and have the X11R6 version of X Window, called XFree86, installed on your machine.
- You have played at least a little with Linux or UNIX, and know the syntax of using some basic UNIX commands such as find, cpio, tar, and ln.

> **CAUTION**
>
> As you did with XFree86, please read this entire chapter thoroughly before proceeding with the installation.

A Brief Introduction to Window Managers and Motif

How the windows in an X session are arranged is a function of a special program called the *window manager*. The window manager controls the look and feel of all the windows on a particular display. The window manager enables the user to move, restack, resize, and iconify windows (that is, reduce windows to an icon).

X Window comes with three window managers by default. These managers are called the Freeware Window Manager (fvwm), the Tab Window Manager (twm) and the Open Look Window Manager (olwm). The twm is also referred to as Tom's Window Manager, after its author, Tom LaStrange. Earlier versions of X also offered the Universal Window Manager (uwm); however, this is no longer offered because it does not conform to the X Consortium's *Inter-Client Communications Conventions Manual* (ICCCM) standards. Please see Chapter 24, "OPEN LOOK and OpenWindows."

Window managers in X are different from other windowing system managers because you are allowed to choose whichever manager you like. As long as a manager follows the ICCCM standard, it can serve as your window manager.

The most prevalent commercial Linux (or UNIX-based) window manager today is the Motif Window Manager (mwm) from the OSF/Motif distribution. In fact, if you use fvwm, you see the similarities between fvwm and mwm. The Motif Window Manager is more important now than ever before, because it has been adopted by Common Open Software Environment (COSE) as the standard interface for future UNIX GUIs. It's most famous for its borders around all the windows it displays.

Motif applications look more like a Mayan temple than a menu system. Almost every item on the screen is rectangular. A rectangular button rests on a rectangular menu bar, which may rest on another rectangular form, which sits on a square window. We will discuss Motif in great detail in this chapter.

NOTE

The latest version at the time of writing was Motif 2.0. There are several updates to Motif (1.2.3, 1.2.4, and so on), but Motif 2.0 is a major release from the last major release 1.2.4. The 2.0 release includes a lot of bug fixes, and adds Widgets to its list of convenience functions. Get an upgrade if you are running an older version, and you may be surprised to see some of your existing bugs disappear!

Getting Motif for Linux

Unlike most of the software for Linux, Motif is not free and is not shareware. You have to pay for a Motif license. The cost is approximately $150. I have listed three vendors here that can sell you Motif for Linux. Due to lack of time before going to press, there was no time to research other vendors; you can check the Internet resources listed in Appendix A, "Linux FTP Sites and Newsgroups," for more information.

Metrolink Incorporated
4711 North PowerLine Rd.
Fort Lauderdale, FL 33309
(305) 938-0283
sales@metrolink.com

SWiM $149.95 (US)
ACC Bookstore
136 Riverside
Westport, CT 06880
(800) 546-7274
orders@acc.corp.com

MOO-TIFF
InfoMagic
11950 N. Highway 89
Flagstaff, AZ 86004
(520) 526-9565
`orders@infomagic.com`

General Installation Procedures

Each Motif distribution has its own distinct installation procedure. The documentation provided by each vendor should give you enough to get started. By reading about one vendor's installation procedure, you can get an idea of how other distributions are installed. For this description, I use the MetroLink installation guidelines. Other distributions may follow a different installation procedure, but you will know what to look for when you are done with the installation.

General software requirements for Motif include the following:

- XFree86 2.1 or later
- C library version of libc 4.4.4 or later
- ld.so runtime linker/loader

The Motif version on the CD-ROM at the back of the book satisfies these requirements for you. However, if you have installed from another source, you should confirm that you meet these requirements before installing Motif.

You must do all the installation as `root`. Be sure that you are `root` before proceeding.

Motif requires the following directories to exist in the X11 installation on your machine.

```
/usr/lib/X11
/usr/bin/X11
/usr/include/X11
```

If these directories do not exist, you must create links to them from where equivalent XFree86 directories are kept. The XFree86 distributions are kept in the following directories:

```
/usr/X11R6/lib/X11
/usr/X11R6/bin/X11
/usr/X11R6/include/X11
```

In some cases, the installation program creates the required links to these directories for you. However, if you do not see these directories, you can create them with the following steps:

```
# ln -s /usr/X11R6/lib/X11 /usr/lib/X11
# ln -s /usr/X11R6/bin/X11 /usr/bin/X11
# ln -s /usr/X11R6/include/X11 /usr/include/X11
```

> **NOTE**
>
> Check to see whether you have /lib/libXm.so.1 or /lib/libXm.so.1.2.2 installed on your machine. Remove these files before proceeding.
>
> Also check and remove, if present, the directory (and its contents) /usr/lib/X11/Motif before you start the installation process. This way you will avoid keeping old files around.

The MetroLink distribution consists of five 3.5-inch, high-density disks. They are labeled as follows:

- Runtime 1 and 2
- Developers Disk 1, 2, and 3.

> **TIP**
>
> The floppy disks on Linux are addressed by a syntax that describes how to read and write them. For example, a 3.5-inch, high-density floppy disk in drive A is addressed as /dev/fd0H1440. For a 5.25-inch, high-density disk in drive B, you have to use /dev/fd1H1200. (The fd0 implies the fast floppy disk as a high-density, 3.5-inch, 1.44MB floppy disk drive. For a 5.25-inch, high-density drive as the second drive you would use /dev/fd1H1200.)
>
> Most Motif distributions come on 3.5-inch, high-density floppy disks, so you should use /dev/fd0H1440 or /dev/fd1H1440 for drive A and B, respectively.

Now insert the first Runtime disk into your floppy drive, and issue the following commands if you are using drive A.

```
# cd /tmp
# cpio --extract --verbose --block-size=32 -I /dev/fd0H1440
```

The cpio program prompts you for the second disk. Replace the disk and press the Enter key to continue.

After cpio is finished with the extraction, you have a large file in the tmp directory. This file is called run.tar.z. Now, you have to extract all the files from file into your directory tree. Issue the following commands:

```
# cd /
# gzip -dc /tmp/run.tar.z | tar -xvf -
```

The gzip -dc command extracts all files in the compressed archive and passes the resulting tar file to the tar program. This tar program extracts (x) all the files it receives on its standard input (-), and lets you know what it's doing by being verbose (v) while extracting each file.

Now, remove the temporary file with the following command:

```
# rm /tmp/run.tar.z
```

Do the same procedure for the developers disks. Use `cpio` to copy the `dev.tar.z` file into the `tmp` directory. The use the `gzip` command as before for the runtime libraries, except use the name `dev.tar.z` instead of `run.tar.z`.

Getting Started with X Window

On some systems, you may have to start X from the command line after you log in. On other systems, you may have to interface through the `xdm` client. Let's start with the easy case of the `xdm` manager already running on your system.

> **CAUTION**
>
> The first thing to remember is that X is very flexible. You can customize almost anything in X. Therefore, be warned that even though I attempt to describe the most common features of X, they may not work exactly as described. This is the price of flexibility. *This is especially true for all the different versions of X and window managers offered in X.*

Starting X and *mwm*

If you do not see any windows at all, and you do not see a cursor, you do not have the X server running. In this case, you have to start X yourself.

There are several steps to take before you start X.

1. Confirm that `startx` exists in your PATH. Use the `echo $PATH` command to see whether `/usr/X11R6/bin` is in your path.

    A sample `startx` is shown in Listing 23.1.

2. Look for a file called `XF86Config` in `/usr/X11R6/lib/X11`. This file contains very hardware-specific information about your system. Read Chapters 21 and 22 to ensure that you have installed X correctly.

> **TIP**
>
> Always make a copy of `XF86Config` and save it away before you modify it. Do not edit this file while you are already in X.

3. Type the command `startx` at your prompt.
4. Wait a few seconds (or minutes, depending on your hardware). You should see several messages whisk by, and the screen should change to that of a session without a window manager.

5. At this point, you can run a crippled windowing system without a window manager, or you can start a window manager. For example, to get the Motif Window Manager, use the following command in an xterm. (Of course, you can use fvwm, or whatever manager you fancy and have installed.)

```
mwm &
```

Listing 23.1. A sample `startx` file.

```
$ less /usr/X11R6/bin/startx
#!/bin/sh

# $Xconsortium: startx.cpp,v 1.4 91/108/22 11:41:29 rws Exp $
# $Xfree86: xc/programs/xinit/startx.cpp,v 3.0 1994/05/22 00:02:28 dawes Exp $
#
# This is just a sample implementation of a slightly less primitive
# interface than xinit.  It looks for user .xinitrc and .xserverrc
# files, then system xinitrc should probably do things like check
# for .Xresources file and merge them in, startup in a window manager,
# and pop a clock and serveral xterms.
#
# Site administrators are STRONGLY urged to write nicer versions.
#

userclientrc=$HOME/.xinitrc
userserverrc=$HOME/.xserverrc
sysclientrc=/usr/X11R6/lib/X11/xinit/xinitrc
sysserverrc=/usr/X11R6/lib/X11/xinit/xserverrc
clientargs=""
serverargs=""

if [ -f $userclientrc ]; then
    clientargs=$userclientrc
else if [ -f $sysclientrc]; then
    clientargs=$sysclientc
fi
fi

if [ -f $userserverrc ]; then
    serverargs=$userserverrc
else if [ if $sysserverrc ]; then
    serverargs=$sysserverrc
fi
fi

whoseargs="client"
while [ "x$1" != "x" ]; do
    case "$1" in
        /''*¦\.*)        if [ "$whoseargs" = "client" ]; then
                    clientargs="$1"
            else
                    serverargs="$1"
            fi ;;
        --)        whoseargs="server" ;;
        *)        if [ "$whoseargs" = "client" ]; then
                clientargs="$clientargs $1"
            else
```

continues

Listing 23.1. continued

```
                serverargs="$serverargs $1"
            fi ;;
    esac
    shift
done

xinit $clientargs -- $serverargs
```

By the way, you can run any ol' manager you have, `fvwm`, `twnm`, `olwm`, and so on. I am simply using `mwm` as an example. Also note that you are running the `mwm` in the background. If you do not do this, you can't issue any commands to the `xterm`. See Figure 23.1 for what your display might now look like. Keep in mind that your display may look quite different from the picture in Figure 23.1 because your startup code has different applications.

FIGURE 23.1.

A typical Motif session.

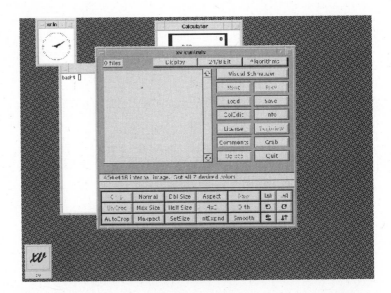

> **TIP**
>
> If you are in the `bash`, KORN, C, or any other common shell at this point, and you forgot the &, type Ctrl-Z to put the job in the background. If you are not running the Korn or C shells, you can kill `mwm` with Ctrl-C, and then restart it with the ampersand.

Congratulations! You are now running Motif.

Note that a lot of things can go wrong while getting to this point. Here are a few of the most common problems:

■ You cannot find the correct files. Ensure that the path includes /usr/X11/bin or the like.

■ You moved the cursor into the window, but now you have to click to be able to type commands to your xterm. By itself, X Window gives the focus to a window when a cursor is moved on to it. mwm, on the other hand, requires that you actually click the left mouse button (Button1) for that window to get focus. *Focus* means that all user input (keyboard and pointer) is now be sent to that window. mwm changes the color of the window border to show that it has received focus.

■ There is not enough memory to run the system. This is especially true if you are on a PC-based platform. Typically, you can get away with 4MB of dynamic RAM for a simple X Window system, but you almost certainly need 8MB or more to be able to get a reasonable response time on a PC. The memory upgrade to 8MB is well worth it, given the performance on a 4MB machine. Only the patient can live with 4MB.

■ The configuration does not look right. You have to modify the default startup parameters. See the "Customizing Motif" section.

■ Exiting the last command in your .xinitrc file terminates your entire X session. If your last command was an xterm and you logged off that xterm, your entire session is terminated. Generally, the last command in your .xinitrc file would be the window manager so that terminating the window manager will also terminate your session.

Working with Motif Windows in *mwm*

Look at the typical xterm window in Motif, shown in Figure 23.2.

FIGURE 23.2.

A typical xterm window.

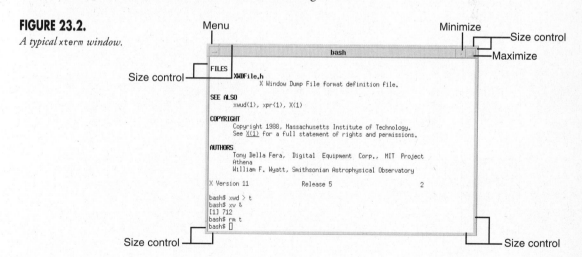

The Title bar is the wide horizontal band on the top of the window. This contains the title for the application itself. In this case, this is the application itself, xterm. You can modify it to your needs. Try the following:

```
xterm -name "I am here" &
```

The minimize button is used to iconify this xterm. The maximize button can be used to resize the window to occupy the entire display area. All corners can be used to resize the window by using the mouse. Note the pseudo–three-dimensional appearance of the borders.

Using the Pointer

You will now work with some of the Motif windows that you have on the screen. Typically, you work with a mouse for the pointer, so the text refers to mice at times. However, you can always substitute your device name for the word *mouse* or *pointer*, and not lose any meaning of the discussion.

Pointers in the mwm environment typically use three buttons, called Button1, Button2, and Button3. As an affront to left-handed individuals, Button1 is usually referred to as the *left button* because it is the most used button of the three. The left button on a mouse is the one that is pressed with your right index finger. When you take the pointer to an item and press a button, you are *clicking* the button.

If you are left-handed, you can map your mouse or pointer buttons differently. See the section entitled, "Help for Left-Handed Users," later in this chapter.

Icons and Windows

The minimize button enables you to iconify an application. An icon is a small symbol that represents an inactive window. The contents of that window are not visible, although they may be updated internally by its process. Icons can be moved around on a screen, but they cannot be resized. Inactive windows that become active may hide icons. Icons save valuable screen space when you're using applications that do not require your constant attention.

Iconifying a Window

Move the cursor to the minimize button, and press the left button on the mouse. The window is removed from the screen, and a smaller icon is seen somewhere on the left of the screen. The minimize button is the one with the smaller square near the right side of the frame. The maximize button is the one with the bigger square and can be found on the right side of the frame.

To restore an icon to a screen, move the cursor to the icon and click on Button1 twice in quick succession. This is known as *double-clicking* the mouse. Some Motif icons are shown in the bottom left side of Figure 23.3.

FIGURE 23.3.

Typical Motif icons.

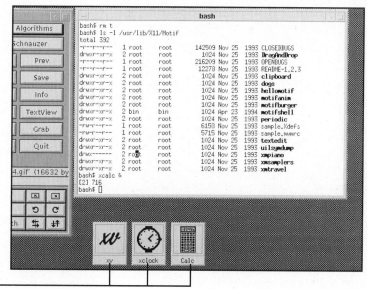

Motif icons

Maximizing a Window

Move the cursor to the maximize button, and press Button1. This enlarges the window to the size of the root window. This way, you can have a huge clock on your screen. Some applications, such as older versions of calc, do not adjust their internal graphic areas when their frame is resized. This leads to annoying blank space on a screen.

Use the maximize button as a toggle. Clicking on an already maximized window causes it to revert to its size and position (also known as geometry) before it was maximized. Clicking on it again remaximizes it.

TIP

Avoid resizing a window when running a vi session under an xterm. This leads to unpredictable results and may cause vi to behave very strangely.

Sizing a Window

The entire frame on a Motif window is a control that enables you to resize the window. See Figure 23.2 for the size controls. The four corners enable you to stretch the window by each corner. The four long bars let you move the edges of the window with the mouse.

To stretch the window using a corner, move the mouse to that corner. Press Button1 and, while keeping it pressed, move the mouse. You should see the cursor change its shape to a double-headed arrow, and a thin border will appear, indicating the size and orientation of the current stretch operation. Size the window by moving the mouse with Button1 pressed. Release the button when you have achieved the desired size.

Note that some applications do not have these sizing controls enabled. An example is the cute, but not very useful, pointer tracking program called xeyes, or the clock program called oclock. (See Figure 23.4.)

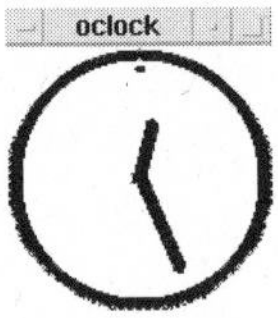

FIGURE 23.4.

The oclock program has a window without resize borders.

To move the edges of the window, move the mouse to that edge. You should see your cursor change shape to a vertical double-headed arrow if you are on a horizontal edge (top or bottom of window). As you move the pointer, a thin border will appear indicating the size and orientation of the current stretch operation. If you are on a vertical edge, the double-headed arrow is horizontal. Press Button1 and, while keeping it pressed, move the pointer around. This moves the edge along with your pointer. Release the button when you have the edge where you want it.

While you are resizing this window, you see a small box come up in the center of the display. This box contains the size of the window in pixels if it's a graphics image, or in rows and columns (in number of characters) if it's an xterm. On some systems, you can use the arrow keys on your keyboard to achieve precision when resizing your windows. Remember to keep the button pressed while you use the arrow keys on your keyboard to do the precise adjustment.

Focus and Selecting a Window

You can select a window or icon to get *focus* by moving the pointer to that item and pressing the left button. This moves the window or icon to the top of the stack. This way, the window or icon isn't obscured by any other screen item.

When a window has focus, it collects all the user input from the pointer and the keyboard. There are two types of focus for a window: click to type and explicit. The click to type focus requires a user to click a pointer button in a window for it to get focus. The explicit focus requires only that the cursor be in the window for the window to get focus. Explicit focus is sometimes referred to as *real estate driven* focus.

In some cases, you want to have the focus where the mouse is, without having to click the pointer button. Sometimes this is not useful for touch typists, because a single movement of the pointer can have the keystroke sent to the wrong window.

TIP

Sometimes it's a good idea to click on the frame to get focus to a window because clicking in the window might accidentally press a button or other control in the window.

After you give the focus to a client, it collects all typed or graphics information until the user clicks elsewhere.

Getting focus also raises the window to the top of the stack. The window frame color changes at this point. You can set the focus to an icon too by selecting it with a mouse. The name of the icon expands at that point, and you see the window menu for that icon. You can move the mouse away from the menu, but the icon retains the focus until you click elsewhere.

The color change scheme depends on your site's default colors. In some cases, you may not see any color change at all if the focused and out-of-focus colors are the same.

Moving a Window or Icon

In order to move a window's location on the screen, complete the following steps:

1. Move the cursor on top of the title bar.
2. Press and hold down pointer Button1.
3. Move the pointer to the desired location. You should see an outline of the window border move with your pointer.
4. Place the outline at the part of the screen where you want your window to be. This is referred to as dragging the window.
5. Release Button1. The window now appears at the new location. It is also the window with the focus by default.

This procedure can be duplicated for an icon. In the case of an icon, you click and drag with the cursor in the icon itself.

While you are moving the window, you see a small box in the center of the screen with two numbers in it. These are positive X and Y offsets of the top left corner of the window from the top left corner of the screen. This is very useful information when trying to precisely place a window on the screen.

You can achieve some fine precision by pressing the arrow keys on the numeric keypad to move the window one step at a time. You must keep the pointer button pressed while you use the arrow keys.

Adding a New Window

Say you want to add a calculator to your screen. Type in

```
$ xcalc &
```

at the prompt in an xterm window. The calculator should appear on the screen. To get another xterm, type the following command:

```
$ xterm &
```

Depending on your site, this can appear anywhere on the screen. Typically, the new window is placed in the upper left corner (x=0,y=0) of the root window, or in the center of the root window.

The size and location of a window is referred to as the window's *geometry*.

> **NOTE**
>
> The reason why you launch applications with an ampersand (&) at the end of the command is to run the application in the background and free up the xterm from which the application is being run. If you do not type the ampersand, the xterm will not accept input until that application is either suspended or killed. Also, the use of the ampersand allows the application to run even after the xterm from which it was run is killed.

Window Geometry

Almost all clients accept the -geometry command line option. This option tells the window manager where to locate the window on the screen. If you do not specify any geometry, the window manager uses its defaults.

The coordinate system for the root window is as follows:

- The origin is top left (0,0).
- The number of display units is in pixels for graphics.
- The number of display units are in character sizes for xterms.

A pixel is the smallest unit available on a screen. Usually, screens are displayed in 1024×768 pixels, 2048×2048 pixels, or something similar. The size of a pixel on screen is very much hardware-dependent. A 200×200 window appears as different sizes on monitors with different resolutions.

The geometry parameter is of the following form:

```
widthxheight[{+-}xoff{-+}yoff]
```

The height and width are usually given in pixels. In the case of xterms, height is given in lines, and width is given in characters per line. It is common to have a 24×80 xterm.

The xoff and yoff are offsets from the start of the left and top edges of the screen respectively. These represent the location of the window on the root window. The curly braces represent either the – or the + character, but not both.

+xoff   A positive offset from the left edge of the screen to the left edge of the window.

-xoff	A negative offset from the right edge of the screen to the right edge of the window.
+yoff	A positive offset from the top edge of the screen to the top edge of the window.
-yoff	A negative offset from the bottom edge of the screen to the bottom edge of the window.

A visual representation of the geometry is shown in Figure 23.5. For example, the line

```
xterm -geometry -50+50 &
```

places the xterm on the top right corner, 50 pixels from the right edge of screen and 50 pixels from the top of the screen.

FIGURE 23.5.

Window geometry.

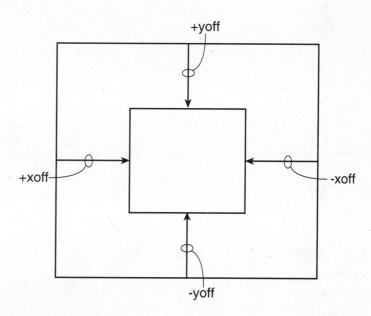

The following parameters specify the edges of the screen:

-0-0	Lower right corner
-0+0	Upper right corner
+0-0	Lower left corner
+0+0	Upper left corner

Using the Window Menu

Using the window menu requires you to have the focus on a window. Let's look at a typical window menu. This also may be different on your screen, but the basic functionality listed here should exist for all later versions of Motif. Take the cursor to the window menu button, and press the left button. The following menu (or something close to it) should appear:

```
Restore      alt-F5
Move         alt-F7
Size         alt-F8
Minimize     alt-F9
Maximize     alt-F10
Lower        alt-F3
Close        alt-F4
```

Using the Keyboard in X and the Meta Key

It's important to bring this point up about the keyboard and its special keys under X. Keyboards come in different types, and the most important key for using keystrokes in X can be radically different from one keyboard to another. On PC-based keyboards, it is usually the Alt key; on Macintoshes, it is the Command key; on Suns, it is Left, Alternate; and other keyboards use other keys. The list goes on.

In short, the *Meta key* is the special key for your keyboard. For a PC-based keyboard, this is the Alt key. So, do not look for a key called Meta on your keyboard. Where it says Meta, use Alt, Command, or whatever key your keyboard is mapped to.

Now you can invoke any item on this window menu in one of two ways:

■ Use the pointer. This way, you click on the window menu and press Button1. Now, move the cursor to the item you want, and release Button1; or, press the Meta key and the character that is underlined in the menu. For moving a window, you press Meta-M. Note that this does not work on some Motif distributions.

> **NOTE**
>
> Alt-key combinations may not always work. In Metro's version of Motif 1.2, the Meta-F7 key allows moving a window, but the Meta-M key does not work at all. You may have a completely different experience with *your* keyboard.

■ While the window has focus, press the Meta-function key combination. Then use the arrow keys on your keyboard to simulate the movement of the cursor, or just use the pointer.

Note that some of these functions may not be available for a menu shown for an icon. You might not be able to size or minimize an icon, but you can move, maximize, or close it.

Using the Root Menu

Click Button3 while the cursor is in the root window. You see a menu pop up on top of all the windows. This is known as the root menu. Keep in mind that this menu is very customizable, and may look radically different on your machine. You will learn all about creating your own menu later in this chapter in the "Customizing Motif" section.

A typical root menu may list the following items. (Your system may have a different list depending on the type of Motif you purchased.)

```
"Root Menu"
New Window
Shuffle Up
Shuffle Down
Refresh
Utils >
Restart
Exit
```

While holding down Button1, move the cursor down the list to the item you want to select. When you get to the menu item you want, release the button. If you do not want to select any items, move the cursor off the menu and release the button.

In the previous list, the functionality can be set to the following:

- New Window starts a new xterm and sets focus to it.
- Refresh redraws the entire screen and all windows.
- Restart kills mwm and restarts it.
- Exit kills mwm and leaves you without a window manager. If this is the last command in your startup script, your windowing session terminates.
- Shuffle Up and Shuffle Down shuffles the stacking order of the windows up or down. The current window with focus is moved down to the bottom when shuffling down, and the next highest window is given the focus. The last window in the stack is brought to the top and given the focus when shuffling up.
- The Utils item brings up another submenu with more choices to select from. See the "Customizing Motif" section, later in this chapter, for details on how to set your menu items.

Now, let's work with Motif clients.

Working with Motif Clients

Most programmers find the X Window system libraries too basic to work with, so they use the next building block called toolkits. The most common interface toolkit is the XtIntrinsics toolkit from MIT. This is called Xt. On top of Xt, you can have other toolkits such as Motif or the Open Look Interface Toolkit (OLIT). When you are working with Motif, you are working with a Motif toolkit. In Motif, you are working with Motif Widgets.

Widgets help developers program consistent user interfaces in Motif. By using Widgets, programmers can quickly put together interfaces that have the same look and feel of all Motif applications.

Some Widgets display information. Some Widgets collect user input (mouse or keyboard) information. Some Widgets react to user input by changing their appearance or performing some programmed function. Some Widgets are simply containers for other Wigdets. All Widgets can be customized in one form or another, whether it is appearance, font size or style, colors, or whatever other parameter is required.

All Widgets of the same type have two data structures with information that describes their attributes: class and instance. The instance data structure contains information for a specific Widget on the screen. The class information contains information required for all Widgets of the class.

Widgets are grouped into several classes. Each class depends on the type of functionality offered by the Widget. Normally, the internal functions of a Widget are hidden from the applications programmer (encapsulation). A Widget class shares a set of functions and data structures for all Widgets in that class. A new Widget class can be derived from an existing Widget class. The newly derived class can inherit all the data structures and functions of the parent class. A Widget is created and destroyed during a Motif program execution.

NOTE

The destruction of a Widget is a bit more complicated, and will be discussed in detail in the next chapter.

NOTE

This should sound familiar to C++ programmers. True polymorphism is somewhat harder to find in Widgets. This is all done in C. For C++ programmers, the class data structure is to the class for an object, as the instance data structure is to the instance of an object.

A Widget is really a pointer to a data structure when viewed in a debugger. This data structure is allocated on the creation of a Widget, and is destroyed when a Widget is destroyed.

Let's look at a typical application screen to see some Widgets in action. You will work with a demo application called xmdialogs, shown in Figure 23.6. The Widgets shown here will be described later in this chapter. The xmdialogs application can be found in the /usr/bin/X11 directory. If you do not have this application, you can still learn about working with Widgets by applying these concepts to different applications.

NOTE

Don't worry if you cannot find this application on your machine. There are plenty of other applications just like this one. If you have the Motif 1.2.3 release or later from Metro Link, you will have this application in your /usr/bin/X11 directory.

FIGURE 23.6.

The xmdialogs *demo application.*

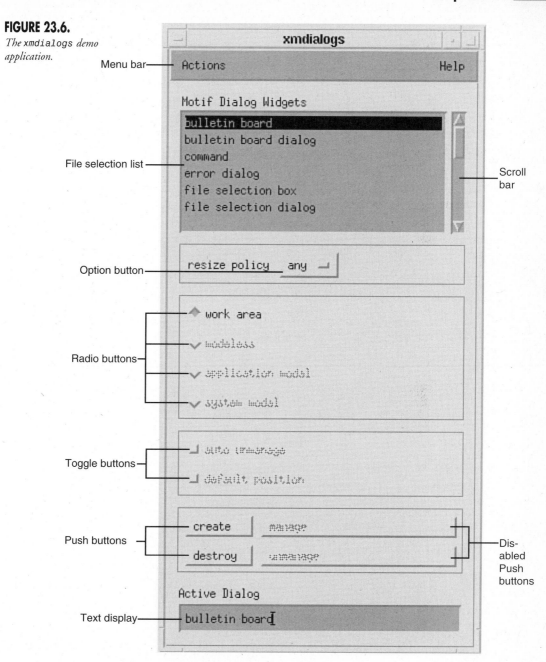

Figure 23.6 shows a Menu bar, a File selection list with scrollbars, an Option button, some Radio and Toggle buttons, some Push buttons, some Labels, and a Text display dialog box.

The Actions and Help items are shown on a menu bar. By moving the pointer to either of these items and pressing Button1, you are presented with a menu of options very similar in operation to the window and root menu.

Underneath this menu bar is a list of items in a scrollable list. This Widget is of the type `XmList`. The `XmList` lets you keep a selection of items in a visible list. It has scroll bars to enable the user to scroll the list if the entire list isn't visible. A programmer can set the number of items that are visible at one time. If you resize the window, and if the list box sizes itself proportionately with the window, the number of visible items in a list may change.

To select an item, move the pointer to the item of your choice and press Button1 once. The item is highlighted in a darker color. Some lists enable you to select more than one item, and others, just one item. In this application, you only select one type of dialog box. (Figure 23.6 shows the bulletin board item to be the selected item.)

The scroll bars on the side of the list Widget are of the class `XmScrollbar`. A scroll bar is either a horizontal or vertical rectangle. There is a raised box in the rectangle called the slider box. This slider moves within the larger rectangle. The movable space for the slider bar is called the scroll region. The ratio of the size of the slider bar to the scroll region is proportional to the size of the work area to the total area being viewed.

The `XmScrollBar` rectangle has two arrows at each end. The arrows point outward relative to the rectangle, and in opposite directions. The arrow keys can be used to move the slider bar within the scroll region.

1. Move the mouse to the slider bar arrow.
2. Click on Button1.
3. The slider bar should move closer to the arrow. The slider moves as close as possible to the arrow being clicked in the scroll area.
4. Release Button1.

Users can also move the slider bar by dragging it with the mouse:

1. Move the pointer on to the slider bar.
2. Press the Button1.
3. Move the pointer up or down for a vertical scroll bar.
4. Move the pointer left or right for a horizontal scroll bar.

   The contents of the work area, as well as the slider bar, scroll with the movement of the pointer. The viewable portion is the work area.
5. Release Button1 when the list area contains the desired viewing data.

Now move your cursor to the selection item of the resize policy button. When you click on this button, you are presented with a pop-up menu of the types of resize policies for the dialog box you want to create. When you press the button, a menu pops out and presents you with a list of options. You make the selection with your pointer by moving the pointer to that button and releasing it. The menu disappears, and your selection is displayed in the box. In Figure 23.6, shown previously, the resize policy is set to *any*. This is known as an *option button*.

Note the diamond-shaped buttons and selections below this current menu. This is a list of one of four possible selections for the dialog box. One of the items is shown in a lighter gray color. This is known as *grayed out*, meaning that the option is a not a valid option at the time. The option for the Work Area is *disabled*. You can select one of the three options. These items are grouped together with a rectangular frame drawn around them. Usually, buttons are grouped together this way in Motif when their functionality falls in the same group of actions. The actions are similar to the buttons on a radio: push one button and the rest of the buttons in the row all come up. This is why these are referred to as *radio buttons*.

Look at the two buttons: *auto manage* and *default position*. These are *toggle buttons* for this application. When you select one button, the other is not influenced at all. The functionality provided by each button is completely independent of the other. Do you see the difference between radio buttons and toggle buttons?

Sometimes a scrollbar is used on each side of a drawing area. This is called a Scrolled Window, and belongs to the `XmScrolledWindow` class. This Widget can hold graphics instead of a list of items. The `XmScrolledWindow` is used primarily to view large graphic items in a small window, whereas `XmList` is used to show items for the user to select from.

Under the toggle buttons, you see four *push buttons*. When a push button is pressed, the colors on the border of the button reverse. Also, the color of the pressed rectangle changes to show the user action. Push buttons are used to invoke some sort of action. When you select the file selection dialog from the list and press the push button to manage it, the display shown in Figure 23.7 appears. This is the standard file selection box under Motif, and you should see it for most applications.

FIGURE 23.7.

A typical File Selection dialog box.

To see a more detailed picture of what types of Widgets are available within Motif, run `/usr/bin/X11/periodic`. (See Figure 23.8.) Note that the menu item for this application can be removed to become a separate application, by dragging on the dashed line. The menu is shown as torn off in Figure 23.9.

FIGURE 23.8.

The Periodic Table of Widgets.

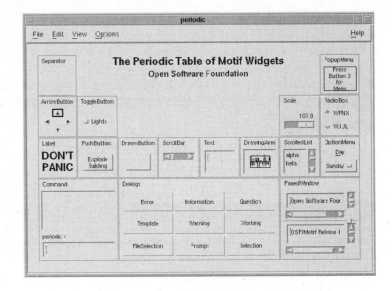

FIGURE 23.9.

A tear-off menu torn off.

Other Types of Widgets

The Motif toolkit also supplies the following Widgets. Please refer to the items in the periodic table in Figure 23.8 to see what each Widget should like on screen.

XmArrowButton   This is a directional arrow with a border around it. A programmer can modify the arrow's direction, thickness, and border color by setting the Widget's parameters. Look at the ends of a scrollbar to see two examples of such a Widget.

XmDrawnButton   A drawn button provides a rectangular area with a border for the programmer. The programmer can size, redraw, or reposition text or graphics within this window. This Widget provides hooks to set parameters for its border appearance, as well as to attach functions for accepting user input.

XmLabel   This is a rectangular box consisting of either text or graphics. It is instantiated, but is also used as a base class for all button Widgets. A label's text can be multiline, multifont, or even multidirectional. In the xmdialogs example, this would be the labels Active Dialog and the Motif Dialog Widgets strings.

Many features of the labels can be modified. This includes the fonts, foreground and background colors, and alignment (left, center, or right justification); in fact, this can even store a pixmap graphic image.

`XmPushButton`   This is a text label or pixmap with a border around it. This Widget accepts keystrokes or mouse button presses. In the `smdialogs` example, these are the *create*, *destroy, manage*, and *unmanage* buttons. When a button has focus, it draws a heavy border around itself.

When you press the Enter key or a pointer on a button, the button has focus. Move the cursor to the button. Press a key or button and hold it down. You have armed the button. The color on the button should change, and the border colors should reverse. This gives the impression that the button has been pressed inward. When you release the button, the button reverts to its original state. When a mouse button is pressed in this Widget the foreground and background colors of the Widget usually also invert.

`XmSeparator`   This is used to create a line between functional sections of a screen. There is really not much that users can do with this Widget except position it on the screen.

`XmText`   This is used to create a fully functional multiline text editor on a screen. The user can select text by dragging the mouse from one location to another while Button1 is pressed. Users can also click anywhere on the Widget to mark the insertion point. If the text Widget is enabled for user input, the user can type at the insertion point and insert the text into the text Widget.

Pull-down menus   These are rectangular areas in the window that enable users to select from a number of items. The items are generally laid out in push buttons. Users can select a push button either by moving the mouse to that selection, or by pressing Alt-K, in which K is the letter of the alphabet that is underlined in the menu button. In the `xmdialogs` function, the Meta-F key selected the file item, and Meta-H selected the Help item.

Pop-up menus   The Motif root window menu is a good example of a pop-up menu. When you press the mouse button, a menu is displayed. You can select an item in the menu by moving the cursor onto the item and pressing Button1.

Scale Widgets   The scale Widget is used to display the value of a data item between two extremes. It can also be used to accept user input. A scale Widget has a scroll region that is very similar to the scroll bar. However, it does not have the arrow buttons at each end.

`XmScrolledWindow`   This is a combination of a horizontal scroll bar, a vertical scroll bar, and a drawing area. If the size of the drawing area fits within the window, you can't see the scrollbars. If the size of the drawing area is greater than the visible area of the scrolled window, you see the horizontal or vertical scrollbars, or both. You can then use the scrollbars to move the visible portion on top of the drawing area. This is known as panning the window.

`XmFrame`   This is a simple Widget used to put a consistent border around one single Widget. Frames can only hold one Widget at a time.

XmRowColumn   This is a general-purpose Widget organizer. The Widget can layout its Widget collection in a variety of ways, including the following:

Row major   In this case, all Widgets on this Row Column Widget are stored until one row fills up, and a new row is created when another Widget is added that doesn't fit on this Widget. The creation of a new row is sometimes called *wrap-around.*

Column major   This is the same as a row major, but it wraps around in a columnar fashion.

In conjunction with this, you can specify the width of each column to be that of the widest Widget; you can also specify the number of fixed columns, the packing (whether all Widgets should be packed as closely as possible), or that the individual Widgets specify their own positions.

There are several other Widgets available in the Motif Widget set. You can see the complete listing and their options in *The Programmers Reference Manual* from the Open Software Foundation.

Gadgets

Motif Widgets create a window in X Window. A complex Motif application can create several X windows very quickly. Each window uses X resources in the server, and many windows can slow your overall system performance.

Gadgets are windowless versions of a Widget. Most Gadgets have the same names as Widgets, but have the string Gadget appended to their name. So, XmLabel has an XmLabelGadget counterpart.

Gadgets do not have all the features of Widgets. For example, Gadgets share the foreground and background colors of their parent. Also, some Gadgets actually turn out to be slower than the Widgets they are trying to replace. Given the troubles that you can get into by using Gadgets, you may be better off not using them.

Customizing with Resources

Now that you are familiar with Widgets, let's talk about the parameters that affect them—resources.

What Are Resources?

As you saw in the previous sections, you can customize some aspects of an application from the command line prompt. X enables you to modify the aspects of an existing application every time a client runs that application. X does this by setting control variables for that client. These control variables are called *resources* and have a value associated with them.

For example, consider the case of an xterm. An xterm's resources are its font size, its pointer shape, the foreground color for all displayed text, its background color, and so on. These are only a few of the resources for an xterm. Most of these resources exist as predefined defaults for all the common clients in a system.

You can specify resources on an application-specific basis, or for all applications on your system. These resources are normally stored in an ASCII file called .Xresources, in your home directory.

This file affects only those applications that you run. This file normally contains only those options that you would like to customize over those values that are set in system files.

You can always override the defaults specified in the system-wide file with defaults in your .Xresources file. In turn, your command line options for a single client override those in the .Xresources file. Keep in mind, however, that the command line default applies only to a specific client. The .Xresources default setting becomes the default for all your clients.

Also, remember that the command line operations override any default resources set in a file. Normally, you set how you want your application to look under normal circumstances, and then override the changes via command line options.

TIP

In some systems, the .Xresources file can also be called .Xdefaults.

To make your resource specifications available to all clients, use the X resource database manager program, xrdb. This stores the resources directly on the server and makes the resource available to all clients on the system. This step takes some care because your change will affect all your clients, regardless of what platform they are running on.

Defining Resources

A resource definition file is basically a line-by-line list of all the resources in the file. Each line consists of two entries: one for the resource type, and the other for the value for the resource. The two entries are colon-separated.

The simplest syntax for a resource definition is as follows:

```
client*variable:  value
```

client is the name of the client. The variable for that client is set to the value. Note that the colon follows the variable without any spaces.

Let's look at the resource declaration for an xterm client.

```
XTerm*foreground: white
XTerm*background: blue
XTerm*font: 10x20
...
```

If you do not already have an .Xdefaults file, you can create one yourself with a text editor.

The values can be Boolean, numeric, or string. Values can be specified for Widgets in an application as well. For example, if you want to set the background color for all PushButtons in an application, myWorld, you set the following resource:

```
myWorld*PushButton.background: red
myWorld*background: blue
```

Note that the asterisk represents the Widgets in between the actual myWorld application and all PushButtons in that application. If you specify

```
myWorld.mainForm.PushButton: blue
```

only the buttons on the Widget mainForm, which in turn must exist on myWorld, are affected. This is *tight binding*. Using the asterisk (*) is *loose binding* because it allows for multiple levels of Widget hierarchy between the objects on either side of the asterisk. If this has a hierarchy of

```
myWorld.mainForm.subForm.PushButton
```

the first two of the following declarations affects the PushButtons on the subForm, and the last does not:

```
myWorld*PushButton.background: red
myWorld*background: blue
myWorld.mainForm.PushButton: blue
```

Another example is the settings for an xterm. If you attempt to set the scrollbars using

```
xterm.scrollbar: true
```

it probably won't work. Most likely, there is a Widget hierarchy between the top-level application and the scrollbar Widgets. In this case, it works if you use the following:

```
xterm*scrollbar: true
```

TIP

When you use a very general setting for a Widget in your resource files, say *labelString, you affect all such occurrences of labelString in all files. Be careful!

After you have modified the .Xresources file, you probably expect to see the changes occur immediately. Not so. You now have to inform the server of your defaults by using the xrdb command. Use the following command:

```
xrdb -load .Xresources
```

This reflects the changes for all subsequent executions of your client. These remain in effect until overridden, or until your session terminates. If you save your .Xresources file in your login directory, these changes are loaded whenever you start X with the following command:

```
xrdb -load .Xresources
```

This command is useful when creating .Xresources for the first time in a session. That is why, in most cases, this command is run when the windowing system is first created. If you want to keep the previous settings, use the -merge command option instead of -load, like so:

```
xrdb -merge .myOwnResources
```

Also, you can use the exclamation point as the comment character at any point in the input line before text begins. So, the following lines are comments:

```
! This is a comment
! another one
! commented*labelString: This resource is not used.
```

You can also use the cpp preprocessor's directives #if, #ifdef, #else, and #endif. This is running through xrdb only. The cpp preprocessor is not run when the .Xresources file is parsed. You can override the run through cpp by using the -nocpp parameter on the command line. No other parameters are required. If you want to remove a resource, use the -remove operation.

```
xrdb -remove .myOldResources
```

User and Class Resource Files

There are two types of resource files: user and class. User files apply to each instance of all applications. These are the resources you set in the .Xresources file. Class files pertain to all the instances of a particular class. These exist in files usually in your home directory or your path. The name of this file is the name of the class. The class name is the name of the application class with the first letter capitalized.

For example, all xterms belong to the class XTerm. Note that the class name is the name of a type of application with the first letter capitalized. XTerm is an exception in this regard because it has XT capitalized instead of only X.

Let's look at setting the resources for a particular class of an application:

```
*labelString:  Hello World
```

This command sets the labelString resource to Hello World for all Widgets in every application in your session. This may not be exactly what you want.

```
Xapp*labelString:  Hello World
```

This command sets the labelString resource to Hello World for all Widgets in every Xapp application in your session. This doesn't affect Widgets within other applications. This effect may be desirable if you are trying to set only one type of application resource.

You can also specify your own class for setting resources. This is done by setting the -name option on a client. For example, you can define all the resources for an xterm with 10×20 font to be of class hugeterm. Then, whenever you run

```
xterm -name hugeterm &
```

it uses the resources in the class hugeterm. Now you can set the foreground color to whatever you want for xterms with a name of hugeterm.

Note that the name resource cannot contain the * or . characters. These values cause your resource setting to be ignored. The mwm environment simply ignores bad syntax, instead of informing the user about these errors.

Customizing Motif

Customizing Motif is very similar to customizing the X resources. However, Motif offers a far greater set of features, and enables the user to customize just about every item on the screen. Without changing a line of code, the resources here can be set to maintain a consistent set of interfaces for all applications. For example, it's easy to change the background color of all the forms in your applications by simply editing the resources file, rather than editing each source file individually. Here are some more methods for setting resources:

- Hard code resource settings.
- Use command line parameters.
- Use the environment variables to specify class files.

Hard-Coded Resource Setting

You can set resources by hard coding the values in your application source code. See Chapter 32, "Motif for Programmers."

Hard coding resource settings is justifiable in the following cases:

- When you do not want to give control to the end user for application-critical resources. A good example is the locations of all buttons on a data entry form. An end user is liable to shuffle them around to the point that the entry application may become unusable.
- When you do not have to worry about locations of resource files. The application is completely standalone.
- When you also do not have to worry about user intervention in your program code.
- When you want to shield users from modifying their UNIX environment variables and having to learn the customization syntax.

Using the Command Line

This was discussed earlier when we talked about customizing X applications and listed some of the resources that can be set from the command line. Motif applications usually list their options in man pages. See the section on `appres` later in this chapter.

Use the `-xrm` command line option to set or override a particular resource. The usage of this option is as follows:

```
xclient -xrm "resource*variable: value"
```

Note that you can concatenate several resource settings using the \ operator.

```
xclient -xrm "resource*variable: value" \
        -xrm "resource*variable: value"     \
        -xrm "resource*variable: value"
```

So, how do you know which resources to set? Look in the *OSF/Motif Programmers Reference Manual* for the description of a Widget's resources.

Looking at the Label Widget, you see resources grouped by the class and all its inherited resources. Some of the resources are declared under the class `Core`, some under `Manager`, and so on. Let's look at some of the resources for a `XmPushButton` Widget. You see these listed with the letters `XmN` in front of them. These letters signify that it is a Motif resource.

```
XmNacctivateback XcCallback    XtCallBackList
   ➥ NULL          C       XmNarmColor XmCarmColor Pixel       Dynamic
   ➥               CSG     XmNarmPixmap       XmCArmPixmap      Pixmap
   ➥        XmUNSPECIFIED_PIXMAP    CSG
XmNdefaultButtonThickness
XmCdefaultButtonShadowThickness Dimension 0 CSG
. . . .
```

Note the letters `CSG` for the access description.

* The C signifies creation. This tells us that
* the resource can be set at creation.
* The S signifies that this value can be set at runtime.
* The G signifies that it can be read (get) at runtime.

So, in the case of the previous `PushButton` Widget, the `XmNactivateCallback` class can only be set at the time it is created: once, at runtime. This is usually done in the code section, where an address to a pointer is set for this Widget.

The other values can be set at runtime. For example, `XmNarmColor` can be set from a resource file because it does have the `S` set for it. Likewise, when programming Widgets, this resource can be read from an application because the `G` value is specified for this resource.

Using Environment Variables

Motif uses several environment variables to hold its pointers to locations for resource files.

The `XENVIRONMENT` environment variable can hold the complete path to a file that holds the resource file. This must be the complete path of the application. If this variable is not set, the `Xt` toolkit looks in `.Xresources-HostName`, in the applications home directory.

The `XUSERFILESEARCHPATH` is a pointer to the locations of application resource files. This is a colon-delimited string. Each field is expanded into meaningful names at runtime. The following are some of the most common fields:

```
%C     Customize Color
%l     Language part
%L     Full lanuguage instruction
%N     Application class name
%S     Suffix
```

The `RESOURCE_MANAGER` variable is set by `xrdb`. This `xrdb` is executed at runtime. This usually happens at startup.

The XFILESEARCH environment variable holds a colon-delimited list of directories for the app-defaults file. Usually, these defaults are in the /usr/lib/X11/app-defaults directory.

Note that some of the classes in the directory have the first two letters of their names capitalized, instead of just one (XTerm, XDbx, XMdemos). So, if your class resource settings do not work as expected, look in this directory for some hints on what the resource class name might look like. Again, the contents of this directory depend on your installation of Motif and X.

The search for the missing .Xresources occurs in the following order:

```
Check in XUSERFILESEARCHPATH,
 if not successful or XFILEUSERSEARCHPATH not set,
         Check in XFILESEARCHPATH,
 if not successful or XFILESEARCHPATH not set,
         Check user HOME directory
```

Now that you have all this information, keep this advice in mind: In all but the most unavoidable cases, you should *not* rely on environments to set your application resources.

The methods are too complicated to learn, especially for the end user. However, they can be a very powerful customization tool. Editing resource files is hard enough on the programmer; it's even worse on the user. However, in order to be a good Motif user, you should know about the environment variables that affect applications that come from other vendors.

Listing an Application's Resources

There are two Motif applications that can assist you in determining an application's resources: appres and editres. Here is the appres program's syntax:

```
appres Class [instance]
```

This lists all the resources in a given class for the named instance of an application. Listing 23.2 shows the manual options of the command appres XTerm for advanced users.

Listing 23.2. Manual options for advanced users.

```
$ appres XTerm
*VT100*font5:
*VT100*font5:        9x15
*VT100*font3:        6x10
*VT100*font4:        7x13
*VT100*font2:        5x7
*VT100*font1:        nil2
*VT100*font6:        10x20
*tekMenu*vtshow*Label:       Show VT Window
*tekMenu*tektextsmall*Label:     Small Characters
*tekMenu*vtmode*Label:       Switch to VT Mode
*tekMenu*tektextlarge*Label:     Large Characters
```

```
*tekMenu*tekpage*Label:      PAGE
*tekMenu*tekreset*Label:     RESET
*tekMenu*tektext2*Label:     #2 Size Characters
*tekMenu*tekhide*Label:      Hide Tek Window
*tekMenu*tekcopy*Label:      COPY
*tekMenu*tektext3*Label:     #3 Size Characters
*tekMenu.Label:      Tek Options
*fontMenu*font5*Label:      Large
*fontMenu*font6*Label:      Huge
*fontMenu*font2*Label:      Tiny
*fontMenu*fontescape*Label:     Escape Sequence
*fontMenu*fontdefault*Label:     Default
*fontMenu*font3*Label:      Small
*fontMenu*fontsel*Label:     Selection
*fontMenu*font1*Label:      Unreadable
*fontMenu*font4*Label:      Medium
*fontMenu.Label:      VT Fonts
*SimpleMenu*menuLabel.font:      -adobe-helvetica-bold-r-normal--*-120-*-*-*-*-
➡iso8859-*
*SimpleMenu*menuLabel.vertSpace:      100
*SimpleMenu*Sme.height:      16
*SimpleMenu*BackingStore:     NotUseful
*SimpleMenu*HorizontalMargins:      16
*SimpleMenu*Cursor:      left_ptr
*mainMenu*terminate*Label:      Send TERM Signal
*mainMenu*securekbd*Label:      Secure Keyboard
*mainMenu*suspend*Label:      Send STOP Signal
*mainMenu*continue*Label:      Send CONT Signal
*mainMenu*allowsends*Label:      Allow SendEvents
*mainMenu*kill*Label:      Send KILL Signal
*mainMenu*interrupt*Label:      Send INT Signal
*mainMenu*logging*Label:      Log to File
*mainMenu*quit*Label:      Quit
*mainMenu*hangup*Label:      Send HUP Signal
*mainMenu*redraw*Label:      Redraw Window
*mainMenu.Label:      Main Options
*vtMenu*hardreset*Label:      Do Full Reset
*vtMenu*scrollbar*Label:      Enable Scrollbar
*vtMenu*scrollkey*Label:      Scroll to Bottom on Key Press
*vtMenu*scrollttyoutput*Label:      Scroll to Bottom on Tty Output
*vtMenu*jumpscroll*Label:      Enable Jump Scroll
*vtMenu*clearsavedlines*Label:      Reset and Clear Saved Lines
*vtMenu*allow132*Label:      Allow 80/132 Column Switching
*vtMenu*reversevideo*Label:      Enable Reverse Video
*vtMenu*tekshow*Label:      Show Tek Window
*vtMenu*cursesemul*Label:      Enable Curses Emulation
*vtMenu*autowrap*Label:      Enable Auto Wraparound
*vtMenu*tekmode*Label:      Switch to Tek Mode
*vtMenu*visualbell*Label:      Enable Visual Bell
*vtMenu*reversewrap*Label:      Enable Reverse Wraparound
*vtMenu*vthide*Label:      Hide VT Window
*vtMenu*marginbell*Label:      Enable Margin Bell
*vtMenu*autolinefeed*Label:      Enable Auto Linefeed
*vtMenu*altscreen*Label:      Show Alternate Screen
```

continues

Listing 23.2. continued

```
*vtMenu*appcursor*Label:      Enable Application Cursor Keys
*vtMenu*softreset*Label:      Do Soft Reset
*vtMenu*appkeypad*Label:      Enable Application Keypad
*vtMenu.Label:     VT Options
*tek4014*fontLarge:       9x15
*tek4014*font2:     8x13
*tek4014*font3:     6x13
*tek4014*fontSmall:      6x10
XTerm.JoinSession:      False
```

> **NOTE**
>
> The appres application sometimes does not run under Motif, use twm.

The second command is a menu-driven GUI program, editres, which enables you to edit the given resources for an application. This is available for X11R5 and later. The program displays a tree-like representation of all the Widget classes in a program, and enables the user to move through the tree node by node. Search your release for this file. If you do not have this file, don't despair; use the find command. See Figure 23.10 for an editres session.

FIGURE 23.10.

The editres *application.*

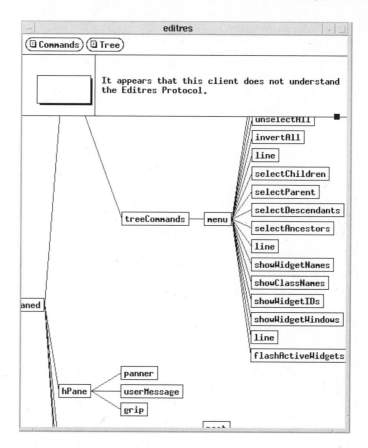

Using the *.mwmrc* File

Create this file from the system.mwmrc file by copying it into your $HOME directory as .mwmrc, and then edit it. (Look in the /var/X11R6/lib directory, and search for the system.mwmrc file using the find command.)

Listing 23.3 shows a sample .mwmrc file. As I stated earlier when working with .Xresources, comments are started with a ! character on a line. Note that, depending on your version of Motif, your listing may look very different than the one shown here. However, you will be able to see the general information presented here.

Listing 23.3. A sample `.mwmrc` file.

```
!!
!!            $HOME/.mwmrc
!!      Modified system.mwmrc for personal changes. kh.
!!
!!
!! Root Menu Description
!!

Menu DefaultRootMenu
{
        "Root Menu"               f.title
        "New Window"              f.exec "xterm &"
        "Shuffle Up"              f.circle_up
        "Shuffle Down"            f.circle_down
        "Refresh"                 f.refresh
        "Pack Icons"              f.pack_icons
!       "Toggle Behavior..."      f.set_behavior
         no-label                 f.separator
        "Restart..."              f.restart
!       "Quit..."                 f.quit_mwm

}

Menu RootMenu_1.1
{
        "Root Menu"               f.title
        "New Window"              f.exec "xterm &"
        "Shuffle Up"              f.circle_up
        "Shuffle Down"            f.circle_down
        "Refresh"                 f.refresh
!       "Pack Icons"              f.pack_icons
!       "Toggle Behavior"         f.set_behavior
         no-label                 f.separator
        "Restart..."              f.restart
}

!!
!! Default Window Menu Description
!!

Menu DefaultWindowMenu
{
        Restore          _R     Alt<Key>F5  f.restore
        Move             _M     Alt<Key>F7  f.move
        Size             _S     Alt<Key>F8  f.resize
        Minimize         _n     Alt<Key>F9  f.minimize
        Maximize         _x     Alt<Key>F10 f.maximize
        Lower            _L     Alt<Key>F3  f.lower
         no-label                           f.separator
        Close            _C     Alt<Key>F4  f.kill
}


!!
!! Key Binding Description
!!8
```

```
Keys DefaultKeyBindings
{
        Shift<Key>Escape    window¦icon      f.post_wmenu
        Alt<Key>space       window¦icon      f.post_wmenu
        Alt<Key>Tab         root¦icon¦window f.next_key
        Alt Shift<Key>Tab         root¦icon¦window    f.prev_key
        Alt<Key>Escape            root¦icon¦window    f.circle_down
        Alt Shift<Key>Escape      root¦icon¦window    f.circle_up
        Alt Shift Ctrl<Key>exclam root¦icon¦window    f.set_behavior
        Alt<Key>F6          window              f.next_key transient
        Alt Shift<Key>F6    window              f.prev_key transient
        Shift<Key>F10            icon           f.post_wmenu
!       Alt Shift<Key>Delete    root¦icon¦window f.restart
}


!!
!! Button Binding Description(s)
!!

Buttons DefaultButtonBindings
{
        <Btn1Down>   icon¦frame  f.raise
        <Btn3Down>   icon¦frame  f.post_wmenu
        <Btn3Down>   root        f.menu      DefaultRootMenu
}

Buttons ExplicitButtonBindings
{
        <Btn1Down>   frame¦icon  f.raise
        <Btn3Down>   frame¦icon  f.post_wmenu
        <Btn3Down>   root        f.menu      DefaultRootMenu
!       <Btn1Up>     icon        f.restore
        Alt<Btn1Down>     window¦icon f.lower
!       Alt<Btn2Down>     window¦icon f.resize
!       Alt<Btn3Down>     window¦icon f.move

}


Buttons PointerButtonBindings
{
        <Btn1Down>   frame¦icon  f.raise
        <Btn3Down>   frame¦icon  f.post_wmenu
        <Btn3Down>   root        f.menu      DefaultRootMenu
        <Btn1Down>   window      f.raise
!       <Btn1Up>     icon        f.restore
        Alt<Btn1Down>     window¦icon f.lower
!       Alt<Btn2Down>     window¦icon f.resize
!       Alt<Btn3Down>     window¦icon f.move
}


!!
!!  END OF mwm RESOURCE DESCRIPTION FILE
!!
```

There are several key features here:

- Key bindings
- Button bindings
- Menu items

A *binding* is a mapping between a user action and a function. The key bindings map keystrokes to actions, and the button bindings map button presses and releases to actions. Menus display the menu items for the user, and let you organize action items into sections.

The format for all the items is as follows:

```
Section_type Section_Title
{
      .. definitions..
      .. definitions..
}
```

In this format, Section_type can be Menu, Keys, or Buttons. The Section_Title is a string defining the variable name. It's a name that can be used to refer to this section in other portions of the file.

The functions shown in the sample file begin with an f. keyword. Some actions are fairly obvious: f.move, f.resize, f.maximize, f.minimize, f.title, f.lower and so on. Some actions are not so obvious: f.separator (displays a line on the menu item), f.circle_up (shuffles window stacking order up), f.circle_down (shuffles window stacking order down).

See Table 23.1 for all the features available for you to work with.

Table 23.1. Motif menu item descriptions.

Function	Description
f.circle_down[*icon¦window*]	Shuffles window stacking order down.
f.circle_up[*icon¦window*]	Shuffles window stacking order up.
f.exec or ! [*command*]	Executes *command*.
f.focus_color	Sets colormap focus of a client window.
f.focus_key	Sets keyboard input focus to a window or icon.
f.goto [*x¦y*]	Hops to a different location on the virtual desktop.
f.kill	Terminates a client window.
f.lower [*-client¦within¦freeFamily*]	Lowers a window to the bottom of the stack.
f.maximize	Maximizes a window.
f.menu	Associates a pull-right menu with the menu pane.
f.minimize	Minimizes a window to an icon.

Function	Description
f.move	Enables the interactive movement of a window.
f.move_constrained	Similar to f.move but restricts movement of the window to within the boundary of the screen.
f.next_cmap	Changes the colormap of the current window to the next colormap in the list.
f.next_key[*icon¦window¦transient*]	Sets keyboard focus to the next window/icon.
f.nop	No operation. It's a filler only.
f.normalize	Restores a window to original size.
f.normalize_and_raise	Restores a window to original size and brings to top of stack.
f.pack_icons	Rearranges the icons on a desktop.
f.pan[*dx¦dy*]	Pans the view of the virtual canvas.
f.pass_keys	Enables/disables (toggles) key bindings.
f.post_wmenu	Posts the window menu.
f.prev_cmap	Changes the colormap of the current window to the previous colormap in the list.
f.prev_key[*icon¦window¦transient*]	Sets keyboard focus to the previous window or icon.
f.quit_mwm	Terminates Motif.
f.raise[*-client¦within¦freeFamily*]	Raises a window to the top of the stack.
f.raise_lower[*within¦freeFamily*]	Raises a window to the top of the stack if it is partially obscured, or lowers it if not at all obscured.
f.refresh	Redraws all windows.
f.refresh_win	Redraws only a specific window.
f.resize	Enables the interactive sizing of a window.
f.restore	Restores the state of an icon/window to its normal state.
f.restore_and_raise	Restores and raises a window to the top of the stack.
f.restart	Restarts mwm.
f.screen [*next¦prev¦backscreen_number*]	Jumps cursor to a specific screen, or to the next, previous, or last visited screen.
f.send_msg *message_number*	Sends a client message.
f.separator	Draws a line.

continues

Table 23.2. continued

Function	Description
f.set_behavior	Restarts Motif, toggling between default or custom behaviors.
f.title	Names the menu.
f.track_pan	Moves the canvas interactively.

You can get more information from the *OSF/Motif Reference* book. In my humble opinion, it's dry but informative; the book will supply you with all the information you could possibly want about these commands.

Adding Your Own Menu Items

Let's see about defining your own menu items. The following could be a sample menu item:

```
Menu MyGames
{
"Kamran Games" f.title
no-label        f.separator
"Tetris"        f.exec "xtetris &"
"Mahhjong"      f.exec "xmahjongg &"
"Chess"         f.exec "xchess &"
}
```

The f.title action specifies a heading for the submenu. The f.separator draws a line under the title. The f.exec fires up the command shown in double quotes.

> **TIP**
>
> Note the ampersand in f.exec for starting these tasks in the background. Do not start a task that may never return and thus hang up your mwm session.

Now, you can add this new menu to the root menu by adding the following line in your DefaultRoot-Menu definitions:

```
"Utils"         f.menu      MyGames
```

More on Button and Key Bindings

The key and button bindings work in the same way as menus. The first obvious difference is the extra column with the words icon, frame, window, and root in it. These words force the bindings on the context. The root applies to any location of the pointer on the root window, the frame or window keywords apply binding only when the pointer is in a window or its frame. The icon bindings apply to icons.

In your .Xdefaults file, refer to these key bindings for the class Mwm:

```
Mwm*keyBindings: DefaultKeyBindings
```

Here are some of the descriptions in the key bindings:

```
Shift<Key>Escape   window¦icon      f.post_wmenu
Alt<Key>space      window¦icon      f.post_wmenu
Alt<Key>Tab        root     f.menu  DefaultRootMenu
```

The syntax for a keystroke binding is

```
modifier<Key>key
```

in which *modifier* is Alt, Control, or Shift. The key can be a keystroke, function key, and so on. The first two declarations describe the same action: show the window menu, but with different keystrokes. The third key binding shows a method for displaying the root menu.

The button bindings are the bindings for your buttons. The three important bindings to remember are as follows:

```
Buttons DefaultButtonBindings
Buttons ExplicitButtonBindings
Buttons PointerButtonBindings
```

In your .Xresource or .Xresources file, refer to one of these button bindings for the class Mwm as

```
Mwm*buttonBindings: DefaultButtonBindings
```

or

```
Mwm*buttonBindings: ExplicitButtonBindings
```

or

```
Mwm*buttonBindings: PointerButtonBindings
```

Customizing Your Desktop with Clients

This is done by using some of the client software that comes with your X11R6 distribution. We will cover the following applications:

*   xsetroot
*   xset
*   xdpyinfo
*   xmodmap

There are several more utilities in the /usr/bin/X11 directory for you to play with: bitmap, xmag, xcalc, and so on. Check each one out to customize your desktop. The ones described here are not so intuitively obvious.

xsetroot

This client customizes the root window characteristics. Here are some of the options available:

- `-cursor cursorfile maskfile`   This option changes the cursor to a displayed mask value. See the sidebar for creating your own cursor using bitmap.
- `-cursor_name name`   This is the name of the standard cursors in the X11 protocol.
- `-bitmap filename`   This option creates a tiled surface on the root window with a bitmap. Check the `/usr/lib/X11/bitmaps` directory for a list of the standard bitmaps.
- `-fg color foreground`   This option sets the color for the bitmap on the root display.
- `-bg color background`   This option sets the color for the bitmap on the root display.
- `-gray or -grey`   This option sets the background to a pleasant (for some) gray background.
- `-rv`   This option reverses the foreground and background colors.
- `-solid color`   This option sets the root window to a solid color; for example, `-solid red` will set a red background.

Look in the `/usr/lib/X11` directory of the file called `rgb.txt` for a list of colors, and look at the later section on colors in this chapter for more information.

See the man pages for additional features for `xsetroot`.

> **NOTE**
>
> The `cursorfile` is an ASCII file with arrays of characters. You create a bitmap using the bitmap utility. Then, run this bitmap through `bmtoa` to convert a bitmap to arrays. There is a reverse utility called `atobm` to convert existing arrays to bitmaps, for use with the bitmap editor.

Using xset

This command sets up some of the basic options on your environment. Some of these options may not work on your particular system. It's worth it to check these out.

Set your bell volume with this command:

```
xset b volume frequency durationInMilliseconds.
```

For example, the command

```
xset b 70 4000 60
```

sets the keyboard bell to about 70 percent of maximum, a frequency of 4000 Hz, and on for 60 milliseconds.

To turn on the speaker, use the following command:

```
xset b on
```

To turn it off, type this:

```
xset b off
```

Turning the speaker back on will return the volume to its default.

Use xset c *volume* to set the keyclick volume in percentages. A volume setting of 0 turns it off. Any other number (1 through 100) turns it on for that percentage. Of course, for this command to work, you must have your speaker turned on.

To set the mouse speed, use the following command at the prompt:

```
xset m acceleration threshold
```

The acceleration is the number of times faster than the threshold that each mouse movement travels. This way, you can zip across the screen with a twitch. Use care in setting this feature unless you are very dexterous.

Invoking the Screen Saver

Use xset s *seconds* to enable the screen saver. You can turn off the screen saver with the off option. The default option reverts to system default time for blanking the screen.

For more options type in xset.

Using Fonts

For example, to load your own fonts, use the following command:

```
$       xset fp /user/home/myfont,/usr/lib/X11/fontsdir
$       xset fp rehash
```

The rehash command forces the server to reread its systems files for your command to take effect.

To restore to normal, use the following command:

```
$       xset fp default
$       xset fp rehash
```

See the section, "Fonts," later in this chapter.

Getting More Information about Your Display: *xdpyinfo*

The xdpyinfo utility gives you more information about your X server. It is used to list the capabilities of your server and all predefined parameters for it. Some of these include the following:

- Name of display
- Version number

- Vendor name
- Extensions

The list is too exhaustive to included here, and will be different for your installation. Pipe its output to a file, and review it for information about the server. Your output may look different. (See Listing 23.4.)

Listing 23.4. Output from `xdpyinfo`.

```
$ xdpyinfo
name of display:    :0.0
version number:    11.0
vendor string:    XFree86
vendor release number:    2110
maximum request size:  262140 bytes
motion buffer size:  0
bitmap unit, bit order, padding:    32, LSBFirst, 32
image byte order:    LSBFirst
number of supported pixmap formats:    2
supported pixmap formats:
    depth 1, bits_per_pixel 1, scanline_pad 32
    depth 8, bits_per_pixel 8, scanline_pad 32
keycode range:    minimum 8, maximum 134
focus:  window 0x200000d, revert to Parent
number of extensions:    6
    XTestExtension1
    SHAPE
    MIT-SHM
    Multi-Buffering
    XTEST
    MIT-SUNDRY-NONSTANDARD
default screen number:    0
number of screens:    1

screen #0:
  dimensions:    800x600 pixels (270x203 millimeters)
8  resolution:    75x75 dots per inch
  depths (2):    1, 8
  root window id:    0x29
  depth of root window:    8 planes
  number of colormaps:    minimum 1, maximum 1
  default colormap:    0x27
  default number of colormap cells:    256
  preallocated pixels:    black 1, white 0
  options:    backing-store YES, save-unders YES
  current input event mask:    0x30003c
    ButtonPressMask          ButtonReleaseMask          EnterWindowMask
    LeaveWindowMask          SubstructureRedirectMask FocusChangeMask
  number of visuals:    6
  default visual id:  0x20
  visual:
    visual id:    0x20
    class:    PseudoColor
    depth:    8 planes
    size of colormap:    256 entries
    red, green, blue masks:    0x0, 0x0, 0x0
    significant bits in color specification:    6 bits
```

```
visual:
   visual id:    0x21
   class:    DirectColor
   depth:    8 planes
   size of colormap:    8 entries
   red, green, blue masks:    0x7, 0x38, 0xc0
   significant bits in color specification:    6 bits
(... this is a very long listing ... )
***END LISTING
```

Help for Left-Handed Users: *xmodmap*

If you are a left-handed user, it might a bit uncomfortable to use the "left" button with your third or second finger. The X designers kept you in mind. If you want to swap the functionality of the pointers on your mouse or pointer, use the xmodmap command. First, display the current mappings like so:

```
xmodmap -pp
```

You see the following display:

```
        Physical    Button
        Button      Code
        1           1
        2           2
        3           3
```

This shows you that button code 1 is mapped to physical button 1, button code 2 is mapped to physical button 2, and button code 3 is mapped to physical button 3.

Now issue this command:

```
xmodmap -e 'pointer =  3 2 1'
```

This reverses the mappings on the buttons. Now, physical button 1 is mapped to button code 3, and so forth. To confirm this, retype the xmodmap -pp command.

```
Physical    Button
Button      Code
1           3
2           2
3           1
```

You can always revert to the default with xmodmap -e 'pointer = default'.

Useful Command Line Options

Some other standard input parameters that can be used to change the behavior of a window from the command line are as follows:

-borderwidth or -bw   Border width of pixels in the frame. This may not be available for all clients.

-foreground or -fg	The foreground color. For example, this can be the text color for an xterm.
-background or -bg	The background color. For example, this can be the text color for an xterm.
-display	Display on which the client runs.
-font or -fn	The font to use for a particular text display.
-geometry	Specifies the geometry.
-iconic	Starts the application in an iconic form.
-rv or -reverse	Swaps foreground and background colors.
-title	The title for the title bar.
-name	The name for the application.

Of course, the man pages on an application can give you more detailed information than one chapter in a book. Explore a little. For example, you can call one terminal name editor, and set your resources in the .Xresources file for name editor.

```
-display nodename:displayname.ScreenName
```

This starts up a remote session on another node. The *displayname* and *ScreenName* are optional and default to zero if not entered.

Logging into Remote Machines

You can log into remote machines by using the xterm -display option, provided you have set your Linux machine up for networks. The remote system must allow you to open a display on its machine. This is done with the xhost + command on its machine. The xhost + command is dangerous because it allows anyone to access your machine, so use it cautiously.

When you want to open an xterm on the remote machine, alma, run this command:

```
xterm -display alma:0.0 &
```

The format for the option into the display parameter is as follows:

```
[host]:[server][:screen]
```

If you are given permission to open a display, you are logged into the remote machine. You can verify this with the uname command. Check the DISPLAY with the echo $DISPLAY command.

When you log out with the exit command, the remote session and the xterm are terminated.

TIP

One of the most common reasons for not being able to open a remote terminal is that the remote host does not allow you to open windows there. Ask the remote users to use the xhost command at the remote machine as a part of their login.

Colors

All the colors in the X Window system are located in the `/usr/lib/X11/rgb.txt` file. This file consists of four columns. The first three columns specify red, green, and blue values; the last entry specifies the name that you can use in your parameters.

A partial listing of the `rgb.txt` file is shown in Listing 23.5.

Listing 23.5. Excerpt from `rgb.txt` file.

```
255 250 250    snow
248 248 255    ghost white
248 248 255    GhostWhite
245 245 245    white smoke
245 245 245    WhiteSmoke
220 220 220    gainsboro
255 250 240    floral white
255 250 240    FloralWhite
253 245 230    old lace
253 245 230    OldLace
250 240 230    linen
250 235 215    antique white
255 239 213    PapayaWhip
255 235 205    blanched almond
255 235 205    BlanchedAlmond
255 218 185    peach puff
255 218 185    PeachPuff
255 222 173    navajo white
255 228 181    moccasin
255 248 220    cornsilk
255 255 240    ivory
255 250 205    lemon chiffon
255 250 205    LemonChiffon
255 245 238    seashell
240 255 240    honeydew
245 255 250    mint cream
255 240 245    LavenderBlush
255 228 225    misty rose
255 228 225    MistyRose
255 255 255    white
  0   0   0    black
 47  79  79    dark slate grey
 47  79  79    DarkSlateGrey
105 105 105    dim gray
105 105 105    DimGray
105 105 105    dim grey
105 105 105    DimGrey
112 128 144    slate gray
112 128 144    SlateGray
112 128 144    slate grey
112 128 144    SlateGrey
119 136 153    light slate gray
119 136 153    LightSlateGray
119 136 153    light slate grey
119 136 153    LightSlateGrey
```

continues

Listing 23.5. continued

```
190 190 190      gray
190 190 190      grey
211 211 211      light grey
```

Because red, green, and blue have 256 values each, the number of possible colors is 16,777,216. Not many workstations can display that many colors at one time. So, X uses a facility to map these colors onto the display, called a *colormap*. A color display uses several bits for displaying entries from this map. The xdpyinfo program gives you the number of bits for the display. This is a frame buffer. A 1-bit frame signifies a black-and-white display. An 8-bit frame buffer signifies 2 to the power of 8 entries, or 256 possible colors.

Unfortunately, due to different phosphors on different screens, your color specification on one monitor may be completely different on another monitor. Tektronix provides a tool called *xtici*, an API, and docs to counter such problems by using the international CIEXYZ standard for color specifications. This is called the Color Management System (CMS), which uses a model called HVC (Hue-Value-Chroma). In the X11R5 (or later) release, look for *Xcms* for more details, or contact Tektronix.

Fonts

Fonts in the X Window system are designed for maximum flexibility. The following are two good utilities to help you sift through some of the 400 or so font types on a basic system:

xlsfonts	Lists the fonts in your system.
xfontsel	Enables you to interactively see what fonts are available on your system and what they look like on the screen.

Using *xlsfonts*

First, let's examine the font names themselves. Use the xlsfonts command to list the fonts on your system. Type the command on an xterm, and because the listing from xlsfonts is very long, be sure to pipe to a text file for review. You should see a listing in which each line is of this form:

`-foundry-family-wt-sl-wd-p-pts-hr-vr-sp-ave-charset-style`

The *foundry* is the company that first developed the font. The most common ones are misc, Adobe, Bitstream, and B&H. You may see more on your system from the results of your xlsfonts command. A *foundry* of misc implies a font with fixed width and height per character; the rest were donated by their respective manufacturers.

The *family* is the general type of font: Courier, Helvetica, New Century Schoolbook, Lucida, and so on. Some families are monospaced, meaning that all their characters have the same width. The other families are proportionally spaced, meaning that each character has a separate width. Courier and Lucida are monospaced fonts. New Century Schoolbook is proportionally spaced.

Use monospaced information for tabular information or running text. This makes your text line up cleanly in running displays. Proportionally spaced fonts are helpful for text in buttons or menu items.

The wt and sl parameters stand for weights and slants, respectively. The common weights are bold and medium. Bold text is drawn with a thicker pen than the normal pen. The common slants are (r) roman, (o) oblique, and (i) italic. The roman text is drawn upright, and oblique text has characters sheared to the right. The italic text is similar to oblique text, but the characters are touched up to show a smoother effect. You may also have reverse oblique (ro) and reverse italic (ri), which make the text lean to the left instead of the right.

The p stands for the point size, which traditionally is 1/72 of an inch. Most monitors support only 75 or 100 dots per inch (dpi) resolution. Because X fonts are bitmaps, it seems logical that the most common fonts within X are of two types: 75dpi and 100dpi.

This number is found in the two fields hr and vr, which stand for the horizontal and vertical resolution, respectively. In almost all cases, you specify either 75 or 100 in each of these fields.

The sp refers to the spacing between two characters on the screen. This can be m for monospaced, p for proportional, or c for fixed fonts that have each character occupy a fixed box.

The ave is 1/10 of the average width of all the characters in the set.

The character set and style is usually set to ISO8859-1. This refers to the ISO Latin-1 character set, which includes characters found in ASCII and other European character sets.

Now that you've seen the large number of options that can define a font, you can rely on using wildcards to specify most of the options for a font. The server matches the first font name that matches your specification with a wildcard. In other words, you only have to specify the parameters you want to change, and use the asterisk for the rest.

For example, *courier-roman gets the first specification for the roman-weighted Courier font. However, *courier gets the bold Courier font. This is because the bold specification exists before the roman specification in the fonts file.

> **TIP**
>
> Use the xset fp=fontpath command to set the directory (75 or 100 dpi) you want searched first in the front of the font path. This guarantees that the correct dpi size directory is searched first.

The font search path is the path used by the server to search for the fonts in your system. This path is usually set to the following value:

```
/usr/lib/X11/fonts/misc,/usr/lib/X11/fonts/75dpi,/usr/lib/X11/fonts/100dpi
```

In each of these directories is a file called fonts.dir. This is a list of all the fonts in the directory, and has two entries per line. The first entry gives a font filename; the second entry gives the complete font description. The first line in the file gives the number of entries in the file.

You can create another file in the font path to alias your own font names by using the file called `fonts.alias`. The server uses only the first one it finds in its path, so just keep one such file in the first directory in your font path. The `fonts.alias` format is very similar to the `fonts.dir` file, except that the first entry is not a filename; it is an alias for a font name. So, if you want to specify a special font type for all your editor `xterms`, you need the following line:

```
editterm    *lucida-medium-r-*-100*
```

Then, you can invoke your `xterm` with this command:

```
xterm -fn editterm &
```

This gets an `xterm` window with the desired font, and is a lot better than typing in the full font specification. Also, by changing the alias once, you can change it for all scripts that use this alias, rather than modifying each script individually.

A good place to start is the `/usr/lib/X11/fonts/misc` directory, where a `fonts.alias` exists from your initial X installation. This file has the fixed and variable aliases defined for you to work with.

Using *xfontsel*

The `xfontsel` program helps you get a better feel for some of the parameters of a particular font. (See Figure 23.11.)

FIGURE 23.11.

Using `xfontsel`.

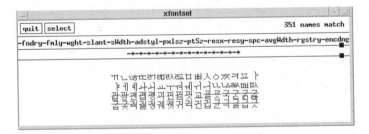

You can move your pointer to any one of the parameters in the first line and click Button1. As you move the pointer on a field, it draws a box around itself to show that it has focus.

If any fonts options exist for your selection, you are presented with a pop-up menu to select from. Move the mouse to a selection, and click on the selection. You see your selection displayed in the font specification string, as well as a sample of what the font will look like on the fonts display screen below that.

Where to Go from Here

In Chapter 32, "Motif for Programmers," you will learn how to program your application.

If you want more information about specific vendors, you can get a wealth of information from the Internet about the latest releases and sources to shareware utilities. Listed in Table 23.3 are some of the newsgroups that can provide you with more information about vendors.

Table 23.3. Some newsgroups with more information.

Newsgroup	Focus
comp.sources.x	Sources for X Window system
comp.windows.x.apps	X Window applications
comp.windows.x.motif	Motif programming issues
comp.os.windows.x.i386	XF86 discussions.

A good starting point for progammers is the site at arachnid.cs.cf.ac.uk/Dave/X_lecture/ X_lecture.

Summary

In this chapter, you have learned the following:

- How to install Motif on Linux.
- How to start an X Window session from the prompt.
- How to use Widgets and the characteristics of these Widgets. This provides the basis for learning how to program your own applications in the Motif environment.
- The basics of the Motif Window Manager, mwm.
- How to move about in mwm and control windows with the keyboard and mouse.
- How to customize your desktop with resource files and client applications.
- How to set your environment to your liking with resources.
- How to use some standard tools available in X to further set up your desktop.
- Where to look next for more information.

OPEN LOOK and OpenWindows

This chapter introduces you to OPEN LOOK on Linux. Ideally, this chapter could be expanded into a book of its own. That being impossible however, we will cover some of the basics of OPEN LOOK in this chapter, including

- What is OPEN LOOK?
- What to install on Linux.
- How to work with a look and feel that's different from Motif.
- How to work with the virtual desktop.
- How to customize your desktop.
- Troubleshooting tips.
- Where to get more information about OPEN LOOK.

If you have not already done so, please read Chapter 23, "Using Motif." This chapter will build on that chapter, so there won't be duplicate information for you to weed through. The information you require from the Motif chapter is the discussion on X Window, working with pointers, and the Motif environment. You will definitely need to know how to use resources in the .Xdefaults files and starting X Window via shell scripts like startx.

What Is OPEN LOOK?

OPEN LOOK is a specification of a *Graphical User Interface* (GUI). A GUI determines the look and feel of a system—the shape of windows, buttons, and scrollbars; how you resize things; how you edit files; and so on. The OPEN LOOK GUI is specified, developed, and maintained primarily by Sun Microsystems Inc. XView is simply the port on Linux. When I talk about OpenWindows, I will refer to XView for Linux in this chapter.

OpenWindows is a windowing environment that conforms to the OPEN LOOK Graphical User Interface Specifications. It's compatible with the X11 window system from MIT as well as (currently) Sun's NeWS and SunView, so you can intermix programs written for any of these systems. It comes from Sun and also with UNIX System V Release 4 from certain vendors.

> **TIP**
>
> OpenWindows should not be called "Windows" or "OPEN LOOK" or "OpenLook," because these terms are either wrong or apply to something else. OpenWindows is sometimes also called openwin or xnews, after the program used to start it and the main executable itself, respectively.

NOTE

The X Window system is a trademark of the Massachusetts Institute of Technology. OPEN LOOK is a trademark of AT&T. OpenWindows is a trademark of Sun Microsystems, Inc.

Portions ©Copyright Bigelow & Holmes 1986, 1985. Lucida is a registered trademark of Bigelow & Holmes. Permission to use the Lucida trademark is hereby granted only in association with the images and fonts described in this file. Portions may be ©1990 Solbourne Computers.

Portions of olvwm not covered under the above copyrights are ©1991 Scott Oaks.

Several toolkits exist for programmers to use in developing programs that conform to the OPEN LOOK specifications:

- OPEN LOOK Intrinsics Toolkit (OLIT)
- XView (This is what you have for Linux.)
- The NeWS Toolkit (TNT)
- C++ User Interface Toolkit (UIT)

OLIT was AT&T's OPEN LOOK Intrinsics Toolkit for the X Window system. OLIT used a widget set and was therefore easy to learn for people who were already X11/Xt programmers. You could buy the source from AT&T, although you didn't get the same version that Sun would ship.

Sun includes the OLIT library in OpenWindows. OLIT is also often included in UNIX System V Release 4. OLIT was written in C. The last release of OLIT in OpenWindows 3.0 was OLIT 3.0. OLIT support passed to USL (UNIX System Laboratories), who replaced it with MoOLIT (see the following Tip).

TIP

You need an OLIT source in order to develop a large application or anything else that uses subclasses.

XView is Sun's toolkit for X11, written in C. It is similar in programmer interface to SunView. There's even a shell script to help migrate source code from SunView to XView. XView is often said to be the easiest toolkit to learn if you are not familiar with X Window.

The XView toolkit is included in OpenWindows, and full source is available by anonymous FTP from export.lcs.mit.edu (and elsewhere). The current version of XView from Sun is 3.2p1.

The NeWS Toolkit (TNT) is an object-oriented programming system based on the PostScript language and NeWS. TNT implements many of the OPEN LOOK interface components required to build the user interface of an application. It's currently included in OpenWindows.

The current version of TNT from Sun is 3.1. Release 3 contains some incompatibilities with TNT 1.0 and TNT 2.0, but Sun is committed to supporting the API, at least until it stops NeWS support some time later this year and replaces it with Display PostScript. Wait. You might ask what "is committed to" means in this context; the answer seems to be that it means absolutely nothing.

Sun currently asserts that it is committed to OLIT, however.

The C++ User Interface Toolkit (UIT) consists of an object-oriented C++ class library layered on top of XView and a tool to generate code from files written in a graphical interface language called DevGuide 2 GIL. The UIT also includes features that simplify event management and the use of PostScript and color. It is said to be compatible with OpenWindows Versions 2 and 3, and presumably Version 3.0.1, as the release mentions that it works on Solaris 2.

UIT is not an official Sun-supported product but an ongoing project of various people within Sun. It can be found on export.lcs.mit.edu in the MIT /R5contrib directory as UITV3.tar.Z (use binary mode!).

> **TIP**
>
> If you cannot decide which GUI to use, consider the MoOLIT interface. MoOLIT is a version of OLIT from AT&T/USL that lets users choose between a Motif- and an OPEN LOOK–type feel at runtime.

olwm and olvwm

There are two window managers for OpenWindows: olwm and olvwm. A *window manager* is responsible for deciding how to lay out windows on the screen, and for managing the user's interaction with the windows.

olwm is the standard OPEN LOOK window manager. It is included with all of the OpenWindows implementations, and you can also get the source via FTP because Sun donated it to the freeware domain.

The olvwm program is a version of olwm that manages a virtual desktop (hence the v in its name). It shows a little map on the screen, with the currently displayed area represented by a small rectangle. You can move around by dragging the rectangle or with the arrow keys. This enables you to run several clients (applications) that occupy the full screen and move the display around from one to the other. Olvwm was derived from the OpenWindows 3.0 olwm by Scott Oaks. You need to have XView 3.0 to compile it.

The olvewm and olwm packages are included on the CD at the back of the book.

Getting Started with OpenWindows

First, confirm that you have installed the XView system on your Linux system. The XView distribution consists of the files in Listing 24.1. You will need to follow the directions included with XView to install these files.

Listing 24.1. `XView` package contents.

```
xv32_a.tgz   Static Libraries for developing Xview 3.2
applications.
xv32_sa.tgz  Static Libraries for debugging Xview 3.2
applications.
xv32_so.tgz  Shared Libraries for Xview 3.2.
xv32exmp.tgz Sample programs for Xview 3.2.
xvinc32.tgz  Include files for Xview 3.2 programming.
xvmenus.tgz  Menus and help files for the OpenLook Window
Manager.
xvol32.tgz   Xview 3.2 Configuration files, programs, and
documentation.
```

Install the packages shown in Listing 24.1 for your `XView` system using the setup program as shown in Chapter 3, "Installing and Updating Linux." If you have already done this installation, you should have at least some files in `/usr/openwin/bin`.

Starting OpenWindows

You need one of two files to get started with OpenWindows: either `.xinitrc` or `.xsessionrc`.

The first time you run OpenWindows, a `.xinitrc` file is created in your login directory (`$HOME`). If it already exists, you might have to edit it somewhat. It's best to move all old X11 files you have to another directory, and then merge the old and new files.

> **TIP**
>
> If you use `xdm`, you should use `.xsessionrc` instead of `.xinitrc`, because `xdm` doesn't look at your `.xinitrc` file.

Please refer to Chapter 23 for a detailed discussion on `.xinitrc` and installing X on your Linux system.

You should take the following steps to convert this `.xinitrc` file into one for using OpenWindows:

- Change the reference to your window manager to either `olwm` or `olvwm` depending on which window manager you want to use.
- Ensure that the `/usr/openwin/bin` directory is in your path.
- You need an environment variable, `OPENWINHOME`, to be set to the directory where the files for your `openwin` system will reside. This variable is usually set to `/usr/openwin` when you log in.
- Copy the `.xinitrc` file into `.xsessionrc` file if you are going to use `xdm`.

There are other optional files you can create in your `$HOME` directory, depending on which version of `olwm` or `olvwm` you use:

■ `.openwin-init`

This file is used to initialize your desktop when you start OpenWindows with `olwm` or
`olvwm`. A sample `.openwin-init` file is shown in Listing 24.2. This sample file shows how
two `xterms` and one clock application are started every time you start a session.
OpenWindows looks at a file called `.openwin-init` in your home directory. If `.openwin-init` is not found in the home directory, OpenWindows looks in the `$OPENWINHOME/lib`
directory. The `.openwin-init` file contains a list of applications to start by default.

Listing 24.2. A sample `.openwin-init` file.

```
#!/bin/sh
#
# Created by 'xtoolplaces' on Fri Dec  9 23:10:23 1994
#

/usr/bin/X11/xterm -sb -sl 500 -j -ls -fn 7x14 -geom 82x24+45+52 &
clock -Wp 4 5 -Ws 172 52 -WP 224 533 +Wi &
xterm -e /bin/bash -geom 80x24+103+89 &
```

■ `.openwin-menu*`

Look in `$OPENWINHOME/lib` (normally `/usr/openwin/lib`) for this and other similarly
named (`openwin-menu-s`, `openwin-menu-d`, and so on) files without the leading period (.).
We will discuss these files in the "Environment Variables" section later in this chapter.

■ `.Xdefaults`

The `.Xdefaults` file applies to OpenWindows as well. You can put X Window resource
specifications in here. In particular, it is a good idea to include at least

```
OpenWindows.FocusLenience:    true
*Input: TRUE
```

These enable non-ICCCM-compliant programs to receive input even if they forget to ask for it.

TIP

`props`, the program that runs when you select Properties from the default root menu under
`olwm` or `olvwm`, writes your choices into `.Xdefaults`.

Don't put comments in `.Xdefaults`, because `props` deletes them.

NOTE

Note that the mouse speed for OpenWindows is best set in your `.xinitrc` with `xset m`.
See the man page for `xset` (`man xset` and `xset -help`) for more information. Do not use
the `.startup.ps` file for setting the mouse speed as suggested by some texts. This is because
the `.startup.ps` method can cause more problems if not used correctly.

Start your program up with the startx support. See Figure 24.1 for what you should see when you start OpenWindows.

FIGURE 24.1.

The Xterm in OpenWindows.

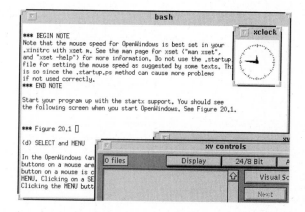

SELECT and MENU

In OpenWindows (and Sun Workstations, for that matter), the left and right buttons on a mouse are referred to as SELECT and MENU, respectively. Clicking the SELECT button in a window selects a window. Clicking the MENU button in a window displays any menu for that application.

> **TIP**
>
> If you have a three-button mouse, the middle button is called the ADJUST button. You can simulate an ADJUST button on a two-button mouse by clicking both buttons together.

> **TIP**
>
> The Shift-Button1 combination is also ADJUST, and Ctrl-Button1 is also MENU. These two combinations are useful if you have a one-button mouse.

Working Within OpenWindows and *olwm*

Let's examine the borders on an Xterm in OpenWindows in greater detail. (See Figure 24.2.) These borders are drawn by olwm and have special functionality.

FIGURE 24.2.

OpenWindows borders.

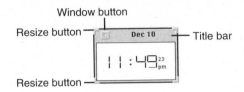

The resize handles (buttons) are the indentations on each window. You can resize a window by pressing and holding SELECT over any of the resize corners and then dragging the mouse to the new location.

Releasing the mouse button sets the new size of the window. If you hold down the Ctrl key while you are dragging, the resize operation is constrained to resize vertically or horizontally, depending on which direction you move first.

The window button is the small box with a downward-pointing triangle near the left end of the title bar. Clicking MENU over the window button brings up the window menu. Clicking SELECT over the left mouse button on the window button executes the window menu's default action. This usually closes the window into an icon. You can change the window menu's default action by holding down the Ctrl key while manipulating the window menu.

An icon represents a closed window. You can still do most of the same operations as with an open window. Moving and selecting icons with SELECT and ADJUST is exactly the same as for open windows. A similar version of the Window menu is available on an icon by pressing MENU. Double-clicking SELECT opens the icon. Icons cannot be resized.

You can select a group of windows and icons by using the left or middle mouse buttons over the *workspace* (the area of the screen outside of all windows and icons, commonly known as the "root window"). Pressing either SELECT or ADJUST and dragging the mouse defines a rubber band rectangle.

When you release the mouse button, you will be operating on the set of windows and icons enclosed by this rectangle. If you created the rectangle using SELECT, the windows and icons within will be selected, and all other objects will be deselected. If you used ADJUST, the objects within will have their selected state toggled, and any other windows and icons already selected will remain selected.

TIP

Some OPEN LOOK pop-up windows have a pushpin instead of a Window button. The pin is either in or out, and you can click SELECT on the pin to change it to the other state. If the pin is out, pressing a command button inside the window executes the command and then dismisses (takes down) the window. If the pin is in, the window is "pinned" to the workspace, and it remains on the screen even after you have pressed a command button in the window. This enables you to press several command buttons in the same window. Pulling the pin out (by clicking SELECT over it) dismisses the window immediately.

Menus

XView supports menus of the form shown in Figure 24.3. This is a sample menu containing options for you to choose. These menus are called *pop-up menus*.

Pop-up menus are operated using the MENU mouse button. There are two methods of operating with an OPEN LOOK menu: the click-move-click method and the press-drag-release method. You choose either method by clicking the MENU button (pressing and releasing it quickly) or by pressing it down and holding it.

If you click the MENU button, a menu pops up and will stay up indefinitely. To continue operating the menu, click the MENU button over a menu item. To dismiss the menu, click the MENU button on an area of the screen outside the menu. To operate menus in press-drag-release mode, press the MENU button and hold it down while you move the mouse. The menu remains on the screen as long as you hold down the MENU button. To execute an action, move the pointer over a menu item and release the mouse button. To dismiss the menu, move the pointer outside the menu and release the MENU button. Some menu items have a submenu. This is indicated by a right-pointing triangle at the right edge of the item. To activate a submenu, click on the item (in click-move-click mode) or move the pointer to the item and then move toward the right edge of the menu (in press-drag-release mode).

Some menus have pushpins. If a menu has a pushpin, it will initially be in the "out" state. If you click on the pin (in click-move-click mode) or move over it and release (in press-drag-release mode), you will pin the menu to the workspace. The menu will remain on the screen indefinitely, and you can execute commands from it by clicking on its items. To remove the menu, move over the pin and click SELECT on it.

The Workspace Menu

Pressing MENU over the workspace brings up the Workspace menu. This menu is customizable, but it typically contains at least the following items. The arrows to the right of any item indicate a submenu for the displayed item. (See Figure 24.3.)

FIGURE 24.3.

*The pinnable Workspace
menu.*

■ Shells This item opens up another submenu with shells to choose from, including color terminals, X Terminals, VT100 emulator, and other assorted shells. (See Figure 24.4.) You can also pin this menu to your desktop. Clicking the MENU button on the menu brings up another submenu enabling you to resize this menu.

FIGURE 24.4.

The Shell selections from the main menu.

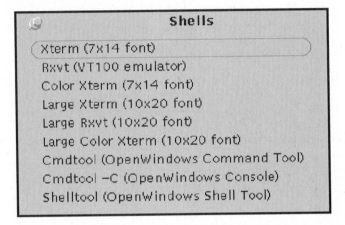

■ Editors This item lets you select many types of editors, including Textedit, the standard OpenWindows text editor. See Figure 24.5 for a view of the Textedit.

FIGURE 24.5.

The Textedit utility.

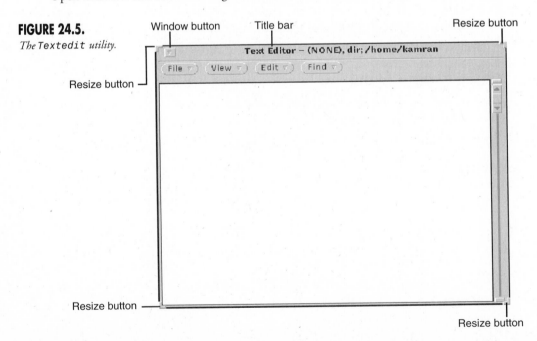

The Cut utility can be used to cut and paste sections between files. You can access any of the menu items by using the SELECT button on any of the menu items.

■ Tools   This opens up the File Manager, manual reader, calculator, spreadsheet, and other assorted items. (See Figure 24.6.)

FIGURE 24.6.

The File Manager utility.

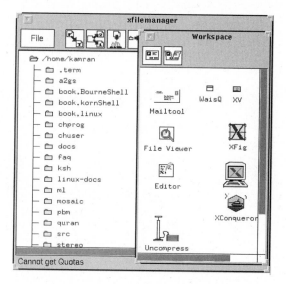

■ Games   This item has a submenu that enables you to invoke games. Check it out.

■ Utilities   This item has a submenu that contains several utility functions for the workspace, including Refresh (redisplay all windows on the screen), Lock Screen, and Save Workspace.

■ Properties   This item brings up the Workspace Properties window, which enables you to view and customize settings of the OpenWindows environment.

■ X11 programs   This item brings up a very long menu of all the X11 programs in `/usr/bin/X11`.

■ XView programs   This item brings up a very long menu of all the X11 programs in `/usr/bin/openwin`.

■ XV 3.00   This brings up the program that I used to capture all the screens for this book.

■ The Window menu   This lets you choose any window on your desktop as your active window.

■ Screen saver option   This item lets you select a screen saver for your session. The Lock screen item is similar to screen saver except that it requires your password to restore the desktop.

■ Exit   This selection shuts down all applications and exits the windowing system. A confirmation notice appears first to give you a chance to cancel the operation.

Configuring Menus for OpenWindows

Look in $OPENWINHOME/lib (normally /usr/openwin/lib) for the file openwin-menu and other files of the form openwin-menu-*. Copy these files into your home directory with a period in front of them. For example, copy openwin-menu as .openwin-menu.

The .openwin-menu file is used to set up your workspace menu. Look at Listing 24.3 for this file.

Listing 24.3. The default .openwin-menu file.

```
#
# @(#)openwin-menu        23.15 91/09/14 openwin-menu
#
#       OpenWindows default root menu file - top level menu
#

"Workspace" TITLE

"Shells " MENU          $OPENWINHOME/lib/openwin-menu-s

"Editors " MENU         $OPENWINHOME/lib/openwin-menu-e

"Tools " MENU           $OPENWINHOME/lib/openwin-menu-t

"Games " MENU           $OPENWINHOME/lib/openwin-menu-g

"Utilities " MENU       $OPENWINHOME/lib/openwin-menu-u

#"Slingshot Examples " MENU    $OPENWINHOME/lib/openwin-ss-ex
#
#"UIT Examples " MENU    $OPENWINHOME/lib/openwin-uit

"Properties "           PROPERTIES

SEPARATOR
"X11 Programs "         DIRMENU     /usr/X11R6/bin

"XView Programs " DIRMENU      $OPENWINHOME/bin
"XV 3.00"         exec /usr/X11R6/bin/xv

"Window Menu "    WINMENU

SEPARATOR

"Screensaver " MENU     $OPENWINHOME/lib/openwin-menu-screensave
```

```
"Lock Screen " MENU       $OPENWINHOME/lib/openwin-menu-xlock

"Exit"          EXIT
```

Let's look at some of the entries in this .openwin-menu file.

- The # signs mark lines as comments.
- The line "Workspace" TITLE defines the name of the menu.
- The next line defines "Shells " as a menu located in a file $OPENWINHOME/lib /openwin-menu-s.
- The "XV 3.00" entry executes the command /usr/X386/bin/xv via the exec command.
- The "Window Menu " entry invokes a special entry for selecting windows via a WINMENU type of window.
- The "XView Programs " entry uses a type DIRMENU to list all the files in $OPENWINHOME/bin.
- The SEPARATOR type draws an empty box at its position.

You can now use different files for customizing your menus differently by adding or deleting items to this file.

The menu specification language has a number of keywords, all of which are in all-uppercase letters.

The syntax for this file is straightforward. Each line typically specifies one menu button. There are three fields per each uncommented line. The first field defines a label, an optional keyword, and an action to take if the item is selected.

The label is either a single word or a string enclosed in double quotes. This string appears in the menu button. If the optional keyword DEFAULT appears next, this menu item becomes the default item for this menu. The rest of the line (excluding leading whitespace) is considered to be a command. It is executed by sending it to bash. Any shell metacharacters are passed through to the shell unchanged.

The command field can be extended onto the next line by placing a backslash (\) at the end of the line. The newline will not be embedded in the command.

A submenu is specified using the special keyword MENU in place of a command. A button is added to the current menu, and clicking or pulling right on this button brings up the submenu. Subsequent lines in the menu file define buttons for the submenu, until a line that has the special keyword END in the command field is encountered. The label of the MENU line must match the label on the END line; otherwise an error is signaled.

Submenus can be nested arbitrarily, bracketed by MENU and END lines with matching labels.

Submenus can be defined in a different file using either the MENU or the INCLUDE keyword. To include a submenu from another file, use a line with a label, either the MENU or the INCLUDE keyword, and then the filename. The file so named is assumed to contain lines that specify menu buttons. The submenu file need not have any MENU or END lines (unless it has submenus itself). The current file need not have a matching END line if the submenu is read from another file. Submenu files included with the MENU keyword are considered to be an integral part of the menu tree, and any error encountered during the reading of the file will cause the entire menu to be considered invalid. A submenu file included with the INCLUDE keyword is considered optional, and any error encountered during reading of the file is not considered fatal. If an error occurs during INCLUDE processing, a disabled (grayed-out) item is inserted in place of the submenu and processing of the current menu file continues.

To make a submenu pinnable, add the special keyword PIN after the END keyword on the line that ends the submenu definition, or after the TITLE directive (I'll discuss that in a minute).

By default, the label in a menu button is used as the title of the submenu.

This can be overridden by specifying a line that has the special keyword TITLE in the command field. The label from this line is used as the submenu's title. This line can appear anywhere in the submenu definition.

It does not add an item to the menu. In addition, if the PIN keyword follows the TITLE keyword on this line, the submenu is made pinnable.

This construct is useful for declaring a submenu defined in a separate file as pinnable.

A line containing only the keyword SEPARATOR adds extra space before the next item.

Table 24.1 lists keywords that can be used in the command field of a menu item. They specify functions that are internal to olwm and that are not invoked by running a shell.

Table 24.1. Special keywords in olwm.

BACK_SELN	Moves the selected windows and icons behind other windows.
EXIT	Kills all applications and exits the window manager after getting confirmation from the user. (This is useful for exiting the entire window system.)
EXIT_NO_CONFIRM	Like EXIT but skips the confirmation notice.
FLIPDRAG	Toggles the state of the DragWindow resource.
FLIPFOCUS	Toggles the state of the SetInput resource.
FULL_RESTORE_SIZE_SELN	Toggles the full-sized/normal-sized states of the selected windows and icons.
NOP	No operation. Don't do anything.
OPEN_CLOSE_SELN	Toggles the opened/closed states of the selected windows and icons.
QUIT_SELN	Quits the selected windows and icons.
PROPERTIES	Brings up Workspace Properties.
REFRESH	Causes all windows on the screen to be repainted.

REREAD_MENU_FILE	Forces an immediate rereading of the workspace menu customization file. Olwm starts a complete search for a menu file and uses the first valid file it finds.
RESTART	Restarts the window manager.
SAVE_WORKSPACE	Takes a snapshot of the set of currently running applications, and put the command lines so obtained into a file $HOME/ .openwin init (in the user's home directory).
	This runs the command specified by the SaveWorkspaceCmd resource.
START_DSDM	Starts providing the DSDM service.
STOP_DSDM	Stops providing the DSDM service.
WMEXIT	Exits the window manager without killing any applications.

The Virtual Desktop

olvwm is a window manager with a virtual desktop. You use the olvwm command to invoke this window manager. Change olwm to olvwm in your .xinitrc file.

olvwm is a virtual window manager for the X Window System that implements parts of the OPEN LOOK graphical user interface. olvwm differs from olwm in that olvwm manages a virtual desktop that is larger than the actual screen.

The Virtual Desktop Manager

When it is started, olvwm displays a *Virtual Desktop Manager* (VDM) window. The VDM is the window that provides a scaled-down version of the entire desktop.

If the desktop is running in default mode, it displays a grid, each square of which maps to the size of the monitor. Each square is termed a *Logical Screen.*

The *Current View* is that part of the desktop that is currently displayed on the screen. A *Virtual Window* is a small rectangle displayed in the VDM. Every window on the desktop has a corresponding virtual window in the VDM.

The VDM always appears on the screen. (See Figure 24.7.)

FIGURE 24.7.
The Virtual Desktop Manager.

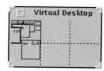

NOTE

"The Virtual Desktop" section was authored by Scott Oaks, scott.oaks@sun.com, who is also responsible for its maintenance. This olwm and olvwm code is not supported by Sun Microsystems in any way. The staff at Sun Microsystems, and especially Stuart Marks, deserve credit as original author(s) of olwm for most of the work contained in XView.

By default, the VDM (and hence the desktop) is divided into a grid. Each square of the grid represents a screen size. The dividing lines between each logical screen are represented by dashed lines in the VDM. This division into logical screens is purely informational. If you like, windows can straddle these boundaries, the current view into the desktop can straddle them also, and windows can be moved at will between them. However, by default, most actions in the VDM keep the current view along these boundary lines.

You can use the resize corners on the VDM to resize the virtual desktop. If you make the virtual desktop smaller, windows that might be off the new virtual desktop are NOT moved (though they are not lost, either, because you can get them back by resizing the desktop). Space added or subtracted is always done so from the right and bottom of the desktop (regardless of which resize corner you used).

Working with Virtual Windows

Events that occur in a particular virtual window behave just as if they were delivered to the corresponding application's frame. Thus, pressing the MENU button over a virtual window brings up the Frame menu and enables the real (and virtual) windows to be opened, closed, resized, and so on.

Pressing the SELECT button selects that real (and virtual) window. Pressing the ADJUST button adds (or subtracts) that window from the selection list.

SELECTing and dragging one or more virtual windows moves the real and virtual windows (just as in olwm). Note that if you drag the mouse outside of the VDM, the window can be moved onto to the screen. Conversely, when dragging a window on the screen, if the mouse moves into the VDM the window's icon moves to another location within the VDM. However, if part of the VDM is obscured, you cannot move a window into that part of the VDM.

NOTE

Note that events are delivered **only** to the real application's frame. Thus, typing characters or using the COPY/CUT/PASTE keys has no effect.

It is possible to drop something onto a virtual window as if it were dropped onto the corresponding application. This enables you to drag a file in one window on the screen to another application on another part of the desktop.

Double-clicking the SELECT button on an area in the VDM background moves the current view to the logical screen containing the point where the mouse was double-clicked.

The MENU button brings up a (pinnable) menu that enables movement based on full screen sizes in the direction indicated. See Figure 24.8.

FIGURE 24.8.

A pinnable menu.

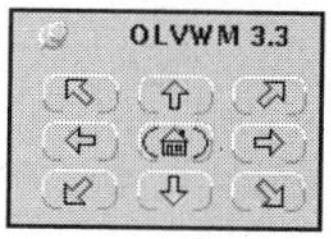

Sticky Windows

You'll notice that the Virtual Desktop Manager never moves on your screen if you change views into the desktop. That's because the VDM is permanently sticky.

Windows that are *sticky* never move position on the screen when you change your view into the desktop. To set a particular window as sticky, simply select Stick in its Frame menu. You may similarly unstick the window via its menu.

Menus for base windows include the Stick and Unstick commands.

> **NOTE**
>
> Only base frames—those that can be iconified, as opposed to those that have a pushpin—are eligible to become sticky. Some frames inherit the stickiness of their base frames. Thus, for most applications, either all windows are sticky or none of them are. The exception to this is applications that create two or more base frames: All base frames are originally created as unsticky (but see the following discussion on the VirtualSticky resource).

Windows that are sticky always appear in the same place on the screen no matter which part of the virtual desktop you're viewing. Windows that are not sticky (by default, all windows except the VDM) move when you change the current view on the virtual desktop.

Like olwm, olvwm uses key bindings for certain actions. All actions are specified in olwm as well as an additional set of actions to control the view into the desktop. You can use the Function keys F1 through F9 with the Alt key to switch virtual screens.

Resources in OpenWindows

You can customize OpenWindows using resources. Resources affect the behavior of applications in olwm. Global resources in olwm consist of two resource components:

- The resource name is taken from the trailing pathname component of argv[0]. This value is typically olwm.
- The second resource component names the global attribute being set.

Thus, to set the `AutoColorFocus` attribute, one would use `olwm.AutoColorFocus` as the resource specification in `.Xdefaults`. `olvwm` will read a resource file (`$HOME/.olvwmrc`) for your resources.

`olwm` automatically picks up changes to many of these resources if the resource database changes at runtime. You can modify `olwm`'s behavior by changing the resource database with `xrdb` or with Workspace Properties.

If a resource value is specified on `olwm`'s command line, it overrides the value in the resource database. Therefore, changing the resource's value in the database has no effect on this resource setting.

Some customizations include the following:

Hot Keys You can specify that when a certain key (or, more likely, key in combination with modifiers) is pressed, certain actions are performed. You can warp to a particular application, and open, raise, close, execute, and quit applications.

Screen Bindings You can specify that certain applications will always start on a particular logical screen.

Menu Options You can alter the behavior of WINMENU selections on a particular window.

More resources are listed in the man pages for `olwm`, `olvwmrc`, and `olvwm`.

Using Text-Editing Features

In general, the editing/moving commands go in the opposite direction when shifted—that is, Ctrl-W deletes a word, and Ctrl-Shift-W deletes the word to the right of the insertion point.

```
Alt-i - include file        Alt-f - find selection (forward/backward)

Ctrl-a - start of line      Ctrl-< - back word
Ctrl-e - end of line        Ctrl-> - forward word
Ctrl-w - delete word        Ctrl-u - delete to start/END of line
Ctrl-Return - move to end/START of document
```

See the `olwm` and `olvwm` man pages for a list of some of the default keys.

You can cut and paste between XTerm and other OpenWindows programs. I will use `textedit` as a sample program.

To go from XTerm to `textedit` (for this example):

1. Select the text you want to copy by dragging the SELECT mouse button in XTerm.

2. Press COPY in the XTerm (this key is Alt-C).

3. Move to the `textedit` window, and press PASTE (Alt-V).

To go the other way, from textedit to XTerm:

1. Select the text in textedit. No need to use COPY.

2. Move to the XTerm window and press the middle mouse button.

(If you have a two-button mouse, press both left and right buttons together.)

NOTE

You can also use the COPY/CUT and PASTE buttons.

For Quick Copy within textedit, mailtool, and similar programs:

1. Click SELECT to get a text caret where you want the copied text to go.

2. Press and hold down the PASTE (or CUT) button.

3. Select the text you want to copy/move. You'll see that it's underlined or crossed out—or even a different color.

4. Let go of the PASTE (or CUT) button. The text you underlined or crossed out appears at the insert caret.

To drag-and-drop to move a selection, follow these steps:

1. Select the text you want to copy or move by dragging or multiple-clicking the SELECT or ADJUST mouse button.

2. Put the mouse pointer anywhere within the selection.

3. Press and hold down the SELECT mouse button and move the mouse pointer a little to the right. You'll see the cursor change into the first three letters of the text (or some other icon).

4. Still holding down the SELECT button, move the mouse over the point where you want to drop the text.

5. You may see the mouse pointer change to a rifle sight or target, to show that it's OK to drop things there.

6. Release SELECT and the text is moved. This works in text fields of dialog boxes as well as in text subwindows.

TIP

To drag-and-drop to copy a selection, you must hold the Ctrl key down as well as the SELECT mouse button.

Support for Left-Handed Users

You can configure OPEN LOOK for a left-handed mouse and keyboard. Use xmodmap to change the mouse buttons. Type man 7 xview for a list of key bindings you can change, at least for XView programs.

> **CAUTION**
>
> Unlike the Motif release, the xmodmap for mouse-key reversal sometimes does not work right. In fact, it may actually reverse some keys on your keyboard or have some other surprising results. You have been warned.

With OpenWindows 2.0, you can use defaultsedit to set the mouse mappings and then let SunView handle them. The status returned by svenv should tell you whether your server is running under SunView or not; put this in your .xinitrc:

```
if eval 'svenv -env'
then
        xmodmap -e "pointer = 1 2 3"
        input_from_defaults
else
        xmodmap -e "pointer = 3 2 1"
fi
```

Troubleshooting

Here are some solutions to problems you might have:

- If man doesn't seem to find OpenWindows commands, even though you are running OpenWindows, try setting the MANPATH environment variable:

  ```
  MANPATH=$OPENWINHOME/share/man:/usr/man; export MANPATH
  ```

  or

  ```
  setenv MANPATH $OPENWINHOME/share/man:/usr/man
  ```

  for csh users. $OPENWINHOME should be /usr/openwin on most systems. Set your path so that $OPENWINHOME/bin (and $OPENWIN/bin/xview for OpenWindows 2) come before /bin (or /usr/bin, they're the same), or you'll get the SunView versions of mailtool, cmdtool, shelltool, and so on.

- Dropped characters when you type into applications.

  In this case, include the following lines in your .Xdefaults file, as these enable non-ICCCM-compliant programs to receive input even if they forget to ask for it.

  ```
  OpenWindows.FocusLenience:     true
  *Input: TRUE
  ```

■ CUT and PASTE just do not work. Add the following either to your `$HOME/.Xdefaults` file or to `$OPENWINHOME/lib/app-defaults/XTerm` instead:

```
XTerm*VT100.Translations: #override \
<Key>L6:select-set(CLIPBOARD)\n\
<Key>L8:insert-selection(CLIPBOARD)
```

If this text is already in the `app-defaults` file, check that `XFILESEARCHPATH` is set to

`/usr/openwin/lib/%T/%N%S`

If it isn't, either set it or copy/merge these lines from `$OPENWINHOME/lib/app-defaults/XTerm` into `/usr/lib/X11/app-defaults/XTerm`.

This version automatically puts each `xterm` selection onto the Clipboard:

```
XTerm*VT100.translations: #override\n\
~Ctrl ~Meta<Btn2Up>: insert-selection(PRIMARY,CUT_BUFFER0)\n\
~Ctrl ~Meta<BtnUp>: select-end(PRIMARY,CUT_BUFFER0,CLIPBOARD)\n\
<KeyPress>L8: insert-selection(CLIPBOARD)
```

TIP

Be sure that the `\n\` is at the very end of all lines in the middle.

■ If you get error messages that look like the following lines,

```
Xlib:  connection to ":0.0" refused by server
Xlib:  Internal error during connection authorization check
Error: Can't Open display
```

try the command `xhost-machine`, where `machine` is the computer on which you ran the command that failed.

If you want to let other users run programs on the same machine as you, using your display, you have to type the command `xhost +'hostname'`, which lets any user on `'hostname'` access your display.

■ Your screen flashes between applications. This is because most hardware can only display a few colors at a time. Try the following steps:

1. Start all the applications with colors that you wish to reserve.

2. Run `cmap_compact save` to create the `.owcolors` file.

3. Put the line `cmap_compact init` near the start of your I `start-up` file (`.xinitrc`).

4. Exit and then restart the window system.

5. `cmap_compact init` pushes those `.owcolors` colors to the end of the colormap and reserves them.

Also note that Ctrl-L2 locks the colors of the current window, and Ctrl-L4 unlocks them—this is described in the `olwm` man page.

See the X*.faq in the /usr/docs/faq directory for detailed information on problems specific to different platforms. The FAQ file can be give you a lot of information about Linux and what problems to expect.

Environment Variables

XView for Linux uses the following environment variables:

- DISPLAY   The name of the X Window display to use :0.0 (on the local machine, the one actually running X11 or xnews) :0.1 (on some machines for a second, monochrome screen) machine-running-unix:0.0 (on other machines). (You may need to do xhost +other-machine to let programs on other machines use your display.)

- HELPPATH   Where XView looks when you press the Help key (or F1): /usr/openwin/lib/locale:/usr/openwin/lib/help.

- LD_LIBRARY_PATH is set to find shared C libraries. It is usually defaulted to this value:

    /usr/lib:/usr/5lib:/usr/openwin/lib:/usr/CC/'arch'

- OPENWINHOME   Where OpenWindows lives (/usr/openwin).

- PATH   Where the shell searches for programs to run.

- Include this line:

    $(OPENWINHOME)/bin:$(OPENWINHOME)/bin/xview

- XFILESEARCHPATH   Where programs look for app-defaults files (/usr/openwin/lib/%T/%N%S). This is usually set to: $OPENWINHOME/lib/%T/%N%S:/usr/lib/X11/%T/%N%S.

Special Help for Sun Workstation Users

If you work with Sun Microsystems Sun Workstations, then the olwm and olvwm managers should make life easier for you. If you want to make life even easier, you can map the function keys to reflect that of Sun workstations. To do this, you have to modify the .Xmodmap file in your home directory. If you do not have a .Xmodmap file, you can create one with a text editor.

The best place to look is in the man pages for .Xmodmap. The man pages are full of examples, some of which I will describe briefly here. For issues specific to your setting, read the man pages.

A typical .Xmodmap file will look like this:

```
keysym F1 = xman
keysym F2 = F19
keysym F3 = F20
keysym F4 = F16
keysym F5 = F18
```

The undo button is ominously absent from the .Xmodmap entries. To get this entry, add the following line. (The text after the ! is a comment and ignored by X.)

```
keysym F6 = F14   ! The undo button.
```

For example, if you hate the location of the shift and control keys on your PC, you can swap the location. Simply put these lines in your .Xmodmap file:

```
remove Lock = Caps_Lock
remove Control = Control_L
keysym Control_L = Caps_Lock
keysym Caps_Lock = Control_L
add Lock = Caps_Lock
add Control = Control_L
```

You can also assign the meta key to a function key using this line:

```
keysym F9 = Meta_L
```

Finally, when you have made your changes, you have to tell the server to use them. It's too cumbersome to shut down the window manager and restart it. Instead, you can use the rdb command:

```
$ xrdb .Xdefaults.
```

You can also invoke specific settings from the command line using xmodmap. For example, type the following line:

```
$ xmodmap -e "keysym F9=Meta_L"
```

Modifying the .Xmodmap file is better in that the changes are preserved for future sessions.

Internet Sites for XView

XView 3.0 is available by anonymous FTP from export.lcs.mit.edu if you want to upgrade the CD-ROM version.

OpenWindows can also be obtained from Sun, or you can get the source from Interactive Systems Inc. It is also included in some vendors' System V Release 4 implementations, although that's not always the latest version.

NOTE

The current release of OpenWindows from Sun for supported architectures is 3.0; for the Sun 3 series it is frozen at OpenWindows 2.0.

Sun includes OpenWindows with SunOS, and it is also included as the windowing system for Solaris.

There are said (by Sun) to be more than 35 ports of OpenWindows either available now or in progress. Unfortunately, none of them seem to be available from anywhere.

Douglas N. Arnold (`dna@math.psu.edu`) keeps an up-to-date FAQ on `ftp.math.psu.edu` (currently `146.186.131.129`) in the file `/pub/FAQ/open-look`.

MoOLIT can be bought from AT&T in source form.

Where To Go for More Information

Nabajyoti Barkakati gives an excellent introduction to X and to OLIT programming, as well as setting up and using X and OpenWindows, in

> *UNIX® Desktop Guide to OPEN LOOK,*
> Sams, 1992, ISBN 0-672-30023-0

The OPEN LOOK Graphical Interface is documented in two books:

> Sun Microsystems Inc., *OPEN LOOK Graphical User Interface Application Style Guidelines,* Addison Wesley, 1989.

> Sun Microsystems Inc., *OPEN LOOK Graphical User Interface Functional Specification,* Addison Wesley, 1989.

David Miller describes programming with OLIT in his book, *An OPEN LOOK At UNIX* (M&T Press).

You could also try *The X Window System: Programming and Applications with* `Xt`*, OPEN LOOK Edition,* by Doug Young and John Pew (Prentice Hall, 1992, ISBN 0-13-982992-X).

Sun Microsystems supplies a large amount of documentation with OpenWindows, although you may have to order it separately. The following list shows what I have; each book is 8.5×11 and vary from about 1 to 2 inches thick. Each manual says "User's Guide" or "Programmer's Guide" on the front cover. The user manuals have a red stripe on the bottom, and the programmer versions have a green stripe:

800-6006-10	*OpenWindows Version 3 Release Manual*
800-6029-10	*OpenWindows Version 3 Installation and Start-Up Guide*
800-6231-10	*OpenWindows Version 3 DeskSet Reference Guide*
800-6618-10	*OpenWindows Version 3 User's Guide*
800-6323-10	*Desktop Integration Guide*
800-6027-10	*Programmer's Guide*
800-6005-10	*OpenWindows Version 3 Reference Manual* (the man pages)

800-6319-10	*The NeWS Toolkit 3.0 Reference Manual*
800-6736-10	*NeWS 3.0 Programming Guide*
800-6055-10	*OLIT 3.0 Widget Set Reference Manual*
800-6198-10	*XView 3.0 Reference Manual: Converting SunView Applications*
800-6854-10	*F3 Font Format Specification*

Sun's AnswerBook CD-ROM contains much of this documentation and can prove to be a valuable source of information if you intend to port applications to Sun Workstations.

Summary

Here is what you should remember from this chapter on OPEN LOOK:

- XView is the OPEN LOOK GUI interface for Linux and is also referred to as OpenWindows. All three terms (XView, OPEN LOOK, and OpenWindows) are used interchangeably, but really refer to the same windowing interface.

- OPEN LOOK is not Motif. Not only are the window decorations different—the terminology used to convey actions is also different. (For example, Close in Motif generally kills an application and its window, whereas Close in OPEN LOOK iconifies a window.)

- You can use two types of OPEN LOOK window managers: olwm and olvwm. The olwm is the base OPEN LOOK window manager and the olvwm extends olwm by providing many virtual screens for your desktop.

- You can use the .Xdefaults files with the olwm keyword to set resources for your applications under olwm. See the man pages for olwm and olvwm for details on all resources for your distribution.

- You can get more information from Sun Microsystems about OPEN LOOK.

- Most OPEN LOOK menus offer a feature that enables you to pin a menu onto your desktop. You must either unpin this menu, or kill its underlying application, to get rid of it.

- On the Virtual Desktop Manager (VDM), you can stick windows on your screen regardless of your virtual desktop by using the Stick/Unstick selection on the Applications menu. All dialog boxes with that menu will stick with it too.

- XView applications enable you to have drag-and-drop capabilities. For example, with the File Manager application you can manage files and directories by dragging them around with the mouse.

- Standard Motif applications should run under XView. XView applications should also run under Motif if you have the shared libraries in your path.

- You can customize dialog box menus to include all executables files in a directory. Check the openwin-menu file for examples.

Ghostscript

25

by Kamran Husain

This chapter covers installation and use of Ghostscript, a PostScript interpreter. Almost everything related to Linux is in PostScript. If you have a PostScript printer, you simply send the file to the printer for a hardcopy.

What Is Ghostscript?

Ghostscript is actually a set of programs. Collectively, these programs provide two important features:

- An interpreter for the PostScript language.
- A library of C functions for implementing primitive PostScript constructs.

> **NOTE**
>
> PostScript is a trademark of Adobe Systems, Incorporated.

Ghostscript has been ported to several platforms from PCs, OS/2, Apple Macintoshes, Ataris, to various flavors of UNIX, for example, Sun workstations, IBM AIX machines, and so on. Since Ghostscript is written in C, chances are that it will be portable to your platform. If you support X11, you will probably be able to run Ghostscript.

Several executable files come with Ghostscript. Some of the executables are also used by other packages under Linux. For example, HylaFAX (Chapter 59, "Using FlexFAX, `sendfax`, and `mgetty`") uses the main Ghostscript program, `gs`. In short, if you use Linux, you will find a need for Ghostscript.

Ghostscript Information

The primary contact for getting information about Ghostscript is:

Aladdin Enterprises
P.O. Box 60264
Palo Alto, CA 94306
voice (415) 322-0103
FAX (415) 322-1734
`ghost@aladdin.com`

In fact, the Ghostscript package that you get with Linux is from Aladdin Enterprises. The information about Ghostscript is best summarized in its README file:

"L. Peter Deutsch, president of Aladdin Enterprises, was the original creator, and is the primary developer and maintainer, of Ghostscript. Aladdin Enterprises owns the copyright on Ghostscript; Ghostscript is distributed with the GNU General Public License, and is also available for commercial licensing."

Installation

To run Ghostscript, you need the executable program and some external initialization files:

```
/usr/lib/ghostscript/bdftops.ps
/usr/lib/ghostscript/decrypt.ps
/usr/lib/ghostscript/font2c.ps
/usr/lib/ghostscript/gs_dbt_e.ps
/usr/lib/ghostscript/gs_dps1.ps
/usr/lib/ghostscript/gs_fonts.ps
/usr/lib/ghostscript/gs_init.ps
/usr/lib/ghostscript/gs_lev2.ps
/usr/lib/ghostscript/gs_statd.ps
/usr/lib/ghostscript/gs_sym_e.ps
/usr/lib/ghostscript/gs_type0.ps
/usr/lib/ghostscript/gslp.ps
/usr/lib/ghostscript/impath.ps
/usr/lib/ghostscript/landscap.ps
/usr/lib/ghostscript/level1.ps
/usr/lib/ghostscript/prfont.ps
/usr/lib/ghostscript/ps2ascii.ps
/usr/lib/ghostscript/ps2epsi.ps
/usr/lib/ghostscript/ps2image.ps
/usr/lib/ghostscript/pstoppm.ps
/usr/lib/ghostscript/quit.ps
/usr/lib/ghostscript/showpage.ps
/usr/lib/ghostscript/type1ops.ps
/usr/lib/ghostscript/wrfont.ps
/usr/lib/ghostscript/uglyr.gsf
/usr/lib/ghostscript/Fontmap
```

The Ghostscript file set includes a set of fonts (`.gsf` files). You should have them online as well.

Installing Ghostscript on a Linux system simply requires getting it from the CD-ROM or Internet. The name of the executable is `gs`.

You can build Ghostscript on your machine if you want to. The makefiles that come with the sources will install all the files and directories under your `/usr/local` directory.

The fonts for Ghostscript are stored in `/usr/lib/ghostscript/fonts`.

The Ghostscript Interpreter

The Ghostscript interpreter is the `gs` command in `/usr/bin/gs`. This is an interactive interpreter that also reads in files for its input. To invoke the `gs` interpreter, use the command

```
gs [filename1] ... [filenameN]
```

The interpreter will read in the files in sequence and interpret them. After doing this, it reads further input from the primary input stream (normally the keyboard). Each line (that is, characters up to a `<return>`) is interpreted separately. To exit from the interpreter, type `quit` and press the Return key. The interpreter also exits gracefully if it encounters end-of-file. Typing the interrupt character (Ctrl-C), is also safe.

426

See Figure 25.1 for the input to the interpreter. (Your version number may be different than that shown in the figure.) The output is shown in a separate window as shown in Figure 25.2 (which shows the FlexFAX FAQ). The file in this example is the FAQ for the HylaFAX program (see Chapter 59) and is called fax-112894.ps. You can get this file via Mosaic (see Chapter 56, "Using Mosaic and Netscape") from www.vix.com from the HylaFAX directory.

FIGURE 25.1.

The gs interpreter.

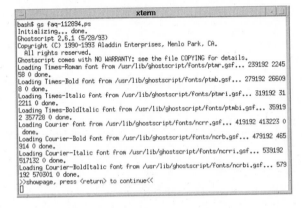

FIGURE 25.2.

The output from gs interpreter.

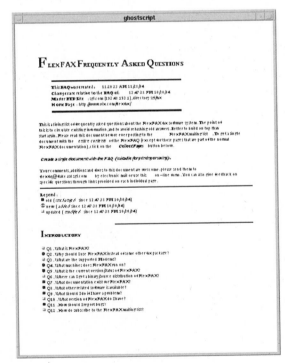

Getting Help While in *gs*

The gs interpreter recognizes several arguments. We will cover most of the important ones in this chapter. However, you can get help from gs too. Either the `-h` or `-?` option tells gs to print out a help screen. The help screen also lists all available devices for gs on your system.

Choosing the Output Device

Ghostscript may be built with multiple output devices. Ghostscript normally opens the first one and directs output to it. To use device Laserjet as the initial output device, include the following argument in the command line:

```
-sDEVICE=laserjet
```

> **NOTE**
>
> Command line arguments to gs can appear anywhere on the command line. Once specified, these arguments apply to all subsequent files listed in the command line. These arguments will not apply to any files specified before the argument. So if you have important arguments like sDEVICE, specify these arguments before you specify the PostScript file.

> **TIP**
>
> PostScript files are usually specified with the `.ps` extension.

For example, for printer output in a normal configuration that includes a Laserjet printer driver, you might use the shell command

```
gs -sDEVICE=laserjet showme.ps
```

Alternatively, in the interpreter you can type

```
(laserjet) selectdevice
(showme.ps) run
```

All output then goes to the printer instead of the display until changed. You can switch devices at any time by using the selectdevice function, for example,

```
(vga) selectdevice  # for VGA screen
```

or

```
(nec) selectdevice   #for NEC printer
```

As yet a third alternative, you can define an environment variable `GS_DEVICE` as the desired default device name. The order of precedence for these alternatives, highest to lowest, is this:

```
selectdevice
(command line)
GS_DEVICE
(first device in build list)
```

To select the density on a printer, use the command

```
gs -sDEVICE=<device> -r<xres>x<yres>
```

For example, on a nine-pin, Epson-compatible printer, you can get the lowest-density (fastest) mode with the command

```
gs -sDEVICE=epson -r60x72
```

For the highest-density mode with Epson printers, use

```
gs -sDEVICE=epson -r240x72.
```

If you select a printer as the output device, Ghostscript also enables you to control where the device sends its output.

```
-sOutputFile=print%d.xyz
```

For compatibility with older versions of Ghostscript, `-sOUTPUTFILE=` also works.

The `%d` is a `printf` format specification. You can use other formats like `%02d`. Each file will receive one page of output. Alternatively, to send the output to a single file `bigfile.xyz`, with all the pages concatenated, use the command line argument: `-sOutputFile=foo.xyz`.

On UNIX-like systems, you can send the output directly to a pipe. For example, to pipe the output to the command `lpr` (which, on many UNIX systems, is the command that spools output for a printer), use the switch

```
-sOutputFile=\¦lpr
```

Don't forget to escape the pipe symbol (¦). You can also send output to `stdout` for piping with the dash as the output file. That is, use the option `-sOutputFile=-`. In this case you must also use the `-q` switch to prevent Ghostscript from writing messages to `stdout`.

To find out what devices are available, type `"devicenames =="` after starting up Ghostscript.

Paper Size Configuration

Ghostscript is normally configured to expect U.S. letter size paper. To select a different paper size as the default, use the argument `-sPAPERSIZE=known_paper_size`. (You can create your own paper sizes with the `devs.mak` file.) Generally, you have a large selection available. The entire list can be found in the file

```
/usr/lib/ghostscript/gs_statd.ps
```

Print this file out if you can, to keep it handy. Some examples of setting the paper size are

```
-sPAPERSIZE=a4
-sPAPERSIZE=legal
-sPAPERSIZE=11x17
-sPAPERSIZE=ledger
```

TIP

A PostScript file may explicitly specify the paper size. In this case, the file's specification will override any command line argument specification.

Environment Variables

Ghostscript uses these environment variables: GS_LIB, GS_LIB_DEFAULT, and GS_FONTPATH.

When looking for the initialization files (gs_*.ps), the files related to fonts, or the file for the run operator, Ghostscript first tries opening the file with the name as given (that is, using the current working directory if none is specified). If this fails, and the filename doesn't specify an explicit directory or drive (that is, doesn't begin with / on UNIX), Ghostscript will try directories in the following order:

- The GS_LIB variable specifies several directories for gs to look in for files if a full path name of an input file is not specified. The directory names are separated by colons (like the PATH command).

- The GS_LIB_DEFAULT variable is similar to the GS_LIB variable and is searched if GS_LIB's directories showed nothing. Both of these variables (GS_LIB and GS_LIB_DEFAULT) can be overridden by the -I argument.

- The GS_FONTPATH environment variable is a list of directories for PostScript fonts. All those files and fonts listed in this directory are added to gs's internal copy of the Fontmap. A Fontmap is a catalog of fonts and the files that contain them.

CAUTION

Ghostscript will create temporary files by using the TEMP environment variable as the location of the /tmp directory. These files are named gs_*XXXXX*, where *XXXXX* is replaced by a number or a string of jumbled characters. Ghostscript doesn't do a very good job of deleting temporary files when it exits. If you see your /tmp space being used by these files you may have to delete them using the rm /tmp/gs_* command.

Configuring for X Window

Ghostscript looks for the resources under the program name ghostscript and class name Ghostscript in the .Xdefaults file. To set a resource, put the resource in .Xdefaults in the following form:

```
Ghostscript*geometry:      -0+0
Ghostscript*xResolution:   72
Ghostscript*yResolution:   72
```

Then load the defaults into the X server:

```
% xrdb -merge ~/.Xdefaults
```

Table 25.1 lists the options available to you.

Table 25.1. Ghostscript resources.

Name	Class	Default
background	Background	white
foreground	Foreground	black
borderColor	BorderColor	black
borderWidth	BorderWidth	1
geometry	Geometry	NULL
xResolution	Resolution	calculated
yResolution	Resolution	calculated
useExternalFonts	UseExternalFonts	true
useScalableFonts	UseScalableFonts	true
logExternalFonts	LogExternalFonts	false
externalFontTolerance	ExternalFontTolerance	10.0
palette	Palette	Color
maxGrayRamp	MaxGrayRamp	128
maxRGBRamp	MaxRGBRamp	5
useBackingPixmap	UseBackingPixmap	true
useXPutImage	UseXPutImage	true
useXSetTile	UseXSetTile	true
regularFonts	RegularFonts	
symbolFonts	SymbolFonts	
dingbatFonts	DingbatFonts	

Here are a few points on these resources:

- The geometry resource only affects window placement. This does not affect the position of the image on the display in the window.
- All resolution numbers are given in pixels per inch.
- The font tolerance gives the largest acceptable difference in the height of the screen font. The tolerance is expressed as a percentage of the height of the desired font.
- The palette resource can be used to restrict Ghostscript to using a grayscale or mono-chrome palette.
- The maxRGBRamp and maxGrayRamp control the maximum number of colors that Ghostscript allocates ahead of time for dithering. Ghostscript will never pre-allocate more than half of the cells in a color map.

To use native X11 fonts, Ghostscript must map PostScript font names to the XLFD font names. The regularFonts, symbolFonts, and dingbatFonts resources give the name mapping for different encodings. The XLFD font name in the mapping must contain seven dashes. The X driver adds the additional size and encoding fields to bring the total number of dashes in the font name to 14. The default font mappings are found in the FontMap file in /usr/lib/ghostscript or check the man pages.

Command-Line Arguments

Ghostscript takes a lot of command-line arguments. Generally you would want to put these in a shell script file instead of having to type them in all the time. Some of the most often used arguments are listed here. For a comprehensive list check out the documents in /usr/lib/ghostscript/doc. Let's look at the most commonly used arguments:

- @filename The filename specified here will contain a list of all the input file names. This beats typing in long names on every execution of gs with lots of input files.
- -Idirectories Adds the list of directories at the head of the library files' search path.
- -ffilename Executes the given file, even if its name begins with a -.
- -Dname=token or -dname=token Defines a name with the given token. The token must not contain any whitespace. You must specify each token with its own -Dname option. -Dname or -dname without the = will set the value to null.
- -Sname=string or -sname=string Defines a string.

NOTE

The differences between -d and -s are these:

-dfoo=hello is equivalent to /foo hello def

-sfoo=hello is equivalent to /foo (hello) def

- ■ -q   Suppresses normal startup messages.
- ■ -gnumber1xnumber2   Number1 is the width, Number2 is the height of the display device. This is for devices that enable width and height to be specified. This is equivalent to -dDEVICEWIDTH=number1 and -dDEVICEHEIGHT=number2.
- ■ -rnumber or -rnumber1xnumber2   This is for the benefit of devices (such as printers) that support multiple X and Y resolutions. You can also use -dDEVICEXRESOLUTION=number1 and -dDEVICEYRESOLUTION=number2.
- ■ -   Uses standard input instead of the file. Ghostscript will read from stdin until reaching end-of-file, and execute it as another file. After the end of file, gs will process any other items as arguments but will not go into interactive mode.
- ■ -dDISKFONTS   This argument causes individual character outlines to be loaded from the disk the first time they are encountered. Normally Ghostscript loads all the character outlines when it loads a font. This may enable loading more fonts into RAM at the expense of slower rendering.
- ■ -dNODISPLAY   Suppresses the normal initialization of the output device. This may be useful when debugging.
- ■ -dNOPAUSE   Disables the prompt and pauses at the end of each page. This is useful for applications where another program is "driving" Ghostscript.
- ■ -dNOPLATFONTS   Disables the use of fonts supplied by your machine. It is needed if the platform fonts look bad when compared to scaleable fonts.
- ■ -dSAFER   Disables the deletefile and renamefile operators and the ability to open files in any mode other than read-only.
- ■ -sDEVICE=device   Selects an alternate initial output device.
- ■ -sOutputFile=filename   Selects an alternate output file instead of the default destination.

PostScript Viewer: Ghostview

Ghostview is used to display encoded PostScript files. Ghostview is free. It was written and copyrighted by Tim Theisen. The ghostview command shows PostScript documents using Ghostscript.

Use the command line below to view a text file.

```
$ ghostview [filename]
```

The ghostview program will create an X window, open the file, and display it. If the filename is '-', ghostview will read from stdin. The ghostview program provides an X11 user interface for the Ghostscript interpreter. ghostview and Ghostscript function as two cooperating programs. ghostview creates the viewing window and Ghostscript draws in it.

Please use Ghostview to view files, especially those that require typesetting before sending them to the printer. You can save a lot of trees this way and get a quicker response about what to expect on the output. There are many programmers who still print out files to see what the output would look like instead of previewing on the screen.

In fact you may not even have to print out a document if you intend to send it to a remote site. If you have to FAX it, use `HylaFAX` (Chapter 59) with your FAX/modem to send it directly. If you have to e-mail it, `uuencode` it and then send it out.

Ghostview has a bewildering number of options. You do not have to use any of these options at all. Most of the options are there to override any `Xresources` that you set in `.Xdefaults`. Let's look at the main window, which consists of a main viewer and control menus (of `HylaFAX`). (See Figure 25.3.)

FIGURE 25.3.

Ghostview main window.

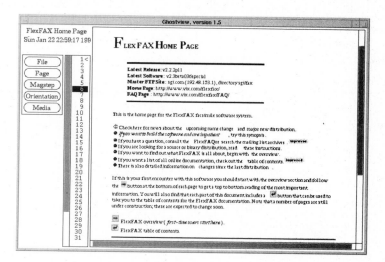

The main viewport is on the right side of the main window. If the page is larger than the viewport, there will be scroll bars along the bottom and right edges of the viewport. To the left of the viewport is the table of contents. If the PostScript file has document structuring convention (DSC) comments, the table of contents will display the page labels (these are usually page numbers). To the left of the table of contents is a menu box. Each push button brings up a pop-up menu.

Above the menu box and table of contents there are three optional labels that contain the title, date, and locator.

The title label contains the `document title` found in the DSC comments. If no title can be found, the filename is used in its place. The date label contains the `document date` found in the DSC comments. If no date can be found, the last modified date of the file is used in its place. Since the title and date labels may be clipped by the main viewport, the date and title labels are pushbuttons that bring up a pop-up window with the title or date. These pop-up windows also show the `document` icon when the displayed string comes from the DSC comments.

The locator shows the location of the cursor in the viewport. The location is expressed in the default user coordinate system. The locator is useful for measuring bounding boxes. Within the main viewport, the mouse cursor is a "target" when Ghostscript is doing work. The cursor is a crosshair when Ghostscript is idle.

> **TIP**
>
> When moving to another page in a document, it is generally best to wait for Ghostscript to become idle. Ghostscript does not handle a series of mouse clicks very well while it's working and can hang. You then have to use the `kill` command to get rid of it, and start over.

Ghostview will always check to see if the file has been modified just before it displays a page or when the application is de-iconified. If the file has changed, it will re-open the file. This causes a bit of an overhead, but is helpful when you are trying to edit a file from another program and need to see your progress.

Clicking anywhere within the viewport will pop up a zoom window. The window is centered on the location that was clicked. Clicking with the left mouse button pops up a low-resolution zoom window. Clicking with the center mouse button pops up a medium-resolution zoom window. Clicking with the right mouse button pops up a high-resolution zoom window.

In the table of contents, the left mouse button selects text and the right mouse button extends selections. However, clicking on a page label with the center mouse button will display that page. The page being displayed is marked with a greater than symbol (>) in the right margin of the table of contents.

There are five buttons in the menu box. These are listed below:

- `File`   This menu enables you to open, reopen, print, show a copyright message, and quit the application. A Select File dialog box will appear when you click the open button. The Select File dialog widget enables you to select a file by typing the path or by browsing in directory listings and selecting entries with the mouse. The Select File dialog box is system modal; that is, no other controls in `ghostview` will be active during this time.

- `Page`   This pop-up menu controls which page you display. `Next` shows the next page, `Redisplay` redraws the current page, `Previous` shows the previous page, `Mark` and `Unmark` set a page in the table of contents as marked and unmarked.

- `Magstep`   This menu controls the magnification of the display. Zero implies no magnification (what you see is what you get). The multiplication factor is 1.2, so with a `magstep` of -1, the document is reduced by -1.2, a `magstep` of 1 zooms in by 1.2.

■ **Orientation** This enables you to select either a landscape or portrait orientation of the display. You can also flip the image with the **Upsidedown** to see FAXed documents. The **Seascape** option rotates the image 90 degrees counterclockwise.

■ **Media** The entries on the **Media** menu set the page media. The standard sizes you can select are: Letter, Tabloid, Ledger, Legal, Statement, Executive, A3, A4, A5, B4, B5, Folio, Quarto, and 10×14.

Keyboard Accelerators

Some of the pop-up menu commands can be executed with the keyboard. The pop-up menu has to be active (in other words, selected by the user for input) for the action to have effect. Some of the bindings are listed in Table 25.2.

Table 25.2. Keyboard shortcuts.

Key	Action
Q	The **Quit** menu button
O	The **Open...** menu button on the **File** menu
R	The **Reopen...** menu button on the **File** menu
S	The **Save marked pages** on the **File** menu
P	The **Print marked pages** on the **File** menu
Shift-P	The **Print all pages** on the **File** menu
BackSpace, B space,	The **Previous** menu button on the **Page** menu
Return, F period,	The **Next** menu button on the **Page** menu
Ctrl-L	The **Redisplay** menu button on the **Page** menu
M	The **Mark** menu button on the **Page** menu
N	The **Unmark** menu button on the **Page** menu
0-5	Selecting the 0 through 5 menu button on the **Magstep** menu
+	Increases the **Magstep** by 1
-	Decreases the **Magstep** by 1
U	Scrolls Up
D	Scrolls Down
H	Scrolls Left
L	Scrolls Right

X Resources

You can set the following resources for Ghostview. Only the most frequently used resources are listed. Please check the lengthy man page for Ghostview script for its long list of resources.

- ■ showTitle (class Labels)   Displays the Title comment. The default is true.
- ■ showDate (class Labels)   Displays the % %% %Data comment. The default is true.
- ■ showLocator (class Labels)   Displays the locator. The default is true.
- ■ autoCenter (class AutoCenter)   Centers the page in the viewport whenever the page size changes. The default is true.
- ■ horizonalMargin (class Margin)   Shows how many pixels ghostview should reserve for horizontal window decorations. The default value is 20.
- ■ verticalMargin (class Margin)   Shows how many pixels ghostview should reserve for vertical window decorations. The default value is 44.
- ■ minimumMagstep (class Magstep)   Sets the smallest magstep to display. The default is -5.
- ■ maximumMagstep (class Magstep)   Sets the largest magstep to display. The default is 5.
- ■ magstep (class Magstep)   Sets the default magstep. The default is 0.
- ■ orientation (class Orientation)   Sets the default orientation. The default is Portrait.
- ■ page (class Page)   Gives the initial page to display.
- ■ pageMedia (class PageMedia)   Sets the default page media. The default is Letter.
- ■ forceOrientation (class Force)   Forces the orientation on the document. The default is false.
- ■ forcePageMedia (class Force)   Forces the page media on the document. The default is false.
- ■ swapLandscape (class SwapLandscape)   Swaps the meaning of Landscape and Seascape. The default is false.
- ■ printCommand (class PrintCommand)   Sets the command used for printing.
- ■ printerVariable (class PrinterVariable)   Gives the name of the printer environment variable. The default value is PRINTER.
- ■ busyCursor (class Cursor)   The cursor shown when Ghostscript is drawing to the window. This is defaulted to a target icon.
- ■ cursor (class Cursor)   The cursor shown when Ghostscript is idle. The default cursor is the crosshair.
- ■ safer (class Safer)   Tells Ghostscript whether to run in safer mode. The default value is true.

Remember that almost all of these resources can be set with the command line argument. For example, the -title argument is equivalent to setting Ghostview.showTitle resource to True, whereas the `-notitle` argument is equivalent to setting the `Title` resource to `False`. Similarly, you can turn the date on or off with the `-date` and `-nodate` arguments, respectively.

Using Other Fonts

The versions of Ghostscript come with a set of default fonts that you can use with any program capable of reading PostScript Type 1 and Type 3 fonts. If you have created your own Type 1 or Type 3 fonts, or have purchased some fonts from another source, you can use these with Ghostscript. Place your fonts in the `lib/ghostscript/fonts` directory. Then edit the `lib/ghostscript/FontMap` file to add a line telling Ghostscript where to find the font. For example,

```
/Helvetica (hlv_xyz.pfb);
```

where `hlv_xyz.pfb` is the name of the font file you have just added. You do not have to reset any X resources for this to work. Simply place the file in the directory, edit the `FontMap` and restart `gs`.

Getting More Help

Aladdin Enterprises, the inventors of Ghostscript, do not have the resources to respond to questions from general users of Ghostscript. There are plenty of other places where you can get very detailed information about Ghostscript.

If you have access to newsgroups, post your questions to `gnu.ghostscript.bug`. There are literally hundreds of Ghostscript users all over the world who are very willing to help you. After all, we all started learning on our own. Using this newsgroup is perhaps the quickest way to get more information on `gs`.

If you have access to Internet mail, but not news, send e-mail to `bug-ghostscript@prep.ai.mit.edu`. If you are having trouble with a specific device driver, look in the file `devs.mak` and see if it is a user-maintained driver. If so, please contact directly the person listed.

There are several files in the `/usr/lib/ghostscript/doc` directory which can provide more information. Some of these files are:

- `readme.doc` Information about problems, major changes, and new features in the current release.
- `NEWS` A detailed history of changes in the most recent Ghostscript releases.
- `use.doc` Information about how to install and use Ghostscript.
- `devices.doc` Detailed information about specific devices that Ghostscript supports.
- `make.doc` How to install, compile, and link Ghostscript.
- `gs.1` The man page for Ghostscript.
- `fonts.doc` Information about the fonts distributed with Ghostscript, including how to add or replace fonts.

- `language.doc` A description of the Ghostscript language and its differences from the documented PostScript language.
- `psfiles.doc` Information about the `.ps` files distributed with Ghostscript other than fonts.
- `drivers.doc` The interface between Ghostscript and device drivers.
- `ps2epsi.doc` Documentation for the PostScript to EPSI conversion utility. Most commercial word processing packages can import EPSI documents for typesetting.
- `hershey.doc` Information about the Hershey fonts, which are the basis of some of the Ghostscript fonts.
- `history.doc` A history of changes in older Ghostscript releases.
- `lib.doc` Information about the Ghostscript library.

Summary

This chapter scratched the surface of a very important PostScript processing program called Ghostscript. The executable file for Ghostscript is called `gs`. You can use `gs` to decode PostScript files for displaying or printing hard copies.

Ghostscript is also used by other programs as a filter for working with PostScript printers that cannot switch from PostScript to text and back just by looking at a document. In this case, the `gs` command is used to convert text to PostScript with an output filter for `lp` before sending the text to a PostScript printer. As another example, `HylaFAX` uses `gs` as its primary PostScript output filter program.

Ghostview is an X Window–based program that provides a canvas for `ghostscript` to write its output to. Ghostview enables you to scroll through a multi-page document, zoom in and out, and save marked pages. The ability to view EPSI or PostScript via Ghostscript saves time and paper when typesetting documents.

PART

V

IN THIS PART

Linux for Programmers

gawk

26

by Tim Parker

The awk programming language was created by the three people who gave their last-name initials to the language: Alfred Aho, Peter Weinberger, and Brian Kernighan. The gawk program included with Linux is the GNU implementation of that programming language.

The awk language is more than just a programming language; it is an almost indispensable tool for many system administrators and UNIX programmers. The language itself is easy to learn, easy to master, and amazingly flexible. Once you get the hang of using awk, you'll be surprised how often you can use it for routine tasks on your system.

To help you understand gawk, I will follow a simple order of introducing the elements of the programming language, as well as showing good examples. You are encouraged, or course, to experiment as the chapter progresses.

I can't cover all the different aspects and features of gawk in this chapter, but we will look at the basics of the language and show you enough, hopefully, to get your curiosity working.

What Is the *awk* Language?

awk is designed to be an easy-to-use programming language that lets you work with information either stored in files or piped to it. The main strengths of awk are its abilities to do the following:

- Display some or all the contents of a file, selecting rows, columns, or fields as necessary.
- Analyze text for frequency of words, occurrences, and so on.
- Prepare formatted output reports based on information in a file.
- Filter text in a very powerful manner.
- Perform calculations with numeric information from a file.

awk isn't difficult to learn. In many ways, awk is the ideal first programming language because of its simple rules, basic formatting, and standard usage. Experienced programmers will find awk refreshingly easy to use.

Files, Records, and Fields

Usually, gawk works with data stored in files. Often this is numeric data, but gawk can work with character information, too. If data is not stored in a file, it is supplied to gawk through a pipe or other form of redirection. Only ASCII files (text files) can be properly handled with gawk. Although it does have the ability to work with binary files, the results are often unpredictable. Since most information on a Linux system is stored in ASCII, this isn't a problem.

As a simple example of a file that gawk works with, consider a telephone directory. It is composed of many entries, all with the same format: last name, first name, address, telephone number. The entire telephone directory is a database of sorts, although without a sophisticated search routine. Indeed, the telephone directory relies on a pure alphabetical order to enable users to search for the data they need.

Each line in the telephone directory is a complete set of data on its own and is called a *record*. For example, the entry in the telephone directory for "Smith, John," which includes his address and telephone number, is a record.

Each piece of information in the record—the last name, the first name, the address, and the telephone number—is called a *field*. For the gawk language, the field is a single piece of information. A record, then, is a number of fields that pertain to a single item. A set of records makes up a *file*.

In most cases, fields are separated by a character that is used only to separate fields, such as a space, a tab, a colon, or some other special symbol. This character is called a *field separator*. A good example is the file /etc/passwd, which looks like this:

```
tparker:t36s62hsh:501:101:Tim Parker:/home/tparker:/bin/bash
etreijs:2ys639dj3h:502:101:Ed Treijs:/home/etreijs:/bin/tcsh
ychow:1h27sj:503:101:Yvonne Chow:/home/ychow:/bin/bash
```

If you look carefully at the file, you will see that it uses a colon as the field separator. Each line in the /etc/passwd file has seven fields: the user name, the password, the user ID, the group ID, a comment field, the home directory, and the startup shell. Each field is separated by a colon. Colons exist only to separate fields. A program looking for the sixth field in any line needs only count five colons across (because the first field doesn't have a colon before it).

That's where we find a problem with the gawk definition of fields as they pertain to the telephone directory example. Consider the following lines from a telephone directory:

```
Smith, John    13 Wilson St.           555-1283
Smith, John    2736 Artside Dr, Apt 123  555-2736
Smith, John    125 Westmount Cr        555-1726
```

We "know" there are four fields here: the last name, the first name, the address, and the telephone number. But gawk doesn't see it that way. The telephone book uses the space character as a field separator, so on the first line it sees "Smith" as the first field, "John" as the second, "13" as the third, "Wilson" as the fourth, and so on. As far as gawk is concerned, the first line when using a space character as a field separator has six fields. The second line has eight fields.

> **NOTE**
>
> When working with a programming language, you must consider data the way the language will see it. Remember that programming languages take things literally.

To make sense of the telephone directory the way we want to handle it, we have to find another way of structuring the data so that there is a field separator between the sections. For example, the following uses the slash character as the field separator:

```
Smith/John/13 Wilson St./555-1283
Smith/John/2736 Artside Dr, Apt 123/555-2736
Smith/John/125 Westmount Cr/555-1726
```

By default, gawk uses blank characters (spaces or tabs) as field separators unless instructed to use another character. If gawk is using spaces, it doesn't matter how many are in a row; they are treated as a single block for purposes of finding fields. Naturally, there is a way to override this behavior, too.

Pattern-Action Pairs

The gawk language has a particular format for almost all instructions. Each command is composed of two parts: a pattern and a corresponding action. Whenever the pattern is matched, gawk executes the action that matches that pattern.

Pattern-action pairs can be thought of in more common terms to show how they work. Consider instructing someone how to get to the post office. You might say, "Go to the end of the street and turn right. At the stop sign, turn left. At the end of the street, go right." You have created three pattern-action pairs with these instructions:

```
end of street: turn right
stop sign: turn left
end of street: turn right
```

When these patterns are met, the corresponding action is taken. You wouldn't turn right before you reached the end of the street, and you don't turn right until you get to the end of the street, so the pattern must be matched precisely for the action to be performed. This is a bit simplistic, but it gives you the basic idea.

With gawk, the patterns to be matched are enclosed in a pair of slashes, and the actions are in a pair of curly braces:

```
/pattern1/{action1}
/pattern2/{action2}
/pattern3/{action3}
```

This format makes it quite easy to tell where the pattern starts and ends, and when the action starts and ends. All gawk programs are sets of these pattern-action pairs, one after the other. Remember these pattern-action pairs are working on text files, so a typical set of patterns might be matching a set of strings, and the actions might be to print out parts of the line that matched.

Suppose there isn't a pattern? In that case, the pattern matches every time and the action is executed every time. If there is no action, gawk copies the entire line that matched without change.

Here are some simple examples. The gawk command

```
gawk '/tparker/' /etc/passwd
```

will look for each line in the /etc/passwd file that contains the pattern tparker and display it (there is no action, only a pattern). The output from the command will be the one line in the /etc/passwd file that contains the string tparker. If there is more than one line in the file with that pattern, they all will be displayed. In this case, gawk is acting exactly like the grep utility!

This example shows you two important things about gawk: It can be invoked from the command line by giving it the pattern-action pair to work with and a filename, and it likes to have single quotes around the pattern-action pair in order to differentiate them from the filename.

The gawk language is literal in its matching. The string cat will match any lines with cat in them, whether the word "cat" by itself or part of another word such as "concatenate." To be exact, put spaces on either side of the word. Also, case is important. We'll see how to expand the matching in the section "Metacharacters" a little later in the chapter.

Jumping ahead slightly, we can introduce a gawk command. The command

```
gawk '{print $3}' file2.data
```

has only an action, so it performs that action on every line in the file file2.data. The action is print $3, which tells gawk to print the third field of every line. The default field separator, a space, is used to tell where fields begin and end. If we had tried the same command on the /etc/passwd file, nothing would have been displayed because the field separator used in that file is the colon.

We can combine the two commands to show a complete pattern-action pair:

```
gawk '/UNIX/{print $2}' file2.data
```

This command will search file2.data line by line, looking for the string UNIX. If it finds UNIX, it prints the second column of that line (record).

> **NOTE**
>
> The quotes around the entire pattern-action pair are very important and should not be left off. Without them, the command might not execute properly. Make sure the quotes match (don't use a single quote at the beginning and a double quote at the end).

You can combine more than one pattern-action pair in a command. For example, the command

```
gawk '/scandal/{print $1} /rumor/{print $2}' gossip_file
```

scans gossip_file for all occurrences of the pattern "scandal" and prints the first column, and then starts at the top again and searches for the pattern "rumor" and prints the second column. The scan starts at the top of the file each time there is a new pattern-action pair.

Simple Patterns

As you might have figured out, gawk numbers all of the fields in a record. The first field is $1, the second is $2, and so on. The entire record is called $0. As a short form, gawk allows you to ignore the $0 in simple commands, so the instructions

```
gawk '/tparker/{print $0}' /etc/passwd
gawk '/tparker/{print}' /etc/passwd
gawk '/tparker/' /etcpasswd
```

result in the same output (the latter one because no action causes the entire line to be printed).

Sometimes you want to do more than match a simple character string. The gawk language has many powerful features, but I'll just introduce a few at the moment. We can, for example, make a comparison of a field with a value. The command

```
gawk '$2 == "foo" {print $3}' testfile
```

instructs gawk to compare the second string ($2) of each record in testfile and check to see if it is equal to the string foo. If it is, gawk prints the third column ($3).

This command demonstrates a few important points. First, there are no slashes around the pattern because we are not matching a pattern but are evaluating something. Slashes are used only for character matches. Second, the == sign means "is equal to." We must use two equal signs, because the single equal sign is used for assignment of values, as you will see shortly. Finally, we put double quotations around foo because we want gawk to interpret it literally. Only strings of characters that are to be literally interpreted must be quoted in this manner.

> **NOTE**
>
> Don't confuse the quotes used for literal characters with those used to surround the pattern-action pair on the command line. If you use the same quote marks for both, gawk will be unable to process the command properly.

Comparisons and Arithmetic

An essential component of any programming language is the ability to compare two strings or numbers and evaluate whether they are equal or different. The gawk program has several comparisons, including ==, which you just saw in an example. Table 26.1 shows the important comparisons.

Table 26.1. The important comparisons.

Comparison	Description
==	Equal to
!=	Not equal to
>	Greater than
<	Less than
>=	Greater than or equal to
<=	Less than or equal to

These are probably familiar to you from arithmetic and other programming languages you may have seen. From this, you can surmise that the command

```
gawk '$4 > 100' testfile
```

will display every line in `testfile` in which the value in the fourth column is greater than 100.

All of the normal arithmetic commands are available, including add, subtract, multiply, and divide. There are also more advanced functions such as exponentials and remainders (also called modulus). Table 26.2 shows the basic arithmetic operations that `gawk` supports.

Table 26.2. Basic arithmetic operators.

Operator	Description	Example
+	Addition	2+6
-	Subtraction	6-3
*	Multiplication	2*5
/	Division	8/4
^	Exponentiation	3^2 (=9)
%	Remainder	9%4 (=1)

You can combine column numbers and math, too. For example, the action

```
{print $3/2}
```

divides the number in the third column by 2.

There is also a set of arithmetic functions for trigonometry and generating random numbers. See Table 26.3.

Table 26.3. Random-number and trigonometric functions.

Function	Description
sqrt(x)	Square root of x
sin(x)	Sine of x (in radians)
cos(x)	Cosine of x (in radians)
atan2(x,y)	Arctangent of x/y
log(x)	Natural logarithm of x
exp(x)	The constant e to the power x
int(x)	Integer part of x
rand()	Random number between 0 and 1
srand(x)	Set x as seed for rand()

The order of operations is important to gawk, as it is to regular arithmetic. The rules gawk follows are the same as with arithmetic: all multiplications, divisions, and remainders are performed before additions and subtractions. For example, the command

```
{print $1+$2*$3}
```

multiplies column two by column three and then adds the result to column one. If you wanted to force the addition first, you would have to use parentheses:

```
{print ($1+$2)*$3}
```

Because these are the same rules you have heard about since grade school, they shouldn't cause you any confusion. Remember, if in doubt, put parentheses in the proper places to force the operations.

Strings and Numbers

If you've used any other programming language, these concepts will be familiar to you. If you are new to programming, you will probably find them obvious, but you'd be surprised how many people get things hopelessly muddled by using strings when they should have used numbers.

A *string* is a set of characters that are to be interpreted literally by gawk. Strings are surrounded by quotation marks. Numbers are not surrounded by quotation marks and are treated as real values.

For example, the command

```
gawk '$1 != "Tim" {print}' testfile
```

will print any line in testfile that doesn't have the word Tim in the first column. If we had left out the quotation marks around Tim, gawk wouldn't have processed the command properly. The command

```
gawk '$1 == "50" {print}' testfile
```

will display any line that has the string 50 in it. It does not attempt to see if the value stored in the first column is different than 50; it just does a character check. The string 50 is not equal to the number 50 as far as gawk is concerned.

Formatting Output

We've seen how to do simple actions in the commands we've already discussed, but you can do several things in an action. For example, the command

```
gawk '$1 != "Tim" {print $1, $5, $6, $2}' testfile
```

will print the first, fifth, sixth, and second columns of testfile for every line that doesn't have the first column equal to "Tim". You can place as many of these columns as you want in a print command.

Indeed, you can place strings in a print command, too, such as in this command

```
gawk '$1 != "Tim" {print "The entry for ", $1, "is not Tim. ", $2}' testfile
```

which will print the strings and the columns as shown. Each section of the print command is separated by a comma. There are also spaces at the end of the strings to ensure there is a space between the string and the value of the column that is printed.

You can use additional formatting instructions to make gawk format the output properly. These instructions are borrowed from the C language, and they use the command printf (print formatted) instead of print.

The printf command uses a placeholder scheme, but the gawk language knows how to format the entry because of the placeholder and looks later in the command line to find out what to put there. An example will help make this obvious:

```
{printf "%5s likes this language\n", $2}
```

The %5s part of the line instructs gawk how to format the string, in this case using five string characters. The value to place in this position is given at the end of the line as the second column. The \n at the end of the quoted section is a newline character. If the second column of a four-line file held names, printf would format the output like this:

```
  Tim likes this language
Geoff likes this language
 Mike likes this language
  Joe likes this language
```

You will notice that the %5s format means to right-justify the column entry. This prevents awkward spacing.

The gawk language supports several format placeholders. They are shown in Table 26.4.

Table 26.4. Format placeholders.

Placeholder	Description
c	If a string, the first character of the string; if an integer, the character that matches the first value
d	An integer
e	A floating-point number in scientific notation
f	A floating-point number in conventional notation
g	A floating-point number in either scientific or conventional notation, whichever is shorter
o	An unsigned integer in octal format
s	A string
x	An unsigned integer in hexadecimal format

Whenever you use one of the format characters, you can place a number before the character to show how many digits or characters are to be used. Therefore, the format 6d would have six digits of an integer. Many formats can be on a line, but each must have a value at the end of the line, as in this example

```
{printf "%5s works for %5s and earns %2d an hour", $1, $2, $3}
```

Here, the first string is the first column, the second string is the second column, and the third set of digits is from the third column in a file. The output would be something like:

```
Joe works for Mike and earns 12 an hour
```

A few little tricks are useful. As you saw in an earlier example, strings are right-justified, so the command

```
{printf "%5s likes this language\n", $2}
```

results in the output

```
  Tim likes this language
Geoff likes this language
 Mike likes this language
  Joe likes this language
```

To left-justify the names, place a minus sign in the format statement:

```
{printf "%-5s likes this language\n", $2}
```

This will result in the output

```
Tim   likes this language
Geoff likes this language
Mike  likes this language
Joe   likes this language
```

Notice that the name is justified on the left instead of on the right.

When dealing with numbers, you can specify the precision to be used, so that the command

```
{printf "%5s earns $%.2f an hour", $3, $6}
```

will use the string in column three and put five characters from it in the first placeholder, and then take the value in the sixth column and place it in the second placeholder with two digits after the decimal point. The output of the command would be like this:

```
Joe earns $12.17 an hour
```

The dollar sign was inside the quotation marks in the `printf` command, and was not generated by the system. It has no special meaning inside the quotation marks. If you want to limit the number of digits to the right of the period, you can do that too. The command

```
{printf "%5s earns $%6.2f an hour", $3, $6}
```

will put six digits before the period and two after.

Finally, we can impose some formatting on the output lines themselves. In an earlier example, you saw the use of \n to add a newline character. These are called *escape codes,* because the backslash is interpreted by gawk to mean something different than a backslash. Table 26.5 shows the important escape codes that gawk supports.

Table 26.5. Escape codes.

Code	Description
\a	Bell
\b	Backspace
\f	Formfeed
\n	Newline
\r	Carriage return
\t	Tab
\v	Vertical tab
\ooo	Octal character ooo
\xdd	Hexadecimal character dd
\c	Any character c

You can, for example, escape a quotation mark by using the sequence \", which will place a quotation mark in the string without interpreting it to mean something special. For example:

```
{printf "I said \"Hello\" and he said "\Hello\"."
```

Awkward-looking, perhaps, but necessary to avoid problems. You'll see lots more escape characters used in examples later in this chapter.

Changing Field Separators

As I mentioned earlier, the default field separator is always a whitespace character (spaces or tabs). This is not often convenient, as we found with the /etc/passwd file. You can change the field separator on the gawk command line by using the -F option followed by the separator you want to use:

```
gawk -F":" '/tparker/{print}' /etc/passwd
```

This command changes the field separator to a colon and searches the etc/passwd file for the lines containing the string tparker. The new field separator is put in quotation marks to avoid any confusion. Also, the -F option (it must be a capital F) is before the first quote character enclosing the pattern-action pair. If it came after, it wouldn't be applied.

Metacharacters

Earlier I mentioned that gawk is particular about its pattern-matching habits. The string cat will match anything with the three letters on the line. Sometimes you want to be more exact in the matching. If you only want to match the word "cat" but not "concatenate," you should put spaces on either side of the pattern:

```
/ cat / {print}
```

What about matching different cases? That's where the or instruction, represented by a vertical bar, comes in. For example

```
/ cat | CAT / {print}
```

will match "cat" or "CAT" on a line. However, what about "Cat?" That's where we also need to specify options within a pattern. With gawk, we use square brackets for this. To match any combination of "cat" in upper- or lowercase, we must write the pattern like this:

```
/ [Cc][Aa][Tt] / {print}
```

This can get pretty awkward, but it's seldom necessary. To match just "Cat" and "cat," for example, we would use the pattern

```
/ [Cc]at / {print}
```

A useful matching operator is the tilde (~). This is used when you want to look for a match in a particular field in a record. For example, the pattern

```
$5 ~ /tparker/
```

will match any records where the fifth field is tparker. It is similar to the == operator. The matching operator can be negated, so

```
$5 !~ /tparker/
```

will find any record where the fifth field is not equal to tparker.

A few characters (called *metacharacters*) have special meaning to gawk. Many of these metacharacters will be familiar to shell users, because they are carried over from UNIX shells. The metacharacters shown in Table 26.6 can be used in gawk patterns.

Table 26.6. Metacharacters.

Metacharacter	Meaning	Example	Meaning of Example
~	The beginning of the field	$3 ~ /^b/	Matches if the third field starts with b
$	The end of the field	$3 ~ /b$/	Matches if the third field ends with b
.	Matches any single character	$3 ~ /i.m/	Matches any record that has a third field value of i, another character, and then m
		Or	/cat|CAT/	Matches cat or CAT

Metacharacter	Meaning	Example	Meaning of Example
*	Zero or more repetitions of a character	/UNI*X/	Matches UNX, UNIX, UNIIX, UNIIIX, and so on
+	One or more repetitions of a character	/UNI+X/	Matches UNIX, UNIIX, and so on, but not UNX
\{a,b\}	The number of repetitions between a and b (both integers)	/UNI\{1,3\}X	Matches only UNIX, UNIIX, and UNIIIX
?	Zero or one repetitions of a string	/UNI?X/	Matches UNX and UNIX only
[ ]	Range of characters	/I[BDG]M/	Matches IBM, IDM, and IGM
[^]	Not in the set	/I[^DE]M/	Matches all three character sets starting with I and ending in M, except IDM and IEM

Some of these metacharacters are used frequently. You will see some examples later in this chapter.

Calling *gawk* Programs

Running pattern-action pairs one or two at a time from the command line would be pretty difficult (and time consuming), so gawk allows you to store pattern-action pairs in a file. A gawk program (called a *script*) is a set of pattern-action pairs stored in an ASCII file. For example, this could be the contents of a valid gawk script:

```
/tparker/{print $6}
$2 != "foo" {print}
```

The first line would look for tparker and print the sixth column, and the second line would start at the top of the file again and look for second columns that don't match the string "foo", then display the entire line. When you are writing a script, you don't need to worry about the quotation marks around the pattern-action pairs as you did on the command line, because the new command to execute this script makes it obvious where the pattern-action pairs start and end.

After you have saved all of the pattern-action pairs in a program, they are called by gawk with the -f option on the command line:

```
gawk -f script filename
```

This command causes gawk to read all of the pattern-action pairs from the file *script* and process them against the file called *filename*. This is how most gawk programs are written. Don't confuse the -f and -F options!

If you want to specify a different field separator on the command line (they can be specified in the script, but use a special format you'll see later), the -F option must follow the -f option:

```
gawk -f script -F":" filename
```

If you want to process more than one file using the script, just append the names of the files:

```
gawk -f script filename1 filename2 filename3 ...
```

By default, all output from the gawk command is displayed on the screen. You could redirect it to a file with the usual Linux redirection commands:

```
gawk -f script filename > save_file
```

There is another way of specifying the output file from within the script, but we'll come back to that in a moment.

BEGIN and END

Two special patterns supported by gawk are useful when writing scripts. The BEGIN pattern is used to indicate any actions that should take place before gawk starts processing a file. This is usually used to initialize values, set parameters such as field separators, and so on. The END pattern is used to execute any instructions after the file has been completely processed. Typically, this can be for summaries or completion notices.

Any instructions following the BEGIN and END patterns are enclosed in curly braces to identify which instructions are part of both patterns. Both BEGIN and END must appear in capitals. Here's a simple example of a gawk script that uses BEGIN and END, albeit only for sending a message to the terminal:

```
BEGIN { print "Starting the process the file" }
$1 == "UNIX" {print}
$2 > 10 {printf "This line has a value of %d", $2}
END { print "Finished processing the file.  Bye!"}
```

In this script, a message is initially printed out, and each line that has the word UNIX in the first column is echoed to the screen. Next, the file is processed again to look for any line with the second column greater than 10, and the message is generated with its current value. Finally, the END pattern prints out a message that the program is finished.

Variables

If you have used any programming language before, you know that a *variable* is a storage location for a value. Each variable has a name and an associated value, which may change.

With gawk, you assign a variable a value using the assignment operator, =:

```
var1 = 10
```

This assigns the value 10 (numeric, not string) to the variable var1. With gawk, you don't have to declare variable types before you use them as you must with most other languages. This makes it easy to work with variables in gawk.

> **NOTE**
>
> Don't confuse the assignment operator, =, which assigns a value, with the comparison operator, ==, which compares two values. This is a common error that takes a little practice to overcome.

The gawk language lets you use variables within actions, so the pattern-action pair

```
$1 == "Plastic" { count = count + 1 }
```

checks to see if the first column is equal to the string "Plastic", and if it is, increments the value of count by one. Somewhere above this line we should set a preliminary value for the variable count (usually in the BEGIN section), or we will be adding one to something that isn't a recognizable number.

> **NOTE**
>
> Actually, gawk assigns all variables a value of zero when they are first used, so you don't really have to define the value before you use it. It is, however, good programming practice to initialize the variable anyway.

Here's a more complete example:

```
BEGIN { count = 0 }
$5 == "UNIX" { count = count + 1 }
END { printf "%d occurrences of UNIX were found", count }
```

In the BEGIN section, the variable count is set to zero. Then, the gawk pattern-action pair is processed, with every occurrence of "UNIX" adding one to the value of count. After the entire file has been processed, the END statement displays the total number.

Variables can be used in combination with columns and values, so all of the following statements are legal:

```
count = count + $6
count = $5 - 8
count = $5 + var1
```

Variables can also be part of a pattern. The following are all valid as pattern-action pairs:

```
$2 > max_value {print "Max value exceeded by ", $2 - max_value}
$4 - var1 < min_value {print "Illegal value of ", $4}
```

Two special operators are used with variables to increment and decrement by one, because these are common operations. Both of these special operators are borrowed from the C language:

count++   increments count by one

count--   decrements count by one

Built-In Variables

The gawk language has a few built-in variables that are used to represent things such as the total number of records processed. These are useful when you want to get totals. Table 26.7 shows the important built-in variables.

Table 26.7. The important built-in variables.

Variable	Description
NR	The number of records read so far
FNR	The number of records read from the current file
FILENAME	The name of the input file
FS	Field separator (default is whitespace)
RS	Record separator (default is newline)
OFMT	Output format for numbers (default is %g)
OFS	Output field separator
ORS	Output record separator
NF	The number of fields in the current record

The NR and FNR values are the same if you are processing only one file, but if you are doing more than one file, NR is a running total of all files, while FNR is the total for the current file only.

The FS variable is useful, because it controls the input file's field separator. To use the colon for the /etc/passwd file, for example, you would use the command

```
FS=":"
```

in the script, usually as part of the BEGIN pattern.

You can use these built-in variables as you would any other. For example, the command

```
NF <= 5 {print "Not enough fields in the record"}
```

gives you a way to check the number of fields in the file you are processing and generate an error message if the values are incorrect.

Control Structures

Enough of the details have been covered to allow us to start doing some real gawk programming. Although we have not covered all of gawk's pattern and action considerations, we have seen all the important material. Now we can look at writing control structures.

If you have any programming experience at all, or have tried some shell script writing, many of these control structures will appear familiar. If you haven't done any programming, common sense should help, as gawk is cleanly laid out without weird syntax. Follow the examples and try a few test programs of your own.

Incidentally, gawk enables you to place comments anywhere in your scripts, as long as the comment starts with a # sign. You should use comments to indicate what is going on in your scripts if it is not immediately obvious.

The *if* Statement

The if statement is used to allow gawk to test some condition and, if it is true, execute a set of commands. The general syntax for the if statement is

```
if (expression) {commands} else {commands}
```

The expression is always evaluated to see if it is true or false. No other value is calculated for the if expression. Here's a simple if script:

```
# a simple if loop
(if ($1 == 0){
        print "This cell has a value of zero"
        }
else {
        printf "The value is %d\n", $1
        })
```

You will notice that I used the curly braces to lay out the program in a readable manner. Of course, this could all have been typed on one line and gawk would have understood it, but writing in a nicely formatted manner makes it easier to understand what is going on, and debugging the program becomes much easier if the need arises.

In this simple script, we test the first column to see if the value is zero. If it is, a message to that effect is printed. If not, the printf statement prints the value of the column.

The flow of the if statement is quite simple to follow. There can be several commands in each part, as long as the curly braces mark the start and end. There is no need to have an else section. It can be left out entirely, if desired. For example, this is a complete and valid gawk script:

```
(if ($1 == 0){
        print "This cell has a value of zero"
        })
```

The gawk language, to be compatible with other programming languages, allows a special format of the if statement when a simple comparison is being conducted. This quick-and-dirty if structure is harder to read for novices, and I don't recommend it if you are new to the language. For example, here's the if statement written the proper way:

```
# a nicely formatted if loop
(if ($1 > $2){
        print "The first column is larger"
        }
else {
        print "The second column is larger"
        })
```

Here's the quick-and-dirty method:

```
# if syntax from hell
$1 > $2{
      print "The first column is larger"
      }
{print "The second column is larger")
```

You will notice that the keywords `if` and `else` are left off. The general structure is retained: expression, true commands, and false commands. However, this is much less readable if you do not know that it is a `if` statement! Not all versions of `gawk` will allow this method of using `if`, so don't be too surprised if it doesn't work. Besides, you should be using the more verbose method of writing `if` statements for readability's sake.

The *while* Loop

The `while` statement allows a set of commands to be repeated as long as some condition is true. The condition is evaluated each time the program loops. The general format of the `gawk` `while` loop is

```
while (expression){
      commands
      }
```

For example, the `while` loop can be used in a program that calculates the value of an investment over several years (the formula for the calculation is value=amount(1+interest_rate)^years):

```
# interest calculation computes compound interest
# inputs from a file are the amount, interest_rate, and years
{var = 1
while (var <= $3) {
      printf("%f\n", $1*(1+$2)^var)
      var++
      }
}
```

You can see in this script that we initialize the variable `var` to 1 before entering the `while` loop. If we hadn't done this, `gawk` would have assigned a value of zero. The values for the three variables we use are read from the input file. The `autoincrement` command is used to add one to `var` each time the line is executed.

The *for* Loop

The `for` loop is commonly used when you want to initialize a value and then ignore it. The syntax of the `gawk` `for` loop is

```
for (initialization; expression; increment) {
      command
      }
```

The initialization is executed only once and then ignored, the expression is evaluated each time the loop executes, and the increment is executed each time the loop is executed. Usually the increment is a counter of some type, but it can be any collection of valid commands. Here's an example of a for loop, which is the same basic program as shown for the while loop:

```
# interest calculation computes compound interest
# inputs from a file are the amount, interest_rate, and years
{for (var=1; var <= $3; var++) {
      printf("%f\n", $1*(1+$2)^var)
      }
}
```

In this case, var is initialized when the for loop starts. The expression is evaluated, and if true, the loop runs. Then the value of var is incremented and the expression is tested again.

The format of the for loop might look strange if you haven't encountered programming languages before, but it is the same as the for loop used in C, for example.

next and exit

The next instruction tells gawk to process the next record in the file, regardless of what it was doing. For example, in this script:

```
{ command1
      command2
      command3
      next
      command4
}
```

as soon as the next statement is read, gawk moves to the next record in the file and starts at the top of the current script block (given by the curly brace). In this example, *command4* will never be executed because the next statement moves back up to *command1* each time.

The next statement is usually used inside an if loop, where you may want execution to return to the start of the script if some condition is met.

The exit statement makes gawk behave as though it has reached the end of the file, and it then executes any END patterns (if any exist). This is a useful method of aborting processing if there was an error in the file.

Arrays

The gawk language supports arrays and enables you to access any element in the array easily. No special initialization is necessary with an array, because gawk treats it like any other variable. The general format for declaring arrays is

```
var[num]=value
```

As an example, consider the following script that reads an input file and generates an output file with the lines reversed in order:

```
# reverse lines in a file
{line[NR] = $0 }  # remember each line
```

```
END {var=NR                # output lines in reverse order
      while (var > 0){
      print line[var]
      var —
      }
}
```

In this simple program (try and do the same task in any other programming language to see how efficient gawk is!), we used the NR (number of records) built-in variable. After reading each line into the array line[ ], we simply start at the last record and print them again, stepping down through the array each time. We don't have to declare the array or do anything special with it, which is one of the powerful features of gawk.

Summary

We've only scratched the surface of gawk's abilities, but you might have noticed that it is a relatively easy language to work with and places no special demands on the programmer. That's one of the reasons gawk is so often used for quick programs. It is ideal, for example, for writing a quick script to count the total size of all the files in a directory. In the C language, this would take many lines, but it can be done in less than a dozen lines in gawk.

If you are a system administrator or simply a power user, you will find that gawk is a great complement to all the other tools you have available, especially because it can accept input from a pipe or redirection. For more information on gawk, check the man pages or one of the few awk books that are available.

Programming in C

27

by
Rick McMullin

IN THIS CHAPTER

Linux is distributed with a wide range of software-development tools. Many of these tools support the development of C and C++ applications. This chapter describes the tools that can be used to develop and debug C applications under Linux. It is not intended to be a tutorial on the C programming language, but rather to describe how to use the C compiler and some of the other C programming tools that are included with Linux. In this chapter you will learn about the following:

■ What C is

■ The GNU C compiler

■ Debugging GCC applications with `gdb`

You also will look at some of the useful C tools that are included with the Linux distribution. These tools include pretty print programs, additional debugging tools, and automatic function prototypers.

> **NOTE**
>
> *Pretty print* programs are programs that automatically reformat code so that it has consistent indenting.

What Is C?

C is a general-purpose programming language that has been around since the early days of the UNIX operating system. It was originally created by Dennis Ritchie at Bell Laboratories to aid in the development of UNIX. The first versions of UNIX were written using assembly language and a language called B. C was developed to overcome some of the shortcomings of B. Since that time, C has become one of the most widely used computer languages in the world.

Why did C gain so much support in the programming world? Some of the reasons that C is so commonly used include the following:

■ It is a very portable language. Almost any computer that you can think of has at least one C compiler available for it, and the language syntax and function libraries are standardized across platforms. This is a very attractive feature for developers.

■ Executable programs written in C are fast.

■ C is the system language with all versions of UNIX.

C has evolved quite a bit over the last 20 years. In the late 1980s, the American National Standards Institute published a standard for the C language known as ANSI C. This further helped to secure C's future by making it even more consistent between platforms. The 1980s also saw an object-oriented extension to C called C++. C++ will be described in the next chapter, "Programming in C++."

The C compiler that is available for Linux is the GNU C compiler, abbreviated GCC. This compiler was created under the Free Software Foundation's programming license and is therefore freely distributable. You will find it on the book's companion CD-ROM.

The GNU C Compiler

The GNU C Compiler (GCC) that is packaged with the Red Hat Linux distribution is a fully functional, ANSI C compatible compiler. If you are familiar with a C compiler on a different operating system or hardware platform, you will be able to learn GCC very quickly. This section describes how to invoke GCC and introduces some of the commonly used GCC compiler options.

Invoking GCC

The GCC compiler is invoked by passing it a number of options and a number of filenames. The basic syntax for invoking gcc is this:

```
gcc [options] [filenames]
```

The operations specified by the command-line options will be performed on each of the files that are specified on the command line. The next section describes the options that you will use most often.

GCC Options

There are more than 100 compiler options that can be passed to GCC. You will probably never use many of these options, but you will use some of them on a regular basis. Many of the GCC options consist of more than one character. For this reason you must specify each option with its own hyphen, and you cannot group options after a single hyphen as you can with most Linux commands. For example, the following two commands are not the same:

```
gcc -p -g test.c
gcc -pg test.c
```

The first command tells GCC to compile test.c with profile information for the prof command and also to store debugging information within the executable. The second command just tells GCC to compile test.c with profile information for the gprof command.

When you compile a program using gcc without any command-line options, it will create an executable file (assuming that the compile was successful) and call it a.out. For example, the following command would create a file named a.out in the current directory.

```
gcc test.c
```

To specify a name other than a.out for the executable file, you can use the -o compiler option. For example, to compile a C program file named count.c into an executable file named count, you would type the following command.

```
gcc -o count count.c
```

NOTE

When you are using the -o option, the executable filename must occur directly after the -o on the command line.

There are also compiler options that allow you to specify how far you want the compile to proceed. The -c option tells GCC to compile the code into object code and to skip the assembly and linking stages of the compile. This option is used quite often because it makes the compilation of multifile C programs faster and easier to manage. Object code files that are created by GCC have a .o extension by default.

The -s compiler option tells GCC to stop the compile after it has generated the assembler files for the C code. Assembler files that are generated by GCC have a .s extension by default. The -E option instructs the compiler to perform only the preprocessing compiler stage on the input files. When this option is used, the output from the preprocessor is sent to the standard output rather than being stored in a file.

TIP

The following file extensions are assumed to be used when using the language compilers, including gcc:

Extension	Type of File
.a	Archive file
.c	C program file
.C, .cc, or .cxx	C++ program file
.h	A preprocessor (include) file
.i	An already preprocessed C file only needing compiling and assembling
.ii	An already preprocessed C++ file only needing compiling and assembling
.m	Objective-C program file
.o	Compiled object file
.s	Assembler source that had been preprocessed
.S	Assembler source which requires preprocessing

Optimization Options

When you compile C code with GCC, it tries to compile the code in the least amount of time and also tries to create compiled code that is easy to debug. Making the code easy to debug means that the sequence of the compiled code is the same as the sequence of the source code, and no code gets optimized out of the compile. There are many options that you can use to tell GCC to create smaller, faster executable programs at the cost of compile time and ease of debugging. Of these options the two that you will typically use are the -o and the -02 options.

The -o option tells GCC to perform basic optimizations on the source code. These optimizations will in most cases make the code run faster. The -02 option tells GCC to make the code as fast and small as it can. The -O2 option will cause the compilation speed to be slower than it is when using the -o option, but will typically result in code that executes more quickly.

In addition to the -o and -O2 optimization options, there are a number of lower-level options that can be used to make the code faster. These options are very specific and should only be used if you fully understand the consequences that using these options will have on the compiled code. For a detailed description of these options, refer to the GCC manual page by typing man gcc on the command line.

Debugging and Profiling Options

GCC supports several debugging and profiling options. Of these options, the two that you are most likely to use are the -g option and the -pg option.

The -g option tells GCC to produce debugging information that the GNU debugger (gdb) can use to help you to debug your program. GCC provides a feature that many other C compilers do not have. With GCC you can use the -g option in conjunction with the -o option (which generates optimized code). This can be very useful if you are trying to debug code that is as close as possible to what will exist in the final product. When you are using these two options together you should be aware that some of the code that you have written will probably be changed by GCC when it optimizes it. For more information on debugging your C programs, refer to the "Debugging GCC Programs with gdb" section in this chapter.

The -pg option tells GCC to add extra code to your program that will, when executed, generate profile information that can be used by the gprof program to display timing information about your program. For more information on gprof, refer to the "gprof" section in this chapter.

Debugging GCC Programs with *gdb*

Linux includes the GNU debugging program called gdb. gdb is a very powerful debugger that can be used to debug C and C++ programs. It enables you to see the internal structure or the memory that is being used by a program while it is executing. Some of the functions that gdb provides for you are these:

- It enables you to monitor the value of variables that are contained in your program.
- It enables you to set breakpoints that will stop the program at a specific line of code.
- It enables you to step through the code, line by line.

You can run gdb by typing gdb on the command line and pressing Enter. If your system is configured properly, gdb should start and you will see a screen that resembles the following:

```
GDB is free software and you are welcome to distribute copies of it
under certain conditions; type "show copying" to see the conditions.
There is absolutely no warranty for GDB; type "show warranty" for details.
GDB 4.15 (i586-unknown-linux), Copyright 1995 Free Software Foundation, Inc.
(gdb)
```

When you start gdb, there are a number of options that you can specify on the command line. You will probably run gdb in the following way:

```
gdb <fname>
```

When you invoke gdb in this way, you are specifying the executable file that you want to debug. This tells gdb to load the executable file with the name fname. There are also ways of starting gdb that tell it to inspect a core file that was created by the executable file being examined, or to attach gdb to a currently running process. To get a listing and brief description of each of these other options, you can refer to the gdb man page or type gdb -h at the command line.

Compiling Code for Debugging

To get gdb to work properly, you must compile your programs so that debugging information will be generated by the compiler. The debugging information that is generated contains the types for each of the variables in your program as well as the mapping between the addresses in the executable program and the line numbers in the source code. gdb uses this information to relate the executable code to the source code.

To compile a program with the debugging information turned on, use the -g compiler option.

gdb Basic Commands

The gdb supports many commands that enable you to perform different debugging operations. These commands range in complexity from very simple file-loading commands to complicated commands that allow you to examine the contents of the call stack. Table 27.1 describes the commands that you will need to get up and debugging with gdb. To get a description of all of the gdb commands, refer to the gdb manual page.

Table 27.1. Basic gdb commands.

Command	Description
file	Loads the executable file that is to be debugged
kill	Terminates the program that you are currently debugging
list	Lists sections of the source code that was used to generate the executable file
next	Advances one line of source code in the current function, without stepping into other functions
step	Advances one line of source code in the current function, and does step into other functions
run	Executes the program that is currently being debugged
quit	Terminates gdb
watch	Enables you to examine the value of a program variable whenever the value changes

Command	Description
break	Sets a breakpoint in the code; this causes the execution of the program to be suspended whenever this point is reached
make	Enables you to remake the executable program without quitting out of gdb or using another window
shell	Enables you to execute UNIX shell commands without leaving gdb

The gdb environment supports many of the same command-editing features as do the UNIX shell programs. You can tell gdb to complete unique commands by pressing the Tab key just as you do when you are using bash or tcsh. If what you have typed in is not unique, you can make gdb print a list of all the commands that match what you have typed in so far by pressing the Tab key again. You can also scroll up and down through the commands that you have entered previously by pressing the up and down arrow keys.

Sample *gdb* Session

This section takes you step by step through a sample gdb session. The sample program that is being debugged is quite simple, but it is sufficient to illustrate how gdb is typically used.

We will start by showing a listing of the program that is to be debugged. The program is called greeting and is supposed to display a simple greeting followed by the greeting printed in reverse order.

```c
#include  <stdio.h>

main ()
{
  void my_print(char *);
  void my_print2(char *);

  char my_string[] = "hello there";

  my_print (my_string);
  my_print2 (my_string);
}

void my_print (char *string)
{
  printf ("The string is %s\n", string);
}

void my_print2 (char *string)
{
  char *string2;
  int size, i;

  size = strlen (string);
  string2 = (char *) malloc (size + 1);
  for (i = 0; i < size; i++)
    string2[size - i] = string[i];
```

```
    string2[size+1] = '\0';
    printf ("The string printed backward is %s\n", string2);
}
```

You should compile the preceding program using the gcc command followed by the filename. To rename the generated binary (instead of using the default a.out filename), use the -o option followed by the binary name:

```
gcc -o greeting greeting.c
```

The program, when executed, displays the following output:

```
The string is hello there
The string printed backward is
```

The first line of output comes out correctly, but the second line prints something that was unexpected. We intended the second line of output to be

```
The string printed backward is ereht olleh
```

For some reason the my_print2 function is not working properly. Let's take a look at the problem using gdb. First you need to start gdb, specifying the greeting program as the one to debug. You do this by typing the following command:

```
gdb greeting
```

NOTE

Remember that you must compile the greeting program with the compiler debug options turned on, by typing gcc -q -o greeting greeting.c.

If you forget to pass the program to debug as a parameter to gdb, you can load it in after gdb is started by using the file command at the gdb prompt:

```
(gdb) file greeting
```

This command will load the greeting executable just as if you had told gdb to load it on the command line.

You can now run greeting by entering the run command from the gdb prompt. When the program is executed from within gdb, the result should resemble the following:

```
(gdb) run
Starting program: /root/greeting
The string is hello there
The string printed backward is
Program exited with code 040
```

The output of the greeting program is the same as when we executed the program outside of gdb. The question is, why is the backward print not working? To find the problem we can set a breakpoint at the line after the for statement in the my_print2 function. To do this, list the source file by entering the list command at the gdb prompt:

```
(gdb) list
```

The first time you enter the list command, you get output that resembles the following:

```
1       #include  <stdio.h>
2
3       void main ()
4       {
5          void my_print(char *);
6          void my_print2(char *);
7
8          char my_string[] = "hello there";
9
10         my_print (my string)
```

If you press Enter, gdb will execute the list command again, giving you the following output:

```
11      my_print2 (my string);
12      {
13
14      void my_print (char *string)
15      {
16         printf ("The string is %s\n", string);
17      }
18
19      void my_print2 (char *string)
20      {
```

Pressing Enter one more time will list the rest of the greeting program:

```
21         char *string2;
22         int size, i;
23
24         size = strlen (string);
25         string2 = (char *) malloc (size + 1);
26         for (i = 0; i < size; i++)
27            string2[size - i] = string[i];
28         string2[size+1] = '\0';
29         printf ("The string printed backward is %s\n", string2);
30      }
```

By listing the file you can see that the place where you want to set the breakpoint is line 27. Now, to set the breakpoint, type the following command at the gdb command prompt:

```
(gdb) break 27
```

gdb should now print a response resembling the following:

```
Breakpoint 1 at 0x8000570: file greeting.c, line 27
(gdb)
```

Now you can run the program again by typing the run command. This command will generate the following output:

```
Starting program: /root/greeting
The string is hello there

Breakpoint 1, my_print2 (string = 0xbffffe14 "hello there") at greeting.c:27
27  string2[size - i]=string[i]
```

You can see what is actually going wrong with your program by setting a watch to tell you the value of the string2[size - i] variable expression.

To do this, type

```
(gdb) watch string2[size - i]
```

gdb will return the following acknowledgment:

```
Hardware watchpoint 2: string2[size - i]
```

Now that a watch has been set, gdb will halt the program and display the new value of variable string2[size - i] each time it changes. But because we already have a breakpoint established at the line where string2[size - i] will be updated, two breaks for each pass through the loop will actually be generated: once for the breakpoint and again for the watch. To eliminate this redundancy, eliminate the breakpoint by typing disable 1 at the gdb prompt.

> **NOTE**
>
> Breakpoints are reset by disabling the number of the breakpoint assigned to the code line. For example, when we previously typed break 27, breakpoint 1 was assigned to that line of code. So to clear the breakpoint, we disable breakpoint number 1 by typing disable 1.

Now you can step through the execution of the for loop using the cont (short for "continue") command:

```
(gdb) cont
```

After the first time through the loop, gdb tells us that string2[size - i] is 'h'. gdb informs you of this by writing the following message on the screen:

```
Hardware watchpoint 2, string2[size - i]

Old value = 0 '\000'
New value = 104 'h'
my_print2(string = 0xbffffe14 "hello there") at greeting.c:26
26 for (i=0; i<size; i++)
```

This is the value that you expected. Continuing through the loop several more times reveals similar results. Everything appears to be functioning normally. When you get to the point where i=10, the value of the `string2[size - i]` expression is equal to `'e'`, the value of the `size - i` expression is equal to 1, and the program is at the last character that is to be copied over into the new string.

> **NOTE**
>
> You can see the current value of a variable or expression at any time from the `gdb` prompt by using the print EXP command. For example, try `print i` or `print (size - i)` while continuing through the loop.

If you continue through the loop one more time, you see that there was not a value assigned to `string2[0]`, which is the first character of the string. Because the `malloc` function initializes the memory it assigns to null, the first character in `string2` is the null character. This explains why nothing was being printed when you tried to print `string2`.

Now that you have found the problem, it should be quite easy to fix. You must write the code so that the first character going into `string2` is being put into `string2` at offset `size - 1` instead of `string2` at offset `size`. This is because the size of `string2` is 12, but it starts numbering at offset zero. The characters in the string should start at offset 0 and go to offset 10, with offset 11 being reserved for the null character.

There are many ways to modify this code so that it will work. One way is to keep a separate size variable that is one smaller than the real size of the original string. This solution is shown in the following code:

```c
#include  <stdio.h>

void main ()
{
  void my_print(char *);
  void my_print2(char *);

  char my_string[] = "hello there";

  my_print (my_string);
  my_print2 (my_string);
}

void my_print (char *string)
{
  printf ("The string is %s\n", string);
}

void my_print2 (char *string)
{
  char *string2;
  int size, size2, i;

  size = strlen (string);
  size2 = size -1;
```

```
  string2 = (char *) malloc (size + 1);
  for (i = 0; i < size; i++)
    string2[size2 - i] = string[i];
  string2[size] = '\0';
  printf ("The string printed backward is %s\n", string2);
}
```

Additional C Programming Tools

The Red Hat Linux distribution includes a number of C development tools that have not yet been described. This section describes many of these additional tools and their typical uses.

xxgdb

xxgdb is an X Window system–based graphical user interface to gdb. All of the features that exist in the command-line version of gdb are present in xxgdb. xxgdb enables you to perform many of the most commonly used gdb commands by pressing buttons instead of typing in commands. It also graphically represents where you have placed breakpoints.

You can start xxgdb by typing the following into an Xterm window.

xxgdb

When you initiate xxgdb you can specify any of the command-line options that were available with gdb. xxgdb also has some of its own command-line options. These are described in Table 27.2.

Table 27.2. The xxgdb command-line options.

Option	Description
=db_name	Specifies the name of the debugger to be used. The default is gdb.
=db_prompt	Specifies the debugger prompt. The default is gdb.
=gdbinit	Specifies the filename of the initial gdb command file. The default is .gdbinit.
=nx	Tells xxgdb not to execute the .gdbinit file.
=bigicon	Uses a large icon size for the xxgdb icon.

When you start xxgdb, a window, depicted in Figure 27.1, opens on your screen.

FIGURE 27.1.

The xxgdb debugging window.

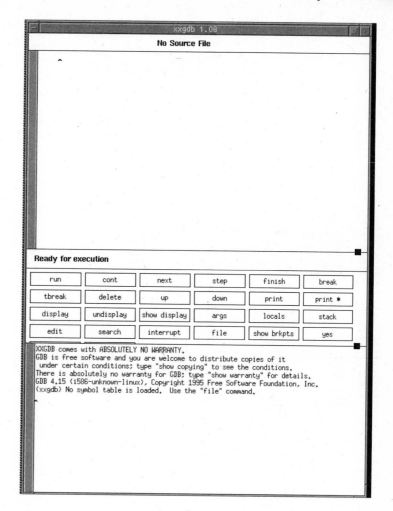

The bottom pane of the window contains a message that is similar to the one displayed on the screen when you started the command-line version of gdb. Use this pane to enter commands to the xxgdb debugger just as you would in gdb. To give the pane focus, left-click anywhere in its region and type:

```
file greeting
```

This should open the file for debugging and display its source code in the upper pane of the window, as shown in Figure 27.2.

FIGURE 27.2.

The xxgdb *window with debug source open.*

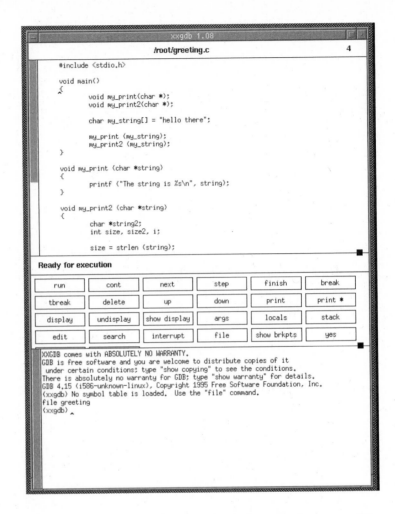

You could have accomplished the same thing by using the File button shown in the center of the window. In addition, you can use the run, break, and cont buttons much in the same way that we have used them before in gdb, only now graphically. To watch a variable (as long as it is within context) you can use the display button.

Try experimenting with the different features that this program provides and refer to the xxgdb and gdb manual pages for information on additional capabilities these tools provide.

calls

calls is a program that is not included on the Linux CD-ROM accompanying this book, but you can obtain a copy from the sunsite FTP site under the directory /pub/Linux/devel/lang/c/calls.tar.Z. Some older CD-ROM distributions of Linux include this file. Because it is a useful tool, we will cover it here. If you think it will be of use to you, obtain a copy from an FTP or BBS site or another CD-ROM. calls runs the GCC preprocessor on the files that are passed to it on the command line, and displays a function call tree for the functions that are in those files.

> **NOTE**
>
> To install calls on your system, perform the following steps while you are logged in as root:
>
> 1. FTP the file sunsite.unc.edu/pub/Linux/devel/lang/c/calls.tar.z.
> 2. Uncompress and untar the file.
> 3. cd into the calls subdirectory that was created by untarring the file.
> 4. Move the file named calls to the /usr/bin directory.
> 5. Move the file named calls.1 to the /usr/man/man1 directory.
>
> This will install the calls program and man page on your system.

When calls prints out the call trace, it includes the filename in which the function was found in brackets after the function name:

```
main [program.c]
```

If the function was not in one of the files that was passed to calls, it does not know where that function lives and prints only the function name:

```
printf
```

calls also makes note of recursive and static functions in its output. Recursive functions are represented in the following way:

```
fact <<< recursive in factorial.c >>>
```

Static functions are represented as follows:

```
total [static in calculate.c]
```

As an example, assume that you executed calls with the following program as input:

```
##include <stdio.h>

void main ()
{
void my_print(char *);
void my_print2(char *);

char my_string[] = "hello there";
my_print (my_string);
my_print2(my_string);
}
```

```
void my_print (char *string)
{
printf ("The string is %s\n", string);
}

void my_print2 (char *string)
{
  char *string2;
  int size, size2, i;

  size = strlen (string);
  size2 = size -1;
  string2 = (char *) malloc (size + 1);
  for (i = 0; i < size; i++)
    string2[size2 - i] = string[i];
  string2[size] = '\0';
  printf ("The string printed backward is %s\n", string2);
}
```

This would generate the following output:

```
1 main [greeting.c]
2        my_print [greeting.c]
3              printf
4        my_print2 [greeting.c]
5              strlen
6              malloc
7              printf
```

`calls` recognizes a number of command-line options that enable you to specify the appearance of the output and what function calls get displayed. For more information on these command-line options, refer to the `calls` manual page or type `calls -h` at the command line.

cproto

`cproto` is a program included on this book's CD-ROM. `cproto` reads in C source files and automatically generates function prototypes for all of the functions. Using `cproto` saves you from having to type in a function definition for all of the functions that you have written in your programs.

If you ran the following code through the `cproto` program

```
#include   <stdio.h>

void main ()
{
  char my_string[] = "hello there";
  my_print (my_string);
  my_print2(my_string);
}

void my_print (char *string)
{
  printf ("The string is %s\n", *string);
}
```

```
void my_print2 (char *string)
{
  char *string2;
  int size, size2, i;

  size = strlen (string);
  size2 = size -1;
  string2 = (char *) malloc (size + 1);
  for (i = 0; i < size; i++)
    string2[size2 - i] = string[i];
  string2[size] = '\0';
  printf ("The string printed backward is %s\n", string2);
}
```

you would get the following output:

```
/* greeting.c */
void main(void);
void my_print(char *string);
void my_print2(char *string);
```

This output could be redirected to an include file and used to define the prototypes for all of the functions.

indent

The indent utility is another programming utility that is included with Linux. This program, in its simplest form, reformats or pretty prints your C code so that it is consistently indented and all opening and closing braces are represented consistently. There are numerous options that enable you to specify how you want indent to format your code. For information on these options, refer to the indent manual page or type indent -h at the command line.

The following example shows the default output of the indent program.

C code before running indent:

```
#include  <stdio.h>

void main () {
void my_print(char *);
void my_print2(char *);
     char my_string[] = "hello there";
  my_print (my_string);
    my_print2(my_string); }

void my_print (char *string)
{
  printf    ("The string is %s\n", *string);
}

void my_print2               (char *string) {
   char *string2;
     int size, size2, i;
```

```
        size = strlen (string);
        size2 = size -1;
        string2 = (char *) malloc (size + 1);
  for (i = 0; i < size; i++)
            string2[size2 - i] = string[i];
        string2[size] = '\0';
        printf ("The string printed backward is %s\n", string2);
}
```

C code after running indent:

```
#include   <stdio.h>

void main ()
{
  void my_print(char *);
  void my_print2(char *);

  char my_string[] = "hello there";
  my_print (my_string);
  my_print2 (my_string);
}

void my_print (char *string)
{
  printf ("The string is %s\n", *string);
}

void my_print2 (char *string)
{
  char *string2;
  int size, size2, i;

  size = strlen (string);
  size2 = size -1;
  string2 = (char *) malloc (size + 1);
  for (i = 0; i < size; i++)
    string2[size2 - i] = string[i];
  string2[size] = '\0';
  printf ("The string printed backward is %s\n", string2);
}
```

Indent does not change how the code compiles; it just changes how the source code looks. It makes the code more readable, which is always a good thing.

gprof

gprof is a program that is installed in the /usr/bin directory on your Linux system. It allows you to profile C, Pascal, or Fortran programs to determine where most of the execution time is being spent.

gprof will tell you how many times each function used by your program is called, and also the percentage of the total execution time the program spent on each function. This information can be very useful if you are trying to improve the performance of a program.

To use gprof on one of your C programs, you must compile the program using gcc's -pg option. This causes the program to create a file called gmon.out each time it is executed. gprof uses the gmon.out file to generate the profile information.

After you run your program and it has created the gmon.out file, you can get its profile by entering the following command:

```
gprof <program_name>
```

The program_name parameter is the name of the program that created the gmon.out file.

TIP

The profile data that gprof displays to the screen is quite large. If you want to examine this data, you should either redirect gprof's output to a file or use the more or less pipes.

---

f2c and p2c

f2c and p2c are two source code conversion programs. f2c converts FORTRAN77 code into either C or C++ code, and p2c converts Pascal code into C code. Both are included in the Linux installation when you install GCC.

If you have some code that has been written using either FORTRAN77 or Pascal that you want to rewrite in C, f2c and p2c can prove to be very useful programs. Both programs produce C code that can typically be compiled directly by gcc without any human intervention.

If you are converting small, straightforward FORTRAN77 or Pascal programs, you should be able to get away with using f2c or p2c without any options. If you are converting very large programs consisting of many files, you will probably have to use some of the command-line options that are provided by the conversion program that you are using.

To invoke f2c on a FORTRAN program, enter the following command:

```
f2c my_fortranprog.f
```

NOTE

f2c requires that the program being converted has either a .f or a .F extension.

To convert a Pascal program to C, enter the following command:

```
p2c my_pascalprogram.pas
```

Both of these commands create C source code files that have the same name as the original file, except with a .c extension instead of .f or .pas.

For more information on the specific conversion options that are available with f2c or p2c, refer to their respective man pages.

Summary

This chapter introduced the GNU C compiler and many of the options that you will typically use when you compile C code. It also introduced the concepts behind debugging code with the GNU debugger, and illustrated the usefulness of some of the other C utility programs that are either included on the Linux CD-ROM, or available via FTP from sunsite.unc.edu.

If you will be writing C code, the time that you spend learning how to use gdb and some of the other tools mentioned in this chapter will be more than worth the eventual time-saving that you will gain.

The next chapter will discuss many of the same topics, but with a focus on C++ development rather than C development.

Programming in C++

28

by
Rick McMullin

Chapter 27, "Programming in C," introduced you to the C programming environment and C programming tools that come with Linux. This chapter describes the same kinds of information for C++. This chapter covers the following topics:

■ What C++ is

■ Why to use C++

■ The GNU C++ compiler

■ Debugging C++ applications

In addition to these topics, this chapter also looks at some of the C++ programming tools and class libraries that are included on the Linux CD.

What Is C++?

C++ is an object-oriented extension to the C programming language. It was developed at Bell Labs in the early 1980s and is quickly becoming the language of choice in the computer industry. Dozens of C++ compilers are available on the market today. The most common of these for PC-based systems are Borland C++, Microsoft's Visual C++, Symantec C++, and Watcom C++. These compilers can compile MS-DOS, MS Windows, OS/2, and Windows NT programs. In addition to the number of C++ compilers that are available on DOS-based machines, a great number are also based on other hardware architectures.

Most UNIX systems have C++ compilers available from the system vendor. Linux also comes with a C++ compiler. This is the GNU C++ compiler. The GNU C++ compiler is very closely related to the GNU C compiler (GCC). In fact, since Release 2.0 of GCC, the GNU C++ compiler has been integrated with GCC. Previous to Release 2.0 of GCC, the GNU C++ compiler was a separate program known as g++. One of the major enhancements in Release 2.0 of GCC was merging these two compilers.

GCC now incorporates a C compiler, a C++ compiler, and an Objective C compiler, although you will still find the g++ executable on your system.

Why C++?

C++ and object-oriented programming (OOP) did not just happen. There were many fundamental reasons for the shift from structured programming to OOP. In the early days of computer programming, back when PDP-8s still roamed the earth in great numbers, there was a shift from machine language coding to assembler language coding. This was done because the computers of the day were a little more powerful than their predecessors. Programmers wanted to make their lives easier by moving some of the burden of programming onto the computer.

As the years went by and computers got even more powerful, new, higher-level languages started to appear. Examples of these languages are FORTRAN, COBOL, Pascal, and C. With these languages came a programming methodology known as structured programming. Structured programming helped to simplify the systems being designed by enabling programmers to break the problem into small pieces and then implement these pieces as functions or procedures in whatever language was being used.

The structured programming approach worked well for small to medium-sized software applications, but it started to fall apart as systems reached a certain size. OOP tried to solve some of the problems that structured programming was causing. It did this by extending some of the structured programming concepts and by introducing some of its own.

The main concepts that OOP focuses on are the following:

- Data encapsulation
- Inheritance
- Polymorphism

Data Encapsulation

In structured programming, problems often arose where there was a data structure that was common to several different pieces of code. One piece of code could access that data without the other piece of code being aware that anything was happening.

Data encapsulation is a process of grouping common data together, storing it into a data type, and providing a consistent interface to that data. This ensures that no one can access that data without going through the user interface that has been defined for that data.

The biggest benefit that this kind of mechanism provides is that it protects code outside the code that is directly managing this data from being affected if the structure of the data changes. This greatly reduces the complexity of large software systems.

C++ implements data encapsulation through the use of classes.

Inheritance

Inheritance is a form of code reuse in which you can inherit or use the data and behavior of other pieces of code. Inheritance is typically used only when a piece of software logically has many of the same characteristics as another piece of software, such as when one object is a specialization of another object.

Inheritance is implemented in C++ by allowing objects to be subclassed by other objects.

Polymorphism

Polymorphism occurs when a language allows you to define functions that perform different operations on objects depending on their type. The true power of this lies in the fact that you can send a message to a base class and that message can be passed down to each of its subclasses and mean different things to each of them.

Polymorphism is implemented in C++ using virtual functions.

Classes of Objects and Methods

In C++, classes can be thought of as C structures that contain not only the data fields but also operations that can be performed on those data fields. A simple example of this concept is a geometric shape. A geometric shape can be many things, such as a rectangle, a triangle, or a circle. All geometric shapes have certain attributes in common, including area and volume. You could define a structure in C called shape in the following way:

```
struct shape{
        float area;
        float volume;
}
```

If you added some common behavior to this structure, you would have the equivalent of a C++ class. This would be written as follows:

```
class shape {
public:
                float area;
                float volume;
                float calc_area();
                float calc_volume():
};
```

You have now defined a C++ class. The calc_area and calc_volume items are known as methods of the class (instead of functions, as in C). If you were to define a variable that was of type shape as

```
shape circle;
```

you would have created a circle object. An object is an instance of a class, or a variable that is defined to be of the type of a class.

GCC Options

This section describes some of the GCC options that are most commonly used. I will first talk about some of the options that can be used both with C and C++ and then talk about C++ specific options. Any of the compiler options that you use with C you can use with C++ as well, but some of them may not make any sense in the context of a C++ compile. If you specify options that don't make sense, the compiler just ignores them.

> **NOTE**
>
> When you are compiling C++ programs, it is easiest to use the g++ script. This sets all the default C++ options so you don't have to.

A great number of compiler options can be passed to GCC. Many of these options are specific to a certain hardware platform or are for making fine-tuning adjustments to the code that is produced. You will probably never use any of these kinds of options. The options covered in this chapter are those that you will use on a regular basis.

Many of the GCC options consist of more than one character. For this reason, you must specify each option with its own hyphen and not group options after a single hyphen as you can with most Linux commands.

When you compile a program using GCC without any command-line options, it creates an executable file (assuming that the compile was successful) and calls it a.out. For example, the following command would create a file named a.out in the current directory:

```
gcc test.C
```

To specify a name other than a.out for the executable file, you can use the -o compiler option. For example, to compile a C++ program file named count.C (the capital C is used to show C++ code, as opposed to a small c for C code) into an executable file named count, you would type the following command:

```
gcc -o count count.C
```

> **NOTE**
>
> When you are using the -o option, the executable filename must occur directly after the -o on the command line.

Other compiler options allow you to specify how far you want the compile to proceed. The -c option tells GCC to compile the code into object code and skip the assembly and linking stages of the compile. This option is used quite often because it makes the compilation of multifile C++ programs faster and easier to manage. Object code files created by GCC have an .o extension by default.

The -S compiler option tells GCC to stop the compile after it has generated the assembler files for the C code. Assembler files generated by GCC have an .s extension by default. The -E option instructs the compiler to perform only the preprocessing compiler stage on the input files. When this option is used, the output from the preprocessor is sent to the standard output rather than being stored in a file.

Debugging and Profiling Options

GCC supports several debugging and profiling options. Of these options, the two that you are most likely to use for C++ programs are the -gstabs+ option and the -pg option.

The -gstabs+ option tells GCC to produce stabs format debugging information that the GNU debugger (gdb) can use to help you debug your program. For more information on debugging your C++ programs, refer to the "Debugging C++ Applications" section later in this chapter.

The -pg option tells GCC to add extra code to your program that will, when executed, generate profile information that can be used by the gprof program to display timing information about your program. For more information on gprof, refer to the "gprof" section in Chapter 27.

GCC C++ Specific Options

The GCC options that control how a C++ program is compiled are listed in Table 28.1.

Table 28.1. GCC options.

Option	Meaning
-fall-virtual	Treats all possible member functions as virtual. This applies to all functions except for constructor functions and new or deleted member functions.
-fdollars-in-identifiers	Accepts $ in identifiers. You can also prohibit the use of $ in identifiers by using the -fno-dollars-in-identifiers option.
-felide-constructors	Tells the compiler to leave out constructors whenever possible.
-fenum-int-equiv	Permits implicit conversion of int to enumeration types.
-fexternal-templates	Produces smaller code for template declarations. This is done by having the compiler generate only a single copy of each template function where it is defined.
-fmemoize-lookups	Uses heuristics to compile faster. These heuristics are not enabled by default because they are effective only for certain input files.
-fno-strict-prototype	Treats a function declaration with no arguments the same way that C would treat it. This means that the compiler treats a function prototype that has no arguments as a function that will accept an unknown number of arguments.
-fnonnull-objects	Assumes that objects reached through references are not null.
-fsave-memoized	Same as -fmemorize-lookups.
-fthis-is-variable	Permits assignment to "this."
-nostdinc++	Does not search for header files in the standard directories specific to C++.
-traditional	This option has the same effect as -fthis-is-variable, but also attempts to support some aspects of traditional C compilers.
-fno-default-inline	Does not assume that functions defined within a class scope are inline functions.
-Wenum-clash	Warns about conversion between different enumeration types.
-Woverloaded-virtual	Warns when derived class function declaration may be an error in defining a virtual function. When you define a virtual function in a derived class, it must have the same

Option	Meaning
	signature as the function in the base class. This option tells the compiler to warn you if you have defined a function that has the same name and a different signature as a function that is defined in one of the base classes.
-Wtemplate-debugging	If you are using templates, this option warns you if debugging is not yet available.
-gstabs+	Tells the compiler to generate debugging information in stabs format, using GNU extensions understood only by the GNU debugger. The extra information produced by this option is necessary to ensure that gdb handles C++ programs properly.

Debugging C++ Applications

A very important part of developing C++ programs is being able to debug them efficiently. The GNU debug application that was introduced in Chapter 27 can also be used to debug C++ applications. This section describes some of the differences between debugging C applications and debugging C++ applications.

The basic gdb commands that were introduced in Chapter 27 are listed again for your convenience in Table 28.2.

Table 28.2. Basic gdb commands.

Command	Description
file	Loads the executable file that is to be debugged.
kill	Terminates the program you are currently debugging.
list	Lists sections of the source code used to generate the executable file.
next	Advances one line of source code in the current function, without stepping into other functions.
step	Advances one line of source code in the current function, and does step into other functions.
run	Executes the program that is currently being debugged.
quit	Terminates gdb.
watch	Enables you to examine the value of a program variable whenever the value changes.

continues

Table 28.2. continued

Command	Description
break	Sets a breakpoint in the code; this causes the execution of the program to be suspended whenever this point is reached.
make	This command enables you to remake the executable program without quitting gdb or using another window.
shell	Enables you to execute UNIX shell commands without leaving gdb.

From the programmer's perspective, you have more details to be aware of when debugging C++ code than when you are debugging C code. This is because of the C++ features such as virtual functions and exception handling. gdb has added features to support debugging both of these C++ specific features.

Debugging Virtual Functions

As described in the "Polymorphism" section of this chapter, virtual functions are C++'s way of implementing polymorphism. This means that there may be more than one function in a program with the same name. The only way to tell these functions apart is by their signatures. The signature of a function is composed of the types of all the arguments to the function. For example, a function with the prototype

```
void func(int, real);
```

has a signature of int,real.

You can see how this could cause gdb a few problems. For example, if you had defined a class that had a virtual function called calculate, and two objects with different definitions for this function were created, how would you set a breakpoint to trigger on this function? You set breakpoints in C by specifying the function name as an argument to the gdb break command, as follows:

```
(gdb) break calculate
```

This does not work in the case of a virtual function because the debugger would not be able to tell which calculate you wanted the breakpoint to be set on. gdb was extended in a few ways so that it could handle virtual functions. The first way to solve the problem is to enter the function name by specifying its prototype as well. This would be done in the following way:

```
break 'calculate (float)'
```

This would give gdb enough information to determine which function the breakpoint was meant for. A second solution that gdb supports is using a breakpoint menu. Breakpoint menus allow you to specify the function name of a function. If there is more than one function definition for that function, it gives you a menu of choices. The first choice in the menu is to abort the break command. The second choice is to set a breakpoint on all the functions that the break command matches.

The remaining choices correspond to each function that matches the break command. The following code shows an example of a breakpoint menu:

```
 (gdb) break shape::calculate
[0] cancel
[1] all
[2] file: shapes.C: line number: 153
[3] file: shapes.C: line number: 207
[4] file: shapes.C: line number: 247
> 2 3
Breakpoint 1 at 0xb234: file shapes.C, line 153
Breakpoint 2 at 0xa435: file shapes.C, line 207
Multiple breakpoints were set
Use the "delete" command to delete unwanted breakpoints
(gdb)
```

Debugging Exception Handlers

Exceptions are errors that occur within your program. Exception handlers are pieces of code that are written to handle errors and potential errors. For example, if you were writing a C program and calling the `malloc` function to get a block of memory, you would typically check `malloc`'s return code to make sure the memory allocation was successful. If C supported exception handling, you could specify a function that would receive or catch exceptions, and the `malloc` function would send or throw an exception to your function if one occurred.

The `gdb` added two new commands to support C++ exception handling: the `catch` command and the `catch info` command. The `catch` command is used to set a breakpoint in active exception handlers. The syntax of this command is as follows:

```
catch exceptions
```

`exceptions` is a list of the exceptions to catch.

The `catch info` command is used to display all the active exception handlers.

Summary of *gdb* C++ Specific Commands

In addition to the `gdb` commands that have been added to support some of the new language features contained in C++, there are also some new `set` and `show` options. These options are listed in Table 28.3.

Table 28.3. gdb's C++ `set` and `show` options.

Command	Description
`set print demangle`	Prints C++ names in their source form rather than in the encoded or mangled form that is passed to the assembler.
`show print demangle`	Shows whether `print demangle` is on or off.

continues

Table 28.3. continued

Command	Description
set demangle-style	Sets the style of demangled output. The options are auto, gnu, lucid, and arm.
show demangle-style	Shows which demangle style is being used.
set print object	When displaying a pointer to an object, identifies the actual type of the object.
show print object	Shows whether print object is turned on or off.
set print vtbl	Pretty prints C++ virtual function tables.
show print vtbl	Shows whether print vtbl is turned on or off.

GNU C++ Class Libraries

GNU C++ comes packaged with an extensive class library. A class library is a reusable set of classes that can be used to perform a specified set of functions. Some typical examples of class libraries are class libraries that handle database access, class libraries that handle graphical user interface programming, and class libraries that implement data structures.

Examples of graphical user interface class libraries include the Microsoft Foundation Classes and Borland's Object Windows Library, both of which are class libraries that are used for developing Windows applications.

This section introduces several of the features that are offered by the GNU C++ class library.

Streams

The GNU iostream library, called libio, implements GNU C++'s standard input and output facilities. This library is similar to the I/O libraries that are supplied by other C++ compilers. The main parts of the iostream library are the input, output, and error streams. These correspond to the standard input, output, and error streams that are found in C and are called cin, cout, and cerr respectively. The streams can be written to and read from using the << operator for output and the >> operator for input.

The following program uses the iostream library to perform its input and output:

```
#include <iostream.h>
int main ()
{
        char name[10];
        cout << "Please enter your name.\n";
        cin >> name;
        cout << "Hello, " << name << ", how is it going?\n";
}
```

Strings

The GNU `string` class extends GNU C++'s string manipulation capabilities. The `string` class essentially replaces the character array definitions that existed in C and all the `string` functions that go along with the character arrays.

The `string` class adds UNIX shell type string operators to the C++ language, as well as a large number of additional operators. Table 28.4 lists many of the operators that are available with the `string` class.

Table 28.4. String class operators.

Operator	Meaning
`str1 == str2`	Returns TRUE if `str1` is equal to `str2`
`str1 != str2`	Returns TRUE if `str1` is not equal to `str2`
`str1 < str2`	Returns TRUE if `str1` is less than `str2`
`str1 <= str2`	Returns TRUE if `str1` is less than or equal to `str2`
`str1 > str2`	Returns TRUE if `str1` is greater than `str2`
`str1 >= str2`	Returns TRUE if `str1` is greater than or equal to `str2`
`compare(str1,str2)`	Compares `str1` to `str2` without considering the case of the characters
`str3 = str1 + str2`	Stores the result of `str1` concatenated with `str2` into `str3`

A number of other operators are available in the `string` class for performing different types of string comparisons, concatenations, and substring extraction and manipulation.

Random Numbers

Classes are provided in the GCC C++ class library that allow you to generate several different kinds of random numbers. The classes used to generate these numbers are the `Random` class and the `RNG` class.

Data Collection

The class library provides two different classes that perform data collection and analysis functions. The two classes are `SampleStatistic` and `SampleHistogram`. The `SampleStatistic` class provides a way of collecting samples and also provides numerous statistical functions that can perform calculations on the collected data. Some of the calculations that can be performed are mean, variance, standard deviation, minimum, and maximum.

The `SampleHistogram` class is derived from the `SampleStatistic` class and supports the collection and display of samples in bucketed intervals.

Linked Lists

The GNU C++ library supports two kinds of linked lists: single linked lists, implemented by the SLList class, and doubly linked lists, implemented by the DLList class. Both of these types of lists support all the standard linked list operations. A summary of the operations that these classes support is shown in Table 28.5.

Table 28.5. List operators.

Operator	Description
list.empty()	Returns TRUE if list is empty
list.length()	Returns the number of elements in list
list.prepend(a)	Places a at the front of list
list.append(a)	Places a at the end of list
list.join(list2)	Appends list2 to list, destroying list2 in the process
a = list.front()	Returns a pointer to the element that is stored at the head of the list
a = list.rear()	Returns a pointer to the element that is stored at the end of the list
a = list.remove_front()	Deletes and returns the element that is stored at the front of the list
list.del_front()	Deletes the first element without returning it
list.clear()	Deletes all items from list
list.ins_after(i, a)	Inserts a after position i in the list
list.del_after(i)	Deletes the element following position i in the list

Doubly linked lists also support the operations listed in Table 28.6.

Table 28.6. Doubly linked list operators.

Operator	Description
a = list.remove_rear()	Deletes and returns the element stored at the end of the list
list.del_real()	Deletes the last element, without returning it
list.ins_before(i, a)	Inserts a before position i in the list
list.del(i, dir)	Deletes the element at the current position and then moves forward one position if dir is positive and backward one position if dir is 0 or negative

Plex Classes

Plex classes are classes that behave like arrays but are much more powerful. Plex classes have the following properties:

- They have arbitrary upper and lower index bounds.
- They can dynamically expand in both the lower and upper bound directions.
- Elements may be accessed by indices. Unlike typical arrays, bounds checking is performed at runtime.
- Only elements that have been specifically initialized or added can be accessed.

Four different types of Plexes are defined: the FPlex, the XPlex, the RPlex, and the MPlex. The FPlex is a Plex that can grow or shrink only within declared bounds. An XPlex can dynamically grow in any direction without any restrictions. An RPlex is almost identical to an XPlex, but it has better indexing capabilities. Finally, the MPlex is the same as an RPlex except that it allows elements to be logically deleted and restored.

Table 28.7 lists some of the operations that are valid on all four of the Plexes.

Table 28.7. Operations defined for Plexes.

Operation	Description
Plex b(a)	Assigns a copy of Plex a to Plex b
b = a	Copies Plex a into b
a.length()	Returns the number of elements in a
a.empty()	Returns TRUE if a has no elements
a.full()	Returns TRUE if a is full
a.clear()	Removes all the elements from a
a.append(b)	Appends Plex b to the high part of a
a.prepend(b)	Prepends Plex b to the low part of a
a.fill(z)	Sets all elements of a equal to z
a.valid(i)	Returns TRUE if i is a valid index into a
a.low_element()	Returns a pointer to the element in the lowest position in a
a.high_element()	Returns a pointer to the element in the highest position in a

Plexes are a very useful class on which many of the other classes in the GNU C++ class library are based. Some of the Stack, Queue, and Linked list types are built on top of the Plex class.

Stacks

The stacks class implements the standard version of a last-in-first-out (LIFO) stack. Three different implementations of stacks are offered by the GNU C++ class library: the VStack, the XPStack, and the SLStack. The VStack is a fixed-size stack, meaning that you must specify an upper bound on the size of the stack when you first create it. The XPStack and the SLStack are both dynamically sized stacks that are implemented in a slightly different way.

Table 28.8 lists the operations that can be performed on the Stack classes.

Table 28.8. Stack class operators.

Operator	Description
Stack st	Declares st to be a stack
Stack st(sz)	Declares st to be a stack of size sz
st.empty()	Returns TRUE if stack is empty
st.full()	Returns TRUE if stack is full
st.length()	Returns the number of elements in stack
st.push(x)	Puts element x onto the top of the stack
x = st.pop()	Removes and returns the top element from the stack
st.top()	Returns a pointer to the top element in the stack
st.del_top()	Deletes the top element from the stack without returning it
st.clear()	Deletes all elements from stack

Queues

The Queue class implements a standard version of a first-in-first-out (FIFO) queue. Three different kinds of queue are provided by the GNU C++ class library: the VQueue, the XPQueue, and the SLQueue. The VQueue is a fixed-size queue, so you must specify an upper bound on the size of this kind of queue when you first create it. The XPQueue and the SLQueue are both dynamically sized queues, so no upper bound is required. The operations supported by the Queue classes are listed in Table 28.9.

Table 28.9. Queue class operators.

Operator	Description
Queue q	Declares q to be a queue
Queue q(sz)	Declares q to be a queue of size sz
q.empty()	Returns TRUE if q is empty
q.full()	Returns TRUE if q is full

Operator	Description
q.length()	Returns the number of elements in q
q.enq(x)	Adds the x element to q
x = q.deq()	Removes and returns an element from q
q.front()	Returns a pointer to the front of q
q.del_front()	Removes an element from q and does not return the result
q.clear	Removes all elements from the queue

In addition to the normal kind of queue that is discussed in this section, the GNU C++ class library also supports double-ended queues and priority queues. Both of these types of queues have similar behavior to the regular queue. The double-ended queue adds operators for returning a pointer to the rear of the queue and deleting elements from the rear of the queue. The priority queues are arranged so that a user has fast access to the least element in the queue. They support additional operators that allow for searching for elements in the queue.

Sets

The Set class is used to store groups of information. The only restriction on this information is that no duplicate elements are allowed. The class library supports several different implementations of sets. All of the implementations support the same operators. These operators are shown in Table 28.10.

Table 28.10. Set operators.

Operator	Description
Set s	Declares a set named s that is initially empty
Set s(sz)	Declares a set named s that is initially empty and has a set maximum size of sz
s.empty()	Returns TRUE if s is empty
s.length()	Returns the number of elements in s
i = s.add(z)	Adds z to s, returning its index value
s.del(z)	Deletes z from s
s.clear()	Removes all elements from s
s.contains(z)	Returns TRUE if z is in s
s.(i)	Returns a pointer to the element indexed by i
i = a.first()	Returns the index of the first item in the set
s.next(i)	Makes i equal to the index of the next element in s

continues

Table 28.10. continued

Operator	Description
`i = s.seek(z)`	Sets `i` to the index of `z` if `z` is in `s`, and 0 otherwise
`set1 == set2`	Returns TRUE if `set1` contains all the same elements as `set2`
`set1 != set2`	Returns TRUE if `set1` does not contain all the same elements as `set2`
`set1 <= set2`	Returns TRUE if `set1` is a subset of `set2`
`set1 ¦= set2`	Adds all elements of `set2` to `set1`
`set1 -= set2`	Deletes all the elements that are contained in `set2` from `set1`
`set1 &= set2`	Deletes all elements from `set1` that occur in `set1` and not in `set2`

The class library contains another class that is similar to sets. This class is known as the bag. A bag is a group of elements that can be in any order (just as is the case with sets) but in which there can also be duplicates. Bags use all the operators that sets use except for the ==, !=, ¦=, <=, ¦=, -=, and &= operators. In addition, bags add two new operators for dealing with elements that are in the bag more than once. These new operators are shown in Table 28.11.

Table 28.11. Additional operators for bags.

Operator	Description
`b.remove(z)`	Deletes all occurrences of `z` from `b`
`b.nof(z)`	Returns the number of occurrences of `z` that are in `b`

Many other classes available in the GNU C++ class library provide functions other than those listed here. In addition to what comes with the compiler, many other freely available class libraries can be useful as well.

Summary

C++ offers many advantages over C. Some of these advantages come from the concepts of object-oriented programming, and others come from the highly flexible class libraries that are available to C++ programmers. This chapter gave a brief introduction to object-oriented programming and also talked about the C++ features that exist in the GNU C compiler and the GNU debugger.

Perl

29

by Kamran Husain

IN THIS CHAPTER

Perl stands for *Practical Extraction and Report Language* and is a free utility that comes with Linux versions. Perl was developed by Larry Wall. The -v option will print the version number of Perl you are running. This book is written for Perl 5.002, and not for 5.001m which comes with your Linux system, since the later version has fewer bugs and more features. The full release of 5.002 is available at the FTP site `ftp.mox`. The latest release is available from the Web site `http://mox.perl.com/perl/info/software.html` as `perl5.002.tar.gz`. Installation is very easy if you follow the read me directions.

Perl is a program just like any other program on your system, only it's more powerful than most other programs because it combines the features of `awk`, `grep`, `sed`, and C all in one language! To run Perl, you can simply type `perl` at the prompt and type in your code. In almost all cases, though, you will want to keep your Perl code in files just like shell scripts. A Perl program is referred to as a *script*.

Perl programs are interpreted and compiled by the Perl program before executing the program. To create a Perl program you use the syntax of `#!program_name` as the first line of an executable file to create a Perl script. The following two lines are a valid Perl script:

```
#!/usr/bin/perl
print "I be Perl\n";
```

On some Linux systems, the path to Perl is `/sbin/perl`, and on some it's `/usr/local/bin/perl`. The libraries for the Perl program on some other machines will be located in the `/usr/bin/perl5`, `/usr/lib/perl5`, or the `/usr/local/lib/perl5` directory. Use a `find` command to see if you can locate Perl on your system.

You can run programs via the command line with the -e switch to `perl`. For example, entering the following command at the prompt will print `"Howdy!"`.

```
$ perl -e 'print "Howdy";\n'
```

In all but the shortest of Perl programs, you will use a file to store your Perl code as a script. Using a script file offers you the ease of not having to type commands interactively and thus not being able to correct typing errors easily. A script file also provides a written record of which commands to use to do some task.

To fire off a command on all lines in the input, use the -p option. Thus,

```
$perl -p -e 's/old/new/g' test.txt
```

will run the command to substitute all strings `old` with `new` on each line from the file `test.txt`. If you use the -p option, it will print each line as it is read in.

Let's start with an introduction to the Perl language.

Variables in Perl

Perl has three basic types of variables: scalars, arrays, and associative arrays. A scalar variable is anything that can hold one number or a string. An array stores many scalars in a sequence, where each scalar can be indexed using a number starting from 0. An associative is like an array in that it stores strings in sequenceb but uses another string as an index to address individual items instead of a number.

Let's start with scalar variables.

The syntax for a scalar variable is $variable_name. A variable name is set up and addressed in the same way as Bourne shell variables. To assign values to a scalar, you use statements like these:

```
$name = "Kamran";
$number= 100;
$phone_Number = '555-1232';
```

A variable in Perl is evaluated at runtime to derive a value that is one of the following: a string, a number, or a pointer to scalar. It's important to place a $ sign in front of the variable name, or it will be interpreted as a file handle.

To print out the value of a variable, you would use a print statement. To print the value of $name, you would make a call:

```
print $name;
```

The value of $name is printed to the screen. Perl scripts expect input from a standard input (the keyboard) and write to the standard output.

Code Blocks in Loops

Variables and assignment statements exist in code blocks. Each code block is a section of code between two curly braces. The loop construct and conditional expressions used in Perl delimit code blocks with curly braces. The following are some examples of code blocks available in Perl:

```
while(condition) {
    ... execute code here while condition is true;
}

until(condition) {  # opposite of while statement.
    ... execute code here while condition is false;
}

do {
    ... do this at least once ...
    ... stop if condition is false ...
```

```
} while(condition);

do {
    ... do this at least once ...
    ... stop if condition is true ...
} until(condition);

if (condition1) {
condition1_code true;
} else {
    ...no condition1 up to conditionN  is true;
}

if (condition1) {
...condition1_code true;
} elsif (condition2) {
    condition1_code true;
....
} elsif (conditionN) {
    conditionN_code true;
} else {
    ...no condition from 1 up to N  is true;
}

unless (condition1) { # opposite of "if" statement.
                do this if condition is false;
}
```

The condition in the preceding blocks of code is anything from a Perl variable to an expression that returns either a true or false value. A true value is a nonzero or a nonempty string.

Code blocks can be declared within code blocks to create levels of code blocks. Variables declared in one code block are usually global to the rest of the program. To keep the scope of the variable limited to the code block in which it is declared, use the my $variableName syntax. If you declare with local $variableName syntax, the $variableName will be available to all lower levels but not outside the code block. So if your code calls another subroutine, any variables declared with the word local could be modified by the called subroutine; however, those variables declared by the my keyword will not be visible to the called subroutine.

Variables in code blocks are also declared the first time they are assigned a value. This creation includes arrays and strings. Variables are then evaluated by the parser when they appear in code, and even in strings. There are times when you do not want the variable to be evaluated. This is the time when you should be aware of quoting rules in Perl.

Quoting Rules

Three different types of quotes can be used on Perl. Double quotes (" ") are used to enclose strings. Any scalars in double quoted strings are evaluated by Perl. To force Perl not to evaluate anything in a quote, you will have to use single quotes ('). Finally, to run some values in a shell program and get its return value back, use the back quote (`) symbol. To see an example of how it works, see the sample Perl script in Listing 29.1.

Listing 29.1. Quoting in a Perl script.

```
1    #!/usr/bin/perl
2    $folks="100";
3    print "\$folks = $folks \n";
4    print '\$folks = $folks \n';
5    print "\n\n BEEP! \a  \LSOME BLANK \ELINES HERE \n\n";
6    $date = 'date +%D';
7    print "Today is [$date] \n";
8    chop $date;
9    print "Date after chopping off carriage return: [".$date."]\n";
```

The output from the code in Listing 29.1 is shown here. The line numbers shown in the listing are for the benefit of illustration only and are not present in the actual file.

```
$folks = 100
$folks = $folks \n

 BEEP!   some blank LINES HERE

Today is [03/29/96
]
Date after chopping off carriage return: [03/29/96]
```

Let's go over the code shown in Listing 29.1.

Line 1 is the mandatory first line of the Perl script.

Line 2 assigns a string value to $folks variable. Note that you did not have to declare the variable $folks; it was created when used for the first time.

Line 3 prints the value of $folks in between double quotes. The $ sign in $folks has to be escaped with the \ character to prevent Perl from evaluating the value of $folks instead of printing the word $folks verbatim in the output like this:

```
$folks = 100
```

In line 4, Perl does not evaluate anything between the single quotes. The entire contents of the line are left untouched and printed out here:

```
\$folks = $folks \n
```

Perl has several special characters to format text data for you. Line 5 prints multiple blank lines with the \n character and beeps at the terminal. Two \n characters are needed to proceed from the end of the current line, skip line and position the cursor at the next line. Notice how the words SOME BLANK are printed in lowercase? This is because they are encased between the \L and \E special characters, which forces all characters to be lowercase. Some of these special characters are listed in Table 29.1.

Table 29.1. Special characters in Perl.

Character	Meaning
\n	New line (line feed)
\r	Carriage return (MSDOS)
\t	Tab
\a	Beep
\b	Backspace
\L \E	Lowercase all characters in between \L and \E
\l	Lowercase next character
\U \E	Uppercase all characters in between \U and \E
\u	Uppercase next character
\cC	Insert control character "C"
\x##	Hex number in ##, such as \x1d
\0ooo	Octal number in ooo, such as \0213
\\	A backslash
\c	Insert the next character literally, such as \$ puts $

In line 6, the script uses the back quotes (') to execute a command and then returns the results in the $date variable. The string in between the two back quotes is what you would type at the command line, with one exception: if you use Perl variables in the command line for the back quotes, Perl will evaluate these variables before passing it off to the shell for execution. For example, line 6 could be rewritten as

```
$parm = "+%D";
$date = '$date $parm';
```

The returned value in $date is printed out in line 7. Note that there is an extra carriage return in the text for data. To remove it, use the chop command as shown in line 8.

Then in line 9, the $date output is shown to print correctly. Note how the period (.) is used to concatenate three strings together for the output.

It's easy to construct strings in Perl with the (.) operator. Given two strings $first and $last, you can construct the string $fullname like this to get "Jim Smith":

```
$first = "Jim";
$last = "Smith";
$fullname = $first . " " . $last;
```

Numbers in Perl are stored as floating point numbers; even variables used as integers are really stored as floating point numbers. There are a set of operations you can do with numbers. These operations are listed in Table 29.2.

Table 29.2 also lists Boolean operators.

Table 29.2. Numeric operations with Perl.

Operations	Comparisons
$r = $x + $y	Add $x to $y and assign result to $r
$r = $x - $y	Subtract $y from $x and assign result to $r
$r = $x * $y	Multiply $y and $x and assign result to $r
$r = $x / $y	Divide $x by $y and assign result to $r
$r = $x % $y	Modulo. Divide $x by $y and assign remainder to $r
$r = $x ** $y	Raise $x to power of $y and assign result to $r
$r = $x << $n	Shift bits in $x left $n times and assign to $r
$r = $x >> $n	Shift bits in $x right $n times and assign to $r
$r = ++$x	Increment $x, and assign $x to $r
$r = $x++	Assign $x to $r, then increment $x
$r += $x;	Add $x to $r, then assign to $r
$r = --$x	Decrement $x, and assign $x to $r
$r = $x--	Assign $x to $r, then decrement $x
$r -= $x;	Subtract $x from $r, then assign to $r
$r /= $x;	Divide $r by $x, then assign to $r
$r *= $x;	Multiply $r by $x, then assign to $r
$r = $x <=> $y	$r is 1 if $x > $y; 0 if $x == $y; -1 if $x < $y
$r =~ $x	Bind $x to $r
$r = $x || $y	$r = $x logical or $y
$r = $x && $y	$r = $x logical and $y
$r = ! $x	$r = logical not $x

You can compare values of variables to check results of operations. Table 29.3 lists the comparison operators for numbers and strings.

Table 29.3. Comparison operations with Perl.

Operations	Comparisons
$x == $y	True if $x is equal to $y
$x != $y	True if $x is not equal to $y
$x < $y	True if $x is less than $y
$x <= $y	True if $x is less than or equal to $y

continues

Table 29.3. continued

Operations	Comparisons
`$x > $y`	True if `$x` is greater than `$y`
`$x >= $y`	True if `$x` is greater than or equal to `$y`
`$x eq $y`	True if string `$x` is equal to string `$y`
`$x ne $y`	True if string `$x` is not equal to string `$y`
`$x lt $y`	True if string `$x` is less than string `$y`
`$x le $y`	True if string `$x` is less than or equal to string `$y`
`$x gt $y`	True if string `$x` is less than string `$y`
`$x ge $y`	True if string `$x` is less than or equal to string `$y`
`$x x $y`	Repeat `$x`, `$y` times
`$x . $y`	Return the concatenated value of `$x` and `$y`
`$x cmp $y`	Return 1 if `$x` gt `$y`, 0 if `$x` eq `$y`, -1 if `$x` lt `$y`
`$w ? $x : $y`	Return `$x` if `$w` is true, `$y` if `$w` is false
`($x..$y)`	Return a list of numbers from `$x` to `$y`

Arrays and Associative Arrays

Perl has arrays to let you group items using a single variable number. Perl offers two types of arrays: those whose items are indexed by number (arrays) and those whose items are indexed by a string (associative arrays).

An index into an array is referred to as the *subscript* of the array.

> **TIP**
>
> An associative array is referred to as "hash" because of the way it's stored *internally* in Perl.

Arrays are referred to with the @ symbol. Individual items in an array are derived with a $ and the subscript. For example, the first item in an array `@count` would be `$count[0]`, the second item would be `$count[1]`, and so on. See Listing 29.2 for some usage of arrays.

Listing 29.2. Using arrays.

```
1 #!/usr/bin/perl
2 #
3 # An example to show how arrays work in Perl
```

```
 4 #
 5 @amounts = (10,24,39);
 6 @parts = ('computer', 'rat', "kbd");
 7
 8 $a = 1; $b = 2; $c = '3';
 9 @count = ($a, $b, $c);
10
11 @empty = ();
12
13 @spare = @parts;
14
15 print '@amounts = ';
16 print "@amounts \n";
17
18 print '@parts = ';
19 print "@parts \n";
20
21 print '@count = ';
22 print "@count \n";
23
24 print '@empty = ';
25 print "@empty \n";
26
27 print '@spare = ';
28 print "@spare \n";
29
30
31 #
32 # Accessing individual items in an array
33 #
34 print '$amounts[0] = ';
35 print "$amounts[0] \n";
36 print '$amounts[1] = ';
37 print "$amounts[1] \n";
38 print '$amounts[2] = ';
39 print "$amounts[2] \n";
40 print '$amounts[3] = ';
41 print "$amounts[3] \n";
42
43 print "Items in \@amounts  = $#amounts \n";
44 $size = @amounts; print "Size of Amount  = $size\n";
45 print "Item 0 in \@amounts = $amounts[$[]\n";
46
@amounts = 10 24 39
@parts = computer rat kbd
@count = 1 2 3
@empty =
@spare = computer rat kbd
$amounts[0] = 10
$amounts[1] = 24
$amounts[2] = 39
$amounts[3] =
Items in @amounts  = 2
Size of Amount  = 3
Item 0 in @amounts = 10
```

In line 5, three integer values are assigned the @amounts array. In line 6, three strings are assigned to the @parts array. In line 8, the script assigns both string and numeric values to variables and then assigns the values of the variable to the @count array. An empty array is created in line 11. In line 13, the @spare array is assigned the same values as those in @parts.

Lines 15 through 28 print out the first five lines of the output. In lines 34 to 41, the script addresses individual items of the @amounts array. Note that $amount[3] does not exist; it is therefore printed as an empty item.

The $#array syntax is used in line 43 to print the last index in an array, so the script prints 2. The size of the amounts array would be ($#amounts + 1). If an array is assigned to a scalar, as shown in line 44, the size of the array is assigned to the scalar. Line 45 shows the use of a special Perl variable called $[, which is the base subscript (zero, unless you redefine it) of an array.

Associative Arrays

An associative array is really an array with two items per index. The first item at each index is called a *key* and the other item is called the *value*. You index into an associative array using keys to get values. An associative array name is preceded with a percent sign (%), and indexed items are with curly braces ({}).

See Listing 29.3 for some sample uses of associative arrays.

Listing 29.3. Using associative arrays.

```
 1  #!/usr/bin/perl
 2  #
 3  # Associative Arrays.
 4  #
 5
 6  %subscripts = (
 7          'bmp', 'Bitmap',
 8          "cpp", "C++ Source",
 9          "txt", 'Text file' );
10
11  $bm = 'asc';
12  $subscripts{$bm} = 'Ascii File';
13
14  print "\n =========== Raw dump of hash   ========= \n";
15  print %subscripts;
16
17  print "\n =========== using foreach   ========= \n";
18  foreach $key (keys (%subscripts)) {
19      $value = $subscripts{$key};
20      print "Key = $key, Value = $value \n";
21      }
22
23  print "\n === using foreach with sort ========= \n";
24  foreach $key (sort keys (%subscripts)) {
25      $value = $subscripts{$key};
26      print "Key = $key, Value = $value \n";
```

```
27      }
28
29 print "\n =========== using each()  ========= \n";
30 while (($key,$value) = each(%subscripts)) {
31     print "Key = $key, Value = $value \n";
32     }
33
```

```
=========== Raw dump of hash  =========
txtText filecppC++ SourceascAscii FilebmpBitmap
=========== using foreach  =========
Key = txt, Value = Text file
Key = cpp, Value = C++ Source
Key = asc, Value = Ascii File
Key = bmp, Value = Bitmap

=== using foreach with sort =========
Key = asc, Value = Ascii File
Key = bmp, Value = Bitmap
Key = cpp, Value = C++ Source
Key = txt, Value = Text file

=========== using each()  =========
Key = txt, Value = Text file
Key = cpp, Value = C++ Source
Key = asc, Value = Ascii File
Key = bmp, Value = Bitmap
```

An associative array called %subscripts is created in line 6 up to line 9. Three items of (key,value) pairs are added to %subscripts as a list. At line 11, a new item is added to the %subscript array by assigning $bm to a key and then using $bm as the index. We could just as easily add the string 'Ascii File' with the hard-coded statement:

```
$subscripts{'asc'} = 'Ascii File';
```

Look at the output from line 15 which dumps out the associative array items.

In line 17, the script uses a foreach statement to loop over the keys in the %subscripts array. The keys() function returns a list of keys for a given hash. The value of the item at $subscripts{$key} is assigned to $value at line 19. You could combine lines 18 and 19 into one statement like this without loss of meaning:

```
print "Key = $key, Value = $subscripts{$key} \n";
```

Using the keys alone did not list the contents of the %subscripts hash in the order you want. To sort the output, you should sort the keys into the hash. This is shown in line 24. The sort() function takes a list of items and returns a text-sorted version. The foreach function takes the output from the sort() function applied to the value returned by the keys() function. To sort in decreasing order, you can apply the reverse function to the returned value of sort() to get this line:

```
foreach $key (reverse sort keys (%subscripts)) {
```

It's more efficient to use the each() function when working with associative arrays, because only one lookup is required per item to get both the key and its value. See line 30 where the ($key,$value) pairs assigned to the value are returned by the each() command.

The code in line 30 is important and deserves some explaining. First of all, the while() loop is used here. The format for a while loop is defined as:

```
while( conditionIsTrue) {
    codeInLOOP
}
..
codeOutOfLOOP
```

While the condition in the while loop is a nonzero number, a nonempty string, or a nonempty list, the code in the area codeInLOOP will be executed. Otherwise, the next statement outside the loop (for instance, after the curly brace) will be executed.

Secondly, look at how the list ($key,$value) is mapped onto the list returned by the each function. The first item of the returned list is assigned to $key, the next item to $value. This is part of the array slicing operations available in Perl.

Array Operations

When working with arrays in Perl, you are really working with lists. You can add or remove items from the front or back of the list. Items in the middle of the list can be indexed using subscripts or keys. Sublists can be created from lists. Lists can be concatenated to create new lists. Got all that?

Let's look at some examples of how they fit together. See Listing 29.4, which uses some of these concepts.

Listing 29.4. Array operations.

```
 1 #!/usr/bin/perl
 2 #
 3 # Array operations
 4 #
 5
 6 $a = 'RFI';
 7 $b = 'UPS';
 8 $c = 'SPIKE';
 9
10 @words = ('DC','AC','EMI','SURGE');
11
12 $count = @words;   # Get the count
13
14 #
15 # Using the for operator on a list
16 #
17 print "\n \@words = ";
18 for $i (@words) {
```

```
19        print "[$i] ";
20        }
21
22 print "\n";
23 #
24 # Using the for loop for indexing
25 #
26 for ($i=0;$i<$count;$i++) {
27        print "\n Words[$i] : $words[$i];";
28        }
29 #
30 # print 40 equal signs
31 #
32 print "\n";
33 print "=" x 40;
34 print "\n";
35 #
36 # Extracting items into scalars
37 #
38 ($x,$y) = @words;
39 print "x = $x, y = $y \n";
40 ($w,$x,$y,$z) = @words;
41 print "w = $x, x = $x, y = $y, z = $z\n";
42
43 ($anew[0], $anew[3], $anew[9], $anew[5]) = @words;
44
45 $temp = @anew;
46
47 #
48 # print 40 equal signs
49 #
50 print "=" x 40;
51 print "\n";
52
53 print "Number of elements in anew = ". $temp, "\n";
54 print "Last index in anew = ". $#anew, "\n";
55 print "The newly created Anew array is: ";
56 $j = 0;
57 for $i (@anew) {
58        print "\n \$anew[$j] = is $i ";
59        $j++;
60        }
61 print "\n";
62
63
```

```
@words = [DC] [AC] [EMI] [SURGE]

Words[0] : DC;
Words[1] : AC;
Words[2] : EMI;
Words[3] : SURGE;
========================================
x = DC, y = AC
w = AC, x = AC, y = EMI z = SURGE
========================================
Number of elements in anew = 10
Last index in anew = 9
```

continues

Listing 29.4. continued

```
The newly created Anew array is:
 $anew[0] = is DC
 $anew[1] = is
 $anew[2] = is
 $anew[3] = is AC
 $anew[4] = is
 $anew[5] = is SURGE
 $anew[6] = is
 $anew[7] = is
 $anew[8] = is
 $anew[9] = is EMI
```

Lines 6, 7, and 8 assign values to scalars $a, $b and $c. In line 10, four values are assigned to the @words array. Line 12 gives a count of the number of elements in the array.

The for loop statement is used to cycle through each element in the list. Perl takes each item in the @words array, assigns it to $i and then executes the statements in the block of code between the curly braces. We could rewrite line 18 as the following and get the same result:

```
for $i ('DC','AC','EMI','SURGE') {
```

In the case of the sample in Listing 29.4, you print the value of each item with square brackets around them. Line 22 simply prints a new line.

Now look at line 26, where the for loop is defined. The syntax in the for() loop will be very familiar to C programmers:

```
for (startingCondition; endingCondition; at_end_of_every_loop) {
      execute_statements_in_this_block;
   }
```

Line 26 sets $i to zero when the for loop is started. Before Perl executes the next statement within the block, it checks to see if $i is less than $count. If $i is less than $count, the print statement is executed. If $i is greater than or equal to $count, the next statement following the ending curly brace will be executed. After executing the last statement in a for() loop code block, line 28, Perl increments the value of with the end of loop statement: $i++. So $i is incremented. Perl goes back to the top of the loop to test for the ending condition to see what to do next.

In the next lines 32 through 34, we print an output delimiting line with 40 equals signs. The x operator in line 33 will cause the = to be repeated by the number following it. Another way to print a somewhat fancier line would be to do the following in lines 32-34:

```
32 print "\n[";
  33 print "-=" x 20;
  34 print "]\n";
```

Next, line 38 takes the first two items in @words and assigns them to variables $x and $y, respectively. The rest of the items in @words are not used. Line 40 assigns four items from @words to four variables. The mapping of items from @words to variables is done on a one-to-one basis based on the type of parameter on the left-hand side of the = sign..

Had you used the following line in place of line 40, you would get the value of $word[0] in $x and the rest of @word in @sublist:

```
($x,@sublist) = @words;
```

Line 43 creates a new array, @anew, and assigns it values from the @words array—but not on a one-to-one basis. In fact, you will see that the @anew array is not even the same size as @words. Perl automatically resizes the @anew array to be at least as large as the largest index. In this case, since $anew[9] is being assigned a value, @anew will be at least 10 items long to cover items from 0 to 9.

In lines 53 and 54, the script prints out the value of the number of elements in the array and the highest valid index in the array. Lines 57 through 60 print out the value of each item in the anew area. Notice that items in the @new array are not assigned any values.

You can create other lists from lists as well. See the example in Listing 29.5.

Listing 29.5. Creating sublists.

```perl
 1 #!/usr/bin/perl
 2 #
 3 # Array operations
 4 #
 5
 6 $a = 'RFI';
 7 $b = 'UPS';
 8 $c = 'SPIKE';
 9
10 @words = ('DC','AC','EMI','SURGE');
11
12 $count = @words;  # Get the count
13 #
14 # Using the for operator on a list
15 #
16 print "\n \@words = ";
17 for $i (@words) {
18     print "[$i] ";
19     }
20
21 print "\n";
22 print "=" x 40;
23 print "\n";
24
25 #
26 # Concatenate lists together
27 #
28 @more = ($c,@words,$a,$b);
29 print "\n  Putting a list together: ";
30 $j = 0;
31 for $i (@more) {
32     print "\n \$more[$j] = is $i ";
```

continues

Listing 29.5. continued

```
33      $j++;
34      }
35 print "\n";
36
37 @more = (@words,($a,$b,$c));
38 $j = 0;
39 for $i (@more) {
40      print "\n \$more[$j] = is $i ";
41      $j++;
42      }
43 print "\n";
44
45
46 $fourth = ($a x 4);
47 print " is $fourth\n";
@words = [DC] [AC] [EMI] [SURGE]
=========================================

  Putting a list together:
$more[0] = is SPIKE
$more[1] = is DC
$more[2] = is AC
$more[3] = is EMI
$more[4] = is SURGE
$more[5] = is RFI
$more[6] = is UPS

$more[0] = is DC
$more[1] = is AC
$more[2] = is EMI
$more[3] = is SURGE
$more[4] = is RFI
$more[5] = is UPS
$more[6] = is SPIKE

$more[0] = is RFIRFIRFIRFI
```

Listing 29.5 creates one list from another list. In line 10, the script creates and fills the @words array. In lines 16 through 19, the script prints out the array. Lines 21-23, which print equal signs to create a divider, are repeated again (which you will soon convert into a subroutine).

At line 28, the @more array is created by placing $c, the entire @words array, $a, and $b together. The size of the @more array will be 6. The items in the @more array are printed out in lines 31 through 35.

The code at line 37 creates another @more array with different ordering. The previously created @more array is freed back to the memory pool. The newly ordered @more list is printed from lines 38 through 43.

The script then uses the x operator in line 46 to create another item by concatenating four copies of $a into the variable $fourth.

If you are like me, you probably don't want to type the same lines of code again and again. For example, the code in lines 21-23 of Listing 29.5 could be made into a function that looks like this:

```
sub printLine {
  print "\n";
  print "=" x 40;
  print "\n";
}
```

Now when you want to print the lines, call the subroutine with this line of code:

```
&printLine;
```

The section "Subroutines" covers other aspects of subroutines. For now, let's get back to some of the things you can do with arrays using the functions supplied with Perl. See Listing 29.6 for a script that uses the array functions discussed here.

Listing 29.6. Using array functions.

```
 1 #!/usr/bin/perl
 2 #
 3 # Functions for Arrays
 4 #
 5 sub printLine {
 6 print "\n"; print "=" x 60; print "\n";
 7 }
 8
 9 $quote= 'Listen to me slowly';
10
11 #
12 # USING THE SPLIT function
13 #
14 @words = split(' ',$quote);
15
16 #
17 # Using the for operator on a list
18 #
19 &printLine;
20 print "The quote from Sam Goldwyn: $quote ";
21 &printLine;
22 print "The words \@words = ";
23 for $i (@words) {
24     print "[$i] ";
25     }
26
27 #
28 # CHOP
29 #
30 &printLine;
31 chop(@words);
32 print "The chopped words \@words = ";
33 for $i (@words) {
34     print "[$i] ";
35     }
```

continues

Listing 29.6. continued

```
36 print "\n .. restore";
37 #
38 # Restore!
39 #
40 @words = split(' ',$quote);
41
42 #
43 # Using PUSH
44 #
45 @temp = push(@words,"please");
46 &printLine;
47 print "After pushing \@words = ";
48 for $i (@words) {
49     print "[$i] ";
50     }
51
52 #
53 # USING POP
54 #
55 $temp = pop(@words);  # Take the 'please' off
56 $temp = pop(@words);  # Take the 'slowly' off
57 &printLine;
58 print "Popping twice \@words = ";
59 for $i (@words) {
60     print "[$i] ";
61     }
62 #
63 # SHIFT from the from the top of  the array.
64 #
65 $temp = shift @words;
66 &printLine;
67 print "Shift $temp off, \@words= ";
68 for $i (@words) {
69     print "[$i] ";
70     }
71 #
72 # Restore words
73 #
74 @words = ();
75 @words = split(' ',$quote);
76 &printLine;
77 print "Restore words";
78 #
79 # SPLICE FUNCTION
80 #
81 @two = splice(@words,1,2);
82 print "\n Words after splice = ";
83 for $i (@words) {
84     print " [$i]";
85     }
86 print "\n Returned from splice = ";
87 for $i (@two) {
88     print " [$i]";
89     }
90 &printLine;
91
92 #
```

```
93 # Using the join function
94 #
95 $joined = join(":",@words,@two);
96 print "\n Returned from join = $joined ";
97 &printLine;
```

The `split` function is used in line 14 to split the items in the string `$quote` into the `@words` array.

Then the script uses `chop()` on a list. This function removes a character from a string. When applied to an array, `chop` removes a character from each item on the list. See lines 31 through 35.

You can add or delete items from an array using the `pop(@Array)` or `push(@Array)` functions. The `pop()` function removes the last item from a list and returns it as a scalar. In the `push(ARRAY,LIST);`, the `push()` function takes an array as the first parameter and treats the rest of the parameters as items to place at the end of the array. In line 45, the `push` function pushes the word `please` into the back of the `@words` array. In lines 55 and 56, two words are popped off the `@words` list. The size of the array `@word` changes with each command.

Let's look at how the shift function in used in line 65. The `shift(ARRAY)` function returns the first element of an array. The size of the array is decreased by 1. You can use `shift` in one of three ways listed here:

```
shift (@mine); # return first item of @mine
shift @mine; # return first item of @mine
shift; # return first item in @ARGV
```

The special variable `@ARGV` is the argument vector for your Perl program.

TIP

The `push`/`pop` routines work on the back of an array and the `shift`/`unshift` routines work on the front of an array.

The number of elements in `@ARGV` are easily found by assigning a scalar to `$ARGC`, which is equal to `@#ARGV` before any operations are applied to `@ARGV`.

Then, after restoring `@words` to its original value, the script uses the `splice()` function to remove items from the `@words` array. The `splice` function is very important function and is really the key behind the `pop()`, `push()`, and `shift()` functions. The syntax for the `splice()` function is:

```
splice(@array,$offset,$length,$list)
```

The `splice` function will return the items removed in the form of a list. It will replace the `$length` items in `@array` starting from `$offset` with the contents of `$list`. If you leave out the `$list` parameter, and just use `splice(@array,$offset,$length)`, then nothing will be inserted in the original array. Any removed items will be returned from splice().If you leave out the $length paramater to splice and use it as splice(@array,$offset), then $length will be set the length of the @array from the offset.

File Handles and Operators

Now that we have covered basic array and numeric operations, let's cover some of the input/output operations where files are concerned. A Perl program has three file handles when it starts up: STDIN (for standard input), STDOUT (for standard output) and STDERR (for standard error message output). Note the use of capitals and the lack of the $ sign to signify that these are file handles. For a C/C++ programmer, the three handles would be akin to stdin, stdout and stderr.

To open a file for I/O you have to use the open statement. The syntax for the open call is:

```
open(HANDLE, $filename);
```

The HANDLE is then used for all the operations on a file. To close a file, you would use the function close HANDLE;

For writing text to a file given a handle, you can use the print statements to write to the file:

```
print HANDLE $output;
```

The HANDLE defaults to STDIN if no handle is specified. To read one line from the file given a HANDLE you will use the <> operators:

```
$line = <HANDLE>
```

In the preceding code, $line will be assigned all the input until a carriage return or eof. When writing interactive scripts, you normally use the chop() function to remove the end-of-line character. To read from the standard input into a variable $response, you would use the statements in sequence:

```
$response = <STDIN>;
chop $response; # remove offensive carriage return.
```

You can do binary read and write operations on a file using the read() and write functions. The syntax for each type of function is:

```
read(HANDLE,$buffer,$length[,$offset]);
```

The read function will read from HANDLE into $buffer, up $length bytes from the $offset in bytes from the start of the file. The $offset is optional and read() defaults reading to the current location in the file if $offset is left out. The location in the file to read from is advanced $length bytes. To check if you have reached the end of file, use the command:

```
eof(HANDLE);
```

A nonzero value returned will signify the end of the file, and a zero returned will indicate that there is more to read in the file. You can move to a position in the file using the seek function.

```
seek(HANDLE,$offset,$base)
```

The $offset is from the location specified in $base. The seek function behaves exactly like the C function call. If $base is 0, the $Offset is from the start of the file.

There can be errors associated with opening files, so to print out error messages before a script crashes the die() function is used. A call to open a file called "test.data" would look like this:

```
open(TESTFILE,"test.data") ¦¦ die "\n $0 Cannot open $! \n";
```

The preceding line literally reads, "Open test.data for input or die if you cannot open it". The $0 is the Perl special variable for the process name and $! is the errno from the system as a string.

The filename signifies the type of operation you intend to perform with the file. Table 29.4 lists some of the ways you can open a file.

Table 29.4. File open types.

File	Action
"test.data"	Opens test.data for reading. File must exist.
"<test.data"	Opens test.data for reading. File must exist.
">test.data"	Opens test.data for writing. Creates file if it does not exist. Appends to any existing file called test.data.
"+>test.data"	Opens test.data for reading and writing. Creates file if it does not exist.
"+<test.data"	Opens test.data for reading and writing. Creates file if it does not exist. Preferred way in Perl 5.
"¦ cmd"	Opens a pipe to write to.
"cmd ¦"	Opens a pipe to read from.
"-"	Opens STDIN.
">-"	Opens STDOUT.

When working with multiple files, you can have more than one unique handle to write to or read from. Use the select HANDLE; call to set the default file handle to use when using print statements. For example, say you have two file handles, LARRY and CURLY. Here's how to switch between handles:

```
select LARRY;
print "Whatsssa matter?\n"; # write to LARRY
select CURLY;
print "Whoop, whoop, whoop!"; # write to CURLY
select LARRY;
print "I oughta.... "; # write to LARRY again
```

Of course, by explicitly stating the handle name you could get the same result with these three lines of code:

```
print LARRY "Whatsssa matter?\n"; # write to LARRY
print CURLY "Whoop, whoop, whoop!"; # write to CURLY
print LARRY "I oughta.... "; # write to LARRY again
```

This is a very brief introduction to using file handles in Perl. The use of file handles is covered throughout the rest of the book, so don't worry if this pace of information is too quick. You will see plenty of examples throughout the book.

You can also check for the status of a file given a filename. The available tests are listed in the source test file in Listing 29.7.

Listing 29.7. Testing file parameters.

```perl
#!/usr/bin/perl

$name = "test.txt";
print "\nTesting flags for $name \n";
print "\n========= Effective User ID tests ";
print "\n is readable" if ( -r $name);
print "\n is writeable" if ( -w $name);
print "\n is executeable" if ( -x $name);
print "\n is owned " if ( -o $name);
print "\n========= Real User ID tests ";
print "\n is readable" if ( -R $name);
print "\n is writeable" if ( -W $name);
print "\n is executeable" if ( -X $name);
print "\n is owned " if ( -O $name);

print "\n========= Reality Checks ";
print "\n exists " if ( -e $name);
print "\n has zero size " if ( -z $name);
print "\n has some bytes in it " if ( -s $name);

print "\n is a file " if (-f $name);
print "\n is a directory " if (-d $name);
print "\n is a link " if (-l $name);
print "\n is a socket " if (-S $name);
print "\n is a pipe " if (-p $name);

print "\n is a block device " if (-b $name);
print "\n is a character device " if (-c $name);


print "\n has setuid bit set " if (-u $name);
print "\n has sticky bit set " if (-k $name);
print "\n has gid bit set " if (-g $name);
```

```
print "\n is open to terminal " if (-t $name);
print "\n is a Binary file " if (-B $name);
print "\n is a Text file " if (-T $name);

print "\n is Binary to terminal " if (-t $name);
print "\n is open to terminal " if (-t $name);
print "\n age of file is ".(int(-M $name)+1)." day(s) old" if (-e $name);
print "\n access time of file is ".(-A $name) if (-e $name);
print "\n inode change time of file is ".(-C $name) if (-e $name);



printf "\n";
```

Working with Patterns

Perl has a very powerful regular expression parser and string `search` and `replace` functions. To search for a substring, you would use the following syntax normally within an `if` block:

```
if ($a =~ /menu/) {
    printf "\n Found menu in $a! \n";
}
```

The value in `$a` is the number of matched strings. To search in a case-insensitive manner, use an `'i'` at the end of the search statement like this:

```
if ($a =~ /mEnU/i) {
    printf "\n Found menu in $a! \n";
}
```

You can even search for items in an array. For example, if `$a` was an array `@a`, then the returned value from the search operation will be an array with all the matched strings. If you do not specify the "`@a =~`" portion, then Perl will use the `$_` default name space to search on.

To search and replace strings, use the following syntax:

```
$expr =~ s/old/new/gie
```

The `'g'`, `'i'`, and `'e'` are optional parameters. If the `'g'` is not specified, only the first match to the "old" string will be replaced with "new." The `'i'` flag specifies a case-insensitive search. The `'e'` forces Perl to use the "new" string as a Perl expression. So, in the following example, the value of `$a` will be "HIGHWAY":

```
$a = "DRIVEWAY";
$a =~ s/HIGH/DRIVE/
print $a;
```

Perl has a `grep()` function very similar to the `grep` function in UNIX, Perl's `grep` function takes a regular expression and a list. The return value from `grep` can be handled one of two ways: if assigned to a scalar, it is the number of matches found, and if assigned to a list, it's a sublist of all the items found via `grep`.

Please check the man pages for using grep(). Some of the main types of predefined patterns are shown in Table 29.5.

Table 29.5. Main types of predefined patterns.

Code	Pattern
.	Any character
\d	Digits [0-9]
\D	Anything but digits
\w	[a-zA-Z]
\W	Anything but \w
\s	Space or tab
\S	Anything but \s
\n	Newline
\r	Carriage return
\t	Tab
\f	Formfeed
\0	Null
\000	Octal
\X00	Hex
\cX	ASCII Control Character
*	Zero or more of previous pattern
+	One or more of previous pattern
?	Zero or one of previous pattern

Perl uses the special variable called $_. This is the default variable to use by Perl if you do not explicitly specify a variable name and Perl expects a variable. For example, in the grep() function, if you omit the LIST, grep() will use the string in the variable $_. The $_ variable is Perl's default string to search, assign input, or read for data for a number.

Subroutines

Perl 5 supports subroutines and functions with the sub command. You can use pointers to subroutines, too. The syntax for subroutines is

```
sub Name {

}
```

The ending curly brace does not require a semicolon to terminate it. If you are using a reference to a subroutine it can be declared without a Name, as shown here:

```
$ptr = sub {

};
```

Note the use of the semicolon to terminate the end of the subroutine. To call this function you would use the following line:

```
&\$ptr(argument list);
```

Parameters to subroutines are passed in the @_ array. To get the individual items in the array, we can use $_[0], $_[1], and so on. You can define your own local variables with the 'local' keyword.

```
sub sample {
local ($a, $b, @c, $x) = @_
    &lowerFunc();
}
```

In the preceding subroutine, you will find that $a = $_[0], $b = $_[1] and @c will point to the rest of the arguments as one list with $x empty. Generally, an array is the last assignment in such an assignment since it chews up all your parameters.

The 'local' variables will all be available for use in the lowerFunc() function. To hide the $a, $b, @c, and $x from lowerFunc, use the 'my' keyword like this:

```
my ($a, $b, @c, $x) = @_
```

Remember, $x will be empty. Now, the code in localFunc() will not be able to access $a, $b, @c, or $x.

Parameters in Perl can be in form, from the looks of it. Since Perl 5.001m, you can define prototypes for subroutine arguments as well with the syntax

```
sub    Name (parameters) {

}
```

If the parameters are not what the function expects, Perl will bail out with an error. The parameter format is as follows: $ for a scalar, @ for an array, % for hash, & for a reference to a subroutine, and * for anything. So, if you want your function to accept only three scalars, you would declare it as

```
sub func1($$$) {
    my ($x,$y,$z) = @_;
    code here
}
```

To pass the value of an array by reference (by pointer), you would use a backslash (\). If you pass two arrays without the backslash specifier, the contents of the two arrays will be concatenated into one long array in @_. The function prototype to pass three arrays, a hash, and the rest in an array would look like this:

```
sub func2(\@\@\@\%@)
```

More Features in Perl 5

Perl 5 offers a vast array of new features when compared with Perl 4. In fact, the new Perl 5 is a complete rewrite of the Perl 4 interpreter. The new features in Perl include object-oriented programming, dynamically loaded packages, and a rich set of Perl modules designed for a specific task. Modules for Perl include those for networking, interprocess communications, World Wide Web applications, mathematical applications, and so on. The list goes on. You can even extend Perl with your own C modules!

The topics are too vast to cover in one chapter alone and require a book. For more information, please consult the following books:

- *Perl 5 Unleashed*, by Kamran Husain (Indianapolis: Sams Publishing, 1996). This book covers the advanced features of Perl, including object-oriented programming, Web development, module development, extensions in C and C++, and so on.
- *Teach Yourself Perl 5 in 21 Days*, by Dave Till (Indianapolis: Sams Publishing, 1995). A good book on the basics of Perl for the new user.
- *Teach Yourself CGI Programming with Perl in a Week*, by Eric Herrmann (Indianapolis: Sams.net Publishing, 1996). A good book for learning how to create interactive Web pages with the Common Gateway Interface.

The following two classics offer a good base and will serve as a good reference to Perl 4 and its internals:

- *Programming Perl*, by Larry Wall and Randall Schwartz, O'Reilly & Associates, 1990.
- *Learning Perl*, by Randall Schwartz, O'Reilly & Associates, 1993.

Also, refer to the Perl man and documentation pages at the Web site at http://www.metronet.com/perlinfo/doc/manual.

Summary

This chapter has been a whirlwind introduction to Perl and, sadly, could not cover every aspect of Perl programming basics. As you work with Perl, though, you will learn more from practice than anything else. Do not despair. Read the man pages and ask lots of questions in the comp.lang.perl newsgroup.

Introduction to Tcl and Tk

30

by
Rick McMullin

IN THIS CHAPTER

This chapter introduces the Tcl programming language and its most popular extension, Tk. This chapter covers the following topics:

- What Tcl is
- What Tk is
- The Tcl language
- The Tk language extensions

By the end of this chapter, you should understand what Tcl and Tk are, and also how to write simple applications using Tcl and Tk.

What Is Tcl?

Tcl stands for Tool Command Language. (It is pronounced "tickle.") It is a scripting language similar to the shell scripting languages introduced in Chapter 13, "Shell Programming." Tcl can be used to quickly write text-based application programs.

Tcl was developed by John Ousterhout, then of the University of California at Berkeley. Tcl is an interpreted language and therefore has the usual advantages and disadvantages of all interpreted languages. The key disadvantage of interpreted languages is that they execute much slower than compiled languages. The biggest advantage of interpreted languages is that developing applications using them is usually much faster than using compiled languages. This is because you don't have to wait for code to compile and can see any changes you make to the code almost instantly.

Tcl has a core set of built-in functions that provide the basic features of its programming language. The true power of Tcl, however, is that it is easily extendible. Application programmers can add functions to Tcl and can even imbed the Tcl function library directly into their applications. This gives programmers the power to include an interpretive scripting language directly in their own application without having to do any of the work of developing the language. This means that you can provide users of your application with all the commands that exist within Tcl and also any that you create and add to the Tcl library.

Invoking Tcl commands is done by starting up the Tcl shell, called `tclsh`. Once you have started `tclsh`, you can type Tcl commands directly into it. Straying slightly from the "hello world" example that you find in almost every introductory language text, the following example shows you how to write `Hello there` instead to the screen:

```
puts stdout "Hello there"
```

This command contains three separate words. The first word in the command is the actual command name, `puts`. The `puts` command is an abbreviation for put string; it simply writes something to the device that is specified in the second word of the command. In this case the second word tells `puts` to write to the standard output device, which is typically the screen. The third word in the `puts` command is `"Hello there"`. The quotation marks tell Tcl to interpret everything contained within them as a single word.

> **NOTE**
>
> The default output device is `stdout` (standard output, usually the screen), so if you intend to write something to `stdout` using the `puts` command, the second argument is optional.

Even though this is a very simple example, it illustrates the basic command syntax of the Tcl language. There are obviously many more commands contained within Tcl, but the basic syntax of all Tcl commands is the same:

```
command parameter1 parameter2 ...
```

The command can be any of the built-in Tcl commands, or it can be a user-defined extension to the Tcl command set in the form of a Tcl procedure. In either case, the fundamental syntax remains unchanged.

What Is Tk?

Tk, which was also developed by Ousterhout, is a graphical user interface extension to Tcl. Tk is based on the X Window system and allows application developers to develop X Window-based applications much faster than they could using other X Window toolkits, such as Motif or OPEN LOOK.

Like Tcl, Tk also has a shell that enables you to enter commands to be interpreted. The Tk shell is a superset of the Tcl command shell. This means that anything you can do in the Tcl command shell you can also do in the Tk command shell. The big difference between the two is that the Tk command shell was designed to enable you to build X Window front ends to your applications.

The Tk command shell is called `wish`, which stands for windowing shell. You must be running X Window when you invoke `wish`. This is because when `wish` is invoked, it brings up a window to display the results of any of the graphical commands it interprets. When you invoke `wish`, a window should appear on your screen.

Let's try enhancing the earlier "Hello there" example by displaying `Hello there` in a button in the `wish` window. To accomplish this, you must first ensure that `wish` has been started. This is easily done by typing the following command into an Xterm window:

```
wish
```

This command brings up the `wish` window and also executes the Tk interpreter in the Xterm window. You can now type Tcl or Tk commands directly in the Xterm window. The commands necessary to print `Hello there` in a button in the `wish` window are as follows:

```
button .b -text "Hello there" -command exit
pack .b
```

The syntax of the command on the first line contains the command name followed by a number of arguments. The first argument is the name you are giving to the new button. The rest of the arguments passed to the button command are slightly different from the arguments you saw in the Tcl version of the "Hello there" example. These arguments each consist of two parts. The first part tells Tk what the argument name is, and the second part tells Tk the value of the argument.

The second argument has the name text, and the value of the argument is the string you want to display in the button. The third argument has the name command and is used to specify the command that you want to execute when that button is pushed. In this example, you do not really want anything to happen if the button is pushed, so you just tell wish to exit from the current script.

The button command created a button widget that you called .b. To get the button to show up in the wish window, you must tell Tk to display the button. This is done by the pack command.

In this example, the pack command has only one argument: the name of the button that you created in the first command. When the pack command is executed, a button with the string Hello there displayed in it appears in the wish window.

Two things about this example are worth discussing in more detail. The first is why you called the button .b instead of b, bob, or button1. The significance is not the actual text in the button name (this in fact could be bob or button1), but the period (.) preceding the name of the button.

The period notation is used to represent the widget hierarchy. Each widget is contained in another widget. The root widget, or the highest level widget, is contained in the wish window and is called . (this is analogous to the Linux directory structure, in which each directory has an owner or a parent directory and the root or highest level directory is named /). Each time you create a new widget, you must tell Tk which widget the new widget should be contained in. In the "Hello there" example, the container specified for the button widget was ., the root widget.

The second item of interest is the resizing of the wish window that occurs after you enter the pack command. The wish window shrinks down to a size that is just large enough to hold the button you created. Tk causes the wish window to default to a size just large enough to hold whatever it has in it. Many commands can be used to change this behavior and customize how things are displayed on the screen. You will see some of these commands later in this chapter.

The Tcl Language

Now that you have seen examples of both Tcl and Tk in action, it is appropriate to take a step back and look at the underlying Tcl language in more detail. Tcl contains a rich set of programming commands that support all the features found in most high-level languages. This section discusses many of these features and gives examples that explain how to use them.

Tcl Variables and Variable Substitution

Like the UNIX shell programming languages, Tcl supports the concept of variables. Variables are temporary storage places used to hold information that will be needed by a program at some later point in time. In Tcl, variable names can consist of any combination of printable characters.

Typically, variable names are meaningful names that describe the information being stored in them. For example, a variable that is being used to hold the monthly sales of a product might have one of the following names:

```
Monthly_sales
"Monthly sales"
```

> **NOTE**
>
> Quotation marks cause Tcl to ignore the whitespace characters (spaces and tabs) in the variable name and treat it as one word. This is discussed in the "Quotes" section of this chapter.

The value that is placed into a variable can also be any combination of printable characters. Possible values for the `Monthly_sales` variable are

```
"40,000"
40000
"refer to table 3"
```

The Tcl `set` command is used to assign values to variables. The `set` command can pass either one or two arguments. When two arguments are passed to the `set` command, the first one is treated as the variable name and the second is the value to assign to that variable.

When the `set` command is used with only one argument, Tcl expects the argument to be the name of a variable, and the `set` command returns the value of that variable. The following command assigns the value of 40000 to the variable `Monthlysales` and then echoes the value to the screen:

```
set Monthlysales 40000
```

To print the value of the `Monthlysales` variable to the screen, you would type

```
set Monthlysales
```

All values that are assigned to variables are stored as character strings. If you defined a variable to be equal to the integer 40, as in the following command

```
set num 40
```

the value 40 would be represented as the character string `40`, not as an integer.

So far you have seen how to set variables and how to display their values to the screen, but you have not seen how they are used with commands other than the `set` command. To use the value of a variable in another command, you must precede the variable name with an unquoted dollar sign ($). This tells Tcl to expect a variable name and to substitute the value of that variable for the variable name. The following example shows a simple use of variable substitution:

```
set Monthlysales 40000
expr $Monthlysales * 12
```

The first command assigns the value of 40000 to the variable `Monthlysales`. The `expr` command is used to perform mathematical evaluations of expressions. In this case it takes the value of the variable `Monthlysales` and multiplies it by 12.

Tcl Command Substitution

Command substitution provides a way of substituting the result of a Tcl command (or commands) into an argument of another command. The syntax for command substitution is to include the commands that are being substituted in square brackets, as follows:

```
set Monthlysales 40000
set Yearlyforecast [ expr $Monthlysales * 12 ]
```

The first command once again sets the variable `Monthlysales` to the value of 40000. The second command makes use of command substitution to set the value of `Yearlyforecast` equal to the result of the command in the square braces.

In this example the substitute consisted of only one command. Tcl allows the substitute to consist of any valid Tcl script, meaning that it can contain any number of Tcl commands.

Quotes

Often you want to use commands containing special characters that you don't want Tcl to interpret. By quoting these characters, you hide the special characters from the Tcl interpreter.

Three kinds of quoting can be used in Tcl scripts. The first is quoting with double quotation marks (""). This kind of quoting is used to hide whitespace characters and command separators from the Tcl interpreter.

Whenever you have two or more words that you want Tcl to treat as a single word, you can do so by surrounding the words with quotation marks. A good example of this type of quoting is when you want to create variable names that contain more than one word, or you want to assign a value that contains more than one word to a variable, as follows:

```
set "Monthly sales" 40000

set Heading1 "Description of item"
```

The second kind of quoting uses the backslash character (\). This type of quoting can hide any single character from the interpreter. This form of quoting is most commonly used to hide special characters, such as $, from the Tcl interpreter. The following example illustrates the need for backslash quoting:

```
set Header1 "The cost is \$3.50"
```

In this example the Header1 variable is being assigned the value The cost is $3.50. The quotation marks are necessary to hide the fact that there are four separate words contained in the character string. The backslash in this command tells the Tcl interpreter to treat the $ as a regular character instead of the variable substitution character. If the backslash was not used in the command, the interpreter would attempt to substitute the variable named 3.50 into the command. This would result in an error, because there is no variable with that name defined.

The third type of quoting available in Tcl uses curly braces ({}). This quoting is more powerful than quoting using quotation marks or backslashes. Quoting using braces hides not only whitespace and command separators from the Tcl interpreter but also any other kind of special character. This type of quoting can be used to eliminate the need for backslash quoting in character strings. The example used for backslash quoting could be written using brace quotation as follows:

```
set Header1 {The cost is $3.50}
```

The most important use of curly brace quoting is to defer the evaluation of special characters. This means that special characters are not processed immediately by the Tcl interpreter but are instead passed to a command that processes the special characters on its own. An example of when deferred evaluation is used is in the while command:

```
set count 0
while {$count < 3} {
    puts "count equals $count"
    set count [expr $count + 1]
}
```

The while command has to evaluate both of its arguments each time it iterates through the loop. It is therefore necessary for the interpreter to ignore the special characters in both of these arguments and leave the evaluation of these characters up to the while command.

Now that you have all the language basics out of the way, you can move on to some of the more advanced Tcl commands.

The *if* Command

The if command, just like in other languages, evaluates an expression and, based on the results of the expression, executes a set of commands. The syntax of the if command is the following:

```
if {expr} {commands}
```

The if command expects two arguments. The first argument is an expression that is used to determine whether to execute the commands contained in the second argument. The expression argument is typically an expression that evaluates to either True or False. For example:

```
$i < 10
$num = 2
```

Expressions such as the following, although valid, do not make much sense in the context of an `if` command:

```
$i + $b
10 * 3
```

The second argument to the `if` command is a Tcl script, which can contain any number of Tcl commands. This script is executed if the expression contained in the first argument evaluates to True.

The `if` commands can have one or more `elseif` commands and one `else` command associated with them. The syntax for these commands is shown here:

```
if {expr} {
      commands }
elseif {expr} {
      commands }
elseif {expr} {
      commands }
else {
      commands }
```

The commands associated with the first `if` or `elseif` whose expression evaluates to True are executed. If none of these expressions evaluate to True, the commands associated with the `else` command are executed.

The *for* Command

The `for` command in Tcl provides a way of implementing `for` loops. Tcl `for` loops are very similar to `for` loops in other languages, such as C. The `for` command expects four arguments. The first argument is a script that is used to initialize the counter. The second argument is an expression that is evaluated each time through the loop to determine whether to continue. The third argument is used to define the increment to be used on the counter. The fourth argument is the set of commands to be executed each time through the loop.

```
for { set i 0} {$i < 10} {incr i 1} {
    puts [expr 2 * $i]
}
```

The preceding loop executes ten times. The counter i is initially set to 0. The for loop executes while i is less than 10, and the value of i is increased by 1 each time through the loop. The command that is executed each time through the loop is the puts command. This evaluates 2 × i each time through the loop and prints the result to the screen. The output that results from running this command is listed here:

```
0
2
4
6
8
10
12
14
16
18
```

The *while* Command

The while command is used to implement while loops in Tcl. while loops are very similar to for loops. The only real difference between them is that the for loop provides more enhanced features for controlling entrance and exit criteria for the loop. The syntax for the while loop is shown in the following example:

```
set i 0
while {$i < 10} {
    puts [expr 2 * $i]
    set i [expr $i + 1]
}
```

This while loop performs the same function as the example that was presented in the section describing the for loop. It calculates 2 × i each time through the loop and prints the result to the screen. Notice that in this example you have to handle incrementing the counter yourself. With the for loop, the counter incrementing was taken care of by the for command.

The *switch* Command

The switch command provides the same function as an if statement that has multiple elseif clauses associated with it. The switch command compares a value (this value is usually stored in a variable) with any number of patterns, and if it finds a match it executes the Tcl code associated with the matching pattern.

```
switch $thing {
    car {puts "thing is a car"}
    truck {puts "thing is a truck"}
    default {puts "I don't know what this thing is"}
}
```

> **NOTE**
>
> The Tcl `switch` command is equivalent to the `case` statement found in Pascal and some other languages.

This `switch` command compares the value that is stored in the `thing` variable (which must be set prior to these statements, of course) with the string `car` and the string `truck` to see if it matches either of them. If the value of the `thing` variable is equal to `car`, then `thing is a car` is displayed on the screen. If the value of the `thing` variable is equal to `truck`, then `thing is a truck` is displayed on the screen. If neither of these cases are true, the default clause is executed and `I don't know what this thing is` displays on the screen.

> **TIP**
>
> Whenever you need to check to see if a variable is equal to one of a number of values, you should use a `switch` command instead of an `if` command with multiple `elseif` clauses. This makes your code much easier to read and understand.

Comments

It is always a good idea to include comments in any Tcl code you write—or code you write in any other language, for that matter. This becomes especially important if any of the following situations are possible:

- Someone else needs to look at or maintain your code.
- Your programs get large.
- You won't be looking at code that you have written for long periods of time after you write it.

Chances are that at least one of these situations will come up with Tcl code you have written.

Comments cannot be placed in the middle of a command. They must occur between commands. The pound sign (#) is used to inform Tcl to expect a comment.

```
# This is a valid comment

set a 1 ;   # This is a valid comment

set a 1        # This is an invalid comment
```

The third comment shown here is invalid because it occurs in the middle of a command.

> **NOTE**
>
> Recall that Tcl interprets everything up to a newline character or a semicolon to be part of the command.

The Tk Language Extensions

Earlier in this chapter, a simple example of Tk displayed `Hello there` in a button in the `wish` window. Tk is much more powerful than that example showed. Along with the button widget are many other widgets provided by Tk. These include menus, scrollbars, and list boxes. This section gives you an overview of some of the other Tk widgets and gives short examples explaining how these widgets can be used.

Frames

Frame widgets are containers for other widgets. They do not have any interesting behavior like the other Tk widgets. The only visible properties of frame widgets that you can set are their color and their border appearance. You can give three different border appearances to a frame widget: flat, raised, and sunken. You can experiment with the different frame widgets to see how they look.

The flat border frame widget is not too exciting. It looks exactly the same as the default `wish` window (because the default border appearance is flat).

Buttons

Button widgets are used to get specific input from a user. A button can be turned on or activated by the user of a Tk program by moving the mouse pointer over the button and then pressing the left mouse button. Tk provides the following three kinds of button widgets:

- Button
- Check button
- Radio button

The button widget is used to initiate some specific actions. The button usually has a name such as "Load file" that describes the action that results if you press the button.

Check button widgets are used to allow users of a program to turn program options on or off. When the check button is shaded the program option is on, and when the check button is not shaded the program option is off.

Radio buttons are similar to check buttons except that they are defined in groups, where only one member of a group of radio buttons is allowed to be on at one time. This means that if one radio button in a group of radio buttons is on, none of the other radio buttons in that group can be turned on. When the radio button is shaded it is on, and when the radio button is not shaded it is off.

Menus and Menu Buttons

Menu widgets are used to implement pull-down menus, cascading menus, and pop-up menus. A menu is a top-level widget that contains a set of menu entries that have values or commands associated with them. Five kinds of entries can be used in menus:

- Cascade entries display a submenu when the mouse pointer passes over them. The cascade entry is similar in function to the menu button widget.

- Command entries invoke a Tcl script when activated. The command entry is similar to the button widget in function.

- Check button entries toggle a program option between on and off. When the check button is shaded the option is on, and when the check button is not shaded it is off. The check button entry is similar in function to the check button widget.

- Radio button entries toggle a program option. The difference between the radio button entry and the check button entry is that radio buttons are typically defined in groups, with the restriction that only one of the radio buttons in the group can be active at once. The radio button entry is similar in function to the radio button widget.

- Separator entries display a horizontal line in the menu. This is used for appearance purposes only. There is no behavior associated with a separator entry.

The main difference between the menu entries and the button widgets is that the button widgets can exist by themselves, but the menu entries must exist within the context of a menu widget.

Menu button widgets are similar to button widgets. The only real difference between the two is that when menu buttons are invoked they bring up menus instead of executing Tcl scripts as button widgets would. The menu button name usually describes the types of menu entries contained in the menu that the menu button activates. This means that you should find menu entries that perform some kind of file operations contained within the File menu.

You can activate a menu by moving the mouse pointer to the menu button widget and pressing the left mouse button. This activates the menu associated with the menu button and displays the menu entries that are contained in that menu to the screen. You can now move the mouse pointer down through the list of menu entries and select the one you want.

The File menu contains two command entries (the Open entry and Quit entry), one cascade entry (the Save As entry), and one separator entry. The menu that comes up as a result of clicking the mouse pointer on the Save As cascade entry contains three command entries: the Text entry, the Ver 1 file entry, and the Ver 2 file entry.

List Boxes

The list box widget enables users of a Tk application to select items from a list of one or more items. If the number of items to be displayed in the list box is larger than the number of lines in the list box, you can attach scrollbars to make the extra items accessible.

Scrollbars

Scrollbar widgets are used to control what is displayed in other widgets. Scrollbar widgets are attached to other widgets to allow users to scroll up and down through the information contained in the widget. You typically put scrollbars on any widget that is designed to contain an arbitrary number of lines of information (such as a list box) or on widgets that contain more lines of information than the widget can display, given its size.

Summary

This chapter started off by introducing Tcl and the Tk tool kit and describing the uses of both. Although this chapter contained a lot of information, it barely scratched the surface of the programming tools provided by Tcl and the Tk tool kit.

Tcl has many more programming features than were described in this book. Some of the most notable are arrays, lists, and procedures.

Not all of the Tk widgets were described here, either. Some of the widgets that were not described are canvasses, scales, labels, messages, and `textedit` widgets.

Tk is just one example of an extension to Tcl. There are many other extensions available that extend the behavior of Tcl in different ways. Some of these extensions are as follows:

- Ak: An audio extension for Tcl, Ak provides numerous commands for sound recording and playback.
- XF: This is an interactive graphical user interface developer for Tk.
- Tcl-DP: This is a Tcl extension that helps programmers develop distributed applications using Tcl.

If you would like to learn more about Tcl and Tk, a good place to start is the manual pages for Tcl, Tk, and any of the specific commands you want information about. There are also a few books available that are devoted to Tcl and Tk programming.

Other Compilers and Languages Ported to Linux

This chapter gives you a brief introduction to some languages other than those that have been assigned whole chapters in this book. You will learn details about the following languages and how to get packages for them:

- Ada
- FORTRAN
- Digital Signal Processing
- Modula-3
- OGI
- Eiffel
- COBOL
- LISP
- Scheme

All the packages here have accompanying documentation and "how-to-use" instructions for them.

The list of programming languages covered here is not complete. As Linux becomes more and more acceptable in the programming community, you will see more languages being ported to Linux.

Ada

The Ada programming language was named after Ms. Ada Lovelace, a member of the original Ada software development team. Ada is the choice of many real-time system software developers and has been enhanced significantly for this purpose. Needless to say, some greatly enthused individuals have ported this language over to Linux. The Ada package is referred to as the GNAT (for GNu Ada Translator). The authors therefore appropriately belong to the GNAT project at New York University.

The latest update at the time of this writing was in March 1996. The Ada95 standard of the Ada language is covered in this release. The Ada for Linux package comes in the following files:

- `gnat-3.03-src.tar.gz`
- `gnat-3.03-i486-linux-elf-bin.tar.gz`
- `gnat-3.01-linuxaout.tar.gz`
- `gnat-3.01-linuxaout.README`

For more information, you can contact the support folks via e-mail at `gnat-request@cs.nyu.edu`. The FTP site at `tsx-11.mit.edu` has the latest information and release of this software in the directory `/pub/linux/packages/Ada`.

FORTRAN

The FORTRAN programming language is also ported to Linux. Only versions up to FORTRAN 77 have been ported over. There are only commercial ports of FORTRAN 90 as of this publication. The package in the `tsx-11.mit.edu` archives under the `/pub/linux/packages/fortran` directory contains the following files:

- `ftnchek-2.7.lsm`
- `ftnchek-2.7.tgz`
- `libf2c-0.9.lsm`
- `libf2c-0.9.tar.gz`
- `mpfun-1.0.lsm`
- `mpfun-1.0.tar.gz`
- `toolpack-1.2.lsm`
- `toolpack-1.2.tar.gz`

For a more up-to-date description of the files, check the INDEX file in the same directory as the above files. The `libf2c-0.9.tar.gz` contains the functions for converting FORTRAN code to C. Actually, the program `f2c` does a pretty decent job on all my class assignments at the university. The output is not idiot-proof, but it does the major portion of the job of translation.

The `toolpack` files are tools for FORTRAN programmers. Functions include printing aids for clean output listings and some sort of lint checker. Tools in this package include those for portability testing and dynamic programming analysis. All the script files in the toolpack are written for the C shell, so you will need to have the `tcsh` program installed on your system.

You will use at least 5–10MB of your disk space depending on which package you install.

The `mpfun` package is a multiple precision (FORTRAN MP) library and translator. This package performs multiprecision floating-point arithmetic with up to 16 million decimal digits, using advanced, recent algorithms and automatic translation from FORTRAN 77 code to FORTRAN multiprocessor code. The translation is done via directives within comment fields.

Digital Signal Processing

The ObjectProDSP package is an X Window system, object-oriented tool for Digital Signal Processing design development and implementation. The package contains the basics for building interactive scientific and engineering applications. The package was developed by Paul P. Budnik, Jr. (mtnmath@mtnmath.com). The amount of disk space required is about 5MB. You can get it from `tsx-11.mit.edu` archives in the `/pub/linux/packages/dsp` directory.

Modula-3

The Modula-3 language is available from Digital Equipment Corporation's research center SRC. Modula-3 is an object-oriented language designed for multiprocess, distributed application development. Modula-3 resembles Pascal in many ways but is more suited for building large applications.

The key features of the Modula-3 package include a full-blown GUI interface, runtime typing, support for multithreaded applications, garbage collection, and exception handling. The garbage collection and storage reallocation features of the language are of keen interest to object-oriented programmers. After all, what frees an object—the portion of the code that created it, or the portion to which the object was passed? The garbage collector for removing a large number of these problems is built into the language.

Modula-3 uses threads to process its incoming messages. Unlike other X-based applications, where one event queue has to be managed between several listening applications, Modula-3 allows the invocation of threads to perform message handling. A good example of the usage of this feature is the Trestle package—the interface package to X. With Trestle you can create threads to run in the background while you're doing other processing.

You can get Modula-3 from the Internet from the FTP site at: `tsx-11.mit.edu` in the `/pub/linux/packages/modula-3` directory.

OGI

The OGI Speech Tools version 1.0.1 for Linux are speech data manipulation research tools. These tools are primarily used for signal manipulation, phonetic, phonemic, and word analysis. This package has the capability to build audio databases that can be used to train neural networks, with a neural network trainer (NN) also in the package. The OGI speech tools were developed at the Center for Spoken Language Understanding (CSLU-OGI). You can get more information about them from `tools@cse.ogi.edu`.

The FTP site for this package is `sunsite.unc.edu` in the file `/pub/Linux/apps/sound/ogi-speech.tar.gz` or in `tsx-11.mit.edu` in the directory `/pub/linux/packages/ogi`.

You need some sort of sound card that is capable of digitizing sound under Linux. A good package for digitizing sound would be the Sox package.

If you are into computational linguistics, or are interested in speech compression, recognition, or applications of neural networks, this is one great research package to check out. The documentation in this package consists of man pages, and TeX source. Check `ogi-doc-PS.tar.gz` for TeX documentation in PostScript format. For the document in DVI format, try using the file `ogi-doc-dvi.tar.gz`.

Eiffel

Eiffel is a nonproprietary object-oriented language developed by Dr. Bertrand Meyer and his colleagues. An excellent reference book for Eiffel is Dr. Meyer's Book *Object-Oriented Software Construction*, Prentice Hall, 1988. In 1994, Dr. Meyer's company ported Eiffel to Linux.

The most advertised feature of Eiffel is its capability to reuse code without modifications. In conventional C++ and some other object-oriented languages, code reuse is still in its infancy. Eiffel is a new language primarily written with reuse in mind. Polymorphism, garbage collection, dynamic binding, multiple inheritance, and templates are built into the language. Even so, Eiffel code is interoperable with C and C++.

The design of Eiffel has been placed in the public domain. The Eiffel trademark is owned by the Nonprofit International Consortium for Eiffel (NICE). You should really have no fear using this trademark because NICE is quite nice about using the Eiffel trademark. The official language description is *Eiffel: The Language*, by Dr. Meyers, Prentice Hall, 1992. The formal syntax is included in the 600-plus page book along with examples, source code, and application guidelines.

Tower Technologies Corporation is promoting its commercial release of Eiffel, called TowerEiffel. Visit the web site at `http://www.twr.com`. This site is a bit slow to get access to at times.

COBOL

Though not the preferred choice of "real" systems programmers, COBOL is a very widely used language in the business community. Naturally, there are ports to Linux in this database-oriented language. A good commercial port worth looking into is the ACUCOBOL-85 port by the Acucobol, Inc., company. Check the Web site at `http://www.acucobol.com` for more information about COBOL.

The ACUCOBOL-85 version of COBOL offers programmable hot keys, advanced windows capabilities (not X), its own file system, and a source = level debugger. Acucobol, Inc., also offers more than 600 tools to work with the Linux compiler. The COBOL code on Linux is portable to other platforms running COBOL-85.

LISP

LISP stands for LISt Processing. LISP was developed around 1958 and has been used in all areas of computer science research (for example, in artificial intelligence), as well as being the basis for products, such as `emacs` and AutoCAD. (Actually, AutoCAD uses AutoLISP, an enhanced version of LISP.)

The Common LISP language interpreter and compiler (`clisp`) package is in the Red Hat Linux distribution. As the name suggests, the package contains both an interpreter and a compiler for generating machine-executable code. Invoked without arguments, `clisp` executes a `read-eval-print` loop, in which expressions are read from standard input, evaluated by the LISP interpreter, and their results output to standard output. When invoked with the -c option, the specified LISP files are compiled to a machine-readable code that can be executed more efficiently.

To get more information about the clisp package, type clisp -h at the prompt. If you are short of RAM on your machine, specify the amount of memory that clisp will use with the -m *XXX*K option, where *XXX* is the amount of memory to use in kilobytes. The clisp package has support for three languages: English, German, and French.

If you are an emacs user, you will want to use the -I option to make clisp ILISP compatible. ILISP is the LISP interface for the emacs editor.

The language implemented conforms to the book by Guy L. Steele Jr., *Common LISP—The Language*, Digital Press, First edition, 1984.

Scheme

Another language closely related to LISP is the Scheme language. A Scheme programmer has at his or her disposal the power of C and LISP. Scheme allows free data-typing of variables by offering lists, arrays of lists, associative lists, and arrays, in addition to the numeric and string data types.

Scheme, like clisp, is available in compiled or interpreted form. You can create output files from Scheme using two of three types of options: fast, cheap, and algorithmically correct. The fast option produces a large executable, the "correct" version has more error checking, and the cheap version produces a smaller, though (maybe) slower version of the program.

The interpreted environment produces a rapid development front end because there is no edit-compile-run cycle. You simply edit what you have changed and reexecute, just like in LISP.

Several versions of Scheme are available on various sites on the Internet:

▨ bigloo-bin.tar.gz:	The Bigloo version, which is the de facto standard for Scheme
▨ bigloo-ELF-bin.tar.gz:	The ELF version of the Bigloo version
▨ scheme2c-bin.tar.gz:	The Scheme to C converter libraries for converting Scheme code to C code
▨ scm-bin.tar.gz and slib.tar.gz:	The SCM package by Aubrey Jaffer (jaffer@ai.mit.edu) contains sockets, I/O, POSIX interfaces, and a curses screen-management library
▨ stk-bin.tar.gz:	The Tk compatible library

Summary

The number of languages and software packages available for Linux continues to grow with Linux's popularity. This chapter has given you a snapshot of some of the languages available for Linux. Time and space have limited us to introducing in detail only a few of the more common languages, such as Fortran, LISP, Scheme and so on. There are, however, many more languages which may be ideal for your project. It might be worth your while to check out some of these languages and get that ideal fit.

Motif for Programmers

This chapter will cover the following topics:

- The basics of writing Motif applications for Linux
- Special naming conventions in Motif and X
- Writing and compiling your first Motif application
- Revisiting the widget hierarchy
- Using labels and strings in Motif
- Using various common widgets
- Designing layout
- Using menus
- Dialog boxes
- Event handling and other sources of input
- Colors in X
- Drawing lines, points, arcs, and polygons

A question you might be asking is "Why include a topic on a development system that you have to pay for when just about everything for Linux is free?" Well, if you want to develop any applications for the Common Desktop Environment (CDE), you should know how to program Motif applications. Linux is a mature enough system to enable you this luxury of building portable applications. (Plus, the $150 or so (U.S.) you pay for the Motif license will well pay for itself if you can do the work at home on your Linux system rather than commuting!)

Writing Motif Applications

This chapter introduces you to writing Motif applications. The information here will not be limited to writing applications for Linux alone, because the concepts in this chapter can be applied to other UNIX systems as well.

In programming Motif applications, you have to get used to programming in an event-driven environment. A typical C application runs from start to finish at its own pace. When it needs information, the application looks for this information from a source such as a file or the keyboard and (almost always) gets the information as soon as it asks for it. If the information is not available when the application asks for it, the application either waits for it or displays an error message. Also, the order of the incoming data is important for such applications; pieces of data that are out of sequence may cause the application to behave strangely.

In the case of event-driven programming, an application must wait for events on an input queue. The queue orders all incoming events in the order they are received. The first message to come in from one end of a queue is the first one to leave the queue. (Such queues are often called *FIFOs*, for First In, First Out.) An *event* can be anything from a mouse click, key button, or other event such as a timeout notification.

Because events can come in at any time, and in no predefined order, they are referred to as asynchronous events. That is, the order and time of arrival of each event is not deterministic. The application must wait for an event to occur and then proceed based on that event. Thus the term *event-driven programming.*

In the case of X Window, each X Window application has one input queue for all of its incoming events. The application must wait for events on this input queue. Similarly, a server waits for an event from a client and then responds based on the type of event received. This event handling and other aspects of X programming are handled by a toolkit called XtIntrinsics, or Xt for short.

In Xt, an application will typically run in a loop forever. This loop is called an *event loop.* An application enters the loop by calling a function XtAppMainLoop(). While in this event loop, an application will always wait for an event, When the application receives an event, the application handles the event itself or almost always "dispatches" the event to a window or *Widget.*

A Widget registers functions that it wants called when a type of event is received. This function is called a *callback* function. In most cases, a callback function is independent of the entire application. For example, some Widgets will redraw themselves when a pointer button is clicked in their display area. In this case, they would register a redraw callback function on a button click.

Xt also supports *actions*, which enable applications to register a function with Xt. An action is called when one or more sequences of specific event types are received. For example, pressing Ctrl-X would call the exit function. The mapping of the action to an event is handled via a translation table within Xt. Functions that handle specific events are referred to as *event handlers.*

Look at Figure 32.1 to see how the toolkit exists with Motif. As you can see from the connections in the figure, an application can get to the core Xlib functions through three means: via Motif, via the Xt library, or directly. This flexible hierarchy gives you many options when developing Motif applications because you are at liberty to take full advantage of all functions in all three libraries.

FIGURE 32.1.

The toolkit hierarchy for X, Xt, Motif.

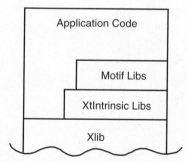

Naming Conventions

By default, most Xlib functions begin with the letter X, but you should not always rely on this being true for all functions. Several macros and functions in the X Window system do not begin with X. For example, BlackColor and WhiteColor are not macros. In general, though, if a name in

Xlib begins with X, it's probably a function. If a name begins with a capital letter (A through Z), it's a macro.

With Xt, the naming conventions get better, but only slightly. In Xt, macros are not differentiated from functions in any way.

> **TIP**
>
> Do not rely on the name of a toolkit function to give you information about whether it's a macro. Read the manual to be absolutely sure.

In Motif, almost all declarations begin with Xm. Therefore, XmC refers to a class, XmR refers to a resource, XmN refers to a name, and XtN refers to Xt resources used by Motif. Declarations ending with the words WidgetClass define the base class for a type of Widget. A few conventions to remember about parameters for most Xlib functions are

- Width always to the left of height
- X always to the left of y
- Source always to the left of destination
- Display usually is the first parameter

With practice, you will be able to identify the type of parameters to pass and which toolkit a function belongs to, and be able to make some educated guesses as to what parameters an unknown function might expect.

Writing Your First Motif Application

Let's look at the basic format for a Motif application, shown in Listing 32.1. (I added line numbers for your benefit.) I will discuss this application in detail. You will build other Motif applications based on the structure in this particular application as you progress through this chapter.

> **NOTE**
>
> The line numbers are for reference only.

Listing 32.1. A sample Motif application.

```
1      /*
2      ** This is a typical Motif application with one button that
3      ** exits it.
4      */

5      #include <X11/Intrinsic.h>
```

```
 6       #include <Xm/Xm.h>
 7       #include <Xm/Form.h>
 8       #include <Xm/PushB.h>
 9       void  bye(Widget w, XtPointer clientdata, XtPointer calldata);
10       int main(int  argc, char **argv)
11       {
12       Widget top;
13       XtAppContext app;
14       Widget aForm;
15       Widget aButton;
16       Arg   args[5];

17       /**
18       *** Initialize the toolkit.
19       **/
20       top = XtAppInitialize(&app, "KBH", NULL, 0, (Cardinal *)&argc,
21                   argv, NULL, args, 0);

22       /**
23       *** Create a Form on this top level Widget. This is a nice Widget
24       *** to place other Widgets on top of.
25       **/
26       aForm = XtVaCreateManagedWidget("Form1",
27             xmFormWidgetClass, top,
28             XmNheight,90,
29             XmNwidth,200,
30             NULL);

31       /**
32       *** Add a button on the form you just created. Note how this Button
33       *** Widget is connected to the form that it resides on. Only
34       *** left, right, and bottom edges are attached to the form. The
35       *** top edge of the button is not connected to the form.
36       **/
37       aButton = XtVaCreateManagedWidget("Push to Exit",
38             xmPushButtonWidgetClass, aForm,
39             XmNheight,20,
40             XmNleftAttachment,XmATTACH_FORM,
41             XmNrightAttachment,XmATTACH_FORM,
42             XmNbottomAttachment,XmATTACH_FORM,
43             NULL);

44       /**
45       *** Call the function "bye" when the PushButton receives
46       *** an activate message; i.e. when the pointer is moved to
47       *** the button and Button1 is pressed and released.
48       **/
49       XtAddCallback( aButton, XmNactivateCallback,
50          bye, (XtPointer) NULL);
51       XtRealizeWidget(top);
52       XtAppMainLoop(app);
53       return(0);
54       }

55       void  bye(Widget w, XtPointer clientdata, XtPointer calldata)
56       {
57       exit(0);
58       }
```

The listing shows an application in which a button attaches itself to the bottom of a form. See Figure 32.2.

FIGURE 32.2.

The output of
`l32_1.c`.

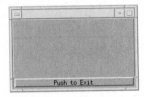

No matter how you resize the window, the button will always be on the bottom. The application does the following things in the order listed:

1. Initializes the toolkit to get a shell Widget.
2. Makes a Form Widget.
3. Manages all Widgets as they are created.
4. Makes the Button Widget on top of the Form Widget.
5. Attaches a callback function to the button.
6. Realizes the Widget (that is, makes the hierarchy visible).
7. Goes into its event loop.

Let's look at the application in more detail. The `include` files in the beginning of the listing are required for most applications. Notably, the two files shown in lines 5 and 6 are required for just about any Motif application you'll ever write.

```
#include <X11/Intrinsic.h>
#include <Xm/Xm.h>
```

These two lines declare the definitions for `XtIntrinsics` and Motif, respectively. In some systems, you may not require the first inclusion, but it's harmless to put it in there because multiple inclusions of `Intrinsic.h` are permitted. In addition, each Motif Widget requires its own header file. In Listing 32.1, the Widgets Form and PushButton are included via statements in lines 7 and 8:

```
#include <Xm/Form.h>
#include <Xm/PushB.h>
```

The variables in the program are declared in lines 12 through 16:

```
Widget top;
XtAppContext app;
Widget aForm;
Widget aButton;
int    n;
```

The `top`, `aForm`, and `aButton` represent Widgets. Even though their functions are different, they can all be referred to as Widgets.

The `XtAppContext` type is an *opaque* type, which means that a Motif programmer does not have to be concerned about how the type is set up. Widgets are opaque types as well; only the items that are required for the programmer are visible.

The first executable line of the program calls the `XtAppInitialize()` function (in line 20) to initialize the `Xt` toolkit and create an application shell and context for the rest of the application. This value is returned to the Widget *top* (for top-level shell). This Widget will provide the interface between the window manager and the rest of the Widgets in this application.

The application then creates a Form Widget on this top-level Widget. A *form widget* is used to place other Widgets on top of itself. It is a *manager widget* because it "manages" other Widgets.

There are two steps required for displaying a Widget: First you have to *manage* (with `XtVaCreateManagedWidget`) it and then you have to *realize* (with `RealizeWidget`) it.

Managing a Widget enables it to be visible. If a Widget is unmanaged, it will never be visible. By managing a Widget, the program gives the viewing control over to the windowing system to enable it to display it. Any child Widgets remain invisible, even if they are managed, if the parent Widget is unmanaged.

Realizing a Widget actually creates all the subwindows under an application and displays them. Normally only the top-level Widget is realized after all the Widgets are managed. This call will realize all the children of this Widget.

Note that realizing a Widget takes time. A typical program will manage all the Widgets except the topmost one. This way the application will only have to realize the topmost Widget when the entire tree has to display only the topmost parent. You have to realize a Widget at least once, but you can manage and "unmanage" Widgets as you want to display or hide them.

You can always create and manage a Widget to call `XtCreate` and `XtManageChild` in two separate calls. However, the samples in this chapter will use a single call to create and manage a Widget: `XtVaCreateManagedWidget`.

Note the parameters in this call to create the Form Widget shown in lines 26 through 30:

```
aForm = XtVaCreateManagedWidget("Form1",
          xmFormWidgetClass, top,
          XmNheight,90,
          XmNwidth,200,
          NULL);
```

The first parameter is the name of the new Widget. The second parameter describes the class of the Widget being created. Recall that this is simply the Widget name sandwiched between `xm` and `WidgetClass`. So, in this case, it is `xmFormWidgetClass`. Note the lowercase x for the class pointer. This class pointer is declared in the header files included at the beginning of the file, `Form.h`.

TIP

As another example, the class pointer for a Label would be called `xmLabelWidgetClass` and would require the `Label.h` file. Motif programmers have to be especially wary of the case of all variables.

The next argument is the parent Widget of this new Widget. In this case, `top` is the parent of `Form1`. The `top` Widget is returned from the call to `XtAppInitialize`.

The remaining arguments specify the parameters of this Widget. In this case you are setting the width and height of the Widget. This list is terminated by a `NULL` parameter.

After the form is created, a button is placed on top of it. A Form Widget facilitates placement of other Widgets on top of it. In this application you will cause the button to "attach" itself to the bottom of the form. The following three lines (40–42) attach themselves to the form:

```
XmNleftAttachment,XmATTACH_FORM,
XmNrightAttachment,XmATTACH_FORM,
XmNbottomAttachment,XmATTACH_FORM,
```

The class of this button is included in the `PushB.h` file and is called `xmPushButtonWidgetClass`. The name of this Widget is also the string that is displayed on the face of the button. Note that the parent of this button is the `aForm` Widget. The hierarchy is as follows:

```
top -> is the parent of aForm -> is the parent of -> aButton.
```

The next step is to add a callback function when the button is pressed. This is done with the call to `XtAddCallback`, as shown in the following:

```
XtAddCallback( aButton, XmNactivateCallback, bye, (XtPointer) NULL);
```

Here are the parameters for this call:

- `aButton` is the PushButton Widget.
- `XmNactivateCallback` is the action that will trigger a call to this function.
- `bye` is the name of the function that will be called when the action is triggered. (You should declare this function before making this function call, or you will get a compiler error.)
- `NULL` is a pointer. This pointer could point to some structure meaningful to function `bye`.

This will register the callback function `bye` for the Widget. Now the topmost Widget, `top`, is realized. This causes all managed Widgets below `top` to be realized. The application then goes into a loop that processes all incoming events.

The `bye` function of this program simply exits the application.

Compiling This Application

Now comes the tough part of compiling this application into a working application. You will use the gcc compiler that comes with Linux for this purpose.

First, check the location of the libraries in your system. Check the /usr/lib/X11 directory for the following libraries: libXm.a, libXt.a, and libX11.a. If possible, use the shared library versions of these libraries with .so extensions followed by some numbers. The advantage of using shared libraries is a smaller Motif application; a typical application like the one you've been working on can be up to 1MB in size because of Motif's overhead.

The disadvantage of shared libraries is that your end user may not have the correct version of the library in his path. This does annoy some end users, especially if no fast method of acquiring this resource is available. Also, shipping a shared library with your application may cause you to pay some licensing fees to the original library vendor. From a programmer's perspective, shared libraries are sometimes impossible to use with your debugger. Of course, if your debugger supports them, use it. Check your compiler documentation. In most cases, if you intend to use shared libraries, use the static versions to do your debugging and testing, and then compile the shared version. Always check your vendor's licensing agreement for details on how to ship shared libraries.

The application can be compiled with this command:

```
gcc 132_1.c -o list1 -lXm -lXt -lX11 -I/usr/x11/include -L/usr/x11/lib
```

The program can be run from a command line if you create a script file:

```
$ cat mk
gcc $1.c -o $1 -lXm -lXt -lX11 -I/usr/x11/include -L/usr/x11/lib
```

and pass it just the filename without the extension. The best way is to create a makefile, but this script file will work with the examples in this text. So, to compile 132_1.c, you would use the script as follows:

```
$ mk 132_1
```

You should see the output in Figure 32.2 on your screen. Your application is the one with 132_1 in its frame.

The Widget Hierarchy

The Motif Widget set is a hierarchy of Widget types. (See Figure 32.3.) Any resources provided by a Widget are inherited by all its derived classes. Consider the three most important base classes: Core, XmPrimitive, and XmManager.

FIGURE 32.3.
The partial Motif hierarchy.

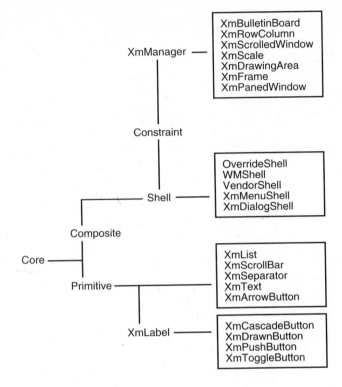

Core

The Core Widget class provides the basis for all classes. It provides at least the following resources for all Widgets:

XmNx,XmNy: A Widget's position on the display.

XmNheight, XmNwidth: A Widget's size.

XmNborderWidth: Set to 1 by default.

XmNsensitive: A Boolean resource that specifies whether this Widget can receive input.

XmNcolorMap: The default color map.

XmNbackground: The background color.

Check the Motif Programmer's reference manual for a complete listing.

XmPrimitive

The XmPrimitive Widget class inherits all the resources from Core and adds more functionality.

XmNforeground: The foreground color.

XmNhighlightOnEnter: Changes color when the pointer is within a displayed area of Widget.

XmNhighlightThickness: If XmNhighlightOnEnter is TRUE, changes the border to this thickness.

XmNhighlightColor: The color it changes to when highlighted.

XmNshadowThickness: This is the thickness to show the pseudo-three-dimensional look for which Motif is famous. The default value is 2.

XmNtopShadowColor and XmNbottomShadowColor: Sets the color for top and bottom lines around a Widget.

XmNuserData: A pointer available for the programmer's use.

The XmPrimitive Widget also provides the XmNdestroyCallback resource. This can be set to a function that would do clean-up when a Widget is destroyed. In Motif 1.2.*x* or later, the XmPrimitive class also provides a XmNhelpCallback that is called when the F1 key is pressed in the Widget's window. This is to allow specific help information for a button, for example.

XmManager

The XmManager class provides support for all Motif Widgets that contain other Widgets. This is never used directly in an application, and it works in a manner similar to the XmPrimitive class. It provides the following resources:

XmNforeground: The color of the pixels in the foreground.

XmNshadowThickness: For the three-dimensional effect.

XmNtopShadowColor: For the three-dimensional effect. This is automatically defaulted to a color derived from the background color. This color is used on the left and top borders of a Widget.

XmNbottomShadowColor: For the three-dimensional effect. This is automatically defaulted to a color derived from the background color. This color is used on the right and bottom borders of a Widget.

XmNuserData: For storing user data. Could be used as a void pointer.

The Label Widget

The Label Widget is used to display strings or pixmaps. Include the Xm/Label.h file in your source file before using this Widget. Some of the resources for this Widget include the following:

XmNalignment: Determines the alignment of the text in this Widget. The acceptable values are XmALIGNNMENT_END, XmALIGNMENT_CENTER, and XmALIGNEMENT_BEGIN for right, center, and left justification, respectively.

XmNrecomputeSize: A Boolean resource. If set to TRUE, the Widget will resize should the size of the string or pixmap change dynamically. This is the default. If set to FALSE, the Widget will not attempt to resize itself.

XmNlabelType: The default value of this type is XmSTRING to show strings. However, it can also be set to XmPIXMAP when displaying a pixmap specified in the XmNpixmap resource.

XmNlabelPixmap: This is used to specify which pixmap to use when the XmNlabelType is set to XmPIXMAP.

XmNlabelString: This is used to specify which XmString compound string to use for the label. This defaults to the name of the label. See the section, "Strings in Motif: Compound Strings."

To get acquainted with left and right justification on a label, see Listing 32.2. The listing also shows how the resources can be set to change Widget parameters programmatically and via the .Xresource files.

Listing 32.2. How to use a Label Widget.

```
/*
** This application shows how to use a Label Widget.
*/

#include <X11/Intrinsic.h>
#include <Xm/Xm.h>
#include <Xm/Form.h>
#include <Xm/PushB.h>
#include <Xm/Label.h>    /** <---- for the label **/


void  bye(Widget w, XtPointer clientdata, XtPointer calldata);

int main(int  argc, char **argv)
{
Widget top;
XtAppContext app;
Widget aForm;
Widget aLabel;             /** <---- for the label ***/
Widget aButton;
Arg    args[5];

/**
*** Initialize the toolkit.
**/
top = XtAppInitialize(&app, "KBH", NULL, 0, (Cardinal *)&argc,
           argv, NULL, args, 0);

/**
*** Create a Form on this top-level Widget. This is a nice Widget
*** to place other Widgets on top of.
**/
aForm = XtVaCreateManagedWidget("Form1",
      xmFormWidgetClass, top,
      XmNheight,90,
      XmNwidth,200,
      NULL);

/**
*** Add a button on the form you just created. Note how this Button
*** Widget is connected to the form that it resides on. Only
```

```
*** left, right, and bottom edges are attached to the form. The
*** top edge of the button is not connected to the form.
**/
aButton = XtVaCreateManagedWidget("Push to Exit",
     xmPushButtonWidgetClass, aForm,
     XmNheight,20,
     XmNleftAttachment,XmATTACH_FORM,
     XmNrightAttachment,XmATTACH_FORM,
     XmNbottomAttachment,XmATTACH_FORM,
     NULL);

/**
*** Now let's create the label for us.
*** The alignment is set to right-justify the label.
*** Note how the label is attached to the parent form.
**/

aLabel = XtVaCreateManagedWidget("This is a right justified Label",
     xmLabelWidgetClass, aForm,
     XmNalignment, XmALIGNMENT_END,
     XmNleftAttachment,XmATTACH_FORM,
     XmNrightAttachment,XmATTACH_FORM,
     XmNtopAttachment,XmATTACH_FORM,
     NULL);

/**
*** Call the function "bye" when the PushButton receives
*** an activate message; i.e. when the pointer is moved to
*** the button and Button1 is pressed and released.
**/
XtAddCallback( aButton, XmNactivateCallback, bye, (XtPointer) NULL);
XtRealizeWidget(top);
XtAppMainLoop(app);
return(0);
}

void  bye(Widget w, XtPointer clientdata, XtPointer calldata)
{
exit(0);
}
```

Output is shown in Figure 32.4.

FIGURE 32.4.

Using the Label Widget.

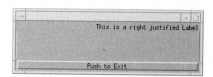

Avoid using the \n in the label name. If you have to create a multistring Widget, use the
XmStringCreate calls to create a compound string (see the next section). Another way to set the
string is by specifying it in the resource file and then merging the resources.

The listing shows the Label to be right-justified. You could easily center the string horizontally by not specifying the alignment at all and letting it default to the center value. Alternatively, try setting the alignment parameter to `XmALIGNMENT_BEGINNING` for a left-justified label.

Strings in Motif: Compound Strings

A compound string is Motif's way of representing a string. In a typical C program, a NULL-terminated string is enough to specify a string. In Motif, a string is also defined by the character set it uses. Strings in Motif are referred to as *compound strings* and are kept in opaque data structures called `XmString`.

In order to get a compound string from a regular C string, use this function call:

```
XmString XmStringCreate( char *text, char *tag);
```

This function will return an equivalent compound string given a pointer to a NULL-terminated C string and a tag. The tag specifies which fontlist to use and is defaulted to `XmFONTLIST_DEFAULT_TAG`.

New lines in C strings have to be handled by special separators in Motif. So to create a string and preserve the newlines, use the call

```
XmString XmStringCreateLtoR( char *text, char *tag);
```

The compound strings have to be created and destroyed just like any other object. They persist long after that function call that created them returns. Therefore, it's a good idea to free all locally used `XmStrings` in a function before returning, or else all references to the strings will be lost. The definition of a call to free `XmString` resources is

```
XmStringFree( XmString s);
```

You can run similar operations on strings as you would in a C program, except that these string operations are called by different names. Use the function

```
Boolean XmStringByteCompare( XmString s1, XmString s2);
```

for a strict byte-for-byte comparison, and for a just the text comparison, use

```
Boolean XmStringCompare( XmString s1, XmString s2);
```

To check if a string is empty, use

```
Boolean XmStringEmpty( XmString s1);
```

To string two strings together, use

```
XmString XmStringConcat( XmString s1, XmString s2);
```

`XmString Concat()` creates a new string by concatenating s2 to s1 and returns it. This returned string has to be freed just like s1 and s2.

If you want to use `sprintf`, use it on a temporary buffer and then create a new string. For example:

```
char str[32];
XmString xms;
......
sprintf(str," pi = %lf, Area = %lf", PI, TWOPI*r);
xms = XmStringCreateLtoR( str, XmFONTLIST_DEFAULT_TAG);
......
n = 0;
XtSetArg(arg[n],XmNlabelString,xms); n++;
XtSetValues(someLabel, arg, n);
XmStringFree(xms);
```

If a string value becomes corrupted without your performing any direct actions on it, check to see whether the Widget is not making a copy for its use of the passed `XmString`. Sometimes a Widget might be keeping only a pointer to the `XmString`. If that string were freed, the Widget might wind up pointing to bad data.

One good way to check is to set an `XmString` resource, then use the `XtGetValues` function to get the same resource from the Widget. If the values of the `XmStrings` are the same, the Widget is not making a copy for itself. If they are not the same, it is safe to free the original because the Widget is making a local copy. The default course of action is to assume that a Widget makes a copy of such resources for itself.

A similar test could be used to determine whether a Widget returns a copy of its resource or to a pointer to it. Use the same listing shown previously, but this time use a `getValue` to get the same resource twice. Then do the comparison to see whether the address for the original string matches the address of the returned value from `getValue()`: If the values match, the Widget keeps a pointer. If the values do not match, the Widget keeps an internal copy.

```
/**
*** This is a sample partial listing of how to check if the
*** data returned on an XtGetValues and an XtSetValues
*** call is a copy or a reference.
***/

#include "Xm/Text.h"
..
Widget w;
XmString x1, x2, x3;

x3 = XmStringCreateLtoR("test", XmFONTLIST_DEFAULT_TAG);
XmTextSetString(w,x3);
...
x1 = XmTextGetString(w);
x2 = XmTextGetString(w);

XtWarning(" Checking SetValues");
if (x1 != x3)
     XtWarning("Widget keeps a copy ! Free original!");
else
     XtWarning("Widget does not keep a copy! Do NOT free original");
```

```
XtWarning(" Checking GetValues");
if (x1 == x2)
      XtWarning("Widget returns a copy! Do NOT free");
else
      XtWarning("Widget does not return a copy! You should free it ");
```

The XtWarning() message is especially useful for debugging the progress of programs. The message is relayed to the stderr of the invoking application. If this is an xterm, you will see an error message on that terminal window. If no stderr is available for the invoke mechanism, the message is lost.

TIP

The XtSetArg macro is defined as

```
#define XtSetArg(arg,n,d) \
((void)((arg).name = (n).(arg).value = (XtArgVal)(d)))
```

Do *not* use XtSetArg(arg[n++]... as this will increment n twice.

The *XmPushButton* Widget Class

The XmPushButton is perhaps the most heavily used Widget in Motif. Listings 32.1 and 32.2 show the basic usage for PushButton. When a button is pressed in the PushButton area, the button goes into an *armed state* (a state between not pressed and going to pressed). The color of the button changes to reflect this state, and you can set this color by using XmNarmColor. This color is shown when the XmNfillOnArm resource is set to TRUE.

TIP

If the armColor for a PushButton does not seem to be working, try setting the XmNfillOnArm resource to TRUE.

The callback functions for a PushButton are the following:

> XmNarmCallback: Called when a PushButton is armed.

> XmNactivateCallback: Called when a button is released in the Widgets area while the Widget is armed. This is not invoked if the pointer is outside the Widget when the button is released.

> XmNdisarmCallback: Called when a button is released with the pointer outside the Widget area while the Widget was armed.

If a callback has more than one function registered for a Widget, all of the functions will be called, but not necessarily in the order they were registered. Also, do not rely on the same order being preserved on other systems. If you want more than one function performed during a callback, sandwich them in one function call.

In Listing 32.2, you saw how a callback function was added to a PushButton with the `XtAddCallback` function. The same method can be used to call other functions for other actions such as the `XmNdisarmCallback`.

The *XmToggleButton* Widget Class

This class is a subclass of the `XmLabel` Widget class. You can have two types of buttons: one of many or *n* of many. When using *one of many*, the user can make only one selection from many items. (See Figure 32.5.) When using *n of many*, the user can select many options. (See Figure 32.6.) Note the way the buttons are drawn, with one of many shown as diamonds and *n* of many shown as boxes.

FIGURE 32.5.

One of many toggle buttons.

FIGURE 32.6.

Using n *of many toggle buttons.*

The resources for this Widget include the following:

`XmNindicatorType`: Determines the style. Can be set to `XmN_OF_MANY` or `XmONE_OF_MANY` (the default).

`XmNspacing`: The number of pixels between the button and its label.

`XmNfillOnSelect`: The color of the button changes to reflect a set when the `XmNfillOnArm` resource is set to TRUE.

XmNfillColor: The color to show when set.

XmNset: A Boolean resource indicating whether the button is set or not. If this resource is set from a program, the button will automatically reflect the change.

It's easier to use the convenience functions:

XmToggleButtonGetState(Widget w)

to get the Boolean state for a Widget, and to use

XmToggleButtonSetState(Widget w, Boolean b)

to set the value for a ToggleButton Widget.

Similar to the PushButton class, the ToggleButton class has three callbacks:

XmNarmCallback: Called when the ToggleButton is armed.

XmNvalueChangedCallback: Called when a button is released in the Widgets area while the Widget is armed. This is not invoked if the pointer is outside the Widget when the button is released.

XmNdisarmCallback: Called when a button is released with the pointer outside the Widget area while the Widget was armed.

For the callbacks, the data passed into the Callback function is a structure of type:

```
typedef struct {
    int     reason;
    Xevent      *event;
    int     set;
} XmToggleButtonCallbackStruct;
```

The reason for the callback is one of the following events: XmCR_ARM, XmCR_DISARM, or XmCR_ACTIVATE. The event is a pointer to XEvent, which caused this callback. The set value is 0 if the item is not set, or nonzero if set. Look at Listing 32.3, which shows the use of ToggleButton. The ToggleButtons are arranged in one column via the RowColumn Widget, discussed later in this chapter.

Listing 32.3. Using ToggleButton in Motif.

```
/*
** This is a typical Motif application that demonstrates the use of
** a ToggleButton Widget(s) stored on a RowColumn Widget.
*/

#include <X11/Intrinsic.h>
#include <Xm/Xm.h>
#include <Xm/Form.h>
#include <Xm/ToggleB.h>
#include <Xm/RowColumn.h>
```

```
#include <Xm/PushB.h>


void  bye(Widget w, XtPointer clientdata, XtPointer calldata);

#define MAX_BTNS 4

int main(int  argc, char **argv)
{
Widget top;
XtAppContext app;
Widget aForm;
Widget aButton;
Widget aRowCol;
char  str[32];
Widget      aToggle[MAX_BTNS];
Arg         args[5];
int   i;

/**
*** Initialize the toolkit.
**/
top = XtAppInitialize(&app, "KBH", NULL, 0, (Cardinal *)&argc,
            argv, NULL, args, 0);

/**
*** Create a Form on this top-level Widget. This is a nice Widget
*** to place other Widgets on top of.
**/
aForm = XtVaCreateManagedWidget("Form1",
      xmFormWidgetClass, top,
      XmNheight,150,
      XmNwidth,100,
      NULL);



/**
*** Add a button on the form you just created. Note how this Button
*** Widget is connected to the form that it resides on. Only
*** left, right, and bottom edges are attached to the form. The
*** top edge of the button is not connected to the form.
**/
aButton = XtVaCreateManagedWidget("Push to Exit",
      xmPushButtonWidgetClass, aForm,
      XmNheight,20,
      XmNleftAttachment,XmATTACH_FORM,
      XmNrightAttachment,XmATTACH_FORM,
      XmNbottomAttachment,XmATTACH_FORM,
      NULL);

#define DO_RADIO
/**
*** A quick intro to the hierarchy in Motif.
*** Let's create a RowColumn Widget to place all ToggleButtons.
```

continues

Listing 32.3. continued

```
*** Note how the RowColumn button attaches itself to
*** the top of the button.
**/
aRowCol = XtVaCreateManagedWidget("rowcol",
      xmRowColumnWidgetClass, aForm,
#ifdef DO_RADIO
      XmNradioBehavior, TRUE,
      XmNradioAlwaysOne, TRUE,
#endif
      XmNleftAttachment,XmATTACH_FORM,
      XmNrightAttachment,XmATTACH_FORM,
      XmNtopAttachment,XmATTACH_FORM,
      XmNbottomAttachment,XmATTACH_WIDGET,
      NULL);
/**
*** Make ToggleButtons on this form called RowCol. Attach them all to the
*** RowColumn Widget on top of the form.
***
*** Note the radioBehavior setting
**/

for (i=0; i< MAX_BTNS; i++)
     {
     sprintf(str,"Button %d",i);
     aToggle[i] = XtVaCreateManagedWidget(str,
          xmToggleButtonWidgetClass, aRowCol,
          XmNradioBehavior, TRUE,
          NULL);
     }

XmToggleButtonSetState(aToggle[0],TRUE, FALSE);
/**
*** Call the function "bye" when the PushButton receives
*** an activate message; i.e. when the pointer is moved to
*** the button and Button1 is pressed and released.
**/
XtAddCallback( aButton, XmNactivateCallback, bye, (XtPointer) NULL);
XtRealizeWidget(top);
XtAppMainLoop(app);
return(0);
}

void  bye(Widget w, XtPointer clientdata, XtPointer calldata)
{
exit(0);
}
```

See Figure 32.6, shown previously, for the output of this listing with the #define DO_RADIO line commented out. By defining the DO_RADIO label, you can make this into a Radio Button application. That is, only one of the buttons can be selected at one time. See Figure 32.5, shown previously, for the radio behavior of these buttons.

Convenience Functions

Usually the way to set resources for a Widget is at the time of the Widget's creation. This is done either with the XtVaCreateManagedWidget call or with the XmCreateYYY call, where YYY is the name of the Widget you are creating.

This test uses the variable argument call to create and manage Widgets. I do it simply because it's easier for me to see what resources I am setting and create them all in one function call. You might have a personal preference to do it in two steps. Either way is fine. Keep in mind, though, that if you do use the XmCreateYYY call, you have to set the resource settings in a list of resource sets. Listing 32.4 is an example of creating a Label Widget. This is a function that creates a Label Widget on a Widget given the string x.

Listing 32.4. Sample convenience function for creating a Label on a form.

```
/**
*** This is a sample convenience function to create a label
*** Widget on a parent. The string must be a compound string.
**/
Widget makeLabel( Widget onThis, XmString x)
{
Widget   lbl;
Cardinal n;
Arg      arg[5];

n = 0;
XtSetArg(arg[n], XmNalignment, XmALIGNMENT_BEGIN); n++;
XtSetArg(arg[n], XmNlabelString, x); n++;
lbl = XmCreateLabel("A Label", onThis, arg, n);
XtManageChild(lbl);
return(lbl);
}
```

Or you could use the variable argument lists in creating this Label, as shown in Listing 32.5.

Listing 32.5. Creating a label.

```
/**
*** Another way of making a label on a parent.
**/
Widget makeLabel( Widget onThis, XmString x)
{
Widget   lbl;
lbl = XmCreateManagedWidget("A Label",
      xmLabelWidgetClass, onThis,
      XmNalignment, XmALIGNMENT_BEGIN,
      XmNlabelString, x,
      NULL);

return(lbl);
}
```

In either case, it's your judgment call as to which one to use. The variable list method of creating is a bit easier to read and maintain. But what about setting values after a Widget has been created? This would be done via a call to `XtSetValue` with a list and count of resource settings. For example, to change the alignment and text of a Label, you would use

```
n = 0;
XtSetArg(arg[n], XmNalignment, XmALIGNMENT_BEGIN); n++;
XtSetArg(arg[n], XmNlabelString, x); n++;
XtSetValues(lbl,arg,n);
```

Similarly, to get the values for a Widget, you would use `XtGetValues`:

```
Cardinal n; /* usually an integer or short... use Cardinal to be safe */
int align;
XmString x;
...
n = 0;
XtSetArg(arg[n], XmNalignment, &align); n++;
XtSetArg(arg[n], XmNlabelString, &x); n++;
XtGetValues(lbl,arg,n);
```

In the case of other Widgets, let's use the Text Widget. This setting scheme is hard to read, quite clumsy, and prone to typos. For example, when you get a string for a Text Widget, should you use x or address of x?

For this reason, Motif provides convenience functions. For example, in the ToggleButton Widget class, rather than using the combination of `XtSetValue` and `XtSetArg` calls to get the state, you would use one call, `XmToggleButtonGetState(Widget w)`, to get the state. These functions are valuable code savers when writing complex applications. In fact, you should write similar convenience functions whenever you can't find one that suits your needs.

The List Widget

This displays a list of items from which the user selects. The list is created from a list of compound strings. Users can select either one or many items from this list. The resources for this Widget include the following:

> `XmNitemCount`: Determines the number of items in the list.
>
> `XmNitems`: An array of compound strings. Each entry corresponds to an item in the list. Note that a List Widget makes a copy for all items in its list when using `XtSetValues`; however, it returns a pointer to its internal structure when returning values to a `XtGetValues` call. Therefore, do *not* free this pointer from `XtGetValues`.
>
> `XmNselectedItemCount`: The number of items currently selected.
>
> `XmNselectedItems`: The list of selected items.
>
> `XmNvisibleItemCount`: The number of items to display at one time.
>
> `XmNselectionPolicy`: Used to set single or multiple selection capability. If set to `XmSINGLE_SELECT`, the user will be able to only select one item. Each selection will invoke the `XmNsingleSelectionCallback`. Selecting one item will deselect a previously selected

item. If set to XmEXTENDED_SELECT, the user will be able to select a block of contiguous items in a list. Selecting a new item or more will deselect another previously selected item and will invoke the XmNmultipleSelection callback. If set to XmMULTIPLE_SELECT, the user will be able to select multiple items in any order. Selecting one item will not deselect another previously selected item but will invoke the XmNmultipleSelection callback. If set to XmBROWSE_SELECT, the user can move the pointer (with the button pressed) across all the selections, but only one item will be selected. Unlike the XmSINGLE_SELECT setting, the user does not have to press and release the button on an item to select it. The XmbrowseSelectionCallback will be invoked when the button is finally released on the last item browsed.

It is easier to create the List Widget with a call to XmCreateScrolledList() because this will automatically create a scrolled window for you. However, scrolled windows may prove to be slow when compared to XtSetValues() calls. If you feel that speed is important, consider using XtSetValues(). You should create the list for the first time by using XtSetValues.

The following convenience functions will make working with List Widgets easier.

> XmListAddItem(Widget w, XmString x, int pos)
> This will add the compound string x to the List Widget w at the one relative position pos. If pos is 0, the item is added to the back of the list. This function is very slow, so do not use it to create a newlist, because it rearranges the entire list before returning.

> XmListAddItems(Widget w, XmString *x, int count, int pos);
> This will add the array of compound strings x of size count to the List Widget w from the position pos. If pos is 0, the item is added to the back of the list. This function is slow, too, so do not use it to create a newlist.

> XmDeleteAllItems(Widget w)
> This will delete all the items in a list. It's better to write a convenience function to do
> n = 0; XtSetArg(arg[n], XmNitems, NULL); n++; XtSetArg(arg[n], XmNitemCount, 0); n++; XtSetValues(mylist,arg,n);

> XmDeleteItem(Widget w, XmString x)
> Deletes the item x from the list. This is a slow function.

> XmDeleteItems(Widget w, XmString *x, int count)
> Deletes all the count items in x from the list. This is an even slower function. You might be better off installing a new list.

> XmListSelectItem(Widget w, XmString x, Boolean Notify)
> Programmatically selects x in the list. If Notify is True, the appropriate callback function is also invoked.

> XmListDeselectItem(Widget w, XmString x)
> Programmatically deselects x in the list.

> XmListPos(Widget w, XmString x)
> Returns the position of x in the list. Returns 0 if not found.

Let's use the List Widget for a sample application. See Listing 32.6.

Listing 32.6. Using List Widgets.

```
/*
** This is a typical Motif application for using a list Widget
*/

#include <X11/Intrinsic.h>
#include <Xm/Xm.h>
#include <Xm/Form.h>
#include <Xm/PushB.h>

#include <Xm/List.h>     /*** for the list Widget ***/
#include <Xm/ScrolledW.h> /*** for the scrolled window Widget ***/

/*** Some items for the list ***/
#define NUMITEMS 8
char *groceries[NUMITEMS] = {
     "milk",
     "eggs",
     "bread",
     "pasta",
     "cd-rom",    /** I don't go out often!**/
     "bananas",
     "yogurt",
     "oranges",
     };
/* For the list Widget, we need compound strings */
XmString xarray[NUMITEMS];

#define USE_SCROLL

void  bye(Widget w, XtPointer clientdata, XtPointer calldata);

int main(int   argc, char **argv)
{
Widget top;
XtAppContext app;
Widget aForm;
Widget aList;
Widget aButton;
Arg    args[15];
int    i;

/**
*** Initialize the toolkit.
**/
top = XtAppInitialize(&app, "KBH", NULL, 0, (Cardinal *)&argc,
          argv, NULL, args, 0);

/**
*** Create a Form on this top-level Widget. This is a nice Widget
*** to place other Widgets on top of.
**/
aForm = XtVaCreateManagedWidget("Form1",
     xmFormWidgetClass, top,
```

```
        XmNheight,90,
        XmNwidth,200,
        NULL);

/**
*** Add a button on the form you just created. Note how this Button
*** Widget is connected to the form that it resides on. Only
*** left, right, and bottom edges are attached to the form. The
*** top edge of the button is not connected to the form.
**/
aButton = XtVaCreateManagedWidget("Push to Exit",
        xmPushButtonWidgetClass, aForm,
        XmNheight,20,
        XmNleftAttachment,XmATTACH_FORM,
        XmNrightAttachment,XmATTACH_FORM,
        XmNbottomAttachment,XmATTACH_FORM,
        NULL);
/**
*** Now create a list of items for this Widget.
**/
for (i=0; i < NUMITEMS; i++)
        xarray[i] = XmStringCreateLtoR(groceries[i],
                    XmSTRING_DEFAULT_CHARSET);

#ifndef USE_SCROLL
/**
*** Then create the list Widget itself. Note this will not
*** put up a scroll bar for you.
**/
aList = XtVaCreateManagedWidget("Push to Exit",
        xmListWidgetClass, aForm,
        XmNitemCount, NUMITEMS,
        XmNitems, xarray,
        XmNvisibleItemCount, 4,
        XmNscrollBarDisplayPolicy, XmAS_NEEDED,
        XmNleftAttachment,XmATTACH_FORM,
        XmNrightAttachment,XmATTACH_FORM,
        XmNtopAttachment,XmATTACH_FORM,
        XmNbottomAttachment,XmATTACH_WIDGET,
        XmNbottomWidget,aButton,
        NULL);

#else
/**
*** Alternatively, use the scrolled window with the following code:
**/
 i = 0;
 XtSetArg(args[i], XmNitemCount, NUMITEMS); i++;
 XtSetArg(args[i], XmNitems, xarray); i++;
 XtSetArg(args[i], XmNvisibleItemCount, 4); i++;
 XtSetArg(args[i], XmNscrollBarDisplayPolicy, XmAS_NEEDED); i++;
 XtSetArg(args[i], XmNleftAttachment,XmATTACH_FORM); i++;
 XtSetArg(args[i], XmNrightAttachment,XmATTACH_FORM); i++;
 XtSetArg(args[i], XmNtopAttachment,XmATTACH_FORM); i++;
 XtSetArg(args[i], XmNbottomAttachment,XmATTACH_WIDGET); i++;
```

continues

Listing 32.6. continued

```
XtSetArg(args[i], XmNbottomWidget,aButton); i++;
aList =  XmCreateScrolledList(aForm,"groceryList",args,i);
XtManageChild(aList);
#endif

/**
*** Call the function "bye" when the PushButton receives
*** an activate message; i.e. when the pointer is moved to
*** the button and Button1 is pressed and released.
**/
XtAddCallback( aButton, XmNactivateCallback, bye, (XtPointer) NULL);
XtRealizeWidget(top);
XtAppMainLoop(app);
return(0);
}

void  bye(Widget w, XtPointer clientdata, XtPointer calldata)
{
exit(0);
}
```

The output is shown in Figure 32.7.

FIGURE 32.7.

Using the List Widget.

XmScrollBar

The ScrollBar Widget enables the user to select a value from a range. Its resources include the following:

XmNvalue: The value representing the location of the slider.

XmNminimum and XmNmaximum: The range of values for the slider.

XmNshowArrows: Boolean value if set shows arrows at either end.

XmNorientation: Set to XmHORIZONTAL for a horizontal bar or XmVERTICAL (default) for a vertical bar.

XmNprocessingDirection: Set to either XmMAX_ON_LEFT or XmMAX_ON_RIGHT for XmHORIZONTAL orientation, or XmMAX_ON_TOP or XmMAX_ON_BOTTOM for XmVERTICAL orientation.

XmNincrement: The increment per move.

XmNpageIncrement: The increment if a button is pressed in the arrows or the box. This is defaulted to 10.

XmNdecimalPoint: Shows the decimal point from the right.

Note that all values in the ScrollBar Widget's values are given as integers. Look at the radio station selection example in Listing 32.7. A point to note in this listing is that the exit button for the application is offset on the left and right by 20 pixels. This is done via the XmATTACH_FORM value for each side (left or right) being offset by the value in XmNleftOffset and XmNrightOffset, respectively. See Listing 32.3 on how to attach items to a Form.

Listing 32.7. Using the Scale Widget.

```
/*
** An application to show the radio station selection via a scale.
*/

#include <X11/Intrinsic.h>
#include <Xm/Xm.h>
#include <Xm/Form.h>
#include <Xm/PushB.h>
#include <Xm/Scale.h>


#define MAX_SCALE 1080
#define MIN_SCALE 800
void  bye(Widget w, XtPointer clientdata, XtPointer calldata);
void myfunction(Widget w, XtPointer dclient,  XmScaleCallbackStruct *p);

int main(int  argc, char **argv)
{
Widget top;
XtAppContext app;
Widget aForm;
Widget aScale;
Widget aButton;
XmString xstr; /* for the scale title */
Arg   args[5];

/**
*** Initialize the toolkit.
**/
top = XtAppInitialize(&app, "ScaleMe", NULL, 0, (Cardinal *)&argc,
          argv, NULL, args, 0);

/**
*** Create a Form on this top-level Widget. This is a nice Widget
*** to place other Widgets on top of.
**/
aForm = XtVaCreateManagedWidget("Form1",
    xmFormWidgetClass, top,
```

continues

Listing 32.7. continued

```
        XmNheight,90,
        XmNwidth,240,
        NULL);

/**
*** Add a button on the form you just created. Note how this Button
*** Widget is connected to the form that it resides on. Only
*** left, right, and bottom edges are attached to the form. The
*** top edge of the button is not connected to the form.
**/
aButton = XtVaCreateManagedWidget("Push to Exit",
        xmPushButtonWidgetClass, aForm,
        XmNheight,20,
        XmNleftAttachment,XmATTACH_FORM,
        XmNleftOffset,20,
        XmNrightAttachment,XmATTACH_FORM,
        XmNrightOffset,20,
        XmNbottomAttachment,XmATTACH_FORM,
        NULL);
/**
***    Create the radio FM selection scale here.
***    Note that since we have to work with integers,
***    we have to set the frequency scale to 10x actual
***    value and then set the decimal point explicitly
***    for the display. No provision is made for selecting
***    odd frequencies.
**/

xstr = XmStringCreateLtoR("Radio Stations", XmSTRING_DEFAULT_CHARSET);
aScale =  XtVaCreateManagedWidget("sample it",
        xmScaleWidgetClass, aForm,
        XmNheight,40,
        XmNminimum, 800,
        XmNvalue, 1011,
        XmNmaximum, 1080,
        XmNdecimalPoints,1,
        XmNtitleString,xstr,
        XmNshowValue,TRUE,
        XmNorientation,XmHORIZONTAL,
        XmNprocessingDirection,XmMAX_ON_RIGHT,
        XmNleftAttachment,XmATTACH_FORM,
        XmNrightAttachment,XmATTACH_FORM,
        XmNtopAttachment,XmATTACH_FORM,
        XmNbottomAttachment,XmATTACH_WIDGET,
        XmNbottomAttachment,aButton,
        NULL);
XmStringFree(xstr);


/**
*** Call the function "bye" when the PushButton receives
*** an activate message; i.e. when the pointer is moved to
*** the button and Button1 is pressed and released.
**/
XtAddCallback( aButton, XmNactivateCallback, bye, (XtPointer) NULL);
XtAddCallback( aScale, XmNvalueChangedCallback, myfunction, (XtPointer) NULL);
```

```
XtRealizeWidget(top);
XtAppMainLoop(app);
return(0);
}

void  bye(Widget w, XtPointer clientdata, XtPointer calldata)
{
exit(0);
}

void myfunction(Widget w, XtPointer dclient,  XmScaleCallbackStruct *p)
{
int k;

k = p->value;
if ((k & 0x1) == 0)  /** % 2  is zero ** check limits and increase **/
     {
     k++;
     if (k >= MAX_SCALE) k = MIN_SCALE + 1;
     if (k <= MIN_SCALE) k = MAX_SCALE - 1;
     XmScaleSetValue(w,k);  /** this will redisplay it too **/
     }
}
```

In the case of FM selections, you would want the bar to show odd numbers. A good exercise for you would be to allow only odd numbers in the selection. Hint: Use `XmNvalueChangedCallback` as follows:

```
XtAddCallback(aScale, XmNvalueChangedCallback, myfunction);
```

Output is shown in Figure 32.8.

FIGURE 32.8.

Using the Scale Widget.

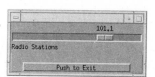

The callback sends a pointer to the structure of type `XmScaleCallbackStruct` to a function called `myfunction`. A sample function, `myfunction()`, follows:

```
/**
*** Partial listing for not allowing even numbers for FM selection.
**/
#define MAX_SCALE 1080
#define MIN_SCALE 800
static void myfunction(Widget w, XtPointer dclient,  XmScaleCallbackStruct *p)
{
int k;

k = p->value;
```

```
if ((k & 0x1) == 0)  /** % 2  is zero ** check limits and increase **/
    {
    k++;
    if (k >= MAX_SCALE) k = MIN_SCALE + 1;
    if (k <= MIN_SCALE) k = MAX_SCALE - 1;
    XmScaleSetValue(w,k);  /** this will redisplay it too **/
    }
}
```

Text Widgets

This Widget enables the user to type in text and provides full text-editing capabilities. This text could be multiline or single-line. If you are sure you want only single-line input from the user, you can specify the TextField Widget. This is simply a scaled-down version of the Text Widget. The resources for both are the same unless explicitly stated. They include the following:

XmNvalue: A character string, just like in C. This is different from Motif 1.1 or older, in which this value used to be a compound string. If you have Motif 1.2 or later, this will be C string.

XmNmarginHeight and XmNmarginWidth: The number of pixels on either side of the Widget. The default is five pixels.

XmNmaxLength: Sets the limit on the number of characters in the XmNvalue resource.

XmNcolumns: The number of characters per line.

XmNcursorPosition: The number of characters at the cursor position from the beginning of the text file.

XmNeditable: Boolean value. If set to TRUE, enables the user to insert text.

The callbacks for this Widget are

XmNactivateCallback: Called when the user presses the Enter key.

XmNfocusCallback: Called when the Widget receives focus from the pointer.

XmNlosingFocusCallback: Called when the Widget loses focus from the pointer.

This Widget has several convenience functions:

XmTextGetString(Widget w) returns a C string (char *).

XmTextSetString(Widget w, char *s) sets a string for a Widget.

XmTextSetEditable(Widget w, Boolean TRUEOrFALSE) sets the Widget's editable string.

XmTextInsert(Widget w, XmTextPosition pos, char *s) sets the text at the position defined by pos. This XmTextPosition is an opaque item defining the index in the text array.

XmTextShowPosition(Widget w, XmTextPosition p) scrolls to show the rest of the string at position p.

`XmTextReplace(Widget w, XmTextPosition from, XmTextPosition to, char *s)` replaces the string starting from the location `from` inclusive to the position `to`, inclusive with the characters in string `s`.

`XmTextRemove(Widget w)` clears the text in a string.

`XmTextCopy(Widget w, Time t)` copies the currently selected text to the Motif clipboard. The `Time t` value is derived from the most recent `XEvent` (usually in a callback), which is used by the clipboard to take the most recent entry.

`XmTextCut(Widget w, Time t)` is similar to `XmTextCopy` but removes the selected text from the text's buffer.

`XmTextPaste(Widget w)` pastes the contents of the Motif clipboard onto the text area at the current cursor (insertion) position.

`XmTextClearSelection(Widget w, XmTextPosition p, XmTextPosition q, Time t)` selects the text from location p to location q.

In the following example, you could construct a sample editor application using the Text Widget. For the layout of the buttons, you would want to use Widgets of the `XmManager` class to manage the layout for you rather than having to do it in your own application. These Manager Widgets are

```
XmBulletinBoard
XmRowColumn
XmForm
```

XmBulletinBoard Widgets

The `BulletinBoard` class enables the programmer to lay out Widgets by specifying their `XmNx` and `XmNy` resources. These values are relative to the top-left corner of the `BulletinBoard` Widget. The `BulletinBoard` will not move its child Widgets around by itself. If a Widget resizes, it's the application's responsibility to resize and restructure its Widgets on the bulletin board.

The resources for the Widget are as follows:

`XmNshadowType`: Specifies the type of shadow for this Widget. It can be set to `XmSHADOW_OUT` (the default), `XmSHADOW_ETCHED_IN`, `XmSHADOW_ETCHED_OUT`, or `XmSHADOW_IN`.

`XmNshadowThickness`: The number of pixels for the shadow. This is defaulted to 0 to not see a shadow.

`XmNallowOverlap`: Enables the children to be overlapped as they are laid on the Widget. This is a Boolean resource and is defaulted to TRUE.

`XmNresizePolicy`: Specifies the resize policy for managing itself. If set to `XmRESIZE_NONE`, it will not change its size. If set to `XmRESIZE_ANY`, the default, it will grow or shrink to attempt to accommodate all of its children automatically. If set to `XmRESIZE_GROW`, it will grow only, never shrink, automatically.

`XmNbuttonFontList`: Specifies the font for all `XmPushButton` children.

XmNlabelFontList: Specifies the default font for all Widgets derived from XmLabel.

XmNtextFontList: Specifies the default font for all Text, TextField, and XmList children.

It also provides the callback XmNfocusCallback, which is called when any children of the BulletinBoard receive focus.

XmRowColumn Widgets

The XmRowColumn Widget class orders its children in a row-and-column (or row major) fashion. This is used to set up menus, menu bars, and radio buttons. The resources provided by this Widget include the following:

XmNorientation: XmHORIZONTAL for a row major layout of its children; XmVERTICAL for a column major layout.

XmNnumColumns: Specifies the number of rows for a vertical Widget and the number of columns for a horizontal Widget.

XmNpacking: Determines how the children are packed. XmPACK_TIGHT enables the children to specify their own size. It fits children in a row (or column if XmHORIZONTAL) and then starts a new row if no space is available. XmPACK_NONE forces BulletinBoard-like behavior. XmPACK_COLUMN forces all children to be the size of the largest child Widget. This uses the XmNnumColumns resource and places all of its children in an organized manner.

XmNentryAlignment: Specifies which part of the children to use in its layout alignment. Its default is XmALIGNMENT_CENTER, but it can be set to XmALIGNMENT_BEGINNING for left or XmALIGNMENT_END for right side. This is on a per-column basis.

XmNverticalEntryAlignment: Specifies the alignment on a per-row basis. It can be assigned a value of XmALIGNMENT_BASELINE_BOTTOM, XmALIGNMENT_BASELINE_TOP, XmALIGNMENT_CONTENTS_BOTTOM, XmALIGNMENT_CONTENTS_TOP, or XmALIGNMENT_CENTER.

XmNentryBorder: The thickness of a border drawn around all children. Defaulted to 0.

XmNresizeWidth: A Boolean variable. If set to TRUE, will enable the RowColumn Widget to resize its width when necessary.

XmNresizeHeight: A Boolean variable. If set to TRUE, will enable the RowColumn Widget to resize its height when necessary.

XmNradioBehaviour: Works with ToggleButtons only. It enables only one ToggleButton of a group of buttons to be active at time. The default is FALSE.

XmNisHomogeneous: If set to TRUE, specifies that only children of the type of class in XmNentryClass can be children of this Widget. The default is FALSE.

XmNentryClass: Specifies the class of children allowed in this Widget if XmNisHomogeneous is TRUE.

A sample radio button application was shown in Listing 32.5. To see another example of the same listing but with two columns, see Listing 32.8.

Listing 32.8. Using RowColumn Widgets.

```
/*
** This is another Motif application that demonstrates the use of
** a ToggleButton Widget(s) stored on a multicolumn RowColumn Widget.
*/

#include <X11/Intrinsic.h>
#include <Xm/Xm.h>
#include <Xm/Form.h>
#include <Xm/ToggleB.h>
#include <Xm/RowColumn.h>
#include <Xm/PushB.h>


void  bye(Widget w, XtPointer clientdata, XtPointer calldata);

#define MAX_BTNS 8
#define NUM_COL  2

int main(int  argc, char **argv)
{
Widget top;
XtAppContext app;
Widget aForm;
Widget aButton;
Widget aRowCol;
char   str[32];
Widget      aToggle[MAX_BTNS];
Arg         args[5];
int    i;

/**
*** Initialize the toolkit.
**/
top = XtAppInitialize(&app, "KBH", NULL, 0, (Cardinal *)&argc,
          argv, NULL, args, 0);

/**
*** Create a Form on this top-level Widget. This is a nice Widget
*** to place other Widgets on top of.
**/
aForm = XtVaCreateManagedWidget("Form1",
     xmFormWidgetClass, top,
     XmNheight,150,
     XmNwidth,200,
NULL);


/**
*** Add a button on the form you just created. Note how this Button
*** Widget is connected to the form that it resides on. Only
*** left, right, and bottom edges are attached to the form. The
*** top edge of the button is not connected to the form.
**/
```

continues

Listing 32.8. continued

```
aButton = XtVaCreateManagedWidget("Push to Exit",
      xmPushButtonWidgetClass, aForm,
      XmNheight,20,
      XmNleftAttachment,XmATTACH_FORM,
      XmNrightAttachment,XmATTACH_FORM,
      XmNbottomAttachment,XmATTACH_FORM,
      NULL);

#define DO_RADIO
/**
*** A quick intro to the hierarchy in Motif.
*** Let's create a RowColumn Widget to place all Toggle
*** Buttons.
*** Note how the RowColumn button attaches itself to
*** the top of the button.
**/
aRowCol = XtVaCreateManagedWidget("rowcol",
      xmRowColumnWidgetClass, aForm,
#ifdef DO_RADIO
      XmNradioBehavior, TRUE,
      XmNradioAlwaysOne, TRUE,
#endif
      XmNnumColumns,NUM_COL,
      XmNleftAttachment,XmATTACH_FORM,
      XmNrightAttachment,XmATTACH_FORM,
      XmNtopAttachment,XmATTACH_FORM,
      XmNbottomAttachment,XmATTACH_WIDGET,
      NULL);
/**
*** Make ToggleButtons on this form called RowCol. Attach them all
*** RowColumn Widget on top of the form.
***
*** Note the radioBehavior setting
**/

for (i=0; i< MAX_BTNS; i++)
      {
      sprintf(str,"Button %d",i);
      aToggle[i] = XtVaCreateManagedWidget(str,
            xmToggleButtonWidgetClass, aRowCol,
            XmNradioBehavior, TRUE,
            NULL);
      }

XmToggleButtonSetState(aToggle[0],True, False);
/**
*** Call the function "bye" when the PushButton receives
*** an activate message; i.e. when the pointer is moved to
*** the button and Button1 is pressed and released.
**/
XtAddCallback( aButton, XmNactivateCallback, bye, (XtPointer) NULL);
XtRealizeWidget(top);
XtAppMainLoop(app);
return(0);
}
```

```
void  bye(Widget w, XtPointer clientdata, XtPointer calldata)
{
exit(0);
}
```

See Figure 32.9.

FIGURE 32.9.

Using the RowColumn Widget.

XmForm Widgets

The beginning of this chapter introduced you to the workings of a Form Widget. This is the most flexible, but complex, Widget in Motif.

Its resources include

■ XmNtopAttachment

■ XmNleftAttachment

■ XmNrightAttachment

■ XmNbottomAttachment

These values specify how a child is assigned in position. The following values correspond to each of the sides of the Widget:

XmATTACH_NONE: Does not attach this side to Form.

XmATTACH_FORM: Attaches to the corresponding side on Form.

XmATTACH_WIDGET: Attaches this side to the opposite side of a reference Widget—for example, the right side of this Widget to the left side of the reference Widget. A reference Widget is another child on the same form.

XmATTACH_OPPOSITE_WIDGET: Attaches this side to the same side of a reference Widget. This is rarely used.

XmATTACH_POSITION: Attaches a side by the number of pixels shown in XmNtopPosition, XmNleftPosition, XmNrightPosition, and XmNbottomPosition resources, respectively.

XmATTACH_SELF: Uses the XmNx,XmNy,XmNheight, and XmNwidth resources.

■ XmNtopWidget

■ XmNleftWidget

■ `XmNrightWidget`

■ `XmNbottomWidget`

These resources are set to the corresponding Widgets for each side for the `XmATTACH_WIDGET` setting in an attachment.

■ `XmNtopOffset`

■ `XmNleftOffset`

■ `XmNrightOffset`

■ `XmNbottomOffset`

These resources are the number of pixels a side of a child is offset from the corresponding Form side. The offset is used when the attachment is `XmATTACH_FORM`.

> **TIP**
>
> Sometimes it's hard to get the settings for a Form Widget just right, or the Form Widget doesn't lay out the Widgets in what seems to be the proper setting for a child Widget. In these cases, try to manage and lay out the children in ascending or descending order from the origin of the Form Widget. That is, create the top-left Widget first and use it as an anchor to create the next child, then the next one to its right, and so on. There is no guarantee that this will work, so try from the bottom right, bottom left, or top right for your anchor positions.
>
> If this technique doesn't work, try using two forms on top of the form with which you are working. Forms are cheap; your time is not. It's better to just make a form when two or more Widgets have to reside in a specific layout.

While trying a new layout on a Form Widget, if you get error messages about failing after 10,000 iterations, you have conflicting layout requests to a child or children Widgets. Check the attachments very carefully before proceeding. This error message results from the Form Widget trying different layout schemes to accommodate your request.

> **TIP**
>
> At times, conflicting requests to a Form will cause your application to slow down while it's trying to accommodate your request, not show the form, or both. At this time, try to remove your Form settings one at a time until the errors disappear. You should then be able to weed out the offending resource setting for that Form.

Designing Layouts

When designing layouts, think about the layout before you start writing code. Let's try an order entry example. See Listing 32.9.

Listing 32.9. Setting up a simple hierarchy.

```
/*
** This listing shows how to set up a hierarchy.
*/

#include <X11/Intrinsic.h>
#include <Xm/Xm.h>
#include <Xm/Form.h>
#include <Xm/PushB.h>
#include <Xm/Label.h>
#include <Xm/Text.h>
#include <Xm/RowColumn.h>

/*** Some items for the list ***/
#define NUMITEMS 4

char *thisLabel[NUMITEMS] = { "Name", "User Id", "Home", "Usage" };
/* For the list Widget, we need compound strings */
XmString xarray[NUMITEMS];

#define USE_SCROLL

void  bye(Widget w, XtPointer clientdata, XtPointer calldata);

int main(int  argc, char **argv)
{
Widget top;
XtAppContext app;
Widget masterForm;
Widget buttonForm;
Widget labelForm;
Widget inputForm;
Widget labelRC;
Widget textRC;
Widget buttonRC;
Widget inputText[NUMITEMS];
Widget inputLabel[NUMITEMS];
Widget searchBtn;
Widget cancelBtn;
Arg    args[15];
int    i;

/**
*** Initialize the toolkit.
**/
top = XtAppInitialize(&app, "KBH", NULL, 0, (Cardinal *)&argc,
          argv, NULL, args, 0);
```

continues

Listing 32.9. continued

```
/**
*** Create a Form on this top-level Widget. This is a nice Widget
*** to place other Widgets on top of.
**/
masterForm = XtVaCreateManagedWidget("MasterForm",
      xmFormWidgetClass, top,
      XmNheight,150,
      XmNwidth,200,
      NULL);

buttonForm = XtVaCreateManagedWidget("ButtonForm",
      xmFormWidgetClass, masterForm,
      XmNtopAttachment,XmATTACH_POSITION,
      XmNtopPosition, 75,
      XmNheight,30,
      XmNbottomAttachment,XmATTACH_FORM,
      XmNleftAttachment,XmATTACH_FORM,
      XmNrightAttachment,XmATTACH_FORM,
      NULL);

labelForm = XtVaCreateManagedWidget("LabelForm",
      xmFormWidgetClass, masterForm,
      XmNtopAttachment,XmATTACH_FORM,
      XmNbottomAttachment,XmATTACH_POSITION,
      XmNbottomPosition, 75,
      XmNleftAttachment,XmATTACH_FORM,
      XmNrightAttachment,XmATTACH_POSITION,
      XmNrightPosition,50,
      NULL);

inputForm = XtVaCreateManagedWidget("InputForm",
      xmFormWidgetClass, masterForm,
      XmNtopAttachment,XmATTACH_FORM,
      XmNbottomAttachment,XmATTACH_POSITION,
      XmNbottomPosition, 75,
      XmNrightAttachment,XmATTACH_FORM,
      XmNleftAttachment,XmATTACH_POSITION,
      XmNleftPosition,50,
      NULL);

/**
*** Now create the RowColumn manager Widgets
**/

buttonRC = XtVaCreateManagedWidget("buttonRC",
      xmRowColumnWidgetClass, buttonForm,
      XmNbottomAttachment,XmATTACH_FORM,
      XmNtopAttachment,XmATTACH_FORM,
      XmNleftAttachment,XmATTACH_FORM,
      XmNrightAttachment,XmATTACH_FORM,
      XmNorientation, XmHORIZONTAL,
      NULL);
```

```
labelRC = XtVaCreateManagedWidget("buttonRC",
        xmRowColumnWidgetClass, labelForm,
        XmNbottomAttachment,XmATTACH_FORM,
        XmNtopAttachment,XmATTACH_FORM,
        XmNleftAttachment,XmATTACH_FORM,
        XmNrightAttachment,XmATTACH_FORM,
        XmNorientation, XmVERTICAL,
        NULL);

textRC = XtVaCreateManagedWidget("buttonRC",
        xmRowColumnWidgetClass, inputForm,
        XmNbottomAttachment,XmATTACH_FORM,
        XmNtopAttachment,XmATTACH_FORM,
        XmNleftAttachment,XmATTACH_FORM,
        XmNrightAttachment,XmATTACH_FORM,
        XmNorientation, XmVERTICAL,
        NULL);

for (i = 0; i < NUMITEMS; i++)
        {
        inputLabel[i] = XtVaCreateManagedWidget(thisLabel[i],
            xmLabelWidgetClass, labelRC,  NULL);
        inputText[i] = XtVaCreateManagedWidget(thisLabel[i],
            xmTextWidgetClass, textRC,  NULL);
        }

searchBtn = XtVaCreateManagedWidget("Search",
            xmPushButtonWidgetClass, buttonRC,  NULL);
cancelBtn = XtVaCreateManagedWidget("Cancel",
            xmPushButtonWidgetClass, buttonRC,  NULL);

XtAddCallback( cancelBtn, XmNactivateCallback, bye, (XtPointer) NULL);

/** Add the handler to search here. **/
XtRealizeWidget(top);
XtAppMainLoop(app);
return(0);
}

void  bye(Widget w, XtPointer clientdata, XtPointer calldata)
{
exit(0);
}
```

The output of this application is shown in Figure 32.10. Notice how the labels do not line up with the Text Widget. There is a problem in the hierarchy of the setup. See the hierarchy of the application in Figure 32.11.

FIGURE 32.10.
The output of Listing 32.9.

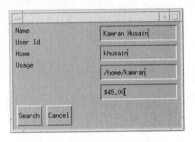

FIGURE 32.11.
The hierarchy of Listing 32.9.

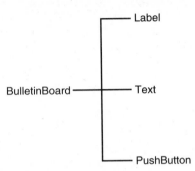

The Form Widgets are created to maintain the relative placements of all of the Widgets that correspond to a type of functionality. The RowColumn Widgets allow the placement of items on themselves. The best route to take in this example would be to lay one text and one label on one RowColumn Widget and have three RowColumn Widgets in all, one for each instance up to NUM_ITEMS. This will ensure that each label lines up with its corresponding text Widget.

Here are a few points to note about laying out applications:

- Think about what the form or dialog is trying to achieve. Draw it on paper if you have to. Coding is the easy part; determining what to do is much harder.

- Be consistent. Users will love you for it. If Alt-X is a shortcut for Exit in one screen, do not make it a Cut operator in another. Keep controls on the same side of all dialogs and forms. Use separators to separate different functions on the same window.

- Choose a color scheme for your end users. What may be cool to you may be grotesque to the end user. They may not even be using a color monitor in some rare cases. A combination of white, gray, and black may be your best bet in this case if you do not want to deal with different color schemes in your code.

- Colors on your monitor may not be the same on the end user's monitor.

- Do not assume that the user has the same resolution monitor as yourself. Keep fonts clean, and buttons big enough for a large cursor. Allow windows to be resized as much as possible to enable users to customize their desktops.

- Assume nothing. If the user can size your window to an unworkable size, either limit the size in the resize callback to the lowest size or do not allow sizing at all.

- Offer some help for the user. In the future, Help will be required as a standard option on menu bars, so plan ahead.

- Avoid clutter. Too many options and entries on one huge form tend to confuse and baffle the user. Consider a two-or-more-tiered approach via dialogs. Default everything as much as possible.

- Allow the program to be more forgiving. Sometimes an "Are you sure?" dialog with an option to change a list of parameters can be endearing to the user. On the other hand, some users hate this type of checking.

Menus

Designing a Widget hierarchy is especially important when working with Motif menus. Motif menus are a collection of Widgets, so there is no "menu" Widget for a menu. You create menus using a hierarchy of different types of Widgets: RowColumn, PushButton, CascadeButton, ToggleButton, Label, and Separator.

There are three kinds of menus in Motif:

- Pop-up: This appears as a list of items when a pointer button is pressed on a Widget.
- Pull-down: This appears when a button on an existing menu is pressed.
- Option: This enables the user to select from a list of options with the current selection visible at all times.

The procedure to create a menu is different for each type of menu.

Pop-Up Menus

To create a pop-up menu, follow these steps:

1. Include the correct header files. You will need the header files for the menu:

   ```
   Label.h
   RowColumn.h
   PushB.h
   Separator.h
   BulletinB.h
   CascadeB.h
   ```

2. Create the menu pane with a call to XmCreatePopupMenu. This is a convenience call to create RowColumn and MenuShell Widgets with the proper settings.

3. Create the buttons on the menu pane. Use XmPushbuttons, XmToggleButtons, XmSeparator, and XmCascadeButtons.

4. Attach callback functions to the Widgets.

Listing 32.10 shows how to set up a simple pop-up menu.

Listing 32.10. Using pop-up menus.

```c
/*
** This listing shows how to set up a pop-up menu.
** Use the left mouse button on the area below the label.
*/

#include <X11/Intrinsic.h>
#include <Xm/Xm.h>
#include <Xm/BulletinB.h>
#include <Xm/PushB.h>
#include <Xm/Label.h>
#include <Xm/Text.h>
#include <Xm/RowColumn.h>
#include <Xm/CascadeB.h>
#include <Xm/Separator.h>

void  showSelection(Widget w, XtPointer clientdata, XtPointer calldata);
XtEventHandler  showMenu(Widget w, XtPointer menu, XEvent *x, Boolean f);

/*** Some items for the list ***/
#define NUMITEMS 3

char *thisLabel[NUMITEMS] = { "CD", "Developer", "Release" };
/* For the list widget, we need compound strings */
XmString xarray[NUMITEMS];
Widget menu; /* <-- for the menu */
Widget menuBtn[NUMITEMS];  /* <-- for the menu */

#define USE_SCROLL

void  bye(Widget w, XtPointer clientdata, XtPointer calldata);

int main(int  argc, char **argv)
{
Widget top;
XtAppContext app;
Widget masterForm;
Widget masterLabel;
Arg    args[15];
Widget tmp;
int    i;

/**
*** Initialize the toolkit.
**/
top = XtAppInitialize(&app, "KBH", NULL, 0, (Cardinal *)&argc,
          argv, NULL, args, 0);

/**
*** Create a Bulletin Board on this-top level widget. This is a nice widget
*** to place other widgets on top of.
**/
masterForm = XtVaCreateManagedWidget("bb1",
      xmBulletinBoardWidgetClass, top,
      XmNheight,150,
```

```
        XmNwidth,200,
        NULL);

masterLabel = XtVaCreateManagedWidget("Click Me",
        xmLabelWidgetClass, masterForm,
        XmNheight,50,
        XmNwidth,200,
        NULL);

/* XtAddCallback( cancelBtn, XmNactivateCallback, bye, (XtPointer) NULL);   */

menu = XmCreatePopupMenu(masterLabel, "menu", NULL, 0);
XtRealizeWidget(menu);

/** Add the event handler for managing the popup **/
tmp  = XtCreateManagedWidget("Sample", xmLabelWidgetClass, menu, NULL, 0);
tmp  = XtCreateManagedWidget("Swp1", xmSeparatorWidgetClass, menu, NULL, 0);
tmp  = XtCreateManagedWidget("Btn1", xmPushButtonWidgetClass, menu, NULL, 0);
XtAddCallback(tmp,XmNactivateCallback, showSelection, NULL);
tmp  = XtCreateManagedWidget("Btn2", xmPushButtonWidgetClass, menu, NULL, 0);
XtAddCallback(tmp,XmNactivateCallback, showSelection, NULL);
tmp  = XtCreateManagedWidget("Btn3", xmPushButtonWidgetClass, menu, NULL, 0);
XtAddCallback(tmp,XmNactivateCallback, showSelection, NULL);

XtAddEventHandler( masterForm, ButtonPressMask, True, (XtEventHandler)showMenu,
    menu);
tmp  = XtCreateManagedWidget("Quit", xmPushButtonWidgetClass, menu, NULL, 0);
XtAddCallback(tmp,XmNactivateCallback, bye, NULL);


/** Add the handler to search here. **/
XtRealizeWidget(top);
XtAppMainLoop(app);
return(0);
}

/**
*** This function will display the pop-up menu on the screen
**/
XtEventHandler  showMenu(Widget w, XtPointer menu, XEvent *event, Boolean f)
{

printf ("\n showing position ");
switch  (event->xbutton.button)
     {
     case Button1: printf(" button 1");  break;
     case Button2: printf(" button 2");  break;
     case Button3: printf(" button 3");  break;
     default: printf(" %d",  event->xbutton.button); break;
     }
if((event->xbutton.button == Button1)
  || (event->xbutton.button == Button2))
     {
     XmMenuPosition(menu, (XButtonPressedEvent *)event);
      printf(" Managing %ld",       (long)menu);
```

continues

588

Listing 32.10. continued

```
      XtManageChild(menu);
      }
}

/**
*** This echos the selection on the controlling terminal
**/
void  showSelection(Widget w, XtPointer clientdata, XtPointer calldata)
{
printf("\n %s ",  XtName(w));
}

void  bye(Widget w, XtPointer clientdata, XtPointer calldata)
{
exit(0);
}
```

Note three important items about this listing:

- You can use `printf` functions within Motif applications. The output goes to the controlling terminal by default. This is invaluable in debugging.

- The menu is not visible by itself. An event handler on the menu's parent is registered before the menu can be displayed. This enables the menu to be displayed whenever a button is pressed.

- The `XmMenuPosition` call sets the position of the pop-up menu. It is then managed (that is, after placement).

The Menu Bar

A menu bar is a horizontal bar that is always available to the user. Motif uses the `RowColumn` Widget as a bar with cascading buttons on it for each option.

The procedure for creating a menu bar is as follows:

1. Include the correct header files. You will need the header files for the menu:

   ```
   Label.h
   RowColumn.h
   PushB.h
   Separator.h
   BulletinB.h
   CascadeB.h
   ```

2. Create the menu bar with a call to `XmCreateMenuBar()`.

3. Create the pull-down menu panes with a call to `XmCreatePulldownMenu()`.

4. For each pull-down pane, create a cascade button on the menu bar. Use the menu bar as the parent. A cascade button is used to link the items in a menu with the menu bar itself.

5. Attach the menu pane to its corresponding cascade button. Use the XmNsubMenuId resource of the cascade button to the appropriate menu pane.

6. Create the menu entries in the menu panes.

Listing 32.11 shows you how to set up a simple menu application.

Listing 32.11. Creating a menu bar.

```
/*
** This listing shows how to set up a menu bar and pulldown menus
*/

#include <X11/Intrinsic.h>
#include <Xm/Xm.h>
#include <Xm/Form.h>
#include <Xm/PushB.h>
#include <Xm/Label.h>
#include <Xm/Text.h>
#include <Xm/RowColumn.h>
#include <Xm/CascadeB.h>
#include <Xm/Separator.h>

void doBackup(Widget w, XtPointer x, XtPointer c)
{
printf("\n Start backup ");
}
void doRestore(Widget w, XtPointer x, XtPointer c)
{
printf("\n Start restore ");
}
void bye(Widget w, XtPointer x, XtPointer c)
{
exit(0);
}
void selectTape(Widget w, XtPointer x, XtPointer c)
{
printf("\n Select tape drive...");
}
void selectDisk(Widget w, XtPointer x, XtPointer c)
{
printf("\n Select Floppy disks...");
}

void helpBtn(Widget w, XtPointer x, XtPointer c)
{
printf("\n ... No help available ");
}

int main (int argc, char*argv[])
{
Widget top;
XtAppContext app;
Widget masterForm;
Widget menu;        /* for the menu bar */
```

continues

Listing 32.11. continued

```
Widget submenu; /* for pulldown menus */
Widget cascade; /* for cascade button on the menu bar */
Widget filler;
Arg    args[10];
int    n;
/**
*** Initialize the toolkit.
**/
top = XtAppInitialize(&app, "KBH", NULL, 0, (Cardinal *)&argc,
          argv, NULL, args, 0);


/**
*** Create a Form on this top-level Widget. This is a nice Widget
*** to place other Widgets on top of.
**/
masterForm = XtVaCreateManagedWidget("Form1",
      xmFormWidgetClass, top,
      XmNheight,150,
      XmNwidth,200,
      NULL);


n = 0;
XtSetArg(args[n],XmNheight, 50); n++;
menu = XmCreateMenuBar(masterForm,"mastermenu",
      args, n);
submenu = XmCreatePulldownMenu(menu,"submenupane1", NULL, 0);
cascade = XtVaCreateManagedWidget("File",
      xmCascadeButtonWidgetClass, menu,
      XmNsubMenuId, submenu,
      NULL);

filler = XtVaCreateManagedWidget("Backup",
      xmPushButtonWidgetClass, submenu,  NULL);
XtAddCallback( filler, XmNactivateCallback, doBackup, (XtPointer) NULL);

filler = XtVaCreateManagedWidget("Restore",
      xmPushButtonWidgetClass, submenu,  NULL);
XtAddCallback( filler, XmNactivateCallback, doRestore, (XtPointer) NULL);

filler = XtVaCreateManagedWidget("Quit",
      xmPushButtonWidgetClass, submenu,  NULL);
XtAddCallback( filler, XmNactivateCallback, bye, (XtPointer) NULL);


submenu = XmCreatePulldownMenu(menu,"submenupane2", NULL, 0);

cascade = XtVaCreateManagedWidget("Options",
      xmCascadeButtonWidgetClass, menu,
      XmNsubMenuId, submenu,
      NULL);

filler = XtVaCreateManagedWidget("Tape",
      xmPushButtonWidgetClass, submenu,  NULL);
XtAddCallback( filler, XmNactivateCallback, selectTape, (XtPointer) NULL);
```

```
filler = XtVaCreateManagedWidget("Floppy",
        xmPushButtonWidgetClass, submenu,  NULL);
XtAddCallback( filler, XmNactivateCallback, selectDisk, (XtPointer) NULL);

submenu = XmCreatePulldownMenu(menu,"submenupane3", NULL, 0);

cascade = XtVaCreateManagedWidget("Help",
        xmCascadeButtonWidgetClass, menu,
        XmNsubMenuId, submenu,
        NULL);
filler = XtVaCreateManagedWidget("Floppy",
        xmPushButtonWidgetClass, submenu,  NULL);
XtAddCallback( filler, XmNactivateCallback, selectDisk, (XtPointer) NULL);


XtVaSetValues( menu,
        XmNmenuHelpWidget, cascade,
        NULL);
XtAddCallback( cascade, XmNactivateCallback, helpBtn ,NULL);


XtManageChild(menu);
/** Add the handler to search here. **/
XtRealizeWidget(top);
XtAppMainLoop(app);
return(0);

}
```

Note that the Motif programming style requires you to provide the Help button (if you have any) to be right-justified on the menu bar. This Help Cascade button should then be set to the XmNmenuHelpWidget of a menu bar. The menu bar will automatically position this Widget to the right-hand side of the visible bar. See Listing 32.12 on how to create pull-down menu items on a menu items on a menu bar.

Listing 32.12. Creating menu bars with pull-down menu items.

```
/*
** This listing shows how to set up a menu bar and pull-down menus
*/

#include <X11/Intrinsic.h>
#include <Xm/Xm.h>
#include <Xm/Form.h>
#include <Xm/PushB.h>
#include <Xm/Label.h>
#include <Xm/Text.h>
#include <Xm/RowColumn.h>
#include <Xm/CascadeB.h>
#include <Xm/Separator.h>

void doBackup(Widget w, XtPointer x, XtPointer c)
```

continues

Listing 32.12. continued

```
{
printf("\n Start backup ");
}
void doRestore(Widget w, XtPointer x, XtPointer c)
{
printf("\n Start restore ");
}
void bye(Widget w, XtPointer x, XtPointer c)
{
exit(0);
}
void selectTape(Widget w, XtPointer x, XtPointer c)
{
printf("\n Select tape drive...");
}
void selectDisk(Widget w, XtPointer x, XtPointer c)
{
printf("\n Select Floppy disks...");
}

void helpBtn(Widget w, XtPointer x, XtPointer c)
{
printf("\n ... No help available ");
}

int main (int argc, char*argv[])
{
Widget top;
XtAppContext app;
Widget masterForm;
Widget menu;      /* for the menu bar */
Widget submenu; /* for pull-down menus */
Widget cascade; /* for CascadeButton on the menu bar */
Widget filler;
Arg    args[10];
int    n;
/**
*** Intialize the toolkit.
**/
top = XtAppInitialize(&app, "KBH", NULL, 0, (Cardinal *)&argc,
          argv, NULL, args, 0);

/**
*** Create a Form on this top-level Widget. This is a nice Widget
*** to place other Widgets on top of.
**/
masterForm = XtVaCreateManagedWidget("Form1",
     xmFormWidgetClass, top,
     XmNheight,150,
     XmNwidth,200,
     NULL);


n = 0;
XtSetArg(args[n],XmNheight, 50); n++;
```

```
menu = XmCreateMenuBar(masterForm,"mastermenu",
      args, n);

/********************* The change is here ******************/
n = 0;
XtSetArg(args[n],XmNtearOffModel, XmTEAR_OFF_ENABLED); n++;
submenu = XmCreatePulldownMenu(menu,"submenupane1", args, n);
/********************* The change is here ******************/
cascade = XtVaCreateManagedWidget("File",
      xmCascadeButtonWidgetClass, menu,
      XmNsubMenuId, submenu,
      NULL);

filler = XtVaCreateManagedWidget("Backup",
      xmPushButtonWidgetClass, submenu,  NULL);
XtAddCallback( filler, XmNactivateCallback, doBackup, (XtPointer) NULL);

filler = XtVaCreateManagedWidget("Restore",
      xmPushButtonWidgetClass, submenu,  NULL);
XtAddCallback( filler, XmNactivateCallback, doRestore, (XtPointer) NULL);

filler = XtVaCreateManagedWidget("Quit",
      xmPushButtonWidgetClass, submenu,  NULL);
XtAddCallback( filler, XmNactivateCallback, bye, (XtPointer) NULL);


submenu = XmCreatePulldownMenu(menu,"submenupane2", NULL, 0);

cascade = XtVaCreateManagedWidget("Options",
      xmCascadeButtonWidgetClass, menu,
      XmNsubMenuId, submenu,
      NULL);

filler = XtVaCreateManagedWidget("Tape",
      xmPushButtonWidgetClass, submenu,  NULL);
XtAddCallback( filler, XmNactivateCallback, selectTape, (XtPointer) NULL);

filler = XtVaCreateManagedWidget("Floppy",
      xmPushButtonWidgetClass, submenu,  NULL);
XtAddCallback( filler, XmNactivateCallback, selectDisk, (XtPointer) NULL);

submenu = XmCreatePulldownMenu(menu,"submenupane3", NULL, 0);

cascade = XtVaCreateManagedWidget("Help",
      xmCascadeButtonWidgetClass, menu,
      XmNsubMenuId, submenu,
      NULL);
filler = XtVaCreateManagedWidget("Floppy",
      xmPushButtonWidgetClass, submenu,  NULL);
XtAddCallback( filler, XmNactivateCallback, selectDisk, (XtPointer) NULL);


XtVaSetValues( menu,
      XmNmenuHelpWidget, cascade,
      NULL);
```

continues

Listing 32.12. continued

```
XtAddCallback( cascade, XmNactivateCallback, helpBtn ,NULL);


XtManageChild(menu);
/** Add the handler to search here. **/
XtRealizeWidget(top);
XtAppMainLoop(app);
return(0);


}
```

The Options Menu

An Options menu enables the user to select from a list of items while displaying the most recently selected item. The procedure for creating an Options menu is similar to creating menu bars:

1. Include the correct header files. You will need the header files for the menu:

    ```
    Label.h
    RowColumn.h
    PushB.h
    Separator.h
    BulletinB.h
    CascadeB.h
    ```

2. Create the menu bar with a call to `XmCreateOptionMenu()`.
3. Create the pull-down menu panes with a call to `XmCreatePulldownMenu()`.
4. For each pull-down pane, create a CascadeButton on the menu bar.
5. Attach the menu pane to its corresponding CascadeButton. Use the `XmNsubMenuId` resource of the CascadeButton to the appropriate menu pane.
6. Create the menu entries in the menu panes.

Accelerators and Mnemonics

An accelerator for a command is the keystroke that invokes the callback for that particular menu item. For example, for opening a file, you could use Ctrl-O. The resource for this accelerator could be set in the resource file as

```
*Open*accelerator: Ctrl<Key>O
```

The corresponding menu item should read "Open Ctrl+O" to let the user know about this short-cut. Note the + instead of -. You can also set this resource via the command in the .Xresources file:

```
*Open*acceleratorText: "Ctrl+O"
```

Using the .Xresource file is the preferred way of setting these resources.

Mnemonics are a short form for letting the user select menu items without using the mouse. For example, the user could press <meta>F to invoke the File menu. These are also usually set in the .Xresource file. The syntax for the File menu to use the <meta>F key would be:

```
*File*mnemonic:F
```

> **TIP**
>
> With Linux on your PC, *meta* means the Alt key.

Dialog Boxes

A *dialog box* is used to convey information about something to the user and requests a canned response in return. For example, a dialog box might say "Go ahead and Print" and present three buttons—OK, Cancel, and Help. The user must then select one of the three buttons to process the command.

A typical dialog box displays an icon, a message string, and usually three buttons (OK, Cancel, and Help). Motif provides predefined dialog boxes for the following categories:

- Errors
- Information
- Warnings
- Working
- Questions

Each of these dialog box types displays a different icon: a question mark for the Question dialog box, an exclamation mark for an Information dialog box, and so on. Convenience functions ease the creation of dialog boxes. These are

- `XmCreateErrorsDialog`
- `XmCreateInformationDialog`
- `XmCreateWarningDialog`
- `XmCreateWorkingDialog`
- `XmCreateQuestionDialog`

The infamous "OK to quit?" dialog box can be implemented as shown in Listing 32.13. There is another example in Listing 32.17.

Listing 32.13. Code fragment to confirm quit command.

```
/*
** Confirm quit one last time
*/
void reallyQuit(Widget w, XtPointer clientdata, XtPointer calldata)
{
exit(0);
}
void confirmQuit(Widget w, XtPointer clientdata, XtPointer calldata)
{
static Widget quitDlg = NULL;
static char *msgstr = "Really Quit?"

if (quitDlg != NULL)
    {
    /* first time called */
    quitDlg = XmCreateQuestionDialog(w,"R U Sure",NULL,0);
    XtVaSetValues(quitDlg, XtVaTypedArg,
            XmNmessageString,
            XmRString,
            msgstr,
            strlen(msgstr),
            NULL);

    XtAddCallback(quitDlg, reallyQuit, NULL);
    }
XtManageChild(quitDlg);
}
```

Append this code fragment to the end of any sample listings in this chapter to get instant checking before you actually quit the application. Note that the quitDlg dialog box is set to NULL when the function is first called. It does not have to be re-created on every call after the first one; it is only managed for all subsequent calls to this function.

Modes of a Dialog Box

A dialog box can have four modes of operation, called *modality*. The mode is set in the XmNdialogStyle resource. The possible values are

- Nonmodal: The user can ignore the dialog box and work with any other window on the screen. Resource value is XmDIALOG_MODELESS.

- Primary Application Modal: All input to the window that invoked the dialog box is locked out. The user can use the rest of the windows in the application. Resource value is XmDIALOG_PRIMARY_APPLICATION_MODAL.

- Full Application Modal: All input to all the windows in the application that invoked the dialog box is locked out. The user cannot use the rest of the windows in the application. Resource value is XmDIALOG_FULL_APPLICATION_MODAL.

- System Modal: All input is directed to the dialog box. The user cannot interact with any other window in the system. Resource value is XmDIALOG_SYSTEM_MODAL.

The dialog boxes provided by Motif are based on the XmMessageBox Widget. Sometimes it is necessary to get to the Widgets in a dialog box. This is done with a call to XmMessageBox GetChild(Widget dialog, typeOfWidget); where typeOfWidget can be one of the following:

XmDIALOG_HELP_BUTTON XmDIALOG_CANCEL_BUTTON

XmDIALOG_SEPARATOR XmDIALOG_MESSAGE_LABEL

XmDIALOG_OK_BUTTON XmDIALOG_SYMBOL_LABEL

The dialog box may have more Widgets that can be addressed. Check the man pages for the descriptions of these Widgets. For example, to hide the Help button on a dialog box, use the call

XtUnmanageChild(XmMessageBoxGetChild(dlg, XmDIALOG_HELP_BUTTON));

or, in the case of adding a callback, use

XtAddCallback(XmMessageBoxGetChild(dlg, XmDIALOG_OK_BUTTON),
        XmNactivateCallback, yourFunction);

A typical method of creating custom dialog boxes is to use existing ones. Then, using the XmMessageBoxGetChild function, you can add or remove any function you want. For example, by replacing the message string Widget with a Form Widget, you have a place for laying out Widgets however you need to.

Events

An *event* is a message sent from the X server to the application that some condition in the system has changed. This could be a button press, a keystroke, requested information from the server, or a timeout. An event is always relative to a window and starts from the bottom up. It propagates up the window hierarchy until it gets to the root window, where the root window application makes the decision to either use or discard it. If an application in the hierarchy does use the event or does not allow upward propagation of events, the message is used at the window itself. Only device events are propagated upward (such as keyboard or mouse)—not configuration events.

An application must request an event of a particular type before it can begin receiving events. Each Motif application calls XtAppInitialize to create this connection automatically.

Events contain at least the following information :

- The type of event
- The display where it happened
- The window of the event, called the *event window*
- The serial number of the last event processed by the server

Look in the file <X11/Xlib.h> for a description of the union called XEvent, which enables access to these values. The file <X11/X.h> contains the descriptions of constants for the types of events. All event types share the header:

```
typedef struct {
      int type;
      unsigned long serial;   /* # of last request processed by server */
      Bool send_event;  /* true if this came from a SendEvent request */
      Display *display;/* display the event was read from */
      Window window;      /* window on which event was requested in event mask */
} XAnyEvent;
```

Expose Events

The server generates an Expose when a window that was covered by another is brought to the top of the stack, or even partially exposed. The structure for this event type is

```
typedef struct {
      int type;          /* type of event */
      unsigned long serial;   /* # of last request processed by server */
      Bool send_event;  /* true if this came from a SendEvent request */
      Display *display; /* display the event was read from */
      Window window;
      int x, y;
      int width, height;
      int count;         /* if nonzero, at least this many more */
} XExposeEvent;
```

Note how the first five fields are shared between this event and XAnyEvent. Expose events are guaranteed to be in sequence. An application may get several Expose events from one condition. The count field keeps a count of the number of Expose events still in the queue when the application receives this one. Thus, it can be up to the application to wait to redraw until the last Expose event is received (that is, count == 0).

Pointer Events

A Pointer event is generated by a mouse press, release, or movement. The type of event is called XButtonEvent. Recall that the leftmost button is Button1, but it can be changed. The structure returned by this button press and release is

```
typedef struct {
      int type;          /* of event */
      unsigned long serial;   /* # of last request processed by server */
      Bool send_event;  /* true if this came from a SendEvent request */
      Display *display; /* display the event was read from */
      Window window;               /* "event" window it is reported relative to */
      Window root;                 /* root window that the event occured on */
      Window subwindow; /* child window */
      Time time;         /* milliseconds */
      int x, y;          /* pointer x, y coordinates in event window */
```

```
        int x_root, y_root;     /* coordinates relative to root */
        unsigned int state;     /* key or button mask */
        unsigned int button;    /* detail */
        Bool same_screen;       /* same screen flag */
} XButtonEvent;

typedef XButtonEvent XButtonPressedEvent;
typedef XButtonEvent XButtonReleasedEvent;
```

The event for a movement is called XMotionEvent, with the type field set to MotionNotify.

```
typedef struct {
        int type;               /* MotionNotify */
        unsigned long serial;   /* # of last request processed by server */
        Bool send_event;   /* true if this came from a SendEvent request */
        Display *display;  /* display the event was read from */
        Window window;              /* "event" window reported relative to */
        Window root;                /* root window that the event occured on */
        Window subwindow;  /* child window */
        Time time;              /* milliseconds */
        int x, y;               /* pointer x, y coordinates in event window */
        int x_root, y_root;        /* coordinates relative to root */
        unsigned int state;        /* key or button mask */
        char is_hint;              /* detail */
        Bool same_screen;  /* same screen flag */
} XMotionEvent;

typedef XMotionEvent XPointerMovedEvent;
```

Keyboard Events

A keyboard event is generated when the user presses or releases a key. Both types of events, KeyPress and KeyRelease, are returned in a XKeyEvent structure.

```
typedef struct {
        int type;               /* of event */
        unsigned long serial;   /* # of last request processed by server */
        Bool send_event;   /* true if this came from a SendEvent request */
        Display *display;  /* display the event was read from */
        Window window;              /* "event" window it is reported relative to */
        Window root;                /* root window that the event occured on */
        Window subwindow;  /* child window */
        Time time;              /* milliseconds */
        int x, y;               /* pointer x, y coordinates in event window */
        int x_root, y_root;        /* coordinates relative to root */
        unsigned int state;        /* key or button mask */
        unsigned int keycode;   /* detail */
        Bool same_screen;  /* same screen flag */
} XKeyEvent;

typedef XKeyEvent XKeyPressedEvent;
typedef XKeyEvent XKeyReleasedEvent;
```

The keycode field gives information on whether the key was pressed or released. These constants are defined in <X11/keysymdef.h> and are vendor-specific. These are called KeySym and are generic across all X servers. For example, the F1 key could be described as XK_F1. The function XLookupString converts a KeyPress event into a string and a KeySym (a portable key symbol). The call is

```
int XLookupString(XKeyEvent *event,
            char *returnString,
             int max_length,
          KeySym  *keysym,
          XComposeStatus *compose);
```

The returned ASCII string is placed in returnString for up to max_length characters. The keysym contains the key symbol. Generally, the compose parameter is ignored.

Window Crossing Events

The server generates crossing EnterNotify events when a pointer enters a window and LeaveNotify events when a pointer leaves a window. These are used to create special effects for notifying the user that the window has focus. The XCrossingEvent structure looks like the following:

```
typedef struct {
      int type;           /* of event */
      unsigned long serial;   /* # of last request processed by server */
      Bool send_event; /* true if this came from a SendEvent request */
      Display *display; /* display the event was read from */
      Window window;              /* "event" window reported relative to */
      Window root;                /* root window that the event occured on */
      Window subwindow; /* child window */
      Time time;          /* milliseconds */
      int x, y;           /* pointer x, y coordinates in event window */
      int x_root, y_root;     /* coordinates relative to root */
      int mode;               /* NotifyNormal, NotifyGrab, NotifyUngrab */
      int detail;
      /*
       * NotifyAncestor, NotifyVirtual, NotifyInferior,
       * NotifyNonlinear, NotifyNonlinearVirtual
       */
      Bool same_screen; /* same screen flag */
      Bool focus;       /* boolean focus */
      unsigned int state;     /* key or button mask */
} XCrossingEvent;
typedef XCrossingEvent XEnterWindowEvent;
typedef XCrossingEvent XLeaveWindowEvent;
```

These are generally used to color a window on entry and exit to provide feedback to the user as he moves the pointer around.

Event Masks

An application requests events of a particular type by calling a function named XAddEventHandler(). The prototype for this function is

```
XAddEventHandler( Widget ,
            EventMask ,
            Boolean maskable,
            XtEventHandler handlerfunction,
            XtPointer clientData);
```

The handler function is of the form

```
void handlerFunction( Widget w, XtPointer clientData,
                XEvent *ev, Boolean *continueToDispatch);
```

The first two arguments are the `clientdata` and Widget passed in `XtAddEventHandler`. The `ev` argument is the event that triggered this call. The last argument enables this message to be passed to other message handlers for this type of event. This should be defaulted to TRUE.

You would use the following call on a `Widget` `w` to be notified of all pointer events of the type `ButtonMotion` and `PointerMotion` on this Widget.

```
extern void handlerFunction( Widget w, XtPointer clientData,
                XEvent *ev, Boolean *continueToDispatch);

XAddEventHandler( w, ButtonMotionMask ¦ PointerMotionMask, FALSE,
            handlerFunction, NULL );
```

The possible event masks are

- NoEventMask
- KeyPressMask
- KeyReleaseMask
- ButtonPressMask
- ButtonReleaseMask
- EnterWindowMask
- LeaveWindowMask
- PointerMotionMask
- PointerMotionHintMask
- Button1MotionMask
- Button2MotionMask
- Button3MotionMask
- Button4MotionMask
- Button5MotionMask
- ButtonMotionMask
- KeymapStateMask
- ExposureMask
- VisibilityChangeMask
- StructureNotifyMask
- ResizeRedirectMask
- SubstructureNotifyMask
- SubstructureRedirectMask

- FocusChangeMask
- PropertyChangeMask
- ColormapChangeMask
- OwnerGrabButtonMask

Listing 32.14 is a sample application that shows how to track the mouse position.

Listing 32.14. Tracking a pointer.

```
/*
** This application shows how to track a pointer
*/

#include <X11/Intrinsic.h>
#include <Xm/Xm.h>
#include <Xm/Form.h>
#include <Xm/PushB.h>
#include <Xm/Label.h>

static int track;

void  upMouse(Widget w, XtPointer clientdata, XEvent *x, Boolean *f)
{
track = 0;
}
void  moveMouse(Widget w, XtPointer clientdata, XEvent *x, Boolean *f)
{
if (track == 1)
     {
     printf("\n x: %d, y: %d", x->xmotion.x, x->xmotion.y);
     }
}
void  downMouse(Widget w, XtPointer clientdata, XEvent *x, Boolean *f)
{
track = 1;
}

void  bye(Widget w, XtPointer clientdata, XtPointer calldata);

int main(int  argc, char **argv)
{
Widget top;
XtAppContext app;
Widget aForm;
Widget aLabel;
Widget aButton;
Arg    args[5];

/**
*** Initialize the toolkit.
**/
top = XtAppInitialize(&app, "KBH", NULL, 0, (Cardinal *)&argc,
          argv, NULL, args, 0);

/**
```

```
*** Create a Form on this top-level Widget. This is a nice Widget
*** to place other Widgets on top of.
**/
aForm = XtVaCreateManagedWidget("Form1",
      xmFormWidgetClass, top,
      XmNheight,90,
      XmNwidth,200,
      NULL);

/**
*** Add a button on the form you just created. Note how this Button
*** Widget is connected to the form that it resides on. Only
*** left, right, and bottom edges are attached to the form. The
*** top edge of the button is not connected to the form.
**/
aButton = XtVaCreateManagedWidget("Push to Exit",
      xmPushButtonWidgetClass, aForm,
      XmNheight,20,
      XmNleftAttachment,XmATTACH_FORM,
      XmNleftOffset,20,
      XmNrightAttachment,XmATTACH_FORM,
      XmNrightOffset,20,
      XmNbottomAttachment,XmATTACH_FORM,
      NULL);

/**
*** Now let's create the label for us.
*** The alignment is set to right-justify the label.
*** Note how the label is attached to the parent form.
**/

aLabel = XtVaCreateManagedWidget("This is a Label",
      xmLabelWidgetClass, aForm,
      XmNalignment, XmALIGNMENT_END,
      XmNleftAttachment,XmATTACH_FORM,
      XmNrightAttachment,XmATTACH_FORM,
      XmNtopAttachment,XmATTACH_FORM,
      XmNbottomAttachment,XmATTACH_WIDGET,
      XmNbottomWidget,aButton,
      NULL);

/**
*** Now add the event handlers for tracking the mouse on the
*** label. Note that the LeaveWindowMask is set to release
*** the pointer for you should you keep the button pressed
*** and leave the window.
**/
XtAddEventHandler( aLabel, ButtonPressMask, FALSE, downMouse, NULL);
XtAddEventHandler( aLabel, ButtonMotionMask, FALSE, moveMouse, NULL);
XtAddEventHandler( aLabel, ButtonReleaseMask | LeaveWindowMask,
            FALSE, upMouse, NULL);
/**
*** Call the function "bye" when the PushButton receives
*** an activate message; i.e. when the pointer is moved to
*** the button and Button1 is pressed and released.
**/
```

continues

Listing 32.14. continued

```
XtAddCallback( aButton, XmNactivateCallback, bye, (XtPointer) NULL);
XtRealizeWidget(top);
XtAppMainLoop(app);
return(0);
}

void  bye(Widget w, XtPointer clientdata, XtPointer calldata)
{
exit(0);
}
```

Managing the Queue

Managing the X server is critical if you have to handle lots of incoming events. The `XtAppMainLoop()` function handles all the incoming events via the following functions:

- `XtAppPending` checks the queue to see if any events are pending.

- `XtAppNextEvent` removes the next event from the queue.

- `XtDispatchEvent` passes the message to the appropriate window.

The loop can do something else between checking and removing messages via the replacement code segment:

```
while (!done)
        {
        while (XtAppPending( applicationContext))
                {
                XtAppNextEvent( applicationContext, &ev));
                XtDispacthEvent( &ev));
                }
        done = interEventFunction();
        }
```

There are some caveats with this scheme:

- This is a nonblocking function. It must be fed at all times with events, or it will take over all other applications' time.

- There is no guarantee when your inter-event function will be run if the queue is flooded with events.

- Note the `while` loop for checking messages. It's more efficient to flush the queue first and then call your function rather than calling it once every time you check for messages.

- The inter-event function must be fast or you will see the user interface slow down. If you want to give some response back to your user about what's going on while in a long inter-event function, you can make a call to `XmUpdateDisplay( Display *)`. This will handle only the Expose events in the queue so that you can update some status display.

Consider using the select call to handle incoming events of file descriptors. This is a call that enables an application to wait for events from various file descriptors on read-ready, write-ready, or both. The file descriptors can be sockets, too!

See the man page for more information on the select call.

Open all the files with an open call.

Get the file descriptor for the event queue.

Use the Select macros to set up the parameters for select call ret = return from the select function:

switch (ret)

    case 0:

        process the event queue

    case 1: ...

        process the file descriptor

Work Procedures

These are functions called by the event-handler loop whenever no events are pending in the queue. The function is expected to return a Boolean value indicating whether it has to be removed from the loop after it is called. If TRUE, it wants to be removed; if FALSE, it wants to be called again. For example, you could set up a disk file transfer to run in the background, which will keep returning FALSE until it is done, at which time it will return TRUE.

The work procedures are defined as

```
Boolean yourFunction(XtPointer clientdata);
```

The way to register a work procedure is to call

```
XtWorkProcId     XtAppAddWorkProc ( XtAppContext app,
                     XtWorkProc   functionPointer,
                     XtPointer    clientData);
```

The return ID from this call is the handle to the work procedure. It is used to remove the work procedure with a call to the function `XtRemoveWorkProc( XtWorkProcId id);`.

Using Timeouts

A *timeout* is used to perform some task at (almost) regular intervals. Applications set up a timer callback function that is called when a requested time interval has passed. This function is defined as

```
void thyTimerCallback( XtPointer clientdata, XtInterval *tid);
```

where clientdata is a pointer to client-specific data. The setup function for the timeout returns the timer ID and is defined as

```
XtIntervalId XtAddTimeOut ( XtAppContext app,
                    int milliseconds,
                    XtTimerCallback TimerProcedure,
                    XtPointer clientdata);
```

This call sets up a timer to call the TimerProcedure function when the requested milliseconds have passed. It will do this only once. If you want cyclic timeouts—for example, in a clock application—you have to explicitly set up the next function call in the timer handler function itself. So generally, the last line in a timer handler is a call to set a timeout for the next time the function wants to be called.

Linux is not designed for real-time applications, and you can't expect a deterministic time interval between successive timer calls. Some heavy graphics updates can cause delays in the timer loop. For user-interface applications, the delays are probably not a big drawback; however, consult your vendor before you attempt to write a time-critical control application. Depending on your application, your mileage may vary. See Listing 32.15 for an example of setting up cyclic timers.

Listing 32.15. Setting up cyclic timers.

```
/*
** This application shows how to set a cyclic timer
*/

#include <X11/Intrinsic.h>
#include <Xm/Xm.h>
#include <Xm/Form.h>
#include <Xm/PushB.h>
#include <Xm/Text.h>

int counter;
char buf[32];
#define ONE_SECOND 1000L  /* **APPROXIMATELY** 1000 milliseconds..*/

/* Timing is *not* precise in Motif... so do not rely on this time
** for a time-critical application. Use interrupt handlers instead.
*/
void makeTimer(Widget w, XtIntervalId id);

void  bye(Widget w, XtPointer clientdata, XtPointer calldata);

int main(int  argc, char **argv)
{
Widget top;
XtAppContext app;
Widget aForm;
Widget aText;
Widget aButton;
Arg    args[5];

/**
*** Initialize the toolkit.
**/
```

```
top = XtAppInitialize(&app, "KBH", NULL, 0, (Cardinal *)&argc,
            argv, NULL, args, 0);

/**
*** Create a Form on this top-level Widget. This is a nice Widget
*** to place other Widgets on top of.
**/
aForm = XtVaCreateManagedWidget("Form1",
      xmFormWidgetClass, top,
      XmNheight,90,
      XmNwidth,200,
      NULL);

/**
*** Add a button on the form you just created. Note how this Button
*** Widget is connected to the form that it resides on. Only
*** left, right, and bottom edges are attached to the form. The
*** top edge of the button is not connected to the form.
**/
aButton = XtVaCreateManagedWidget("Push to Exit",
      xmPushButtonWidgetClass, aForm,
      XmNheight,20,
      XmNleftAttachment,XmATTACH_FORM,
      XmNleftOffset,20,
      XmNrightAttachment,XmATTACH_FORM,
      XmNrightOffset,20,
      XmNbottomAttachment,XmATTACH_FORM,
      NULL);

/**
*** Now let's create the label for us.
*** The alignment is set to right-justify the label.
*** Note how the label is attached to the parent form.
**/

aText = XtVaCreateManagedWidget("This is a Label",
      xmTextWidgetClass, aForm,
      XmNalignment, XmALIGNMENT_CENTER,
      XmNleftAttachment,XmATTACH_FORM,
      XmNrightAttachment,XmATTACH_FORM,
      XmNtopAttachment,XmATTACH_FORM,
      XmNbottomAttachment,XmATTACH_WIDGET,
      XmNbottomWidget,aButton,
      NULL);

/**
*** Now add the timer handler
**/

counter = 0;
makeTimer(aText, (XtIntervalId )NULL);
/**
*** Call the function "bye" when the PushButton receives
*** an activate message; i.e. when the pointer is moved to
*** the button and Button1 is pressed and released.
**/
```

continues

Listing 32.15. continued

```
XtAddCallback( aButton, XmNactivateCallback, bye, (XtPointer) NULL);
XtRealizeWidget(top);
XtAppMainLoop(app);
return(0);
}

void  bye(Widget w, XtPointer clientdata, XtPointer calldata)
{
exit(0);
}

/** This function creates the timer code. **/
void makeTimer(Widget w, XtIntervalId id)
{
Widget tmp;
extern int counter;

sprintf(buf,"%4d",counter++);
XmTextSetString(w,buf);

if (counter < 10) /** reinvoke yourself if < 10 times **/
XtAppAddTimeOut( XtWidgetToApplicationContext(w), ONE_SECOND,
            (XtTimerCallbackProc)makeTimer, (XtPointer)w);

}
```

Handling Other Sources

The XtAddInput function is used to handle inputs from sources other than the event queue. The definition is

```
XtInputId XtAddInput( XtAppContext  app,
                int         LinuxfileDescriptor,
                XtPointer   condition,
                XtInputCallback   inputHandler,
                XtPointer   clientdata);
```

The return value from this call is the handle to the inputHandler function. This is used to remove the call via the call

```
XtRemoveInput( XtInput Id);
```

The inputHandler function itself is defined as

```
void InputHandler(XtPointer clientdata, int *fd, XtInputId *id);
```

Unlike timers, you have to register this function only once. Note that a pointer to a file descriptor is passed in to the function. The file descriptor must be a Linux file descriptor. You do not have support for Linux IPC message queues or semaphores through this scheme. The IPC mechanism is considered dated and is limited to one machine. Consider using sockets instead.

NOTE

AIX enables pending on message queues via the select call. Look at the AIX man pages for this call.

The Graphics Context

Each Widget draws itself on the screen using its set of drawing parameters called the *graphics context* (GC). For drawing on a Widget, you can use the X primitive functions if you have its window and its graphics context. It's easier to limit your artwork to the DrawingArea Widget, which is designed for this purpose. You can think of the GC as your paintbrush and the Widget as the canvas. The color and thickness of the paintbrush are just some of the factors that determine how the paint is transferred to the canvas.

The function call to create a GC is to use

```
GC XCreateGC (Display dp, Drawable d, unsigned long mask, XGCValue *values);
```

For use with a Widget w, this call would look like this:

```
GC gc;
XGCVvalue gcv;
unsigned long mask;

gc = XCreate(XtDisplay(w), DefaultRootWindow(XtDisplay(w)),
            mask, gcv);
```

Also, you can create a GC for a Widget directly with a call to XtGetGC(). The prototype for this function is

```
gc = XtGetGC (Widget w, unsigned long mask, XGCValue *values);
```

The values for the mask parameter are defined as an ORed value of the following definitions:

- GCFunction
- GCPlaneMask
- GCForeground
- GCBackground
- GCLineWidth
- GCLineStyle
- GCCapStyle
- GCJoinStyle
- GCFillStyle
- GCFillRule

- GCTile

- GCStipple

- GCTileStipXOrigin

- GCTileStipYOrigin

- GCFont

- GCSubWindowMode

- GCGraphicsExposures

- GCClipXOrigin

- GCClipYOrigin

- GCClipMask

- GCDashOffset

- GCDashList

- GCArcMode

So, if a call is going to set the Font and Clipping mask, the value of the mask will be (GCFont |
GCClipMask). The data structure for setting the graphics context is as follows:

```
typedef struct {
      int function;              /* logical operation */
      unsigned long plane_mask;/* plane mask */
      unsigned long foreground;/* foreground pixel */
      unsigned long background;/* background pixel */
      int line_width;            /* line width */
      int line_style;            /* LineSolid, LineOnOffDash, LineDoubleDash */
      int cap_style;             /* CapNotLast, CapButt,
                            CapRound, CapProjecting */
      int join_style;            /* JoinMiter, JoinRound, JoinBevel */
      int fill_style;            /* FillSolid, FillTiled,
                            FillStippled, FillOpaeueStippled */
      int fill_rule;             /* EvenOddRule, WindingRule */
      int arc_mode;              /* ArcChord, ArcPieSlice */
      Pixmap tile;               /* tile pixmap for tiling operations */
      Pixmap stipple;            /* stipple 1 plane pixmap for stipping */
      int ts_x_origin;  /* offset for tile or stipple operations */
      int ts_y_origin;
        Font font;                 /* default text font for text operations */
      int subwindow_mode;        /* ClipByChildren, IncludeInferiors */
      Bool graphics_exposures;/* boolean, should exposures be generated */
      int clip_x_origin;         /* origin for clipping */
      int clip_y_origin;
      Pixmap clip_mask; /* bitmap clipping; other calls for rects */
      int dash_offset;  /* patterned/dashed line information */
            char dashes;
} XGCValues;
```

If you want to set a value in a GC, you have to take two steps before you create the GC:

1. Set the value in the XGCValue structure.

2. Set the mask for the call.

Let's look at the values of the functions in a bit more detail.

GCFunction

This determines how the GC paints to the screen. The dst pixels are the pixels currently on the screen, and the src pixels are those that your application is writing using the GC.

```
GXclear dst = 0
GXset   dst = 1
GXand       dst = src AND dst
Gxor  dst = src OR dst
GXcopy      dst = src
GXnoop      dst = dst
Gxnor dst = NOT(src OR dst)
Gxxor dst = src XOR dst
GXinvert dst = NOT dst
GxcopyInverted dst = NOT src
```

The function for a GC is changed via a call to XSetFunction (Display *dp, GC gc, int function), where function is set to one of the values just mentioned. The default value is GXcopy. There are several other masks that you can apply. They are listed in the <X11/X.h> file.

GCPlaneMask

The plane mask sets which planes of a drawable can be set by the GC. This is defaulted to AllPlanes, thereby enabling the GC to work with all planes on a Widget.

GCForeground & GCBackground

These are the values of the pixels to use for the foreground and background colors, respectively. The call to manipulate these is

```
XSetForeGround(Display *dp, GC gc, Pixel pixel);
XSetBackGround(Display *dp, GC gc, Pixel pixel);
```

GCLineWidth

This is the number of pixels for the width of all lines drawn via the GC. It is defaulted to zero, which is the signal to the server to draw the thinnest line possible.

GCLineStyle GCDashOffset GCDashList

This determines the style of the line drawn on-screen. LineSolid draws a solid line using the foreground color, LineOnOffDash draws an intermittent line with the foreground color, and LineDoubleDash draws a line that is composed of interlaced segments of the foreground and background colors. The GCDashOffset and GCDashList values determine the position and length of these dashes.

GCCapStyle

This determines how the server draws the ends of lines. CapNotLast draws up to, but does not include, the endpoint pixels of a line; CapButt draws up to the endpoints of a line (inclusive); CapRound tries to round off the edges of a thick line (three or more pixels wide); and CapProjecting extends the endpoint a little.

`GCJoinStyle`

This is used to draw the endpoints of a line. It can be set to `JointMiter` for a 90-degree joint, `JoinBevel` for a beveled joint, or `JoinRound` for a rounded joint.

`GCFillStyle, GCTile, GCStipple`

The fill style can be set to `FillSolid`, which specifies the fill color to be the foreground color; `FillTiled` specifies a pattern of the same in the Tile attribute; and `FillStipple` specifies a pattern in the Stipple attribute. `FillStipple` uses the foreground color where a bit is set to 1 and nothing when a bit is set to 0, whereas `FillOpaqueStippled` uses the foreground color when a bit is set to 1 and the background color when a bit is set to 0.

`GCFont`

This specifies the fontlist to use. (See the section, "Using Fonts and FontLists," later in this chapter.)

`GCArcMode`

This defines the way an arc is drawn on-screen (see the next section).

Drawing Lines, Points, Arcs, and Polygons

Motif applications can access all the graphics primitives provided by `Xlib`. All `Xlib` functions must operate on a window or a pixmap; both are referred to as *drawable*. Widgets have a window after they are realized. You can access this window with a call to `XtWindow()`. An application can crash if `Xlib` calls are made to a window that is not realized. The way to check is via a call to `XtIsRealized()` on the Widget, which will return TRUE if it is realized and FALSE if it is not. Use the XmDrawingArea Widget's callbacks for rendering your graphics, because it is designed for this purpose. The callbacks available to you are

- `XmNresizeCallback`: Invoked when the Widget is resized.
- `XmNexposeCallback`: Invoked when the Widget receives an Expose event.
- `XmNinputCallback`: Invoked when a button or key is pressed on the Widget.

All three functions pass a pointer to the XmDrawingAreaCallbackStruct.

Drawing a Line

To draw a line on-screen, use the `XDrawLine` or `XDrawLines` function call. Consider the example shown in Listing 32.16.

Listing 32.16. Drawing lines and points.

```
/*
** This application shows how to draw lines and points
** by tracking the pointer
*/
```

```c
#include <X11/Intrinsic.h>
#include <Xm/Xm.h>
#include <Xm/Form.h>
#include <Xm/PushB.h>
#include <Xm/DrawingA.h>

/**
*** used for tracking and drawing via the mouse
**/
static int track;
static int lastx;
static int lasty;
static GC thisGC;
XGCValues gcv;
Widget aForm;
Widget aDraw;
Widget aButton;


/**
*** Connect the mouse down and up movements
**/
void  upMouse(Widget w, XtPointer clientdata, XEvent *e, Boolean *f)
{
if (track == 1)
      {
      XDrawLine(XtDisplay(w),XtWindow(w),
            thisGC, lastx, lasty, e->xbutton.x, e->xbutton.y);
      }
track = 0;
}


void  lostMouse(Widget w, XtPointer clientdata, XEvent *x, Boolean *f)
{
track = 0;
}
/**
*** This function tracks the movement of the mouse by
*** drawing points on its location while a button is
*** pressed.
**/
void  moveMouse(Widget w, XtPointer clientdata, XEvent *e, Boolean *f)
{
if (track == 1)
      {
      printf("\n x: %d, y: %d", e->xmotion.x, e->xmotion.y);
      XDrawPoint(XtDisplay(w),XtWindow(w),
            thisGC, e->xmotion.x, e->xmotion.y);
      }
}
void  downMouse(Widget w, XtPointer clientdata, XEvent *e, Boolean *f)
{
track = 1;
lastx = e->xbutton.x;
lasty = e->xbutton.y;
}
```

continues

Listing 32.16. continued

```
void  bye(Widget w, XtPointer clientdata, XtPointer calldata);

int main(int  argc, char **argv)
{
Widget top;
XtAppContext app;
Arg    args[5];

/**
*** Initialize the toolkit.
**/
top = XtAppInitialize(&app, "KBH", NULL, 0, (Cardinal *)&argc,
          argv, NULL, args, 0);

/**
*** Create a Form on this top-level Widget. This is a nice Widget
*** to place other Widgets on top of.
**/
aForm = XtVaCreateManagedWidget("Form1",
      xmFormWidgetClass, top,
      XmNheight,200,
      XmNwidth,200,
      NULL);

/**
*** Add a button on the form you just created. Note how this Button
*** Widget is connected to the form that it resides on. Only
*** left, right, and bottom edges are attached to the form. The
*** top edge of the button is not connected to the form.
**/
aButton = XtVaCreateManagedWidget("Push to Exit",
      xmPushButtonWidgetClass, aForm,
      XmNheight,20,
      XmNleftAttachment,XmATTACH_FORM,
      XmNleftOffset,20,
      XmNrightAttachment,XmATTACH_FORM,
      XmNrightOffset,20,
      XmNbottomAttachment,XmATTACH_FORM,
      NULL);

/**
*** Now let's create the label for us.
*** The alignment is set to right-justify the label.
*** Note how the label is attached to the parent form.
**/

aDraw = XtVaCreateManagedWidget("paperusitto",
      xmDrawingAreaWidgetClass, aForm,
      XmNalignment, XmALIGNMENT_END,
      XmNleftAttachment,XmATTACH_FORM,
      XmNrightAttachment,XmATTACH_FORM,
      XmNtopAttachment,XmATTACH_FORM,
      XmNbottomAttachment,XmATTACH_WIDGET,
      XmNbottomWidget,aButton,
      NULL);
```

```
gcv.foreground = BlackPixel(XtDisplay(aDraw), DefaultScreen(XtDisplay(aDraw)));
gcv.background = WhitePixel(XtDisplay(aDraw), DefaultScreen(XtDisplay(aDraw)));
gcv.line_width = 2;
thisGC = XtGetGC( aDraw,
 GCForeground | GCBackground | GCLineWidth,
            (XGCValues *) &gcv);
/**
*** Now add the event handlers for tracking the mouse on the
*** label. Note that the LeaveWindowMask is set to release
*** the pointer for you should you keep the button pressed
*** and leave the window and disables tracking.
**/
XtAddEventHandler( aDraw, ButtonPressMask, FALSE, downMouse, NULL);
XtAddEventHandler( aDraw, ButtonMotionMask, FALSE, moveMouse, NULL);
XtAddEventHandler( aDraw, ButtonReleaseMask,FALSE, upMouse, NULL);
XtAddEventHandler( aDraw, LeaveWindowMask, FALSE, lostMouse, NULL);
/**
*** Call the function "bye" when the PushButton receives
*** an activate message; i.e. when the pointer is moved to
*** the button and Button1 is pressed and released.
**/
XtAddCallback( aButton, XmNactivateCallback, bye, (XtPointer) NULL);

XtRealizeWidget(top);
XtAppMainLoop(app);
return(0);
}

void reallyQuit(Widget w, XtPointer clientdata, XtPointer calldata)
{
exit(0);
}


/**
*** pesky quit routine
**/
void  bye(Widget w, XtPointer clientdata, XtPointer calldata)
{
static Widget quitDlg = NULL;
static char *msgstr = "Are you sure you want to Quit?";

if (quitDlg != (Widget )NULL)
     {
     /* first time called */
     quitDlg = XmCreateQuestionDialog(w,"R U Sure", (XtPointer *)NULL,0);
     XtVaSetValues(quitDlg,
               XmNdialogStyle, XmDIALOG_FULL_APPLICATION_MODAL,
          XtVaTypedArg, XmNmessageString, XmRString,
               msgstr,
 strlen(msgstr),
          NULL);

     XtAddCallback(quitDlg, XmNokCallback, reallyQuit, NULL);
     }
XtManageChild(quitDlg);
}
```

The output from Listing 32.16 is shown in Figure 32.12.

FIGURE 32.12.
Drawing points and lines.

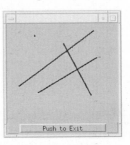

This is an example of the primitives required to draw one line on the Widget. Note the number of GCValues that have to be set to achieve this purpose. The XDrawLine function definition is as follows:

```
XDrawLine( Display *dpy,
      Drawable d,
      GC gc,
      int x1,
      int y1,
      int x2,
      int y2);
```

It's more efficient to draw multiple lines in one call. Use the XDrawLines function with a pointer to an array of points and its size.

The mode parameter can be set to

■ CoorModeOrigin to use the values relative to the drawables' origin.

■ CoorModePrevious to use the values as deltas from the previous point. A *delta* is the change in x and y coordinates between this coordinate and the previous one.

The first point is always relative to the drawables' origin. To draw boxes, use the XDrawRectangle function:

```
XDrawRectangle( Display *display, Drawable dwindow,
            GC    gc,int   x,int     y,
            unsigned int width, unsigned int height);
```

will draw a rectangle at (x,y) of geometry (width, height). To draw more than one box at a time, use the XDrawRectangles() function. This function is declared as

```
XDrawRectangles( Display *display, Window dwindow,
            GC    gc,  XRectangle *xp, int number);
```

where xp is a pointer to an array of number rectangle definition structures.

For filled rectangles, use the XFillRectangle and XFillRectangles calls, respectively.

Drawing a Point

To draw a point on-screen, use the XDrawPoint or XDrawPoints function call. This is similar to line-drawing functions. (Refer to Listing 32.16.)

Drawing an Arc

To draw circles, arcs, and similar shapes, use the XDrawArc function:

```
XDrawArc(Display *display, Window dwindow,
         GC   gc, int x, int y,
         unsigned int width, unsigned int height,
         int         a1, int a2);
```

This function is very flexible. It draws an arc from an angle a1 starting from the 3 o'clock position to angle a2. The units for angles are in one sixty-fourths (1/64) of a degree. The arc is drawn counterclockwise. The largest value is (64×360) units because the angle arguments are truncated. The width and height define the bounding rectangle for the arc. The XDrawArcs() function is used to draw multiple arcs, given pointers to the array. The prototype for this function is

```
XDrawArcs (Display *display, Window dwindow,
           GC gc, XArc *arcptr, int number);
```

To draw polygons, use the call

```
XDrawSegments( Display *display, Window dwindow, GC gc,
          XSegment *segments, int number);
```

The XSegment structure includes four short members—x1,y1,x2, and y2—which define the starting and ending points of all segments. For connected lines, use the XDrawLines function shown earlier. For filled polygons, use the XFillPolygon() function call.

Using Fonts and FontLists

Fonts are perhaps the trickiest aspect of Motif to master. See the section on fonts in Chapter 23, "Using Motif," before reading this section to familiarize yourself with font definitions.

The function XLoadQueryFont(Display *dp, char *name) returns an XFontStruct structure. This structure defines the extents for the character set. This is used to set the values of the Font field in a GC.

To draw a string on the screen, use

```
XDrawString ( Display *dp, Drawable dw, GC gc,
         int x, int y, char *str, int len);
```

which uses only the foreground color. To draw with the background and foreground colors, use

```
XDrawImageString ( Display *dp, Drawable dw, GC gc,
          int x, int y, char *str, int len);
```

The X Color Model

The X Color Model is based on an array of colors called a *colormap*. Applications refer to a color by its index into this colormap. The indices are placed in the application's frame buffer, which contains an entry for each pixel of the display. The number of bits in the index defines the number of bitplanes. The number of bitplanes defines the number of colors that can be displayed on-screen at one time. For example, one bit per pixel gives two colors, four bits per pixel gives 16 colors, and eight bits per pixel gives 256 colors.

Applications generally inherit the colormap of their parent. They can also create their own colormap using the XCreateColormap call. The call is defined as

```
Colormap XCreateColormap( Display *display, Window   dwindow,
                Visual   *vp, int requested);
```

This allocates the number of requested color entries in the colormap for a window. Generally, the visual parameter is derived from the macro

```
DefaultVisual (Display *display, int screenNumber);
```

where screenNumber = 0 in almost all cases. Colormaps are a valuable resource in X and must be freed after use. This is done via the call XFreeColormap(Display *display, Colormap c);

Applications can get the standard colormap from the X server by using the XGetStandardColormap() call, and set it via the XSetStandardColormap() call. These are defined as

```
XGetStandardColormap( Display *display, Window   dwindow,
        XStandardColormap *c, Atom property);
```

and

```
XSetStandardColormap( Display *display, Window   dwindow,
XStandardColormap *c, Atom property);
```

Once applications have a Colormap to work with, they have to follow two steps:

1. Define the colormap entries.

   The property atom can take the values of RGB_BEST_MAP, RGB_GRAY_MAP, or 2RGB_DEFAULT_MAP. These are names of colormaps stored in the server. They are not colormaps in themselves.

2. Set the colormap for a window via the call

   ```
   XSetWindowColormap ( Display *display, Window   dwindow,   Colormap c );
   ```

For setting or allocating a color in the Colormap, use the XColor structure defined in <X/Xlib.h>.

To see a bright blue color, use the segment

```
XColor color;
color.red = 0;
color.blue = 0xffff;
color.green = 0;
```

Then add the color to the `Colormap` using the call to the function:

```
XAllocColor(Display *display,
            Window dwindow,
            XColor *color );
```

See Listing 32.17 for a sample function to set the color of a Widget.

Listing 32.17. Convenience function for getting colors.

```
/**
*** Convenience function to get colors
**/
Pixel GetPixel( Widget w, int r, int g, int b)
{
Display *dpy;
int     scr;
Colormap cmp;
XColor          clr;

dpy = XtDisplay(w);
scr = DefaultScreen(dpy);
cmp = DefaultColormap(dpy);

clr.red = (short)r;
clr.green = (short)g;
clr.blue = (short)b;
clr.flags = DoRed ¦ DoGreen ¦ DoBlue;

/**
*** Note that the default black pixel of the display and screen
*** is returned if the color could not be allocated.
**/
return(XAllocColor(dpy,cmp,&clr) ? clr.pixel : BlackPixel(dpy,scr));
}
```

The default white and black pixels are defined as

```
Pixel BlackPixel( Display *dpy, int screen);
Pixel WhitePixel( Display *dpy, int screen);
```

and will work with any screen as a fallback.

The index (`Pixel`) returned by this function is not guaranteed to be the same every time the application runs. This is because the colormap could be shared between applications requesting colors in different orders. Each entry is allocated on a next-available-entry basis. Sometimes, if you overwrite an existing entry in a cell, you might actually see a change in a completely different application. So be careful.

Applications can query the RGB components of a color by calling the function

```
XQueryColor( Display *display, Colormap *cmp, Xcolor   *clr);
```

For many colors at one time, use

```
XQueryColors( Display *display, Colormap *cmp,
          Xcolor     *clr,      int number);
```

At this time the application can modify the RGB components. Then you can store them in the colormap with the call

```
XStoreColor( Display *display, Colormap *cmp,XColor *clr);
```

Recall that X11 has some strange names for colors in the /usr/lib/rgb.txt file. Applications can get the RGB components of these names with a call to

```
XLookupColor( Display *display, Colormap cmp,
         char *name,XColor *clr, XColor  *exact);
```

The name is the string to search for in the rgb.txt file. The returned value clr contains the next closest existing entry in the colormap. The exact color entry contains the exact RGB definition in the entry in rgb.txt. This function does not allocate the color in the colormap. To do that, use the call

```
XAllocNamedColor( Display *display, Colormap cmp,
            char *name, Xcolor      *clr, XColor  *exact);
```

Pixmaps, Bitmaps, and Images

A Pixmap is like a window, but is off-screen and therefore invisible to the user. This is usually the same depth of the screen. You create a Pixmap with the call

```
XCreatePixmap (Display *dp,
            Drawable dw,
            unsigned int width,
            unsigned int height,
            unsigned int depth);
```

A drawable can be either a Window (on-screen) or a Pixmap (off-screen). *Bitmaps* are Pixmaps of a depth of one pixel. Look in

```
/usr/include/X11/bitmaps
```

for a listing of se of the standard bitmaps.

The way to copy Pixmaps from memory to the screen is via the call to XCopyArea. The prototype for this call is

```
XCopyArea( Display dp,
     Drawable Src, Drawable Dst,
     GC gc, int src_x, int src_y,
     unsigned int width, unsigned int height,
     int dst_x, int dst_y);
```

The caveat with this XCopyArea is that the depth of the Src and Dst drawables have to be of the same depth. To show a bitmap on a screen with depth greater than 1 pixel, you have to copy the bitmap one plane at a time. This is done via the call

```
XCopyPlane( Display dp,
     Drawable Src, Drawable Dst,
     GC gc, int src_x, int src_y,
     unsigned int width, unsigned int height,
     int dst_x, int dst_y, unsigned long plane);
```

where the plane specifies the bit plane to which this one-bit-deep bitmap must be copied. The actual operation is largely dependent on the modes set in the GC.

For example, to show the files in the /usr/include/bitmaps directory that have three defined values for a sample file called gumby.h:

- gumby_bits = pointer to an array of character bits.
- gumby_height and gumby_width = integer height and width.

First, create the bitmap from the data using the XCreateBitmapFromData() call. To display this one-plane-thick image, copy the image from this plane to plane 1 of the display. You can actually copy to any plane in the window. A sample call could be set for copying from your Pixmap to the Widget's plane 1 in the following manner:

```
XCopyPlane( XtDisplay(w), yourPixmap, XtWindow(w), gc,
     0,0, your_height, your_width, 0,0,1);
```

where it copies from the origin of the pixmap to the origin of plane 1 of the window.

There are other functions for working with images in X. These include the capability to store device-dependent images on disk and the Xpm format.

Summary

This chapter covered the following topics:

- The basics of writing Motif applications
- The special naming conventions in Motif and X
- Writing and compiling your first Motif application
- An overview of the Motif Widget hierarchy
- Working with various common Widgets
- Designing layouts
- Creating pop-up menus and menu bars
- Creating simple dialog boxes
- How to use the mouse in event handling
- How to use colors in X
- How to draw lines and points

This chapter could easily expand into a book. (Please do not tempt me!) I have only covered the basics of writing Motif applications. However, given the vast number of tools in Linux, you can see how you can port any existing Motif application code to and from a Linux machine. Similarly, a Linux machine can also prove to be a good development platform for developing Motif applications.

Programming XView Applications

33

by
Kamran Husain

In this chapter you will learn how to program in an older, but still widely found, OPEN LOOK–based user interface manager called XView. You will find this distribution helpful when you work with older code or when you port code from the OPEN LOOK style to Motif.

A Note About CDE

In March 1993, the Common Open Software Environment (COSE) committees adopted the Common Desktop Environment (CDE). CDE is based on the Motif interface. Sun Microsystems Inc., the primary developer of OPEN LOOK applications, agreed to conform to CDE as well. In short, this means that OPEN LOOK interface–based applications will soon be out of style. However, applications with an OPEN LOOK interface still exist and have to be ported to Motif eventually. A good knowledge of how OPEN LOOK applications work will be very beneficial to you if you ever have to port old existing code to conform to CDE.

Overview

To a programmer, the XView toolkit is an object-oriented toolkit. Think of XView objects as building blocks from which the user can create complicated applications, and think of each block as part of a package. Each package provides properties that you can modify to configure the object.

The XView toolkit consists of the objects shown in Figure 33.1. The subclasses are derived from the classes to their left. For example, Icon is a subclass of Window. Each class is also referred to as a package.

FIGURE 33.1.

XView class hierarchy.

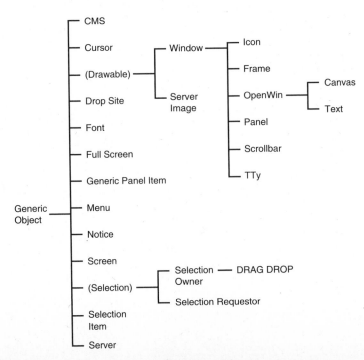

Some objects are visible and some are not. The visible objects provide the windows, scrollbars, and so on. The invisible objects, such as the font, display, or server, provide frameworks that aid in the display or layout of visible objects.

When you create an object, you get a handle to the object back from the XView libraries. Handles are opaque pointers to structures. This means that you can pass information via functions to these objects via their handles but you cannot see their structures directly.

The following functions enable you to manipulate all XView objects:

- `xv_init()` Establishes the connection to the server, initializes the notifier (message handler), and loads the resource databases
- `xv_create()` Creates an object
- `xv_destroy()` Destroys an object
- `xv_find()` Finds an object with given criteria; if not found, creates the object
- `xv_get()` Gets an attribute value
- `xv_set()` Sets an attribute value

There are three categories of attributes: generic attributes apply to all objects; common attributes are shared by some, but not all, objects; and specific attributes belong to one class of objects only. Attributes that are specific to a type of object are prefixed with the name of the object; for example, `FRAME_*`, `ICON_*`, `MENU_*`, and so on. Common and generic attributes are prefixed by `XV_`. For example, `XV_HEIGHT` applies to all objects, but `FRAME_HEIGHT` applies only to frame objects.

Each attribute may have different types of values. For example, the following code sets a `panel_item`.

```
panel_item = (Panel_item) xv_create( masterpanel, PANEL_CYCLE,
    XV_HEIGHT,        100,
    XV_WIDTH,         50,
    PANEL_LABEL_X,       100,
    PANEL_LABEL_Y,       100,
    PANEL_LABEL_STRING, "Help",
    PANEL_CHOICE_STRINGS, "About ... ",
                "How to use Help",
               "Search Index",
              NULL,

    NULL);
```

Note how the types of values are mixed in this function call. All attributes except `PANEL_CHOICE_STRINGS` take a single argument. The `PANEL_CHOICE_STRINGS` attribute takes a list of arguments. The list is terminated with a `NULL` value.

We will go over the details of each object in this chapter.

Requirements

To create an XView program you must link in the XView and OPEN LOOK graphics library, which includes all the toolkit functions for you. You will also need the X11 library. The command line to use the gcc compiler for a simple XView application is

```
$ gcc sample.c -lxview -lolgx -lX11 -o sample
```

However, this compile command relies on the fact that your libraries are located in /usr/lib or you have links to this location. The XView libraries are located in the /usr/openwin/lib directories.

See the sample makefile in Listing 33.1 that you can use with the applications in this chapter. To compile a listing from this book, type make *filename*. For example, type make list33_2.

Listing 33.1. Sample `makefile` for creating XView applications.

```
CC=gcc
LIBPATH=-L/usr/openwin/lib -L/usr/X11/lib
INCPATH=/usr/openwin/include
LIBS= -lxview -lolgx -lX11

list33_2: list 33_2.c
        $(CC) $< -I$(INCPATH) $(LIBPATH) $(LIBS) -o $@

list33_3: list 33_3.c
        $(CC) $< -I$(INCPATH) $(LIBPATH) $(LIBS) -o $@

list33_4: list 33_4.c
        $(CC) $< -I$(INCPATH) $(LIBPATH) $(LIBS) -o $@

list33_5: list 33_5.c
        $(CC) $< -I$(INCPATH) $(LIBPATH) $(LIBS) -o $@

list33_6: list 33_6.c
        $(CC) $< -I$(INCPATH) $(LIBPATH) $(LIBS) -o $@

list33_7: list 33_7.c
        $(CC) $< -I$(INCPATH) $(LIBPATH) $(LIBS) -o $@

list33_8: list 33_8.c
        $(CC) $< -I$(INCPATH) $(LIBPATH) $(LIBS) -o $@

list33_9: list 33_9.c
        $(CC) $< -I$(INCPATH) $(LIBPATH) $(LIBS) -o $@

list33_10: list 33_10.c
        $(CC) $< -I$(INCPATH) $(LIBPATH) $(LIBS) -o $@
```

The -lxview in LIBS refers to the libxview.a library. The libxview.a library contains the code for all the windows manipulation and libolgx.a contains the OPENLOOK graphics library. The libX11.a is required by the libxview.a library, and libolgx.a is required by the libxview.a library.

Header Files

The basic definitions you must use for XView are located in two files: xview/generic.h and xview/xview.h in the /usr/openwin/include directory tree. The header files required by other packages, such as FONT or FRAME, are declared in files of the same name as the package. For example, for the FONT package you must use the xview/font.h header file. You can include these files more than once.

> **NOTE**
>
> In some source distributions, the file generic.h is not explicitly called out in the source files. In order to compile source files under Linux, you will need the generic.h file.

Sample Application

Take a look at the simple application shown in Listing 33.2, which places a window with a Quit button on it.

Listing 33.2. A simple application.

```
/*
** A sample program to show you how to present items for
** selection to the user.
**
*/
#include <xview/generic.h>
#include <xview/xview.h>
#include <xview/frame.h>
#include <xview/panel.h>
#include <xview/cms.h>

Frame frame;

#define FORE 0
#define BACK 2

int main(int argc, char *argv[])
{
Cms    cms;
Panel panel;
void quit();

printf("\n 0\n");
xv_init(XV_INIT_ARGC_PTR_ARGV, &argc, argv, NULL);


cms = (Cms ) xv_create((int)NULL,CMS, /* NULL -> use the default Frame*/
    CMS_SIZE, CMS_CONTROL_COLORS + 4,
    CMS_CONTROL_CMS, True,
    CMS_NAMED_COLORS, "LightBlue", "Blue", "Red", "Green", NULL,
    NULL);

frame = (Frame)xv_create((int)NULL, FRAME,
    FRAME_LABEL, argv[0],
    XV_WIDTH, 200,
    XV_HEIGHT, 100,
    NULL);

xv_set(frame,
    WIN_CMS, cms,
    WIN_FOREGROUND_COLOR, CMS_CONTROL_COLORS + FORE,
```

continues

Listing 33.2. continued

```
    WIN_BACKGROUND_COLOR, CMS_CONTROL_COLORS + BACK,
    NULL);

panel = (Panel)xv_create(frame, PANEL,NULL);

(void) xv_create(panel, PANEL_BUTTON,
    PANEL_LABEL_STRING, "Quit",
    PANEL_NOTIFY_PROC, quit,
    NULL);

xv_main_loop(frame);
exit(0);
}

void quit()
{
xv_destroy_safe(frame);
}
```

> **NOTE**
>
> At the chance of being too literal, don't forget to run the applications in this chapter from an X terminal. The programs will not run without the X server.

The output from this application is shown in Figure 33.2. There are several things that you should note about this sample application.

- The XV toolkit is initialized as soon as possible in the application with the xv_init call.
- All attribute values to the xv_create() function call are terminated with a NULL parameter.
- The (Frame) cast is used to override the default returned value from xv_create().
- The <xview/generic.h> header file is used to get all the required definitions for the file.

> **NOTE**
>
> The figures shown in this chapter depict the program being run from the dwm window manager.

Initialization

You should initialize the XView system as soon as possible in any application. The xv_init() call does this for you. By default, xv_init() uses the DISPLAY environment variable for you. By passing the argc and argv values you can override the default values for the application from the command line. You can use xv_init() only once in an application; the libraries ignore all other calls.

Normally you'd override the DISPLAY variable if you wanted to display the window on a different machine.

FIGURE 33.2.

A sample XView application.

Sample application ——

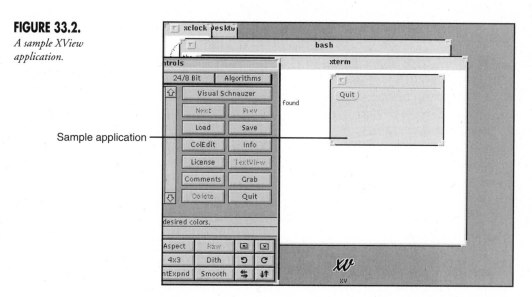

You can use two types of parameters for the first argument to xv_init(): XV_INIT_ARGS, which leaves the argc and argv unchanged, or XV_INIT_ARGC_PTR_ARGV, which modifies argc and argv to remove all XView-specific arguments. With XV_INIT_ARGS, you pass argc into xv_init and with XV_INIT_ARGC_PTR_ARGV you pass the address of argc to xv_init().

Creating Objects

The xv_create function is used to create all the objects in an application. The syntax for the xv_create function is

```
xv_object xv_create(xv_object owner, xv_package pkg, void *attr)
```

where the owner is the parent of the object being created, and of type *pkg* given the attributes listed in variable length arguments starting with attr. Sometimes you can use a NULL value in place of the owner parameter to indicate that the owner value can be substituted for screen or server as appropriate. However, in some calls the owner parameter must point to a valid object, so the NULL value will generate an error.

The attributes for the newly created object inherit their behavior from their parents. The attributes can be overridden by values included in the variable list specified in attr.

The values of attributes are set in the following decreasing order of precedence:

■ A call to xv_set will override any other type of setting

■ Any command-line arguments

- Values in the .Xdefaults file
- Values in the attributes of an xv_create call
- Window Manager defaults

Exiting an Application

The best way to get out of an XView application is to destroy the topmost object. Use the xv_destroy_safe() function call, which waits for the destruction of all derived objects and cleans up after itself. You can also use xv_destroy() to get out immediately with the risk of not giving up system resources but be able to exit very quickly. If you don't give up resources, they will not be freed for use by any other applications in the system and will use up valuable memory space.

Frames

A *frame* is a container for other windows. A frame manages the geometry of subwindows that do not overlap. Some examples include canvases, text windows, panels, and scrollbars. You saw a base frame in the output of LIST33_1.c (refer to Figure 33.2 and Listing 33.2).

Frames enable you to specify three types of outputs on three areas. The topmost area is the name on the top of the frame called the header. The bottom of the frame is divided into two sections; one is left-justified and the other is right-justified. Figure 33.3 shows the output from Listing 33.3, which shows you how to write to these areas.

Listing 33.3. Header and footer frames.

```
/*
**
** Listing to show headers and footers.
**
*/
#include <xview/generic.h>
#include <xview/xview.h>
#include <xview/frame.h>
#include <xview/panel.h>


/*
**
*/
Frame frame;

/*
**
*/
int main(int argc, char *argv[])
{

Panel panel;
void quit();
```

```
xv_init(XV_INIT_ARGC_PTR_ARGV, &argc, argv, NULL);

frame = (Frame)xv_create(NULL, FRAME,
    FRAME_LABEL, "Title Here",
    FRAME_SHOW_FOOTER, TRUE,
    FRAME_LEFT_FOOTER, "left side",
    FRAME_RIGHT_FOOTER, "right side",
    XV_WIDTH, 200,
    XV_HEIGHT, 100,
    NULL);

panel = (Panel)xv_create(frame, PANEL,NULL);

(void) xv_create(panel, PANEL_BUTTON,
    PANEL_LABEL_STRING, "Quit",
    PANEL_NOTIFY_PROC, quit,
    NULL);

xv_main_loop(frame);
exit(0);
}

void quit()
{
xv_destroy_safe(frame);
}
```

FIGURE 33.3.

Header and footer frames.

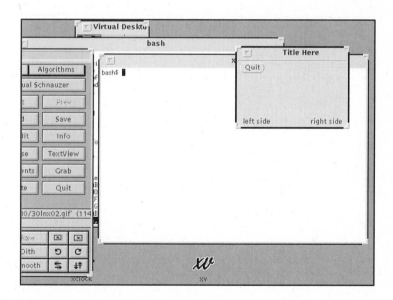

The parameters used to create these headers are shown in the following lines:

```
Frame frame;
frame = (Frame) xv_create(NULL, FRAME,
        FRAME_LABEL, argv[0],
        FRAME_SHOW_FOOTER, TRUE,
```

```
        FRAME_LEFT_FOOTER, "left side",
        FRAME_RIGHT_FOOTER, "right side",
        FRAME_LABEL, "Title Here",
        NULL);
```

You have to turn the footer display on with the FRAME_SHOW_FOOTER attribute set to TRUE. The other values in this call actually set the values of the header and footer.

Command Frames

Command frames are usually used to perform a quick function and then disappear. These frames are usually pop-up frames like the pushpin dialog boxes you saw in Chapter 24, "OPEN LOOK and OpenWindows." If the pushpin is pressed in, the dialog box remains "pinned" to the screen; otherwise, the dialog box will go away after the user performs the section.

Listing 33.4 shows you a program to create command frames.

Listing 33.4. Using command frames.

```
/*
** Sample Application to show command frames.
**
*/
#include <xview/generic.h>
#include <xview/xview.h>
#include <xview/frame.h>
#include <xview/panel.h>

/*
** Global Frames
*/
Frame frame;
Frame popup;


/*
**
** Declare the used functions here
**
*/
void show_greeting(Frame *fp);
int  show_popup();
int  push_it();
void quit();

/*
** The main function
*/
int main(int argc, char *argv[])
{
Panel panel;
Panel fpanel;


    /*
    **  Initialize the toolkit
```

```
*/
xv_init(XV_INIT_ARGC_PTR_ARGV, &argc, argv, NULL);

/*
**  Create top level frame.
*/
frame = (Frame)xv_create(NULL, FRAME,
FRAME_LABEL, "Title Here",
FRAME_SHOW_FOOTER, TRUE,
FRAME_LEFT_FOOTER, "Popup",
FRAME_RIGHT_FOOTER, argv[0],
XV_WIDTH, 200,
XV_HEIGHT, 100,
NULL);

/*
** Create the popup Frame.
*/
popup = (Frame) xv_create(frame, FRAME_CMD,
FRAME_LABEL, "Popup",
XV_WIDTH, 100,
XV_HEIGHT, 100,
NULL);

/*
** Create panel for popup
*/
fpanel = (Panel)xv_get(popup, FRAME_CMD_PANEL,NULL);

/*
** Add buttons to popup
*/
(void) xv_create(fpanel, PANEL_BUTTON,
PANEL_LABEL_STRING, "Greet",
PANEL_NOTIFY_PROC,  show_greeting,
NULL);

(void) xv_create(fpanel, PANEL_BUTTON,
PANEL_LABEL_STRING, "Push Me",
PANEL_NOTIFY_PROC,  push_it,
NULL);

/*
** Create panel
*/
panel = (Panel)xv_create(frame, PANEL,NULL);

/*
** Add buttons to main application frame
*/
(void) xv_create(panel, PANEL_BUTTON,
PANEL_LABEL_STRING, "Hello",
PANEL_NOTIFY_PROC,  show_popup,
NULL);


(void) xv_create(panel, PANEL_BUTTON,
PANEL_LABEL_STRING, "Quit",
```

continues

Listing 33.4. continued

```
    PANEL_NOTIFY_PROC, quit,
    NULL);

    xv_main_loop(frame);
exit(0);
}

void quit()
{
xv_destroy_safe(frame);
}


void show_greeting(Frame *fp)
{
printf ("\n Greet you? How?");
}


show_popup(Frame item, Event *ev)
{
xv_set(popup, XV_SHOW, TRUE, NULL);
}

push_it(Panel_item item, Event *ev)
{
int ret;

ret = (int)xv_get(popup, FRAME_CMD_PIN_STATE) ;
if (ret == FRAME_CMD_PIN_IN)
    {
    printf("Pin already in.. bye\n");
    xv_set(popup, XV_SHOW, TRUE, NULL);  /* refresh anyway */
    }
    else
    {
    printf("Pin out.. pushing it in\n");
    xv_set(popup, FRAME_CMD_PIN_STATE, FRAME_CMD_PIN_IN, NULL);
    xv_set(popup, XV_SHOW, TRUE, NULL);  /* refresh anyway */
    }
}
```

The output from Listing 33.4 is shown in Figure 33.4.

Look at the important lines of the program in Listing 33.4 in detail. By examining these lines you will learn the following:

- How to create pop-up menus
- How to add buttons to a panel
- How to handle callback functions for xview objects

FIGURE 33.4.

Using command frames.

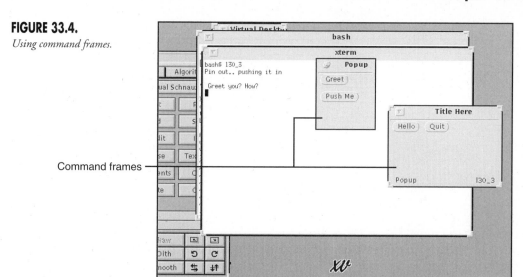

Command frames

There are two frames in this application: `frame` and `popup`. These frames are declared at the top of the application with the statements

```
Frame frame;
Frame popup;
```

We also declared the following functions in this application:

- `void show_greeting(Frame *fp);` This function is called when the Greeting button is pressed.
- `int show_popup();` This function is called when the Hello button is pressed.
- `int push_it();` This function is called when the Push Me button is pressed.
- `void quit();` This function is called when the Quit button is pressed.

The main `xv_init()` and frame creation for the program is as in Listing 33.3. Let's concentrate on the pop-up menu examples.

First, the pop-up frame is created with the following lines:

```
popup = (Frame) xv_create(frame, FRAME_CMD,
FRAME_LABEL, "Popup",
XV_WIDTH, 100,
XV_HEIGHT, 100,
NULL);
```

This call will create the pop-up frame with `frame` as the owner. The pop-up frame is not displayed immediately. You can create several pop-up frames this way and display them only when they are needed.

NOTE

Note that if you do not set the XV_WIDTH and XV_HEIGHT parameters for this xv_create()
call, the pop-up screen will occupy the entire screen.

Next we create a panel for this pop-up with the call

```
fpanel = (Panel)xv_get(popup, FRAME_CMD_PANEL,NULL);
```

Then we add the Greet and Push Me buttons to this new fpanel. This is done by the xv_create
calls, which are shown next:

```
(void) xv_create(fpanel, PANEL_BUTTON,
PANEL_LABEL_STRING, "Greet",
PANEL_NOTIFY_PROC,  show_greeting,
NULL);

(void) xv_create(fpanel, PANEL_BUTTON,
PANEL_LABEL_STRING, "Push Me",
PANEL_NOTIFY_PROC,  push_it,
NULL);
```

At this point you are ready to create the main application frame, show it, and go into the main loop.
The important call that does this is shown next. The function show_popup() is assigned to be called
when the Hello button is pressed.

```
(void) xv_create(panel, PANEL_BUTTON,
    PANEL_LABEL_STRING, "Hello",
    PANEL_NOTIFY_PROC,  show_popup,
    NULL);
```

Now look at the functions that are called when each button is pressed. The show_greeting function simply prints out a string. (You can use your imagination here for the contents of the string for
your own application.) The show_popup() function will use the call to the xv_set() function to
actually make the pop-up frame visible.

```
xv_set(popup, XV_SHOW, TRUE, NULL);
```

Now for the function that will emulate the behavior of pushing in the pin. This is the push_it()
function. The FRAME_CMD_PIN_STATE parameter requests the state of the pushpin on the dialog box.
The state for the pin is defined as FRAME_CMD_PIN_IN if the pushpin is already pushed in. This is the
state for which you check. If the pushpin is not in this state, it is pushed in with the xv_set(popup,
FRAME_CMD_PIN_STATE, FRAME_CMD_PIN_IN, NULL); function call.

TIP

A command frame has no resize corners by default. To turn these corners on, set
FRAME_SHOW_RESIZE_CORNERS to TRUE.

Setting Colors on Frames

The colors on an XView frame object are defaulted to the OpenWindows.WindowColor resource. This resource is inherited by all subframes as well. You can override these colors with the CMS package. The CMS package is created by a call to xv_create():

```
cms = (Cms *) xv_create(parent, CMS, attrs, NULL);
```

A CMS can contain as many colors as are allowed in the largest color map you can create. You can have several color maps referencing the same color; in fact, the system can share the location of colors between two independent applications. For this reason, you should allocate all your colors once, at cms creation, to allocate all the colors in your color map to prevent another application from changing the colors you absolutely need.

For example, to create a cms with four named colors, you would use the following function call:

```
cms = (Cms  *)xv_create(parent, CMS,
    CMS_SIZE, 4,
    CMS_NAMED_COLORS, "Violet", "Yellow", "Blue", "Orange",
    NULL);
```

The CMS_SIZE value asks for a four-entry color table that is indexed from 0 to 3, with the values of the named colors "Violet", "Yellow", "Blue", and "Orange". The foreground color for a frame is the first indexed color in a Cms and the background color for a frame is the last indexed (n-1) color in a Cms. Setting a CMS_SIZE will give you either an error or a monochromatic display. Of course, to avoid runtime errors you must know that the colors you just specified by name do exist in the /usr/lib/rgb.txt file.

Listing 33.5 is an example of an application that sets the colors. This will let you set the foreground and background colors of a frame and all its children.

Listing 33.5. Using CMS.

```
#include <xview/generic.h>
#include <xview/xview.h>
#include <xview/frame.h>
#include <xview/panel.h>
#include <xview/cms.h>

Frame frame;

#define FORE 3
#define BACK 0

int main(int argc, char *argv[])
{
Cms    cms;
Panel panel;
void quit();

printf("\n 0\n");
xv_init(XV_INIT_ARGC_PTR_ARGV, &argc, argv, NULL);
```

continues

Listing 33.5. continued

```
cms = (Cms ) xv_create((int)NULL,CMS, /* NULL -> use the default Frame*/
    CMS_SIZE, CMS_CONTROL_COLORS + 4,
    CMS_CONTROL_CMS, True,
    CMS_NAMED_COLORS, "LightBlue", "Blue", "Red", "Green", NULL,
    NULL);

frame = (Frame)xv_create((int)NULL, FRAME,
    FRAME_LABEL, argv[0],
    XV_WIDTH, 200,
    XV_HEIGHT, 100,
    NULL);

xv_set(frame,
    WIN_CMS, cms,
    WIN_FOREGROUND_COLOR, CMS_CONTROL_COLORS + FORE,
    WIN_BACKGROUND_COLOR, CMS_CONTROL_COLORS + BACK,
    NULL);

panel = (Panel)xv_create(frame, PANEL,NULL);

(void) xv_create(panel, PANEL_BUTTON,
    PANEL_LABEL_STRING, "Quit",
    PANEL_NOTIFY_PROC, quit,
    NULL);

xv_main_loop(frame);
exit(0);
}

void quit()
{
xv_destroy_safe(frame);
}
```

> **TIP**
>
> You cannot use xv_get with the CMS_NAMED_COLORS attribute.

> **CAUTION**
>
> Use xv_set() to override the colors on a frame. Any color requests on a frame at the time of creation are overridden by values of the .Xdefaults resources values.

Canvases

A *canvas* is an XView object that is used to display items that are too large to fit on a window. The viewable portion of the image is seen through a viewport or view window of the object. You can have multiple views of the same data that is stored on a canvas by splitting each scrollable portion into two or more views. The split views must all reside on the same canvas because you cannot have multiple views of canvas data that are not on the same frame.

There are three components of a canvas object:

- The Paint window, which contains the actual painted data
- The View window, which has the scrollbars but no painted data
- The canvas subwindow, which contains the union of the View window and Paint window

Look at a simple example in Listing 33.6 of how to use scrollbars and how to paint on a paint window. (I have added line numbers for readability.)

Listing 33.6. Using canvases and scrollbars.

```
1    /*
2    ** An example of a scrolled window
3    */

4    #include <X11/Xlib.h>
5    #include <xview/generic.h>
6    #include <xview/xview.h>
7    #include <xview/frame.h>
8    #include <xview/panel.h>
9    #include <xview/canvas.h>
10   #include <xview/scrollbar.h>
11   #include <xview/xv_xrect.h>

12   /*
13   ** Declare our callback functions for this application.
14   */
15   Frame frame;
16   void redraw(Canvas c, Xv_Window pw, Display *dp, Window xwin,
17           Xv_xrectlist *rp) ;

18   int main(int argc, char *argv[])
19   {
20   Canvas canvas;
21   Panel panel;
22   Scrollbar h_s, h_v;
23   void quit();

24       xv_init(XV_INIT_ARGC_PTR_ARGV, &argc, argv, NULL);

25   frame = (Frame)xv_create(NULL, FRAME,
26       FRAME_LABEL, argv[0],
27       XV_WIDTH, 400,
28       XV_HEIGHT, 200,
29       (int)NULL);

30   /*
31   ** Create the canvas.
32   */
33   canvas = (Canvas) xv_create(frame, CANVAS,
34       CANVAS_REPAINT_PROC, redraw,
```

continues

Listing 33.6. continued

```
35          CANVAS_X_PAINT_WINDOW, TRUE,
36          CANVAS_AUTO_SHRINK, FALSE,
37          CANVAS_AUTO_EXPAND, TRUE,
38          CANVAS_WIDTH, 500,
39          CANVAS_HEIGHT, 500,
40          XV_WIDTH, 400,
41          XV_HEIGHT, 200,
42          NULL);

43     /*
44     ** Create the splittable scrollbars
45     */
46          h_s = (Scrollbar)xv_create(canvas, SCROLLBAR,
47          SCROLLBAR_DIRECTION, SCROLLBAR_HORIZONTAL,
48          SCROLLBAR_SPLITTABLE, TRUE,
49          NULL);

50          h_v = (Scrollbar)xv_create(canvas, SCROLLBAR,
51          SCROLLBAR_DIRECTION, SCROLLBAR_VERTICAL,
52          SCROLLBAR_SPLITTABLE, TRUE,
53          NULL);

54     xv_main_loop(frame);
55     exit(0);
56     }

57     void redraw(Canvas c, Xv_Window pw, Display *dp, Window xwin,
58             Xv_xrectlist *rp)
59     {
60          GC gc;
61          int wd, ht;
62          int i;
63          int j;
64          int dx;
65          int dy;

66          gc = DefaultGC(dp, DefaultScreen(dp));
67          wd = (int)xv_get(pw, XV_WIDTH);
68          ht = (int)xv_get(pw, XV_HEIGHT);

69          dx = ht / 10;
70          for (i = 0; i < ht; i += dx)
71              XDrawLine(dp,xwin,gc, i,0,i,ht);

72
73          dx = wd / 10;
74          for (i = 0; i < wd; i += dx)
75              XDrawLine(dp,xwin,gc, 0,i,wd,i);
76     /* XDrawLine(dp,xwin,gc, 0,0,wd,ht);   */

77     }
78     void quit()
79     {
80     xv_destroy_safe(frame);
81     }
```

Lines 33 through 42 create the canvas. The CANVAS_AUTO_EXPAND and CANVAS_AUTO_SHRINK parameters maintain the relation of the canvas subwindow and the paint subwindow. These values default to TRUE. When both values are TRUE, the canvas and paint subwindows will expand or shrink based on the size of the window on which they are being displayed.

Setting the CANVAS_AUTO_EXPAND value to TRUE enables the paint subwindow to expand larger than the canvas subwindow. If the canvas subwindow expands to a bigger size than the paint subwindow, the paint subwindow is expanded to at least that size as well. If the canvas subwindow size shrinks, the paint subwindow does not shrink because it is already at the same size or bigger than canvas subwindows at that time.

Setting the CANVAS_AUTO_SHRINK value to TRUE forces the canvas object to always confirm that the paint subwindow's height and width are never greater than the canvas subwindow. In other words, the size of the paint subwindow is always changed to be at least the same or less than the size of the canvas subwindow.

You can explicitly set the size of the canvas window with the CANVAS_WIDTH and CANVAS_HEIGHT parameters. (See lines 38 and 39.) These canvas dimensions can be greater than the viewing window dimensions set with XV_WIDTH and XV_HEIGHT (lines 40 and 41).

We have to add the include file <xview/scrollbar.h> to get the definitions for the scrollbar package. These are created in lines 46 through 53. Note how we have to create two separate scrollbars, one vertical and one horizontal.

The scrollbars in this example show how they can split to provide multiple, tiled views of the data in the canvas window. To split a view, press the right mouse button on a scrollbar and you will be presented with a pop-up menu. Choose the Split View option to split the view or the Join View option to join two views together. You will not see a Join View option if a scrollbar does not dissect a view.

You can programmatically split a canvas view even if scrollbars are not present. Use the OPENWIN_SPLIT attribute in an xv_set() function call. For example:

```
xv_window xv;
xv = (xv_window)xv_get(canvas,OPENWIN_NTH_VIEW,0);

xv_set(canvas,
    OPENWIN_SPLIT,
    OPENWIN_SPLIT_VIEW, xv,
    OPENWIN_SPLIT_DIRECTION,
    OPENWIN_SPLIT_HORIZONTAL,
    NULL);
```

TIP

You may want to group your xv_set() function calls into distinct logical calls to set each type of parameter instead of one long convoluted list of parameters to one xv_set() function. Splitting the code into these groups makes the code easier to read and debug.

Note that only `OPENWIN_*` type of attributes are allowed in the `xv_set()` call with the `OPENWIN_SPLIT` parameter. Do not mix other types of attributes. To get the first view you can use a value of `0` to the `OPENWIN_NTH_VIEW` parameter. For the next view, use `1`, and so on. To get an idea of how many views there are for this canvas use the call

```
int number;
number = (int)xv_get(canvas, OPENWIN_NVIEWS);
```

To get the paint window to do your own drawing, perhaps in response to other user input, you can use the `xv_get()` function to get the paint window. For example,

```
xv_window xv_paint;
xv_paint = (xv_window)xv_get(canvas, CANVAS_VIEW_PAINT, null);
```

Listing 33.6 shows how to use the standard `Xlib` function calls to draw on the canvas. (See Figure 33.5.) You must use the include file `<X/Xlib.h>` for all the definitions and declarations. The `XDrawLine` function used in this example is somewhat simple. However, this example shows you how to set up your Graphics Context and use the standard `XDrawLine` function to draw a grid. You can use other X drawing functions just as easily.

FIGURE 33.5.

The scrolled window example.

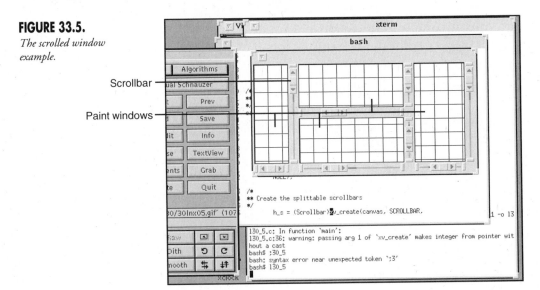

Buttons

A *button* item enables a user to select an action. Several types of buttons are available to you as a programmer. Figure 33.6 shows how various buttons are used. There are four distinct examples shown in Figure 33.6:

- ▪ The Menu Item is shown as "Y/N/Q".
- ▪ The 1 of N choice of items from four items.

- The M of N choice of items from three items to match others.
- Choosing via four checkboxes.

The listing for generating Figure 33.6 is shown in Listing 33.7. We will go over this listing in detail.

FIGURE 33.6.

Using buttons.

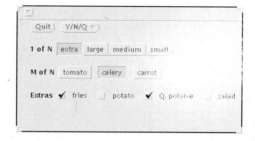

Listing 33.7. Using menus, buttons, and choices.

```c
/*
** A sampler of some of the choices to present to a user
*/
#include <xview/generic.h>
#include <xview/xview.h>
#include <xview/frame.h>
#include <xview/panel.h>
#include <xview/openmenu.h>

Frame frame;
int menuHandler( Menu item, Menu_item selection);
int selected( Panel_item item, Event *ev);
void quit();

int main(int argc, char *argv[])
{
Rect   *rt;
Rect   *qrt;
Panel panel;
Panel quitbtn;
Panel oneN;
Panel manyN;
Panel chooser;
Menu  menu1;


    xv_init(XV_INIT_ARGC_PTR_ARGV, &argc, argv, NULL);

frame = (Frame)xv_create(NULL, FRAME,
    FRAME_LABEL, argv[0],
    XV_WIDTH, 400,
    XV_HEIGHT, 200,
    NULL);

panel = (Panel)xv_create(frame, PANEL,NULL);
```

continues

Listing 33.7. continued

```
quitbtn =    (Panel)xv_create(panel, PANEL_BUTTON,
    PANEL_LABEL_STRING, "Quit",
    PANEL_NOTIFY_PROC, quit,
    XV_X, 20,
    NULL);


menu1 = (Menu) xv_create(NULL, MENU,
    MENU_STRINGS, "Yes", "No", "Maybe", "Bye", NULL,
    MENU_NOTIFY_PROC, menuHandler,
    NULL);

xv_create (panel, PANEL_BUTTON,
    PANEL_LABEL_STRING, "Y/N/Q",
    PANEL_ITEM_MENU, menu1,
    PANEL_NOTIFY_PROC, selected,
    NULL);

qrt = (Rect *) xv_get(quitbtn, XV_RECT);

oneN =   (Panel) xv_create(panel, PANEL_CHOICE,
    PANEL_LABEL_STRING, "1 of N",
    PANEL_CHOICE_STRINGS,
        "extra", "large", "medium", "small", NULL,
    XV_X, 20,
    XV_Y, rect_bottom(qrt) + 20,
    NULL);

rt = (Rect *) xv_get(oneN, XV_RECT);

manyN = (Panel) xv_create(panel, PANEL_CHOICE,
    PANEL_LABEL_STRING, "M of N",
    PANEL_CHOICE_STRINGS,
        "tomato", "celery", "carrot" , NULL,
    PANEL_CHOOSE_ONE, FALSE,
    XV_X, 20,
    XV_Y, rect_bottom(rt) + 20,
    NULL);

rt = (Rect *) xv_get(manyN, XV_RECT);

chooser = (Panel) xv_create(panel, PANEL_CHECK_BOX,
    PANEL_LAYOUT, PANEL_HORIZONTAL,
    PANEL_LABEL_STRING, "Extras",
    PANEL_CHOICE_STRINGS,
        "fries", "potato", "Q. potato", "salad" , NULL,
    PANEL_CHOOSE_ONE, FALSE, /* Let 'em have it all */
    XV_X, 20,
    XV_Y, rect_bottom(rt) + 20,
    NULL);

xv_main_loop(frame);
exit(0);
}

/*
```

```
** This function is called when you select an item
*/
int selected( Panel_item item, Event *ev)
{
printf(" %s .. \n ", xv_get(item, PANEL_LABEL_STRING));
}


/*
** This function handles the menu selection item.
** Shows you how to exit via menu item too.
*/
int menuHandler(Menu item, Menu_item thing)
{
printf("%s .. \n", xv_get(thing, MENU_STRING));
if (!strcmp((char *)xv_get(thing,MENU_STRING), "Bye")) quit();
}


/*
** Make a clean exit.
*/
void quit()
{
xv_destroy_safe(frame);
}
```

Take a look at the part where the "Y/N/Q" menu button was created. First we created the menu items on the menu as menu1. Note that we did not display all of the choices in the menu, just its header.

```
menu1 = (Menu) xv_create(NULL, MENU,
    MENU_STRINGS, "Yes", "No", "Maybe", "Bye", NULL,
    MENU_NOTIFY_PROC, menuHandler,
    NULL);
```

Then we created the panel button that will house this menu with the following lines:

```
xv_create (panel, PANEL_BUTTON,
    PANEL_LABEL_STRING, "Y/N/Q",
    PANEL_ITEM_MENU, menu1,
    PANEL_NOTIFY_PROC, selected,
    NULL);
```

That was it. Now you can click the right button on the "Y/N/Q" button to get the selection items as a pull-down menu. If you click the left button, the first item in the menu item will be displayed momentarily and selected. Two functions are assigned as callbacks in the previous code segments:

- menuHandler(): This function will show on your terminal the menu item selected.
- selected(): This function merely displays the menu item string. You could just as easily display another menu or other items instead of this simple example.

Now look at the example for the "1 of N" selection. As the name of this item suggests, you can choose only one of a given number of items. This is called an *exclusive selection*.

The following lines are used to create this exclusive selection item:

```
oneN =  (Panel) xv_create(panel, PANEL_CHOICE,
    PANEL_LABEL_STRING, "1 of N",
    PANEL_CHOICE_STRINGS,
        "extra", "large", "medium", "small", NULL,
    XV_X, 20,
    XV_Y, rect_bottom(qrt) + 20,
    NULL);
```

Note how we used the core class's XV_X and XV_Y attributes to position this box below the Quit button. We got the position as a rectangle (typedef Rect) of the Quit button via the xv_get call given the XV_RECT attribute:

```
qrt = (Rect *) xv_get(quitbtn, XV_RECT);
```

The position given by XV_X and XV_Y was relative to the top-left position of the panel. This given position is known as absolute positioning because we are using hard-coded numbers to position items.

> **NOTE**
>
> To position items generally we can use two functions: xv_row() and xv_col(). These functions use the WIN_ROW_GAP and WIN_COLUMN_GAP to set the spaces between the items. The following example shows you how to position twelve items on a panel:
>
> ```
> #define ROW 3
> #define COL 4
> extern char *name[ROW][COL];
> int i, j;
> for (i = 0; i < ROW; i++)
>         for (j = 0; j < COL; j++)
>         {
>         xv_create(panel, PANEL_BUTTON,
>             XV_X, xv_col(panel,j),
>             XV_Y, xv_row(panel,i),
>             PANEL_LABEL_STRING, name[i][j],
>             NULL);
>         }
> ```

All items presented in this list are shown with the NULL-terminated list passed in with the PANEL_CHOICE_STRINGS attribute. The default function of PANEL_CHOICE is to enable only one selection. To get more than one selection if you have a list of choices, you can follow the same procedure you used for the exclusive selection panel. The difference between 1 of M and M of N lies in setting the value of the PANEL_CHOOSE_ONE to FALSE. This usage creates the M of N items shown in the following lines:

```
manyN = (Panel) xv_create(panel, PANEL_CHOICE,
    PANEL_LABEL_STRING, "M of N",
    PANEL_CHOICE_STRINGS,
        "tomato", "celery", "carrot" , NULL,
    PANEL_CHOOSE_ONE, FALSE,
    XV_X, 20,
```

```
    XV_Y, rect_bottom(rt) + 20,
    NULL);
```

With 1 of M, we use the XV_RECT call to position this choice of many item's button on the screen.

Finally, this example showed you how to use check boxes to create the input items shown for our choices of a side order. Checkboxes are always non-exclusive. The text to do this is shown in the following lines:

```
chooser = (Panel) xv_create(panel, PANEL_CHECK_BOX,
    PANEL_LAYOUT, PANEL_HORIZONTAL,
    PANEL_LABEL_STRING, "Extras",
    PANEL_CHOICE_STRINGS,
        "fries", "potato", "Q. potato", "salad" , NULL,
    XV_X, 20,
    XV_Y, rect_bottom(rt) + 20,
    NULL);
```

This set of checkboxes was also positioned to align with the qv_get and rect_bottom() calls.

List Items

Use the PANEL_LIST attribute to show lists of items. An example is shown in Figure 33.7. The corresponding listing is shown in Listing 33.8. Lists enable you to insert text (and graphics as glyphs) in them. You can have duplicates in a list. If you do not want to allow duplicates, set the PANEL_LIST_INSERT_DUPLICATE to FALSE.

FIGURE 33.7.

Using lists to display data.

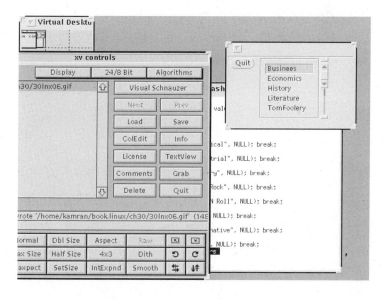

Listing 33.8. Using lists to display data.

```c
/*
** Using Lists
*/
#include <xview/generic.h>
#include <xview/xview.h>
#include <xview/frame.h>
#include <xview/panel.h>

Frame frame;

int main(int argc, char *argv[])
{

Panel panel;
void quit();

    xv_init(XV_INIT_ARGC_PTR_ARGV, &argc, argv, NULL);

frame = (Frame)xv_create(NULL, FRAME,
    FRAME_LABEL, argv[0],
    XV_WIDTH, 200,
    XV_HEIGHT, 100,
    NULL);

panel = (Panel)xv_create(frame, PANEL,NULL);

(void) xv_create(panel, PANEL_BUTTON,
    PANEL_LABEL_STRING, "Quit",
    PANEL_NOTIFY_PROC, quit,
    NULL);

(void) xv_create(panel, PANEL_LIST,
    PANEL_LIST_STRINGS,
        "Business", "Economics", "History",
"Literature", "TomFoolery", "Math",
        "Computer Sci.", "Engineering", NULL,
    NULL);



xv_main_loop(frame);
exit(0);
}

void quit()
{
xv_destroy_safe(frame);
}
```

Lists are ordered from 0 and up, so the first row is 0, the second row is 1, and so on. To delete the rows 7 through 9 from a long list, use the xv_set function:

```c
xv_set(list_item,
    PANEL_LIST_DELETE_ROWS, 6, 3
    NULL);
```

In the preceding example you are requesting that 3 rows be deleted starting from row index number 6 (which is the seventh row). All other rows are adjusted upward after these rows are deleted.

To insert items into this list you can use PANEL_LIST_INSERT and PANEL_LIST_STRING calls. If you wanted to replace the third row with a string pointed to by a pointer called buffer, you would use the following function call:

```
xv_set(list_item,
    PANEL_LIST_DELETE, 2,
    PANEL_LIST_INSERT, 2,
    PANEL_LIST_STRING, buffer,
    NULL);
```

The PANEL_NOTIFY_PROC function for a list is called when an item is selected, deselected, added, or deleted. The prototype for this function call is

```
listCallBack(
    Panel_item      item,
    char            *string,
    Xv_opaque       client_data,
    Panel_list_op   op,
    Event           *event,
    int             row);
```

The item is the panel list itself in this function call. The string is the label for the row, or NULL if no item is defined in the list for the row. The opaque client_data is a user-specified value specified at list creation time with the PANEL_LIST_CLIENT_DATA parameter. For example, the line

```
PANEL_LIST_CLIENT_DATA, 2, "Hello",
```

will assign the value of client_data to 2 for the row with the string "Hello" in it. Each client_data value must be assigned one line at a time.

The op parameter can be one of the following values:

- PANEL_LIST_OP_SELECT when the row is selected
- PANEL_LIST_OP_DESELECT when the row is deselected
- PANEL_LIST_OP_VALIDATE when a new row is added
- PANEL_LIST_OP_DELETE when the row has been deleted

You can take action based on the value of the op parameter in one handy function or have this function call other functions. For example, the following pseudocode illustrates how you could handle the op parameter:

```
switch (op)
    {
    case    PANEL_LIST_OP_SELECT: selectHandler();
    break;
    case    PANEL_LIST_OP_DESELECT: unSelectHandler();
    break;
    case    PANEL_LIST_OP_VALIDATE: addRowHandler();
    break;
    case    PANEL_LIST_OP_DELETE: deleteRowHandler();
    break;
    }
```

Scale Bars

Now look at how you create slider bars so the user can set the value of a variable. An example of this application is shown in Figure 33.8 and a corresponding listing is given in Listing 33.9.

FIGURE 33.8.

Using sliders.

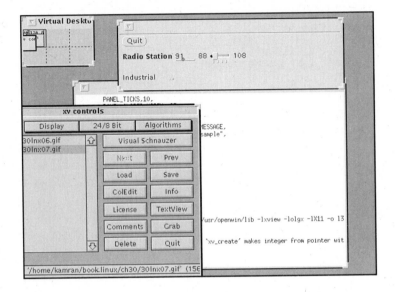

Listing 33.9. Using slider control.

```c
#include <xview/generic.h>
#include <xview/xview.h>
#include <xview/frame.h>
#include <xview/panel.h>

Frame frame;
Panel_item stationName;

void display_setting(Panel_item, int value, Event *ev);

int main(int argc, char *argv[])
{
Panel panel;
Panel_item slider;
void quit();

    xv_init(XV_INIT_ARGC_PTR_ARGV, &argc, argv, NULL);

frame = (Frame)xv_create(NULL, FRAME,
    FRAME_LABEL, argv[0],
    XV_WIDTH, 400,
    XV_HEIGHT, 100,
    NULL);
panel = (Panel)xv_create(frame, PANEL,
        PANEL_LAYOUT, PANEL_VERTICAL,
        NULL);
```

```
(void) xv_create(panel, PANEL_BUTTON,
    PANEL_LABEL_STRING, "Quit",
    PANEL_NOTIFY_PROC, quit,
    NULL);

slider = xv_create (panel, PANEL_SLIDER,
    PANEL_LABEL_STRING, "Radio Station",
    PANEL_MIN_VALUE, 88,
    PANEL_MAX_VALUE, 108,
    PANEL_NOTIFY_PROC, display_setting,
    PANEL_VALUE,99,
    PANEL_NOTIFY_LEVEL, PANEL_ALL, /* not just at the end */
    PANEL_SHOW_RANGE, TRUE,
    PANEL_TICKS,10,
    PANEL_SLIDER_WIDTH, 100,
    NULL);

stationName = xv_create(panel, PANEL_MESSAGE,
        PANEL_LABEL_STRING, "sample",
        NULL);

xv_main_loop(frame);
exit(0);
}

void quit()
{
xv_destroy_safe(frame);
}

/*
** This function is called when the slider value is changed.
*/
void display_setting(Panel_item item, int value, Event *ev)
{
switch (value)
    {
    case 89: xv_set(stationName,
        PANEL_LABEL_STRING,"Classical", NULL); break;
    case 91: xv_set(stationName,
        PANEL_LABEL_STRING,"Industrial", NULL); break;
    case 93: xv_set(stationName,
        PANEL_LABEL_STRING,"Country", NULL); break;
    case 95: xv_set(stationName,
        PANEL_LABEL_STRING,"Soft Rock", NULL); break;
    case 101: xv_set(stationName,
        PANEL_LABEL_STRING,"Roll N Roll", NULL); break;
    case 104: xv_set(stationName,
        PANEL_LABEL_STRING,"Pop", NULL); break;
    case 107: xv_set(stationName,
        PANEL_LABEL_STRING,"Alternative", NULL); break;
    default: xv_set(stationName,
        PANEL_LABEL_STRING,"bzzz", NULL); break;
    }

}
```

To create a slider, assign the PANEL_SLIDER value to the xv_create() function call. How the slider is used and displayed is governed by the following attributes:

■ PANEL_MIN_VALUE and PANEL_MAX_VALUE: The range of values that this slider can take. These values have to be integers. For the example in this book we used 88 and 108.

■ PANEL_SHOW_RANGE: Sets the slider to show the value of the ranges allowed for the selection.

■ PANEL_NOTIFY_LEVEL: Can be set to one of two values: PANEL_ALL if the callback procedure is called while the slider is moving, or PANEL_DONE only when the pointer button is released.

■ PANEL_DIRECTION: Can be used to set the orientation of the slider to either horizontal or vertical.

■ PANEL_TICKS: The number of ticks that show on the display. Set it to 0 if you do not want ticks to be shown. The number of ticks are adjusted as you size the slider. You fix the width of the slider by setting the PANEL_SLIDER_WIDTH to 100 (refer to Listing 33.8).

You can edit the selection value by clicking it and using the keyboard. This value will change the location of the slider as soon as you press the Enter key. Error values will be ignored.

Note how a message label displays the station name as the slider is being moved. To set the value of this label, make a call to xv_set() and give the attribute PANEL_LABEL_STRING a string value. For example, if the value of the slider is 89, you can set the message to "Classical", as shown in the following lines:

```
case 89: xv_set(stationName,
    PANEL_LABEL_STRING,"Classical", NULL); break;
```

TIP

You can create a gauge by using the PANEL_GAUGE package instead of PANEL_SLIDER. The dimensions of the gauge are set by the PANEL_GAUGE_WIDTH and PANEL_GAUGE_HEIGHT attributes. A user cannot change the value of the slider on a gauge because a gauge can be used only as a feedback item.

Text Windows

XView has a lot of options for displaying data. This section will only cover a few portions of this feature. Please refer to the man pages for Text in /usr/openwin/man. Let's get started with some of the basics, though. A sample application is shown in Listing 33.10 and its corresponding output is shown in Figure 33.9.

Listing 33.10. Using text items.

```
#include <xview/generic.h>
#include <xview/xview.h>
#include <xview/frame.h>
#include <xview/panel.h>
```

```
Frame frame;

int main(int argc, char *argv[])
{

Panel panel;
void quit();

    xv_init(XV_INIT_ARGC_PTR_ARGV, &argc, argv, NULL);

frame = (Frame)xv_create(NULL, FRAME,
    FRAME_LABEL, argv[0],
    XV_WIDTH, 300,
    XV_HEIGHT, 300,
    NULL);

panel = (Panel)xv_create(frame, PANEL,NULL);

(void) xv_create(panel, PANEL_BUTTON,
    PANEL_LABEL_STRING, "Quit",
    PANEL_NOTIFY_PROC, quit,
    NULL);

    xv_create(panel, PANEL_TEXT,
        PANEL_LABEL_STRING, "Single",
        PANEL_VALUE, "Single Line of Text",
        NULL);

    xv_create(panel, PANEL_MULTILINE_TEXT,
        PANEL_LABEL_STRING, "Multi",
        PANEL_DISPLAY_ROWS, 3,
        PANEL_VALUE_DISPLAY_LENGTH, 30,
        PANEL_VALUE, "Multiple  Lines of Text \
    in this example \
    This is a line 1\
    This is a line 2\
    This is a line 3\
    of some long string",
        NULL);

xv_main_loop(frame);
exit(0);
}

void quit()
{
xv_destroy_safe(frame);
}
```

We created a single panel text entry item with the following lines using the PANEL_TEXT package:

```
xv_create(panel, PANEL_TEXT,
    PANEL_LABEL_STRING, "Single",
    PANEL_VALUE, "Single Line of Text",
    NULL);
```

FIGURE 33.9.

Using text items.

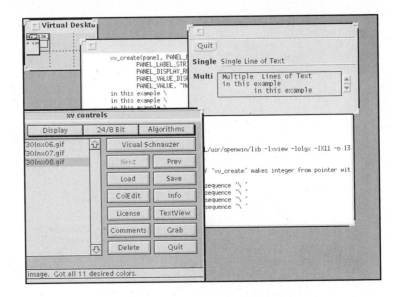

If the PANEL_LAYOUT value is set to PANEL_VERTICAL, the value will be placed below the label. The default is PANEL_HORIZONTAL. The number of characters is set with the PANEL_VALUE_DISPLAY_LENGTH attribute. This value should not be less than 4. (This is not in the listing and is only for your information.)

If you want the user to enter private data such as password information, you can set the PANEL_MASK_CHAR value to something like an asterisk. This setting displays an asterisk for each character that the user types in. The value of the text remains what the user typed in.

You can have notification procedures for four types of input for a text item with the PANEL_NOTIFY_LEVEL. (See Table 33.1.)

Table 33.1. Notification procedures.

Notification	Action to take on input
PANEL_NONE	Never inform this package.
PANEL_NON_PRINTABLE	On each non-printable character.
PANEL_SPECIFIED	If the input character is found in a string specified by the attribute PANEL_NOTIFY_STRING.
PANEL_ALL	On all characters input.

You can also have multiple lines of text on a display. A sample of this is shown in Listing 33.10. Look at the following excerpted lines:

```
xv_create(panel, PANEL_MULTILINE_TEXT,
    PANEL_LABEL_STRING, "Multi",
    PANEL_DISPLAY_ROWS, 3,
    PANEL_VALUE_DISPLAY_LENGTH, 30,
    PANEL_VALUE, "Multiple  Lines of Text \
in this example\
This is a line 1\
This is a line 2\
This is a line 3\
of some long string",
    NULL);
```

The PANEL_MULTILINE_TEXT package can have the following attributes set for it: PANEL_DISPLAY_ROWS sets the number of lines that the viewing window will display, and PANEL_VALUE_DISPLAY_LENGTH is the number of characters wide you want the display to be.

Where To Go from Here

This chapter is a very brief introduction to the XView packages available under Linux. In this section you have learned a little about putting user interface items together on a panel. You should now have enough knowledge to start creating your own interfaces in XView.

Some cool binaries to look for in the /usr/openwin/bin directory are props for setting window parameters and textedit, a pretty good editor.

Summary

You use objects to build XView applications. Each object is a class and is referred to as a package. Each package has attributes that can have values. Attributes can be shared among other objects, be common to a few objects only, or be specific to one object.

You can retrieve an attribute's values by calling xv_get() and set a value by calling xv_set. An attribute may be assigned more than one value. Each attribute can have a different type of value attached to it.

You can use standard Xlib function calls to perform drawing operations. This gives you tremendous flexibility in rendering your custom graphics on screens and XView packages.

The XView packages enable you to create and place objects on panels. You can place these objects using absolute positioning from the top left corner of a panel, relative to other objects, or in row/column order.

The xv_create() call passes the type of object as a parameter to create XView objects. You can set other attributes by passing a NULL-terminated list to xv_create(). Default attribute values that are not explicitly set by xv_create() are inherited from the object's parent.

Smalltalk/X

34

by
Rick McMullin

This chapter describes Smalltalk/X (ST/X), a fairly complete implementation of the Smalltalk-80 programming environment. Anyone who has used Smalltalk-80 or any other version of Smalltalk will be impressed with this freely available implementation. In this chapter we will see

- What Smalltalk/X is
- How to install Smalltalk/X
- Invoking Smalltalk/X
- Getting around in Smalltalk/X

This chapter gives you an overview of the Smalltalk/X application. After reading the chapter you should be familiar with the facilities that Smalltalk/X provides and be able to navigate your way through the Smalltalk/X user interface.

What Is Smalltalk/X?

When describing Smalltalk/X, it is probably appropriate to start with a description of Smalltalk itself. Smalltalk is an object-oriented programming language that has been a continuing development project at ParcPlace Systems since the early 1970s. Although it was not the first object-oriented language, it was the first object-oriented language to gain wide use in the industry.

Smalltalk has been around for about 15 years now but it was not until recently that it started to become popular. Many universities now teach a Smalltalk course as part of their standard computer science curriculum, and many companies have seen the value that Smalltalk adds in terms of quick development.

Smalltalk/X was developed by Claus Gittinger and was first released in 1988. It is almost identical to the behavior of the Smalltalk 80 implementation of the Smalltalk language. Smalltalk/X comes complete with an application launcher, several different browsers for browsing through the Smalltalk class hierarchy, and a very powerful debugging utility. The unique aspect of Smalltalk/X is that it can also behave as a Smalltalk-to-C translation utility. This is a very useful feature because this means that you will be able to combine the speed of development that Smalltalk provides with the speed of execution that C provides.

How To Install Smalltalk/X

Before installing Smalltalk/X, you must first retrieve it from `sunsite.unc.edu` in the `/pub/Linux/devel/lang/smalltalkx` directory. Once there, you will find the following files:

- `COPYRIGHT`   As the filename suggests, this is the SmallTalk/X copyright information document.
- `INDEX`   Provides a list of files in the directory.
- `LICENSE`   The distribution license for SmallTalk/X.
- `README`   Contains a brief discription of how to get SmallTalk/X running.
- `bitmaps.tar.Z`   Contains sample graphics that can be used to dress up the visual appeal of your programs.

- ■ `doc.tar.Z` The documentation set for SmallTalk/X. This package also includes several demos.
- ■ `exe.tar.Z` The executable archive. Although this is really the only file you need to download to get SmallTalk/X up and running, installing the bitmap, documentation, goodies, and source files is also highly recommended.
- ■ `goodies.tar.Z` Various extras thrown in for your enjoyment.
- ■ `source.tar.Z` Support and library files needed to get the most out of SmallTalk/X.

To install Smalltalk/X, perform the following steps as `root`.

1. Create a directory called `/usr/local/lib/smalltalk`.
2. Copy the following files into the `/usr/local/lib/smalltalk` directory.

   `bitmaps.tar.Z`

   `doc.tar.Z`

   `exe.tar.Z`

   `goodies.tar.Z`

   `source.tar.Z`

3. Uncompress and untar these files by entering the following commands from the `/usr/local/lib/smalltalk` directory.

   `uncompress *.Z`

   `tar -xf bitmaps.tar`

   `tar -xf doc.tar`

   `tar -xf exe.tar`

   `tar -xf goodies.tar`

   `tar -xf source.tar`

4. You can now delete all of the `tar` files by typing the following command:

   `rm -f *.tar`

5. Finally, create the following links:
   ```
   ln /usr/i486-linuxaout/lib/libc.so.4 /usr/lib/libc.so.4
   ln /usr/i486-linuxaout/lib/libXt.so.3 /usr/lib/libXt.so.3
   ln /usr/i486-linuxaout/lib/libxll.so.3 /usr/lib/libxll.so.3
   ln /usr/i486-linuxaout/lib/libm.so.4 /usr/lib/libm.so.4
   ```

The Smalltalk/X program should now be installed and ready to go.

NOTE

If you do not have write access to the `/usr/local/lib` directory, install Smalltalk/X in some other directory by following the same steps listed above. If you do this you must set the `SMALLTALK_LIBDIR` variable to be equal to the new directory.

Invoking Smalltalk/X

You invoke Smalltalk/X by typing

`smalltalk`

in an Xterm window from the `/usr/local/lib/smalltalk` directory. When ST/X starts, it checks to see if there is an image file for it to use. If it cannot find an image file, it uses a file called `smalltalk.rc` to set up the default behavior for your environment. The image file that is loaded by default is called `st.img`, and contains a snapshot of what your ST/X environment looked like the last time you exited. This allows you to resume exactly where you left off. You can save a snapshot under any name with the extension `.img`. To invoke ST/X with an image other than `st.img`, type the following command at the prompt:

`smalltalk -i nameofImage.img`

Getting Around in ST/X

Once ST/X is invoked, two windows or views will appear. The Transcript view and the Launcher menu. The Transcript view is shown in Figure 34.1.

FIGURE 34.1.

The Transcript view.

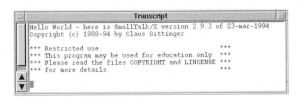

The Transcript is the console where relevant systems information is shown. The Launcher menu is shown in Figure 34.2.

FIGURE 34.2.

The Launcher menu.

The Launcher allows access to the tools you will need to program your application. Table 34.1 gives the options available from the Launcher and a brief description of each.

Table 34.1. The Launcher menu options.

Option	Description
Browsers	The pull-right menu of this option gives you access to browsers, senders, and implementors.
Workspace	This option brings up a workspace view.
FileBrowser	This browser allows inspection and manipulation of files and directories.
Projects	This option allows you to choose an existing or new project.
Utilities	This contains tools specific to your programming needs.
Goodies	This contains other non-programming related tools.
Games & Demos	This contains some sample programs and games to play.
info & help	This contains topics that give you help and information on the ST/X environment and programming in Smalltalk.
snapshot	This option takes a snapshot of your present ST/X environment and asks for the name of the image file you wish to store the snapshot in.
exit	This option allows you to exit ST/X immediately or exit and save a snapshot of the current environment.

The following sections describe most of these options in more detail.

The Browsers Options

The Browsers option in the Launcher menu gives you access to different browsers or editors that let you read and manipulate classes, methods, changes, senders, and implementors. The sub-options available are

- System Browser
- Class Hierarchy Browser
- Implementors
- Senders
- Changes Browser
- Directory Browser

Each of these sub-options will be discussed in detail in this section.

The System Browser

The standard System Browser contains five subviews:

- Class category list
- Class list
- Method category list
- Method list
- Code view

The System Browser is shown in Figure 34.3.

FIGURE 34.3.

The System Browser.

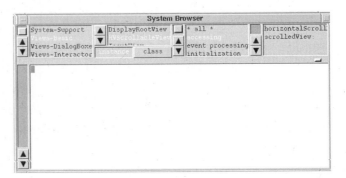

Within the ST/X system, classes are assigned to a category. A *category* is simply an attribute used for grouping classes to make them easier to handle. To select a class category, click on the name of the category in the class category list. This is the leftmost section of the top half of the System Browser. This will display, in the class list subview, all classes belonging to that category. The class list subview is the second section from the far left of the system browser. You can also select one of two special categories: * all *, which selects all classes and lists them alphabetically; and * hierarchy *, which lists all classes in a tree by inheritance.

If you select a class in the class list, all method categories for that class will be displayed in the method category list, which is the second section from the right in the top half of the System Browser. Like class categories, method categories are simply for grouping methods according to their function. When you select a method category, all methods in that category are shown in the method list view in the far right section of the browser. The special * all * category will show all methods in alphabetical order. Selecting a method from the method list will show the corresponding method's source code in the code view which is the bottom half of the System Browser.

The browser enables you to change either a class or its metaclass. There are two toggle buttons, *class* and *instance*, in the same section of the browser as the class list view. *Instance*, which is the default, makes the changes affect the class. Selecting *class* makes the changes affect the metaclass.

A pop-up menu is available in each view by pressing the middle or menu mouse button while the pointer is in that view. The pop-up menu available in the class category view is shown in Figure 34.4, and the purpose of each function is shown in Table 34.2.

FIGURE 34.4.

The Class Category pop-up menu.

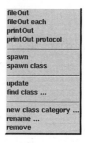

Table 34.2. Class Category pop-up menu functions.

Function	Description
fileOut	Saves all classes in the currently selected class category into one source file named classCategory.st
fileOut each	Saves all classes but puts each class into a separate file called className.st
printOut	Sends a printed representation of all classes selected to the printer including the method source code
printOut protocol	Sends a protocol-only representation of all classes in the category to the printer without the method's source code
spawn	Starts a class category browser without a class category list on the currently selected class category
spawn class	Starts a full class browser which allows you to edit all code for the selected class in one view
update	Re-scans all classes in the system and updates the lists shown
find class...	Pops up a dialog box to enter the name of a class you wish to search for and have displayed
new class category...	Displays a dialog for the creation of a new class category.
rename...	Renames a category and changes the category attribute of all classes in the currently selected class category
remove	Removes all classes and subclasses in the current class category

The class list pop-up menu appears when you press the menu mouse button with the pointer in the class list view. The functions available from this menu are shown in Figure 34.5 and are explained in Table 34.3.

FIGURE 34.5.

The Class List pop-up menu.

Table 34.3. Class List pop-up menu functions.

Function	Description
fileOut	Saves the source code of the currently selected class in a file named `className.st`.
printOut	Sends the source code of the currently selected class to the printer.
printOut protocol	Sends a protocol description of the currently selected class to the printer. The output will contain the class description, class comment, and the classes protocol and method comments.
spawn	Starts a class browser on the currently selected class.
spawn hierarchy	Starts a browser on all subclasses of the currently selected class.
hierarchy	Shows the hierarchy of the currently selected class in the code view.
definition	Shows the class definition in the code view and allows you to change the class definition.
comment	Shows the class comment in the code view and allows you to edit it.
class instvars	Shows the class-instance-variables for the selected class and allows you to edit them.
variable search	Provides a search facility to find different variable references and all methods referencing the searched-for variable.
new class	Allows you to create a new class using as a template the currently selected class.
new subclass	Same as new class but it will create a subclass of the currently selected class.
rename	Changes the name of the currently selected class.
remove	Removes the currently selected class and all of its subclasses.

The method category pop-up menu appears when you press the menu mouse button while the pointer is in the method category view. The functions available from this menu are shown in Figure 34.6 and explained in Table 34.4.

FIGURE 34.6.

The Method Category pop-up menu.

Table 34.4. Method Category pop-up menu functions.

Function	Description
fileOut	Saves the source code of the currently selected method category in a file named className-category.st
printOut	Sends the source code of the currently selected method category to the printer
spawn	Starts a method category browser on the currently selected method category of the currently selected class
spawn category	Starts a browser on all methods of the class which have the same category as the currently selected one
find method here...	Searches for the method that implements a specified selector
find method...	Searches in the class hierarchy for the first class implementing the selector you specify in the dialog box
new category...	Enables you to add a new category to the list
copy category...	Enables you to copy all methods in a class category to the currently selected class
create access methods	Creates methods to access instance variables
rename...	Renames the currently selected method category
remove	Removes all methods in the currently selected class that are members of the currently selected method category

The method list pop-up menu appears when you press the menu mouse button while the pointer is in the method list view. The functions available from this menu are shown in Figure 34.7 and explained in Table 34.5.

FIGURE 34.7.
The Method List pop-up menu.

Table 34.5. Method List pop-up menu functions.

Function	Description
`fileOut`	Saves the currently selected method in a file named `className-selector.st`
`printOut`	Sends the source code of the currently selected method to the printer
`spawn`	Starts a browser for editing this method
`senders...`	Starts a new browser on all methods sending a specific message
`implementors...`	Starts a new browser on all methods implementing a specific message
`globals...`	Starts a new browser on all methods that are accessing a global that is either a global variable or a symbol, as well as all methods sending a corresponding message
`local senders...`	Same as `senders` but limits the search to the current class and its subclasses
`local implementors...`	Same as `implementors...` but limits the search to the current class and its subclasses
`new method`	Enables you to create a new method from a template in the code view
`change category...`	Enables you to change the category of the selected method
`remove`	Removes the currently selected method

When you add or remove instance variables to or from a system class description and *accept* (that is, save the changes), the system creates a new class instead of changing the old one. The original class still exists to give existing instances of the class a valid class even though it is no longer accessible by name. After the change, you can no longer edit the old class.

It is recommended that you don't change the definition of system classes but only private ones. It is safer to use the copy category function to copy an existing class and its methods to a new class and modify the new class. This is especially important for classes which are used by the system itself since changes can lead to problems in the operation of the ST/X environment.

The code view is the lower half of the System Browser. It is here that you can modify the class or instance definitions as well as methods. The pop-up menu for this area is the edit menu that appears in every text editing view in ST/X. The functions in this menu are discussed in the "Editing in Browsers" section of this chapter.

The Class Hierarchy Browser

When the Class Hierarchy Browser is selected, a dialog box appears which asks for the *name of class*. If you enter a valid class, the Class Hierarchy Browser appears for that class. This is the same as the System Browser except there is no class category list since this is for one specific class. The pop-up menus for each of the four subviews are the same as in the System Browser.

Implementors

When the Implementors option is selected, a dialog box appears which asks for a selector. A selector is the name of the type of operation a message requests of its receiver.

If you enter a valid selector, an Implementors view will be displayed. This view is similar to the one shown in Figure 34.8.

FIGURE 34.8.

The Implementors view.

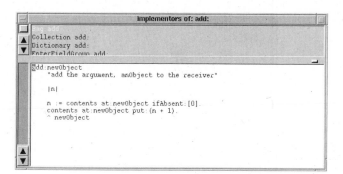

The Implementors view contains a list of the methods that implement the method specified by the selector. The pop-up menu for the top half of the Implementor view is the same as the pop-up menu for the method list subview which was discussed in the "System Browser" section of this chapter.

Senders

When the Senders option is selected, a dialog box appears that asks for a selector. If you enter a valid selector, then a Senders view will be displayed. This view is similar to the one shown in Figure 34.9.

The Senders view contains a list of the methods that send the selected message. The pop-up menu for the top half of the Senders view is the same as the pop-up menu for the method list subview which was discussed in the "System Browser" section.

FIGURE 34.9.

Senders view.

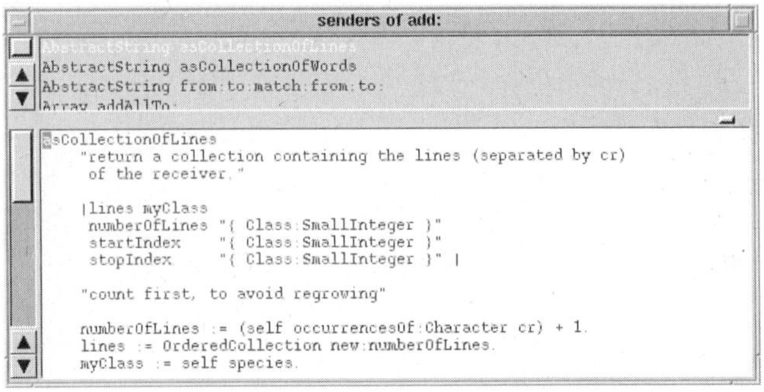

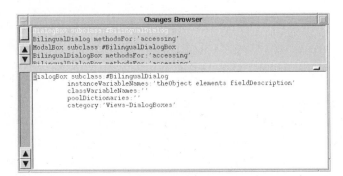

The Changes Browser

Each time you make a change to either the class hierarchy or to a method, ST/X writes a record to a changes file. The Changes Browser enables you to inspect and manipulate the changes file. There are two subviews in the Changes Browser; the change list and the contents view. The change list gives a list of all changes in chronological order. A sample Changes Browser is shown in Figure 34.10.

To display a change, select one of the changes from the change list. The change browser then displays the contents of the change in the contents view.

FIGURE 34.10.

The Changes Browser.

The pop-up menu for the change list has the functions described in Table 34.6.

Table 34.6. The Change List pop-up menu.

Function	Description
apply change	Applies the currently selected change.
apply to end	Applies all the changes from the currently selected change to the end of the changes file.
apply all changes	Applies all the changes in the file.
delete	Deletes the currently selected change from the list.
delete to end	Deletes all changes from the currently selected change to the end of the file.
delete changes for this class	Deletes all changes affecting the same class as the currently selected change to the end of the changes file.
delete all changes for this class	Deletes all changes in the file for the same class as the currently selected change.
update	Rereads the changes file.
compress	Compresses the change list and removes multiple changes of a method and leaves the most recent change compared to current.
compare with current version	Compares a method's source code in a change with the current version of the method and outputs a message in the Transcript view.
make change a patch	Appends the change to the end of the patches file which will be run and automatically applied at ST/X startup.
save change a file	Saves any changes made to the current file.
update sourcefile from change	This function is not currently implemented.
writeback changefile	Writes the change list back to the changefile changes file. All delete/compress operations performed in the Change Browser will not affect the changes file unless this operation is performed.

The Change Browser can be used to recover from a system crash by re-applying all changes that were made after the last snapshot entry.

NOTE

To control the size of the changes file, it is a good idea to apply a compress periodically. This will remove all old changes for a method leaving the newest one.

Directory Browser

When you select the Directory Browser option, a browser with five subviews is displayed. The top half of the browser displays the current directory and all subdirectories and files contained in it. If you select a directory, it is expanded in the next section to the right across the top half of the browser. If you select a file, the contents of the file are displayed in the lower half of the Browser. The pop-up menu for the directory area has only two functions:

- `up`—Moves up to the directory above the one selected
- `goto directory`—Enables you to go to a specified directory

The content view has the same edit menu as all the other text editors and is discussed in the "Editing in Browsers" section in this chapter. A typical Directory Browser is shown in Figure 34.11.

FIGURE 34.11.

The Directory Browser.

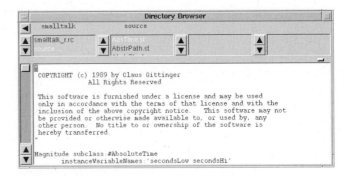

The Workspace Option

The Workspace option displays a view from which you can enter and compile Smalltalk code. The Workspace is usually used as a testing area or scratch pad when coding. You can use it to test your Smalltalk code before building it into the code library using the System Browser code view.

The File Browser Option

The File Browser gives you the ability to inspect and manipulate files and directories. The File Browser is shown in Figure 34.12.

It consists of four subviews that are described in Table 34.7.

Table 34.7. The File Browser subviews.

Subview	Purpose
path-label field	Shows the name of the current directory
file pattern field	Allows a search pattern to be entered for choosing files for the file list

Subview	Purpose
file list	Shows a list of file and directory names
contents view	Shows the contents of a selected file

FIGURE 34.12.

The File Browser.

Path Label field

Contents view

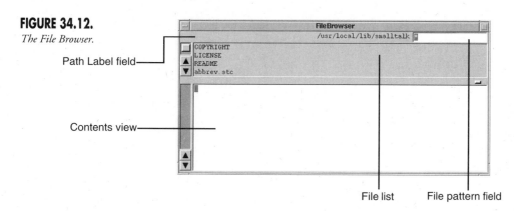

File list   File pattern field

To inspect the contents of a file, double-click the left mouse button on the name of the file in the file list. To change directories, double-click on the directory name. Directory names are always shown in the file list.

You can use the file pattern field to display the list of files matching the specified pattern. The default is *, which shows all files. The search pattern can be changed by moving the pointer to the field, editing the pattern, and then pressing enter or choosing accept from the file pattern pop-up menu.

As in the other browsers we have discussed, each subview has a pop-up menu that is activated by the menu mouse button. The path-label pop-up menu is shown in Figure 34.13.

FIGURE 34.13.

The Path-Label pop-up menu.

The functions available in this menu are described in Table 34.8.

Table 34.8. The Path-Label pop-up menu functions.

Function	Purpose
copy path	Copies the current pathname into the cut and paste buffer
change directory...	Opens a dialog box to enter the name of the directory you wish to change to
change to home directory	Changes the file list to your home directory

The file list pop-up menu is shown in Figure 34.14.

FIGURE 34.14.

The File List pop-up menu.

The functions available in this menu are described in Table 34.9.

Table 34.9. The File List pop-up menu functions.

Function	Purpose
spawn	Starts another file browser on the current directory or the directory selected in the file list.
get contents	Shows the contents of the currently selected file in the contents view.
show info	Displays a view with type, size, access, and owner information for the currently selected file or directory.
show full info	Displays the same as above with more details such as the last access, last modification date, and time.
fileIn	Loads the selected file into the system by reading and evaluating Smalltalk expressions from it.
update	Rereads the directory and updates the file list.
execute unix command…	Allows execution of any UNIX command through a pop-up box.
remove	Removes the selected file(s) or directory(s).
rename...	Renames the selected file.
display long list	Shows file information in the file list. This option toggles with display short list which is the default.
show all files	Displays all the files including hidden files. This option toggles with hide hidden files which is the default.
create directory...	Creates a new directory.
create file...	Creates a new file.

The pop-up menu for the contents view is the same edit menu as the other text editors and is discussed in the "Editing in Browsers" section of this chapter.

The Projects Option

The Projects option of the Launcher menu enables you to create a new project or select a previously created project. When the new project function is selected, a new project is automatically created for you and the new project object appears on your screen. If you select the select project function, a dialog box appears with a list of existing projects from which to choose. Simply select a project and it will be loaded in to the environment.

The Utilities Option

The Utilities option provides thirteen tools that assist you in programming in the ST/X environment. Table 34.10 gives you a brief description of each tool.

Table 34.10. The Utilities option.

Utility	Description
Transcript	Opens the Transcript view.
Window tree	Displays a graphical tree representation of the window hierarchy of all windows that are active or in wait state at the time it was requested.
Class tree	Displays a graphical tree representation of the class hierarchy of the system.
Event monitor	Displays a view that monitors events.
Process monitor	Displays a view that gives information about all currently active or waiting processes. This information changes as the state of the processes change.
Memory monitor	Displays a graph that tells you the present memory usage and changes as the memory usage changes.
Memory usage	Displays a table of the classes and the number of instances of each, average size, bytes, and percentage of memory used by each.
collect Garbage	Runs a Generation Scavenge algorithm to collect short term objects and destroy them. If an object survives long enough, it is moved to an area of memory where it remains until the user requests its collection.
collect Garbage & compress	Same as Collect Garbage but also compresses to recover space.

continues

Table 34.10. continued

Utility	Description
full screen hardcopy	Takes a picture of the screen and asks you for a name of a file with a .tiff extension in which to save the image.
screen area hardcopy	Same as Fullscreen hardcopy but for only a specific area of the screen.
view hardcopy	Same as Fullscreen hardcopy but for one specific view only.
ScreenSaver	Enables you to choose from one of three different screen savers to use in the ST/X environment.

The Goodies Option

The Goodies option of the Launcher menu provides a pull-right menu of six different tools that are useful at any time, not just when you program in Smalltalk. The Goodies are described in Table 34.11.

Table 34.11. The Goodies.

Tool	Description
Clock	Displays an analog clock in a square with a toggle for the second hand.
Round Clock	Same as the clock but it's round and remains visible when it is minimized.
Directory View	Displays a pictorial representation of files and directories. A folder represents a directory and a document is a file.
Mail Tool	A tool for managing electronic mail.
News Tool	A repository for news, information and documents.
Draw Tool	A fairly comprehensive tool for drawing diagrams, charts, pictures, and so on.

The Games & Demo Option

Contained in the pull-right menu of this option are games for your enjoyment and example applications that may be useful. The Games & Demos option menu is shown in Figure 34.15.

FIGURE 34.15.

The Games & Demos option menu.

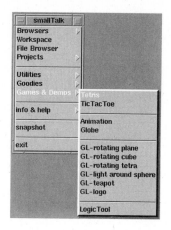

Editing in Browsers

All views that show text allow the usual editing functions of that text through a pop-up menu. The functions available in this menu are described in Table 34.12.

Table 34.12. Editing functions.

Function	Description
again	Repeats the last edit.
copy	Copies the selected text.
cut	Cuts the selected text out of the file.
paste	Pastes the text that was copied or cut prior to choosing the paste option to the current position of the pointer.
doIt	Evaluates the highlighted text.
printIt	Prints a representation of the result of the evaluation at the current cursor position.
inspectIt	Invokes the Inspector view on the result.
accept	Once you have completed editing, you must use this option to save the changes to the file; otherwise, the changes will not be written to the file.
search...	Enables you to search for a specific string.
goto...	Enables you to move to a specific location in the file.
font...	Enables you to change the font of the file.
indent...	Enables you to change the indenting of the file.
save as...	Enables you to save the file under a different name.
print	Prints the file.

To select or highlight text, press the left mouse button over the first character and move the mouse (while pressing the mouse button) to the end of the text you wish to select and then release the mouse button. If you press the left mouse button again, the highlighting is removed and you can select something else.

To scroll through the text, use the scroll bars on the left of the view. By clicking the mouse below or above the thumb, the text scrolls one page for every click. If you press the Shift key at the same time as you click, the text scrolls to the position of the pointer in the scroll bar. This is useful for scrolling rapidly through long documents.

Using the Inspector

The Inspector enables you to inspect an object. It consists of two subviews, one showing the names of the object's instance variables and the other showing the value of the selected instance variable. You can start an inspector by using the `inspectIt` function on the edit menu or by sending one of the following messages to an object:

```
anObject inspect
```

or

```
anObject basicInspect
```

The `basicInspect` command will open a general inspector that shows instance variables as they are physically present in the object. The `inspect` command is redefined in some classes to open an inspector showing the logical contents of the object.

Using the Debugger

The Debugger is displayed whenever an error occurs in your Smalltalk code. It shows you where the error occurred and how the system got there. The Debugger runs in one of three modes: `normal`, `modal`, and `inspecting`.

When in normal mode and an error occurs in a process, which is not the event handler process, the debugger will start up on top of the erroneous process. This blocks all interaction with the affected process and its views. Other views are still active and respond as usual.

When an error occurs in the Smalltalk event handler process, the debugger starts in modal mode. While a modal debugger is active you cannot interact with any other view.

The inspecting mode can be entered from the ProcessMonitor by the pop-up menu and allows inspection of the state of other processes. But since the debugged process may continue to run, it is only possible to inspect a snapshot of the affected process.

The Debugger contains four subviews:

- The Context Walkback List shows the context chain that led to the error
- The Method Source View shows the method that caused the error

■ The Receiver Inspector allows inspection of the receiver of the selected message

■ The Context Inspector provides information about the arguments and local variables of this context.

The Debugger is shown in Figure 34.16.

FIGURE 34.16.

The Debugger.

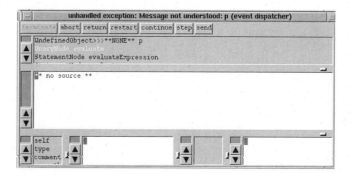

The functions that are common to each view appear as a set of buttons below the context walkback list. These functions are described in Table 34.13.

Table 34.13. The Debugger function buttons.

Button	Description
terminate	Terminates the erroneous process
abort	Aborts the current activity if possible
return	Continues execution as if the selected context returned
restart	Continues execution by restarting the selected context
continue	Continues execution
step (single step)	Lets the process continue execution until the next send is executed in the currently selected context
send (single send)	Lets the process continue execution for one message send

The walkback subview has a pop-up menu with the functions described in Table 34.14.

Table 34.14. Walkback Subview pop-up menu function.

Function	Description
exit smalltalk	Leaves ST/X without saving an image
show more	Shows 50 more contexts of the walk-back

continues

Table 34.14. continued

Function	Description
breakpoints	Not yet available
trace on/off	Not yet available
trace step	Not yet available

A miniDebugger is entered if an error occurs within the Debugger itself. This is a line-by-line debugger that allows limited debugging without the use of a graphical user interface. It is controlled by entering commands in the Xterm window where ST/X was started. If you type ? at the miniDebugger prompt, you will get a list of commands that are available for use in this stripped down debugger.

Summary

This chapter introduced you to the Smalltalk environment that is provided by the Smalltalk/X application. If you are interested in learning how to program using Smalltalk and do not have access to one of the commercial versions of Smalltalk, then Smalltalk/X is perfect for you. Not only does Smalltalk/X come with all the tools and programming aids that were talked about in this chapter, but it also comes with many examples and some fairly complete documentation that will make learning Smalltalk easier for you.

Mathematics on Linux

35

by Kamran Husain

This book has dealt with many issues regarding the tools available for Linux. Now, let's look at some of the mathematics tools for Linux. Specifically, we will work with tools for doing mathematical and statistical applications under Linux. One such tool we will be working with is Scilab, an interactive math and graphics package. Another tool for symbolic math is Pari. For statistical operations using LISP choose LISP-STAT.

Scilab

The Scilab application was developed by the Institut National de Recherche de Informatique et en Automatique (INRIA) in France. Although this application is not as formidable as MATLAB, a commercial product with more bells and whistles, Scilab is still powerful enough to provide decent graphics and solutions to math problems.

With Scilab you can do matrix multiplication, plot graphs, and so on. Using its built-in functions, Scilab enables you to write your own functions. With its toolbox, you can build your own signal-processing functions in addition to those provided by Scilab.

Added to all its features, the help file is quite voluminous. If you want to find out how to do a math problem with Scilab, you will probably find it in the docs. Added to the good documentation are sample programs to get you started.

How To Get and Install Scilab

Now that you are probably interested in Scilab, you will want to know where to get it. Scilab is free via the Internet. The primary site is `ftp.inria.fr`, and the directory for this is in `INRIA/Projects/Meta2/Scilab`. Look for the zipped file with the latest date. Each zipped file is complete in itself.

The file you are looking for is called `scilab-2.2-Linux-elf.tar.gz`. In its unzipped form, the file is about 15MB in size. After moving `scilab-2.2-Linux-elf.tar.gz` to the directory you want it installed in (such as `/usr/local`), untar by typing `gunzip scilab-2.2-Linux-elf.tar.gz ¦ tar xvf-`.

After you have installed it (into the `/usr/local/scilab-2.2` directory), go to the `/usr/local/scilab-2.2/bin` subdirectory and modify the `scilab` shell script file. Replace the assignment of the `SCI` variable with the path to the location of your `scilab` files. For example, in my case I set the value to

```
SCI="/home/khusain/scilab-2.1.1"
```

> **NOTE**
>
> If Scilab does not show up in color the first time you invoke it, try `*customization: -color` in your `.Xdefaults` file. Don't forget to run `xrdb .Xdefaults` to enforce the change.

Running Scilab

To invoke scilab, type `scilab` in an Xterm window while in the `/usr/local/scilab-2.2/bin` directory.

The prompt for Scilab is -->. You will see responses to your commands immediately below where you type in entries.

A healthy example of how to use Scilab would probably be beneficial. Let's see how to declare values:

```
-->x=1.0
```

This sets x equal to 1.0. To declare an array, use square brackets:

```
-->x=[1 2 3]
x =
! 1. 2. 3. !
```

See Figure 35.1 to see what it looks like on your screen.

To declare a large array you can use indices of the form [*start:end*]. Use a semicolon at the end of the line to indicate that you really do not want Scilab to echo the results back to you. So, the following statement

FIGURE 35.1.

Main screen for Scilab.

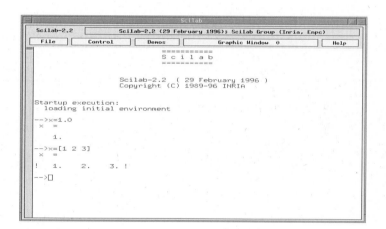

```
-->x=[1:100];
```

declares x as a vector of values from 1 to 100 and does not display the contents of x back to you. If you want to give staggered values of x, you can use an increment operator in the form [start:increment:stop]. So, this statement declares x to contain five odd numbers from 1:

```
-->x=[1:2:10]
x =
! 1. 3. 5. 7. 9. !
```

Let's try an example of a simple matrix multiplication problem of ax=b. First declare the a matrix, separating all the rows with semicolons. If you do not use semicolons, the values in matrix a will be interpreted as a 25×1 vector instead of a 5×5 matrix.

```
-->a=[ 1 1 0 0 0; 1 1 1 0 0; 0 1 1 1 0; 0 0 1 1 1; 0 0 0 1 1]
a =
! 1.  1.  0.  0.  0. !
! 1.  1.  1.  0.  0. !
! 0.  1.  1.  1.  0. !
! 0.  0.  1.  1.  1. !
! 0.  0.  0.  1.  1. !
```

Then declare X as a vector.

```
-->X=[ 1 3 5 7 9 ]
X =
! 1.  3.  5.  7.  9. !
```

To get the dimensions right for the multiplication, you have to use the single quote operator (") to get the transpose of X. Then put the results of the multiplication of a and X transpose into b.

```
-->b= a * X'
b =
!  4. !
!  9. !
! 15. !
! 21. !
! 16. !
-->
```

The results look right. In fact, Scilab displayed the dimensions correctly too, since the results of the multiplication are a matrix of size 5×1.

More Information on Scilab

The documentation for the Scilab application is available from `ftp.inria.fr` in the `/INRIA/Projects/Meta2/Scilab/doc` directory. It contains a PostScript document called `intro.ps` which contains the user's manual titled *Introduction to Scilab*. Take time to read this manual carefully.

Pari

The Pari package is useful for doing symbolic mathematical operations. Its primary features include an arbitrary precision calculator, its own programming facilities, and interfaces to C libraries.

Where To Get Pari

To get Pari, use the FTP site `megrez.math.u-bordeaux.fr`, and from the `/pub/pari/unix` directory get the `gplinux.tar.gz` file. The binaries may not work with a later version of Linux because the binaries are built with older versions of shared libraries. If you have a newer version of Linux than the one supported by Pari, either you can edit the sources yourself or wait until the authors of Pari catch up. Sorry.

With the version of Linux on the CD-ROM, you need to compile your own version of Pari. The source files are in the `pari-1.39.03.tar.gz` file. The source `tar` file unpacks into three directories: `src`, `doc`, and `examples`. You will find the examples very useful indeed.

To compile the sources, run the `Makemakefile` command in the `src` directory. When creating this version, remove the definition of the option `-DULONG_NOT_DEFINED` from the `CFLAGS` macro in the newly created `Makefile`. Then type `make` at the prompt. Be prepared to wait awhile for this package to compile.

Running Pari

After you have compiled the source files for Pari, type `gp` at the console prompt. Your prompt will be a question mark (?). Start by typing simple arithmetic expressions at this prompt. You should be rewarded with answers immediately. Let's look at the following sample session:

```
? 4*8
%1 = 32
? 4/7*5/6
%2 = 10/21
```

The answer was returned to us in fractions. To get real numbers, introduce just one real number in the equation. You will then get the answer as a real number. The percent signs identify the returned line numbers.

```
? 4.0/7 * 5/6
%3 = 0.4761904761904761904761904761
```

To set the precision in number of digits, you use the `?\precision` command. The maximum number of digits is 315,623, a large number for just about all users. For a modest precision of 10 digits to the right of the decimal point, use

```
?\precision = 10
  precision = 10 significant digits
? 4.0/7*5/6
%4 = 0.47619004761
```

You can even work with expressions, as shown in the following example:

```
? (x+2)*(x+3)
%5 = x^2+5*x + 6
```

You can assign values to variables to get the correct answer from evaluating an expression.

```
? x = 3
%6 = 3
? eval(%5)
%7 = 60
```

This is not where the power of Pari ends, though. You can factor numbers, solve differential equations, and even factor polynomials. The FTP site for Pari contains a wealth of information and samples. See `megrez.math.u-bordeaux.fr`. Also, the `examples` and `docs` directories contain samples and the manual to help you get started.

Using LISP-STAT

For statistical computing, consider using LISP-STAT. Written by Luke Tierney at the University of Minnesota, LISP-STAT is a very powerful, interactive, object-oriented LISP package.

Where To Get LISP-STAT

The LISP-STAT package is available from `ftp.stat.umn.edu` in the `/pub/xlispstat` directory. Get the latest `tar` file version you can—currently, `xlispstat-3-44.tar.gz`. In order to build this file you need the `dld` library for Linux. This `dld` library is found in `tsx-11.mit.edu` in the `/pub/linux/binaries/libs` directory as `dld-3.2.5.bin.tar.gz`. Install this `dld` library in the `/lib` directory first.

Running *xlispstat*

At the command prompt in an Xterm, type `xlispstat`. You will be presented with a > prompt. Type commands at this prompt. For example, to multiply two matrices together, use the command:

```
> (def a (matrix '(3 3) '(2 5 7 1 2 3 1 1 2)))
A
> (def b (matrix '(3 1) '(4 5 6)))
B
> (matmult a b)
#2A((75.0) (32.0) (21))
```

The variables in LISP-STAT are not case-sensitive. Note the single quote (') before the list of numbers for the matrix. If you omit the quote, the list will be evaluated and replaced with the result of the evaluation. By leaving the single quote in there, you are forcing the interpreter to leave the list in its place.

Let's try solving a simple set of linear equations using LISP-STAT. The following would be a simple example to solve:

```
3.8x + 7.2y = 16.5
1.3x - 0.9y = -22.1
```

The following script would set up and solve this linear equation problem:

```
> (def a (matrix '(2 2) '(3.8 7.2 1.3 -0.9)))
A
> (def b (matrix '(2 1) '(16.5 -22.1)))
B
> (matmult (inverse a) b)
#2A((-11.288732394366198) (8.249608763693271))
```

You can do other math operations on lists of numbers as well. See the following example for calculating the mean of a list of numbers:

```
> (def sm (list 1.1 2.3 4.1 5.7 2.1))
SM
> (mean SM)
3.06
```

There are many plotting functions available for LISP-STAT. For plotting one variable, try the function `plot-function`. For (x,y) pairs of numbers, use the `plot-lines` function. For a function of two variables, use the `spin-function`. For 3-D plots, use the `spin-plot` function.

Plots are not limited to lines. You can do histograms, planar plots, and so on. (See Figure 35.2.) See the help pages for details on specifics of how to generate these plots. Two or more plots can be linked together so that changes in one set of data can be reflected in another. You can add points to a plot using the `add-points` function. For reconfiguring how the points are displayed, you can `send` commands to the plot windows. Plots can be linked together to enable more than one view of the same data.

FIGURE 35.2.

A Histogram sample.

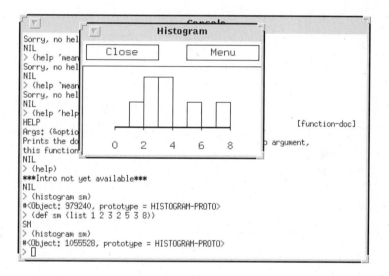

Each plot is displayed in an X window. You can move the mouse cursor over a point, and it will echo back a value for you.

To get help on this system, use the `help` command. The help documentation for this command should be visible. If nothing shows up, check the environment variables to see if the binaries are in the PATH. For example, the command to get help on EIGENVALUES and its invocation is shown in Figure 35.3.

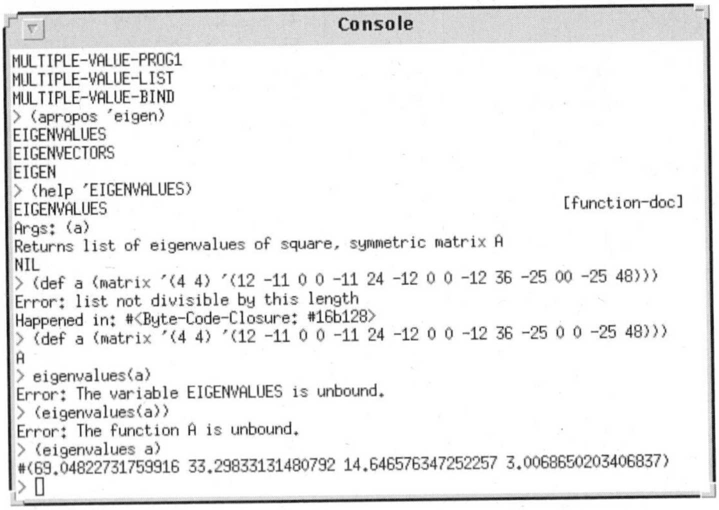

FIGURE 35.3.

Sample of using EIGEN-VALUES.

```
                           Console
  ▽
MULTIPLE-VALUE-PROG1
MULTIPLE-VALUE-LIST
MULTIPLE-VALUE-BIND
> (apropos 'eigen)
EIGENVALUES
EIGENVECTORS
EIGEN
> (help 'EIGENVALUES)
EIGENVALUES                                        [function-doc]
Args: (a)
Returns list of eigenvalues of square, symmetric matrix A
NIL
> (def a (matrix '(4 4) '(12 -11 0 0 -11 24 -12 0 0 -12 36 -25 00 -25 48)))
Error: list not divisible by this length
Happened in: #<Byte-Code-Closure: #16b128>
> (def a (matrix '(4 4) '(12 -11 0 0 -11 24 -12 0 0 -12 36 -25 0 0 -25 48)))
A
> eigenvalues(a)
Error: The variable EIGENVALUES is unbound.
> (eigenvalues(a))
Error: The function A is unbound.
> (eigenvalues a)
#(69.04822731759916 33.29833131480792 14.646576347252257 3.0068650203406837)
>
```

A Last Note

For simple math operations involving spreadsheets, you can always use the xspread program provided with the X package. (The CD-ROM at the back of the book has version 2.1.) For more powerful spreadsheet functions, you might want to resort to a commercial spreadsheet package and take advantage of its support, too. The XESS spreadsheet is available for Linux from Applied Information systems, (919) 942-7801 or http://www.ais.com/Xess. You can share data between spreadsheets, or use the API to develop and have access to a full suite of math functions available on spreadsheets that run under DOS or UNIX.

Wolfram Research has released its Mathematica program for Linux. The Mathematica package has extensive numeric and symbolic capabilities, 2-D and 3-D graphics, and a very large library of application programs. With an additional feature called MathLink, you can exchange information between other applications on a network. You can get more information about Mathematica from info@wri.com or http://www.wri.com.

Summary

You have several options when it comes to performing mathematical operations or writing such applications under Linux. You can either write the code yourself using C, FORTRAN, or other available languages—or you can use a package. If you are familiar with MATLAB, consider using Scilab. For regular expressions and polynomials, try using Pari. If you are a LISP user or want to do vector operations or statistics, consider using the LISP-STAT package.

Database Products for Linux

36

by
Kamran Husain

IN THIS CHAPTER

This chapter covers some common database applications for Linux. The two applications we focus on in this chapter are FlagShip and dbMAN V. We also briefly cover LINCKS, a free, object-oriented database management system (DBMS).

What Is XBASE?

XBASE is a generic term for implementations of what was originally the dBASE programming language. The main players in the MS-DOS version of this database are FoxPro (now owned by Microsoft), dBASE V (now owned by Borland), and Clipper (owned by Computer Associates).

XBASE is a language that has statements normally found in programming languages, such as IF, ELSE, ENDIF, and WHILE. The programming language structure is designed for accessing records in databases and not for general purpose programming. For example, the GOTO statement in XBASE refers to a record in a database, not a location in the program code. XBASE has some powerful statements for processing files and getting data from forms and screens.

In addition, setting up relations between files is easy to do with XBASE. The names of all fields in a file, and their types and lengths, are recorded in the file header. New fields can be added to a file without changing programs that use the file. The scheme allows for having different, disjointed programs all accessing the database file in their own way and all using the fields in the header.

The three major manufacturers of databases have largely ignored Linux as a platform for their products. What we have instead for Linux are products called FlagShip (by WorkGroup Solutions) and dbMAN (from Versasoft Corporation). Both of these products run on several implementations of UNIX. dbMAN also runs on MS-DOS.

Comparing the two products is like comparing apples and oranges. FlagShip is patterned after Clipper Version 5. The dbMAN package resembles dBASE III+ or FoxPlus. FlagShip, like Clipper, is a compiler. dbMAN is primarily an interpreter, although it is possible to "compile" dbMAN programs.

FlagShip is also an object-oriented language, which makes it philosophically different from dbMAN, as well as from FoxPro and dBASE. Clipper and FlagShip have several C-like features. Actually, the resemblance is a plus for Linux users.

The target markets of the two are also different. dbMAN is targeted primarily at individual users. If you want a program you can run on your desk to keep track of time billed to clients or that maintains a phone list of customers or your sales record, dbMAN can do the job.

By contrast, FlagShip might be overkill for simple database operations such as mailing or customer tracking lists, in other words, the casual user, not programmer. This is not to say that you cannot use it for simple applications, but you may have to learn a bit of programming to really use FlagShip's wonderful and powerful features. FlagShip is more realistically aimed at people who want to develop or port software packages. Traditionally, dBASE files always have separate data (.DBF) and index files. The format of data files is pretty much uniform for all XBASEs. It is hard to find two products that use the same index file formats. I was able to use the same .DBF files with FlagShip and dbMAN.

FlagShip

FlagShip is available from Red Hat (http://www.redhat.com/acc/product-pages) and WorkGroup Solutions. Download an evaluation version from WGS at ftp://ftp.wgs.com/pub2/wgs (see http://www.wgs.com/fsdemo.html for instructions), or see http://www.wgs.com/flagship.html for more information.

FlagShip is a compiler. It translates the XBASE code into C. The generated code can be linked with the gcc compiler. This means that you can link functions written in C or assembler into FlagShip programs. You can even mix XBASE and C code in a program. The compiled binaries may be distributed without paying royalties to MultiSoft.

FlagShip has no equivalent of the "dot prompt" or interactive command interface found in other XBASE products. However, there is a public-domain program in their WorkGroup Solutions's FTP area named dbu. This program will provide the capability to create files and indexes, add, change, or locate records, and browse files.

The FlagShip feature has an online reference program called fsman. The fsman contains the entire FlagShip manual—more than 1,000 pages worth of material. This means that you do not have thick manuals all over your desk. The samples can be saved as text files on disk. This makes it easy to incorporate programming examples in the manual into whatever program you are working on at the time. Of course, you could also use the mouse to copy text from fsman into your program by cutting and pasting between windows.

FlagShip uses the curses toolkit for its user interface. During installation, you get a set of terminfo files specifically for FlagShip. Because of a problem with ncurses 1.8.5, they are compiled with ncurses 1.8.1.

FlagShip doesn't have a function specifically for managing pull-down menus. What FlagShip and Clipper programmers normally do is use @PROMPT/MENU TO statements to create the horizontal menu, and use a function called ACHOICE() for the vertical menus.

FlagShip has functions for managing windows that work very nicely, but the functions are not part of the basic package. You have to buy the FStools library. As the name suggests, the FStools library is a clone of the Clipper Tools library. There are also windowing functions in the NanForum library (containing mathematical and statistics functions), which is public domain.

You can set hot keys with the statement SET KEY keyid TO statement. Normally, the statement would be a function invocation. Within this function, you can call the function READVAR() to find out which field the cursor was in when the key was pressed. An input field can be validated by adding the VALID statement parameter to the @SAY/GET statement. Again, the statement would normally be a function invocation. Within the function, the value the user typed in could be looked up in a database file.

To determine how compatible FlagShip is with Clipper, I downloaded a couple of programs from a local BBS. I ran into two problems. The programs contained function calls that looked like this:

```
IF (expr, true_result,)
```

FlagShip complained about the absence of the third parameter. Adding .f. for the third parameter solved the problem. The other problem was a reference to a function named FT_Shadow(), which FlagShip simply doesn't know about. Get rid of this problem by commenting it out.

A key feature of FlagShip is the TBROWSE() object. You use this in place of the BROWSE command that exists in other languages. If you don't have any previous experience with object-oriented programming, setting up TBROWSE() for the first time is not easy. The best course of action is to use the examples and samples in the fsman pages.

When running a FlagShip program in an xterm, you may get hieroglyphics instead of line drawing characters. Fiddling with the acsc parameter in the fslinxterm terminfo entry may not help. Try using the vga font that comes with DOSemu package. See Chapter 57, "DOSemu," for more information. Instead of using the acsc parameter, FlagShip uses another file named Fschrmap.def which maps the character codes generated by the program to the character codes displayed on the screen. Using the vga font is actually a better solution because it's possible to display double line drawing characters.

FlagShip is picky about reserved words. If you have a filename such as browse, you are liable to run into problems running programs. Keep a list of all the reserved words in FlagShip and avoid using these as file or program names. Check the list of reserved words in the fsman pages.

FlagShip programs could be attached to WWW pages. This makes it possible for net surfers to access and update databases. This feature, plus the ability to link in your C and C++ programs, makes FlagShip a very powerful data management tool.

Currently, the enhancements to FlagShip include GUI support. This should further increase the visual appeal of the product.

dbMAN

The dbMAN program is an interpreter. When you start dbMAN, you get a CMD: prompt. This is where you enter all your commands to dbMAN. You can think of this a . prompt in dBASE. For starters, you can type in ASSIST, at the CMD: prompt. ASSIST starts up a menu-driven interface similar to ones available with FoxPro or dBASE.

The menu-driven interface is not very elaborate. ASSIST only enables one file to be open at a time. This means that it is not possible to set up relations. It is possible to start up a simple program generator from ASSIST. Again, it has a single file limitation.

You can compile programs in dbMAN. Compiling a program does not produce an executable binary. It produces a .run file, which still requires dbMAN to execute it.

It is also possible to enter CREATE REPORT or MODIFY REPORT at the CMD: prompt. This puts you in dbMAN's report writer. The report writer enables display of data by using the relational operators. dbMAN provides a function called PMENU() to create pull-down menus. PMENU doesn't have any mechanism for temporarily disabling a menu choice.

dbMAN handles windows differently from other XBASE products. Prior to defining a window, you call PUSHWIND() to push the current window onto a stack. When a program is in its initial state, the entire screen is considered to be a window. You then call WINDOW() to create the window. When you are finished with it, you call POPWIND(), which removes the window and makes the previous window active.

dbMAN enables you to define only one hot key. You do so by invoking the ONKEY() function. This will have no effect until you execute the ON KEY statement. The statement will normally be DO hot-key-handler.

The BROWSE command has a long list of options. You can browse only specified fields, and you can specify the width of each field, and whether it is editable. The list of fields can include fields in other files, which is great if you have relationships set up.

dbMAN does not use either termcap or terminfo. Instead, it includes a file named dbmterm.dbm. This file looks similar to termcap. There are no entries for either xterm or console. You have to create your own entries using the existing entries.

dbMAN has no facility for executing functions written in C or assembler. So you have to use what they offer. There were a couple of nasty bugs in the version of dbMAN I evaluated, which was version 5.32. The main one bug I found was that procedure files simply didn't work if the procedure file was a .prg. If you compiled the procedure file into a .run file, it worked OK.

You can get dbMAN from

VERASOFT Corp.
4340 Alamaden Expressway, #110
San Jose, CA 95118
(408) 723-9044

LINCKS

LINCKS is an object-oriented database management system. LINCKS is a good system if you intend to use this system on a network and share data via RPC calls. You need to have some experience with networks, as well as an existing network to fully benefit from this package. This package is not for a single node system just because it would be an overkill for such a platform.

You can get LINCKS from sunsite.unc.edu in the /pub/Linux/apps/databases/lincks directory.

LINCKS is based on an append-only object-oriented structure. Objects are derived from other objects. Links can be set between objects to define relationships. You define views to an object. A view is used to specify how the data in the object is presented to a user. Multiple views can exist for the same object. Views can be inherited.

The main interface is xlincks program. Using commands similar to emacs, you can interactively browse through databases. The interface resembles the hypertext functions of a Web page. You click on a highlighted item, and the program leads to a page with more information about the topic.

Help is available in two forms: context sensitive or as a browseable database. The help file is always a button away—to access help, simply press the Help button. The contents of the help file are well organized and are a good starting place to learn about LINCKS. The manual is also available in PostScript for the sunsite archives.

LINCKS comes with a few programs in its distribution package. You can create new databases using the dbroot command. To prune databases of unreferenced objects, use the cutoff command. The main server for the application is the netserv program which fires off a dbs process for each connected client.

Other Database Products

This is a quick overview of some other database management systems for Linux. Most of these are free and can be found on the Internet.

mbase v5.0 is a relational database system originally written for the Amiga and ported to other platforms. It uses a format similar to C to do the database programming. To compile using mbase, you need ncurses and time. My efforts to compile the package failed miserably until I made several modifications to the Makefile. If you really want cheap, C-like access to your DBMS, use this package. Otherwise get FlagShip or dbMAN.

onyx is a database prototype program based on a format like the C language. The make config command starts the process and a series of questions pop up. Answering all these questions results in configuring Linux.

DBF is an XBASE manipulation package and is a collection of utility programs that manipulate dbf files. Some of the utilities, such as dbfadd, add a record or layer of information in the database. dbflist lists the records in the database, dbft lists the structure of each database and its items.

typhoon is yet another RDBMS. The package is in Beta form. The "most notable" feature for this RDBMS (depending on your point of view) is that it's entirely like C. The problem is that the product still has to mature before being considered a viable RDBMS.

Summary

This chapter has given you a brief introduction to the various database management systems for Linux. There are many more products for Linux which can provide DBMS solutions. Hopefully, the major manufacturers will soon catch on and provide the database solutions for this market.

PART

Linux for System Administrators

System Administration Basics

37

by Tim Parker

So far in this book, you've seen how to use Linux for many different tasks. However, there are some issues we haven't dealt with because they are used rarely, or only by a single administrator (who may be the only user). This chapter looks at simple system administration tasks, including the following:

- Starting and shutting down the system properly
- Managing the disk partitions
- Making backups
- `gzip`, `compress`, and `tar`
- Message of the day
- Emergency boot floppies

Of course, we can't cover everything you need to know to run a system efficiently. Instead, we will look at the basic information and utilities and leave you to experiment. For more details, check the documentation files with your Linux operating system. Better yet, consider purchasing a good UNIX system administration book, such as *Linux System Administrator's Survival Guide* (Sams Publishing, 1995). Much of the information in a UNIX book will be applicable to Linux.

The *root* Account

The `root` login, as you probably know, has no limitations at all. It can do anything anywhere, access any files it wants, and control any processes. This power has its price, though: Any mistake can be disastrous, sometimes resulting in damage to the entire operating system.

A mystique has built up in the UNIX community about the `root` login, because it holds unlimited power over the system. The tendency to want to use this superuser login is overwhelming for many. However, a simple `rm` command in the wrong place can spell many hours of trouble.

For this reason, the `root` account should be employed only for limited system use, and then only when its power is necessary (such as when rebuilding a kernel, installing new software, or setting up new file systems). As a general rule, you should not use the `root` account for routine tasks.

Naturally, many people use `root` for their daily Linux sessions, ignoring any advice because they think they won't make mistakes. In truth, everyone makes a mistake occasionally. Check with any UNIX system administrator and you'll find that accidents happen with the `root` account. (I have managed to delete entire file systems more than once while trying to do two things at the same time.) Although many people will ignore the rule about using `root` only when necessary, most of them eventually find out why this rule is important!

Starting and Stopping the System

There are several ways of booting the Linux operating system, as well as a few ways to safely shut it down. Some were mentioned earlier in this book. Because Linux can be installed in many different ways, there is no single "right" method of booting the operating system, so we must look at both hard-disk-based and floppy-disk-based boot procedures.

Booting from a Floppy

A boot floppy, as its name implies, is a floppy disk that boots the Linux kernel. A boot floppy has the `root` partition installed on the floppy itself instead of the hard drive (although both may co-exist). Without the `root` partition, Linux would be unable to find the hard drives for the rest of the operating system.

You can create Linux boot floppies with the setup routine included in most distributions of the operating system. Check the documentation or information files that came with your Linux distribution, if there are any. Alternatively, most Linux setup utilities have a menu-driven interface that prompts you for a boot floppy setup when you rebuild or reconfigure the kernel. You should use this procedure to make a boot floppy, which is also useful for emergencies.

In most cases, a boot floppy is used only in emergencies when your system won't start up normally. The boot floppy enables you to load Linux, and then mount the hard drives that are causing the problem to check for damage. Luckily, this is not required very often. If you haven't used LILO to choose the partition to boot or set your boot sequence to Linux by default, you may need the boot floppy to start up Linux. In this case, the boot floppy is much like a DOS boot floppy.

You can create a boot floppy from scratch by copying over the kernel image from the hard drive. The kernel image is usually in the file `vmlinuz`, `vmlinux`, `Image`, or `/etc/Image`, depending on the distribution of Linux. The Red Hat distribution uses `vmlinuz`, which is a compressed kernel (hence the `z` in the name). Compressed kernels uncompress themselves as they are loaded into memory at boot time. The `vmlinuz` image expands to `vmlinux`. (Compressed kernels take up less disk space; that's why they are used.)

After you have identified the kernel, you can set the `root` device in the kernel image to point to the `root` partition on either the floppy or hard drive. In this case, we want the floppy. The root partition is set with the `rdev` command, whose format is as follows:

```
rdev kernelname device
```

where `kernelname` is the name of the kernel image, and `device` is the name of the Linux `root` partition. To set a floppy boot device with the file `vmlinuz`, the command would be

```
rdev vmlinuz /dev/fd0
```

for the first floppy on the system. You can set other parameters with `rdev` as well if you want to change system defaults during boot. Check the `rdev` man page for the `rdev` help file for complete information.

As a final step in creating the boot floppy, copy the kernel image to the floppy disk. You should use a preformatted diskette (format with DOS if necessary) to allow the Linux routines to identify the type of diskette and its density. To copy the `vmlinuz` kernel to the first floppy drive, use this command:

```
cp vmlinuz /dev/fd0
```

The floppy should now be ready to boot the system. You might not be able to boot the system without the floppy if you changed the location of the `root` partition. You can change the `root` partition back to the hard drive with the rdev command after completing the boot floppy, which enables you to boot from either. This can be useful when you have diskettes for several different boot configurations. You can also create the boot floppy from the Linux setup program.

Using LILO To Boot

LILO is a program that resides in the boot sector of your hard drive and allows Linux to be booted from the hard disk either after you tell it to or after a default number of seconds has elapsed.

LILO can also be used with other operating systems such as OS/2 and DOS. If you have LILO set to autoboot Linux, you must interrupt the process by pressing the Ctrl, Alt, or Shift keys when the bootup is started if you want to boot into another operating system. This displays a boot prompt that enables you to specify another operating system.

If LILO is set to allow a given time before it boots into Linux, you can use the Ctrl-Alt-Shift sequence to interrupt the boot process before the timer expires and Linux starts loading. Finally, if LILO is set to not autoboot into Linux, but to wait for explicit instructions, you must press Enter to boot Linux or type the name of the other operating system.

Some Linux distributions have a configuration file in the directory /etc/lilo that can be edited to provide boot information, while other versions of Linux configure LILO during the installation process. If the latter is the case, you can change the settings with the setup utility. Some versions of Linux use the configuration file /etc/lilo.conf instead of /etc/lilo.

Shutting Down Linux

You can't just turn off the power switch! This can cause damage to the file system, sometimes irreversibly. Because Linux keeps many files open at once, as well as several processes, they must all be closed down properly before you cycle the power to the unit.

There are a few ways to shut the Linux system down, but the formal method is to use the shutdown command. The syntax for shutdown is

```
shutdown [minutes] [warning]
```

where *minutes* is the number of minutes to wait before shutting the system down and *warning* is an optional message displayed for all users currently logged in. Some versions of shutdown allow the word now instead of a time, while others require either no argument or the number 0 to shut the system down immediately without waiting. You can have shutdown reboot the system after the shutdown by adding the argument -r (for reboot).

Using shutdown is best if you have other users on your system, because it gives them a warning that they should log out, and it prevents loss of information. It can also be used to automate a shutdown much later (such as at midnight), with messages just before that time warning any users still logged in.

If you can't wait and want to shut the system down immediately, use the `halt` command or the "three-finger salute" of Ctrl-Alt-Delete. This immediately shuts down all the processes and halts the system as quickly as possible. Then the power can be shut off.

> **WARNING**
>
> Some Linux distributions don't support Ctrl-Alt-Delete, and a couple of older distributions use it to halt the system immediately without terminating processes properly. This can cause damage. Check the documentation or man pages for information.

Mounting File Systems

File systems are not available until they are mounted onto the Linux main file system. Even hard drives must be mounted, because only the `root` file system is available in the `/` directory until the rest are mounted. The `mount` command is used to mount a file system.

During the boot process, the `mount` command is used from the startup files (such as the `/etc/rc` file or files under the `/etc/rc.d` directory) to mount all the File Systems maintained in the file `/etc/fstab`. You can look at the file to see the type of information maintained there. Every file system that is mounted during the boot process has an entry giving its device name, its mount directory (called the mount point), the type of file system it is, and any options that apply.

You can add a new file system from a hard disk, a CD-ROM, a floppy, or any other type of device that provides a file system supported by Linux, using the `mount` command. The format is

```
mount filesystem mountpoint
```

where `filesystem` is the name of the device and `mountpoint` is where in the Linux file system it should be mounted. For example, if you want to mount a SCSI CD-ROM to the file system as `/usr/cdrom`, issue the following command:

```
mount /dev/scd0 /usr/cdrom
```

The directory `/usr/cdrom` must be created before the command is given, or the `mount` command will generate an ambiguous error. You should replace `/dev/scd0` with the name of your CD-ROM device driver (`/dev/cd0` for most non-SCSI CD-ROM drives, and `/dev/scd0` for SCSI CD-ROM drivers). When the file system has been mounted properly, changing to `/usr/cdrom` lets you access all the files on the CD-ROM as if they were part of the normal file system.

If your `/etc/fstab` file doesn't have any entries in it already, you have to mount the file system with a slightly different syntax:

```
mount -t fstypefilesystem mountpoint
```

where fstype is the type of file system (such as ISO9660, MSDOS, and so on). The rest of the arguments are the same as the previous example. The -t option is used when the file system to be mounted doesn't already have an entry in the /etc/fstab file.

Mounting a Floppy

You can mount a floppy disk with a command similar to the one in the CD-ROM example just discussed. To mount a floppy in the first floppy drive on the directory /mnt, issue the following command:

```
mount /dev/fd0 /mnt
```

If the file system is not the default value used by Linux, the type of file system must be specified. For example, to mount a floppy using the ext2 file system, use the -t option of the mount command:

```
mount -t ext2 /dev/fd0 /mnt
```

Creating a New File System

To create a file system on a floppy (so it can be mounted), you should use the utility mke2fs or the command mkdev fs, depending on the version of Linux. To use mke2fs, for example, issue the command

```
mke2fs /dev/fd0 1440
```

to create a floppy file system on a 1.44MB 3.5-inch diskette.

Unmounting File Systems

To detach a mounted file system from your Linux file system, use the umount command with the name of the device. For example, to unmount a floppy in /dev/fd0, issue the command

```
umount /dev/fd0
```

and the floppy will be removed from the mounted point. Be sure to type umount instead of unmount!

If you want to remove the current floppy and replace it with another, you can't simply swap them. The current floppy must be unmounted, and then the new one must be mounted. Failure to follow this process can result in corruption or erroneous directory listings.

Checking File Systems

Every now and again a file might get corrupted or a file system's inode table might get out of sync with the disk's contents. For these reasons, it is a good idea to check the file system at regular intervals. Several utilities can check file systems, depending on the version of Linux. The utility fsck is available for some systems, while the utility e2fsck is designed for Linux's ext2fs file system. Many

Linux versions include other utilities such as `xfsck` and `efsfck` for different file systems. In many cases, the `fsck` command is linked to the individual file system versions.

To use `e2fsck` to check a file system, issue the command with the device name and the options a (automatically correct errors) and v (verbose output):

```
e2fsck -av /dev/hda1
```

This command checks and repairs any problems on the `/dev/hda1` (or whatever device driver you specify) partition. If any corrections have been made to a partition, you should reboot the machine as soon as possible to allow the system to resync its tables.

Whenever possible, it is a good idea to unmount the file system before checking it, because this can prevent problems with open files. Of course, you can't unmount the primary `root` partition while running from it, so you can boot from a boot floppy that contains the check utilities, and start them from the floppy.

Using a File as Swap Space

When you installed Linux, your setup program probably set up a partition specifically for the swap space. You can, when the original installation has been completed, set Linux to use a file instead of the partition, thus freeing up the partition's disk space.

Generally, there is a performance degradation with using a file because the file system is involved, although the effect can be small on fast disks and CPUs. However, this is a useful technique when you need to add more swap space, such as when you temporarily want to run a swap-space-intensive application such as a compiler.

To create a file used as the swap space, issue the following command:

```
dd if=/dev/zero of=/swap bs=1024 count=16416
```

This creates a file (called swap) for swap space that is about 16MB (in this case, 16416 blocks). If you want a different size, replace the number after count with the correct value in bytes. Next, physically create the file swap file with the command

```
mkswap /swap 16416
```

(the number should match the blocks determined earlier) and turn the swap space on with the command

```
swapon /swap
```

If you want to remove the swap file and use the swap partition, use the command

```
swapoff /swap
```

followed by a standard `rm` command to remove the file.

Swap files can't be larger than 16MB with most Linux versions, but you can have up to eight swap files and partitions on your system.

Compressing Files with *gzip* and *compress*

Files abound on a UNIX system, adding up to a large chunk of disk real estate. Instead of deleting files, an alternative is to compress them so that they take up less space. Several compression utilities are available for UNIX and Linux systems. The most commonly used are `compress` and the newer GNU `gzip`.

When run on a file, `compress` creates a smaller file with the extension `.Z`, which immediately identifies the file as being compressed. To compress a file, use the following command:

```
compress filename
```

You can also use wildcards to compress several files at once. `compress` supports a number of options, but most aren't used often. By default, when a file is compressed, the uncompressed original is deleted, although this can be changed with a command-line option.

To uncompress a compressed file, run the `uncompress` program:

```
uncompress filename
```

Alternatively, you can use a wildcard such as `*.Z` to uncompress all the compressed files. Remember to include the `.Z` suffix when specifying the filename.

The `gzip` utility is a new compression tool that uses different algorithms than `compress`. The `gzip` program has a few extra features that were added since `compress` was released, such as adjustable compression (the more compression required, the longer it takes to compress). To use `gzip`, specify the filename to be compressed and the compression type:

```
gzip -9 filename
```

The `-9` option, which tells `gzip` to use the highest compression factor, will probably be the option you use the most. Alternatively, leave this option off and let `gzip` work with its default settings. A `gzip` compressed file has the extension `.gz` appended, and the original file is deleted. To uncompress a gzipped file, use either the `gunzip` utility or `gzip -d filename`.

Using *tar*

The `tar` (tape archiver) utility has been used with UNIX systems for many years. Unfortunately, it's not very friendly and can be quite temperamental at times, especially when you're unfamiliar with the syntax required to make `tar` do something useful.

The `tar` program is designed to create a single archive file, much as the ZIP utilities do for DOS. With `tar`, you can combine many files into a single larger file, which makes it easier to move the collection or back it up to tape. The general syntax used by `tar` is as follows:

```
tar [options] [file]
```

The options available are lengthy and sometimes obtuse. Files can be specified with or without wildcards. A simple example of creating a `tar` archive file is

```
tar cvf archive1.tar /usr/tparker
```

which combines all the files in /usr/tparker into a tar archive called archive1.tar. The c option tells tar to create the archive; the v tells it to be verbose, displaying messages as it goes; and the f tells it to use the filename archive1.tar as the output file.

The extension .tar is not automatically appended by tar, but is a user convention that helps identify the file as an archive. This convention isn't widely used, though, although it should be as it helps identify the file.

The c option creates new archives. (If the file existed before, it is deleted.) The u (update) option is used to append new files to an existing archive, or to create the archive if it doesn't exist. This is useful if you keep adding files. The x option is used to extract files from the archive. To extract with the tar command all the files in the archive in the earlier example, you would use the command

```
tar xvf archive1.tar
```

There's no need to specify a filename, because the filenames and paths will be retained as the archive is unpacked. It's important to remember that the path is saved with the file. So if you archived /usr/tparker and then moved into /usr/tparker and issued the extract command, the files would be extracted relevant to the current directory, which would place them in /usr/tparker/usr/tparker. You must be very careful to extract files properly. If you want to force a new directory path on extracted files, a command-line option allows this.

The tar system does not remove the original files as they are packed into the archive, nor does it remove the archive file when files are extracted. These steps must be performed manually.

You can use tar to copy files to tapes or floppies by specifying a device name and the f option as a device name. To archive files in /usr/tparker to a floppy disk in the first drive, you could use the following command:

```
tar cvf /dev/fd0 /usr/tparker
```

This can cause a problem if the floppy doesn't have enough capacity, however, so tar lets you specify the capacity with the k option. In this case, the command for a 1.44MB floppy is as follows:

```
tar cvfk /dev/fd0 1440 /usr/tparker
```

If the floppy is full before the entire archive has been copied, tar prompts you for another one. It's important to keep the arguments in the right order. You see that the f is before the k, so the device name must be before the capacity. All the argument keyletters are gathered together instead of issued one at a time followed by their value, which is one aspect of tar that can be very confusing.

As a last issue for backing up to floppy, it is sometimes necessary to tell the tar program about the blocking used (blocking identifies how many blocks are used for each chunk of information on the device). A floppy usually has a blocking factor of 4, so the command becomes the following:

```
tar cvfkb /dev/fd0 1440 4 /usr/tparker
```

A final problem with tar is that it can't always handle a generic device such as /dev/fd0, and must be specifically told the disk type.

For more complete information on all the options used by `tar`, check the man pages or, even better, a good system administration book.

You can use `tar` to archive compressed files, too, in the same manner. You can also compress a `tar` file without any problems. In these cases, you might get filenames such as

```
filename.tar.gz
```

which show that you should run `gunzip` first to recover the `tar` file, and then run `tar` to extract the files in the archive. You can run the commands together with pipes:

```
gunzip filename.tar.gz ¦ tar xvf -
```

The hyphen as the `tar` filename after the pipe symbol is standard UNIX terminology for taking the input from the pipe (`stdin`).

Backups

The three rules of system administration are back up, back up, and back up. This might sound silly and trite, but a backup can save you whenever you do something silly to the file system, or when problems occur. With UNIX, most backups are made to a tape device using `tar`, although many Linux users don't have tape units available and have to resort to floppies.

Backups are made with the `tar` utility, as I mentioned earlier. The procedure is exactly the same as I showed you earlier. To back up the entire system on floppy, the command is

```
tar -cvfbk /dev/fd0 1440 4 /
```

To back up to a high-capacity tape device larger than the file system (and hence not needing a capacity limit) called `/dev/rct0`, the command is

```
tar -cvfk /dev/rct0 20 /
```

In many cases, you won't want to back up the entire system, because it's easier to reinstall off a CD-ROM. However, you should back up your user files by either backing up the entire `/usr` directory or specifically backing up your own home directory.

To restore a backup, you use the `tar` command again:

```
tar -xvf /dev/rct0
```

This recovers all files from the tape device `/dev/rct0`. You can explicitly restore specific files if you need to.

Several commercial products offer automated backups, although you can do this quite easily with the `cron` command.

Setting Up Your System

You can perform several little tasks to tweak or optimize your Linux system, although in many cases they are dependent on the version you are running and other applications coexisting. We can look at a few of the miscellaneous tasks here.

Setting the System Name

The system name is contained in a file called /etc/HOSTNAME. It is simply the name the system calls itself for identification, which is especially useful if you are networking your Linux machine with others. You can call the system anything you want.

To set your system name (also called a host name), you can either edit the system files (which should be followed by a reboot to make the changes effective) or use the hostname command. The command

```
hostname hellfire
```

sets the machine's name to hellfire.

Using a Maintenance Disk

Every system should have a maintenance disk that enables you to check the root file system, recover from certain disk problems, and solve simple problems (such as forgetting your root password). The emergency disks, also called the boot/root floppies, are created with the setup program in most distributions of Linux when the configuration is changed.

You can usually create an emergency boot disk from the CD-ROM that the system came on, as well as obtain the necessary files from FTP sites.

After you have booted your machine with the emergency disk, you can mount the disk partitions with the mount command.

Forgetting the *root* Password

This is an embarrassing and annoying problem, but luckily one easily fixed with Linux. (If only other UNIX systems were so easy!) To recover from a problem with the root password, use a boot floppy and boot the system. Mount the root partition, and edit the /etc/passwd file to remove any password for root; then, reboot from the hard disk.

After the system has booted, you can set a password again.

WARNING

This points out one major security problem with Linux: Anyone with a boot floppy can get unrestricted access to your system!

Setting the Login Message

If you have more than one user on the system, you can display information about the system, its maintenance, or changes in a file called /etc/motd (message of the day). The contents of this file are displayed whenever someone logs in.

To change the /etc/motd file, use any text editor and save the contents as ASCII. You can make the contents as long as you want, but readers usually appreciate brevity. The /etc/motd file is useful for informing users of downtime, backups, or new additions. You can also use it to give a more personal feel to your system.

Summary

System administration is not a complicated subject, unless you want to get into the nitty-gritty of your operating system and its configuration. For most Linux users who use the operating system for their personal experimentation, the administration steps explained in this chapter should be sufficient for most purposes. If you want to get into more detail, check out a good UNIX system administration book.

Devices and Device Administration

38

by Tim Parker

This chapter is devoted to devices that might be attached to your Linux system, such as terminals, modems, and printers. It shows you how to add and manage the different devices, and it also looks at many of the Linux commands you will need to properly administer your system.

In this chapter, you will learn the following:

- What a device driver is
- The difference between block mode and character mode devices
- Major and minor device numbers
- The mknod command
- How to manage printers and the print spooler
- How to add a printer
- How to add a terminal and modem
- The configuration files used by terminals
- The startup sequence used to permit logins

All of this information is necessary if you are to have a smoothly running system. Even if you don't intend to add terminals or modems, you should know about the startup process and how the configuration files are handled.

Character and Block Mode Devices

Everything attached to the computer you are using to run Linux is treated as a device by the operating system. It doesn't matter whether the device is a terminal, a hard disk, a printer, a CD-ROM drive, or a modem. Everything that accepts or sends data to the operating system is a device.

The concept of treating everything on the system as a device is one of the benefits of the UNIX architecture. Each device has a special section in the kernel, called a device driver, which includes all the instructions necessary for Linux to communicate with the device. When a new device is developed, it can be used with Linux by writing a device driver, which is usually a set of instructions that explains how to send and receive data.

Device drivers allow the Linux kernel to include only the operating system and support software. By having the instructions for talking to devices within a set of files, they can be loaded as needed (in the case of rarely used devices), or kept in memory all the time when the operating system boots. As refinements are made to a peripheral, small changes to the device driver file can be linked into the kernel to keep the operating system informed of the new features and capabilities.

When an application instructs a device to perform an action, the Linux kernel doesn't have to worry about the mechanism. It simply passes the request to the device driver and lets it handle the communications. Similarly, when you're typing at the keyboard, your terminal's device driver accepts the keystrokes and passes them to the shell or application, filtering out any special codes that the kernel doesn't know how to handle by translating them into something the kernel can perform.

Linux keeps device files in the /dev directory by default and convention. It is permissible to keep device files anywhere on the file system, but keeping them all in /dev makes it obvious that they are device files.

Every type of device on the Linux system communicates in one of two ways: character by character or as a set of data in a predefined chunk or block. Terminals, printers, and asynchronous modems are character devices, using characters sent one at a time and echoed by the other end. Hard drives and most tape drives, on the other hand, use blocks of data, because this is the fastest way to send large chunks of information. These peripherals are called either character mode or block mode devices, based on the way they communicate.

> **NOTE**
>
> Another way to differentiate between character and block mode devices is by how the buffering to the device is handled. Character mode devices want to do their own buffering. Block mode devices, which usually communicate in chunks of 512 or 1,024 bytes, have the kernel perform the buffering.
>
> Some devices can be both character and block mode devices. Some tape drives, for example, can handle both character and block modes, and therefore have two different device drivers. The device driver that is used depends on how the user wants to write data to the device.

The device file has all the details about whether the device is a character mode or block mode device. There is an easy way to tell which type of device a peripheral is: Look at the output of the listing command that shows file permissions (such as ls -l). If the first character is a b, the device is a block mode device; a c indicates a character mode device.

Device files are usually named to indicate the type of device they are. Most terminals, for example, have a device driver with the name tty followed by two or more letters or numbers, such as tty1, tty1A, or tty04. The letters tty identify the file as a terminal (tty stands for teletype), and the numbers or letters identify the specific terminal referred to. When coupled with the directory name /dev, the full device driver name becomes /dev/tty01.

Major and Minor Device Numbers

There might be more than one device of the same type on a system. For example, your Linux system might have a multiport card (multiple serial ports) with 10 Wyse 60 terminals hanging off it. Linux can use the same device driver for each of the terminals because they are all the same type of device.

However, there must be a method for the operating system to differentiate which one of the 10 terminals you want to address. That's where device numbers are used. Each device is identified by two device numbers: The major number identifies the device driver to be used, and the minor number identifies the device number. For example, the 10 Wyse 60 terminals on the multiport card can all use a device file with the same major number, but each will have a different minor number, thereby uniquely identifying it to the operating system.

Every device on the system has both major and minor device numbers assigned in such a way as to ensure that they are unique. If two devices are assigned the same number, Linux can't properly communicate with them.

Some devices use the major and minor device numbers in a strange way. Some tape drives, for example, use the minor number to identify the density of the tape and adjust its output in that manner.

Device files are created with the command mknod (make node) and removed with the standard rm command.

The *mknod* Command

The mknod (make node) command is used for several different purposes in Linux. It can create a FIFO (first in first out) pipe or a character or block mode device file. The format of this command is

```
mknod [options] device b¦c¦p¦u major minor
```

The options can be one of the following:

--help	displays help information and then exits.
-m [mode]	sets the mode of the file to mode instead of the default 0666 (only symbolic notation is allowed).
--version	displays version information, then exits.

The argument after the device or pathname specifies whether the file is a block mode device (b), character mode device (c), FIFO device (p), or unbuffered character mode device (u). One of these arguments must be present on the command line.

Following the type of file argument are two numbers for the major and minor device numbers assigned to the new file. Every device on a UNIX system has a unique number that identifies the type of device (the major number) and the specific device itself (the minor number). Both a major and a minor number must be specified for any new block, character, or unbuffered mode device. Device numbers are not specified for a type p device.

Examples of using the mknod command are shown in several sections later in this chapter, when devices are added to the system.

Printer Administration

Printers are commonly used devices that can cause a few problems for system administrators. They are quite easy to configure as long as you know something about the hardware. Managing printer queues is also quite easy, but like many things in Linux, you must know the tricks to make the system work easily for you.

Linux is based on the BSD version of UNIX, which unfortunately is not the most talented UNIX version when it comes to printer administration. However, because it's unlikely that the Linux system will be used on very large networks with many printers, administration tasks can be reduced to the basics. Be warned, though, that the BSD UNIX printer administration and maintenance commands have a reputation for quirky and inconsistent behavior!

The *lpd* Printing Daemon

All printing on the Linux system is handled by the lpd daemon, which is usually started when the system boots. During the startup process, the lpd daemon reads through the file /etc/printcap to identify the sections that apply to any of the printers known to be attached to the system. The lpd daemon uses two other processes, called *listen* and *accept*, to handle incoming requests for printing and to copy them to a spooling area.

In most cases, you won't have to modify the lpd daemon. However, there might be times when you have to stop it manually and restart it. The command to load lpd is

```
lpd [-l] [port]
```

The -l option invokes a logging system that notes each print request. This option can be useful when you're debugging the printer system. The port number allowed in the lpd command line is used to specify the Internet port number if the system configuration information is to be overridden. You will probably never have to use it.

The size of the print spool area is set by an entry in the file minfree in each spool directory (each printer has its own spool directory). The contents of minfree show the number of disk blocks to keep reserved so that spooling large requests doesn't fill up the hard drive. The contents of the file can be changed with any editor.

Access to the lpd daemon to allow printing of a user request must pass a quick validation routine. Two files are involved: /etc/hosts.equiv and /etc/hosts.lpd. If the machine name of the sending user is not in either file, the print requests are refused. Because the local machine is always in hosts.equiv (as localhost), users on the Linux machine should always have their print requests granted.

Following a Print Request

To understand how the print daemon works, as well as how print requests are managed by Linux, it is instructive to follow a print request. When a user requests a print job with the lpr command, lpr assembles the data to be printed and copies it into the spooling queue, where lpd can find it.

NOTE

The lpr program is the only one in the Linux system that can actually queue files for printing. Any other program that offers printing capabilities does so by calling lpr.

As part of its spooling task, lpr also checks for instructions on how to print the file. It can get the information from three sources: the command line (supplied as arguments), environment variables (set by the shell or the user), or the system's default values.

The lpr program knows which spool to put the print request in because of the destination printer designation. The printer destination can be specified on the lpr command line, or through an environment variable. When the destination printer name has been determined, lpr checks the file /etc/printcap to look up the printer's information, including the spool directory. The spool directory is usually of the form /usr/spool/printer_name, such as /usr/spool/lp1.

Within the spool directory, lpr creates two files. The first has the letters cf (control file) followed by a print ID number. The cf file contains information about the print job, including the owner's name. The second file starts with df (data file) and has the actual contents of the file to be printed with it. When lpr has finished creating the df file, it sends a signal to lpd that informs the daemon that a print job is waiting in the spool directory.

When lpd gets the signal from lpr, it checks the file /etc/printcap to see whether the printer is for a local or remote printer. If the print job is for a remote printer (one attached to another machine on the network), lpd opens a connection to the remote machine, transfers both the control and data files, and deletes the local copies.

If the print job is for a local printer, lpd checks to make sure the printer exists and is active, and then sends the print request to the printing daemon running that queue.

The /etc/printcap File and Spooling Directories

The /etc/printcap file is consulted by both the user's print command lpr and the lpd print daemon. It contains information about every printer that is accessible from the Linux machine.

The format of /etc/printcap is straightforward (and similar to the /etc/termcap file for terminal descriptions). The following is an extract from /etc/printcap:

```
# HP Laserjet
lp|hplj|laserjet-acctng|HP LaserJet 4M in Room 425:\
        :lp=/dev/lp0:\
        :sd=/usr/spool/lp0:\
        :lf=/usr/spool/errorlog:\
        :mx#0:\
        :of=/usr/spool/lp0/hpjlp:\
```

The first field in each entry is a list of all the allowable names for the printer. These can be used with the environment variables set by a user's shell or by the system, as well as with options on the lpr command line with a destination printer specified. Valid names are separated by a vertical bar.

Usually, each entry includes at least three names: a short name that is four characters or less (such as hplj); a more complete name with an owner, if necessary (such as laserjet-acctng); and a full, descriptive name with any other information necessary to identify the printer (such as HP LaserJet 4M in Room 425).

NOTE

If a print job is submitted without a destination name, and one can't be determined from environment variable values, it is routed to the printer lp. Therefore, one of the printers (usually the system default printer) should also have the name lp as part of its identifier.

A comment in the file is shown with a pound symbol (sometimes called a hash mark) as the first character. Following the printer name is a set of two-character parameters and values used by the printer. The format of these entries is always one of the following:

NN	A Boolean value
NN=string	Set equal to string
NN#number	Set not equal to number

When a Boolean value is used (no assignment follows the two-character identifier), the value is set to True by default. If the value of False was required, the two-character identifier would not be included in the description.

Most assignments are shown with colons beginning and ending each definition to enhance readability and make the file easier for the print utilities to parse. Null values are valid assignments employed by putting two colons together.

A few of the parameters in the /etc/printcap file are worth highlighting because they are useful for administration purposes. Not all of these parameters might be present in every printer definition in the /etc/printcap file, but most appear:

sd	The spool directory
lf	The log directory for error messages
af	Accounting log file
mx	Determines the type of files that can be printed
of	Output filter program to be used when printing

All printers should have their own spool directories, usually under the printer name in /usr/spool, such as /usr/spool/hplj. Spool directories are necessary for both remote and local printers. When a new printer is added to the system, the spool directory might have to be created manually (using mkdir). The permissions for the spool directory should be set to 775. The directory must be owned by root or daemon. The group ID should be set to root or daemon, too. In both cases, daemon theoretically is the better ID for user and group, although root will work also.

The error log file can be located anywhere on the system. It can be shared by all printers, if desired, because each log entry includes the name of the printer.

The accounting log file is used to record printouts for systems in which users are charged. If accounting records are not to be used on the system, ignore the entry entirely in the /etc/printcap file. The file can also be used for generating statistics, however. Some heavily used systems might want to have the accounting file for those purposes even when charges are not incurred by the users. An entry is written to the accounting log file after a print job has completed. Account information can be displayed with the Linux pac command. (Use the man pac command to display the man pages for more information about pac.)

The mx character enables you to identify the types of files to be printed. Usually this is set to mx#0, meaning that there are no restrictions on the types of files.

Output filters modify the format of the outgoing file to the printer to fit its requirements. For example, many laser printers can't handle 66 lines per page, so the output filter repaginates to 60 lines (or whatever the number of lines per page is set to). Sometimes, special codes must be added to force line feeds, font changes, or paper bin selections. All these items are part of the output filter. Several other types of filters are available, but the output filter is the one most commonly encountered.

Within each spool directory, there may be two status files: status and lock. Each file is one line long and can be modified with an editor. These files contain a description of the current state of the printer. They are created and managed by the lpd printer daemon and used by several printer commands for status information.

Adding Printer Devices with *mknod*

Linux supports both parallel and serial printer devices. Both parallel and serial printers are character mode devices. Unfortunately, most Linux distributions do not have an easy-to-use printer installation and configuration utilities like many UNIX versions. Instead, the printer devices must be created and set up manually.

Parallel printers are referred to as devices lp0, lp1, or lp2, depending on the address of the parallel port they are used with. (The most common is the single parallel port on a PC, which is /dev/lp0.) Valid parallel port devices, their addresses, and their usual equivalents under MS-DOS are as follows:

```
/dev/lp0    0x03bc    LPT1
/dev/lp1    0x0378    LPT2
/dev/lp2    0x0278    LPT3
```

> **NOTE**
>
> To determine the address of a parallel port, you can use a diagnostic utility (such as DOS's MSD.EXE). Some BIOS versions display port addresses when the system is booting. If you are unsure, try the ports starting with /dev/lp0, and wait to see whether a printout is possible. The first parallel port on a PC is typically set to address 0x03bc.

Linux uses the mknod (make node) command to create a parallel printer device file. After the device has been made, the ownership of the device driver file must be altered to root or daemon.

The following is a command to make a parallel printer device on the first parallel port (`/dev/lp0`):

```
mknod -m 620 /dev/lp0 c 6 0
chown root.daemon /dev/lp0
```

In this example, the file permissions are set to mode `620`, the device `/dev/lp0` is created, and it is set to be a character mode device with a major device number of `6` and a minor device number of `0`. Usually, minor device numbers start at `0` and are incremented upward; therefore, because this is the first printer added, the minor device number is set to `0`.

> **NOTE**
>
> The ownership `root.daemon` is a special Linux convention for the daemons run by root. The entry `root.daemon` does not appear in the `/etc/passwd` file. This uses a convention that lets the first part of the entry (before the period) indicate the user and the second part (after the period) represent the group.

If a different device is configured, the device name itself must be changed to the device number. For each possible parallel port, the `mknod` commands are as follows:

```
mknod -m 620 /dev/lp0 c 6 0
mknod -m 620 /dev/lp1 c 6 1
mknod -m 620 /dev/lp2 c 6 2
```

In these examples, the minor device numbers have been incremented to correspond to the port number. This is not necessary, but it can help with identification.

After the `mknod` and `chown` commands have been issued, it is advisable to manually check to ensure that the ownerships are set properly and that a spool directory has been created. If the spool directory doesn't exist, you have to create it manually. The permissions and ownership requirements of the spool directory were given earlier, in the section "The `/etc/printcap` File and Spooling Directories."

Managing Printers with *lpc*

Printers are controlled through a utility called `lpc`. The `lpc` program lets you perform several important functions pertaining to the printers used on your Linux system:

- Display printer status information
- Enable or disable the printer
- Enable or disable the printer queue
- Remove all print requests from a printer's queue
- Promote a particular print request to the top of the queue
- Make changes to the `lpd` printer daemon

The `lpc` program can't be used for remote printers. It affects only those directly attached and configured on the local machine.

> ### WARNING
>
> Be warned that lpc is one of the most unpredictable and unreliable programs included with the Linux operating system! It can hang up for no obvious reason, and it can also display erroneous status messages. In some cases, the only way to fix a severely screwed-up printer system is to reset the machine completely!

When used without any arguments, lpc prompts you for a command. The following are several valid lpc commands and their arguments (a vertical bar indicates a choice of arguments):

abort *printer_name* ¦ all   Is similar to the stop command, except it doesn't allow any print job that is currently being printed to finish before stopping the printer. When used with the all argument, all printers are stopped. Any job that is abnormally terminated by the abort command is requeued when the printer is started again. See the stop command for more details about the printer daemon and lock files.

clean *printer_name* ¦ all   Removes all print jobs that are queued, including any active print jobs. In many cases, the currently printing job proceeds normally because it has been passed to the printer daemon or the printer's buffer. All other jobs are removed, though. If the all argument is used, all printers have their print queues cleaned.

disable *printer_name* ¦ all   Disables the spooling of print requests to the printer (or all printers, depending on the argument). Any jobs that are already queued are unaffected. Any user trying to send a print job to the disabled printer receives a message indicating that the printer is disabled, and the print job is refused. Printers are enabled and disabled through changes in the lock file in the spool directory.

down *printer_name message*   Is used to take a printer completely offline, usually for an extended period. If a message is included, it can be as long as you want. It is placed in the status file in the spool directory and displayed to users trying to queue to the printer. The down command is usually used when a printer has serious problems and must be removed from the system for more than a day.

enable *printer_name* ¦ all   Enables the spooling of print requests to the printer or all printers.

exit   Exits from lpc (the same as quit).

help or ?   Shows a short list of all lpc commands. If an argument is supplied, it displays a one-line description of that command (such as help abort).

quit   Exits from lpc (the same as exit).

restart *printer_name* ¦ all   Restarts the printer daemon, and is usually used after it has died for an inexplicable reason (which the BSD printer daemons tend to do). If the argument all is supplied, all printer daemons are restarted.

`start` *printer_name*   Starts the printer, allowing it to print requests. This command starts the printer queue daemon for that printer.

`status` *printer_name*   Displays the printer name, whether it has the spool queue enabled, whether printing is enabled, the number of entries in the print queue, and the status of the daemon for that printer. If there are no entries in the queue, no printer daemon will be active. However, if there are entries in the queue and the printer daemon shows as `no daemon present`, the daemon has died and must be started again with the `restart` command.

`stop` *printer_name*   Stops the printer. Print requests can still be spooled, but they are not printed until the printer is started. If a job is being printed when the `stop` command is issued, the job completes the print process and then stops printing. The `start` and `stop` commands alter the contents of the lock file in the print spool directories. The `stop` command also kills the daemon for spooling to that printer.

`topq` *printer_name print_ID*   Moves the print request with *print_ID* to the top of the print queue.

`topq` *printer_name username*   Moves all print requests owned by *username* to the top of the queue. (This is very handy for system administrators who don't want to wait!)

`up` *printer_name*   Is used to reactivate a printer that was taken down. See the `down` command for more information.

The `lpc` utility isn't very user-friendly, but it's the only way to handle printers and their queues in Linux. Several front-end menu-driven utilities are beginning to appear that simplify this task.

Managing the Printer Queue with *lpq* and *lprm*

Several commands help you administer the printer queue specifically, instead of relying on the `lpc` command. Two tasks are commonly required by a system administrator: displaying the current queue and removing print jobs in a queue.

To display the current print queue for any printer, use the `lpq` command. It has the following syntax:

```
lpq [-l] [-Pprinter_name] [job_ID ...] [username ...]
```

With no arguments at all, `lpq` displays information about the current printer queues. The `lpq` command normally displays information about who queued the print job, where it is in the queue, the files being printed, and the total size of the files. The `-l` option displays more information about each entry in the printer queue. Usually, only one line of information is displayed.

A specific printer can be displayed with the `-P` option, followed by the printer's name. If no name is supplied, the default system printer is displayed. If one or more *job_IDs* or *usernames* are provided, only information about the job or jobs queued by the user is shown.

NOTE

Because users can't access the Linux printer spooling directories, they can remove queued print jobs only with the lprm command. If you are a system administrator, you might want to let all system users know how to use this command to keep unwanted print jobs from printing.

The lprm command is used to remove files from a printer queue. This command is often mistyped as lpr, which doesn't remove the file from the queue. To use lprm, you must know the print job ID; or, if you are logged in as root, you can remove all jobs for a particular printer. The syntax of the lprm command is as follows:

```
lprm [-Pprinter_name] [-] [job_ID ...] [username ...]
```

If the single hyphen argument is used, lprm removes all jobs owned by the user who issues the command. If you are logged in as root, all print jobs are removed. A particular printer's jobs can be removed by using the -P option. For example, the command

```
lprm -Phplj -
```

removes all print jobs queued on the printer hplj by the user who issues the command, or all print jobs for that printer if issued by root.

WARNING

It is easy to accidentally remove all print jobs for a printer when you use the lprm command as root. Take care to use the proper syntax, or you may get frustrated at having to requeue all the jobs!

If a print job ID or a username is supplied as an argument, lprm removes that job or all jobs submitted by the user. If no arguments are supplied at all, the currently active job submitted by the user is deleted.

When lprm removes files from the queue, it echoes a message to the display. If there are no files to remove, nothing is echoed (and you will be left wondering what, if anything, happened).

If you try to use lprm on a job that is currently being printed, it might not be terminated properly because the file might already reside in the printer's buffer. In some cases, terminating a job that is currently printing can cause the printer to lock, because some output format files can't handle the termination instructions and freeze when the lock file in the spool directory changes. In cases such as this, the ps command must be used to find the output filter process ID, and then it must be killed.

> **NOTE**
>
> In cases of printer lockup that don't seem to solve themselves with the lpc utility, try killing the lpd daemon and restarting it. If that doesn't work, you will probably have to reboot the entire system.

Terminals

Most Linux systems use only the system console that came with the PC (the PC's screen and keyboard act as the system console). You won't have to make any configuration changes to Linux to use the system console effectively.

Some system administrators want to add remote terminals to allow other users to work with Linux simultaneously (it *is* a multiuser system, after all). New terminals can be added to the system in one of two ways: through a serial port on the back of the PC or through a multiport card with many serial ports on it.

Using Multiport Cards

Multiport cards provide an easy and effective method of adding many serial ports to your system. Multiport cards are offered by dozens of vendors in different configurations. They provide from two to 32 additional serial ports per card (for terminals, modems, or printers), and can use several different types of connectors (such as DB25 connectors, DB9 connectors, or RJ11 wide telephone-style jacks).

If you are going to use a multiport card, make sure you can find one with software device drivers that are designed to work with Linux. You can't use any multiport card designed for other versions of UNIX (or Xenix) without modification. Because multiport card device drivers are complex binaries, modification is beyond the scope of most people's programming abilities.

Multiport cards come with complete instructions for installing the device drivers for the multiport card, as well as configuring the terminals. Because the details of the configurations change depending on the manufacturer of the multiport card, you should consult the documentation accompanying the card for more information.

Adding Serial Port Terminals

You can use the serial ports on the PC to add remote terminals. The terminal can be a dedicated terminal or another PC running terminal emulation software. Linux doesn't really care about the identity of the remote machine, except when it comes to sending instructions for screen displays.

The wiring of cables between the remote terminal and the PC hosting the Linux operating system depends on the type of connectors at both ends. In most cases, the cable is a DTE- (Data Terminal

Equipment) to-DTE type, although some terminals and PC serial ports require DCE (Data Communications Equipment) cabling. As a general rule, terminals and remote computers use DTE, and modems use DCE. The difference between DTE and DCE cabling is in the way the wires run from each end connector.

A typical DCE cable (such as for a modem) uses straight-through wiring, meaning that pin 1 on the PC end goes to pin 1 on the modem end, pin 2 goes through to pin 2, and so on. This is called a *straight* cable (also called a *modem* cable by some).

When connecting a terminal, however, some of the pins must be crossed to permit signals to pass properly. The wiring of such a cable (often called a *null modem* cable or *hard-wired* cable) requires several crosses or shorts to make the connection valid. Serial port connectors on a PC are either a DB9 (9-pin) or a DB25 (25-pin) connector. Not all of the wires in the 25-pin (or the 9-pin, for that matter) are required for a terminal device. A complete terminal cable can be made of only three pins (send, receive, and ground), although Linux also uses the Carrier Detect wire to tell when a terminal is attached and active.

The important pins and their meanings for DTE (computer to terminal) 25-pin cables are shown in Table 38.1. The cable numbers are changed for 9-pin connectors, but the crossings are the same.

Table 38.1. DTE cables for a 25-pin connector.

Terminal Pin	Computer Pin	Meaning
1	1	Ground
2	3	Transmit data / receive data
3	2	Receive data / transmit data
4	4	Ready to send
5	5	Clear to send
6	20	Data set ready / data terminal ready
7	7	Ground
8	20	Carrier detect / data terminal ready
20	6, 8	Data terminal ready / data set ready, carrier detect

Because most users want to purchase premade cables to connect remote terminals, we won't deal with building your own cables. Instead, simply visit your local computer store and explain the equipment at both ends, as well as whether you have DB9 (9-pin) or DB25 (25-pin) connectors at each end. Also note whether the connectors at each end are male (pins sticking out) or female (no pins). Usually, the PC has male serial port connectors (requiring a female end on the cable), and a terminal has female connectors (requiring a male connector on the cable); but, if you're connecting a remote PC, you need female connectors at both ends.

> **NOTE**
>
> If the wiring of a cable isn't clearly indicated and the vendor doesn't know whether it's a straight-through or null modem cable, you might need to purchase a null modem device. A null modem is a short connector that has the pin crossings within it, effectively converting a straight-through cable to a null modem cable, and vice versa.

The Login Process

To understand the files involved in a terminal configuration, it is useful to look at the process that occurs whenever a login occurs.

The process begins with the /etc/init daemon executing when the Linux system is booted. The init daemon is responsible for running the /etc/getty program for each terminal that is connected to the system. The init daemon knows whether a terminal is connected because of entries in two files: /etc/ttys and /etc/inittab. The /etc/ttys file lists all ports on the system and the type of terminal that is connected. The /etc/inittab file has a compete list of all terminals and their parameters. We'll look at both files in more detail later, in the section "Terminal Files: /etc/ttys and /etc/inittab."

When the /etc/ttys and /etc/inittab files indicate that a terminal is connected and active, the init daemon runs the /etc/getty program for that terminal. The getty program sets the communications parameters for the terminal and displays the login prompt on the screen.

When a user logs in on the terminal, the getty process executes the login program to request a password. The login program then validates the username and password against the entries in the /etc/passwd file. If the login is valid, the login program displays the message of the day (stored in the file /etc/motd) and executes whatever shell the user is supposed to run (as specified in /etc/passwd). Finally, login sets the TERM environment variable and exits.

When the login process terminates, the shell continues to execute and reads the startup files; then, it generates the shell prompt and waits for the user to issue instructions.

As you have seen, many files are involved in the startup process, all in the /etc directory. We can look at the important files (at least for terminal characteristics) in more detail.

What Are /sbin/getty and /etc/gettydefs?

The /sbin/getty (/etc/getty on some systems) program is referred to quite a lot when dealing with terminals, but people often don't clearly understand what the program does. Quite simply, /sbin/getty is a binary program that sets the communications parameters between Linux and a terminal, including the speed, protocol, and any special handling of the cable.

The /sbin/getty program is called by /etc/init when a user is logging in. When called, /sbin/getty then opens the serial port or other connection to the terminal and sets the communications parameters based on information in the file /etc/gettydefs (getty definitions). The getty process then generates the login prompt on the remote terminal.

Many special handling and command options are available with the getty process, but most of them are of little interest to users and casual system administrators. If you want complete information on the getty command, consult the man pages that accompany Linux.

The /etc/gettydefs file is used to supply the settings getty uses for communications. The format of each line in the gettydefs file is as follows:

```
label:initial flags: final flags: login prompt: next label
```

The *label* is used to identify each line, so that when /sbin/getty is started with an argument (as it usually is, transparent to the user), the argument is used to match the *label* and provide the configuration information. The *initial* and *final* flags are used to set any behavior for the connection before and after the login program has executed.

The *login* prompt is the prompt to be displayed on the terminal. Usually it is just login:, but it can be any string. Finally, the *next label* is used to send getty to another line, in case it can't use the current one. This is typically used with modem lines, which start at a high speed (such as 9600 baud) and go to 4800, 2400, and 1200 in sequence, trying to connect at each step. For terminals, the *next label* is usually a pointer back to the line's first *label*.

An extract from a sample /etc/gettydefs file looks like this:

```
console# B19200 OPOST ONLCR TAB3 BRKINT IGNPAR ISTRIP IXON IXANY PARENB ECHO
ECHOE ECHOK ICANON ISIG CS8 CREAD # B19200 OPOST ONLCR TAB3 BRKINT IGNPAR ISTRIP
IXON IXANY PARENB ECHO ECHOE ECHOK ICANON ISIG CS8 CREAD #Console Login: #console

9600H# B9600 # B9600 SANE IXANY PARENB TAB3 HUPCL #login: #4800H

4800H# B4800 # B4800 SANE IXANY PARENB TAB3 HUPCL #login: #2400H

2400H# B2400 # B2400 SANE IXANY PARENB TAB3 HUPCL #login: #1200H

1200H# B1200 # B1200 SANE IXANY PARENB TAB3 HUPCL #login: #300H

300H# B300 # B300 SANE IXANY PARENB TAB3 HUPCL #login: #9600H
```

If you look at the file that accompanies your Linux system, you see that there are many more lines, but they all have the same format as the preceding samples. The easiest lines to look at are the shorter ones (the last five lines in the preceding extract), but they all have the same format as the preceding samples.

These lines are for a modem, starting at 9600 baud. The initial flag is set to B9600, which sets the baud rate at 9600 baud. The final flags, used when a connection has been established, set the characteristics of the line (such as a TAB meaning three spaces). Finally, the field at the end points to the next lower speed to provide checks for slower modems or poor lines that prevent fast logins.

The first line in the preceding extract is typical for a terminal. It sets many initial and final flags that control how the terminal behaves. The reference at the end of the line is back to the same definition, because the terminal is hardwired to the system.

You shouldn't have to change the entries in the `gettydefs` file, because the default file contains many different configurations. You should examine the file carefully to find an entry that will work with the terminal you are using. If you do make changes to the `gettydefs` file, you should run the command `getty -c gettydefs` to make the changes effective.

Terminal Files: */etc/ttys* and */etc/inittab*

Terminal configuration information is stored in the files `/etc/ttys` and `/etc/inittab`. These files can be modified by any editor. Some menu-driven programs are now appearing that perform changes to the files for you.

Before making any changes to the terminal configuration files, make a safe copy in case the changes aren't effective and the file can't be returned to its original state easily. Simply copy the two files to new names such as `/etc/tty.original` and `/etc/inittab.original`.

The `/etc/ttys` file has two columns. The first shows the type of terminal, and the second shows the device name. A typical `/etc/ttys` file from a new installation of Linux looks like this:

```
console tty1
console tty2
console tty3
console tty4
console tty5
console tty6
vt100 ttyp0
vt100 ttyp1
vt100 ttyp2
vt100 ttyp3
```

The terminal type in the first column is used to set the TERM environment variable when you log in, unless you override the value.

The `/etc/inittab` file is used to set the behavior of each terminal. The format of the `/etc/inittab` file follows this pattern:

ID:runlevel:action:process

The *ID* is a one- or two-character string that uniquely identifies the entry. In most cases, this corresponds to the device name, such as 1 for `tty1`.

The *runlevel* decides the capabilities of the terminal with the various states that the Linux operating system can be in (run levels vary from 0 to 6, and A, B, and C). If no entry is provided, all *runlevels* are supported. Multiple *runlevels* may be mentioned in the field.

The *action* section shows how to handle the *process* field. The *action* field has several valid entries:

boot	Runs when inittab is first read.
bootwait	Runs when inittab is first read.
initdefault	Sets initial run level.
off	Terminates the process if it is running.
once	Starts the process once.
ondemand	Always keeps the process running (the same as respawn).
powerfail	Executes when init gets a power fail signal.
powerwait	Executes when init gets a power fail signal.
sysinit	Executes before accessing the console.
respawn	Always keeps the process running.
wait	Starts the process once.

The *action* indicates the behavior of the terminal device when the system starts and when a getty process is terminated on it.

A simple /etc/inittab file (taken from an earlier version of Linux for clarity's sake because the latest version complicates the lines a little) looks like this:

```
# inittab for Linux
id:1:initdefault:
rc::bootwait:/etc/rc
1:1:respawn:/etc/getty 9600 tty1
2:1:respawn:/etc/getty 9600 tty2
3:1:respawn:/etc/getty 9600 tty3
4:1:respawn:/etc/getty 9600 tty4
```

The first two lines (after the comment) are used when the system boots. The second line tells the system to run /etc/rc in order to boot. The rest of the lines indicate that a getty process should be started for tty1 through tty4 at 9600 baud.

Terminal Definitions: The /etc/termcap File

The /etc/termcap file holds the instructions for communicating with different terminals. Most terminals that are supported by the operating system have an entry inside this file. The termcap (terminal capabilities) file can be quite large. If you are going to make changes, copy a version to a safe filename first.

The contents of the termcap file are similar to the printer definition file /etc/printcap. Each entry in the termcap file has a name with several variations, as well as a set of codes and values for different terminal characteristics. Because terminals use many different codes for different actions, many codes can be used with some of the more talented terminals.

An extract from a termcap file shows the definitions for two fairly simple terminals, the Wyse 30 and Wyse 85:

```
w0¦wy30-vb¦wyse30-vb¦wyse 30 Visible bell:\
        :vb=\E'8\E'\072\E'9:\
        :tc=wy30:
wc¦wy85¦wyse85¦Wyse 85 in 80 column mode, vt100 emulation:\
        :is=\E[61"p\E[13l\E>\E[?1l\E[?3l\E[?7h\E[?16l\E[?5W:\
        :co#80:li#24:am:cl=\E[;H\E[2J:bs:cm=\E[%i%d;%dH:nd=2\E[C:up=2\E[A:\
        :ce=\E[0K:cd=\E[0J:so=2\E[7m:se=2\E[m:us=2\E[4m:ue=2\E[m:\
        :ku=\E[A:kd=\E[B:kr=\E[C:kl=\E[D:\
        :kh=\E[H:xn:\
        :im=:CO=\E[?25h:CF=\E[?25l:ic=\E[1@:dc=\E[1P:\
        :dl=\E[1M:al=\E[1L:GS=\EF:GE=\EG:pt:
```

The meaning of each set of codes is not really of interest to most users and system administrators. You have to start changing or rewriting terminal entries only if you are adding a terminal type that doesn't exist in the termcap file already.

> **NOTE**
>
> Most terminals offer multiple emulations. If you can't find the terminal type in the termcap file, look for an emulation that is supported. It's easier to emulate a different terminal than to write a termcap entry for a new type.

The terminal characteristics in the /etc/termcap file are used by the /etc/ttys file. The first column of the ttys file gives the default terminal type used to set the TERM environment variable. Essentially, the startup routine uses a pattern-matching utility to find a matching line in the termcap file, and then reads the codes that follow.

Adding a Terminal

Terminals are added to Linux in much the same manner as printers: using the mknod command. To add a terminal, you must decide which port the terminal will be connected to. The serial ports on a PC are referred to by Linux as /dev/ttyS0 (for COM1 in DOS terms), /dev/ttyS1 (for COM2), and so on.

Most PC systems have one or two serial ports, although up to four can be accommodated (ttyS0 to ttyS3). Linux uses the serial ports based on their addresses in the BIOS. The usual addresses for the serial ports are as follows:

ttyS0 (COM1)	0x03f8
ttyS1 (COM2)	0x02f8
ttyS2 (COM3)	0x03e8
ttyS3 (COM4)	0x02e8

If you're not sure which serial port is which, you might have to either use a DOS-based diagnostic utility (such as MS-DOS's MSD.EXE) or start at the lowest address and work up, testing the terminal each time. If the PC has only one port, it is almost always configured as COM1.

To create a new terminal device, you must run the mknod (make node) command to create the new device driver file, and then change the permissions on the file to let it be run by root or daemon. Most Linux distributions include the terminal devices already.

> **NOTE**
>
> The mknod command was covered in detail earlier in this chapter. Check out the section "The mknod Command."

A typical command for creating a new terminal device is

```
mknod -m 660 /dev/ttyS0 c 4 64
```

The -m 660 sets the permissions on the file. /dev/ttyS0 specifies the first serial port on the machine (COM1). The c indicates that the terminal is a character device (almost all terminals, except very high-speed high-end models, are character devices). The major device number is set to 4, while the minor device number is set to 64. For the other serial ports on the PC (COM1 through COM4), the commands would be as follows:

```
mknod -m 660 /dev/ttyS1 c 4 65
mknod -m 660 /dev/ttyS2 c 4 66
mknod -m 660 /dev/ttyS3 c 4 67
```

The changes in the minor device number with the preceding different commands are not required, but there must be a unique minor device number for each terminal.

After the mknod command has been executed, the device driver must be set to the proper ownership. Issue the command

```
chown root.tty /dev/ttyS0
```

replacing the /dev/ttyS0 with whatever device the command applies to. The ownership is set to root.tty.

You also want to change the entry in the /etc/ttys file to include the terminal type and device that you have added so that the startup of the terminal can be performed properly. Because the /etc/inittab file already contains entries for the standard serial ports, you can edit the entry for your new terminal's port (if necessary) to set the baud rate and other parameters that may be required.

Using *stty* and *tset*

The stty command enables you to change and query a terminal option. The stty command is very complex, with dozens of options that modify the behavior of the terminal device driver. Luckily, only the most intense system administrators have to use the many options, so in this chapter we will ignore most of the details.

To see the current settings of a terminal, use the `stty` command without any arguments. It displays a set of parameters. You can use this to verify that the terminal has read the configuration information properly from the `/etc/inittab` and `/etc/gettydefs` files.

Like `stty`, the `tset` command has many options, most of which are seldom used (especially if you are not dealing with strange terminals and weird connectors). The `tset` command is used to initialize the terminal driver. If the `tset` command is given with a specific argument, it uses that. Otherwise, the value in the `TERM` environment variable is used.

You can use `tset` within the startup files of a user who always logs in from a remote terminal (through a modem). If you put the command

```
tset -m dialup:vt100
```

in the shell startup file (`.profile`, `.cshrc`, and so on), the terminal type will be set to `vt100` every time a connection is made through the modem. Of course, this sets the terminal type even if someone isn't using a VT100 terminal, so you can use the command

```
tset -m dialup:?vt100
```

to have the user connecting through the modem prompted for the terminal type. The prompt looks like this:

```
TERM=(vt100)?
```

If the user presses Enter, the `TERM` variable is set to `vt100`. If the user doesn't want to use that value, she can enter the correct string at the prompt.

So far, `tset` seems to be quite simple, but in fact it has a very complex structure when dealing with hard wired terminals. To properly configure a terminal connected through a serial port, you need a command such as this:

```
eval 'tset -s -Q -m dialup:?vt100 -m switch:z29'
```

The full details of this type of command are unimportant for most system administrators. If you want more information, check the man pages for `tset` and `stty` that came with your Linux system.

Resetting a Screwy Terminal

Every now and then a terminal connected through a serial port starts acting screwy, either not showing a prompt or generating garbage. There are two quick ways to try to reset the terminal. If they don't work, the terminal should be shut down and restarted. (You might have to kill the processes that were running on the terminal.)

The first approach is to issue a set of Ctrl-J characters on the screwy terminal, and then type `stty sane` followed by another Ctrl-J. The command `stty sane` should reset the terminal characteristics to normal. You probably won't see the letters you are typing, so enter them carefully.

If the terminal isn't behaving at this point, try typing reset and pressing Enter or Ctrl-J. If this doesn't work, the terminal has hung and should be reset manually.

Adding a Modem

The process for adding a modem is very similar to that for adding a terminal. In most cases, the procedure outlined earlier in "Adding a Terminal" can be followed.

Modems are used for several purposes on a Linux system, such as networking, connecting to remote systems, and accepting incoming calls. If the modem is to act as a conduit into the Linux system for remote terminals to connect, the procedure given in "Adding a Terminal" is followed, except for the entries that will be selected in the /etc/inittab file. In the case of a modem, find a set of lines that move through the different baud rates the modem supports.

Modems that are to be used for networking through the UUCP utility are dealt with in Chapter 42, "Networking," and Chapter 43, "UUCP." It includes information on setting the different configuration files properly.

For modems used to call out of the system, Linux has a menu-driven configuration utility as part of the setup command, which can set the proper configuration information automatically.

Summary

This chapter has shown you the basics of devices, device management, and how to add new devices to your Linux system. The information presented applies to most distributions of Linux, although there might be some slight changes in options and arguments as the different utilities are enhanced or streamlined. If you want more information about any of the commands, refer to the man pages that came with Linux, or consult a comprehensive system administration book.

Users and Logins

39

by Tim Parker

All access to a Linux system is through a user account. Every user must be set up by the system administrator, with the sole exception of the root account (and some system accounts that users seldom, if ever, use). While many Linux systems only have one user, that user should not use the root account for daily access. Most systems allow several users to gain access, either through multiple users on the main console, through a modem or network, or over hard-wired terminals. Knowing how to set up and manage user accounts and their associated directories and files is an important aspect of Linux system administration.

This chapter looks at the the following subjects:

- The root (superuser) account
- How to create new users
- The files a new user requires
- What is a group of users
- Managing groups

The Superuser Account

When the Linux software is installed, one master login is created automatically. This login, called root, is known as the superuser because there is nothing the login can't access or do. While most user accounts on a Linux system are set to prevent the user from accidentally destroying all the system files, for example, the root login can blow away the entire Linux operating system with one simple command. Essentially, the root login has no limitations.

> **WARNING**
>
> The sheer power of the root login can be addictive. When you log in as root you don't have to worry about file permissions, access rights, or software settings. You can do anything at anytime. This power is very attractive to newcomers to the operating system, who tend to do everything while logged in as root. It's only after the system has been damaged that the root login's problems become obvious: There are no safeguards! As a rule, you should only use the root login for system maintenance functions. Do not use the superuser account for daily usage!

The root login should be kept only for those purposes where you really need it. It's a good idea to change the login prompt of the root account to clearly show that you are logged in as root, and hopefully you will think twice about the commands you issue when you use that login. You can change the login prompt with the PS environment variable, discussed in Chapter 13, "Shell Programming." If you are on a standalone system and you destroy the entire file system, it's only you that is inconvenienced. If you are on a multiuser system and you insist on using root for common access, you will have several very mad users after you when you damage the operating system.

So after all those dire warnings, the first thing you should do on a new system is create a login for your normal daily usage. Set the root password to something other users of the system (if there are any) will not easily guess, and change the password frequently to prevent snooping.

You can also create special logins for system administration tasks that do not need wide-open access, such as for tape backups. You can set a login to have root read-only access to the entire file system, but not the potential for damage. This lets you back up the system properly, but not erase the kernel by accident. Similar special logins can be set up for e-mail access, gateways to the Internet, and so on. Think carefully about the permissions each task requires and create a special login for that task—your system will be much more secure and have less chance of accidental damage.

To be precise, the superuser account doesn't have to be called root. It can have any name. The superuser account is always defined as the account with a user ID number of zero. User ID numbers are defined in the /etc/passwd file.

User Accounts: /etc/passwd

Even if you are the only user on your Linux system, you should know about user accounts and managing users. This is because you should have your own account (other than root) for your daily tasks. You therefore need to be able to create a new user. If your system lets others access the operating system, either directly or through a modem, you should create user accounts for everyone who wants access. You may also want a more generic guest account for friends who just want occasional access.

Every person using your Linux system should have his or her own unique user name and password. The only exception is a guest account, or perhaps an account that accesses a specific application, such as a read-only database. By keeping separate accounts for each user, your security is much tighter, and you have a better idea of who is accessing your system and what they are doing. A one-to-one correspondence between users and accounts makes tracking activities much easier.

All the information about user accounts is kept in the file /etc/passwd. The /etc/passwd file should be owned only by root and have the group ID set to zero (usually root or system group, as defined in the /etc/group file). The permissions of the /etc/passwd file should be set to allow write access only by root, but all others can have read access. (We deal with groups and permissions later in this section.) The lines in the /etc/passwd file are divided into a strict format:

username:password:user ID:group ID:comment:home directory:login command

This format can best be seen by looking at a sample /etc/passwd file. The /etc/passwd file created when a Linux system is newly installed is shown in Listing 39.1.

Listing 39.1. The /etc/passwd file created when Linux is first installed.

```
root::0:0:root:/root:/bin/bash
bin:*:1:1:bin:/bin:
daemon:*:2:2:daemon:/sbin:
adm:*:3:4:adm:/var/adm:
```

continues

Listing 39.1. continued

```
lp:*:4:7:lp:/var/spool/lpd:
sync:*:5:0:sync:/sbin:/bin/sync
shutdown:*:6:0:shutdown:/sbin:/sbin/shutdown
halt:*:7:0:halt:/sbin:/sbin/halt
mail:*:8:12:mail:/var/spool/mail:
news:*:9:13:news:/usr/lib/news:
uucp:*:10:14:uucp:/var/spool/uucppublic:
operator:*:11:0:operator:/root:/bin/bash
games:*:12:100:games:/usr/games:
gopher:*:13:30:gopher:/usr/lib/gopher-data:
ftp:*:14:50:ftp user:/home/ftp:
nobody:*:-1:100:nobody:/dev/null:
```

Each line in the /etc/passwd file is composed of seven fields, separated by a full colon. If there is nothing to be entered in a field, the field is left blank, but the colons are retained to make sure each line has seven fields (which also means each line will have six colons). The seven fields (from left to right on each line) are:

user name	A unique identifier for the user.
password	The user's password (encrypted).
user ID (UID)	A unique number that identifies the user to the operating system.
group ID (GID)	A unique number that identifies the user's group (for file permissions).
comment	Usually the user's real name, but sometimes phone numbers, departments, and so on.
home directory	The directory in which users are placed when they log in.
login command	The command executed when the user logs in, normally a shell.

We can look at each field in a little more detail. You should know what each field does and how it is used by other programs on your Linux system. Note that this type of user file is used with almost every UNIX system in the world, so once you know it for Linux, you know it for most UNIX versions.

User Names

The user name is a single string, usually eight characters or less, that uniquely identifies each user. Since the user name is the basis of most communications between users and other machines, the user name you use (or assign to others) should be simple and obvious. Usually, this means a permutation of the user's real name. A typical user name may be a combination of the user's first and last names, such as tparker or timp. The former example, composed of the first initial and last name, is fairly common in large networks.

Note that the characters in these examples are all lowercase. Case is important in Linux (as with all UNIX versions), so tparker and Tparker are two different logins. Since most Linux commands are lowercase, convention is to also keep user names lowercase. Underscores, periods, numbers, and some special characters are allowed, but should be avoided.

Small systems, such as on a single machine, may use more familiar names, such as the user's first name only. A small system may have users with the names tim, bill, yvonne, and so on. If two users have the same name, then there must be some method found to differentiate between the two (such as bill and billy).

A few users like to create cryptic user names that reflect their hobbies, nicknames, pets, lifestyle, or personality. You may find user names such as vader, grumpy, wizard, and hoops. This type of naming is fine on small systems that are used by one or two users, but quickly becomes awkward on larger systems where other users may not know their coworkers' user names. On the whole, if your system is used by more than a couple of friends, discourage this type of user name.

Passwords

The system stores the user's encrypted password in this field. (Actually, the password is encoded, not encrypted, although the convention has always been to use the term encrypted.) This field is very sensitive to changes, and any modification whatsoever can render the login useless until the system administrator performs a password change. A user's password can only be changed by the system administrator by using the passwd command when logged in as root (or by the users themselves).

> **NOTE**
>
> Some versions of UNIX do not keep the passwords in the /etc/passwd file because of potential security problems. If the password fields on your system are all set to x, then another file (called a *shadow password* file) is in use. However, all versions of Linux currently available do use this field normally.
>
> Systems running either Yellow Pages or NIS (Network Information Service), both of which rely on a central file of user names and passwords, do not use this field. However, few Linux systems will use either YP or NIS, so this distinction can be ignored for the moment.

When a user logs in, the login program logically compares the password the user typed to a block of zeros, and then compares that result to the entry in the password field. If they match, the user is granted access. Any deviation causes login to refuse access.

This field can be used to restrict access to the system. If you want a login to never be used for access, such as a system login like lp or sync, place an asterisk between the two colons for this field. This restricts all access. In the example /etc/passwd file shown earlier, you can see that many system logins have an asterisk as their password, effectively blocking access.

This field can also be used to allow unrestricted access by leaving it blank. If there is no password, anyone using the user name is granted access immediately, with no password requested. This is a very bad habit to get into! Do not leave passwords open unless you are using your Linux system for your own pleasure and have nothing of value on the file system.

Don't attempt to put a password in the password field—you cannot recreate the encryption method, and you'll end up locking the user out. Then, only the system administrator is able to change the password and allow access.

User ID

Every user name has an associated, unique user ID. The user ID, also called the UID, is used by Linux to identify everything associated with the user. The user ID is preferable to the user name because numbers are easier to work with than the characters in a name, and they take up much less space. Linux tracks all processes started by a user, for example, by the user ID and not the user name. A translation can take place in some utilities to display the user name, but the utility generally examines the /etc/passwd file to match the UID to the name.

The user ID numbers are usually assigned in specific ranges. Most UNIX systems, for example, allocate the numbers from zero to 99 for machine-specific logins, and the user ID numbers from 100 and up for users. This is a good working model and makes your system consistent with others. In the example /etc/passwd file shown earlier, you can see that root has a UID of 0, while the other system-created logins have numbers ranging upward. The login nobody is a special login used for NFS (Network File System) and has a UID of -1, an invalid number. When you assign user ID numbers, it is a good idea to assign them sequentially, so the first user is 100, the second 101, and so on.

Group ID

The group ID (GID) is used to track the users' startup group (in other words, the ID of the group the users belongs to when they log in). A group, as you will see later, is used for organization purposes to set file permissions, although many organizations don't bother with them. Group ID numbers range from zero and upwards. Linux systems assign a group called users with the group number 100 for this purpose.

The GID is used by the system when tracking file permissions, access, and file creation and modification specifications. If your system has only a single user group, then you need not worry about the GID. If you work with several groups (as might be implemented on a large system), then you need to examine the /etc/group file.

Comments

This field is used for the system administrator to add any information necessary to make the entry more self-explanatory. Typically, this area is used to enter the user's full name, although some system administrators like to add department or extension numbers for convenience. (This field is sometimes called the GECOS field, after the operating system that first used it.)

The comment field is used by some utilities to display information about users, so make sure you don't place any sensitive information there. Electronic mail systems, for example, can access this field to show who is sending mail. While you don't have to use the field, on larger systems it can make things much easier for administrators and other users when they can discover the real name of the person the user name belongs to.

Home Directory

The home directory field indicates to the login process where to place users when they log in. This is usually their home directory. Each user on the system should have her own dedicated home directory, and then the startup files will initialize the environment variable HOME to this value. The directory indicated in this field is the user's initial working directory only, and places no restrictions on the user (unless file permissions have been set to restrict movement).

For the most part, user home directories are located in a common area. Linux tends to use the /home directory, so you will find home directories such as /home/tparker, /home/ychow, and so on. Other versions use /usr, /user, or /u as user home directories. In some cases where the system administrator has experience with another type of UNIX that uses an alternate directory structure, you may find the home directories changed to make life easier (and more familiar) for that administrator. As far as Linux is concerned, it doesn't care what the name of the home directory is, as long as it can be entered.

Login Command

The login command is the command to be executed when login terminates. In most cases this is a shell command that is started, such as the C Shell or Bourne Shell, to provide the user with a shell environment. In some cases, it may be a single application or front-end system that restricts what the user can do. For example, the uucp login (used for e-mail and other simple networking tasks) executes the uucp command only. If the login command field is left empty, the operating system usually defaults to the Bourne shell (although this may change depending on the manner in which the operating system is set up).

Many versions of Linux enable users to change their login shell with the command chsh or passwd -s. When either command is used, the file /etc/shells is searched for a match. Only those commands in the /etc/shells file are allowed as valid entries when the user tries to change his startup shell. (You can add or remove lines in the /etc/shells file using any editor.) This helps you keep tighter security on the system. The superuser account has no restrictions on the entry in this field (or any other user's field). If your system uses the /etc/shells file, make sure it has the same file permissions and ownership as the /etc/passwd file, or a user can sneak through the system security by modifying the startup command for her login.

Default System User Names

The extract from the /etc/passwd file shown in the preceding section lists over a dozen system-dependent user names. These all serve special purposes on the Linux system. A few of these logins are worth noting because they have specific uses for the operating system and for system administrators:

root	The superuser account (UID 0) with unrestricted access and owns many system files.
daemon	Used for system processes. This login is used only to own the processes and set their permissions properly.

bin	Owns executables.
sys	Owns executables.
adm	Owns accounting and log files.
uucp	Used for UUCP communication access and files.

The other system logins are used for specific purposes (`postmaster` for mail, and so on) that are usually self-explanatory. You should not change any of the system logins. In most cases, they have an asterisk in the password field preventing their use for entry purposes.

Adding Users

There are two ways to add users to your system: manually edit the /etc/passwd file, or use an automated script that prompts you for the new user's details and writes a new line to the /etc/passwd file for you. The automated approach is handy for new system administrators who are uneasy about editing a file as important as /etc/passwd, or for those occasions when you have to add several users and the risk of error is thus increased. You must modify the /etc/passwd file when you are logged in as root.

> **CAUTION**
>
> Before making changes to your /etc/passwd file, make a copy of it! If you corrupt the /etc/passwd file you will not be able to log in, even as root, and your system is effectively useless except in system administration mode. Keep a copy of the /etc/passwd file on your emergency floppy or boot floppy in case of problems.

To add an entry to the /etc/passwd file, use any editor that saves information in ASCII. Add the new users to the end of the file, using a new line for each user. Make sure you use a unique user name and user ID (UID) for each user. For example, to add a new user called bill to the system with a UID of 103 (remember to keep UIDs sequential for convenience) and a GID of 100 (the default group), a home directory of /home/bill, and a startup shell of the Bourne shell, add the following line to the /etc/passwd file:

```
bill::103:100:Bill Smallwood:/home/bill:/bin/sh
```

Note that we have left the password blank because you can't type in an encrypted password yourself. As soon as you have saved the changes to /etc/passwd, set a password for this account by running the command:

```
passwd bill
```

This command prompts you for an initial password. Set the password to something that Bill will be able to use, and ask him to change the password the first time he works on the system. Many system administrators set the initial password to a generic string (such as "password" or the login name) and then force the new user to change the password the first time they log in. Using generic strings is usually acceptable if the user logs in quickly, but don't leave accounts with generic login strings sitting around too long—someone else may use the account.

After you have added the necessary line to the /etc/passwd file, you should create the user's home directory. Once created, you must set the ownership to have that user own the directory. For the preceding example, you would issue the following commands:

```
mkdir /home/bill
chown bill /home/bill
```

All users must belong to a group. If your system has only one group defined, then add the user's user name to the line in the /etc/group file that represents that group. If the new user should belong to several groups, add the user name to each group in the /etc/group file. The /etc/group file and groups in general are discussed in the "Groups" section later in the chapter.

Finally, the configuration files for the users' shells should be copied into their home directory and set to allow them access for customization. For example, if you copy the Bourne shell's .profile file from another user called yvonne, you would issue the following commands:

```
cp /home/yvonne/.profile /home/bill/.profile
chown bill /home/bill/.profile
```

You should also manually check the configuration file to ensure there are no environment variables that will be incorrectly set when the user logs in. For example, there may be a line defining the HOME environment variable or the spool directories for printer and mail. Use any ASCII editor to check the configuration file. If you are using the Korn or C shell, there are other configuration files that need to be copied over and edited. Bourne shell compatibles need only a .profile, while the C shell and compatibles need .login and .cshrc. The Korn shell and compatibles need a .profile and usually another file with environment variables embedded in it.

In general, the process for manually adding a new user to your system is:

1. Add an entry for the user in the /etc/passwd file.
2. Create the user's home directory and set the ownership.
3. Copy the shell startup files and edit their settings and ownerships.

The command vipw invokes the vi editor (or whatever the default system editor has been set to) and edits a temporary copy of the /etc/passwd file. The use of a temporary file and file lock acts as a lock mechanism to prevent two different users from editing the file at the same time. When the file is saved, vipw does a simple consistency check on the changed file, and if all appears proper, the /etc/passwd file is updated.

The automated scripts for Linux tend to have the names useradd or adduser. When run, they prompt you for all the information that is necessary in the /etc/passwd file. Both versions let you exit at any time to avoid changing the /etc/passwd file. The automated scripts also tend to ask for an initial password, which you can set to anything you want or leave blank. One advantage of the automated scripts is that they copy all the configuration files for the supported shells automatically, and in some cases, make environment variable changes for you. This can significantly simplify the process of adding users.

A quick note on passwords—they are vitally important to the security of your system. Unless you are on a standalone Linux machine with no dial-in modems, every account should have a secure password. Passwords are assigned and changed with the passwd command. The superuser can change any password on the system, but a user can only change his own password.

Deleting Users

Just like adding new users, deleting users can be done with an automated script or manually. The automated scripts deluser or userdel asks which user you want to delete, and then removes the entry from the /etc/passwd file. Some scripts also clean out the spool and home directory files, if you want. You must make any deletions to the /etc/passwd file when logged in as root.

If you delete users manually, simply remove their entries from the /etc/passwd file. Then you can clean up their directories to clear disk space. You can completely delete all their files and their home directory with the command:

```
rm -r -f /home/userdir
```

where /home/userdir is the full pathname of the user's home directory. Make sure there are no files you want to keep in that directory before you blow them all away!

Next, you should remove the user's mail spool file, which is usually kept in /usr/spool/mail/ username. For example, to remove the user walter's mail file, issue the command:

```
rm /usr/spool/mail/walter
```

The spool file is a single file, so this command cleans up the entries properly. To finish off the mail clean-up, check that the user has no entries in the mail alias files (usually /etc/aliases) or you can force all mail for that user to another login (such as root). To make any changes to the /etc/aliases file effective, you must run the newaliases command.

Finally, clean up the user's cron and at jobs. You can display the user's crontab file using the crontab command.

If you need to retain the user for some reason (such as file ownerships, a general access account, or accounting purposes), you can disable the login completely by placing an asterisk in the password field of the /etc/passwd file. That login can never be used once an asterisk is in the password field. If you need to reactivate the account, simply run the passwd command.

The process for manually deleting a user (or using an automated script that doesn't clean up directories and files) is:

1. Remove the user's entry from /etc/passwd and /etc/group.
2. Remove the user's mail file and any mail aliases.
3. Remove any cron or at jobs.
4. Remove the home directory if you don't want any files it holds.

Occasionally, you may want to temporarily disable a user's account, such as when he or she goes on extended leave, vacation, or because you are mad at them! If you want to temporarily disable the login but be able to recover it at any time in the future, add an asterisk as the first character of the encrypted password. Don't alter any characters in the existing password, but just add the asterisk to the front. When you want to reactivate the account, remove the asterisk and the password is back to whatever it was set at before you made the changes.

Groups

Every user on a UNIX and Linux system belongs to a group. A group is a collection of individuals lumped together for some reason. The users in a group may all work in the same department, may need access to a particular programming utility, or they may all have access to use a special device, such as a scanner or color laser printer. Groups can be set up for any reason, and users can belong to any number of groups. However, a user can only be a member of one group at a time, because groups are used for determining file permissions and Linux only allows one group ID per user at any point in time.

Groups can have their permissions set so that members of that group have access to devices, files, file systems, or entire machines that other users who do not belong to that group may be restricted from. For example, this can be useful when you have an accounting department, all members of which need access to the company's accounts. However, you wouldn't want non-accounting people to go snooping through financial statements, so creating a special group that has access to the accounting system makes sense.

Many small Linux systems have only one group, the default group, because that is the simplest way to manage a system. Then, each user's access to devices and files is controlled by the devices' or files' permissions, not the group. When you start to get several different users in logical groupings, though, groups start to make more sense. You can even use groups to control your friends' or children's access to areas on your home Linux system.

Group information is maintained in the file /etc/group, which is similar in layout to the /etc/passwd file. The default /etc/group file from a newly installed Linux system is shown in Listing 39.2.

Listing 39.2. The default /etc/group file.

```
root::0:root
bin::1:root,bin,daemon
daemon::2:root,bin,daemon
sys::3:root,bin,adm
adm::4:root,adm,daemon
tty::5:
disk::6:root,adm
lp::7:lp
mem::8:
kmem::9:
wheel::10:root
floppy::11:root
mail::12:mail
news::13:news
uucp::14:uucp
```

continues

Listing 39.2. continued

```
man::15:man
users::100:games
nogroup::-1:
```

Each line in the file has four fields separated by colons. Two colons together mean that the field is empty and has no value specified. Each line in the file follows this format:

group name:group password:group ID:users

Each group has a line of its own in the file. The fields in the /etc/group file (from left to right) are listed as follows:

- group name—A unique name usually of eight characters or less (usually standard alphanumeric characters only).
- password—Usually left as an asterisk or blank, but a password can be assigned that a user must enter to join the group. Not all versions of Linux or UNIX use this field, and it is left in the file for backward compatibility reasons.
- group ID (GID)—A unique number for each group, used by the operating system.
- users—A list of all user IDs that belong to that group.

Every Linux system has a number of default groups which belong to the operating system, usually called bin, mail, uucp, sys, and so on. You can see the system-dependent groups in the default /etc/group file as shown in Listing 39.2. In that file, all but the last two entries are system groups. You should never allow users to belong to one of these groups because it gives them access permissions that can be the same as root's. Only system logins should have access to these operating system groups.

Default System Groups

You may have noticed in the startup /etc/group file shown in Listing 39.2 that there are several groups defined. These groups are used to set file permissions and access rights for many utilities. It's worth taking a quick look at some of the most important groups and their functions:

root/wheel/system	Usually used to enable a user to employ the su command to gain root access, it owns most system files.
daemon	Used to own spooling directories (mail, printer, and so on).
kmem	Used for programs that need to access kernel memory directly (including ps).
sys	Owns some system files; on some systems this group behaves the same as kmem.
tty	Owns all special files dealing with terminals.

The default group for the Slackware Linux version /etc/group file, shown previously, is called users, and has a GID of 100. (Many UNIX systems have the default group called group with a group ID of 50 which is the convention.)

Adding a Group

You can edit the information in the /etc/group file manually, using any ASCII editor, or you can use a shell utility such as addgroup or groupadd which go through the process for you. As a system administrator, you may find it easier to do the changes manually because you can see the entire group file at the time you are editing it. Not all versions of Linux have an addgroup or groupadd utility.

To manually add a group to the /etc/group file, first make a backup copy of the file. Use any ASCII editor and add one line to the file for each new group you want to create. Make sure you follow the syntax of the file carefully because incorrect entries prevent users from belonging to that group. In the following lines, two new groups have been created:

```
accounts::101:bill
scanner::102:yvonne
```

The two groups have GIDs of 101 and 102, and like user IDs, the GIDs should be assigned sequentially for convenience. The users that are in the group are appended. In these cases, only one user is in each group. You'll see how to assign multiple users to a group in the next section. The groups do not have to be in order of the GID or group name, although for convenience you usually have the file ordered by GID. You could add new lines anywhere in the file.

The /etc/group file should be checked for file permissions and ownership after you have made changes to it. The file should be owned by root and have a group owner of root (or system, depending on the group with GID 0). The file permissions should prevent anyone but root from writing the file.

Adding a User to New Groups

Users can belong to many groups, in which case their user IDs should be on each group line that they belong to in the file /etc/group. Each user name on a line in the /etc/group file is separated by a comma. There is no limit to the number of users that can belong to a group, in theory, but in practice, the line length of the Linux system (255 characters) acts as an effective limiter. There are ways around this limit, but few systems will require it.

The following excerpt from a /etc/group file shows several groups with multiple members:

```
accounts::52:bill,yvonne,tim,roy,root
prgming::53:bill,tim,walter,gita,phyliss,john,root
cad::54:john,doreen,root
scanner::55:john,root,tim
```

The user names on each line do not have to be in any particular order. Linux searches along each line to find the user names it wants.

A user can be a member of only one group at a time while logged in, so they must use the command newgrp to change between groups they are members of. The starting group a user belongs to when they log in is given by the GID field in the /etc/passwd file.

Deleting a Group

If you decide you don't want a particular group to exist anymore, you can simply remove the group name from the /etc/group file. You should also check the /etc/passwd file to see if any users have that group ID as their startup GID, and change it to another group of which they are members. If you don't change the GIDs, those users will not be able to log in because they have no valid group membership. You should also scan the entire file system for files and directories that are owned by that group and change them to another group. Failure to make this change may prevent access to the file or directory.

Some Linux versions have shell scripts that remove group lines from the /etc/group file for you. The utility is generally called delgroup or groupdel. However, most versions of Linux don't bother with this utility.

The *su* Command

Sometimes you want to execute a command as another user. If you are logged in as superuser and want to create files with bill's permissions and ownership set, it is easier to log in as bill than work as root and then reset all the parameters. Similarly, if you are logged in as a user and need to be superuser for a little while, you would have to log out and back in to make the change. An alternative is the su command.

The su command changes your effective user name and grants you the permissions that user name has. The su command takes the user name you want to change to as an argument. For example, if you are logged in as a typical user and want to be root, you can issue the command:

```
su root
```

and the Linux system prompts you for the root password. If you supply it correctly, you will be root until you issue a Ctrl-D to log out of that account and back to where you started. Similarly, if you are logged in as root and want to be a user, you can issue the command with the user name, such as:

```
su tparker
```

You won't be prompted for a password when changing from root to another user because you have superuser powers. When you Ctrl-D out of the login, you are back as root. If you are logged in as a normal user and want to switch to another non-root login, you have to supply the password, though.

Summary

In this chapter we've looked at the basics of the /etc/passwd and /etc/group files, the two files intimately connected with user access to Linux. As you have seen, these are simple files and can easily be modified by a system administrator to add users and groups at any time. Always bear in mind that these are vital files, and they should be copied to a backup filename, then edited carefully and their permissions checked after each edit.

Processes

40

by Tim Parker

Everything that runs on a Linux system is a process—every user task, every system daemon—*everything* is a process. Knowing how to manage the processes running on your Linux system is an important (indeed even critical) aspect of system administration. This chapter looks processes in some detail. In this chapter you will see:

- How to find out what processes are running
- Determine when a process is hogging the system
- How to find out which processes are locked up
- How to terminate a process
- How to properly manage processes

In the course of discussing processes, we don't bother with the mechanics behind how processes are allocated, or how the Linux kernel manages to time-slice all the processes to run a multitasking operating system. Instead, we'll look at the nitty-gritty aspects of process control that you need in order to keep your system running smoothly.

You may come across the terms *process* and *job* used when dealing with multitasking operating systems. For most purposes, both terms are correct. However, a *job* is usually a process started by a shell (and may involve many processes), while a *process* is a single entity that is executing. To be correct, we'll use the term process throughout.

Processes

A formal definition of a process is that it is a single program running in its own virtual address space. This means that everything running under Linux is a process. This is compared to a job, which may involve several commands executing in series. Alternatively, a single command line issued at the shell prompt may involve more than one process, especially when pipes or redirection are involved. For example, the command

```
nroff -man ps.1 ¦ grep kill ¦ more
```

will start three processes, one for each command.

Types of Processes

There are several types of processes involved with the Linux operating system. Each has its own special features and attributes. The processes involved with Linux are:

- Interactive processes: A process initiated from (and controlled by) a shell. Interactive processes may be in foreground or background.
- Batch processes: Processes that are not associated with a terminal but are submitted to a queue to be executed sequentially.
- Daemon processes: Processes usually initiated when Linux boots and that run in the background until required.

Using the *ps* Command

The easiest method of finding out what processes are running on your system is to use the ps (process status) command. The ps command has a number of options and arguments, although most system administrators use only a couple of common command-line formats. We can start by looking at the basic usage of the ps command, and then examine some of the useful options.

The ps command is available to all system users, as well as root, although the output changes a little depending on whether you are logged in as root when you issue the command.

When you are logged in as a normal system user (in other words, any login but root) and issue the ps command on the command line by itself, it displays information about every process you are running. For example, you might see the following output when you issue the command:

```
$ ps
  PID TTY STAT   TIME COMMAND
   41 v01 S      0:00 -bash
  134 v01 R      0:00 ps
```

ps Command Output

The output of the ps command is always organized in columns. Every process on the system has to have a unique identifier so Linux can tell which processes it is working with. Linux handles processes by assigning a unique number to each process, called the "Process ID" number (or PID). PIDs start at zero when the system is booted and increment by one for each process run, up to some system-determined number (such as 65,564) at which point it starts numbering from zero again, ignoring those that are still active. Usually, the lowest-number processes are the system kernel and daemons, which start when Linux boots and remain active as long as Linux is running. When you are working with processes (such as terminating them), you must use the PID.

The TTY column in the ps command output shows you which terminal the process was started from. If you are logged in as a user, this will usually be your terminal or console window. If you are running on multiple console windows, you will see all the processes you started in every window displayed.

The STAT column in the ps command output shows you the current status of the process. The two most common entries in the status column are S for sleeping and R for running. A running process is one that is currently executing on the CPU. A sleeping process is one which isn't currently active. Processes may switch between sleeping and running many times every second.

The TIME column shows the total amount of system (CPU) time used by the process so far. These numbers tend to be very small for most processes because they require only a short time to complete. The numbers under the TIME column are a total of the CPU time, not the amount of time the process has been alive.

Finally, the COMMAND column contains the name of the command line you are running. This is usually the command line you used, although some commands start up other processes. These are called "child" processes, and they show up in the ps output as if you had entered them as commands.

Login Shells

As a general convention, a login shell has a hyphen placed before its name (such as -bash in the previous output) to help you distinguish the startup shell from any shells you may have started afterwards. Any other shells that appear in the output do not have the hyphen in front of the name, as the following example shows:

```
$ ps
 PID TTY STAT   TIME COMMAND
  46 v01 S      0:01 -bash
  75 v01 S      0:00 pdksh
  96 v01 R      0:00 bash
 123 v01 R      0:00 ps
```

This output shows that the user's startup shell is bash (PID 46), and that he or she started up the Korn shell (pdksh, PID 75) and another Bourne shell (bash, PID 96) afterward.

Notice in the preceding outputs that the command that actually showed you the process status, ps, appears on the output because it was running when you issued the command. The ps command always appears on the output.

For the Superuser

When normal users issue the ps command, they see only their own processes. If you issue the ps command when you are logged in as the superuser (usually root, although you can change the name), you will see all the processes on the system, because the root login owns everything running. This can produce very long outputs, especially on a system with several users, so you probably want to pipe the output from the ps command to a page filter (such as more or less), or save the output in a file for further examination. Both commands are shown here:

```
ps ¦ more
ps > /tmp/ps_file
```

Useful *ps* options

A useful ps option for checking user processes is -u, which adds several columns to the output of the ps command. The output from a user (not root) command using this option looks like this:

```
$ ps -u
USER         PID %CPU %MEM SIZE  RSS TTY STAT START    TIME COMMAND
bill          41  0.1  6.8  364  472 v01 S    23:19    0:01 -bash
bill         138  0.0  3.3   72  228 v01 R    23:34    0:00 ps -u
```

The most important addition to the output is the USER column, which shows who started and owns the process. The name listed under the USER column is the user's login name, as found in the /etc/passwd file. (ps does a look-up in the /etc/passwd file to convert the user ID number—UID—to the proper user name.)

This option also adds the column labeled %CPU which shows the percentage of CPU time that has been used by the process so far. The column %MEM shows the percentage of your system's memory currently used by the process. These numbers can be handy for finding processes that consume far too much CPU or memory, called "CPU hogs" and "memory hogs" by most administrators. If you see a user process that has very high usage, it is worth checking to make sure it is a valid process and not a run-away that will continue to grind at your system's resources.

When you issue this command logged in as root, you see all the processes running on the system. As before, you should consider paginating the output to make it readable. With some versions of Linux's ps command, you can also use the -u option to specify a user's processes by adding each username. For example, if you are logged in as root and want to see only Yvonne's processes, you could issue the command:

```
ps -u yvonne
```

This format of the -u option works with System V versions of ps, but not the BSD-based version of ps included with most Linux distributions (including the one of the CD-ROM). You can obtain other versions of ps on FTP and BBS sites. Most users can issue this command to examine other users' processes, as well. This lets them find out who is hogging all the CPU time! It also lets the superuser see the processes that users are running when they report problems, without having to wade through all the system processes as well.

Users can also see all the processes running on the system (instead of just the processes started by them) by using the -a option. Because the superuser sees all the processes on the system anyway, the root login doesn't have to use this option, although it is still legal to use it. This output doesn't change, though. When issued by a user (not root), the -a option produces the following output:

```
$ ps -a
 PID TTY STAT TIME COMMAND
   1 psf S   0:00 init
   6 psf S   0:00 update (sync)
  23 psf S   0:00 /usr/sbin/crond -110
  29 psf S   0:00 /usr/sbin/syslogd
  31 psf S   0:00 /usr/sbin/klogd
  33 psf S   0:00 /usr/sbin/lpd
  40 psf S   0:00 selection -t ms
  42 v02 S   0:01 -bash
  43 v03 S   0:00 /sbin/agetty 38400 tty3
  44 v04 S   0:00 /sbin/agetty 38400 tty4
  45 v05 S   0:00 /sbin/agetty 38400 tty5
  46 v06 S   0:00 /sbin/agetty 38400 tty6
  41 v01 S   0:01 -bash
 140 v01 R   0:00 ps -a
```

This is a relatively short output showing a very lightly loaded system. Most of the entries are the Linux operating system kernel and daemons, as well as serial port getty processes. Only the last two commands were started by the user who issued the ps command. Of course, you can't tell who started each process with this output, so you can combine the -u and -a options (note that you use only one hyphen, followed by the option letters):

```
$ ps -au
USER       PID %CPU %MEM SIZE  RSS TTY STAT START    TIME COMMAND
root        64  0.0  1.5   41  224 v02 S    22:25    0:00 /sbin/agetty 38400 tty2
root        65  0.0  1.5   41  224 v03 S    22:25    0:00 /sbin/agetty 38400 tty3
root        66  0.0  1.5   41  224 v04 S    22:25    0:00 /sbin/agetty 38400 tty4
```

```
root          67  0.0  1.5   41  224 v05 S   22:25  0:00 /sbin/agetty 38400 tty5
root          68  0.0  1.5   41  224 v06 S   22:25  0:00 /sbin/agetty 38400 tty6
root          69  0.0  1.5   56  228 s00 S   22:25  0:00 gpm -t mman
root          71  0.3  3.6  388  532 pp0 S   22:26  0:02 -bash
root         155  0.0  1.5   77  220 pp0 R   22:37  0:00 ps -au
tparker      119  0.4  3.5  372  520 v01 S   22:32  0:01 -bash
tparker      132  0.1  2.2  189  324 v01 S   22:33  0:00 vi test
```

The -au options produce a list with all the same columns as the -u option, but shows all the processes running on the system. The order in which you enter the options doesn't matter, so -au is functionally the same as -ua. When you are adding several options, this can be handy.

A few other ps command-line options are occasionally useful. The -l option adds information about which processes started each process (useful when you want to identify child processes):

```
$ ps -l
F  UID  PID  PPID  PRI  NI  SIZE  RSS  WCHAN   STAT  TTY  TIME  COMMAND
0  501  41   1     15   0   364   472  114d9c  S     v01  0:00  -bash
0  501  121  41    29   0   64    208  0       R     v01  0:00  ps -l
```

The PPID (Parent Process ID) column shows which process started that particular process. You will see in the extract from the preceding output, that the ps command itself was started by a bash process, because the shell is the entity that is the parent of all user commands. You also see that the PPID for the login Bourne shell is PID "1", which is the init process of the operating system. (If you think about what this means, it implies that if init ever terminates, all other processes die, too. Simply put, when init dies, the entire system is off.)

> **NOTE**
>
> The Linux version of the ps command has a few idiosyncrasies. The hyphen before any options is not strictly necessary, so ps u would work in the same manner as ps -u. However, because UNIX convention (and most UNIX versions) require hyphens, you should use them.

For System Administrators

Most system administrators get by with three versions of the ps command (when logged in as root). To display information about the system as a whole, the following command lines show practically everything there is to know about processes:

```
ps -ax
ps -aux
ps -le
```

The meaning of the primary columns in the output from the two commands has been mentioned earlier in this section. The rest of the columns are either evident from their shortform or not that important. For complete information, see the ps man page (which is not entirely accurate or complete, unfortunately).

Using *kill*

Occasionally you will find a process that has locked up a terminal or isn't doing anything, which is generally referred to as a "hung" process. Sometimes a user will have a process that doesn't terminate properly (especially common with programmers). These are "run-away" processes. In both cases, the only way to get rid of the process and restore some normality to the system is to terminate the process entirely. This is done with the `kill` command.

To use `kill`, you have to have access to another window or console where you can issue commands. If your terminal is completely locked up, you have to find another one to log in on. As a user, you can only `kill` your own processes—you cannot affect any process another user or the system is running. As root, you can terminate any process with the `kill` command.

In order to use the `kill` command, you need the process ID number (PID) of the process to be terminated. You have to obtain the PID with the `ps` command and note the PID. Next, use the `kill` command with the PID as an argument. For example, the following terminal session shows a user process started by Walter called `bad_prog`, that has hung up and needs to be killed. The PID is obtained by displaying all of the system's processes with their user names (we've cut the other lines from the `ps` command output for simplicity's sake):

```
$ ps -u
USER    PID %CPU %MEM SIZE RSS TTY STAT START  TIME COMMAND
walter  561 0.1  6.8  364  472 v01 S    13:19  0:01 -bash
walter  598 9.3  4.1  2736 472 v01 R    15:26  2:01 bad_prog
$ kill 598
```

When you issue the `kill` command, you don't get any return message if it works properly. The only way to verify that the process termination has been properly conducted is to issue another `ps` command and look for the PID or process name.

*kill*ing Child Processes

Because some processes spawn child processes with different PIDs, you must be sure to check that all the child processes are terminated. The best way to do this is to watch the names of the executing processes for a few minutes to ensure the child isn't dormant, only to return later. This problem usually happens when the child processes are being generated by a parent. You should check the `PPID` column (use the `ps -l` option) to see which process is the parent and terminate that.

> **WARNING**
>
> When you are `kill`ing processes and logged in as root, make sure you type the correct PID or you may inadvertently terminate another process. Check the PID carefully! Also, don't `kill` any system processes unless you know what they do and why they need to be terminated.

If the process doesn't terminate properly with the `kill` command, you need to use sterner measures. The `kill` command actually has several levels of operation. When issued with no arguments other than the PID, `kill` tries to gracefully terminate the process (which means any open files are closed, and generally, `kill` is polite to the process). If this doesn't work, you should use the `-9` option, which is a little more forceful in its attempt to terminate the process. For example, to forcefully terminate the process with PID 726, issue the following command:

```
kill -9 726
```

If that doesn't work, then the process may be unkillable. This does happen occasionally with Linux, and the only solution is to shut down and reboot the machine.

killing Rights

To help prevent a user from killing another user's processes, `ps` checks for the process owner. If a user tries to `kill` another user's process, a message like this one is displayed:

```
kill: - Not owner
```

The superuser doesn't get this message because the superuser login can `kill` anything.

Summary

This chapter has shown you how to obtain listings of the processes currently executing on your Linux system and how to terminate them when they require it. Although you may not have to use this knowledge often, every operating system has occasions where something gets out of hand and you need to control it. The problems multiply as the number of users increases. Instead of rebooting the Linux system, process commands enable you to correct the problem without terminating the operating system.

SCSI Device Support

41

by Tim Parker

This chapter will look at SCSI devices. More specifically, you will see:

- What a SCSI device is
- What kind of SCSI devices can be attached to Linux
- How to configure SCSI devices
- Typical problems and solutions for SCSI users

SCSI (Small Computer Systems Interface), pronounced "scuzzy," is a standard method of interfacing between a computer and peripherals. It has many advantages over other interconnect systems such as IDE, albeit generally at a higher price.

SCSI uses a dedicated controller card within the computer, from which a chain of devices can be connected. All the SCSI devices are coupled using a flat-ribbon cable (internally) or a shielded cable (externally). Each SCSI chain can support seven devices. Each device has a SCSI ID number from 0 to 7. Usually the controller card is set to use number 7, while bootable SCSI hard drives are set to use SCSI ID 0. The other numbers are available for other devices, although each ID can be used by only one device.

The advantages of SCSI are primarily in its high speed. Also, with most SCSI devices, all the electronics needed to control them are attached to the device, making it easier for devices to talk to each other. The other major advantage of SCSI is that you don't have to do anything special to configure the system. When you plug in a new SCSI device (such as a scanner) with a unique SCSI ID, the system controller card recognizes it because the on-board electronics identify the type of device to the card automatically.

SCSI devices must have a terminator at each end of the chain. Terminators are a set of resistors that provide an electrical indication that the chain ends at that point. There should only be two terminators on each SCSI chain, one at each end. Most SCSI controller cards have a set of switches or a block of removable resistors that terminate one end, while SCSI devices have a switch or resistors that allow that device to automatically terminate the chain. Some devices are clever enough to sense that they are the last SCSI device in a chain, and they terminate without any intervention from you.

SCSI devices can communicate with each other quickly over the chain. A scanner can send instructions straight to a hard drive, and a tape drive can dump information straight to another SCSI device without involving the operating system too much. This helps the speed and makes SCSI devices particularly flexible.

I won't go into all the details of SCSI connectivity and architecture, because you don't need to know these details for most purposes. If you need more information, most SCSI controller cards include a good description of the theory.

Supported SCSI Devices

You can't assume that since Linux supports SCSI, any SCSI device will work. Most versions of the operating system have a hardware compatibility file in the distribution set that lists all devices that have been tested and are known to work properly with the SCSI system. Check this file carefully before you buy a new device or controller card! Some devices and cards simply don't work with Linux.

Some SCSI devices are shipped with their own kernel patches. You will have to make sure the patches correspond to the version of the Linux kernel you are using, then rebuild the kernel with the new drivers in place. If the devices don't have a Linux kernel patch, check with the manufacturer or Linux distribution sites.

SCSI Device Drivers

Every device on the Linux system must have a device file, and SCSI devices are no different. In many cases, Linux is distributed with a complete set of SCSI device files that only need to be configured properly. You should know a little about device drivers, device files, and major and minor device numbers. See Chapter 38, "Devices and Device Administration," for more information.

Hard Drives

SCSI disk drives are always block devices and should always use major device number 8. No "raw" SCSI devices are usually supported by Linux, despite its similarity to BSD UNIX, which does support raw SCSI devices.

Sixteen minor device numbers are allocated to each SCSI disk device. Minor device number 0 represents the whole disk drive, minor numbers 1 through 4 are the four primary partitions, and minor numbers 5 through 15 are used for any extended partitions.

With Linux, SCSI disk minor device numbers are assigned dynamically, starting with the lowest SCSI ID numbers. The standard naming convention for SCSI hard drives is /dev/sd{*letter*} for the entire disk device (such as /dev/sda or /dev/sdb), and /dev/sd{*letter*}{*partition*} for the partitions on that device (such as /dev/sda1 or /dev/sda2).

Linux presents a few problems when partitioning SCSI disks, because Linux talks directly to the SCSI interface. Each disk drive is viewed as the SCSI host sees it, with block numbers from 0 up to the highest block number. They are all assumed to be error-free. This means there is an easy way to get at the disk geometry. (For comparison, DOS requires head-cylinder-sector mapping, which is not as efficient but does allow direct manipulation.)

To partition the drive, you will either have to use the entire disk for Linux (in which case the installation takes care of it), or you can use DOS or Linux's fdisk program to create partitions for other operating systems first. Also, with systems that support both SCSI hard drives and IDE hard drives, you might have to reconfigure the system in the machine's BIOS to recognize the SCSI drive as the primary (boot) device.

CD-ROM Devices

SCSI CD-ROM drives with a block size of 512 or 2048 bytes will work with Linux, but any other block size will not. Since most CD-ROM drives and CD-ROM discs have either 512- or 2048-

byte blocks, this shouldn't cause a problem unless the drive is from a source where other block sizes are the norm.

CD-ROM discs are offered in several different formats, not all of which might be readable on a Linux system. The international standard is called ISO 9660, but not all CD-ROMs conform to this standard because it was adopted long after CD-ROMs became popular.

SCSI CD-ROMs use the major device number 11, and minor device numbers are allocated dynamically. The first CD-ROM drive found is minor 0, the second is minor 1, and so on. The naming convention used with Linux is /dev/sr{*digit*}, such as /dev/sr0 and /dev/sr1 for the first and second CD-ROM drives installed. Alternatively, some Linux distributions name the devices /dev/scd0, /dev/scd1, and so on.

After you set the CD-ROM SCSI address properly (the system should recognize the device when the SCSI card boots), the CD-ROM device must be mounted. This can be done manually or embedded in the startup sequence so that the drive is always available.

To mount a CD-ROM device, the general command is

```
mount /dev/sr0 /mount_point
```

where *mount_point* is a directory that can be used. You must create the directory beforehand in order for the mount to work. For convenience, most systems that use CD-ROMs should create a directory called /cdrom, which is always the mount point.

If your CD-ROM doesn't mount properly with this command, the reason might be the disc type or the lack of an entry in the file /etc/fstab which identifies the CD as an ISO 9660 device. The correct syntax to mount an ISO 9660 CD-ROM (also called High-Sierra) is

```
mount -t iso9660 /dev/sr0 /mount_point
```

For this to work correctly, you must have the kernel set to support the ISO 9660 file system. If this hasn't been done, rebuild the kernel with this option added.

Linux attempts to lock the CD-ROM drive door when a disc is mounted. This is done to prevent file system confusion due to a media change. Not all CD-ROM drives support door locking, but if you find yourself unable to eject a CD-ROM, it is probably because the disc is mounted (it doesn't have to be in use).

Tape Drives

Linux supports several SCSI tape drives. You should check the hardware configuration guide before purchasing one, though, to ensure compatibility. The most popular SCSI tape models, including the Archive Viper QIC drives, Exabyte 8mm drives, and Wangtek 5150S and DAT tape drives, are all known to work well.

SCSI tapes use character device major number 9, and the minor numbers are assigned dynamically. Usually, rewinding tape devices are numbered from 0, so the first tape drive is /dev/rst0 (character mode, major number 9, minor number 0), the second device is /dev/rst1 (character mode, major number 9, minor number 1), and so on. Non-rewinding devices have the high bit set in the minor number so that the first non-rewinding tape drive is /dev/nrst0 (character mode, major device 9, minor device 128).

The standard naming convention for SCSI tape drives is /dev/nrst{*digit*} for non-rewinding devices (such as /dev/nrst0, /dev/nrst1, and so on), and /dev/rst{*digit*} for rewinding devices (such as /dev/rst0 and /dev/rst1).

Generally, Linux supports tape devices that use either fixed or variable-length blocks, as long as the block length is smaller than the driver buffer length, which is set to 32KB in most Linux distribution sources (although this can be changed). Tape drive parameters such as block size, buffering process, and tape density are set with ioctls, which can be issued by the mt program.

Other Devices

Many other SCSI devices are available, such as scanners, printers, removable cartridge drives, and so on. These are handled by the Linux generic SCSI device driver. The generic SCSI driver provides an interface for sending commands to all SCSI devices.

SCSI generic devices use character mode and major number 21. The minor device numbers are assigned dynamically from 0 for the first device, and so on. The generic devices have the names /dev/sg0, /dev/sg1, /dev/sg2, and so on.

Troubleshooting SCSI Devices

Many common problems with SCSI devices are quite easy to solve. Finding the cause of the problem is often the most difficult step. It's usually helpful to read the diagnostic message that the operating system displays when it boots or attempts to use a SCSI device.

The following are the most common problems encountered with SCSI devices, their probable causes, and possible solutions:

SCSI devices show up at all possible SCSI IDs   You have configured the device with the same SCSI address as the controller, which is typically set at SCSI ID 7. Change the jumper settings to another SCSI ID.

A SCSI device shows up with all possible LUNs   The device probably has bad firmware. The file /usr/src/linux/drivers/scsi/scsi.c contains a list of bad devices under the variable blacklist. You can try adding the device to this list and see if it affects the behavior. If not, contact the device manufacturer.

Your SCSI system times out   Make sure the controller card's interrupts are enabled correctly and that there are no IRQ, DMA, or address conflicts with other boards in your system.

You get "sense errors" from error-free devices   This is usually caused by either bad cables or improper termination on the chain. Make sure the SCSI chain is terminated at both ends using external or onboard terminators. Don't terminate in the middle of the chain, because this can also cause problems. You can probably use passive termination, but for long chains with several devices, try active termination for better behavior.

The tape drive is not recognized at boot time Try booting with a tape in the drive.

A networking kernel does not work with new SCSI devices The autoprobe routines for many network drivers are not passive and can interfere with some SCSI drivers. Try to disable the network portions to identify the guilty program, and then reconfigure it.

A SCSI device is detected, but the system is unable to access it You probably don't have a device file for the device. Device drivers should be in /dev and configured with the proper type (block or character) and unique major and minor device numbers. Run mkdev for the device.

The SCSI controller card fails when it uses memory-mapped I/O This problem is common with Trantor T128 and Seagate boards and is caused when the memory-mapped I/O ports are incorrectly cached. You should have the board's address space marked as uncacheable in the XCMOS settings. If you can't mark them as such, disable the cache and see if the board functions properly.

Your system fails to find the SCSI devices and you get messages when the system boots, such as scsi : 0 hosts *or* scsi%d : type: The autoprobe routines on the controller cards rely on the system BIOS autoprobe and can't boot properly. This is particularly prevalent with these SCSI adapters: Adaptec 152*x*, Adaptec 151*x*, Adaptec AIC-6260, Adaptec AIC-6360, Future Domain 1680, Future Domain TMC-950, Future Domain TMC-8*xx*, Trantor T128, Trantor T128F, Trantor T228F, Seagate ST01, Seagate ST02, and Western Digital 7000. Check that your BIOS is enabled and not conflicting with any other peripheral BIOSes (such as on some adapter cards). If the BIOS is properly enabled, find the board's "signature" by running DOS's DEBUG command to check if the board is responding. For example, use the DEBUG command d=c800:0 to see if the board replies with an acknowledgment (assuming you have set the controller card to use address 0xc8000; if not, replace the DEBUG command with the proper address). If the card doesn't respond, check the address settings.

Sometimes the SCSI system locks up completely There are many possible solutions, including a problem with the host adapter. Check the host adapter with any diagnostics that came with the board. Try a different SCSI cable to see if that is the problem. If the lockups seem to occur when multiple devices are in use at the same time, there is probably a firmware problem. Contact the manufacturer to see if upgrades are available that would correct the problem. Finally, check the disk drives to ensure that there are no bad blocks that could affect the device files, buffers, or swap space.

Summary

SCSI has a reputation for being difficult to work with, but in fact it is one of the easiest and most versatile systems available. Once you get used to the nomenclature, SCSI offers many useful features to the Linux user. Indeed, most veteran UNIX people prefer working with SCSI because it is easy to use with the UNIX kernel, and the same applies to Linux.

Networking

by Tim Parker

IN THIS CHAPTER

In this chapter, you will look at the world of networking. In particular, you will learn the following:

- What is TCP/IP?
- How do you set up Linux to use TCP/IP and Ethernet?
- What changes are necessary to your configuration files?
- How can you test and troubleshoot Ethernet connections?
- What is necessary for a SLIP and PPP connection?

Linux offers a complete implementation of Transmission Control Protocol/Internet Protocol (TCP/IP), the protocol used extensively on the Internet and that is commonly found in local area networks involving UNIX machines. All you need to create a network, or to add your existing machine to a TCP/IP network, is a network card or network interface and some modifications to files already on your Linux system.

Whether you are setting up two machines in your room to talk to each other, or adding your Linux machine to an existing network of 5,000 workstations, the process is the same.

What Is TCP/IP?

TCP/IP is an *open* networking protocol, which simply means that the technical description of all aspects of the protocol have been published. They are available for anyone to implement on their hardware and software. This open nature has helped make TCP/IP very popular. Versions of TCP/IP are now available for practically every hardware and software platform in existence, which has helped make TCP/IP the most widely used networking protocol in the world. The advantage of TCP/IP for a network operating system is simple: Interconnectivity is possible for any type of operating system and hardware platform that you might want to add.

TCP/IP is not a single protocol but a set of more than a dozen protocols. Each protocol within the TCP/IP family is dedicated to a different task. All the protocols that make up TCP/IP use the primary components of TCP/IP to send packets of data.

Transmission Control Protocol and Internet Protocol are two of the primary protocols in the TCP/IP family. The different protocols and services that make up the TCP/IP family can be grouped according to their purposes. The groups and their protocols are the following:

Transport: These protocols control the movement of data between two machines.

> TCP (Transmission Control Protocol): A connection-based service, meaning that the sending and receiving machines communicate with each other through a stream of messages. TCP has message delivery assurance routines incorporated into it.

UDP (User Datagram Protocol): A connectionless service, meaning that the data is sent without the sending and receiving machines being in contact with each other. It's like sending snail-mail (regular postal service) with an address but no guarantee it will arrive.

Routing: These protocols handle the addressing of the data and determine the best routing to the destination. They also handle the way large messages are broken up and reassembled at the destination.

IP (Internet Protocol): Handles the actual transmission of data.

ICMP (Internet Control Message Protocol): Handles status messages for IP, such as errors and network changes that can affect routing.

RIP (Routing Information Protocol): One of several protocols that determine the best routing method.

OSPF (Open Shortest Path First): An alternative protocol for determining routing.

Network Addresses: These services handle the way machines are addressed, both by a unique number and a more common symbolic name.

ARP (Address Resolution Protocol): Determines the unique network hardware addresses of machines on the network based on their IP address.

DNS (Domain Name System): Determines numeric addresses from machine names.

RARP (Reverse Address Resolution Protocol): Determines IP addresses of machines on the network based on their network address (the opposite of ARP).

BOOTP (Boot Protocol): This starts up a network machine by reading the boot information from a server. BOOTP is commonly used for diskless workstations.

User Services: These are applications users have access to.

FTP (File Transfer Protocol): This protocol efficiently transfers files from one machine to another. FTP uses TCP as the transport.

TFTP (Trivial File Transfer Protocol): A simple file transfer method that uses UDP as the transport.

TELNET: Allows remote logins so that a user on one machine can connect to another machine and behave as though they are sitting at the remote machine's keyboard.

Gateway Protocols: These services help the network communicate routing and status information, as well as handle data for local networks.

EGP (Exterior Gateway Protocol): Transfers routing information for external networks.

GGP (Gateway-to-Gateway Protocol): Transfers routing information between Internet gateways.

IGP (Interior Gateway Protocol): Transfers routing information for internal networks.

Others: These are services that don't fall into the categories just mentioned but that provide important services over a network.

NFS (Network File System): Allows directories on one machine to be mounted on another, and then accessed by users as though the directories were on the local machine.

NIS (Network Information Service): Maintains user accounts across networks, simplifying logins and password maintenance.

RPC (Remote Procedure Call): Allows remote applications to communicate with each other using function calls.

SMTP (Simple Mail Transfer Protocol): A protocol for transferring electronic mail between machines.

SNMP (Simple Network Management Protocol): An administrator's service that sends status messages about the network and devices attached to it.

All the TCP/IP protocol definitions are maintained by a standards body that is part of the Internet organization. Although changes to the protocols occasionally occur when new features or better methods of performing older functions are developed, the new versions are almost always backward compatible.

Hardware Requirements

You can actually configure Linux to use TCP/IP without any network card or connection to a network, using a technique called *loopback*. Loopback is a method of instruction that enables part of TCP/IP to talk to another part without leaving the machine. Essentially, you are creating a loop between a software exit and a software entry. Loopbacks are frequently used to test TCP/IP configurations, and some software requires a loopback to be in place for proper operation.

If you want to connect your Linux machine to a network, you need a network card. Linux uses Ethernet, a network system that was designed to provide TCP/IP support. A term you'll see often is *packet*, which is the bundle of data and routing instructions that is assembled by TCP/IP and Ethernet to be sent over the network cables. All messages are broken into packets, then reassembled properly at the destination.

Linux requires an Ethernet card that is compatible with one of the network cards in the following list:

3Com 3C505
3Com 3C503/16
Novell NE1000
Novell NE2000

Western Digital WD8003
Western Digital WD8013
Hewlett-Packard HP27245
Hewlett-Packard HP27247
Hewlett-Packard HP27250

Most Ethernet cards available are compatible with one of these cards, but you should carefully check the documentation with the card to ensure you don't buy a network card that won't work properly.

If you plan to do your networking over the telephone (using a serial port and a modem), you don't need a network card, but you *will* need a fast modem compatible with the service you are planning to use. For example, to use SLIP (Serial Line Interface Protocol), you generally need a modem supporting at least V.32bis speeds (14.4kbps).

Configuring Linux Files

Let's assume you have a typical PC and an Ethernet card, and you want to set up your machine to run TCP/IP over the network. In most cases, the procedure described next will work. However, because there are many versions of Linux, many potential conflicts with other cards and software, and unique software requirements for some systems, this should be considered a guide.

If, after following these instructions, your TCP/IP network doesn't work properly, it's time to carefully scan all the configuration files and error messages for a clue to the problem. Also, don't forget about the Linux UseNet newsgroups, Linux User Groups, and other sources of information about Linux from which you can get help.

To configure the TCP/IP files, you must have installed the networking software on your system. If you haven't installed the networking portions of the distribution, you must do so before proceeding. Your kernel must also have been configured and recompiled with network support added. This is usually done during the installation process, although some users will have to force the kernel recompilation manually if they installed their software in a nonstandard manner.

First we'll deal with the use of a network card, and then look at how to change the basic process to handle SLIP over a serial port and modem.

What You Need Before You Start

Before you start modifying system files, take a few minutes to determine a few basic pieces of information you'll need. It is advisable to write these down somewhere so that they will be handy when you need them, and also so that you won't enter two different values in two files, thereby causing major problems for the system.

IP Address

First you need an IP address, a unique number for your machine. Every machine on the network has to be identified uniquely to allow proper routing. TCP/IP-based networks use 32-bit addresses to uniquely identify networks and all the devices that reside within that network. These addresses are called *Internet addresses* or *IP addresses.*

The 32 bits of the IP address are broken into four 8-bit parts. Each 8-bit part can then have valid numbers ranging from 0 to 255. In IP addresses, the four 8-bit numbers are separated by a period, a notation called *dotted quad.* Examples of dotted quad IP addresses are 255.255.255.255 and 147.14.123.8.

For convenience, IP addresses are divided into two parts: the network number and the device number within that network. This separation into two components allows devices on different networks to have the same host number. However, because the network number is different, the devices are still uniquely identified.

For connection to the Internet, IP addresses are assigned by the Internet Network Information Center (NIC) based on the size of the network. Anyone who wants to connect to the Internet must register with the NIC to avoid duplication of network addresses. If you don't plan to connect to the Internet, you are free to create your own numbering scheme, although future expansion and integration with Internet-using networks can cause serious problems.

For maximum flexibility, IP addresses are assigned according to network size. Networks are divided into three categories: C*lass A, Class B*, and *Class C.* The three network classes break the 32-bit IP addresses into different sizes for the network and host identifiers.

A Class A address uses one byte for the network address and three bytes for the device address, allowing more than 16 million different host addresses. Class B networks use two bytes for the network and two bytes for the host. Because 16 bits allows more than 65,000 hosts, only a few large companies will be limited by this type of class. Class C addresses have three bytes for the network and one for the number of hosts. This provides for a maximum of 254 hosts (the numbers 0 and 255 are reserved) but many different network IDs. The majority of networks are Class B and Class C.

You do have a limitation as to the first value. A Class A network's first number must be between 0 and 127, Class B addresses are between 128 and 191, and Class C addresses are between 192 and 223. This is because of the way the first byte is broken up, with a few of the bits at the front saved to identify the class of the network. Also, you can't use the values 0 and 255 for any part, because they are reserved for special purposes.

Messages sent using TCP/IP use the IP address to identify sending and receiving devices, as well as any routing information put within the message headers. If you are going to connect to an existing network, you should find out what their IP addresses are and what numbers you can use. If you are setting up a network for your own use but plan to connect to the Internet at some point, contact the Network Information Center for an IP address. On the other hand, if you are setting up a network for your own use and don't plan to have more than a telephone connection to other networks (including the Internet), you can make up your own IP addresses.

If you are only setting up a loopback driver, you don't even need an IP address. The default value for a loopback driver is 127.0.0.1.

Network Mask

Next, you need a network mask. This is pretty easy if you have picked out an IP address. The network mask is the network portion of the IP address set to the value 255, and it's used to blank out the network portion to determine routing.

If you have a Class C IP address (three bytes for network and one for devices), your network mask is 255.255.255.0. A Class B network has a network mask of 255.255.0.0, and a Class A network mask is 255.0.0.0.

If you are configuring only a loopback driver, your network mask is 255.0.0.0 (Class A). If you have a complex network setup with subnets or shared IP addresses, you should consult your network administrator for more information about setting your network mask and IP address.

Network Address

The network address is, strictly speaking, the IP address bitwise-ANDed to the netmask. In English, what this means is that it's the network portion of your IP address, so if your IP address is 147.120.46.7 and it's a Class B network, the network address is 147.120.0.0.

To get your own network address, just drop the device-specific part of the IP address and set it to zero. A Class C network with an IP address of 201.12.5.23 has a network address of 201.12.5.0.

If you're only working with a loopback address, you don't need a network mask.

Broadcast Address

The broadcast address is used when a machine wants to send the same packet to all devices on the network. To get your broadcast address, you set the device portion of the IP address to 255. Therefore, if you have the IP address 129.23.123.2, your broadcast address will be 129.23.123.255. Your network address will be 129.23.123.0.

If you are configuring only a loopback driver, you needn't worry about the broadcast address.

Gateway Address

The gateway address is the IP address of the machine that is the network's gateway out to other networks (such as the Internet). You need a gateway address only if you have a network that has a dedicated gateway out. If you are configuring a small network for your own use and don't have a dedicated Internet connection, you don't need a gateway address.

Normally, gateways have the same IP address as your machines, but they have the digit 1 as the device number. For example, if your IP address is `129.23.123.36`, chances are that the gateway address is `129.23.123.1`. This convention has been used since the early days of TCP/IP.

Loopback drivers do not require a gateway address, so if you are configuring your system only for loopback, ignore this address.

Nameserver Address

Many larger networks have a machine whose purpose is to translate IP addresses into English-like names, and vice versa. It is a lot easier to call a machine `bobs_pc` instead of `123.23.124.23`. This translation is done with a system called the Domain Name System (DNS). If your network has a name server, that's the address you need. If you want to have your own machine act as a name server (which requires some extra configuration not mentioned here), use the loopback address `127.0.0.1`.

Loopback drivers don't need a name server because the machine only talks to itself. Therefore, you can ignore the nameserver address if you are only configuring a loopback driver.

Setting Up the Dummy Interface

What's a dummy interface? It's a bit of a trick to give your machine an IP address to work with when it uses only SLIP and PPP interfaces. A dummy interface solves the problem of a stand-alone machine (no network cards connecting it to other machines) whose only valid IP address to send data to is the loopback driver (`127.0.0.1`). While SLIP and PPP may be used for connecting your machine to the outside world, when the interface is not active you have no internal IP address that applications can use.

The problem arises with some applications that require a valid IP address to work. Some word processors and desktop layout tools, for example, require the TCP/IP system to be operational with an IP address for the target machine. The dummy interface essentially sets an IP address for your local machine that is valid as far as TCP/IP is concerned, but doesn't really get used except to fool applications.

Creating a dummy interface is very simple. If your machine has an IP address already assigned for it in the `/etc/hosts` file, all you need to do is set up the interface and create a route. The two commands required are

```
ifconfig dummy machine_name
route add machine_name
```

where machine_name is your local machine's name (such as darkstar). This will create a link to your own IP address. If you do not have an IP address for your machine in the /etc/hosts file, add one before you create the dummy interface.

Configuration Files

Configuring Linux for TCP/IP is not difficult because only a few configuration files need to have the information about IP address and such added to them. You can do this with any editor as long as it saves the files in ASCII format. It is advisable to make copies of the configuration files before you modify them, just in case you damage the format in some way.

Many of these files are similar in every version of UNIX, including most versions of Linux, except for one or two slight naming variations. If you've ever set up a UNIX system (or snooped around one in detail), these files and steps might seem familiar. If you haven't done anything with Linux or UNIX before, just take it one step at a time and follow the instructions!

rc Files

Linux reads the rc (run command) files when the system boots. The init program initiates the reading of these files, and they usually serve to start processes such as mail, printers, cron, and so on. They are also used to initiate TCP/IP connections. Most Linux systems have the rc command files in the directory /etc/rc.d.

The files of interest to TCP/IP, at least as far as Red Hat Linux is concerned, are under the /etc/rc.d/rc2.d directory. The files in this directory start different TCP/IP services. The names of most of the files identify their purposes. For example, the file K20nfs deals with starting the NFS service.

If you want to change services that are started when Red Hat Linux boots, you can edit these files with as ASCII editor. Identify the file that is involved with the service you need to modify (you can often use grep to find the right file, or you can look through them all with more). Whichever file is involved, look for a line that refers to the service. In some cases, this line or lines will be commented out (have a pound sign as the first character) to prevent the system from trying to run them. If the lines are commented out, remove the comment symbol.

/etc/hosts

The /etc/hosts file is a simple list of IP addresses and the hostnames to which they correspond. This is a good location to list all your favorite machines so that you can use the name and have the system look up the IP address. On very small networks, you can add all the machines in the network here and avoid the need to run the nameserver.

Every /etc/hosts file will have an entry for localhost (also called loopback, IP address 127.0.0.1) and probably one for your machine if you named it when you installed the software. If you didn't supply a name and there is no line other than localhost, you can add it now. Use an editor and set your IP address and machine name. Don't bother adding too many other machines until you're sure the network works properly! Here's a sample /etc/hosts file:

```
127.0.0.1        localhost
147.12.2.42      merlin.tpci merlin
```

You will notice that the format is quite simple: an IP address in one column and the name in another column, separated by tabs. If the machine may have more than one name, supply them all. In the example, which uses random numbers for the IP address, the machine 147.12.2.42 has the name merlin. Since it is also part of a larger network called tpci, the machine can be addressed as merlin.tpci. Both names on the line ensure that the system can resolve either name to the same address.

You can expand the file a little if you want by adding other machines on your local network, or those you will communicate with regularly:

```
127.0.0.1        localhost
147.12.2.42      merlin.tpci merlin
147.12.2.43      wizard.tpci wizard
147.12.2.44      arthur.tpci arthur bobs_machine
147.12.2.46      lancelot.tpci lancelot
```

In this example, there are several machines from the same network (the same network mask). One has three different names.

If you are only using the loopback driver, the only line that should be in the file is for the IP address 127.0.0.1 with the name localhost and your machine's name after it.

/etc/networks

The /etc/networks file lists names and IP address of your own network and other networks you connect to frequently. This file is used by the route command. One advantage of this file is that it lets you call remote networks by name, so instead of typing 149.23.24, you can type eds_net.

The /etc/networks file should have an entry for every network that will be used with the route command if you plan on using the network name as an identifier. If there is no entry, errors will be generated, and the network won't work properly. On the other hand, if you don't need to use a network name instead of its IP address, then you can skip the /etc/networks file.

A sample /etc/networks file using random IP addresses is shown next. Remember that you need only the network mask and not the device portion of a remote machine's IP address, although you must fill in the rest with zeroes.

```
loopback              127.0.0.0
localnet              147.13.2.0
eds_net               197.32.1.0
big_net               12.0.0.0
```

At a minimum, you should have a loopback and `localnet` address in the file.

/etc/host.conf

The system uses the `host.conf` file to resolve hostnames. It usually contains two lines that look like this:

```
order hosts, bind
multi on
```

These tell the system to first check the `/etc/hosts` file, then check the nameserver (if one exists) when trying to resolve a name. The `multi` entry lets you have multiple IP addresses for a machine in the `/etc/hosts` file (which happens with gateways and machines on more than one network).

If your `/etc/host.conf` file looks like these two lines, you don't need to make any changes at all.

resolv.conf

The `resolv.conf` file is used by the name resolver program. It gives the address of your name server (if you have one) and your domain name (if you have one). You will have a domain name if you are on the Internet.

A sample `resolv.conf` file for the system `merlin.tpci.com` has an entry for the domain name, which is `tpci.com` (`merlin` is the name of an individual machine):

```
domain tpci.com
```

If a name server is used on your network, you should add a line that gives its IP address:

```
domain tpci.com
nameserver  182.23.12.4
```

If there are multiple name servers, which is not unusual on a larger network, each name server should be specified on its own line.

If you don't have a domain name for your system, you can safely ignore this file for the moment.

/etc/protocols

UNIX systems use the `/etc/protocols` file to identify all the transport protocols available on the system and their respective protocol numbers. (Each protocol supported by TCP/IP has a special number, but that's not really important at this point.) Usually, this file is not modified but is maintained by the system and updated automatically as part of the installation procedure when new software is added.

The /etc/protocols file contains the protocol name, its number, and any alias that may be used for that protocol. A sample /etc/protocols file looks like this:

```
# Internet protocols (IP)
ip       0    IP
icmp     1    ICMP
ggp      3    GGP
tcp      6    TCP
egp      8    EGP
pup      12   PUP
udp      17   UDP
hello    63   HELLO
```

If your entries don't match this, don't worry. You shouldn't have to make any changes to this file at all, but you should know what it does.

/etc/services

The /etc/services file identifies the existing network services. This file is maintained by software as it is installed or configured.

This file consists of the service name, a port number, and the protocol type. The port number and protocol type are separated by a slash, following the conventions mentioned in previous chapters. Any optional service alias names follow. Here's a short extract from a sample /etc/services file:

```
# network services
echo      7/tcp
echo      7/udp
discard   9/tcp    sink   null
discard   9/udp    sink   null
ftp       21/tcp
telnet    23/tcp
smtp      25/tcp   mail mailx
tftp      69/udp
# specific services
login     513/tcp
who       513/udp  whod
```

You shouldn't change this file at all, but you do need to know what it is and why it is there to help you understand TCP/IP a little better.

/etc/hostname or /etc/HOSTNAME

The file /etc/HOSTNAME is used to store the name of the system you are on. (Red Hat Linux uses the uppercase version of the name.) This file should have your local machine's name in it:

```
merlin.tpci
```

That's all it needs. The host name is used by most protocols on the system and many applications, so it is important for proper system operation. The host name can be changed by editing the system file and rebooting the machine, although many operating systems provide a utility program to ensure that this process is performed correctly.

Linux systems have a utility called hostname, which displays the current setting of the system name, as well as the uname program, which can give the node name with the command uname -n. When issued, the hostname and uname commands echo the local machine name, as the following sample session shows:

```
$ hostname
merlin.tpci.com
$ uname -n
merlin
```

All the configuration files necessary for TCP/IP to function have now been set properly, so you should be able to reboot the machine and see what happens.

Testing and Troubleshooting

To try out TCP/IP, reboot your machine and carefully watch the messages displayed on-screen. If you see any error messages, they may help guide you to the faulty file or process. Otherwise, you will see the TCP/IP daemons load one after another.

The *netstat* Command

Probably the best approach to checking on TCP/IP is to use the netstat command, which gives you many different summaries of all network connections and their status. The netstat program provides comprehensive information. It's the program most commonly used by administrators to quickly diagnose a problem with TCP/IP.

There are many more netstat options than the ones mentioned in the next sections. For more information on netstat, start with the man page on the Linux system, then check a good UNIX networking book.

Communications End Points

The netstat command with no options shows information on all active communications end points (where data is actually being transferred or communications are established). To display all end points (active and passive), netstat uses the -a option.

The netstat output is formatted in columns that show the protocol (Proto), the amount of data in the receive and send queues (Recv-Q and Send-Q), the local and remote addresses, and the current state of the connection. Here's a truncated sample output:

```
merlin> netstat -a
Active Internet connections (including servers)
```

```
Proto Recv-Q Send-Q  Local Address        Foreign Address        (state)
ip        0      0    *.*                  *.*
tcp       0   2124    tpci.login           oscar.1034             ESTABL.
tcp       0      0    tpci.1034            prudie.login           ESTABL.
tcp   11212      0    tpci.1035            treijs.1036            ESTABL.
tcp       0      0    tpci.1021            reboc.1024             TIME_WAIT
tcp       0      0    *.1028               *.*                    LISTEN
tcp       0      0    *.*                  *.*                    CLOSED
udp       0      0    localhost.1036       localhost.syslog
udp       0      0    *.1034               *.*
udp       0      0    *.*                  *.*
udp       0      0    *.*                  *.*
```

This excerpt has three active TCP connections, as identified by the state ESTABL., with one that has data being sent (as shown in the Send-Q column). An asterisk means that no end point is yet associated with that address.

Network Interface Statistics

The behavior of the network interface (such as the network interface card) can be shown with the netstat -i option. This quickly shows administrators whether there are major problems with the network connection. The meaning of each column in the netstat command output is intuitive from the title, but if you need clarification check the man page on netstat.

Routing tables are continually updated to reflect connections to other machines. To obtain information about the routing tables (if there are any on your system), the netstat -r option is used.

ping

The ping (Packet Internet Groper) program is used to query another system and ensure a connection is active. The ping program operates by sending a request to the destination machine for a reply. If the destination machine's IP software receives the request, it issues a reply immediately.

The sending machine will continue to send requests until the ping program is terminated with a break sequence. After termination, ping displays a set of statistics. A sample ping session is shown as follows:

```
prudie> ping merlin
PING merlin: 64 data bytes
64 bytes from 142.12.130.12: icmp_seq=0  time=20.0  ms
64 bytes from 142.12.130.12: icmp_seq=1  time=10.1  ms
64 bytes from 142.12.130.12: icmp_seq=2  time=10.3  ms
64 bytes from 142.12.130.12: icmp_seq=3  time=20.2  ms
64 bytes from 142.12.130.12: icmp_seq=4  time=10.1  ms
64 bytes from 142.12.130.12: icmp_seq=5  time=10.2  ms
64 bytes from 142.12.130.12: icmp_seq=6  time=10.1  ms
--- merlin PING Statistics ---
7 packets transmitted, 7 packets received, 0% packet loss
round-trip (ms) min/avg/max = 10/12/20
```

If ping was unable to reach the remote machine, it will display error messages. You can also ping the localhost, which will show if there is an error in the loopback driver configuration files.

The ping program is useful because it provides four important pieces of information: whether the TCP/IP software is functioning correctly, whether a local network device can be addressed (validating its address), whether a remote machine can be accessed (again validating the address and testing the routing), and verifying the software on the remote machine.

SLIP Connections

SLIP connections are configured in much the same manner as the TCP/IP connections described earlier. SLIP is one method of using a modem (or other serial port device) to communicate instead of a network card. SLIP is especially useful for connecting to the Internet through service providers such as UUNET Technologies or NetCom.

For SLIP connections, two Linux programs are involved: dip and slattach. Both programs are used to initiate the SLIP connection. One of the two must be used to initiate the connection. You cannot dial into a SLIP line with a standard communications program because of the special system calls SLIP uses.

dip and slattach have different purposes. The slattach program, which simply connects to the serial device, is used when there is a permanent connection to the SLIP server (no modem or setup handshaking is required). The dip program handles the initiation of the connection, the login, and connection handshaking. If you use a modem to connect to a SLIP server, you should use dip. The dip program can also be used to configure your own system as a SLIP server, allowing others to call in to it.

SLIP is a fairly simple network protocol because only two devices are involved: yours and the server's. When the connection is established, SLIP sends an IP address that will be used for that connection. Some systems use the same IP address (static), while others will have a different IP address each time a connection is made (dynamic). The configuration is slightly different for each type.

Static IP Addresses

A static connection requires that the IP addresses be included in the same files as for an Ethernet network connection. Your machine's IP address should be in the files /etc/hosts, host.conf, and resolv.conf. The gateway address should be the IP address of the SLIP server. The SLIP device files used are sl0, sl1, sl2, and so on.

The only difference in configuration between Ethernet and SLIP is that you only want to execute the ifconfig and route programs for the loopback driver with SLIP. If you use dip to establish the SLIP connection, it will probably take care of this for you, although some problems are occasionally encountered. In these cases, manual changes to the file should be made to allow ifconfig and route to be executed manually from the shell, or from inside a shell script.

The ifconfig routine might need to be modified with the argument pointopoint. SLIP is a variation of Point-to-Point Protocol (PPP). The line would look like this:

```
ifconfig sl0 147.123.12.2 pointopoint 121.12.234.2
```

The first IP address (147.123.12.2) is your machine's IP address, and the numbers following the argument (121.12.234.2) are the IP address of the SLIP server.

Dynamic IP Addresses

If the SLIP server you are connecting to allocates IP addresses dynamically, you can't put an IP address in the configuration files, because it will change each time. Most SLIP servers display a message with the IP address when you connect, and dip can capture these numbers and use them to alter the system parameters appropriately.

dip

The dip program greatly simplifies the connection to a SLIP server. To use it, you need a *chat script* that contains all the commands used to establish communications with the SLIP server during login. The chat script usually includes your login and password too, automating the login process.

A sample dip chat script is included in the man pages for dip, so you should display the man page and read the contents, then save the file (by redirection or copying the man page source) and edit the script. Here's a sample chat script that you can enter by hand if necessary, making sure you put in your own data:

```
# Connection script for SLIP
# Fetch the IP address of our target host.
main:
  # Set the desired serial port and speed.
  port /dev/cua0
  speed 38400
  # Reset the modem and terminal line.
  reset
  # Prepare for dialing.
  send ATZ1\r
  wait OK 4
  if $errlvl != 0 goto error
  dial 666-0999                     ## Change to your server's number!
  if $errlvl != 0 goto error
  wait CONNECT 60
  if $errlvl != 0 goto error
  # We are connected.  Log in to the system.
 login:
  sleep 3
```

```
      send \r\n\r\n
      wait merlin> 20                    ## Change to your server's prompt
      if $errlvl != 0 goto error
      send login\n
      wait name: 10                      ## Wait username: prompt
      if $errlvl != 0 goto erro
      send login_name\n                     ## Change to your own
      wait ord: 10                          ## Wait password prompt
      if $errlvl != 0 goto error
      send my_password\n                    ## Change to your own!
      wait merlin> 10
      if $errlvl != 0 goto error
      send slip\n                           ## Change to suit your server
      wait SLIP 30                          ### Wait for SLIP prompt
      if $errlvl != 0 goto error
      get $local remote 10                  ## Assumes the server sends your IP..
      if $errlvl != 0 goto error            ## address as soon as you enter slip.
      get $remote merlin                    ## slip server address from /etc/hosts
done:
   print CONNECTED to $remote with address $rmtip we are $local
   default
   mode SLIP
   goto exit
error:
   print SLIP to $host failed.
exit:
# End dip script
```

Several different variations of the chat scripts are currently available, including a few on most CD-ROM distributions. If you have access to the Internet, you can find them on some FTP sites or posted on a Linux newsgroup.

Setting Up PPP

PPP is a more talented and faster protocol than SLIP and is preferable for most uses. The configuration, however, is a little more complex than SLIP's. Linux divides the PPP functions into two parts: one for the High-Level Data Link Control (HLDC) protocol which helps define the rules for sending PPP datagrams to between the two machines, and one for the PPP daemon, called pppd, which handles the protocol once the HLDC system has established communications parameters. In addition, Linux includes a program called chat that can be used to call a remote system, although there are several other applications that make use of PPP for the same reason. One popular communications package for this purpose is Kermit.

As with SLIP, PPP establishes a modem link between the two machines, and then hands over the control of the line to PPP. As the user, you never get to see a shell prompt or login, as PPP handles it all for you. Both HLDC and pppd are complex utilities with many options available to fine-tune their behavior. Because you will never use most of these options, we can safely ignore all but the most important aspects necessary to get a PPP connection up and running properly.

Prior to establishing a PPP link, you must have a loopback driver established. You should also have a name resolution system in operation, even if it's the /etc/hosts file or a simple DNS cache-only name server.

Setting Up a PPP Account

It is best to use PPP with a special user account called PPP for optimum protection and behavior. This is not necessary, and you can easily use PPP from any user account, but for more secure operation, you should consider creating a ppp user. The process is simple. First, you need to add a new user to the /etc/passwd file. You can use whatever script your system normally uses to add new users, or edit the /etc/passwd file yourself.

A sample /etc/passwd entry for the ppp account (with UID set to 201 and GID set to 51) looks like this:

```
ppp:*:201:51:PPP account:/tmp:/etc/ppp/pppscript
```

In this case, the account is set with no password (so that no one can log into the account) and a home directory of /tmp (because no files are created). The startup program is set to /etc/ppp/pppscript, a file you create with the configuration information in it (you can use any filename, of course). A sample contents for the pppscript file looks like this:

```
#!/bin/sh
mesg n
stty -echo
exec pppd -detach silent modem crtscts
```

The first line forces execution of the script into the Bourne shell. The second command turns off all attempts to write to the ppp account's tty. The stty command is necessary to stop everything the remote sends being echoed again. Finally, the exec command runs the pppd daemon (which handles all PPP traffic). You will see the pppd daemon and the options later in this section.

Dialing Out: *chat*

PPP requires you to establish a modem connection to the remote machine before it can take over and handle the communications. Several utilities are available to do this, the most commonly used of which is chat. The chat program is popular because it uses a scripting style similar to that used by UUCP (see Chapter 43, "UUCP").

To use chat, you have to assemble a command line that looks almost the same as a UUCP /etc/Systems file entry. For example, to call a remote machine with a Hayes-compatible modem (using the AT command set) at the number 555-1234, you use the following command, which is all formatted as a "chat script," UUCP style:

```
chat "" ATZ OK ATDT5551234 CONNECT "" ogin: ppp word: secret1
```

If you read the UUCP chapter, this may look familiar. If not, all the entries are in a "send-expect" format, with what you send to the remote specified after what you receive from it. The chat script always starts with an expect string, which we must set to be empty because the modem won't talk to us without any signal to it. After the empty string, we send the ATZ (reset) command, wait for an "OK" back from the modem, and then send the dial command. Once a CONNECT message is received back from the modem, the login script for the remote machine is executed: we send a blank character, wait for the ogin: (login) prompt, send the login name ppp, wait for word: (password) prompt, and then send our password. After the login is complete, chat terminates but leaves the line open.

If you want to see all the activity that goes on with the chat program, you can force all messages to the syslog daemon for future study. The -v option forces the messages to syslog, so the command would be:

```
chat -v "" ATZ OK ATDT5551234 CONNECT "" ogin: ppp word: secret1
```

If the other end of the connection doesn't answer with a login script as soon as their modem answers, you may have to force a BREAK command down the line to jog the remote end. This is done in the same way as with UUCP:

```
chat -v "" ATZ OK ATDT5551234 CONNECT "" ogin:-BREAK-ogin: ppp word: secret1
```

There's a security problem with this type of chat entry, as any user doing a ps -ef command will see the entire command line (with its passwords). If you are the only user of your system, this isn't a concern, but to save yourself any problems you can embed the script portion of the command in a file and read the file into chat. The script will not appear on a ps output, then. To call a file for use with chat, use the -f option:

```
chat -f chat_file
```

The chat_file will contain the string:

```
"" ATZ OK ATDT5551234 CONNECT "" ogin: ppp word: secret1
```

The chat script can help you detect common error conditions such as a line busy or no connection established. The messages from your modem (Hayes uses BUSY and NO CARRIER) are embedded in the chat script with the ABORT option, which allows you to exit gracefully from the chat script if one of these error conditions occurs.

To handle these abort conditions, you embed the chat keyword ABORT, followed by the message that should trigger an abort, prior to your normal chat script. For example, to modify the chat script above to abort on a BUSY or NO CARRIER message from the modem, the script would look like this:

```
ABORT BUSY ABORT 'NO CARRIER' "" ATZ OK ATDT5551234 CONNECT "" ogin: ppp word:
secret1
```

We needed two ABORT commands, as each takes only one argument. The rest of the chat script is as usual. Note the need to put quotation marks around the NO CARRIER message as the space in the middle would confuse the script otherwise.

Running *pppd*

To set up a PPP connection, you need to invoke the pppd daemon. If you have a PPP connection already established and your machine is logged into a remote using the ppp account, you can start the pppd daemon. If we assume your local machine is using the device /dev/cua1 for its PPP connection at 38,400 baud, you would start up the pppd daemon with this command:

```
pppd /dev/cua1 38400 crtscts defaultroute
```

This command tells the Linux kernel to switch the interface on /dev/cua1 to PPP, and to establish an IP link to the remote machine. The crtscts option, which is usually used on any PPP connection about 9,600 baud, switches on hardware handshaking. The IP address the local system will use is taken from the local hostname unless one is specified on the pppd command line (which you will seldom need to do, as the local host IP address should be correct for the PPP line).

Other than the machine's default values, you can add the addresses with an option to pppd. The general format is to specify the local IP address, a colon, and then the remote IP address. For example, the option

```
147.23.43.1:36.23.1.34
```

when added to the pppd command line sets the local IP address as 147.23.43.1 and the remote IP address to 36.23.1.34, regardless of that the local values are. If you only want to modify one IP address, leave the other portion blank. The command

```
147.23.43.1:
```

sets the local IP address and accepts the remote IP address as whatever the machine sends.

Because you need chat to establish the connection in the first place, you can embed the chat command as part of the pppd command. This is best done when reading the contents of the chat script from a file (using the -f option). For example, you could issue the following pppd command:

```
pppd connect "chat -f chat_file" /dev/cua1 38400 -detach crtscts modem defaultroute
```

You will notice a few modifications to the pppd command other than the addition of the chat command in quotation marks. The connect command specifies the dialup script that pppd should start with, while the -detach command tells pppd not to detach from the console and move to background. The modem keyword tells pppd to monitor the modem port (in case the line drops prematurely) and hang up the line when the call is finished.

The pppd daemon begins setting up the connection parameters with the remote by exchanging IP addresses, then setting communications values. Once that is done, pppd sets the network layer on your Linux kernel to use the PPP link by setting the interface to /dev/ppp0 (if it's the first PPP link active on the machine). Finally, pppd establishes a kernel routing table entry to point to the machine on the other end of the PPP link.

If you want to change the default behavior of the pppd daemon, you can do it through command line options or a control file. The file is a better approach if you want to change the parameters for every connection established using PPP.

Before completing the command line, pppd scans a number of possible options files. The more common file is /etc/ppp/options, which usually is used to set global defaults. An example of a /etc/ppp/options file looks like this:

```
# /etc/ppp/options: global definitions
domain merlin.com
auth  # force authentication
usehostname  # use local hostname for authentication
lock   # use file locking UUCP-style
```

The domain is established with the domain keyname followed by the full domain name (minus the machine name). The next two lines above (auth and usehostname) deal with authentication of the PPP line, preventing unwanted usage and access. We will look at authentication later in this section. The lock keyword tells pppd to use UUCP-style file locking to prevent device clashes. Locking should be used on all PPP systems to prevent problems.

Checking Problems

The pppd daemon echoes all warnings and error messages to the syslog facility. If you used the -v option with the chat script, chat's messages are also sent to syslog. If you are having trouble with your PPP connections, you can check the syslog for details and try to isolate the problem.

Unless there is an entry in the /etc/syslog.conf file that redirects incoming error and warning messages to another file, the messages are discarded by syslog. To save the messages from pppd and chat, add this line to the /etc/syslog.conf file:

```
daemon.*   /tmp/ppp-log
```

This entry tells syslog to save any incoming messages from a daemon to the /tmp/ppp-log file. You can use any filename you want instead of /tmp/ppp-log. Many Linux versions of the syslog.conf file insist on tabs to separate the columns instead of spaces. Once your script is working, remember to remove this line or the log file will grow quite large!

If you really want to watch what is going on with pppd, you can invoke a debugging option with the kdebug command followed by a number. There are three values for debugging, which are:

1	general debug messages
2	display incoming HLDC data
4	display outgoing HLDC data

The numbers are added together to give the debug level you want. For example, the command `kdebug 5` will display all general debug messages and all outgoing HLDC data. A value of 7 displays everything (this display gets very long!). You can send the output to a file or the console.

PPP Authentication

PPP is a wonderful protocol for modem-based communications, but it has one major problem: it has security holes large enough to drive a bus through. If even slightly incorrectly configured, anyone can use the PPP line to get into your machine, or use the PPP line to get out to other systems. To help prevent this, authentication is often used. Authentication essentially makes sure that each end of the connection is who they say they are and are allowed to use the link. Authentication can also be used with SLIP, but not many systems support it.

There are two authentication schemes used by PPP: the Password Authentication Protocol (PAP) and the Challenge Handshake Authentication Protocol (CHAP). PAP is much like a login procedure. When one machine sends the login name and password to the other, the receiving machine verifies the information with a database on its end. While simple, PAP has the problem that anyone can tap into the line and monitor the passwords being sent.

CHAP solves this problem, and hence is the most favored form of authentication for PPP links. CHAP allows one machine to send a random string to the other, along with its hostname. The other end uses the hostname to look up the proper reply, combine it with the first string, encrypt it, then resend it to the first machine along with its hostname. The first machine performs the same sort of manipulation on the random string it first sent, and if the two replies match, the authentication is complete. CHAP doesn't authenticate only a start time, but at random intervals throughout the connection, which adds to its power.

When two machines connect they don't use authentication unless explicitly instructed to do so (see the `auth` entry in the `/etc/ppp/options` file, discussed earlier). When authentication is active, one end will try to use CHAP first, then, if that fails because the other end doesn't support CHAP, it will use PAP. If neither authentication scheme is supported by the other end, the connection is terminated. If you are going to use authentication for all your PPP connections, put the `auth` entry in the `/etc/ppp/options` file. If not all your connections support authentication, then those connections will fail if `auth` is specified.

The information needed for both CHAP and PPP are kept in two files called `/etc/ppp/chap-secrets` and `/etc/ppp/ppp-secrets` respectively. When authentication is active, one end will check the other for these files, trying CHAP first. If you are going to use authentication for all your connections (which is a very good idea), you can build up the `chap-secrets` and pap-secrets files. If you configure both chap-secrets and pap-secrets and specify the auth option in /etc/ppp/options, no unauthenticated host can connect to your machine.

The /etc/ppp/chap-secrets file consists of four columns for the client name, the server name, the secret password string, and an optional list of IP addresses. The behavior of the system is different depending on whether the local machine is being challenged to authenticate itself, or is issuing a challenge to the remote. When the local machine has to authenticate itself, pppd examines the /etc/ppp/chap-secrets file for an entry in the client field that matches the local host name and the server field equal to the remote hostname, then uses the string to build the authentication message. Such as entry in the /etc/ppp/chap-secrets file looks like this:

```
#   client    server      string  addresses
merlin.tpci.com big_guy.big_net.com   "I hate DOS"
```

This entry will use the string "I hate DOS" to build an authentication message back to big_guy.big_net.com. The quotations are necessary to surround the string in the file. (We will look at the addresses column in a moment.) If you are setting up your system to connect to three different PPP remotes, you will want an entry for each server, so your file may look like this:

```
#   client    server      string  addresses
merlin.tpci.com big_guy.big_net.com "I hate DOS"
merlin.tpci.com chatton.cats.com  "Meow, Meow, Meow"
merlin.tpci.com roy.sailing.ca    "Hoist the spinnaker"
```

When your machine is sending the challenge, the process is reversed. The pppd daemon looks for the remote hostname in the client field, the local hostname in the server field, and uses the string to compare the encryption results with the string sent back by the remote. Entries in the /etc/ppp/chap-secrets file for this purpose look like this:

```
#   client    server      string  addresses
big_guy.big_net.com     merlin.tpci.com   "Size isn't everything"
```

Again, you will have an entry for each remote machine you may need to authenticate. You can see that you will end up having mirror image entries for the client and server fields for each machine you connect to (as either end may require authentication at any time). A simple /etc/ppp/chap-secrets file really looks like this:

```
#   client    server      string  addresses
merlin.tpci.com big_guy.big_net.com   "I hate DOS"
big_guy.big_net.com merlin.tpci.com   "Size isn't everything"
merlin.tpci.com chatton.cats.com    "Meow, Meow, Meow"
chatton.cats.com    merlin.tpci.com   "Here, Kitty, Kitty"
merlin.tpci.com roy.sailing.ca      "Hoist the spinnaker"
roy.sailing.ca      merlin.tpci.com   "Man overboard"
```

The size of the file could get quite large, so CHAP allows you to use a wildcard match, usually only for your local machine. For example, in the /etc/ppp/chap-secrets file below:

```
#   client    server      string  addresses
merlin.tpci.com big_guy.big_net.com   "I hate DOS"
big_guy.big_net.com merlin.tpci.com   "Size isn't everything"
```

```
merlin.tpci.com chatton.cats.com     "Meow, Meow, Meow"
chatton.cats.com    merlin.tpci.com   "Here, Kitty, Kitty"
merlin.tpci.com roy.sailing.ca      "Hoist the spinnaker"
*          merlin.tpci.com    "Man overboard"
```

The last entry allows any other machine connecting to the local host and requiring authentication to use the same string. Of course, the remote must have the same string in its chap-secrets file. This is a little less secure that a dedicated string for each remote, but can be a handy time-saver when using a number of machines only rarely.

The addresses field, which wasn't used in the samples above, lets you list either symbolic names or IP addresses for the clients. This is necessary if the remote wants to use another IP address than its normal one, which would cause the authentication to fail normally. If the addresses field is empty (as they all are in the samples), any IP address is allowed. A hyphen in the field disallows all IP addresses with that client.

The /etc/ppp/pap-secrets file is much the same as the chap-secrets file. The fields in the pap-secrets file are the client (called a user in the pap-secrets format) and server names, a secret string, and valid address aliases. However, the look of the file is different because the client and server names are not full domain names and the secret string is a single block of text. A sample pap-secrets file looks like this:

```
# /etc/ppp/pap-secrets
#   user   server    string  addresses
merlin  darkstar   yG55Sj29 darkstar.big_net.com
darkstar  merlin    5Srg7S merlin.tpci.com
merlin  chatton    MeowMeow chatton.cats.com
chatton  merlin    73wrh6s merlin.tpci.com
```

In this example, the first two lines show a connection to the machine darkstar. The first line is how we authenticate a request from darkstar, and the second how we authenticate a request from us to them. The user name in the first column is the name we send to the remote, while the server field is their identification to us. This poses a problem: The pppd daemon has no way of knowing the remote hosts name, as all it gets is an IP address. You can put the IP address in the addresses column of the file, or you can specify the remote host name at the end of the pppd command line like this:

```
pppd ..... remotename chatton user merlin
```

This shows that the remote is called chatton, and our local host is merlin. The last portion giving the local host name override the default values, if specified.

Summary

In this chapter, you've seen how to install, configure, and test Ethernet connections to your Linux machine. You've also seen how to set up a SLIP or PPP connection. The only other networking process usually found on a Linux box uses UUCP (UNIX-to-UNIX Copy), which is described in Chapter 43, "UUCP."

If you want to install a network to connect several of your machines (assuming you have more than one), you will find it quite easy and useful. If you have two machines, it is fast and efficient to connect a Linux machine and a DOS machine, as long as the DOS machine is running TCP/IP. There are shareware versions of TCP/IP for Windows and many commercial implementations for both DOS and Windows, and TCP/IP is built into both Windows 95 and Windows NT.

UUCP

43

by Tim Parker

UUCP (UNIX to UNIX CoPy) was developed to provide a simple dial-up networking protocol for UNIX systems. It is most often used today as an e-mail transfer system, allowing non-networked machines to transfer e-mail easily over a modem connection. It can also be used for Usenet news and access to similar services that do not require a dedicated connection. UUCP is a two-machine connection, between your Linux machine and another machine running UUCP. UUCP cannot be used as a remote system access system (like FTP or Telnet), nor can it be used as a standard login because the protocols do not support this type of interactive behavior. UUCP does have security features that are adequate for most purposes, but UUCP is the primary source of break-ins for many systems because most system administrators don't bother to set the security system up properly.

Linux can run any of several different versions of UUCP, most of which are compatible with each other to a reasonable extent, except when it comes to configuration and installation procedures. Many Linux versions offer you a choice between the Taylor UUCP version (included on the Red Hat distribution accompanying this book) and the HDB (HoneyDanBer) UUCP. You can use whichever single version came with your Linux software, or if you have both, you can choose between the two (or use both versions as the mood strikes you). Many Linux users prefer the Taylor UUCP implementation, while users who have worked on other UNIX systems prefer HDB because it is more recent. We'll look at both versions in this chapter. (There are even more UUCP versions, but we will ignore them because they are seldom used under Linux.) The first part of the chapter deals with configuring UUCP, while the rest covers using it.

UUCP Configuration

Most of the configuration required for UUCP takes place under the /usr/lib/uucp directory. There are several files used by UUCP, most of which need direct administrator modification to set up properly. While the configuration process can seem awfully complex to someone who has never done it before, there are really only a few files that need changing, and only one or two entries in each file.

The configuration process for Taylor UUCP and HDB UUCP are completely different, so we will look at them separately. However, you don't have to worry which version of UUCP is being run at the remote end of the connection because both can talk to each other (at least that's usually the case), as long as the configuration files are set up properly.

Some versions of Linux have semiautomated UUCP configuration scripts. These are more common with HDB UUCP than Taylor UUCP, but a few helpful scripts are also available for the latter. If you have one of these scripts, by all means use it, but do check the files manually afterwards.

For the configuration processes discussed in the following section, we will assume that our host machine's name is merlin, and we want to connect via UUCP to another Linux system called arthur. As you go through the process, take care to enter the information in the same format as the examples, but don't mix Taylor and HDB UUCP information.

Taylor UUCP Configuration

We can begin with a quick look at the configuration files involved in the Taylor UUCP system. These are the filenames and their primary purposes:

- `/usr/lib/uucp/config`—Defines the local machine name.
- `/usr/lib/uucp/sys`—Defines the remote systems and how to call them.
- `/usr/lib/uucp/port`—Describes each port for calling out and its parameters.
- `/usr/lib/uucp/dial`—Describes the dialers for calling out.
- `/usr/lib/uucp/dialcode`—Used to contain expansions for symbolic dialcodes, but is rarely used when a straight-out telephone connection exists.
- `/usr/lib/uucp/call`—Can contain the login name and password for remote systems, but it is rarely used now.
- `/usr/lib/uucp/passwd`—Contains the login names and passwords used when remote systems connect to your local machine. Used only when `uucico` is password checking instead of using the login process.

To make the configuration process easier, we will ignore all the theory and background information and proceed with a sample configuration. You need only modify the entries to suit your own names, telephone numbers, device files, and so on, and the configuration process will be the same. It can then be repeated for as many systems as you want to connect to.

The first file to modify holds your system name and other general parameters. The file `/usr/lib/uucp/config` needs a single line entry for your system name such as this one:

```
nodename    merlin
```

The keyword `nodename` must be first on the line followed by whitespace (spaces or tabs), then your machine name. The information in this file may have been completed when you installed Linux, but you should manually check the contents to make sure. If your system's name isn't set correctly, the connection to the remote system won't work properly.

> **NOTE**
>
> To use UUCP, you must have a system name. For compatibility with most versions of UUCP, keep the name to seven characters or less. Ideally, the UUCP name is the same name you assigned to your host during configuration. The name doesn't have to follow a convention (such as the system name used by TCP/IP for Internet access), but if you use other network protocols, keep a consistent name. If you have a domain name (for TCP/IP access) use the first component of the machine's full TCP/IP name as the UUCP name. For example, if your full domain name is `merlin.wizards.com`, use the UUCP name `merlin`.

You also need information about the remote system you want to connect to. The /usr/lib/uucp/ sys file holds all the information about remote systems. This file usually has a few sample entries in it, which you can copy or modify. Make sure you don't leave comment marks (pound or hash marks) in the first column or the entries will be ignored. A /usr/lib/uucp/sys entry for the remote machine merlin looks like this:

```
# system: arthur (Bill Smallwood's Linux system)
system    arthur
time      Any
phone     555-1212
port      com1
speed     9600
chat      login: merlin password: secret1
```

The first line in the preceding extract is a comment line. Most system administrators like to put a comment line in to identify each system. The next lines identify the different aspects of the remote system, including its name (arthur), times at which it can be called (Any in this case, meaning no restrictions), the telephone number (including any area code or special digits that have to be dialed), the serial port to be used for the connection (in this case, com1), the speed at which to connect (9600 baud), and the chat script or login process. In this case, the chat script tells UUCP to wait until it sees the string login: then to send merlin, then wait for the prompt password: and then to send secret1.

Most login scripts will require a login and password, and they must be placed in the configuration file because UUCP doesn't allow interactive sessions. This can be a bit of a problem because it allows other users on your system to see the login password for the remote machine, but since it can only be used by UUCP, this is not a major concern. Also, the file permissions on the UUCP configuration files can be set to prevent any system users (other than root) from looking into the file.

NOTE

Not all remote sites need a password for entry through UUCP. For example, some public archives let you log in and retrieve files using the uucp login with no password. Some sites use readily available passwords, such as uucp.

The port name used in the /usr/lib/uucp/sys entry does not have to match a device name on the Linux system, because another file is used to match the entry to a physical device. This file is /usr/ lib/uucp/port, and it requires an entry similar to this for a 9600 baud modem:

```
# com1 device port
port      com1
type      modem
device    /dev/cua0
speed     9600
dialer    Hayes
```

In the /usr/lib/uucp/port file, the name of the port used in the /usr/lib/uucp/sys file is identified on the first line. The type of connection to be used (usually modem) is on the next. The actual Linux device that corresponds to the port name is specified as a device driver (for many Linux systems this can be /dev/modem, which is linked to the serial port device driver).

The modem connection speed comes next, and shows the maximum speed the modem can be used at. Finally, the name of a dialer is entered. This is a throwback to the days when modems couldn't dial themselves, but used another device (called a dialer) to make the connection.

The dialer entry in the /usr/lib/uucp/port file is then matched to an entry in the file /usr/lib/uucp/dial, which tells the modem how to dial the phone. Here's a simple entry:

```
# Hayes modem
dialer      Hayes
chat        "" ATZ OK ATDT\T CONNECT
```

This shows the script that the system uses to communicate to the Hayes modem. In this case, the \T in the command line is replaced with the telephone number to be called. Some Linux systems simplify the use of the /usr/lib/uucp/port and /usr/lib/uucp/dial files into one single entry in the /usr/lib/uucp/sys file, which names the modem file directly.

The remote end of the connection (in this case, the system arthur) must have corresponding entries for merlin. The files will be similar with only name, telephone number, and (possibly) device name and chat script changes. Until both ends are configured properly, you can't get a connection between the two machines.

Some Linux systems with Taylor UUCP have a utility called uuchck that verifies the syntax in the UUCP configuration files and prints out summary information. If you don't have the uuchck utility, it can be downloaded from many FTP and BBS sites. Check Appendix A for some of the possible sites.

By default, Taylor UUCP allows a remote system to execute only a limited number of commands when they log into your system. Typically, the remote is only allowed to execute rmail and rnews, to transfer mail and news, respectively. If you want to allow extra programs to be executed, add a line to the /usr/lib/uucp/sys file that includes all the commands the remote system can execute. For example, the entry:

```
system      chatton
....
commands        rmail rnews rsmtp rdataupdate
```

specifies that the system chatton can execute any of the four commands given after the commands keyword. Note that all four commands must be in the usual search path used by the UUCP utilities (actually by uuxqt).

If you intend to transfer files between two machines, you must also modify the configuration files. When a remote system sends a file to your machine, the files usually should be stored in the directory /usr/spool/uucppublic (some systems use /var/spool/uucppublic) as a safety precaution. You don't want to allow a remote system to write files anywhere on your file system, or they could overwrite critical system files. The convention for most UUCP systems is to use either /usr/spool/uucppublic or /usr/spool/uucp/*system* (where *system* is the remote system's name) as the transfer directories.

You can specify transfer and receive directories in the `/usr/lib/uucp/sys` file. For example, the following entry for the remote system `chatton` has been modified to include specific directories for file transfers:

```
system      chatton
...
local-send    ~/send
local-receive    ~/receive
```

In this configuration, the users on your local machine can send any file that is in the `send` directory under the uucp directory (`~/send`, which means that any file to be sent to a remote system must be transferred there first), and any file incoming from a remote system is stored in the `receive` directory under the uucp directory. If you want to allow transfers from a user's home directory, you can specify the `/usr` directory as a starting point. Multiple entries are separated by spaces, so the entry

```
local-send     ~/send /usr
```

allows transfers from the `send` directory under the uucp directory, or from any directory under `/usr`.

The preceding two lines deal only with file transfers requested or sent from your machine. If you want to enable requests for transfers from the remote machine, you need to add two more lines:

```
remote-send     /usr/lib/uucppublic
remote-request    /usr/lib/uucppublic
```

This forces the remote machine to request files and send them only to the `/usr/lib/uucppublic` directory. Again, you can offer several choices if you want, as long as they are separated by spaces.

Finally, UUCP allows machines to forward data through other machines, a process called *hopping*. In other words, if you want to send mail to the system `warlock` but can only get there through the system `wizard`, you have to instruct UUCP that your local system can get to `warlock` through `wizard`. You add a forward command to the `/usr/lib/uucp/sys` file:

```
system      wizard
...
forward      warlock
```

You should then add an entry for the `warlock` system that tells UUCP that any mail for you will be coming back through `wizard`. The matching entry would be:

```
system      warlock
...
forward-to      merlin
```

The `forward-to` entry is necessary so that any files returned by `warlock` are passed to `merlin`, the local host machine. Otherwise, they would be discarded by UUCP as not being routable.

By default, Taylor UUCP does not allow forwarding, and most system administrators should think carefully about allowing it because the potential for abuse is high.

HDB UUCP Configuration

HDB UUCP is a more recent version of UUCP and its configuration files are different. In many ways, the HDB configuration is easier than Taylor UUCP's, although neither is difficult once you know the basic process.

The name of the local system is not set in the UUCP configuration files but by the Linux hostname itself. To set the system name use the hostname command.

The names of the remote systems are stored in the file /usr/lib/uucp/Systems (some older versions used the name /usr/lib/uucp/L.sys). There is a single line for each remote system that you will be connected to. The format of each line is as follows:

```
sitename   schedule   device_type   speed   phone   login_script
```

where *sitename* is the name of the remote machine, *schedule* is when it can be connected to, *device_type* is the type of device to use to call the remote system, *speed* is the speed (or range of speeds) that can be used to connect, *phone* is the telephone number, and *login_script* is the script used when a connection is made (such as the chat script in Taylor UUCP). For example, to call the remote system arthur, the /usr/lib/uucp/Systems file would have a line like this:

```
arthur Any ACU 9600 555-1212 login: uucp password: secret1
```

The Any entry in the schedule field tells UUCP that it can call at any time. The ACU entry in the device field tells UUCP to use the ACU (automatic calling unit) defined in the /usr/lib/uucp/Devices file.

The /usr/lib/uucp/Devices file (or /usr/lib/uucp/L-devices file in some older versions) contains information about the devices that can be used to call the remote systems. The Devices file follows this syntax:

```
devicetype   ttyline   dialerline   speed   dialer   [token Dialer ...]
```

where *devicetype* is the name of the device (which should match the device name in the /usr/lib/uucp/Systems file), *ttyline* is the device driver to be used for the connecting port (usually a serial line, such as /dev/tty2a or /dev/modem), *dialerline* is an obsolete field left as a hyphen, *speed* is the speed range of the device, and *dialer* is the name of the file that tells UUCP how to use the device. A sample line for a Hayes 9600 baud modem used to connect on the second serial port of the system might have an entry in the /usr/lib/uucp/Devices file like this:

```
ACU tty2A - 9600 dialHA96
```

This identifies the ACU entry as a 9600 baud connection through /dev/tty2A (the /dev portion of the name is not needed with HDB UUCP), and it uses a program called dialHA96 to handle the setup and dialing of the modem. There are usually programs available for most popular modems that set the modem configuration parameters automatically, leaving Linux out of that process.

If a modem program is not available to handle the modem, an entry in the file /usr/lib/uucp/ Dialers can be used. The format of the Dialers entries is:

```
dialer translation  expect  send  ...
```

where *dialer* is the name of the dialer (matching the Devices file), *translation* is the translation table to use for the phone number (converting characters where needed to pauses, beeps, and so on), and the *expect*/*send* entries are the chat script to set up the modem. A sample line in the Dialers file looks like this:

```
hayes1200 =,-,    "" AT\r\c OK\r \EATDT\T\r\c CONNECT
```

This is the entry for a Hayes 1200 Smartmodem, identified by the name hayes1200, with translations for the = and - characters, followed by the AT commands used to set up the modem. Since these entries are usually supplied in the Dialers file for most popular modems, we won't bother going into detail about them.

Permissions for file transfers are a little more convoluted with HDB UUCP than Taylor UUCP, because HDB UUCP adds many features for special handling. Instead of looking at all the file transfer permissions, you are better advised to consult a specialty book on UUCP, because the subject can easily consume 100 pages by itself! For this reason, we'll look at the fundamentals—just enough to get you set up properly.

Permissions for remote system access and file transfers are handled by the file /usr/lib/uucp/ Permissions. The general format of the entries in this file is:

```
MACHINE=remotename LOGNAME=uucp \
    COMMANDS=rmail:rnews:uucp \
    READ=/usr/spool/uucppublic:/usr/tmp \
    WRITE=/usr/spool/uucppublic:/usr/tmp \
    SENDFILES=yes REQUEST=no
```

where MACHINE identifies the remote machine's name, LOGNAME is the name they use to log in (or you use to log in to their system), COMMANDS are the commands they can execute on your local system, READ is the list of directories they can read files from, WRITE is the list of directories where they can write files, SENDFILES means they can send files (yes or no), and REQUEST means they can request files from your system (yes or no). Notice the use of slashes at the end of the first four lines, to indicate this is really a single long line broken up for readability. This is a typical UNIX convention.

A complete entry for the remote system wizard shows that it is allowed to both send and receive files, but only from the /usr/spool/uucppublic directory, and it can only execute mail and uucp commands (the later transfers files):

```
MACHINE=wizard LOGNAME=uucp1 \
    COMMANDS=rmail: uucp \
    READ=/usr/spool/uucppublic: \
    WRITE=/usr/spool/uucppublic: \
    SENDFILES=yes REQUEST=yes
```

To prevent the remote system from sending files, change SENDFILES to no. To prevent the remote system from requesting files, change REQUEST to no.

A UUCP Connection

When UUCP connects to a remote machine, it follows a particular series of steps. You can better understand the configuration files used by UUCP, and the processes that are involved, by following through a typical session. UUCP uses a process called uucico (UUCP Call In/Call Out) to handle the process of connecting and sending information. A UUCP connection can be started with the uucico command followed by the remote system name, such as:

```
uucico -s arthur
```

When uucico starts, it examines the /usr/lib/uucp/sys file (Taylor UUCP) or /usr/lib/uucp/ Systems (HDB UUCP) to see if the remote system name exists there. When it finds the proper remote system name, uucico reads the rest of the entries for that system, including the port to be used. From there, uucico uses /usr/lib/uucp/port and /usr/lib/uucp/dial (Taylor UUCP) or /usr/lib/uucp/Devices and /usr/lib/uucp/Dialers (HDB UUCP) to start the modem connection (assuming it is a modem used to establish the session, of course). When the modem is in use, uucico creates a lock on the device so no other application can use it (the lock is a file starting with LCK.. and followed by the device name, such as LCK..cua0).

Once the chat scripts for setting up and dialing the modem have been executed and the remote system is connected, uucico uses the chat script in the /usr/lib/uucp/sys or /usr/lib/uucp/Systems file to log into the remote. Once logged in, the remote machine starts up its copy of uucico, and the two uucico processes establish handshaking between themselves. Finally, after the handshaking has been established, uucico goes ahead and handles any transfers that are queued.

When completed with the session, the local machine checks to make sure that the remote has nothing further to send and then breaks the connection. Finally, uucico terminates.

Direct Connections

If your two machines are directly connected through a serial port, for example (no modems involved in the connection), you can use UUCP as a simple network protocol for file transfer. The only changes to the configuration files mentioned earlier are in the port specification. Instead of using a modem device, you specify a direct connection. For example, in the /usr/lib/uucp/sys file (Taylor UUCP), you would have an entry like this:

```
port      direct1
```

with a matching entry in the /usr/lib/uucp/port file that looks like this:

```
port      direct1
type      direct
speed     38400
device    /dev/cua1
```

with the speed of the direct connection and the port which uses it specified. The entries in the HDB UUCP version are similar, using the /usr/lib/uucp/Systems and /usr/lib/uucp/Devices files.

Login Scripts

The login scripts that form part of the /usr/lib/uucp/sys or /usr/lib/uucp/Systems file can be the most difficult part of a UUCP connection to get correct. If the machine you are logging into is a typical UNIX system, there should be only the usual login and password prompts to worry about. Other systems may require some special handling to gain access. For this reason, the login script is worth a quick look.

Generally, the layout of the login script is in a pattern-action pair, with the pattern coming from the remote machine and the action from the local. A simple login is:

```
login: merlin password: secret1
```

In this case, the local system waits until it sees the string login: coming from the remote, sends merlin, waits for password:, then sends secret1. You can simplify the script a little by cutting out extra letters from the remote, because all you really need are the last couple of characters and the colon. The script could have been written like this:

```
gin: merlin word: secret1
```

This type of script has a good use. Suppose the remote system sends Login: instead of login:; then the shortened form will work and the longer match won't.

One useful feature of the uucico login script is the ability to wait for the remote machine to reset itself (or start a getty process, more likely). This is implemented by using a hyphen and the word BREAK in the script, which tells uucico to send a break sequence if the remote site hasn't responded in a timely manner. For example, the script would be similar to this:

```
ogin:-BREAK-ogin: merlin sword: secret1
```

In this case, if the remote machine doesn't respond with an ogin: prompt after a short period of time, the local machine sends a break sequence and waits for the prompt again.

A few special characters can be used in the login script. The most important ones for most UUCP purposes are the following:

\c	Suppresses sending carriage return (send only)
\d	Delays one second (send only)
\p	Pauses for a fraction of a second (send only)
\t	Sends a tab (send and receive)
\r	Sends a carriage return (send and receive)
\s	Sends a space (send and receive)
\n	Sends a newline (send and receive)
\\	Sends a backslash (send and receive)

Sometimes you need to use one or more of the characters to get the remote machine to respond to a modem login. For example, the following script

```
\n\r\p ogin: merlin word: secret1
```

sends a carriage return-line feed pair before starting to match characters. This is usually enough to get the remote machine to start a `getty` on the port.

Changing Access Times

Both Taylor and HDB UUCP versions let you specify a time to call the remote systems. While the examples so far show `Any` (meaning the system can be called at any time, day or night), you may want to restrict calls to local-cost times, or on certain days of the week. The reason for limiting calls may be at your end (costs, for example), or at the remote (limited access times during the day, for example).

To specify particular days of the week to allow calls, use a two-digit abbreviation of the day (`Mo`, `Tu`, `We`, `Th`, `Fr`, `Sa`, `Su`), or `Wk` for weekdays (Monday through Friday), `Any` (for any time), or `Never` (for not allowed to connect). Any combination of the days may be used, as you will see in a moment. The times for connecting are specified as a range, in 24-hour format, when a time span is required. If no time is given, it is assumed that any time during the day is allowed.

Dates and times are run together without spaces, while subsequent entries are separated by commas. Examples of restricted access times are as follows:

```
Wk1800-0730
MoWeFi
Wk2300-2400, SaSu
```

The first example allows connection only on weekdays between 6 p.m. and 7:30 a.m. The second allows connection any time on Monday, Wednesday, or Friday. The last example allows connections only between 11 p.m. and midnight on weekdays, and any time on weekends. You can build up any time and date specifications you want. These apply to both Taylor and HDB UUCP versions.

UUCP Security

The permissions of the UUCP configuration files must be carefully set to allow UUCP to function properly, as well as to allow better security for the system. Simply stated, the files should all be owned by uucp, and the group should be uucp on most systems that have that group in the `/etc/group` file. The ownerships can be set either by making all the file changes while logged in as uucp, or by setting the changes as root and then issuing the following commands when you are in the `/usr/lib/uucp` directory:

```
chown uucp *
chgrp uucp *
```

As a security precaution, you should set a strong password for the uucp login if there is one on your system. Some versions of Linux do not supply a password by default, leaving the system wide open for anyone who can type uucp at the login prompt!

The file permissions should be set very tightly, preferably to read-write (and execute for directories) only for the owner (uucp). The group and other permissions should be blanked because a read access can give valuable login information, as well as passwords to someone.

When UUCP logs into a remote system it requires a password and login. This information is contained in the /usr/lib/uucp/sys or /usr/lib/uucp/Systems files, and should be protected to prevent unauthorized snooping by setting file ownerships and permissions as mentioned.

If you have several systems connecting into yours, they can all use the same uucp login and password, or you can assign new logins and passwords as you need them. All you need to do is create a new /etc/passwd entry for each login (with a different login name from uucp, such as uucp1, uucp_arthur, and so forth) and a unique passwd. The remote system can then use that login to access your system. When you create new UUCP users in the /etc/passwd, force them to use uucico only to prevent access to other areas of your system. For example, the login uucp1, shown here, forces uucico as the startup command:

```
uucp1::123:52:UUCP Login for Arthur:/usr/spool/uucppublic:/usr/lib/uucp/uucico
```

The home directory is set to the uucppublic directory, and uucico is the only startup program that can be run. Using different logins for remote machines also allows you to grant different access permissions for each system, preventing unwanted access.

You should also carefully control the commands that remote systems can execute on your local machine. This is done through the permissions fields of the local access file and should be monitored carefully to prevent abuse and unauthorized access. In a similar manner, if you are allowing forwarding of files through your system, you should control who is allowed to forward, and where they are forwarded to.

Most important of all is to ensure that whoever accesses your system on a regular basis is someone you want access to be granted to. Don't leave your system wide open for anyone to enter because you are guaranteeing yourself disaster. Carefully watch logins and make sure file permissions and ownerships are properly set at all times.

Using UUCP

Once you have configured UUCP, you can use it to transfer files and e-mail. In order to use UUCP, you have to know the addressing syntax, which is different than what you may know from the Internet. The UUCP address syntax is:

machine!*target*

where *machine* is the remote machine name and *target* is the name of the user or file that you are trying to get to. For example, to send mail to the user yvonne on machine arthur, you would use the mail command with the destination user name:

```
mail arthur!yvonne
```

UUCP lets you move through several machines to get to a target. This can help save on telephone bills, or make a much wider network available to you from a small number of connections. Suppose you want to send mail to a user called `bill` on a system called `warlock`, which isn't in your configuration files but can be connected to through `arthur`. If you have permission to send mail through the system `arthur` (called a "hop"), you could send the mail with this command:

```
mail arthur!warlock!bill
```

When UUCP decodes this address, it reads the first system name (`arthur`) and sends it to that system. The UUCP processes on `arthur` then examines the rest of the address and realizes the mail is to be sent on to `warlock`. If you have permission to forward through `arthur`, UUCP on `arthur` sends the mail through to `warlock` for you. You can have many hops in an address, as long as each system you are connecting to allows the pass-through and can connect to the next machine on the list. For example, the address:

```
arthur!warlock!chatton!vader!alex
```

would send data through `arthur`, `warlock`, `chatton`, and `vader` in order, and then to the user `alex`. The addresses must be specified in the proper hop order or the address will fail. This multihop addressing can be very useful if a number of friends have local connections to other machines, allowing you to easily set up a complex network. The hard part is usually tracking the names of the systems involved. (The exclamation mark in the address is called a *bang*, so the address above is spoken as "arthur-bang-warlock-bang-chatton-bang-vader-bang-alex.")

> **NOTE**
>
> Some shells don't like the bang character because they are interpreted as a special shell command. Shells, such as the C Shell, use the exclamation mark to recall previous commands, so you must escape the bang with a slash to prevent the shell's interpretation. Addresses then become `arthur\!chatton\!yvonne`. This looks funny, but you get used to it.

Depending on how you have your UUCP system set, it may call out to the other systems in an address whenever something is submitted to it, or if callout times are limited, the data may be spooled until a call is allowed. You have already seen how to set callout times in the `/usr/lib/uucp/sys` and `/usr/lib/uucp/Systems` files.

A quick caution about relying on UUCP for delivery of information: If the systems that are being used are not set to call immediately when there is something queued, your data can take a long time to get to its destination. For example, if one of the hops in your address calls the next machine in the address only once a day, you may have a 24-hour delay in delivery. This can be exacerbated by each machine in the network.

> **CAUTION**
>
> Don't rely on the contents of your data sent through UUCP to be kept confidential. Once on a remote system, any user with access privileges to the queue could snoop into your data. Ideally, the file permission prevents anyone but the superuser accessing the data, but not all systems keep tight security. If you must send sensitive data, encrypt it and let the recipient know the decryption key through another format (not in a mail message!).

UUCP deals with all transfers as *jobs*, a term you'll encounter often when working with UUCP and its documentation. A job is a command that is to be executed on the remote system, a file that is to be transferred to or from the remote, or any other task that you want performed between the two systems.

Sending E-Mail with UUCP

Most utilities like mail packages understand the UUCP addresses, so that you don't have to worry about e-mail not reaching the proper destination. You don't usually have to make any changes at all to applications running under Linux to get them to understand this UUCP address format. In the last section you saw how the mail package can be used with UUCP addresses.

You can use any of the usual `mail` command options to modify the behavior of the package. For example, to send the contents of the file `data_1` to yvonne on system `chatton` through the system `arthur`, and tag the mail with a subject heading, you would issue the command:

```
mail -s "Data file" arthur\!chatton\!yvonne < data_1
```

Most mail packages available for Linux, including X-based mailers, work perfectly well with UUCP addresses, as well as the more common Internet addresses, but you may want to check before adopting a new mail package.

Transferring Files with UUCP

UUCP's most common use is to transfer files from one machine to another. To transfer files using UUCP, you use the uucp command. The syntax of the uucp command is:

```
uucp [options] source destination
```

The options supported by UUCP vary a little depending on the version and type of UUCP implementation, but most versions support the following useful options:

-c	Do not copy the file to a spool directory before sending. The default action is to copy to a spool directory, and using the -c option explicitly specifies it.

-f   Don't create directories on the remote system, if needed. The default action is to create directories as needed and can be explicitly specified with the -d option.

-m   Sends mail to the person who issued the uucp command when the copy is complete.

-n   user   Sends mail to the user on the remote system when the copy is complete.

The default behaviors are usually sufficient for most users, although you may want the mail options when you need confirmation of an action.

Both source and destination are the names of files or directories as appropriate, much like the cp command. However, when you are dealing with a remote system for the source or destination, you need to format the file or directory in valid UUCP address formats. For example, to send the file data_1 from your local machine's current directory to the directory /usr/spool/uucppublic on the machine arthur, you would use the command:

```
uucp data_1 arthur\!/usr/spool/uucppublic
```

Notice that the remote machine name was prepended to the full target directory name. In most cases, when transferring files to remote systems you will want to use the uucppublic directories as you likely will not have permission to transfer files anywhere else in the file system. Once on the remote system in the /usr/spool/uucppublic directory, it is up to the remote system's users to find the file and copy it to its intended destination directory.

If you want to send the same file to the user bill on the remote machine, and store it in a subdirectory called /usr/spool/uucppublic/bill and send mail to both yourself and bill when the copy is completed, you would issue the command:

```
uucp -m -nbill data_1 arthur\!/usr/spool/uucppublic/bill/
```

To copy a file from a remote machine to yours, you need to specify the location of the remote. Remember, you must have access to the directory that the files reside in (as well as read permission on the file), or have the sender copy them to uucppublic. The command

```
uucp chatton\!/usr/tmp/bigfile /usr/tparker/
```

would transfer the bigfile file from the directory /usr/tmp on the machine chatton to your /usr/tparker directory.

UUCP allows wildcards to be used, although you must escape them in quotation marks to prevent the shell from interpreting them. For example, to copy all the files starting with chap on the remote machine warlock's /usr/bill/book directory (assuming you have permission) to your own /usr/bigbook directory, you would issue the command

```
uucp "warlock!/usr/bill/book/chap*" /usr/bigbook/
```

You can also specify hops in the machine transfers by adding the extra machine names to the command. This requires permissions to be set on all the machines that the hop will pass through, and is seldom done. Although you probably don't want to do this either, you could transfer files from one remote system to another by specifying their names on the command line like this:

```
uucp arthur\!/usr/lib/uucppublic/bigfile warlock\!/usr/lib/uucppublic/
```

This sends the file from the arthur system to the warlock system. In most cases, the users on either of the two remote systems would issue the commands, relieving some of the file permission problems.

Checking on Transfers

You can check on the status of transfers that are scheduled but haven't taken place yet using the uustat command. When you issue the uustat command, all the UUCP transfers that are queued are listed. The format of the list is:

```
jobID system user date command size
```

where *jobID* is the ID of the UUCP job, *system* is the name of the system to transfer to (the first system in an address when multiple hops are taking place), *user* is the user name who queued the job, *date* is when the job was queued, *command* is the exact command to be executed, and *size* is the size of the transfer in bytes.

If you issue the command as a user (not superuser), only your jobs are listed. The superuser lists all jobs that are queued. If you are logged in as a regular user and want to see all jobs, use the -a option:

```
uustat -a
```

To cancel a queued job, use the -k option of the uustat command along with the job ID. For example, to cancel job 17, issue the command:

```
uustat -k 17
```

You can only cancel your own jobs, unless you are logged in as superuser, in which case you can cancel any jobs.

Summary

UUCP is quite easy to set up, as long as you follow the rules. Once the configuration files are properly set, UUCP offers an easy way to transfer e-mail, news, and files to other systems. UUCP is also one of the easiest methods to establish a low-volume network because all you need is a modem or a direct connection. Using UUCP to transfer mail and files is as easy as using the usual mail and cp commands.

Although UUCP is less popular nowadays because of the LAN craze, it does provide a simple, very low-cost network for those who need to connect only a couple of machines. It's also great for connecting your machine to those of your friends, allowing e-mail back and forth, and really making your Linux system feel like a well-connected workstation.

Installing Mail and News

44

by Tim Parker

If you have access to other machines through a local area network or through the Internet, you will probably want to install the mail and news software. Both offer a lot of interaction with other users and add a whole new dimension to your Linux system.

To handle electronic mail, most systems rely on *UUCP* (UNIX-to-UNIX Copy). Setting up UUCP is covered in many different online guides and documents, as well as in most UNIX books. You can exchange e-mail with other users, or with the world at large, by connecting to an Internet service provider such as UUNET Technologies.

Reading Usenet newsgroups is a little more complicated, because you have to download the news yourself (100MB per day!) or connect to a site that offers news—a *news server*. Linux includes the software to connect you, although most users will find it easier to use an online service such as CompuServe or Delphi for news access.

In this chapter we look at the following:

- The types of mail software you can use
- Simple UUCP-based configuration of e-mail systems
- Setting your machine to access Usenet newsgroups

Mail

If you installed Linux from a CD-ROM (such as the Red Hat distribution included with this book), one of the installation options was to install the e-mail systems. Some Linux distributions give you a choice of mail packages, whereas others default to one particular type.

During the installation, most Linux setup procedures will install the software properly except for some configuration information about the network. With this kind of installation, there is little you have to do with the mail system except add your host name and configure UUCP (if you are using it to connect to other systems to transfer Mail).

Mail software for most UNIX systems (including Linux) has two components: a transport and a mailer. The *transport* is the low-level software that takes care of delivering the mail, both locally and across other machines. Users never work with the transport, although system administrators must configure it and understand the basic principles. The *mailer* is the user interface that presents mail to the user and accepts new mail. Many mailers are available.

Mail Transport Agents

Transport agents are the underlying software that connects your local machine to remote systems. Several transport agents are available with Linux, but the most commonly used are called *smail* (for send mail) and *sendmail.* You can find sendmail on the CD that accompanies this book.

The smail and sendmail programs are ideally suited for sites that rely on UUCP for mail (either between other machines or to an Internet service provider), and they can be used with some *SMTP* (Simple Mail Transfer Protocol) sites. smail and sendmail are usually provided as an executable binary form with most Linux distributions, although only one of the transport agents is usually supplied.

The configuration changes needed to set up smail or sendmail on your Linux system depend on the type of connection you have to the outside world.

smail

If you are running a UUCP-based mail system and you use a remote system for all processing to other sites (usually used with local area networks that employ a communications server), the changes to your system configuration files are minimal.

The changes occur in the files /usr/local/lib/smail/config and /usr/local/lib/smail/paths. Look for the lines that have to do with hostname and subdomain names and perform the following changes:

- Replace subdomain.domain with your machine's domain name.
- Replace myhostname with your "undomainized" hostname.
- Replace my_uucp_neighbor with the UUCP name of your upstream site.

For example, the following extract shows the settings for a machine called vader that attached to the machine deathstar in the domain starwars.com, first for the file /usr/local/lib/smail/config:

```
#/usr/local/lib/smail/config
# domains we belong to
visible_domain=deathstar.starwars:uucp
# who we're known as (fully-qualified-site-name)
visible_name=vader.starwars
# who we go through
smart_path=deathstar
```

The changes for /usr/local/lib/smail/paths are the machine name only:

```
#/usr/local/lib/smail/paths
# we're a domainized site, make sure we accept mail to both names
vader          %s
vader.starwars.com      %s
```

If you want to run the smail program as an SMTP daemon, you must add the following line to the file /etc/inetd.conf (or whatever the equivalent file is called in your distribution):

```
smtp stream tcp nowait  root  /usr/bin/smtpd smtpd
```

When this is added, any outgoing mail gets sent automatically when using a mailer like elm.

sendmail

The sendmail program is quite popular with small Linux installations. It is included with the Red Hat distribution of Linux.

To configure sendmail, change to the /etc directory and edit the sendmail.cf file. This file has enough information to help you determine which lines to replace with your system values. Usually you will edit the hostname, aliases, and smarthost settings.

Local Delivery Agents

Unlike most UNIX versions, Linux does not have a mail-delivery package built in. Mail-delivery packages send the received mail to the proper user. One of the most widely used is called deliver.

In most cases, you don't have to do anything to install and configure deliver. When you installed the mail software using the Linux installation routine, the necessary software was installed and configured properly.

Mail User Agents

Mail user agents are the mailreaders you use to see your e-mail. Many newsreaders are available. Your choice of mailreaders is more a personal preference than a feature-based decision.

elm is probably the most widely used mailreader with Linux. It uses the configuration file /usr/lib/elm.rc to provide basic information about the machine name and its connections. You should edit the elm.rc file to replace the names with proper values.

Another popular mailreader is mailx, which has been available for UNIX systems for many years. Versions of mailx are available for Linux on many archive sites. Make sure you get version 5.3b or higher because there are security problems in version 5.3a.

Other interesting and popular mailreaders are pine and metamail, both of which are freely available from Linux archive sites and user groups.

News

Usenet is a service provided over the Internet. It's composed of more than 14,000 newsgroups on every subject imaginable. If you want to set your system to download the entire day's news, you must dedicate a lot of money to hardware and telephone lines. Such a connection is beyond the scope of most users.

However, accessing newsgroups from another machine that downloads them is quite easy, using software provided with Linux.

There are two parts to the News software: the server and the client. The *server* is the software that controls the newsgroups and handles delivering articles to other machines. The *client* or newsreader software is the user interface.

You do not have to hook up to the Internet to use News. You can run News locally (on your own machine for all the users) or across a small network. In this case, you don't have to worry about connecting to the Internet's Usenet newsfeed, which generally is expensive and very time-consuming.

News Transport Software

News transport software, as its name implies, carries the news to your system and its newsreaders and helps your users post news to Usenet. Two main news transport software packages are used with Linux: Cnews and INN. The two should not be mixed. Use one or the other, or major hassles will result!

If you plan to use News locally only, much of the configuration required for connecting to the Internet or other newsfeed can be ignored. News normally is stored in the directory /usr/spool/news, so all the news transport and client software should be set to point to this location.

The most popular news transport software is Cnews, which has been available for almost a decade. Cnews runs on many different machines, and many people understand it very well, providing technical resources should you need them. Cnews is designed primarily for capturing news over a UUCP connection and a standard telephone modem, so it requires additional software to provide access to the Internet. This additional software is called *NNTP* (Network News Transfer Protocol). NNTP isn't necessary for local news support.

Installing Cnews is straightforward, as long as you follow the directions in the accompanying documentation files. Configuration involves editing several files, which usually reside in /usr/ lib/news. The files of primary interest are as follows:

- active: The active file
- batchparms: Batch parameters
- explist: Article expiration
- mailname: Header names for mailed replies
- mailpaths: Path to mail moderated postings
- organization: Your company name
- sys: Controls what you take and feed
- whoami: Your hostname

Most of Cnews is configured with shell scripts or utility programs (such as addgroup to change the active file and addfeed to change newsfeed information). Again, check the documentation for complete information.

To download news automatically, cron makes an excellent choice. A sample cron entry for the Cnews newsfeed is

```
20 * * * * /usenet/sw/news/bin/input/newsrun
0 * * * * /usenet/sw/news/bin/batch/sendbatches feedsite
59 0 * * * /usenet/sw/news/bin/expire/doexpire
10 5 * * * /usenet/sw/news/bin/newsdaily
00 5 * * * /usenet/sw/new/bin/newswatch
```

This sample does things every hour, which is fine for a large site but considerable overkill for a small network or single machine where you might want to connect only once a day. Modify the files as necessary to meet your requirement.

InterNetNews (*INN*)

INN is newer than Cnews but is faster and has NNTP built in, making it easier to use for direct newsfeeds. Unfortunately, it is a little harder to install and configure than Cnews. INN uses a daemon (sometimes two) that runs continually, whereas Cnews is invoked by the user (or cron). Novices to Linux should probably stick with Cnews at the beginning until they gain more experience.

Installation is a little more complex than with Cnews, but following the documentation helps. INN is very particular about its file permissions, so make sure you set them properly. Configuration is a matter of making sure all of the site information is correct. Once correctly installed and configured, though, INN requires virtually no maintenance.

Newsreaders

Many newsreaders are available for Linux. A newsreader presents the messages in a newsgroup and lets you step through them or reply to them, as well as create new messages. Some of the most popular newsreaders are tin, trn, and rtin.

Choosing a newsreader is essentially a personal choice. Experiment with several and stay with the one you find easiest to work with and that offers the features you need. They all have some slight twist that gives you different methods of looking at news or moving through newsgroups.

Summary

Both e-mail and news extend the Linux system to be a full-featured UNIX implementation, and make your machine part of a much larger network. Even if you are using your Linux machine only for yourself and have no interest in connecting to the outside world, e-mail is simple and easy to install, configure, and use. Once you've used e-mail, you'll probably never go back to the paper-based kind!

If you have several users on your Linux system or plan to connect to a network, News is a great way to get discussions and information flowing amongst the users. On top of that, News is just plain fun!

Network Security

45

by Tim Parker

IN THIS CHAPTER

Covering everything about security would take several volumes of books, so we can only look at the basics. We can take a quick look at the primary defenses you need in order to protect yourself from unauthorized access through telephone lines (modems), as well as some aspects of network connections. We won't bother with complex solutions that are difficult to implement because they can require a considerable amount of knowledge and they apply only to specific configurations.

Instead, we can look at the basic methods of buttoning up your Linux system, most of which are downright simple and effective. Many system administrators either don't know what is necessary to protect a system from unauthorized access, or they have discounted the chances of a break-in happening to them. It happens with alarming frequency, so take the industry's advice: Don't take chances. Protect your system.

In this chapter, we look at the following topics:

- File permissions
- Protecting modem access
- UUCP's holes
- Tracking an intruder
- What to do if you get broken into

Weak Passwords

Believe it or not, the most common access method of breaking into a system through a network, over a modem connection, or sitting in front of a terminal is through weak passwords. Weak (which means easily guessable) passwords are very common. When these are used by system users, even the best security systems can't protect against intrusion.

If you're managing a system that has several users, you should implement a policy requiring users to set their passwords at regular intervals (usually six to eight weeks is a good idea), and to use non-English words. The best passwords are combinations of letters and numbers that are not in the dictionary.

Sometimes, though, having a policy against weak passwords isn't enough. You might want to consider forcing stronger password usage by using public domain or commercial software that checks potential passwords for susceptibility. These packages are often available in source code, so they can be compiled for Linux without a problem.

File Security

Security begins at the file permission level and should be carried out carefully. Whether you want to protect a file from snooping by an unauthorized invader or another user, you should carefully set your umask (file creation mask) to set your files for maximum security.

Of course, this is really only important if you have more than one user on the system or have to consider hiding information from certain users. However, if you are on a system with several users, consider forcing umask settings for everyone and set read-and-write permissions only for the user, and no permissions for everyone else. This is as good as you can get with file security.

For very sensitive files (such as accounting or employee information), consider encrypting them with a simple utility. There are many such programs available. Most require only a password to trigger the encryption or decryption.

Modem Access

For most Linux users, protecting your system from access through an Internet gateway isn't important because few users have an Internet access machine directly connected to their Linux boxes. Instead, the concern should be about protecting yourself from break-in through the most accessible method open to system invaders: modems.

Modems are the most commonly used interface into every Linux system (unless you're running completely stand-alone, or on a closed network). Modems are used for remote user access, as well as for network and Internet access. Securing your system's modem lines from intrusion is simple and effective enough to stop casual browsers.

Callback Modems

The safest technique to prevent unauthorized access through modems is to employ a callback modem. A callback modem lets a user connect to the system as usual; it then hangs up and consults a list of valid users and their telephone numbers before calling the user back to establish the call. Callback modems are quite expensive, so this is not a practical solution for many systems.

Callback modems have some problems, too, especially if users change locations frequently. Also, callback modems are vulnerable to abuse because of call-forwarding features of modern telephone switches.

Modem-Line Problems

The typical telephone modem can be a source of problems if it doesn't hang up the line properly after a user session has finished. Most often, this is a problem with the wiring of the modem or the configuration setup.

Wiring problems might sound trivial, but there are many systems with hand-wired modem cables that don't properly control all the pins. In this case, the system can be left with a modem session not properly closed and a logout not completed. Anyone calling that modem continues where the last user ended.

To prevent this kind of problem, make sure the cables connecting the modem to the Linux machine are complete. Replace hand-wired cables that you are unsure of with properly constructed commercial ones. Also, watch the modem when a few sessions are completed to make sure the line hangs up properly.

Configuration problems can also prevent line hangups. Check the modem documentation to make sure your Linux script can hang up the telephone line when the connection is broken. This is seldom a problem with the most commonly used modems, but off-brand modems that do not have true compatibility with a supported modem can cause problems. Again, watch the modem after a call to make sure it is hanging up properly.

One way to prevent break-ins is to remove the modem from the circuit when it's not needed. Because access through modems by unwanted intruders is usually attempted after normal business hours, you can control the serial ports that the modems are connected to by using cron to change the status of the ports or disable the ports completely after-hours.

For most systems this is not practical, but for many businesses it is a simple-enough solution. If late-night access is required, one or two modem lines out of a pool can be kept active. Some larger systems keep a dedicated number for the after-hours modem line, usually different from the normal modem line numbers.

How a Modem Handles a Call

In order for a user to gain access to Linux through a modem line, the system uses the getty process. The getty process itself is spawned by the init process for each serial line. The getty program is responsible for getting user names, setting communications parameters (baud rate and terminal mode, for example), and controlling time-outs. With Linux, the serial and multiport board ports are controlled by the /etc/ttys file.

Some Linux systems enable a dialup password system to be implemented. This forces a user calling on a modem to enter a second password that validates access through the modem. If it is supported on your system, dialup passwords are usually set in a file called /etc/dialups.

The Linux system uses the file /etc/dialups to supply a list of ports that offer dialup passwords, while a second file (such as /etc/d_passwd) has the passwords for the modem lines. Access is determined by the type of shell utilized by the user. The same procedure can be applied to UUCP access.

UUCP

The UUCP program was designed with good security in mind. However, it was designed many years ago, and security requirements have changed considerably since then. A number of security problems have been found over the years with UUCP, many of which have been addressed with changes and patches to the system. Still, UUCP requires some system administration attention to ensure that it is working properly and securely.

If you don't plan to use UUCP, remove the uucp user entirely from the /etc/password file or provide a strong password that can't be guessed (putting an asterisk as the first character of the password field in /etc/passwd effectively disables the login). Removing uucp from the /etc/passwd file won't affect anything else on the Linux system.

You should set permissions to be as restrictive as possible in all UUCP directories (usually /usr/lib/uucp, /usr/spool/uucp, and /usr/spool/uucppublic). Permissions for these directories tend to be lax with most systems, so use chown, chmod, and chgrp to restrict access only to the uucp login. The group and user name for all files should be set to uucp. Check the file permissions regularly.

UUCP uses several files to control who is allowed in. These files (/usr/lib/uucp/Systems and /usr/lib/uucp/Permissions, for example) should be owned and accessible only by the uucp login. This prevents modification by an intruder with another login name.

The /usr/spool/uucppublic directory can be a common target for break-ins because it requires read and write access by all systems accessing it. To safeguard this directory, create two subdirectories: one for receiving files and another for sending files. Further subdirectories can be created for each system that is on the valid user list, if you want to go that far.

Local Area Network Access

Most LANs are not thought of as a security problem, but they tend to be one of the easiest methods of getting into a system. However, if any of the machines on the network has a weak access point, all of the machines on the network can be accessed through that machine's network services. PCs and Macintoshes usually have little security, especially over call-in modems, so they can be used in a similar manner to access the network services. A basic rule about LANs is that it's impossible to have a secure machine on the same network as nonsecure machines. Therefore, any solution for one machine must be implemented for all machines on the network.

The ideal LAN security system forces proper authentication of any connection, including the machine name and the user name. A few software problems contribute to authentication difficulties. The concept of a *trusted host*, which is implemented in Linux, enables a machine to connect without hassle, assuming its name is in a file on the host (Linux) machine. A password isn't even required in most cases! All an intruder has to do is determine the name of a trusted host and then connect with that name. Carefully check the /etc/hosts.equiv, /etc/hosts, and .rhosts files for entries that might cause problems.

One network authentication solution that is now widely used is *Kerberos*, a method originally developed at MIT. Kerberos uses a "very secure" host, which acts as an authentication server. Using encryption in the messages between machines to prevent intruders from examining headers, Kerberos authenticates all messages over the network.

Because of the nature of most networks, most Linux systems are vulnerable to a knowledgeable intruder. There are literally hundreds of known problems with utilities in the TCP/IP family. A good first step to securing a system is to disable the TCP/IP services you don't use at all because other people can use them to access your system.

Tracking Intruders

Many intruders are curious about your system but don't want to do any damage. They might get on your system with some regularity, snoop around, play a few games, and leave without changing anything. This makes it hard to know that you are being broken into, and it leaves you at the intruder's mercy should he decide he wants to cause damage or use your system to springboard to another.

You can track users of your system quite easily by invoking *auditing*, a process that logs every time a user connects and disconnects from your system. Not all Linux versions support auditing, so consult your man pages and system documentation for more information.

If you do rely on auditing, you should scan the logs often. It might be worthwhile to write a quick summary script program that totals the amount of time each user is on the system so that you can watch for anomalies and numbers that don't mesh with your personal knowledge of the user's connect times. A simple shell script to analyze the log can be written in gawk. In addition, some audit reporting systems are available in the public domain.

Preparing for the Worst

Assuming someone does break in, what can you do? Obviously, backups of the system are helpful because they let you recover any damaged or deleted files. But beyond that, what should you do?

First, find out how the invader got in, and secure that method of access so it can't be used again. If you're not sure of the access method, close down all modems and terminals and carefully check all the configuration and setup files for holes. There has to be one, or the invader couldn't have gotten in. Also check passwords and user lists for weak or outdated material.

If you are the victim of repeated attacks, consider enabling an audit system to keep track of how intruders get in and what they do. As soon as you see an intruder log in, force him off.

Finally, if the break-ins continue, call the local authorities. Breaking into computer systems (whether in a large corporation or a home) is illegal in most countries, and the authorities usually know how to trace the users back to their calling points. They're breaking into your system and shouldn't get away with it!

Summary

Following the simple steps outlined in this chapter will give you enough security to protect your systems against all but the most determined and knowledgeable crackers. You can't do any harm with the steps mentioned, so you may as well perform them for all Linux systems that have modems or network connections.

PART

VII

Setting Up an Internet Site

Setting Up an Internet Site

46

by Tim Parker

Linux is well suited for connecting to the Internet and for using many of the Internet services. This chapter looks at the ways you can connect to the Internet. The following chapters in this section show you how to set up your Linux system as a server for four popular services.

If you only want to use your Linux system to access other servers, you don't have to worry about any of the material in the next four chapters (although you might want to read this chapter to find out how to connect to the Net). On the other hand, sharing your system's resources with others, whether in a local area network, a small circle of friends, or the worldwide Internet community, can be most of the fun.

If you intend to use your Linux system to offer some of the Internet services (such as FTP, WWW, or Gopher) but you don't want to let everyone gain access (maybe just a few friends), you might not need to worry about connecting to the Internet. You still have to set up the server software, though.

Connecting to the Internet

There are many different ways to connect to the Internet. Your choice of method depends primarily on your usage habits and the services you want access to. It may seem as though an overwhelming number of companies offer Internet access or services. Luckily, there are really only four ways to connect to the Internet.

Briefly, your options for connecting to the Internet are as follows:

- A direct connection to the Internet—This method uses a dedicated machine (a gateway) to connect into the Internet backbone. This method gives you full access to all services but is expensive to set up and maintain.

- Connecting through someone else's gateway—This usually involves getting permission to use someone else's machine for full access to all Internet services.

- Using a direct service provider—Uses a specialty company's gateway that your machine can access to offer limited or full access to Internet services. These companies are not the same as online services, because all they do is act as a gateway to the Internet. Usually, this type of service provider uses modem or dedicated telephone connections with high-speed lines to provide fast service.

- Using an indirect service provider—Using an online company (such as Delphi or CompuServe) to access some or all of the Internet's services. This is usually suitable only for low-volume usage, and doesn't take advantage of Linux at all.

If you are part of a company or sharing the costs with a number of friends, online service providers seldom are able to offer the level of performance you need for support of e-mail, FTP, and other Internet services. As a further reason against online services, most do not allow you to have your own domain name.

It is rare to find a gateway that you can "borrow" for access of your own, unless you are willing to share the costs of the gateway. Most companies that have a gateway will be reluctant to allow many outsiders to use their systems.

That leaves only a direct gateway of your own to the Internet or the use of a service provider. The choice between these two options usually comes down to an issue of the costs to connect both ways. Setting up your own gateway is expensive, but may be cheaper than arranging accounts with a service provider if the volume of traffic is high.

If you want access for yourself or for a very small company, it is unreasonable to have your own dedicated gateway. Setting up an account with a service provider is possible for individuals, but sometimes the costs and machine overhead are too high. Service providers are typically used by small companies, but there is no reason why you can't use a service provider if you anticipate a high Internet usage.

Services You Need

When deciding which method you will use to access the Internet, one of the important items to consider is the type of services you want from the Internet. If all you need is e-mail, then any kind of access will provide it, but some may be ridiculously expensive for what you get.

As a starting point, decide which of the following services are necessary and which are less important:

- Electronic mail—Sending mail to and from other Internet users.
- Telnet—Remote logins to other machines on the Internet.
- FTP—File transfers between machines.
- World Wide Web (WWW) access—A popular hypertext-based (and usually graphical) information service.
- Usenet newsgroups—A set of bulletin boards for conversations on many different subjects.
- Gopher—An information search and retrieval system.
- WAIS—A menu-based document search and retrieval system
- Archie—A method for finding files to transfer.
- Internet Relay Chat (IRC)—A conversation system much like CB radio.

Any system that is directly connected to the Internet through a gateway (yours, a borrowed gateway, or most direct service providers) will provide complete access to all the services listed. Some direct service providers support all the services, but at a slower speed than a gateway. Slower speeds may be a limitation for the World Wide Web if you intend to use and offer graphics (instead of just text). Some service providers limit their access to e-mail and newsgroups, so a little research is necessary.

Direct Connection Through a Gateway

A direct connection (often called a dedicated connection) is one in which you attach into the Internet backbone through a dedicated machine called a gateway or IP router. The connection is over a dedicated telephone line capable of high-speed transfers (usually at 1.44 megabits per second or faster). The gateway becomes part of the Internet architecture and must remain online at all times. You can then use any other computer on the gateway's network to access the Internet services.

Typically, dedicated connections mean high volumes of traffic and require systems with an absolute minimum line speed of 9,600 baud, although high-speed fiber-optic lines with speed capabilities of 45Mbps are not unusual. It is very unlikely an individual or small company would have direct gateway access, primarily because of the high cost of installation and maintenance requirements.

To create a direct access system, you must work with the Internet Network Information Center (NIC) to set up the proper gateways on the Internet backbone for your domain. The capital expense of such a system is high, both for the initial hardware and software and for continuing support. High costs may also be involved with a dedicated telephone line capable of supporting high-speed data transfer.

Connecting Through Another Gateway

An alternative method of connecting to the Internet through a gateway relies on using a "friendly" machine or network. In such a system, a corporation or educational institution that has an Internet gateway may allow you to access the Internet through their system. Because this type of access gives you freedom on their networks, many organizations now refuse this type of piggyback access.

If you are lucky enough to find a company or school that will let you use their network, you simply call into a communications port on the network or gateway, then route through the gateway to the Internet. In many ways, it is as though you are a machine on the provider's network. Typically, you have unlimited access to the Internet's services, although some companies do set restrictions.

Using a Service Provider

Service providers are companies that have an Internet gateway that they share, although the gateway is often transparent to the users. This type of connection is often called "dialup" and uses SLIP (serial line interface protocol) or PPP (point-to-point protocol). Some service providers offer UUCP connections for e-mail.

Service providers usually charge a flat fee for membership with an additional charge based on the amount of time or the number of characters transferred. Joining one of these services is quite easy. Domain names can be registered through many service providers, too, allowing you to use your own domain even though you use a provider.

The primary advantage of direct service providers is that effectively you are directly connected to the Internet. All of the interworking with the service provider's gateway is hidden inside your operating system's setup, making it transparent. A disadvantage is that you cannot always arrange full access to the Internet. Some services do not allow you to FTP through their gateway to another Internet site, for example.

If you are considering using a direct service provider, you should ask the providers in your area about the services they offer, whether special hardware or software is needed, what the fees are, and whether they are based on a flat monthly rate or based on usage, and the kind of technical support available in case you have trouble.

An alternative to using a commercial service provider is to rely on one of the command-line access systems that are springing up in major cities. Such systems provide Internet access through their own gateways as a free service (subsidized by a corporation or government) or at a minimal cost. One popular access provider of this type is FreeNet, an international organization that gives users a unique user name through the FreeNet domain. FreeNet is currently only available in some cities, but it does provide an extremely inexpensive and easy access method to the Internet. All you need is an account (which is usually just a telephone call away), a modem, and communications software.

Summary

Choosing the method with which you connect to the Internet is up to you, but most individuals find a direct service provider the best balance between cost and features, as long as you plan to keep your system running most of the time. Once you have a connection to the Internet, you can set up your server, as explained in the next four chapters.

Setting Up an FTP and Anonymous FTP Site

47

by Tim Parker

Snap question: What is the most widely used TCP/IP and Internet service? If you answered FTP, you're right. (If you didn't choose FTP, this may come as a bit of a surprise. The fact is, FTP remains the most widely used service; although the World Wide Web is quickly catching up.) FTP's popularity is easy to figure: The FTP software is supplied with every version of UNIX and Linux, it's easy to install, configure, and use, and it gives users access to a wealth of information with very little effort.

If all you want to use FTP for is connecting to another machine and transferring files, then you don't have to do much more than enable the FTP service on your system. Much more interesting to many users is turning your Linux machine into an FTP site, where others can connect and obtain files you make available. That's the primary focus of this chapter—setting up an FTP site on your Linux machine. We'll begin, though, with a quick look at using FTP and the way FTP runs on TCP. This information should help you understand how FTP works and what it does with TCP/IP.

What Is FTP?

The File Transfer Protocol (FTP) is one protocol in the TCP/IP family used to transfer files between machines running TCP/IP. (FTP-like programs are also available for some other protocols.) The File Transfer Protocol allows you to transfer files back and forth and manage directories. FTP is not designed to allow you access to another machine to execute programs, but it is the best utility for file manipulation. To use FTP, both ends of a connection must be running a program that provides FTP services. The end that starts the connection (the client) calls the other end (the server) and establishes the FTP protocol through a set of handshaking instructions.

Usually, when you connect to a remote system via FTP, you must log in. This means you must be a valid user, with a user name and password for that remote machine. Because it is impossible to provide logins for everyone who wants to access a machine that enables anyone to gain access, many systems use "anonymous FTP" instead. Anonymous FTP enables anyone to log in to the system with the login name of "ftp" or "anonymous" with either no password, or an e-mail address for their local system.

Using FTP

Using FTP to connect to a remote site is easy. You have access to the remote machine either through the Internet (directly or through a service provider) or through a local area network if the remote machine is directly reachable. To use FTP, you start the FTP client software and provide the name of the remote system you want to connect to. For example, assuming you can get to the remote machine through a LAN or the Internet (which knows about the remote machine thanks to Domain Name Service), you issue the following command:

```
ftp chatton.com
```

This will instruct your FTP software to try to connect to the remote machine `chatton.com` and establish an FTP session.

When the connection is completed (and assuming the remote system allows FTP logins), the remote will prompt for a user ID. If anonymous FTP is supported on the system, a message will usually tell you exactly that. The following is for the Linux FTP archive site sunsite.unc.edu:

```
ftp sunsite.unc.edu
331 Guest login ok, send your complete e-mail address as password.
Enter username (default: anonymous): anonymous
Enter password [tparker@tpci.com]:
¦FTP¦ Open
230-      WELCOME to UNC and SUN's anonymous ftp server
230-            University of North Carolina
230-            Office FOR Information Technology
230-              SunSITE.unc.edu
230 Guest login ok, access restrictions apply.
FTP>
```

After the login process is completed, you will see the prompt FTP> indicating the remote system is ready to accept commands.

When you log on to some systems, you may see a short message that contains instructions for downloading files, any restrictions that are placed on you as an anonymous FTP user, or information about the location of useful files. For example, you may see messages like these (taken from the Linux FTP site):

```
To get a binary file, type: BINARY and then: GET "File.Name" newfilename
To get a text file, type:  ASCII and then: GET "File.Name" newfilename
Names MUST match upper, lower case exactly. Use the "quotes" as shown.
To get a directory, type: DIR. To change directory, type: CD "Dir.Name"
To read a short text file, type: GET "File.Name" TT
For more, type HELP or see FAQ in gopher.
To quit, type EXIT or Control-Z.

230- If you email to info@sunsite.unc.edu you will be sent help information
230- about how to use the different services sunsite provides.
230- We use the Wuarchive experimental ftpd. if you "get" <directory>.tar.Z
230- or <file>.Z it will compress and/or tar it on the fly. Using ".gz" instead
230- of ".Z" will use the GNU zip (/pub/gnu/gzip*) instead, a superior
230- compression method.
```

Once you are logged on the remote system, you can use familiar Linux commands to display file contents and move around directories. To display the contents of a directory, for example, use the ls command (some systems support the DOS equivalent dir). To change to a subdirectory, use the cd command. To return to the parent directory (the one above the current directory), use the command cd ... As you can see, these commands are the same as you would use on your local machine, except you are now navigating on the remote system.

There are no keyboard shortcuts (such as pressing the Tab key to fill in names that match) available with FTP. This means you have to type in the name of files or directories in their entirety (and correctly). If you misspell a file or directory name, you will get error messages and have to try again. Luckily, if you are performing the FTP session through X Window, you can cut and paste lines from earlier in your session.

Transferring files is the whole point of FTP, so you need to know how to retrieve a file from the remote system, as well as how to put a new file there. When you have moved through the remote system's directories and have found a file you want to transfer back to your local system, use the get command. This is followed by the filename. For example:

```
get "soundcard_driver"
```

This will transfer the file soundcard_driver from the remote machine to the current directory on your local machine. When you issue a get command, the remote system will transfer data to your local machine and display a status message when it is completed. There is no indication of progress when a large file is being transferred, so be patient. (Most versions of FTP allow you to use the hash option, which displays pound signs every time a kilobyte of information has been transferred. This can be used to show that the transfer is underway, but it doesn't offer a time to completion.)

```
FTP> get "file1.txt"
200 PORT command successful.
150 BINARY data connection for FILE1.TXT (27534 bytes)
226 BINARY Transfer complete.
27534 bytes received in 2.35 seconds (12 Kbytes/s).
```

If you want to transfer a file the other way (from your machine to the remote, assuming you are allowed to write to the remote machine's file system), use the put command in the same way. The command:

```
put "comments"
```

will transfer the file comments from your current directory on the local machine (you can specify full pathnames) to the current directory on the remote machine (unless you change the path).

The commands get (download) and put (upload) are always relative to your home machine. You are telling your system to get a file from the remote and put it on your local machine, or to put a file from your local machine onto the remote machine. (This is the exact opposite of telnet, which has everything relative to the remote machine. It is important to remember which command moves in which direction, or you could overwrite files accidentally.)

The quotation marks around the filenames in the preceding examples are optional for most versions of FTP, but they do prevent shell expansion of characters, so it's best to use them. For most files, the quotation marks are not needed, but using them is a good habit to get into.

Some FTP versions provide a wildcard capability using the commands mget and mput. Both the FTP get and put commands usually transfer only one file at a time, which must be completely specified (no wildcards). The mget and mput commands enable you to use wildcards. For example, to transfer all the files with a .doc extension, you could issue the command:

```
mget *.doc
```

You will have to try the mget and mput commands to see if they work on your FTP version. (Some FTP get and put commands allow wildcards, too, so you can try wildcards in a command line to see if they work, instead.)

FTP allows file transfers in several formats, which are usually system dependent. The majority of systems (including Linux systems) have only two modes: ASCII and binary. Some mainframe installations add support for EBCDIC, while many sites have a local type that is designed for fast transfers between local network machines (the local type may use 32- or 64-bit words).

The difference between the binary and ASCII modes is simple. Text transfers use ASCII characters separated by carriage return and new-line characters. Binary mode allows transfer of characters with no conversion or formatting. Binary mode is faster than text and also allows for the transfer of all ASCII values (necessary for non-text files). FTP cannot transfer file permissions because these are not specified as part of the protocol.

Linux' FTP provides two modes of file transfer: ASCII and Binary. Some systems automatically switch between the two when they recognize a file is binary format, but you shouldn't count on the switching unless you've tested it before and know it works. To be sure, it is a good idea to manually set the mode. By default, most FTP versions start up in ASCII mode, although a few start in Binary.

To set FTP in binary transfer mode (for any executable file or file with special characters embedded for spreadsheets, word processors, graphics, and so on), type the command

```
binary
```

You can toggle back to ASCII mode with the command `ascii`. Since you will most likely be checking remote sites for new binaries or libraries of source code, it is a good idea to use binary mode for most transfers. If you transfer a binary file in ASCII mode, it will not be usable on your system.

ASCII mode includes only the valid ASCII characters and not the 8-bit values stored in binaries. Transferring an ASCII file in Binary mode does not affect the contents except in very rare instances.

To quit FTP, type the command `quit` or `exit`. Both will close your session on the remote machine, and then terminate FTP on your local machine. Users have a number of commands available within most versions of FTP. The following list outlines the ones most frequently used:

ascii	Switches to ASCII transfer mode
binary	Switches to binary transfer mode
cd	Changes directory on the server
close	Terminates the connection
del	Deletes a file on the server
dir	Displays the server directory
get	Fetches a file from the server
hash	Displays a pound character for each block transmitted
help	Displays help
lcd	Changes directory on the client
mget	Fetches several files from the server
mput	Sends several files to the server
open	Connects to a server
put	Sends a file to the server
pwd	Displays the current server directory
quote	Supplies an FTP command directly
quit	Terminates the FTP session

For most versions, FTP commands are case sensitive, and using upper case will display error messages. Some versions perform a translation for you, so it doesn't matter which case you use. Since Linux uses lower case as its primary character set for everything else, you should probably use lower case with all versions of FTP, too.

How FTP Uses TCP

The File Transfer Protocol uses two TCP channels: TCP port 20 is used for data, and port 21 is for commands. Both these channels must be enabled on your Linux system for FTP to function. The use of two channels makes FTP different from most other file transfer programs. By using two channels, TCP allows simultaneous transfer of FTP commands and data. FTP works in the foreground and does not use spoolers or queues.

FTP uses a server daemon that runs continuously and a separate program that is executed on the client. On Linux systems, the server daemon is called ftpd. The client program is ftp.

During the establishment of a connection between a client and server, and whenever a user issues a command to FTP, the two machines transfer a series of commands. These commands are exclusive to FTP and are known as the internal protocol. FTP's internal protocol commands are four-character ASCII sequences terminated by a new-line character, some of which require parameters. One primary advantage of using ASCII characters for commands is that users can observe the command flow and understand it easily. This helps in a debugging process. Also, the ASCII commands can be used directly by a knowledgeable user to communicate with the FTP server component without invoking the client portion (in other words, communicating with ftpd without using ftp on a local machine); this is seldom used except when debugging (or showing off).

After logging into a remote machine using FTP, you are not actually on the remote machine. You are still logically on the client, so all instructions for file transfers and directory movement must be with respect to your local machine and not the remote one. The process followed by FTP when a connection is established is:

1. Login—Verify user ID and password
2. Define directory—Identify the starting directory
3. Define file transfer mode—Define the type of transfer
4. Start data transfer—Allow user commands
5. Stop data transfer—Close the connection

These steps are performed in sequence for each connection.

A debugging option is available from the FTP command line by adding -d to the command. This displays the command channel instructions. Instructions from the client are shown with an arrow as the first character, while instructions from the server have three digits in front of them. A PORT in the command line indicates the address of the data channel on which the client is waiting for the server's reply. If no PORT is specified, channel 20 (the default value) is used. Unfortunately, the progress of data transfers cannot be followed in the debugging mode. A sample session with the debug option enabled is shown here:

```
$ ftp -d tpci_hpws4
Connected to tpci_hpws4.
220 tpci_hpws4 FTP server (Version 1.7.109.2
➥Tue Jul 28 23:32:34 GMT 1992) ready.
Name (tpci_hpws4:tparker):
--> USER tparker
331 Password required for tparker.
Password:
--> PASS qwerty5
230 User tparker logged in.
--> SYST
215 UNIX Type: L8
Remote system type is UNIX.
--> Type I
200 Type set to I.
Using binary mode to transfer files.
ftp> ls
--> PORT 47,80,10,28,4,175
200 PORT command successful.
--> TYPE A
200 Type set to A.
--> LIST
150 Opening ASCII mode data connection for /bin/ls.
total 4
-rw-r---- 1 tparker tpci  2803 Apr 29 10:46 file1
-rw-rw-r-- 1 tparker tpci  1286 Apr 14 10:46 file5_draft
-rwxr---- 2 tparker tpci 15635 Mar 14 23:23 test_comp_1
-rw-r---- 1 tparker tpci    52 Apr 22 12:19 xyzzy
Transfer complete.
--> TYPE I
200 Type set to I.
ftp> <Ctrl-d>
$
```

You may have noticed in the preceding listing how the mode changed from binary to ASCII to send the directory listing, and then back to binary (the system default value).

Configuring FTP

Whether you decide to provide an anonymous FTP site or a user-login FTP system, you need to perform some basic configuration steps to get the FTP daemon active and get the directory system and file permissions properly set to prevent users from destroying or accessing files they shouldn't. The process can start with choosing an FTP site name. You don't really need a site name, although it can be easier for others to access your machine with one (especially anonymously). The FTP site name is of the format:

`ftp.domain_name.domain_type`

where *domain_name* is the domain name (or an alias) of the FTP server's domain, and *domain_type* is the usual DNS extension. For example, you could have an FTP site name of

`ftp.tpci.com`

showing that this is the anonymous FTP access for anyone accessing the tpci.com domain. It is usually a bad idea to name your FTP site with a specific machine name, such as:

```
ftp.merlin.tpci.com
```

because this makes it difficult to move the FTP server to another machine in the future. Instead, use an alias to point to the actual machine on which the FTP server sits. This is not a problem if you are a single machine connected to the Internet through a service provider, for example, but it is often necessary with a larger network. The alias is easy to set up if you use DNS. Set the alias in the DNS databases with a line like this:

```
ftp    IN    CNAME    merlin.tpci.com
```

This line points anyone accessing the machine `ftp.tpci.com` to the real machine `merlin.tpci.com`. If the machine `merlin` has to be taken out of its FTP server role for any reason, a change in the machine name on this line will point the `ftp.tpci.com` access to the new server. (A change in the alias performed over DNS can take a while to become active because the change must be propagated through all the DNS databases.)

Setting Up *ftpd*

The FTP daemon, `ftpd`, must be started on the FTP server. The daemon is usually handled by `inetd` instead of the `rc` startup files, so `ftpd` is only active when someone needs it. This is the best approach for all but the most heavily loaded FTP sites. When started using `inetd`, the `inetd` daemon watches the TCP command port (channel 21) for an arriving data packet requesting a connection, and then spawns `ftpd`.

Make sure the `ftpd` daemon can be started by `inetd` by checking the `inetd` configuration file (usually `/etc/inetd.config` or `/etc/inetd.conf`) for a line that looks like this:

```
ftp    stream    tcp    nowait    root    /usr/etc/ftpd    ftpd -l
```

If the line doesn't exist, add it to the file. With most Linux systems, the line is already in the file, although it may be commented out. Remove the comment symbol if this is the case. The FTP entry essentially specifies to `inetd` that FTP is to use TCP, and that it should spawn `ftpd` every time a new connection is made to the FTP port. In the preceding example, the `ftpd` daemon is started with the `-l` option, which enables logging. You can ignore this option if you want. You should replace the pathname `/usr/etc/ftpd` with the location of your FTP daemon.

There are several `ftpd` daemon options that you can add to the `/etc/inetd.config` line to control `ftpd`'s behavior. The following list contains the most commonly used options:

- ■ `-d`   Adds debugging information to the `syslog`.
- ■ `-l`   Activates a logging of sessions (only failed and successful logins, not debug information). If the `-l` option is specified twice, all commands are logged, too. If specified three times, the size of all `get` and `put` file transfers are added as well.
- ■ `-t`   Sets the timeout period before `ftpd` terminates after a session is concluded (default is 15 minutes). The value is specified in seconds after the `-t` option.

■ -T   Sets the maximum timeout period (in seconds) that a client can request. The default is two hours. This lets a client alter the normal default timeout for some reason.

■ -u   Sets the umask value for files uploaded to the local system. The default umask is 022. Clients can request a different umask value.

FTP Logins

If you are going to set up a user-based FTP service where each person accessing your system has a valid login name and password, then you must create an account for each user in the /etc/passwd file. If you are not allowing anonymous FTP access, do not create a generic login that anyone can use.

To set up an anonymous FTP server, you must create a login for the anonymous user ID (if one doesn't already exist; many versions of Linux have the entry already completed upon installation). This is done in the normal process of adding a user to the /etc/passwd file. The login name is whatever you want people to use when they access your system, such as anonymous or ftp. You need to select a login directory for the anonymous users that can be protected from the rest of the file system. A typical /etc/passwd entry looks like this:

```
ftp:*:400:51:Anonymous FTP access:/usr/ftp:/bin/false
```

This sets up the anonymous user with a login of ftp. The asterisk password prevents anyone gaining access to the account. The user ID number (400) is, of course, unique to the entire system. For better security, it is a good idea to create a separate group just for the anonymous FTP access (edit the /etc/group file to add a new group), then set the ftp user to that group. Only the anonymous FTP user should belong to that group because it can be used to set file permissions to restrict access and make your system more secure. The login directory in the preceding example is /usr/ftp, although you could choose any directory as long as it belongs to root (for security reasons, again). The startup program shown in the preceding example is /bin/false, which helps protect your system from access to accounts and utilities that do not have a strong password protection.

Setting Up the Directories

As you will see in the next section, "Setting Permissions," you can try to make the entire anonymous FTP subdirectory structure a file system unto itself, with no allowance for the anonymous user to get anywhere other than /usr/ftp (or whatever directory you use for anonymous access). For this reason, you need to create a mini-file system just for the anonymous FTP access which holds the usual directory names and basic files that anyone logging in will need.

The process for setting up the directories that your anonymous FTP login will need is simple, requiring you to create a number of directories and copy files into them. Here's the basic procedure:

1. Create the bin directory (/usr/ftp/bin, for example) and copy the directory listing command ls that users will need to view directory and file details.

2. Create the etc directory (usr/ftp/etc, for example) and copy your passwd file (/etc/passwd) and group file (/etc/group) into it. We'll edit these files in a moment.

3. Create the `lib` directory (`/usr/ftp/lib`, for example) and copy the files `/lib/ld.so` and `/lib/libc.so.X` (where *X* is the version number of the `libc` file) into it. These files are used by `ls`. Do this step only if your `ls` command requires these files; most versions of Linux do not have this dependency.

4. Create the `pub` directory (`/usr/ftp/pub`, for example) to hold your accessible files. We'll look at this directory in more detail in a moment.

5. Create the `dev` directory (`/usr/ftp/dev`, for example) and use the `mknod` command to copy the `/dev/zero` file. You need to retain the same major and minor device numbers as the `/dev/zero` file in `/dev`. This device file is used by `ld.so` (and hence `ls`). Do this step only if `ls` requires the `/lib` directory files mentioned earlier.

The copies of the `/etc/passwd` and `/etc/group` files are copied into the `~ftp/etc` directory. You should edit these files to remove all passwords and replace them with an asterisk. Remove all entries in both `/etc/passwd` and `/etc/group`, except those used by the anonymous FTP login (usually just `anonymous` and `bin`).

The `~ftp/pub` directory structure can be used to store the files you want to allow anonymous users to access. Copy them into this directory. You can create subdirectories as you need them for organizational purposes. It may be useful to create an upload directory somewhere in the `~ftp/pub` directory structure which has write permission, so that users can upload files to you only into this upload area.

Setting Permissions

You can use the `chroot` command to help protect your system. The `chroot` command makes the root directory appear to be something other than / on a file system. For example, since `chroot` is always set for the anonymous FTP login, any time anonymous users type a `cd` command, it can always be relative to their home directory. In other words, when they type `cd /bin` they will really be changing to `/usr/ftp/bin` if the root has been set to `/usr/ftp`. This helps prevent access to any other areas of the file system than the FTP directory structure.

If you do create an upload area, you may want to set the permissions to allow execute and write, but not read (to prevent another user downloading the files someone else has uploaded).

Set all permissions for directories under `~ftp/` to prevent write access by user, group, or other. Make sure the directories and files under `~ftp` are set to allow the anonymous login to read them (set their ownership and group permissions to the root login and group ID), and set only read permission. The directories will need execute and read permission to enable the anonymous users to enter them and obtain directory listings. This provides pretty good security. All directories in the `~ftp` directory structure should have the permissions set with the command

```
chmod 555 dir_name
```

which sets read-execute permission only. The exception is the `upload` directory, which can have write permission as noted earlier.

Test the System

Before you let anyone else onto your Linux FTP system, log into it yourself and try to access files you shouldn't be able to access, move into directories out of the ~ftp structure, and write files where you shouldn't be able to. This will provide a useful test of the permissions and directory structure. Spend a few minutes trying to read and write files. Make sure your system is buttoned up: If you don't, someone else will find the holes and exploit them.

It is a useful idea to set up a mailbox for the FTP administrator so users on other systems who need help or information can send mail to you. Create a mail alias such as `ftp-admin` in the file `/etc/aliases` (and run `newaliases` to make it effective).

Since this is a system administration book, we won't go into much detail about how to organize your directory structure, but a few useful tips may help you. To begin, decide what you want to store in your FTP directories and organize the structure logically. For example, if you are making available programs you have written, set up separate directories for each. A `README` file in each directory will help show browsers what it contains. A master `README` or `INSTRUCTIONS` file in the ~ftp directory can help explain how your site is set up and what its contents are.

A More Secure FTP

The FTP system discussed in the preceding sections, which is the basic one supplied with practically every Linux distribution, requires a bit of work to make it secure. However, it is still vulnerable to very experienced crackers. There's a better alternative if you are paranoid about your system's security: WU FTP. Developed at Washington University, WU FTP adds some extra features to the standard FTP system:

- Better control of user and group IDs
- Better tracking of uploads and downloads
- Automatic shutdown
- Automatic compression and decompression of files

If these features sound useful, you can obtain a copy of the source code of WU FTP from several sites, although the primary site is `wuarchive.wustl.edu`. Check for the file `/packages/wuarchive-ftpd/wu-ftpd-2.4.tar.Z`. You will get the source code which needs to be compiled on your Linux system.

WU FTP uses a number of environment variables to control the service, and the accompanying documentation helps you set it up properly. Setting up WU FTP is much more complex than standard FTP, and the extra security, while useful, may be unnecessary for many FTP site machines that you may set up at home or work (unless you have sensitive information).

Summary

The information in this chapter enables you to set up your system as a full anonymous FTP site or just a site for the users you want to gain access. Although the process is simple, you have to take care to ensure the file permissions are properly set. Once your FTP site is up, you can let others on the Internet or your local area network know that you are running, as well as the type of material you store on your system. Then sit back and share!

Checklist: Protecting an Anonymous FTP System

Anonymous FTP is fast, relatively easy to use, and a huge security problem if you don't carefully set up your system. The following list summarizes a few simple steps to setting up a better anonymous FTP site:

1. Create a user account called `ftp`. Edit the `/etc/passwd` file manually and replace the password with an asterisk in the second field. This prevents anyone from gaining access through the `ftp` account.

2. If a home directory wasn't created for the `ftp` user when you created the account, set up a home directory for the `ftp` user's sole use (such as `/home/ftp`).

3. Set the `ftp` home directory so that the `root` user is the owner:

   ```
   chown root /usr/ftp
   ```

4. Make the `ftp` home directory unwritable to anyone with the command:

   ```
   chmod ugo-w /usr/ftp
   ```

5. Create a `bin` directory under the `ftp` home directory:

   ```
   mkdir ~ftp/bin
   ```

6. Make the `~ftp/bin` directory owned by `root` and unwritable to anyone else:

   ```
   chown root ~ftp/bin
   chmod ugo-w ~ftp/bin
   ```

7. Place a copy of the listing commands (and any others that you want anonymous FTP users to use) in the `bin` directory:

   ```
   cp /bin/ls ~ftp/bin
   ```

8. Create an `etc` directory under the `ftp` home directory and make it owned by `root` and unwritable:

   ```
   mkdir ~ftp/etc
   chown root ~ftp/etc
   chmod ugo-w ~ftp/etc
   ```

9. Copy the `/etc/passwd` and `/etc/group` files into the `~ftp/etc` directory. Edit both files to remove all user accounts except `ftp` (and `ftp`'s group). (At the very least, remove all passwords for other accounts by placing asterisks in the password field.)

10. Create the directory ~ftp/pub/incoming, and make it owned by root. Then, make the directory writable by anyone:

    ```
    mkdir ~ftp/pub/incoming
    chown root ~ftp/pub/incoming
    chmod ugo+w ~ftp/pub/incoming
    ```

11. Place any files you want accessible by anonymous FTP into the ~ftp/pub directory. Users logging in through anonymous FTP will be able to transfer the files out. Allowing users to write files into the directory may not be desirable, so change the permissions or check the files frequently.

By following these steps (modified for your own particular needs), you can create a secure site that lets you breathe a little easier.

Configuring a WAIS Site

48

by Tim Parker

WAIS (Wide Area Information Service) is a menu-based tool that enables users to search for key-words in a database of documents available on your system and show the results. WAIS was developed by Thinking Machines but spun off to a separate company called WAIS Inc., when it became immensely popular and was then purchased by AOL Productions. A free version of WAIS was made available to the Clearinghouse for Networking Information Discovery and Retrieval (CNIDR) as freeWAIS, which is the version most often found on Linux systems.

WAIS lets a user enter some keywords or phrases, and then searches a database for those terms. A typical WAIS search screen is shown in Figure 48.1. (This screen is from the primary WAIS server at `http://www.wais.com`. This server is a good place to look for examples of how WAIS can be used.) In this example, we searched for the keywords `hubble` and `magnitude` (WAIS usually ignores case). After searching all the database indexes it knows about, WAIS shows its results, as shown in Figure 48.2.

FIGURE 48.1.

You can enter complex or simple search criteria on a WAIS search line.

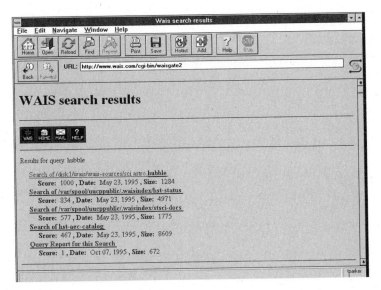

The display generated by WAIS, often displayed in a WWW browser or a WAIS browser as in these figures, lists each match along with its score from 0 to 1000, indicating the manner in which the keywords match the index (the higher numbers are better matches). Users can then refine the list, expand it, or examine documents listed. In Figure 48.3, one of the documents listed in the search results is displayed in the WWW browser window. WAIS can handle many file formats, including text and documents, audio, JPEG and GIF files, and binaries.

The version of WAIS used commonly with Linux is called freeWAIS. This chapter looks at how you can set up a freeWAIS server on your Linux machine. WAIS is a useful service to provide if you deal with a considerable amount of information that you want to make generally available. This could be product information, details about a hobby, or practically any other type of data. All you have to want to do is make it available to others, either on your local area network or to the Internet as a whole.

FIGURE 48.2.

WAIS displays the search results with a score.

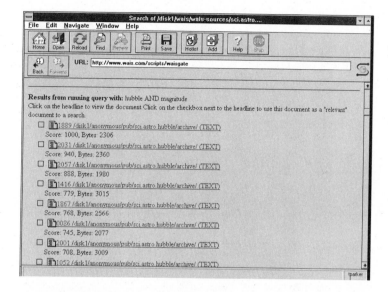

FIGURE 48.3.

Selecting any entry on the WAIS search results lets you see the file.

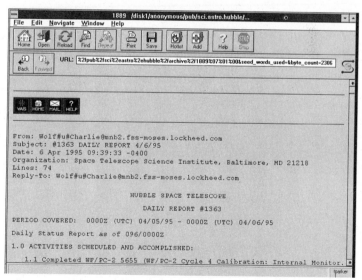

The freeWAIS package has three parts to it: an indexer, a WAIS server, and a client. The indexer handles database information and generates an index that contains keywords and a table indicating the words' occurrences. The server component does the matching between a user's requests and the indexed files. The client is the user's vehicle to access WAIS, and is usually a WAIS or WWW browser. WWW browsers usually have an advantage over WAIS browsers in that the latter cannot display HTML documents.

A follow-up backwards-compatible WAIS system is currently available in a beta version called ZDIST. ZDIST's behavior will be much like freeWAIS, with any changes noted in the documentation. ZDIST adds some new features and is a little smaller and faster than freeWAIS. Because of the unstable beta nature of ZDIST, we'll concentrate on freeWAIS here.

Compiling and Installing freeWAIS

The freeWAIS software is often included in a complete Linux distribution CD-ROM but is also readily available from many FTP and BBS sites. Alternatively, it can be obtained by anonymous FTP from the CNIDR site as `ftp.cnidr.org`. The freeWAIS system resides in the directory `/pub/ NDIR.tools/freewais/freeWAIS-X.X.tar.Z` where `X.X` is the latest version number. The CNIDR site has many binaries available for different machines, as well as generic source code that can be tailored to many different systems.

One of the files in the distribution software, which should be placed in the destination directory, is the `Makefile` used to create the program. If you are compiling the freeWAIS source yourself, examine the `Makefile` to ensure the variables are set correctly. Most are fine by default, pointing to standard Linux utilities. The following lists some of the exceptions that you may have to tweak:

- `CC`   The name of the C compiler you use (usually `cc` or `gcc`).
- `CURSELIB`   Set to the current version of the `curses` library on your system.
- `TOP`   The full path to the freeWAIS source directory.

The `CFLAGS` options let you specify compiler flags when the freeWAIS source is compiled. Many options are supported, all explained in the documentation files that accompany the source. Most of the flag settings can be left as their default values in Linux systems. A few of the specific flags you may want to alter are worth mentioning, though. The most useful are the indexer flags, two of which are potentially useful:

- `-DBIO`   Used to allow indexing on biological symbols and terms. Use only if your site deals with biological documents.
- `-DBOOLEANS`   Enables you to use Booleans as AND and NOT. This flag can be handy for extending the power of searches.

The `-DBOOLEANS` flag handles logical searches. For example, if you are looking for the keywords "green leaf," WAIS by default searches for the words green and leaf separately and judges matches on the two words independently. With the `-DBOOLEANS` flag set, the two words can be ANDed together so a match has to be with the two-word term "green leaf."

A couple of other flags that may be useful for freeWAIS sites deal with the behavior of the system as a whole:

- `-DBIGINDEX`   Should be set when there are many (thousands) of documents to index.
- `-DLITERAL`   Allows a literal search for a string, as opposed to using partial hits on the string's component words.

◼ `-DPARTIALWORD`   Allows searches with asterisks as wildcards (such as auto*).

◼ `-DRELEVANCE_FEEDBACK`   Set to ON, enables clients to use previous search results as search criteria for a new search. This is a useful option.

A number of directories are included in the distribution software, most of which are of obvious intent (`bin` for binaries, `man` for man pages, and so on). The directories used by freeWAIS in its default configuration are as follows:

◼ `bin`   Binaries

◼ `config.c`   C source code for configuration

◼ `doc`   Doc files, help files, and FAQs

◼ `include`   Header files used by the compiler

◼ `lib`   Library files

◼ `man`   Man pages

◼ `Srcfree`   WAIS source code

◼ `Wais-Sources`   Directory of Internet servers

◼ `Wais-Test`   Sample indexer and service scripts

Once you have fine-tuned the configuration file information, you can compile the freeWAIS source with the `make` command:

```
make linux
```

By default, the `make` utility compiles two clients called `swais` and `waisq`. If you want to compile an X version of WAIS called `xwais` (useful if you want to allow access from X terminals or consoles), uncomment the line in the `Makefile` that ends with `makex`.

Setting Up freeWAIS

When you have the compiled freeWAIS components installed and configured properly, you can begin setting up the WAIS index files to documents available on your system. This is usually done by creating an index directory with the default name of `wsindex`. The directory usually resides just under the root of the file system (`/wsindex`) but many administrators like to keep it in a reserved area for the WAIS software (such as `/usr/wais/wsindex`). If the index files are difficult to locate, users may have problems when they try to find them.

The `wais-test` directory created when you installed freeWAIS contains a script called `test.waisindex` that creates four WAIS index files automatically for you. These are used to test the WAIS installation for proper functionality, as well as to show you how you can use the different search and index capabilities of freeWAIS. The following are the four index files:

◼ `test-BOOL`   Index of three example documents using the Boolean capabilities and synonyms

◼ `test-Comp`   Index demonstrating compressed source file handling

- ■ `test-Docs` Index of files in the `doc` directory showing recursive directory search
- ■ `test-Multi` Index of GIF images and multi-document capabilities

Only graphically based (usually X-based) browsers can handle the `Multi` document formats, although any type of browser should be able to handle the other three index formats.

Once you have verified that the indexing system works properly and all the components of freeWAIS are properly installed, you need to build an index file for the documents available on your system. Do this with the `waisindex` command. The `waisindex` command enables you to index files two ways using the `-t` option, followed by one of these keywords:

- ■ `one_line` Index each line of a document so a match can show the exact line the match occurred in.
- ■ `text` Index so a match shows the entire document with no indication of the exact line the match occurred in. This is the default option.

The `waisindex` command takes arguments for the name of the destination index file (`-d` followed by the filename), and the directory or files to be indexed. For example, to index a directory called `/usr/sales/sales_lit` into a destination index file called `sales`, using the `one_line` indexing approach, you would issue the command:

```
waisindex -d sales -t one_line /usr/sales/sales_lit
```

Because there is no path provided for the `sales` index file in this example, it would be stored in the current directory.

Once your WAIS server is running (see the section entitled "Starting freeWAIS"), you can test the indexes by using the `waissearch` command. For example, to look for the word "WAIS" in the index files, issue the command:

```
waissearch -p 210 -d index_file WAIS
```

where `-p` gives the port number (default value is 210), and `-d` is the path to the index file. If the search is successful (and you have something that matches) you will see messages about the number of records returned and the scores of each match. If you see error messages or nothing, check the configuration information and the index files.

A final step you can take if you want your freeWAIS system to be accessible by Internet users is to issue the command:

```
waisindex -export -register Filenames
```

where *Filenames* is the name of the index. This will be registered with the Directory of Servers at `cnidr.org` and `quake.think.com`. These addresses are reached automatically with the `-register` option. Only do this step if you want all Internet users to access your WAIS service. (We will look at the `waisindex` command in much more detail shortly.)

If you want to enable clients to connect to your freeWAIS system with a WWW browser (such as Mosaic or Netscape), you must issue the command:

```
waisindex -d WWW -T HTML -contents -export /usr/resources/*html
```

Replace the /usr/resources path with the path to your HTML files. This line allows WAIS clients to perform keyword searches on HTML documents, as well.

If you want, you can set WAIS to allow only certain domains to connect to it. This is done in the ir.h file, which has a line like this:

```
#define SERVSECURITYFILE    "SERV_SEC"
```

You have to place a copy of an existing SERV_SEC file or one you create yourself in the same directory as the WAIS index files. If there is no SERV_SEC file accessible to WAIS, all domains are allowed access. (You can change the name of the file, of course, as long as the entry in ir.h matches the filename with quotation marks around it.)

Each ASCII entry in the SERV_SEC file follows a strict format for defining the domains that are granted access to WAIS. The format of each line is:

```
domain    [IP address]
```

Each line has the domain name of the host that you want to grant access to with its IP address as an optional add-on to the line. If the domain name and IP address do not match, it doesn't matter because WAIS allows access to a match of either name or address. A sample SERV_SEC file looks likes this:

```
chatton.com
roy.sailing.org
bighost.bignet.com
```

Each of these three domain names can access WAIS, while any connection from a host without these domain names is refused.

The SERV_SEC file should be owned and accessible only by the user that the freeWAIS system is running as (it should not be run as root to avoid security problems), and the file should be modifiable only by root.

Similar to the SERVSECURITYFILE variable is DATASECURITYFILE, which controls access to the databases. There is a line in the ir.h file that looks like this:

```
#define DATASECURITYFILE    "DATA_SEC"
```

where DATA_SEC is a file listing each database file and the domains that have access to it. The file should reside in the same directory as the index files. The format of the DATA_SEC file is:

```
database    domain    [IP address]
```

where database is the name of the database the permissions refer to, and domain and the optional IP address are the same as the SERV_SEC file. A sample DATA_SEC file looks like this:

```
primary    chatton.com
primary    bignet.org
primary    roy.sailing.org
sailing    roy.sailing.org
```

In this example, three domains are granted access to a database called primary (note that primary is just a filename and has no special meaning), while one domain has specific access to the database called `sailing` as well as `primary`. If you want to allow all hosts with access to the system (controlled by `SERV_SEC`) to access a particular database, you can use asterisks in the domain name and IP address fields. For example, the entries:

```
primary    *    *
sailing    roy.sailing.org
```

allow anyone with access to WAIS to use the `primary` database, with only one domain allowed access to the `sailing` database.

In both the `SERV_SEC` and `DATA_SEC` files, you have to be careful with the IP addresses to avoid inadvertently granting access to hosts you really don't want on your system. For example, if you specify the IP address 150.12 in your file, then any IP addresses from 150.12 through 150.120, 151.121, and so on, are also granted access because they match the IP components. Specify IP addresses explicitly to avoid this problem.

Starting freeWAIS

As with the FTP services, you can set freeWAIS to start up when the system boots, by using the `rc` files from the command line at any time, or you can have the processes started by `inetd` when a service request arrives. If you want to start freeWAIS from the command line, you need to specify a number of options. A sample startup command line looks like this:

```
waisserver -u username -p 210 -l 10 -d /usr/wais/wais_index
```

The `-u` option tells `waisserver` to run as the user `username` (which has to be a valid user in `/etc/passwd`, of course), the `-p` option tells `waisserver` what port to use (the default is 210, as shown in the `/etc/services` file), and the `-d` option shows the default location of WAIS indexes. If you want to invoke logging of sessions to a file, use the `-e` option followed by the name of the logfile.

You should run `waisserver` as another user instead of root to prevent holes in the WAIS system from being exploited by a hacker. If the service is run as a standard user (such as `wais`), only the files that the user would have access to would be in jeopardy.

If the port for `waisserver` is set to 210, the service corresponds to the Internet standards for access. If you set the value to another port, you can configure the system for local area access only. If the port number is less than 1023, the WAIS service must be started and managed by root, but any port over 1023 can be handled by a normal user. If you intend to use port 210, you don't have to specify the number in the command line, although the `-p` option still must be used.

If you want to let inetd handle the `waisserver` startup, you need to ensure the file `/etc/services` has an entry for WAIS. The line in the `/etc/services` file looks like this:

```
z3950    210/tcp    #WAIS
```

where `210` is the port number WAIS uses, and `tcp` is the protocol. After modifying or verifying the entry in `/etc/services`, you need to add a WAIS entry to the `inetd.conf` file to start up `waisserver` whenever a request is received on port 210 (or whatever other port you are using). The entry looks like this:

```
z3950   stream   tcp   nowait   root/usr/local/bin/waisserver/waisserver.d
-u  username -d /usr/wais/wais_index
```

where the options are the same as for the command line startup mentioned above. The daemon `waisserver.d` is used when starting up in `inetd` mode, instead of `waisserver`. Again you can use the `-e` option to log activity to a file.

Building Your WAIS Indexes

Once you have the freeWAIS server ready to run and everything seems to be working, it's time to provide some content for your WAIS system. Usually, documents are the primary source of information for WAIS, although you can index any type of file. The key step to providing WAIS service is to build the WAIS index using the `waisindex` command. The `waisindex` command can be a bit obtuse at times, but a little practice and some trial-and-error fiddling will help you master its somewhat awkward behavior.

The `waisindex` program works by examining all the data in the files in which you want to create an index. From its examination, `waisindex` usually generates seven different index files (depending on the content and your commands). Each file holds a list of unique words in the documents. The different index files are then combined into one large database, often called the "source" (or "WAIS source"). Whenever a client WAIS package submits a search, the search strings are compared to the source, and the results displayed with accuracy analysis (the match score).

> **NOTE**
>
> The use of `waisindex` enables a client search to proceed much more quickly because the keywords in the data files have already been extracted. However, the mass of data in the index files can be sizable, so allow plenty of disk space for a WAIS server to work with. (For a typical WAIS site, assume at least double the amount of room needed for the source files.)

WAIS Index Files

The freeWAIS index files are not usually readable by a system user (although one or two files can be read with some success). Usually, `waisindex` creates seven index files, although the number may vary depending on requirements. Each index file has a specific file extension to show its purpose, based on a root name (specified on the `waisindex` command line, or defaulting to `index`). The index files and their purposes are as follows:

`index.doc`	A document file that contains a table with the filename, a headline (title) from the file, the location of the first and last characters of an entry, the length of the document, the number of lines in the document, and the time and date the document was created.
`index.dct`	A dictionary file that contains a list of every unique word in the files cross-indexed to the inverted file.

`index.fn`	A filename file that contains a table with a list of the filenames, the date they were created in the index, and the type of file.
`index.hl`	A headline file that contains a table of all headlines (titles). The headline is displayed in the search output when a match occurs.
`index.inv`	Inverted files that contain a table associating every unique word in all the files with a pointer to the files themselves and the word's importance (determined by how close the word is to the start of the file, the number of times the word occurs in the document, and the percentage of times the word appears in the document).
`index.src`	A source description file that contains descriptions of the information indexed, including the host name and IP address, the port watched by WAIS, the source filename, any cost information for the service, the headline of the service, a description of the source, and the e-mail address of the administrator. The source description file is editable by ASCII editors. We will look at this file in a little more detail shortly.
`index.status`	A status file containing user-defined information.

The source description file is a standard ASCII file that is read by `waisindex` at intervals to see if information has changed. If the changes are significant, `waisindex` updates its internal information. A sample source file looks like this:

```
(:source
 :version 2
 :ip-address "147.120.0.10"
 :ip-name: "wizard.tpci.com"
 :tcp-port 210
 :database-name "Linux stuff"
 :cost 0.00
 :cost-unit: free
 :maintainer "wais_help@tpci.com"
 :subjects "Everything you need to know about Linux"
 :description "If you need to know something about Linux, it's here."
```

You should edit this file when you set up freeWAIS because the default descriptions are rather sparse and useless.

The *waisindex* Command

The `waisindex` command allows a number of options, some of which you have seen earlier in this chapter. The following list contains the primary `waisindex` options of interest to most users:

■ `-a`	Appends data to an existing index file (used to update index files instead of regenerating them each time a new document is added).
■ `-contents`	Indexes the file contents (default action).
■ `-d`	Gives the filename root for index files (for example, `-d /usr/wais/foo` named all index files as `/usr/wais/foo.xxx`).

- -e   Gives the name of the log file for error information (default is stderr—usually the console—although you can specify -s for /dev/null).

- -export   Adds the host name and TCP port to descriptions for easier Internet access.

- -l   Gives the level of log messages. Valid values are 0—no log, 1—log only high priority errors and warnings, 5—log medium priority errors and warnings, as well as index filename information, and 10—log every event.

- -M   Links multiple types of files.

- -mem   Limits memory usage during indexing (the higher the number specified, the faster the indexing process and the more memory used).

- -nocontents   Prevents a file from being indexed (indexes only the document header and filename).

- -nopairs   Instructs waisindex to ignore adjacent capitalized words from being indexed together.

- -nopos   Ignores the location of keywords in a document when determining scores.

- -pairs   Indexes adjacent capitalized words as a single entry.

- -pos   Determines scores based on locations of keywords (proximity of keywords increases scores).

- -r   Recursive subdirectory indexing.

- -register   Registers your indexes with the WAIS Directory of Services.

- -stdin   Uses a filename from the keyboard instead of a filename on the command line.

- -stop   Indicates a file containing stopwords (words too common to be indexed), usually defined in src/ir/stoplist.c.

- -t   Data file type indicator.

- -T   Sets the type of data to whatever follows.

The waisindex program has to be told the type of information in a file, otherwise it may not be able to generate an index properly. Many file types are currently defined with freeWAIS, and you can display them by entering the command:

```
waisindex
```

with no argument. Although many different types are supported by freeWAIS, only a few are really in common use. The most common file types supported by freeWAIS are the following:

- filename   Same as text, except the filename is used as the headline.

- first_line   Same as text, except the first line in the file is used as the headline.

- ftp   Contains FTP code that users can use to retrieve information from another machine.

- GIF   GIF images, one image per file. The filename is used as the headline.
- mail_or_rmail   Indexes the mbox mailbox contents as individual items.
- mail_digest   Standard e-mail, indexed as individual messages. The subject field is the headline.
- netnews   Standard Usenet news, each article a separate item. The subject field is the headline.
- one_line   Indexes each sentence in a document separately.
- PICT   PICT image, one image per file. The filename is used as the headline.
- ps   A PostScript file with one document per file.
- text   Indexes the file as one document, the pathname as the heading.
- TIFF   TIFF image, one image per file. The filename is used as the headline.

To tell waisindex the type of file to be examined, use the -t option followed by the proper type. For example, to index standard ASCII text, you could use the command:

```
waisindex -t text -r /usr/waisdata/*
```

This command indexes all the files in /usr/waisdata recursively, assuming they are all ASCII files.

> **NOTE**
>
> When a document has been indexed, any changes in the document will not be reflected in the WAIS index unless a complete reindex is performed. Using the -a option does not update existing index entries. Instead, start the index process again. You should do this at periodic intervals as a matter of course.

Getting Fancy

You can provide some extra features for users of your freeWAIS service in a number of ways. Although this section is not exhaustive by any means, it shows you two of the easily implementable features that make a WAIS site more attractive.

To begin, suppose you want to make video, graphics, or audio available on a particular subject. Suppose, for example, your site deals with musical instruments, and you have several documents on violins. You may want to provide an audio clip of a violin being played, a video of the making of a violin body, or a graphic image of a Stradivarius violin. To make these extra files available, you should have all the files with the same filename but different extensions. For example, if your primary document on violins is called violins.txt, you may have the following files in the WAIS directories:

- `violins.TEXT`   Document describing violins
- `violins.TIFF`   Image of a Stradivarius
- `violins.MPEG`   Video of the making of a violin body
- `violins.MIDI`   MIDI file of a violin being played

All these files should have the same root name (`violins`) but different types (recognized by `waisindex`). Then, you have to associate the multimedia files with the document file. You can do this with the following command:

```
waisindex -d violin -M TEXT,TIFF,MPEG,MIDI -export /usr/waisdata/violin/*
```

This tells `waisindex` that all four types of files are to be handled. When a user searches for the keyword "violin," all four types of files will be matched, and options on the browser may let them play, view, or hear the non-text components.

Another common feature is the use of synonyms to account for different methods of specifying a subject. For example, a scientist may use the keyword "feline" when a non-scientist may use "cat." You want to be able to match these two words to the same thing. This is done through a file called `SOURCE.syn`, which is automatically read by the search engine when it is working. The `SOURCE.syn` file has the following format:

```
word    synonym [synonym ...]
```

where *word* is the word to be used to search the databases, and *synonym* is the word(s) that should match it. For example, if you are dealing with domestic pets in your WAIS site, you may have the following entries in the `SOURCE.syn` file:

```
cat    feline
dog    canine hound pooch
bird   parrot budgie
```

The synonym file can be very useful when people use different terms to refer to the same thing. An easy way to check for the need for synonyms is to set the logging option for `waisindex` to `10` for a while, and see what words people are using on your site. Don't keep it on too long, though, because the logfiles can become enormous with a little traffic.

Summary

Now that WAIS is up and running on your server, you can go about the process of building your index files and letting others access your server. WAIS is quite easy to manage, and offers a good way of letting other users access your system's documents. The alternative approach, for text-based systems, is Gopher, which we examine in the next chapter.

Setting Up a Gopher Service

49

by Tim Parker

Gopher is one of the most useful Internet services available, because it is widely used by beginners and veterans alike. Gopher is a text-based file location system that leads you through a series of hierarchical menus to find specific files you want. Setting up a Gopher site is really just a matter of configuring the Gopher server software and creating a number of logical directory structures with files indexed in a Gopher format.

Gopher works by having a client program (started by a user) connect to a Gopher server and retrieve information about files available on the Internet (or local area network, if the Gopher server is limited to that area). At the end of 1995, there were more than 6,000 Gopher servers on the Internet, all accessible by anyone with a Gopher client. Those servers contain information about more than 10 million items, ranging from text files to movies, sounds, images, and many types of application binaries. Gopher enables you to display and manipulate lists of files, looking for items of interest to you.

If you or the users of your Linux system want to connect to another Gopher server, you need a Gopher client. There are several clients available with Linux distributions, on FTP and BBS sites, and through several other sources. If you don't want to allow users (or yourself) to start a Gopher client, you can use telnet to connect to sites known as public Gopher clients. These sites allow you to log in as an anonymous user and access the Gopher system. Most Gopher client packages offer more than just Gopher programs. Typical Gopher clients enable you to access WAIS indexes, use FTP, and to some extent, interwork with the World Wide Web.

This chapter looks at how you can set up a Gopher server, allowing others to access your machine's Gopher listings. Although we won't go into detail about how you should structure your Gopher service, you will see how to configure your software.

Gopher and Linux

There are currently two versions of Gopher available for Linux systems: Gopher and Gopher+ (Gopher Plus). Gopher is freely available, but Gopher+ is a commercial product. The difference between the two is functionality. If the additional capabilities of Gopher+ are important to you and your Gopher site, you may want to consider purchasing the product. Essentially, Gopher+ adds the following features:

- Makes extended file information available
- Offers a description of a file
- Can retrieve multiple versions of a file at one time (such as ASCII and PostScript simultaneously)
- Allows file retrieval based on search criteria determined by the user

Gopher+ works with Gopher, but Gopher cannot use the advanced features of Gopher+. Gopher+ and Gopher both work with WWW browsers. Gopher+ licenses tend to cost about $100 or $500, depending on the site's conditions.

The versions of Gopher usually offered with Linux come from one of two sources: University of Minnesota Gopher and Gopher+, or GN Public License Gopher. The most recent public version of UM Gopher is version 1.3 (version 2.13 is free only to educational institutions), but the university is no longer working on the freeware Gopher product, instead concentrating on the commercial Gopher+ product. The GN Public License Gopher includes a WWW service but does not provide full functionality at present.

Gopher uses a TCP/IP family protocol known, surprisingly enough, as the Gopher protocol. This is a fairly simple request-answer protocol that is implemented for speed. When Gopher transfers information about a file it knows about (called a Gopher menu file), it follows a set format. The format used by Gopher is:

```
<type><display_name><selector_string><hostname><port>
```

The fields in the Gopher menu file have the following meanings:

- `type`—A one-character description of the item (see the next bulleted list for valid codes).
- `display_name`—The menu or display name, followed by a tab character.
- `selector_string`—A unique identifier for a document on each server (usually based on the filename). The selector string is followed by a tab character.
- `hostname`—The host where the file resides, followed by a tab character.
- `port`—The port to access the host, followed by a carriage return/line feed pair (usually port 70).

The Gopher+ version of the system adds a few new attributes to each line, including the name of the system administrator responsible for the service, a simple description of the document type (text, for example), the language the file is written in, the last date the file was updated, and the size in bytes.

When a user wants to retrieve a file through the Gopher system, the hostname and port are used to create the connection to the remote server, while the selector string can be used to identify the file to be downloaded.

There are several types of files supported by Gopher, all given a unique one-character type code. The following is a list of valid codes:

- 0   Plain text file
- 1   Directory
- 2   CSO phonebook server (the hostname is the machine to connect to, the selector string is blank)
- 3   Error
- 4   BinHex Macintosh file
- 5   Binary DOS archive file
- 6   UNIX uuencoded file
- 7   Index-search server

- 8   Pointer to text-based telnet session (hostname is the machine name to connect to and selector string is the name to log in as)

- 9   Binary file

- g   GIF file

- h   HTML document

- I   Graphic image

- i   Unselectable inline text

- M   MIME-encapsulated mail document

- P   Adobe PDF file

- s   Sound

- T   Pointer to 3270 telnet session (hostname is machine to connect to and selector string is login name)

The Gopher system uses a number of other files on a Linux system, all of which must exist. The files necessary for Gopher are as follows:

- `tn3270` or similar 3270 emulator—Used for telnet 3270 connections.

- `kermit` or `zmodem` communications programs—Used for downloading files. The binaries are usually called `kermit`, `sz`, `sb`, and `sx`.

- graphics utility—If you allow the display of graphics, you need a graphics utility such as `xv`.

You can modify these requirements if you have a private site (such as for your local area network), but if you are offering open access you should have all the components.

Configuring Gopher

Installing and configuring Gopher (and Gopher+) is a matter of setting a number of configuration options prior to compiling the system software (it is usually not precompiled for you) and configuring some standard files. Gopher+ is done in the same manner, although with some extra parameters. Since Gopher is more likely to be on a Linux site than Gopher+, we'll concentrate on that.

Throughout this section, we will use filenames without full path extensions because it really doesn't matter where you install the Gopher software, as long as the directory paths are set correctly. There is no real standard configuration for directory locations, so feel free to choose whatever works best for you.

The *gopherd.conf* File

The configuration parameters for Gopher (and Gopher+) are in a file called `gopherd.conf`, which is read by the Gopher daemon `gopherd`. The default settings generally need a little modification, although many changes are simply changing commented lines to uncommented, and vice versa.

The first step is to create an alias for the Gopher service on your machine. Perform this step with the line that defines the `hostalias`. There should be a line in the file that looks like this:

```
hostalias: tpci
```

The alias is used to find the Gopher server on your system and should not be directly tied to a real machine, so you can make changes whenever you wish. The best approach is to create an alias and tie it to a physical machine with DNS. If you are running a stand-alone machine, you can either use an alias tied to your machine name or use your machine name directly.

You can also control the number of Gopher connections allowed at one time. This is sometimes necessary to prevent a system from bogging down due to excessive user load. The maximum number of connections Gopher allows is given in a file, usually in the directory `PIDS_Directory`. A line in the `gopherd.conf` file usually has this variable commented out because early versions didn't implement it properly, or it was unstable. If you want to allow this feature, remove the comment symbol and make sure the directory it points to has the necessary files for your version of Gopher. The line usually looks like this:

```
#PIDS_Directory: /pids
```

A better way to handle the load on your system is to use the `MaxConnections` keyword, which sets the number of clients you support concurrently. You have to experiment to determine the best balance between system load and user service. A good starting point for a fast Linux system (80486 or Pentium CPU) is 15 to 25 users. This variable is set like this:

```
MaxConnections: 15
```

If the number of users is exceeded, an error message is generated when the connection is attempted. You can set a number of file decoders for your system. This is used when a user requests a file from Gopher and adds an extension (such as `.Z`, `.gz`, or `.zip`) for a compression or archive utility. The decoders recognize the extension the user supplies and invoke the proper utility to send the file properly decoded. Most `gopherd.conf` files have the following decoder lines already in the setup:

```
decoder: .Z /usr/ucb/zcat
decoder: .gz /usr/gnu/bin/zcat
#decoder: .adpcm /usr/openwin/bin/adpcm_dec
#decoder: .z /usr/gnu/bin/zcat
```

The last two decoders are commented out and can be uncommented, if you want to offer files in these formats through Gopher. You can also add other extensions by adding new lines with the binary name (and its full path).

In addition, the amount of time a cache file stays valid should be set. This is controlled by the line using the keyword `Cachetime`. Set this value to a reasonable value, such as 180 seconds. You should have a line that looks like this in the `gopherd.conf` file:

```
Cachetime: 180
```

You can use the `gopherd.conf` file to restrict access to some files on your system by using the `ignore` keyword. Usually the `gopherd.conf` file will have a number of defined `ignores`, such as these:

```
ignore: lib
ignore: bin
ignore: etc
ignore: dev
```

Any file with this type of extension is ignored. If you have a particular file extension you want to protect, add it to the list. For example, if your accounting system uses the extension `.acct`, you could have the Gopher clients ignore all these files by adding this line:

```
ignore: acct
```

Note that these `ignore` statements only work with file extensions. To be more broad, you can use wildcards and the keyword `ignore_patt` (for ignore pattern). For example, the line:

```
ignore_patt: ^usr$
```

ignores any file with the letters `usr` at the beginning of the name.

The *gopherdlocal.conf* File

In the file `gopherdlocal.conf`, you have to make two small changes to identify the system administrator, otherwise your system generates many annoying notes. The lines in the `gopherdlocal.conf` file look like this by default:

```
Admin: blank
AdminEmail: blank
```

If you do not change these entries to actual values, Gopher can generate all kinds of weird error messages. The `Admin` field usually has the administrator's name and sometimes a telephone number. For example, the file could be filled out as follows:

```
Admin: Yvonne Chow, 555-1212
AdminEmail: ychow@chatton.com
```

Another setting you should provide in the `gopherdlocal.conf` file is the `Abstract`, a short description of what your particular Gopher service provides. If you don't change the default setting, users get a message prompting them to request the Abstract, so you may as well do it right away. Multiple lines in an abstract value are followed by a backslash to show the continuation. A sample Abstract setting looks like this:

```
Abstract: This server provides sound and graphics files \
collected by the administrator on a recent trip to Outer \
Mongolia.
```

General information about your site is provided with a number of general settings for the site name, the organization that runs the site, your machine's geographic location, the latitude and longitude of your site, and a time zone setting. You can leave these blank if you want, but providing the information leads to a more complete Gopher site. The settings in a sample `gopherdlocal.conf` file look like this:

```
Site: Explore_Mongolia
Org: Mongolia Tourist Bureau
Loc: North Bay, Ontario, Canada
Geog: blank
TZ: EDT
```

The setting of `blank` for `Geog` leaves the setting with no value. Obviously, the system administrator didn't know the latitude and longitude settings.

You can set a language option used by Gopher clients to show what language most of the documents available on your site are written in. This is done like this:

```
Language: En_US
```

which refers to American English.

The setting `BummerMsg` is used to display a brief text string to a user who exceeds your maximum number of concurrent users or causes an error when accessing the system. The default value is this:

```
BummerMsg: Sorry, we have exceeded the number of permissible users
```

You can change this to whatever message you want. Try not to be rude or obnoxious because you never know who will get this message.

The last step in modifying the `gopherdlocal.conf` file is to set access procedures for users who log in to your Gopher server. Limiting the users who can get to your server is done through entries with the keyword `access`. The general format of the access line is:

```
access: hostname permissions num_users
```

where *hostname* is either the name or IP address of the host that is connecting to your server, *permissions* is the permission set for those users, and *num_users* is the maximum number of users that can be connected to the service concurrently.

The permissions are set using any combination of the following four words, either as they are or preceded by an exclamation mark to mean "not allowed." The permission keywords are as follows:

- `browse`—Can examine directory contents. If this is forbidden, users can access entries, but they can't get directory contents.
- `ftp`—Allows server to act as gateway to FTP services.
- `read`—Can access a file. If forbidden, the users get the `BummerMsg` when they ask for the file.
- `search`—Can access indexes (type 7 items). If forbidden, access to the indexes is not allowed. This is used primarily with Gopher+.

For example, to set access permissions to allow up to 10 users from the network `chatton.com` to access your Gopher server with full rights, you would add a line like this:

```
access: chatton.com     browse ftp read search 10
```

There is at least one space between each entry, even between permissions. This access entry:

```
access: bignet.org !browse !ftp read search 3
```

allows three concurrent users from `bignet.org` to access the Gopher server and read and search, but not use FTP gateways or browse the directory listings.

If you are using IP addresses, you can use a subset of the IP address to indicate the entire network. For example, if `bignet.com`'s network address is 147.12, you can indicate the entire network with a line like this:

```
access: 147.12. !browse !ftp read search 3
```

You must follow the last quad of numbers specified in the IP address with a period, otherwise 147.120 through 147.129 will also have the same permissions (because they match the digits specified).

If you want to enable access from a particular machine, you can do that, too. For example, to allow your friend's `darkstar` machine to access your Gopher server with full permissions, you would add a line like this:

```
access: darkstar.domain.name browse ftp read search 1
```

Most general Gopher servers tend to allow anyone to connect, so they use a default entry to refer to anyone not explicitly defined by another access entry. The default setting is usually like this:

```
access: default !browse !ftp read search 15
```

which allows anyone to read and search Gopher directories, but not move through them or use your machine as an FTP gateway.

Setting Up the *Makefile*

Two files need modification for the compilation process to proceed properly. These two files are `Makefile.config` and `conf.h`. With many versions of Gopher available on Linux systems, the configuration parameters these files need have already been set, but you should check the values carefully to prevent problems.

The `Makefile.config` file (used by `Makefile` to build the executables) is a lengthy file, so you should be careful while moving through it to avoid accidental changes. The important areas to examine are the directory definitions and server and client settings. These are dealt with individually in the following sections.

One setting you may wish to alter is the debugging utility, which is enabled by default in most systems. This can help you get the system running properly, but when the operation is correct, you should recompile the source with the debugging features removed to make the process faster and smaller, as well as to reduce debug information overhead. To remove debugging features, comment out the DEBUGGING line so it looks like this:

```
#DEBUGGING = -DDEBUGGING
```

By default, this line is probably not commented out.

The directory definitions are usually in a block with five to seven entries, depending on the number of entries for the man pages. A typical directory definition block looks like this:

```
PREFIX = /usr/local
CLIENTDIR = $(PREFIX)/bin
CLIENTLIB = $(PREFIX)/lib
SERVERDIR = $(PREFIX)/etc

MAN1DIR = $(PREFIX)/man/man1
MAN5DIR = $(PREFIX)/man/man5
MAN8DIR = $(PREFIX)/man/man8
```

The primary change to most `Makefile.config` files will be the PREFIX, which is used to set the basic directory for Gopher. The default value is usually `/usr/local`, although you can change it to anything you want (such as `/usr/gopher`). The rest of the variables define subdirectories under the primary Gopher directory and are usually acceptable as they are. Each of the subdirectories can be left the way it is, or you can change it to suit your own needs. You can place all the files in one directory, if you want. The meaning of each variable appears in the following list:

CLIENTDIR	Gopher client software
CLIENTLIB	Client help file (`gopher.hlp`)
MAN1DIR	Man pages for gopher client
MAN8DIR	Man pages for `gopherd`
SERVERDIR	Gopher server (`gopherd`) and configuration file (`gopherd.conf`)

For a Gopher client to run properly on your system, you must modify the CLIENTOPTS line in the `Makefile.config` file. The two options for the CLIENTOPTS line to control its behavior are as follows:

-DNOMAIL	Forbids remote users from mailing files.
-DAUTOEXITONU	Allows the Gopher client to be exited with the u command as well as q command.

To use either or both or these options, add them to the CLIENTOPS line like this:

```
CLIENTOPTS = -DNOMAIL -DAUTOEXITONU
```

Four variables relating to the Gopher server must also be set. These specify the host domain name, the port Gopher should use to listen for connections, the location of the data files, and option flags.

The domain name is set with the DOMAIN variable. It should have a leading period in the name, such as:

```
DOMAIN = .tpci.com
```

You do not need to set this variable, if the hostname command returns the fully qualified domain name of the server. In this case, leave the value blank.

The SERVERPORT variable defines the port Gopher uses to wait for services and is usually set for TCP port 70. This line usually looks like this:

```
SERVERPORT = 70
```

If you are not allowing general access to your Gopher site by Internet users, you can change this value. However, if you want to allow Internet users (even a very small subset) to gain access, you should leave this as port 70. If you are setting up your Gopher site for a small network only, then choose any port number you want (between 1024 and 9999) and make sure all the Gopher clients use that number, too.

The SERVERDATA variable defines the location of the data your Gopher server offers. Its default setting is usually as follows:

```
SERVERDATA = /gopher-data
```

Set the variable to point to the file location you use for your Gopher items.

The SERVEROPTS variable accepts a number of keywords that change the behavior of the Gopher service. A typical entry looks like this:

```
SERVEROPTS = -DSETPROCTITLE -DCAPFILES # -DBIO -DDL
```

Any keywords after the pound sign are ignored when Makefile runs, so you can adjust its location to set the options you want if the order of the variables allows such a simple approach. The following lists the meaning of the different keywords allowed in the SERVEROPTS entry:

-DADD_DATE_AND_TIME	Adds dates and times to titles.
-DBIO	Used only with the WAIS versions developed by Don Gilbert (wais8b5).
-DDL	Provides support for the dl database utility (requires the dl system in a directory variable called DLPATH and the DLOBJS line uncommented out to show the files getdesc.o and enddesc.o locations).
-DCAPFILES	Offers backwards compatibility with the cap directory.
-DLOADRESTRICT	Restricts user access based on the number of concurrent users (see the following section).

-DSETPROCTITLE   Sets the name displayed by ps command
                            (BSD UNIX-based systems only).

The conf.h file is used during the compilation to set other parameters about the Gopher service. The important settings, at least when setting up a Gopher service, are those that relate to the number of queries and timeout variables. These tend to occur at the end of the conf.h file.

The WAISMAXHITS variable defines the maximum number of hits a query to a WAIS database can offer, usually set to around 40. This variable is defined like this:

```
#define WAISMAXHITS 40
```

Note that the pound sign is not a comment symbol because this is written in C. The pound sign is an important part of the processor directive and should be left in place. There is no equal sign in the definition, either.

The MAXLOAD variable is used if the -DLOADRESTRICT keyword was used in the SERVEROPTS variable of Makefile.config. The MAXLOAD defines the maximum load average the Gopher service will respond to requests under (this value can be overridden on the command line). The usual definition is like this:

```
#define MAXLOAD 10.0
```

The READTIMEOUT and WRITETIMEOUT variables set the amount of time a service waits for a network read or write operation before timing out. The default settings are usually adequate. These lines look like the following:

```
#define READTIMEOUT (1*60)
#define WRITETIMEOUT (3*60)
```

The Gopher clients configuration is straight-forward. Begin by defining the Gopher servers the local machine connects to with the CLIENT1_HOST and CLIENT2_HOST entries. The Gopher client chooses one of the two (if both are defined) when it is started. The entries look like this:

```
#define CLIENT1_HOST "gopher_serv.tpci.com"
#define CLIENT2_HOST "other_gopher_serv.tpci.com"
```

The ports to be used to connect to the hosts are defined with these options:

```
#define CLIENT1_PORT 70
#define CLIENT2_PORT 70
```

If you have a local service and don't want to use port 70 (to prevent access from the Internet, for example), set the proper port values. If only one Gopher server is used, set the second value to 0.

Define the language the Gopher client will use by choosing one value out of a number of options. The default is American English, set by this command:

```
#define DEFAULT_LANG "En_US"
```

Other language defines are commented out below this one. If you want to change the default language, comment the American English setting and uncomment the one you want.

When all the configuration changes have been made, you can invoke the compilation process for the client and server with these commands:

```
make client
make server
```

Or you can do both client and server systems at once by using the make command with no argument. The programs and data files must be installed, too, using the command:

```
make install
```

WAIS and Gopher

Gopher clients have the ability to use WAIS indexes to search for documents, but the system must be configured to allow this. We looked at WAIS in Chapter 48, "Configuring a WAIS Site," so for the sake of providing WAIS index access to Gopher, we will assume you have installed WAIS properly and have WAIS indexes ready for Gopher.

To provide WAIS services through Gopher, you may have to make a change in the WAIS source code. Examine the WAIS source code for a line that looks like this:

```
if (gLastAnd) printf("search_word: boolean 'and' scored/n:);
```

This line should be commented out to provide Gopher services, so if it is not, add C comment symbols before and after the line, like this:

```
/* if (gLastAnd) printf("search_word: boolean 'and' scored/n:); */
```

If the line was already commented out (or didn't exist) then you need not make any change. If you changed the line, though, you have to recompile WAIS by changing into the WAIS top directory and running the makefile (type the command make).

Next, examine the Gopher Makefile.config file and look for the WAISTYPE variable. It should be defined on a line like this:

```
WAISTYPE = #-DFREEWAIS_0_4
```

Then, you have to link the Gopher and WAIS services. Suppose your Gopher source directory is /usr/gopher/source and the WAIS source directory is /usr/wais/source. You can link these services by entering the following commands:

```
cd /usr/gopher/source
ln -s /usr/wais/source/include ./ir
ln -s /usr/wais/source/client/ui .
ln -s /usr/wais/source/bin .
```

When Gopher is recompiled, it will make the links between Gopher and freeWAIS and allow the two services to interwork.

Setting Up Your Gopher Directories

Gopher directories and files are quite simple to set up and follow standard naming conventions for the most part. Before you begin, though, you should know which documents and files are to be provided through Gopher to other users, and you should be able to write a short description of each. (If you don't know the contents of a file, either read it or get the author to summarize the file for you.) To begin, we'll assume you will use only a single directory for all your Gopher documents.

Begin by changing to the top directory you use for your Gopher directories (which you may have to create if you haven't already done so). This directory should not be where the Gopher source and configuration files are located, for convenience. Simply choose a useful name and create the directory. For example, to create the Gopher home directory /usr/gopher/data, you would issue a standard mkdir command:

```
mkdir /usr/gopher/data
```

Change into your Gopher directory and copy the files you want to make available into it. When you have done that, you can create a descriptive filename for each file (instead of the more obtuse filenames usually used) up to 80 characters long. For example, if you have a filename called q1.sales you may want to rename it to Company_Sales_1887_Q1 to help users identify the contents a little more easily.

The process for providing better filenames is to first create a .cap directory under your Gopher main directory (such as /usr/gopher/data/.cap). For each file in the main directory, you want to create a file in the .cap directory with the same name, but with a name and number. For example, suppose you have a file called q1.sales in /usr/gopher/data. In /usr/gopher/data/.cap you would create a file with the same name, q1.sales, which has the following contents:

```
Name=Company Sales for the First Quarter, 1887
Numb=1
```

The Name entry can have spaces or other special symbols in it, because it is echoed as a complete string. The Numb entry is for the location of the entry on your Gopher menu. For example, suppose you had the preceding entry and two other files, shown by using cat to display their contents:

```
$ cat q1.sales
Name=Company Sales for the First Quarter, 1887
Numb=1

$ cat q2.sales
Name=Company Sales for the Second Quarter, 1887
Numb=2

$cat q3.sales
Name=Company Sales for the Third Quarter, 1887
Numb=3
```

When these entries are displayed in a Gopher menu they will look like this:

```
1. Company Sales for the First Quarter, 1887
2. Company Sales for the Second Quarter, 1887
3. Company Sales for the Third Quarter, 1887
```

The order of filenames in the .cap directory doesn't matter, but you shouldn't have the same Numb entry more than once.

An alternative to using the .cap directory approach (which allows for easy addition of new files) is to use a single master file for each document you are making available. This file goes in your Gopher top directory and is called .names. Here's the .names file for the same three files just mentioned:

```
$ cd /usr/gopher/data
$ cat .names
# My Gopher main .names file

Path=./q1.sales
Name=Company Sales for the First Quarter, 1887
Numb=1

Path=./q2.sales
Name=Company Sales for the Second Quarter, 1887
Numb=2

Path=./q3.sales
Name=Company Sales for the Third Quarter, 1887
Numb=3
```

As you can see, this format contains the same information but adds the filename (which was not needed in .cap since the filenames were the same). One advantage to using a .names file is that you can reorder your menu entries much more easily because you only have one file to work with instead of several. Also, the .names file enables you to add an abstract describing the file. For example, you could have the following entry in a .names file:

```
Path=./gopher
Name=How to Set up A Gopher Service
Numb=16
Abstract=This document shows the steps you need to take to
set up a Gopher service.
```

You can get a little fancier with Gopher and have a menu item lead to another menu, or to another machine entirely. This is done with links, controlled by a link file, which ends with .link. A .link file has five pieces of information in it, in the same format as this example:

```
Name=More Sales Info
Type=1
Port=70
Path=/usr/gopher/data/more_sales
Host=wizard.tpci.com
```

The `Name` entry is what a user sees on the Gopher menu, and can be any type of description you want, regardless of what else is in the link file. The `Type` field has a code showing the type of document the file links to. The following are all valid codes:

0	Text
1	Directory
2	CSO name server
7	Full text index
8	telnet session
9	Binary
h	HTML file
I	Image file
M	MIME file
s	Sound file

These types are the same as the list shown earlier in this chapter for the types of files Gopher supports, although it's a little shorter here.

The `Port` field is the port for a connection to a remote system (if that's where the link leads), and the `Path` field is where the file is on the local or remote server. The `Host` field, not surprisingly, is the name of the host the file resides on. If you are setting up a link to another machine via FTP or WAIS, you need to specify the path to include the service name and any arguments. For example, if your Gopher menu leads users to a file on another machine through FTP, your link file may look like this:

```
Name=More Sales Info
Type=1
Port=+
Path=ftp:chatton.bigcat.com@/usr/gopher/cats
Host=+
```

The plus signs used in the `Port` and `Host` fields instruct the FTP service on the remote machine to return results to this machine using default ports (such as TCP port 21 for FTP). For a link to a WAIS directory, the format would be:

```
Name=More Sales Info
Type=7
Port=+
Path=waisrc:/usr/wais/data
Host=+
```

Finally, you may want to have a menu item execute a program. You can do this by having the `Path` field use the `exec` command:

```
Path=exec: "args" : do_this
```

where `do_this` is the program you want to execute and `args` are any arguments to be passed to `do_this`. If you have no arguments to pass, leave the quotation marks empty. This format is a little awkward, but it does work.

Starting Gopher

A Gopher server can be started either from the rc startup files, from the command line, or from the inetd daemon. From the command line or the rc files, you need a command line similar to this:

```
/usr/local/etc/gopherd /usr/gopher/gopher-data 70
```

which starts the daemon with the directory the startup Gopher menus reside in and the port number for connections.

The gopherd command line accepts a number of optional flags to control its behavior, although most mirror entries in the configuration files. Valid flags are as follows:

- -C   Disables directory caching
- -c   Runs without chroot restrictions
- -D   Enables debugging
- -I   inetd is used to invoke gopherd
- -L   Followed by a value for the maximum load average
- -l   Log file to record connections (filename follows the option)
- -o   Specifies an alternate configuration file from gopherd.conf (filename follows the option)
- -u   Sets the name of the owner running gopherd (valid username must follow the option)

To help secure your system, use chroot to create a separate file system structure for the Gopher area (as you did with FTP: see Chapter 47, "Setting Up an FTP and Anonymous FTP Site"). The -c option is not as secure as running gopherd with chroot active. Also, the -u option should be used to make gopherd run as a standard user's process, instead of as root. This helps protect against holes in the daemon that a hacker could exploit.

If you want to run Gopher under inetd (started whenever a request for the service arrives), modify the /etc/services and /etc/inetd.conf file to include a line for Gopher. Normally, the entry in /etc/services looks like this:

```
gopher      70/tcp
```

and the entry in /etc/inetd.conf looks like this:

```
gopher    stream    tcp    nowait    root
    /usr/local/etc/gopherd gopherd -I -u username
```

where *username* is the name of the user to run gopherd as (you can set up a specific account for gopher in /etc/passwd with standard permissions).

Once the Gopher server process is up and running, you can test your Gopher installation. You will need a Gopher client. Use the Gopher client to connect to your Gopher server (using your host name), and you should see the top directory of your Gopher resources. Another way to test your Gopher system is to use telnet. Use telnet to connect to the Gopher port, using a command like this:

```
telnet gopher 70
```

If the connection is properly made, you will see your Gopher system on the screen.

Yet another alternative to test your system is to use the program `gopherls`, which requires the name of the directory your Gopher source resides in. To start `gopherls`, you would issue a command as follows:

```
gopherls /usr/wais/gopher/data
```

specifying your Gopher data directory. You can use this technique to test new Gopher directories as you develop them.

Letting the World Know

Because you have spent a lot of time setting up your Gopher service, you can now let everyone else on the Internet know about it. (Of course, you should only do this when your Gopher service is ready, and if you want to allow general access. Don't follow these steps if you are granting access only to a few people or your local area network.)

To have your Gopher service listed in the main Gopher service directories, send an e-mail message to the address:

```
gopher@boombox.micro.umn.edu
```

and include the Gopher service's full name as it appears on your main menu, your host's name and IP address, the port number Gopher uses (which should be TCP port 70 for general Internet access), the e-mail account of the Gopher administrator, and a short paragraph describing your service. If you want, you can also provide a string that gives the path to the data directory, although since most Gopher systems start in the root directory, this string isn't necessary unless you have sub-menus for different purposes.

Summary

After all that, your Gopher service should be ready to use. You do need to set up the Gopher file entries, but that is beyond the scope of this chapter. Consult a good Internet or Gopher book for more information on Gopher directories, files, and entries. Gopher is a handy utility if you have volumes of information you want to share, and although the configuration process can take a while, once it's completed, the Gopher system tends to work very well.

Configuring a
WWW Site

50

by Tim Parker

Just about everyone on the planet knows about the World Wide Web. It's the most talked about aspect of the Internet. With the Web's popularity, more system users are getting into the game by setting up their own WWW servers and home pages. There are now sophisticated packages that act as Web servers for many operating systems. Linux, based on UNIX, has the software necessary to provide a Web server.

You don't need fancy software to set up a Web site, only a little time and the correct configuration information. That's what this chapter is about. We look at how you can set up a World Wide Web server on your Linux system—whether for friends, your LAN, or the Internet as a whole.

The major aspect of the Web that attracts users and makes it so powerful, aside from its multimedia capabilities, is the use of hyperlinks. A hyperlink lets one mouse click move you from document to document, site to site, graphic to movie, and so on. All the instructions of the move are built into the Web code.

There are two main aspects to the World Wide Web: server and client. Client software, such as Mosaic and Netscape, is probably the most familiar. However, many different Web client packages other than these two are also available, some specifically for X or Linux.

> **NOTE**
>
> The Red Hat distribution that accompanies this book already includes the Apache Web server software that is preconfigured on your Linux system during the installation process. However, this chapter provides an overview on manually setting up server software so that you can become more familiar with generic `httpd` server configurations.

Web Server Software

There are three primary versions of Web server software that will run under Linux. They are from NCSA, CERN, and Plexus. The most readily available system is from NCSA, which also produces Mosaic. NCSA's Web system is fast and quite small, can run under `inetd` or as a stand-alone daemon, and provides pretty good security. For this chapter, we will use NCSA's Web software, although you can easily use either of the other two packages instead (although the configuration information will be different, of course).

> **NOTE**
>
> The Web server software for one of the three is available via anonymous FTP or WWW from one of the sites listed here, depending on the type of server software you want:
> CERN: `ftp//ftp.w3.org/pub/httpd` (FTP)
> NCSA: `ftp.ncsa.uiuc.edu/web/httpd/unix/ncsa_httpd` (FTP)
>   `http://hoohoo.ncsa.uiuc.edu` (WWW)
> Plexus: `ftp://austin.bsdi.com/plexus/2.2.1/dist/Plexus-2.2.1.tar.Z` (WWW).

The NCSA Web software is available for Linux in both compiled and source code forms. Using the compiled version is much easier because you don't have to configure and compile the source code for the Linux platform. The binaries are often provided compressed and tarred, so you will have to uncompress and then extract the `tar` library. Alternatively, many CD-ROMs provide the software ready to go. If you do obtain the compressed form of the Web server software, follow the installation or `README` files to place the Web software in the proper location.

Unpacking the Web Files

If you have obtained a library of source code or binaries from an FTP or BBS site, you probably have to untar and uncompress them first. (Check with any `README` files, if there are any, before you do this; otherwise you may be doing this step for nothing.) Usually, you will proceed by creating a directory for the Web software, and then changing into it and expanding the library with a command such as this:

```
zcat httpd_X.X_XXX.tar.Z ¦ tar xvf -
```

The software is often named by the release and target platform, such as `httpd_1.5_linux.tar.Z`. Use whatever name your `tar` file has in the preceding line. Installation instructions are sometimes in a separate `tar` file, such as `Install.tar.z`, which you have to obtain and uncompress with the command:

```
zcat Install.tar.z
```

Make sure you are in the target directory when you issue these commands, though, or you will have to move a lot of files. You can place the files anywhere; however, it is often a good idea to create a special area for the Web software that can have its permissions controlled, such as `/usr/web`, `/var/web`, or a similar name.

Once you have extracted the contents of the Web server distribution and the library files are in their proper directories, you can look at what has been created automatically. You should find the following subdirectories:

`cgi-bin`	Common gateway interface binaries and scripts
`conf`	Configuration files
`icons`	Icons for home pages
`src`	Source code and (sometimes) executables
`support`	Support applications

Compiling the Web Software

If you don't have to modify the source and recompile for Linux (because your software is the Linux version), you can skip the configuration details mentioned in the rest of this section. On the other hand, you may want to know what is happening in the source code anyway, because you can better understand how Linux works with the Web server code. If you obtained a generic, untailored version of the NCSA Web server, you have to configure the software.

Begin by editing the `src/Makefile` file to specify your platform. There are several variables that you have to check for proper information:

AUX_CFLAGS	Uncomment the entry for Linux (identified by comment lines and symbols, usually).
CC	The name of the C compiler (usually cc or gcc).
EXTRA_LIBS	Add any extra libraries that need to be linked in (none are required for Linux).
FLAGS	Add any flags you need for linking (none are required for most Linux linkers).

Finally, look for the `CFLAGS` variable. Some of the values for `CFLAGS` may be set already. The following are valid values for `CFLAGS`:

-DSECURE_LOGS	Prevents CGI scripts from interfering with any log files written by the server software.
-DMAXIMUM_DNS	Provides a more secure resolution system at the cost of performance.
-DMINIMAL_DNS	Doesn't allow reverse name resolution, but speeds up performance.
-DNO_PASS	Prevents multiple children from being spawned.
-DPEM_AUTH	Enables PEM/PGP authentication schemes.
-DXBITHACK	Provides a service check on the execute bit of an HTML file.
-O2	Optimizing flag.

It is unlikely that you will need to change any of the flags in the `CFLAGS` section, but at least you now know what they do. Once you have checked the `src/Makefile` for its contents, you can compile the server software. Issue the command:

```
make linux
```

If you see error messages, check the configuration file carefully. The most common problem is the wrong platform (or multiple platforms) selected in the file.

Configuring the Web Software

Once the software is in the proper directories and compiled for your platform, it's time to configure the system. Begin with the `httpd.conf-dist` file. Copy it to the filename `httpd.conf`, which is what the server software looks for. This file handles the `httpd` server daemon. Before you edit the file, you have to decide whether you will install the Web server software to run as a daemon, or whether it will be started by `inetd`. If you anticipate frequent use, run the software as a daemon. For occasional use, either is acceptable.

There are several variables in `httpd.conf` that need to be checked or have values entered for them. All the variables in the configuration file follow the syntax:

```
variable value
```

with no equals sign or special symbol between the variable name and the value assigned to it. For example, a few lines would look like this:

```
FancyIndexing on
HeaderName Header
ReadmeName README
```

Where pathnames or filenames are supplied, they are usually relative to the Web server directory, unless explicitly declared as a full pathname. You need to supply the following variables in httpd.conf:

AccessConfig | The location of the access.conf configuration file. The default value is conf/access.conf. You can use either absolute or relative pathnames.

AgentLog | The log file to record details of the type and version of browser used to access your server. The default value is logs/agent_log.

ErrorLog | The name of the file to record errors. The default is /logs/error_log.

Group | The Group ID the server should run as (used only when server is running as a daemon). Can be either a group name or group ID number. If a number, it must be preceded by #. The default is #-1.

MaxServers | The maximum number of children allowed.

PidFile | The file where you want to record the process ID of each httpd copy. The default is /logs/httpd.pid. Used only when the server is in daemon mode.

Port | Port number httpd should listen to for clients. Default port is 80. If you don't want the Web server generally available, choose another number.

ResourceConfig | The path to the srm.conf file, usually conf/srm.conf.

ServerAdmin | E-mail address of the administrator.

ServerName | The fully qualified host name of the server.

ServerRoot | The path above which users cannot move (usually the Web server top directory or usr/local/etc/httpd).

ServerType | Either stand-alone (daemon) or inetd.

StartServers | The number of server processes that are started when the daemon executes.

TimeOut | The amount of time in seconds to wait for a client request, after which it is disconnected (default is 1800, which should be reduced).

TransferLog | The path to the location of the access log. Default is logs/access_log.

TypesConfig | The path to the location of the MIME configuration file. Default is conf/mime.conf.

User | Defines the user ID the server should run as (only valid if running as daemon). Can be name or number, but must be preceded by # if a number. Default is #-1.

The next configuration file to check is `srm.conf`, which is used to handle the server resources. The variables that have to be checked or set in the `srm.conf` file are as follows:

AccessFileName	The file that gives access permissions (default is `.htaccess`).
AddDescription	Provides a description of a type of file. For example, an entry could be `AddDescription PostScript file *.ps`. Multiple entries are allowed.
AddEncoding	Indicates that files with a particular extension are encoded somehow, such as `AddEncoding compress Z`. Multiple entries are allowed.
AddIcon	Gives the name of the icon to display for each type of file.
AddIconType	Uses `MIME` type to determine the icon to use.
AddType	Overrides `MIME` definitions for extensions.
Alias	Substitutes one pathname for another, such as `Alias data /usr/www/data`.
DefaultType	The default `MIME` type, usually `text/plain`.
DefaultIcon	The default icon to use when `FancyIndexing` is on (default is `/icons/unknown.xbm`).
DirectoryIndex	Filename to return when the URL is for your service only. Default value is `index.html`.
DocumentRoot	Absolute path to the HTML document directory. Default is `/usr/local/etc/httpd/htdocs`.
FancyIndexing	Adds icons and filename information to the file list for indexing. Default is on. (This option is for backward compatibility with the first release of HTTP.)
HeaderName	The filename used at the top of a list of files being indexed. Default is `Header`.
IndexOptions	Indexing parameters (including `FancyIndexing`, `IconsAreLinks`, `ScanHTMLTitles`, `SuppressLastModified`, `SuppressSize`, and `SuppressDescription`).
ReadmeName	The footer file is displayed with directory indexes. Default is `README`.
Redirect	Maps a path to another URL.
ScriptAlias	Similar to `Alias` but for scripts.
UserDir	Directory users can use this for `httpd` access. Default is `public_html`. Usually set to a user's home page directory. Can be set to `DISABLED`.

The third file to examine and modify is `access.conf-dist`, which defines the services available to WWW browsers. Usually, everything is accessible to a browser, but you may want to modify the file to tighten security or disable some services not supported on your Web site. The format of the `conf-dist` file is different than the two preceding configuration files. It uses a set of "sectioning directives" delineated by angle brackets. The general format of an entry is

```
<Directory Dir_Name>
...
</Directory>
```

and anything between the beginning and ending delimiters (<Directory> and </Directory>, respectively) are directives. It's not quite that easy, because there are several variations that can exist in the file. The best way to customize the access.conf-dist file is to follow these steps for a typical Web server installation:

1. Locate the Options directive and remove the Indexes option. This prevents users from browsing the httpd directory. Valid Options entries are discussed shortly.

2. Locate the first Directory directive and check the path to the cgi-bin directory. The default path is /usr/local/etc/httpd/cgi-bin.

3. Find the AllowOverride variable and set it to None (this prevents others from changing the settings). The default is All. Valid values for the AllowOverride variable are discussed shortly.

4. Find the Limit directive and set to whichever value you want.

The Limit directive controls access to your server. The following are valid values for the Limit directive:

allow	Allows specific host names following the allow keyword to access the service.
deny	Denies specific host names following the deny keyword from accessing the service.
order	Specifies the order in which allow and deny directives are evaluated (usually set to deny,allow but can also be allow,deny).
require	Requires authentication through a user file specified in the AuthUserFile entry.

The Options directive can have several entries, all of which have a different purpose. The default entry for Options is

```
Options Indexes FollowSymLinks
```

You removed the Indexes entry from the Options directive in the first step of the preceding customization procedure. These entries all apply to the directory the Options field appears in. The valid entries for the Options directive are:

All	All features enabled.
ExecCGI	cgi scripts can be executed from this directory.
FollowSymLinks	Allows httpd to follow symbolic links.
Includes	Include files for the server are enabled.
IncludesNoExec	Include files for the server are enabled but the exec option is disabled.
Indexes	Enables users to retrieve server-generated indexes (doesn't affect precompiled indexes).

None	No features enabled.
SymLinksIfOwnerMatch	Follows symbolic links only if the user ID of the symbolic link matches the user ID of the file.

The `AllowOverride` variable is set to `All` by default, and this should be changed. There are several valid values for `AllowOverride`, but the recommended setting for most Linux systems is `None`. The valid values for `AllowOverride` are as follows:

All	Access controlled by a configuration file in each directory.
AuthConfig	Enables some authentication routines. Valid values: `AuthName` (sets authorization name of directory); `AuthType` (sets authorization type of the directory, although there is only one legal value: `Basic`); `AuthUserFile` (specifies a file containing user names and passwords); and `AuthGroupFile` (specifies a file containing group names).
FileInfo	Enables `AddType` and `AddEncoding` directives.
Limit	Enables `Limit` directive.
None	No access files allowed.
Options	Enables `Options` directive.

After all that, the configuration files should be properly set. While the syntax is a little confusing, reading the default values shows you the proper format to use when changing entries. Next, you can start the Web server software.

Starting the Web Software

With the configuration complete, it's time to try out the Web server software. In the configuration files, you made a decision as to whether the Web software will run as a daemon (stand-alone) or will start from `inetd`. The startup procedure is a little different for each method (as you would expect), but both startup procedures can use one of the following three options on the command line:

-d	The absolute path to the root directory of the server files (used only if the default location is not valid).
-f	The configuration file to read if not the default value of `httpd.conf`.
-v	Displays the version number.

If you are using `inetd` to start your Web server software, you need to make a change to the `/etc/services` file to permit the Web software. Add a line similar to this to the `/etc/services` file:

```
http     port/tcp
```

where *port* is the port number used by your Web server software (usually 80).

Next, modify the `/etc/inetd.conf` file to include the startup commands for the Web server where the last entry is the path to the `httpd` binary:

```
httpd stream tcp nowait nobody /usr/web/httpd
```

Once this is done, restart `inetd` by killing and restarting the `inetd` process or by rebooting your system, and the service should be available through whatever port you specified in `/etc/services`.

If you are running the Web server software as a daemon, you can start it at any time from the command line with the command:

```
httpd &
```

Even better, add the startup commands to the proper `rc` startup files. The entry usually looks like this:

```
# start httpd
if [ -x /usr/web/httpd ]
then
 /usr/web/httpd
fi
```

substituting the proper paths for the `httpd` binary, of course. Rebooting your machine should start the Web server software on the default port number.

To test the Web server software, use any Web browser and type in the URL field:

```
http://machinename
```

where *machinename* is the name of your Web server. If you see the contents of the root Web directory or the `index.html` file, all is well. Otherwise, check the log files and configuration files for clues as to the problem.

If you haven't installed a Web browser yet, you can still check to see if the Web server is running by using `telnet`. Issue a command like this, substituting the name of your server (and your Web port number if different than 80):

```
telnet www.wizard.tpci.com 80
```

You should get a message similar to this if the Web server is responding properly:

```
Connected to wizard.tpci.com
Escape character is '^]'.
HEAD/HTTP/1.0
HTTP/1.0 200 OK
```

You'll also see some more lines showing details about the date and content. You may not be able to access anything, but this shows that the Web software is responding properly.

Setting Up Your Web Site

Having a server with nothing for content is useless, so you need to set up the information you will share through your Web system. This begins with Uniform Resource Locators (URLs), which are an address to file locations. Anyone using your service only has to know the URL. You don't need to have anything fancy. If you don't have a special home page, anyone connecting to your system will get the contents of the Web root directory's `index.html` file, or failing that, a directory listing of the Web root directory. That's pretty boring, though, and most users want fancy home pages. To write a home page, you need to use HTML (HyperText Markup Language).

A home page is like a main menu. Many users may not ever see it because they can enter into any of the subdirectories on your system, or obtain files from another Web system through a hyperlink, without ever seeing your home page. However, many users want to start at the top, and that's where your home page comes in. A home page file is usually called `index.html`. It is usually at the top of your Web source directories.

Writing an HTML document is not too difficult. The language uses a set of tags to indicate how the text is to be treated (such as headlines, body text, figures, and so on). The tricky part of HTML is getting the tags in the right place, without extra material on a line. HTML is rather strict about its syntax, so errors must be avoided to prevent problems.

In the early days of the Web, all documents were written with simple text editors. As the Web expanded, dedicated Web editors that understand HTML and the use of tags began to appear. Their popularity has driven developers to produce dozens of editors, filters, and utilities—all aimed at making a Web documenter's life easier (as well as to ensure that the HTML language is properly used). There are HTML editors for many operating systems.

HTML Authoring Tools

You can write HTML documents in many ways: You can use an ASCII editor, a word processor, or a dedicated HTML tool. The choice of which method you use depends on personal preference and your confidence in HTML coding, as well as which tools you can easily obtain. Because many HTML-specific tools have checking routines or filters to verify that your documents are correctly laid out and formatted, they can be appealing. They also tend to be more friendly than non-HTML editors. On the other hand, if you are a veteran programmer or writer, you may want to stick with your favorite editor and use a filter or syntax checker afterward.

> **NOTE**
>
> One of the best sites to look for new editors and filters is `http://www.ncsaa.uiuc.edu/SDG/Software/Mosaic/Docs/FAQ-Software.html` which contains an up-to-date list of offerings.

You can use any ASCII editor to write HTML pages, including simple screen-oriented editors based on `vi` or `emacs`. They all enable you to enter tags into a page of text, but the tags are treated as words with no special meaning. There is no validity checking performed by simple editors, because they simply don't understand HTML. There are some extensions for `emacs` and similar full-screen editors that provide a simple template check, but they are not rigorous in enforcing HTML styles.

If you wish to use a plain editor, you should carefully check your document for the valid use of tags. One of the easiest methods of checking a document is to import it into an HTML editor that has strong HTML tag checking. Another easy method is to simply call up the document on your Web browser and carefully study its appearance.

You can obtain a dedicated HTML authoring package from some sites, although they are not as common for Linux as for DOS and Windows. If you are running both operating systems, you can always develop your HTML documents in Windows, and then import them to Linux. There are several popular HTML tools for Windows, such as HTML Assistant, HTMLed, and HoTMetaL. A few of the WYSIWYG editors are also available for X, and hence run under Linux, such as HoTMetaL. Some HTML authoring tools are fully WYSIWYG, while others are character-based. Most offer strong verification systems for generated HTML code.

An alternative to using a dedicated editor for HTML documents is to enhance an existing WYSIWYG word processor to handle HTML properly. The most commonly targeted word processor for these extensions is Word for Windows, WordPerfect, and Word for DOS. Several extension products are available in varying degrees of complexity. Most run under Windows; although a few have been ported to Linux.

The advantage to using one of these extensions is that you retain a familiar editor and make use of the near-WYSIWYG features it can provide for HTML documents. Although it can't show you the final document in Web format, it can be close enough to prevent all but the most minor problems.

CU_HTML is a template for Microsoft's Word for Windows that gives a very-near-to WYSIWYG view of HTML documents. Graphically, CU_HTML looks much the same as Word, but with a new toolbar and pull-down menu item. CU_HTML provides a number of different styles and a toolbar of oft-used tasks. Tasks such as linking documents are easy, as are most tasks that tend to worry new HTML document writers. Dialog boxes are used for many tasks, simplifying the interface considerably.

The only major disadvantage to CU_HTML is that it can't be used to edit existing HTML documents if they are not in Word format. When CU_HTML creates an HTML document, there are two versions produced, one in HTML and the other as a Word DOC file. Without both, the document can't be edited. An existing document can be imported, but it loses all the tags.

Like CU_HTML, ANT_HTML is an extension to Word. There are some advantages and disadvantages of ANT_HTML over CU_HTML. The documentation and help is better with ANT_HTML, and the toolbar is much better. It also has automatic insertion of opening and closing tags as needed.

One system that has gained popularity among Linux users is tkWWW. tkWWW is a tool for the Tcl language and its Tk extension for X. tkWWW is a combination of a Web browser and a near-WYSIWYG HTML editor. Although originally UNIX based, tkWWW has been ported to several other platforms, including Windows and Macintosh.

NOTE

tkWWW can be obtained through anonymous FTP to `harbor.ecn.purdue.edu` in the directory `/pub/tcl/extensions`. Copies of Tcl and Tk can be found in several sites depending on the platform required, although most distributions of Linux have Tcl and Tk included in the distribution set. As a starting point, try anonymous FTP to `ftp.aud.alcatel.com` in the directory `tcl/extensions`.

When you create a Web page with tkWWW in editor mode, you can then flip modes to browser to see the same page properly formatted. In editor mode, most of the formatting is correct, but the tags are left visible. This makes for fast development of a Web page.

Unfortunately, tkWWW must rely on Tk for its windowing, which tends to slow things down a bit on average processors. Also, the browser aspect of tkWWW is not impressive, using standard Tk frames. However, as a prototyping tool, tkWWW is very attractive, especially if you know the Tcl language.

Another option is to use an HTML filter. HTML filters are tools that let you take a document produced with any kind of editor (including ASCII text editors) and convert the document to HTML. Filters are useful when you work in an editor that has its own proprietary format, such as Word.

HTML filters are attractive if you want to continue working in your favorite editor and simply want a utility to convert your document with tags to HTML. Filters tend to be fast and easy to work with, because they take a filename as input and generate an HTML output file. The degree of error checking and reporting varies with the tool.

There are filters available for most types of documents, many of which are available directly for Linux, or as source code that can be recompiled without modification under Linux. Word for Windows and Word for DOS documents can be converted to HTML with the CU_HTML and ANT_HTML extensions mentioned earlier. A few stand-alone conversion utilities have also begun to appear. The utility WPTOHTML converts WordPerfect documents to HTML. WPTOHTML is a set of macros for WordPerfect versions 5.1 and 6.0. The WordPerfect filter can also be used with other word processor formats that WordPerfect can import.

FrameMaker and FrameBuilder documents can be converted to HTML format with the tool FM2HTML. FM2HTML is a set of scripts that converts Frame documents to HTML, while preserving hypertext links and tables. It also handles GIF files without a problem. Because Frame documents are platform independent, Frame documents developed on a PC or Macintosh could be moved to the Linux platform and FM2HTML executed there.

> **NOTE**
>
> A copy of FM2HTML is available by anonymous FTP from bang.nta.no in the directory /pub. The UNIX set is called fm2html.tar.v.0.n.m.Z.

LaTeX and TeX files can be converted to HTML with several different utilities. There are quite a few Linux-based utilities available, including LATEXTOHTML, which can even handle inline LaTeX equations and links. For simpler documents, the utility VULCANIZE is faster but can't handle mathematical equations. Both LATEXTOHTML and VULCANIZE are Perl scripts.

> **NOTE**
>
> LATEXTOHTML is available through anonymous FTP from `ftp.tex.ac.uk` in the directory `pub/archive/support` as the file `latextohtml`. VULCANIZE can be obtained from the Web site `http://www.cis.upenn.edu/~mjd/vulcanize.html`.

RTFTOHTML is a common utility for converting RTF format documents to HTML. Many word processors handle RTF formats, so an RTF document can be saved from your favorite word processor and then RTFTOHTML run to convert the files.

> **NOTE**
>
> RTFTOHTML is available through `http:\\www.w3.org/hypertext/www/tools/rtftohtml-2.6.html`.

Maintaining HTML

Once you have written a Web document and it is available to the world, your job doesn't end. Unless your document is a simple text file, you will have links to other documents or Web servers embedded. These links must be verified at regular intervals. Also, the integrity of your Web pages should be checked at intervals, to ensure that the flow of the document from your home page is correct.

There are several utilities available to help you check links and also to scan the Web for other sites or documents you may want to provide a hyperlink to. These utilities tend to go by a number of names, such as robot, spider, or wanderer. They are all programs that move across the Web automatically, creating a list of Web links that you can access. (Spiders are similar to the Archie and Veronica tools for the Internet, although neither of these cover the Web.)

Although they are often thought of as utilities for users only (to get a list of sites to try), spiders and their kin are useful for document authors, too, because they show potentially useful and interesting links. One of the best known spiders is the World Wide Web Worm, or WWWW. WWWW enables you to search for keywords or create a Boolean search, and can cover titles, documents, and several other search types (including a search of all known HTML pages).

A similarly useful spider is WebCrawler, which is similar to WWWW except it can scan entire documents for matches of any keywords. It displays the result in an ordered list from closest match to least likely match.

NOTE

A copy of World Wide Web Worm can be obtained from
`http://www.cs.colorado.edu/home/mcbryan/WWWW.html`.
WebCrawler is available from
`http://www.biotech.washington.edu/WebCrawler/WebCrawler.html`.

A common problem with HTML documents as they age is that links that point to files or servers may no longer exist (because either the locations or the documents have changed). It is therefore good practice to validate the hyperlinks in a document on a regular basis. A popular hyperlink analyzer is HTML_ANALYZER. It examines each hyperlink and the contents of the hyperlink to ensure that they are consistent. HTML_ANALYZER functions by examining a document for all links, and then creating a text file that has a list of the links in it. HTML_ANALYZER uses the text files to compare the actual link content to what it should be.

HTML_ANALYZER actually does three tests: It validates the availability of the documents pointed to by hyperlinks (called validation); it looks for hyperlink contents that occur in the database but are not themselves hyperlinks (called completeness); and it looks for a one-to-one relation between hyperlinks and the contents of the hyperlink (called consistency). Any deviations are listed for the user.

HTML_ANALYZER users should have a good familiarity with HTML, their operating system, and the use of command-line driven analyzers. The tool must be compiled using the make utility prior to execution. There are several directories that must be created prior to running HTML_ANALYZER, and when it runs, it creates several temporary files when that are not cleaned up, so this is not a good utility for a novice.

Summary

Setting up your home page requires you to either use an HTML authoring tool or write HTML code directly into an editor. The HTML language is beyond the scope of this book, but you should find several good guides to HTML at your bookstore. HTML is rather easy to learn. With the information in this chapter, you should be able to set up your Web site to enable anyone on the Internet to connect to you. Enjoy the Web!

PART

VIII

IN THIS PART

Advanced Programming Topics

Source Code Control

51

by Peter MacKinnon

A large-scale software project involving numerous files and programmers can present logistical nightmares if you happen to be the poor soul responsible for managing it:

"How do I know whether this file of input/output routines that Sue has been working on is the most current one?"

"Oh, no—I have to recompile my application, but I can't remember which of these 50 files I changed since the last compile!"

Even small applications typically use more than one source code file. When compiling and linking C applications, you usually must deal with not only source code, but also header files and library files. Fortunately, Linux features a software development environment that, for the most part, can greatly simplify these concerns.

In this chapter, we will look at the following software development utilities for Linux:

- ■ `make`
- ■ RCS (Revision Control System)

make

Perhaps the most important of all the software development utilities for Linux, `make` is a program that keeps a record of dependencies between files and only updates those files that have been changed since the last update. The term *update* usually refers to a compile or link operation, but it may also involve the removal of temporary files. This updating process can sometimes be repeated dozens of times in the course of a software project. Instead of managing these tasks manually, `make` can be your automatic dependency manager, giving you more time to do other important things such as coding or watching TV.

`make` generates commands using a description file known as a `makefile`. These commands are then executed by the shell. The `makefile` is basically a set of rules for `make` to follow whenever performing an update of your program. These rules usually relate to the definition of the dependencies between files. In the case of creating a Linux executable of C code, this usually means compiling source code into object files, and linking those object files together, perhaps with additional library files. `make` also can figure some things out for itself, such as the fact that the modification times (or timestamps) for certain files may have changed.

> **NOTE**
>
> `makefile` or `Makefile` is literally the name that the `make` program expects to find in the current directory.

`make` is certainly best suited for C programming, but it can be used with other types of language compilers for Linux, such as assembler or FORTRAN.

A Sample *makefile*

Let's look at a simple application of make. The command

```
$ make someonehappy
```

tells Linux that you want to create a new version of someonehappy. In this case, someonehappy is an executable program; thus, there will be compiling and linking of files. someonehappy is referred to as the *target* of this make operation. The object files that are linked together to create the executable are known as someonehappy's *dependents*. The source code files that are compiled to create these object files are also indirect dependents of someonehappy.

The files that are used to build someonehappy are the following (the contents of these files are unimportant to the example):

> Two C source code files: main.c, dothis.c
>
> Three header files: yes.h, no.h, maybe.h
>
> One library file: /usr/happy/lib/likeatree.a
>
> An assembly language file: itquick.s

It appears that this is a small project, so you could choose to manually compile and link these files to build your executable. Instead, create a makefile for your someonehappy project to help automate these tedious tasks.

In your favorite editor, write the following:

```
someonehappy: main.o dothis.o itquick.o /usr/happy/lib/likeatree.a
        cc -o someonehappy main.o dothis.o itquick.o /usr/happy/lib/likeatree.a
main.o: main.c
        cc -c main.c
dothis.o: dothis.c
        cc -c dothis.c
itquick.o: itquick.s
        as -o itquick.o itquick.s
fresh:
        rm *.o
maybe.h: yes.h no.h
        cp yes.h no.h /users/sue/
```

Basic *makefile* Format

So, assuming that these files are in the same directory as the makefile, what do you have? The format of a makefile such as the one you have made is a series of entries. Your makefile has six entries: the first line of an entry is the dependency line, which lists the dependencies of the target denoted at the left of the colon; the second line is one or more command lines, which tells make what to do if the target is newer than its dependent (or dependents). An entry basically looks like this:

```
target: dependents
(TAB) command list
```

The space to the left of the command list is actually a tab. This is part of the makefile syntax: each command line must be indented using a tab. A dependency line can have a series of commands associated with it. make executes each command line as if the command had its own shell. Thus, the command

```
cd somewhere
mv *.c anotherwhere
```

will not behave the way you may have intended. To remedy this kind of situation, you must use the following syntax whenever you need to specify more than one command:

```
dependency line
command1;command2;command3;...
```

or

```
dependency line
        command1; \
        command2; \
        command3;
```

and so on. If you use a backslash to continue a line, it must be the last character before the end-of-line character.

> **TIP**
>
> You can specify different kinds of dependencies for a target by placing the same target name on different dependency lines.

The first entry in our makefile is the key one for building our executable. It states that someonehappy is to be built if all the dependent object files and library files are present, and if any are newer than the last version of someonehappy. Of course, if the executable is not present at all, make merrily performs the compile command listed, but not right away. First, make checks to see which object files need to be recompiled in order to recompile someonehappy. This is a recursive operation as make examines the dependencies of each target in the hierarchy, as defined in the makefile.

The last entry is a little goofy. It copies the header files yes.h and no.h (somehow related to maybe.h) to the home directories of the user named sue if they have been modified. This is somewhat conceivable if Sue was working on related programs that used these header files and needed the most recent copies at all times. More importantly, it illustrates that make can be used to do more than compiling and linking, and that make can execute several commands based on one dependency.

The fresh target is another example of a target being used to do more than just compiling. This target lacks any dependents, which is perfectly acceptable to the make program. As long as there are no files in the current directory named fresh, make executes the supplied command to remove all object files. This works because make treats any such entry as a target that must be updated.

So, if you enter the command

```
$ make someonehappy
```

make starts issuing the commands it finds in the makefile for each target that must be updated to achieve the final target. make echoes these commands to the user as it processes them. Simply entering

```
$ make
```

would also work in this case, because make always processes the first entry it finds in the makefile. These commands are echoed to the screen, and the make process halts if the compiler finds an error in the code.

If all of someonehappy's dependencies are up to date, make does nothing except inform you of the following:

```
'someonehappy' is up to date
```

You can actually supply the name (or names) of any valid target in your makefile on the command line for make. It performs updates in the order that they appear on the command line, but still applies the dependency rules found in the makefile. If you supply the name of a fictional target (one that doesn't appear in your makefile and is not the name of a file in the current directory), make will complain something like this:

```
$ make fiction
make: Don't know how to make fiction. Stop.
```

Building Different Versions of Programs

Suppose that you want to have different versions of your someonehappy program that use most of the same code, but require slightly different interface routines. These routines are located in different C files (dothis.c and dothat.c), and they both use the code found in main.c. Instead of having separate makefiles for each version, you can simply add targets that do different compiles. Your makefile would look like the following one. Note the first line that has been added. It is a comment about the makefile, and is denoted by a # character followed by the comment text.

```
# A makefile that creates two versions of the someonehappy program
someonehappy1: main.o dothis.o itquick.o /usr/happy/lib/likeatree.a
        cc -o someonehappy main.o dothis.o itquick.o /usr/happy/lib/likeatree.a
someonehappy2: main.o dothat.o itquick.o /usr/happy/lib/likeatree.a
        cc -o someonehappy main.o dothat.o itquick.o /usr/happy/lib/likeatree.a
main.o: main.c
        cc -c main.c
dothis.o: dothis.c
        cc -c dothis.c
dothat.o: dothat.c
        cc -c dothat.c
itquick.o: itquick.s
        as -o itquick.o itquick.s
fresh:
        rm *.o
maybe.h: yes.h no.h
        cp yes.h no.h /users/sue/
```

Thus, your `makefile` is now equipped to build two variations of the same program. Issue the command

```
$ make someonehappy1
```

to build the version using the interface routines found in `dothis.c`. Build your other program that uses the `dothat.c` interface routines with the following command:

```
$ make someonehappy2
```

Forcing Recompiles

It is possible to trick `make` into doing (or not doing) recompiles. An example of a situation in which you may not want `make` to recompile is when you have copied files from another directory. This operation updates the modification times of the files, though they may not need to be recompiled. You can use the `touch` utility or `make` with the `-t` option to update the modification times of all target files defined in the `makefile`.

> **TIP**
>
> Do you want to test your `makefile`? Use `make` with the `-n` option. It will echo the commands to you without actually executing them.

Macros

`make` lets you define macros within your `makefile`, which are expanded by `make` before the program executes the commands found in your `makefile`. Macros have the following format:

```
macro identifier = text
```

The text portion can be the name of a file, a directory, a program to execute, or just about anything. Text can also be a list of files, or a literal text string enclosed by double quotes. The following is an example of macros that you might use in your `someonehappy` makefile:

```
LIBFILES=/usr/happy/lib/likeatree.a
objects = main.o dothis.o
CC = /usr/bin/cc
1version="This is one version of someonehappy"
OPTIONS =
```

As a matter of convention, macros are usually in uppercase, but they can be typed in lowercase as in the previous example. Notice that the `OPTIONS` macro defined in the list has no text after the equal sign. This means that you have assigned the `OPTIONS` macro to a null string. Whenever this macro is found in a command list, `make` will generate the command as if there were no `OPTIONS` macro at all. By the same token, if you try to refer to an undefined macro, `make` will ignore it during command generation.

Macros can also include other macros, as in the following example:

```
BOOK_DIR = /users/book/
```

```
MY_CHAPTERS = ${BOOK_DIR}/pete/book
```

Macros must be defined before they are used on a dependency line, although they can refer to each other in any order.

make has internal macros that it recognizes for commonly used commands. The C compiler is defined by the CC macro, and the flags that the C compiler uses are stored in the CFLAGS macro.

Macros are referred to in the makefile by enclosing the macro name in curly brackets and preceding the first bracket with a $. If you use macros in the first someonehappy makefile, it might look like this:

```
# Time to exercise some macros
CC = /usr/bin/cc
AS = /usr/bin/as
OBJS = main.o dothis.o itquick.o
YN = yes.h no.h
# We could do the following if this part of the path might be used elsewhere
LIB_DIR = /usr/happy/lib
LIB_FILES = ${LIB_DIR}/likeatree.a
someonehappy:  ${OBJS} ${LIB_FILES}
      ${CC} -o someonehappy ${OBJS} ${LIB_FILES}
main.o: main.c
      cc -c main.c
dothis.o: dothis.c
      cc -c dothis.c
itquick.o: itquick.s
      ${AS} -o itquick.o itquick.s
fresh:
      rm *.o
maybe.h: ${YN}
      cp yes.h no.h /users/sue/
```

make also recognizes shell variables as macros if they are set in the same shell in which make was invoked. For example, if a C shell variable named BACKUP is defined by

```
$ setenv BACKUP /usr/happy/backup
```

you can use it as a macro in your makefile. The macro definition

```
OTHER_BACKUP = ${BACKUP}/last_week
```

would be expanded by make to be

```
/usr/happy/backup/last_week
```

You can reduce the size of your makefile even further. For starters, you don't have to specify the executables for the C and assembler compilers because these are known to make. You can also use two other internal macros, referred to by the symbols $@ and $?. The $@ macro always denotes the current target; the $? macro refers to all the dependents that are newer than the current target. Both of these macros can only be used within command lines. Thus, the makefile command

```
someonehappy: ${OBJS} ${LIB_FILES}
      ${CC} -o $@ ${OBJS} ${LIB_FILES}
```

will generate

```
/usr/bin/cc -o someonehappy main.o dothis.o itquick.o /usr/happy/lib/likeatree.a
```

when using the following:

```
$ make someonehappy
```

The `$?` macro is a little trickier to use, but quite powerful. Use it to copy the `yes.h` and `no.h` header files to Sue's home directory whenever they are updated. The `makefile` command

```
maybe.h: ${YN}
       cp $? /users/sue/
```

evaluates to

```
cp no.h /users/sue/
```

if only the `no.h` header file has been modified. It also evaluates to

```
cp yes.h no.h /users/sue/
```

if both header files have been updated since the last `make` of `someonehappy`.

So, with a little imagination, you can make use of some well-placed macros to shrink your `makefile` further, and arrive at the following:

```
# Papa's got a brand new makefile
OBJS = main.o dothis.o itquick.o
YN = yes.h no.h
LIB_DIR = /usr/happy/lib
LIB_FILES = ${LIB_DIR}/likeatree.a
someonehappy:  ${OBJS} ${LIB_FILES}
       ${CC} -o $@ ${OBJS} ${LIB_FILES}
main.o: main.c
       cc -c $?
dothis.o: dothis.c
       cc -c $?
itquick.o: itquick.s
       ${AS} -o $@ $?
fresh:
       rm *.o
maybe.h: ${YN}
       cp $? /users/sue/
```

Suffix Rules

As mentioned earlier in the "Macros" section, `make` does not necessarily require everything to be spelled out for it in the `makefile`. Because `make` was designed to enhance software development in Linux, it has knowledge about how the compilers work, especially for C. For example, `make` knows that the C compiler expects to compile source code files having a `.c` suffix, and that it generates object files having an `.o` suffix. This knowledge is encapsulated in a suffix rule: `make` examines the suffix of a target or dependent to determine what it should do next.

There are many suffix rules that are internal to `make`, most of which deal with the compilation of source and linking of object files. The default suffix rules that are applicable in your `makefile` are as follows:

```
.SUFFIXES: .o .c .s

.c.o:
     ${CC} ${CFLAGS} -c $<

.s.o:
     ${AS} ${ASFLAGS} -o $@ $<
```

The first line is a dependency line stating the suffixes that make should try to find rules for if none are explicitly written in the makefile. The second dependency line is terse: Essentially, it tells make to execute the associated C compile on any file with a .c suffix whose corresponding object file (.o) is out of date. The third line is a similar directive for assembler files. The new macro $< has a similar role to that of the $? directive, but can only be used in a suffix rule. It represents the dependency that the rule is currently being applied to.

These default suffix rules are powerful in that all you really have to list in your makefile are any relevant object files. make does the rest: If main.o is out of date, make automatically searches for a main.c file to compile. This also works for the itquick.o object file. After the object files are updated, the compile of someonehappy can execute.

You can also specify your own suffix rules in order to have make perform other operations. Say, for instance, that you want to copy object files to another directory after they are compiled. You could explicitly write the appropriate suffix rule in the following way:

```
.c.o:
     ${CC} ${CFLAGS} -c $<
     cp $@  backup
```

The $@ macro, as you know, refers to the current target. Thus, on the dependency line shown, the target is a .o file, and the dependency is the corresponding .c file.

Now that you know how to exploit the suffix rule feature of make, you can rewrite your someonehappy makefile for the last time (I'll bet you're glad to hear that news).

```
# The final kick at the can
OBJS = main.o dothis.o itquick.o
YN = yes.h no.h
LIB_FILES = /usr/happy/lib/likeatree.a
someonehappy:  ${OBJS} ${LIB_FILES}
     ${CC} -o $@ ${OBJS} ${LIB_FILES}
fresh:
     rm *.o
maybe.h: ${YN}
     cp $? /users/sue/
```

This makefile works as your first one did, and you can compile the entire program using the following:

```
$ make somonehappy
```

Or, just compile one component of it as follows:

```
$ make itquick.o
```

This discussion only scratches the surface of make. You should refer to the man page for make to further explore its many capabilities.

RCS

One of the other important factors involved in software development is the management of source code files as they evolve. On any type of software project, you might continuously release newer versions of a program as features are added or bugs are fixed. Larger projects usually involve several programmers, which can complicate versioning and concurrency issues even further. In the absence of a system to manage the versioning of source code on your behalf, it would be very easy to lose track of the versions of files. This could lead to situations in which modifications are inadvertently wiped out or redundantly coded by different programmers. Fortunately, Linux provides just such a versioning system, called *RCS* (*Revision Control System*).

RCS can administer the versioning of files by controlling access to them. For anyone to update a particular file, the person must record in RCS who she is and why she is making the changes. RCS can then record this information along with the updates in an RCS file separate from the original version. Because the updates are kept independent from the original file, you can easily return to any previous version if necessary. This can also have the benefit of conserving disk space because you don't have to keep copies of the entire file around. This is certainly true for situations in which versions differ only by a few lines; it is less useful if there are only a few versions, each of which is largely different from the next.

Deltas

The set of changes that RCS records for an RCS file is referred to as a delta. The version number has two forms. The first form contains a release number and a level number. The release number is normally used to reflect a significant change to the code in the file. When you first create an RCS file, it is given a default release of 1 and level of 1 (1.1). RCS automatically assigns incrementally higher integers for the level number within a release (for example, 1.1, 1.2, 1.3, and so on). RCS enables you to override this automatic incrementing whenever you want to upgrade the version to a new release.

The second form of the version number also has the release and level components, but adds a branch number followed by a sequence number. You might use this form if you were developing a program for a client that required bug fixes, but you don't want to place these fixes in the next "official" version. Although the next version may include these fixes anyway, you may be in the process of adding features that would delay its release. For this reason, you would add a branch to your RCS file for this other development stream, which would then progress with sequence increments. For example, imagine that you have a planned development stream of 3.1, 3.2, 3.3, 3.4, and so on. You realize that you need to introduce a bug fix stream at 3.3, which will not include the functionality proposed for 3.4. This bug fix stream would have a numbering sequence of 3.3.1.1, 3.3.1.2, 3.3.1.3, and so on.

> **TIP**
>
> As a matter of good development practice, each level or sequence should represent a complete set of changes. That implies that the code in each version is tested to be free of any obvious bugs.

> **NOTE**
>
> Is any code completely bug-free? This certainly isn't the case for complex programs in which bugs might become apparent only when code is integrated from different developers. Your aim is to at least make your own part of the world bug-free.

Creating an RCS File

Let's assume that you have the following file of C code, called `finest.c`:

```c
/* A little something for RCS */
#include <stdio.h>
main()
{
        printf("Programming at its finest...\n");
}
```

The first step in creating an RCS file is to make an RCS directory:

```
$ mkdir RCS
```

This is where your RCS files will be maintained. You can then check a file into RCS by issuing the `ci` (check-in) command. Using your trusty `finest.c` program, enter the following:

```
$ ci finest.c
```

This operation prompts for comments, and then creates a file in the RCS directory called `finest.c,v`, which contains all the deltas on your file. After this, RCS transfers the contents of the original file and denotes it as revision 1.1. Anytime that you check in a file, RCS removes the working copy from the RCS directory.

Retrieving an RCS File

To retrieve a copy of your file, use the `co` (check-out) command. If you use this command without any parameters, RCS gives you a read-only version of the file, which you can't edit. You need to use the `-l` option in order to obtain a version of the file that you can edit.

```
$ co -l finest.c
```

Whenever you finish making changes to the file, you can check it back in using `ci`. RCS prompts for text that is entered as a log of the changes made. This time the `finest.c` file is deposited as revision 1.2.

RCS revision numbers consist of release, level, branch, and sequence components. RCS commands typically use the most recent version of a file, unless they are instructed otherwise. For instance, say that the most recent version of `finest.c` is 2.7. If you want to check in `finest.c` as release 3, issue the `ci` command with the `-r` option, like this:

```
$ ci -r3 finest.c
```

This creates a new release of the file as 3.1. You could also start a branch at revision 2.7 by issuing the following:

```
$ ci -r2.7.1 finest.c
```

You can remove out-of-date versions with the `rcs` command and its `-o` option.

```
$ rcs -o2.6 finest.c
```

Using Keywords

RCS lets you enter keywords as part of a file. These keywords contain specific information about such things as revision dates and creator names that can be extracted using the `ident` command. Keywords are embedded directly into the working copy of a file. When that file is checked in and checked out again, these keywords have values attached to them. The syntax is

```
$keyword$
```

which is transformed into

```
$keyword: value$
```

Some keywords used by RCS are shown in the following list.

`$Author$`	The user who checked in a revision
`$Date$`	The date and time of check-in
`$Log$`	Accumulated messages that describe the file
`Revision$`	The revision number

If your `finest.c` file used the keywords from the previous table, the command

```
$ ident finest.c
```

produces output like this:

```
$Author: pete $
$Date: 95/01/15 23:18:15 $
$Log: finest.c,v $
# Revision 1.2 95/01/15 23:18:15 pete
# Some modifications
#
```

```
# Revision 1.1 95/01/15 18:34:09 pete
# The grand opening of finest.c!
#
$Revision: 1.2 $
```

Retrieving Version Information from an RCS File

Instead of querying the contents of an RCS file based on keywords, you might be interested in obtaining summary information about the version attributes using the `rlog` command with the `-t` option. On the `finest.c` RCS file, the output from

```
$ rlog -t finest.c
```

would produce output formatted like this:

```
RCS file:       finest.c,v;  Working file:    finest.c
head:           3.2
locks:          pete: 2.1;  strict
access list: rick tim
aymbolic names:
comment leader:   " * "
total revisions: 10;
description:
You know...programming at its finest...
=========================================================
```

`head` refers to the version number of the highest revision in the entire stream. `locks` describes which users have versions checked out and the type of lock (strict or implicit for the RCS file owner). `access list` is a list of users who have been authorized to make deltas on this RCS file. The next section illustrates how user access privileges for an RCS file can be changed.

Administering Access

One of the most important functions of RCS is to mediate the access of users to a set of files. For each file, RCS maintains a list of users who have permission to create deltas on that file. This list is empty to begin with, so that all users have permission to make deltas. The `rcs` command is used to assign user names or group names with delta privileges. The command

```
$ rcs -arick,tim finest.c
```

enables the users Rick and Tim to make deltas on `finest.c` and simultaneously restricts all other users (except the owner) from that privilege.

Perhaps you change your mind and decide that the user Rick is not worthy of making deltas on your wonderful `finest.c` program. You can deny him that privilege using the `-e` option:

```
& rcs -erick finest.c
```

Suddenly, in a fit of paranoia, you can trust no one to make deltas on `finest.c`. Like a software Mussolini, you place a global lock (which applies to everyone, including the owner) on release 2 of `finest.c` using the `-e` and `-L` options:

```
$ rcs -e -L2 finest.c
```

so that no one can make changes on any delta in the release 2 stream. Only the file owner could make changes, but this person still would have to explicitly put a lock on the file for every check-out and check-in operation.

Comparing and Merging Revisions

Revisions can be compared to each other to discover what, if any, differences lie between them. This can be used as a means of safely merging together edits of a single source file by different developers. The `rcsdiff` command is used to show differences between revisions existing in an RCS file, or between a checked-out version and the most current revision in the RCS file. To compare the `finest.c` 1.2 version to the 1.5 version, enter

```
$ rcsdiff -r1.2 -r1.5 finest.c
```

The output would appear something like

```
RCS file: finest.c,v
retrieving revision 1.1
rdiff  -r1.2 -r1.5 finest.c
6a7,8
>
> /* ...but what good is this? */
```

This output indicates that the only difference between the files is that two new lines have been added after the original line six. To just compare your current checked-out version with that of the "head" version in the RCS file, simply enter

```
$ rcsdiff finest.c
```

Once you have determined if there are any conflicts in your edits with others, you may decide to merge together revisions. You can do this with the `rcsmerge` command. The format of this command is to take one or two filenames representing the version to be merged, and a third filename indicating the working file (in the following example, this is `finest.c`).

The command

```
$ rcsmerge -r1.3 -r1.6 finest.c
```

produces output like this:

```
RCS file: finest.c,v
retrieving revision 1.3
retrieving revision 1.6
Merging differences between 1.3 and 1.6 into finest.c
```

If any lines between the two files overlapped, rcsmerge would indicate which lines originated from which merged file in the working copy. You would have to resolve these overlaps by explicitly editing the working copy to remove any conflicts before checking the working copy back into RCS.

> **NOTE**
>
> There is an implied order in which the files to be merged are placed in the rcsmerge command. If you are placing a higher version before a lower one at the -r options, this is essentially undoing the edits that have transpired from the older (lower) version to the newer (higher) version.

Tying It All Together: Working with *make* and RCS

The make program supports interaction with RCS, enabling you to have a largely complete software development environment. However, the whole issue of using make with RCS is a sticky one if your software project involves several people sharing source code files. Clearly, it may be problematic if someone is compiling files that you need to be stable in order to do your own software testing. This may be more of a communication and scheduling issue between team members than anything else. At any rate, using make with RCS can be very convenient for a single programmer, particularly in the Linux environment.

make can handle RCS files through the application of user-defined suffix rules that recognize the ,v suffix. RCS interfaces well with make because its files use the ,v suffix, which works well within a suffix rule. You could write a set of RCS-specific suffix rules to compile C code as follows:

```
CO = co
.c,v.o:
        ${CO} $<
        ${CC} ${CFLAGS} -c $*.c
        - rm -f $*.c
```

The CO macro represents the RCS check-out command. The $*.c macro is necessary because make automatically strips off the .c suffix. The hyphen preceding the rm command instructs make to continue, even if the rm fails. For main.c stored in RCS, make generates these commands:

```
co main.c
cc -O -c main.c
rm -f main.c
```

Summary

Linux offers two key utilities for managing software development: make and RCS. make is a program that generates commands for compilation, linking, and other related development activities. make can manage dependencies between source code and object files so that an entire project can be recompiled as much as is required for it to be up-to-date. RCS is a set of source code control programs that enables several developers to work on a software project simultaneously. It manages the use of a source code file by keeping a history of editing changes that have been applied to it. The other benefit of versioning control is that it can, in many cases, reduce disk space requirements for a project. CVS is an enhancement to the RCS programs. It automatically provides for the merging of revisions. This capability enables several developers to work on the same source code file at once, with the caveat that they are responsible for any merging conflicts that arise.

Working with the Kernel

52

by Kamran Husain and Tim Parker

IN THIS CHAPTER

This chapter will look at:

- How to install and recompile the kernel of Linux
- How to add new software to the kernel
- How to install new versions of the shared libraries
- The steps necessary to create a new Linux kernel

Usually, you will want to leave the kernel alone, except when you are performing a major upgrade or installing a new device driver that has special kernel modifications. The details of the process are usually supplied with the software. However, this chapter gives you a good idea of the general process.

Few people will want to change the details in the kernel source code, because they lack the knowledge to do so (or have enough knowledge to know that hacking the kernel can severely damage the system). However, most users will want to install new versions of Linux, add patches, or modify the kernel's behavior a little.

> **CAUTION**
>
> Don't modify the kernel unless you know what you are doing. If you damage the source code, your kernel may be unusable—and in the worst cases, your file system may be affected. Take care and follow instructions carefully. You need to know several things about kernel manipulation, and this chapter looks at only the basics.

Several versions of Linux are commonly used, with a few inconsistencies between them. For that reason, the exact instructions given here may not work with your version of Linux. However, the general approach is the same, and only the directory or utility names may be different. Most versions of Linux supply documentation that lists the recompilation process and the locations of the source code and compiled programs.

Before you do anything with the kernel or utilities, make sure you have a good set of emergency boot disks, and preferably, a complete backup on tape or diskette. Although the process of modifying the kernel is not difficult, every now and then it does cause problems that can leave you stranded without a working system. Boot disks are the best way to recover, so make at least one extra set.

Upgrading and Installing New Kernel Software

Linux is a dynamic operating system. New releases of the kernel, or parts of the operating system that can be linked into the kernel, are made available at regular intervals to users. Whether or not you want to upgrade to the new releases is up to you and usually depends on the features or bug fixes that the new release offers. You will probably have to recompile and relink the kernel when new software is added, unless it is loaded as a utility or device driver.

You should avoid upgrading your system with every new release, for a couple of reasons. The most common problem with constant upgrades is that you may be stuck with a new software package that causes backward compatibility problems with your existing system or that has a major problem with it that was not patched before the new software was released. This can cause you no end of trouble. Most new software releases wipe out existing configuration information, so you have to reconfigure the packages that are being installed from scratch.

Another problem with constant upgrades is that the frequency with which new releases are made available is so high that you can probably spend more time simply loading and recompiling kernels and utilities than actually using the system. This becomes tiresome after a while. Because most major releases of the Linux operating system are available, the number of changes to the system is usually quite small. Therefore, you should read the release notes carefully to ensure that the release is worth the installation time and trouble.

The best advice is to upgrade only once or twice a year, and only when there is a new feature or enhancement to your system that will make a significant difference in the way you use Linux. It's tempting to always have the latest and newest versions of the operating system, but there is a lot to be said for having a stable, functioning operating system.

If you do upgrade to a new release, bear in mind that you don't have to upgrade everything. The last few Linux releases have changed only about five percent of the operating system with each new major package upgrade. Instead of replacing the entire system, just install those parts that will have a definite effect, such as the kernel, compilers and their libraries, and frequently used utilities. This saves time and reconfiguration.

Compiling the Kernel from Source Code

Upgrading, replacing, or adding new code to the kernel is usually a simple process: you obtain the source for the kernel, make any configuration changes, compile it, and then place it in the proper location on the file system to run the system properly. The process is often automated for you by a shell script or installation program, and some upgrades are completely automated— you don't need to do anything except start the upgrade utility.

Kernel sources for new releases of Linux are available from CD-ROM distributions, FTP sites (see Appendix A, "Linux FTP Sites and Newsgroups"), user groups, and many other locations. Most kernel versions are numbered with a version and a patch level, so you will see kernel names such as 1.12.123, where 1 is the major release, 12 is the minor version release, and 123 is the patch number. Most sites of kernel source code maintain several versions simultaneously, so check through the source directories for the latest version of the kernel.

Patch releases are sometimes numbered differently and do not require the entire source of the kernel to install. They just require the source of the patch. In most cases, the patch overlays a section of existing source code, and a simple recompilation is all that's necessary to install the patch. Patches are released quite frequently.

Most kernel source programs are maintained as a gzipped tar file. Unpack the files into a subdirectory called /usr/src, which is where most of the source code is kept for Linux. Some versions of Linux keep other directories for the kernel source, so you may want to check any documentation supplied with the system or look for a README file in one of the three /usr/src subdirectories, linux, linux-1.2.13, or redhat for more instructions.

Often, unpacking the gzipped tar file in /usr/src creates a subdirectory called /usr/src/linux, which can overwrite your last version of the kernel source. Before starting the unpacking process, rename or copy any existing /usr/src/linux (or whatever name is used with the new kernel) so you have a backup version in case of problems.

After the kernel source has been unpacked, you need to create two symbolic links to the /usr/include directory, if they are not created already or set by the installation procedure. Usually, the link commands required are

```
ln -sf /usr/src/linux/include/linux /usr/include/linux
ln -sf /usr/src/linux/include/asm /usr/include/asm
```

If the directory names shown are different from your version of Linux, substitute the new directory names for /usr/src/linux. Without these links, the upgrade or installation of a new kernel cannot proceed.

After the source code has been ungzipped and untarred and the links have been established, the compilation process can begin. You must have a version of gcc or g++ (the GNU C and C++ compilers) or some other compatible compiler available for the compilation. You may have to check with the source-code documentation to make sure you have the correct versions of the compilers; occasionally, new kernel features are added that are not supported by older versions of gcc or g++.

Check the file /usr/src/linux/Makefile (or whatever path the Makefile is in with your source distribution). There will be a line in the file that defined the ROOT_DEV, which is the device that is used as the root file system when Linux boots. Usually the line looks like this:

```
ROOT_DEV = CURRENT
```

If you have any other value, make sure it is correct for your file-system configuration. If the Makefile has no value, set it as shown in the preceding code line.

TIP

It's a good idea to run make clean; make depend; make mrproper before rebuilding the kernel to make sure all old files are removed.

The compilation process begins when you change to the `/usr/src/linux` directory and issue the following command:

```
make config
```

This command invokes the `make` utility for the C compiler. The process may be slightly different for some versions of Linux, so you should check with any release or installation notes supplied with the source code.

> **NOTE**
>
> Be sure that you are running either `/bin/bash` or `/bin/sh` before you run `make`. Running another shell such as `tcsh` may cause you problems with the make files.

The `config` program issues a series of questions and prompts that you need to answer to indicate any configuration issues that need to be completed before the actual compilation begins. These may be about the type of disk drive you are using, the CPU, any partitions, or other devices, such as CD-ROMs. Answer the questions as well as you can. If you are unsure, choose the default values or the choice that makes the most sense. The worst case is that you might have to redo the process if the system doesn't run properly. (You do have an emergency boot disk ready, don't you?)

Next, you have to set all the source dependencies. This is a step that is commonly skipped, and it can cause several problems if it is not performed for each software release. Issue the command

```
make dep
```

If the software you are installing does not have a `dep` file, check with the release or installation notes to ensure that the dependencies are correctly handled by the other steps.

After that, you can finally compile the new kernel. The command to start the process is

```
make zImage
make zdisk
make zlilo
```

This compiles the source code and leaves the new kernel image file in the current directory (usually `/usr/src/linux`). The `make zdisk` is really necessary for creating a boot disk, and therefore expects a blank, unformatted disk in the floppy drive and will ask you for one as it runs. Not all releases or upgrades to the kernel support compressed image compilation.

The last step in the process is to copy the new kernel image file to the boot device or a boot floppy. Use the following command to place the file on a floppy:

```
cp Image /dev/fd0
```

To be safe, copy the old kernel to a known image and then copy the newly created image to the root. This would be accomplished with these two commands:

```
mv /vmlinuz /vmlinuz.old
cp /usr/src/linux/arch/i386/boot/zImage /vmlinuz
```

Now all that remains is to reboot the system and see if the new kernel loads properly. If there are any problems, boot from a floppy, restore the old kernel, and start the process again. Check the documentation supplied with the release source code for any information about problems you may encounter or steps that may have been added to the process.

Adding Drivers to the Kernel

You may want to link in new device drivers or special software to the kernel without going through the upgrade process of the kernel itself. This is often necessary when you add a new device to the system, such as a multiport board or an optical drive, that should be loaded during the boot process. Alternatively, you may be adding special security software that must be linked into the kernel.

The add-in kernel software usually has installation instructions provided, but the general process is to locate the source in a directory that can be found by the kernel-recompilation process (such as the /usr/src directory). To instruct the make utility to add the new code to the kernel, you often need to modify the Makefile. These modifications may be performed manually or by an installation script. Some software has its own Makefile supplied for this reason.

At this point, it's time to begin the kernel recompilation with the new software added into the load. The process is the same as shown in the preceding section; the kernel is installed in the boot location or set by LILO. Typically, the entire process takes about 10 minutes and is quite trouble-free, unless the vendor of the kernel modification did a sloppy job. Make sure that the source code provided for the modification will work with your version of the Linux kernel by reading any text files that accompany the code and software-compatibility files included with most distributions of Linux.

The latest version numbers to look for are found in the newsgroup discussions. To see the version of kernel source tree to build your kernel, use the command: uname -a. The version number of your kernel should be 1.2.13 or higher.

Upgrading Libraries

Most of the software on a Linux system is set to use shared libraries (a set of subroutines used by many programs). When you see the message

```
Incompatible library version
```

displayed after you have performed an upgrade to the system and you try to execute a utility, it means that the libraries have been updated and need to be recompiled. Most libraries are backward compatible, so existing software should work properly even after a library upgrade.

Library upgrades occur less frequently than kernel upgrades, and you can find them in the same places. There are usually documents that guide you to the latest version of a library, or there may be a file explaining which libraries are necessary with new versions of the operating system kernel.

Most library upgrades are `gzipped` `tar` files, and the process for unpacking them is the same as for kernel source code—except that the target directories are usually `/lib`, `/usr/lib`, and `/usr/include`. Usually, any files that have the extension `.a` or `.aa` go in the `/usr/lib` directory. Shared library image files, which have the format `libc.so.version`, are installed into `/lib`.

You may have to change symbolic links within the file system to point to the latest version of the library. For example, if you are running library version `libc.so.4.4.1` and upgrade to `libc.so.5.2.18`, you must remove the old link and reset the symbolic link set in `/lib` to this `libc.so.5.2.18` file. The command is:

```
ln -sf /lib/libc/so/4/4/1 /lib/libc.so.5.2.18
```

where the last filename in the link command is the name of the current library file in `/lib`. Your library name may be different, so check the directory and release or installation notes first.

You would also need to change the symbolic link for the file `libm.so.version` in the same manner. Do not delete the symbolic links; all programs that depend on the shared library (including `ls`) would be unable to function without them.

Developing Modules

A module is an object file that is loaded at runtime by the Linux kernel. Modules offer a bit of functionality that does not have to be loaded in memory all the time. When a particular function in a module is found, the Linux kernel will load it in. Types of modules include, but are not limited to, the following:

- Tape module via the `ftape` module
- PPP/SLIP modules
- CD-ROM modules

First check to see if your kernel supports modules. To do this, run the `make config` command and see what the default response to the question of "dynamic loading support" is. If the answer to this question is not Yes, you should answer Yes, and then rebuild, install, and boot from a new kernel. If the system already supports modules, you can begin with the next step of making modules.

To make the modules on your system, go to /usr/src/linux directory and run the two commands:

```
make modules
```

```
make modules_install.
```

Be prepared to wait a while.

To list the current modules in your kernel, use the lsmod command. To insert a module, use the command insmod moduleName. To remove a module, use the command rmmod moduleName. Modules can be loaded automatically by placing the commands to load them in the /etc/rc.d/ rc.sysinit file.

The Red Hat Live File System

Red Hat offers a "live" file system on CD-ROM. If you are short on disk space or do not want the entire Red Hat distribution on your hard drive, you can run off the CD-ROM with the "live" file system. It's easy to mount the CD-ROM as an extension of the file system with the command:

```
mount -t iso9660 /dev/cdrom /mntFS
```

From then on the CD-ROM will be accessed under the /mntFS directory. To check out the source files, and so on for your Red Hat distribution you would look in the directory /mntFS/live/usr/src/linux. The Red Hat subdirectory under the /mntFS/live/usr/src/ directory is empty. (An oversight you ask? No, if you buy the official version from Red Hat you get a second CD with the source tree on it!)

There are only a few subdirectories under the live file system. These directories are listed here relative to the /mntFS/live tree:

```
total 145
drwxrwxr-x  16 root      root          2048 Mar  6 13:53 .
drwxr-xr-x   6 root      root          2048 Mar  6 13:32 ..
-r--r--r--   1 root      root           586 Mar  6 14:10 TRANS.TBL
drwxr-xr-x   2 root      root          8192 Mar  6 13:45 bin
drwxr-xr-x   2 root      root          2048 Mar  6 13:45 boot
drwxr-xr-x   3 root      root         77824 Mar  6 13:45 dev
drwxr-xr-x  11 root      root         12288 Mar  6 13:45 etc
drwxr-xr-x   6 root      root          2048 Mar  6 13:45 home
drwxr-xr-x   3 root      root          6144 Mar  6 13:45 lib
drwxr-xr-x   2 root      root          2048 Mar  6 13:32 lost+found
drwxr-xr-x   4 root      root          2048 Mar  6 13:45 mnt
dr-xr-xr-x  29 root      root          6144 Mar  6 13:46 proc
drwxr-xr-x   4 root      root          2048 Mar  6 13:46 root
drwxr-xr-x   2 root      root         10240 Mar  6 13:46 sbin
drwxrwxrwx   3 root      root          2048 Mar  6 13:46 tmp
drwxr-xr-x  19 root      root          4096 Mar  6 13:45 usr
drwxr-xr-x  13 root      root          2048 Mar  6 13:46 var
```

Most of these subdirectories are not as heavily populated as the root directory of a hard disk installed system.

Running off the CD-ROM may save you disk space, but it certainly does not save you time. Also, you cannot configure some important files in directories off the mount point. The inability to read/write certain directories even as root may cause some system administrative scripts to fail.

Also, the performance of the system when run from the CD-ROM on a 486 DX4, with 32MB of RAM, was slow. Really, there should be no need to run any serious application by running off the CD-ROM. You can install fewer components if you have to. Actually running off the CD-ROM is very slow and really intended for trying out packages and loading files from your CD-ROM. Do not attempt to run off the CD-ROM even if you have a 6X drive since the performance will be very slow.

Also, keep in mind that to run off the CD-ROM you will need to create boot disks as described in the first three chapters of this book. The image to use for CD-ROM boot capability for the RAM disk is called `liveram.img`. In addition to the RAM disk, you will have to have a blank, formatted disk to use as your data repository. Please refer to the installation sections in the first three chapters of this book on how to create boot and ram disks. Please see Chapter 4, "LILO," for more information.

An Introduction to the Linux Source Tree

The Linux source code can be found in the `/usr/src/linux` directory.

You will need to look at the source code if you want to make enhancements to the kernel. For the reader interested in kernels, this directory is a very good reference.

The first point to start is to look in the `/usr/src/include` directory and see what header files you have available. This way you can tell what system services are available. (See Table 52.1.) I have deliberately left out redundant, old, or unused headers files. By examining the header files, you can see what files and systems are available in Linux.

Table 52.1. Linux header files.

FILE	Description
a.out.h	Generated for the GNU C compilers.
autoconf.h	Automatically generated C config file, don't edit it!
aztcd.h	Definitions for an AztechCD268 CD-ROM interface.
binfmts.h	Binary formats for the files.
bios32.h	BIOS32, PCI BIOS functions and defines.

continues

Table 52.1. continued

FILE	Description
blkdev.h	Block device information.
busmouse.h	Header file for Logitech Bus Mouse driver.
cdrom.h	General header for all CD-ROM drives.
cdu31a.h	Definitions for a Sony interface CD-ROM drive.
coff.h	The COFF file format definitions.
config.h	Linux kernel configuration header.
ctype.h	Standard C types header.
cyclades.h	For the Cyclades devices.
debugreg.h	Debug registers header file.
delay.h	Delay routines for precomputed loops_per_second value.
elf.h	The Executable and Linking format definitions.
errno.h	The standard error return definitions.
etherdevice.h	Ethernet device handlers declarations.
ext2_fs.h	The new extended filesystem (e2fs) declarations.
ext_fs.h	The ext filesystem (efs) definitions, older linux.
fcntl.h	The standard file control declaration.
fd.h	Floppy disk software control definitions.
fdreg.h	Some defines for the floppy disk controller itself.
fs.h	Definitions for some important file table structures.
genhd.h	Generic hard disk header declarations.
hdreg.h	Declarations for the AT hard disk controllers.
head.h	Intel's Global and Interrupt Descriptor Table.
hpfs_fs.h	The HP file system information.
icmp.h	Definitions for the ICMP protocol.
if.h	Definitions for the INET interface module.
if_arp.h	Definitions for the ARP (RFC 826) protocol.
if_ether.h	Definitions for the Ethernet IEEE 802.3 interface.
if_plip.h	PLIP tuning facilities for the new Niibe PLIP.
if_slip.h	Special use with the SLIP/CSLIP/KISS TNC driver.
igmp.h	Internet Gateway Management Protocol (IGMP).
in.h	Definitions of the Internet Protocol.
in_systm.h	Miscellaneous internetwork definitions for kernel.

FILE	Description
inet.h	Internet Protocol headers.
interrupt.h	For Linux interrupt drivers.
ioctl.h	Standard IO control definitions.
ioport.h	For detecting, reserving, allocating system resources.
ip.h	Definitions for the IP protocol.
ipc.h	For Interprocess communication
ipx.h	For sockets in network programming.
iso_fs.h	The ISO file system headers.
kd.h	Kernel development declarations.
kernel.h	Kernel header file declarations.
kernel_stat.h	More Kernel statistics header file declarations.
keyboard.h	Declaration for using the keyboard.
ldt.h	Definitions for use with Inter Local Descriptor Tables.
limits.h	Limits for the kernel to use.
linkage.h	Linking declarations for the kernel.
locks.h	File locking definitions.
lp.h	Line Printer support header.
major.h	Major device number header.
malloc.h	Standard memory management function header.
math_emu.h	Math emulation declarations.
mc146818rtc.h	Register definitions for RealTime Clock and CMOS RAM.
mcd.h	Definitions for a Mitsumi CD-ROM interface.
minix.h	The minix filesystem constants/structures.
mm.h	Memory manager for kernel.
mman.h	Memory Mapping definitions.
module.h	Dynamic loading of modules into the kernel.
mouse.h	Serial mouse.
msdos_fs.h	The MS-DOS file system constants/structures.
msg.h	For message processing in Linux IPC.
param.h	Internal Linux parameters header.
pci.h	PCI bus defines and function prototypes.
personality.h	Linux file personality declarations.

continues

Table 52.1. continued

FILE	Description
pipe_fs_i.h	For use with Linux file pipes.
ppp.h	For use with Point-To-Point Protocol with Linux.
proc_fs.h	The *proc* file system constants/structures.
ptrace.h	Defines to help the user use the ptrace system call.
resource.h	Resource control/accounting header file for Linux.
route.h	Global definitions for the IP router interface.
sbpcd.h	For Panasonic CD-ROMs.
sched.h	The Linux task scheduler.
scsicam.h	SCSI RAM support functions, use for HDIO_GETGEO, and so on.
sem.h	For use with semaphores on Linux.
serial.h	Linux serial IO definitions.
serial_reg.h	For the UART port assignments.
shm.h	For shared memory use on Linux.
signal.h	For Linux signal information.
skbuff.h	For the 'struct sk_buff' memory handlers.
socket.h	The socket-level I/O control calls.
sockios.h	More of the socket-level I/O control calls.
sonycd535.h	Commands for the CD-ROMs by Sony (CDU-531-5).
soundcard.h	For interfacing with Soundcards.
stat.h	Standard C and UNIX definitions.
stddef.h	Standard C definitions.
string.h	String functions declarations for C programmers.
symtab_begin.h	Symbol table entries.
symtab_end.h	Symbol table entries.
sys.h	All system call entry points.
sysv_fs.h	The SystemV/Coherent file system definitions.
tasks.h	Specifying the max number of tasks at one time in Linux.
tcp.h	Definitions for the TCP protocol.
termios.h	Terminal IO declarations.
time.h	Standard declarations for use with timers.
timer.h	Do not modify this timer declarations file.
times.h	For use with Linux kernel timers.

FILE	Description
timex.h	For TIMEX devices.
tpqic02.h	Include file for QIC-02 driver for Linux.
tqueue.h	The task queue handling information for Linux.
tty.h	Defines some structures used by tty_io.c.
tty_driver.h	Interface between low-level tty driver and kernel.
types.h	Standard Linux types.h file.
udp.h	Definitions for the UDP protocol.
ultrasound.h	For Ultrasound CD-ROM devices.
umsdos_fs.h	The UMSDOS file system header.
un.h	Linux header for socket programming.
unistd.h	Standard UNIX file header.
user.h	For use with core dumps and user segments.
utime.h	Time information.
utsname.h	Time information and structures.
version.h	Linux version information.
vfs.h	Virtual file system headers.
vm86.h	Virtual memory management routines.
vt.h	For use with virtual terminals.
xd.h	Definitions for IO ports, and so on, for XT hard controllers.

Let's give an example of how you would use this header file information. Let's say that in the default kernel for the sbcpd (Panasonic CD-ROM) drive, it takes very long for it boot since it probes the IO ports to see where the drive is in the IO port memory space. You know you have set your jumpers on the drive to 0x260, why not just have it look there and keep going. You are sick of typing in the sequence every time you boot: sbpcd=0x260,SoundBlaster Sounds good. Let's look at the sbpcd.h file in /usr/src/linux/include/linux. First become root and make sure that you have write privileges to this header file to save your changes to. Look at the part of the file where it says to define your CD-ROM port base address as CDROM_PORT and specify the type of your interface card as SBPRO. So you can change the address lines in file after line 90 as the following:

```
#undef CDROM_PORT   /* get rid of previous declarations.   */
#undef SBPRO        /* get rid of previous declarations.          */
#undef SOUND_BASE   /* get rid of previous declarations. */
```

```
/* override these values. */
#define CDROM_PORT 0x230 /* <<< port address                          */
#define SBPRO      0      /* <<< interface type                       * /
#define SOUND_BASE 0x220 /* <<< sound address of this card or 0   */
```

Now get out of the editor after making the changes. Rebuild the kernel and install it as discussed earlier in this chapter. Reboot and there you have it—a fast boot.

This is only a quick example of how to use the valueable resource of information to customize your Linux system. I am sure that with some exploring you can come across some more examples.

A Brief Introduction to ELF

The *Executable and Linking Format* (ELF) has become a hot topic for Linux users lately. All major releases of the Linux kernel and libraries will support the ELF format in the future. The general idea is that ELF will be the common object file format for all Linux binaries. The public release of all ELF file format compatible compilers are here with the kernel on the CD-ROM, and hopefully with the future releases of Linux.

First of all, the current shared libraries are a bit bulky to manage. When you are dealing with large packages such as the X Window System that span a big tree hierarchy, building and maintaining such a library is a formidable task. Also, the a.out shared library scheme does not support the dynamic load function: dlopen().

So what's the big deal about ELF? The general UNIX programming community seems to like this file format. In fact, several commercial versions of UNIX, such as Solaris and Unixware already use ELF. More vendors such as SCO, HP are moving to towards supporting it in the future. (By the way, Microsoft's NT is not based on ELF.) There is no reason why the Linux community should be left behind.

There are three basic types of ELF files: object (.o) files, a.out executables and shared libraries. Even though functionally the three types of files perform different functions, internally they are very similar in structure. One common part in all different ELF file types (including a.out and other executable file formats) is the idea of a section. A section represents a portion of the file containing a set of related information. A binary image of a file consists of many sections. For example, executable code is always placed in a section known as .text, all data variables initialized by the user are placed in a section known as .data, and uninitialized data is placed in a section known as .bss (historically known as *Below Stack Segment*).

Dividing executables into sections has many important advantages. For example, once you have loaded the executable portions of an executable into memory, the values at these memory locations need not change. Unless of course you happen to be of the twisted mentality that actually modifies code while it's executing. Executable code which could modify itself is considered a dispicable programming practice in most cases.

Given this set of code segments, the memory manager on a machine can set aside portions of memory as read-only. Thereafter any attempt to modify a read-only memory location will result in a core dump. So all attempts to modify read-only memory are considered fatal errors. Rather than set individual bits of memory and slow the computer down, you can set bits on portions of memory known as pages. (On an Intel 386 machine, a page is 4096 bytes long.) Pages are normally set at 1024 byte multiples since most paging systems work on 1024 byte boundaries. This was the reason to switch from the ZMAGIC file format to the QMAGIC format in ELF files. Both formats have a 32-byte header at the start of the file, but with ZMAGIC the .text section starts at byte offset 1024 followed by a header. The QMAGIC .text section includes the header and starts at the beginning of the file. ZMAGIC took up more space than QMAGIC and did not page easily since it was not on a 1024 byte boundary. A 1024 byte boundary makes items easily cache-able with the current Linux buffering scheme.

For program security and consistency, we want all executable parts in read-only memory and all modifiable data locations in writable memory. The read-only memory is therefore sacrosanct from erroneous memory updates. It's efficient to group all of the executable portions together in one section (.text) and all modifiable data areas together into another area of memory (.data). Data sections are further divided into two sections: uninitialized data (.bss) and initialized data (.data). The .bss section is different from .data because .bss doesn't take up space in the file, it only tells how much space will be needed for uninitialized variables.

When the kernel starts to load and run an executable, it looks at the image header on what to do when loading the image. First the kernel locates the .text section within the executable, then loads them into memory and then marks these executeable memory pages as read-only to prevent self-modifying code The kernel then locates the .data section in read-write memory. After that loading and initializing .data, the kernel allocates space for, and loads the .bss section. (The Linux kernel will zero out the .bss section by default.)

Each a.out or ELF file also includes a symbol table, which is a list of all of the symbols in the program. A symbol is a named address of a program entry point or a variable, and more. Symbols are defined or referenced within the file. Information about a symbol in the symbol table contains the address associated with the symbol, and some kind of tag indicating the type of the symbol at the minimum. ELF files have considerably more information per symbol than a.out file.

Symbol information is critical when debugging files. However, the size of the executeable file is greater than it has to be. You can remove symbol tables the strip utility. The advantage is that the final executable is smaller once stripped. The disadvantage is that you lose the ability to debug the stripped binary. With a.out it is always possible to remove the symbol table from a file, but with ELF you typically need some symbolic information in the file for the program to load and run. So in an ELF image, the strip program will always leave some symbolic information behind.

Now let's see the topic of relocation. First compile a program with the following line in it:

```
printf("Hello World\n");
```

The compiler will generate an object file which contains a reference to the function `printf`. Since your program has not defined this symbol, it is an *external reference*. The executable object code for program will contain an instruction to call `printf`, but in the object code we do not yet know the actual location to call to perform this function. The compiler will generate assembler code which in turn will be passed to the assembler portion for conversion where a relocation reference will be generated.

A relocation reference contains three major components: One is an index into the symbol table, so the kernel loader will symbol to what is being referenced and the other is an offset into the `.text` section, which refers to the address of the operand of the call instructions. The third component is a tag of the type of relocation. When `gcc` links this file, its linker will resolve the relocations by patching the external references into library text sections. The output from this process after the linker will be the `a.out` file (unless you specified a different name with `-o name` option). An `a.out` executable will therefore not have any relocations. The kernel loader, `ld`, cannot resolve such symbols and will not run such a binary.

So how's the ELF format different from the `a.out` format? Let's look at `a.out` formats first. First, the header of an `a.out` file (look at `struct exec`, defined in `/usr/src/linux/include/linux/a.out.h`) contains only allows the `.text`, `.data`, and `.bss` sections and does not directly support any additional sections. Two, a.out contains only the sizes of the various sections not the offsets of where they are in the file since the offsets are predefined constants. Also, there is no built-in shared library support. The `a.out` format was developed before shared library technology was developed, so shared libraries are not very cleanly supported. It is not impossible to design shared library implementations that work with `a.out`. ELF allows us to discard some of the hacks that were required to piggyback a shared library implementation onto `a.out`.

Now let's look a little bit at what a shared library is. Non-shared libraries (also known as *static* libraries) contain common useful procedures callable from programs. When you link against a static library, the linker must extract all library functions you require and make them part of your executable making it bulky.

A shared library lets you take a static version of library and pre-link it into some kind of special type of executable. When you link your program against the shared library, the linker does not extract the binary code from shared library into your executeable, rather it simply adds a reference to the code's offset and the library to use. After linking, when the loader runs your program, it knows where to get the code from which library to fill in any memory gaps.

With the current `a.out` scheme, shared libraries must be loaded in predefined locations in memory. ELF shared libraries are position independent. This means that you can load them at just about any location in memory to get them to work. ELF shared libraries have to be compiled with `-fPIC` switch to generate position independant code. When you compile something to be `-fPIC`, the compiler reserves one machine register (register `ebx` on the i386) to point to the start of a global offset table (GOT). The cost is that this register is reserved by the compiler and results in less flexibility in optimizing code. `ebx` register in an i386 machine is not very popular so it's not that big a loss in speed.

Another ELF feature is that its shared libraries resolve symbols and externals at run time by using a symbol table and a list of relocations. Symbol resolution is performed before the image executes. The ELF support in Linux makes it very efficient since all symbols are referenced off the same global variable for the ELF library, rather than a fixed location in memory. Basically each global variable defined or referenced in the shared library means that the kernel uses the `ebx` register to compute and load the address of the variable from the GOT to get the address. The advantage of using one global variable is that when the loader `ld` moves an entire `.text` or `.data` section, you need only resolve one global address and do no address resolutions.

A similar setup is used for functions with the use of a *Procedure Link Table* (PLT). The use of the PLT enables the programmer to redefine (override) functions which might be in the shared library. Then the PLT entry for the function can be used instead of the regular library entry. A PLT is only an array of jump instructions, one for each function that you might need to go to. Thus if a particular function is called from many positions within the shared library, the call will always pass through one jump instruction. You can then control all calls to this file by setting or resetting this one location register. Efficient and clean.

This chapter cannot possibly cover all you need to know about the ELF format. For more information about the ELF file format, obtain the ELF specifications from a number of sources—for example `ftp.intel.com` in `pub/tis/elf11g.zip`.

The specifications are also available in a printed format. See SYSTEM V Application Binary Interface (ISBN 0-13-100439-5) and SYSTEM V Application Binary Interface, Intel386 Architecture Processor Supplement (ISBN 0-13-104670-5).

Summary

Recompiling kernel source and adding new features to the kernel proceeds smoothly, as long as you know what you are doing. Don't let the process scare you, but always keep boot disks on hand. Follow instructions wherever available, because most new software has special requirements for linking into the kernel or replacing existing systems.

Writing Device Drivers

53

by Tim Parker

IN THIS CHAPTER

This chapter will look at:

- What a device driver is
- How Linux uses device drivers
- Interrupts and device drivers
- How a device driver is written

Device drivers provide an interface between the operating system and the peripherals attached to the machine. A typical device driver consists of a number of functions that accept I/O requests from the operating system and instruct the device to perform those requests. In this manner, a uniform interface between devices and the operating system kernel is provided.

We can't cover everything there is to know about device drivers in a single chapter. Indeed, several sizable books have been written on the subject. Since device drivers are not written by casual users, but mostly by talented programmers, the information supplied here is mainly an introduction to the subject.

The code snippets in this chapter were taken from a set of simple device drivers written in C. They are portable and designed for a UNIX system, but they also execute properly under Linux. Use them only as a guide, if you decide you want to write device drivers. Obtain one of the specialty books on the subject if you get serious about programming device drivers.

Device Drivers

Linux uses a device driver for every device attached to the system. The basic device driver instructions are part of the kernel or loaded during the boot process. By using a device driver, the devices appear to the operating system as files that can addressed, redirected, or piped as normal files.

Each device attached to the Linux system is described in a device driver program file, and some parameters about the device are described in a *device file* which is usually stored in the /dev directory. When you add a new peripheral to the system, a device driver must either be attached to the Linux operating system to control the device, or you must write or supply a device driver. You also need a device file in the /dev directory for each device. Otherwise, the device can't be used.

Each device file has an assigned device number that uniquely identifies the device to the operating system. Linux device numbers consist of two parts. The *major number* identifies what general type the device driver handles, while the *minor number* can specify a particular unit for that general type of device. For example, multiple hard disk drives will use the same device driver (the same major number), but each has unique minor numbers to identify the specific drives to the operating system.

There are two major types of device drivers: character mode and block mode. Any UNIX device uses one or both of the driver types. Block mode drivers are the most common type. They deal with I/O in blocks of data to and from the kernel's buffer cache (which copies to memory the data from the cache). Originally designed for use with disk drives, block mode is used with virtually all mass storage devices, such as disk drives, high-capacity tape drives, magneto-optical drives, synchronous modems, and some high-speed printers.

Character mode devices differ from block mode devices in two significant ways. I/O can be processed directly to and from the process's memory space, without using the kernel's cache. In addition, I/O requests are usually passed directly to the character mode device. Terminals and printers are obvious character mode devices, as are asynchronous modems and some tape drives.

Block mode devices perform a "strategy" function that reads or writes a block of data to the device. A series of special device control functions called ioctl() functions are available with character mode devices. In order to use these ioctl() functions, block mode devices will sometimes use character mode. An example is a tape drive that can use either a character or block mode driver, depending on the type of data being written.

Regardless of the type of device driver, the driver itself performs a series of basic tasks whenever a request is made of the device. First, the device is checked to ensure that it is ready and available for use. If so, it is "opened" to allow the calling process access. Read or write commands are usually executed, and then the device is "closed" to allow other processes access to the device.

Interrupts

Interrupts are signals from the devices to the operating system to indicate that attention is required. Interrupts are generated whenever an I/O is processed and the device is ready for another process. The interrupts used by Linux are similar to those used by DOS, so if you are familiar with DOS interrupts, you know most of the story already.

Upon receipt of an interrupt, the operating system suspends whatever it was executing and processes the interrupt. In most cases, interrupts are handled by the device driver. Interrupts must be checked to ensure that they are valid and will not affect operation of a process underway, except to suspend it momentarily.

A problem with handling interrupts is that the interrupt should not suspend the Linux kernel's operation or that of the device drivers themselves, except under controlled conditions. Interrupts that are not properly handled or carefully checked can cause suspension of a device driver that was processing the I/O that the interrupt requested.

The processing of an interrupt is usually suspended during the stages where critical operation would be affected. The areas of device driver code that should not allow an interrupt to stop their processing are termed *non-stoppable* or *critical* code. Typically, interrupt suspension during critical code segments is performed by raising the CPU priority equal to or greater than the interrupt priority level. After critical code execution, the CPU priority level is lowered again.

Interrupt priority is usually manipulated with four functions: spl5(), spl6(), spl7(), and splx(). Calling one of the first three will cause interrupts *not* to be acknowledged during processing. spl5() disables disk drives, printer, and keyboard interrupts. spl6() disables the system clock, while spl7() disables all interrupts, including serial devices. These three functions always return a code indicating the previous value of the interrupt level. splx() is used to restore interrupts to their previous values.

Therefore, before processing critical code, embedding the command

```
old_level = spl5();
```

in the device driver source disables interrupts until the following command is issued:

```
splx(old_level);
```

Multiple level changes are combined into device drivers as in the following example:

```
int level_a, level_b;
level_a = spl5();
/* do any code that can't be  */
/* interrupted by disk drives */
level_b = spl7();
/* do all code that can't be  */
/* interrupted by anything    */
splx(level_b);
/* any final code that's not  */
/* interrupted by disk drives */
splx(level_a);
```

This seemingly awkward method of bouncing between levels is necessary to avoid freezing the device driver and kernel, which prevents the system from operating normally. The protection mechanisms must be invoked only for as short a time as necessary.

It is usually unwise to use the `spl6()` and `spl7()` functions. `spl6()` can cause the system clock to lose time in some cases, and `spl7()` causes loss of characters in serial I/O, unless they are used for very short time spans. Even then, it is usually sufficient to use `spl5()` for all interrupts in critical code.

Anatomy of a Linux Device Driver

Device driver code is similar to normal code in its structure. In Linux, drivers are generally written in C, although assembler and C++ are still occasionally used.

Headers

A typical device driver has a header that consists of `include` statements for system functions, device register addresses, content definitions, and driver global variable definitions. Most device drivers use a standard list of `include` files, such as:

`param.h`	Kernel parameters
`dir.h`	Directory parameters
`user.h`	User area definitions
`tty.h`	Terminal and `clist` definitions
`buf.h`	Buffer header information

The `tty.h` file is used for character mode drivers, while `buf.h` is used by all block mode devices.

Device registers are defined in the device driver header and are based on the device. For a character mode device, these registers commonly refer to port addresses, such as I/O address, status bits, and control bits. Toggle commands for the device are defined as their device codes.

An example of device register's initialization is shown in the device driver for a standard screen terminal (UART) device:

```
/* define the registers */
#define RRDATA       0x01      /* receive */
#define RTDATA       0x02      /* transmit */
#define RSTATUS      0x03      /* status */
#define RCONTRL      0x04      /* control */
...etc

/* define the status registers */
#define SRRDY        0x01      /* received data ready */
#define STRDY        0x02      /* transmitter ready */
#define SPERR        0x08      /* parity error */
#define SCTS         0x40      /* clear to send status */
...etc
```

The functions the device driver must perform are dependent on the nature of the device. All devices have an `open()` and `close()` routine that allows the device to perform I/O.

Opening the Device

The `open()` routine must check to ensure a valid device has been specified, validate the device request (permission to access the device or device not ready), then initialize the device. The `open()` routine is run every time a process uses the device.

The `open()` routine presented here is for a generic terminal device, td.

```
tdopen(device,flag)
int device,flag;
{
        /* definitions for local variables ignored */
        /* details and definitions ignored in code */

        /* check device number */
        if (UNMODEM(device) >= NTDEVS)
        {
            seterror(ENXIO);
            return;
        }

        /* check if device in use */
        /* if so, see if superuser (suser) for override */
        tp = &td_tty[UNMODEM(device)];
        address = td_address[UNMODEM(device)];
        if((tp->t_lflag & XCLUDE) && !suser())
        {
            seterror(EBBUSY);
            return;
        }
```

```
        /* if not open, initialize by calling ttinit() */
        if((tp->t_state & (ISOPEN|WOPEN)) == 0)
        {
            ttinit(tp);
            /* initialize flags, and call tdparam() to set line */
            tdparam(device);
        }

        /* if a modem is used, check carrier status */
        /* if direct, set carrier detect flags */
        /* set interrupt priority to avoid overwrite */
        /* wait for carrier detect signal */
        /* code eliminated from example */
```

Closing the Device

The close() routine is used only after the process is finished with the device. The routine disables interrupts from the device and issues any shut-down commands. All internal references to the device will be reset. close() routines are not usually required in many device drivers because the device is treated as being available throughout. Exceptions are removable media and exclusive-use devices. Some modems require closing (close()) to allow the line to be hung up.

Again, the terminal device example is used for the close() routine sample:

```
        tdclose(device)
        {
            register struct tty *tp;
            tp = &td_tty[UNMODEM(device)];
            (*linesw[tp->t_line].l_close)(tp);
            if(tp->t_cflag & HUPCL)
                tdmodem(device,TURNOFF);
            /* turn off exclusive flag bit */
            ip->t_lflag & =~XCLUDE
        }
```

Strategy Functions

Strategy functions (block mode devices only) are issued with a parameter to the kernel buffer header. The buffer header contains the instructions for a read or write along with a memory location for the operation to occur to or from. The size of the buffer is usually fixed at installation and varies from 512 to 1024 bytes. It can be examined in the file param.h as the BSIZE variable. A device's block size may be smaller than the buffer block size, in which case, the driver executes multiple reads or writes.

The strategy function can be illustrated in a sample device driver for a hard disk. No code is supplied, but the skeleton explains the functions of the device driver in order:

```
        int hdstrategy(bp)
        register struct buf *bp;
        {
            /* initialize drive and partition numbers */
            /* set local variables */

            /* check for valid drive & partition */
            /* compute target cylinder */
```

```
/* disable interrupts */
/* push request into the queue */
/* check controller: if not active, start it */
/* reset interrupt level */
}
```

Write Functions

Character mode devices employ a write() instruction that checks the arguments of the instruction for validity, and then copies the data from the process memory to the device driver buffer. When all data is copied, or the buffer is full, I/O is initiated to the device until the buffer is empty, at which point the process is repeated. Data is read from the process memory using a simple function (cpass) that returns a -1 when end of memory is reached. The data is written to process memory using a complementary function (passc). The write() routine is illustrated for the terminal device:

```
tdwrite(device)
    {
        register struct tty *tp;
        tp=&td_tty[UNMODEM(device)];
        (*linesw[tp->t_line].l_write)(tp);
    }
```

Large amounts of data are handled by a process called copyio which takes the addresses of source and destination, a byte count, and a status flag as arguments.

Read Functions

The read() operation for character mode devices transfers data from the device to the process memory. The operation is analogous to that of the write procedure. For the terminal device, the read() code becomes:

```
tdread(device)
{
    register struct tty *tp;
    tp=&td_tty[UNMODEM(device)];
    (*linesw[tp->t_line].l_read)(tp);
}
```

A small buffer is used when several characters are to be copied at once by read() or write(), rather than continually copying single characters. clist implements a small buffer used by character mode devices as a series of linked lists that use getc and putc to move characters on and off the buffer respectively. A header for clist maintains a count of the contents.

start and *ioctl* Routines

A start routine is usually used for both block and character mode devices. It takes requests or data from device queues and sends them in order to the device. Block mode devices queue data with the *strategy* routine, while character mode devices use clist. The start routine maintains busy flags automatically as instructions are passed to the device. When a device has finished its process, it executes an intr routine which reinitializes the device for the next process.

The character mode ioctl() routine provides a special series of instructions to drivers. These include changes in the communications method between the driver and the operating system, as well as device-dependent operations (tape load or rewind, or memory allocation, for example).

The ioctl() function can be illustrated with the terminal device example. The ioctl() routine, in this case, calls another function that sets the device parameters. No code is supplied for the called function, but the skeleton explains the process of the device driver in order:

```
tdioctl(device,cmd,arg,mode)         int device;
int cmd;
int mode;
faddr_t arg;
{
    if(ttiocom(&td_tty[UNMODEM(device)],cmd,arg,mode))
        tdparam(device)
}

tdparam(device)
{
    /* initialize variables */
    /* get address and flags for referenced line */
    addr=td_addr[UNMODEM(device)];
    cflag=td_tty[UNMODEM(device].t_cflag;

    /* check speed: if zero hang up line */
    /* set up speed change */
    /* set up line control */
    /* manage interrupts */
}
```

Using a New Device Driver

Drivers are added to Linux systems in a series of steps. First the interrupt handler is identified, and then the device driver entry points (such as open) are added to a driver entry point table. The entire driver is compiled and linked to the kernel, and then placed in the /dev directory. (See Chapter 52, "Working with the Kernel," for more information on adding to the Linux kernel.) Finally, the system is rebooted and the device driver tested. Obviously, changes to the driver require the process to be repeated, so device driver debugging is an art that minimizes the number of machine reboots!

CAUTION

Two basic don'ts are important for device driver programming. Don't use sleep() or seterror() during interrupt suspensions, and don't use floating-point operations.

Interrupt suspensions must be minimized, but they must be used to avoid corruption of clist (or other buffer) data. Finally, it is important to minimize stack space.

You can simplify debugging device drivers in many cases by using judicious `printf` or `getchar` statements to another device, such as the console. Statements like `printf` and `getchar` enable you to set up code that traces the execution steps of the device driver. If you are testing the device when logged in as root, the `adb` debugger can be used to allow examination of the kernel's memory while the device driver executes. Careful use of `adb` allows direct testing of minor changes in variables or addresses, but be careful as incorrect use of `adb` may result in system crashes!

One of the most common problems with device drivers (other than faulty coding) is the loss of interrupts or the suspension of a device while an interrupt is pending. This causes the device to hang. A time-out routine is included in most device drivers to prevent this. Typically, if an interrupt is expected and has not been received within a specified amount of time, the device is checked directly to ensure the interrupt was not missed. If an interrupt was missed, it can be simulated by code. You can use the `spl` functions during debugging usually helps to isolate these problems.

Block mode-based device drivers are generally written using interrupts. However, more programmers are now using *polling* for character mode devices. Polling means the device driver checks at frequent intervals to determine the device's status. The device driver doesn't wait for interrupts but this does add to the CPU overhead the process requires. Polling is not suitable for many devices, such as mass storage systems, but for character mode devices it can be of benefit. Serial devices generally are polled to save interrupt overhead.

A 19,200 baud terminal will cause approximately 1,920 interrupts per second, causing the operating system to interrupt and enter the device driver that many times. By replacing the interrupt routines with polling routines, the interval between CPU demands can be decreased by an order of magnitude, using a small device buffer to hold intermediate characters generated to or from the device. Real time devices also benefit from polling, since the number of interrupts does not overwhelm the CPU. If you want to use polling in your device drivers, you should read one of the books dedicated to device driver design, as this is a complex subject.

Summary

Most Linux users will never have to write a device driver, as most devices you can buy already have a device driver available. If you acquire brand new hardware, or have the adventurous bug, you may want to try writing a driver, though. Device drivers are not really difficult to write (as long as you are comfortable coding in a high-level language like C), but drivers tend to be very difficult to debug. The device driver programmer must at all times be careful of impacting other processes or devices. However, there is a peculiar sense of accomplishment when a device driver executes properly.

Network Programming

54

by Kamran Husain and Tim Parker

IN THIS CHAPTER

This chapter will look at the basic concepts you need for network programming:

- Ports and sockets
- Record and file locking
- Interprocess communications

It is impossible to tell you how to program applications for a network in just a few pages. Indeed, the best reference to network programming available takes almost 800 pages in the first volume alone! If you really want to do network programming, you need a lot of experience with compilers, TCP/IP, network operating systems, and a great deal of patience.

For information on details of TCP/IP, check the book *Teach Yourself TCP/IP in 14 Days* by Tim Parker (Sams).

Ports and Sockets

Network programming relies on the use of sockets to accept and transmit information. Although there is a lot of mystique about sockets, the concept is actually very simple to understand.

Most applications that use the two primary network protocols, Transmission Control Protocol (TCP) or User Datagram Protocol (UDP) have a port number that identifies the application. A *port number* is used for each different application the machine is handling, so it can keep track of them by numbers instead of names. The port number makes it easier for the operating system to know how many applications are using the system and which services are available.

In theory, port numbers can be assigned on individual machines by the system administrator, but some conventions have been adopted to allow better communications. This convention enables the port number to identify the type of service that one system is requesting from another. For this reason, most systems maintain a file of port numbers and their corresponding services.

Port numbers are assigned starting from the number 1. Normally, port numbers above 255 are reserved for the private use of the local machine, but numbers between 1 and 255 are used for processes requested by remote applications or for networking services.

Each network communications circuit that goes into and out of the host computer's TCP application layer is uniquely identified by a combination of two numbers, together called the *socket*. The socket is composed of the IP address of the machine and the port number used by the TCP software.

Because there are at least two machines involved in network communications, there will be a socket on both the sending and receiving machine. The IP address of each machine is unique, and the port numbers are unique to each machine, so socket numbers will also be unique across the network. This enables an application to talk to another application across the network based entirely on the socket number.

The sending and receiving machines maintain a port table that lists all active port numbers. The two machines involved have reversed entries for each session between the two, a process called *binding*. In other words, if one machine has the source port number 23 and the destination port number set at 25, then the other machine will have its source port number set at 25 and the destination port number set at 23.

Socket Programming

Linux supports BSD style socket programming. Both connection-oriented and connectionless types of sockets are supported. In connection-oriented communication, the server and client establish a connection before any data is exchanged. In connectionless communication, data is exchanged as part of a message. In either case, the server always starts up first, binds itself to a socket, and listens to messages. How the server attempts to listen depends on the type of connection for which you have programmed it.

You need to know about only a few system calls:

- `socket()`
- `bind()`
- `accept()`
- `listen()`
- `connect()`
- `sendto()`
- `recvfrom()`

We will cover these in the following examples.

socket()

The `socket()` system call creates a socket for the client or the server. The socket function is defined as follows:

```
#include<sys/types.h>
#include<sys/socket.h>

int socket(int family, int type, int protocol)
```

For Linux, you will have `family` = `AF_UNIX`. The type is either `SOCK_STREAM` for reliable, though slower communications or `SOCK_DGRAM` for faster, but less reliable communications. The protocol should be `IPPROTO_TCP` for `SOCK_STREAM` and `IPPROTO_UDP` for `SOCK_DGRAM`.

The return value from this function is `-1` if there was an error; otherwise, it's a socket descriptor. You will use this socket descriptor to refer to this socket in all subsequent calls in your program.

Sockets are created without a name. Clients use the name of the socket in order to read or write to it. This is where the bind function comes in.

The *bind()* System Call

The bind() system call assigns a name to an unnamed socket.

```
#include<sys/types.h>
#include<sys/socket.h>
```

```
int bind(int sockfd, struct sockaddr *saddr, int addrlen)
```

The first item is a socket descriptor. The second is a structure with the name to use, and the third item is the size of the structure.

Now that you have bound an address for your server or client, you can connect() to it or listen on it. If your program is a server, then it sets itself up to listen and accept connections. Let's look at the function available for such an endeavor.

The *listen()* System Call

The listen() system call is used by the server. It is defined as follows:

```
#include<sys/types.h>
#include<sys/socket.h>
```

```
int listen(int sockfd, int backlog);
```

The sockfd is the descriptor of the socket. The backlog is the number of waiting connections at one time before rejecting any. Use the standard value of 5 for backlog. A returned value of less than 1 indicates an error.

If this call is successful, you can accept connections.

The *accept()* System Call

The accept() system call is used by a server to accept any incoming messages from clients' connect() calls. Be aware that this function will not return if no connections are received.

```
#include<sys/types.h>
#include<sys/socket.h>
```

```
int accept(int sockfd, struct sockaddr *peeraddr, int addrlen)
```

The parameters are the same as that for the bind call, with the exception that the peeraddr points to information about the client that is making a connection request. Based on the incoming message, the fields in the structure pointed at by peeraddr are filled out.

So how does a client connect to a server. Let's look at the connect() call.

The *connect()* System Call

The connect() system call is used by clients to connect to a server in a connection-oriented system. This connect() call should be made after the bind() call.

```
#include<sys/types.h>
#include<sys/socket.h>
```

```
int connect(int sockfd, struct sockaddr *servsaddr, int addrlen)
```

The parameters are the same as that for the bind call, with the exception that the servsaddr points to information about the server that the client is connecting to. The accept call creates a new socket for the server to work with the request. This way the server can fork() off a new process and wait for more connections. On the server side of things, you would have code that looks like that shown in Listing 54.1.

Listing 54.1. Server side for socket-oriented protocol.

```
#include    <sys/types.h>
#include    <sys/socket.h>
#include <linux/in.h>
#include <linux/net.h>

#define MY_PORT 6545

main(int argc, char *argv[])
{
int sockfd, newfd;
int cpid; /* child id */
struct sockaddr_in servaddr;
struct sockaddr_in clientInfo;

if ((sockfd = socket(AF_INET, SOCK_STREAM, 0) < 0)
    {
    myabort("Unable to create socket");
    }

bzero((char *)&servaddr, sizeof(servaddr));

servaddr.sin_family = AF_INET;
servaddr.sin_addr.s_addr = htonl(INADDR_ANY);
servaddr.sin_family = htons(MY_PORT);

/*
* The htonl(for a long integer) and htons(for short integer) convert
* a host oriented byte order * into a network order.
*/

if (bind(sockfd,(struct sockaddr *)&servaddr,sizeof(struct sockaddr)) < 0)
    {
```

continues

Listing 54.1. continued

```
    myabort("Unable to bind socket");
    }

listen(sockfd,5);
for (;;)
    {
    /* wait here */
    newfd=accept(sockfd,(struct sockaddr *)&clientInfo,
            sizeof(struct sockaddr);
    if (newfd < 0)
        {
        myabort("Unable to accept on socket");
        }

    if ((cpid = fork()) < 0)
        {
        myabort("Unable to fork on accept");
        }
    else if (cpid == 0) {  /* child */
        close(sockfd); /* no need for original */
        do_your_thing(newfd);
        exit(0);
        }
        close(newfd); /* in the parent */
    }
}
```

In the case of connection-oriented protocols, the server performs the following functions:

- Creates a socket with a call to the socket() function.
- Binds itself to an address with the bind() function call.
- Listens for connections with the listen() function call.
- Accepts any incoming requests with the accept() function call.
- Gets incoming messages with the read() function and replies back with the write() call.

Now let's look at the client side of things in Listing 54.2.

Listing 54.2. Client side function.

```
#include    <sys/types.h>
#include    <sys/socket.h>
#include <linux/in.h>
#include <linux/net.h>

#define MY_PORT 6545
#define MY_HOST_ADDR "204.25.13.1"

int getServerSocketId()
{
    int fd, len;
    struct sockaddr_in   unix_addr;
```

```
                    /* create a Unix domain stream socket */
    if ( (fd = socket(AF_UNIX, SOCK_STREAM, 0)) < 0)
        {
        return(-1);
        }

                    /* fill socket address structure w/our address */
    memset(&unix_addr, 0, sizeof(unix_addr));
    unix_addr.sin_family = AF_INET;

    /* convert internet address to binary value*/
    unix_addr.sin_addr.s_addr = inet_addr(MY_HOST_ADDR);
    unix_addr.sin_family = htons(MY_PORT);

    if (bind(fd, (struct sockaddr *) &unix_addr, len) < 0)
        return(-2);
    memset(&unix_addr, 0, sizeof(unix_addr));
    if (connect(fd, (struct sockaddr *) &unix_addr, len) < 0)
        return(-3);

    return(fd);
}
```

The client for connection-oriented communication also takes the following steps:

- Creates a socket with a call to the socket() function.
- Attempts to connect to the server with a connect() call.
- If a connection is made, requests for data with the write() call, and reads incoming replies with the read() function.

Connectionless Socket Programming

Now let's consider the case of a connectionless exchange of information. The principle on the server side is different from the connection-oriented server side in that the server calls recvfrom() instead of the listen and accept calls. Also, to reply to messages, the server uses the sendto() function call. See Listing 54.3 for the server side.

Listing 54.3. The server side.

```
#include     <sys/types.h>
#include     <sys/socket.h>
#include <linux/in.h>
#include <linux/net.h>

#define MY_PORT 6545
#define MAXM    4096
char mesg[MAXM];

main(int argc, char *argv[])
```

continues

Listing 54.3. continued

```
{
int sockfd, newfd;
int cpid; /* child id */
struct sockaddr_in servaddr;
struct sockaddr_in clientInfo;

if ((sockfd = socket(AF_INET, SOCK_STREAM, 0) < 0)
    {
    myabort("Unable to create socket");
    }

bzero((char *)&servaddr, sizeof(servaddr));

servaddr.sin_family = AF_INET;
servaddr.sin_addr.s_addr = htonl(INADDR_ANY);
servaddr.sin_family = htons(MY_PORT);

/*
* The htonl(for a long integer) and htons(for short integer) convert
* a host oriented byte order * into a network order.
*/


if (bind(sockfd,(struct sockaddr *)&servaddr,sizeof(struct sockaddr)) < 0)
    {
    myabort("Unable to bind socket");
    }


for (;;)
    {
    /* wait here */
                    n = recvfrom(sockfd, mesg, MAXM, 0,
                    (struct sockaddr *)&clientInfo,
                     sizeof(struct sockaddr));

                doSomethingToIt(mesg);

                sendto(sockfd,mesg,n,0,
                (struct sockaddr *)&clientInfo,
                 sizeof(struct sockaddr));
    }
}
```

As you can see, the two function calls to process each message make this an easier implementation than a connection-oriented one. However, you have to process each message one at a time because messages from multiple clients can be multiplexed together. In a connection-oriented scheme, the child process always knows where each message originated.

The client does not have to call the connect() system call either. Instead, the client can call the sendto() function directly. The client side is identical to the server side, with the exception that the sendto call is made before the recvfrom() call.

```
#include <sys/types.h>
#include <sys/socket.h>

int sendto((int sockfd,
 const void *message__,  /* the pointer to message */
 int  length, /* of message */
 unsigned  int type, /* of routing, leave 0 *
 const struct sockaddr * client, /* where to send it */
 int length ); /* of sockaddr);
```

> **NOTE**
>
> If you are a BSD user, use the `sendto()` call, do not use `sendmsg()` call. The `sendto()` call is more efficient.

Any errors are indicated by a return value of -1. Only local errors are detected.

The `recvfrom()` system call is defined as follows:

```
#include <sys/types.h>
#include <sys/socket.h>

int recvfrom(int sockfd,
 const void *message__,  /* the pointer to message */
 int  length, /* of message */
 unsigned  int flags, /* of routing, leave 0 *
 const struct sockaddr * client, /* where to send it */
 int length ); /* of sockaddr);
```

If a message is too long to fit in the supplied buffer, the extra bytes are discarded. The call may return immediately or wait forever, depending on the type of the flag being set. You can even set time out values. Check the man pages for `recvfrom` for more information.

There you have it: the very basics of how to program applications to take advantage of the networking capabilities under Linux. We have not even scratched the surface of all the intricacies of programming for networks. A good starting point for more detailed information would be *UNIX Network Programming* by W. Richard Stevens, published in 1990 by Prentice Hall. This book is a classic used in universities and is, by far, *the* most detailed book to date.

Record and File Locking

When two processes want to share a file, the danger exists that one process might affect the contents of the file, and thereby affect the other process. For this reason, most operating systems use a mutually exclusive principle: When one process has a file open, no other process can touch it. This is called *file locking*.

The technique is simple to implement. What usually happens is that a "lock file" is created with the same name as the original file but with the extension `.lock`, which tells other processes that the file is unavailable. This is how many Linux spoolers, such as the print system and UUCP, implement file locking. It is a brute-force method, perhaps, but effective and easy to program.

Unfortunately, this technique is not good when you must have several processes access the same information quickly because the delays waiting for file opening and closing can grow to be appreciable. Also, if one process doesn't release the file properly, other processes can hang there, waiting for access.

For this reason, record locking is sometimes implemented. With record locking, a single part of a larger file is locked to prevent two processes from changing its contents at the same time. Record locking enables many processes to access the same file at the same time, each updating different records within the file, if necessary. The programming necessary to implement record locking is more complex than file locking, of course.

Normally, to implement record locking, you use a file offset, or the number of characters from the beginning of the file. In most cases, a range of characters are locked, so the program has to note the start of the locking region and the length of it, and then store that information somewhere other processes can examine it.

Writing either file locking or record locking code requires a good understanding of the operating system, but is otherwise not difficult, especially because there are thousands of programs readily available from the Internet, in networking programming books, and on BBSes to examine for example code.

Interprocess Communications

Network programming always involves two or more processes talking to each other (interprocess communications), so the way in which processes communicate is vitally important to network programmers. Network programming differs from the usual method of programming in a few important aspects. A traditional program can talk to different modules (or even other applications on the same machine) through global variables and function calls. That doesn't work across networks.

A key goal of network programming is to ensure that processes don't interfere with each other. Otherwise, systems can get bogged down or lock up. Therefore, processes must have a clean and efficient method of communicating. UNIX is particularly strong in this regard, because many of the basic UNIX capabilities, such as pipes and queues, are used effectively across networks.

Writing code for interprocess communications is quite difficult compared to single application coding. If you want to write this type of routine, you should study sample programs from a network programming book or a BBS site to see how they accomplish the task.

Summary

Few people need to write network applications, so the details of the process are best left to those who want them. Experience and lots of examples are the best way to begin writing network code, and mastering the skills can take many years.

Adding Server Support for PEX

This chapter is really two chapters in one. I will discuss two topics here:

- Building a new server for X.
- To build this new server, we will add PEX support to it. This will serve as an example of how to add more capabilities to the X server.

After you read this chapter, you will have an idea of how to draw to an X drawable, and use Motif and PEX together. This chapter is not a tutorial on PEX, nor will you become the world's expert on writing additions to X servers. This chapter will introduce you to techniques that you can use to add features to the X server. You will also learn where to look for more information about PEX and X servers.

What Is PEX?

The X Window system is primarily a two-dimensional graphical system. Due to the lack of standards in the three-dimensional (3-D) area, there hasn't been an evolution of good 3-D developmental tool libraries. However, PEX is supposed to alleviate this problem by providing a consistent set of toolkit calls, which enables a user to support 3-D software with little effort.

PEX originally stood for *PHIGS Extensions to X*. PHIGS stands for *Programmer's Hierarchical Interactive Graphics System*. PEX has been adopted by the Common Open Software Environment (COSE) for X11 releases that are later than 2.2.

However, PEX is simply historical at this point, because the last version of the PEX protocol (Version 6.0) is not designed specifically for PHIGS at all. PEX is now designed to support 3-D application programs. PEX is an extension to the Core X Protocol to provide 3-D graphics support within the X Window environment. Included in the X11R5 distribution is code for the Sample Implementation of the extensions to the X Window server, which implements the functionality defined by the PEX Protocol Extensions.

In order to access the PEX functional extensions to the X server, one must use an application that generates PEX Protocol. The application can either generate the Protocol bytestream itself, or use something called an Application Protocol Interface (API). One such API provided with the X11R5 distribution is the PHIGS 3D graphics standard. This is a port of the PHIGS C language binding onto an internal layer, which generates the PEX Protocol enabling this particular PHIGS implementation to work within the X Window environment. Other alternate APIs are available via anonymous FTP from export.lcs.mit.edu.

When discussing PEX, it is important not to confuse the protocol with the API. The API is the conceptual model of 3-D graphics that the application developer sees when developing a client program. The PEX protocol is generated by the API, and is interpreted by the X server to perform graphics requests on behalf of the client program.

One API provided with the R5 PEX-SI is a PHIGS/PHIGS-PLUS API. The PHIGS/PHIGS-PLUS standards are specified in two parts. First, a functional description explains each operation conceptually, in a language-independent manner. Second, language bindings are used to bind the particular PHIGS functions to the semantics of the language. The PEX-SI comes with an application programmer interface that conforms to the latest revision of the PHIGS/PHIGS-PLUS C language binding.

If your version of R5 is patched through patch number 22, you have a second MIT-supplied API called PEXlib. PEXlib is to the PEX protocol what Xlib is to the core X protocol. PEXlib provides an interface that is as close as possible to a one-to-one correspondence between functions and protocol requests. It is intended to be a systems programming interface (so, people developing graphics toolkits and graphics systems will implement their system on top of PEXlib). It is proposed that the PHIGS API be ported to PEXlib when PEXlib is finalized. This change would not affect programs written to the existing PHIGS API.

However, because PEXlib is intimately tied to the protocol, it is expected that there will be changes between the current PEXlib (which supports Version 5.0 and 5.1 of the PEX protocol) and the PEXlib that supports the next major version of the PEX protocol, Version 6.0. Naturally, every attempt will be made to make the changes to the API minimal. The nature of the changes from 5.1 to 6.0 are not such that every primitive will be affected; rather the changes deal with the sticky problems of subsets, multibuffering, and other issues of global rendering semantics.

PEX Server

Find out whether you have PEX available on your X server first. By default, PEX support is *not* built into the servers you received for Linux. The xdpyinfo command displays all the extensions supported by a server.

Output from the PEX command should contain strings of the following form:

```
number of extensions:    7
XTestExtension1
SHAPE
MIT-SHM
X3D-PEX       (<— This is the line you are looking for)
Multi-buffering
MIT-SUNDRY-NONSTANDARD
```

If one of the extensions listed is X3D-PEX, your server supports PEX. If you do not see this line, you must build the server yourself.

Building a Server

To build a server that only includes the drivers you need, use the LinkKit instead of compiling the complete X system. Using the LinkKit package is much easier. The LinkKit package can be found in /usr/X386/lib/Server.

The LinkKit package contains a file called site.def for you to edit. The site.def file contains the site-specific information for your system. Edit the site.def file to define which servers you want to build, and the drivers and font *renderers* (programs that generate fonts for display) you want to include.

> **NOTE**
>
> You must run all the commands in this section as root.

Let's examine the `site.def` file in a bit of detail. See Listing 55.1 for the `site.def` file that I used to create a PEX server for my machine.

Listing 55.1. Sample `site.def` file.

```
XCOMM $XFree86: mit/server/ddx/x386/LinkKit/site.def.LK,v 2.11
      1994/04/10 05:49:56 dawes Exp $

/* Configuration file for Server Link Kit */

#ifdef BeforeVendorCF

/*
 * Change these definitions if you need to override the defaults:
 */

/*
 * HasGcc: defaults:
 *         SVR3,4:         YES
 *         Mach, 386bsd:   YES
 */
/* #define HasGcc          NO */

/*
 * HasGcc2: (should also set HasGcc)
 *      defaults:
 *         SVR3,4:         YES
 *         Mach:      YES
 *         386bsd:         NO
 */
/* #define HasGcc2         NO */

/*
 * If the link kit you are using was built with gcc2, and you are using
 * a different compiler:
 *   1. Install libgcc.a in a directory searched by your 'ld'
 *   2. Set NeedLibGcc to YES
 */
#define NeedLibGcc         NO

/*
 * Uncomment this if you want to link with the Gnu malloc library
 */
/* #define GnuMalloc    YES */

/*
 * GnuMallocLib: link-time flags to include the Gnu malloc library.
 * this is only used when GnuMalloc is set to YES.
 *      defaults:
 *         386bsd:          -lgnumalloc
```

```
     *           others:               -lgmalloc
     */
    /* #define GnuMallocLib          -L/usr/local/gnu -lmalloc */

    /*
     * Server configuration parameters
     */

    #define FontRenderers            Speedo Type1
    #define X386Vga2Drivers          et4000 et3000 pvga1 gvga tvga8900 ncr \
                        compaq oak generic
    #define X386Vga16Drivers         et4000 tvga8900 generic
    #define X386Vga256Drivers        et4000 et3000 pvga1 gvga ati tvga8900 cirrus \
                        ncr compaq oak
    #define X386Hga2Drivers          /**/
    /* To enable the hga2 driver, replace the above line with the following */
    /* #define X386Hga2Drivers          hga6845 */

    /*
     * To include the generic banked monochrome driver in the monochrome server,
     * uncomment this with one of the following low level drivers
     *    hgc1280           [Hyundai HGC-1280 1280x1024]
     *    sigma      [Sigma L-View]
     *    visa       [???]
     *    apollo           [???]
     *    ...
     *    (list is subject to grow)
     */
    /* #define X386Bdm2Drivers    hgc1280 sigma visa apollo */

    /* #define XF86S3Drivers             mmio_928 s3_generic */
    /*
     * Set which servers to build.  Change the YES to NO for servers you don't
     * want to build.
     */

    /* The SVGA color server */
    #define XF86SVGAServer         YES

    /* The 16-color VGA server */
    #define XF86VGA16Server        NO

    /* The VGA mono server */
    #define XF86MonoServer         NO

    /* The S3 server */
    #define XF86S3Server           NO

    /* The IBM 8514/A server */
    #define XF86I8514Server        NO

    /* The Mach8 server */
    #define XF86Mach8Server        NO

    /* The Mach32 server */
    #define XF86Mach32Server       NO

    /* Set the default server (ie the one that gets the sym-link to "X") */
```

continues

Listing 55.1. continued

```
/* #define XFree86DefaultServer      XF86_S3 */

/*
 * If you want PEX (and this link kit was built with PEX support), uncomment
 * the following
 */
/* #define BuildPexExt          YES */
#define BuildPexExt          YES

#endif /* BeforeVendorCF */

#ifdef AfterVendorCF

/* If you are using a different ProjectRoot, set it here */

/*
#ifdef ProjectRoot
#undef ProjectRoot
#endif
#define ProjectRoot /usr/X11R5
*/

#endif /* AfterVendorCF */
```

Note the following items about this `site.def` file:

- The `HasGcc` and `HasGcc2` definitions have been commented out for Linux.
- If the LinkKit was built with gcc-2.x and you are using some other compiler, you must install `libgcc.a` and set `NeedLibGcc` to YES.

For Linux, `NeedLibGcc` is set to NO.

The servers available to you via LinkKit are shown in Table 55.1. To create any of these servers, you have to set the value of the corresponding variable to YES.

Table 55.1. Server types in `site.def`.

Server Type	Variable To Set
256-color server	XF86SVGAServer
16-color server	XF86VGA16Server
Monochrome server	XF86MonoServer
S3 server	XF86S3Server
Mach8 server	XF86Mach8Server
Mach32 server	XF86Mach32Server
IBM 8514/A server	XF86I8514Server

In the sample `site.def` in Listing 55.1, I have set only the 256-color SVGA server to be built. All other servers will not be built.

> **NOTE**
>
> The PEX extensions you have do not support the Monochrome server.

The `Drivers` variables define the video drivers that you want to include in a server. The order of drivers determines the order in which the server probes the video card to determine which driver to use. The `generic` driver should be the last one included in the monochrome and 16-color servers because its probe always succeeds.

The `generic_s3` driver should be the last one included in the S3 servers for similar reasons.

After you have edited the `site.def` file, you must create the `Makefile`.

To build the `Makefile`, run this command:

```
# ./mkmf
```

Then, run make to link the servers that you have configured in the `site.def` file. This command takes a while. After this command is done, run the `make install` command to install the new servers:

```
# make install
```

> **TIP**
>
> Run `make clean` to remove the files that were created by this procedure.
>
> This frees the directory structures of any unnecessary files, which is important because disk space is at a premium under Linux.

Now start X, run the window manager, and in an `xterm` use the `xdpyinfo` command to see whether the PEX extensions are there. It is possible to see which drivers are included in the server by running the X server with the `-showconfig` flag.

Writing Your Own Driver

If you are including a driver that it not part of the standard distribution, make a directory in `drivers/vga256` (`drivers/vga2` if it is for the monochrome server; `drivers/vga16` if it is for the 16-color server; or `drivers/bdm2` if it is for the bdm2 monochrome server's bdm2 screen). Copy either the source or the `.o` file, and a suitable `Imakefile`, into that directory. The name of the directory should be the same as the name of the driver. If you are adding an additional font renderer, put the library in `./renderers`. Look at the `VGADriver.Doc` file for more details.

Getting PEX

You have PEX files on the CD-ROM at the back of this book.

There are several examples of PEX code available on the Internet. One sample library can be found at the site export.lcs.mit.edu in the /R5contrib/R5contrib-fixes directory as the file PEX.examples.tar.Z.

Sample PEX Source File

Let's look at an example of a simple PEX program that prints the line Howdy World. (Hello World is a bit overused.) The following is the listing for printing this line:

```
#include "phigs/phigs.h"
#include "X11/Xlib.h"
#include "X11/Xatom.h"
#include "strings.h"

char windowName[] = "PEX in Linux";
char HelloStr[] = "Howdy World";

main()
{
    Pconnid_x_drawable      connid;
    Display                 *display;
    int                 screen;
    Ppoint                  text_pt;

      popen_phigs(NULL,0); /* open a conn. to PHIGS server */
          /*
          ** Set the error file name to NULL
          ** Set default memory size to zero
          */

    connid.display = display = XOpenDisplay( NULL );
    screen = DefaultScreen( display );
    connid.drawable_id =
       XCreateSimpleWindow( display,
           RootWindow( display, screen ),
           0, 0, 600, 600, 4,
           WhitePixel( display, screen ),
           BlackPixel( display, screen ) );

    XChangeProperty( display, connid.drawable_id, XA_WM_NAME,
```

```
        XA_STRING, 8, PropModeReplace,
        (unsigned char *) windowName , strlen(windowName) );

    XMapWindow( display, connid.drawable_id );

    popen_ws( 1, &connid, phigs_ws_type_x_drawable );

    popen_struct( 1 );

    text_pt.x = 0.2;
    text_pt.y = 0.5;
    pset_char_ht( 0.05 );
    ptext( &text_pt, HelloStr, strlen(HelloStr)):
    pclose_struct( );

    ppost_struct( 1, 1, 1.0 );

    printf("Hit return to exit");
    getchar();

    pclose_ws( 1 );
    pclose_phigs( );
}
```

The first executable line in this file opens a connection to the PEX server with a call to popen_phigs(NULL,0). The NULL parameter sets the error filename to nothing, and the 0 sets the default memory size to 0.

The next lines set the display, screen, and window IDs for this application. The window ID is set to point to the root window for the application with a call to the XCreateSimpleWindow function. The display and screen IDs are set to the defaults. Note that you are using low-level X Window system function calls to create the root window. This example tells you that it's possible to access all the low-level X Window functions, in addition to the PEX functions.

The XChangeProperty function call sets the window name to the one desired. The display and window ID (connid.drawable_id) are set to that of the root window of the application.

The XMapWindow function maps your display to the current window ID.

The popen_ws() call opens the workspace for the display for you to be able to draw on. You then set the test position for the Howdy World string. Then, open a structure for writing with PEX primitives to set the text_pt structure with the text. It is necessary to call the pclose_struct() function when done with the drawing area buffer. Lastly, post the structure to ppost_struct.

Wait until the user gives the keystroke you want, and then end the application. In this case, you must call two functions before ending the application. One is a call to pclose_ws(1) for closing the workspace, and the other is a call to pclose_phigs( ) for shutting down the PEX server.

PEXlib and Motif

In the previous example, the drawable was used to create the drawing patterns on a drawing area widget. PEXlib by itself is intended to be an interface into the lower-level Xlib. PEXlib gives you the capability to do 3-D mappings, shading, and so on, along with other geometric transformations.

This section covers the basic act of combining PEXlib with Motif. This way, you can get a drawable area under Motif and be able to use PEX functions on it. In addition to this, you still have the Motif framework to add your own menus to it. The steps to combine Motif and PEXlib are as follows:

- Initialize an X Window, and get the best visual you can for PEX.
- Initialize PEX with a call to PEXInitialize.
- Create a top-level shell.
- Create a drawing area interface for PEX.
- Map the drawing area to the screen.
- Create a PEX renderer (just like the GC) for this drawing area.
- Draw to your heart's delight.

Initializing the Toolkit

For initializing the toolkit, you must use a long method instead of XtAppInitialize. This long method enables you to select the best visual you can get for PEX. The following code segment will suffice:

```
XtToolkitInitialize();
app_context = XtCreateApplicationContext();
cp_argc     = argc;
argv_sz = argc * sizeof(char *);
cp_argv = (char **)XtMalloc(argv_sz);
memcpy(cp_argv, argv, argv_sz); /* copy the pointers */

display = XtOpenDisplay(app_context,
            argv[0], argv[0],
            "pEX", /* Class Name */
            NULL, 0, /* no resource options */
            &argc, argv);


if (display == (Display *) NULL)
        abort("Unable to open display");
```

You are making a copy of argc and argv to preserve their values, because the call to XtOpenDisplay() mangles these original values. It's necessary to check whether the display pointer is set to a valid value when you return from XtOpenDisplay() because the display may not have been opened for a variety of reasons, and you do not want to work a NULL pointer for the display.

Initialize the PEXlib functions with a call to the function PEXInitialize(). The syntax for this call is as follows:

```
#include <X11/PEX5/PEXlib.h>

int PEXInitialize(Display *dp,
        PEXExtensionInfo *info_ptr,
        int message_length,
        char *msg);
```

The `PEXExtensionInfo` pointer should point to a structure to which you want this function to return information about the PEX server. The message array should be about 80 characters long, and contain the text for any returned error messages. The function returns 0 if no errors occurred; otherwise, it returns one of the following values:

- `PEXBadExtension` if the X server does not support PEX
- `PEXBadProtocolVersion` if your X server and the PEXlib you are using are of different versions
- `PEXBadLocalAlloc` if you are out of memory
- `PEXBadFloatConversion` if the X server does not support the PEX floating point

Also, note that I used PEX5 as the location of the include files. When PEX 6.0 comes along, you may have to change this PEX5 reference to PEX6 in all the code you have to date. A bummer indeed, but necessary for an upgrade.

The returned `PEXExtensionInfo` structure is of the following form:

```
typedef struct {
unsigned_short    major_version;
unsigned_short    minor_version;
unsigned long release;
unsigned long subset_info;
char *vendor_name;
int    major_opcode;
int    first_event;
int    first_error;
} PEXExtensionInfo;
```

The major version is usually 5 or 6, and the minor version either 0 or 1. The vendor name and release are vendor-specific. The subset information contains information about the features in your PEX server, and can have the following values:

`PEXImmediateMode`   Enables drawing primitives that are sent directly to the display.

`PEXWorkstationOnly`   Enables workstation resources.

`PEXStructureMode`   Enables drawing primitives to be stored in a structure before being sent to the display.

`PEXCompleteImplementation`   Enables all of these functions.

Check this value to see what features your X server supports. If your server does not have either the complete or Immediate mode graphics (the Linux server is and should be complete), you should exit the application with an error message.

Creating the Window

Now create the window with the `colormap` and the best visual for PEX. The way to do this is as follows:

```
XStandardColormap        colormap;
Colormap     PEX_colormap;
```

```
/* open display as before */

screen = DefaultScreen(display);
visual = DefaultVisual(display,screen);
depth  = DefaultDepth(display,screen);
status = GetStdColormap(display, screen,
              visual, depth,
              &colormap);
if (status == True)
      PEX_colormap = colormap;


blue = AllocNamedColor(display, PEX_colormap,
        "Blue", 0L);

white = AllocNamedColor(display, PEX_colormap,
        "White", 0L);


n = 0;
XtSetArg(args[n],XmNvisual, visual); n++;
XtSetArg(args[n],XmNdepth, depth); n++;
XtSetArg(args[n],XmNcolormap, colormap); n++;
XtSetArg(args[n],XmNallowResize, True); n++;
XtSetArg(args[n],XmNmapWhenManaged, False); n++;
XtSetArg(args[n],XmNbackground, blue); n++;
XtSetArg(args[n],XmNforeground, white); n++;
XtSetArg(args[n],XmNargc, cp_argc); n++;
XtSetArg(args[n],XmNargv, cp_argv); n++;
XtSetArg(args[n],XmNheight, 400); n++;
XtSetArg(args[n],XmNwidth, 400); n++;

toplevel = XtAppCreateShell(NULL, "peX",
      applicationShellWidgetClass, display, args, n);


mainWindow = XmCreateMainWindow(toplevel, "mainWin", NULL, 0);

drawMe = XmCreateDrawingArea(mainWindow,
              "pexdraw", args, n);
```

> **TIP**
>
> If you are unfamiliar with programming in Motif or X, please refer to Chapter 32, "Motif for Programmers."

The application requires the toplevel shell. For this shell, you have to manually set its visual, screen, display, and colormap. Note that the resize resource is set to True and mapWhenManaged is set to False. You have to set these values via the XtArgs args array at creation time for this to work. The toplevel shell is where you create the main window to place your Motif widgets. After you have created the main window with the XmCreateMainWindow function call, you create the drawing area called drawMe on top of this window.

Next, you add callbacks to the drawing area widget to allow for redrawing. Add the callbacks to the drawing area for the following types of events: `resize`, `expose`, and `input`.

The complete code for a very simple application is shown in Listing 55.2.

Listing 55.2. A sample PEX application with Motif.

```
#include <Xm/Xm.h>
#include <Xm/DrawingA.h>
#include <Xm/MainW.h>
#include <Xm/RowColumn.h>
#include <X11/PEX5/PEXlib.h>
#include <stdio.h>

int bailout(char *str)
{
printf ("\n %s", str);
exit(1);
}

int pex_set_line_color(Display *dpy, PEXRenderer p,
        float r, float g, float b)
{
PEXColor pc;

pc.rgb.red = r;
pc.rgb.green = g;
pc.rgb.blue = b;

PEXSetLineColor(dpy, p, PEXOCRender, PEXColorTypeRGB, &pc);
}

void doSamplePEX( Display *dpy, Window win, PEXRenderer ren)
{
PEXCoord     coords[10];

PEXBeginRendering(dpy, win, ren);

PEXSetLineWidth(dpy, ren, PEXOCRender, 8.0);

pex_set_line_color(dpy, ren, 0.5, 0.5, 1.0);

coords[0].x = 0.3; coords[0].y = 0.3; coords[0].z = 0.0;
coords[1].x = 0.3; coords[1].y = 0.6; coords[1].z = 0.0;
coords[2].x = 0.6; coords[2].y = 0.6; coords[2].z = 0.0;
coords[3].x = 0.6; coords[3].y = 0.3; coords[3].z = 0.0;

PEXPolyline(dpy, ren, PEXOCRender, 4, coords);

pex_set_line_color(dpy, ren, 1.5, 0.5, 1.5);

coords[0].x = 0.3; coords[0].y = 0.3; coords[0].z = 0.5;
coords[1].x = 0.3; coords[1].y = 0.6; coords[1].z = 0.5;
coords[2].x = 0.6; coords[2].y = 0.6; coords[2].z = 0.5;
coords[3].x = 0.6; coords[3].y = 0.3; coords[3].z = 0.5;
```

continues

Listing 55.2. continued

```
PEXPolyline(dpy, ren, PEXOCRender, 4, coords);

PEXEndRendering(dpy, win, ren);
XFlush(dpy); /* important */

}


void quitBtn( Widget w, void *p, void *pp)
{
     exit(0);
}


void drawBtn( Widget w, XmDrawingAreaCallbackStruct *sp,
          XtPointer *client_data)
{
     Dimension   wd, ht;
     PEXRenderer *rp;

     if (sp == NULL) return;

     switch(sp->reason)
     {
     case XmCR_EXPOSE:
          if (sp->event->xexpose.count == 0)
          {
          rp = (PEXRenderer *)client_data;
          doSamplePEX(XtDisplay(w), XtWindow(w), *rp);
          }
          break;
     case XmCR_INPUT:
          break;
     }
}

int
pexInit(Display *dpy, PEXExtensionInfo **pexparms)
{
int    err;
char   errorMsg[PEXErrorStringLength+1];
PEXExtensionInfo *pex_info;

     err = PEXInitialize(dpy, pexparms,
          PEXErrorStringLength, errorMsg);

     if (err) return False;

     pex_info = (PEXExtensionInfo *)(*pexparms);

     if( (pex_info->subset_info & PEXImmediateMode) ||
     ((pex_info->subset_info & 0xffff) == PEXCompleteImplementation))
     {
     return True;
     }
```

```
        return False;
}

int main(int argc, char *argv[])
{
        Widget parent;
        XtAppContext        app_context;
        int cp_size;
        int cp_argc;
        int cp_argv;
        int status;
        int screen;
        int depth;
        int fore;
        int bkg;
        int n;
        Arg wars[20];
        Visual *visual;
        Colormap colormap;
        XStandardColormap std_cmp;
        PEXRendererAttributes pex_attr;
        Display        *dpy;
        PEXExtensionInfo *pexParms;
        PEXRenderer   ren;
        Widget mainw;
        Widget filemenu;
        Widget menubar;
        Widget exitBtn;
        Widget drawme;


        XtToolkitInitialize();
        app_context = XtCreateApplicationContext();

        cp_argc = argc;
        cp_size = argc * (sizeof(char *));
        cp_argv = (char **)XtMalloc(cp_size);
        memcpy(cp_argv, argv, cp_size);

        dpy = XtOpenDisplay(app_context, NULL, NULL,
            "pexSample", NULL, 0, &argc, argv);

        if (dpy == (Display *) NULL)
            bailout("Cannot open display");

        status = pexInit(dpy,&pexParms);
        if (status == False) bailout("Cannot use PEX");


        screen = DefaultScreen(dpy);
        visual = DefaultVisual(dpy, screen);
        depth = DefaultDepth(dpy,screen);

        status = GetStdColormap(dpy, screen, visual, depth, &std_cmp);
        colormap = std_cmp.colormap;
        bkg = BlackPixel(dpy,screen);
        fore = WhitePixel(dpy,screen);
```

continues

Listing 55.2. continued

```
n = 0;
XtSetArg(wars[n], XmNvisual, visual); n++;
XtSetArg(wars[n], XmNdepth, depth); n++;
XtSetArg(wars[n], XmNcolormap, colormap); n++;
XtSetArg(wars[n], XmNbackground, bkg); n++;
XtSetArg(wars[n], XmNborderColor, fore); n++;
XtSetArg(wars[n], XmNargc, cp_argc); n++;
XtSetArg(wars[n], XmNargv,cp_argv); n++;
XtSetArg(wars[n], XmNallowResize, True); n++;
XtSetArg(wars[n], XmNmappedWhenManaged, False); n++;
XtSetArg(wars[n], XmNwidth, 300); n++;
XtSetArg(wars[n], XmNheight, 300); n++;
parent = XtAppCreateShell(NULL,"pexSample",
        applicationShellWidgetClass, dpy, wars, n);

n = 0;
mainw = XmCreateMainWindow(parent, "mainwindow", wars, n);

n = 0;
XtSetArg(wars[n], XmNresizePolicy, XmRESIZE_ANY); n++;
XtSetArg(wars[n], XmNbackground, bkg); n++;
XtSetArg(wars[n], XmNborderColor, fore); n++;

drawme = XmCreateDrawingArea(mainw, "da", wars, n);

XtAddCallback(drawme, XmNexposeCallback,
(XtCallbackProc)drawBtn, (XtPointer) &ren);
XtAddCallback(drawme, XmNinputCallback,
(XtCallbackProc)drawBtn, (XtPointer) &ren);
XtAddCallback(drawme, XmNresizeCallback,
(XtCallbackProc)drawBtn, (XtPointer) &ren);

XtManageChild(drawme);
XtManageChild(mainw);
XtRealizeWidget(parent);

pex_set_color_approx(dpy,XtWindow(drawme), &std_cmp, &pex_attr);

XtMapWidget(parent);

ren = PEXCreateRenderer(XtDisplay(mainw), XtWindow(drawme),
        PEXRAColorApproxTable, &pex_attr);
if (ren == 0) {
        printf("\n Bad renderer \n"); exit (1);
}

XtAppMainLoop(app_context);
return(0);

}
```

A few points to note about Listing 55.2 are that the immediate mode was used for rendering on the screen. PEX-SI provides no support for double buffering. This is a serious bug because lack of double buffering hinders performance.

Even worse, the PEX-SI API assumes that the client desires an XClearArea on the window before each frame is drawn. This causes unnecessary flickering while the screen is cleared and redrawn on all primitive drawing calls. What should have been done was to provide an end-of-render procedure hook, with the default hook installed to do a clear area function call.

Individual vendors (because of market pressure) have provided their own solutions to the double buffering problem. (Most PHIGS workstations do double buffering. If you do immediate mode you get single buffering along with the PEX-SI's XClearArea call.)

A final word about adding too many features in an X server. The more you add to the X server, the more memory it chews up in your system. Unless you absolutely require PEX (or other) support, do not add it to your X server, especially if RAM is 8MB or less. The PEX support for Linux added about 420KB on my system, which is not a lot, but it does start adding up. Also, the overhead of PEX applications tend to make my 8MB, 486/33 somewhat slow when running PEX demos, which leads me to believe that PEX on Linux with less than 16MB is not worth the hassle. If you are serious about PEX on Linux, get a faster machine and put gobs of memory on it. The performance improved very dramatically on a 486/66 with 32MB of RAM.

Where To Look for More Information

If you would like more information and examples of source code for PEX, check out these FTP sites:

- export.lcs.mit.edu in /R5contrib/contrib-R5fixes has several tar files of source code for PHIGS and PEX including a 3-D drawing program.
- http://www.x.org is a good place to start looking for more information on X.

Summary

This chapter has been a whirlwind tour of PEX. The topic of PEX could be a book in itself. In fact, there are several texts available that go into excruciating detail about PEX. You should have learned the following information from this chapter:

- How to create a new X server with your specifications. Building your own server with LinkKit is far easier than trying to re-create the entire X distribution. There are fewer memory requirements, and the build takes up less disk space and time to compile and link.
- How to install the new server. The LinkKit does this for you automatically and gives you options to clean your directories, and so on.
- How to check for the extensions in the current server.
- How to interface Motif with PEX.
- The trade-offs of having too many extensions in X server, such as loss of memory and speed for added functionality.
- Where to look for more information about PEX and Linux.

Using Mosaic and Netscape

IN THIS CHAPTER

This chapter is a brief introduction to the World Wide Web and Mosaic and Netscape. We will cover the following topics in this chapter:

- A brief introduction to the Web.
- How to get Mosaic for Linux.
- How to set up Mosaic on your Linux machine.
- How to get and set up Netscape for your Linux machine.
- How to configure a SLIP connection for dialup and dedicated lines using Linux.
- Getting started with an HTML document. You will learn the basics of writing your own Web documents.

Introduction to the Web

The World Wide Web (WWW) is a fairly new invention. In 1989, researchers at CERN (a European Lab for Particle Physics) wanted to share information between nodes on their network. The researchers automated the process of locating files on remote machines and then copying the required information to their local machines. This retrieval process had to be done with a standard interface, regardless of the type of data or the means of getting this data. This meant that the interface had to include almost all the data retrieval tools such as FTP, Gopher, and so on, and be able to handle graphical, text, and binary files with a consistent interface.

The resulting network was such a success that the method caught on with users worldwide and gave us the World Wide Web. The letters *WWW* are now synonymous with the word *Internet*. The number of sites offering Web services is growing every day.

> **NOTE**
>
> Although the Red Hat distribution that accompanies this book includes a copy of the Arena Web browser, Arena lacks much of the functionality provided by browsers such as Mosaic and Netscape. This chapter is included to show you how to download and install these more powerful browsers so that you can take advantage of the capabilities they offer.

Introduction to Mosaic

To access the services on the Web, you need a browser. A browser is an application that knows how to interpret and display documents it finds on the Web. Documents on the Web are encoded in the HyperText Markup Language (HTML). Hypertext documents contain special codes that tell the browser how to locate information on the Web. How the browser interprets the codes is left as a local issue. Some browsers such as Lynx ignore any requests for inline images; some older Mosaic browsers ignore the interactive Forms that a user can fill in while online.

> **NOTE**
>
> The hypertext Home Page about NCSA has the following information:
>
> "Established in 1985 with a National Science Foundation grant, the National Center for Supercomputing Applications (NCSA) opened to the national research community in January 1986. NCSA is a high-performance computing and communications facility designed to serve U.S. computational science and engineering communities. Located on the campus of the University of Illinois at Urbana-Champaign (UIUC), NCSA is funded by the National Science Foundation, the Advanced Research Projects Agency, other federal agencies, the state of Illinois, the University of Illinois, and industrial partners."
>
> Enough said.

Mosaic includes the following features:

- The capability to display plain text, HTML documents, and audio
- The capability to display inline graphics and images
- A customizable graphical user interface
- The capability to track previous sites with lists in a History and Hotlist
- The capability to find items via search commands within a document and over the Internet
- Extendability via third-party viewers for a type of graphical data format

Where To Get Mosaic for Linux

The latest version is available from the Internet at the following FTP sites:

- `sunsite.unc.edu` in the directory `/pub/Linux/system/Network/info-systems/Mosaic`.
- There are several files in here with version numbers 2.0 and higher. The 2.5 version was the most recent stable one on my system at the time I wrote this chapter. Your mileage may vary. I used the file `Mosaic-2.5.bin.tar.gz` as my starting point. FTP to this site and get the latest version for yourself.
- `tsx-11.mit.edu` is a mirror site for `sunsite`. Use this site if `sunsite` appears to be very busy.
- Another excellent site for Web documents is the FTP site `ftp.ncsa.uiuc.edu`. Look under the `/Web` directory tree for a whole forest of documents on the Web, source code, and versions of Mosaic.

■ If you have access to the Web already through another source, you should look at `http://www.w3.org` for information about the Web, latest source code, and other Web-related documents.

After you get the files from these sources, you have to unzip the files via GNU's `gunzip` program. The `gunzip` program removes the `.gz` extension after it unzips a file.

The commands to do this are shown next. Substitute the name of the Mosaic version you get for the word *myfile* here.

```
$ ls myfile*
myfile.tar.gz
$ gunzip file.tar.gz
$ ls myfile*
myfile.tar
$ tar -xf myfile.tar
...
```

After the dust settles from the `tar` extraction command (the `-x` option is for extract), you have the file `Mosaic` in your directory. Along with these files, you also have some `app-defaults` files that you can use to customize your copy of Mosaic. As with other X applications, almost all of Mosaic's features can be customized using the `Xdefaults` file with the `Mosaic` resource. For example, to set the home page use this line:

```
Mosaic*HomePage : "http://www.another.nicer.site.com/myfile"
```

Alternatively, you can set the `WWW_HOME` environment variable to the path shown above. Using the environment variable is more consistent with other UNIX platforms.

The distributions from NCSA include the `app-defaults` files for each version of Mosaic. After you have installed Mosaic on your machine, edit these files to customize your own files. Read the `app-defaults` files for all the resources that are available to you for your version of Mosaic.

Now, you can fire up Mosaic from within an `xterm` with the command `Mosaic`. (It's probably best to have Mosaic run in the background so as not to tie up your `xterm`.) When Mosaic is up, it attempts to load its default hypertext document called the Home Page. Basically, the Home Page is the first document you start off with and the one document that you know that you can always load if you get lost while browsing the Web.

Before you go browsing the Web, let's first talk about hypertext documents. Once you know how hypertext documents work, you'll find it easier to browse the Web. Be patient; the next section is worth your time to read.

Hypertext Document and HTML Basics

Hypertext documents contain links to other documents on the Web. Links are often called hyperlinks. They enable you to access other documents and services on the Internet. You *surf the Net* by accessing other documents through these links. It's fairly easy to create these hypertext documents with links, so you can create your own documents with sites that you regularly visit and find interesting.

To create a hypertext document for display on a Web server, you have to learn the HyperText Markup Language (HTML), which is a collection of styles that define the various components of a document. HTML is based on SGML (Standardized General Markup Language), a superset standard of marking documents.

> **NOTE**
>
> So why write your own Web page?
>
> There are many reasons that you would want to create your own HTML documents. The first reason is for exposure. Your own document on the Internet can have information about you or topics that you find interesting. You can have a page about your business, because a Web address on a business card does look cool. Just remember not to *spam* your page's address on the Internet; it's not polite. (*Spamming* is the slang word for posting multiple copies of a message to many unrelated newsgroups.)
>
> Second, a Web page can be a repository of your favorite sites on the Internet. While cruising the Net, if you come across a decent page or two, you can simply edit your own Web page to add this site. Then, it's simply a matter of bringing up your favorite page to get back to the old sites again.
>
> Last, you may decide to dump Mosaic and go with a newer, better browser that doesn't read the hotlists you created from Mosaic. For example, you have to jump through hoops to get your Windows browsers' hotlists into UNIX Mosaic, or vice versa. When all your data is in a Web document, all you have to do is load the document in there, and you are done—no formats, hoops, and magic potions.

Mosaic can display ASCII text files. Therefore, you really don't need to know HTML to write up an HTML document. Any old file will do. However, if you want to have a document formatted when accessed by a viewer such as Mosaic, you must code it with HTML. HTML documents are also called source files. Source files are in plain text format and can be created using any text editor.

Let's get into a bit more detail about HTML formatting codes, called tags. HTML tags consist of a left angle bracket (<), followed by some coding (called the directive), and closed by a right angle bracket (>). HTML tags are generally paired, as with <H1> and </H1>. The ending tag looks just like the starting tag except a slash (/) precedes the directive within the brackets. For example, <H1> tells the viewer to start formatting a top-level heading, and </H1> tells the viewer that the heading is complete.

HTML tags are inserted in the source files to tell Mosaic (or some other Web viewer) how to interpret or display the coded information. For example, citation tags are defined by Mosaic to be displayed in italics. Each time you enclose a book title between `<cite>` and `</cite>` tags, Mosaic automatically displays the text in italics. This is known as a logical style, because it is configured by the viewer. Viewers can interpret a logical style in different ways.

Hyperlinks

The chief power of HTML comes from its capability to link regions of text (and also images) to another document (or an image, movie, or audio file). These regions are highlighted to indicate that they are hypertext links. To create a hyperlink, a special HTML code is entered that includes the Uniform Resource Locator (URL). A URL is the way of telling your Web browser where and how to get the information. You can jump directly to URLs to see whether they are valid by using the URL command from the File menu. Enter the URL in the dialog box, and Mosaic attempts to get it for you. (See Figure 56.1.)

FIGURE 56.1.

Jumping hyperlinks via URLs.

At the same time, text or a graphic is designated to serve as the anchor (the information that is displayed in color or underlined and clicked on). A hyperlink may be made to a remote or local server, depending on how the URL is encoded.

You can keep a history of information space navigation, which tracks where you've been. You now have quick access to frequently used documents via a personal list. (See Figure 56.2.) History lists are valid for a current session only. Hotlists are those lists that you want to keep for all future sessions. (See Figure 56.3.) You should enter those places here that you may like to visit in a future session.

FIGURE 56.2.

The Mosaic History dialog box.

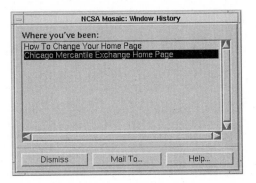

FIGURE 56.3.

The Mosaic Hotlist dialog box.

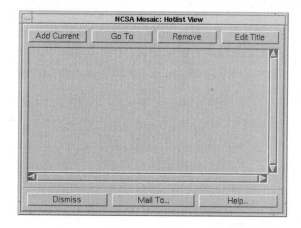

Inline Images

Mosaic can display images inside documents, making it a highly visual medium for your information. However, each image requires processing time, which slows down the initial display of the document. Using a particular image multiple times in a document causes very little performance degradation compared to using the image only once.

An image is sized before it is included in a document. Images can fill a screen. Or, they can be small images that save time when Mosaic displays the document, but are still large enough to present information and be a teaser for the larger image displayed in a separate window.

An image tag is coded into the source file to tell Mosaic that an image is to be displayed. The image tag is an HTML extension, first implemented in Mosaic. You can test your Web pages by loading this file locally to see how it looks. You don't necessarily have to be connected to the Internet to do this.

Where To Get More Help on HTML

When you have Mosaic, you have access to online help for writing your own HTML documents. To get *The Beginner's Guide to HTML* select On HTML... from the help menu. You have to be on the Internet for this to work, because Mosaic accesses the Web to get the latest copy for you. This file provides up-to-date information in far greater detail than what you are reading right now. You should print this guide out for future reference. See also *Teach Yourself Web Publishing with HTML in 14 Days* (Sams Publishing).

Netscape

The authors of the first NCSA Mosaic have formed their own company called Netscape Communications. Their new brainchild is called Netscape, and you can get a Linux version of it for yourself.

The format for using Netscape is very similar to that of Motif. You can use URLs to type your destination name or use the point-and-click method to navigate HTML documents.

The options buttons include the ability to turn on and off the button bar, URL locator, and the bottom status bars. This way, you can customize your screens to suit your preferences. A sample of the preferences file is shown in Listing 56.1.

Listing 56.1. A sample Netscape preferences file.

```
# Netscape Preferences File
# Version: 1.1N
# This is a generated file!  Do not edit.
SHOW_TOOLBAR:     True
SHOW_URL:     True
SHOW_DIRECTORY_BUTTONS:     False
AUTOLOAD_IMAGES:     True
FTP_FILE_INFO:     True
SHOW_SECURITY_BAR:     False
TOOLBAR_ICONS:     False
TOOLBAR_TEXT:     True
HOME_DOCUMENT:     http://www.ikra.com/
FONT_SIZE:     2
UNDERLINE_LINKS:     True
HISTORY_FILE:     /home/khusain/.netscape-history
HISTORY_EXPIRATION:     30
BOOKMARKS_FILE:     /home/khusain/.netscape-bookmarks.html
TMPDIR:     /tmp
TN3270:     xterm -e tn3270 %h
TELNET:        xterm -e telnet %h %p
RLOGIN:     xterm -e rlogin %h
RLOGIN_USER:     xterm -e rlogin %h -l %u
NNTPSERVER:     news
NEWSRC_DIR:     /home/khusain
NEWS_MAX_ARTICLES:     100
REAL_NAME:     Jonathan Doe Husain
EMAIL_ADDRESS:     khusain@ikra.com
ORGANIZATION:     Hardly any mps inc.
SIGNATURE_FILE:     /home/khusain/.signature
SIGNATURE_DATE:     0
8BIT_MAIL_AND_NEWS:     True
MAILHOST:     localhost
SOCKS_HOST:
FTP_PROXY:
HTTP_PROXY:
HTTPS_PROXY:
GOPHER_PROXY:
WAIS_PROXY:
NO_PROXY:
MEMORY_CACHE_SIZE:     2000
DISK_CACHE_SIZE:     5000
SOCKET_BUFFER_SIZE:     32
MAX_CONNECTIONS:     4
CACHE_DIR:     /home/khusain/.netscape-cache
```

```
LICENSE_ACCEPTED:     501 1.1N
DITHER_IMAGES:      True
STREAMING_IMAGES:      True
VERIFY_DOCUMENTS:      0
MIME_TYPES:        /usr/local/lib/netscape/mime.types
PERSONAL_MIME_TYPES:      /home/khusain/.mime.types
MAILCAP:      /usr/local/lib/netscape/mailcap
PERSONAL_MAILCAP:      /home/khusain/.mailcap
WARN_ENTER_SECURE:      False
WARN_LEAVE_SECURE:      False
WARN_MIXED_SECURE:      False
WARN_SUBMIT_INSECURE:      False
ADD_URLS:
BOOKMARK_MENU:
PRINT_COMMAND:      lpr
PRINT_REVERSED:      False
PRINT_COLOR:      True
PRINT_LANDSCAPE:      False
PRINT_PAPER:      0
```

Even though this file states "do not edit," you can get away with a few changes via a text editor. Keep in mind though, that any changes you make through the preferences dialog in the main screen may override what you edited manually.

The "N" display at the top right-hand corner of your display shows shooting stars as files are downloaded. If you want to stop any further transfers, you can click your mouse on this icon.

The bookmark feature is a bit more intuitive than for Mosaic. In fact, for some people, it's a bit easier to use and edit.

Netscape creates a .netscape_cache directory in your home directory, primarily for keeping track of images for HTML files. The size of this directory can get quite big after a few sessions of Netscape. Once in a while, if you are short of disk space, delete the files in this directory and the history file called .netscape-history file.

Another file of interest would be the .netscape-history file. This file can get large, too, after a few months of Web browsing, because this is where Netscape tracks where you have been. You can use this file as a guide to hunt for that special location that you just cannot remember now. If only my memory were this easily accessible.

Where To Get Netscape

You can get netscape from www.netscape.com, the home site for Netscape Communications. Read the license agreements carefully. All you get is a 90-day evaluation period if you are not a student or are using it for commercial, as opposed to personal, reasons.

Installation is easy. Get the file from the www.netscape.com site and un-tar it. You will have all the executables and associated files in a subdirectory.

> **NOTE**
>
> If you are using Netscape Version 1.1, you will get an error or warning message that the environment variable XNLSPATH does not contain the correct config files. This causes the program to crash if you cut and paste text in its text fields. The included files have to be placed in /usr/X386/lib/X11/nls, or you should set XNLSPATH to the nls subdirectory where you installed netscape.
>
> Your best course of action would be to get Netscape 2.01 (or the latest version) from the Web site at http://www.mcom.com/comprod/mirror/index.html.

SLIP Connections

Setting up a SLIP connection is necessary if you are not already on the Internet. To get a dialup SLIP connection you have to use the /sbin/dip program. The dip stands for Dialup Internet Protocol. For a dedicated connection you should use the slattach program.

If you are already connected to the Internet through another means, skip this section entirely.

dip

The dip program uses a script file to connect you to a SLIP account. You need a SLIP account to use Mosaic. Using dip with a -t option can also let you run in interactive mode for debugging, but in most cases you use it with a script file.

A script file is basically a file that handles your login and setup for you. You invoke /sbin/dip with the script name as an argument. A sample script file to work with my Internet SLIP account is shown in Listing 56.2. Your Internet provider should provide a script for you. If it does not provide one, ask for it.

Let's look at this sample script file in Listing 56.2.

Listing 56.2. A sample dip script file.

```
main:
#
# Get the local and remote names for the network
#
get $remote remote

#
#
#
default
get $mtu 1500
port cua1
speed 38400
modem HAYES
flush
```

```
reset
send +++
sleep 1
send ate1v1m1q0\r
wait OK 2
if $errlvl != 0 goto error
send atdt5551212\r

if $errlvl != 0 goto error
# wait CONNECT 60

login:
sleep 3
wait login: 30
if $errlvl != 0 goto error
send johndoe\r

wait ord: 5
send  doa+sol!\r

wait TERM 10
send  dumb\r

wait $ 10
send dslip\r

wait Your 10
#
# get $remote remote
#
get $local remote
#
# Ask for the remote site's IP address interactively from the user
#
get $remote ask

# cannot do this dec $remote

done:
print LOCAL address is $local
print CONNECTED to $remote
print GATEWAY address $remote
default
mode CSLIP
goto exit

error:
        print SLIP to $remote failed
exit:
```

Listing 56.2 shows how to access an Internet service provider via a dialup SLIP account. This script gives you an example of how to log into the remote system and get your local address, and even asks you for the remote IP address.

Normally, you run the SLIP script as root. You can set the permissions on the files in /etc/dip for all user access and not have to run as root. For debugging purposes, the -v option echoes all the script lines as they are executed. The echo on and echo off commands in script files turn the echoing on or off while executing. The -v option is like having the echo on command set as the first line in the script file.

The modem command in the scripts for dip only supports the HAYES parameter. You can set the speed with the speed command. For other parameters of your modem, use the Hayes command set. For example, send ate1v1m1q0\r sends the accompanying string to the modem to initialize it.

You can send output to the modem (and remote host) with the send command. To wait for a specific string, use the wait command with part of the string you are waiting for. Beware though, that if the string you are waiting for never appears, you can hang forever. The sleep command simply pauses the shell execution for the specified number of seconds. All variables for dip must be lower-case and preceded with a dollar sign. The dip program recognizes the following special variables:

```
$remote for remote host name
$rmtip          for remote host IP address
$local for local host name
$locip          for local host IP address
$mtu    contains the MTU value for the connection.
➡ You get this value from your internet provider.
```

The get command is dip's way of setting a variable. The following line requests the name of the remote host from the user. The ask parameter tells dip to prompt the user for the input.

```
        get $remote ask
```

The local address for this script is derived when you log into your service provider. The remote host prints out a string of the form *Your IP address is zzz.yyy.xxx.www*. So the script waits for the Your string and then gets the last word on the line. Some SLIP service providers assign you a different address every time you log in, so you have to do this. The way to do this is as follows:

```
#
# Get local address from this string.
#
wait Your 10
get $local remote
```

The default command tells dip to route all default message traffic points to the SLIP link. The default command should be executed just before the mode command.

The mode command recognizes either SLIP or CSLIP as a parameter. CSLIP is the compressed SLIP mode. If all goes well, the dip program goes into daemon mode. The dip program executes the ifconfig program to automatically configure your interface as a point-to-point link.

Finally, to kill an existing dip process, you can use /sbin/dip with the -k option. You should do this when you turn off your machine or log out to free up your phone line.

NOTE

Read Chapter 42, "Networking," to set your `/etc/hosts` file. Also, if you are not familiar with the `ifconfig` and `traceroute` commands, read the man pages for them. The `ifconfig` program configures and maintains kernel resident network interfaces. The `traceroute` command is useful in tracking messages as they come and go from your machine on the SLIP link. It is an invaluable tool for debugging.

slattach

The `slattach` file is used to connect on a dedicated line to a remote server. If your modem is on `/dev/cua2`, the command to configure a CSLIP connection is run as root:

```
# slattach /dev/cua2 &
```

You can put this in your `rc.inet` files if you like. If your service provider does not support CSLIP, you can use the `-p slip` option to get the uncompressed SLIP mode. Just make sure that you run the same mode as your service provider.

Then, you execute the following commands:

```
# ifconfig sl0 localhost pointtopoint myrichISP
# route add myrichISP
# route add default gw myrichISP
```

The first command connects you as a point-to-point to a SLIP connection. (The `sl0` is *ess el zero*.) The next two commands add the node `myrichISP` (the Internet service provider) as the default route.

To kill this connection, you must issue the following commands:

```
# route del default
# route del myrichISP
# ifconfig sl0 down
# kill -9 (slAttachPID)
```

In this case, `slAttachPID` is the process ID of the `slattach` process. For more information on setting up SLIP connections, see Chapter 42.

Using Mosaic

The Mosaic Document View screen is where you see all the HTML documents on the Web. (See Figure 56.4.)

FIGURE 56.4.

The Mosaic main screen.

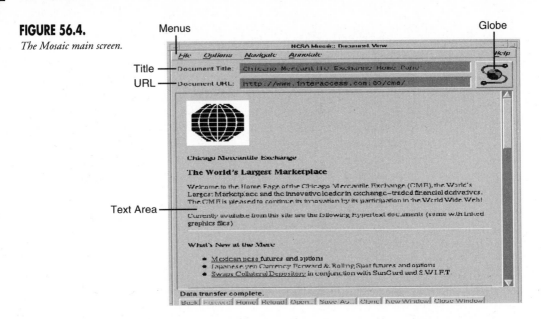

The Document View window has five pull-down menus: File, Options, Navigate, Annotate, and Help. The main portion of the screen is taken up by the viewing area for the data. Mosaic shows the title of the document and its URL under the menu bar.

> **NOTE**
>
> To navigate the Web of information, a single click of your left mouse button on the words or images shown in color or underlined, which are the hyperlinks between documents, starts the transfer.

Document Title, URL, and Globe

The Document Title field displays the title assigned to the document you are viewing. Not all authors include document titles when they prepare files. Therefore, sometimes there is a default entry in the Document Title field showing basic information about the document and its source.

Under the title is the Document URL field, which lists the server type and location, and the path of the document currently being viewed. In the upper-right corner of the Mosaic screen is a globe superimposed on a stylized *S*. This is the official logo for NCSA Mosaic.

This globe icon serves two purposes:

1. When a hyperlink is activated by clicking on the word or image, the globe spins and beams of light travel along the segments of the *S* toward the globe. This movement signifies that your document is being retrieved.

2. You can abort any current document retrieval process by clicking on the globe. The beams of light usually stop when you do this, which in turn indicates that the current transfer has been aborted.

The status line then displays the message. If part of the file was already retrieved without the inline images, the Document View window contains the new document; click the Back button at the bottom of the window to return to the document containing the hyperlink.

Viewing Area

Below the Document URL field is the viewing area, which displays the contents of the current document file. The highlighted or underlined words or images within the viewing area are actually hyperlinks to other files. Use the scroll bar on the right side of the viewing area to move up and down in the file contents.

Some hyperlinks open in separate windows because they depend on external viewers to display the file contents. This is generally true for movies and for some graphics. To alert you that this is the case, Mosaic displays the message `Spawning external viewer` in the information line at the bottom of the window.

If Mosaic attempts to spawn an external viewer that is not installed, an error message may be displayed on the console (`xterm`) from which Mosaic was executed. NCSA Mosaic may ask you to enter a filename to save the current unidentifiable document.

The Document View window also displays the status of the current retrieval process in the information line.

Somewhere between the document viewing area and the bottom row of control buttons is an area that Mosaic uses to let you know specific information such as the status of your retrieval of a file, the use of an external viewer, and the URL of a linked file.

Bottom Control Panel

Nine buttons form the bottom control panel: Back, Forward, Home, Reload, Open, Save As, Clone, New Window, and Close Window. The buttons provide shortcut access to items contained within the five pull-down menus.

If your Document View window is not wide enough, all nine buttons are not displayed. Because the function of each button is also offered in a pull-down menu, no functionality is lost if you open a narrow Document View window. The following list discusses each button, and notes the corresponding pull-down menu option.

Back   Returns to the previous document in the Document View window history (such as you have followed a hyperlink or selected a menu item). No action can be performed if you have only viewed one document so far. Also available on the Navigate menu.

Forward	Returns to the document that preceded the current document. This button is dimmed if you have not moved backward yet. For example, if you move from Document 1 to Document 2 and return to Document 1 with Back, Forward brings up Document 2 again. Also available on the Navigate menu.
Home	Moves to your home document or home page. The default home document is the Mosaic Home Page. Also available on the Navigate menu.
Reload	Reloads the current document from the server, thus displaying any file changes made and saved since the last loading. (This is particularly useful if you are editing a document file.) Also available on the File menu as Reload Current.
Open	Opens the Open Document window to enter the URL for a file to be viewed. Also available as Open URL... on the File menu.
Save As	Opens the Save Document window that lets you save the current document to your local system in different formats. Also available on the File menu.
Clone	Opens a duplicate of the window being viewed. This is a useful choice if you want to keep a window open for reference but also want to select another hyperlink or open another file. Also available on the File menu as Clone Window.
New Window	Opens a new Document View window. The content of the new window is your default home page. There is no limit on the number of windows you can open. Also available on the File menu.
Close Window	Closes the current Document View window. If you only have one window open, the entire application exits. Also available on the File menu.

The Cursor and Displaying Hyperlink URLs

The cursor in Mosaic is generally a standard short arrow pointing slightly to the left of twelve o'clock. The cursor changes its configuration depending on where you are in the Document View window. It is the arrow configuration unless it is pointing to a hyperlink.

When the cursor rests on a hyperlink, it changes to a small hand icon pointing to the left. At the same time that the cursor changes its configuration, the hyperlink's URL is displayed in the information line. This tells you what will be retrieved if you select the hyperlink. The URL may also tell you the format of the document.

For example, suppose the URL http://www.ncsa.uiuc.edu/Pubs/access/accessDir.html is displayed in the information line. This tells you that the document will be retrieved from the NCSA WWW server (www.ncsa.uiuc.edu).

If you see the CERN WWW server (info.cern.ch) and an image file extension (.gif), you can surmise that the hyperlink is an image being retrieved from Switzerland and might take longer to download than a local text file. (Of course, your access to the Internet plays a part in the retrieval speed; but in general, you should expect links from overseas, as well as image files, to take slightly longer to display.)

Shortcuts and Keyboard Options

Each underlined letter is a shortcut to the same action as the corresponding menu item after the menu is open on your screen. You must have first selected a menu for the underlined shortcuts to work.

While your mouse pointer is in the hypertext viewing area, the following hotkeys (keyboard shortcuts for common actions) are active. As Table 56.1 shows, in most instances Mosaic accepts either case for the hotkey.

Table 56.1. Mosaic hotkeys.

Equivalent	Action
a or A	Annotate this window
b or B	Back to previous URL
c or C	Clone this window (make a new copy for reference)
d or D	Document source; shows the HTML document
f or F	Forward to next URL
H	Show the Hotlist
m or M	Mail to; you are better off using mailx or pine
n or N	New window starts a new session
l or L	Open a local HTML file
o or O	Open URL
p or P	Print
R	Refresh
r	Reload
s or S	Search/find in document
h	Window history
EXC	Close current window

You can select text from the viewing area as though you are in a normal workstation or editor window. Cut and paste into other X Window system windows as usual by pressing the left mouse button to begin selecting text, and then holding the button down and dragging. Alternatively, release the left mouse button and use the right mouse button to complete the selection.

The Fancy Selections setting under the Options menu causes the paste function to imitate the formatted display in the NCSA Mosaic viewing area.

Writing a Hypertext Document

Writing a document in HTML is fairly easy if you are a programmer. All you need is a text editor to create and edit a file. From then on, it's a matter of putting the Uniform Resource Locators (URLs) in the file and testing it out.

URLs

A URL is a way of specifying where a resource exists in the Internet. A resource can be a file, FTP site, database, image, newsgroup, archive, and other such goodies. Pointing to a document means telling your local program, such as Mosaic, the location and name of a resource and how to get it. See Appendix A, "Linux FTP Sites and Newsgroups," for a list of Web pages for Linux.

> **TIP**
>
> Try to edit an existing HTML document instead of writing one from scratch. Save an interesting Web document with the File menu and then edit it with your favorite text editor. You'll save a lot of time writing an HTML document this way.

A URL is composed of three parts:

action://sitename/pathname

The `action` part can be at least one of the following. It's not limited to these, of course, but these are the most common ways of getting the files that you see:

`http`	For HTML documents
`gopher`	For starting a gopher session
`ftp`	For starting an `ftp` session
`file`	For getting a raw file that may or may not be an HTML file

A browser program then attempts to use this action on the `sitename` and `pathname` in the URL. Given this information, you can also write your own HTML documents.

You use text anchors to attach links to an HTML document. An anchor is simply a region of text that is reserved as a pointer to another place. In Mosaic these anchors are displayed as underlined text. Other Web viewers may display a link in a different font, a different color, or both. The beauty of HTML is that different viewers can show an HTML document in their own style. You are not limited to one type of display with all viewers.

HTML anchors take the following form:

```
<a href="htmlfile">GoDocument</a>
```

In this form, <a and /a> are tags that mark the location pointed to by this HTML anchor. Tags are usually paired, with the ending tag having an extra /. The href token specifies the file to get, and the text between the > and < is what you see in dashed boxes. Tags are not case-sensitive, so <a> is equal to <A>.

In a hypertext document, you can use the following example to mark a link to the "official" list of WWW servers at CERN:

```
For List servers at CERN, <a
href="http://www.w3.org/hypertext/DataSources/WWW/Servers.html"
>GoCERN</a>
```

With a browser you see the following line:

```
For List servers at CERN, GoCERN.
```

In this example, the GoCERN text is underlined when it appears on-screen.

An HTML document uses tags to specify special areas of the text. The format of an HTML document is loosely described as follows:

```
<HTML>
        <HEAD>
    <TITLE>This is a Home Page</TITLE>
    <HEAD>
    <BODY>
            .... tags ... text .... etc. etc.
    </BODY>
    </HTML>
```

There can be only one pair of <BODY> and </BODY> tags in the entire HTML document. These are used to store the text for the HTML document. The <HEAD> and </HEAD> tags show the title in the heading section of a viewer. You generally have only one such pair in an HTML document because the text in the </HEAD> applies to the whole document.

For example, to show the title in an HTML document, use the following tag:

```
<TITLE>This is a Home Page For Mosaic!</TITLE>
```

Tags are not case-sensitive, and any formatting in between the tags is almost always ignored. So the previous title could also be written as follows:

```
<TITLE>
This is

      a Home

Page
For
        Mosaic!
</TITLE>
```

Paragraphs in an HTML document are introduced with a <P> tag and ended with a </P> tag. To break a line in the middle, you use the <BR> tag to add a line break.

HTML enables you to use up to six levels of headings, numbered H1 through H6; H1 is the leftmost (highest) heading, and H6 is the lowest heading. To define a heading use the following:

```
<H1>heading 1</H1>
```

Most Mosaic servers define a different point size for the level of heading you are supposed to be on. Don't skip heading titles when writing a document (for instance, don't use level 5 after level 1). It's not considered a good writing style and does not show up well on Mosaic viewers. You won't get any errors, but the document will look sloppy.

The following tags can be used to specify how to display the text on a viewer:

```
<I> </I>  italicize the text in between
    <B> </B>  bold face the text in between
    <U> </U>  underline the text in between
```

HTML supports unordered lists of items with the <UL>, <LI>, </LI>, and </UL> tags. To specify such a list, use the following construct:

```
<UL>
    <LI> Eat the  cake</LI>
    <LI> Swim with the fish</LI>
    <LI> Start the BBQ </LI>
    <LI> Write a chapter </LI>
    </UL>
```

This list is displayed with each item between the <LI> and </LI> as a bulleted item. Unordered lists are generally used as menu items from which a user can choose an item.

To display a numbered list, use an ordered list with <OL> and </OL> to enclose the list. Technically, you do not need to use the </LI> for each item, but some browsers may not support it. The previous list could be shown as follows:

```
<OL>
    <LI> Eat the  cake</LI>
    <LI> Swim with the fish</LI>
    <LI> Start the BBQ </LI>
    <LI> Write a chapter </LI>
    </OL>
```

HTML documents enable you to keep a glossary between <DL> and </DL> tags. Each glossary item contains a pair of <DT> and <DD> tags. The syntax for the glossary is as follows:

```
<DL>
    <DT>Item<DD>Description of this item in one line.
    <DT>Another item <DD>Another One Line Description
    </DL>
```

The <DT> tag indicates the beginning of an element within a glossary, followed by the description after the <DD> tag. The glossary item is displayed flushed left on a line by itself, followed by the description with a tab in front of it.

If you really want to include source listings and the like, you can put the text between <PRE> and </PRE> tags. The text between these two tags is displayed literally by your browser.

Other types of tags supported by Mosaic include the following:

```
<BR>        Produce a line break
  <HR>        Draw a horizontal line
  <EM> </EM> Emphasize in different font (italics in Mosaic)
  <STRONG> </STRONG>  Boldface in Mosaic, another font with other browsers.
```

You can also place images in your document with the `<IMG>` tag. For example, the construct

```
<IMG SRC=http://dont.inhale.com/graphics/billy.gif>
```

gets the image `billy.gif` from the site `dont.inhale.com` and has the browser display it for you. (If you want to get a better image editor for HTML documents, try `mapedit` at `sunsite.unc.edu` in the `/pub/packages/info-systems` directory.) If you do not specify a full address for the image, the browser uses the current page's directory and site.

Images that are declared one after another are placed side by side on the user's screen. You can introduce line breaks with the `<BR>` or `<P>` tags. You can also annotate the images with the text `ALIGN` keyword:

```
<IMG SRC="local.gif" ALIGN="bottom"> annotation
```

The keywords for the `ALIGN` keyword are `top`, `middle`, and `bottom` for aligning the annotation text position. In the previous example, the text will be shown on the bottom of the figure.

Some text-based browsers are not capable of displaying images that enable you to specify a special character that is displayed instead of the image. The attribute for this special character is the `ALT` keyword.

```
<IMG SRC="local.gif" ALIGN="middle" ALT="$"> annotation
```

This shows a dollar sign where the image would be shown on a graphic browser.

You can link images to actions within a link pair. For example, the following action gets you an HTML document by clicking or selecting the figure:

```
<A HREF="bozo.html" <IMG SRC="clown.gif"> </A>
```

That's about all I can put in this space about writing HTML documents. You can always find more interesting documents on the Web as you surf. Save these and see how others do their documents. Most of the information on the Web is very helpful in teaching you how to write your own Web documents.

TIP

Avoid the temptation to put large GIF images in your HTML documents. The time needed to download these large GIF files on 14.4 modems (still a limitation for a lot of dialup users) is very long. No one wants to wait 12 minutes or so for a pretty 1MB image to come down, when he or she could be looking at other sites with a faster download. Be considerate of your reader's time and keep the sizes of any included images to a reasonable size, say not more than 20KB. You'll still have enough resolution to put your pictures in there.

Using Other Browsers

If you can use Mosaic, you can use just about any other browser. All browsers are based on the same basic principles of retrieving and displaying a file by checking the type of data in it. Once you know how to navigate using URLs, surfing the Net becomes a task of learning how to use the special keys for your browser to help you customize its functions to best suit your needs.

There are many browsers already available for surfing the Net. Also, enhancements are being made to those that already have been out for a while. For example, as we go to print the Netscape 2.0 port to Linux is being completed. You will then have access to more features, including Sun Microsystems' JAVA language with multimedia support.

Summary

After a brief introduction to the Web, the following items were covered in this chapter:

- Where to get Mosaic for Linux, which versions to use, and how to debug common problems in Mosaic.
- How to install Mosaic on your machine after you have FTPed it.
- How to surf the Web with Mosaic and use its controls to get around documents.
- A brief introduction to connecting your Linux node via SLIP to an Internet service provider.
- Some of the basics on HTML and how to write your own HTML documents for the Web. After reading this chapter, you should be able to write your own files and read HTML documents from other sites.

Happy surfin'.

DOSemu

by R
Kan

IN THIS CHAPTER

DOSemu stands for DOS emulator. This is a bit of a misnomer, because DOSemu does not actually emulate MS-DOS. Instead, it provides an environment in Linux under which MS-DOS and MS-DOS applications can be run. DOSemu enables you to run MS-DOS sessions

- On a virtual console
- Within an `xterm`
- As an X Window application
- Over a serial or network connection

The development of DOSemu is not yet complete. A small but growing number of MS-DOS applications will run under DOSemu. The most impressive application reported to run under DOSemu is the real mode of MS Windows 3.0.

MS-DOS applications will not run as fast under DOSemu as they would under native MS-DOS, but most applications are fast enough. You have the added advantage of being able to run Linux and MS-DOS applications side by side.

The design of DOSemu will always cause some speed degradation, but the same design also provides the capability to virtualize a PC. The disk drives, serial ports, and memory configurations configured under DOSemu do not need to match the hardware that actually exists on your PC.

> **CAUTION**
>
> There are a few things you need to be wary of when you first start using DOSemu. DOSemu is considered to be alpha software. Major disk corruption is unlikely to happen when you run DOSemu, but you should take normal precautions. You should back up anything valuable on your DOS and Linux hard-drive partitions before actually running DOSemu.
>
> Although DOSemu is strictly user-level code, some unexpected results may occur. When you first configure and test DOSemu you should shut down any critical Linux applications and be prepared to reboot your machine. This may seem like an unnecessary precaution for an experienced Linux user. However, my first attempt at DOSemu caused my modem to hang up because DOSemu reset the configured serial ports.

Installing DOSemu from Source Distributions

DOSemu is available on some CD-ROM distributions and on most major Linux BBSs and FTP sites such as `sunsite.unc.edu` (in directory `/pub/Linux/system/Emulators/dosemu`). The latest version available as of this writing was 0.53pl39 (pre-release 0.53, patch level 39). DOSemu is dependent on the version of the Linux kernel installed. Version 0.52 will not work with kernels newer than 1.1.30, nor will version 0.53 work with Linux kernels prior to 1.1.30.

For the truly adventuresome, the latest development version of DOSemu is available on the Internet via anonymous FTP at `dspsun.eas.asu.edu:/pub/dosemu/`. As with the development version of any software, it is not as thoroughly tested, and may have some serious bugs. Stick to the released versions if at all possible.

The latest released version at the time of writing that is stable was /pub/linux/ALPHA/dosemu/dosemu0.60.4.tgz from tsx-11.mit.edu. Be cautious with later releases.

The DOSemu distribution needs to be installed in a directory under /usr/src. DOSemu will not build correctly if the distribution is installed elsewhere. A DOSemu distribution consists of a compressed tar file that is unpacked by a shell command such as

```
bash# tar -zxvf filename.tar.gz
```

DOSemu is undergoing constant revisions. Review the QuickStart and other README files before proceeding.

Building an Executable Version of DOSemu

DOSemu is distributed as source code that needs to be compiled and linked before you use it. This is not a very complicated task because the process is automated. To build DOSemu, you need the following software installed:

- GNU C compiler version 2.5.8 or later
- GNU make
- libc 4.5.21 or later
- ncurses

To build DOSemu, log in as root, change directory (cd) to the directory created by unpacking the tar archive and type the following commands:

```
bash# make config
bash# make depend
bash# make most
```

The DOSemu distribution includes a reference manual written in TeX. If you have TeX installed and want to create a typeset version of the manual, use make everything instead of make most.

To properly compile DOSemu, you need to be logged in as root, and have approximately 12MB of virtual memory free. Use the top command to check how much free memory is available. You can increase the free memory by either installing an additional swap file or by killing unnecessary processes. Fortunately, you only need excess memory to compile DOSemu.

The full build of DOSemu takes approximately 10 minutes on a 90 MHz Pentium. When the build is complete, you are ready to configure and run DOSemu.

Configuring DOSemu

DOSemu can be configured to boot MS-DOS from a floppy or hard drive. As when configuring a real PC, you usually start by booting from a floppy and work up to booting from a hard drive.

Making a DOS Boot Floppy

The simplest and safest way to initially configure DOSemu is by using a boot floppy. Create a bootable DOS floppy from your favorite DOS distribution. DOSemu supports MS-DOS Versions 3.3 through 6.22, as well as DR-DOS 6.0.

In addition to bootable DOS, the disk should have the following DOS files:

- `format.com`
- `sys.com`
- DOS mouse driver for your mouse
- A simple file editor such as `edit`, `edlin`, or `ted`

From the `dosemu` subdirectory, copy the following device drivers onto the floppy:

- `emufs.sys`
- `ems.sys`
- `cdrom.sys`

From the command subdirectory copy the following file:

`exitemu.com`

> **TIP**
>
> The easiest way to copy files from a Linux directory to an MS-DOS formatted floppy is to use the mcopy command. For example:
>
> `mcopy filename a:`

Configuring Parameters in /etc/dosemu.conf

Everything you need to configure DOSemu exists in the file `/etc/dosemu.conf`. A user-specific configuration file can be created in a user's home directory named `~/.dosrc`. Both of these files have the same format. I will refer to these files interchangeably as `dosemu.conf`. A sample configuration file is in the `examples/` subdirectory of the standard DOSemu distribution. Look for the file named `dosemu.dist`.

The example file is several hundred lines long. Most of this configuration file contains comments to help explain the configuration options. Anything to the right of a # character is a comment. A # in the first column means that the entire line is a comment. Sample configuration lines for nearly all supported hardware and software options are contained in this file. Most DOSemu configurations can be expressed in 25 to 30 lines.

Configuration parameters in /etc/dosemu.conf have two basic formats. A parameter that needs just one value has the form *parameter value*. A parameter that needs multiple values has the form *parameter { value1 value2 ... }*.

Getting DOSemu To Run for the First Time

One way to configure DOSemu is to copy the example configuration file to /etc/dosemu.conf, and then edit the parameters based on information in the comments. Another way is to create a simple dosemu.conf file and add to it as needed. A bare-bones file looks like the following:

```
timint on
keyboard {  layout us  keybint on  rawkeyboard on  }
video { vga  console }
cpu 80486
bootA
floppy { device /dev/fd0 threeinch }
```

Use a text editor to make the following customizations to dosemu.conf based on your actual hardware:

- Change the video line to cga, ega, or ma if you don't have VGA.
- Change the cpu to 80386 if you do not have a 80486 or Pentium.
- If your boot floppy is a 5.25, replace threeinch with fiveinch.

Make sure your drive A floppy is not mounted under Linux and insert your boot floppy into drive A. Start DOSemu from a virtual console by typing DOS. Your version of DOS will boot from drive A, and you should be at the familiar A:> prompt. If you are using an empty MS-DOS disk, you will soon run out of things to do. To exit DOSemu prompt press Alt-Ctrl-PgDn, or use the exitemu.com command provided on your boot floppy.

Configuring Disk Options

Most Linux users have DOS partitions on a hard drive. Some may even have a separate hard drive dedicated to DOS. This section shows several ways to configure DOSemu to access these drives as native DOS disks. You can abandon your boot floppy and boot from a hard drive, even if you do not have an MS-DOS formatted drive or partition anywhere.

Accessing a Dedicated MS-DOS Disk or Partition

The easiest way to access a hard drive is to configure the drive in your dosemu.conf file. The disk or partition in question must be formatted for MS-DOS and be a primary partition. Extended DOS partitions are not yet supported. The format of the parameter entry to access a hard drive is

```
disk { type "device"  readonly }
```

The *type* parameter can be partition or wholedisk, and the *device* is the Linux device being accessed. Typical names would be /dev/hda1 for a partition or /dev/sda for an entire disk. The readonly qualifier is optional, and like the name infers, it write-locks the disk or partition in question. If you boot Linux from a hard drive using LILO, do not access that drive using `wholedisk`. When DOSemu boots from that drive, it will give you a LILO prompt. Unfortunately, neither LILO nor Linux will run from within a DOSemu session.

The following are some examples of valid entries for disks:

```
disk { partition "/dev/sda4" }                   # mount 4th partition
disk { partition "/dev/hda1" readonly}  # mount 1st IDE partition readonly
disk { wholedisk "/dev/sda" }                    # mount the whole 1st SCSI disk
```

> **CAUTION**
>
> Linux may have other tasks also accessing disks. To avoid problems with file corruption, disks mounted as read/write under Linux should be configured as read-only. Use `umask=022` in the `/etc/fstab` entry for the dos partition:
>
> ```
> /dev/hda1  /dos  messydos  umask=022
> ```

How To Access Any Linux Directory from DOSemu

A much safer way to access a DOS directory is through the `emufs.sys` device driver. This driver enables you to access any Linux subdirectory as a logical device under DOS. In your `config.sys` of your boot device, simply add the lines

```
device = emufs.sys /c
```

where `/c` is the Linux directory you want to mount. The next available drive letter is used for this logical drive.

Any disk or device mounted in the Linux file system can be made available to DOSemu as a logical disk through the `emufs` driver. Disks and directories do not need to be DOS formatted and can include CD-ROMs as well as NFS and IPX mounted disks. However, files in these directories must be in the MS-DOS 6.0 format to be visible under DOSemu.

With a logical device you can do typical operations such as read, write, and delete files, and run executables. Utilities such as `drvspace`, `undelete`, and `defrag` will not work on disks accessed through `dosemufs`.

Creating Diskimages

DOSemu has an additional abstraction called a diskimage. A *diskimage* is a Linux file that appears to DOS as a logical device. Either a floppy or a hard disk is supported as a diskimage. A diskimage makes an ideal boot device because the size can be set just large enough to boot MS-DOS. Unlike drives accessed by `dosemufs`, drives configured by diskimages work with utilities like `undelete`, `scandisk`, and `defrag`.

Creating Floppy Image Files

A floppy disk file is easy to create under Linux. The floppy image file does not need to do anything except exist initially. To create an initial floppy image file use the `touch` command; for example,

```
touch filename
```

This new floppy will appear as an unformatted floppy when you boot DOSemu. Because the size of the floppy is configured in DOSemu, formatting the floppy will expand the image file to the expected size (1.44MB for a high-density, 3.5-inch floppy).

Accessing a Floppy Image Under DOSemu

To use a floppy disk, you need to specify the floppy geometry for the benefit of DOS.

```
floppy { heads 2 sectors 18 tracks 80 threeinch file /usr/dos/hdimage }
```

This simulates a 1.44MB, 3.5-inch floppy. A diskimage floppy can be used in the same way as any floppy, except that it cannot be removed. Expect the diskimage floppy to operate significantly faster than a real floppy, with formatting taking only a few seconds.

> **TIP**
>
> Some DOS utilities that like to reboot MS-DOS, such as `DRVSPACE`, will check to see if you have a floppy in drive A before allowing you to continue. Because you cannot eject a floppy diskimage, you need to remove the floppy configuration and restart DOSemu.

Creating Hard Diskimage Files Under Linux

Hard diskimage files are more confusing to configure than floppies. To initially create the hard disk file, use the command `mkhdimage` found in the `periph` directory of the DOSemu distribution. Instead of specifying the size of the image, you need to specify the number of heads, sectors, and cylinders of the disk to create. The following is an example `mkhdimage` command that creates a 10MB disk:

```
mkhdimage -h 8 -s 20 -c 128 > /usr/dos/hdimage
```

To compute the size of a disk based on disk geometry, multiply heads×sectors×cylinders×512 (number of bytes per sector under MS-DOS). Because these parameters do not represent the real characteristics of a disk, the ratio of heads to sectors to cylinders does not matter to DOSemu. However, MS-DOS will only recognize the first 1024 cylinders of a disk.

Because `mkhdimage` only creates a file of 128 bytes, no other check of available space for the configured amount takes place. Do not configure a diskimage drive larger than the available disk space.

Accessing a Diskimage Under DOS

To use a diskimage as a logical hard drive, use the disk parameter with a type of image rather than `wholedisk` or `partition`, as well as the name of the Linux file used.

```
disk { image "/usr/dos/hdimage" }
```

Like floppy diskimages, hard diskimages are not initially formatted. When a diskimage file is initialized it is also unpartitioned. Use the MS-DOS `fdisk` utility to create a partition on the drive you configure. To avoid confusion and data loss, configure DOSemu with only one real floppy and only the new hard diskimage for a hard drive. Sometimes a new diskimage will appear to `fdisk` to have a partition created, but MS-DOS is unable to access the partition. The easy fix is to delete the existing partition and re-create it.

Hard diskimages are different than floppies in that disk space used under Linux is allocated on demand. A newly formatted diskimage of any size takes up enough disk space to store FAT information. The disk file grows as disk space is used under DOS. An interesting observation is if a diskimage is `drvspaced` under MS-DOS, `drvspace` will allocate the entire amount of space for its drive mapping.

Configuring Video Options for the Virtual Consoles of Linux

Linux's virtual console can support more than just text-mode virtual consoles. Due to the direct-access nature of most DOS-based video, this is perhaps DOSemu's biggest weakness. Not all video boards will work correctly with DOSemu, and even fewer will work perfectly. The basic configuration for the video section with graphics looks like the following:

```
video { type console graphics chipset  chipset_type memsize kb vbios_seg address
          vbios_size=hex }
```

If your video board is 100 percent VGA–compatible, omitting everything past the keyword `graphics` might work.

The following chipset keywords are supported:

- █ `et4000`
- █ `s3` (801, 805, and 928)
- █ `diamond`
- █ `trident`

Video boards that do not have the BIOS configured at 0×C000 need the `vbios_seg` to be set to the actual address. When in doubt, the video BIOS starting address (`vbios_seg`) as well as the video BIOS size (`vbios_size`) can be determined by the Microsoft Diagnostics (MSD) utility that comes with MS-DOS and Windows.

The following line will allow DOS access to known video ports directly, and will help compatibility:

```
allowvideoaccess on
```

Using DOSemu from Other Than a Virtual Console

DOSemu does not need to run under just a Linux virtual console. DOSemu can run in an `xterm`, on a remote (network or dial-up) connection, or within its own X Window interface. Remote connections and `xterms` are configurable in exactly the same way as are virtual consoles, except that no levels of graphics are possible. Remote sessions typically cannot generate a Ctrl-Alt-PgDn to end the session; using the `exitemu.com` is the quickest way to end a remote DOS session.

The X Window interface to DOSemu is called *xdos*. Xdos is a relatively recent development for DOSemu, and has only a few additional features over running DOSemu in an `xterm`. Xdos has built-in mouse support so that a mouse supported under X Window also works within the xdos window. Graphics support does not yet exist for xdos, but may be eventually possible—development work is underway. Figure 57.1 shows an example xdos session running within X Window. Configuration parameters available for xdos are listed in Table 57.1.

FIGURE 57.1.

*Example xdos session
running under X Window.*

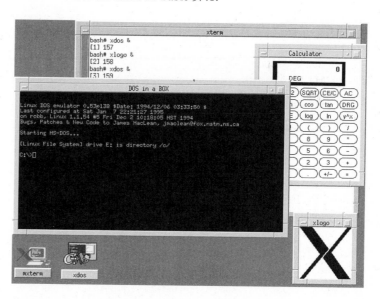

Parameters specific to xdos take the form

```
X { param1 value1 param2 value2}
```

Table 57.1. Xdos-specific `dosemu.conf` parameters.

Parameter	Sample	Meaning
title	"DOS box"	X Window–specific title.
display	"mybox:0"	X server to use if xdos is to be displayed on another X server.
font	"vga"	Monospaced font to be used.
icon_name	"xdos"	Icon name to use when DOSemu iconized.
updatelines	25	Number of text lines in the display.
updatefreq	8	How often X updates the xdos screen. 20 is approximately once per second.
blinkrate	8	How often the cursor blinks.

A starting point for configuring xdos is the following line:

```
X { title "DOS box" icon_name "xdos" updatelines 25 updatefreq 8}
```

Configuring Keyboards

The DOSemu keyboard can be configured to handle a number of different keyboard layouts for international keyboards. If a given layout is available in the Linux kernel configuration, it is probably available to DOSemu. The following is the default configuration for a keyboard:

```
keyboard { layout us keybint on rawkeyboard off }
```

The `keybint` option enables DOSemu to handle keyboard interrupts more accurately but is a bit unstable.

The normal keyboard handlers should suffice for simpler DOS tasks, but will not handle more complicated keystrokes. Keyboard-intensive packages like WordPerfect that make heavy use of Alt and Ctrl keys need to be represented better. The `rawkeyboard` option offers a nearly complete representation of the PC keyboard by bypassing all key translations. This is known as *raw mode*. To use raw mode simply turn it on in the keyboard configuration. Raw mode is only possible when you are running DOSemu from a virtual console.

> **CAUTION**
>
> If DOSemu unexpectedly exits while a keyboard is in raw mode, you may be stuck with a disabled keyboard. The only option may be to reboot your PC.

If you are running xdos the keyboard mapping is controlled mainly by your ~/.Xmodmap file. Because the backspace and delete keys are typically reversed under X Window, the following Linux commands will restore the expected keystrokes:

```
xmodmap -e "keycode 107 = 0xffff"
xmodmap -e "keycode 22 = 0xff08"
```

Changing this mapping may cause the same problem with other X Window applications.

TIP

Sometimes keystrokes are echoed in duplicate. This phenomenon happens on consoles that have the istrip setting turned on. To turn istrip off, use stty.

Configuring Serial Ports

To configure serial ports you simply need to make them known to DOSemu. The basic configuration looks like the following:

```
serial { com1 device /dev/cua0 }
```

This example maps DOSemu's com1 to Linux's serial port 0 (which maps to COM1 under native DOS). You can specify additional parameters, such as the port address and IRQ. All of the serial port parameters except the Linux port apply only to ports configured under DOSemu. DOSemu accesses the real serial ports as Linux devices that are configured by the kernel. The IRQ, com port number, and port addresses are what you want DOSemu to simulate, and do not need to match the actual hardware. The same IRQ restrictions between COM 1/3 and COM 2/4 still exist under DOSemu. If you cannot use two ports simultaneously under Linux, you cannot do so under DOSemu.

The following example configures the hardware com1 as com3 with a different IRQ and base address:

```
serial { com3 base 0x3e8 iq 5 device /dev/cua0 }
```

It is generally less confusing if you configure ports as they really exist.

Configuring Printers

Printers under DOSemu can print to a device or file, or you can let a Linux program such as lpr handle the output. Each printer statement in dosemu.conf is assigned an LPT device number in the order in which it occurs in the file. Multiple printers can be declared to DOSemu; however, MS-DOS has a set limit of three LPT devices.

To configure a printer to save to a file or device, simply specify the `file` keyword and the name of the file or device. A time-out value will specify how long DOSemu waits in seconds after the last character is received before flushing data and closing the file or device. The following are some example printer configurations using a file and device designation:

```
printer { file "/usr/tmp/dos-print-1" timeout 10 }
printer { file "/dev/lp1" timeout 10 }
```

> **CAUTION**
>
> Direct access to a printer using the device name can cause problems if other Linux tasks also access that device. Avoid this method if possible.

To configure a printer to send data through an external program such as `lpr`, specify the command to use and any options to include on the print line. The option parameter must contain the string `%s` in the same place you would specify the filename if you were using this command under Linux (for example, `lpr -p %s`). An example of configuring the printer to print using `lpr` is as follows:

```
printer { command "lpr" options "-p %s" timeout 10 }
```

DOSemu implements printing as a two-step process:

- Save the file to temporary disk file.
- Issue a command to print the file.

When the time-out expires, DOSemu closes the temporary file and issues the specified command. The directory `/usr/tmp` needs to exist to save the temporary files, and should have world access. Setting the sticky bit on this directory will help speed up printing. The sticky bit speeds up file access by maintaining the files in memory rather than only on disk.

Using Debug Parameters

A large level of debugging information is available under DOSemu. This information is sent to `stderr`, but can be sent to a file using redirection; for example,

```
dos 2> dbg.out
```

or through a DOS command-line option,

```
dos -p dbg.out
```

There are approximately 20 different debug message types that can be turned on. When you are configuring DOSemu, the most useful message type is the `config` parameter. This points out syntax problems in the configuration file. Turning on debug information is most helpful when DOSemu returns to the shell prompt without any error messages.

The following example debug configuration shows all the available debug parameters :

```
debug { config off    disk off    warning off   hardware off
   port   off          read off    general off   IPC    off
   video  off          write off   xms    off    ems    off
   serial off          keyb off    dpmi   off     printer off
   mouse off}
```

Other Configuration Parameters

There are several miscellaneous parameters that can be adjusted for DOSemu. Table 57.2 shows the various parameters and their meanings.

Table 57.2. Other DOSemu configuration parameters.

Parameter	Possible Values	Meaning
dosbanner	on or off	Turns on/off welcome banner when booting DOSemu.
mathco	on or off	Tells MS-DOS if a coprocessor is available. Because Linux already emulates a math coprocessor, set this to "on".
dpmi	on or off	Turns on DPMI support. This is a bit unstable, so use with caution.
FastFloppy	number	Turns on higher speed floppy access. Use with caution.
speaker	off native	Turns on access to speaker by direct access, emulated or by a speaker emulation mode.
EmuSYS	File extension	Uses an alternative config.sys file with this file extension. A good value might be "EMU". Alternative to DOS 6 boot menus.
EmuBat	File extension	Uses an alternative autoexec.bat file with this file extension. Similar to EmuSYS.
Cpu	80286, 80386	CPU type to emulate. Because you won't fool all programs, use what you really have.
ipxsupport	on or off	Allows IPX access through the Linux kernel.
xms	Size in kilobytes	Amount of XMS memory to make available.
ems	Size in kilobytes	Amount of EMS memory to make available.
Hogthreshold	Number	The higher the number, the longer DOS can "hog" the CPU waiting for a keystroke. An initial setting of 5000 is a good starting point. Set to 0 to turn off hog detection.

continues

Table 57.2. continued

Parameter	Possible Values	Meaning
bootB	~	Specifies that DOS is to boot from the floppy configured as B.
port{ }		Allows DOSemu access to specific hardware ports. List the hex values of hardware ports desired.
mouse	Type of mouse you have	Microsoft, Logitech, mmseries, Mouseman, Hitachi, busmouse, Mousesystems, and PS2 are supported.

Runtime Options of DOSemu

Table 57.3 shows command options supported on the DOSemu command line. Options specified here will override conflicting parameters specified in the dosemu.conf file. A few other options are available, but are either intended for development use or are not completely supported as of yet. Use the -? option to get a complete list of the command options.

Table 57.3. DOSemu command-line options.

Option	Meaning
-A	Boot from floppy drive A
-C	Boot from hard drive C
-D	Set debug options
-F	Number of floppy disks to use from dosemu.conf (1-4)
-H	Number of hard disks to use from dosemu.conf (1 or 2)
-P	Copy debug information to file, same as using 2>
-V	Turn on VGA emulation
-c	Optimize video performance under virtual consoles
-e	Specify the amount of EMS memory to make available
-f	Flip definition of A: and B: floppy drives
-k	Use raw keyboard console (rawkeyboard in dosemu.conf)
-t	Deliver time interrupt 9
-x	Specify the amount of XMS memory to make available

Option	Meaning
-?	Print command summary only
-2	Emulate a 286
-3	Emulate a 386
-4	Emulate a 486

Limitations of DOSemu

DOSemu is not perfect yet. Development is underway, with many known opportunities for speed optimizations and improvements.

Notable Software That Won't Run Under DOSemu

Perhaps the most significant application that does not run under DOSemu is Windows 3.1. As with Linux in general, volunteers are working to correct this. Other software that requires DOS Protected Mode Interface (DPMI) is also likely to cause problems. To find an up-to-date list of software that has been successfully used under DOSemu, look for the file /doc/EMUsucess.txt in the DOSemu distribution.

Hardware Limitations for DOSemu

Not all video cards are currently supported under DOSemu. More popular cards are supported simply because developers are more likely to have them. Some non-typical hardware is reported to work under DOSemu with some patches.

Sound cards are problematic under DOSemu. They have the potential to perform DMA (direct memory access) to memory the Linux kernel had allocated elsewhere. A generic sound-card interface that interacted with the kernel's built-in sound card support would solve this problem.

Performance Limitations

DOSemu runs slower than a native MS-DOS session. I have successfully run a few older benchmark programs under DOSemu to compare the performance degradation to native MS-DOS. Benchmark results are not a perfect measure, but they do demonstrate potential performance in some distinct areas. I measured three different areas: CPU performance, disk performance, and video performance, each of which produced strangely different results.

CPU Performance

DOSemu's raw CPU speed depends on what else is happening under Linux. With an otherwise idle Linux box, DOSemu's compute speed is close to that of a native MS-DOS session. The Landmark Version 2.0 and PC-Bench Version 5.6 show similar performance, with perhaps a 10 to 20 percent performance penalty under DOSemu for the instruction mix, CPU, and FPU measurements.

Disk Performance

Determining the disk speed degradation under DOSemu proved to be difficult. In some cases there was a performance decrease, and in others a performance increase. This discrepancy seems directly related to the quality of support of the controller and disk drive from the underlying Linux kernel, as well as the built-in caching provided by Linux.

Linux runs as a pure 32-bit operating system, and handles I/O operations to disk controllers in bait mode. This, combined with much better SCSI support, can lead to equal or better disk benchmark numbers under DOSemu than under native DOS. Not all disks are as fast under DOSemu, with performance degradation ranging from small to huge. As with CPU speed, disk speed depends on what other Linux tasks are doing.

Video Performance

Video support is Linux's Achilles' heel. Text performance is much slower when not running DOSemu under a virtual console. Under a virtual console, benchmarked text speed approaches that of native MS-DOS. When you are using real-world applications, the text speed is dramatically slower, with an observed speed as low as 20 percent of the speed under native MS-DOS. Graphics speed is even worse.

Mouse Support

For mouse support, you can get Microsoft compatible mouse drivers from oak.oakland.edu:/Simtel/msdos/mouse/mouse701.zip (mscmouse). Make sure you have the correct port assigned to the mouse. Even so, some mice do not get recognized for up to 60 seconds, so be patient.

Another known problem is that DOSemu is not able to use COM4 after DOSemu finishes execution. This port is at 0x2E8, /dev/cua3 in Linux and uses interrupt 5. You can run the command:

```
setserial /dev/cua3 irq 5
```

Another cure is to disable the allowvideoportaccess on line in the config file.

Optimizing DOSemu

There are a few changes that will help DOS performance under DOSemu short of buying a faster PC.

Using Garrot

Garrot is an MS-DOS based Terminate and Stay Resident (TSR) program written by Thomas G. McWilliams that releases CPU time from a DOSemu process back to Linux. Some MS-DOS applications poll endlessly on events such as keyboard input. Garrot keeps track of how long a DOS application has been running without giving control back to Linux. After a threshold of time has expired, control returns to Linux. The Garrot threshold is best determined by trial and error. A good initial value is half the *bogo-mips* value. Bogo-mips is the value that the Linux kernel assigns for internal delay loops, and is displayed when booting the Linux kernel.

For CPU-intensive DOS applications, Garrot will cause a minor degradation in CPU speed. For non-CPU–intensive applications, Garrot will show a dramatic decrease in overall CPU usage, as measured by the Linux utility `top`.

Other Optimization Suggestions

The following parameters in `dosemu.conf` will help speed up various aspects of DOSemu:

- `Hogthreshold`. Set this to half the value shown in boot up messages for BogoMIP message.
- `fastfloppy`
- X parameters `"updatefreq"` and `"updatelines"`
- `-c` option on the DOS command line

Because DOSemu runs as a Linux process, any general Linux optimizations should also help performance under DOSemu. Typical optimizations include having enough swap space, optimizing the kernel, and killing unneeded Linux processes.

Sources for More Documentation About DOSemu

The DOSemu manual (`dosemu.texinfo`) written by Robert Sanders has not been updated in some time but is still a good source of information. It is distributed with DOSemu.

The "dosEMU Novice's Altering Guide" or DANG is a road map to the inner workings of DOSemu. It is designed for the adventurous, those people who wish to modify the source code themselves. DANG is maintained by Alistair MacDonald (`am20@unix.york.ac.uk`) and is posted periodically to the MSDOS channel of Linux Activists.

The EMU success list (`EMUsuccess.txt`) is a list of all programs that have been reported to work with DOSemu. It is posted periodically to the mailing list. The most recent version can be found on `dspsun.eas.asu.edu:/pub/dosemu`.

Of course, there is the DOSemu FAQ/HOWTO. But you already know about that, don't you? It is also posted frequently to the mailing list. The most recent version can be found on `dspsun.eas.asu.edu:/pub/dosemu`.

Where To Get More Information About DOSemu

Try subscribing to the `linux-msdos-digest` mailing list. To subscribe, send e-mail to `Majordomo@vger.rutgers.edu` with the following command in the body of your e-mail message:

```
subscribe linux-msdos-digest your_username@your.email.address
```

To get rid of these messages, send e-mail to `Majordomo@vger.rutgers.edu` with the following command in the body of your e-mail message:

```
unsubscribe linux-msdos-digest your_username@your.email.address
```

> **TIP**
>
> The `Netware-HOWTO` by Lauri Tischler (`ltischler@fipower.pp.fi`) is now a separate document. It is included with the DOSemu distribution and may also be found at `sunsite.unc.edu`.

How DOSemu Works

DOSemu works similar to the DOS feature of MS Windows in that it uses the virtual 86 (vm86) feature of the i386 and above chips. Under vm86, a process runs under a private 80x86 environment that is isolated by the i386 processor from any other process.

In addition to private access to an 80×86 processor, MS-DOS and MS-DOS applications need to interact with PC hardware through port accesses and interrupt functions. In vm86 mode, both port access and interrupts return vm86 back to the DOSemu.

For port access attempts, DOSemu tries to recognize the port, and either simulates its function or passes the request to the real hardware. Ports that DOSemu are allowed to map are configured by the `Port` parameter in `dosemu.conf`. Direct access to hardware ports is possible under Linux through `/dev/kmem` support.

DOS interrupt functions are widely understood and well-documented. Interrupts are caught from virtual 86 mode, and are implemented by executing the equivalent functionality as Linux system calls.

A Brief History of DOSemu and Its Contributing Authors

The first release of DOSemu was written by Matthias Lautner in September 1992. Since that time, many other people have contributed major pieces of functionality. There are too many authors to name, but some of the more significant contributors include Robert Sanders, James MacLean, Andres Tridgell, Stephen Tweedie, and Andreas Kies. Other parts of DOSemu functionality were borrowed from Carnegie Mellon's MACH DOS emulator.

The Wine Project

58

by Robert Pfister

IN THIS CHAPTER

Wine stands for Windows Emulator. It enables Microsoft Windows programs to run under a UNIX X Windows environment. Like DOSemu, Wine takes direct advantage of the Intel 386 architecture to actually run the MS Windows application. Wine simply translates any MS Windows API calls into appropriate UNIX and X Windows calls. Like OS/2, MS Windows programs running under Wine get to take advantage of features of the underlying operating system. Wine is simply another user-mode Linux process that is protected from corruption by other process. This is dubbed *crash-protection* under OS/2. Because Linux uses preemptive multitasking, Wine processes can co-exist with other processes without some of the problems experienced by applications running under native MS Windows.

Current Status of Wine

As with most of the Linux community, developers of Wine are volunteers. Wine is currently Alpha or pre-release code. Only a few of the simplest MS Windows applications run without incident. My favorite MS Windows Entertainment Pack game, Pipe Dream by Lucas Arts, runs acceptably under Wine, as shown in Figure 58.1.

FIGURE 58.1.

Pipe Dream running under Wine.

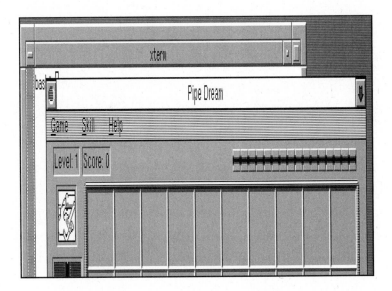

Although Pipe Dream and other simple games are certainly playable under Wine, everything is not perfect. Some speed degradation is noticeable, as is the occasional screen glitch.

Sun Soft has implemented a similar product, called WABI, for its UNIX-based workstations. WABI has been on the market for over a year and supports some of the more complex MS Windows applications such as Microsoft Excel and Lotus Smart Suite. Given enough development time, it is reasonable to expect that Wine will be capable of running general MS Windows applications as well.

Setting Up Wine

Wine is available only as source code. If you have the prerequisite software and a little patience, setting Wine up is not very difficult—even if you are not a programmer.

System Requirements

Any Linux machine suitable for running X Window will run Wine applications at a reasonable speed. In theory, Wine should have some advantages running under Linux as opposed to under MS Windows, which is confined to the MS-DOS environment. Experiences with current versions of Wine show that an application running under Wine is slower on the same machine running MS-DOS and MS Windows.

To make full use of Wine, you need MS Windows 3.1 installed on a disk partition that is accessible under Linux. It is also convenient to run existing MS Windows applications from the same directory in which they are installed under native MS-DOS and MS Windows. The typical Linux user also has MS-DOS and MS Windows installed on a hard drive; thus it is only a matter of making the directories available under Linux. Linux kernels as of Version 1.1.83 do not support compressed MS-DOS file systems made by MS-DOS utilities such as `stacker` and `drvspace`.

> **TIP**
>
> Some Linux installation programs will prompt you through setting up an MS-DOS partition as a Linux subdirectory. If you did not set up such a partition, add the following line to your `/etc/fstab`,
>
> ```
> /dev/hda1 /c MSDOS defaults
> ```
>
> where `hda1` is the partition that contains MS-DOS, and `/c` is the Linux subdirectory to use. In this example it is assumed that the `/c` subdirectory exists. Otherwise, use `mkdir` to create the subdirectory.

Wine is distributed as source code, and must be compiled before use. It requires approximately 10MB of disk space. 3.5MB of that disk space is the source code alone. To build Wine, you need to have the following:

- GCC
- LibC
- XFree with development parts loaded
- Linux kernel newer than 99.13

Where To Get the Wine Distribution

A new version of Wine is released approximately once a week. Major Linux FTP sites on the Internet contain the most recent release. On `sunsite.unc.edu`, look in the `/pub/Linux/ALPHA/wine/development` directory. Wine releases are named after the date they are released. Wine-950727.tar.gz was released on 7/27/95. The most current release is the one with the latest date. For more information, check out the Web page at `http://daedalus.dra.hmg.gb/gale/wine/wine.html`.

How To Install Wine

Unlike DOSemu, the Wine distribution is not sensitive to where it is installed. For brevity, make a symbolic link from the actual directory (say `/usr/src/Wine950122`) to `/usr/wine` using the `ln` command as follows:

```
# ln -s /usr/src/Wine950122 /usr/wine
```

A Wine distribution consists of a compressed `tar` file. To unpack the distribution, use a shell command such as

```
# tar -zxvf filename.tar.gz
```

How To Configure Wine Before Building

Wine must be configured before being built. The `Configure` utility prompts the user for the necessary information, and automatically builds the appropriate configuration files. There are three major steps to configuring Wine:

1. Compilation configuration
2. Run-time parameters
3. Automatic system specific configuration

The configure script begins with the following questions.

```
Build Wine as emulator or library (E/L) [E]?
Short filenames (Y/N) [N]?
Use the XPM library (Y/N) [N]?
Language [En/De/No] ?
Global configfile name  /usr/local/etc/wine.conf
```

It is safe to press Enter and accept the defaults for these questions. These parameters are added to a global configuration file, `autoconf.h`. If parameter changes are necessary, re-run `Configure`. To avoid errors, do not attempt to edit this file.

Initially Configuring Runtime Parameters with *Configure*

The questions in this section relate to lines in the global configuration file `/usr/local/etc/wine.conf`. Following each question is an explanation of its meaning.

```
Which directory do you want to use as A:
Which directory do you want to use as C:
```

Answer these questions with the Linux directory where the MS-DOS A: and C: drive are mounted. If your disk partition on which MS Windows is mounted is `/c`, then use `/c`. If you do not plan on using a floppy disk, do not worry if A: does not point to a valid directory.

```
Where is the Windows directory 'c:\windows\'
Where is the System directory 'c:\windows\system'
Where should Windows apps store temp files 'c:\windows\temp'
Which path should be used to find progs/DLL's 'c:\windows;c:\windows\system'
```

These directories should match where MS Windows is installed on your MS-DOS partition. Because the default MS Windows installation is in c:\windows, the default answers are usually sufficient.

```
Where is sysres.dll  /usr/wine/sysres.dll'
```

The sysres.dll is a DLL that contains Wine specific resources. These resources include bitmaps and dialog boxes for things like the About Wine menu item. The default value is sufficient here as well.

```
Where is COM1" CF_Com1 '/dev/cua0'
Where is COM2" CF_Com2 '/dev/cua1'
Where is LPT1" CF_Lpt1 '/dev/lp0'
```

As with DOSemu, the communication and printer ports under Wine can be configured as any similar port under Linux. For simplicity, it is best to map the COM and LPT ports to the same ones that would appear under native MS-DOS.

```
Log messages to which file (CON = stdout) 'CON'
```

This defines where the system messages generated by Wine will go. Sending messages to CON will send them to stdout. This is the most useful place, as these messages can easily be redirected elsewhere. By default, Wine generates a lot of informational messages, which slows things down a bit. A casual user will likely want to redirect these messages to /dev/null. To make this be the default action, use /dev/null for the log file.

Configure displays a long list of message types and asks the following question:

```
Exclude which messages from the log  'WM_SIZE;WM_TIMER'
```

If you don't care about any status messages from Wine, leave this as the default. Individual error messages can be turned on or off as well as redirected from the command line.

At this point, Configure will display the global configuration file based on your responses to the questions. You will be asked if you want to edit the file using your default editor:

```
Do you want to edit it using vi (Y/N) [N]?
```

You can always edit this file later with your favorite text editor, so it is safe to answer no to this question.

Automatic System-Specific Configuration

After the wine.conf file has been successfully built, the Configure utility proceeds to make changes to the source tree via the xmkmf. Xmkmf is a utility that creates makefiles for X Window and creates a Makefile from an Imakefile taking into account the peculiarities of different X Window installations across UNIX-like platforms.

How To Build Wine

To build Wine, simply type

```
make
```

You're done with the hard part of configuring Wine. However, building Wine seems like the longest part. To build Wine from scratch takes approximately eight minutes on a 90MHz Pentium. You will also need the `-lXext` libraries for the final link to work, so install it from your CD-ROM first.

Using Wine

Using Wine can be as simple as typing wine *filename*. Wine can be configured and used with a number of different options—including a debugger for tracking down internal errors in Wine itself.

Specifying Configuration Parameters

Wine's global configuration file is typically `/usr/local/etc/wine.conf`. The configuration parameters match mostly with the above questions and are organized in the format of MS Windows `.ini` files. A sample file follows, with some comments on the usage of each section.

The following statements map MS-DOS drive letters to the matching subdirectory under Linux:

```
[drives]
A=/a
C=/c
```

These parameters tell Wine where to find Windows- and Wine-specific DLLs and directories:

```
[wine]
Windows=c:\windows
System=c:\windows\system
Temp=c:\temp
Path=c:\windows;c:\windows\system
SystemResources=/users/wine/wine950122/sysres.dll
```

The following section applies to the mapping of MS Windows fonts to X font (note that the * is used for wildcard matching of X fonts):

```
[fonts]
system=*-helvetica
mssansserif=*-helvetica
msserif=*-times
fixedsys=*-fixed
arial=*-helvetica
helv=*-helvetica
roman=*-times
default=*-*
```

The following section maps serial ports available under Wine with corresponding Linux serial port identifiers:

```
[serialports]
Com1=/dev/cua0
Com2=/dev/cua1
```

The following section maps printer ports available under Wine with the corresponding printer port under Linux

```
[parallelports]
Lpt1=/dev/lp0
```

These parameters determine the amount of logging and the destination:

```
[spy]
File=CON
Exclude=WM_SIZE;WM_TIMER
```

Using Command-Line Options

The Wine command line has the following format: wine wine_*options program program_options*. For example:

```
bash# /usr/wine/wine -debugmsg +all /c/windows/winmine.exe
```

Table 58.1 shows command-line options available with Wine.

Table 58.1. Wine command-line options.

Option	Meaning
-depth n	Change the depth to use for multiple-depth screens. This configures Wine to use other than the default number of colors. (8 bitplanes is 256 colors and usually the only acceptable answer.)
-desktop geom	Run an MS Windows application with a desktop of the size specified. For example, 850×620 would create a window of 850 by 620. Running with a desktop also eliminates the modal, or stuck-on-top, behavior of Wine applications.
-display name	Use an X display other than the default. This enables users to run an MS Windows application on another X device over an attached network.
-iconic	Start application as an icon rather than full-screen. This is same functionality as run minimized from the Program Manager under native MS Windows.
-debug	Enter debugger before starting application
-name name	Set the application name. This is useful for telling the X Window manager a meaningful name for the application. The default name is wine.
-privatemap	Use a private color map. This is useful for applications that make extensive use of color. Running an application this way causes the colors of other X applications to look weird while the Wine session is the selected window.

continues

Table 58.1. continued

Option	Meaning
-synchronous	Turn on synchronous display mode. This can severely slow down applications, as it causes X Window to wait for the completion of each command before sending the next one. X applications can send commands to an X server that may or may not be on the same machine. Under some applications, synchronization is necessary so that graphics operations do not get optimized away by the X server.
-backingstore	This is an optimization that enables an X server to handle expose events without interrupting the client program.
-spy *file*	Turn on message spying to the specified file. This can also be done by output redirection.
-debugmsg *name*	Turn specific debugging information on or off. To get a current list of debug message types, type the following command: wine -debugmsg help help.

The Wine Debugger

Wine has a built-in debugger that is useful for uncovering problems within the program. When an MS Windows program exits due to a problem, the debugger starts in the xterm from which Wine was started. If you are not interested in troubleshooting Wine, you need only type quit at the prompt and skip to the next section of this chapter.

The Wine debugger is similar to the GNU debugger gdb. Breakpoints can be set; examination and modification of registers as well as memory locations are possible. However, this is a minimal debugger that includes only the commands listed in Table 58.2.

Table 58.2. Wine debugger commands.

Command	Meaning
break	Set a breakpoint at a specified address or symbolic value. Wine will stop before executing instructions at this address. For example, break * GDI_Ordinal_24 sets a breakpoint at the start of Windows *Ellipse* function known internally as GDI.24.
bt	Backtrace, or show the history of Wine calls leading to the current place. The addresses shown are the return addresses, not the calling addresses.
cont	Continue program execution until a breakpoint or error condition is reached.
define	Equates a symbol to a value. For example: define *myproc* 0x000001c6.

Command	Meaning
disable	Disable a specific breakpoint. Breakpoints defined by the break command are stored by breakpoint numbers. To disable a breakpoint, you need to find the breakpoint number with the info command. To disable breakpoint number 1, simply type disable 1.
enable	Enables a breakpoint number, the opposite of disable. To enable the previously disabled breakpoint number 1, simply type enable 1.
help	Prints a help text of the available commands.
info	Provides information on the following: reg registers information. stack dumps the current stack. break shows the current breakpoints and if they are enabled. segments shows information about memory segments in use.
mode	Switches between 16- and 32-bit modes.
print	Prints out values of expressions given.
quit	Exits debugger and ends any MS Windows program in progress.
set	Enables depositing of values in registers and memory.
symbolfile	Loads a symbol file containing symbolic values. The file wine.sym is created as part of the Wine build.
x	Examines memory values in several different formats. The format of x is x / *format address*, where *format* can be one of the following: x　longword hexadecimal (32-bit integer) d　longword decimal w　word hexadecimal b　byte c　single character s　null-terminated ASCII string I　i386 instruction A number can be specified before the *format* to indicate a repeating group. For example, listing 10 instructions after a given address would be x / 10 I *0x000001cd*.

In order to benefit from using the Wine debugger, an understanding of debugging i386 assembly is essential. If you are serious about debugging Wine, an assembly language output from GCC is essential.

How Wine Works

Wine is composed of a MS Windows program loader and a library of MS Windows functions.

How Wine Loads Programs

Wine's first duty is to load an MS Windows executable image into memory. This also includes any DLL files and other resources that the application needs. MS Windows uses a different executable image type than does DOS that is called NE, or new executable. DLLs and font files also use this NE format, which makes Wine's job easier.

Individual segments of the NE image must be load into memory, and references to other DLL and Windows calls need to be resolved. Calls to functions outside an image are referred to by the module name and function number. A call to *Ellipse* is actually stored as GDI.24.

After an executable image is loaded into memory, Wine simply jumps to the WinMain() function defined in the image. A call to MS Windows graphics function *Ellipse* is stored as *GDI.24. GDI* is the name of the MS Windows graphics library, and 24 is the position in that DLL where *Ellipse* starts. Wine does not need to do any instruction emulation because both Linux and MS Windows use the i386 instruction set. When an MS Windows primitive function is called, Wine intercepts that call and passes it to a matching library routine.

The Wine Library

Wine converts the MS Windows API to the matching X or UNIX API calls. A call to the MS Windows Ellipse function to draw an ellipse in a window has the following format:

```
Ellipse (hdc, xLeft, yTop, xRight, yBottom);
```

The definitions are of xLeft, yTop, xRight, and yBottom are a bounding box for an ellipse as shown in Figure 58.2.

FIGURE 58.2.

MS Windows ellipse coordinates.

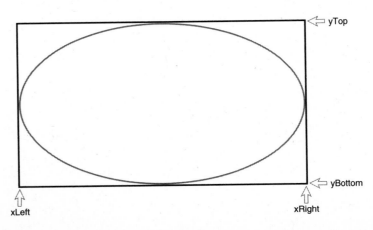

The same ellipse is drawn under the X API `XDrawArc` function:

`XDrawArc(display, d, gc, x, y, width, height, angle1, angle2);`

The definitions of `x`, `y`, `width`, `height`, `angle1`, and `angle2` are shown in Figure 58.3.

FIGURE 58.3.

XDrawArc coordinates.

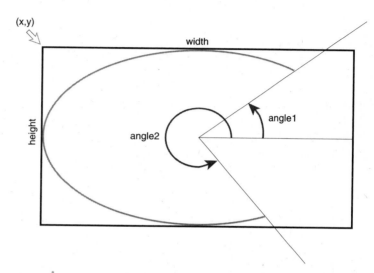

Wine needs to do a little math to convert the coordinates from an `Ellipse` call to that of an `XDrawArc` call. Other parameters of the `XDrawArc` call are a bit easier to map. The *d* refers to a drawable area, which is typically a handle to a window. Under MS Windows, this is contained in the `hdc` structure. The *gc* is a graphics context and is analogous in functionality to the *hdc* under MS Windows. As X is capable of displaying on different machines over a network, the *display* parameter describes which display to use. The *display* parameter remains constant over the life of a Wine session. The last thing Wine has to consider is that an MS Windows `Ellipse` call can also specify a filled ellipse. Wine checks the `hdc`, and possibly uses `XFillArc` instead.

There are nearly 300 graphics primitives available under MS Windows that need to undergo similar translations. While this might seem to be a bit of work, the graphics conversions are among the simpler things to emulate under MS Windows.

Where Does Wine End and MS Windows Begin?

As Wine currently requires parts of MS Windows to operate, it is a bit confusing to know where Wine ends and MS Windows begins. Wine currently provides API calls for the following parts of a typical MS Windows installation:

`commdlg`	Common Windows Dialogs
`gdi`	Graphics Device Interface

kernel	Kernel Interface
keyboard	Keyboard Interface
mmsystem	Multimedia System Interface
mouse	Mouse Interface
shell	Windows 3.1 Shell API Library
sound	Windows sound system
toolhelp	Debugging and tools helper calls
user	Microsoft Windows User Interface
win87em	Coprocessor/Emulator Library
winsock	Windows Socket interface (TCP/IP)

Wine requires access to some parts of MS Windows to use features that are not implemented by Wine. One example is the MS Windows dynamic link library OLECLI, which implements the OLE client. The Wine team has made significant headway in reducing the amount of files needed. The Wine project charter includes removing any dependency on MS Windows files. This includes utilities and file organizations to install MS Windows applications.

Some of the simplest MS Windows applications run today under Wine without need of any MS Windows code or access to any MS Windows directories. WINMINE.EXE and SOL.EXE are examples of such applications. Although no suggested directory organization exists to support this, a quick example of doing this is the following:

1. Copy winmine.exe and win.ini to a Linux directory such as /users/windows.
2. Change the Windows path options in wine.conf, such as to /users/windows.
3. Dismount your MS-DOS partition.
4. Run Wine.

Limitations of Wine

Only a few MS Windows software packages run correctly under Wine. Luckily it is possible to estimate how likely a program is to run correctly without actually running it. Unfortunately there are some classes of applications that are unlikely to ever run under Wine.

Software That Works

The most recent versions of Wine support a good number of the MS Windows applets and games included with the stock MS Windows 3.1. There are considerable variations between each release of Wine. Changes that help some applications often break others. But here are some of the accessories and games that work reasonably well under Wine:

- calc.exe
- clock.exe
- cruel.exe
- golf.exe

- ■ notepad.exe
- ■ pipe.exe
- ■ pegged.exe
- ■ reversi.exe
- ■ winmine.exe

Using *winestat* To Analyze Windows Programs

Part of Wine is the winestat utility. This is actually the same program as Wine, but instead of running an MS Windows executable, winestat simply attempts to load a Windows executable and reports on how successful the load was. In loading an executable, winestat also loads any DLLs necessary, and reports if any are missing. winestat looks for Windows API calls that are used by either the executable or any DLL, and verifies their existence. A sample winestat run on the MS Windows Paintbrush applet pbrush yields the following:

```
KERNEL.1 not implemented
KERNEL.54 not implemented
KERNEL.113 not implemented
KERNEL.114 not implemented
KERNEL.121 not implemented
KERNEL.154 not implemented
KERNEL.178 not implemented
KERNEL.207 not implemented
KERNEL: 52 of 60 (86.7 %)
USER: 150 of 150 (100.0 %)
GDI.151 not implemented
GDI.307 not implemented
GDI.366 not implemented
GDI.439 not implemented
GDI: 80 of 84 (95.2 %)
SHELL: 9 of 9 (100.0 %)
KEYBOARD: 2 of 2 (100.0 %)
TOTAL: 293 of 305 winapi functions implemented (96.1 %)
```

winestat calls out the individual functions by number and module that are not implemented by Wine. If you are curious as to the function name, rather than number, look at the Wine sources in the if1632 directory for the given module name's spec file. A sample kernel.spec file is as follows:

```
#1 FATALEXIT
#2 EXITKERNEL
3   pascal GetVersion() GetVersion()
...
...
...
#54 pascal16 GETINSTANCEDATA
```

Any line in a .spec file that starts with a # is considered a comment, not an implemented function. In this example, both 1 and 54 are commented, with the respective names of FATALEXIT, and GETINSTANCEDATA. FATALEXIT is used for debugging MS Windows programs under error conditions and is not important for most MS Windows users. GETINSTANCEDATA copies configuration data from a previous instance of an application. If you are running only one instance of an application, this does not apply.

The final percentage shows which MS Windows API calls are implemented. This is often a good measure of how much of an application could work under Wine. Unfortunately, if a single, unimplemented API call is needed to initialize your MS Windows application, anything less than 100 percent is not good enough.

MS Windows applications to which `winestat` gives an overall implementation rating over 95 percent are worth a try. Unlike DOSemu, Wine is not as prone to leaving Linux in an unusable state. However it is not always a trivial matter to kill an errant Wine session. The easiest thing to do is to start Wine with a separate desktop: `wine -desktop 800×600 filename`. Normal methods of killing a Windows process from your window manager should work.

> **TIP**
>
> When all else fails trying to stop an errant Wine session, switch to a free virtual console and kill the errant Wine process.
>
> For example, Alt-Ctrl and F2 would switch to virtual console number 2. You can log into a virtual console and use `ps -ax ¦ grep wine` to find your Wine sessions. Use `kill -15 pid` where `pid` is the process id returned by `ps` to stop the process. You can return to your X session by switching to the virtual console that is running X. If you don't know what console number that is, hold down the Alt and Ctrl keys, and press F1 through F8 until you find it.

Major Pieces That Are Missing from Wine

Perhaps the most obvious omission from Wine is the lack of a printer interface. As this is a complex process, work on a printer interface is little more than a few ideas. It would be a huge task to support all of the types of printers supported under MS Windows. Wine will likely implement only a PostScript driver. Existing Linux utilities such as `GhostScript` are already capable of converting PostScript to other types of printer types, such as HP laser and inkjet printers.

The 32-bit Windows API (`win32`) is mostly unsupported. This is the executable image format for Windows NT and Windows 95, and is known as PE (portable executable). Wine currently supports the loading of resource files, such as fonts, that are in PE format, but is unable to handle executables or DLLs.

Software Unlikely to Ever Work

The Wine project has no plans to support Windows Virtual Device Drivers. (VDDs). VDDs use a different image format, called LE for linear executable, that the Wine loader is unable to handle. Because VDDs do things like direct hardware manipulation, coexistence of a VDD with Linux device drivers would be a tough problem indeed. One of the uses of VDDs in commercial MS Windows is for TCP/IP stacks. Wine supports TCP/IP through the `winsock` DLL, which uses the TCP/IP inherent in the Linux kernel.

History of Wine

The first parts of Wine were made available in July 1993. The first versions had problems running the MS Windows Solitaire game, and were quite limited. Notably missing was support for menus. Since then a huge number of changes have been made by many dedicated people. It would be nearly impossible to mention everyone who contributed to Wine, or to parts of Linux that make Wine possible, but here is a list of people anyway:

Bob Amstadt, Dag Asheim, Martin Ayotte, Ross Biro, Uwe Bonnes, Erik Bos, Fons Botman, John Brezak, Andrew Bulhak, John Burton, Niels de Carpentier, Roman Dolejsi, Frans van Dorsselaer, Paul Falstad, Olaf Flebbe, Peter Galbavy, Ramon Garcia, Hans de Graaff, Charles M. Hannum, John Harvey, Cameron Heide, Jochen Hoenicke, Onno Hovers, Jeffrey Hsu, Miguel de Icaza, Jukka Iivonen, Alexandre Julliard, Jochen Karrer, Andreas Kirschbaum, Albrecht Kleine, Jon Konrath, Alex Korobka, Greg Kreider, Anand Kumria, Scott A. Laird, Martin von Loewis, Kenneth MacDonald, Peter MacDonald, William Magro, Juergen Marquardt, Marcus Meissner, Graham Menhennitt, David Metcalfe, Steffen Moeller, Philippe De Muyter, Itai Nahshon, Michael Patra, Jim Peterson, Robert Pouliot, Keith Reynolds, John Richardson, Johannes Ruscheinski, Thomas Sandford, Constantine Sapuntzakis, Daniel Schepler, Ulrich Schmid, Bernd Schmidt, Yngvi Sigurjonsson, Rick Sladkey, William Smith, Erik Svendsen, Tristan Tarrant, Andrew Taylor, Duncan C. Thomson, Goran Thyni, Jimmy Tirtawangsa, Jon Tombs, Linus Torvalds, Gregory Trubetskoy, Michael Veksler, Sven Verdoolaege, Eric Warnke, Manfred Weichel, Morten Welinder, Jan Willamowius, Carl Williams, Karl Guenter Wuensch, Eric Youngdale, and James Youngman.

For more information about the Wine project, get the FAQ at `http://www.asgardpro.com/dave/wine-faq.html` or visit the project's home page at `http://daedalus.dra.hmg.gb/gale/wine/wine.html`.

Using HylaFAX, sendfax, and mgetty

59

by Kamran Husain

IN THIS CHAPTER

This chapter deals with a fax application for Linux: HylaFAX. Though there are other fax facilities for UNIX systems, such as `netfax`, in this chapter, I concentrate on HylaFAX because it may be the most comprehensive. You also have access to the C++ source code to make any necessary modifications to the application to adapt it to your PC.

HylaFAX was invented by Sam Leffler. You can send thanks and an "Atta boy" to him via e-mail at `sam@sgi.com`. HylaFAX is indeed a great piece of work.

HylaFAX is a system for sending and receiving fax documents. Some of the notable features of HylaFAX include the following:

- ■ Queued fax transmission by date and time
- ■ Asynchronous fax reception via a daemon
- ■ Most programs are part of a tool kit. You can update portions of the application by updating the executable file.

Installing HylaFAX

> **NOTE**
>
> The Display PostScript interpreter, Ghostscript, is supplied in binary form for Silicon Graphics machines. There is information on obtaining and setting up Ghostscript (see Chapter 25, "Ghostscript").

Where To Get HylaFAX

HylaFAX can be obtained via public FTP on the Internet. It is also available on a number of public domain and shareware-style CD-ROMs. The master distribution site for HylaFAX is the host `ftp.sgi.com`. (See the `/sgi/fax/binary` directory at that site.)

> **NOTE**
>
> HylaFax is essentially the same program as FlexFAX, but with a new name and many more features.

All the HylaFAX documentation is online on the World Wide Web (WWW). This documentation describes how to unpack and install the source distribution images. The HylaFAX home page at `sgi.com` is the place to go for all the HylaFAX documentation.

The HylaFAX source code is available for public FTP on `ftp.sgi.com` as `/sgi/fax/source HylaFAX-v3.0.pl0-tar.gz`.

You can get more information about HylaFAX from the WWW by accessing the Web page `http://www.vix.com/hylaFAX`. Check out the FAQs at this site for the most up-to-date information.

Types of Modems

HylaFAX comes with detailed information on specific modems and configuration instructions in a file called MODEMS. Read this file carefully to see whether your modem is listed. If it is, you should have no problems with HylaFAX. If you cannot find your exact modem, choose the one that best fits the description you have. Chances are that a close enough setting will work fine.

Most of the modems on the list are either Class 1 or 2, and both types are supported by HylaFAX. Do not confuse the fax Group I, II, or III standards with Class 1 or 2. The groups discuss how faxes are encoded, and classes explain how you "talk" to a modem.

Installation Steps

First, unzip and untar the source files from the distribution in a local directory. After you get the source file for HylaFAX, the first installation steps are to configure your system and then do a make install command.

The source code is in a compressed tar file. To extract the software

```
$ mkdir fax
$ cd fax
$ uncompress $(DOWNLOAD_DIR)/v2.3.src.tar.Z
$ tar -xf  $(DOWNLOAD_DIR)/v2.3.src.tar
```

The DOWNLOAD_DIR is the directory you downloaded the tar file to. Because the software is written mostly in C++, you need gnu C++. The versions guaranteed to work with gcc 2.5.8 and libg++ 2.5.3 are the current recommended versions of the GNU tools.

To build and install executables from the sources, look first for any port/target/README file that has target-specific information. In this case, look at port/linux/README.

Then, enter the following commands.

```
$ su
    # configure
    # make clean
    # make install
```

I have deliberately not shown output from the configure and make commands because I discuss them in detail in this section. You have to run the make commands as root because they access the /usr/local tree, and you will need write permissions when you write files to that tree.

The output from a sample configure command is shown in Listing 59.1.

Listing 59.1. The output from the `configure` command.

```
$ configure
...(Extraneous text deleted here)...
this means that only a crummy built-in font will be available for imaging text.

Warning, /usr/local/bin/gs does not seem to be an executable program;
you'll need to correct this before starting up the fax server.

HylaFAX configuration parameters are:

Directory for applications:      /usr/local/bin
Directory for lib data files:    /usr/local/lib/fax
Directory for lib executables:   /usr/local/lib/fax
Directory for servers:           /usr/local/etc
Directory for manual pages:      /usr/local/man
Directory for documentation:     /usr/local/doc/HylaFAX
Directory for spooling:          /usr/spool/fax
Type of uucp lock files:         ascii
Directory for uucp lock files:   /usr/spool/uucp
Mode for uucp lock files:        0444
Type of PostScript imager:       gs
PostScript imager program:       /usr/local/bin/gs
Default page size:               North American Letter
Default vertical res (lpi):      98
Directory for font metrics:      /usr/local/lib/afm
Location of sendmail program:    /usr/lib/sendmail

Are these ok [yes]?
```

It's important to maintain the locations of all the listed files. Changing these locations is not a good idea because they are the default values for other applications. For example, the `sendfax` command did not work with any other location of the afm tree other than at `/usr/local/lib/afm`. Changing the location via `configure` did not help at all.

The `make` install process takes a while because the `make` install script has to traverse several directories and build source files in each sub-directory. The files are placed in different parts of your system based on the output of the `configure` command.

You may have to copy the files `mkfifo`, `chown`, and `chgrp` from the `/bin` directory to the `/usr/local/bin` directory. The `make` files exclusively use these files to set the file permissions. You have to edit the location of the `echo` command in the `make` files to reflect the correct location for your echo command. If you see `/usr/local/bin/echo not found` error messages, either copy `echo` to `/usr/local/bin`, or edit the `make` files to point to the correct location. To get rid of the message `Warning, /usr/local/bin/gs does not ...` in the previous listing, you create a link to `gs` from `/usr/local/bin/gs`.

After the installation is done, check `/usr/local/bin/fax` for executable files. At a minimum, you should have `faxcover`, `faxd`, and `sendfax` in this directory.

Once you have HylaFAX installed, you can add modems with the `faxaddmodem` shell script. This script is interactive and steps you through the configuration and installation of a new or existing modem.

> **TIP**
>
> Even if you have a previous version of this software installed, run the faxaddmodem script to update the configuration information for your modems. Running faxaddmodem twice will not ruin anything.

> **TIP**
>
> If your modem is configured to communicate to the host at a fixed baud rate, use the -s option with faxaddmodem. See the faxaddmodem manual page for details.

A sample configuration session for my machine is shown in Listing 59.2. Note that I ran as root while I did this. I pressed the Enter key after each [yes] command to accept the default responses. If you do not like what you see, type n and then press Enter.

Listing 59.2. Sample configuration for HylaFAX.

```
# faxaddmodem
Verifying your system is set up properly for fax service...

There is no entry for the fax user in the password file.
The fax software needs a name to work properly; add it [yes]?

  Added user "fax" to /etc/passwd.
  Added fax user to "/etc/passwd.sgi".

There does not appear to be an entry for the fax service in
either the yellow pages database or the /etc/services file;
should an entry be added to /etc/services [yes]?

There is no entry for the fax service in "/usr/etc/inetd.conf";
should one be added [yes]?

Poking inetd so that it rereads the configuration file.

There does not appear to be an entry for the FaxMaster in
either the yellow pages database or the /usr/lib/aliases file;
should an entry be added to /usr/lib/aliases [yes]?
Users to receive fax-related mail [root]?

Rebuilding /usr/lib/aliases database.
41 aliases, longest 81 bytes, 823 bytes total

Done verifying system setup.

Serial port that modem is connected to []? cua1
```

continues

Listing 59.2. continued

```
Ok, time to set up a configuration file for the modem.  The manual
page config(4F) may be useful during this process.  Also be aware
that at any time you can safely interrupt this procedure.

No existing configuration. Let's do this from scratch.

Phone number of fax modem []? +1.713.265.1539

This is the phone number associated with the modem being configured.
It is passed as an "identity" to peer fax machines and it may
also appear on tag lines created by the fax server.
The phone number should be a complete international dialing specification
in the form +&ltcountry code&gt; &ltarea code&gt; &ltlocal part&gt;.
Any other characters included for readability are automatically
removed if they might cause problems.

Area code []? 713
Country code [1]?
Long distance dialing prefix [1]?
International dialing prefix [011]?
Tracing during normal server operation [1]?
Tracing during send and receive sessions [11]?
Protection mode for received fax [0600]?
Rings to wait before answering [1]?
Modem speaker volume [off]?

The server configuration parameters are

    FAXNumber:              +1.713.265.1539
    AreaCode               713
    CountryCode            1
    LongDistancePrefix:    1
    InternationalPrefix:   011
    ServerTracing:         1
    SessionTracing:        11
    RecvFileMode:          0600
    RingsBeforeAnswer:     1
    SpeakerVolume:         off

Are these ok [yes]? n

Phone number of fax modem [+1.713.265.1539]?
Area code [713]?
Country code [1]?
Long distance dialing prefix [1]?
International dialing prefix [011]?
Tracing during normal server operation [1]?
Tracing during send and receive sessions [11]?
Protection mode for received fax [0600]?
Rings to wait before answering [1]?
Modem speaker volume [off]? low

The server configuration parameters are

    FAXNumber:              +1.713.265.1539
    AreaCode               713
```

```
CountryCode              1
LongDistancePrefix:      1
InternationalPrefix:     011
ServerTracing:           1
SessionTracing:          11
RecvFileMode:            0600
RingsBeforeAnswer:       1
SpeakerVolume:           low

Are these ok [yes]?

Now we are going to probe the tty port to figure out the type
of modem that is attached.  This takes a few seconds, so be patient.
Note that if you do not have the modem cabled to the port, or the
modem is turned off, this may hang (just go and cable up the modem
or turn it on, or whatever).

Hmm, this looks like a Class 1 modem.
Product code is "1444".
Modem manufacturer is "USRobotics".
Modem model is "Courier".

Using prototype configuration file config.usr-courier...

The modem configuration parameters are:

ModemRate:               19200
ModemFlowControl:        xonxoff
ModemFlowControlCmd:     &H2
ModemSetupDTRCmd:        S13=1&D2
ModemSetupDCDCmd:        &C1
ModemDialCmd:            DT%s@
ModemResultCodesCmd      X4

Are these ok [yes]?

Startup a fax server for this modem [yes]
/usr/etc/faxd -m /dev/cua1
#
```

HylaFAX requires that a fax user exist in the password file on the server machine. This user should have the same user ID as uucp so that lock files can be easily shared.

Client applications communicate with the server machine via the faxd.recv program. This program is designed to be started by the inetd program. If the appropriate entry is not present in inetd's configuration file, confirming this prompt causes it to be added. Note that there must also be a fax service already set up for this step to succeed (see above).

A fax server entry must exist so that the inetd program can set up the fax job submission server, faxd.recv, on the appropriate port. If the server machine is running NIS (formerly known as Yellow Pages), it may be necessary to create the entry in the appropriate map. Otherwise the entry is installed in the /etc/services file.

The fax server sends mail notices to a well-known user called the `FaxMaster` when certain events occur. Some examples are when faxes are received or when modems appear to be on the blink. This step sets up a mail alias for this the `FaxMaster`. The alias lists those system administrators that handle HylaFAX-specific problems. I chose `root` because I have a small system and I usually wind up doing all my administrative stuff as root anyway. If you have a large user base, perhaps a specific user could handle all the fax-related problems.

This completes the collection of server-related parameters. The remaining steps identify and configure the modem. Note that if you do not specify a fixed rate for modem communications, `faxaddmodem` will probe for a good speed. The `faxaddmodem` command is good at finding what type of modem you have and configuring it. Unless you have a compelling reason to change the responses to settings other than the defaults, leave them.

The fax daemon is now started for you. This is done with `/usr/etc/faxd -m /dev/cua1`. You may want to put this command in your `/etc/rc.d` file for subsequent boots so that you don't have to remember to start it yourself.

Troubleshooting

You are bound to run into difficulties while installing HylaFAX. Despite my assertions in the last section about two simple steps to complete the installation, you still have the potential of running into problems. Here is a brief list of problems and their solutions. The list is by no means complete, nor is it guaranteed the examples will apply to you, but at least it will give you an idea of what could be wrong.

- You need the `afm-tar.Z` file for the Adobe Font Metric (AFM) fonts required by the `sendfax` program. You can get this file via FTP from `sgi.com`. Some HylaFAX distributions do not include these Metric files. A subset of these fonts is available via FTP from `sgi.com` in the file `/sgi/fax/afm-tar.Z`. If you do not install the AFM files, you get error messages about `fonts not found`.

- Add a user called `fax` to the same group as uucp. The `faxaddmodem` call may not work and bomb with errors about `too many arguments`. If this happens, make sure your modem works. If you cannot use cu on your modem, fix that problem first. Check the cables, initialization strings, and so on. For external modems, check to see whether the cable has the relevant signals for doing hardware flow control if necessary and that it passes the DCD and DTR signals appropriately.

- If you have a Class 1 modem, you cannot use hardware flow control. Class 2 modems do support hardware control. Ensure that you have the correct cables for the type of external modem you plan to connect to.

Setting Up a Send and Receive Daemon

The `faxd` daemon is the main processing agent of the HylaFAX package. You need one `faxd` process and FIFO for each fax modem on your system. `faxd` listens to its own FIFO for all its command directives. When you start `faxd`, you can use the following options:

- ■ `-m` to specify the terminal device the fax modem is attached to. For example, `/dev/cua1` is a mandatory argument to `faxd`.

- ■ `-q` to specify a spooling area in which to operate other than `/var/spool/HylaFAX`.

- ■ `-i` to specify the interval in seconds that a job should be held between transmission attempts. By default, this interval is 900 seconds.

- ■ `-g` option can be used to indicate that `faxd` should act like the `getty` program if it receives a call from a data modem. See the `getty` man page for details. If this option is not specified and the server is not configured to support incoming data connections, incoming data connections will be rejected.

- ■ `-d` stops `faxd` from detaching itself from the terminal. This is useful for debugging.

- ■ `-1` option causes `faxd` to generate only 1D-encoded fax when sending.

> **CAUTION**
>
> There is no way to abort an incoming fax. Just sit back and wait until it's over.

The `faxd.recv` daemon is the program that implements the server side of the fax job submission protocol. It also implements extensions to this protocol to support job removal and the return of status information. `faxd.recv` is normally invoked by `inetd` with a line in the following form:

```
fax stream tcp nowait fax /usr/libexec/faxd.recv  faxd.recv
```

The `faxd.recv` daemon accepts requests for transmitting faxes and creates the appropriate queue and document files in the HylaFAX spooling area. If a job is received properly, a request to process the job is then sent to a fax server by writing to a FIFO special file named `FIFO` in the spooling directory. The `faxd.recv` daemon then returns a message to the sender indicating the Job ID (an integer number associated with the job). This Job ID can be used later to remove the job from the queue and to query the job's status.

Diagnostics generated by `faxd.recv` are logged with the `syslog` facility. The user is always informed of any problem that affects the status of the queued job. Check the man pages for a list of these error messages.

Sending a Fax

To send a fax, you will use the `sendfax` program. The syntax for this command from the man page is

```
sendfax [ -a transmit-time ]
            [ -c comments ]
            [ -r regarding ]
            [ -x to-company ]
            [ -y to-location ]
            [ -d destination ]
            [ -f from ]
```

```
[ -h host[:modem] ]
[ -i identifier ]
[ -k kill-time ]
[ -lm ]
[ -n ]
[ -p ]
[ -s pagesize-name     ]
[ -t tries ]
[ -v ]
[ -DR ]
[ files...   ]
```

sendfax queues up fax requests to a faxd server. These requests normally are processed immediately, although they may also be queued for later transmission using a syntax identical to the at command. For each job that is queued, Sendfax prints on the standard output a job identifier. This number can be supplied to the faxrm command to remove the job or to the faxalter(1) command to alter some of its parameters.

Fax documents are made from the concatenation of files specified on the command line. If no files are supplied, sendfax reads data from the standard input unless polling is requested. sendfax passes PostScript and TIFF documents directly to the fax server for transmission and attempts to convert other file formats to either PostScript or TIFF. In normal operation, sendfax automatically converts ASCII-text or troff output before transmission.

By default, sendfax will generate a cover page for each fax that is transmitted. This cover page is created by the faxcover program using information determined by sendfax and by information supplied on the command line. The -x option is used to specify the receiver's company; the -y option to specify the receiver's geographical location; the -c option to specify a comments field; and the -r option to specify a Re: subject. If a destination is specified as user@fax-number, the user string is passed to faxcover as the identity of the recipient.

NOTE

The preceding options must precede the -d option on the command line. Note also that multiword names must be enclosed in quote marks (").

TIP

If you don't want a cover page, specify the -n option.

Here are a few other things about sending faxes:

- You can use *70, on the -d parameter of sendfax when you want to disable call waiting.
- By default, a fax is sent at low resolution (98 lines per inch). Medium resolution (196 lines per inch), often called *fine mode*, is requested with the -m option. Low resolution is requested with the -1 option.

- Faxes are on 8.5×11 pages unless otherwise configured. Other sizes include A3, ISO A4, ISO A5, ISO A6, ISO B4, North American Letter, American Legal, American Ledger, American Executive, Japanese Letter, and Japanese Legal.

- By default, `sendfax` uses the `FAXSERVER` environment variable to identify the fax server to which the job should be directed. This can be overridden with a `-h` option. The server specified with the `-h` option, and by the environment variable, is a host name or address and optionally, a modem identifier. The syntax for the latter is either `host:modem` or `modem@host`. For example, `cua2@no.inhale.edu`. If no modem is specified, the job will be submitted to any available modem.

If the first attempt to send a fax is unsuccessful, HylaFAX periodically tries to resend the fax. By default, HylaFAX tries to transmit the fax for one day from the time of the initial transmission. The `-k` option is used to specify an alternate time for killing the job. This time is specified using notation compatible with `at` and as a time relative to the time of the initial transmission attempt.

If an error is encountered while HylaFAX is processing a job, the fax server sends an electronic mail message to the account submitting the job. If the `-D` option is specified, HylaFAX also notifies the account by mail when the job is completed. In addition, if the `-R` option is specified, notification also is returned any time the job must be queued for retransmission.

Notification messages identify a job by its job identifier.

An arbitrary identification string can be specified instead with the `-i` option.

If the `-v` option is specified, `sendfax` prints information on the standard output about what `sendfax` does. If you specify `---v -v`, even `faxd.recv` displays its status messages as it works.

See the man pages for more information on the options available with this `sendfax` command.

Only two types of files are accepted by the fax server for transmission: PostScript files or TIFF Class F (bi-level Group 3-encoded) files. All other types of files must be converted to one of these two formats. The `sendfax` program applies a set of rules against the contents of each input file to identify the file's type and to figure out how to convert the file to a format that is suitable for transmission. These rules are stored in the `/usr/local/lib/HylaFAX/typerules` file, an ASCII file similar to `/etc/magic`. See the man pages on type rules for a detailed look at how these type rules work.

Receiving Faxes

Server processes can be configured to answer incoming phone calls and automatically receive faxes. Received documents are placed in the `recvq` subdirectory as TIFF Class F files. The server can be configured to make these files publicly accessible, or they can be made private, in which case an administrator must manage their delivery.

When a fax is received, the server process invokes the `bin/faxrcvd` command. The default command is a shell script that sends a mail message to a well-known user, the `FaxMaster`, but you might also, for example, automatically spool the document for printing.

Actually the man pages for HylaFAX are well written (for man pages). In the man pages for `faxd`, you get a lot of detailed information about how received faxes are handled.

Special Features

HylaFAX comes with several features from creating cover pages and receiving incoming data calls to handling polling requests. In each of these cases you can get more information for the man pages for each command discussed in the remainder of this chapter.

Cover Pages

You generate PostScript cover sheets for your outgoing faxes with the `faxcover` command. The syntax for this command from the man page is

```
$ faxcover [ -t to-name ]
           [ -l to-location ]
           [ -x to-company ]
           [ -v to-voice-number ]
           [ -c comments ]
           [ -r regarding ]
           [ -p page-count ]
           [ -s pagesize-name ]
           [ -C  template-file ]
           -f from-name -n fax-number
```

To generate the cover page for each outgoing fax, `faxcover` is invoked by the `sendfax` program. `Faxcover` generates a PostScript cover-page document on the standard output. The cover page fills the entire area of the default page and is created according to the information supplied on the command line and a cover sheet template file. The default template file is named `faxcover.ps`. You can override the default cover sheet with the `-C` option by specifying a file in the `FAXCOVER` environment variable.

If the cover sheet's filename is not an absolute path, `faxcover` looks first for this file in the sender's home directory. If no such file is present, `faxcover` looks in the library directory where the HylaFAX client application data is installed. If no template file is located, `faxcover` terminates without generating a cover page.

Polling

HylaFAX supports the polled retrieval of fax documents. Documents received because of a poll request are stored in the `recvq` subdirectory and also delivered directly to the requester using the `bin/pollrcvd` command. This script typically encodes the binary fax data and returns it to the recipient via e-mail.

Receiving Data Calls

Most fax modems also support non-fax communications. HylaFAX uses the locking mechanism employed by `uucp` and `cu`. Therefore, HylaFAX transparently relinquishes the serial port when an application uses the modem for an outgoing call. In addition, HylaFAX attempts to deduce whether an incoming call is for fax or data use. If an incoming call comes from a data modem and the `-g` argument is specified in the configuration file (or on the command line when the fax server process is started), HylaFAX invokes the `getty` program so that the caller may log in to the system.

Checking Status

HylaFAX maintains status information in several forms. General status information for each server process can be displayed by the `faxstat(1)` program. The server processes may also be configured to log various kinds of debugging and tracing information. For more information about configuration, see the section entitled "Installation Steps" in this chapter. The `faxstat` utility provides information such as the remote status of jobs queued for transmission, jobs received, and the general status of server processes. See Listing 59.3.

Listing 59.3. Output of the `faxstat` command.

```
# faxstat
Server on localhost:cua1 for C: Running and idle.

Job  Modem Destination   Time-To-Send   Sender      Status
2    any   5551212                      root        Queued and waiting
1    any   5551212                      kamran      Being processed
Server on localhost:cua1 for C: Sending job 1 to 5796555.
```

Any problems encountered during fax transmission are reported to the user by e-mail. A user may also request notification by mail when a job is requeued. The server process uses the `/bin/notify` command to inform the user via e-mail.

The file `etc/xferlog` contains status information about all faxes sent and received. This file is in a simple ASCII format that is easy to manipulate with programs such as `vi` or `emacs`.

To get more accounting information, use the following commands.

- ◼ `xferlog`—A log file of all transmitted files
- ◼ `xferstats`—Accounting information about all faxes sent or received

E-Mail Setup

It is easy to set up a simple mail-to-fax gateway facility with HylaFAX. If your system uses `sendmail` to deliver mail, follow the instructions in the `faxmail/mailfax.sh-sendmail` document. If your system uses `smail` (Linux users), follow the instructions in `faxmail/mailfax.sh-smail`. Restart your mail software.

Now, mail to `user@dest.fax` will be formatted and submitted as a facsimile job to `user` at the specified destination. By writing a more involved `mailfax` script, you can add options and display parameters such as different resolutions by parsing the user string. See the `faxgateway` documentation on www.vix.com in HylaFAX/faxgateway.html or the /sgi/fax/contrib/dirks-faxmailer/README on sgi.com for more information.

Files Used

HylaFAX stores its data, configuration, and faxes in several places on the file system in Linux. Here is a list of the important files and directories:

- HylaFAX uses a spool area on the disk for sending and receiving faxes. The spooling area is located under the directory /var/spool/HylaFAX.

- The /usr/local/bin directory has the commands used by the HylaFAX package. The commands are fax2ps, faxaddmodem, faxalter, faxanswer, faxcover, faxmail, faxquit, faxrm, faxstat, and sendfax.

- The ./etc directory stores all the configuration, access control, and accounting information.

- The ./sendq directory has all the outgoing fax jobs.

- The ./recvq directory contains a copy of all received faxes.

- The ./docq and ./temp subdirectories are used in fax transmission also.

- The info subdirectory contains files that describe the capabilities of fax machines called by HylaFAX. This information is used in preparing documents for transmission.

- The cinfo subdirectory contains files with per-machine control parameters to use when sending faxes.

- The status subdirectory contains files to which server processes write their current status.

- The log subdirectory contains logging information about send and receive sessions.

Multiple Modems

HylaFAX supports multiple fax modems on a single host. Associated with each modem is a server process that handles transmission and asynchronous reception. Server processes operate independently of each other and use file-locking to avoid conflicts when handling jobs submitted for transmission. All modems are treated equally at the same priority. A HylaFAX server process accepts messages and commands through FIFOs. A FIFO is basically a communications data channel where the first data in (FI) is the first data out (FO).

Another Fax Solution

The mgetty+sendfax+vgetty package is a set of programs to send and receive faxes in a UNIX environment. The package only supports Class 2 modems. The filename is called mgetty+sendfax-0.98.tar.gz, and you can get it from tsx-11.mit.edu in the /pub/linux/sources/sbin directory. There are three parts to this package: sendfax, vgetty, and mgetty. The program mgetty is for receiving faxes and handling external logins without killing any outgoing calls. sendfax is a program that sends fax files. vgetty is an extended version of mgetty that can answer the telephone like an answering machine and record voice-mail messages in addition to mgetty's fax or data call handling capabilities. The entire package lets you manage faxes and voice messages.

So what's the difference between mgetty and the regular versions of getty? Unlike traditional versions of getty or uugetty, which will put a modem into auto-answer mode, mgetty does not. When a call comes in, mgetty tells the modem to answer and tell mgetty what kind of call is being received. If it is fax, mgetty will receive the fax itself. If the modem is getting data, mgetty prompts for a user ID, and then hands the open line off to login for a normal data login.

It's the modem's job to distinguish a fax call from a data call. Not all fax modems can do this, so if yours does not do this, there is no way for mgetty to do this for you. mgetty can be used with modems that cannot distinguish a fax call from a data call, but you must tell it ahead of time what type of call to expect. You can configure mgetty to allow for uucp and other connections.

> **NOTE**
>
> Note that mgetty also supports caller ID and can be programmed to deny connections based on originating telephone number.

If you have a voice-capable modem, then you can use vgetty. The vgetty program is an extension to mgetty that provides additional call-handling capabilities. When the modem reports an incoming call, vgetty has the modem pick up the line and play a greeting. Then, as with mgetty, the modem reports the type of call. If it hears "human voices" (stuff it can't identify), the modem reports a voice connection and vgetty records the noise as an incoming voice message. If the modem reports that it identifies a fax tone, vgetty acts like mgetty and receives a fax or answers a poll. If instead, the modem hears nothing following the greeting (a certain level of silence that continues for a certain number of seconds), the modem assumes the caller is a data modem and attempts a data connection.

> **TIP**
>
> Do not use vgetty if you expect a large number of voice calls and very few data calls on the phone line you hook up. Most modems will hang up during the incoming message.

Basically the sendfax portion does the following:

- Send faxes directly or using shell scripts.
- Do fax polling. The *polling* means that you can call another fax machine and request data from it.
- Create a fax queue: outgoing faxes get sent automatically, and the user is informed by mail about the result.

You will need the Portable Bitmap Toolkit (pbmplus) for converting from the standard G3 fax format to printable images. The reason is that mgetty itself can only send or receive G3 (raster) format. However, the distribution includes tools to convert raw G3 files to or from the format used by pbmplus. The pbmplus toolkit is available from tsx-11 or sunsite archives. You will have to use the pbmtog3 and g3topbm utilities in mgetty to convert between PBM and G3. Also, the Ghostscript interpreter can convert PostScript to G3, but not vice versa.

To compile the package, copy the policy.h-dist over to the policy.h file. Then run make all to make all the packages.

To enable logins with fax capability, replace the getty with mgetty (or vgetty if your modem can handle voice) for the /dev/tty device you have configured for incoming calls. To send faxes, you have to use sendfax. The syntax for the command is:

```
sendfax [-p]    [-xdebuglevel]   [-v]    [-lmodemlines]
[-minitstring]] [-dpolldirectory] [-Cmodemclass] [-S]
[-n] phone-number [g3file]
```

The options for this command are as follows:

- **-p** Tells sendfax to try fax polling, that is, get any documents queued in the remote fax machine for you.

- **-x** Uses the given level of verbosity for logging—0 means no logging, 5 is really noisy.

- **-v** Gives some progress report on stdout.

- **-l** Uses the given modem lines. Multiple lines can be separated by a colon. Example: sendfax -l tty1a:tty2a

- **-m** Sends an additional init string. This string is sent right after initializing the modem and setting it into Class 2 mode. You can use this to set the speaker value, some special registers, and so on.

  The modem must return "OK." If it returns "ERROR," sendfax prints an error message and aborts. You do not have to prepend the "AT" prefix, but it won't do any harm either.

- **-d** Specifies the directory where polled fax files should go to. Defaults to the directory from which the program was invoked for the current directory. Unused if not polling a fax.

- **-C** The values for class are the type of modem: "auto" (the default), or "cls2."

- **-S** Assumes modem connection on stdin, do not try to lock or initialize anything. To take over existing connections use with a dial string of T1. The T1 command sends out a short beep and no phone number at all. Such a behavior would confuse many modems. In the case of a pulse dialed number, this action may confuse the telco switch. You may also use the -m ATX1 option with the -S option if you do not wait for dial tone.

- **-n** Tells sendfax to send the fax pages in "normal" (204×98 dpi) mode. Default is "fine" mode (204×196 dpi).

Now that we have discussed all these options, you may be happy to know that none of these options are required to send a fax. So the following command by itself will send out a fax:

```
$ sendfax 5551212 sample.g3
```

will send the G3 encoded file fax to the number 5551212. For sending graphic images in the popular PBM format, you can also pipe the output of the pbm2g3 command to sendfax:

```
$ pbm2g3 sample.pbm ¦ sendfax 555-1212
```

The Sticky Copyright Issue

From the FAQ, the note about the copyright is as follows:

"The mgetty +sendfax package is Copyright © 1993 Gert Doering. You are permitted to do anything you want with this program—redistribute it, use parts of the code in your own programs, ..., but you have to give me credit—do not remove my name.

"If the program works for you, and you want to honour my efforts, you are invited to donate as much as you want.

"If you make money with mgetty, I want a share. What I mean by that is: it's perfectly OK with me to get paid for mgetty installation or support, but if you want to actually sell mgetty, or pack mgetty with a modem and sell it as "UNIX FAX package," contact me first."

> ### WARNING
>
> This package is still BETA software. Use it at your own risk, there is NO warranty. If it erases all the data on your hard disk, damages your hardware, or kills your dog, that is entirely your problem. Anyway, the program works for me and quite a lot of other people.
>
> For more info on the copyright issue, please contact Mr. Doering directly.

Troubleshooting the Modems

The FAQ has some interesting questions and answers to the commonly found bugs, "features," and fixes. In most cases, if your modem is not supported, twiddling with a few files here or there will not do the trick. I tried four different types of known name-brand modems before a cheap clone modem worked. I have no idea why this modem, which by the way has no visible markings, worked whereas the others did not. You may have better luck than I did.

In short, trying to fax out of Linux may not be as easy as you think. It's possible, but will take time and effort on your part.

Summary

This is a brief introduction to HylaFAX, a complete fax-handling package for UNIX and Linux. I covered the following items in this chapter.

- How to get HylaFAX for your machine.

- HylaFAX installation involves untarring the source files in a local directory. Then it's a matter of running `configure` to customize the program for your machine and running `make install`. You have to be `root` to install HylaFAX.

- How to check the `MODEMS` file to see whether your modem is supported.

- HylaFAX requires a background daemon `faxd` to handle incoming and outgoing faxes. You have to start the daemon with the `-m` option to specify where your modem exists. You need a FIFO and daemon for each modem on your system.

- The sendfax program requires the Adobe Font Metric files (in `/usr/local/lib/afm`) for converting from text to fax.

- Install Ghostscript before you install the HylaFAX package. This saves you a lot of time and gets rid of most installation problems.

- How to check the status of received or sent faxes with the `faxstat` program.

- The fax daemon, `faxd`, can be configured to answer either data or fax transmissions if `faxd` is invoked with the `-g` argument.

- HylaFAX supports polling via fax machines.

- How to get more information about HylaFAX via the WWW by accessing the Web page `http://www.vix.com/hylafax`.

The source code for HylaFAX is available for public FTP on `ftp.sgi.com` as `/sgi/fax/source/hylaFAX-v3.0.pl0-tar.gz`.

I have also introduced you to `sendfax`, `mgetty`, and `vgetty`. These three programs enable you to send faxes, receive faxes, and even set up voice mail on your Linux box, provided your modem is supported.

Linux Games

60

by Ed Trejis

A variety of games comes with Linux. The games can be roughly divided between those that require the X Window system to run and those that will run in plain text mode. In this chapter, you will learn about both types. The chapter provides a reasonably complete list of both X- and character-based games.

This is the final chapter in the book. We decided to save the most fun and addictive Linux programs for last!

Which Games Have You Installed?

The games listed in this chapter come in several different installation packages, so you might not have one or more of these games on your system. For instance, the graphical version of Tetris, GNU Chess, and Xfractint are each installed separately.

If one of the listed games sounds intriguing, you might want to install it if you haven't done so already.

> **NOTE**
>
> Many more games are available from Internet sites.

X Games

The following games require X Window to run.

As X Window is a graphical, windowing environment, you might guess that X games are graphically oriented. You would be right! Almost all of the following games use color and bitmapped graphics. Often, you can specify the palette of colors the game will use.

However, you should keep in mind the following:

- Arcade games, and home video game systems, have dedicated hardware that is designed specifically for running games. X Window is a generic environment. Even today's powerful personal computers can't match the speed and smoothness of movement of a game machine.

- Games work your hardware and operating system software harder than any other application. For best performance, games are often programmed to run "close to the edge" and do various software and hardware tricks. You might find that one or more of these games will crash your system or have strange side effects.

- The X games that come with Linux are personal efforts. The individuals who wrote the games, and allowed free distribution, appreciate suggestions and help in further development. Don't hold these games to commercial standards—they are not commercial products.

■ The Red Hat version on the CD-ROM will let you install two types games. The "Y" set contains the BSD games collection and the other set "XAP" contains the games with X Window support. Install both versions and then remove the ones you don't like.

> **NOTE**
>
> It's tempting to put new games in /usr/games, though the most common area for user installed games is in /usr/local/games. The /usr/games directory is usually reserved for games that come with the system.

Following is a discussion of the X games you should find on your system. Keep in mind that installation differences might mean that you have more or fewer games.

Games in the *fvwm* Root Menu

If you use the X display manager fvwm, the fvwm Root menu (usually accessed by holding down the left mouse button while the cursor is in the root screen area) has a Games submenu choice. If you use a different window manager, such as Motif, your menus will be correspondingly different.

The menu choices are listed here. Some of the games they start are described in detail later in this chapter.

The Games menu features the following entries:

■ Hextris
■ Xbill
■ Chess (GNU Chess)
■ Xchomp
■ Minesweeper
■ Backgammon
■ Xjewel
■ Xlander
■ Xsnow
■ Tetris (Xtetris)
■ Trojka

X Games Not in the Menus

The following games can be started by typing the appropriate command at the Linux prompt in a command-line window. These, and any other games you may install, can be added to the Games menu if you desire. See Chapter 21, "Installing X Window on Linux," for more information.

- Spider
- Xboing
- Xpaint
- Xcannon
- Xgal
- Xcurling
- attraction
- Xsnooker
- Xcarrom
- Xpool
- Xhockey
- hopalong
- Xdino
- Xevil

Look in the /usr/x11/bin directory for still more games not listed here.

Spider (Small and Large)

This is double-deck solitaire. To see this game's man page, type man spider. To start this game, type spider in a command-line window.

This game requires a fair bit of thought, planning, and skill. The aim is to arrange cards of the same suit in descending order. You can also, however, have cards of different suits arranged in descending order. Sometimes this can help you immediately, but hinder you in the long run! Note that, if you do have two or more consecutive cards of the same suit, the cards will move as a group. Spider is challenging; don't try to play it just to pass the time!

GNU Chess

This is a graphical version of GNU Chess that uses the xboard display system.

> **WARNING**
>
> Running GNU Chess under xboard is very resource-intensive. It may crash your system.
>
> Adding more swap space may correct an agonizingly long response time. Do not worry, it's not your system, it's GNU Chess.

Xtetris

If you've never been hooked on Tetris, here's your chance. This is a nice X implementation of a game that always seems to suffer when taken from the video arcade and placed on a home computer.

To see this game's man page, type `man xtetris`.

To start this game, type `xtetris` in a command-line window.

The colors are nicely done, and the movement is relatively smooth. However, if you're used to the arcade version of Tetris, watch out for the following:

- Left and right arrow keys move from side to side; up and down arrow keys rotate clockwise and counterclockwise. Most people have a preferred direction of rotation for the pieces; experiment to find out which way is right for you.

- The spacebar, as is usual on home-computer implementation, slam-dunks the piece to the bottom rather than just hauling it down faster.

- The colors of the pieces, though attractive, are sometimes confusing. For instance, the L-shaped piece that is yellow in the arcade version is purple in xtetris, and the L-shaped piece that is purple in the arcade version is light blue in xtetris. Again, very confusing if you're used to the arcade version.

The purpose of the game? Arrange the pieces so they interlock without gaps. As soon as you create a (horizontal) row that's completely filled, it vaporizes. This is good, because when the pieces stack up to the top, the game is over. (Pity the Cossack doesn't come out and tap his feet when things start to get a little out of control.)

Xlander

This is an update of the old arcade game, Lunar Lander. You get a bird's-eye view from the window of your lunar lander. By operating the main and directional thruster engines, you attempt to touch down softly on the landing pad. If things go wrong, instead of a bird's-eye view, you get a meteorite's-eye view!

To see this game's man page, type `man xlander`.

To start this game, type `xlander` in a command-line window.

You may have problems getting the game to respond to your keyboard input. In that case, the moon's surface is only a short plummet away.

Ico

Ico sets a polyhedron (a solid, multisided geometric shape) bouncing around your screen. Depending on the options specified, this three-dimensional polygon can occupy its own window or use the entire root window.

To see this game's man page, type `man ico`. It can be started from the command line (within X Window) by typing `ico`. In fact, you *should* start it from the command line because of the options available. If you start it from the Demo/Gadgets menu, you will only get a wireframe polygon in its own, small window.

One interesting option you can use from the command line is `-colors`. If you specify more than one color, you get a multicolored polyhedron, with each face a different color.

With the `-colors` option, you must type in the colors to be used in the following format: `rgb:<red intensity>/<green intensity>/<blue intensity>`. The intensities have to be specified in hexadecimal notation; `000` is the lowest value and `fff` is the highest. For example, the complete command might be

```
ico -colors rgb:000/888/fff rgb:e00/400/b80 rgb:123/789/def
```

This program is fairly resource-intensive and might slow down your system.

Maze

This draws a maze, and then solves it. There is no way you can solve it for yourself. Maze is a demo, not a game. On a fast system, it solves it too quickly to follow!

Xeyes

Not really a game, but cute anyway. Whenever you start Xeyes, you get a large pair of bodiless eyes that follow your cursor's movements. Running four or five copies of Xeyes at once gives your system a surrealistic touch.

To see this game's man page, type `man xeyes`.

To start this game, type `xeyes` in a command-line window.

Xlogo

This displays the official X logo.

Xhextris

This is a version of Tetris that uses pieces made up of hexagons. To start the game, type `xhextris` on an X Window command line. No man page is available.

Minesweeper

You are given a large grid. Some of the squares contain mines. Your job is to flag all of the mines.

This game is started by typing `xdemineur` at the Linux prompt in a command-line window.

Starting Minesweeper brings up the playing field, which is a dark gray grid, and a Score window.

You uncover a square by clicking on it with the left mouse button. If you uncover a mine, you are blown up and the game is over!

It's more likely, though, that you will either uncover a number or open up several light gray, blank squares (with no numbers or mines). The number tells you how many mines are found adjacent to that square, horizontally, vertically, or diagonally. For example, a "1" means there is only one mine adjacent to that square. If you've already determined the location of one mine adjacent to a "1" square, then it's safe to uncover all other squares next to the "1" square because they can't possibly contain a mine! In this fashion, you try to deduce the location of the mines. If you happen to uncover a square that has no number (and therefore no mines next to it), the game will automatically uncover the entire numberless area and its border.

When you think you've located a mine, you "sweep" or mark it by clicking on it with the *right* mouse button (if you click the left button accidentally, and there is indeed a mine there, the game is over). The right button toggles on and off a flag marker. Note that the game does not tell you whether you have correctly placed the flag.

You will soon discover that certain patterns of numbers let you place a mine without any doubt; other times, you have to make an educated guess.

Of course, sometimes you miscalculate and blow up. To restart the game, click with either mouse button in the Score window. If you complete the game successfully, your time will be recorded.

Xpaint

This is a color drawing-and-painting program. Start it from the Linux prompt in a command-line window by typing xpaint. A Tool menu will appear. Start a new canvas from the File menu. The Tool menu holds your drawing and painting implements (brushes, pencils, spray cans, and so on); the palette of colors and patterns is found underneath the canvas.

To see the man page, type man xpaint.

Character-Based Games

There is a long history of games being written for the UNIX operating system. Your Linux /usr/games directory contains a number of these games, from various time periods.

Many of these games were written before color, bitmapped windowing systems became common. Most of the games in /usr/games (except for Tetris, for instance) are character-based. This means that graphics (if there are any!) are displayed on your screen using standard screen characters: A, *, ¦, x, and so on. In addition, all input is from the keyboard.

An advantage of character-based games is that they do not require a graphical or windowing environment to run. A monochrome display is fine.

The character-based nature of some games, such as Hangman or Bog (Boggle), takes nothing away from the play; you don't really wish for fancy color graphics when playing them. Other character-based games might strike you as interesting historical curiosities: they show you what their ingenious programmers could manage with such a simple display system, but clearly would be better served by color graphics.

A Summary of Games in */usr/games*

The games found in /usr/games can be roughly categorized into the following types:

- Text adventure: Battlestar; Paranoia; Wump
- Word games: Bog (Boggle); Hangman
- Card games: Canfield; Cribbage; Go Fish
- Board games: Backgammon; GNU Chess; Mille Miglia; Monop (Monopoly)
- Simulations: ATC (air traffic control); Trek
- Character-based "video" games: Robots, Snake, Tetris, Worm
- Math games/utilities: arithmetic; bcd, Morse, and ppt; Factor; Primes
- Full graphics games: DOOM
- Miscellaneous demos and utilities: Caesar; Fortune; Number; Rain; and Worms

---

TIP

Two of the more interesting character-based games, Rogue and Hack, do not come with the Linux distribution. These games use the screen to display the rooms and corridors of a dungeon. You (and, in Hack, your trusty dog) move around the dungeon, mapping out the corridors, entering the rooms (be careful when you explore dark, unlit rooms), picking up treasure and magical items—and, last but not least, fighting monsters (or running from them!). After you have fully explored the level you're on, you can descend to a lower, more difficult level.

Every time you run Hack or Rogue, the dungeons are different. Every monster has different fighting skills, and some monsters have special talents. The magical items, which include rings, wands, scrolls, and potions, have a variety of effects. Some of the items you find, such as armor, might be enchanted or magically enhanced; but if you find a cursed item, you may have been better off not picking it up at all!

Both Rogue and Hack have their enthusiasts, but Hack is a later, more elaborate version that is generally preferred. If you come across either game on the Internet, pick it up and try it! There are also versions of Hack available for MS-DOS-based computers.

Text Adventure Games

These games follow the classic text-based formula: the system informs you that "you are in a maze of small twisty passages, all alike" or something similar; you type in your actions as go forward, east, take sword, and so on. If you like solving puzzles, these games will appeal to you. With text-based games, the adventure follows a defined path, and your responses are usually limited.

The following example is the start of the text-based game Battlestar, which you will learn about in the next section. Your commands are typed at the >-: prompt:

```
Version 4.2, fall 1984.
First Adventure game written by His Lordship, the honorable
Admiral D.W. Riggle


             This is a luxurious stateroom.
The floor is carpeted with a soft animal fur and the great wooden furniture
is inlaid with strips of platinum and gold.  Electronic equipment built
into the walls and ceiling is flashing wildly.  The floor shudders and
the sounds of dull explosions rumble though the room.  From a window in
the wall ahead comes a view of darkest space.  There is a small adjoining
room behind you, and a doorway right.

>-: right
           These are the executive suites of the battlestar.
Luxurious staterooms carpeted with crushed velvet and adorned with beaten
gold open onto this parlor. A wide staircase with ivory banisters leads
up or down. This parlor leads into a hallway left. The bridal suite is right.
Other rooms lie ahead and behind you.

>-: up
         You are at the entrance to the dining hall.
A wide staircase with ebony banisters leads down here.
The dining hall is to the ahead.

>-: quit
Your rating was novice.
```

Battlestar

Type battlestar at the command prompt. A sample session is shown in the code in the previous section. A man page is available by typing man battlestar.

Paranoia

Type paranoia at the command prompt. In this humorous game, you play a secret agent on a desperate mission. Unlike most text-based adventure games, Paranoia lets you choose your actions from a menu. This is useful if you hate having to find a command that the game will understand. There is no man page for Paranoia.

Wump

Type wump at the command prompt. You are out hunting the Wumpus, armed with some custom arrows and relying on your wit and sense of smell. When you start the game, you are given the choice of seeing the instructions.

Type man wump to see the man page.

Word Games

The following two games are versions of popular word-finding and word-guessing games.

Boggle

Type bog at the command prompt. This is a version of the Parker Brothers game Boggle Deluxe. You are given a 5×5 grid of letters. In the allotted time of three minutes, you type in words made up from the given letters. By default, you must use letters that adjoin horizontally, vertically, and diagonally, without reusing any letters. Plurals and different tenses count as different words—for instance, "use," "uses," "used," and "user" are all allowed in your word list. This follows the official Boggle rules. You can change these defaults, if you want.

At the end, the computer displays the list of words which it found. You can never beat the computer, because it only allows you to type in real words. You will discover that the Boggle dictionary has some odd omissions; this can be annoying, but it isn't very serious.

This game works well without color graphics, although the small size of the letter grid makes your eyes blur after a while.

Hangman

Type hangman at the command prompt. You won't miss the color graphics. The game is self-explanatory, but just in case, a man page is available; type man hangman. Hangman picks its words at random; sometimes the choices seem quite impossible to guess.

Card Games

Because of the lack of graphics, the following games are not as successful as the character-based word games.

Canfield

Type canfield at the command prompt. This is a version of solitaire. A man page is available by typing man canfield. This game does not have the time-wasting potential of graphics and mouse-based solitaire games.

Cribbage

Type `cribbage` at the command prompt. If you're a cribbage fan, this game is for you. A man page is available by typing `man cribbage`.

Go Fish

Type `fish` at the command prompt. It's you against the computer at Go Fish. A man page is available by typing `man fish`. One confusing aspect is that sometimes several actions are displayed all together on the screen (for instance, you have to go fish, the computer has to go fish, and it's back to you, all in one block).

Board Games

These are character-based versions of board games. The play quality is variable; Backgammon is probably the best of the lot.

Backgammon

Type `backgammon` at the command prompt; or, for an easy-to-follow tutorial on how to play Backgammon, type `teachgammon`. These games don't suffer from lack of graphics, but the lack of a pointing device such as a mouse means that specifying your moves is a cumbersome task, requiring entries such as `8-12,4-5`. Typing `?` at the game prompt gives you help on entering your moves.

Typing `man backgammon` will give you the manual entry for both Backgammon and Teachgammon.

Chess

Several chess and chess-related programs come in the GNU Chess package. Type `gnuchess` at the prompt to play chess against the computer. There is an analysis program, `gnuan`. The game utility prints the chessboard position to a PostScript printer or file.

Enter your moves using standard algebraic notation—for instance, e2-4.

This is an elaborate package; you should start by reading the man page.

> **NOTE**
>
> There seem to be some problems with startup messages overwriting parts of the chessboard.

Mille Miglia

Type `mille` at the command prompt. This is the Linux version of a Parker Brothers racing game. You should read the man page before starting, because the game's commands are not very intuitive. To see the man page, type `man mille`.

Monopoly

Type monop at the command prompt. This is a character-based version of the Parker Brothers game Monopoly. The computer does not actually play; it simply keeps track of who owns what and how much money each player has. You can play by yourself, but it's pretty obvious that you will, eventually, win! Unfortunately, the board is not displayed in any form, making it quite difficult to keep track of what's happening. This is an interesting effort, but the play is poor. A man page is available.

Simulations

The following games let you try your hand at being in charge. They are open-ended, in that each game is different and does not follow a canned plot. They combine character graphics, for instance, a radar display, with text readouts and text-based commands.

Air Traffic Control

Type atc at the command prompt. Type man atc and read the man page first; otherwise, you will be responsible for one or more air tragedies! This game runs in real time. A good supply of caffeine will probably help you do well.

Trek

Type trek at the command prompt. You can "go where no one has gone before," hunt (and be hunted by) Klingons, and so on. A man page is available by typing man trek; read it before playing to avoid being a disgrace to the Federation.

"Video" Games

The following games all rely on a full-screen display, although all graphics are assembled from the standard character set.

Robots

Type robots at the command prompt. Robots on the screen pursue you; your only hope is to make two robots collide, at which point the robots explode. The resulting junk heap destroys any robots that run into it. You move about the screen using the hjkl keys, as used by the vi editor (diagonal movement is allowed, using yubn). Moves are simultaneous: each time you move, so do the robots. Sometimes, though, you have to teleport to get out of an impossible situation. You die if a robot touches you; otherwise, after clearing the screen, you go on to a bigger and better wave of robots. A man page is available by typing man robots.

> **NOTE**
>
> Some Linux distributions might include a version of Robots that has been hacked or modified so that you can't make a misstep that brings you in contact with a robot (thus leading to your demise). This takes away from the challenge of the game.

Tetris

Type `tetris` at the command prompt. Ironically, although it does not look anywhere near as professional as Xtetris or other full-graphics versions, it plays very well—especially if you're used to the arcade version of Tetris. Use the arrow keys for piece movement and rotation.

Worm

Type `worm` at the command prompt. You are a worm, moving about the screen and eating numbers. As you eat the numbers, you grow in length. Do not run into yourself or into the wall! How long can you get before you (inevitably) run into something? Note that you still slowly crawl forward, even if you don't enter a move command.

A man page is available by typing `man worm`.

Math Games and Utilities

The following programs are small and interesting, although perhaps not that exciting.

Arithmetic

Type `arithmetic` at the command prompt. You are asked the answer to simple addition questions. This goes on until you type Ctrl-C to exit. A man page is available by typing `man arithmetic`.

BCD Punch Card Code, Morse Code, Paper Tape Punch Code

Type `bcd` at the command line to convert text you type to a punched card, type `morse` to see your text converted to Morse code, or type `ppt` for paper punch tape output. If the command line doesn't contain any text to encode, the programs go into interactive mode. Note that the Enter character you must use to finish each line of input gets coded as well. The `bcd` man page covers all three programs.

Factor

Type `factor` at the command line. This command provides you with the prime factors of any number you supply. You can type `factor <number>` to factor just the one number, or `factor` without any number to go into interactive mode. Numbers can range from –2,147,483,648 to 2,147,483,648. The following is a sample run of Factor:

```
d$ factor
123
123: 3 41
36
36: 2 2 3 3
1234567
1234567: 127 9721
6378172984028367
factor: ouch
d$
```

Primes

Type primes at the command prompt. If you include a range on the command line, Primes displays all prime numbers in the range. If no range is included, Primes waits for you to enter a number, and then starts displaying primes greater than that number. The program is surprisingly fast! A man page is available by typing man primes.

Other Thinking Games

The following programs might actually be a bit frustrating to play with initially, but they can also provide hours of addiction!

Sokoban

Imagine yourself in charge of a warehouse containing a maze and lots of bales of cotton. Each bale is so heavy that you can only push it and not pull it. So don't push a bale into a spot where you cannot push it out. Each level in this game gets more and more challenging as you attempt to collect all the bales into a loading area where you can move to the next level. The source code is available from sunsite.unc.edu in the file sokoban-src.tar.gz.

DOOM

This exciting, though controversially gory, game is now ported to Linux as well. Complete with sound support and exquisite graphics, this Linux port does its DOS counterpart justice. One problem to keep in mind though, is that your colormaps in X may be mixed up once your cursor moves out of the X terminal you run DOOM under. Two other things to keep in mind—you have to rebuild your kernel to add the sound support, and the version 1.666 of DOOM will not run external WAD files. (I recommend that you get the registered version.)

Conquest

This is an elaborate game of global conquest with equally complex instructions and display. At least the files are in an executable form, and you do not have to build them. One thing to remember is to use the xconq file and run xset fp rehash to bring up the correct fonts. A comparable game, called Empire, is also available in source from tsx-11.mit.edu, but you need a network connection to run this game.

Miscellaneous Demos and Utilities

The following programs might interest you.

Caesar

Type caesar at the command line. This program attempts to decrypt encoded words. Type man caesar to see the man page.

Fortune

Type fortune at the command line for your Linux fortune-cookie message.

Number

Type number *<number>* at the command line. Converts the Arabic number given as *<number>* (for example, 41) to its equivalent in English (forty-one).

Rain

Type rain at the command prompt. Your screen becomes rippled like a puddle in a rainstorm. On most Linux console screens, the program runs too fast to look even remotely convincing. Press Ctrl-C to exit.

Worms

Type worms at the command prompt (do not confuse with the Worm program described previously). This fills your screen with squirming worms. Like Rain, the program runs much too fast on a Linux console screen. A man page is available by typing man worms.

Summary

You should now be able to while away the time by sitting at your machine and playing your favorite games. If you haven't installed the X Window system yet, maybe this is an extra incentive!

PART

IN THIS PART

Appendixes

Linux FTP Sites and Newsgroups

If you have access to the Internet, either directly or through an online service provider such as CompuServe, Delphi, or America Online, you can access additional sources of Linux software and information. There are two popular sources of Linux software and help available, one through FTP and the other through Linux-specific Usenet newsgroups.

If you don't have access to the Internet, you may still be able to get some of the information available through other sources, such as Bulletin Board Systems (BBSes) and CD-ROMs published by companies specializing in redistributing public domain material.

FTP Sites

FTP is a method of accessing remote systems and downloading files. It is quite easy to use and provides users with Internet access and a fast method for updating their list of binaries.

For those without FTP access, but who can use electronic mail through the Internet, the utility `ftpmail` can provide access to these FTP sites.

What Is FTP?

File Transfer Protocol (FTP) is one protocol in the TCP/IP family of protocols. TCP/IP is used extensively as the communications protocol of the Internet, as well as in many Local Area Networks (LANs). UNIX systems almost always use TCP/IP as their protocol.

FTP is used to transfer files between machines running TCP/IP. FTP-like programs are also available for some other protocols.

To use FTP, both ends of a connection must be running a program that provides FTP services. To download a file from a remote system, you must start your FTP software and instruct it to connect to the FTP software running on the remote machine.

The Internet has many FTP *archive sites*. These are machines that are set up to allow anyone to connect to them and download software. In some cases, there are FTP archive sites that mirror each other. A *mirror site* is one that maintains exactly the same software as another site, so you simply connect to the one that is easiest for you to access, and you have the same software available for downloading as if you had connected to the other site.

Usually, when you connect to a remote system, you must log in. This means you must be a valid user, with a username and password for that remote machine. Because it is impossible to provide logins for everyone who wants to access a public archive, many systems use anonymous FTP. *Anonymous FTP* enables anyone to log into the system with the login name of `guest` or `anonymous` and either no password or the login name for the user's local system (used for auditing purposes only).

Connecting and Downloading Files with FTP

Using FTP to connect to a remote site is quite easy. Assuming you have access to the Internet either directly or through a service provider, you must start FTP and provide the name of the remote system to which you want to connect. If you are directly connected to the Internet, the process is simple: you enter the ftp command with the name of the remote site:

```
ftp sunsite.unc.edu
```

If you are using an online service, such as Delphi, you must access its Internet services menus and invoke FTP from that. Some online services allow you to enter the name of any FTP site at a prompt, whereas others have some menus that list all available sites. You may have to hunt through the online documentation for your service provider to find the correct procedure.

After you issue the FTP command, your system will attempt to connect to the remote machine. When it does (and assuming the remote system allows FTP logins), the remote will prompt you for a user ID. If anonymous FTP is supported on the system, a message will usually tell you that. The login below is shown for the Linux FTP archive site sunsite.unc.edu:

```
$ ftp sunsite.unc.edu
Connected to fddisunsite.oit.unc.edu.
220 helios FTP server (Version wu-2.4(39) Tue May 16 01:34:21 EDT 1995) ready.
Name (sunsite.unc.edu:username): anonymous
331 Guest login ok, send your complete e-mail address as password.
Password:
230 Guest login ok, access restrictions apply.
Remote system type is UNIX.
Using binary mode to transfer files.
ftp>
```

After the login process is completed, you will see the prompt ftp>, indicating the system is ready to accept commands. When you log into some systems, you will see a short message that might contain instructions for downloading files, any restrictions that are placed on you as an anonymous FTP user, or information about the location of useful files. For example, you might see messages like this:

```
To get a binary file, type:  BINARY and then: GET "File.Name" newfilename
To get a text file, type:    ASCII  and then: GET "File.Name" newfilename
Names MUST match upper, lower case exactly. Use the "quotes" as shown.
To get a directory, type: DIR. To change directory, type: CD "Dir.Name"
To read a short text file, type: GET "File.Name" TT
For more, type HELP or see FAQ in gopher.
To quit, type EXIT or Control-Z.

230- If you email to info@sunsite.unc.edu you will be sent help information
230- about how to use the different services sunsite provides.
230- We use the Wuarchive experimental ftpd. if you "get" <directory>.tar.Z
230- or <file>.Z it will compress and/or tar it on the fly. Using ".gz" instead
230- of ".Z" will use the GNU zip (/pub/gnu/gzip*) instead, a superior
230- compression method.
```

After you are connected to the remote system, you can use familiar Linux commands to display file contents and move around the directories. To display the contents of a directory, for example, use the command ls or the DOS equivalent dir. To change to a subdirectory, use the cd command. To return to the parent directory (the one above the current directory), use the command cdup or cd ... There are no keyboard shortcuts available with FTP, so you have to type in the name of files or directories in their entirety.

When you have moved through the directories and have found a file you want to move back to your home system, use the get command:

```
get "file1.txt"
```

The commands get (download) and put (upload) are relative to your home machine. You are telling your system to get a file from the remote location and put it on your local machine, or to put a file from your local machine onto the remote machine. This is the exact opposite of another commonly used TCP/IP protocol, telnet, which has everything relative to the remote machine. It is important to remember which command moves in which direction, or you could overwrite files accidentally.

The quotation marks around the filename are optional for most versions of FTP, but they do provide specific characters to the remote version (preventing shell expansion), so the quotation marks should be used to avoid mistakes. FTP provides two modes of file transfer: ASCII and binary. Some systems will automatically switch between the two, but it is a good idea to manually set the mode to ensure you don't waste time. To set FTP in binary transfer mode (for any executable file), type the command

```
binary
```

You can toggle back to ASCII mode with the command ASCII. As you will most likely be checking remote sites for new binaries or libraries of source code, it is a good idea to use binary mode for most transfers. If you transfer a binary file in ASCII mode, it will not be executable (or understandable) on your system. ASCII mode includes only the valid ASCII characters and not the Ctrl-key sequences used within binaries. Transferring an ASCII file in binary mode does not affect the contents, although spurious noise may cause a problem in rare instances.

When you issue a get command, the remote system will transfer data to your local machine and display a status message when it is finished. There is no indication of progress when a large file is being transferred, so be patient.

```
ftp> get file1.txt
200 PORT command successful.
150 BINARY data connection for FILE1.TXT (27534 bytes)
226 BINARY Transfer complete.
27534 bytes received in 2.35 seconds (12 Kbytes/s).
```

To quit FTP, type the command quit, which will close your session on the remote machine and then terminate FTP on your local machine.

Using *ftpmail*

If you don't have access to a remote site through FTP, all is not lost. If you have electronic mail, you can still get files transferred to you. Some online systems allow Internet mail to be sent and received, but do not allow direct access to FTP. Similarly, some Internet service providers offer UUCP accounts that do not allow direct connection but do provide e-mail. To get to FTP sites and transfer files, you use the ftpmail utility.

The site mentioned previously, `sunsite.unc.edu`, is a major Linux archive site that supports `ftpmail`. All of the sites listed in this appendix as Linux FTP sites also support `ftpmail`. To find out how to use `ftpmail`, send an e-mail message to the login `ftpmail` at one of the sites, such as `ftpmail@sunsite.unc.edu`, and have the body of the message contain only one word: `help`.

By return mail, the `ftpmail` utility will send instructions for using the service. Essentially, you send the body of the FTP commands you want executed in a mail message, so you could get back a directory listing of the Linux directory in a mail message with this text:

```
open sunsite.unc.edu
cd /pub/Linux
ls
quit
```

You could transfer a file back through e-mail with a similar mail message:

```
open sunsite.unc.edu
cd /pub/Linux
binary
get README
quit
```

The `ftpmail` system is relatively slow, as you must wait for the e-mail to make its way to the target machine and be processed by the remote, then for the return message to make its way back to you. It does provide a useful access method for those without FTP connections, though, and a relatively easy way to check the contents of the Linux directories on several machines.

Linux FTP Archive Sites

The list of Linux FTP archive sites changes slowly, but the sites listed in Table A.1 were all valid and reachable when this book was written. Many of these sites are mirror sites, providing exactly the same contents.

To find the site nearest you, use the country identifier at the end of the site name (`fi`=Finland, `fr`=France, and so on). Most versions of FTP allow either the machine name or the IP address to be used, but if the name cannot be resolved by the local Internet gateway, the IP address is the best addressing method.

Table A.1. Linux FTP archive sites.

Site Name	IP Address	Directory
tsx-11.mit.edu	18.86.0.44	/pub/linux
sunsite.unc.edu	152.2.254.81	/pub/Linux
nic.funet.fi	128.214.248.6	/pub/Linux
ftp.dfv.rwth-aachen.de	137.226.4.111	/pub/linux
ftp.ibp.fr	132.227.77.2	/pub2/linux

continues

Table A.1. continued

Site Name	IP Address	Directory
`ftp.uu.net`	`192.48.96.9`	`/`
`wuarchive.wustl.edu`	`128.252.135.4`	`/systems/linux`
`ftp.win.tue.nl`	`131.155.70.19`	`/pub/linux`
`ftp.ibr.cs.tu-bs.de`	`134.169.34.15`	`/pub/linux`
`ftp.denet.dk`	`129.142.6.74`	`/pub/OS/Linux`

The primary home sites for the Linux archives are `tsx-11.mit.edu`, `sunsite.unc.edu`, and `nic.funet.fi`. *Home sites* are where most of the new software loads begin. The majority of sites in Table A.1 mirror one of these three sites.

Bulletin Boards

There are literally hundreds of Bulletin Board Systems (BBSes) across the world that offer Linux software. Some download new releases on a regular basis from the FTP home sites, whereas others rely on the users of the BBS to update the software.

A complete list of BBSes with Linux software available would be too lengthy (as well as out-of-date almost immediately) to include here. Zane Healy maintains a complete list of BBSes offering Linux material. To obtain the list, send e-mail requesting the Linux list to `healyzh@holonet.net`.

If you don't have access to e-mail, try posting messages on a few local bulletin board systems asking for local sites that offer Linux software, or ask someone with Internet access to post e-mail for you.

LINUX-related BBSes

Zane Healy (`healyzh@holonet.net`) maintains this list. If you know of or run a BBS that provides Linux software but isn't on this list, you should get in touch with him.

You can also get an up-to-date list on BBSes from `tsx-11.mit.edu` in the `/pub/linux/docs/bbs.list` file. The lists shown below were up-to-date at the time we went to print.

United States BBSes

Here is a list of some of the BBSes in the United States that carry Linux or information about Linux:

> 1 Zero Cybernet BBS, (301) 589-4064. MD.
>
> AVSync, (404) 320-6202. Atlanta, GA.
>
> Allentown Technical, (215) 432-5699. 9600 v.32/v.42bis Allentown, PA. WWIVNet 2578
>
> Acquired Knowledge, (305) 720-3669. 14.4k v.32bis Ft. Lauderdale, FL. Internet, UUCP

Atlanta Radio Club, (404) 850-0546. 9600 Atlanta, GA.

Brodmann's Place, (301) 843-5732. 14.4k Waldorf, MD.
RIME ->BRODMANN, Fidonet

Centre Programmers Unit, (814) 353-0566. 14.4k V.32bis/HST Bellefonte, PA.

Channel One, (617) 354-8873. Boston, MA. RIME ->CHANNEL

Citrus Grove Public Access, (916) 381-5822. ZyXEL 16.8/14.4 Sacramento, CA.

CyberVille, (817) 249-6261. 9600 TX. FidoNet 1:130/78

Digital Designs, (919) 423-4216. 14.4k, 2400 Hope Mills, NC.

Digital Underground, (812) 941-9427. 14.4k v.32bis IN. Usenet

Dwight-Englewood BBS, (201) 569-3543. 9600 v.42 Englewood, NJ. Usenet

EchoMania, (618) 233-1659. 14.4k HST Belleville, IL. Fidonet 1:2250/1

Enlightend, (703) 370-9528. 14.4k Alexandria, VA. Fidonet 1:109/615

Flite Line, (402) 421-2434. Lincoln, NE. RIME ->FLITE, DS modem

Georgia Peach BBS, (804) 727-0399. 14.4k Newport News, VA.

Harbor Heights BBS, (207) 663-0391. 14.4k Boothbay Harbor, ME.

Horizon Systems, (216) 899-1293. 2400 Westlake, OH.

Information Overload, (404) 471-1549. 19.2k ZyXEL Atlanta, GA. Fidonet 1:133/308

Intermittent Connection, (503) 344-9838. 14.4k HST v.32bis Eugene, OR. 1:152/35

Horizon Systems, (216) 899-1086. USR v.32 Westlake, OH.

Legend, (402) 438-2433. Lincoln, NE. DS modem

Lost City Atlantis, (904) 727-9334. 14.4k Jacksonville, FL. Fidonet

MAC's Place, (919) 891-1111. 16.8k, DS modem Dunn, NC. RIME ->MAC

MBT, (703) 953-0640. Blacksburg, VA.

Main Frame, (301) 654-2554. 9600 Gaithersburg, MD. RIME ->MAINFRAME

MegaByte Mansion, (402) 551-8681. 14.4 V,32bis Omaha, NE.

Micro Oasis, (510) 895-5985. 14.4k San Leandro, CA.

My UnKnown BBS, (703) 690-0669. 14.4k V.32bis VA. Fidonet 1:109/370

Mycroft QNX, (201) 858-3429. 14.4k NJ.

NOVA, (703) 323-3321. 9600 Annandale, VA. Fidonet 1:109/305

North Shore BBS, (713) 251-9757. Houston, TX.

PBS BBS, (309) 663-7675. 2400 Bloomington, IL.

Part-Time BBS, (612) 544-5552. 14.4k v.32bis Plymouth, MN.

Programmer's Center, (301) 596-1180. 9600 Columbia, MD. RIME

Programmer's Exchange, (818) 444-3507. El Monte, CA. Fidonet

Programmer's Exchange, (818) 579-9711. El Monte, CA.

Rebel BBS, (208) 887-3937. 9600 Boise, ID.

Rem-Jem, (703) 503-9410. 9600 Fairfax, VA.

Rocky Mountain HUB, (208) 232-3405. 38.4k Pocatello, ID.
Fidonet, SLNet, CinemaNet

Ronin BBS, (214) 938-2840. 14.4 HST/DS Waxahachie (Dallas), TX.

S'Qually Holler, (206) 235-0270. 14.4k USR D/S Renton, WA.

Slut Club, (813) 975-2603. USR/DS 16.8k HST/14.4K Tampa, FL. Fidonet 1:377/42

Steve Leon's, (201) 886-8041. 14.4k Cliffside Park, NJ.

Tactical-Operations, (814) 861-7637. 14.4k V32bis/V42bis State College, PA.
Fidonet 1:129/226, tac_ops.UUCP

Test Engineering, (916) 928-0504. Sacramento, CA.

The Annex, (512) 575-0667. 2400 TX. Fidonet 1:3802/216

The Annex, (512) 575-1188. 9600 HST TX. Fidonet 1:3802/217

The Computer Mechanic, (813) 544-9345. 14.4k v.32bis

The Laboratory, (212) 927-4980. 16.8k HST, 14.4k v.32bis NY. Fidonet 1:278/707

The Mothership Connection, (908) 940-1012. 38.4k Franklin Park, NJ.

The OA Southern Star, (504) 885-5928. New Orleans, LA. Fidonet 1:396/1

The Outer Rim, (805) 252-6342. Santa Clarita, CA.

The Sole Survivor, (314) 846-2702. 14.4k v.32bis St. Louis, MO.
WWIVnet, WWIVlink, and so on.

Third World, (217) 356-9512. 9600 v.32 IL.

Top Hat BBS, (206) 244-9661. 14.4k WA. Fidonet 1:343/40

UNIX USER, (708) 879-8633. 14.4k Batavia, IL. Usenet, Internet mail

Unix Online, (707) 765-4631. 9600 Petaluma, CA. Usenet access

VTBBS, (703) 231-7498. Blacksburg, VA.

VWIS Linux Support BBS, (508) 793-1570. 9600 Worcester, MA.

Valhalla, (516) 321-6819. 14.4k HST v.32 Babylon, NY.
Fidonet (1:107/25 5), Usenet

Walt Fairs, (713) 947-9866. Houston, TX. Fidonet 1:106/18

WaterDeep BBS, (410) 614-2190. 9600 v.32 Baltimore, MD.

WayStar BBS, (508) 480-8371. 9600 V.32bis or 14.4k USR/HST Marlborough, MA.
Fidonet 1:333/16

WayStar BBS, (508) 481-7147. 14.4k V.32bis USR/HST Marlborough, MA.
Fidonet 1:333 /14

WayStar BBS, (508) 481-7293. 14.4k V.32bis USR/HST Marlborough, MA.
Fidonet 1:333 /15

alaree, (512) 575-5554. 14.4k Victoria, TX.

hip-hop, (408) 773-0768. 19.2k Sunnyvale, CA. Usenet access

hip-hop, (408) 773-0768. 38.4k Sunnyvale, CA.

splat-ooh, (512) 578-2720. 14.4k Victoria, TX.

splat-ooh, (512) 578-5436. 14.4k Victoria, TX.

victrola.sea.wa.us, (206) 838-7456. 19.2k Federal Way, WA. Usenet

Outside of the United States

If you live outside the United States, you can get information about Linux from these BBSes:

500cc Formula 1 BBS, +61-2-550-4317. V.32bis Sydney, NSW, Australia.

A6 BBS, +44-582-460273. 14.4k Herts, UK. Fidonet 2:440/111

Advanced Systems, +64-9-379-3365. ZyXEL 16.8k Auckland, New Zealand.

BOX/2, +49.89.601-96-77. 16.8 ZYX Muenchen, BAY, Germany.

Baboon BBS, +41-62-511726. 19.2k Switzerland.

Basil, +33-1-44670844. v.32bis Paris, Laurent Chemla, France.

BigBrother / R. Gmelch, +49.30.335-63-28. 16.8 Z16 Berlin, BLN, Germany.

Bit-Company / J. Bartz, +49.5323.2539. 16.8 ZYX MO Clausthal-Zfd., NDS, Germany

CRYSTAL BBS, +49.7152.240-86. 14.4 HST Leonberg, BW, Germany.

CS-Port / C. Schmidt, +49.30.491-34-18. 19.2 Z19 Berlin, BLN, Germany.

Cafard Naum, +33-51701632. v.32bis Nantes, Yann Dupont, France.

DUBBS, +353-1-6789000. 19.2 ZyXEL Dublin, Ireland. Fidonet 2:263/167

DataComm1, +49.531.132-16. 14.4 HST Braunschweig, NDS, Germany.
Fidonet 2:240/55

DataComm2, +49.531.132-17. 14.4 HST Braunschweig, NDS, Germany.
Fidonet 2:240/55

Die Box Passau 2+1, +49.851.555-96. 14.4 V32b Passau, BAY, Germany.

Die Box Passau ISDN, +49.851.950-464. 38.4/64k V.110/X.75 Passau, BAY, Germany.

Die Box Passau Line 1, +49.851.753-789. 16.8 ZYX Passau, BAY, Germany.

Die Box Passau Line 3, +49.851.732-73. 14.4 HST Passau, BAY, Germany.

DownTown BBS Lelystad, +31-3200-48852. 14.4k Lelystad, Netherlands.

Echoblaster BBS #1, +49.7142.213-92. HST/V32b Bietigheim, BW, Germany.

Echoblaster BBS #2, +49.7142.212-35. V32b Bietigheim, BW, Germany.

FORMEL-Box, +49.4191.2846. 16.8 ZYX Kaltenkirchen, SHL, Germany.

Fiffis Inn BBS, +49-89-5701353. 14.4-19.2 Munich, Germany.

Fractal Zone BBS /Maass, +49.721.863-066. 16.8 ZYX Karlsruhe, BW, Germany.

Galaktische Archive, 0043-2228303804. 16.8 ZYX Wien, Austria.
Fidonet 2:310/77 (19:00-7:00)

Galway Online, +353-91-27454. 14.4k v32b Galway, Ireland.

Gunship BBS, +46-31-693306. 14.4k HST DS Gothenburg, Sweden.

Hipposoft /M. Junius, +49.241.875-090. 14.4 HST Aachen, NRW, Germany.

Le Lien, +33-72089879. HST 14.4/V32bis Lyon, Pascal Valette, France.

Linux Server /Braukmann, +49.441.592-963. 16.8 ZYX Oldenburg, NDS, Germany.

Linux-Support-Oz, +61-2-418-8750. v.32bis 14.4k Sydney, NSW, Australia.

LinuxServer / P. Berger, +49.711.756-275. 16.8 HST Stuttgart, BW, Germany.

Logical Solutions, 403 299-9900 through 9911. 2400 AB, Canada.

Logical Solutions, 403 299-9912, 299-9913. 14.4k AB, Canada.

Logical Solutions, 403 299-9914 through 9917. 16.8k v.32bis AB, Canada.

MM's Spielebox, +49.5323.3515. 14.4 ZYX Clausthal-Zfd., NDS, Germany.

MM's Spielebox, +49.5323.3516. 16.8 ZYX Clausthal-Zfd., NDS, Germany.

MM's Spielebox, +49.5323.3540. 9600 Clausthal-Zfd., NDS, Germany.

MUGNET Intl-Cistron BBS, +31-1720-42580. 38.4k Alphen a/d Rijn, Netherlands.

Magic BBS, 403-569-2882. 14.4k HST/Telebit/MNP Calgary, AB, Canada.
Internet/Usenet

Modula BBS, +33-1 4043 0124. HST 14.4 v.32bis Paris, France.

Modula BBS, +33-1 4530 1248. HST 14.4 V.32bis Paris, France.

Nemesis' Dungeon, +353-1-324755 or 326900. 14.4k v32bis Dublin, Ireland.

On the Beach, +444-273-600996. 14.4k/16.8k Brighton, UK. Fidonet 2:441/122

Pats System, +27-12-333-2049. 14.4k v.32bis/HST Pretoria, South Africa.

Public Domain Kiste, +49.30.686-62-50. 16.8 ZYX BLN, Germany. Fidonet 2:2403/17

Radio Free Nyongwa, 514-524-0829. v.32bis ZyXEL Montreal, QC, Canada.
Usenet, Fidonet

Rising Sun BBS, +49.7147.3845. 16.8 ZYX Sachsenheim, BW, Germany.
Fidonet 2:2407/4

STDIN BBS, +33-72375139. v.32bis Lyon, Laurent Cas, France.

Synapse, 819-246-2344. 819-561-5268 Gatineau, QC, Canada. RIME->SYNAPSE

The Controversy, (65)560-6040. 14.4k V.32bis/HST Singapore.

The Field of Inverse Chaos, +358 0 506 1836. 14.4k v32bis/HST Helsinki, Finland.

The Purple Tentacle, +44-734-590990. HST/V32bis Reading, UK. Fidonet 2:252/305

The Windsor Download, (519)-973-9330. v32bis 14.4 ON, Canada.

Thunderball Cave, 472567018. Norway.

UB-HOFF /A. Hoffmann, +49.203.584-155. 19.2 ZYX+ Duisburg, Germany.

V.A.L.I.S., 403-478-1281. 14.4k v.32bis Edmonton, AB, Canada. Usenet

bakunin.north.de, +49.421.870-532. 14.4 D 2800 Bremen, HB, Germany.

nonsolosoftware, +39 51 432904. ZyXEL 19.2k Italy. Fidonet 2:332/417 nonsolosoftware, +39 51 6140772. v.32bis, v.42bis Italy. Fidonet 2:332/407

r-node, 416-249-5366. 2400 Toronto, ON, Canada. Usenet

Usenet Newsgroups

Usenet is a collection of discussion groups (called *newsgroups*) that is available to Internet users. There are more than 14,000 newsgroups with over 2GB of traffic posted every single day. Of all of these newsgroups (which cover every conceivable topic), several are dedicated to Linux.

You can access Usenet newsgroups through special software called a *newsreader* if you have access to a site that downloads the newsgroups on a regular basis. Alternatively, most online services such as CompuServe, America Online, and Delphi also offer access to Usenet. Some BBSes also are providing limited access to newsgroups.

Usenet newsgroups fall into three categories: primary newsgroups, which are readily available to all Usenet users; local newsgroups with a limited distribution; and alternate newsgroups that may not be handled by all news servers. The primary newsgroups of interest to Linux users are

alt.os.linux	alt.os.linux.caldera
alt.uu.comp.os.linux.questions	at.fido.linux
comp.os.linux.advocacy	comp.os.linux.announce
comp.os.linux.answers	comp.os.linux.development.apps
comp.os.linux.development.system	comp.os.linux.hardware
comp.os.linux.m68k	comp.os.linux.misc
comp.os.linux.networking	comp.os.linux.setup
comp.os.linux.x	linux.act.680x0
linux.act.admin	linux.act.apps
linux.act.bbsdev	linux.act.chaos_digest
linux.act.compression	linux.act.configs
linux.act.c-programming	linux.act.debian
linux.act.dec_alpha	linux.act.doc
linux.act.fido	linux.act.fsf
linux.act.fsstnd	linux.act.ftp
linux.act.gcc	linux.act.hams
linux.act.ibcs2	linux.act.ibsc2
linux.act.interviews	linux.act.japanese
linux.act.kernel	linux.act.laptops
linux.act.linux-bbs	linux.act.linuxbsd
linux.act.linuxnews	linux.act.linuxss
linux.act.localbus	linux.act.lugnuts
linux.act.mca	linux.act.mgr
linux.act.mips	linux.act.msdos
linux.act.mumail	linux.act.net
linux.act.newbie	linux.act.new-channels
linux.act.normal	linux.act.nys

```
linux.act.oasg-trust            linux.act.oi
linux.act.pkg                   linux.act.postgres
linux.act.ppp                   linux.act.promotion
linux.act.qag                   linux.act.scsi
linux.act.serial                linux.act.seyon
linux.act.sound                 linux.act.svgalib
linux.act.sysvpkg-project       linux.act.tape
linux.act.term                  linux.act.tktools
linux.act.userfs                linux.act.uucp
linux.act.wabi                  linux.act.word
linux.act.x11                   linux.admin.isp
linux.appletalk                 linux.apps.bbsdev
linux.apps.flexfax              linux.apps.linux-bbs
linux.apps.seyon                linux.apps.seyon.development
linux.bbs.rocat                 linux.debian
linux.debian.announce           linux.debian.user
linux.dev.680x0                 linux.dev.admin
linux.dev.apps                  linux.dev.atm
linux.dev.bbs                   linux.dev.config
linux.dev.c-programming         linux.dev.debian
linux.dev.diald                 linux.dev.doc
linux.dev.fido                  linux.dev.fsf
linux.dev.fsstnd                linux.dev.ftp
linux.dev.gcc                   linux.dev.hams
linux.dev.ibcs2                 linux.dev.interviews
linux.dev.ipx                   linux.dev.japanese
linux.dev.kernel                linux.dev.laptop
linux.dev.linuxbsd              linux.dev.linuxnews
linux.dev.linuxss               linux.dev.localbus
linux.dev.lugnuts               linux.dev.mca
linux.dev.mgr                   linux.dev.msdos
linux.dev.net                   linux.dev.newbie
linux.dev.new-lists             linux.dev.normal
linux.dev.nys                   linux.dev.oasg
linux.dev.oi                    linux.dev.pkg
linux.dev.ppp                   linux.dev.qag
linux.dev.scsi                  linux.dev.serial
linux.dev.seyon                 linux.dev.sound
linux.dev.standards             linux.dev.svgalib
linux.dev.tape                  linux.dev.term
linux.dev.uucp                  linux.dev.wabi
linux.dev.word                  linux.dev.x11
linux.fido.ifmail               linux.free-widgets.announce
linux.free-widgets.bugs         linux.free-widgets.development
```

```
linux.largesites              linux.local.chicago
linux.local.nova-scotia       linux.local.silicon-valley
linux.motif.clone             linux.news.groups
linux.new-tty                 linux.ports.alpha
linux.ports.hp-pa             linux.ports.powerpc
linux.samba                   linux.samba.announce
linux.sdk                     linux.sources.kernel
linux.test                    linux.wine.users
```

Newsgroups specific to the X-windows environment installed with the Linux distribution include:

```
comp.windows.x
comp.windows.x.announce
comp.windows.x.apps
comp.windows.x.i386unix
comp.windows.x.intrinsics
comp.windows.x.motif
```

These newsgroups should be available at all Usenet sites unless the system administrator filters them out for some reason.

There are also regional newsgroups that usually are not widely distributed, or that have specific issues which may be in a language other than English. Some sample regional newsgroups carried by Usenet are

```
dc.org.linux-users

de.comp.os.linux

fr.comp.os.linux

tn.linux
```

If you do have access to Usenet newsgroups, it is advisable to regularly scan the newsgroup additions and deletions to check for new Linux newsgroups or existing groups that have folded. Most online services that provide access to Usenet maintain lists of all active newsgroups, which can be searched quickly.

The traffic on most of these Linux newsgroups deals with problems and issues people have when installing, configuring, or using the operating system. Usually, there is a lot of valuable information passing through the newsgroups, so check them regularly. The most interesting messages that deal with a specific subject (called *threads*) are collected and stored for access through an FTP site.

Commercial Vendors for Linux

This appendix lists all the commercial vendors that sell Linux distributions. See Appendix A, "Linux FTP Sites and Newsgroups," for a list of FTP sites that have Linux for free. The advantage of getting Linux from a commercial vendor is that you get a lot of software bundled in one package instead of having to do it yourself. You can also get a list of these vendors from the *Linux Journal,* a monthly periodical:

> *Linux Journal*
> P.O. Box 85867
> Seattle, WA 98145-1867
> Phone: (206) 527-3385
> Fax: (206) 527-2806

The `Linux Distribution-HOWTO` file contains up-to-date information on Linux vendors that bundle packages together for sale. This list is maintained by Matt Welsh, `mdw@sunsite.unc.edu`. The `HOWTO` file can be found in `/pub/linux/docs/HOWTO/Distribution-howto` at `tsx-11.mit.edu`.

Debian Linux Distribution

> The Debian Linux Association
> Station 11
> P.O. Box 3121
> West Lafayette, IN 47906

Full releases are available at `ftp.debian.org`.

Yggdrasil Plug-and-Play Linux CD-ROM and the Linux Bible

> Yggdrasil Computing, Incorporated
> 4880 Stevens Creek Blvd., Suite 205
> San Jose, CA 95129-1034
> Toll free: (800) 261-6630
> Phone: (408) 261-6630
> Fax: (408) 261-6631
> E-mail: `info@yggdrasil.com`
> WWW: `http://www.yggdrasil.com`

InfoMagic Developer's Resource CD-ROM Kit

> InfoMagic, Inc.
> 11950 N. Hwy. 89
> Flagstaff, AZ 86004
> Toll free: (800) 800-6613

Phone: (602) 526-9565
Fax: (602) 526-9573
WWW: http://www.infomagic.com

Linux Quarterly CD-ROM

Morse Telecommunication, Inc.
26 East Park Avenue, Suite 240
Long Beach, NY 11561
Orders: (800) 60-MORSE
Tech Support: (516) 889-8610
Fax: (516) 889-8665
E-mail: Linux@morse.net

Sequoia International Motif Development Package

Sequoia International, Inc.
600 West Hillsboro Blvd., Suite 300
Deerfield Beach, FL 33441
Phone: (305) 480-6118

Takelap Systems Ltd.

The Reddings
Court Robin Lane, Llangwm
Usk, Gwent, United Kingdom NP5 1ET
Phone: +44 (0)291 650357
E-mail: info@ddrive.demon.co.uk

Trans-Ameritech Linux Plus BSD CD-ROM

Trans-Ameritech Enterprises, Inc.
2342A Walsh Ave.
Santa Clara, CA 95051
Phone: (408) 727-3883
E-mail: roman@trans-ameritech.com

Red Hat Software

Red Hat Software
25 Sylvan Road South
Suite F1
Westport, CT 06880
Phone: (800) 454-5502
E-mail: sales@redhat.com
WWW: http://www.redhat.com

Caldera Internet Office Systems

Caldera, Inc.
633 South 550 East
Provo, UT 84606
Phone: (800) 850-7778
E-mail: info@caldera.com
WWW: http://www.caldera.com

The Linux
Documentation Project

The Linux Documentation Project is a loose team of writers, proofreaders, and editors who are working on a set of definitive Linux manuals. The overall coordinator of the project is Matt Welsh, aided by Lars Wirzenius and Michael K. Johnson.

Welsh maintains a Linux home page on the World Wide Web at `http://sunsite.unc.edu/mdw/ linux.html`.

They encourage anyone who wants to help to join them in developing any Linux documentation. If you have Internet e-mail access, you can join the DOC channel of the Linux-Activists mailing list by sending mail to `linux-activists-request@niksula.hut.fi` with the following line as the first line of the message body:

```
X-Mn-Admin: join DOC
```

Feel free to get in touch with the author and coordinator of this manual if you have questions, postcards, money, or ideas. Welsh can be reached via Internet e-mail at `mdw@sunsite.unc.edu` or at the following phone number: (607) 256-7372.

The GNU General Public License

Linux is licensed under the GNU General Public License (the GPL or copyleft), which is reproduced here to clear up some of the confusion about Linux's copyright status.

Linux is not shareware, nor is it in the public domain. The bulk of the Linux kernel has been copyrighted since 1993 by Linus Torvalds, and other software and parts of the kernel are copyrighted by their authors. Thus, Linux is copyrighted. Everyone is permitted to copy and distribute verbatim copies of this license document, but changing it is not allowed.

However, you may redistribute it under the terms of the GPL, which follows.

> **NOTE**
>
> The following copyright applies to the Red Hat Linux/Intel compilation and any portions of Red Hat Linux/Intel it does not conflict with. Whenever this policy does conflict with the copyright of any individual portion of Red Hat Linux/Intel, it does not apply.
>
> This copyright does conflict with the Metro X Server copyright. By purchasing Official Red Hat Linux, you automatically receive a single user license for the Metro X server. This license entitles you to install Metro X on one machine for every Official Red Hat Linux CD you purchase. Purchase of this book does not entitle you to a Metro X license.
>
> Note that the various archive CDs you purchase (including an archive CD you purchase directly from Red Hat Software) does not constitute Official Red Hat Linux and does not entitle you to a Metro X license. Any product that does not include Metro X Server program binaries does not include such a license.

> **NOTE**
>
> The GNU agreement shown in this chapter is available on the CD-ROM as COPYING in the root directory (or in /usr/src/linux).

GNU GENERAL PUBLIC LICENSE, Version 2, June 1991

Copyright 1989, 1991
Free Software Foundation, Inc.
675 Mass Ave.
Cambridge, MA 02139
USA

Everyone is permitted to copy and distribute verbatim copies of this license document, but changing it is not allowed.

E.1. Preamble

The licenses for most software are designed to take away your freedom to share and change it. By contrast, the GNU General Public License is intended to guarantee your freedom to share and change free software—to make sure the software is free for all its users. This General Public License applies to most of the Free Software Foundation's software and to any other program whose authors commit to using it. (Some other Free Software Foundation software is covered by the GNU Library General Public License instead.)

You can apply it to your programs, too.

When we speak of free software, we are referring to freedom, not price. Our General Public Licenses are designed to make sure that you have the freedom to distribute copies of free software (and charge for this service if you wish); that you receive source code or can get it if you want it; that you can change the software or use pieces of it in new free programs, and that you know you can do these things.

To protect your rights, we need to make restrictions that forbid anyone to deny you these rights or to ask you to surrender the rights.

These restrictions translate to certain responsibilities for you if you distribute copies of the software, or if you modify it.

For example, if you distribute copies of such a program, whether gratis or for a fee, you must give the recipients all the rights that you have. You must make sure that they, too, receive or can get the source code. And you must show them these terms so they know their rights.

We protect your rights with two steps:

1. Copyright the software, and
2. Offer you this license which gives you legal permission to copy, distribute and/or modify the software.

Also, for each author's protection and ours, we want to make certain that everyone understands that there is no warranty for this free software. If the software is modified by someone else and passed on, we want its recipients to know that what they have is not the original, so that any problems introduced by others will not reflect on the original authors' reputations.

Finally, any free program is threatened constantly by software patents. We wish to avoid the danger that redistributors of a free program will individually obtain patent licenses, in effect making the program proprietary. To prevent this, we have made it clear that any patent must be licensed for everyone's free use or not licensed at all.

The precise terms and conditions for copying, distribution, and modification follow.

E.2. GNU General Public License: Terms and Conditions for Copying, Distribution, and Modification

0. This License applies to any program or other work which contains a notice placed by the copyright holder saying it may be distributed under the terms of this General Public License. The "Program," below, refers to any such program or work, and "a work based on the Program" means either the Program or any derivative work under copyright law: that is to say, a work containing the Program or a portion of it, either verbatim or with modifications and/or translated into another language. (Hereinafter, translation is included without limitation in the term "modification.") Each licensee is addressed as "you."

Activities other than copying, distribution, and modification are not covered by this License; they are outside its scope. The act of running the Program is not restricted, and the output from the Program is covered only if its contents constitute a work based on the Program (independent of having been made by running the Program).

Whether that is true depends on what the Program does.

1. You may copy and distribute verbatim copies of the Program's source code as you receive it, in any medium, provided that you conspicuously and appropriately publish on each copy an appropriate copyright notice and disclaimer of warranty; keep intact all the notices that refer to this License and to the absence of any warranty; and give any other recipients of the Program a copy of this License along with the Program.

   You may charge a fee for the physical act of transferring a copy, and you may at your option offer warranty protection in exchange for a fee.

2. You may modify your copy or copies of the Program or any portion of it, thus forming a work based on the Program, and copy and distribute such modifications or work under the terms of Section 1 above, provided that you also meet all of these conditions:

   a. You must cause the modified files to carry prominent notices stating that you changed the files and the date of any change.

   b. You must cause any work that you distribute or publish, that in whole or in part contains or is derived from the Program or any part thereof, to be licensed as a whole at no charge to all third parties under the terms of this License.

   c. If the modified program normally reads commands interactively when run, you must cause it, when started running for such interactive use in the most ordinary way, to print or display an announcement including an appropriate copyright notice and a notice that there is no warranty (or else, saying that you provide a warranty) and that users may redistribute the program under these conditions, and telling the user how to view a copy of this License. (Exception: if the Program itself is interactive but does not normally print such an announcement, your work based on the Program is not required to print an announcement.)

   These requirements apply to the modified work as a whole. If identifiable sections of that work are not derived from the Program, and can be reasonably considered independent and separate *works in themselves, then this License, and its terms, do not apply to those sections when you distribute them as separate works. But when you distribute the same sections as part of a whole which is a work based on the Program, the distribution of the whole must be on the terms of this License, whose permissions for other licensees extend to the entire whole, and thus to each and every part regardless of who wrote it.*

Thus, it is not the intent of this section to claim rights or contest your rights to work written entirely by you; rather, the intent is to exercise the right to control the distribution of derivative or collective works based on the Program.

In addition, mere aggregation of another work not based on the Program with the Program (or with a work based on the Program) on a volume of a storage or distribution medium does not bring the other work under the scope of this License.

3. *You may copy and distribute the Program (or a work based on it, under Section 2) in object code or executable form under the terms of Sections 1 and 2 above provided that you also do one of the following:*

   a. *Accompany it with the complete corresponding machine-readable source code, which must be distributed under the terms of Sections 1 and 2 above on a medium customarily used for software interchange; or,*

   b. *Accompany it with a written offer, valid for at least three years, to give any third party, for a charge no more than your cost of physically performing source distribution, a complete machine-readable copy of the corresponding source code, to be distributed under the terms of Sections 1 and 2 above on a medium customarily used for software interchange; or,*

   c. *Accompany it with the information you received as to the offer to distribute corresponding source code. (This alternative is allowed only for noncommercial distribution and only if you received the program in object code or executable form with such an offer, in accord with Subsection b above.)*

The source code for a work means the preferred form of the work for making modifications to it. For an executable work, complete source code means all the source code for all modules it contains, plus any associated interface definition files, plus the scripts used to control compilation and installation of the executable. However, as a special exception, the source code distributed need not include anything that is normally distributed (in either source or binary form) with the major components (compiler, kernel, and so on) of the operating system on which the executable runs, unless that component itself accompanies the executable.

If distribution of executable or object code is made by offering access to copy from a designated place, then offering equivalent access to copy the source code from the same place counts as distribution of the source code, even though third parties are not compelled to copy the source along with the object code.

4. *You may not copy, modify, sublicense, or distribute the Program except as expressly provided under this License. Any attempt otherwise to copy, modify, sublicense, or distribute the Program is void, and will automatically terminate your rights under this License. However, parties who have received copies, or rights, from you under this License will not have their licenses terminated so long as such parties remain in full compliance.*

5. You are not required to accept this License, since you have not signed it. However, nothing else grants you permission to modify or distribute the Program or its derivative works. These actions are prohibited by law if you do not accept this License. Therefore, by modifying or distributing the Program (or any work based on the Program), you indicate your acceptance of this License to do so, and all its terms and conditions for copying, distributing, or modifying the Program or works based on it.

6. Each time you redistribute the Program (or any work based on the Program), the recipient automatically receives a license from the original licenser to copy, distribute, or modify the Program subject to these terms and conditions. You may not impose any further restrictions on the recipients' exercise of the rights granted herein. You are not responsible for enforcing compliance by third parties to this License.

7. If, as a consequence of a court judgment or allegation of patent infringement or for any other reason (not limited to patent issues), conditions are imposed on you (whether by court order, agreement, or otherwise) that contradict the conditions of this License, they do not excuse you from the conditions of this License. If you cannot distribute so as to satisfy simultaneously your obligations under this License and any other pertinent obligations, then as a consequence you may not distribute the Program at all. For example, if a patent license would not permit royalty-free redistribution of the Program by all those who receive copies directly or indirectly through you, then the only way you could satisfy both it and this License would be to refrain entirely from distribution of the Program.

If any portion of this section is held invalid or unenforceable under any particular circumstance, the balance of the section is intended to apply and the section as a whole is intended to apply in other circumstances.

It is not the purpose of this section to induce you to infringe any patents or other property right claims or to contest validity of any such claims; this section has the sole purpose of protecting the integrity of the free software distribution system, which is implemented by public license practices. Many people have made generous contributions to the wide range of software distributed through that system in reliance on consistent application of that system; it is up to the author/donor to decide if he or she is willing to distribute software through any other system and a licensee cannot impose that choice.

This section is intended to make thoroughly clear what is believed to be a consequence of the rest of this License.

8. If the distribution and/or use of the Program is restricted in certain countries either by patents or by copyrighted interfaces, the original copyright holder who places the Program under this License may add an explicit geographical distribution limitation excluding those countries, so that distribution is permitted only in or among countries not thus excluded. In such case, this License incorporates the limitation as if written in the body of this License.

9. The Free Software Foundation may publish revised and/or new versions of the General Public License from time to time. Such new versions will be similar in spirit to the present version but may differ in detail to address new problems or concerns.

Each version is given a distinguishing version number. If the Program specifies a version number of this License which applies to it and "any later version," you have the option of

> *following the terms and conditions either of that version or of any later version published by the Free Software Foundation. If the Program does not specify a version number of this License, you may choose any version ever published by the Free Software Foundation.*

10. *If you wish to incorporate parts of the Program into other free programs whose distribution conditions are different, write to the author to ask for permission. For software which is copyrighted by the Free Software Foundation, write to the Free Software Foundation; we sometimes make exceptions for this. Our decision will be guided by the two goals of preserving the free status of all derivatives of our free software and of promoting the sharing and reuse of software generally.*

NO WARRANTY

11. *BECAUSE THE PROGRAM IS LICENSED FREE OF CHARGE, THERE IS NO WARRANTY FOR THE PROGRAM, TO THE EXTENT PERMITTED BY APPLICABLE LAW. EXCEPT WHEN OTHERWISE STATED IN WRITING, THE COPYRIGHT HOLDERS AND/OR OTHER PARTIES PROVIDE THE PROGRAM "AS IS" WITHOUT WARRANTY OF ANY KIND, EITHER EXPRESSED OR IMPLIED, INCLUDING, BUT NOT LIMITED TO, THE IMPLIED WARRANTIES OF MERCHANTABILITY AND FITNESS FOR A PARTICULAR PURPOSE. THE ENTIRE RISK AS TO THE QUALITY AND PERFORMANCE OF THE PROGRAM IS WITH YOU. SHOULD THE PROGRAM PROVE DEFECTIVE, YOU ASSUME THE COST OF ALL NECESSARY SERVICING, REPAIR, OR CORRECTION.*

12. *IN NO EVENT, UNLESS REQUIRED BY APPLICABLE LAW OR AGREED TO IN WRITING, WILL ANY COPYRIGHT HOLDER, OR ANY OTHER PARTY WHO MAY MODIFY AND/OR REDISTRIBUTE THE PROGRAM AS PERMITTED ABOVE, BE LIABLE TO YOU FOR DAMAGES, INCLUDING ANY GENERAL, SPECIAL, INCIDENTAL, OR CONSEQUENTIAL DAMAGES ARISING OUT OF THE USE OR INABILITY TO USE THE PROGRAM (INCLUDING BUT NOT LIMITED TO LOSS OF DATA OR DATA BEING RENDERED INACCURATE OR LOSSES SUSTAINED BY YOU OR THIRD PARTIES OR A FAILURE OF THE PROGRAM TO OPERATE WITH ANY OTHER PROGRAMS), EVEN IF SUCH HOLDER OR OTHER PARTY HAS BEEN ADVISED OF THE POSSIBILITY OF SUCH DAMAGES.*

END OF TERMS AND CONDITIONS

How To Apply These Terms to Your New Programs

If you develop a new program and you want it to be of the greatest possible use to the public, the best way to achieve this is to make it free software that everyone can redistribute and change under these terms.

To do so, attach the following notices to the program. It is safest to attach them to the start of each source file to most effectively convey the exclusion of warranty. Each file should have at least the "copyright" line and a pointer to where the full notice is found:

```
<one line to give the program's name and a brief idea of what it does.>
    Copyright (C) 19yy  <name of author>
```

```
This program is free software; you can redistribute it and/or modify it under
the terms of the GNU General Public License as published by the Free Software
Foundation; either version 2 of the License, or (at your option) any later
version.
```

```
This program is distributed in the hope that it will be useful, but WITHOUT ANY
WARRANTY; without even the implied warranty of MERCHANTABILITY or FITNESS FOR
A PARTICULAR PURPOSE. See the GNU General Public License for more details.
```

```
You should have received a copy of the GNU General Public License along with
this program; if not, write to the Free Software Foundation, Inc., 675 Mass
Ave, Cambridge, MA 02139, USA.
```

Also add information on how to contact you by electronic and paper mail.

If the program is interactive, make it output a short notice like this when it starts in an interactive mode:

```
Gnomovision version 69, Copyright (C) 19yy name of author Gnomovision comes
with ABSOLUTELY NO WARRANTY; for details type ' show w' . This is free software,
and you are welcome to redistribute it under certain conditions; type ' show c'
for details.
```

The hypothetical commands ' show w' and ' show c' should show the appropriate parts of the General Public License. Of course, the commands you use may be called something other than ' show w' and ' show c' ; they could even be mouse-clicks or menu items—whatever suits your program.

You should also get your employer (if you work as a programmer) or your school, if any, to sign a "copyright disclaimer" for the program, if necessary. Here is a sample; alter the names:

> *Yoyodyne, Inc., hereby disclaims all copyright interest in the program ' Gnomovision' (which makes passes at compilers) written by James Hacker.*
>
> *<signature of Ty Coon>, 1 April 1989*
>
> *Ty Coon, President of V.*

This General Public License does not permit incorporating your program into proprietary programs. If your program is a subroutine library, you may consider it more useful to permit linking proprietary applications with the library. If this is what you want to do, use the GNU Library General Public License instead of this License.

Copyright Information

E

The Linux kernel is Copyright 1991, 1992, 1993, 1994 Linus Torvalds (others hold copyrights on some of the drivers, file systems, and other parts of the kernel) and is licensed under the terms of the GNU General Public License (see `COPYING` in `/usr/src/linux`).

Many other software packages included in Red Hat Linux are licensed under the GNU General Public License, which is included in the file `COPYING`.

This product includes software developed by the University of California, Berkeley and its contributors:

Copyright © 1980, 1983, 1986, 1988, 1990, 1991 The Regents of the University of California. All rights reserved.

Redistribution and use in source and binary forms, with or without modification, are permitted, provided that the following conditions are met:

1. Redistributions of source code must retain the above copyright notice, this list of conditions, and the following disclaimer.

2. Redistributions in binary form must reproduce the above copyright notice, this list of conditions, and the following disclaimer in the documentation and/or other materials provided with the distribution.

3. All advertising materials mentioning features or use of this software must display the following acknowledgment:

    This product includes software developed by the University of California, Berkeley and its contributors.

4. Neither the name of the university nor the names of its contributors may be used to endorse or promote products derived from this software without specific prior written permission.

THIS SOFTWARE IS PROVIDED BY THE REGENTS AND CONTRIBUTORS "AS IS" AND ANY EXPRESS OR IMPLIED WARRANTIES, INCLUDING, BUT NOT LIMITED TO, THE IMPLIED WARRANTIES OF MERCHANTABILITY AND FITNESS FOR A PARTICULAR PURPOSE ARE DISCLAIMED. IN NO EVENT SHALL THE REGENTS OR CONTRIBUTORS BE LIABLE FOR ANY DIRECT, INDIRECT, INCIDENTAL, SPECIAL, EXEMPLARY, OR CONSEQUENTIAL DAMAGES (INCLUDING, BUT NOT LIMITED TO, PROCUREMENT OF SUBSTITUTE GOODS OR SERVICES; LOSS OF USE, DATA, OR PROFITS; OR BUSINESS INTERRUPTION) HOWEVER CAUSED AND ON ANY THEORY OF LIABILITY, WHETHER IN CONTRACT, STRICT LIABILITY, OR TORT (INCLUDING NEGLIGENCE OR OTHERWISE) ARISING IN ANY WAY OUT OF THE USE OF THIS SOFTWARE, EVEN IF ADVISED OF THE POSSIBILITY OF SUCH DAMAGE.

The Red Hat Linux distribution contains Info-ZIP's compression utilities. Info-ZIP's software (Zip, Unzip, and related utilities) is free and can be obtained as source code or executables from various anonymous-FTP sites, including `ftp.uu.net:/pub/archiving/zip/*`. This software is provided free—there are no extra or hidden charges resulting from the use of this compression code. Thanks, Info-ZIP! :^)

Zip/Unzip source can also be found in the `RedHat_source/a/base` directory.

The Red Hat installation scripts; RPM, the Red Hat packaging system; and GLINT, the Red Hat graphical installation system, are Copyright 1995, 1996, Red Hat Software, Inc., Durham, N.C.

Linux and Red Hat Linux are copyrighted under the terms of the GNU Public License.

Sams Publishing supplies this software as a convenience only without warranties or technical support. Technical support for Linux is available from many suppliers, some of whom are mentioned in the text of this book. This is not an "official" copy of Red Hat Linux as that term is defined by Red Hat Software, Inc. (See `http://www.redhat.com`.)

Redistribution and use of this software, with or without modification, is permitted provided that the following condition is met:

1. Redistributions of this software must retain the above copyright notice, this list of conditions, and the following disclaimer.

THIS SOFTWARE IS PROVIDED BY THE AUTHOR "AS IS" AND ANY EXPRESS OR IMPLIED WARRANTIES, INCLUDING, BUT NOT LIMITED TO, THE IMPLIED WARRANTIES OF MERCHANTABILITY AND FITNESS FOR A PARTICULAR PURPOSE ARE DISCLAIMED. IN NO EVENT SHALL THE AUTHOR BE LIABLE FOR ANY DIRECT, INDIRECT, INCIDENTAL, SPECIAL, EXEMPLARY, OR CONSEQUENTIAL DAMAGES (INCLUDING, BUT NOT LIMITED TO, PROCUREMENT OF SUBSTITUTE GOODS OR SERVICES; LOSS OF USE, DATA, OR PROFITS; OR BUSINESS INTERRUPTION) HOWEVER CAUSED AND ON ANY THEORY OF LIABILITY, WHETHER IN CONTRACT, STRICT LIABILITY, OR TORT (INCLUDING NEGLIGENCE OR OTHERWISE) ARISING IN ANY WAY OUT OF THE USE OF THIS SOFTWARE, EVEN IF ADVISED OF THE POSSIBILITY OF SUCH DAMAGE.

For more information on this subject, please check `http://www.redhat.com`.

Copyright notice for XView3.2-X11R6:

©Copyright 1989, 1990, 1991 Sun Microsystems, Inc. Sun design patents pending in the U.S. and foreign countries. OPEN LOOK is a trademark of USL. Used by written permission of the owners.©

©Copyright Bigelow & Holmes 1986, 1985. Lucida is a registered trademark of Bigelow & Holmes. Permission to use the Lucida trademark is hereby granted only in association with the images and fonts described in this file.

SUN MICROSYSTEMS, INC., USL, AND BIGELOW & HOLMES MAKE NO REPRESENTATIONS ABOUT THE SUITABILITY OF THIS SOURCE CODE FOR ANY PURPOSE. IT IS PROVIDED "AS IS" WITHOUT EXPRESS OR IMPLIED WARRANTY OF ANY KIND. SUN MICROSYSTEMS, INC., USL AND BIGELOW & HOLMES, SEVERALLY AND INDIVIDUALLY, DISCLAIM ALL WARRANTIES WITH REGARD TO THIS SOURCE CODE, INCLUDING ALL IMPLIED WARRANTIES OF MERCHANTABILITY AND FITNESS FOR

A PARTICULAR PURPOSE. IN NO EVENT SHALL SUN MICROSYSTEMS, INC., USL OR BIGELOW & HOLMES BE LIABLE FOR ANY SPECIAL, INDIRECT, INCIDENTAL, OR CONSEQUENTIAL DAMAGES, OR ANY DAMAGES WHATSOEVER RESULTING FROM LOSS OF USE, DATA OR PROFITS, WHETHER IN AN ACTION OF CONTRACT, NEGLIGENCE OR OTHER TORTIOUS ACTION, ARISING OUT OF OR IN CONNECTION WITH THE USE OR PERFORMANCE OF THIS SOURCE CODE.

***Various other copyrights apply. See the documentation accompanying the software packages for full details.

Although every effort has been made to provide a complete source tree for this project, it's possible that something may have been forgotten. If you discover anything is missing, we will provide copies—just ask!

> **NOTE**
>
> We are required to provide any missing source to GPLed software for three years, per the following section (E.2.3.b) of the GNU General Public License.
>
> b. *Accompany it with a written offer, valid for at least three years, to give any third party, for a charge no more than your cost of physically performing source distribution, a complete machine-readable copy of the corresponding source code, to be distributed under the terms of Sections 1 and 2 above on a medium customarily used for software interchange;*

Furthermore, if you find something is missing (even if you don't need a copy), please point it out to sales@redhat.com so it can be fixed.

INDEX

SYMBOLS

Add to Your Sams Library Today with the Best Books for Programming, Operating Systems, and New Technologies

The easiest way to order is to pick up the phone and call

1-800-428-5331

between 9:00 a.m. and 5:00 p.m. EST.
For faster service please have your credit card available.

ISBN	Quantity	Description of Item	Unit Cost	Total Cost
0-672-30850-9		Linux System Administrator's Survival Guide (Book/CD-ROM)	$49.99	
0-672-30840-1		Understanding Local Area Networks, 5th Edition	$29.99	
0-672-30537-2		The Waite Group's UNIX Communications and the Internet, 3rd Edition	$35.00	
0-672-30584-4		Networking UNIX	$35.00	
0-672-30745-6		HTML & CGI Unleashed (Book/CD-ROM)	$49.99	
0-672-30542-9		X Windows System Programming, 2nd Edition (Book/Disk)	$39.99	
0-672-30540-2		Teach Yourself the UNIX C Shell in 14 Days	$29.99	
0-672-30586-0		Teach Yourself Perl in 21 Days	$29.99	
1-57521-030-4		Teach Yourself Java in 21 Days (Book/CD-ROM)	$39.99	
1-57521-049-5		Java Unleashed (Book/CD-ROM)	$49.99	
1-57521-014-2		Teach Yourself Web Publishing with HTML in 14 Days, Premier Edition (Book/CD-ROM)	$39.99	
1-57521-071-1		Building an Intranet Web (Book/CD-ROM)	$55.00	
1-57521-051-7		Web Publishing Unleashed (Book/CD-ROM)	$49.99	
		Shipping and Handling: See information below.		
		TOTAL		

❏ 3 ½" Disk

❏ 5 ¼" Disk

Shipping and Handling: $4.00 for the first book, and $1.75 for each additional book. Floppy disk: add $1.75 for shipping and handling. If you need to have it NOW, we can ship product to you in 24 hours for an additional charge of approximately $18.00, and you will receive your item overnight or in two days. Overseas shipping and handling adds $2.00 per book and $8.00 for up to three disks. Prices subject to change. Call for availability and pricing information on latest editions.

201 W. 103rd Street, Indianapolis, Indiana 46290

1-800-428-5331 — Orders   1-800-835-3202 — FAX   1-800-858-7674 — Customer Service

Book ISBN 0-672-30962-5

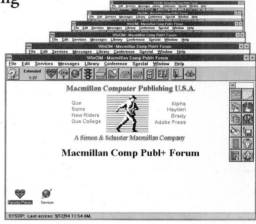

A V I A C O M S E R V I C E

The Information SuperLibrary™

Bookstore

Search

What's New

Reference

Software

Newsletter

Company Overviews

Yellow Pages

Internet Starter Kit

HTML Workshop

Win a Free T-Shirt!

Macmillan Computer Publishing

Site Map

Talk to Us

CHECK OUT THE BOOKS IN THIS LIBRARY.

You'll find thousands of shareware files and over 1600 computer books designed for both technowizards and technophobes. You can browse through 700 sample chapters, get the latest news on the Net, and find just about anything using our massive search directories.

All Macmillan Computer Publishing books are available at your local bookstore.

We're open 24-hours a day, 365 days a year.

You don't need a card.

We don't charge fines.

And you can be as **LOUD** as you want.

The Information SuperLibrary

http://www.mcp.com/mcp/   ftp.mcp.com

The CD-ROM

The companion CD-ROM contains the latest Red Hat (3.0.3) Linux release. It includes a variety of Linux kernels, including version 1.3.18. Plus, you'll find hundreds of additional programs and tools for Linux. See Part I, "Introduction," of this book for detailed instructions on installing Linux.

The version of Red Hat included on the CD-ROM does not allow users (including root) to execute binaries or access files directly from the current directory unless that directory is specifically included in the PATH environment variable or the user types the full directory name as part of the command—regardless of the permissions set on the file. Attempts to access a file while in a directory that is not included in the PATH will result in Linux complaining that it is unable to find the file. To circumvent this, make one of the following changes:

1. To effect a global change to enable all users (and root) to access files from the current directory, modify the PATH line in /etc/profile to read as follows:

   PATH="$PATH:/usr/X11R6/bin:/usr/bin/mh:./"

2. To allow only specific users to access files from the current directory, modify the PATH line in .bash_profile of the user's home directory (that is, /home/*username*/.bash_profile) to read as follows:

   PATH="$PATH:$HOME:./"

If you are unsure about how to edit files in Linux, see Chapter 16, "Text Editors," for instructions on using vi or emacs.

Having made the changes, log out of your current session and log in again for the changes to take effect. Of course, the appropriate permissions on each file must still be set because they are always enforced by the Linux operating system. (See the section "File Permissions and Ownership" in Chapter 8, "The Linux File System.")

Sams Publishing Support

If you have a damaged CD-ROM, or if you're having a problem with the book, you can contact our support department.

E-mail:	support@mcp.com	*Telephone:*	(317) 581-3833
Mail:	Macmillan Computer Publishing Support Department 201 West 103rd Street Indianapolis, IN 46290	*Fax:*	(317) 581-4773

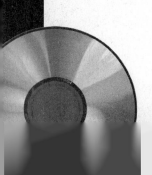